JAVA
HOW TO PROGRAM

WITH AN INTRODUCTION TO
VISUAL J++™

Deitel & Deitel
Books and Cyber Classrooms
published by
Prentice Hall

How to Program **Series**
C How to Program, Second Edition
C++ How to Program
Java How to Program
Java How to Program with an Introduction to Visual J++

Multimedia Cyber Classroom **Series**
C & C++ Multimedia Cyber Classroom
Java Multimedia Cyber Classroom

For continuing updates on Prentice Hall and Deitel & Associates, Inc. publications visit the Prentice Hall web site

`http//www.prenhall.com/deitel`

To communicate with the authors, send email to:

`deitel@deitel.com`

For information on corporate on-site seminars and public seminars offered by Deitel & Associates, Inc. worldwide, visit:

`http://www.deitel.com`

JAVA HOW TO PROGRAM

WITH AN INTRODUCTION TO VISUAL J++™

H. M. Deitel
Deitel & Associates, Inc.

P. J. Deitel
Deitel & Associates, Inc.

PRENTICE HALL, Upper Saddle River, NJ 07458

Library of Congress Cataloging-in-Publication Data

Deitel, Harvey M.
   Java how to program : with an introduction to Visual J++ / H.M.
Deitel, P.J. Deitel. -- Special ed.
      p. cm.
   Includes bibliographical references and index.
   ISBN 0-13-632589-0
   1. Java (Computer program language) 2. Microsoft Visual J++.
   I. Deitel, Paul J. II Title.
   QA76.73.J38D45 1997
   005.13'3--dc21   97-3526
                                                            CIP

Acquisitions Editor: *Alan Apt*
Development Editor: *Sondra Chavez*
Production Editor: *Camille Trentacoste*
Copy Editor: *Michael Schiaparelli*
Chapter Opener and Cover Designer: *Tamara Newnam*
Manufacturing Manager: *Alexis R. Heydt*

© 1997 by Prentice-Hall, Inc.
A Simon & Schuster Company/A Viacom Company
Upper Saddle River, New Jersey 07458

The authors and publisher of this book have used their best efforts in preparing this book. These efforts include the development, research, and testing of the theories and programs to determine their effectiveness. The authors and publisher make no warranty of any kind, expressed or implied, with regard to these programs or to the documentation contained in this book. The authors and publisher shall not be liable in any event for incidental or consequential damages in connection with, or arising out of, the furnishing, performance, or use of these programs.

Java and JavaScript are trademarks of Sun Microsystems, Inc. Sun, Sun Microsystems, Sun Microsystems Computer Corporation, the Sun logo, the Sun Microsystems logo, Sun Microsystems Computer Corporation logo, Java and HotJava are trademarks or registered trademarks of Sun Microsystems, Inc. Micorsoft and Visual J++ are either registered trademarks or trademarks of Microsoft Corporation in the United States and/or other countries.Portions reprinted with permission from Microsoft Corporation. UNIX is a registered trademark in the United States and other countries, exclusively licensed through X/Open Company, Ltd. Many of the designations used by manufacturers and sellers to distinguish their products are claimed as trademarks. Where those designations appear in this book, and Prentice-Hall and the authors were aware of a trademark claim, the designations have been printed in initial caps or all caps.

Printed in the United States of America

10 9 8 7 6 5 4 3

ISBN 0-13-632589-0

Prentice-Hall International (UK) Limited, *London*
Prentice-Hall of Australia Pty. Limited, *Sydney*
Prentice-Hall Canada Inc., *Toronto*
Prentice-Hall Hispanoamericana, S.A., *Mexico*
Prentice-Hall of India Private Limited, *New Delhi*
Prentice-Hall of Japan, Inc., *Tokyo*
Simon & Schuster Asia Pte. Ltd., *Singapore*
Editora Prentice-Hall do Brasil, Ltda., *Rio de Janeiro*

TO

Susanne Peterson, Academic Program Manager at Microsoft
Nancy Beals, Textbook Publishing Program Manager at Microsoft
and to the members of Microsoft's Visual J++ development team.

Thank you for the vision of a textbook that would introduce Visual J++ to computer science students worldwide. Thank you also for giving us the privilege of writing that book and providing the extraordinary support we needed to ensure its timely completion.

H. M. D.
P. J. D.
March, 1997

TO

Sondra Chavez, our project manager at Prentice Hall
Camille Trentacoste, our production manager at Prentice Hall and
Tamara Newnam, our cover and icon designer.

We wrote Java How to Program *in seven months—evenings, weekends, and on airplanes. We were working full-time and traveling extensively, teaching C++ and Java courses to our industry clients. Sondra, Camille and Tammy reached into our minds to understand our vision for* Java How to Program *and devoted themselves tirelessly to helping us realize that vision under an impossible schedule.*

It is to these special people that we dedicate this book.

H. M. D.
P. J. D.
September, 1996

Contents

*Summary • Terminology • Common Programming Errors • Performance Tips •
Testing and Debugging Tips • Self-Review Exercises • Answers to Self-Review
Exercises • Exercises*

Illustrations

Preface

Live in fragments no longer. Only connect.
Edward Morgan Forster

Welcome to Java, Microsoft Visual J++[1] and the exciting world of Internet, Intranet and World Wide Web programming! This book is by an old guy and a young guy. The old guy (HMD; Massachusetts Institute of Technology 1967) has been programming and/or teaching programming for 36 years. The young guy (PJD; MIT 1991) has been programming for 17 years and has caught the teaching and writing "bug." The old guy programs and teaches from experience; the young guy does so from an inexhaustible reserve of energy. The old guy wants clarity; the young guy wants performance. The old guy appreciates elegance and beauty; the young guy wants results. We got together to produce a book we hope you will find informative, challenging and entertaining.

In November 1995 we attended an Internet/World Wide Web conference to hear a Sun Microsystems representative discuss Java. *Java How to Program* was born at that moment, published in September 1996 and went on to become the world's best-selling Java computer science textbook.

In November of 1996, Microsoft asked us to write a special edition of *Java How to Program* that would introduce and include Microsoft's *Visual J++ Publisher's Edition* software on CD-ROM. We formed *Java How to Program with an Introduction to Visual J++* by adding to *Java How to Program* the detailed Appendix G, "Getting Started with Visual J++."

Please take a moment now and read the back cover and inside back cover to learn more about the Microsoft *Visual J++ Publisher's Edition* software included on the enclosed CD-ROM.

Why We Wrote Java How to Program

Dr. Harvey M. Deitel taught introductory programming courses in universities for 20 years with an emphasis on developing clearly written, well-structured programs. Much of what is taught in these courses is the basic principles

---

1. Micorsoft and Visual J++ are either registered trademarks or trademarks of Microsoft Corporation in the United States and/or other countries.

of programming with an emphasis on the effective use of control structures and function-alization. We present these topics in *Java How to Program* exactly the way HMD has done in his university courses. Our experience has been that students handle the material in the early chapters on control structures and methods (Java's term for functions) in about the same manner as they handle introductory Pascal or C courses. There is one noticeable dif-ference though: students are highly motivated by the fact that they are learning a leading-edge language (Java) and a leading-edge programming paradigm (object-oriented pro-gramming) that will be immediately useful to them as they leave the university environ-ment and head into a world in which the Internet has a massive new prominence. This increases their enthusiasm for the material—a big help when you consider that there is much more to learn in a Java course given that students must now master both the base lan-guage and substantial class libraries as well. But students quickly discover that they can do great things with Java, so they are willing to put in the extra effort.

Our goal was clear: produce a Java textbook for introductory university-level courses in computer programming for students with little or no programming experience, yet offer the depth and the rigorous treatment of theory and practice demanded by traditional, upper-level C and C++ courses and that satisfies professionals' needs. To meet these goals, we produced a comprehensive book because our text also patiently teaches the principles of control structures, object-oriented programming, the Java language and Java class libraries.

Java How to Program is the first college textbook on Java. We wrote it fresh on the heels of *C How to Program,* Second Edition and *C++ How to Program*, each of which has become the world's leading introductory textbook in its respective field. Approximately 200,000 students worldwide have learned C and/or C++ from these texts. We taught 25 Java courses to approximately 400 students as we were writing *Java How to Program* and monitored student reaction to Java and to our materials. We have prepared a Windows-based, interactive CD-ROM multimedia edition of this book, the *Java Multimedia Cyber Classroom* (available November 1996). [Prentice Hall offers a "value pack" edition of both *Java How to Program* and the *Java Multimedia Cyber Classroom* at a discount for people who want to use both the book and the multimedia CD.]

We believe in Java. Its conceptualization by Sun Microsystems, the creators of Java, is brilliant: base a new language on two of the world's most widely used implementation languages, C and C++. This immediately gives Java a huge pool of highly skilled program-mers who are currently responsible for implementing most of the world's new operating systems, communications systems, database systems and personal computer applications systems software. Remove the messier, more complex and error-prone features (such as pointers, templates, operator overloading and multiple inheritance, among others). Keep the language as concise as is reasonable by removing special-purpose features that are used by only small segments of the programming community. Make the language truly portable so it is appropriate for implementing Internet-based and World-Wide-Web-based applica-tions, and build in the features people really need such as strings, graphics, graphical user interface components, exception handling, multithreading, multimedia (audio, images, ani-mation—and eventually video), file processing, Internet-based client/server networking and prepackaged data structures. Then make the language available at *no charge* to tens of millions of potential programmers worldwide.

Java was originally promoted as a means of adding "dynamic content" to World-Wide-Web pages. Instead of Web pages with only text and static graphics, people's Web pages "come alive" with audios, animations, interactivity—and soon, video and three-dimensional imaging. But we saw much more than this. These features are precisely what businesses and organizations really need to meet today's information processing requirements. So we immediately viewed Java as having the potential to become one of the world's key general-purpose programming languages.

There are a number of for-sale Java products available. However, you do not need them to get started with Java. We intentionally wrote *Java How to Program* using only the free Java software available from Sun Microsystems over the Internet. We have seen many excellent Java for-sale products that will certainly be attractive to businesses and individuals programming in Java.

Java is empowering people and organizations to unleash their creativity. We have seen this in the 25 Java courses we taught prior to publishing *Java How to Program.* Once our students enter lab, we can't hold them back. They are eager to experiment and explore portions of the Java class libraries that we haven't as yet covered in class. They produce applications that go well beyond anything we've ever tried in our introductory C and C++ courses. And they tell us about projects they "can't wait" to try after the course.

Java has weaknesses that we discuss frankly. But we should not lose sight of the fact that Java is "just a baby"—it needs time to mature. Interest in Java is huge. People really want the "Java model" to work. The apparent weaknesses are being addressed and solutions are forthcoming. For example, organizations and individuals want to transact business over the Internet. The Internet is a fundamentally insecure communications channel. But techniques exist and are being refined for performing secure transmission over insecure channels—a contradiction in terms, perhaps, but nevertheless soon to be reality.

The computer field has never seen anything like the Internet/World Wide Web/Java "explosion" occurring today. People want to communicate. People need to communicate. Sure they have been doing that since the dawn of civilization, but computer communications have been mostly limited to digits, alphabetic characters and special characters passing back and forth. The next major wave is surely multimedia. People want to transmit pictures and they want those pictures to be in color. They want to transmit voices, sounds and audio clips. They want to transmit full motion color video. And at some point, they will insist on three-dimensional, moving-image transmission. Our current flat, two-dimensional televisions will eventually be replaced with three-dimensional versions that turn our living rooms into "theaters-in-the-round." Actors will perform their roles as if we were watching live theater. Our living rooms will be turned into miniature sports stadiums. Our business offices will enable video conferencing among colleagues half a world apart as if they were sitting around one conference table. The possibilities are intriguing and Java is sure to play a key role in making many of these possibilities become reality.

There have been predictions that the Internet could eventually replace the telephone system. Well, why stop there? It could also replace radio and television as we know them today. It's not hard to imagine the Internet replacing the newspaper with completely electronic news media. This textbook you are reading may someday appear in a museum alongside radios, TVs and newspapers in an "early media of ancient civilization" exhibit.

Teaching Approach

Java How to Program contains a rich collection of examples, exercises, and projects drawn from many fields to provide the student with a chance to solve interesting real-world problems. The book concentrates on the principles of good software engineering and stresses program clarity. We avoid arcane terminology and syntax specifications in favor of teaching by example. Each of our code examples has been carefully tested on several Java platforms including those for Sun's Solaris and Microsoft's Windows 95 and Windows NT.

This book is written by two educators who spend most of their time teaching edge-of-the-practice topics in industry classrooms worldwide. The text emphasizes pedagogy.

Introducing Object Orientation and Applets from Chapter One!
Java How to Program "jumps right in" with object-oriented programming, applets and even basic graphical user interface design from Chapter 1! People tell us this is a "gutsy" move. But Java students really want to "cut to the chase." There is great stuff to be done in Java so let's get right to it! Java is not trivial by any means, but it's fun and students can see immediate results. Students can get graphical, animated, multimedia-based, audio-intensive, multithreaded, network-based programs running quickly through Java's extensive class libraries of "reusable components." They can implement impressive projects. They can be much more creative and productive in a one- or two-semester course than is possible in C and C++ introductory courses.

Live-Code Teaching Approach
The book is loaded with live-code examples. This is the focus of the way we teach and write about programming, and the focus of each of our multimedia *Cyber Classrooms* as well. Virtually every new concept is presented in the context of a complete, working Java program (applet or application) immediately followed by a window showing the program's output. We call this style of teaching and writing our **live-code approach**. *We use the language to teach the language.* Reading these programs is much like entering and running them on a computer.

World Wide Web Access
All of the code for *Java How to Program* is on the Internet at the Prentice Hall Web site **http://www.prenhall.com/deitel** and at the Deitel & Associates, Inc. Web site **http://www.deitel.com**. Please download all the code then run each program as you read the text. Make changes to the code examples and see what happens. See how the Java compiler "complains" when you make various kinds of errors. Immediately see the effects of making changes to the code. It's a great way to learn programming by doing programming. [You must respect the fact that this is copyrighted material. Feel free to use it as you study Java, but you may not republish any portion of it without explicit permission from the authors and Prentice Hall.]

Objectives
Each chapter begins with a statement of *Objectives*. This tells the student what to expect and gives the student an opportunity, after reading the chapter, to determine if he or she has met these objectives. It is a confidence builder and a source of positive reinforcement.

Quotations

The learning objectives are followed by quotations. Some are humorous, some are philo-
sophical, and some offer interesting insights. Our students enjoy relating the quotations to
the chapter material. The quotations are worth a "second look" after you read each chapter.

Outline

The chapter *Outline* helps the student approach the material in top-down fashion. This, too,
helps students anticipate what is to come and set a comfortable and effective learning pace.

12,087 lines of code in 200 Example Programs (with Program Outputs)

We present Java features in the context of complete, working Java programs. This is the
focus of our teaching and our writing. We call it our "live-code" approach. Each program
is followed by a window with the output produced when the program runs. This enables the
student to confirm that the programs run as expected. Reading the book carefully is much
like entering and running these programs on a computer. The programs range from just a
few lines of code to substantial examples with several hundred lines of code. Students
should download all the code for the book from our Web sites and run each program while
studying that program in the text. The programs are available at both **http://www.dei-
tel.com** and **http://www.prenhall.com/deitel**.

166 Illustrations/Figures

An abundance of charts, line drawings and program outputs is included. The discussion of
control structures, for example, features carefully drawn flowcharts. [Note: We do not
teach the use of flowcharting as a program development tool, but we do use a brief, flow-
chart-oriented presentation to specify the precise operation of Java's control structures.]

369 Programming Tips

We have included programming tips to help students focus on important aspects of program
development. We highlight hundreds of these tips in the form of *Good Programming Practices, Common Programming Errors, Testing and Debugging Tips, Performance Tips,
Portability Tips*, and *Software Engineering Observations*. These tips and practices represent the best we have been able to glean from a combined four-and-one-half decades of programming and teaching experience. One of our students—a mathematics major—told us
recently that she feels this approach is like the highlighting of axioms, theorems, and cor-
ollaries in mathematics books; it provides a basis on which to build good software.

62 Good Programming Practices

When we teach introductory courses, we state that the "buzzword" of each course is "clarity," and we highlight as *Good Programming Practices* techniques for writing programs
that are clearer, more understandable, more debuggable, and more maintainable.

139 Common Programming Errors

Students learning a language tend to make certain errors frequently. Focusing the students'
attention on these *Common Programming Errors* helps the student avoid making the same
errors. It also helps reduce the long lines outside instructors' offices during office hours!

29 Testing and Debugging Tips

When we first designed this "tip type," we thought we would use it strictly to tell people how to test and debug Java programs. In fact, many of the tips describe aspects of Java that reduce the likelihood of "bugs" and thus simplify the testing and debugging process for Java programs compared to that required for C and C++ programs.

50 Performance Tips

In our experience, teaching students to write clear and understandable programs is by far the most important goal for a first programming course. But students want to write the programs that run the fastest, use the least memory, require the smallest number of keystrokes, or dazzle in other nifty ways. Students really care about performance. They want to know what they can do to "turbo charge" their programs. So we have included 50 *Performance Tips* that highlight opportunities for improving program performance.

8 Portability Tips

Some programmers assume that if they implement an application in Java, the application will automatically be "perfectly" portable across all Java platforms. Unfortunately, this is not always the case. We include *Portability Tips* to help students write portable code and also to provide insights on how Java achieves its high degree of portability. We had many more portability tips in *C How to Program* and *C++ How to Program*. We needed fewer *Portability Tips* in *Java How to Program* because Java is designed to be portable top-to-bottom, so much less conspicuous effort is required on the Java programmer's part to achieve portability than with either C or C++.

81 Software Engineering Observations

The object-oriented programming paradigm requires a complete rethinking about the way we build software systems. Java is an effective language for performing good software engineering. The *Software Engineering Observations* highlight architectural and design issues that affect the construction of software systems, especially large-scale systems. Much of what the student learns here will be useful in upper-level courses and in industry as the student begins to work with large, complex real-world systems.

Summary

Each chapter ends with additional pedagogical devices. We present a thorough, bullet-list-style *Summary* of the chapter. On average, there are 34 summary bullets per chapter. This helps the students review and reinforce key concepts.

Terminology

We include in a *Terminology* section an alphabetized list of the important terms defined in the chapter—again, further reinforcement. On average, there are 87 terms per chapter.

Summary of Tips, Practices, and Errors

For ease of reference, we collect and reiterate the *Good Programming Practices*, *Common Programming Errors*, *Testing and Debugging Tips*, *Performance Tips*, *Portability Tips*, and *Software Engineering Observations*.

346 Self-Review Exercises and Answers (Count Includes Separate Parts)
Extensive self-review exercises and answers are included for self-study. This gives the student a chance to build confidence with the material and prepare for the regular exercises. Students should be encouraged to do all the self-review exercises and check their answers.

879 Exercises (Solutions in Instructor's Manual; Count Includes Separate Parts)
Each chapter concludes with a substantial set of exercises including simple recall of important terminology and concepts; writing individual Java statements; writing small portions of Java methods and classes; writing complete Java methods, classes, applets and applications; and writing major term projects. The large number of exercises across a wide variety of areas enables instructors to tailor their courses to the unique needs of their audiences and to vary course assignments each semester. Instructors can use these exercises to form homework assignments, short quizzes, and major examinations. The solutions for the exercises are included in the *Instructor's Manual* and on the disks available only to instructors through their Prentice-Hall representatives. Solutions to approximately half of the exercises are included on the *Java Multimedia Cyber Classroom* CD (available November 1996 in bookstores and computer stores; it can be ordered from Prentice Hall at 1-800-922-0579).

4613 Index Entries (with a Total of 7824 Page References)
We have included an extensive *Index* at the back of the book. This helps the student find any term or concept by keyword. The *Index* is useful to people reading the book for the first time and is especially useful to practicing programmers who use the book as a reference. Each of the 1584 terms in the *Terminology* sections appears in the *Index* (along with many more index items from each chapter). Students can use the *Index* in conjunction with the *Terminology* sections to be sure they have covered the key material of each chapter.

"Double Indexing" of All Java Live-Code Examples and Exercises
Java How to Program has 200 live-code examples and 1225 exercises (including parts). Many of the exercises are challenging problems or projects requiring substantial effort. We have "double indexed" all of the live-code examples and most of the more challenging projects. For every Java source-code program in the book, we took the file name with the **.java** extension, such as **LoadAudioAndPlay.java** and indexed it both alphabetically (in this case under "L") and as a subindex item under "Examples. This makes it easier to find examples using particular features. The more substantial exercises, such as "Maze Generator and Walker," are indexed both alphabetically (in this case under "M") and as subindex items under "Exercises."

Bibliography
An extensive bibliography is included to encourage further reading.

A Tour of the Book

Chapter 1—Introduction to Computers and Java Applets—discusses what computers are, how they work and how they are programmed. The chapter gives a brief history of the development of programming languages from machine languages, to assembly languages, to high-level languages. The origin of the Java programming language is discussed. The chapter includes an introduction to a typical Java programming environment and gives a concise introduction to writing Java programs. A detailed treatment of decision making and arithmetic operations in Java is presented. After studying this chapter, the student will understand how to write simple, but complete, Java programs. A distinguishing feature of Chapter 1 is that we "jump right in" with object-oriented programming in Java; our first program uses inheritance to create a Java applet, then displays the applet window. We introduce some basics of HTML programming and discussion the relationship among HTML, the World Wide Web and the Internet. We waste no time in getting to **Label**s and **TextField**s to prompt for inputs and read them from the keyboard. With Java you can write two kinds of programs namely, *applets* designed to be transported over the Internet and executed in World Wide Web browsers like Netscape Navigator, and stand-alone *applications* designed to execute on your own computer. Because of the intense interest in Java applets and the World Wide Web, we present Java programs as applets whenever possible. Because of certain stringent security restrictions related to file processing and networking the examples in those chapters (15 and 16) are presented as Java applications.

Chapter 2—Developing Java Applications—focuses on the program development process. The chapter discusses how to take a *problem statement* (i.e., a *requirements document*) and from it develop a working Java program, including performing intermediate steps in pseudocode. The chapter introduces some fundamental data types and simple control structures used for decision making (**if** and **if/else**) and repetition (**while**). We examine counter-controlled repetition, sentinel-controlled repetition, and introduce Java's increment, decrement and assignment operators. We have had a positive experience assigning problems 2.11 through 2.14 in our introductory courses. Since these four problems have similar structure, doing all four is a nice way for students to "get the hang" of the program development process. Students will enjoy the challenges of the "mystery programs." The more mathematically inclined students will enjoy problems on palindromes, binary-to-decimal conversion, encryption and decryption, and calculating factorials.

Chapter 3—Control Structures—discusses much of the C portion of Java, especially the sequence, selection (**if**, **if/else** and **switch**) and repetition (**while**, **for** and **do/while**) control structures. The chapter uses simple flowcharts to show the flow of control through each of the control structures. The techniques discussed in Chapter 2 and Chapter 3 constitute a large part of what has been traditionally taught in the universities under the topic of structured programming. With Java we do object-oriented programming. In doing so, we discover that the insides of the objects we build make abundant use of control structures. Chapter 3 examines repetition in detail and compares the alternatives of counter-controlled loops and sentinel-controlled loops. This chapter helps the student develop good programming habits in preparation for dealing with the more substantial programming tasks in the remainder of the text. The chapter clearly explains the labeled **break** and **continue** statements with live-code examples. The chapter concludes with a discussion of logical operators—**&&** (logical AND), **&** (boolean logical AND), **||** (logical OR), **|** (boolean logical inclusive OR), **^** (boolean logical exclusive OR) and **!** (NOT). There is a substantial exercise set including mathematical, graphical business applications. Students will enjoy Exercise 3.26 that asks them to write a program with repetition and decision structures that prints the iterative song, "The Twelve Days of Christmas." The more mathematically inclined students will enjoy problems on binary, octal, decimal and hexadecimal number systems, calculating the mathematical constant π with an infinite series, Pythagorean triples and De Morgan's Laws. Our students particularly enjoy the challenges of triangle-printing and diamond-printing in Exercises 3.10 and 3.21; these problems really help students learn to deal with nested repetition structures—a complex topic to master in introductory courses.

Chapter 4—Methods—takes a deeper look inside objects. Objects contain data which we will generally refer to as *instance variables* and executable units called *methods* (these are often called *functions* in non-object-oriented procedural programming languages like C). We explore methods in depth and include a discussion of methods that "call themselves," so-called *recursive* methods. We discuss class library methods, programmer-defined methods, recursion, call-by-value and call-by-reference capabilities. The techniques presented in Chapter 4 are essential to the production of properly structured programs, especially the kinds of larger programs and software that system programmers and application programmers are likely to develop in real-world applications. The "divide and conquer" strategy is presented as an effective means for solving complex problems by dividing them into simpler interacting components. Students enjoy the treatment of random numbers and simulation, and they appreciate the discussion of the dice game of craps that makes elegant use of control structures (this is one of our most successful lectures in our introductory courses). The chapter offers a solid introduction to recursion and includes a table summarizing the dozens of recursion examples and exercises distributed throughout the remainder of the book. Some texts leave recursion for a chapter late in the book; we feel this topic is best covered gradually throughout the text. The topic of method overloading (i.e., allowing multiple methods to have the same name as long as they have different "signatures") is motivated and explained clearly. The extensive collection of exercises at the end of the chapter includes several classical recursion problems such as the Towers of Hanoi; we revisit this problem later in the text where we employ graphics, animation and sound to make the problem "come alive." There are many mathematical and graphical examples. Our students particularly enjoy the development of a "Computer-Assisted Instruction" system in exercises 4.31 and 4.32; we ask students to develop a multimedia version of this system later in the book.

Chapter 5—Arrays—explores the processing of data in lists and tables of values. Arrays in Java are processed as objects, further evidence of Java's commitment to almost 100% object-orientation. We discuss the structuring of data into arrays, or groups, of related data items of the same type. The chapter presents numerous examples of both single-subscripted arrays and double-subscripted arrays. It is widely recognized that structuring data properly is just as important as using control structures effectively in the development of properly structured programs. Examples in the chapter investigate various common array manipulations, printing histograms, sorting data, passing arrays to functions and an introduction to the field of survey data analysis (with simple statistics). A feature of this chapter is the discussion of elementary sorting and searching techniques and the presentation of binary searching as a dramatic improvement over linear searching. The 44 end-of-chapter exercises include a variety of interesting and challenging problems such as improved sorting techniques, the design of an airline reservations system, an introduction to the concept of turtle graphics (made famous in the LOGO programming language) and the Knight's Tour and Eight Queens problems that introduce the notions of heuristic programming so widely employed in the field of artificial intelligence. The exercises conclude with a series of recursion problems including the selection sort, palindromes, linear search, binary search, the eight queens, printing an array, printing a string backwards and finding the minimum value in an array. The chapter exercises include a delightful simulation of the classic race between the tortoise and the hare, card shuffling and dealing algorithms, recursive quicksort and recursive maze traversals. A special section entitled "Building Your Own Computer" explains machine language programming and proceeds with the design and implementation of a computer simulator that allows the reader to write and run machine language programs. This unique feature of the text will be especially useful to the reader who wants to understand how computers really work. Our students enjoy this project and often implement substantial enhancements; many enhancements are suggested in the exercises. In Chapter 17, another special section guides the reader through building a compiler; the machine language produced by the compiler is then executed on the machine language simulator produced in Chapter 5. Information is communicated from the compiler to the simulator in sequential files (which the students will master in Chapter 15).

Chapter 6—Object-Based Programming—begins our deeper discussion of classes. The chapter represents a wonderful opportunity for teaching data abstraction the "right way"—through a language (Java) expressly devoted to implementing abstract data types (ADTs). The chapter focuses on the essence and terminology of classes and objects. What is an object? What is a class of objects? What does the inside of an object look like? How are objects created? How are they destroyed? How do objects communicate with one another? Why are classes such a natural mechanism for packaging software as reusable componentry? The chapter discusses implementing ADTs as Java-style classes, accessing class members, enforcing information hiding with **private** instance variables, separating interface from implementation, using access methods and utility methods, initializing objects with constructors (and using overloaded constructors). The chapter discusses declaring and using constant objects, composition—the process of building classes that have references to objects as members, the **this** reference that enables an object to "know itself," dynamic memory allocation, static class members for containing and manipulating class-wide data and examples of popular abstract data types such as stacks and queues. The chapter exercises challenge the student to develop classes for complex numbers, rational numbers, times, dates, rectangles, huge integers, a class for playing Tic-Tac-Toe, a savings account class and a class for holding sets of integers.

Chapter 7—Object-Oriented Programming—discusses the relationships among classes of objects and programming with related classes. How can we exploit commonality between classes of objects to minimize the amount of work it takes to build large software systems? What is polymorphism? What does it mean to "program in the general" rather than "programming in the specific?" How does programming in the general make it easy to modify systems and add new features with minimal effort? How can we program for a whole category of objects rather than programming individually for each type of object? The chapter deals with one of the most fundamental capabilities of object-oriented programming languages, inheritance, which is a form of software reusability in which new classes are developed quickly and easily by absorbing the capabilities of existing classes and adding appropriate new capabilities. The chapter discusses the notions of superclasses and subclasses, **protected** members, direct superclasses, indirect superclasses, use of constructors in superclasses and subclasses, and software engineering with inheritance. The chapter compares inheritance ("is a" relationships) with composition ("has a" relationships). A feature of the chapter is its several substantial case studies. In particular, a lengthy case study implements a point, circle and cylinder class hierarchy. The exercises ask the student to compare the creation of new classes by inheritance vs. composition; to extend the inheritance hierarchies discussed in the chapter; to write an inheritance hierarchy for quadrilaterals, trapezoids, parallelograms, rectangles and squares; and to create a more general shape hierarchy with two-dimensional shapes and three-dimensional shapes. The chapter explains polymorphic behavior. When many classes are related through inheritance to a common superclass, each subclass object may be treated as a superclass object. This enables programs to be written in a general manner independent of the specific types of the subclass objects. New kinds of objects can be handled by the same program, thus making systems more extensible. Polymorphism enables programs to eliminate complex **switch** logic in favor of simpler "straight-line" logic. A screen manager of a video game, for example, can simply send a "draw" message to every object in a linked list of objects to be drawn. Each object knows how to draw itself. A new type of object can be added to the program without modifying that program as long as that new object also knows how to draw itself. This style of programming is typically used to implement today's popular graphical user interfaces. The chapter distinguishes between abstract classes (from which objects cannot be instantiated) and concrete classes (from which objects can be instantiated). Abstract classes are useful for providing an inheritable interface to classes throughout the hierarchy. A feature of the chapter is its two major polymorphism case studies—a payroll system and shape, point, circle, cylinder hierarchy headed up by an abstract class. The chapter exercises ask the student to discuss a number of conceptual issues and approaches, work with abstract classes, develop a basic graphics package, modify the chapter's employee class—and pursue all these projects with polymorphic programming.

   Chapter 8—Strings and Characters—deals with processing words, sentences, characters and groups of characters. The key difference between Java and C here is that Java strings are objects. This makes string manipulation more convenient and much safer than in C where string and array manipulations are based on dangerous pointers. We present classes **String**, **StringBuffer**, **Character** and **StringTokenizer**. For each we provide extensive live-code examples demonstrating most of their methods "in action." In all cases we show output windows so the reader can see the precise effects of each of the string and character manipulations we discuss. Students will enjoy the card shuffling and dealing example (which they will enhance in the exercises to the later chapters on graphics and multimedia). A key feature of the chapter is an extensive collection of challenging string manipulation exercises related to limericks, pig Latin, text analysis, word processing, printing dates in various formats, check protection, writing the word equivalent of a check amount, Morse Code and metric-to-English conversions. Students will enjoy the challenges of developing their own spell checker and crossword puzzle generator.

Advanced Topics

Chapters 9, 10 and 11 were co-authored with our colleague, Mr. Tem Nieto of Deitel & Associates, Inc. Tem's infinite patience, attention to detail, illustration skills and creativity are apparent throughout these chapters. [Take a fast peek at Figure 10.27 to see what happens when we turn Tem loose!] **Chapter 9—Graphics**—begins a run of chapters that present the multimedia "sizzle" of Java. We consider Chapters 9 through 18 to be the book's advanced material. Professors who have been teaching C and/or C++ at the introductory level will find that the Java topics open all kinds of opportunities to explore new areas. This is "fun stuff." Traditional C and C++ programming are pretty much confined to character-mode input/output. Some versions of C++ are supported by platform-dependent class libraries that can do graphics, but using these libraries makes your applications nonportable. Java's graphics capabilities are platform independent and hence, portable—and we mean portable in a worldwide sense. You can develop graphics-intensive Java applets and distribute them over the World Wide Web to colleagues everywhere and they will run nicely on the local Java platforms. We discuss graphics contexts and graphics objects; drawing strings, characters and bytes; color and font control; screen manipulation and paint modes; and drawing lines, rectangles, rounded rectangles, 3-dimensional rectangles, ovals, arcs and polygons. The chapter has 39 figures that painstakingly illustrate each of these graphics capabilities with live-code examples, appealing screen outputs, detailed features tables and detailed line art. Some of the 33 exercises challenge students to develop graphical versions of their solutions to previous exercises on Turtle Graphics, the Knight's Tour, the Tortoise and the Hare simulation, Maze Traversal and the Bucket Sort.

   Chapter 10—Basic Graphical User Interface Components—introduces the creation of applets and applications with user-friendly graphical user interfaces (GUIs). Once again, the key to Java's treatment of these subjects is that Java is platform independent. A GUI-based applet or application developed once will run on all Java platforms. Actually, the user interface components will appear a bit different on each platform, because Java "ties into" the local GUI system, be it Microsoft's Windows, Apple's Macintosh, Motif, Sun's OpenWindows, OS/2's Warp or any other system. So Java applications running on a platform with which you are familiar will take on the appearance of GUI applications running on that platform. GUI development is a huge topic, so we divided into two chapters. These chapters truly cover the material in depth to enable you to build "industrial-strength" GUI interfaces. Through its 49 programs, tables and line drawings, the chapter illustrates GUI design principles, the **java.awt** (Abstract Windowing Toolkit) hierarchy, labels, push buttons, lists, text fields, choice buttons, check boxes, radio buttons, panels, handling mouse events, handling keyboard events and using three of Java's simpler GUI layout managers, namely **FlowLayout**, **BorderLayout** and **GridLayout**. The 26 exercises challenge the student to create specific GUIs, exercise various GUI features, develop drawing programs that let the user draw with the mouse and control fonts.

   Chapter 11—Advanced Graphical User Interface Components—continues the discussion started in Chapter 10. Here, we continue the detailed walkthrough of Java's GUI capabilities. The 30 figures walk the reader through the creation and manipulation of more advanced GUI components including text areas, canvases, scrollbars, custom components, frames, menus and dialog boxes. The chapter concludes with discussions of Java's more sophisticated layout managers, namely **CardLayout** and **GridBagLayout**, and shows how to develop custom layout mangers. The exercises encourage the reader to develop more substantial GUIs with the advanced components presented in the chapter.

Chapter 12—Exception Handling—is one of the most important chapters in the book from the standpoint of building so-called "mission-critical" or "business-critical" applications that require high degrees of robustness and fault tolerance. Things do go wrong, and at today's computer speeds—commonly 100 million operations per second— if they can go wrong they will, and rather quickly at that. Programmers are often a bit naive about using components. They ask, "How do I request that a component do something for me?" They also ask "What value(s) does that component return to me to indicate it has performed the job I asked it to do?" But programmers also need to be concerned with, "What happens when the component I call on to do a job experiences difficulty? How will that component signal that it had a problem?" In Java, when a component (i.e., a class object) encounters difficulty, it can "throw an exception." The environment of that component is programmed to "catch" that exception and deal with it. Java's exception handling capabilities are geared to an object-oriented world in which programmers construct systems largely from reusable, prefabricated components built by other programmers. To use a Java component, you need to know not only how that component behaves when "things go well," but also what exceptions that component throws when "things go poorly." The chapter distinguishes between rather serious system **Error**s (normally beyond the control of most programs) and **Exception**s that programs generally want to deal with to ensure robust operation. The chapter discusses the vocabulary of exception handling. The **try** block executes program code that may execute properly or may **throw** an exception if something goes wrong. Associated with each **try** block are one or more **catch** blocks that handle thrown exceptions attempting to restore order and keep systems "up and running" rather than letting them "crash." Even if order can not be fully restored, the **catch** blocks may perform operations that enable a system to continue executing, albeit at reduced levels of performance—such activity is often referred to as "graceful degradation." Regardless of whether exceptions are thrown or not, a **finally** block accompanying a **try** block will always execute; the **finally** block normally performs cleanup operations like closing files and releasing resources acquired in the **try** block. The chapter does contain several nice live-code examples, but its material is more crucial to many of the live-code examples in Chapters 13 through 18. A feature of the chapter is the enumeration of the various **Error**s and **Exception**s of the various Java packages. The chapter has some of the most appropriate quotes in the book thanks to the painstaking research performed by Barbara Deitel. You recall that we added *Testing and Debugging Tips* as a new feature to *Java How to Program* over the set of tips we had used in our C and C++ books. The vast majority of these *Testing and Debugging Tips* fell naturally out of the material in Chapter 12 which has 16 of the 29 mentioned in the entire text. Please take exception handling seriously. The mechanism chosen by Java's designers is similar to that used by C++. It is certain to be widely employed in the object-oriented programming community.

Chapter 13—Multithreading—deals with how to program applets and applications that can perform multiple activities in parallel. Although our bodies are quite good at this (breathing, eating, blood circulation, vision, hearing, etc. can all occur in parallel), our conscious minds have trouble with this. Computers used to be built with a single rather expensive processor. Today processors are becoming so inexpensive that it is possible to build computers with many processors that work in parallel—such computers are called multiprocessors. The trend is clearly towards computers that can perform many tasks in parallel. Most of today's programming languages, including C and C++, do not include features for expressing parallel operations. These languages are often referred to as "sequential" programming languages or "single-thread-of-control" languages. Java includes capabilities to enable multithreaded applications, i.e., applications that can specify that multiple activities are to occur in parallel. This makes Java better prepared to deal with the more sophisticated multimedia, networked-based multiprocessor-based applications programmers will be introducing in the mid-to-late 1990s. As we will see, multithreading is even effective on single-processor systems. This is one of the key capabilities of Java that convinced us to invest in this language and write *Java How to Program.* For years, the "old guy" taught operating systems courses and wrote operating systems textbooks, but he never had a multithreaded language like Java available to demonstrate the concepts. In this chapter, we really enjoyed presenting multithreaded programs that demonstrate clearly the kinds of problems that can occur in parallel programming. There are all kinds of subtleties that develop in parallel programs that you simply never think about when writing sequential programs. A feature of the chapter is the extensive set of examples that show these problems and how to solve them. Another feature is the implementation of the "circular buffer," a popular means of coordinating control between asynchronous, concurrent "producer" and "consumer" processes that, if left to run without synchronization, would cause data to be lost and/or duplicated incorrectly, most likely with devastating results. We discuss the monitor construct developed by C. A. R. Hoare and implemented in Java; this is a standard topic in operating systems courses. The chapter discusses threads and thread methods. It walks through the various thread states and state transitions with a detailed line drawing showing the life-cycle of a thread. We discuss thread priorities and thread scheduling and use a line drawing to show Java's fixed-priority scheduling mechanism. We examine a producer/consumer relationship without synchronization, observe the trouble it causes and then solve the problem with thread synchronization. We implement a producer/consumer relationship with a circular buffer and proper synchronization with a monitor. We discuss daemon threads that kind of "hang around" and do useful work (like "garbage collection" of discarded memory) when excess processor time is available. We discuss the **Runnable** interface that enables you to run objects as threads without having to subclass them from class **Thread** and we indicate that the notion of "interface" is Java's replacement for the dangerous (albeit powerful) feature of C++ called multiple inheritance. We close with a discussion of thread groups which, for example, enable separation to be enforced between system threads like the garbage collector and user threads. The chapter has a nice complement of 26 exercises. The featured exercise is the classic readers and writers problem, a favorite in upper-level computer science courses in operating systems; citations appear in the exercises for students who wish to research this topic. This is an important problem in database-oriented transaction-processing systems. It raises subtle issues of solving problems in concurrency control while ensuring that every separate activity that needs to receive service does indeed do so without the possibility of "indefinite postponement" which could cause some activities never to receive service—a condition also referred to as "starvation." Operating systems professors will enjoy having Java-literate students. We can expect all kinds of progress in the field of parallel programming as Java's multithreading capabilities enable large numbers of computing students to pursue parallel-programming class projects. When these students enter industry over the next several years, we expect a surge in parallel systems programming and parallel applications programming. We have been predicting this for decades—Java will make it a reality.

If this is your first Java book and you are an experienced computing professional, you may well be thinking, "Hey, this just keeps getting better and better. I can't wait to get started programming in this language. It will let me do all kinds of stuff I'd like to do, but that was never easy for me to do with the other languages I've used." You've got it right. Java is an enabler. So if you liked the multithreading discussion, hold onto your hat, because Java will let you program multimedia applications and make them available instantaneously over the World Wide Web. **Chapter 14—Multimedia: Images, Animation and Audio**—deals with Java's capabilities for making computer applications come alive. It is remarkable that students in first programming courses will be writing applications with all these capabilities. The possibilities are intriguing. Imagine having access (over the Internet and through CD-ROM technology) to vast libraries of graphics images, audios and videos and being able to weave your own together with those in the libraries to form creative applications. Already more than half the new computers sold come "multimedia equipped." Within just a few years, new machines equipped for multimedia will be as common as machines with floppy disks today. We can't wait to see the kinds of term papers and classroom presentations students will be making when they have access to vast public domain libraries of images, drawings, voices, pictures, videos, animations and the like. A "paper" when most of us were in the earlier grades was a collection of characters, possibly handwritten, possibly typewritten. A "paper" in just a few short years will become a multimedia "extravaganza" that makes the subject matter come alive. It will hold your interest, pique your curiosity, make you feel what the subjects of the paper felt when they were making history. Multimedia will make your science labs much more exciting. Textbooks will come alive. Instead of looking at a static picture of some phenomenon, you will watch that phenomenon occur in a colorful, animated, presentation with sounds, videos and various other effects. It will leverage the learning process. People will be able to learn more, learn it in more depth and experience more viewpoints. The chapter discusses images and image manipulation, audios, animation, flicker elimination and the monitoring of "media clips" with **MediaTracker** objects. When we first learned Java, we decided to put a spinning Deitel & Associates, Inc. logo up on our Web site. We enjoyed using Java's features to do this and rapidly ran into the kinds of flicker problems than can hurt the effectiveness of animations. We evolved a sequence of programs that incrementally applied Java's flicker-elimination techniques. So the programs in this chapter are genuine hands-on, real-world solutions by real programmers solving a common problem (flicker elimination) in multimedia applications. A feature of the chapter is the discussion of image maps that enable a program to sense the presence of the mouse cursor over a region of an image, even without clicking the mouse. We present a live-code image map application with the icons Prentice Hall artists created for our *Java Multimedia Cyber Classroom* programming tips. As the user moves the mouse cursor across the six icon images of our bug character, the type of tip is displayed, either "Good Programming Practice" for the thumbs-up icon, "Portability Tip" for the bug with the suitcase icon, and so on. Once you have read the chapter, you will be eager to try out all these techniques, so we have included 67 (!) problems to challenge and entertain you. Here are the exercises that you may want to turn into term projects:

Analog Clock	Flight Simulator	Physics Demo: Bouncing Ball
Animation	Floor Planner	Physics Demo: Kinetics
Arithmetic Tutor	Game of Pool	Player Piano
Artist	Horse Race	Random Inter-Image Transition
Automated Teller Machine	Image Flasher	Randomly Erasing an Image
Background Audio	Image Zooming	Reaction Time Tester
Bubble Help	Jigsaw Puzzle Generator	Rotating Image
Calendar/Tickler File	Juggling Teacher	Roulette
Calling Attention to an Image	Karaoke	Screensaver
Coloring B/W Photographs	Knight's Tour Walker	Scrolling Image Marquee
Craps	Limericks	Scrolling Test Marquee
Crossword	Maze Generator and Walker	Sheet Music Generator/Player
Digital Clock	Multimedia Aerobics	Shuffleboard
Dynamic Kaleidoscope	Multimedia Authoring System	Story Teller
Dynamic Customized Newsletter	Multimedia Simpletron Simulator	Synthesizer
Dynamic Stock Evaluator	Music Teacher	Text Flasher
Fashion Designer	One-Armed Bandit	Tortoise and the Hare
15 Puzzle	Pendulum,	Towers of Hanoi
Fireworks Designer	Pinball Machine	Video Games

You are going to have a great time attacking some of these problems! Some will take a few hours, some are great term projects and some will probably seem unconquerable. We see all kinds of opportunities for multimedia electives starting to appear in the university computing curriculum. We really hope that you will have contests with your classmates to develop the best solutions to several of these problems.

Chapter 15—Files and Streams—deals with input/output that is accomplished through streams of data directed to and from files. This is one of the most important chapters for programmers who will be developing commercial applications. The chapter begins with an introduction to the data hierarchy from bits, to bytes, to fields, to records, to files. Next, Java's simple view of files and streams is presented. We then present a walkthrough of the 23 classes of Java's extensive input/output files and streams class hierarchy. We put many of these classes to work in live-code examples in this chapter and in Chapter 16, "Networking." We show how programs pass data to secondary storage devices like disks and how programs retrieve data already stored on those devices. Sequential-access files are discussed using a series of three programs that show how to open and close files, how to store data sequentially in a file and how to read data sequentially from a file. Random-access files are discussed using a series of four programs that show how to sequentially create a file for random access, how to read and write data to a file with random access, and how to read data sequentially from a randomly accessed file. The fourth random-access program combines many of the techniques of accessing files both sequentially and randomly into a complete transaction processing program. We discuss buffering and how it helps programs that do significant amounts of input/output perform better. We discuss class **File** that programs use to obtain a variety of information about files and directories. We explain how objects can be output to, and input from, secondary storage devices. Students in our industry seminars have told us that after studying the material on file processing, they were able to produce substantial file-processing programs that were immediately useful to their organizations. The exercises ask the student to implement a variety of programs that build and process both sequential-access files and random-access files.

Chapter 16—Networking—deals with applets and applications that can communicate over computer networks. What is a client? What is a server? How do clients ask servers to perform their services? How do servers give results back to clients? What is a URL (uniform resource locator)? How can a Java program load other World Wide Web pages? How can I use Java to develop collaborative applications? This chapter gives you what you need to begin implementing client/server networked Java programs immediately. We show how to write programs that "walk the Web." We discuss manipulating URLs, using a URL stream connection to read a file on a server, establishing simple clients and servers using stream sockets, client/server interaction with stream sockets, connectionless client/server interaction with datagrams, security and the network, and forthcoming networking and security APIs. A key feature of the chapter is the live-code implementation of a collaborative client/server Tic-Tac-Toe game in which two clients play Tic-Tac-Toe with one another arbitrated by multithreaded server—great stuff! The multithreaded server architecture is exactly what is used today in popular UNIX, OS/2 and Windows NT network servers. The chapter has a nice collection of exercises including several suggested modifications to the multithreaded server example.

Chapter 17—Data Structures—is particularly valuable in second- and third-level university courses. The chapter discusses the techniques used to create and manipulate dynamic data structures such as linked lists, stacks, queues (i.e., waiting lines) and trees. The chapter begins with discussions of self-referential classes and dynamic memory allocation. We proceed with a discussion of how to create and maintain various dynamic data structures. For each type of data structure, we present live-code programs and show sample outputs. Although it is valuable to know how these classes are implemented, Java programmers will quickly discover that many of the data structures they need are already available in class libraries such as Java's own **java.util** that we discuss in Chapter 18. The chapter helps the student master Java-style references (i.e., Java's replacement for the more dangerous pointers of C and C++). One problem when working with references is that students may have trouble visualizing the data structures and how their nodes are linked together. So we have included illustrations that show the links and sequence in which they are created. The binary tree example is a nice capstone for the study of references and dynamic data structures. This example creates a binary tree; enforces duplicate elimination; and introduces recursive preorder, inorder and postorder tree traversals. Students have a genuine sense of accomplishment when they study and implement this example. They particularly appreciate seeing that the inorder traversal prints the node values in sorted order. The chapter includes a substantial collection of exercises. A highlight of the exercises is the special section "Building Your Own Compiler." This exercise is based on earlier exercises that walk the student through the development of an infix-to-postfix-conversion program and a postfix-expression-evaluation program. We then modify the postfix evaluation algorithm to generate machine-language code. The compiler places this code in a file (using techniques the student mastered in Chapter 15). Students then run the machine language produced by their compilers on the software simulators they built in the exercises of Chapter 5! The 34 exercises include a supermarket simulation using queueing, recursively searching a list, recursively printing a list backwards, binary tree node deletion, level-order traversal of a binary tree, printing trees, writing a portion of an optimizing compiler, writing an interpreter, inserting/deleting anywhere in a linked list, analyzing the performance of binary tree searching and sorting and implementing an indexed list class.

Chapter 18—Java Utilities Package and Bit Manipulation—walks through the classes of the **java.util** package and discuss each of Java's bitwise operators. This is a nice chapter for reinforcing the notion of reuse. When classes already exist, it is much faster to develop software by simply reusing these classes than by "reinventing the wheel." Classes are included in class libraries because the classes are generally useful, correct, performance tuned, portability certified and/or for a variety of other reasons. Someone has invested considerable work in preparing these classes so why should you write your own? We believe the world's class libraries will grow at a phenomenal rate. If this is the case, then your skill and value as a programmer will depend on your familiarity with what classes exist and how you can reuse them cleverly to develop high-quality software rapidly. University data structures courses will be changing drastically over the next several years because most important data structures are already implemented in widely available class libraries. This chapter discusses many classes. Two of the most useful are **Vector** (a dynamic array that can grow and shrink as necessary) and **Stack** (a dynamic data structure that allows insertions and deletions from only one end—called the top—thus ensuring last-in-first-out behavior). The beauty of studying these two classes is that they are related through inheritance as discussed in Chapter 7, so the **java.util** package itself implements some classes in terms of others thus avoiding reinventing that wheel and taking advantage of reuse. We also discuss classes **Dictionary**, **Hashtable**, **Date**, **Observable**, **Observer** (actually an interface), **Properties** (for creating and manipulating persistent **Hashtable**s), **Random** and **BitSet**. The discussion of **BitSet** include live code for one of the classic applications of **BitSet**s, namely the *Sieve of Eratosthenes* used for determining prime numbers. The chapter discusses in detail Java's powerful bit manipulation capabilities that enable programmers to exercise lower-level hardware capabilities. This helps programs process bit strings, set individual bits on or off and store information more compactly. Such capabilities—inherited from C—are characteristic of low-level assembly languages and are valued by programmers writing system software such as operating systems and networking software. The chapter concludes with 19 exercises

Appendix A—Java Demos—presents a huge collection of the best Java demos Abbey Deitel was able to track down on the Web. Many of these sites make their source code available to you, so you can download the code and add your own features—a truly great way to learn Java! We encourage our students to do this and we're amazed at the results! Abbey has requested that you send her the URLs of your favorite sites that you would like to share with others. Please write to Abbey c/o **deitel@deitel.com**. She will put links to them in our "Best Java Demos" list on our Web sites. You should start your search by checking out Gamelan's treasure trove at **http://www.gamelan.com.** You can save time finding the best demos by checking out the Java Applet Rating Service at **http://www.jars.com**. Here's a list of Abbey's current recommendations (the URLs and descriptions of each are in Appendix A):

Angry Fish	*Dethtris Game by Ultramaster*	*Pong*
Animated Netscape Logo	*Drive a Tank*	*Rubik's Cube*
Animated SDSU Logo	Featured Games of the Week	*San Francisco Subway Map*
Animation	*15 Puzzle*	*Santa's Jolly Laughter*
ASTERNOID!	*Froggie*	*Slot Machine*
Ataxx Game	*Graffitti*	*Solitaire*
Audio Files	*Iceblox Game*	*Starbase*
Black Jack	*Java Piano*	*Stereoscopic 3D Hypercube*
Celebrity Painter	*Java Slider*	*Tennis*
Centipedo	*Jigsaw Puzzle*	*3-D Cube*
Chat	*Knight's Tour*	*Traffic Simulation*
Chess	*Marble Solitaire Game*	*3D Tetris*
Cool Beans Java Programming	*Mazda Miata Animation*	*Video Movie Clips*
Connect4	*Missile Commando*	*Visible Human Body Sections*
Crazy Counter	*Mr. Potato Head*	

Appendix B—Java Resources—presents the best resources Abbey was able to track down on the Web. This is a great way for you to get into the "world of Java." The appendix lists various Java resources (such as consortia, journals and companies that make various key Java-related products).

animated applets	documentation	learning Java
applets	downloadable applets	links to Java sites
applications	examples	lists of resources
arts and entertainment	events	lists of what is new and cool
audio sites	exercises	live chat sessions on Java
books	FAQs (frequently asked ?s)	mailing lists
Café Del Sol Java resource	Gamelan (3000 java resources)	message exchange center
Candle-Web (links to Java sites)	games	news
class hierarchy diagrams	graphics	**news:comp.lang.java**
class libraries	hottest new Java sites	newsgroups
conferences	Hot Java documentation	newsletters
consultants	HotJava newsgroup	products
contests	IDEs	projects
current information	information	publications
databases	Java Applet Rating Service	puzzles
demos (many with source code)	java@java.sun.com (get help)	reference materials
developer's kit	JavaSoft	resources
development tools	Java tools	search for applets by keywords
Digital Espresso (resources)	Java Users Group (JUGs)	seminars
discussion groups	*Java World* magazine	sites

software	tutorials for learning java	VRML browsers
Sun Microsystems	URLs for Java applets	VRML sites
SunWorld magazine online	user interface	VRML 3D graphics animations.
"The Java Developer"	utility classes	**www.gamelan.com**
trade shows	video sites	**www.javasoft.com**
training (please call us!)	Yahoo (Web search engine)	**www.javaworld.com**
tutorial called "Brewing Java"	VRML (Virtual Reality)	

Appendix C—Operator Precedence Chart—lists each of the Java operators and indicates their relative precedence and associativity. We list each operator on a separate line and include the full name of the operator.

Appendix D—ASCII Character Set—lists the characters of the ASCII (American Standard Code for Information Interchange) character set and indicates the character code value for each. Java uses the Unicode character set with 16-bit characters for representing all of the characters in the world's "commercially significant" languages. Unicode includes ASCII as a subset. Currently, most English-speaking countries are using ASCII and just beginning to experiment with Unicode. We will say more about Unicode in the Second Edition of *Java How to Program*.

Appendix E—Number Systems—discusses the binary (base 2), decimal (base 10), octal (base 8) and hexadecimal (base 16) number systems. This material is valuable for introductory courses in computer science and computer engineering. The appendix is presented with the same pedagogic learnings aids as the chapters of the book. A nice feature of the appendix is its 32 exercises, 19 of which are self-review exercises with answers.

Appendix F—Object-Oriented Elevator Simulator—walks the student through a carefully paced and substantial term project. The appendix begins with a simple introduction to object-oriented thinking so the instructor can assign the elevator case study in parallel with the early chapters of the book. These sections introduce the concepts and terminology of object orientation to help students become familiar with what objects are and how they behave. Next we present a requirements specification for a substantial object-oriented system project, namely building the elevator simulator, and we carefully guide the student through the typical phases of the object-oriented design process. By the time the student has finished the early assignments, he or she has completed a careful object-oriented design of the elevator simulator and is ready—if not anxious—to begin programming the elevator in Java.

This appendix forms the basis of a carefully paced term project that many instructors will choose to assign. A complete, multimedia-based implementation of the elevator with graphics, animation and audios is in the *Instructor's Manual* (that even has the elevator play "elevator music" when it's moving between floors!).

This appendix is one of the most important components of the *Java How to Program* learning experience. It is intended as a term project for intense first programming courses and for most second-level programming courses. We have divided the appendix into 12 carefully paced assignments that enable the student to develop the elevator in parallel with reading the appropriate chapters of the textbook. *Section F.1* begins with an introduction to object orientation. We will see that object orientation is a natural way of thinking about the world and writing computer programs. Section F.2 presents the elevator "requirements document" that describes the elevator in sufficient detail for the student to begin the design process. In Elevator Assignment 1 (Prerequisites: Chapters 1–3) the student begins the object-oriented design process by identifying the classes in the requirements document.

Classes have attributes and behaviors. Class attributes are represented in Java programs by data. In Elevator Assignment 2 (Prerequisite: Chapter 4) the student concentrates on determining the attributes of the classes needed to implement the elevator simulator. In **Elevator Assignment 3** (Prerequisite: Chapter 6) we concentrate on determining the behaviors of the classes needed to implement the elevator simulator. Behaviors are implemented in Java as methods—Java's term for the member functions with which C++ programmers are familiar. **Elevator Assignment 4** (Prerequisite: Chapter 6) concentrates on the interactions between class objects.

In **Elevator Assignment 5** (Prerequisite: Chapter 6) you begin programming the elevator simulator. For each of the classes you identified in the previous assignments, you write an appropriate class definition. Each class definition is written in a separate file with the **.java** extension. You then write a "driver" applet that tests each of these classes and attempts to run the complete elevator simulation. For this first version of the simulator, you design only a simple, text-oriented output that displays a message for each significant event that occurs. **Elevator Assignment 6** (Prerequisite: Chapter 6) discusses composition, a capability that allows you to create classes that have as members references to objects. Composition enables you to create a building class that contains references to the elevator and to the floors, and, in turn, create an elevator class that contains references to buttons.

Elevator Assignment 7 (Prerequisites: Chapters 9–11) focuses on enhancing the elevator's graphical user interface. **Elevator Assignment 8** (Prerequisites: Chapters 9–11) builds on the GUI you developed in Assignment 7; you will add to the GUI and begin graphically representing the events occurring in your simulation. **Elevator Assignment 9** (Prerequisite: Chapter 13) covers the steps necessary to provide interaction between the GUI and events generated by your simulator. The interaction in many cases will be done with multithreading. **Elevator Assignment 10** (Prerequisite: Chapter 13) covers the steps necessary to provide animation for your simulator. **Elevator Assignment 11** (Prerequisite: Chapter 14) covers the steps necessary to provide additional animation as well some audio for your simulator. **Elevator Assignment 12** (Prerequisite: Chapter 14) enhances the animation of the previous assignment. In **Section F.15** we list nine significant modifications that can be made to your elevator simulator; some of these require the data structures techniques of Chapters 17 and 18.

The Java Multimedia Cyber Classroom

We have implemented an interactive, CD-ROM-based, Windows version of *Java How to Program* called the *Java Multimedia Cyber Classroom*. It is loaded with features for learning and reference. The *Cyber Classroom* is available separately from the textbook, and is available wrapped with the textbook at a discount.

There is an introductory video with the authors overviewing the Cyber Classroom's features. The 200 live-code example Java programs in the textbook truly "come alive" in the Cyber Classroom. We have placed executables for all these examples "under the hood" of the Cyber Classroom, so if you are viewing a program and want to execute it, you simply click on the lightning bolt icon and the program will run. You will immediately see—and hear for the audio-based multimedia programs—the program's outputs. If you want to modify a program and see and hear the effects of your changes, simply click on the floppy-disk icon that causes the source code to be "lifted off" the CD and "dropped into" one of your own directories so you can edit the text, recompile the program and try out your new version. Click on the audio icon and Paul Deitel will talk about the program and "walk you through" the code. [You will not hear Harvey Deitel's voice in these audios—our friends at Prentice Hall like Paul's voice better!]

The Cyber Classroom also provides all kinds of navigational aids including extensive hyperlinking. The Cyber Classroom remembers in a "history list" recent sections you have visited and allows you to move forward or backward in that history list. The thousands of index entries are hyperlinked to their text occurrences. You can key in a term and the Cyber Classroom will locate its occurrences throughout the text. The Table of Contents entries are "hot," so clicking on a chapter name immediately takes you to that chapter. You can insert "bookmarks" at places to which you may want to return. You can even add "notes" just as you would in the margin of a textbook.

Students and professional users of our *Cyber Classrooms* tell us they like the interactivity and that the *Cyber Classroom* is an effective reference because of the extensive hyperlinking and other navigational features. We recently had an email from a person who said that he lives "in the boonies" and can not take a live course at a university, so the *Cyber Classroom* was the solution to his educational needs.

Professors have sent us emails indicating their students enjoy using the *Cyber Classroom*, spend more time on the course and master more of the material than in textbook only courses. Also, the *Cyber Classroom* helps shrink lines outside professors' offices during office hours. We have published the *C & C++ Multimedia Cyber Classroom* and hope to publish *Cyber Classroom* editions of our forthcoming *Visual Basic How to Program* and *Visual C++ How to Program* textbooks.

Acknowledgments

One of the great pleasures of writing a textbook is acknowledging the efforts of many people whose names may not appear on the cover, but whose hard work, cooperation, friendship, and understanding were crucial to the production of the book.

Three other people at Deitel & Associates, Inc. devoted long hours to this project. We would like to acknowledge the efforts of Tem Nieto, Barbara Deitel and Abbey Deitel.

Tem Nieto, a graduate of the Massachusetts Institute of Technology, is one of our full-time colleagues at Deitel & Associates, Inc. Tem teaches C, C++ and Java seminars and works with us on textbook writing, course development and multimedia authoring efforts. He is co-authoring our next book, *Visual Basic How to Program*. Tem co-authored Chapters 9, 10 and 11; Appendix F on the object-oriented, multimedia-based elevator simulator project and the Special Section entitled "Building Your Own Compiler" in Chapter 17.

Barbara Deitel managed the preparation of the manuscript and coordinated with Prentice Hall all the efforts related to production of the book. Barbara's efforts are by far the most painstaking of what we do to develop books. She has infinite patience. She handled the endless details involved in publishing an 1100-page, two-color book; a 500-page instructor's manual and the 650 megabyte CD *Cyber Classroom.* She used FrameMaker page-layout software to prepare the book. Barbara mastered this complex software package and did a marvelous job giving the book its clean style. She spent several months researching the quotes that appear at the beginning of each chapter. Barbara prepared every one of the 7824 page references in the 45-page index. She did all of this in parallel with handling her extensive responsibilities at Deitel & Associates, Inc.

Abbey Deitel, a recent graduate of Carnegie Mellon University's industrial management program, and now pursuing a management career in fashion and retailing, wrote Appendix A, "Java Demos," and Appendix B, "Java Resources" and suggested the title for the book. We asked Abbey to surf the World Wide Web and track down the best Java sites. She didn't have to go far. She immediately discovered Gamelan, a wonderful site that at the time of this writing already listed approximately 3000 significant Java resources including many nice demos. She used every major Web search engine and collected this information for you in Appendices A and B. For each resource and demo, Abbey has provided a brief explanation. She rejected hundreds of sites and has listed for you the best she could find. Abbey will be maintaining current versions of these resources and demo listings on our Web sites `http://www.prenhall.com/deitel` and `http://www.deitel.com`. She asks that you send URLs for your favorite sites to her by email at `deitel@deitel.com` and she will post links to these on our sites.

We are fortunate to have been able to work on this project with a talented and dedicated team of publishing professionals at Prentice Hall. This book happened because of the encouragement, enthusiasm, and persistence of our publisher, Alan Apt, and his boss—one of the best friends we've ever had in publishing—Marcia Horton, Vice President and Editor-in-Chief of Prentice-Hall's Engineering and Computer Science Division. Laura Steele coordinated the complex reviewer effort on the manuscript. Sondra Chavez served as developmental editor and was always incredibly helpful when we needed assistance— her ebullience and good cheer are sincerely appreciated. Camille Trentacoste did a marvelous job as production manager.

The *Java Multimedia Cyber Classroom* is being developed in parallel with *Java How to Program.* We sincerely appreciate the multimedia insight, savvy and technical expertise of our editor Mark Taub. He did a remarkable job bringing Prentice Hall's first multimedia textbook, the *C & C++ Multimedia Cyber Classroom,* to publication under a tight schedule. We also want to thank Logan Campbell, President of the Prentice Hall Professional and Technical Reference Division, for his trust and confidence in us, and for making impressive resources available to our projects. Logan, too, is one of the best friends we've had in publishing.

We owe special thanks to the creativity of Tamara Newnam who did the art work for our programming tips icons and the cover. She created the delightful creature who shares with you the book's programming tips. Please help us name this endearing little bug. Some early suggestions: D. Bug, InterGnat, DeetleBug (an unfortunate moniker that was attached to the old guy in high school) and the "drunk bug on the cover."

We sincerely appreciate the efforts of our reviewers:

Peter Jones (JavaSoft)

Ian Smith (Georgia Institute of Technology)

Jim Roberts (Carnegie-Mellon University)
Andrew M. Brown (Bell Laboratories)
Gordon Bradley (Naval Postgraduate School)
Richard Enbody (Michigan State University)
Ken Merson (Borland)
Mark Ellis (Reuters)

Under an impossibly tight time schedule, they scrutinized every aspect of the text and made countless suggestions for improving the accuracy and completeness of the presentation.

We would sincerely appreciate your comments, criticisms, corrections, and suggestions for improving the text. Please send your suggestions for improving and adding to our list of *Good Programming Practices, Common Programming Errors, Testing and Debugging Tips, Performance Tips, Portability Tips,* and *Software Engineering Observations.* We will acknowledge all contributors in the next edition of our book. Please address all correspondence to our email address:

deitel@deitel.com

or write us as follows:

Harvey M. Deitel (author)
Paul J. Deitel (author)
c/o Computer Science Editor
College Book Editorial
Prentice Hall
1 Lake Street
Upper Saddle River, New Jersey 07458

We will respond immediately. Well, that's it for now. Welcome to the new and exciting world of Java programming. We hope you enjoy this look at contemporary applications development using the Internet, the World Wide Web, multimedia and multithreading. Good luck!

Dr. Harvey M. Deitel
Paul J. Deitel

About the Authors

Dr. Harvey M. Deitel, CEO of Deitel & Associates, Inc., has 35 years experience in the computing field including extensive industry and academic experience. He is one of the world's leading computer science instructors and seminar presenters. Dr. Deitel earned B.S. and M.S. degrees from the Massachusetts Institute of Technology and a Ph.D. from Boston University. He worked on the pioneering virtual memory operating systems projects at IBM and MIT that developed techniques widely implemented today in systems like UNIX, OS/2, and Windows NT. He has 20 years of college teaching experience including earning tenure and serving as the Chairman of the Computer Science Department at

Boston College. He is author or co-author of more than a dozen books and is currently writing five more. With translations published in Japanese, Russian, Spanish, Chinese, Korean, and French, Dr. Deitel's texts have earned international recognition.

Paul J. Deitel, Executive Vice President of Deitel & Associates, Inc., is a graduate of the Massachusetts Institute of Technology's Sloan School of Management where he received a B.S. in Management with a specialization in Information Technology. Through Deitel & Associates, Inc. he has delivered Java, C and C++ courses for industry clients including Digital Equipment Corporation, Sun Microsystems, Rogue Wave Software, Software 2000, Computervision, Cambridge Technology Partners, Open Environment Corporation, One Wave, Hyperion Software, Lucent Technologies, Adra Systems, Entergy, CableData Systems and IBM. He has lectured on C++ for the Boston Chapter of the Association for Computing Machinery and will be delivering intermediate and advanced Java courses at the C++ World conference presented by SIGS Publications. He teaches Java internationally. He is the co-author of nine books with Harvey Deitel and is currently writing five more.

The Deitels are co-authors of the world's best-selling introductory college computer science textbooks, *C How to Program:* Second Edition and *C++ How to Program* (both published in 1994 by Prentice Hall). The Deitels are also co-authors of the *C & C++ Multimedia Cyber Classroom*—Prentice Hall's first multimedia-based textbook—and the forthcoming *Java Multimedia Cyber Classroom.*

About Deitel & Associates, Inc.

Deitel & Associates, Inc. is an internationally recognized firm specializing in programming languages and object technology education. The company provides courses on Java, C++, C, Visual Basic, and Object-Oriented Analysis and Design. The principals of Deitel & Associates, Inc. are Dr. Harvey M. Deitel and Paul J. Deitel. The company's clients include some of the world's largest computer companies and business organizations. Through its publishing partnership with Prentice Hall, Deitel & Associates, Inc. publishes leading-edge programming textbooks, professional books and interactive, CD-ROM based multimedia *Cyber Classrooms*. Deitel & Associates, Inc. can be reached via email at

`deitel@deitel.com`

To learn more about Deitel & Associates, Inc. and its on-site course curriculum, visit:

`http://www.deitel.com`

To learn more about Deitel & Deitel Prentice Hall publications, visit:

`http://www.prenhall.com/deitel`

1

Introduction to Computers and Java Applets

Objectives

- To understand basic computer science concepts.
- To become familiar with different types of programming languages.
- To understand the Java program development environment.
- To be able to write simple Java programs.
- To be able to use simple input and output statements.
- To become familiar with fundamental data types.
- To be able to use arithmetic operators.
- To understand the precedence of arithmetic operators.
- To be able to write simple decision-making statements.

Our life is frittered away by detail ... Simplify, simplify.
Henry Thoreau

High thoughts must have high language.
Aristophanes

My object all sublime
I shall achieve in time.
W. S. Gilbert

Get hold of portable property.
Charles Dickens, *Great Expectations*

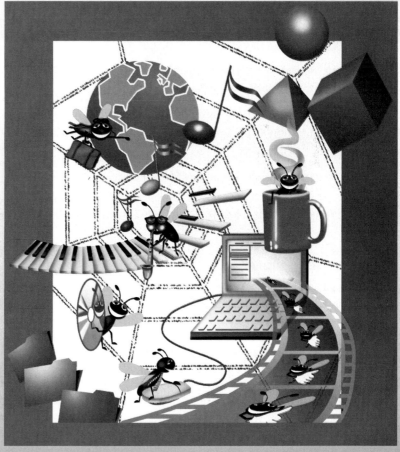

Outline

Summary • Terminology • Common Programming Errors • Good Programming Practices • Performance Tip • Portability Tips • Software Engineering Observations • Self-Review Exercises • Answers to Self-Review Exercises • Exercises

1.1 Introduction

Welcome to Java! We have worked hard to create what we hope will be an informative, entertaining and challenging learning experience for you. Java is a powerful computer programming language that is fun to use for novices while simultaneously being appropriate for experienced programmers bulding substantial information systems. *Java How to Program* is designed to be an effective learning tool for each of these audiences.

How can one book appeal to both groups? The answer is that the common core of the book emphasizes achieving program *clarity* through the proven techniques of *structured programming* and *object-oriented programming*. Nonprogrammers will learn programming the right way from the beginning. We have attempted to write in a clear and straightforward manner. The book is abundantly illustrated. Perhaps most importantly, the book presents a huge number of working Java programs and shows the outputs produced when those programs are run on a computer.

The early chapters introduce the fundamentals of computers, computer programming, and the Java computer programming language. Novices who have taken our courses tell us that the material in those chapters presents a solid foundation for the deeper treatment of Java in the later chapters. Experienced programmers typically read the early chapters quickly and find that the treatment of Java in the later chapters is rigorous and challenging.

Many experienced programmers have told us that they appreciate our treatment of structured programming. Often they have been programming in structured languages like C or Pascal, but because they were never formally introduced to structured programming, they are not writing the best possible code in these languages. As they review structured programming in the chapter, "Control Structures," they are able to improve their C and Pascal programming styles as well. So whether you are a novice or an experienced programmer, there is much here to inform, entertain, and challenge you.

Most people are familiar with the exciting things computers do. Using this textbook, you will learn how to command computers to do those things. It is *software* (i.e., the instructions you write to command the computer to perform *actions* and make *decisions*) that controls computers (often referred to as *hardware*), and Java is one of today's most popular software development languages. Java was developed by Sun Microsystems and is available free over the Internet from the Sun site `http://www.javasoft.com`.

The use of computers is increasing in almost every field of endeavor. In an era of steadily rising costs, computing costs have been decreasing dramatically because of the rapid developments in both hardware and software technology. Computers that might have filled large rooms and cost millions of dollars two decades ago can now be inscribed on the surfaces of silicon chips smaller than a fingernail, and that cost perhaps a few dollars each. Ironically, silicon is one of the most abundant materials on the earth—it is an ingredient in common sand. Silicon chip technology has made computing so economical that approximately 200 million general-purpose computers are in use worldwide helping people in business, industry, government, and their personal lives. That number could easily double in a few years.

This book will challenge you for several reasons. Your peers over the last few years probably learned C or Pascal as their first programming language. They probably learned the programming methodology called *structured programming*. You will learn both structured programming and the exciting newer methodology, *object-oriented programming*. Why do we teach both? We certainly anticipate that object-orientation will be the key programming methodology for the mid-to-late 1990s. So you will build and work with many *objects* in this course. But you will discover that the internal structure of those objects is often best built using structured programming techniques. Also, the logic of manipulating objects is occasionally best expressed with structured programming.

Another reason we present both methodologies is that over the next decade there will be a massive migration from C-based systems (built primarily with structured programming techniques) to C++ and Java-based systems (built primarily with object-oriented programming techniques). There is a huge amount of so-called "legacy C code" in place because C has been in use for a quarter of a century and its use in recent years has been increasing dramatically. Once people learn C++ and/or Java, they find these languages to be more powerful than C, and these people often choose to move their programming project to C++ and/or Java. They begin converting their legacy systems, a process that is relatively straightforward. Then they begin employing the object-oriented programming capabilities of C++ and/or Java to realize the full benefits of these languages.

Java is certain to become the implementation language of choice in the 1990s for implementing Internet-based applications. Why is Java an attractive first programming language? There are many reasons. Each of them individually may seem attractive, but perhaps not attractive enough to justify switching from "main-line," industry-proven languages like C and C++. But taken as a whole, Java provides a very attractive package for advancing the state of programming language education especially at the introductory and intermediate levels. Over the near term C, and especially C++, are secure as the "heavy-duty" implementation languages programmers need to build the complex, large-scale systems to support their day-to-day operations. For the near term, Java will seem to many people a nice language for making web pages "come alive." But as Java evolves, people will start to see it as a perfectly viable, if not preferred language, for meeting most of an organizations programming needs.

For many years languages like C and C++ appealed to universities because of their portability. Introductory courses could be offered in these languages on any hardware/operating system combination as long as a C/C++ compiler was available.

But the programming world has become more complex and more demanding. Today users want applications with graphical user interfaces (GUIs). They want applications that enable them to use the multimedia capabilities of graphics, images, animation, audio, and even video. They want applications that can run on computer networks like the Internet and communicate with other applications. They want applications that can take advantage of the flexibility and performance improvements of multithreading. They want applications with richer file processing than C or C++. They want these applications that are not limited to their desktop or even to some local organization network, but that can integrate Internet components as well. They want applications that can be written quickly and correctly in a manner that takes advantage of a world of "reuse, reuse, reuse." They want access to a growing universe of reusable software components. And programmers want all these benefits in a truly portable manner so that applications written on one platform will run without modification on any other. Java offers all these benefits to the programming community.

Another reason Java is attractive for university courses is that it is fully object oriented. One reason that C++ use has grown so quickly is that it extends C programming into the arena of object orientation. For the huge community of C programmers this has been a powerful advantage. C++ includes ANSI/ISO C and offers the ability to do object-oriented programming as well. C has been around since 1969. During that time, an enormous amount of C code has been written. Because C++ includes C, many organizations find it to be an ideal next step. They can take their C code, compile it, often with little or few nominal changes, in a C++ compiler and continue writing C-like code while their programmers master the object paradigm. Then the programmers can gradually migrate portions of the legacy C code into C++ as time permits. New systems can be entirely written in object-oriented C++. Initially, such strategies have been very appealing to many organizations. The downside is that even after adopting this strategy, companies tend to continue producing C-like code for many years. This, of course, means that they do not quickly realize the full benefits of object-oriented programming. Many organizations wish they could plunge 100% into object-oriented development, but the realities of mountains of legacy code often prevent this.

Java is a fully object-oriented language. You cannot write C-like so called procedural programs in Java. You must create and manipulate objects. For universities this is power-fully appealing. Students will learn object-oriented programming from the start. They will simply think in an object-oriented manner.

Here, too, there is a trade-off. Organizations turning to Java for new applications development do not want to convert all their legacy code to Java. So Java allows for so-called *native code.* This means that existing C code and C++ code can be integrated with Java code. Although this may seem a bit awkward (and it certainly is), it presents a prag-matic solution to a problem most organizations face.

Java is currently available from Sun Microsystems at no charge. Anyone can download over the Internet the complete Java Developer's Kit (JDK) from the Sun Microsystems World Wide Web site **http://www.javasoft.com** (don't wait until the last minute to do so however, because, as you can guess this is a busy site). The fact that Java is free is appealing to universities facing tight budgets and lengthy budget planning cycles. Also, as bug fixes and new versions of Java become available, these become available immediately over the Internet, so universities can keep their Java software literally up to the minute.

Can Java be taught in a first programming course—the intended audience for this book? We think so. Prior to writing this book, Deitel & Associates, Inc. instructors taught 24 Java courses to over 350 people at all levels of expertise including many nonprogram-mers. We found that nonprogrammers become productive faster with Java than with C or C++. They were anxious to experiment with Java's powerful features for graphics, graph-ical user interfaces, multimedia, animation, multithreading, networking and the like—and they were successful building substantial Java programs even in their first courses.

For many years, the programming language Pascal was the preferred vehicle for use in introductory and intermediate programming courses. Many people said that C was too dif-ficult a language for these courses. In 1992, we published the first edition of *C How to Pro-gram,* in an attempt to get the universities to try C instead of Pascal in these courses. We used the exact same pedagogic approach we had used in our university courses for a dozen years, but wrapped the concepts in C rather than Pascal. We found that students were able to handle the C at about the same level as the Pascal. But there was one noticeable differ-ence. Students expressed their appreciation that they were learning a language (C) likely to be valuable to them in industry.

Our industry clients appreciated the availability of C-literate graduates who could be put to work immediately on substantial projects rather than having to first go through costly and time-consuming educational programs.

The first edition of *C How to Program* included a 60-page introduction to C++ and object-oriented programming. We saw C++ coming on strong, but we felt it would be at least a few more years before the universities would be ready to teach C++ and OOP in introductory courses.

During 1993 we saw a tremendous surge in interest in C++ and OOP among our industry clients. But we still did not sense that the universities were ready to switch to C++ and OOP en masse. So in January 1994 we published the Second Edition of C *How to Program* with a 300-page section on C++ and OOP. In May 1994 we published the first edition of *C++ How to Program,* a 950-page book devoted to the premise that C++ and OOP were now ready for prime time in introductory university courses for many schools that wanted to be at the leading edge of programming languages education.

In 1995, we were following the introduction of Java carefully. In November 1995 we attended an Internet conference in Boston. A representative from Sun Microsystems gave a presentation on Java that filled one of the large ballrooms at the Hynes Convention Center. As the presentation proceeded, it became very clear to us that Java would play a significant part in the development of interactive, multimedia web pages. But we immediately saw a much greater potential for the language. We saw Java as the proper language for many universities to teach first year programming language students in this modern world of graphics, images, animation, audio, video, networking, multithreading, and collaborative computing. At the time, we were busy writing the second edition of *C++ How to Program.* We contacted our publisher, Prentice Hall, and told them of our vision of Java making a strong impact in the university curriculum. We all agreed to delay the second edition of *C++ How to Program* a bit so that we could get the first edition of *Java How to Program* to the market in time for fall 1996 courses. We sincerely hope this book makes it possible for many universities to experiment successfully with Java in their introductory and intermediate programming courses.

This first chapter has two parts. The first part introduces the basics of computers and computer programming. The second part gets you started immediately writing some simple Java programs.

So there you have it! You are about to start on a challenging and rewarding path. As you proceed, please share your thoughts on Java and *Java How to Program* with us via email over the Internet at **deitel@deitel.com**. We will make every effort to respond quickly. Prentice Hall maintains **http://www.prenhall.com/deitel**—a World Wide Web site dedicated to our Prentice Hall textbooks and multimedia products *Java How to Program, Java Multimedia Cyber Classroom, C How to Program, C++ How to Program* and *C & C++ Multimedia Cyber Classroom.* The site contains frequently asked questions (FAQs), errata, updates, additional text and examples, and new developments in programming languages and object-oriented programming technologies. If you would like to learn more about the authors or Deitel & Associates, Inc. please visit our World Wide Web site at **http://www.deitel.com**. Thank you and good luck!

1.2 What is a Computer?

A *computer* is a device capable of performing computations and making logical decisions at speeds millions, and even billions, of times faster than human beings can. For example, many of today's personal computers can perform tens of millions of additions per second. A person operating a desk calculator might require decades to complete the same number of calculations a powerful personal computer can perform in one second. (Points to ponder: How would you know whether the person added the numbers correctly? How would you know whether the computer added the numbers correctly?) Today's fastest *supercomputers* can perform hundreds of billions of additions per second—about as many calculations as hundreds of thousands of people could perform in one year! And trillion-instruction-per-second computers are already functioning in research laboratories.

Computers process *data* under the control of sets of instructions called *computer programs*. These computer programs guide the computer through orderly sets of actions specified by people called *computer programmers*.

The various devices (such as the keyboard, screen, disks, memory, and processing units) that comprise a computer system are referred to as *hardware*. The computer programs that run on a computer are referred to as *software*. Hardware costs have been declining dramatically in recent years, to the point that personal computers have become a commodity. Unfortunately, software development costs have been rising steadily as programmers develop ever more powerful and complex applications, without being able to improve the technology of software development. In this book you will learn proven software development methods that can reduce software development costs—top-down stepwise refinement, functionalization and object-oriented programming.

1.3 Computer Organization

Regardless of differences in physical appearance, virtually every computer may be envisioned as being divided into six *logical units* or sections. These are:

1. *Input unit.* This is the "receiving" section of the computer. It obtains information (data and computer programs) from various *input devices* and places this information at the disposal of the other units so that the information may be processed. Most information is entered into computers today through typewriter-like keyboards and "mouse" devices. In the future, perhaps most information will be entered by speaking to computers and by electronically scanning images.

2. *Output unit.* This is the "shipping" section of the computer. It takes information processed by the computer and places it on various *output devices* to make the information available for use outside the computer. Information output from computers is displayed on screens, printed on paper or used to control other devices.

3. *Memory unit.* This is the rapid access, relatively low-capacity "warehouse" section of the computer. It retains information that has been entered through the input unit so that the information may be made immediately available for processing when it is needed. The memory unit also retains information that has already been processed until that information can be placed on output devices by the output unit. The memory unit is often called either *memory* or *primary memory.*

4. *Arithmetic and logic unit (ALU).* This is the "manufacturing" section of the computer. It is responsible for performing calculations such as addition, subtraction, multiplication, and division. It contains the decision mechanisms that allow the computer, for example, to compare two items from the memory unit to determine whether or not they are equal.

5. *Central processing unit (CPU).* This is the "administrative" section of the computer. It is the computer's coordinator and is responsible for supervising the oper-

ation of the other sections. The CPU tells the input unit when information should be read into the memory unit, tells the ALU when information from the memory unit should be utilized in calculations, and tells the output unit when to send information from the memory unit to certain output devices.

6. *Secondary storage unit.* This is the long-term, high-capacity "warehousing" section of the computer. Programs or data not being used by the other units are normally placed on secondary storage devices (such as disks) until they are needed, possibly hours, days, months, or even years later. Information in secondary storage takes longer to access than information in primary memory. The cost per unit of secondary storage is much less than the cost per unit of primary memory.

1.4 Evolution of Operating Systems

Early computers were capable of performing only one *job* or *task* at a time. This form of computer operation is often called single-user *batch processing.* The computer runs a single program at a time while processing data in groups or *batches.* In these early systems, users generally submitted their jobs to the computer center on decks of punched cards. Users often had to wait hours or even days before printouts were returned to their desks.

Software systems called *operating systems* were developed to help make it more convenient to use computers. Early operating systems managed the smooth transition between jobs. This minimized the time it took for computer operators to switch between jobs, and hence increased the amount of work, or *throughput,* computers could process.

As computers became more powerful, it became evident that single-user batch processing rarely utilized the computer's resources efficiently. Instead, it was thought that many jobs or tasks could be made to *share* the resources of the computer to achieve better utilization. This is called *multiprogramming.* Multiprogramming involves the "simultaneous" operation of many jobs on the computer—the computer shares its resources among the jobs competing for its attention. With early multiprogramming operating systems, users still submitted jobs on decks of punched cards and waited hours or days for results.

In the 1960s, several groups in industry and the universities pioneered *timesharing* operating systems. Timesharing is a special case of multiprogramming in which users access the computer through *terminals*, typically devices with keyboards and screens. In a typical timesharing computer system, there may be dozens or even hundreds of users sharing the computer at once. The computer does not actually run all the users simultaneously. Rather, it runs a small portion of one user's job and then moves on to service the next user. The computer does this so quickly that it may provide service to each user several times per second. Thus the users' programs *appear* to be running simultaneously. An advantage of timesharing is that the user receives almost immediate responses to requests rather than having to wait long periods for results as with previous modes of computing.

1.5 Personal, Distributed, and Client/Server Computing

In 1977, Apple Computer popularized the phenomenon of *personal computing.* Initially, it was a hobbyist's dream. Computers became economical enough for people to buy them for their own personal or business use. In 1981, IBM, the world's largest computer vendor, introduced the IBM Personal Computer. Almost overnight, personal computing became legitimate in business, industry, and government organizations.

But these computers were "standalone" units—people did their work on their own machines and then transported disks back and forth to share information. Although early personal computers were not powerful enough to timeshare several users, these machines could be linked together in computer networks, sometimes over telephone lines and sometimes in *local area networks (LANs)* within an organization. This led to the phenomenon of *distributed computing* in which an organization's computing, instead of being performed strictly at some central computer installation, is distributed over networks to the sites at which the real work of the organization is performed. Personal computers were powerful enough to handle the computing requirements of individual users, and to handle the basic communications tasks of passing information back and forth electronically.

Today's most powerful personal computers are as powerful as the million dollar machines of just a decade ago. The most powerful desktop machines—called *workstations*—provide individual users with enormous capabilities. Information is easily shared across computer networks where some computers called *file servers* offer a common store of programs and data that may be used by *client* computers distributed throughout the network, hence the term *client/server computing*. C and C++ have become the programming languages of choice for writing software for operating systems, for computer networking and for distributed client/server applications. Java is rapidly becoming the language of choice for developing Internet-based applications. Today's popular operating systems such as UNIX, OS/2, Windows 95 and Windows NT provide the kinds of capabilities discussed in this section.

1.6 Machine Languages, Assembly Languages, and High-level Languages

Programmers write instructions in various programming languages, some directly understandable by the computer and others that require intermediate *translation* steps. Hundreds of computer languages are in use today. These may be divided into three general types:

1. Machine languages
2. Assembly languages
3. High-level languages

Any computer can directly understand only its own *machine language.* Machine language is the "natural language" of a particular computer. It is defined by the hardware design of that computer. Machine languages generally consist of strings of numbers (ultimately reduced to 1s and 0s) that instruct computers to perform their most elementary operations one at a time. Machine languages are *machine-dependent,* i.e., a particular machine language can be used on only one type of computer. Machine languages are cumbersome for humans, as can be seen by the following section of a machine language program that adds overtime pay to base pay and stores the result in gross pay.

```
+1300042774
+1400593419
+1200274027
```

As computers became more popular, it became apparent that machine-language programming was simply too slow and tedious for most programmers. Instead of using the strings of numbers that computers could directly understand, programmers began using English-like abbreviations to represent the elementary operations of the computer. These English-like abbreviations formed the basis of *assembly languages. Translator programs* called *assemblers* were developed to convert assembly language programs to machine language at computer speeds. The following section of an assembly language program also adds overtime pay to base pay and stores the result in gross pay, but more clearly than its machine language equivalent:

```
LOAD  BASEPAY
ADD   OVERPAY
STORE GROSSPAY
```

Although such code is clearer to humans, it is incomprehensible to computers until translated to machine language.

Computer usage increased rapidly with the advent of assembly languages, but these still required many instructions to accomplish even the simplest tasks. To speed the programming process, *high-level languages* were developed in which single statements could be written to accomplish substantial tasks. The translator programs that convert high-level language programs into machine language are called *compilers.* High-level languages allow programmers to write instructions that look almost like everyday English and contain commonly used mathematical notations. A payroll program written in a high-level language might contain a statement such as:

```
grossPay = basePay + overTimePay
```

Obviously, high-level languages are much more desirable from the programmer's standpoint than either machine languages or assembly languages. C, C++, and Java are among the most powerful and most widely used high-level languages.

The process of compiling a high-level language program into machine language can take a considerable amount of computer time. *Interpreter* programs were developed to directly execute high-level language programs without the need for compiling those programs into machine language. Although compiled programs execute much faster than interpreted programs, interpreters are popular in program development environments in which programs are recompiled frequently as new features are added and errors are corrected. Once a program is developed, a compiled version can be produced to run most efficiently.

1.7 History of C++

C++ evolved from C which evolved from two previous languages, BCPL and B. BCPL was developed in 1967 by Martin Richards as a language for writing operating systems software and compilers. Ken Thompson modeled many features in his language B after their counterparts in BCPL and used B to create early versions of the UNIX operating system at Bell Laboratories in 1970 on a DEC PDP-7 computer. Both BCPL and B were "typeless" languages—every data item occupied one "word" in memory. For example, it was the programmer's responsibility to treat a data item as a whole number or a real number.

The C language was evolved from B by Dennis Ritchie at Bell Laboratories and was originally implemented on a DEC PDP-11 computer in 1972. C uses many important concepts of BCPL and B while adding data typing and other features. C initially became widely known as the development language of the UNIX operating system. Today, virtually all new major operating systems are written in C and/or C++. Over the past two decades, C has become available for most computers. C is hardware independent. With careful design, it is possible to write C programs that are *portable* to most computers.

By the late 1970s, C had evolved into what is now referred to as "traditional C," or "Kernighan and Ritchie C." The publication by Prentice Hall in 1978 of Kernighan and Ritchie's book, *The C Programming Language,* brought wide attention to the language (Ke78). This publication became one of the most successful computer science books ever.

The widespread use of C with various types of computers (sometimes called *hardware platforms*) led to many variations. These were similar, but often incompatible. This was a serious problem for programmers who needed to write portable programs that would run on several platforms. It became clear that a standard version of C was needed. In 1983, the X3J11 technical committee was created under the American National Standards Committee on Computers and Information Processing (X3) to "provide an unambiguous and machine-independent definition of the language." In 1989, the standard was approved. ANSI cooperated with the International Standards Organization (ISO) to standardize C worldwide; the joint standard document was published in 1990 and is referred to as ANSI/ISO 9899: 1990. The second edition of Kernighan and Ritchie, published in 1988, reflects this version called ANSI C, a version of the language now used worldwide (Ke88).

C++, an extension of C, was developed by Bjarne Stroustrup in the early 1980s at Bell Laboratories. C++ provides a number of features that "spruce up" the C language, but more importantly, it provides capabilities for *object-oriented programming.*

There is a revolution brewing in the software community. Building software quickly, correctly, and economically remains an elusive goal, and this at a time when demands for new and more powerful software are soaring. *Objects* are essentially reusable software *components* that model items in the real world. Software developers are discovering that using a modular, object-oriented design and implementation approach can make software development groups much more productive than is possible with previous popular programming techniques such as structured programming. Object-oriented programs are easier to understand, correct and modify.

Many other object-oriented languages have been developed, including Smalltalk, developed at Xerox's Palo Alto Research Center (PARC). Smalltalk is a pure object-oriented language—literally everything is an object. C++ is a hybrid language—it is possible to program in either a C-like style, an object-oriented style, or both.

1.8 History of Java

Perhaps the microprocessor revolution's most important contribution to date is that it made possible the development of personal computers which may soon number 300 million worldwide. Personal computers have had a profound impact on people and the way organizations conduct and manage their business.

Many people believe that the next major area in which microprocessors will have a profound impact is in intelligent consumer electronic devices. Recognizing this, Sun Microsystems funded an internal corporate research project code-named Green in 1991. The project resulted in the development of a C and C++ based language which its creator, James Gosling, called Oak after an oak tree outside his window at Sun. It was later discovered that there already was a computer language called Oak. When a group of Sun people visited a local coffee place, the name Java was suggested and it stuck.

But the Green project ran into some difficulties. The marketplace for intelligent consumer electronic devices was not developing as quickly as Sun had anticipated. Worse yet, a major contract for which Sun competed was awarded to another company. So the project was in danger of being cancelled. By sheer good fortune, the World Wide Web exploded in popularity in 1993 and Sun people saw the immediate potential of using Java to create Web pages with so-called dynamic content. This breathed new life into the project.

Sun formally announced Java at a major conference in May 1995. Ordinarily, an event like this would not have generated that much attention. However, Java generated immediate interest in the business community because of the phenomenal commercial interest in the World Wide Web. Java was not an academic language like Pascal or a language designed by one person or a small group for their own local use like C or C++. Rather, Java was designed for commercial reasons and it generated mammoth interest in the business community because of another Internet related development, the World Wide Web.

1.9 Java Class Libraries

Java programs consist of pieces called *classes* and *methods*. You can program each piece you may need to form a Java program. But most Java programmers take advantage of rich collections of existing classes and methods in Java class libraries. Thus, there are really two pieces to learning the Java "world." The first is learning the Java language itself so that you can program your own classes and methods, and the second is learning how to use the classes and methods in the extensive Java class libraries. Throughout the book, we discuss many library classes and methods. Class libraries are provided primarily by compiler vendors, but many class libraries are supplied by independent software vendors.

Software Engineering Observation 1.1

Use a building block approach to creating programs. Avoid reinventing the wheel. Use existing pieces—this is called software reuse and it is central to object-oriented programming.

Software Engineering Observation 1.2

When programming in Java you will typically use the following building blocks: classes and methods from class libraries, classes and methods you create yourself, and classes and methods other people create and make available to you.

The advantage of creating your own classes and methods is that you will know exactly how they work. You will be able to examine the Java code. The disadvantage is the time-consuming and complex effort that goes into designing and developing new classes and methods.

Performance Tip 1.1

Using library classes and methods instead of writing your own versions can improve program performance because these classes and methods are carefully written to perform efficiently.

Portability Tip 1.1

Using library classes and methods instead of writing your own versions can improve program portability because these classes and methods are included in virtually all Java implementations.

Software Engineering Observation 1.3

Extensive class libraries of reusable software components are available over the Internet in general and the World Wide Web in particular. Many of these libraries are available at no charge.

1.10 Other High-level Languages

Hundreds of high-level languages have been developed, but only a few have achieved broad acceptance. *FORTRAN* (FORmula TRANslator) was developed by IBM Corporation between 1954 and 1957 to be used for scientific and engineering applications that require complex mathematical computations. FORTRAN is still widely used, especially in engineering applications.

COBOL (COmmon Business Oriented Language) was developed in 1959 by a group of computer manufacturers and government and industrial computer users. COBOL is used primarily for commercial applications that require precise and efficient manipulation of large amounts of data. Today, more than half of all business software is still programmed in COBOL. Approximately one million people are actively writing COBOL programs.

Pascal was designed at about the same time as C. It was created by Professor Nicklaus Wirth and was intended for academic use. We say more about Pascal in the next section.

1.11 Structured Programming

During the 1960s, many large software development efforts encountered severe difficulties. Software schedules were typically late, costs greatly exceeded budgets, and the finished products were unreliable. People began to realize that software development was a far more complex activity than they had imagined. Research activity in the 1960s resulted in the evolution of *structured programming*—a disciplined approach to writing programs that are clearer than unstructured programs, easier to test and debug, and easier to modify. Chapter 3, "Control Structures," discusses the principles of structured programming.

One of the more tangible results of this research was the development of the Pascal programming language by Nicklaus Wirth in 1971. Pascal, named after the seventeenth-century mathematician and philosopher Blaise Pascal, was designed for teaching structured programming in academic environments and rapidly became the preferred programming language in most universities. Unfortunately, the language lacks many features needed to make it useful in commercial, industrial, and government applications, so it has not been widely accepted in these environments.

The Ada programming language was developed under the sponsorship of the United States Department of Defense (DOD) during the 1970s and early 1980s. Hundreds of separate languages were being used to produce DOD's massive command-and-control software systems. DOD wanted a single language that would fulfill most of its needs. Pascal was chosen as a base, but the final Ada language is quite different from Pascal. The language was named after Lady Ada Lovelace, daughter of the poet Lord Byron. Lady Lovelace is generally credited with writing the world's first computer program in the early 1800s (for the Analytical Engine mechanical computing device designed by Charles Babbage). One important capability of Ada is called *multitasking;* this allows programmers to specify that many activities are to occur in parallel. The other widely used high-level languages we have discussed—including C and C++—generally allow the programmer to write programs that perform only one activity at a time. Java, again, supports multithreading.

1.12 Basics of a Typical Java Environment

Java systems generally consist of several parts: an environment, the language, the Java Applications Programming Interface, and various class libraries. The following discussion explains a typical Java program development environment as shown in Fig. 1.1.

Java programs normally go through five phases to be executed (Fig. 1.1). These are: *edit, compile, load, verify* and *execute.* If you are not using UNIX, Windows 95 or Windows NT, refer to the manuals for your system, or ask your instructor how to accomplish these tasks in your environment, although your environment will probably be quite similar to that in Fig. 1.1.

Phase 1 consists of editing a file. This is accomplished with an *editor program.* The programmer types a Java program using the editor and makes corrections if necessary. The program is then stored on a secondary storage device such as a disk. Java program file names end with the **.java** extension. Two editors widely used on UNIX systems are **vi** and **emacs**. On Windows 95 and Windows NT simple edit programs like the DOS Edit command and the Windows Notepad will suffice. Java development environments have built-in editors that are smoothly integrated into the programming environment. We assume the reader knows how to edit a program.

In Phase 2, the programmer gives the command **javac** to *compile* the program. The Java compiler translates the Java program into *bytecodes*—the language understood by the Java interpreter. To compile a program called **Welcome.java**, type

```
javac Welcome.java
```

If the program compiles correctly, a file called **Welcome.class** will be produced. This is the file containing the bytecodes that will be interpreted during the execution phase.

Phase 3 is called *loading.* Before a program can be executed, the program must first be placed in memory. This is done by the *class loader* which takes the **.class** file (or files) containing the bytecodes and transfers it to memory. The **.class** file can be loaded from a disk on your system or over a network. The class loader begins loading **.class** files in two situations. For example, the command

```
java Welcome
```

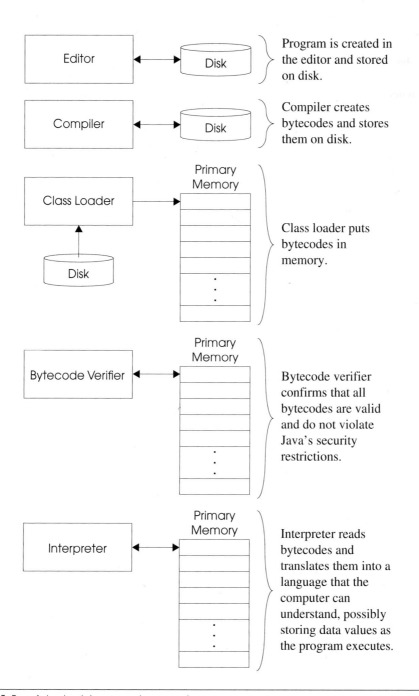

Fig. 1.1   A typical Java environment.

invokes the *java interpreter* for the **Welcome** program and causes the class loader to load information used in the **Welcome** program. The **Welcome** program is referred to as an *application*. Applications are programs that are executed by the Java interpreter. The class loader is also executed when a Java *applet* is loaded into a World Wide Web browser such as Netscape's Navigator browser or Sun's HotJava browser. Applets are Java programs that are typically loaded from the Internet by a browser. Applets are loaded when the user browses an *HTML (Hypertext Markup Language)* document containing the applet. Applets can also be executed from the command-line using the *appletviewer command* provided with the *Java Developer's Kit (JDK)*—a set of tools including the compiler (**javac**), interpreter (**java**), **appletviewer** and other tools used by Java programmers. Like Netscape Navigator and HotJava, the **appletviewer** requires an HTML document to invoke an applet. For example, if the **Welcome.html** file refers to the **Welcome** applet, the **appletviewer** command is used as follows:

```
appletviewer Welcome.html
```

This causes the class loader to load the information used in the **Welcome** applet. The **appletviewer** is commonly referred to as the minimum browser—it only knows how to interpret applets.

Before the bytecodes are executed by the Java interpreter or the **appletviewer**, they are verified by the *bytecode verifier* in Phase 4. This ensures that the bytecodes are valid and that they do not violate Java's security restrictions. Java must enforce strong security because Java programs arriving over the network could potentially cause damage to your files and your system.

Finally, in Phase 5, the computer, under the control of its CPU, interprets the program one bytecode at a time.

Programs rarely work on the first try. Each of the preceding phases can fail because of various types of errors that we will discuss in this text. For example, an executing program might attempt to divide by zero (an illegal operation on computers just as it is in arithmetic). This would cause the computer to print an error message. The programmer would return to the edit phase, make the necessary corrections, and proceed through the remaining phases again to determine that the corrections work properly.

 Common Programming Error 1.1

Errors like division-by-zero errors occur as a program runs, so these errors are called runtime errors or execution-time errors. Fatal run-time errors cause programs to terminate immediately without having successfully performed their jobs. Nonfatal run-time errors allow programs to run to completion, often producing incorrect results.

Most programs in Java input and/or output data. When we say that a program prints a result, we normally mean that the result is displayed on a screen. Data may be output to other devices such as disks and hardcopy printers.

1.13 A Tour of the Book

In Chapter 1, "Introduction to Computers and Java Applets," we present some historical information and we introduce some simple Java applets. The book uses a technique we call the *live-code approach.* Every concept is presented in the context of a complete working Java program which is immediately followed by the screen output produced when that program is executed on a computer. With Java you can write two kinds of programs namely, *applets* designed to be transported over the Internet and executed in World Wide Web browsers like Netscape Navigator, and stand-alone *applications* designed to execute on your own computer. Because of the intense interest in Java applets and graphical user interfaces, we work almost exclusively with applets in the early chapters. Throughout the book, we introduce various graphical user interface components. These components are discussed in detail in Chapters 10 and 11.

In Chapter 2, "Developing Java Applications," we focus on the program development process. The chapter discusses how to take a *problem statement* (i.e., a *requirements document*) and from it develop a working Java program. The chapter introduces some fundamental data types and some simple control structures used for decision making.

Chapter 3, "Control Structures," discusses much of the C portion of Java, especially the sequence, selection, and repetition control structures. The chapter uses simple flowcharts to show the flow of control through each of the control structures. The chapter concludes with a structured programming summary that enumerates each of the control structures. The techniques discussed in Chapter 2 and Chapter 3 constitute a large part of what has been traditionally taught in the universities under the topic of structured programming. With Java we seek to do so-called object-oriented programming. In doing so, we will discover that the insides of the objects we build make abundant use of control structures.

In Chapter 4, "Methods," we take a deeper look inside objects. Objects contain data which we will generally refer to as instance variables, and executable units called methods (these are often called *functions* in non-object-oriented procedural programming languages like C). We explore methods in depth and include a discussion of methods that call themselves, so-called recursive methods.

Chapter 5, "Arrays," explores the processing of data in lists and tables of values. Arrays in Java are processed as objects, further evidence of Java's commitment to almost 100% object-orientation.

Chapter 6, "Object-Based Programming," focuses on the essence and terminology of objects. What is an object? What is a class of objects? What does the inside of an object look like? How are objects created? How are they destroyed? How do objects communicate with one another? Why are classes such a natural mechanism for packaging software as reusable componentry?

Chapter 7, "Object-Oriented Programming," discusses the relationships among classes of objects and programming with related classes. How can we exploit commonality between classes of objects to minimize the amount of work it takes to build large software systems? What does it mean to "program in the general" rather than "programming in the specific?" How does programming in the general make it easy to modify systems and add new features with minimal effort? How can we program for a whole category of objects rather than programming individually for each type of object?

Chapter 8 "Strings and Characters," deals with the processing of words, sentences, characters and groups of characters. The key difference between Java and C here is that Java treats strings as objects thus making string manipulation more convenient than in C, but more importantly, safer than in C where string manipulation, like array manipulation, is based on dangerous pointers.

Chapter 9, "Graphics," begins to introduce the multimedia "sizzle" of Java. Traditional C and C++ programming are pretty much confined to character mode input/output. Some versions of C++ are supported by platform-dependent class libraries that can do graphics, but using one of these libraries makes your applications nonportable. The beauty of Java's graphics capabilities is that they are platform independent and hence, portable.

Chapter 10, "Basic Graphic User Interface Components," introduces the creation of applets and applications with user-friendly graphical user interfaces (GUIs). Chapter 11, "Advanced Graphical User Interface Components," continues the discussion started in Chapter 10. Once again, the key to Java's treatment of these subjects is that it is platform independent. A GUI-based applet or application developed once will run on all Java platforms. Actually, although no rewriting is required to run Java GUI applications on different platforms, the user interface components will appear a bit different on different platforms. The reason for this is that Java actually "ties into" the local GUI system, be it Microsoft's Windows, Apple's Macintosh, Motif, Sun's OpenWindows, OS/2's Warp, or any other system. So Java applications running on a platform with which you are familiar will take on the appearance of GUI applications running on that platform.

Chapter 12, "Exception Handling," is one of the most important chapters in the book from the standpoint of building so-called mission-critical or business-critical applications. Things do go wrong, and in fact at today's computer speeds—commonly 100 million operations per second—if it can go wrong they will, and rather quickly at that. Programmers are often a bit naive about using components. They ask, "How do I ask a component to do something for me?" They also ask "What value(s) does that component return to me to indicate it has performed the job I asked it to do?" But programmers also need to be concerned with, "What happens when the component I call upon to do a job for me experiences difficulty? How will that component signal to me that it had a problem?" In Java, when a component (i.e., a class object) encounters difficulty, it can throw an exception. The environment of that component is programmed to catch that exception and deal with it. Java's exception handling capabilities are especially geared to an object-oriented world in which programmers construct systems largely from reusable prefabricated components built by other programmers. To use a Java component, you need to know not only how that component behaves when "things go well," but what exceptions that component throws when "things go poorly."

Chapter 13, "Multithreading," deals with how to program applets and applications that can perform multiple activities in parallel. Although our bodies are quite good at this (breathing, eating, blood circulation, vision, hearing, etc. can all occur in parallel), our conscious minds have trouble with this. Computers used to be built with a single rather expensive processor. Today processors are becoming so inexpensive that it is possible to build computers with many processors that work in parallel—such computers are called multiprocessors. The trend is clearly towards computers that can perform many tasks in parallel. Most of today's programming languages, including C and C++, do not include features for expressing parallel operations. These languages are often referred to as sequential programming languages or single thread of control languages. Java includes capabilities to enable multithreaded applications, i.e., applications that can specify that multiple activities are to occur in parallel. This makes Java better prepared to deal with the more sophisticated multimedia, networked-based multiprocessor-based applications programmers will be introducing in the mid-to-late 1990s. As we will see, multithreading is even effective on single-processor systems.

Chapter 14, "Multimedia," deals with Java's capabilities for images, animation, audio, and eventually video. It is remarkable that students in first programming courses will be writing applications with all these capabilities. The possibilities are intriguing and endless. Imagine having access (over the Internet and through CD-ROM technology) to vast libraries of graphics images, audios and videos and being able to weave your own together with those in the libraries to form creative applications. Already more than half the new computers sold come multimedia equipped. Within just a few years, new machines equipped for multimedia will be as common as machines with floppy disks today.

Chapter 15, "Files and Streams," deals with input/output which is accomplished through streams of data directed from and to files. This is one of the most important chapters for programmers who will be developing commercial applications. How does a program pass data to a secondary storage device like a disk? How does a program retrieve data already stored on disk? What are sequential files? What are random access files? What is buffering and how does it help programs that do significant amounts of input/output perform better?

Chapter 16, "Networking," deals with applets and applications that can communicate over computer networks. What is a client? What is a server? How do clients ask servers to perform their services? How do servers give results back to clients? What is a URL (uniform resource locator)? How can a Java program load other World Wide Web pages? How can I use Java to develop collaborative applications?

Chapter 17, "Data Structures," deals with arranging elements of data into useful aggregations such as linked lists, stacks, queues and trees. Each data structure has certain important properties that are useful in a wide variety of applications. We walk through the details of building each of these popular data structures. This is a particularly valuable experience in crafting useful classes, certainly a crucial skill for Java programmers. Much of the value of this chapter is in general principles that are useful to the Java programmers in implementing a very wide variety of classes. Although it is useful to know how these classes work on the inside, Java programmers will quickly discover that most of the data structures they need are already available in class libraries such as Java's own **java.util** which we discuss in the next chapter. Chapter 17 reinforces much of the class crafting discussed in Chapters 6 and 7 on object-based programming and object-oriented programming.

Chapter 18, "Java Utilities Package and Bit Manipulation," walks through the classes of the **java.util** package. This is a nice chapter for reinforcing the notion of reuse, reuse, reuse. When classes already exist, it is much faster to develop software by reusing these classes than by reinventing the wheel. Classes are included in class libraries because the classes are generally useful, correct, performance tried, portability certified and/or for a variety of other reasons. Someone has invested considerable work in preparing these classes so why reinvent the wheel? Our belief is that the world's class libraries will grow at a phenomenal rate. If this is the case, then your skill and value as a programmer will depend in large measure on your familiarity with what classes already exist and how to reuse them cleverly to develop high-quality software rapidly. This chapter discusses many classes. Two of the most useful are **Vector** (a dynamic array that can grow and shrink as necessary) and **Stack** (a dynamic data structure that allows insertions and deletions from only one end—called top—thus ensuring last-in-first-out behavior). The beauty of studying these two classes is that they are related through inheritance as discussed in Chapter 7, so the **java.util** package itself implements some classes in terms of others thus avoiding reinventing that wheel and taking advantage of reuse, reuse, reuse.

Well, that's it for now. Welcome to the new and exciting world of Java programming. We hope you enjoy this look at contemporary applications development using the Internet, the World Wide Web, multimedia and multithreading.

1.14 General Notes About Java and this Book

Java is a powerful language. Experienced Java programmers sometimes take pride in being able to create some weird, contorted, convoluted usage of the language. This is a poor programming practice. It makes programs more difficult to read, more likely to behave strangely, more difficult to test and debug, and more difficult to adapt to changing requirements. This book is also geared for novice programmers, so we stress *clarity*. The following is our first "good programming practice."

Good Programming Practice 1.1

Write your Java programs in a simple and straightforward manner. This is sometimes referred to as KIS ("keep it simple"). Do not "stretch" the language by trying bizarre usages.

We will include many of these tips throughout the text to highlight those practices that can help you write programs that are clearer, more understandable, more maintainable, and easier to test and debug. These practices are only guidelines; you will, no doubt, develop your own preferred programming style. We will also highlight Common Programming Errors (problems to watch out for so you do not make these errors in your programs), Performance Tips (techniques that will help you write programs that run faster and use less memory), Portability Tips (techniques that will help you write programs that can run, with little or no modifications, on a variety of computers; these tips also include general observations about how Java achieves its high degree of portability), and Software Engineering Observations (thoughts and concepts that affect and improve the overall architecture of a software system, and particularly, of large software systems).

You have heard that Java is a portable language, and that programs written in Java can run on many different computers. *Portability is an elusive goal.* The ANSI C standard document (An90) contains a lengthy list of portability issues, and complete books have been written that discuss portability (Ja89) (Ra90).

Portability Tip 1.2

Although it is easier to write portable programs in Java than in most other programming languages, there are differences among compilers, interpreters and computers that can make portability difficult to achieve. Simply writing programs in Java does not guarantee portability in all cases. The programmer will occasionally need to deal directly with compiler and computer variations.

We have done a careful walkthrough of Sun's Java documentation and audited our presentation against it for completeness and accuracy. However, Java is a rich language, and there are some subtleties in the language and some topics we have not covered. If you need additional technical details on Java, we suggest that you read the most current Java documentation available over the Internet at **http://www.javasoft.com**. Our book contains an extensive bibliography of books and papers on the Java language in particular and on object-oriented programming in general.

Good Programming Practice 1.2

Read the documentation for the version of Java you are using. Refer to this documentation frequently to be sure you are aware of the rich collection of Java features and that you are using these features correctly.

Good Programming Practice 1.3

Your computer and compiler are good teachers. If after carefully reading your Java documentation manual you are not sure how a feature of Java works, experiment and see what happens. Study each message you get when you compile your programs and correct the programs to eliminate the messages.

In this book we explain how Java works in its current implementations. Perhaps the most striking problem with the early versions of Java is that the Java programs execute interpretively on the client's machine. Interpreters execute slowly compared to fully compiled machine code. Actually, interpreters have one huge advantage over compilers for the Java world, namely that an interpreted program can begin execution immediately as soon as it is downloaded to the client's machine, whereas a source program to be compiled must first suffer a potentially long delay as the program is compiled before it can be executed.

For the moment, only Java interpreters are available at the client's site. But compilers are being written for the most popular platforms. These compilers will take the Java bytecodes and compile them into the native machine code of the client's machine. These compiled programs will run just as fast as compiled C or C++ code. Thus, there will be some trade-offs in various Java applets and applications. Java applications designed to run locally will be prime candidates for these new compilers.

Applets present some more interesting issues. Remember, the applet could be coming from virtually any Web server in the world. So the applet will have to be able to run on any possible Java platform. Short, fast executing Java applets can certainly still be interpreted. But what about more substantial, compute-intensive applets. Here the user may be willing to suffer the compilation delay in favor of getting better execution performance. For some especially performance-intensive applets the user may have no choice; interpreted code would simply run too slowly for the applet to perform properly, so the applet would have to be compiled.

An intermediate step between interpreters and compilers is an intelligent interpreter that, through clever study of the program code as the interpreter runs, can produce compiled code for the performance intensive portions of the program and execute those portions in machine language (in loops, for example) rather than reinterpreting them.

The point of all this discussion is simply that although Java bytecodes are currently interpreted, it is likely that better performance will be achieved through a number of means currently under development. Strategists should take this into consideration when evaluating Java's potential for developing more substantial information systems.

For organizations wanting to do heavy-duty information systems development, Integrated Development Environments (IDEs) are beginning to appear from the major software suppliers. The IDEs provide many tools for supporting the software development process. Several Java IDEs on the market today are just as powerful as those available for C and C++ systems development. This is a strong signal that these major IDE suppliers view Java as a viable language for developing an abundance of substantial applications.

Sun has announced its Java Database Connectivity (JDBC) standard. This is intended for people developing industrial strength database applications. It signals Sun's intention to make Java effective for developing enterprise information systems. This is a more comprehensive mission for Java than simply developing Web pages with active content.

Another indication from Sun Microsystems about its commitment to Java was the announcement of several microprocessors designed to run Java bytecode programs directly. This would offer a huge performance increase over interpreting Java bytecode programs. Initially, three different Java microprocessors were announced varying in price from only a few dollars to as much as $100 each. Sun envisions substantial markets for these microprocessors including the originally intended Java market—intelligent consumer electronic devices such as television set-top boxes, VCRs, security systems, and the like.

1.15 Introduction to Java Programming

The Java language facilitates a disciplined approach to computer program design. We now introduce Java programming and present several examples that illustrate many important features of Java. Each example is analyzed one statement at a time. In Chapter 2 and Chapter 3 we present a detailed treatment of *program development* and *program control* in Java.

1.16 A Simple Program: Printing a Line of Text

Java uses notations that may appear strange to nonprogrammers. We begin by considering a simple *applet* that displays a line of text. An applet is a program that runs in a World Wide Web browser like Netscape's Navigator browser or Sun's HotJava browser. The program and its screen output are shown in Fig. 1.2.

This program illustrates several important features of the Java language. We consider each line of the program in detail. We have inserted line numbers for the reader's convenience; those line numbers are not part of Java programs. Line 8 does the "real work" of the program, namely displaying the phrase **Welcome to Java Programming!** on the screen. But let us consider each line in order. The line

        `// A first program in Java`

begins with `//` indicating that the remainder of the line is a *comment*. Programmers insert comments to *document* programs and improve program readability. Comments also help other people read and understand your program. Comments do not cause the computer to perform any action when the program is run. Comments are ignored by the Java compiler and do not cause any bytecodes to be generated. The comment **A first program in**

```
 1   // A first program in Java
 2   import java.applet.Applet;   // import Applet class
 3   import java.awt.Graphics;    // import Graphics class
 4
 5   public class Welcome extends Applet {
 6      public void paint( Graphics g )
 7      {
 8         g.drawString( "Welcome to Java Programming!", 25, 25 );
 9      }
10   }
```

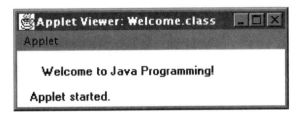

Fig. 1.2   A first program in Java.

Java simply describes the purpose of the program. A comment that begins with **//** is called a *single-line comment* because the comment terminates at the end of the current line. Later, we will discuss two alternate comment notations that facilitate writing multiple-line comments. Note that a **//** comment can begin in the middle of a line and continue until the end of that line (as in lines 2 and 3).

Good Programming Practice 1.4

Every program should begin with a comment describing the purpose of the program.

Java contains many predefined pieces called *classes* that are grouped by directories on disk into categories of related classes called *packages*. The packages are referred to as the *Java class library* or the *Java applications programming interface (Java API)*. The lines

```
import java.applet.Applet;   // import Applet class
import java.awt.Graphics;    // import Graphics class
```

are **import** statements, which load classes required to compile a Java program. These specific lines tell the compiler to load the **Applet** class from the **java.applet** package and the **Graphics** class from the **java.awt** package. When you create an applet in Java, the **Applet** class must be imported. The **Graphics** class is imported so the program can display information on the screen.

One of the great strengths of Java is the large number of classes in the packages of the Java API that programmers can reuse rather than "reinventing the wheel." We exercise a large number of these classes in this book. We will discuss classes and packages in detail throughout the book.

The line

```
public class Welcome extends Applet {
```

begins an *applet **class** definition* for the **Welcome** class. The **class** keyword introduces a class definition in Java and is immediately followed by the class name (**Welcome** in this program). Every Java program is composed of at least one class definition. When you create a class definition, you always use pieces of an existing class definition. For this reason, you never really create a class definition "from scratch." Java provides a mechanism called *inheritance* for creating new classes that use pieces of existing class definitions. The ***extends** keyword* followed by a class name indicates the class from which our new class inherits pieces. In this example, using inheritance results in a new class definition which has the capabilities defined in the Java API's **Applet** class as well as the new features we are adding in our **Welcome** class definition. The inheritance mechanism is easy to use; the programmer does not need to know much about the class from which the new class is inherited. All Java applets must inherit from the **Applet** class, but the programmer does not need to know how to use the entire **Applet** class (which is described throughout the text). In the inheritance relationship, **Applet** is called the *superclass* or *base class* and **Welcome** is called the *subclass* or *derived class*. We will discuss inheritance in detail in Chapter 7, "Object-Oriented Programming."

Good Programming Practice 1.5

Investigate the capabilities of any class in the Java API documentation carefully before inheriting a subclass from it.

Classes are used to *instantiate* (or *create*) *objects* in memory for use in a program. An object is a region in the computer's memory in which information is stored for use by the program. Our **Welcome** class is used to create an object that executes the applet. The browser in which we run the applet is actually responsible for creating an instance of the **Welcome** class for us. The keyword ***public*** enables the browser to create and execute our applet. In Java, the main applet class (i.e., the one that inherits from **Applet**) is always a **public** class. The **public** keyword is discussed in detail in Chapter 6, "Object-Based Programming."

When you save your applet in a file, the applet's class name is used as part of the file name. For our applet, the file name would be **Welcome.java**.

Common Programming Error 1.2

It is an error if the file name is not identical in both spelling and capitalization to the class name.

Common Programming Error 1.3

*It is an error not to end a file name with the .**java** extension for a file containing an applet's class definition.*

The *left brace,* **{**, begins the *body* of every class definition. A corresponding *right brace,* **}**, must end each class definition. The line

```
public void paint( Graphics g )
```

introduces a program building block called a *method*. Methods are explained in detail in Chapter 4. Java programs contain at least one method that performs tasks during the applet's execution. The program in Fig. 1.2 contains the definition for method **paint** (lines 6 through 9). The **paint** method is called automatically for you during an applet's execution and is used to display information on the screen. Methods are able to perform tasks and return information when they complete their tasks. The **void** keyword indicates that this method will perform a task, but will not return any information when it completes its task. The set of parentheses after **paint** define the method's *parameter list*. The parameter list is where methods receive information required to complete their tasks. The **paint** method's parameter list indicates that it requires a **Graphics** object (that is named **g**) to perform its task. The **public** keyword is required so the browser can automatically call your **paint** method. For now, all method definitions will begin with the **public** keyword.

The left brace, **{**, on line 7 begins the method definition's body. A corresponding right brace, **}**, must end the method definition's body (line 9 of the program).

The line

```
g.drawString( "Welcome to Java Programming!", 25, 25 );
```

instructs the computer to perform an *action*, namely to use the **drawString** method of **Graphics** object **g** to draw the *string* of characters contained between the quotation marks. A string is sometimes called a *character string*, a *message*, or a *literal*. The entire line, including **g.drawString**, its *arguments* in the parentheses, and the *semicolon* (**;**) is called a *statement*. Every statement must end with a semicolon (also known as the *statement terminator*). When the preceding statement is executed, it displays the message **Welcome to Java Programming!** on the screen at the *coordinates* 25 and 25. Coordinates are measured from the upper-left corner of the applet in *pixels*. A pixel ("picture element") is the unit of display for your computer's screen. On a color screen a pixel appears as one colored dot on the screen. For example, many personal computers have 640 pixels for the width of the screen and 480 pixels for the height of the screen for a total of 640 times 480 or 307,200 displayable picture elements. Many other computers have higher screen resolutions. The higher the screen resolution, the smaller the applet appears on the screen. The first coordinate is always the *x coordinate* representing the number of pixels from the left side of the applet and the second coordinate is always the *y coordinate* representing the number of pixels from the top of the applet. Most drawing methods from the **Graphics** class require at least one set of coordinates to specify where to draw on the applet.

Common Programming Error 1.4

Omitting the semicolon at the end of a statement is a syntax error. A syntax error is caused when the compiler cannot recognize a statement. The compiler normally issues an error message to help the programmer locate and fix the incorrect statement. Syntax errors are violations of the language. Syntax errors are also called compile errors, compile-time errors, or compilation errors because they appear during the compilation phase.

Good Programming Practice 1.6

Place a space after each comma (,) to make programs more readable.

Good Programming Practice 1.7

Indent the entire body of each method one level of indentation within the braces that define the body of the method. This makes the structure of a program stand out and helps make programs easier to read.

Good Programming Practice 1.8

Set a convention for the size of indent you prefer and then uniformly apply that convention. The tab key may be used to create indents, but tab stops may vary. We recommend using either 1/4-inch tab stops or (preferably) three spaces to form a level of indent.

After compiling the program of Fig. 1.2, it is necessary to create an *HTML (Hypertext Markup Language)* file to load the applet into a browser to execute. Browsers read text files. Figure 1.3 contains the simple HTML file **Welcome.html** that can be used to load the applet defined in Fig. 1.2.

Many HTML codes (referred to as *tags*) come in pairs. For example, lines 1 and 4 of Fig. 1.3 indicate the start and end of the HTML encodings in the file. All HTML tags begin with a left angle bracket **<** and end with a right angle bracket **>**. Lines 2 and 3 are special HTML tags for Java applets. They tell the browser to load a specific applet and define the size of the applet in the browser. The **applet** *tag* is composed of several pieces. The first piece (**code="Welcome.class"**) indicates the file containing the compiled applet class that you defined. When you compile your Java programs, every class is compiled into a separate file that has the same name as the class and ends with the **.class** extension. The second and third pieces of the **applet** tag indicate the **width** and the **height** of the applet in pixels. The upper left corner of the applet is always at x-coordinate 0 and y-coordinate 0. The width of this applet is 275 pixels and the height of this applet is 35 pixels. On line 3, the **</applet>** tag terminates the **<applet>** tag that began on line 2. On line 4, the **</html>** tag terminates the **<html>** tag that began on line 1.

To demonstrate our applet, we use the **appletviewer** command from Sun's Java Developer's Kit (JDK). In the appendices, we discuss how to obtain the JDK from Sun's **java.sun.com** site (or **www.javasoft.com**), and we explain how to use each of the pieces of software in the JDK. The **appletviewer** is a program that tests Java applets. It only understands the **applet** HTML tag so it is sometimes referred to as the "minimal browser" (it ignores all other HTML tags). The **appletviewer** is invoked for the **Welcome** applet from your computer's command line as follows:

```
appletviewer Welcome.html
```

Note that the **appletviewer** requires an HTML file to load an applet.

```
1   <html>
2   <applet code="Welcome.class" width=275 height=35>
3   </applet>
4   </html>
```

Fig. 1.3   The **Welcome.html** file that loads the **Welcome** applet class of Fig. 1.2 into a browser.

Common Programming Error 1.5

Running the **appletviewer** *with a file name that does not end with* **.html** *prevents the* **appletviewer** *from loading your applet for execution.*

Welcome to Java Programming! can be printed several ways. Two **draw-String** statements in the **paint** method can print multiple lines as in Fig. 1.4.

1.17 Another Java Program: Adding Integers

Our next program inputs integers typed by a user at the keyboard, computes the sum of these values and displays the result. As the user types each integer and presses the *Enter key*, the integer is read into the program and added to the total.

This program uses some *Graphical User Interface (GUI) components* of the Java API. GUI components are pieces that facilitate data entry by the user of your program and data outputs by your program. For example, Fig. 1.5 contains a Netscape Navigator window. In the window, there is a bar containing *menus* (File, Edit, View, etc.). Below the menu bar there is a set of *buttons* that each have a defined task in Netscape Navigator. Below the buttons there is a *text field* in which the user can type the name of the World Wide Web site to visit. To the left of the text field is a *label* that indicates the purpose of the text field. The menus, buttons, text fields and labels are part of Netscape Navigator's GUI. They enable you to interact with the Navigator program. Java contains classes that implement the GUI components described here and others that will be described in the Basic Graphical User Interfaces and Advanced Graphical User Interfaces chapters. Our next applet (Fig. 1.6) uses a label and a text field to enable you to interact with the applet.

```
1    // Displaying multiple strings
2    import java.applet.Applet;   // import Applet class
3    import java.awt.Graphics;    // import Graphics class
4
5    public class Welcome extends Applet {
6       public void paint( Graphics g )
7       {
8          g.drawString( "Welcome to", 25, 25 );
9          g.drawString( "Java Programming", 25, 40 );
10      }
11   }
```

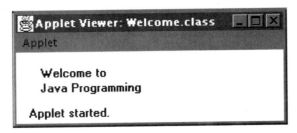

Fig. 1.4   Displaying multiple strings.

Fig. 1.5   A sample Netscape Navigator window with GUI components.

The comment

        // Addition program

states the purpose of the program.
    The line

        import java.awt.*;   // import the java.awt package

imports the **java.awt** package so the compiler can compile this applet. The asterisk (*****) indicates that all the classes in the **java.awt** package should be available to the compiler for compilation. Remember that our last two programs only imported the **Graphics** class from the **java.awt** package. In this program, we use the **TextField** and **Label** classes of the **java.awt** package. When an entire package is imported into a program, the compiler will only import those classes that are used in the program.

    As stated earlier, every Java program is based on at least one class definition that uses pieces of an existing class definition via inheritance. Remember that applets must inherit from the **Applet** class. The line

        public class Addition extends Applet {

```
1   // Addition program
2   import java.awt.*;     // import the java.awt package
3   import java.applet.Applet;
4
5   public class Addition extends Applet {
6       Label prompt;        // prompt user to input
7       TextField input;     // input values here
8       int number;          // store input value
9       int sum;             // store sum of integers
10
11      // setup the graphical user interface components
12      // and initialize variables
13      public void init()
14      {
15          prompt = new Label( "Enter integer and press Enter:" );
16          input = new TextField( 10 );
17          add( prompt );  // put prompt on applet
18          add( input );   // put input on applet
19          sum = 0;        // set sum to 0
20      }
21
22      // process user's action on the input text field
23      public boolean action( Event e, Object o )
24      {
25          number = Integer.parseInt( o.toString() ); // get number
26          input.setText( "" );  // clear data entry field
27          sum = sum + number;     // add number to sum
28          showStatus( Integer.toString( sum ) );  // show result
29          return true;  // indicates user's action was processed
30      }
31  }
```

Fig. 1.6   An addition program "in action." (part 1 of 2)

Fig. 1.6   An addition program "in action." (part 2 of 2)

says that class **Addition** inherits from **Applet**. All class definitions start with a left brace, **{**, and end with a right brace, **}**.

The following lines

```
Label prompt;        // prompt user to input
TextField input;     // input values here
int number;          // store input value
int sum;             // store sum of integers
```

are *declarations*. The words **prompt** and **input** are *references*—names that are used to refer to our **Label** and **TextField** *objects* in the program. An object contains information for use by a program. We will define object more precisely later when we study object-based programming and object-oriented programming. The words **number** and **sum** are the names of *variables*. A variable is similar to an object. The main difference between a variable and an object is that an object is defined by a class definition which can contain both information and methods whereas a variable is defined by a *primitive (or built-in) data type* such as **int** (integer values, i.e., whole numbers such as 7, −11, 0, 31914). Every piece of data in a Java program is an object except for variables of the primitive types. We discuss the other primitive data types in Chapter 2.

Each declaration declares one or more *references* or *variables* and ends with a semicolon. The reference **input** is of type **TextField**. Text fields are used to get information from the user at the keyboard or display information on the screen. The reference **prompt** is of type **Label**. A **Label** contains a string literal to display on the screen. Normally, a label is associated with another graphical user interface element on the screen (such as the text field in this program). The variables **number** and **sum** are of primitive data type *int*. All variables and references must be declared with a name and a type before they can be used in a program. Variables or references of the same type may be declared in one declaration or in multiple declarations. If more than one name is declared in a declaration, the names are separated by *commas* (**,**). This is referred to as a *comma-separated list*.

A variable or reference name is any valid *identifier.* An identifier is a series of characters consisting of letters, digits, underscores (_), and dollar signs (**$**) that does not begin
with a digit. Java allows identifiers of any length. Java is *case sensitive*—uppercase and
lowercase letters are different, so **a1** and **A1** are different identifiers.

Good Programming Practice 1.9

*Choosing meaningful variable names helps a program to be "self-documenting," i.e., it be-
comes easier to understand the program simply by reading it rather than having to read manuals or use excessive comments.*

The declarations on lines 6 through 9 are for names that can be used throughout the
class definition (i.e., in all methods of the class). It is also possible to place declarations in
a method definition. However, the declaration of a variable in a method definition must
appear before the variable is used in the method. A variable declared in a method cannot be
accessed directly by other methods. We will consider methods in depth in Chapter 4.

Good Programming Practice 1.10

*Always place a blank line before a declaration that appears between executable statements.
This makes the declarations stand out in the program and contributes to program clarity.*

Good Programming Practice 1.11

*If you prefer to place declarations at the beginning of a method, separate those declarations
from the executable statements in that method with one blank line to highlight where the declarations end and the executable statements begin.*

This applet contains two methods—**init** (definition begins on line 13) and **action**
(definition begins on line 23). The **init** method is normally supplied in an applet to initialize variables and references that are used in the applet. The **init** method is automatically called for you when the applet begins executing and is guaranteed to be the first
method called. In fact, applets always begin with a series of three method calls—**init**,
start (discussed in a later example), and **paint**. If you do not define any one (or more)
of these three methods, you get a "free" version of that method from the **Applet** class that
does nothing. This is one of the reasons we inherit all applets from the **Applet** class. The
action method processes interactions between the user and the *graphical user interface
(GUI) components* on the applet.

The first line of the **init** method always appears as

```
public void init()
```

which states that **init** is a **public** method that returns no information (**void**) when it
completes and receives no arguments (empty parentheses after **init**) to perform its task.

The line

```
prompt = new Label( "Enter integer and press Enter:" );
```

creates a **Label** object that is initialized to the string literal **"Enter integer and
press Enter:"**. This is used to label the text field **input** on the applet. This message
is called a *prompt* because it tells the user to take a specific action. The ***new*** *operator* cre-

ates an object while the program executes by asking the computer for enough memory to store an object of the type specified to the right of **new**. The value in parentheses after the type is used to *initialize* (give a value to) the object created. The reference **prompt** is given the result of the **new** operation using the *assignment operator* **=**. The statement is read as, "**prompt** *gets* the value of **new Label("Enter integer and press Enter:")**." The **=** operator is called a *binary operator* because it has two *operands*—**prompt** and the value of the expression **new Label("Enter integer and press Enter:")**.

The line

```
input = new TextField( 10 );
```

creates a **TextField** object using the **new** operator and assigns the result to **input**. The number **10** specifies the size in characters of the text field on the screen.

The lines

```
add( prompt );
add( input );
```

place the **Label** and **TextField** components on the applet so the user can interact with them. The **add** method is one of the many methods from the **Applet** class that are inherited when we define the **Addition** class. The line

```
sum = 0;
```

is an assignment statement that sets **sum** to **0**. Note that the variables **value** and **sum** are not created with the **new** operator. Only class type objects must be allocated dynamically (with **new**). Primitive type variables are allocated automatically by Java.

Next we explain the **action** method—one of several methods we discuss over the course of this text that processes interactions between the user and the applet's GUI components. An interaction between a user and a GUI component generates an *event*. Events tell the applet that the user is interacting with one of the applet's GUI components. For example, when you type a number from the keyboard into the text field in this program and press the *enter key* (or *return key*), an event (which happens to be an object of the **Event** class in the **java.awt** package) is sent to the applet indicating that the user pressed the enter key in the text field. This automatically causes the **action** method to execute. In this program, the **action** method is only called when the user presses the enter key in the text field. The processing of user interactions with GUI components is often referred to as *event-driven programming*.

The first line of the **action** method

```
public boolean action( Event event, Object o )
```

indicates that action is a **public** method that returns a *boolean* (a primitive data type that always has the value **true** or **false**) value when it completes its task. For the early examples in the text, the **action** method will always return **true**. The **action** method receives two arguments—an **Event** and an **Object**. The **Event** argument is used to determine what event occurred. We will revisit the **Event** argument in the next example.

The **Object** argument contains event-specific information. For example, when the user presses the enter key after typing in the text field, the **Object** argument contains the text that was in the text field. The **Object** argument can be an object of any type (except the primitive data types)—it is the most generic type in the Java language (we will discuss **object** in depth in Chapters 6 and 7). One nice feature of Java is that any object of any class type can be converted into a **String** using the **toString** method. A **String** is an object that can store a string literal (strings are discussed in detail in Chapter 8).

Once in the **action** method, we must process the information typed in the text field by the user. In the body of the **action** method, the line

```
number = Integer.parseInt( o.toString() );  // get number
```

assigns to **number** the result of the **Integer.parseInt** method which converts its **String** argument to an integer. The string it converts is the result of the **o.toString()** method which converts the **Object** called **o** into a **String**. Any subsequent references to **number** in the program use this same integer value.

The line

```
input.setText( "" );   // clear data entry field
```

uses the **setText** method of the **TextField** class to set the **input** text field to the empty string—i.e., the string with no characters in it. This clears (or erases) the text that the user typed in the text field.

The assignment statement

```
sum = sum + number;    // add number to sum
```

calculates the sum of the variables **sum** and **number**, and assigns the result to variable **sum** using the assignment operator **=**. The statement is read as, "**sum** *gets* the value of **sum + number**." Most calculations are performed in assignment statements.

After performing the calculation, we display the result in the *status bar* at the bottom of the **appletviewer** window (or your browser). In the four outputs of Fig. 1.6, the **appletviewer** status bar is at the bottom of the window where "applet started," "45," "72," and "117" are displayed, respectively. In Fig. 1.5, the Netscape Navigator status bar is at the bottom of the screen where "Document: Done" is displayed. The line

```
showStatus( Integer.toString( sum ) );   // show result
```

uses the **Applet** class's **showStatus** method to put a **String** in the status bar. The **String** displayed is the result of the method **Integer.toString(sum)** which takes the integer **sum** and converts it to a **String**.

Finally, the line

```
return true;   // indicates user's action was processed
```

tells **action** to return **boolean** value **true** to the applet when it completes its task. This tells the applet that the user's action that caused the event has been processed. As mentioned earlier, the **action** method will return **true** in our early examples.

Good Programming Practice 1.12

Place spaces on either side of a binary operator. This makes the operator stand out and makes the program more readable.

1.18 Memory Concepts

Variable names such as **sum** and **number** actually correspond to *locations* in the computer's memory. Every variable has a *name*, a *type*, a *size* and a *value*.

In the addition program of Fig. 1.6, when the statement

```
number = Integer.parseInt( o.toString() );
```

is executed, the value typed by the user in the text field is placed into a memory location to which the name **number** has been assigned by the compiler. Suppose the user enters the number **45** as the value for **number**. The computer will place **45** into location **number** as shown in Fig. 1.7.

Whenever a value is placed in a memory location, this new value replaces the previous value in that location. The previous value is destroyed.

Once the program has obtained a value, it adds the value to the sum and places the result into variable **sum**. The statement

```
sum = sum + number;
```

that performs the addition also involves destroying a value. This occurs when the calculated sum of **sum** and **number** is placed into location **sum** (without regard to what value may already be in **sum**). After **sum** is calculated, memory appears as in Fig. 1.8. Note that the value of variable **number** appears exactly as it did before it was used in the calculation of **sum**. The value was used, but not destroyed, as the computer performed the calculation. Thus, when a value is read out of a memory location, the process is nondestructive.

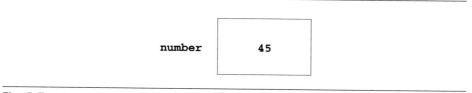

| number | 45 |

Fig. 1.7   A memory location showing the name and value of a variable.

| number | 45 |
| sum | 45 |

Fig. 1.8   Memory locations after a calculation.

1.19 Arithmetic

Most programs perform arithmetic calculations. The *arithmetic operators* are summarized in Fig. 1.9. Note the use of various special symbols not used in algebra. The *asterisk (*)* indicates multiplication and the *percent sign (%)* is the *modulus* operator which is discussed shortly. The arithmetic operators in Fig. 1.9 are binary operators. For example, the expression **sum + value** contains the binary operator **+** and the two operands **sum** and **value**.

Integer division yields an integer quotient; for example, the expression **7 / 4** evaluates to **1**, and the expression **17 / 5** evaluates to **3**. Note that any fractional part in integer division is simply discarded (i.e., truncated)—no rounding occurs. Java provides the modulus operator, **%**, which yields the remainder after integer division. The modulus operator is an integer operator that can be used only with integer operands. The expression **x % y** yields the remainder after **x** is divided by **y**. Thus, **7 % 4** yields **3**, and **17 % 5** yields **2**. In later chapters, we consider many interesting applications of the modulus operator such as determining if one number is a multiple of another.

> **Common Programming Error 1.6**
>
> *Attempting to use the modulus operator, %, with noninteger operands is a syntax error.*

Arithmetic expressions in Java must be written in *straight-line form* to facilitate entering programs into the computer. Thus, expressions such as "**a** divided by **b**" must be written as **a / b** so that all constants, variables, and operators appear in a straight line. The algebraic notation

$$\frac{a}{b}$$

is generally not acceptable to compilers, although some special-purpose software packages do exist that support more natural notation for complex mathematical expressions.

Parentheses are used in Java expressions in the same manner as in algebraic expressions. For example, to multiply **a** times the quantity **b + c** we write:

      a * (b + c)

Java operation	Arithmetic operator	Algebraic expression	Java expression
Addition	**+**	$f + 7$	**f + 7**
Subtraction	**–**	$p - c$	**p - c**
Multiplication	*****	bm	**b * m**
Division	**/**	$x / y \ or \ \dfrac{x}{y} \ or \ x \div y$	**x / y**
Modulus	**%**	$r \bmod s$	**r % s**

Fig. 1.9　Arithmetic operators.

Java applies the operators in arithmetic expressions in a precise sequence determined by the following *rules of operator precedence,* which are generally the same as those followed in algebra:

1. Operators in expressions contained within pairs of parentheses are evaluated first. Thus, *parentheses may be used to force the order of evaluation to occur in any sequence desired by the programmer.* Parentheses are said to be at the "highest level of precedence." In cases of *nested,* or *embedded,* parentheses, the operators in the innermost pair of parentheses are applied first.

2. Multiplication, division, and modulus operations are applied next. If an expression contains several multiplication, division, and modulus operations, operators are applied from left to right. Multiplication, division, and modulus are said to be on the same level of precedence.

3. Addition and subtraction operations are applied last. If an expression contains several addition and subtraction operations, operators are applied from left to right. Addition and subtraction also have the same level of precedence.

The rules of operator precedence enable Java to apply operators in the correct order. When we say operators are applied from left to right, we are referring to the *associativity* of the operators. We will see that some operators associate from right to left. Fig. 1.10 summarizes these rules of operator precedence. This table will be expanded as additional Java operators are introduced. A complete precedence chart is included in the appendices.

Now let us consider several expressions in light of the rules of operator precedence. Each example lists an algebraic expression and its Java equivalent.

The following is an example of an arithmetic mean (average) of five terms:

Algebra: $m = \dfrac{a + b + c + d + e}{5}$

Java: `m = (a + b + c + d + e) / 5;`

Operator(s)	Operation(s)	Order of evaluation (precedence)
( )	Parentheses	Evaluated first. If the parentheses are nested, the expression in the innermost pair is evaluated first. If there are several pairs of parentheses "on the same level" (i.e., not nested), they are evaluated left to right.
*, /, or %	Multiplication Division Modulus	Evaluated second. If there are several, they are evaluated left to right.
+ or −	Addition Subtraction	Evaluated last. If there are several, they are evaluated left to right.

Fig. 1.10 Precedence of arithmetic operators.

The parentheses are required because division has higher precedence than addition. The entire quantity **(a + b + c + d + e)** is to be divided by **5**. If the parentheses are erroneously omitted, we obtain **a + b + c + d + e / 5** which evaluates as

$$a + b + c + d + \frac{e}{5}$$

The following is an example of the equation of a straight line:

Algebra: $y = mx + b$

Java: **y = m * x + b;**

No parentheses are required. The multiplication is applied first because multiplication has a higher precedence than addition.

The following example contains modulus (%), multiplication, division, addition, and subtraction operations:

Algebra: $z = pr\%q + w/x - y$

The circled numbers under the statement indicate the order in which Java applies the operators. The multiplication, modulus, and division are evaluated first in left-to-right order (i.e., they associate from left to right) since they have higher precedence than addition and subtraction. The addition and subtraction are applied next. These are also applied left to right.

Not all expressions with several pairs of parentheses contain nested parentheses. For example, the expression

a * (b + c) + c * (d + e)

does not contain nested parentheses. Rather, the parentheses are said to be "on the same level."

To develop a better understanding of the rules of operator precedence, consider how a second-degree polynomial is evaluated.

y = a * x * x + b * x + c;

The circled numbers under the statement indicate the order in which Java applies the operators. There is no arithmetic operator for exponentiation in Java, so we have represented x^2 as **x * x**.

Suppose variables **a, b, c,** and **x** are initialized as follows: **a = 2, b = 3, c = 7,** and **x = 5**. Figure 1.11 illustrates the order in which the operators are applied in the preceding second-degree polynomial.

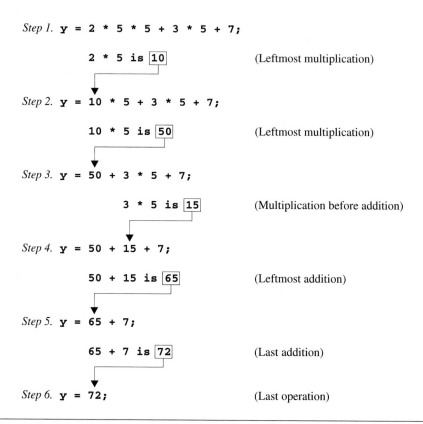

Step 1. **y = 2 * 5 * 5 + 3 * 5 + 7;**

2 * 5 is 10   (Leftmost multiplication)

Step 2. **y = 10 * 5 + 3 * 5 + 7;**

10 * 5 is 50   (Leftmost multiplication)

Step 3. **y = 50 + 3 * 5 + 7;**

3 * 5 is 15   (Multiplication before addition)

Step 4. **y = 50 + 15 + 7;**

50 + 15 is 65   (Leftmost addition)

Step 5. **y = 65 + 7;**

65 + 7 is 72   (Last addition)

Step 6. **y = 72;**   (Last operation)

Fig. 1.11 Order in which a second-degree polynomial is evaluated.

As in algebra, it is acceptable to place unnecessary parentheses in an expression to make the expression clearer. These unnecessary parentheses are also called *redundant parentheses.* For example, the preceding assignment statement might be parenthesized as

y = (a * x * x) + (b * x) + c;

1.20 Decision Making: Equality and Relational Operators

This section introduces a simple version of Java's **if** *structure* that allows a program to make a decision based on the truth or falsity of some *condition.* If the condition is met, i.e., the condition is *true,* the statement in the body of the **if** structure is executed. If the condition is not met, i.e., the condition is *false,* the body statement is not executed. We will see an example shortly.

Conditions in **if** structures can be formed by using the *equality operators* and *relational operators* summarized in Fig. 1.12. The relational operators all have the same level of precedence and associate left to right. The equality operators both have the same level of precedence, which is lower than the precedence of the relational operators. The equality operators also associate left to right.

Standard algebraic equality operator or relational operator	Java equality or relational operator	Example of Java condition	Meaning of Java condition
Equality operators			
=	==	x == y	**x** is equal to **y**
≠	!=	x != y	**x** is not equal to **y**
Relational operators			
>	>	x > y	**x** is greater than **y**
<	<	x < y	**x** is less than **y**
≥	>=	x >= y	**x** is greater than or equal to **y**
≤	<=	x <= y	**x** is less than or equal to **y**

Fig. 1.12 Equality and relational operators.

Common Programming Error 1.7

A syntax error will occur if the operators ==, !=, >=, *and* <= *contain spaces between their symbols.*

Common Programming Error 1.8

Reversing the operators !=, >=, *and* <= *as in* =!, =>, *and* =<, *respectively causes a syntax error.*

Common Programming Error 1.9

Confusing the equality operator == *with the assignment operator* =. *The equality operator should be read "is equal to" and the assignment operator should be read "gets" or "gets the value of." Some people prefer to read the equality operator as "double equals."*

The following example uses six **if** statements to compare two numbers input into text fields by the user. If the condition in any of these **if** statements is satisfied, the **draw-String** statement associated with that **if** is executed. When the user presses the enter key (or return key) in the second text field, the numbers are read into variables **num1** and **num2**. The comparisons are performed in the **paint** method. The program and four sample outputs are shown in Fig. 1.13.

Note that the program in Fig. 1.13 uses two separate **TextField** objects to input two integers. When the user presses the enter key in the *second* text field, the **action** method is called and the **if** structure beginning at line 55 is executed. The line

```
    if ( event.target == input2 ) {
```

determines if the user pressed return in the **input2** text field. Remember that when the user presses the enter key in a text field, an event is generated that results in a call to the **action** method. The **Event** object that is passed to the **action** method contains many pieces of information that enable the programmer to process the event. The most important

```
1   // Using if statements, relational
2   // operators, and equality operators
3   import java.awt.*;
4   import java.applet.Applet;
5
6   public class Comparison extends Applet {
7      Label prompt1;      // prompt user to input first value
8      TextField input1;   // input first value here
9      Label prompt2;      // prompt user to input second value
10     TextField input2;   // input second value here
11     int num1, num2;     // store input values
12
13     // setup the graphical user interface components
14     // and initialize variables
15     public void init()
16     {
17        prompt1 = new Label( "Enter an integer" );
18        input1 = new TextField( 10 );
19        prompt2 =
20           new Label( "Enter an integer and press Enter" );
21        input2 = new TextField( 10 );
22        add( prompt1 );  // put prompt1 on applet
23        add( input1 );   // put input1 on applet
24        add( prompt2 );  // put prompt2 on applet
25        add( input2 );   // put input2 on applet
26     }
27
28     // display the results
29     public void paint( Graphics g )
30     {
31        g.drawString( "The comparison results are:", 70, 75 );
32
33        if ( num1 == num2 )
34           g.drawString( num1 + " == " + num2, 100, 90 );
35
36        if ( num1 != num2 )
37           g.drawString( num1 + " != " + num2, 100, 105 );
38
39        if ( num1 < num2 )
40           g.drawString( num1 + " < " + num2, 100, 120 );
41
42        if ( num1 > num2 )
43           g.drawString( num1 + " > " + num2, 100, 135 );
44
45        if ( num1 <= num2 )
46           g.drawString( num1 + " <= " + num2, 100, 150 );
47
48        if ( num1 >= num2 )
49           g.drawString( num1 + " >= " + num2, 100, 165 );
50     }
```

Fig. 1.13 Using equality and relational operators (part 1 of 3).

```
51
52      // process user's action on the input2 text field
53      public boolean action( Event event, Object o )
54      {
55          if ( event.target == input2 ) {
56              num1 = Integer.parseInt( input1.getText() );
57              num2 = Integer.parseInt( input2.getText() );
58              repaint();
59          }
60
61          return true;   // indicates user's action was processed
62      }
63  }
```

Fig. 1.13 Using equality and relational operators (part 2 of 3).

Fig. 1.13 Using equality and relational operators (part 3 of 3).

piece is the *target* of the event. The **target** is the graphical user interface component with which the user interacted to generate the event. The condition in the **if** structure—**event.target == input2**—asks, "is the target of the event the **input2** text field?" If the preceding condition is true, the body of the **if** structure is executed. The body begins on line 55 with the opening left brace, **{**, and ends on line 59 with the closing right brace, **}**. The braces in the **if** structure are required if there is more than one statement in the body. The statements

```
num1 = Integer.parseInt( input1.getText() );
num2 = Integer.parseInt( input2.getText() );
```

read the text entered by the user in the text fields **input1** and **input2**, convert the text into integers and store the values in variables **num1** and **num2**. The **getText** method of the **TextField** class is used to read the text from each text field. When **input1.get-Text()** is executed, the text from the **input1** text field is retrieved. Similarly, when **input2.getText()** is executed, the text from the **input2** text field is retrieved.

In the first two programs, we used the **paint** method to display information on the screen. Remember that the **paint** method is special in that it is automatically called once for you when the applet executes. However, in this example we want to display different information on the screen each time the user enters new values into the text fields and presses the enter key in the **input2** text field. The line

```
repaint();
```

results in a call to the **paint** method for us. The **repaint** method is one of the many methods inherited when we define our **Comparison** class to extend the **Applet** class. When called, **repaint** first invokes (calls) another inherited method called **update**. The update method erases any information on the applet that was displayed previously with **paint**, then calls **paint** again for you.

The **if** structure from line 33 in **paint**

```
if ( num1 == num2 )
    g.drawString( num1 + " == " + num2, 100, 90 );
```

compares the values of the variables **num1** and **num2** for equality. If they are equal, the **drawString** method displays the result of the expression **num1 + " == " + num2** on the screen. This expression is interesting because it adds an integer to a string literal, then adds another integer to the result of the first addition. Java has a special version of the **+** operator that enables a string and a value of another data type (including another string) to be added together—the result of this operation is always a new string. If we assume that **num1** and **num2** both have the value 1000, the expression evaluates as follows: First **num1** is converted to a string and added to the string **" == "** which results in the string **"1000 == "**. Next, **num2** is converted to a string and added to **"1000 == "** which results in the string **"1000 == 1000"**. This string is displayed on the screen. Note that the automatic conversion of integers **num1** and **num2** only occurs because they are added to the string literal **" == "**. The process of adding strings to other strings is called string concatenation and is discussed in Chapter 8, "Strings and Characters."

Common Programming Error 1.10

*Confusing the **+** operator used for string concatenation with the **+** operator used for addition can lead to strange results. For example, assuming **y** has the value **5**, the Java statement **g.drawString("y + 2 = " + y + 2, 30, 30);** displays **y + 2 = 52** not **y + 2 = 7** because the value of **y** gets concatenated with the **2** instead of added to it.*

Common Programming Error 1.11

*Adding values with the **+** operator for display on the screen with the **drawString** method when none of the values is a string results in a syntax error. To automatically convert values of other types to strings, at least one operand of the **+** operator must be a string.*

Common Programming Error 1.12

*Replacing == in the condition of an **if** structure such as **if (x == 1)** statement; with = as in **if (x = 1)** statement; is a syntax error.*

Notice the indentation in the **if** statements throughout the program. Such indentation enhances program readability.

Good Programming Practice 1.13

*Indent the statement in the body of an **if** structure to make the body of the structure stand out and to enhance program readability.*

Good Programming Practice 1.14

There should be no more than one statement per line in a program.

Common Programming Error 1.13

*Placing a semicolon immediately after the right parenthesis after the condition in an **if** structure is normally an error. The semicolon would cause the body of the **if** structure to be empty, so the **if** structure itself would perform no action regardless of whether or not its condition is true. Worse yet, the original body statement of the **if** structure would now become a statement in sequence with the **if** structure and would always be executed.*

Notice the use of spacing in Fig. 1.13. In Java statements, *white space* characters such as tabs, newlines, and spaces are normally ignored by the compiler. So, statements may be split over several lines and may be spaced according to the programmer's preferences. It is incorrect to split identifiers and string literals. Ideally, statements should be kept small, but it is not always possible to do so.

Good Programming Practice 1.15

A lengthy statement may be spread over several lines. If a single statement must be split across lines, choose breaking points that make sense such as after a comma in a comma-separated list, or after an operator in a lengthy expression. If a statement is split across two or more lines, indent all subsequent lines.

The chart in Fig. 1.14 shows the precedence of the operators introduced in this chapter. The operators are shown top to bottom in decreasing order of precedence. Notice that all these operators, with the exception of the assignment operator **=**, associate from left to right. Addition is left associative, so an expression like **x + y + z** is evaluated as if it had been written **(x + y) + z**. The assignment operator **=** associates from right to left, so an expression like **x = y = 0** is evaluated as if it had been written **x = (y = 0)** which, as we will soon see, first assigns the value **0** to variable **y** and then assigns the result of that assignment—**0**—to **x**.

Good Programming Practice 1.16

Refer to the operator precedence chart when writing expressions containing many operators. Confirm that the operators in the expression are performed in the order you expect. If you are uncertain about the order of evaluation in a complex expression, use parentheses to force the order, exactly as you would do in algebraic expressions. Be sure to observe that some operators such as assignment (=) associate right to left rather than left to right.

Operators				Associativity	Type
( )				left to right	parentheses
*	/	%		left to right	multiplicative
+	-			left to right	additive
<	<=	>	>=	left to right	relationals
==	!=			left to right	equalities
=				right to left	assignment

Fig. 1.14 Precedence and associativity of the operators discussed so far.

We have introduced many important features of Java including printing data on the screen, inputting data from the keyboard, performing calculations, and making decisions. In Chapter 2, we build on these techniques as we introduce *structured programming*. You will become more familiar with indentation techniques. We will study how to specify and vary the order in which statements are executed—this order is called *flow of control*.

Summary

- The various devices (such as the keyboard, screen, disks, memory, and processing units) that comprise a computer system are referred to as hardware.

- The computer programs that run on a computer are referred to as software.

- Operating systems are software systems that make it more convenient to use computers and to get the best performance from computers.

- With distributed computing, an organization's computing is distributed via networking to the sites where the real work of the organization is performed.

- File servers store programs and data that may be shared by client computers distributed throughout the network, hence the term client/server computing.

- Any computer can directly understand only its own machine language.

- Machine languages generally consist of strings of numbers (ultimately reduced to 1s and 0s) that instruct computers to perform their most elementary operations one at a time. Machine languages are machine-dependent.

- English-like abbreviations form the basis of assembly languages. Assemblers translate assembly language programs into machine language.

- Compilers translate high-level language programs into machine language programs. High-level languages (like Java) contain English words and conventional mathematical notations.

- Interpreter programs directly execute high-level language programs without the need for compiling those programs into machine language. An advantage of interpreted programs is that they can begin executing without the delay associated with compilation.

- Although compiled programs execute faster than interpreted programs, interpreters are popular in program development environments in which programs are recompiled frequently as new features are added and errors are corrected. Once a program is developed, a compiled version can then be produced to run most efficiently.

- Structured programming is a disciplined approach to writing programs that are clearer than unstructured programs, easier to test and debug, and easier to modify.

- Java systems consist of the environment, the language, and the class libraries.

- Errors like division-by-zero errors occur as a program runs, so these errors are called run-time errors or execution-time errors.

- Fatal errors cause programs to terminate immediately without successful completion. Nonfatal errors allow programs to run to completion, often producing incorrect results.

- Objects are essentially reusable software components that model items in the real world.

- An applet is a program that runs in a World Wide Web browser like Netscape's Navigator browser or Sun's HotJava browser.

- Comments are used to *document* programs and improve program readability. Comments do not cause the computer to perform any action when the program is run. Comments are ignored by the Java compiler.

- A comment that begins with **//** is called a single-line comment because the comment terminates at the end of the current line.

- Java contains predefined pieces called classes that are grouped by directories on disk into categories of related classes called packages. The packages together are referred to as the Java class library or the Java applications programming interface (Java API).

- The **import** statement loads classes required to compile a Java program.

- The **Graphics** class enables the program to display information on the screen.

- The **class** keyword introduces a class definition.

- The **extends** keyword enables new classes to inherit from existing class definitions.

- All Java applets must inherit from the **Applet** class.

- Classes are used to instantiate objects in memory for use in a program. An object is a region in the computer's memory in which information is stored for use by the program.

- The class that inherits from **Applet** is always a **public** class.

- The applet's class name is used as part of the file name (which must end with **.java**).

- The left brace, **{**, begins the body of every class definition. A corresponding right brace, **}**, must end each class definition.

- The **paint** method is called automatically and is used to display information.

- The **void** keyword indicates that a method does not return any information when it completes its task.

- The parameter list is where a method receives information required to complete its task.

- The left brace, **{**, begins every method definition's body. A corresponding right brace, **}**, must end each method definition's body.

- A string is sometimes called a character string, a message, or a literal.

- Every statement must end with a semicolon (the statement terminator).

- Coordinates are measured from the upper-left corner (x-coordinate 0 and y-coordinate 0) of the applet in pixels. Most drawing methods from the **Graphics** class require at least one set of coordinates to specify where to draw on the applet.

- It is necessary to create an HTML (Hypertext Markup Language) file to load an applet into a browser to execute.

- Every class is compiled into a separate file that has the same name as the class and ends with the **.class** extension.

- The HTML **applet** tag invokes a Java applet. The applet tag must specify the **.class** file for the applet and the **_width_** and the **_height_** of the applet in pixels.

- The **appletviewer** is a program that tests Java applets. The **appletviewer** requires an HTML file to load an applet.

- Graphical User Interface (GUI) components are pieces that can be added to your programs to facilitate data entry and data output.

- A variable is defined by a primitive (or built-in) data type such as **int**. Every piece of data in a Java program is an object except for variables of the primitive types.

- **TextField**s are used to get information from the user at the keyboard or display information on the screen.

- A **Label** contains a string literal to display on the screen. Normally, a label is associated with another graphical user interface component.

- All variables and references must be declared with a name and a type before they can be used in a program.

- An identifier is a series of characters consisting of letters, digits, underscores (_), and dollar signs (**$**) that does not begin with a digit. Java allows identifiers of any length. Java is case sensitive—uppercase and lowercase letters are different.

- The declaration of a variable in a method definition must appear before the variable is used in the method.

- The **init** method is supplied in an applet to initialize variables and references in the applet. The **init** method is automatically called for you when the applet begins executing and is guaranteed to be the first method called.

- Applets always begin with a series of three method calls—**init**, **start**, and **paint**. If you do not define any one (or more) of these three methods, you get a "free" version of that method from the **Applet** class that does nothing.

- A prompt tells the user to take a specific action.

- The assignment **=** operator is called a binary operator because it has two operands.

- The **add** method is used to place GUI components on an applet.
- Variables of primitive data types are not created with the **new** operator. Only class type objects must be allocated dynamically with **new**.
- An interaction between a user and a GUI component generates an event.
- Processing user interactions with GUI components is referred to as event-driven programming.
- The **action** method is called when the user presses the enter key in a text field. The **Object** argument of the **action** method contains the text that was in the text field.
- The **Event** argument of the **action** contains the **target** of the event—the graphical user interface component with which the user interacted to generate the event.
- A **String** is an object that can store a string literal. Any object of any class type can be converted into a **String** using the **toString** method.
- The **Integer.parseInt** method converts its **String** argument to an integer.
- The **setText** method of the **TextField** class places text in the specified text field.
- Most calculations are performed in assignment statements.
- The status bar is located at the bottom of the **appletviewer** or browser window.
- The **Applet** class's **showStatus** method puts a **String** in the status bar.
- Every variable has a name, a type, a size and a value.
- Whenever a value is placed in a memory location, this new value replaces the previous value in that location. The previous value is destroyed.
- When a value is read out of a memory location, the process is nondestructive.
- The arithmetic operators are all binary operators.
- Integer division yields an integer result.
- The modulus operator, **%**, yields the remainder after integer division.
- Java applies the operators in arithmetic expressions in a precise sequence determined by the rules of operator precedence. Parentheses may be used to force the order of evaluation to occur in any sequence.
- The **if** structure allows a program to make a decision based on the truth or falsity of some condition. If the condition is true, the statement in the body of the **if** structure is executed. If the condition is false, the body statement is not executed.
- Conditions in **if** structures can be formed by using the equality and relational operators.
- The **getText** method of the **TextField** class reads the text from a text field.
- The **repaint** method calls the **update** method which erases any information on the applet, then calls **paint**.
- Java has a special version of the **+** operator that enables a string and a value of another data type (including another string) to be added together to produce a new string. The process of adding strings to other strings is called string concatenation.

- White space characters such as tabs, newlines, and spaces are normally ignored by the compiler. Statements may be split over several lines and may be spaced according to the programmer's preferences. It is incorrect to split identifiers and string literals.

Terminology

abstraction
action
action method
add method
ANSI C
applet
Applet class
appletviewer
application
arithmetic and logic unit (ALU)
arithmetic operators
assembly language
assignment operator (**=**)
associativity of operators
base class
binary operators
body of a method
boolean primitive type
bytecodes
C
C standard library
C++
C++ class libraries
case sensitive
central processing unit (CPU)
character string
class
.class file extension
class keyword
client/server computing
comment (**//**)
compile error
compile-time error
compiler
computer
computer program
condition
CPU
decision
declaration
derived class
distributed computing

drawString method
editor
equality operators
    == "is equal to"
    != "is not equal to"
Event class
execution-time error
extends keyword
false value
fatal error
file server
flow of control
getText method
Graphics class
hardware
high-level language
HTML (Hypertext Markup Language)
identifier
if structure
import statement
information hiding
inheritance
input device
input/output (I/O)
int primitive type
integer (**int**)
Integer class
integer division
interface
interpreter
Java
Java Developer's Kit (JDK)
.java file extension
Java Virtual Machine
Label class
logic error
machine dependent
machine independent
machine language
main
memory
memory location

message

method

modulus operator (%)

multiplication operator (*)

multiprocessor

multiprogramming

multitasking

multithreading

Netscape browser

nested parentheses

nonfatal error

object

Object class

object-oriented design (OOD)

object-oriented programming (OOP)

operand

operator

output device

paint method

parentheses ()

parseInt method

precedence

primary memory

procedural programming

programming language

public keyword

reference

relational operators

    > "is greater than"

    < "is less than"

    >= "is greater than or equal to"

    <= "is less than or equal to"

repaint method

reserved words

right-to-left associativity

rules of operator precedence

run-time error

semicolon (**;**) statement terminator

software

statement

statement terminator (**;**)

string

structured programming

syntax error

target instance variable

Textfield class

true value

update method

variable

variable name

variable value

void keyword

white space characters

World Wide Web

Common Programming Errors

1.1   Errors like division-by-zero errors occur as a program runs, so these errors are called run-time errors or execution-time errors. Fatal run-time errors cause programs to terminate immediately without having successfully performed their jobs. Nonfatal run-time errors allow programs to run to completion, often producing incorrect results.

1.2   It is an error if the file name is not identical in both spelling and capitalization to the class name.

1.3   It is an error not to end a file name with the **.java** extension for a file containing an applet's class definition.

1.4   Omitting the semicolon at the end of a statement is a syntax error. A syntax error is caused when the compiler cannot recognize a statement. The compiler normally issues an error message to help the programmer locate and fix the incorrect statement. Syntax errors are violations of the language. Syntax errors are also called compile errors, compile-time errors, or compilation errors because they appear during the compilation phase.

1.5   Running the **appletviewer** with a file name that does not end with **.html** prevents the **appletviewer** from loading your applet for execution.

1.6 Attempting to use the modulus operator, **%**, with noninteger operands is a syntax error.

1.7 A syntax error will occur if the operators **==**, **!=**, **>=**, and **<=** contain spaces between their symbols.

1.8 Reversing the operators **!=**, **>=**, and **<=** as in **=!**, **=>**, and **=<**, respectively causes a syntax error.

1.9 Confusing the equality operator **==** with the assignment operator **=**. The equality operator should be read "is equal to" and the assignment operator should be read "gets" or "gets the value of." Some people prefer to read the equality operator as "double equals."

1.10 Confusing the **+** operator used for string concatenation with the **+** operator used for addition can lead to strange results. For example, assuming **y** has the value **5**, the Java statement **g.drawString("y + 2 = " + y + 2, 30, 30);** displays **y + 2 = 52** not **y + 2 = 7** because the value of **y** gets concatenated with the **2** instead of added to it.

1.11 Adding values with the **+** operator for display on the screen with the **drawString** method when none of the values is a string results in a syntax error. To automatically convert values of other types to strings, at least one operand of the **+** operator must be a string.

1.12 Replacing **==** in the condition of an **if** structure such as **if (x == 1) statement;** with **=** as in **if (x = 1) statement;** is a syntax error.

1.13 Placing a semicolon immediately after the right parenthesis after the condition in an **if** structure is normally an error. The semicolon would cause the body of the **if** structure to be empty, so the **if** structure itself would perform no action regardless of whether or not its condition is true. Worse yet, the original body statement of the **if** structure would now become a statement in sequence with the **if** structure and would always be executed.

Good Programming Practices

1.1 Write your Java programs in a simple and straightforward manner. This is sometimes referred to as KIS ("keep it simple"). Do not "stretch" the language by trying bizarre usages.

1.2 Read the documentation for the version of Java you are using. Refer to this documentation frequently to be sure you are aware of the rich collection of Java features and that you are using these features correctly.

1.3 Your computer and compiler are good teachers. If after carefully reading your Java documentation manual you are not sure how a feature of Java works, experiment and see what happens. Study each message you get when you compile your programs and correct the programs to eliminate the messages.

1.4 Every program should begin with a comment describing the purpose of the program.

1.5 Investigate the capabilities of any class in the Java API documentation carefully before inheriting a subclass from it.

1.6 Place a space after each comma (**,**) to make programs more readable.

1.7   Indent the entire body of each method one level of indentation within the braces that define the body of the method. This makes the structure of a program stand out and helps make programs easier to read.

1.8   Set a convention for the size of indent you prefer and then uniformly apply that convention. The tab key may be used to create indents, but tab stops may vary. We recommend using either 1/4-inch tab stops or (preferably) three spaces to form a level of indent.

1.9   Choosing meaningful variable names helps a program to be "self-documenting," i.e., it becomes easier to understand the program simply by reading it rather than having to read manuals or use excessive comments.

1.10   Always place a blank line before a declaration that appears between executable statements. This makes the declarations stand out in the program and contributes to program clarity.

1.11   If you prefer to place declarations at the beginning of a method, separate those declarations from the executable statements in that method with one blank line to highlight where the declarations end and the executable statements begin.

1.12   Place spaces on either side of a binary operator. This makes the operator stand out and makes the program more readable.

1.13   Indent the statement in the body of an **if** structure to make the body of the structure stand out and to enhance program readability.

1.14   There should be no more than one statement per line in a program.

1.15   A lengthy statement may be spread over several lines. If a single statement must be split across lines, choose breaking points that make sense such as after a comma in a comma-separated list, or after an operator in a lengthy expression. If a statement is split across two or more lines, indent all subsequent lines.

1.16   Refer to the operator precedence chart when writing expressions containing many operators. Confirm that the operators in the expression are performed in the order you expect. If you are uncertain about the order of evaluation in a complex expression, use parentheses to force the order, exactly as you would do in algebraic expressions. Be sure to observe that some operators such as assignment (**=**) associate right to left rather than left to right.

Performance Tip

1.1   Using library classes and methods instead of writing your own versions can improve program performance because these classes and methods are carefully written to perform efficiently.

Portability Tips

1.1   Using library classes and methods instead of writing your own versions can improve program portability because these classes and methods are included in virtually all Java implementations.

1.2   Although it is easier to write portable programs in Java than in most other programming languages, there are differences among compilers, interpreters and computers that can make portability difficult to achieve. Simply writing programs in Java does not guarantee portability in all cases. The programmer will occasionally need to deal directly with compiler and computer variations.

Software Engineering Observations

1.1   Use a building block approach to creating programs. Avoid reinventing the wheel. Use existing pieces—this is called software reuse and it is central to object-oriented programming.

1.2   When programming in Java you will typically use the following building blocks: classes and methods from class libraries, classes and methods you create yourself, and classes and methods other people create and make available to you.

1.3   Extensive class libraries of reusable software components are available over the Internet in general and the World Wide Web in particular. Many of these libraries are available at no charge.

Self-Review Exercises

1.1   Fill in the blanks in each of the following:
   a) The company that popularized personal computing was _____.
   b) The computer that made personal computing legitimate in business and industry was the _____.
   c) Computers process data under the control of sets of instructions called _____.
   d) The six key logical units of the computer are the _____, _____, _____, _____, _____, and the _____.
   e) The three classes of languages discussed in the chapter are _____, _____, and _____.
   f) The programs that translate high-level language programs into machine language are called _____.
   g) The _____ language was developed by Wirth for teaching structured programming in universities.
   h) The Department of Defense developed the Ada language with a capability called _____ which allows programmers to specify that many activities can proceed in parallel.

1.2   Fill in the blanks in each of the following sentences about the Java environment.
   a) The _____ command from the Java Developer's Kit executes a Java applet.
   b) The _____ command from the Java Developer's Kit executes a Java application
   c) The _____ command from the Java Developer's Kit compiles a Java program.
   d) An _____ file is required to invoke a Java applet.
   e) A Java program file must end with the _____ file extension.
   f) When a Java program is compiled, the file produced by the compiler ends with the _____ file extension.
   g) The file produced by the Java compiler contains _____ that are interpreted to execute a Java applet or application.

1.3   Fill in the blanks in each of the following.
   a) The _____ begins the body of every method and the _____ ends the body of every method.
   b) Every statement ends with a _____.
   c) The _____ structure is used to make decisions.

1.4   State whether each of the following is true or false. If false, explain why.
   a) Comments cause the computer to print the text after the **//** on the screen when the program is executed.
   b) All variables to be used in a method must be declared before they are used.
   c) All variables must be given a type when they are declared.
   d) Java considers the variables **number** and **NuMbEr** to be identical.
   e) Declarations can appear almost anywhere in the body of a Java method.
   f) The modulus operator (**%**) can be used only with integer operands.
   g) The arithmetic operators *****, **/**, **%**, **+**, and **–** all have the same level of precedence.

1.5   Write Java statements to accomplish each of the following:
   a) Declare the variables **c**, **thisIsAVariable**, **q76354**, and **number** to be of type **int**.
   b) Prompt the user to enter an integer. Hint: Declare a **Label** reference, create a **Label** object, and specify how to place the **Label** on the applet.
   c) Read an integer from the keyboard and store the value entered in integer variable **age**. Assume that the **TextField** called **input** exists and that the **action** method's **Object** argument **o** contains the text the user entered.
   d) If the variable **number** is not equal to **7**, display **"The variable number is not equal to 7"** at x-coordinate 10 and y-coordinate 10 from the **paint** method. Assume **Graphics** object **g** as the argument to the **paint** method.
   e) Print the message **"This is a Java program"** on one line from the **paint** method. Assume **Graphics** object **g** as the argument to the **paint** method and choose your own coordinates.
   f) Print the message **"This is a Java program"** on two lines where the first line ends with **Java**. Assume **Graphics** object **g** as the argument to the **paint** method and choose your own coordinates.

1.6   Identify and correct the errors in each of the following statements:
```
a) if ( c < 7 );
        g.drawString( "c is less than 7", 25, 25 );
b) if ( c => 7 )
        g.drawString( "c is equal to or greater than 7", 25, 25 );
```

Answers to Self-Review Exercises

1.1   a) Apple.   b) IBM Personal Computer.   c) programs.   d) input unit, output unit, memory unit, arithmetic and logic unit, central processing unit, secondary storage unit. e) machine languages, assembly languages, high-level languages. f) compilers. g) Pascal. h) multitasking.

1.2   a) **appletviewer**. b) **java**. c) **javac**. d) HTML. e) **.java**. f) **.class**. g) bytecodes.

1.3   a) Left brace (**{**), right brace (**}**).   b) Semicolon.   c) **if**.

1.4   a) False. Comments do not cause any action to be performed when the program is executed. They are used to document programs and improve their readability.
   b) True.
   c) True.
   d) False. Java is case sensitive, so these variables are distinct.
   e) True.
   f) True.
   g) False. The operators *****, **/**, and **%** are on the same level of precedence, and the operators **+** and **-** are on a lower level of precedence.

1.5   a) `int c, thisIsAVariable, q76354, number;`
   b) `Label prompt;`
      `prompt = new Label( "Enter an integer" );`
      `add( prompt );`
   c) `age = Integer.parseInt( o.toString() );`
   d) `if ( number != 7 )`
         `g.drawString( "The variable number is not equal to 7.",`
                        `10, 10 );`
   e) `g.drawString( "This is a Java program", 10, 10 );`
   f) `g.drawString( "This is a Java", 10, 10 );`
      `g.drawString( "program", 10, 25 );`

1.6   a) Error: Semicolon after the right parenthesis of the condition in the **if** statement. Correction: Remove the semicolon after the right parenthesis. Note: The result of this error is that the output statement will be executed whether or not the condition in the **if** statement is true. The semicolon after the right parenthesis is considered an empty statement—a statement that does nothing. We will learn more about the empty statement in the next chapter.
   b) Error: The relational operator **=>**. Correction: Change **=>** to **>=**.

Exercises

1.7   Categorize each of the following items as either hardware or software:
   a) CPU
   b) Java compiler
   c) ALU
   d) Java interpreter
   e) input unit
   f) an editor program

1.8   Why might you want to write a program in a machine-independent language instead of a machine-dependent language? Why might a machine-dependent language be more appropriate for writing certain types of programs?

1.9   Fill in the blanks in each of the following statements:
   a) Which logical unit of the computer receives information from outside the computer for use by the computer? _____.
   b) The process of instructing the computer to solve specific problems is called_____.

c) What type of computer language uses English-like abbreviations for machine language instructions? _____.

d) Which logical unit of the computer sends information that has already been processed by the computer to various devices so that the information may be used outside the computer? _____.

e) Which logical unit of the computer retains information? _____.

f) Which logical unit of the computer performs calculations? _____.

g) Which logical unit of the computer makes logical decisions? _____.

h) The level of computer language most convenient to the programmer for writing programs quickly and easily is _____.

i) The only language that a computer can directly understand is called that computer's _____.

j) Which logical unit of the computer coordinates the activities of all the other logical units? _____.

1.10   Fill in the blanks in each of the following:

a) _____ are used to document a program and improve its readability.

b) An object of the _____ class is capable of receiving input from the user at the keyboard or displaying information on an applet.

c) A Java statement that makes a decision is _____.

d) Calculations are normally performed by _____ statements.

e) An object of the _____ class is used to display text that is normally associated with another GUI component on an applet.

1.11   Write Java statements that accomplish each of the following:

a) Display the message **"Enter two numbers"** using a **Label**.

b) Assign the product of variables **b** and **c** to variable **a**.

c) State that a program performs a sample payroll calculation (i.e., use text that helps to document a program).

1.12   State which of the following are true and which are false. Explain your answers.

a) Java operators are evaluated from left to right.

b) The following are all valid variable names: **_under_bar_**, **m928134**, **t5**, **j7**, **her_sales**, **his_account_total**, **a**, **b**, **c**, **z**, **z2**.

c) A valid Java arithmetic expression with no parentheses is evaluated from left to right.

d) The following are all invalid variable names: **3g**, **87**, **67h2**, **h22**, **2h**.

1.13   Fill in the blanks in each of the following:

a) What arithmetic operations are on the same level of precedence as multiplication? _____.

b) When parentheses are nested, which set of parentheses is evaluated first in an arithmetic expression? _____.

c) A location in the computer's memory that may contain different values at various times throughout the execution of a program is called a _____.

1.14   What, if anything, prints when each of the following Java statements is performed? If nothing prints, then answer "nothing." Assume **x = 2** and **y = 3**.

a) `g.drawString( Integer.toString( x ), 25, 25 );`

b) `g.drawString( Integer.toString( x + x ), 25, 25 );`

c) `g.drawString( "x =", 25, 25 );`

        d) `g.drawString( "x =" + x, 25, 25 );`
        e) `g.drawString( ( x + y ) + " = " + ( y + x ), 25, 25 );`
        f) `z = x + y;`

1.15   Which of the following Java statements contain variables whose values are destroyed?
        a) `p = i + j + k + 7;`
        b) `g.drawString( "variables values destroyed", 25, 25 );`
        c) `g.drawString( "a = 5", 25, 25 );`

1.16   Given $y = ax^3 + 7$, which of the following are correct statements for this equation?
        a) `y = a * x * x * x + 7;`
        b) `y = a * x * x * (x + 7);`
        c) `y = (a * x) * x * (x + 7);`
        d) `y = (a * x) * x * x + 7;`
        e) `y = a * (x * x * x) + 7;`
        f) `y = a * x * (x * x + 7);`

1.17   State the order of evaluation of the operators in each of the following Java statements, and show the value of **x** after each statement is performed.
        a) `x = 7 + 3 * 6 / 2 - 1;`
        b) `x = 2 % 2 + 2 * 2 - 2 / 2;`
        c) `x = (3 * 9 * (3 + (9 * 3/ (3))));`

1.18   Write a Java applet that asks the user to enter two numbers, obtains the two numbers from the user, and prints the sum, product, difference, and quotient of the two numbers. Use the graphical user interface techniques shown in Fig. 1.13.

1.19   Write a Java applet that asks the user to enter two integers, obtains the numbers from the user, and displays the larger number followed by the words "**is larger**" in the status bar of the applet. If the numbers are equal, print the message "**These numbers are equal.**" Use the graphical user interface techniques shown in Fig. 1.13.

1.20   Write a Java applet that inputs three integers from the keyboard, and prints the sum, average, product, smallest, and largest of these numbers. Use the GUI techniques shown in Fig. 1.13.

1.21   Write a Java applet that reads in the radius of a circle and prints the circle's diameter, circumference, and area. Use the constant value 3.14159 for π. Use the GUI techniques shown in Fig. 1.6.

1.22   Write a Java program that prints a box, an oval, an arrow, and a diamond as follows:

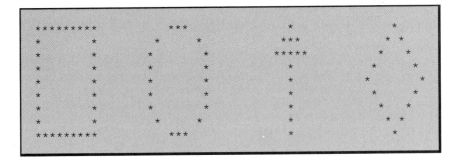

1.23   Here's a peek ahead. Java's **Graphics** class provides many drawing capabilities that will be discussed in detail in Chapter 9, "Graphics." Write a Java applet that uses the following statement to draw a rectangle from the applet's **paint** method.

```
g.drawRect( 10, 10, 50, 50 );
```

The **drawRect** method of the **Graphics** class requires four arguments. The first two are the coordinates of the upper left corner of the rectangle. The third argument is the width of the rectangle in pixels. The fourth argument is the height of the rectangle in pixels.

1.24   Modify the solution to Exercise 1.23 to output a variety of rectangles of different sizes.

1.25   The **Graphics** class contains a **drawOval** method that takes the exact same four arguments as the **drawRect** method. However, the arguments for the **drawOval** method specify the "bounding box" for the oval. The sides of the bounding box are the boundaries of the oval. Write a Java applet that draws an oval and a rectangle with the same four arguments. You will see that the oval touches the rectangle at the center of each side.

1.26   Modify the solution to Exercise 1.25 to output a variety of ovals of different shapes and sizes.

1.27   What does the following code print?

```
g.drawString( "*", 25, 25 );
g.drawString( "***", 25, 55 );
g.drawString( "*****", 25, 85 );
g.drawString( "****", 25, 70 );
g.drawString( "**", 25, 40 );
```

1.28   Write a Java applet that reads integers and determines and prints the largest and the smallest integers in the group. Use only the programming techniques you learned in this chapter.

1.29   Write a Java applet that reads an integer and determines and prints whether it is odd or even. (Hint: Use the modulus operator. An even number is a multiple of two. Any multiple of two leaves a remainder of zero when divided by 2.)

1.30   Write a Java applet that reads in two integers and determines and prints if the first is a multiple of the second. (Hint: Use the modulus operator.)

1.31   Write a Java applet that displays a checkerboard pattern as follows:

```
* * * * * * * *
 * * * * * * * *
* * * * * * * *
 * * * * * * * *
* * * * * * * *
 * * * * * * * *
* * * * * * * *
 * * * * * * * *
```

1.32   Distinguish between the terms fatal error and nonfatal error. Why might you prefer to experience a fatal error rather than a nonfatal error?

1.33   Here's another peek ahead. In this chapter you learned about integers and the type **int**. Java can also represent uppercase letters, lowercase letters, and a considerable variety of special symbols. Every character has a corresponding integer representation. The set of characters a computer uses and the corresponding integer representations for those characters is called that computer's character set. You can indicate a character by simply enclosing that character in single quotes as with **'A'**.

You can determine the integer equivalent of a character by preceding that character with **(int)**—this is called a cast (we will say more about casts in Chapter 2).

```
(int) 'A'
```

The following statement would output a character and its integer equivalent from an applet's paint method

```
g.drawString( "The character " + 'A' +
              " has the value " + (int) 'A', 25, 25 );
```

When the preceding statement executes, it displays the character A and the value 65 (on systems that use the so-called Unicode character set) as part of the string. Write a Java applet that prints the integer equivalents of some uppercase letters, lowercase letters, digits and special symbols. At a minimum, determine the integer equivalents of the following: **A B C a b c 0 1 2 $ * + /** and the blank character.

1.34   Write a Java applet that inputs a five-digit number, separates the number into its individual digits and prints the digits separated from one another by three spaces each. For example, if the user types in **42339**, the program should print

```
4    2    3    3    9
```

1.35   Using only the techniques you learned in this chapter, write a Java applet that calculates the squares and cubes of the numbers from 0 to 10 and prints the following table of values:

```
number   square   cube
0        0        0
1        1        1
2        4        8
3        9        27
4        16       64
5        25       125
6        36       216
7        49       343
8        64       512
9        81       729
10       100      1000
```

2

Developing Java Applications

Objectives

- To understand basic problem solving techniques.
- To be able to develop algorithms through the process of top-down, stepwise refinement.
- To be able to use the **if** and **if/else** selection structures to choose among alternative actions.
- To be able to use the **while** repetition structure to execute statements in a program repeatedly.
- To understand counter-controlled repetition and sentinel-controlled repetition.
- To be able to use the increment, decrement, and assignment operators.

Let's all move one place on.
Lewis Carroll

The wheel is come full circle.
William Shakespeare, King Lear

How many apples fell on Newton's head before he took the hint!
Robert Frost, Comment

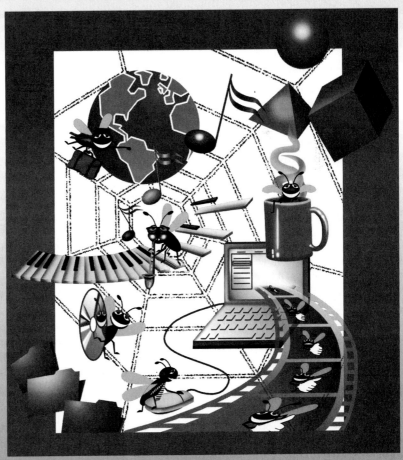

Outline

Summary • Terminology • Common Programming Errors • Good Programming Practices • Performance Tips • Portability Tip • Software Engineering Observations • Self-Review Exercises • Testing and Debugging Tip • Answers to Self-Review Exercises • Exercises

2.1 Introduction

Before writing a program to solve a problem, it is essential to have a thorough understanding of the problem and a carefully planned approach to solving the problem. When writing a program, it is equally essential to understand the types of building blocks that are available and to employ proven program construction principles. In this chapter and in Chapter 3 we discuss these issues in our presentation of the theory and principles of structured programming. The techniques you learn here are applicable to most high-level languages including Java. When we study object-oriented programming in more depth in Chapter 6, we will see that control structures are helpful in building and manipulating objects.

In Chapter 1, we presented an introduction to Java programming using applets which are executed in the Appletviewer or in a World Wide Web browser. In this chapter, we present concepts in the context of Java applications. An application is a stand-alone program that does not require the Appletviewer or a World Wide Web browser to execute.

2.2 Algorithms

Any computing problem can be solved by executing a series of actions in a specific order. A *procedure* for solving a problem in terms of

1. the *actions* to be executed, and

2. the *order* in which these actions are to be executed

is called an *algorithm*. The following example demonstrates that correctly specifying the order in which the actions are to be executed is important.

Consider the "rise-and-shine algorithm" followed by one junior executive for getting out of bed and going to work: (1) Get out of bed, (2) take off pajamas, (3) take a shower, (4) get dressed, (5) eat breakfast, (6) carpool to work.

This routine gets the executive to work well-prepared to make critical decisions. Suppose, however, that the same steps are performed in a slightly different order: (1) Get out of bed, (2) take off pajamas, (3) get dressed, (4) take a shower, (5) eat breakfast, (6) carpool to work.

In this case, our junior executive shows up for work soaking wet. Specifying the order in which statements are to be executed in a computer program is called *program control*. In this chapter and Chapter 3, we investigate the program control capabilities of Java.

2.3 Pseudocode

Pseudocode is an artificial and informal language that helps programmers develop algorithms. The pseudocode we present here is particularly useful for developing algorithms that will be converted to structured portions of Java programs. Pseudocode is similar to everyday English; it is convenient and user-friendly although it is not an actual computer programming language.

Pseudocode programs are not actually executed on computers. Rather, they help the programmer "think out" a program before attempting to write it in a programming language such as Java. In this chapter, we give several examples of pseudocode programs.

The style of pseudocode we present consists purely of characters, so programmers may conveniently type pseudocode programs using an editor program. The computer can produce a fresh printed copy of a pseudocode program on demand. A carefully prepared pseudocode program may be converted easily to a corresponding Java program. This is done in many cases simply by replacing pseudocode statements with their Java equivalents.

Pseudocode consists only of executable statements—those that are executed when the program has been converted from pseudocode to Java and is run. Declarations are not executable statements. For example, the declaration

```
int i;
```

tells the compiler the type of variable **i** and instructs the compiler to reserve space in memory for the variable. This declaration does not cause any action—such as input, output, or a calculation—to occur when the program is executed. Some programmers choose to list variables and mention the purpose of each at the beginning of a pseudocode program.

2.4 Control Structures

Normally, statements in a program are executed one after the other in the order in which they are written. This is called *sequential execution*. Various Java statements we will soon discuss enable the programmer to specify that the next statement to be executed may be other than the next one in sequence. This is called *transfer of control*.

During the 1960s, it became clear that the indiscriminate use of transfers of control was the root of much difficulty experienced by software development groups. The finger of blame was pointed at the ***goto*** *statement* that allows the programmer to specify a transfer of control to one of a very wide range of possible destinations in a program. The notion of so-called *structured programming* became almost synonymous with *"****goto*** elimination."* Java does not have a ***goto*** statement.

The research of Bohm and Jacopini[1] had demonstrated that programs could be written without any ***goto*** statements. The challenge of the era became for programmers to shift their styles to "***goto***-less programming." It was not until the 1970s that programmers started taking structured programming seriously. The results have been impressive as software development groups have reported reduced development times, more frequent on-time delivery of systems, and more frequent within-budget completion of software projects. The key to these successes is that structured programs are clearer, easier to debug and modify, and more likely to be bug-free in the first place.

Bohm and Jacopini's work demonstrated that all programs could be written in terms of only three *control structures*, namely the *sequence structure*, the *selection structure*, and the *repetition structure*. The sequence structure is built into Java. Unless directed otherwise, the computer executes Java statements one after the other in the order in which they are written. The *flowchart* segment of Fig. 2.1 illustrates a typical sequence structure in which two calculations are performed in order.

A flowchart is a graphical representation of an algorithm or of a portion of an algorithm. Flowcharts are drawn using certain special-purpose symbols such as rectangles, diamonds, ovals, and small circles; these symbols are connected by arrows called *flowlines*.

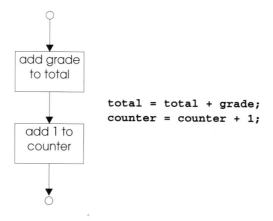

```
total = total + grade;
counter = counter + 1;
```

Fig. 2.1   Flowcharting Java's sequence structure.

---

1. Bohm, C., and G. Jacopini, "Flow Diagrams, Turing Machines, and Languages with Only Two Formation Rules," Communications of the ACM, Vol. 9, No. 5, May 1966, pp. 336-371.

Like pseudocode, flowcharts are useful for developing and representing algorithms, although pseudocode is strongly preferred by most programmers. Flowcharts show clearly how control structures operate; that is all we use them for in this text. The reader should carefully compare the pseudocode and flowchart representations of each control structure.

Consider the flowchart segment for the sequence structure in Fig. 2.1. We use the *rectangle symbol*, also called the *action symbol,* to indicate any type of action including a calculation or an input/output operation. The flowlines in the figure indicate the order in which the actions are to be performed—first, **grade** is to be added to **total** then **1** is to be added to **counter**. Java allows us to have as many actions as we want in a sequence structure. As we will soon see, anywhere a single action may be placed, we may place several actions in sequence.

When drawing a flowchart that represents a *complete* algorithm, an *oval symbol* containing the word "Begin" is the first symbol used in the flowchart; an oval symbol containing the word "End" is the last symbol used. When drawing only a portion of an algorithm as in Fig. 2.1, the oval symbols are omitted in favor of using *small circle symbols* also called *connector symbols*.

Perhaps the most important flowcharting symbol is the *diamond symbol*, also called the *decision symbol,* which indicates that a decision is to be made. We will discuss the diamond symbol in the next section.

Java provides three types of selection structures; we discuss each of these in this chapter and Chapter 3. The **if** selection structure either performs (selects) an action if a condition is true or skips the action if the condition is false. The **if/else** selection structure performs an action if a condition is true and performs a different action if the condition is false. The **switch** selection structure (Chapter 3) performs one of many different actions depending on the value of an expression.

The **if** structure is called a *single-selection structure* because it selects or ignores a single action. The **if/else** structure is called a *double-selection structure* because it selects between two different actions. The **switch** structure is called a *multiple-selection structure* because it selects among many different actions.

Java provides three types of repetition structures, namely **while**, **do/while** and **for** (**do/while** and **for** are covered in Chapter 3) Each of the words **if**, **else**, **switch**, **while**, **do**, and **for** are Java *keywords*. These words are reserved by the language to implement various features such as Java's control structures. Keywords may not be used as identifiers such as for variable names. A complete list of Java keywords is shown in Fig. 2.2.

 Common Programming Error 2.1

Using a keyword as an identifier.

Well, that is all there is. Java has only seven control structures: sequence, three types of selection and three types of repetition. Each program is formed by combining as many of each type of control structure as is appropriate for the algorithm the program implements. As with the sequence structure of Fig. 2.1, we will see that each control structure is flowcharted with two small circle symbols, one at the entry point to the control structure and one at the exit point.

Java Keywords				
abstract	boolean	break	byte	case
catch	char	class	continue	default
do	double	else	extends	false
final	finally	float	for	if
implements	import	instanceof	int	interface
long	native	new	null	package
private	protected	public	return	short
static	super	switch	synchronized	this
throw	throws	transient	true	try
void	volatile	while		

Keywords that are reserved but not used by Java

byvalue	cast	const	future	generic
goto	inner	operator	outer	rest
var				

Fig. 2.2   Java keywords.

Single-entry/single-exit control structures make it easy to build programs—the control structures are attached to one another by connecting the exit point of one control structure to the entry point of the next. This is similar to the way a child stacks building blocks, so we call this *control-structure stacking*. We will learn that there is only one other way control structures may be connected—a method called *control-structure nesting*. Thus, algorithms in Java programs are constructed from only seven different types of control structures combined in only two ways.

2.5 The `if` Selection Structure

A selection structure is used to choose among alternative courses of action in a program. For example, suppose that the passing grade on an examination is 60 (out of 100). Then the pseudocode statement

> *If student's grade is greater than or equal to 60*
> > *Print "Passed"*

determines if the condition "student's grade is greater than or equal to 60" is true or false. If the condition is true, then "Passed" is printed, and the next pseudocode statement in order is "performed" (remember that pseudocode is not a real programming language). If the condition is false, the print statement is ignored, and the next pseudocode statement in order is performed. Note that the second line of this selection structure is indented. Such indentation is optional, but it is highly recommended because it emphasizes the inherent structure of structured programs. The Java compiler ignores *whitespace characters* like blanks, tabs and newlines used for indentation and vertical spacing. Programmers insert these whitespace characters to enhance program clarity.

Good Programming Practice 2.1

Consistently applying reasonable indentation conventions throughout your programs greatly improves program readability. We suggest a fixed-size tab of about 1/4 inch or three spaces per indent.

The preceding pseudocode *If* statement may be written in Java as

```
if ( grade >= 60 )
    System.out.println( "Passed" );
```

Notice that the Java code corresponds closely to the pseudocode. This is one of the properties of pseudocode that makes it such a useful program development tool. The statement in the body of the **if** structure outputs the string literal **"Passed"** to your computer's screen. **System.out.println** will be discussed in more detail in the program of Fig. 2.7.

Good Programming Practice 2.2

Pseudocode is often used to "think out" a program during the program design process. Then the pseudocode program is converted to Java.

The flowchart of Fig. 2.3 illustrates the single-selection **if** structure. This flowchart contains what is perhaps the most important flowcharting symbol—the *diamond symbol,* also called the *decision symbol,* which indicates that a decision is to be made. The decision symbol contains an expression, such as a condition, that can be either true or false. The decision symbol has two flowlines emerging from it. One indicates the direction to be taken when the expression in the symbol is true; the other indicates the direction to be taken when the expression is false. A decision can be made on any expression that evaluates to a value of Java's **boolean** type.

Note that the **if** structure, too, is a single-entry/single-exit structure. We will soon learn that the flowcharts for the remaining control structures also contain (besides small circle symbols and flowlines) only rectangle symbols to indicate the actions to be performed, and diamond symbols to indicate decisions to be made. This is the *action/decision model of programming* we have been emphasizing.

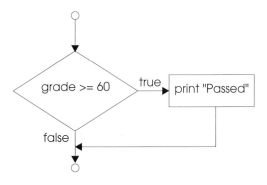

Fig. 2.3   Flowcharting the single-selection **if** structure.

We can envision seven bins, each containing only control structures of one of the seven types. These control structures are empty. Nothing is written in the rectangles or in the diamonds. The programmer's task, then, is assembling a program from as many of each type of control structure as the algorithm demands, combining those control structures in only two possible ways (stacking or nesting), and then filling in the actions and decisions in a manner appropriate for the algorithm. We will discuss the variety of ways in which actions and decisions may be written.

2.6 The `if/else` Selection Structure

The **if** selection structure performs an indicated action only when the condition is true; otherwise the action is skipped. The **if/else** selection structure allows the programmer to specify that a different action is to be performed when the condition is true than when the condition is false. For example, the pseudocode statement

> *If student's grade is greater than or equal to 60*
> > *Print "Passed"*
> *else*
> > *Print "Failed"*

prints *Passed* if the student's grade is greater than or equal to 60 and prints *Failed* if the student's grade is less than 60. In either case, after printing occurs, the next pseudocode statement in sequence is "performed." Note that the body of the *else* is also indented.

> **Good Programming Practice 2.3**
>
> *Indent both body statements of an **if/else** structure.*

Whatever indentation convention you choose should be carefully applied throughout your programs. It is difficult to read programs that do not obey uniform spacing conventions.

> **Good Programming Practice 2.4**
>
> *If there are several levels of indentation, each level should be indented the same additional amount of space.*

The preceding pseudocode *if/else* structure may be written in Java as

```
if ( grade >= 60 )
   System.out.println( "Passed" );
else
   System.out.println( "Failed" );
```

The flowchart of Fig. 2.4 nicely illustrates the flow of control in the **if/else** structure. Once again, note that (besides small circles and arrows) the only symbols in the flowchart are rectangles (for actions) and a diamond (for a decision). We continue to emphasize this action/decision model of computing. Imagine again a deep bin containing as many empty double-selection structures as might be needed to build a Java algorithm. The programmer's job is to assemble the selection structures (by stacking and nesting) with other control structures required by the algorithm, and to fill in the empty rectangles and empty diamonds with actions and decisions appropriate to the algorithm being implemented.

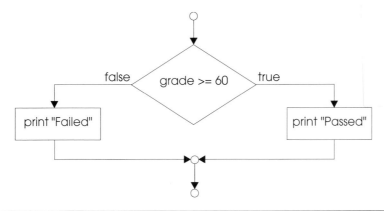

Fig. 2.4 Flowcharting the double-selection **if/else** structure.

The *conditional operator (?:)* is closely related to the **if/else** structure. The **?:** is Java's only *ternary operator*—it takes three operands. The operands together with the **?:** form a *conditional expression*. The first operand is a **boolean** expression, the second is the value for the conditional expression if the condition is true, and the third is the value for the conditional expression if the condition is false. For example, the output statement

```
System.out.println( grade >= 60 ? "Passed" : "Failed" );
```

contains a conditional expression that evaluates to the string **"Passed"** if the condition **grade >= 60** is true and evaluates to the string **"Failed"** if the condition is false. Thus, the statement with the conditional operator performs essentially the same as the preceding **if/else** statement. The precedence of the conditional operator is low, so the entire conditional expression is normally placed in parentheses. We will see that conditional operators can be used in some situations where **if/else** statements cannot.

*Nested **if/else** structures* test for multiple cases by placing **if/else** structures inside **if/else** structures. For example, the following pseudocode statement will print **A** for exam grades greater than or equal to 90, **B** for grades in the range 80 to 89, **C** for grades in the range 70 to 79, **D** for grades in the range 60 to 69, and **F** for all other grades.

> *If student's grade is greater than or equal to 90*
> > *Print "A"*
>
> *else*
> > *If student's grade is greater than or equal to 80*
> > > *Print "B"*
> >
> > *else*
> > > *If student's grade is greater than or equal to 70*
> > > > *Print "C"*
> > >
> > > *else*
> > > > *If student's grade is greater than or equal to 60*
> > > > > *Print "D"*
> > > >
> > > > *else*
> > > > > *Print "F"*

This pseudocode may be written in Java as

```
if ( grade >= 90 )
   System.out.println( "A" );
else
   if ( grade >= 80 )
      System.out.println( "B" );
   else
      if ( grade >= 70 )
         System.out.println( "C" );
      else
         if ( grade >= 60 )
            System.out.println( "D" );
         else
            System.out.println( "F" );
```

If **grade** is greater than or equal to 90, the first four conditions will be true, but only the **System.out.println** statement after the first test will be executed. After that **System.out.println** is executed, the **else**-part of the "outer" **if/else** statement is skipped. Most Java programmers prefer to write the preceding **if** structure as

```
if ( grade >= 90 )
   System.out.println( "A" );
else if ( grade >= 80 )
   System.out.println( "B" );
else if ( grade >= 70 )
   System.out.println( "C" );
else if ( grade >= 60 )
   System.out.println( "D" );
else
   System.out.println( "F" );
```

Both forms are equivalent. The latter form is popular because it avoids the deep indentation of the code to the right. Such indentation often leaves little room on a line, forcing lines to be split and decreasing program readability.

It is important to note that the Java compiler always associates an **else** with the previous **if** unless told to do otherwise by the placement of braces **{}**. This is referred to as the *dangling else problem*. For example,

```
if ( x > 5 )
   if ( y > 5 )
      System.out.println( "x and y are > 5" );
else
   System.out.println( "x is <= 5" );
```

appears to indicate that if **x** is greater than **5**, the **if** structure in its body determines if **y** is also greater than **5**. If so, the string **"x and y are > 5"** is output. Otherwise, it *appears* that if **x** is not greater than **5**, the **else** part of the **if/else** structure outputs the string **"x is <= 5"**.

Beware! The preceding nested **if** structure does not execute as it appears. The compiler actually interprets the preceding structure as

```
if ( x > 5 )
    if ( y > 5 )
        System.out.println( "x and y are > 5" );
    else
        System.out.println( "x is <= 5" );
```

in which the body of the first **if** structure is an **if/else** structure. This structure tests if **x** is greater than **5**. If so, execution continues by testing if **y** is also greater than **5**. If the second condition is true, the proper string—**"x and y are > 5"**—is displayed. However, if the second condition is false, the string **"x is <= 5"** is displayed even though we know **x** is greater than **5**.

To force the preceding nested if structure to execute as it was originally intended, the structure must be written as follows:

```
if ( x > 5 ) {
    if ( y > 5 )
        System.out.println( "x and y are > 5" );
}
else
    System.out.println( "x is <= 5" );
```

The braces (**{}**) indicate to the compiler that the second **if** structure is in the body of the first **if** structure and that the **else** is matched with the first **if** structure. Exercises 2.21 and 2.22 enable you to investigate the dangling else problem further.

The **if** selection structure normally expects only one statement in its body. To include several statements in the body of an **if**, enclose the statements in braces (**{** and **}**). A set of statements contained within a pair of braces is called a *compound statement*.

Software Engineering Observation 2.1

A compound statement can be placed anywhere in a program that a single statement can be placed.

The following example includes a compound statement in the **else** part of an **if/else** structure.

```
if (grade >= 60)
    System.out.println( "Passed" );
else {
    System.out.println( "Failed" );
    System.out.println( "You must take this course again." );
}
```

In this case, if **grade** is less than 60, the program executes both statements in the body of the **else** and prints

```
Failed.
You must take this course again.
```

Notice the braces surrounding the two statements in the **else** clause. These braces are important. Without the braces, the statement

```
System.out.println( "You must take this course again." );
```

would be outside the body of the **else**-part of the **if**, and would execute regardless of whether the grade is less than 60.

Common Programming Error 2.2

Forgetting one or both of the braces that delimit a compound statement can lead to syntax errors or logic errors.

A syntax error (such as when one brace in a compound statement is left out of the program) is caught by the compiler. A *logic error* (such as the one caused when both braces in a compound statement are left out of the program) has its effect at execution time. A *fatal logic error* causes a program to fail and terminate prematurely. A *nonfatal logic error* allows a program to continue executing but the program produces incorrect results.

Software Engineering Observation 2.2

*Just as a compound statement can be placed anywhere a single statement can be placed, it is also possible to have no statement at all, i.e., the empty statement. The empty statement is represented by placing a semicolon (**;**) where a statement would normally be.*

Common Programming Error 2.3

*Placing a semicolon after the condition in an **if** structure leads to a logic error in single-selection **if** structures and a syntax error in double-selection **if** structures (if the **if**-part contains an actual body statement).*

Good Programming Practice 2.5

Some programmers prefer to type the beginning and ending braces of compound statements before typing the individual statements within the braces. This helps avoid omitting one or both of the braces.

In this section, we introduced the notion of a compound statement. A compound statement may contain declarations (as does the body of **main**, for example). If so, the compound statement is called a *block*. The declarations in a block are commonly placed first in the block before any action statements, but declarations may be intermixed with action statements. We will discuss the use of blocks in Chapter 4. The reader should avoid using blocks until that time.

2.7 The `while` Repetition Structure

A *repetition structure* allows the programmer to specify that an action is to be repeated while some condition remains true. The pseudocode statement

While there are more items on my shopping list
  Purchase next item and cross it off my list

describes the repetition that occurs during a shopping trip. The condition, "there are more items on my shopping list" may be true or false. If it is true, then the action, "Purchase next item and cross it off my list" is performed. This action will be performed repeatedly while the condition remains true. The statement(s) contained in the *while* repetition structure constitute the body of the *while*. The *while* structure body may be a single statement or a com-

When the **while** structure is entered, **product** is 2. Variable **product** is repeatedly multiplied by 2, taking on the values 4, 8, 16, 32, 64, 128, 256, 512, and 1024 successively. When **product** becomes 1024, the condition in the **while** structure, **product <= 1000**, becomes false. This terminates the repetition with 1024 as the final value of **product**. Execution continues with the next statement after the **while**. Note: If a **while** structure's condition is initially false the body statement(s) will never be performed.

2.8 Formulating Algorithms: Case Study 1 (Counter-Controlled Repetition)

To illustrate how algorithms are developed, we solve several variations of a class averaging problem. Consider the following problem statement:

> *A class of ten students took a quiz. The grades (one of the letters A, B, C, D, or F) for this quiz are available to you. Determine the class average on the quiz.*

The average is calculated by first associating a grade point value with each letter grade. The letter grade A has the grade point value 4, B has the value 3, C has the value 2, D has the value 1 and F has the value 0. The class average is equal to the sum of the grade point values divided by the number of students. The algorithm for solving this problem on a computer must input each of the grades, perform the averaging calculation, and print the result.

Let us use pseudocode to list the actions to be executed and specify the order in which these actions should be executed. We use *counter-controlled repetition* to input the grades one at a time. This technique uses a variable called a *counter* to specify the number of times a set of statements should execute. In this example, repetition terminates when the counter exceeds 10. In this section, we present a pseudocode algorithm (Fig. 2.6) and the corresponding program (Fig. 2.7). In the next section, we show how pseudocode algorithms are developed. Counter-controlled repetition is often called *definite repetition* because the number of repetitions is known before the loop begins executing.

Note the references in the algorithm to a total and a counter. A *total* is a variable used to accumulate the sum of a series of values. A counter is a variable used to count—in this case, to count the number of grades entered. Variables used to store totals are normally initialized to zero before being used in a program; otherwise the sum would include the previous value stored in the total's memory location. Counter variables are normally initialized to zero or one, depending on their use (we present examples showing each of these uses).

In the program of Fig. 2.7, the Java compiler ensures that variables **counter** and **total** are initialized before they are used in a calculation. Uninitialized variables used in calculations results in error messages from the compiler stating that the variables may not have been initialized.

Common Programming Error 2.6

Not initializing a counter or total results in an error message from the compiler stating that the variable may not have been initialized. You must initialize the variable to allow the compiler to complete compilation of your program.

Good Programming Practice 2.6

Initialize counters and totals.

Set total to zero
Set grade counter to one

While grade counter is less than or equal to ten
    Input the next grade

    If the letter grade is equal to A
        Add grade point value 4 to the total
    else if the letter grade is equal to B
        Add grade point value 3 to the total
    else if the letter grade is equal to C
        Add grade point value 2 to the total
    else if the letter grade is equal to D
        Add grade point value 1 to the total
    else if the letter grade is equal to F
        Add grade point value 0 to the total

    Add one to the grade counter

Set the class average to the total divided by ten
Print the class average

Fig. 2.6   Pseudocode algorithm that uses counter-controlled repetition to solve
the class average problem.

This is our first application in Java, so there are some additional features that must be explained before we can continue. An application begins execution at the **main** method (line 7). Applications are executed using the Java interpreter (**java**) rather than using the Appletviewer or a World Wide Web browser.

The statement

```
import java.io.*;
```

in line 4 imports the Java input/output package to enable our program to read data from the keyboard and output data to the screen.

When creating an application you must still define a class as we did in Chapter 1. However, the class you define does not extend class **Applet** because we are not creating an applet. Method **main** is defined inside class **Average** in this application. Method main must have the following first line:

```
public static void main( String args[] )
```

If **main** does not begin with this line, the Java interpreter will not be able to execute your program. We will explain the key pieces of this line in later chapters. For now, if you are creating an application, simply copy this line when you define your **main** method.

```
1    // Fig. 2.7: Average.java
2    // Class average program with
3    // counter-controlled repetition
4    import java.io.*;
5
6    public class Average {
7       public static void main( String args[] ) throws IOException
8       {
9          int counter, grade, total, average;
10
11         // initialization phase
12         total = 0;
13         counter = 1;
14
15         // processing phase
16         while ( counter <= 10 ) {
17            System.out.print( "Enter letter grade: " );
18            System.out.flush();
19            grade = System.in.read();
20
21            if ( grade == 'A' )
22               total = total + 4;
23            else if ( grade == 'B' )
24               total = total + 3;
25            else if ( grade == 'C' )
26               total = total + 2;
27            else if ( grade == 'D' )
28               total = total + 1;
29            else if ( grade == 'F' )
30               total = total + 0;
31
32            System.in.skip( 1 );     // skip the newline character
33            counter = counter + 1;
34         }
35
36         // termination phase
37         average = total / 10;       // integer division
38         System.out.println( "Class average is " + average );
39      }
40   }
```

Fig. 2.7   Java program for the class average problem with counter-controlled repetition (part 1 of 2).

In Fig. 2.7, method **main** actually begins with the line

```
public static void main( String args[] ) throws IOException
```

which contains some optional information. The user will be typing letter grades at the keyboard that we will read into the program to calculate the average of the grades for the class. When information is read from the keyboard, Java tests for problems during the input (e.g., there is no more data to input). If a problem occurs, Java generates an *exception* that tells

```
Enter letter grade: A
Enter letter grade: A
Enter letter grade: A
Enter letter grade: A
Enter letter grade: A
Enter letter grade: B
Enter letter grade: B
Enter letter grade: C
Enter letter grade: D
Enter letter grade: F
Class average is 2
```

Fig. 2.7   Java program for the class average problem with counter-controlled
repetition (part 2 of 2).

the programmer what went wrong (we cover exceptions in detail in Chapter 12). Exceptions, as their name implies, are exceptional cases during a program's execution—they do not happen frequently, but they can happen. The programmer can process the exception and allow the program to continue or can ignore the exception, in which case the program may terminate.

Java is extremely strict about exception processing. If you compile a program that does input from the keyboard, Java *expects* you to write your program so it handles any input problems that may occur. If you want to ignore the exceptions, you must indicate to the compiler that you are aware of the problems that might occur. At the end of line 7, the words **throws IOException** are our indication to the compiler that we are aware of the fact that an input/output exception can occur when the program attempts to read from the keyboard and that we are consciously ignoring these input/output exceptions in our program. This is referred to as *declaring the exception*. The words **throws IOException** are referred to as the ***throws*** clause of method ***main***.

We have chosen to ignore exceptions at this point in the text so we can focus on the discussion of algorithms and control structures. In Chapter 12, we discuss the process of writing your programs to process these exceptional cases.

Software Engineering Observation 2.3

A program should be written to process exceptional cases that can occur during the execution of the program. This results in programs that are more robust and more likely to execute properly.

Testing and Debugging Tip 2.1

Java is strict about processing exceptional cases in a program. Java has better security and error handling requirements than C or C++. This leads to programs that are easier to debug and maintain.

If we do not declare the exception, the compiler issues the error message, "Exception **java.io.IOException** must be caught, or it must be declared in the throws clause of this method."

The lines

```
System.out.print( "Enter letter grade: " );
System.out.flush();
grade = System.in.read();
```

correspond to the pseudocode statement, *"Input the next grade."* The first two lines display the prompt **Enter letter grade:** on the screen. All output to the screen and input from the keyboard in Java is accomplished with *streams*. Thus, the first line above sends the stream of characters **Enter letter grade:** to the *standard output stream object—***System.out**—which is normally "connected" to the screen. We discuss **System.out** in detail in Chapter 15, "Files and Streams." The method **System.out.print** takes its argument and sends it to the screen to be displayed. When using this method, the characters to be output are sometimes placed in a *buffer* (a temporary holding area in the computer's memory) and not actually displayed on the screen. The method **System.out.flush** forces the characters in the buffer to be displayed before the user types a letter grade.

The third line above uses the *standard input stream object—***System.in**—to obtain one letter grade from the user. The **System.in** object takes input from the standard input stream which is usually the keyboard. The **System.in.read** method reads one character from the keyboard and stores that character in integer variable **grade**. Characters are normally stored in variables of type ***char*** which occupy two bytes or characters can fit in the four-byte **int** type. Thus, we can treat a character as either an integer or a character depending on its use. For example, the statement

```
System.out.println( "The character (" + 'a' +
                    ") has the value " + ( (int) 'a' ) );
```

prints the character **a** and its integer value as follows

```
The character (a) has the value 97
```

The integer 97 is the character's numerical representation in the computer. Java uses the *ISO (International Standards Organization) Unicode character set* in which 97 represents the lowercase letter **'a'**. Many computers today use the *ASCII (American Standard Code for Information Interchange) character set*. The ASCII character set is a subset of the Unicode character set. ASCII characters and their decimal values are shown in the Appendices.

Note the use of the single quotes around the character **a** in the preceding statement. When writing a program that contains a literal character value, the character must be placed in single quotes (**'**). If you place the character in double quotes (**"**), it is interpreted by Java as a string literal. String literals cannot be assigned directly to **char** or **int** variables.

After the grade is entered by the user, it is processed in the **if/else** structure. Notice that each **if** condition tests the variable **grade** for equality with a literal character in single quotes that represents the letter grade.

The program is now ready to increment the variable counter to indicate that a grade has been processed and read the next grade from the user. However, when the user types a character at the keyboard and presses the Enter (or Return) key, two characters are actually sent to the program through the input stream—the letter grade (such as "A") and the *newline* character which is automatically sent to the program when the user presses the Enter key (this also results in a newline character being output to the screen which causes the next characters output to appear at the beginning of the next line on the screen). The line

```
System.in.skip( 1 );     // skip the newline character
```

indicates that the program should skip **1** character (the newline character) in the input stream. This enables the user at the keyboard to enter the next grade when the program returns to line 19 to read the next grade. Without this line, the program will attempt to process the newline character as a valid letter grade. Finally, the line

```
System.out.println( "Class average is " + average );
```

displays the string literal "Class average is" followed by the value of variable **average**. Method **System.out.println** outputs its argument followed by a newline character. Method **System.out.flush** is not required after the preceding statement because **System.out.println** automatically forces its output to be displayed on the screen.

To execute this program (after it has been compiled), type the command

```
java Average
```

at your computer's command line (the DOS prompt on a Windows 95 or Windows NT system or at the shell prompt on a UNIX system) and press the Enter key. This executes the Java interpreter and tells it that the **main** method that begins the execution of this application is in the class **Average**. See your instructor if you have questions about executing commands from the command line of your computer.

Note that the averaging calculation in the program produced an integer result. Actually, the sum of the grade point values in this example is 29 which when divided by 10 should yield 2.9, i.e., a number with a decimal point. We will see how to deal with such numbers (called floating-point numbers) in the next section.

In the programs of Fig. 2.7, Fig. 2.9 and Fig. 2.11, we input individual characters from the user at the keyboard using the **System.in.read** method. This is actually due to Java's limited capabilities for reading information from the standard input stream using object **System.in**—it is only capable of reading one keystroke of information at a time (or a group of keystrokes as we will see in Chapter 15). Often it is necessary to read information such as integers and other data types into a program. For example, grades could be input as integers from 0 to 100. Chapter 1 demonstrated how to read integers from the user via text fields in an applet. Java mechanisms that enable input of miscellaneous data types are demonstrated throughout the text. Chapter 15 discusses how to read various data types using input streams that are connected to files on disk rather than the standard input stream.

2.9 Formulating Algorithms with Top-down, Stepwise Refinement: Case Study 2 (Sentinel-Controlled Repetition)

Let us generalize the class average problem. Consider the following problem:

Develop a class averaging program that will process an arbitrary number of letter grades each time the program is run.

In the first class average example, the number of grades (10) was known in advance. In this example, no indication is given of how many grades are to be entered. The program must process an arbitrary number of grades. How can the program determine when to stop the input of grades? How will it know when to calculate and print the class average?

One way to solve this problem is to use a special value called a *sentinel value* (also called a *signal value*, a *dummy value*, or a *flag value*) to indicate "end of data entry." The user types grades in until all legitimate grades have been entered. The user then types the sentinel value to indicate that the last grade has been entered. Sentinel-controlled repetition is often called *indefinite repetition* because the number of repetitions is not known before the loop begins executing.

Clearly, the sentinel value must be chosen so that it cannot be confused with an acceptable input value. Because grades on a quiz are the letters A, B, C, D and F, Z is an acceptable sentinel value for this problem. Thus, a run of the class average program might process a stream of inputs such as A, A, C, C, B, and Z. The program would then compute and print the class average for the grades A, A, C, C, and B (Z is the sentinel value, so it should not enter into the averaging calculation).

Common Programming Error 2.7

Choosing a sentinel value that is also a legitimate data value results in a logic error and may prevent a sentinel-controlled loop from terminating properly.

We approach the class average program with a technique called *top-down, stepwise refinement*, a technique that is essential to the development of well-structured algorithms. We begin with a pseudocode representation of the *top:*

Determine the class average for the quiz

The top is a single statement that conveys the overall function of the program. As such, the top is, in effect, a complete representation of a program. Unfortunately, the top rarely conveys a sufficient amount of detail from which to write the Java algorithm. So we now begin the refinement process. We divide the top into a series of smaller tasks and list these in the order in which they need to be performed. This results in the following *first refinement*.

Initialize variables
Input, sum, and count the quiz grades
Calculate and print the class average

Here, only the sequence structure has been used—the steps listed are to be executed in order, one after the other.

Software Engineering Observation 2.4

Each refinement, as well as the top itself, is a complete specification of the algorithm; only the level of detail varies.

To proceed to the next level of refinement, i.e., the *second refinement*, we commit to specific variables. We need a running total of the numbers, a count of how many numbers have been processed, a variable to receive the value of each grade as it is input, and a variable to hold the calculated average. The pseudocode statement

Initialize variables

may be refined as follows:

> *Initialize total to zero*
> *Initialize counter to zero*

Notice that only the variables *total* and *counter* need to be initialized before they are used; the variables *average* and *grade* (for the calculated average and the user input, respectively) need not be initialized because their values are written over as they are calculated or input.

The pseudocode statement

> *Input, sum, and count the quiz grades*

requires a repetition structure (i.e., a loop) that successively inputs each grade. Because we do not know in advance how many grades are to be processed, we will use sentinel-controlled repetition. The user will type legitimate grades in one at a time. After the last legitimate grade is typed, the user will type the sentinel value. The program will test for the sentinel value after each grade is input and will terminate the loop when the sentinel value is entered by the user. The second refinement of the preceding pseudocode statement is then

> *Input the first grade (possibly the sentinel)*
> *While the user has not as yet entered the sentinel value*
> > *If the letter grade is equal to A*
> > > *Add grade point value 4 to the total*
> > *else if the letter grade is equal to B*
> > > *Add grade point value 3 to the total*
> > *else if the letter grade is equal to C*
> > > *Add grade point value 2 to the total*
> > *else if the letter grade is equal to D*
> > > *Add grade point value 1 to the total*
> > *else if the letter grade is equal to F*
> > > *Add grade point value 0 to the total*
> >
> > *Add one to the grade counter*
> > *Input the next grade (possibly the sentinel)*

Notice that in pseudocode, we do not use braces around the set of statements that form the body of the *while* structure. We simply indent all these statements under the *while* to show that they all belong to the *while*. Again, pseudocode is only an informal program development aid.

The pseudocode statement

> *Calculate and print the class average*

may be refined as follows:

> *If the counter is not equal to zero*
> > *Set the average to the total divided by the counter*
> > *Print the average*
> *else*
> > *Print "No grades were entered"*

Notice that we are being careful here to test for the possibility of division by zero—a *logic error* that if undetected would cause the program to produce invalid output. The complete second refinement of the pseudocode for the class average problem is shown in Fig. 2.8.

Good Programming Practice 2.7

When performing division by an expression whose value could be zero, explicitly test for this case and handle it appropriately in your program (such as printing an error message) rather than allowing the division by zero to occur.

Figures 2.6 and 2.8, include completely blank lines in the pseudocode to make the pseudocode more readable. The blank lines separate the phases of the programs.

Software Engineering Observation 2.5

Many algorithms can be divided logically into three phases: an initialization phase that initializes the program variables; a processing phase that inputs data values and adjusts program variables accordingly; and a termination phase that calculates and prints the final results.

Initialize total to zero
Initialize counter to zero

Input the first grade (possibly the sentinel)
While the user has not as yet entered the sentinel value
    If the letter grade is equal to A
        Add grade point value 4 to the total
    else if the letter grade is equal to B
        Add grade point value 3 to the total
    else if the letter grade is equal to C
        Add grade point value 2 to the total
    else if the letter grade is equal to D
        Add grade point value 1 to the total
    else if the letter grade is equal to F
        Add grade point value 0 to the total

    Add one to the grade counter
    Input the next grade (possibly the sentinel)

If the counter is not equal to zero
    Set the average to the total divided by the counter
    Print the average
else
    Print "No grades were entered"

Fig. 2.8   Pseudocode algorithm that uses sentinel-controlled repetition to solve the class average problem.

The pseudocode algorithm in Fig. 2.8 solves the more general class averaging problem. This algorithm was developed after only two levels of refinement. Sometimes more levels are necessary.

Software Engineering Observation 2.6

The programmer terminates the top-down, stepwise refinement process when the pseudocode algorithm is specified in sufficient detail for the programmer to be able to convert the pseudocode to a Java algorithm. Implementing the Java algorithm is then normally straight-forward.

The Java program and a sample execution are shown in Fig. 2.9. Although the grade point value for each letter grade is an integer, the averaging calculation is likely to produce a number with a decimal point (i.e., a real number). The type **int** cannot represent real numbers. The program introduces the data type ***double*** to handle numbers with decimal points (also called *floating-point numbers*) and introduces a special operator called a *cast operator* to handle the type conversion we will need for the averaging calculation. These features are explained in detail after the program is presented.

In this example, we see that control structures may be stacked on top of one another (in sequence) just as a child stacks building blocks. The **while** structure is immediately followed by an **if/else** structure in sequence. We also see the only other structured way control structures may be connected in Java, namely through *nesting* of one control structure inside another as shown by the nested **if/else** structure inside the **while** structure.

Notice the compound statement in the **while** loop in Fig 2.9. Without the braces, the last three statements in the body of the loop would fall outside the loop, causing the computer to interpret this code incorrectly as follows

```
while ( grade != 'Z' )
   if ( grade == 'A' )
      total = total + 4;
   else if ( grade == 'B' )
      total = total + 3;
   else if ( grade == 'C' )
      total = total + 2;
   else if ( grade == 'D' )
      total = total + 1;
   else if ( grade == 'F' )
      total = total + 0;

System.in.skip( 1 );
counter = counter + 1;
System.out.print( "Enter letter grade, Z to end: " );
System.out.flush();
grade = System.in.read();
```

This would cause an infinite loop in the program if the user does not input the character "**Z**" for the first grade.

Good Programming Practice 2.8

In a sentinel-controlled loop, the prompts requesting data entry should explicitly remind the user what the sentinel value is.

```
1    // Fig. 2.9: Average.java
2    // Class average program with
3    // sentinel-controlled repetition.
4    import java.io.*;
5
6    public class Average {
7       public static void main( String args[] ) throws IOException
8       {
9          double average;   // number with decimal point
10         int counter, grade, total;
11
12         // initialization phase
13         total = 0;
14         counter = 0;
15
16         // processing phase
17         System.out.print( "Enter letter grade, Z to end: " );
18         System.out.flush();
19         grade = System.in.read();
20
21         while ( grade != 'Z' ) {
22            if ( grade == 'A' )
23               total = total + 4;
24            else if ( grade == 'B' )
25               total = total + 3;
26            else if ( grade == 'C' )
27               total = total + 2;
28            else if ( grade == 'D' )
29               total = total + 1;
30            else if ( grade == 'F' )
31               total = total + 0;
32
33            System.in.skip( 1 );
34            counter = counter + 1;
35            System.out.print( "Enter letter grade, Z to end: " );
36            System.out.flush();
37            grade = System.in.read();
38         }
39
40         // termination phase
41         if ( counter != 0 ) {
42            average = (double) total / counter;
43            System.out.println( "Class average is " + average );
44         }
45         else
46            System.out.println( "No grades were entered" );
47      }
48   }
```

Fig. 2.9   Java program for the class average problem with sentinel-controlled repetition (part 1 of 2).

```
Enter letter grade, Z to end: A
Enter letter grade, Z to end: A
Enter letter grade, Z to end: A
Enter letter grade, Z to end: A
Enter letter grade, Z to end: A
Enter letter grade, Z to end: B
Enter letter grade, Z to end: B
Enter letter grade, Z to end: B
Enter letter grade, Z to end: B
Enter letter grade, Z to end: B
Enter letter grade, Z to end: Z
Class average is 3.5
```

Fig. 2.9   Sample execution for the class average problem (part 2 of 2).

Averages do not always evaluate to integer values. Often, an average is a value such as 3.333 or 2.7 that contains a fractional part. These values are referred to as floating-point numbers and are represented by the data type **double**. The variable **average** is declared to be of type **double** to capture the fractional result of our calculation. However, the result of the calculation **total / counter** is an integer because **total** and **counter** are both integer variables. Dividing two integers results in *integer division* in which any fractional part of the calculation is lost (i.e., *truncated*). Because the calculation is performed first, the fractional part is lost before the result is assigned to **average**. To produce a floating-point calculation with integer values, we must create temporary values that are floating-point numbers for the calculation. Java provides the *unary cast operator* to accomplish this task. The statement

```
average = (double) total / counter;
```

includes the cast operator **(double)** which creates a temporary floating-point copy of its operand, **total**. Using a cast operator in this manner is called *explicit conversion*. The value stored in **total** is still an integer. The calculation now consists of a floating-point value (the temporary **double** version of **total**) divided by the integer **counter**.

The Java compiler only knows how to evaluate expressions in which the data types of the operands are identical. To ensure that the operands are of the same type, the compiler performs an operation called *promotion* (also called *implicit conversion*) on selected operands. For example, in an expression containing the data types **int** and **double**, **int** operands are *promoted* to **double**. In our example, after **counter** is promoted to **double**, the calculation is performed and the result of the floating-point division is assigned to **average**. Later in this chapter we discuss all the standard data types and their order of promotion.

Cast operators are available for any data type. The cast operator is formed by placing parentheses around a data type name. The cast operator is a *unary operator*, i.e., an operator that takes only one operand. In Chapter 1, we studied the binary arithmetic operators. Java also supports unary versions of the plus (**+**) and minus (**-**) operators, so the programmer can write expressions like **−7** or **+5**. Cast operators associate from right to left and have the same precedence as other unary operators such as unary **+** and unary **−**. This precedence is one level higher than that of the *multiplicative operators* *****, **/**, and **%**, and one level lower than that of parentheses. We indicate the cast operator with the notation *(type)* in our precedence charts.

Common Programming Error 2.8

Using floating-point numbers in a manner that assumes they are represented precisely can lead to incorrect results. Floating-point numbers are represented only approximately by most computers.

Good Programming Practice 2.9

Do not compare floating-point values for equality or inequality. Rather, test that the difference is less than a specified small value.

Despite the fact that floating-point numbers are not always "100% precise," they have numerous applications. For example, when we speak of a "normal" body temperature of 98.6 we do not need to be precise to a large number of digits. When we view the temperature on a thermometer and read it as 98.6, it may actually be 98.5999473210643. The point here is that calling this number simply 98.6 is fine for most applications.

Another way floating-point numbers develop is through division. When we divide 10 by 3, the result is 3.3333333… with the sequence of 3s repeating infinitely. The computer allocates only a fixed amount of space to hold such a value, so clearly the stored floating-point value can only be an approximation.

2.10 Formulating Algorithms with Top-down, Stepwise Refinement: Case Study 3 (Nested Control Structures)

Let us work through another complete problem. We will once again formulate the algorithm using pseudocode and top-down, stepwise refinement, and we will write a corresponding Java program.

Consider the following problem statement:

A college offers a course that prepares students for the state licensing exam for real estate brokers. Last year, several of the students who completed this course took the licensing examination. Naturally, the college wants to know how well its students did on the exam. You have been asked to write a program to summarize the results. You have been given a list of these 10 students. Next to each name is written a 1 if the student passed the exam and a 2 if the student failed.

Your program should analyze the results of the exam as follows:

1. Input each test result (i.e., a 1 or a 2). Display the message "Enter result" on the screen each time the program requests another test result.

2. Count the number of test results of each type.

3. Display a summary of the test results indicating the number of students who passed and the number of students who failed.

4. If more than 8 students passed the exam, print the message "Raise tuition."

After reading the problem statement carefully, we make the following observations about the problem:

1. The program must process test results for 10 students. A counter-controlled loop will be used.

2. Each test result is a number—either a 1 or a 2. Each time the program reads a test result, the program must determine if the number is a 1 or a 2. We test for a 1 in our algorithm. If the number is not a 1, we assume that it is a 2. (An exercise at the end of the chapter considers the consequences of this assumption.)

3. Two counters are used to keep track of the exam results—one to count the number of students who passed the exam and one to count the number of students who failed the exam.

4. After the program has processed all the results, it must decide if more than 8 students passed the exam.

Let us proceed with top-down, stepwise refinement. We begin with a pseudocode representation of the top:

Analyze exam results and decide if tuition should be raised

Once again, it is important to emphasize that the top is a complete representation of the program, but several refinements are likely to be needed before the pseudocode can be naturally evolved into a Java program. Our first refinement is

Initialize variables
Input the ten exam grades and count passes and failures
Print a summary of the exam results and decide if tuition should be raised

Here, too, even though we have a complete representation of the entire program, further refinement is necessary. We now commit to specific variables. Counters are needed to record the passes and failures, a counter will be used to control the looping process, and a variable is needed to store the user input. The pseudocode statement

Initialize variables

may be refined as follows:

Initialize passes to zero
Initialize failures to zero
Initialize student to one

Notice only the counters for the number of passes, number of failures and number of students are initialized. The pseudocode statement

Input the ten quiz grades and count passes and failures

requires a loop that successively inputs the result of each exam. Here it is known in advance that there are precisely ten exam results, so counter-controlled looping is appropriate. Inside the loop (i.e., *nested* within the loop) a double-selection structure will determine whether each exam result is a pass or a failure, and will increment the appropriate counter accordingly. The refinement of the preceding pseudocode statement is then

> *While student counter is less than or equal to ten*
>   *Input the next exam result*
>
>   *If the student passed*
>   *Add one to passes*
>   *else*
>   *Add one to failures*
>
>   *Add one to student counter*

Notice the use of blank lines to set off the *if/else* control structure to improve program readability. The pseudocode statement

> *Print a summary of the exam results and decide if tuition should be raised*

may be refined as follows:

> *Print the number of passes*
> *Print the number of failures*
> *If more than eight students passed*
>   *Print "Raise tuition"*

The complete second refinement appears in Fig. 2.10. Notice that blank lines are also used to set off the *while* structure for program readability.

This pseudocode is now sufficiently refined for conversion to Java. The Java program and two sample executions are shown in Fig. 2.11.

> *Initialize passes to zero*
> *Initialize failures to zero*
> *Initialize student to one*
>
> *While student counter is less than or equal to ten*
>   *Input the next exam result*
>
>   *If the student passed*
>   *Add one to passes*
>   *else*
>   *Add one to failures*
>
>   *Add one to student counter*
>
> *Print the number of passes*
> *Print the number of failures*
> *If more than eight students passed*
>   *Print "Raise tuition"*

Fig. 2.10 Pseudocode for examination results problem.

```
1   // Fig. 2.11: Analysis.java
2   // Analysis of examination results
3   import java.io.*;
4
5   public class Analysis {
6      public static void main( String args[] ) throws IOException
7      {
8         // initializing variables in declarations
9         int passes = 0, failures = 0, student = 1, result;
10
11        // process 10 students; counter-controlled loop
12        while ( student <= 10 ) {
13           System.out.print( "Enter result (1=pass,2=fail): " );
14           System.out.flush();
15           result = System.in.read();
16
17           if ( result == '1' )        // if/else nested in while
18              passes = passes + 1;
19           else
20              failures = failures + 1;
21
22           student = student + 1;
23           System.in.skip( 1 );
24        }
25
26        System.out.println( "Passed " + passes );
27        System.out.println( "Failed " + failures );
28
29        if ( passes > 8 )
30           System.out.println( "Raise tuition " );
31     }
32  }
```

```
Enter result (1=pass,2=fail): 1
Enter result (1=pass,2=fail): 2
Enter result (1=pass,2=fail): 2
Enter result (1=pass,2=fail): 1
Enter result (1=pass,2=fail): 1
Enter result (1=pass,2=fail): 1
Enter result (1=pass,2=fail): 2
Enter result (1=pass,2=fail): 1
Enter result (1=pass,2=fail): 1
Enter result (1=pass,2=fail): 2
Passed 6
Failed 4
```

Fig. 2.11 Java program and sample execution for examination results problem
(part 1 of 2).

```
Enter result (1=pass,2=fail): 1
Enter result (1=pass,2=fail): 1
Enter result (1=pass,2=fail): 1
Enter result (1=pass,2=fail): 2
Enter result (1=pass,2=fail): 1
Enter result (1=pass,2=fail): 1
Enter result (1=pass,2=fail): 1
Enter result (1=pass,2=fail): 1
Enter result (1=pass,2=fail): 1
Enter result (1=pass,2=fail): 1
Passed 9
Failed 1
Raise tuition
```

Fig. 2.11 Sample execution for examination results problem (part 2 of 2).

Note that we have taken advantage of a feature of Java that allows variable initialization to be incorporated into declarations. Looping programs may require initialization at the beginning of each repetition; such initialization would normally occur in assignment statements.

Good Programming Practice 2.10

Initializing variables when they are declared in methods helps the programmer avoid compiler messages warning of uninitialized data. Instance variables of primitive data type **int** *are automatically initialized to zero and instance variables of primitive data types* **boolean** *are automatically initialized to* **false**.

Software Engineering Observation 2.7

Experience has shown that the most difficult part of solving a problem on a computer is developing the algorithm for the solution. Once a correct algorithm has been specified, the process of producing a working Java program from the algorithm is normally straightforward.

Software Engineering Observation 2.8

Many experienced programmers write programs without ever using program development tools like pseudocode. These programmers feel that their ultimate goal is to solve the problem on a computer, and that writing pseudocode merely delays the production of final outputs. Although this may work for simple and familiar problems, it can lead to serious errors on large, complex projects.

2.11 Assignment Operators

Java provides several assignment operators for abbreviating assignment expressions. For example the statement

```
c = c + 3;
```

can be abbreviated with the *addition assignment operator* **+=** as

```
c += 3;
```

The **+=** operator adds the value of the expression on the right of the operator to the value of the variable on the left of the operator and stores the result in the variable on the left of the operator. Any statement of the form

       variable **=** *variable operator expression;*

where *operator* is one of the binary operators **+**, **-**, *****, **/**, or **%** (or others we will discuss later in the text), can be written in the form

       *variable operator***=** *expression;*

Thus the assignment **c += 3** adds **3** to **c**. Figure 2.12 shows the arithmetic assignment operators, sample expressions using these operators, and explanations.

Performance Tip 2.1

Programmers can write programs a bit faster and compilers can compile programs a bit faster when the "abbreviated" assignment operators are used. Some compilers generate code that runs faster when "abbreviated" assignment operators are used.

Performance Tip 2.2

Many of the performance tips we mention in this text result in nominal improvements, so the reader may be tempted to ignore them. Significant performance improvement is often realized when a supposedly nominal improvement is placed in a loop that may repeat a large number of times.

2.12 Increment and Decrement Operators

Java provides the unary *increment operator*, **++**, and the unary *decrement operator*, **--**, which are summarized in Fig. 2.13. If a variable **c** is incremented by 1, the increment operator **++** can be used rather than the expressions **c = c + 1** or **c += 1**. If an increment or decrement operator is placed before a variable, it is referred to as the *preincrement* or *predecrement operator,* respectively. If an increment or decrement operator is placed after a variable, it is referred to as the *postincrement* or *postdecrement operator,* respectively. Pre-

Assignment operator	Sample expression	Explanation	Assigns
Assume: `int c = 3, d = 5, e = 4, f = 6, g = 12;`			
+=	c += 7	c = c + 7	10 to c
-=	d -= 4	d = d - 4	1 to d
*=	e *= 5	e = e * 5	20 to e
/=	f /= 3	f = f / 3	2 to f
%=	g %= 9	g = g % 9	3 to g

Fig. 2.12 Arithmetic assignment operators.

Operator	Called	Sample expression	Explanation
++	preincrement	++a	Increment **a** by 1 then use the new value of **a** in the expression in which **a** resides.
++	postincrement	a++	Use the current value of **a** in the expression in which **a** resides, then increment **a** by 1.
--	predecrement	--b	Decrement **b** by 1 then use the new value of **b** in the expression in which **b** resides.
--	postdecrement	b--	Use the current value of **b** in the expression in which **b** resides, then decrement **b** by 1.

Fig. 2.13 The increment and decrement operators.

incrementing (predecrementing) a variable causes the variable to be incremented (decremented) by 1, then the new value of the variable is used in the expression in which it appears. Postincrementing (postdecrementing) the variable causes the current value of the variable to be used in the expression in which it appears, then the variable value is incremented (decremented) by 1.

The applet of Fig. 2.14 demonstrates the difference between the preincrementing version and the postincrementing version of the **++** increment operator. Postincrementing the variable **c** causes it to be incremented after it is used in the **g.drawString** method call (line 13). Preincrementing the variable **c** causes it to be incremented before it is used in the **g.drawString** method call (line 19).

The program displays the value of **c** before and after the **++** operator is used. The decrement operator (**--**) works similarly.

 Good Programming Practice 2.11

Unary operators should be placed next to their operands with no intervening spaces.

The three assignment statements in Fig 2.11

```
passes = passes + 1;
failures = failures + 1;
student = student + 1;
```

can be written more concisely with assignment operators as

```
passes += 1;
failures += 1;
student += 1;
```

with preincrement operators as

```
++passes;
++failures;
++student;
```

```
1    // Fig. 2.14: Increment.java
2    // Preincrementing and postincrementing
3    import java.awt.Graphics;
4    import java.applet.Applet;
5
6    public class Increment extends Applet {
7       public void paint( Graphics g )
8       {
9          int c;
10
11         c = 5;
12         g.drawString( Integer.toString( c ), 25, 25 );
13         g.drawString( Integer.toString( c++ ),  // postincrement
14                    25, 40 );
15         g.drawString( Integer.toString( c ), 25, 55 );
16
17         c = 5;
18         g.drawString( Integer.toString( c ), 25, 85 );
19         g.drawString( Integer.toString( ++c ),  // preincrement
20                    25, 100 );
21         g.drawString( Integer.toString( c ), 25, 115 );
22      }
23   }
```

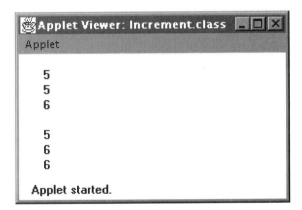

Fig. 2.14 The difference between preincrementing and postincrementing .

or with postincrement operators as

```
passes++;
failures++;
student++;
```

It is important to note here that when incrementing or decrementing a variable in a statement by itself, the preincrement and postincrement forms have the same effect, and the predecrement and postdecrement forms have the same effect. It is only when a variable appears in the context of a larger expression that preincrementing the variable and postincrementing the variable have different effects (and similarly for predecrementing and post-decrementing).

Common Programming Error 2.9

Attempting to use the increment or decrement operator on an expression other than a simple variable name, e.g., writing **++(x + 1)** *is a syntax error.*

The chart in Fig. 2.15 shows the precedence and associativity of the operators introduced to this point. The operators are shown top-to-bottom in decreasing order of precedence. The second column describes the associativity of the operators at each level of precedence. Notice that the conditional operator (**? :**), the unary operators increment (**++**), decrement (**--**), plus (**+**), minus (**-**) and casts, and the assignment operators **=, +=, -=, *=, /=** and **%=** associate from right to left. All other operators in the operator precedence chart of Fig. 2.15 associate from left to right. The third column names the various groups of operators.

2.13 Primitive Data Types

The table in Fig. 2.16 lists the primitive data types in Java. The primitive types are the building blocks for more complicated types. Like its predecessor languages C and C++, Java requires all variables to have a type before they can be used in a program. For this reason, Java is referred to as a *strongly-typed language.*

Unlike C and C++, the primitive types in Java are portable across all computer platforms that support Java. This enables programmers to write programs once without knowing which computer platform will execute the program.

In C and C++ programs, programmers frequently had to write programs multiple times to support the many different computer platforms because the primitive data types were not guaranteed to be identical from computer to computer. For example, an **int** value on one machine might be represented by 16 bits (or 2 bytes) of memory and an **int** value on another machine might be represented by 32 bits (or 4 bytes) of memory. In Java, **int** values are always 32 bits (or 4 bytes).

Operators						Associativity	Type
( )						left to right	parentheses
++	--	+	-	(*type*)		right to left	unary
*	/	%				left to right	multiplicative
+	-					left to right	additive
<	<=	>	>=			left to right	relational
==	!=					left to right	equality
? :						right to left	conditional
=	+=	-=	*=	/=	%=	right to left	assignment

Fig. 2.15 Precedence of the operators encountered so far in the text.

Type	Size in bits	Values	Standard
boolean	1	true or false	
char	16	`'\u0000'` to `'\uFFFF'`	(ISO Unicode character set)
byte	8	-128 to +127	
short	16	-32,768 to +32,767	
int	32	-2,147,483,648 to +2,147,483,647	
long	64	-9,223,372,036,854,775,808 to +9,223,372,036,854,775,807	
float	32	-3.40292347E+38 to +3.40292347E+38	(IEEE 754 floating-point)
double	64	-1.79769313486231570E+308 to +1.79769313486231570E+308	(IEEE 754 floating-point)

Fig. 2.16 The Java primitive data types.

Portability Tip 2.1

All primitive data types in Java are portable across all platforms that support Java.

Each data type in the table is listed with its size in bits (there are 8 bits to a byte) and its range of values. Because the designers of Java want it to be portable, they chose to use internationally recognized standards for both character formats (Unicode) and for floating-point numbers (IEEE 754).

2.14 Common Escape Sequences

When outputting information, it is sometimes helpful to add some formatting with special characters called *escape sequences*. Some common escape sequences are listed in Fig. 2.17.

Escape Sequence	Description
`\n`	Newline. Position the cursor to the beginning of the next line.
`\t`	Horizontal tab. Move the cursor to the next tab stop.
`\r`	Carriage return. Position the cursor to the beginning of the current line; do not advance to the next line.
`\\`	Backslash. Used to print a backslash character.
`\'`	Single quote. Used to print a single quote character.
`\"`	Double quote. Used to print a double quote character.

Fig. 2.17 Some common escape sequences.

In Fig. 2.17, the backslash (\) that starts each escape sequence is called an *escape character*. It indicates that a "special" character is to be output. When a backslash is encountered in a string of characters, the next character is combined with the backslash to form an escape sequence.

Escape sequences can be used as individual characters in single quotes or as characters in a string. The application of Fig. 2.18 demonstrates some common escape sequences. The first output statement (lines 7 and 8) uses **\'** twice to wrap a character in single quotes. The second output statement (lines 9 and 10) uses **\"** twice to wrap a string in double quotes. The third output statement (line 11) uses **** to output a backslash character. The fourth output statement (line 12) uses **\t** twice to output a line of text with two tabs in the middle. Tab characters can be used to output information in columns. The fifth output statement (line 13) uses **\n** twice to output text double-spaced—i.e., with a blank line between lines of text. Note that the **System.out.println** method actually performs the same task as the **System.out.print** method, but it adds a **\n** character to the output automatically. Finally, the last output statement uses a **\r** character to demonstrate repositioning the cursor at the start of the current line. Notice that the **#** characters overwrite some of the ***** characters that were output before the **\r** character.

Note that the escape sequences **\n**, **\t** and **\r** only work when they are output using **System.out** (or the other output capabilties discussed in Chapter 15, Files and Streams).

```
1   // Fig. 2.18: EscapeSequences.java
2   // Demonstrating common escape sequences
3
4   public class EscapeSequences {
5      public static void main( String args[] )
6      {
7         System.out.println( "Displaying single quotes: " +
8                             "\'A\'" );
9         System.out.println( "Displaying double quotes: " +
10                            "\"string\"" );
11        System.out.println( "Displaying a backslash: \\" );
12        System.out.println( "Text separated\t\tby two tabs" );
13        System.out.println( "Here is double\n\nspaced text" );
14        System.out.println( "**********\r#####" );
15     }
16  }
```

```
Displaying single quotes: 'A'
Displaying double quotes: "string"
Displaying a backslash: \
Text separated          by two tabs
Here is double

spaced text
#####*****
```

Fig. 2.18 Demonstrating common escape sequences.

Summary

- A procedure for solving a problem in terms of the actions to be executed and the order in which these actions should be executed is called an algorithm.

- Specifying the order in which statements are to be executed in a computer program is called program control.

- Pseudocode helps the programmer "think out" a program before attempting to write it in a programming language such as Java.

- Declarations are messages to the compiler telling it the names and attributes of variables and telling it to reserve space for variables.

- A selection structure is used to choose among alternative courses of action.

- The **if** selection structure executes an indicated action only when the condition is true.

- The **if/else** selection structure specifies separate actions to be executed when the condition is true and when the condition is false.

- Whenever more than one statement is to be executed where normally only a single statement is expected, these statements must be enclosed in braces forming a compound statement. A compound statement can be placed anywhere a single statement can be placed.

- An empty statement indicating that no action is to be taken is indicated by placing a semicolon (**;**) where a statement would normally be.

- A repetition structure specifies that an action is to be repeated while some condition remains true.

- The format for the **while** repetition structure is

    ```
    while ( condition )
         statement
    ```

- An application begins execution at the **main** method. Applications are executed using the Java interpreter (**java**).

- Method main must have the following first line:

    ```
    public static void main( String args[] )
    ```

- If **main** does not begin with this line, the Java interpreter will not be able to execute your program.

- Exceptions are exceptional cases during a program's execution—they do not happen frequently, but they can happen. Exceptions can be processed to allow the program to continue or can be ignores, in which case the program may terminate.

- Java is extremely strict about exception processing. If you compile a program that does input from the keyboard, Java expects you to write your program so it handles any input problems that may occur. If you want to ignore the exceptions, you must indicate to the compiler that you are aware of the problems that might occur by declaring the exception in the **throws** clause of the method.

- The standard output stream object—**System.out**—outputs information to the standard output stream which is normally "connected" to the screen.

- Method **System.out.print** sends its argument to the screen to be displayed. When using this method, the characters to be output are sometimes placed in a buffer (a temporary holding area in the computer's memory) and not actually displayed on the screen. Method **System.out.flush** forces the characters in the buffer to be displayed.

- Method **System.out.println** sends its argument followed by a newline character to the screen to be displayed.

- The standard input stream object—**System.in**—obtains input from the standard input stream which is usually the keyboard. The **System.in.read** method reads one character from the keyboard and returns it as its integer value which is the character's numerical representation in the computer. Java uses the *ISO (International Standards Organization) Unicode character set* to represent characters in memory. Method **System.in.skip** enables the program to skip characters in the input stream.

- The Java interpreter executes applications written in Java. To run the Java interpreter for an application, at the command line, type **java** followed by the name of the class in which method **main** is defined and press Enter.

- A value that contains a fractional part is referred to as a floating-point number and is represented by the data type **float** or **double**.

- Unary cast operator **(double)** creates a temporary floating-point copy of its operand.

- Java provides the arithmetic assignment operators **+=**, **-=**, ***=**, **/=**, and **%=** that help abbreviate certain common types of expressions.

- The increment operator, **++**, and the decrement operator, **--**, increment or decrement a variable by 1. If the operator is prefixed to the variable, the variable is incremented or decremented by 1 first, then used in its expression. If the operator is postfixed to the variable, the variable is used in its expression, then incremented or decremented by 1.

- The primitive types (**boolean**, **char**, **byte**, **short**, **int**, **long**, **float**, and **double**) are the building blocks for more complicated types in Java.

- Java requires all variables to have a type before they can be used in a program. For this reason, Java is referred to as a strongly-typed language.

- Primitive types in Java are portable across all computer platforms that support Java.

- Java uses internationally recognized standards for both character formats (Unicode) and for floating-point numbers (IEEE 754).

Terminology

-- operator	algorithm
++ operator	application
?: operator	arithmetic assignment operators:
action	**+=**, **-=**, ***=**, **/=**, and **%=**
action/decision model	block

body of a loop   nonfatal error
cast operator   postdecrement operator
compound statement   postincrement operator
conditional operator (**? :**)   predecrement operator
control structure   preincrement operator
counter-controlled repetition   promotion
decision   pseudocode
decrement operator (**--**)   repetition
definite repetition   repetition structures
double   selection
double-selection structure   sentinel value
empty statement (**;**)   sequential execution
exception   single-entry/single-exit control structures
if selection structure   single-selection structure
if/else selection structure   stacked control structures
implicit conversion   standard input stream
increment operator (**++**)   standard output stream
indefinite repetition   structured programming
infinite loop   syntax error
initialization   **System.in**
integer division   **System.in.read**
IOException   **System.in.skip**
ISO Unicode character set   **System.out**
keyword   **System.out.flush**
logic error   **System.out.print**
loop counter   **System.out.println**
loop-continuation condition   top-down, stepwise refinement
main method   unary operator
nested control structures   **while** repetition structure
newline character   whitespace characters

Common Programming Errors

2.1   Using a keyword as an identifier.

2.2   Forgetting one or both of the braces that delimit a compound statement can lead to syntax errors or logic errors.

2.3   Placing a semicolon after the condition in an **if** structure leads to a logic error in single-selection **if** structures and a syntax error in double-selection **if** structures (if the **if**-part contains an actual body statement).

2.4   Not providing in the body of a **while** structure an action that eventually causes the condition in the **while** to become false. Normally, such a repetition structure will never terminate—an error called an "infinite loop."

2.5   Spelling the keyword **while** with an uppercase **W** as in **While** (remember that Java is a case-sensitive language). All of Java's reserved keywords such as **while**, **if**, and **else** contain only lowercase letters.

2.6   Not initializing a counter or total results in an error message from the compiler stating that the variable may not have been initialized. You must initialize the variable to allow the compiler to complete compilation of your program.

2.7   Choosing a sentinel value that is also a legitimate data value results in a logic error and may prevent a sentinel-controlled loop from terminating properly.

2.8   Using floating-point numbers in a manner that assumes they are represented precisely can lead to incorrect results. Floating-point numbers are represented only approximately by most computers.

2.9   Attempting to use the increment or decrement operator on an expression other than a simple variable name, e.g., writing **++(x + 1)** is a syntax error.

Good Programming Practices

2.1   Consistently applying reasonable indentation conventions throughout your programs greatly improves program readability. We suggest a fixed-size tab of about 1/4 inch or three spaces per indent.

2.2   Pseudocode is often used to "think out" a program during the program design process. Then the pseudocode program is converted to Java.

2.3   Indent both body statements of an **if/else** structure.

2.4   If there are several levels of indentation, each level should be indented the same additional amount of space.

2.5   Some programmers prefer to type the beginning and ending braces of compound statements before typing the individual statements within the braces. This helps avoid omitting one or both of the braces.

2.6   Initialize counters and totals.

2.7   When performing division by an expression whose value could be zero, explicitly test for this case and handle it appropriately in your program (such as printing an error message) rather than allowing the division by zero to occur.

2.8   In a sentinel-controlled loop, the prompts requesting data entry should explicitly remind the user what the sentinel value is.

2.9   Do not compare floating-point values for equality or inequality. Rather, test that the difference is less than a specified small value.

2.10   Initializing variables when they are declared in methods helps the programmer avoid compiler messages warning of uninitialized data. Instance variables of primitive data type **int** are automatically initialized to zero and instance variables of primitive data types **boolean** are automatically initialized to **false**.

2.11   Unary operators should be placed next to their operands with no intervening spaces.

Performance Tips

2.1   Programmers can write programs a bit faster and compilers can compile programs a bit faster when the "abbreviated" assignment operators are used. Some compilers generate code that runs faster when "abbreviated" assignment operators are used.

2.2   Many of the performance tips we mention in this text result in nominal improvements, so the reader may be tempted to ignore them. Significant performance improvement is often realized when a supposedly nominal improvement is placed in a loop that may repeat a large number of times.

Portability Tip

2.1   All primitive data types in Java are portable across all platforms that support Java.

Software Engineering Observations

2.1   A compound statement can be placed anywhere in a program that a single statement can be placed.

2.2   Just as a compound statement can be placed anywhere a single statement can be placed, it is also possible to have no statement at all, i.e., the empty statement. The empty statement is represented by placing a semicolon (*;*) where a statement would normally be.

2.3   A program should be written to process exceptional cases that can occur during the execution of the program. This results in programs that are more robust and more likely to execute properly.

2.4   Each refinement, as well as the top itself, is a complete specification of the algorithm; only the level of detail varies.

2.5   Many algorithms can be divided logically into three phases: an initialization phase that initializes the program variables; a processing phase that inputs data values and adjusts program variables accordingly; and a termination phase that calculates and prints the final results.

2.6   The programmer terminates the top-down, stepwise refinement process when the pseudocode algorithm is specified in sufficient detail for the programmer to be able to convert the pseudocode to a Java algorithm. Implementing the Java algorithm is then normally straightforward.

2.7   Experience has shown that the most difficult part of solving a problem on a computer is developing the algorithm for the solution. Once a correct algorithm has been specified, the process of producing a working Java program from the algorithm is normally straightforward.

2.8   Many experienced programmers write programs without ever using program development tools like pseudocode. These programmers feel that their ultimate goal is to solve the problem on a computer, and that writing pseudocode merely delays the production of final outputs. Although this may work for simple and familiar problems, it can lead to serious errors on large, complex projects.

Testing and Debugging Tip

2.1   Java is strict about processing exceptional cases in a program. Java has better security and error handling requirements than C or C++. This leads to programs that are easier to debug and maintain.

Self-Review Exercises

2.1   Answer each of the following questions.
   a) All programs can be written in terms of three types of control structures: _____, _____, and _____.
   b) The _____selection structure is used to execute one action when a condition is true and another action when that condition is false.
   c) Repetition of a set of instructions a specific number of times is called_____ repetition.
   d) When it is not known in advance how many times a set of statements will be repeated, a _____ value can be used to terminate the repetition.

2.2   Write four different Java statements that each add 1 to integer variable **x**.

2.3   Write Java statements to accomplish each of the following:
   a) Assign the sum of **x** and **y** to **z** and increment the value of **x** by 1 after the calculation.
   b) Test if the value of the variable **count** is greater than 10. If it is, print "**Count is greater than 10**"
   c) Decrement the variable **x** by 1 then subtract it from the variable **total**.
   d) Calculate the remainder after **q** is divided by **divisor** and assign the result to **q**. Write this statement two different ways.

2.4   Write a Java statement to accomplish each of the following tasks.
   a) Declare variables **sum** and **x** to be of type **int**.
   b) Assign **1** to variable **x**.
   c) Assign **0** to variable **sum**.
   d) Add variable **x** to variable **sum** and assign the result to variable **sum**.
   e) Print **"The sum is: "** followed by the value of variable **sum**.

2.5   Combine the statements that you wrote in Exercise 2.4 into an application that calculates and prints the sum of the integers from 1 to 10. Use the **while** structure to loop through the calculation and increment statements. The loop should terminate when the value of **x** becomes 11.

2.6   Determine the values of each variable after the calculation is performed. Assume that when each statement begins executing all variables have the integer value 5.
   a) `product *= x++;`
   b) `quotient /= ++x;`

2.7   Identify and correct the errors in each of the following:
```
a) while ( c <= 5 ) {
      product *= c;
      ++c;
b) if ( gender == 1 )
      System.out.println( "Woman" );
   else;
      System.out.println( "Man" );
```

2.8   What is wrong with the following **while** repetition structure:

```
while ( z >= 0 )
    sum += z;
```

Answers to Self-Review Exercises

2.1   a) Sequence, selection, and repetition. b) **if/else**. c) Counter-controlled or definite.   d) Sentinel, signal, flag, or dummy.

2.2
```
x = x + 1;
x += 1;
++x;
x++;
```

2.3   a) `z = x++ + y;`
b) `if ( count > 10 )`
      `System.out.println( "Count is greater than 10" );`
c) `total -= --x;`
d) `q %= divisor;`
   `q = q % divisor;`

2.4   a) `int sum, x;`
b) `x = 1;`
c) `sum = 0;`
d) `sum += x;` or `sum = sum + x;`
e) `System.out.println( "The sum is: " + sum );`

2.5
```
// Calculate the sum of the integers from 1 to 10
public class Calculate {
    public static void main( String args[] )
    {
        int sum, x;
        x = 1;
        sum = 0;
        while ( x <= 10 ) {
            sum += x;
            ++x;
        }
        System.out.println( "The sum is: " + sum );
    }
}
```

2.6   a) `product = 25, x = 6;`
b) `quotient = 0, x = 6;`

2.7   a) Error: Missing the closing right brace of the **while** body.
Correction: Add closing right brace after the statement **++c;**.
c) Error: Semicolon after **else** results in a logic error. The second output statement will always be executed.
Correction: Remove the semicolon after **else**.

2.8   The value of the variable **z** is never changed in the **while** structure. Therefore, if the loop-continuation condition **(z >= 0)** is true, an infinite loop is created. To prevent the infinite loop, **z** must be decremented so that it eventually becomes less than 0.

Exercises

2.9   Identify and correct the errors in each of the following (Note: There may be more than one error in each piece of code):

```
a) if ( age >= 65 );
       System.out.println( "Age greater than or equal to 65" );
   else
       System.out.println( "Age is less than 65 )";
b) int x = 1, total;
   while ( x <= 10 ) {
      total += x;
      ++x;
   }
c) While ( x <= 100 )
      total += x;
      ++x;
d) while ( y > 0 ) {
       System.out.println( y );
       ++y;
   }
```

2.10   What does the following program print?

```
public class Mystery {
   public static void main( String args[] )
   {
      int y, x = 1, total = 0;
      while ( x <= 10 ) {
         y = x * x;
         System.out.println( y );
         total += y;
         ++x;
      }
      System.out.println( "Total is " + total );
   }
}
```

For Exercise 2.11 through 2.14 perform each of these steps:
   a) Read the problem statement.
   b) Formulate the algorithm using pseudocode and top-down, stepwise refinement.
   c) Write a Java program.
   d) Test, debug, and execute the Java program.

2.11   Because of the high price of gasoline, drivers are concerned with the mileage obtained by their automobiles. One driver has kept track of several tankfuls of gasoline by recording miles driven and gallons used for each tankful. Develop a Java applet that will input the miles driven and gallons used (both as integers) for each tankful. The program should calculate and display the miles per gallon obtained for each tankful and print the combined miles per gallon obtained for all tankfuls up to this point. All average calculations should produce floating-point results. Use two text fields to input the data (see Fig. 1.13 for hints).

2.12   Develop a Java applet that will determine if a department store customer has exceeded the credit limit on a charge account. For each customer, the following facts are available:

a) Account number
b) Balance at the beginning of the month
c) Total of all items charged by this customer this month
d) Total of all credits applied to this customer's account this month
e) Allowed credit limit

The program should input each of these facts from text fields as integers, calculate the new balance (= beginning balance + charges - credits), display the new balance and determine if the new balance exceeds the customer's credit limit. For those customers whose credit limit is exceeded, the program should display the message, "Credit limit exceeded."

2.13   A large company pays its salespeople on a commission basis. The salespeople receive $200 per week plus 9 percent of their gross sales for that week. For example, a salesperson who sells $5000 worth of merchandise in a week receives $200 plus 9 percent of $5000, or a total of $650. You have been supplied with a list of items sold by each salesperson. The values of these items are as follows:

Item	Value
A	239.99
B	129.75
C	99.95
D	350.89

Develop a Java application that inputs one salesperson's items sold for last week and calculates and displays that salesperson's earnings. There is no limit to the number of items sold by a salesperson.

2.14   Develop a Java applet that will determine the gross pay for each of several employees. The company pays "straight-time" for the first 40 hours worked by each employee and pays "time-and-a-half" for all hours worked in excess of 40 hours. You are given a list of the employees of the company, the number of hours each employee worked last week, and the hourly rate of each employee. Your program should input this information for each employee, and should determine and display the employee's gross pay. Use text fields to input the data.

```
Enter hours worked (-1 to end): 39
Enter hourly rate of the worker ($00.00): 10.00
Salary is $390.00

Enter hours worked (-1 to end): 40
Enter hourly rate of the worker ($00.00): 10.00
Salary is $400.00

Enter hours worked (-1 to end): 41
Enter hourly rate of the worker ($00.00): 10.00
Salary is $415.00

Enter hours worked (-1 to end): -1
```

2.15   The process of finding the largest value (i.e., the maximum of a group of values) is used frequently in computer applications. For example, a program that determines the winner of a sales contest would input the number of units sold by each salesperson. The salesperson who sells the most units wins the contest. Write a pseudocode program and then a Java program that inputs a series of 10 single digit numbers, and determines and prints the largest of the numbers. Hint: Your program should use three variables as follows:

counter:	A counter to count to 10 (i.e., to keep track of how many numbers have been input, and to determine when all 10 numbers have been processed)

number: The current digit input to the program

largest: The largest number found so far.

2.16   Write a Java application that utilizes looping to print the following table of values:

```
N          10*N       100*N      1000*N

1          10         100        1000
2          20         200        2000
3          30         300        3000
4          40         400        4000
5          50         500        5000
```

2.17   Using an approach similar to Exercise 2.15, find the *two* largest values of the 10 digits entered. Note: You may input each number only once.

2.18   Modify the program in Fig. 2.11 to validate its inputs. On any input, if the value entered is other than 1 or 2, keep looping until the user enters a correct value.

2.19   What does the following program print?

```java
public class Mystery2 {
    public static void main( String args[] )
    {
        int count = 1;
        while ( count <= 10 ) {
            System.out.println( count % 2 == 1 ?
                                "****" : "++++++++" );
            ++count;
        }
    }
}
```

2.20   What does the following program print?

```java
public class Mystery3 {
    public static void main( String args[] )
    {
        int row = 10, column;
        while ( row >= 1 ) {
            column = 1;
            while ( column <= 10 ) {
                System.out.print( row % 2 == 1 ? "<" : ">" );
                ++column;
            }
            --row;
            System.out.println();
        }
    }
}
```

2.21   *(Dangling Else Problem)* Determine the output for each of the following when **x** is **9** and **y** is **11** and when **x** is **11** and **y** is **9**. Note that the compiler ignores the indentation in a Java program. Also, the Java compiler always associates an **else** with the previous **if** unless told to do otherwise by the placement of braces **{}**. Because, on first glance, the programmer may not be sure which **if** an **else** matches, this is referred to as the "dangling else" problem. We have eliminated the indentation from the following code to make the problem more challenging. (Hint: Apply indentation conventions you have learned.)

a)
```java
if ( x < 10 )
if ( y > 10 )
System.out.println( "*****" );
else
System.out.println( "#####" );
System.out.println( "$$$$$" );
```

b)
```java
if ( x < 10 ) {
if ( y > 10 )
System.out.println( "*****" );
}
else {
System.out.println( "#####" );
System.out.println( "$$$$$" );
}
```

2.22   *(Another Dangling Else Problem)* Modify the following code to produce the output shown. Use proper indentation techniques. You may not make any changes other than inserting braces. The compiler ignores indentation in a Java program. We have eliminated the indentation from the following code to make the problem more challenging. Note: It is possible that no modification is necessary.

```java
if ( y == 8 )
if ( x == 5 )
System.out.println( "@@@@@" );
else
System.out.println( "#####" );
System.out.println( "$$$$$" );
System.out.println( "&&&&&" );
```

a)   Assuming **x = 5** and **y = 8**, the following output is produced.

```
@@@@@
$$$$$
&&&&&
```

b)   Assuming **x = 5** and **y = 8**, the following output is produced.

```
@@@@@
```

c)   Assuming **x = 5** and **y = 8**, the following output is produced.

```
@@@@@
&&&&&
```

d) Assuming **x = 5** and **y = 7**, the following output is produced. Note: The last three output statements after the **else** are all part of a compound statement.

```
#####
$$$$$
&&&&&
```

2.23   Write an applet that reads in the size of the side of a square and then prints a hollow square of that size out of asterisks using the **drawString** method inside your applet's **paint** method. Your program should work for squares of all side sizes between 1 and 20. For example, if your program reads a size of 5, it should print

```
*****
*   *
*   *
*   *
*****
```

2.24   A palindrome is a number or a text phrase that reads the same backwards as forwards. For example, each of the following five-digit integers are palindromes: 12321, 55555, 45554 and 11611. Write an applet that reads in a five-digit integer and determines whether or not it is a palindrome.

2.25   Write an applet that inputs an integer containing only 0s and 1s (i.e., a "binary" integer) and print its decimal equivalent. (Hint: Use the modulus and division operators to pick off the "binary" number's digits one at a time from right to left. Just as in the decimal number system where the right-most digit has a positional value of 1, and the next digit left has a positional value of 10, then 100, then 1000, etc., in the binary number system the rightmost digit has a positional value of 1, the next digit left has a positional value of 2, then 4, then 8, etc. Thus the decimal number 234 can be interpreted as 4 * 1 + 3 * 10 + 2 * 100. The decimal equivalent of binary 1101 is 1 * 1 + 0 * 2 + 1 * 4 + 1 * 8 or 1 + 0 + 4 + 8 or 13.)

2.26   Write an application that displays the following checkerboard pattern

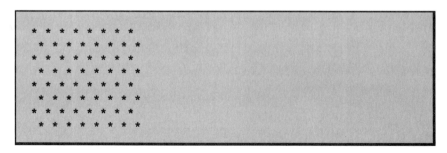

Your program may use only three output statements, one of the form

```
System.out.print( "* " );
```

one of the form

```
System.out.print( " " );
```

and one of the form

```
System.out.println();
```

Note that the preceding statement indicates that the program should output a single newline character to drop to the next line on the output.

2.27   Write an applet that keeps displaying in the status bar the multiples of the integer 2, namely 2, 4, 8, 16, 32, 64, etc. Your loop should not terminate (i.e., you should create an infinite loop). What happens when you run this program?

2.28   What's wrong with the following statement? Provide the correct statement to accomplish what the programmer was probably trying to do.

```
System.out.println( ++(x + y) );
```

2.29   Write an applet that reads three nonzero values entered by the user in text fields and determines and prints if they could represent the sides of a triangle.

2.30   Write an applet that reads three nonzero integers and determines and prints if they could be the sides of a right triangle.

2.31   A company wants to transmit data over the telephone, but they are concerned that their phones may be tapped. All of their data is transmitted as four-digit integers. They have asked you to write a program that will encrypt their data so that it may be transmitted more securely. Your applet should read a four-digit integer entered by the user in a text field and encrypt it as follows: Replace each digit by *(the sum of that digit plus 7) modulus 10.* Then, swap the first digit with the third, and swap the second digit with the fourth. Then print the encrypted integer. Write a separate applet that inputs an encrypted four-digit integer, and decrypts it to form the original number.

2.32   The factorial of a nonnegative integer n is written $n!$ (pronounced "n factorial") and is defined as follows:

$n! = n \cdot (n - 1) \cdot (n - 2) \cdot \ldots \cdot 1$ (for values of n greater than or equal to 1)

and

$n! = 1$ (for $n = 0$).

For example, $5! = 5 \cdot 4 \cdot 3 \cdot 2 \cdot 1$ which is 120.

a)   Write an applet that reads a nonnegative integer from a text field and computes and prints its factorial.

b)   Write an applet that estimates the value of the mathematical constant e by using the formula:

$$e = 1 + \frac{1}{1!} + \frac{1}{2!} + \frac{1}{3!} + \ldots$$

c)   Write an applet that computes the value of e^x by using the formula:

$$e^x = 1 + \frac{x}{1!} + \frac{x^2}{2!} + \frac{x^3}{3!} + \ldots$$

3

Control Structures

Objectives

- To be able to use the **for** and **do/while** repetition structures to execute statements in a program repeatedly.
- To understand multiple selection using the **switch** selection structure.
- To be able to use the **break** and **continue** program control statements.
- To be able to use the logical operators.

Who can control his fate?
William Shakespeare, Othello

The used key is always bright.
Benjamin Franklin

Man is a tool-making animal.
Benjamin Franklin

Intelligence ... is the faculty of making artificial objects, especially tools to make tools.
Henry Bergson

Outline

3.1 Introduction

Before writing a program to solve a particular problem, it is essential to have a thorough understanding of the problem and a carefully planned approach to solving the problem. When writing a program, it is equally essential to understand the types of building blocks that are available and to employ proven program construction principles. In this chapter we discuss all of these issues in our presentation of the theory and principles of structured programming. The techniques that you will learn here are applicable to most high-level languages including Java. When we begin our formal treatment of object-oriented programming in Java in Chapter 6, we will see that the control structures we study here in Chapter 3 are helpful in building and manipulating objects.

3.2 Essentials of Counter-Controlled Repetition

Counter-controlled repetition requires:

1. The *name* of a control variable (or loop counter).

2. The *initial value* of the control variable.

3. The *increment* (or *decrement*) by which the control variable is modified each time through the loop.

4. The condition that tests for the *final value* of the control variable (i.e., whether looping should continue).

Consider the simple program shown in Fig. 3.1, which prints the numbers from 1 to 10. The declaration

```
int counter = 1;
```

```
1   // Fig. 3.1: WhileCounter.java
2   // Counter-controlled repetition
3   import java.awt.Graphics;
4   import java.applet.Applet;
5
6   public class WhileCounter extends Applet {
7      public void paint( Graphics g )
8      {
9         int counter = 1;                // initialization
10        int yPos = 25;
11
12        while ( counter <= 10 ) {       // repetition condition
13           g.drawString( Integer.toString( counter ),
14                         25, yPos );
15           ++counter;                   // increment
16           yPos += 15;
17        }
18     }
19  }
```

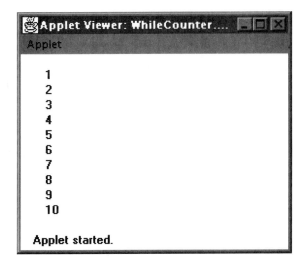

Fig. 3.1   Counter-controlled repetition.

names the control variable (**counter**), declares it to be an integer, reserves space for it in memory, and sets it to an *initial value* of **1**. Declarations that require initialization are, in effect, executable statements.

The declaration and initialization of **counter** could also have been accomplished with the statements

```
int counter;
counter = 1;
```

The declaration is not executable, but the assignment is. We use both methods of initializing variables.

The statement

```
++counter;
```

increments the loop counter by 1 each time the loop is performed. The loop-continuation condition in the **while** structure tests if the value of the control variable is less than or equal to **10** (the last value for which the condition is true). Note that the body of this **while** is performed even when the control variable is **10**. The loop terminates when the control variable exceeds **10** (i.e., **counter** becomes **11**).

The program in Fig. 3.1 can be made more concise by initializing **counter** to **0** and by replacing the **while** structure with

```
while ( ++counter <= 10 ) {     // repetition condition
    g.drawString( Integer.toString( counter ), 25, yPos );
    yPos += 15;
}
```

This code saves a statement because the incrementing is done directly in the **while** condition before the condition is tested. Coding in such a condensed fashion takes practice.

Common Programming Error 3.1

Because floating-point values may be approximate, controlling counting loops with floating-point variables may result in imprecise counter values and inaccurate tests for termination.

Good Programming Practice 3.1

Control counting loops with integer values.

Good Programming Practice 3.2

Indent the statements in the body of each control structure.

Good Programming Practice 3.3

Put a blank line before and after each major control structure to make it stand out in the program.

Good Programming Practice 3.4

Too many levels of nesting can make a program difficult to understand. As a general rule, try to avoid using more than three levels of indentation.

Good Programming Practice 3.5

Vertical spacing above and below control structures, and indentation of the bodies of control structures within the control structure headers gives programs a two-dimensional appearance that greatly improves readability.

3.3 The **for** Repetition Structure

The **for** repetition structure handles all the details of counter-controlled repetition. To illustrate the power of **for**, let us rewrite the program of Fig. 3.1. The result is shown in Fig. 3.2. The program operates as follows.

```
1   // Fig. 3.2: ForCounter.java
2   // Counter-controlled repetition with the for structure
3   import java.awt.Graphics;
4   import java.applet.Applet;
5
6   public class ForCounter extends Applet {
7      public void paint( Graphics g )
8      {
9         int yPos = 25;
10
11        // Initialization, repetition condition, and incrementing
12        // are all included in the for structure header.
13        for ( int counter = 1; counter <= 10; counter++ ) {
14           g.drawString( Integer.toString( counter ), 25, yPos );
15           yPos += 15;
16        }
17     }
18  }
```

Fig. 3.2   Counter-controlled repetition with the **for** structure.

When the **for** structure begins executing, the control variable **counter** is initialized to 1. Note that **counter** is declared inside the **for** and thus is known only within the **for** structure's body. Then, the loop-continuation condition **counter <= 10** is checked. Because the initial value of **counter** is 1, the condition is satisfied, so the body statement prints the value of **counter**, namely 1. Variable **counter** is then incremented in the expression **counter++**, and the loop begins again with the loop-continuation test. Because the control variable is now equal to 2, the final value is not exceeded, so the program performs the body statement again. This process continues until the control variable **counter** is incremented to 11—this causes the loop-continuation test to fail and repetition terminates. The program continues by performing the first statement after the **for** structure (in this case, the implied **return** statement at the end of the program).

Figure 3.3 takes a closer look at the **for** structure of Fig. 3.2. Notice that the **for** structure "does it all"—it specifies each of the items needed for counter-controlled repeti-

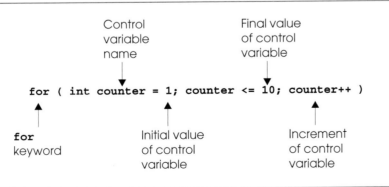

Fig. 3.3   Components of a typical **for** header.

tion with a control variable. If there is more than one statement in the body of the **for** (as in Fig. 3.2), braces are required to define the body of the loop.

Notice that Fig. 3.2 uses the loop-continuation condition **counter <= 10**. If the programmer incorrectly wrote **counter < 10**, then the loop would only be executed 9 times. This is a common logic error called an *off-by-one error*.

Common Programming Error 3.2

*Using an incorrect relational operator or using an incorrect final value of a loop counter in the condition of a **while** or **for** structure can cause off-by-one errors.*

Good Programming Practice 3.6

*Using the final value in the condition of a **while** or **for** structure and using the **<=** relational operator will help avoid off-by-one errors. For a loop used to print the values 1 to 10, for example, the loop-continuation condition should be **counter <= 10** rather than **counter < 10** (which is an off-by-one error) or **counter < 11** (which is also correct).*

The general format of the **for** structure is

```
for ( expression1; expression2; expression3 )
    statement
```

where *expression1* initializes the loop's control variable, *expression2* is the loop-continuation condition, and *expression3* increments the control variable. In most cases the **for** structure can be represented with an equivalent **while** structure as follows:

```
expression1;

while ( expression2 ) {
    statement
    expression3;
}
```

There is an exception to this rule which we will discuss in Section 3.7.

Sometimes, *expression1* and *expression3* in a **for** structure are comma-separated lists of expressions that enable the programmer to use multiple initialization expressions and/or multiple increment expressions. For example, there may be several control variables in a single **for** structure that must be initialized and incremented.

Good Programming Practice 3.7

*Place only expressions involving the control variables in the initialization and increment sections of a **for** structure. Manipulations of other variables should appear either before the loop (if they execute only once like initialization statements) or in the loop body (if they execute once per repetition like incrementing or decrementing statements).*

The three expressions in the **for** structure are optional. If *expression2* is omitted, Java assumes that the loop-continuation condition is true, thus creating an infinite loop. One might omit *expression1* if the control variable is initialized elsewhere in the program. *expression3* might be omitted if the increment is calculated by statements in the body of the **for** or if no increment is needed. The increment expression in the **for** structure acts like a stand-alone statement at the end of the body of the **for**. Therefore, the expressions

```
counter = counter + 1
counter += 1
++counter
counter++
```

are all equivalent in the incrementing portion of the **for** structure. Many programmers prefer the form **counter++** because the incrementing occurs after the loop body is executed. The postincrementing form therefore seems more natural. Because the variable being incremented here does not appear in an expression, both forms of incrementing have the same effect. The two semicolons in the **for** structure are required.

Common Programming Error 3.3

*Using commas instead of the two required semicolons in a **for** header.*

Common Programming Error 3.4

*Placing a semicolon immediately to the right of the right parenthesis of a **for** header makes the body of that **for** structure an empty statement. This is normally a logic error.*

The initialization, loop-continuation condition, and increment portions of a **for** structure can contain arithmetic expressions. For example, assume that **x = 2** and **y = 10**. If **x** and **y** are not modified in the loop body, the statement

```
for ( int j = x; j <= 4 * x * y; j += y / x )
```

is equivalent to the statement

```
for ( int j = 2; j <= 80; j += 5 )
```

The "increment" of a **for** structure may be negative (in which case it is really a decrement and the loop actually counts downwards).

If the loop-continuation condition is initially false, the body of the **for** structure is not performed. Instead, execution proceeds with the statement following the **for**.

The control variable is frequently printed or used in calculations in the body of a **for** structure, but it does not have to be. It is common to use the control variable for controlling repetition while never mentioning it in the body of the **for** structure.

Good Programming Practice 3.8

*Although the value of the control variable can be changed in the body of a **for** loop, avoid doing so because this practice can lead to subtle errors.*

The **for** structure is flowcharted much like the **while** structure. For example, the flowchart of the **for** statement

```
for ( int counter = 1; counter <= 10; counter++ ) {
    g.drawString( Integer.toString( counter ), 25, yPos );
    yPos += 15;
}
```

is shown in Fig. 3.4. This flowchart makes it clear that the initialization occurs only once and that incrementing occurs each time *after* the body statement is performed. Note that

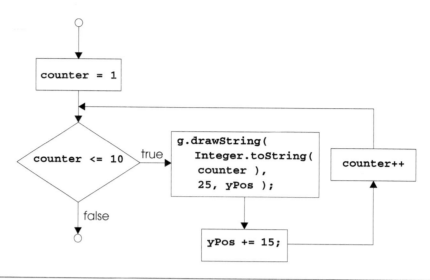

Fig. 3.4   Flowcharting a typical **for** repetition structure.

(besides small circles and arrows) the flowchart contains only rectangle symbols and a diamond symbol. Imagine, again, that the programmer has access to a deep bin of empty **for** structures—as many as the programmer might need to stack and nest with other control structures to form a structured implementation of an algorithm's flow of control. The rectangles and diamonds are then filled with actions and decisions appropriate to the algorithm.

3.4 Examples Using the **for** Structure

The following examples show methods of varying the control variable in a **for** structure. In each case, we write the appropriate **for** header. Note the change in the relational operator for loops that decrement the control variable.

a)   Vary the control variable from **1** to **100** in increments of **1**.

```
for ( int i = 1; i <= 100; i++ )
```

b)   Vary the control variable from **100** to **1** in increments of **-1** (decrements of **1**).

```
for ( int i = 100; i >= 1; i-- )
```

Common Programming Error 3.5

*Not using the proper relational operator in the loop-continuation condition of a loop that counts downwards (such as using **i <= 1** in a loop counting down to 1).*

c)   Vary the control variable from **7** to **77** in steps of **7**.

```
for ( int i = 7; i <= 77; i += 7 )
```

d)   Vary the control variable from **20** to **2** in steps of **-2**.

```
for ( int i = 20; i >= 2; i -= 2 )
```

e) Vary the control variable over the following sequence of values: **2, 5, 8, 11, 14, 17, 20**.

```
for ( int j = 2; j <= 20; j += 3 )
```

f) Vary the control variable over the following sequence of values: **99, 88, 77, 66, 55, 44, 33, 22, 11, 0**.

```
for ( int j = 99; j >= 0; j -= 11 )
```

The next two sample programs demonstrate simple applications of the **for** repetition structure. The program of Fig. 3.5 uses the **for** structure to sum all the even integers from **2** to **100**.

Note that the body of the **for** structure in Fig. 3.5 could actually be merged into the rightmost portion of the **for** header by using the comma operator as follows:

```
for ( int number = 2; number <= 100;
      sum += number, number += 2)
   ;
```

The initialization **sum = 0** could also be merged into the initialization section of the **for** structure.

```
1   // Fig. 3.5: Sum.java
2   // Counter-controlled repetition with the for structure
3   import java.awt.Graphics;
4   import java.applet.Applet;
5
6   public class Sum extends Applet {
7      public void paint( Graphics g )
8      {
9         int sum = 0;
10
11        for ( int number = 2; number <= 100; number += 2 )
12           sum += number;
13
14        g.drawString( "Sum is " + sum, 25, 25 );
15     }
16  }
```

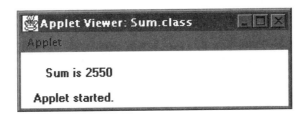

Fig. 3.5 Summation with **for**.

Good Programming Practice 3.9

*Although statements preceding a **for** and statements in the body of a **for** can often be merged into the **for** header, avoid doing so because it makes the program more difficult to read.*

Good Programming Practice 3.10

Limit the size of control structure headers to a single line if possible.

The next example computes compound interest using the **for** structure. Consider the following problem statement:

A person invests $1000.00 in a savings account yielding 5 percent interest. Assuming that all interest is left on deposit, calculate and print the amount of money in the account at the end of each year for 10 years. Use the following formula for determining these amounts:

$$a = p (1 + r)^n$$

where

p is the original amount invested (i.e., the principal)
r is the annual interest rate
n is the number of years
a is the amount on deposit at the end of the nth year.

This problem involves a loop that performs the indicated calculation for each of the 10 years the money remains on deposit. The solution is shown in Fig. 3.6.

```java
1   // Fig. 3.6: Interest.java
2   // Calculating compound interest
3   import java.awt.Graphics;
4   import java.applet.Applet;
5
6   public class Interest extends Applet {
7      public void paint( Graphics g )
8      {
9         double amount, principal = 1000.0, rate = .05;
10        int yPos = 40;
11
12        g.drawString( "Year", 25, 25 );
13        g.drawString( "Amount on deposit", 100, 25 );
14
15        for ( int year = 1; year <= 10; year++ ) {
16           amount = principal * Math.pow( 1.0 + rate, year );
17           g.drawString( Integer.toString( year ), 25, yPos );
18           g.drawString( Double.toString( amount ), 100, yPos );
19           yPos += 15;
20        }
21     }
22  }
```

Fig. 3.6   Calculating compound interest with **for** (part 1 of 2).

Fig. 3.6   Calculating compound interest with **for** (part 2 of 2).

The **for** structure executes the body of the loop 10 times, varying a control variable from 1 to 10 in increments of 1. Although Java does not include an exponentiation operator, we can, however, use the **Math** class method **Math.pow** for this purpose. The method **Math.pow(x, y)** calculates the value of **x** raised to the **y**th power. Method **Math.pow** takes two arguments of type **double** and returns a **double** value. The type **double** is a floating-point type much like **float**, but a variable of type **double** can store a value of much greater magnitude with greater precision than **float**. Constants (like **1000.0** and **.05** in Fig. 3.6) are treated as being type **double** by Java.

Notice that we declared the variables **amount, principal**, and **rate** to be of type **double**. We did this for simplicity because we are dealing with fractional parts of dollars and we need a type that allows decimal points in its values. Unfortunately, this can cause trouble. Here is a simple explanation of what can go wrong when using **float** or **double** to represent dollar amounts (assuming that dollar amounts are displayed with two digits to the right of the decimal point): Two **double** dollar amounts stored in the machine could be 14.234 (which would normally be rounded to 14.23 for display purposes) and 18.673 (which would normally be rounded to 18.67 for display purposes). When these amounts are added, they produce the internal sum 32.907 which would normally be rounded to 32.91 for display purposes. Thus your printout could appear as

```
    14.23
+  18.67
 -------
    32.91
```

but a person adding the individual numbers as printed would expect the sum 32.90! You have been warned!

Good Programming Practice 3.11

*Do not use variables of type **float** or **double** to perform precise monetary calculations. The imprecision of floating-point numbers can cause errors that will result in incorrect monetary values. In the exercises, we explore the use of integers to perform monetary calculations. Note: Class libraries are becoming available for properly performing monetary calculations.*

Note that the calculation **1.0 + rate** which appears as an argument to the **Math.pow** method is contained in the body of the **for** statement. In fact, this calculation produces the same result each time through the loop, so repeating the calculation is wasteful.

Performance Tip 3.1

Avoid placing expressions whose values do not change inside loops. But even if you do, many of today's sophisticated optimizing compilers will automatically place such expressions outside loops in the generated machine language code.

3.5 The `switch` Multiple-Selection Structure

We have discussed the **if** single-selection structure and the **if/else** double-selection structure. Occasionally, an algorithm will contain a series of decisions in which a variable or expression is tested separately for each of the constant integral values it may assume, and different actions are taken. Java provides the **switch** multiple-selection structure to handle such decision making.

The **switch** structure consists of a series of **case** labels, and an optional **default** case. The program in Fig. 3.7 uses **switch** to count the number of each different letter grade that students earned on an exam.

```
1   // Fig. 3.7: SwitchTest.java
2   // Counting letter grades
3   import java.awt.*;
4   import java.applet.Applet;
5
6   public class SwitchTest extends Applet {
7      Label prompt;       // label for text field
8      TextField input;    // text field to enter grades
9
10     int aCount = 0, bCount = 0, cCount = 0,
11         dCount = 0, fCount = 0;
12
13     public void init()
14     {
15        prompt = new Label( "Enter grade" );
16        input = new TextField( 2 );
17        add( prompt );
18        add( input );
19     }
```

Fig. 3.7   An example using **switch** (part 1 of 3).

```
20
21      public void paint( Graphics g )
22      {
23          g.drawString( "Totals for each letter grade:", 25, 40 );
24          g.drawString( "A: " + aCount, 25, 55 );
25          g.drawString( "B: " + bCount, 25, 70 );
26          g.drawString( "C: " + cCount, 25, 85 );
27          g.drawString( "D: " + dCount, 25, 100 );
28          g.drawString( "F: " + fCount, 25, 115 );
29      }
30
31      public boolean action( Event e, Object o )
32      {
33          String val = o.toString();
34          char grade = val.charAt( 0 );
35
36          showStatus( "" );        // clear status bar area
37          input.setText( "" );     // clear input text field
38
39          switch ( grade ) {
40
41             case 'A': case 'a':  // Grade was uppercase A
42                ++aCount;          // or lowercase a.
43                break;
44
45             case 'B': case 'b':  // Grade was uppercase B
46                ++bCount;          // or lowercase b.
47                break;
48
49             case 'C': case 'c':  // Grade was uppercase C
50                ++cCount;          // or lowercase c.
51                break;
52
53             case 'D': case 'd':  // Grade was uppercase D
54                ++dCount;          // or lowercase d.
55                break;
56
57             case 'F': case 'f':  // Grade was uppercase F
58                ++fCount;          // or lowercase f.
59                break;
60
61             default:             // catch all other characters
62                showStatus( "Incorrect grade. Enter new grade." );
63                break;
64          }
65
66          repaint();  // display summary of results
67          return true;
68      }
69  }
```

Fig. 3.7   An example using **switch** (part 2 of 3).

Fig. 3.7   An example using **switch** (part 3 of 3).

In the program, the user enters letter grades for a class into a text field. When the Enter key is pressed, the **action** method is called to read the letter grade and process it. The line

```
String val = o.toString();
```

takes the value entered by the user in the text field and assigns it to **val**. Remember that the **action** method automatically receives the data in the text field (as a **String**) when the user presses the Enter key and that **o.toString()** allows us to use the value as a **String** in our program. However, we actually want to process an individual character typed by the user. The line

```
char grade = val.charAt( 0 );
```

uses the **charAt** method to select the character at position 0 of the string and assign it to the variable **grade**. Java considers the first character in a string to be at position 0. The **charAt** method can be used to select a character at any position in a string. For example, if the string **s** contains "**hello**," the statement

```
char letter = s.charAt( 4 );
```

selects the fifth character ("**o**") and assigns it to variable **letter**.

After clearing the text field and status bar, the **switch** structure is entered. The keyword **switch** is followed by the variable name **grade** in parentheses. This is called the *controlling expression.* The value of this expression is compared with each of the *case labels.* Assume the user has entered the letter **C** as a grade. **C** is automatically compared to each **case** in the **switch**. If a match occurs (**case 'C':**), the statements for that **case** are executed. For the letter **C**, **cCount** is incremented by **1**, and the **switch** structure is exited immediately with the **break** statement.

The **break** statement causes program control to proceed with the first statement after the **switch** structure. The **break** statement is used because the **case**s in a **switch** statement would otherwise run together. If **break** is not used anywhere in a **switch** structure, then each time a match occurs in the structure, the statements for all the remaining **case**s will be executed. (This feature is perfect for programming the iterative song "The Twelve Days of Christmas!") If no match occurs, the **default** case is executed and an error message is printed.

Each **case** can have multiple actions. The **switch** structure is different from other structures in that braces are not required around multiple actions in a **case** of a **switch**. The general **switch** structure (using a **break** in each **case**) is flowcharted in Fig. 3.8.

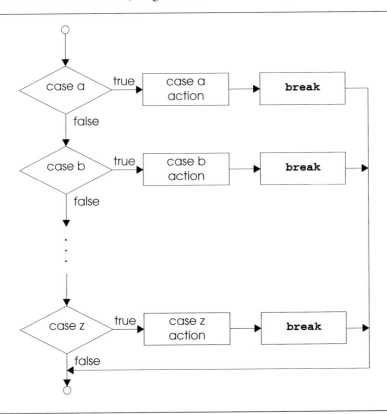

Fig. 3.8   The **switch** multiple-selection structure.

The flowchart makes it clear that each **break** statement at the end of a **case** causes control to immediately exit the **switch** structure. Again, note that (besides small circles and arrows) the flowchart contains only rectangle symbols and diamond symbols. Imagine, again, that the programmer has access to a deep bin of empty **switch** structures—as many as the programmer might need to stack and nest with other control structures to form a structured implementation of an algorithm's flow of control. And again, the rectangles and diamonds are then filled with actions and decisions appropriate to the algorithm. Nested control structures are common, but it is rare to find nested **switch** structures in a program.

Common Programming Error 3.6

*Forgetting a **break** statement when one is needed in a **switch** structure.*

Good Programming Practice 3.12

*Provide a **default** case in **switch** statements. Cases not explicitly tested in a **switch** statement without a **default** case are ignored. Including a **default** case focuses the programmer on the need to process exceptional conditions. There are situations in which no **default** processing is needed.*

Good Programming Practice 3.13

*Although the **case** clauses and the **default** case clause in a **switch** structure can occur in any order, it is considered a good programming practice to place the **default** clause last.*

Good Programming Practice 3.14

*In a **switch** structure when the **default** clause is listed last, the **break** for that **case** statement is not required. Some programmers include this **break** for clarity and symmetry with other cases.*

Note that several **case** labels listed together (such as **case 'D': case 'd':** in Fig. 3.7) simply means that the same set of actions is to occur for each of the cases.

When using the **switch** structure, remember that the expression after each **case** can only be a *constant integral expression,* i.e., any combination of character constants and integer constants that evaluates to a constant integer value. A character constant is represented as the specific character in single quotes such as **'A'**. An integer constant is simply an integer value.

Common Programming Error 3.7

*Omitting the space between the word **case** and the integral value being tested in a **switch** structure can cause a logic error. For example, writing **case3:** instead of writing **case 3:** simply creates an unused label (we will say more about labels later). The problem is that the **switch** structure will not perform the appropriate actions when the **switch**'s controlling expression has a value of 3.*

When we discuss object-oriented programming, we will present a more elegant way to implement **switch** logic. We will use a technique called polymorphism to create programs that are often clearer, easier to maintain, and easier to extend than programs using **switch** logic.

3.6 The do/while Repetition Structure

The **do/while** repetition structure is similar to the **while** structure. In the **while** structure, the loop-continuation condition is tested at the beginning of the loop before the body of the loop is performed. The **do/while** structure tests the loop-continuation condition *after* the loop body is performed, therefore *the loop body is executed at least once.* When a **do/while** terminates, execution continues with the statement after the **while** clause. Note that it is not necessary to use braces in the **do/while** structure if there is only one statement in the body. However, the braces are usually included to avoid confusion between the **while** and **do/while** structures. For example,

> **while** (*condition*)

is normally regarded as the header to a **while** structure. A **do/while** with no braces around the single statement body appears as

```
do
    statement
while ( condition );
```

which can be confusing. The last line—**while(** *condition* **);**—may be misinterpreted by the reader as a **while** structure containing an empty statement. Thus, the **do/while** with one statement is often written as follows to avoid confusion:

```
do {
    statement
} while (condition);
```

Good Programming Practice 3.15

*Some programmers always include braces in a **do/while** structure even if the braces are not necessary. This helps eliminate ambiguity between the **while** structure and the **do/while** structure containing one statement.*

Common Programming Error 3.8

*Infinite loops are caused when the loop-continuation condition in a **while**, **for**, or **do/while** structure never becomes false. To prevent this, make sure there is not a semicolon immediately after the header of a **while** structure. In a counter-controlled loop, make sure the control variable is incremented (or decremented) in the body of the loop. In a sentinel-controlled loop, make sure the sentinel value is eventually input.*

The program in Fig. 3.9 uses a **do/while** structure to print the numbers from 1 to 10. Note that the control variable **counter** is preincremented in the loop-continuation test. Note also the use of the braces to enclose the single-statement body of the **do/while**.

The **do/while** flowchart (Fig. 3.10) makes it clear that the loop-continuation condition is not executed until the action is performed at least once. The flowchart contains only a rectangle and a diamond. Imagine, also, that the programmer has access to a bin of empty **do/while** structures—as many as the programmer might need to stack and nest with other control structures to form a structured implementation of an algorithm. The rectangles and diamonds are filled with actions and decisions appropriate to the algorithm.

```
1   // Fig. 3.9: DoWhileTest.java
2   // Using the do/while repetition structure
3   import java.awt.Graphics;
4   import java.applet.Applet;
5
6   public class DoWhileTest extends Applet {
7      public void paint( Graphics g )
8      {
9         int counter = 1;
10        int xPos = 25;
11
12        do {
13           g.drawString( Integer.toString( counter ), xPos, 25 );
14           xPos += 15;
15        } while ( ++counter <= 10 );
16     }
17  }
```

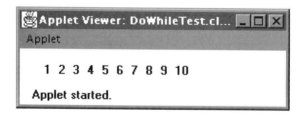

Fig. 3.9   The **do/while** repetition structure.

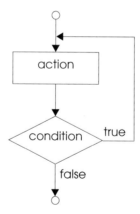

Fig. 3.10 The **do/while** repetition structure.

3.7 The break and continue Statements

The **break** and **continue** statements alter the flow of control. The **break** statement, when executed in a **while**, **for**, **do/while**, or **switch** structure, causes immediate exit from that structure. Execution continues with the first statement after the structure. Common uses of the **break** statement are to escape early from a loop, or to skip the remainder of a **switch** structure (as in Fig. 3.7). Figure 3.11 demonstrates the **break** statement in a **for** repetition structure. When the **if** structure detects that **count** has become **5**, **break** is executed. This terminates the **for** statement and the program proceeds to the second **drawString**, i.e., the one after the **for**. The loop fully executes only four times.

The **continue** statement, when executed in a **while**, **for**, or **do/while** structure, skips the remaining statements in the body of that structure, and proceeds with the next iteration of the loop. In **while** and **do/while** structures, the loop-continuation test is evaluated immediately after the **continue** statement is executed. In the **for** structure, the increment expression is executed, then the loop-continuation test is evaluated. Earlier, we stated that the **while** structure could be used in most cases to represent the **for** structure. The one exception occurs when the increment expression in the **while** structure follows the **continue** statement. In this case, the increment is not executed before the repetition-continuation condition is tested, and the **while** does not execute in the same manner as the **for**. Figure 3.12 uses the **continue** statement in a **for** structure to skip the output statement in the structure when **count** is 5 and begin the next iteration of the loop.

Good Programming Practice 3.16

*Some programmers feel that **break** and **continue** violate structured programming. Because the effects of these statements can be achieved by structured programming techniques we will soon learn, these programmers do not use **break** and **continue**.*

Software Engineering Observation 3.1

There is a tension between achieving quality software engineering and achieving the best performing software. Often, one of these goals is achieved at the expense of the other.

```
1   // Fig. 3.11: BreakTest.java
2   // Using the break statement in a for structure
3   import java.awt.Graphics;
4   import java.applet.Applet;
5
6   public class BreakTest extends Applet {
7      public void paint( Graphics g )
8      {
9         int count, xPos = 25;
10
11         for ( count = 1; count <= 10; count++ ) {
12            if ( count == 5 )
13               break;   // break loop only if count == 5
14
15            g.drawString( Integer.toString( count ), xPos, 25 );
16            xPos += 10;
17         }
18
19         g.drawString( "Broke out of loop at count = " + count,
20                       25, 40 );
21      }
22   }
```

Fig. 3.11 Using the **break** statement in a **for** structure (part 1 of 2).

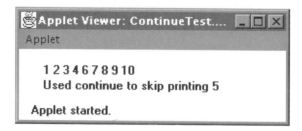

```
1 2 3 4
Broke out of loop at count = 5
```

Fig. 3.11   Using the **break** statement in a **for** structure (part 2 of 2).

```java
1    // Fig. 3.12: ContinueTest.java
2    // Using the continue statement in a for structure
3    import java.awt.Graphics;
4    import java.applet.Applet;
5
6    public class ContinueTest extends Applet {
7       public void paint( Graphics g )
8       {
9          int xPos = 25;
10
11         for ( int count = 1; count <= 10; count++ ) {
12            if ( count == 5 )
13               continue;  // skip remaining code in loop
14                         // only if count == 5
15
16            g.drawString( Integer.toString( count ), xPos, 25 );
17            xPos += 10;
18         }
19
20         g.drawString( "Used continue to skip printing 5",
21                       25, 40 );
22      }
23   }
```

```
1 2 3 4 6 7 8 9 10
Used continue to skip printing 5
```

Fig. 3.12   Using the **continue** statement in a **for** structure.

3.8 The Labeled `break` and `continue` Statements

The **break** statement can only break out of an immediately enclosing **while, for, do/while** or **switch** structure. To break out of a nested set of structures, you can use the *labeled* **break** *statement*. This statement, when executed in a **while, for, do/while** or **switch**, causes immediate exit from that structure and any number of enclosing structures; program execution resumes with the first statement after the enclosing *labeled compound statement* (i.e., a set of statements enclosed in curly braces and preceded by a label). Labeled **break** statements are commonly used to terminate nested looping structures containing **while, for, do/while** or **switch** structures. Figure 3.13 demonstrates the labeled **break** statement in a nested **for** structure. The labeled compound statement (lines 11-28) begins with a label (an identifier followed by a colon); here we use the label **stop**. When the **if** structure at line 18 detects that **row** is equal to **5**, the statement

```
break stop;
```

is executed. This terminates both the **for** structure at line 16 and its enclosing **for** structure at line 12, and the program proceeds to the statement at line 30, i.e., the first statement after the labeled compound statement. The inner **for** structure fully executes only four times. Notice that the **drawString** at line 27 never executes because it is included in the labeled compound statement and the outer **for** structure never completes.

The **continue** statement proceeds with the next iteration (repetition) of the immediately enclosing **while, for** or **do/while** structure. The *labeled* **continue** *statement*, when executed in a repetition structure (**while, for** or **do/while**), skips the remaining statements in that structure's body and any number of enclosing repetition structures, and proceeds with the next iteration of the enclosing *labeled repetition structure* (i.e., a repetition structure preceded by a label). In labeled **while** and **do/while** structures, the loop-continuation test is evaluated immediately after the **continue** statement is executed. In a labeled **for** structure, the increment expression is executed, then the loop-continuation test is evaluated. Figure 3.14 uses the labeled **continue** statement in a nested **for** structure to cause execution to continue with the next iteration of the outer **for** structure. The labeled **for** structure (lines 11-24) starts at the **nextRow** label. When the **if** structure at line 18 in the inner **for** structure detects that **column** is greater than **row**, the statement

```
continue nextRow;
```

is executed and execution continues with the next iteration of the outer **for** loop. Even though the inner **for** structure counts from 1 to 10, the number of **#** characters output on a row never exceeds row number **row**.

3.9 Logical Operators

So far we have studied only *simple conditions* such as **count <= 10, total > 1000**, and **number != sentinelValue**. These conditions were expressed in terms of the relational operators **>, <, >=**, and **<=**, and the equality operators **==** and **!=**. Each decision tested one condition. To test multiple conditions in the process of making a decision, we had to perform these tests in separate statements or in nested **if** or **if/else** structures.

```
1   // Fig. 3.13: BreakLabelTest.java
2   // Using the break statement with a label
3   import java.awt.Graphics;
4   import java.applet.Applet;
5
6   public class BreakLabelTest extends Applet {
7      public void paint( Graphics g )
8      {
9         int xPos, yPos = 0;
10
11        stop: {  // labeled compound statement
12           for ( int row = 1; row <= 10; row++ ) {
13              xPos = 25;
14              yPos += 15;
15
16              for ( int column = 1; column <= 5 ; column++ ) {
17
18                 if ( row == 5 )
19                    break stop; // jump to stop label
20
21                 g.drawString( "#", xPos, yPos );
22                 xPos += 7;
23              }
24           }
25
26           yPos += 15;
27           g.drawString( "Loops terminated normally", 25, yPos );
28        }
29
30        yPos += 15;
31        g.drawString( "End of paint method", 25, yPos );
32     }
33  }
```

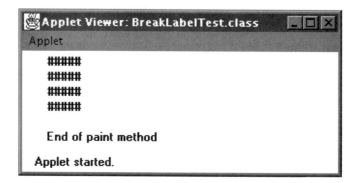

Fig. 3.13 Using a labeled **break** statement in a nested **for** structure.

```
1   // Fig. 3.14: ContinueLabelTest.java
2   // Using the continue statement with a label
3   import java.awt.Graphics;
4   import java.applet.Applet;
5
6   public class ContinueLabelTest extends Applet {
7      public void paint( Graphics g )
8      {
9         int xPos, yPos = 0;
10
11        nextRow:    // target label of continue statement
12           for ( int row = 1; row <= 5; row++ ) {
13              xPos = 25;
14              yPos += 15;
15
16              for ( int column = 1; column <= 10; column++ ) {
17
18                 if ( column > row )
19                    continue nextRow; // jump to nextRow label
20
21                 g.drawString( "#", xPos, yPos );
22                 xPos += 7;
23              }
24           }
25     }
26  }
```

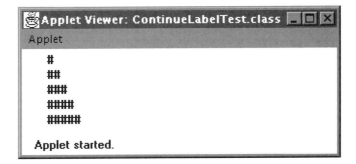

Fig. 3.14 Using a labeled **continue** statement in a nested **for** structure.

Java provides *logical operators* that may be used to form more complex conditions by combining simple conditions. The logical operators are **&&** *(logical AND)*, **&** *(boolean logical AND)*, **| |** *(logical OR)*, **|** *(boolean logical inclusive OR)*, **^** *(boolean logical exclusive OR)* and **!** *(logical NOT also called logical negation)*. We will consider examples of each of these.

Suppose we wish to ensure at some point in a program that two conditions are *both* **true** before we choose a certain path of execution. In this case we can use the logical **&&** operator as follows:

```
if ( gender == 1 && age >= 65 )
   ++seniorFemales;
```

This **if** statement contains two simple conditions. The condition **gender == 1** might be evaluated, for example, to determine if a person is a female. The condition **age >= 65** is evaluated to determine if a person is a senior citizen. The two simple conditions are evaluated first because the precedences of **==** and **>=** are both higher than the precedence of **&&**. The **if** statement then considers the combined condition

```
gender == 1 && age >= 65
```

This condition is **true** if and only if both of the simple conditions are **true**. Finally, if this combined condition is indeed **true**, then the count of **seniorFemales** is incremented by **1**. If either or both of the simple conditions are **false**, then the program skips the incrementing and proceeds to the statement following the **if**. The preceding combined condition can be made more readable by adding redundant parentheses

```
( gender == 1 ) && ( age >= 65 )
```

The table of Fig. 3.15 summarizes the **&&** operator. The table shows all four possible combinations of **false** and **true** values for expression1 and expression2. Such tables are often called *truth tables*. Java evaluates to **false** or **true** all expressions that include relational operators, equality operators, and/or logical operators.

Now let us consider the || (logical OR) operator. Suppose we wish to ensure that either *or* both of two conditions are **true** before we choose a certain path of execution. In this case we use the || operator as in the following program segment:

```
if ( semesterAverage >= 90 || finalExam >= 90 )
   System.out.println ( "Student grade is A" );
```

This statement also contains two simple conditions. The condition **semesterAverage >= 90** is evaluated to determine if the student deserves an "A" in the course because of a solid performance throughout the semester. The condition **finalExam >= 90** is evaluated to determine if the student deserves an "A" in the course because of an outstanding performance on the final exam. The **if** statement then considers the combined condition

```
semesterAverage >= 90 || finalExam >= 90
```

expression1	expression2	expression1 && expression2
false	false	false
false	true	false
true	false	false
true	true	true

Fig. 3.15 Truth table for the **&&** (logical AND) operator.

and awards the student an "A" if either or both of the simple conditions are **true**. Note that the message "**Student grade is A**" is not printed only when both of the simple conditions are **false**. Figure 3.16 is a truth table for the logical OR operator (| |).

The **&&** operator has a higher precedence than the | | operator. Both operators associate from left to right. An expression containing **&&** or | | operators is evaluated only until truth or falsity is known. Thus, evaluation of the expression

```
gender == 1 && age >= 65
```

will stop immediately if **gender** is not equal to **1** (i.e., the entire expression is **false**), and continue if **gender** is equal to **1** (i.e., the entire expression could still be **true** if the condition **age >= 65** is **true**). This performance feature is called *short-circuit evaluation*.

Common Programming Error 3.9

*In expressions using operator **&&**, it is possible that a condition—we will call this the dependent condition—may require another condition to be true for it to be meaningful to evaluate the dependent condition. In this case, the dependent condition should be placed after the other condition or an error might occur.*

Performance Tip 3.2

*In expressions using operator **&&**, if the separate conditions are independent of one another make the condition that is most likely to be **false** the leftmost condition. In expressions using operator | |, make the condition that is most likely to be **true** the leftmost condition. This can reduce a program's execution time.*

The *boolean logical AND (**&**)* and *boolean logical inclusive OR (|)* operators, work identically to the regular logical AND and logical OR operators with one exception—the boolean logical operators always evaluate both of their operands (i.e., there is no short-circuit evaluation). Therefore, the expression

```
gender == 1 & age >= 65
```

evaluates **age >= 65** regardless of whether **gender** is equal to **1**. This is useful if the right operand of the boolean logical AND or boolean logical inclusive OR operator has a needed *side effect*—a modification of a variable's value. For example, the expression

```
birthday == true | ++age >= 65
```

expression1	expression2	expression1		expression2
false	false	false
false	true	true
true	false	true
true	true	true

Fig. 3.16 Truth table for the logical OR (| |) operator.

guarantees that the condition **++age >= 65** will be evaluated. Thus, the variable **age** will be incremented regardless of whether the overall expression is **true** or **false**.

A condition containing the *boolean logical exclusive OR (^)* operator is **true** *if and only if* one of its operands results in a **true** value and one results in a **false** value. If both operands are **true** or both operands are **false**, the result of the entire condition is **false**. Figure 3.17 is a truth table for the boolean logical exclusive OR operator (^). This operator also evaluates both of its operands (i.e., there is no short-circuit evaluation).

Java provides the **!** (logical negation) operator to enable a programmer to "reverse" the meaning of a condition. Unlike the logical operators **&&**, **&**, **||** and **|** operators, which combine two conditions (binary operators), the logical negation operator has only a single condition as an operand (unary operator). The logical negation operator is placed before a condition to choose a path of execution if the original condition (without the logical negation operator) is **false**, such as in the following program segment:

```
if ( ! ( grade == sentinelValue ) )
   System.out.println( "The next grade is " + grade );
```

The parentheses around the condition **grade == sentinelValue** are needed because the logical negation operator has a higher precedence than the equality operator. Figure 3.18 is a truth table for the logical negation operator.

In most cases, the programmer can avoid using logical negation by expressing the condition differently with an appropriate relational or equality operator. For example, the preceding statement may also be written as follows:

```
if ( grade != sentinelValue )
   System.out.println( "The next grade is " + grade );
```

This flexibility can help a programmer express a condition in a more convenient manner.

expression1	expression2	expression1 ^ expression2
false	false	false
false	true	true
true	false	true
true	true	false

Fig. 3.17 Truth table for the boolean logical exclusive OR (^) operator.

expression	!expression
false	true
true	false

Fig. 3.18 Truth table for operator **!** (logical NOT).

The program of Fig. 3.19 demonstrates all the logical operators and boolean logical operators by producing their truth tables.

```
1    // Fig. 3.19: LogicalOperators.java
2    // Demonstrating the logical operators
3    import java.awt.Graphics;
4    import java.applet.Applet;
5
6    public class LogicalOperators extends Applet {
7       public void paint( Graphics g )
8       {
9          g.drawString( "Logical AND (&&)", 10, 25 );
10         g.drawString( "F && F: " + ( false && false ), 10, 40 );
11         g.drawString( "F && T: " + ( false && true ), 10, 55 );
12         g.drawString( "T && F: " + ( true && false ), 10, 70 );
13         g.drawString( "T && T: " + ( true && true ), 10, 85 );
14
15         g.drawString( "Logical OR (||)", 215, 25 );
16         g.drawString( "F || F: " + ( false || false ), 215, 40 );
17         g.drawString( "F || T: " + ( false || true ), 215, 55 );
18         g.drawString( "T || F: " + ( true || false ), 215, 70 );
19         g.drawString( "T || T: " + ( true || true ), 215, 85 );
20
21         g.drawString( "Boolean logical AND (&)", 10, 115 );
22         g.drawString( "F & F: " + ( false & false ), 10, 130 );
23         g.drawString( "F & T: " + ( false & true ), 10, 145 );
24         g.drawString( "T & F: " + ( true & false ), 10, 160 );
25         g.drawString( "T & T: " + ( true & true ), 10, 175 );
26
27         g.drawString( "Boolean logical inclusive OR (|)",
28                       215, 115 );
29         g.drawString( "F | F: " + ( false | false ), 215, 130 );
30         g.drawString( "F | T: " + ( false | true ), 215, 145 );
31         g.drawString( "T | F: " + ( true | false ), 215, 160 );
32         g.drawString( "T | T: " + ( true | true ), 215, 175 );
33
34         g.drawString( "Boolean logical exclusive OR (^)",
35                       10, 205 );
36         g.drawString( "F ^ F: " + ( false ^ false ), 10, 220 );
37         g.drawString( "F ^ T: " + ( false ^ true ), 10, 235 );
38         g.drawString( "T ^ F: " + ( true ^ false ), 10, 250 );
39         g.drawString( "T ^ T: " + ( true ^ true ), 10, 265 );
40
41         g.drawString( "Logical NOT (!)",
42                       215, 205 );
43         g.drawString( "!F: " + ( !false ), 215, 220 );
44         g.drawString( "!T: " + ( !true ), 215, 235 );
45      }
46   }
```

Fig. 3.19 Demonstraing the logical operators (part 1 of 2).

Fig. 3.19 Demonstraing the logical operators (part 2 of 2).

In the output of Fig. 3.19, the letters **F** and **T** indicate **false** and **true** for the operands in each condition. The result of the condition is shown as **true** or **false**.

The chart in Fig. 3.20 shows the precedence and associativity of the Java operators introduced to this point. The operators are shown from top to bottom in decreasing order of precedence.

3.10 Structured Programming Summary

Just as architects design buildings by employing the collective wisdom of their profession, so should programmers design programs. Our field is younger than architecture is, and our collective wisdom is considerably sparser. We have learned that structured programming produces programs that are easier than unstructured programs to understand and hence are easier to test, debug, modify, and even prove correct in a mathematical sense.

Figure 3.21 summarizes Java's control structures. Small circles are used in the figure to indicate the single entry point and the single exit point of each structure. Connecting individual flowchart symbols arbitrarily can lead to unstructured programs. Therefore, the programming profession has chosen to combine flowchart symbols to form a limited set of control structures, and to build structured programs by properly combining control structures in two simple ways. For simplicity, only single-entry/single-exit control structures are used—there is only one way to enter and only one way to exit each control structure.

Operators						Associativity	Type
( )						left to right	parentheses
++	--	+	-	!	(*type*)	right to left	unary
*	/	%				left to right	multiplicative
+	-					left to right	additive
<	<=	>	>=			left to right	relational
==	!=					left to right	equality
&						left to right	boolean logical AND
^						left to right	boolean logical exclusive OR
|						left to right	boolean logical inclusive OR
&&						left to right	logical AND
||						left to right	logical OR
? :						right to left	conditional
=	+=	-=	*=	/=	%=	right to left	assignment

Fig. 3.20 Operator precedence and associativity.

Connecting control structures in sequence to form structured programs is simple—the exit point of one control structure is connected directly to the entry point of the next control structure, i.e., the control structures are simply placed one after another in a program; we have called this "control structure stacking." The rules for forming structured programs also allow for control structures to be nested.

Figure 3.22 shows the rules for forming properly structured programs which assume the rectangle flowchart symbol may be used to indicate any action including input/output.

Applying the rules of Fig. 3.22 to the simplest flowchart (Fig. 3.23) always results in a structured flowchart with a neat, building-block appearance. For example, repeatedly applying rule 2 to the simplest flowchart results in a structured flowchart containing many rectangles in sequence (Fig. 3.24). Notice that rule 2 generates a stack of control structures; so let us call rule 2 the *stacking rule*.

Rule 3 is called the *nesting rule*. Repeatedly applying rule 3 to the simplest flowchart results in a flowchart with neatly nested control structures. For example, in Fig. 3.25, the rectangle in the simplest flowchart is first replaced with a double-selection (**if/else**) structure. Then rule 3 is applied again to both of the rectangles in the double-selection structure, replacing each of these rectangles with double-selection structures. The dashed boxes around each of the double-selection structures represent the rectangle that was replaced.

Rule 4 generates larger, more involved, and more deeply nested structures. The flowcharts that emerge from applying the rules in Fig. 3.22 constitute the set of all possible structured flowcharts and hence the set of all possible structured programs.

The beauty of the structured approach is that we use only seven single-entry/single-exit pieces and assemble them in only two ways. Figure 3.26 shows the some stacked building blocks that emerge from applying rule 2 and the kinds of nested building blocks that emerge from applying rule 3. The figure also shows the kind of overlapped building blocks that cannot appear in structured flowcharts (because of the elimination of the **goto** statement).

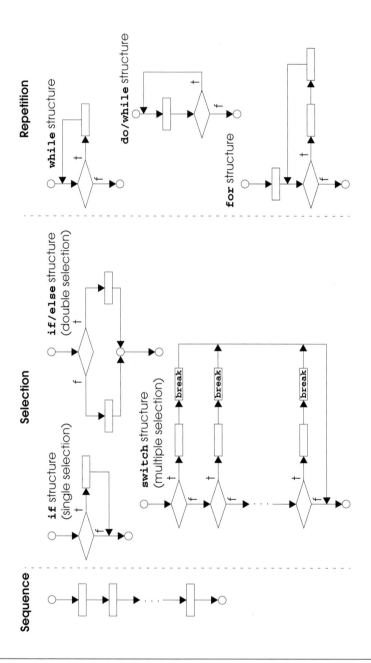

Fig. 3.21 Java's single-entry/single-exit sequence, selection, and repetition structures.

Rules for Forming Structured Programs

1) Begin with the "simplest flowchart" (Fig. 3.23).
2) Any rectangle (action) can be replaced by two rectangles (actions) in sequence.
3) Any rectangle (action) can be replaced by any control structure (sequence, **if**, **if/else**, **switch**, **while**, **do/while**, or **for**).
4) Rules 2 and 3 may be applied as often as you like and in any order.

Fig. 3.22 Rules for forming structured programs.

Fig. 3.23 The simplest flowchart.

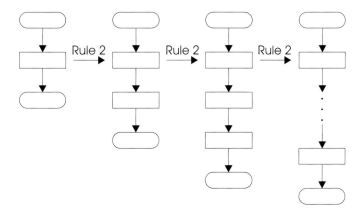

Fig. 3.24 Repeatedly applying rule 2 of Fig. 3.22 to the simplest flowchart.

If the rules in Fig. 3.22 are followed, an unstructured flowchart (such as that in Fig. 3.27) cannot be created. If you are uncertain if a particular flowchart is structured, apply the rules of Fig. 3.22 in reverse to try to reduce the flowchart to the simplest flowchart. If the flowchart is reducible to the simplest flowchart, the original flowchart is structured; otherwise, it is not.

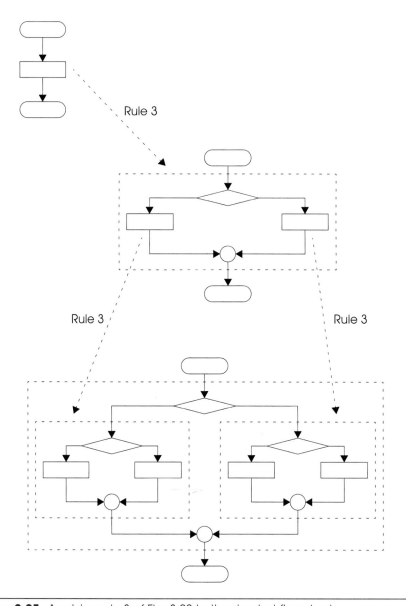

Fig. 3.25 Applying rule 3 of Fig. 3.22 to the simplest flowchart.

Structured programming promotes simplicity. Bohm and Jacopini have given us the result that only three forms of control are needed:

- Sequence
- Selection
- Repetition

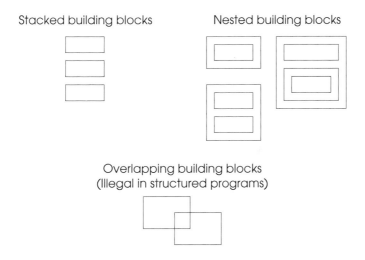

Fig. 3.26 Stacked building blocks, nested building blocks, and overlapped building blocks.

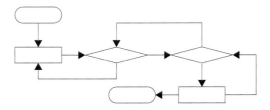

Fig. 3.27 An unstructured flowchart.

Sequence is trivial. Selection is implemented in one of three ways:

- **if** structure (single selection)
- **if/else** structure (double selection)
- **switch** structure (multiple selection)

In fact, it is straightforward to prove that the simple **if** structure is sufficient to provide any form of selection—everything that can be done with the **if/else** structure and the **switch** structure can be implemented by combining **if** structures (although perhaps not as smoothly).

Repetition is implemented in one of three ways:

- **while** structure
- **do/while** structure
- **for** structure

The **while** structure is sufficient to provide any form of repetition; everything that can be done with the **do/while** structure and the **for** structure can be done with the **while** structure (although perhaps not as smoothly).

Combining these results illustrates that any form of control ever needed in a Java program can be expressed in terms of:

- sequence
- **if** structure (selection)
- **while** structure (repetition)

And these control structures can be combined in only two ways—stacking and nesting. Indeed, structured programming promotes simplicity.

In this chapter, we discussed how to compose programs from control structures containing only actions and decisions. In Chapter 4, Methods, we discuss in detail another program structuring unit called the *method* (methods are often called functions or procedures in other programming languages). We will learn to compose large programs by combining methods which, in turn, are composed of control structures. We will also discuss how using methods promotes software reusability. Then we discuss the details of Java's other program structuring unit called the *class*. We will then proceed with our treatment of object-oriented programming. Now, we continue our introduction to objects by introducing a problem that the reader will attack with the techniques of object-oriented design.

Summary

- The **for** repetition structure handles all the details of counter-controlled repetition. The general format of the **for** structure is

  > **for** *(expression1; expression2; expression3)*
  >   *statement*

  where *expression1* initializes the loop's control variable, *expression2* is the loop-continuation condition, and *expression3* increments the control variable.

- The **do/while** repetition structure tests the loop-continuation condition at the end of the loop, so the body of the loop will be executed at least once. The format for the **do/while** structure is

  > **do**
  >   *statement*
  > **while** *(condition)*;

- The **break** statement, when executed in one of the repetition structures (**for**, **while**, and **do/while**), causes immediate exit from the structure.

- The **continue** statement, when executed in one of the repetition structures (**for**, **while**, and **do/while**), skips any remaining statements in the body of the structure, and proceeds with the next iteration of the loop.

- The **switch** statement handles a series of decisions in which a particular variable or expression is tested for values it may assume, and different actions are taken. In most programs, it is necessary to include a **break** statement after the statements for each

case. Several **case**s can execute the same statements by listing the **case** labels together before the statements. The **switch** structure can only test for constant integral expressions.

- Logical operators may be used to form complex conditions by combining conditions. The logical operators are **&&**, **&**, **| |**, **|**, **^**, and **!**, meaning logical AND, boolean logical AND, logical OR, boolean logical inclusive OR, boolean logical exclusive OR and logical NOT (negation), respectively.

Terminology

&& operator	labeled **continue** statement
| | operator	labeled repetition structure
! operator	logical AND (**&&**)
boolean logical AND (**&**)	logical negation (**!**)
boolean logical exclusive OR (**^**)	logical operators
boolean logical inclusive OR (**|**)	logical OR (**| |**)
break	**long**
case label	loop-continuation condition
continue	multiple selection
counter-controlled repetition	nested control structures
default case in **switch**	off-by-one error
definite repetition	repetition structures
do/while repetition structure	short-circuit evaluation
for repetition structure	single-entry/single-exit control structures
infinite loop	stacked control structures
labeled **break** statement	**switch** selection structure
labeled compound statement	**while** repetition structure

Common Programming Errors

3.1   Because floating-point values may be approximate, controlling counting loops with floating-point variables may result in imprecise counter values and inaccurate tests for termination.

3.2   Using an incorrect relational operator or using an incorrect final value of a loop counter in the condition of a **while** or **for** structure can cause off-by-one errors.

3.3   Using commas instead of the two required semicolons in a **for** header.

3.4   Placing a semicolon immediately to the right of the right parenthesis of a **for** header makes the body of that **for** structure an empty statement. This is normally a logic error.

3.5   Not using the proper relational operator in the loop-continuation condition of a loop that counts downwards (such as using $i <= 1$ in a loop counting down to 1).

3.6   Forgetting a **break** statement when one is needed in a **switch** structure.

3.7   Omitting the space between the word **case** and the integral value being tested in a **switch** structure can cause a logic error. For example, writing **case3:** instead of writing **case 3:**

simply creates an unused label (we will say more about labels later). The problem is that the **switch** structure will not perform the appropriate actions when the **switch**'s controlling expression has a value of 3.

3.8   Infinite loops are caused when the loop-continuation condition in a **while**, **for**, or **do/while** structure never becomes false. To prevent this, make sure there is not a semicolon immediately after the header of a **while** structure. In a counter-controlled loop, make sure the control variable is incremented (or decremented) in the body of the loop. In a sentinel-controlled loop, make sure the sentinel value is eventually input.

3.9   In expressions using operator **&&**, it is possible that a condition—we will call this the dependent condition—may require another condition to be true for it to be meaningful to evaluate the dependent condition. In this case, the dependent condition should be placed after the other condition or an error might occur.

Good Programming Practices

3.1   Control counting loops with integer values.

3.2   Indent the statements in the body of each control structure.

3.3   Put a blank line before and after each major control structure to make it stand out in the program.

3.4   Too many levels of nesting can make a program difficult to understand. As a general rule, try to avoid using more than three levels of indentation.

3.5   Vertical spacing above and below control structures, and indentation of the bodies of control structures within the control structure headers gives programs a two-dimensional appearance that greatly improves readability.

3.6   Using the final value in the condition of a **while** or **for** structure and using the **<=** relational operator will help avoid off-by-one errors. For a loop used to print the values 1 to 10, for example, the loop-continuation condition should be **counter <= 10** rather than **counter < 10** (which is an off-by-one error) or **counter < 11** (which is also correct).

3.7   Place only expressions involving the control variables in the initialization and increment sections of a **for** structure. Manipulations of other variables should appear either before the loop (if they execute only once like initialization statements) or in the loop body (if they execute once per repetition like incrementing or decrementing statements).

3.8   Although the value of the control variable can be changed in the body of a **for** loop, avoid doing so because this practice can lead to subtle errors.

3.9   Although statements preceding a **for** and statements in the body of a **for** can often be merged into the **for** header, avoid doing so because it makes the program more difficult to read.

3.10   Limit the size of control structure headers to a single line if possible.

3.11   Do not use variables of type **float** or **double** to perform precise monetary calculations. The imprecision of floating-point numbers can cause errors that will result in incorrect monetary values. In the exercises, we explore the use of integers to perform monetary calculations. Note: Class libraries are becoming available for properly performing monetary calculations.

3.12   Provide a **default** case in **switch** statements. Cases not explicitly tested in a **switch** statement without a **default** case are ignored. Including a **default** case focuses the programmer on the need to process exceptional conditions. There are situations in which no **default** processing is needed.

3.13   Although the **case** clauses and the **default** case clause in a **switch** structure can occur in any order, it is considered a good programming practice to place the **default** clause last.

3.14   In a **switch** structure when the **default** clause is listed last, the **break** statement for that **case** is not required. Some programmers include this **break** for clarity and symmetry with other cases.

3.15   Some programmers always include braces in a **do/while** structure even if the braces are not necessary. This helps eliminate ambiguity between the **while** structure and the **do/ while** structure containing one statement.

3.16   Some programmers feel that **break** and **continue** violate structured programming. Because the effects of these statements can be achieved by structured programming techniques we will soon learn, these programmers do not use **break** and **continue**.

Performance Tips

3.1   Avoid placing expressions whose values do not change inside loops. But even if you do, many of today's sophisticated optimizing compilers will automatically place such expressions outside loops in the generated machine language code.

3.2   In expressions using operator **&&**, if the separate conditions are independent of one another make the condition that is most likely to be false the leftmost condition. In expressions using operator **| |**, make the condition that is most likely to be true the leftmost condition. This can reduce a program's execution time.

Software Engineering Observation

3.1   There is a tension between achieving quality software engineering and achieving the best performing software. Often, one of these goals is achieved at the expense of the other.

Self-Review Exercises

3.1   State whether the following are true or false. If the answer is false, explain why.
   a) The **default** case is required in the **switch** selection structure.
   b) The **break** statement is required in the default case of a **switch** selection structure.
   c) The expression (**x > y && a < b**) is true if either **x > y** is true or **a < b** is true.
   d) An expression containing the **| |** operator is true if either or both of its operands is true.

3.2   Write a Java statement or a set of Java statements to accomplish each of the following:
   a) Sum the odd integers between 1 and 99 using a **for** structure. Assume the integer variables **sum** and **count** have been declared.

b) Calculate the value of **2.5** raised to the power of **3** using the **pow** method.

c) Print the integers from 1 to 20 using a **while** loop and the counter variable **x**. Assume that the variable **x** has been declared, but not initialized. Print only 5 integers per line. Hint: Use the calculation **x % 5**. When the value of this is 0, print a newline character, otherwise print a tab character. Assume this is an application—use the **System.out.println()** method to output the newline character and use the **System.out.print('\t')** method to output the tab character.

d) Repeat Exercise 3.2 (c) using a **for** structure.

3.3   Find the error in each of the following code segments and explain how to correct it.

a)
```
x = 1;

while ( x <= 10 );
   x++;
}
```

b)
```
for ( y = .1; y != 1.0; y += .1 )
      System.out.println( y );
```

c)
```
switch ( n ) {

   case 1:
      System.out.println( "The number is 1" );

   case 2:
      System.out.println( "The number is 2" );
      break;

   default:
      System.out.println( "The number is not 1 or 2" );
      break;
}
```

d) The following code should print the values 1 to 10.
```
n = 1;

while ( n < 10 )
      System.out.println( n++ );
```

Answers to Self-Review Exercises

3.1   a) False. The **default** case is optional. If no default action is needed, then there is no need for a **default** case.

b) False. The **break** statement is used to exit the **switch** structure. The **break** statement is not required when the **default** case is the last case.

c) False. Both of the relational expressions must be true in order for the entire expression to be true when using the **&&** operator.

d) True.

3.2   a)
```
sum = 0;
for ( count = 1; count <= 99; count += 2 )
   sum += count;
```

b) **Math.pow(2.5, 3)**

c) ```
x = 1;

while (x <= 20) {
    System.out.print(x);

    if (x % 5 == 0)
        System.out.println();
    else
        System.out.print('\t');

    x++;
}
```

d) ```
for ( x = 1; x <= 20; x++ ) {
    System.out.print( x );

    if ( x % 5 == 0 )
        System.out.println();
    else
        System.out.print( '\t' );
}
```

or

```
for ( x = 1; x <= 20; x++ )

    if (x % 5 == 0)
        System.out.println( x );
    else
        System.out.print( x + "\t" );
```

3.3   a)   Error: The semicolon after the **while** header causes an infinite loop.
           Correction: Replace the semicolon by a **{** or remove both the **;** and the **}**.
    b)   Error: Using a floating-point number to control a **for** repetition structure.
           Correction: Use an integer, and perform the proper calculation in order to get the values you desire.
```
for ( y = 1; y != 10; y++ )
    System.out.println( (float) y / 10 );
```
    c)   Error: Missing **break** statement in the statements for the first **case**.
           Correction: Add a **break** statement at the end of the statements for the first **case**. Note that this is not necessarily an error if the programmer wants the statement of **case 2:** to execute every time the **case 1:** statement executes.
    d)   Error: Improper relational operator used in the while repetition-continuation condition.
           Correction: Use **<=** rather than **<** or change **10** to **11**.

Exercises

3.4   Find the error in each of the following (Note: there may be more than one error):
    a) ```
For (x = 100, x >= 1, x++)
    System.out.println(x);
```
```

b) The following code should print whether integer **value** is odd or even:

```
switch ( value % 2 ) {

    case 0:
        System.out.println( "Even integer" );

    case 1:
        System.out.println( "Odd integer" );
}
```

c) The following code should output the odd integers from 19 to 1:

```
for ( x = 19; x >= 1; x += 2 )
    System.out.println( x );
```

d) The following code should output the even integers from 2 to 100:

```
counter = 2;
do {
    System.out.println( counter );
    counter += 2;
} While ( counter < 100 );
```

3.5   What does the following program do?

```
public class Printing {
    public static void main( String args[] )
    {
        for ( int i = 1; i <= 10; i++ ) {

            for ( int j = 1; j <= 5; j++ )
                System.out.print( '@' );

            System.out.println();
        }
    }
}
```

3.6   Write an application that finds the smallest of several letters. Assume that the first value read is a digit character that specifies the number of letters remaining.

3.7   Write an applet that calculates and prints the product of the odd integers from 1 to 15.

3.8   The *factorial* method is used frequently in probability problems. The factorial of a positive integer *n* (written *n!* and pronounced "n factorial") is equal to the product of the positive integers from 1 to *n*. Write an applet that evaluates the factorials of the integers from 1 to 5. Display the results in tabular format. What difficulty might prevent you from calculating the factorial of 20?

3.9   Modify the compound interest program of Fig. 3.6 to repeat its steps for interest rates of 5 percent, 6 percent, 7 percent, 8 percent, 9 percent, and 10 percent. Use a **for** loop to vary the interest rate.

3.10   Write an application that prints the following patterns separately one below the other. Use **for** loops to generate the patterns. All asterisks (*****) should be printed by a single statement of the form **System.out.print ('*');** (this causes the asterisks to print side by side). Hint: The last two patterns require that each line begin with an appropriate number of blanks. Extra credit: Combine your code from the four separate problems into a single program that prints all four patterns side by side making clever use of nested **for** loops.

```
(A)                   (B)                   (C)                   (D)
*                     **********            **********                     *
**                    *********             *********                     **
***                   ********              ********                     ***
****                  *******               *******                     ****
*****                 ******                ******                     *****
******                *****                 *****                     ******
*******               ****                  ****                    *******
********              ***                   ***                   ********
*********             **                    **                  *********
**********            *                     *                 **********
```

3.11   One interesting application of computers is drawing graphs and bar charts (sometimes called "histograms"). Write an applet that reads five numbers (each between 1 and 30). For each number read, your program should print a line containing that number of adjacent asterisks. For example, if your program reads the number seven, it should print *******.

3.12   A mail order house sells five different products whose retail prices are product 1 — $2.98, product 2—$4.50, product 3—$9.98, product 4—$4.49, and product 5—$6.87. Write an applet that reads a series of pairs of numbers as follows:

1) Product number
2) Quantity sold for one day

Your program should use a **switch** structure to help determine the retail price for each product. Your program should calculate and display the total retail value of all products sold last week. Use a text field to obtain the product number from the user.

3.13   Modify the program of Fig. 3.7 so that it calculates the grade point average for the class. A grade of 'A' is worth 4 points, 'B' is worth 3 points, etc.

3.14   Modify the program in Fig. 3.6 so that it uses only integers to calculate the compound interest. (Hint: Treat all monetary amounts as integral numbers of pennies. Then "break" the result into its dollar portion and cents portion by using the division and modulus operations respectively. Insert a period.)

3.15   Assume **i = 1, j = 2, k = 3**, and **m = 2**. What does each of the following statements print? Are the parentheses necessary in each case?

```
a) System.out.println( i == 1 );
b) System.out.println( j == 3 );
c) System.out.println( i >= 1 && j < 4 );
d) System.out.println( m <= 99 & k < m );
e) System.out.println( j >= i || k == m );
f) System.out.println( k + m < j | 3 - j >= k );
g) System.out.println( !m );
h) System.out.println( !( j - m ) );
i) System.out.println( !( k > m ) );
```

3.16   Write an application that prints a table of the binary, octal, and hexadecimal equivalents of the decimal numbers in the range 1 through 256. If you are not familiar with these number systems, read the appendix, "Number Systems," first.

3.17   Calculate the value of π from the infinite series

$$\pi = 4 - \frac{4}{3} + \frac{4}{5} - \frac{4}{7} + \frac{4}{9} - \frac{4}{11} + \cdots$$

Print a table that shows the value of π approximated by 1 term of this series, by two terms, by three terms, etc. How many terms of this series do you have to use before you first get 3.14? 3.141? 3.1415? 3.14159?

3.18   *(Pythagorean Triples)* A right triangle can have sides that are all integers. The set of three integer values for the sides of a right triangle is called a Pythagorean triple. These three sides must satisfy the relationship that the sum of the squares of two of the sides is equal to the square of the hypotenuse. Write an application to find all Pythagorean triples for **side1**, **side2**, and the **hypotenuse** all no larger than 500. Use a triple-nested **for**-loop that tries all possibilities. This is an example of "brute force" computing. You will learn in more advanced computer science courses that there are large numbers of interesting problems for which there is no known algorithmic approach other than using sheer brute force.

3.19   A company pays its employees as managers (who receive a fixed weekly salary), hourly workers (who receive a fixed hourly wage for up to the first 40 hours they work and "time-and-a-half," i.e., 1.5 times their hourly wage, for overtime hours worked), commission workers (who receive a $250 plus 5.7% of their gross weekly sales), or pieceworkers (who receive a fixed amount of money per item for each of the items they produce—each pieceworker in this company works on only one type of item). Write an applet to compute the weekly pay for each employee. Each type of employee has its own pay code: Managers have paycode 1, hourly workers have code 2, commission workers have code 3 and pieceworkers have code 4. Use a **switch** to compute each employee's pay based on that employee's paycode. Within the **switch**, prompt the user (i.e., the payroll clerk) to enter the appropriate facts your program needs to calculate each employee's pay based on that employee's paycode.

3.20   *(De Morgan's Laws)* In this chapter, we discussed the logical operators **&&**, **&**, **||**, **|**, and **!**. De Morgan's Laws can sometimes make it more convenient for us to express a logical expression. These laws state that the expression **!**(*condition1* **&&** *condition2*) is logically equivalent to the expression (**!***condition1* **||** **!***condition2*). Also, the expression **!**(*condition1* **||** *condition2*) is logically equivalent to the expression (**!***condition1* **&&** **!***condition2*). Use De Morgan's Laws to write equivalent expressions for each of the following, and then write a program to show that both the original expression and the new expression in each case are equivalent:

    a) !(x < 5) && !(y >= 7)
    b) !(a == b) || !(g != 5)
    c) !((x <= 8) && (y > 4))
    d) !((i > 4) || (j <= 6))

3.21   Write an applet that prints the following diamond shape. You may use an output statement in your **paint** method that prints a single asterisk (*). Maximize your use of repetition (with nested **for** structures) and minimize the number of output statements.

```
    *
   ***
  *****
 *******
*********
 *******
  *****
   ***
    *
```

3.22   Modify the program you wrote in Exercise 3.21 to read an odd number in the range 1 to 19 to specify the number of rows in the diamond. Your program should then display a diamond of the appropriate size.

3.23   A criticism of the **break** statement and the **continue** statement is that each is unstructured. Actually **break** statements and **continue** statements can always be replaced by structured statements, although doing so can be awkward. Describe in general how you would remove any **break** statement from a loop in a program and replace that statement with some structured equivalent. (Hint: The **break** statement leaves a loop from within the body of the loop. The other way to leave is by failing the loop-continuation test. Consider using in the loop-continuation test a second test that indicates "early exit because of a 'break' condition.") Use the technique you developed here to remove the break statement from the program of Fig. 3.11.

3.24   What does the following program segment do?

```
for ( i = 1; i <= 5; i++ ) {

    for ( j = 1; j <= 3; j++ ) {

        for ( k = 1; k <= 4; k++ )
            System.out.print( '*' );
        System.out.println();
    }
    System.out.println();
}
```

3.25   Describe in general how you would remove any **continue** statement from a loop in a program and replace that statement with some structured equivalent. Use the technique you developed here to remove the **continue** statement from the program of Fig. 3.12.

3.26   (*"The Twelve Days of Christmas" Song*) Write an application that uses repetition and **switch** structures to print the song "The Twelve Days of Christmas." One **switch** structure should be used to to print the day (i.e., "First," "Second," etc.). A separate **switch** structure should be used to print the remainder of each verse.

4

Methods

Objectives

- To understand how to construct program modularly from small pieces called methods.
- To introduce the common math methods available in the Java API.
- To be able to create new methods.
- To understand the mechanisms used to pass information between methods.
- To introduce simulation techniques using random number generation.
- To understand how the visibility of identifiers is limited to specific regions of programs.
- To understand how to write and use methods that call themselves.

Form ever follows function.
Louis Henri Sullivan

E pluribus unum.
(One composed of many.)
Virgil

O! call back yesterday, bid time return.
William Shakespeare, *Richard II*

Call me Ishmael.
Herman Melville, *Moby Dick*

When you call me that, smile.
Owen Wister

Outline

4.1 Introduction

Most computer programs that solve real-world problems are much larger than the programs presented in the first few chapters. Experience has shown that the best way to develop and maintain a large program is to construct it from smaller pieces or *modules* each of which is more manageable than the original program. This technique is called *divide and conquer*. This chapter describes many key features of the Java language that facilitate the design, implementation, operation, and maintenance of large programs.

4.2 Program Modules in Java

Modules in Java are called *methods* and *classes*. Java programs are written by combining new methods the programmer writes with "pre-packaged" methods available in the *Java API* (also referred to as the *Java class library*) and by combining new classes the programmer writes with "pre-packaged" classes available in various class libraries. In this chapter, we concentrate on methods; we will discuss classes in detail beginning with Chapter 6.

   The Java API provides a rich collection of classes and methods for performing common mathematical calculations, string manipulations, character manipulations, input/output, error checking, and many other useful operations. This makes the programmer's job easier because these methods provide many of the capabilities programmers need. The Java API methods are provided as part of the Java Developer's Kit (JDK).

Good Programming Practice 4.1

Familiarize yourself with the rich collection of classes and methods in the Java API and with the rich collections of classes available in various class libraries.

Software Engineering Observation 4.1

Avoid reinventing the wheel. When possible, use Java API classes and methods instead of writing new classes and methods. This reduces program development time.

The programmer can write methods to define specific tasks that may be used at many points in a program. These are sometimes referred to as *programmer-defined methods*. The actual statements defining the method are written only once and these statements are hidden from other methods.

A method is *invoked* (i.e., made to perform its designated task) by a *method call*. The method call specifies the method name and provides information (as *arguments*) that the called method needs to do its job. A common analogy for this is the hierarchical form of management. A boss (the *calling method* or *caller*) asks a worker (the *called method*) to perform a task and *return* (i.e., report back) the results when the task is done. The boss method does not know *how* the worker method performs its designated tasks. The worker may call other worker methods, and the boss will be unaware of this. We will soon see how this "hiding" of implementation details promotes good software engineering. Figure 4.1 shows the **main** method communicating with several worker methods in a hierarchical manner. Note that **worker1** acts as a boss method to **worker4** and **worker5**. Relationships among methods may be other than the hierarchical structure shown in this figure.

4.3 Math Class Methods

Math class methods allow the programmer to perform certain common mathematical calculations. We use various **Math** class methods here to introduce the concept of methods. Later in the book, we will discuss many of the other methods in the Java API.

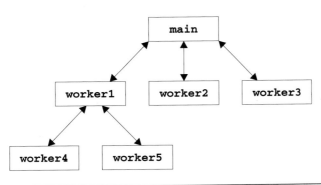

Fig. 4.1   Hierarchical boss method/worker method relationship.

Methods are normally called by writing the name of the method followed by a left parenthesis followed by the *argument* (or a comma-separated list of arguments) of the method followed by a right parenthesis. For example, a programmer desiring to calculate and print the square root of **900.0** might write

```
System.out.println( Math.sqrt( 900.0 ) );
```

When this statement is executed, the method **Math.sqrt** is called to calculate the square root of the number contained in the parentheses (**900.0**). The number **900.0** is the *argument* of the **Math.sqrt** method. The preceding statement would print **30**. The **Math.sqrt** method takes an argument of type **double** and returns a result of type **double**. Note that all **Math** class methods must be invoked by preceding the method name with the class name **Math** and a dot (**.**) operator. Normally we invoke methods through an object or directly as in the following two lines of code from an applet

```
g.drawString( "Welcome to Java programming!", 25, 25 );
showStatus( "hello" );
```

The first statement might appear in your applet's **paint** method. The statement invokes the **drawString** method through the **Graphics** object **g** (also referred to as *sending the drawString message to the object* **g**). The second statement could appear in any method of your applet. The statement invokes the **showStatus** method directly and displays a string in the status bar of your browser or the Appletviewer. In Chapter 6, we discuss in detail the different types of methods associated with classes and how they are invoked.

Software Engineering Observation 4.2

It is not necessary to import the **Math** *class into a program to use* **Math** *class methods. The* **Math** *class is part of the* **java.lang** *package which is automatically imported by the compiler.*

Common Programming Error 4.1

Forgetting to invoke a **Math** *class method by preceding the method name with the class name* **Math** *and a dot operator (.) results in a syntax error.*

Method arguments may be constants, variables, or expressions. If **c1 = 13.0**, **d = 3.0**, and **f = 4.0**, then the statement

```
System.out.println( Math.sqrt( c1 + d * f ) );
```

calculates and prints the square root of **13.0 + 3.0 * 4.0 = 25.0**, namely **5** (because Java does not ordinarily print trailing zeros or the decimal point in a floating-point number that has no fractional part).

Some **Math** class methods are summarized in Fig. 4.2. In the figure, the variables **x** and **y** are of type **double**. The **Math** class also defines two commonly used mathematical constants—**Math.PI** and **Math.E**. Constant **Math.PI** (3.14159265358979323846) is the ratio of a circle's circumference to its diameter. Constant **Math.E** (2.7182818284590452354) is the base value for natural logarithms (performed by the **Math.log** method).

Method	Description	Example
abs(x)	absolute value of *x* This method also has versions **float**, **int**, and **long** values.	if **x** > 0 then **abs(x)** is **x** if **x** = 0 then **abs(x)** is 0 if **x** < 0 then **abs(x)** is -**x**
ceil(x)	rounds *x* to the smallest integer not less than *x*	ceil(9.2) is 10 ceil(-9.8) is -9
cos(x)	trigonometric cosine of x (x in radians)	cos(0.0) is 1
exp(x)	exponential method e^x	exp(1.0) is 2.71828 exp(2.0) is 7.38906
floor(x)	rounds *x* to the largest integer not greater than *x*	floor(9.2) is 9 floor(-9.8) is -10
log(x)	natural logarithm of x (base e)	log(2.718282) is 1 log(7.389056) is 2
max(x, y)	larger value of *x* and *y* This method also has versions **float**, **int**, and **long** values.	max(2.3, 12.7) is 12.7 max(-2.3, -12.7) is -2.3
min(x, y)	smaller value of *x* and *y* This method also has versions **float**, **int**, and **long** values.	min(2.3, 12.7) is 2.3 min(-2.3, -12.7) is -12.7
pow(x, y)	x raised to power y (x^y)	pow(2, 7) is 128 pow(9, .5) is 3
sin(x)	trigonometric sine of *x* (*x* in radians)	sin(0.0) is 0
sqrt(x)	square root of *x*	sqrt(900.0) is 30 sqrt(9.0) is 3
tan(x)	trigonometric tangent of x (x in radians)	tan(0.0) is 0

Fig. 4.2 Commonly used **Math** class methods.

4.4 Methods

Methods allow the programmer to modularize a program. All variables declared in method definitions are *local variables*—they are known only in the method in which they are defined. Most methods have a list of *parameters* that provide the means for communicating information between methods. A method's parameters are also local variables.

There are several motivations for modularizing a program with methods. The divide-and-conquer approach makes program development more manageable. Another motivation is *software reusability*—using existing methods as building blocks to create new programs. With good method naming and definition, programs can be created from standardized methods, rather than being built by using customized code. A third motivation is to avoid repeating code in a program. Packaging code as a method allows that code to be executed from several locations in a program simply by calling the method.

Software Engineering Observation 4.3

Each method should be limited to performing a single, well-defined task, and the method name should effectively express that task. This promotes software reusability.

Software Engineering Observation 4.4

If you cannot choose a concise name that expresses what the method does, it is possible that your method is attempting to perform too many diverse tasks. It is usually best to break such a method into several smaller methods.

4.5 Method Definitions

Each program we have presented has consisted of a class definition that contained at least one method definition that called Java API methods to accomplish its tasks. We now consider how programmers write their own customized methods.

Consider an applet that uses a method **square** (invoked from the applet's **paint** method) to calculate the squares of the integers from 1 to 10 (Fig. 4.3).

Good Programming Practice 4.2

Place a blank line between method definitions to separate the methods and enhance program readability.

Method **square** is *invoked* or *called* in **paint** on line 13 with the call

```
square( x )
```

The **square** method receives a copy of the value of **x** in the *parameter* **y**. Then **square** calculates **y * y**. The result is passed back to the point in **paint** where **square** was invoked, and the result is displayed. This process is repeated ten times using the **for** repetition structure.

The definition of the **square** method (line 20) shows that **square** expects an integer parameter **y**. The keyword **int** preceding the method name indicates that **square** returns an integer result. The **return** statement in **square** passes the result of the calculation back to the calling method. Note that the entire method definition is contained between the braces of the class **SquareInt**. All methods in Java must be defined inside a class definition.

Common Programming Error 4.2

Defining a method outside the braces of a class definition results in a syntax error.

The format of a method definition is

> *return-value-type method-name*(parameter-list)
> {
>   *declarations and statements*
> }

The *method-name* is any valid identifier. The *return-value-type* is the data type of the result returned from the method to the caller. The return-value-type **void** indicates that a method does not return a value.

```
1   // Fig. 4.3: SquareInt.java
2   // A programmer-defined square method
3   import java.awt.Graphics;
4   import java.applet.Applet;
5
6   public class SquareInt extends Applet {
7       // output the squared values of 1 through 10
8       public void paint( Graphics g )
9       {
10          int xPosition = 25;
11
12          for ( int x = 1; x <= 10; x++ ) {
13              g.drawString( String.valueOf( square( x ) ),
14                          xPosition, 25);
15              xPosition += 20;
16          }
17      }
18
19      // square method definition
20      public int square(int y)
21      {
22          return y * y;
23      }
24  }
```

Fig. 4.3   Using a programmer-defined method.

Common Programming Error 4.3
Omitting the return-value-type in a method definition causes a syntax error.

Common Programming Error 4.4
*Forgetting to return a value from a method that is supposed to return a value is a syntax er-ror. If a return-value-type other than **void** is specified, the method must contain a **return** statement.*

Common Programming Error 4.5
*Returning a value from a method whose return type has been declared **void** causes a syntax error.*

The *parameter-list* is a comma-separated list containing the declarations of the param-eters received by the method when it is called. If a method does not receive any values, *parameter-list* is empty (i.e., an empty set of parentheses follows the method name). A type must be listed explicitly for each parameter in the parameter list of a method.

Common Programming Error 4.6

Declaring method parameters of the same type as **float x, y** *instead of* **float x, float y**. *The parameter declaration* **float x, y** *would actually report a compilation error because types are required for each parameter in the parameter list.*

Common Programming Error 4.7

Placing a semicolon after the right parenthesis enclosing the parameter list of a method definition is a syntax error.

Common Programming Error 4.8

Defining a method parameter again as a local variable in the method is a syntax error.

Good Programming Practice 4.3

Although it is not incorrect to do so, do not use the same names for the arguments passed to a method and the corresponding parameters in the method definition. This helps avoid ambiguity.

The *declarations* and *statements* within braces form the *method body*. The method body is also referred to as a *block*. A block is simply a compound statement that includes declarations. Variables can be declared in any block, and blocks can be nested. *A method cannot be defined inside another method.*

Common Programming Error 4.9

Defining a method inside another method is a syntax error.

Good Programming Practice 4.4

Choosing meaningful method names and meaningful parameter names makes programs more readable and helps avoid excessive use of comments.

Software Engineering Observation 4.5

A method should usually be no longer than one page. Better yet, a method should usually be no longer than half a page. Regardless of how long a method is, it should perform one task well. Small methods promote software reusability.

Software Engineering Observation 4.6

Programs should be written as collections of small methods. This makes programs easier to write, debug, maintain and modify.

Software Engineering Observation 4.7

A method requiring a large number of parameters may be performing too many tasks. Consider dividing the method into smaller methods that perform the separate tasks. The method header should fit on one line if possible.

Software Engineering Observation 4.8

The method header and method calls should all agree in the number, type, and order of arguments and parameters, and in the type of return value.

There are three ways to return control to the point at which a method was invoked. If the method does not return a result, control is returned simply when the method-ending right brace is reached, or by executing the statement

```
return;
```

If the method does return a result, the statement

```
return expression;
```

returns the value of *expression* to the caller. When a return statement is executed, control returns immediately to the point at which a method was invoked.

Note that the example of Fig. 4.3 actually contains two method definitions—**paint** (line 8) and **square** (line 20). Remember that the **paint** method is automatically called to enable the applet to display information. In this example, the **paint** method repeatedly invokes the **square** method to perform a calculation, then **paint** outputs the result. Methods in a class definition are allowed to invoke all other methods in the same class definition (there is an exception to this discussed in Chapter 6).

Our second example uses a programmer-defined method called **maximum** to determine and return the largest of three integers (Fig. 4.4). The three integers are input by the user into text fields. When the user presses the Enter key in one of the text fields, the **action** method is invoked, the strings in the text fields are read and converted to integers, and the integers are passed to the **maximum** method which determines the largest integer. This value is returned to the **action** method by the **return** statement in the **maximum** method. The value returned is assigned to the variable **max** which is then displayed in the **result** text field.

Notice the implementation of the method **maximum** (line 35). The first line indicates that the method returns an integer, that the method's name is **maximum** and that the method takes three integer parameters (**x**, **y**, and **z**) to accomplish its task. Also, the body of the method contains the statement

```
return Math.max( x, Math.max( y, z ) );
```

which returns the largest of the three integers using two calls to the **Math.max** method. First, method **Math.max** is invoked with the values of variables **y** and **z** to determine the larger of these two values. Next the value of variable **x** and the result of the first call to **Math.max** are passed to method **Math.max**. Finally, the result of the second call to **Math.max** is returned to the point at which **maximum** was invoked (i.e., the **action** method in this program).

Another important feature of method definitions is the *coercion of arguments,* i.e., the forcing of arguments to the appropriate type to pass to a method. For example, the **Math** class method **sqrt** can be called with an integer argument even though the method is defined in the **Math** class to receive a **double** argument, and the method will still work correctly. The statement

```
System.out.println( Math.sqrt( 4 ) );
```

```
1   // Fig. 4.4: Maximum.java
2   // Finding the maximum of three integers
3   import java.awt.*;
4   import java.applet.Applet;
5
6   public class Maximum extends Applet {
7      Label label1, label2, label3, resultLabel;
8      TextField number1, number2, number3, result;
9      int num1, num2, num3, max;
10
11     // set up labels and text fields
12     public void init()
13     {
14        label1 = new Label( "Enter first integer:" );
15        number1 = new TextField( "0", 10 );
16        label2 = new Label( "Enter second integer:" );
17        number2 = new TextField( "0", 10 );
18        label3 = new Label( "Enter third integer:" );
19        number3 = new TextField( "0", 10 );
20        resultLabel = new Label( "Maximum value is:" );
21        result = new TextField( "0", 10 );
22        result.setEditable( false );
23
24        add( label1 );
25        add( number1 );
26        add( label2 );
27        add( number2 );
28        add( label3 );
29        add( number3 );
30        add( resultLabel );
31        add( result );
32     }
33
34     // maximum method definition
35     public int maximum( int x, int y, int z )
36     {
37        return Math.max( x, Math.max( y, z ) );
38     }
39
40     // get the integers and call the maximum method
41     public boolean action( Event e, Object o )
42     {
43        num1 = Integer.parseInt( number1.getText() );
44        num2 = Integer.parseInt( number2.getText() );
45        num3 = Integer.parseInt( number3.getText() );
46        max = maximum( num1, num2, num3 );
47        result.setText( Integer.toString( max ) );
48        return true;
49     }
50  }
```

Fig. 4.4 Programmer-defined **maximum** method (part 1 of 2).

Fig. 4.4   Programmer-defined **maximum** method (part 2 of 2).

correctly evaluates **Math.sqrt(4)**, and prints the value **2**. The method definition's parameter list causes the integer value **4** to be converted to the **double** value **4.0** before the value is passed to **Math.sqrt**. In many cases, argument values that do not correspond precisely to the parameter types in the method definition are converted to the proper type before the method is called. In some cases, these conversions can lead to compiler errors if

Java's *promotion rules* are not followed. The promotion rules specify how types can be converted to other types without losing data. In our **Math.sqrt** example above, an **int** is automatically converted to a **double** without changing its value. However, a **double** converted to an **int** truncates the fractional part of the **double** value. Converting large integer types to small integer types (e.g., **long** to **int**) may also result in changed values.

The promotion rules apply to expressions containing values of two or more data types; such expressions are also referred to as *mixed-type expressions*. The type of each value in a mixed-type expression is promoted to the "highest" type in the expression (actually a temporary version of each value is created and used for the expression—the original values remain unchanged). Figure 4.5 lists the primitive data types and the types to which each is allowed to be promoted automatically.

Converting values to lower types can result in incorrect values. Therefore, in cases where information may be lost due to conversion, the Java compiler requires the programmer to use a cast operator to force the conversion to occur. To invoke our **square** method that uses an integer parameter (Fig. 4.3) with the **double** variable **y**, the method call is written as **square((int) y)**. This explicitly converts the value of **y** to an integer for use in method **square**. Thus, if **y**'s value is **4.5**, method **square** returns **16** not **20.25**.

 Common Programming Error 4.10

Converting a primitive-data-type value to another primitive data type that is not in the original type's list of allowed promotions can change the data value.

4.6 Java API Packages

As we have seen, Java contains many predefined pieces called classes that are grouped by directories on disk into categories of related classes called packages. Together, these packages are referred to as the Java applications programming interface (Java API).

Throughout the text, **import** statements are used to load classes required to compile a Java program. For example, to tell the compiler to load the **Applet** class from the **java.applet** package, the statement

Type	Allowed promotions
double	None (there are no primitive types larger than **double**)
float	**double**
long	**float** or **double**
int	**long**, **float** or **double**
char	**int**, **long**, **float** or **double**
short	**int**, **long**, **float** or **double**
byte	**short**, **int**, **long**, **float** or **double**
boolean	None (**boolean** values are not considered to be numbers in Java)

Fig. 4.5 Allowed promotions for primitive data types.

```
import java.applet.Applet;
```

is used. One of the great strengths of Java is the large number of classes in the packages of
the Java API that programmers can reuse rather than "reinventing the wheel." We exercise
a large number of these classes in this book. Fig. 4.6 lists alphabetically the packages of the
Java API and a description of each package.

Java API package	Explanation
java.applet	*The Java Applet Package.* This package contains the Applet class and several interfaces that enable the creation of applets, interaction of applets with the browser, and playing audio clips.
java.awt	*The Java Abstract Windowing Toolkit Package.* This package contains all the classes and interfaces required to create and manipulate graphical user interfaces (these classes are discussed in detail in Chapter 10, Basic Graphical User Interface Components and Chapter 11, Advanced Graphical User Interface Components).
java.awt.image	*The Java Abstract Windowing Toolkit Image Package.* This package contains classes and interfaces that enable storing and manipulation of images in a program.
java.awt.peer	*The Java Abstract Windowing Toolkit Peer Package.* This package contains interfaces that enable Java's graphical user interface components to interact with their platform-specific versions (i.e., a button is implemented differently on each computer platform so its peer is used to actually display and manipulate the button in a platform specific manner).
java.io	*The Java Input/Output Package.* This package contains classes that enable programs to input and output data (see Chapter 15, Files and Streams).
java.lang	*The Java Language Package.* This package is automatically imported by the compiler into all programs. The package contains basic classes and interfaces required by many Java programs (these classes are discussed throughout the text).
java.net	*The Java Networking Package.* This package contains classes that enable programs to communicate via the Internet or corporate intranets (see Chapter 16, Networking)
java.util	*The Java Utilities Package.* This package contains utility classes and interfaces such as: date and time manipulations (**Date**), various random number processing capabilities (**Random**), storing and processing large amounts of data, breaking strings into smaller pieces called tokens (**StringTokenizer**), and other capabilities (see Chapter 18, Utilities and Bit Manipulation).

Fig. 4.6   The Java API packages.

4.7 Random Number Generation

We now take a brief and, it is hoped, entertaining diversion into a popular programming application, namely simulation and game playing. In this section and the next section, we will develop a nicely structured game-playing program that includes multiple methods. The program uses most of the control structures we have studied.

There is something in the air of a gambling casino that invigorates people from the high-rollers at the plush mahogany-and-felt craps tables to the quarter-poppers at the one-armed bandits. It is the *element of chance,* the possibility that luck will convert a pocketful of money into a mountain of wealth. The element of chance can be introduced through the *random* method from the **Math** class.

Consider the following statement:

```
double randomValue = Math.random();
```

The **random** method generates a **double** value from 0.0 up to (but not including) 1.0. If **random** truly produces values at random, every value from 0.0 up to (but not including) 1.0 has an equal *chance* (or *probability*) of being chosen each time **random** is called.

The range of values produced directly by **random** is often different than what is needed in a specific application. For example, a program that simulates coin tossing might require only 0 for "heads" and 1 for "tails." A program that simulates rolling a six-sided die would require random integers in range 1 to 6. A program that randomly predicts the next type of spaceship (out of four possibilities) that will fly across the horizon in a video game would require random integers in the range 1 through 4.

To demonstrate **random**, let us develop a program to simulate 20 rolls of a six-sided die and print the value of each roll. We use the multiplication operator (*****) in conjunction with **random** as follows

```
(int) ( Math.random() * 6 )
```

to produce integers in the range 0 to 5. This is called *scaling.* The number 6 is called the *scaling factor.* We then *shift* the range of numbers produced by adding 1 to our previous result. Figure 4.7 confirms that the results are in the range 1 to 6. The integer cast operator is used to truncate the floating-point part (the part after the decimal point) of each value produced by the preceding expression.

To show that these numbers occur approximately with equal likelihood, let us simulate 6000 rolls of a die with the program of Fig. 4.8. Each integer from 1 to 6 should appear approximately 1000 times.

As the program output shows, by scaling and shifting we have utilized the **random** method to realistically simulate the rolling of a six-sided die. Note that *no* **default** case is provided in the **switch** structure. After we study arrays in Chapter 5, we will show how to replace the entire **switch** structure elegantly with a single-line statement. Run the program several times and observe the results. Notice that a *different* sequence of random numbers is obtained each time the program is executed.

The values produced directly by **random** are always in the range:

```
0.0 ≤ Math.random() < 1.0
```

```
1   // Fig. 4.7: RandomInt.java
2   // Shifted, scaled random integers
3   import java.awt.Graphics;
4   import java.applet.Applet;
5
6   public class RandomInt extends Applet {
7      public void paint( Graphics g )
8      {
9         int xPosition = 25;
10        int yPosition = 25;
11        int value;
12
13        for ( int i = 1; i <= 20; i++ ) {
14           value = 1 + (int) ( Math.random() * 6 );
15           g.drawString( Integer.toString( value ),
16                         xPosition, yPosition );
17
18           if ( i % 5 != 0 )
19              xPosition += 40;
20           else {
21              xPosition = 25;
22              yPosition += 15;
23           }
24        }
25     }
26  }
```

Fig. 4.7   Shifted, scaled random integers.

Previously we demonstrated how to write a single statement to simulate the rolling of a six-sided die with the statement:

```
int face = 1 + (int) ( Math.random() * 6 );
```

which always assigns an integer (at random) to variable **face** in the range $1 \le$ **face** ≤ 6. Note that the width of this range (i.e., the number of consecutive integers in the range) is 6 and the starting number in the range is 1. Referring to the preceding statement, we see that the width of the range is determined by the number used to scale **random** with the multiplication operator (i.e., 6), and the starting number of the range is equal to the number (i.e., 1) added to **(int) (Math.random() * 6)**. We can generalize this result as follows

```
1   // Fig. 4.8: RollDie.java
2   // Roll a six-sided die 6000 times
3   import java.awt.Graphics;
4   import java.applet.Applet;
5
6   public class RollDie extends Applet {
7      int frequency1 = 0, frequency2 = 0,
8          frequency3 = 0, frequency4 = 0,
9          frequency5 = 0, frequency6 = 0;
10
11     // summarize results
12     public void start()
13     {
14         for ( int roll = 1; roll <= 6000; roll++ ) {
15             int face = 1 + (int) ( Math.random() * 6 );
16
17             switch ( face ) {
18                 case 1:
19                     ++frequency1;
20                     break;
21                 case 2:
22                     ++frequency2;
23                     break;
24                 case 3:
25                     ++frequency3;
26                     break;
27                 case 4:
28                     ++frequency4;
29                     break;
30                 case 5:
31                     ++frequency5;
32                     break;
33                 case 6:
34                     ++frequency6;
35                     break;
36             }
37         }
38     }
39
40     // display results
41     public void paint( Graphics g )
42     {
43         g.drawString( "Face", 25, 25 );
44         g.drawString( "Frequency", 100, 25 );
45         g.drawString( "1", 25, 40 );
46         g.drawString( Integer.toString( frequency1 ), 100, 40 );
47         g.drawString( "2", 25, 55 );
48         g.drawString( Integer.toString( frequency2 ), 100, 55 );
49         g.drawString( "3", 25, 70 );
50         g.drawString( Integer.toString( frequency3 ), 100, 70 );
```

Fig. 4.8   Rolling a six-sided die 6000 times (part 1 of 2).

```
51        g.drawString( "4", 25, 85 );
52        g.drawString( Integer.toString( frequency4 ), 100, 85 );
53        g.drawString( "5", 25, 100 );
54        g.drawString( Integer.toString( frequency5 ),
55                      100, 100 );
56        g.drawString( "6", 25, 115 );
57        g.drawString( Integer.toString( frequency6 ),
58                      100, 115 );
59     }
60  }
61
```

```
Applet Viewer: RollDie.class

Applet

   Face        Frequency
   1           1020
   2           1008
   3           981
   4           990
   5           995
   6           1006

Applet started.
```

Fig. 4.8   Rolling a six-sided die 6000 times (part 2 of 2).

```
n = a + (int) ( Math.random() * b );
```

where **a** is the *shifting value* (which is equal to the first number in the desired range of consecutive integers), and **b** is the scaling factor (which is equal to the width of the desired range of consecutive integers). In the exercises, we will see that it is possible to choose integers at random from sets of values other than ranges of consecutive integers.

4.8 Example: A Game of Chance

One of the most popular games of chance is a dice game known as "craps," which is played in casinos and back alleys throughout the world. The rules of the game are straightforward:

A player rolls two dice. Each die has six faces. These faces contain 1, 2, 3, 4, 5, and 6 spots. After the dice have come to rest, the sum of the spots on the two upward faces is calculated. If the sum is 7 or 11 on the first throw, the player wins. If the sum is 2, 3, or 12 on the first throw (called "craps"), the player loses (i.e., the "house" wins). If the sum is 4, 5, 6, 8, 9, or 10 on the first throw, then that sum becomes the player's "point." To win, you must continue rolling the dice until you "make your point," (i.e., roll your point value). The player loses by rolling a 7 before making the point.

The program in Fig. 4.9 simulates the game of craps.

```
1   // Fig. 4.9: Craps.java
2   // Craps
3   import java.awt.*;
4   import java.applet.Applet;
5
6   public class Craps extends Applet {
7      // constant variables for status of game
8      final int WON = 0, LOST = 1, CONTINUE = 2;
9
10     // other variables used in program
11     boolean firstRoll = true;    // true if first roll
12     int dieSum = 0;              // sum of the dice
13     int myPoint = 0;    // point if no win/loss on first roll
14     int gameStatus = CONTINUE;   // WON, LOST, CONTINUE
15
16     // graphical user interface components
17     Label die1Label, die2Label, sumLabel, pointLabel;
18     TextField firstDie, secondDie, sum, point;
19     Button roll;
20
21     // setup graphical user interface components
22     public void init()
23     {
24        die1Label = new Label( "Die 1" );
25        firstDie = new TextField( 10 );
26        firstDie.setEditable( false );
27        die2Label = new Label( "Die 2" );
28        secondDie = new TextField( 10 );
29        secondDie.setEditable( false );
30        sumLabel = new Label( "Sum is" );
31        sum = new TextField( 10 );
32        sum.setEditable( false );
33        roll = new Button( "Roll Dice" );
34        pointLabel = new Label( "Point is" );
35        point = new TextField( 10 );
36        point.setEditable( false );
37
38        add( die1Label );
39        add( firstDie );
40        add( die2Label );
41        add( secondDie );
42        add( sumLabel );
43        add( sum );
44        add( pointLabel );
45        add( point );
46        add( roll );
47     }
```

Fig. 4.9   Program to simulate the game of craps (part 1 of 4).

```
48
49      // process one roll of the dice
50      public void play()
51      {
52         if ( firstRoll ) {                    // first roll of the dice
53            dieSum = rollDice();
54
55            switch( dieSum ) {
56               case 7: case 11:              // win on first roll
57                  gameStatus = WON;
58                  point.setText( "" );  // clear point text field
59                  firstRoll = true;       // allow new game to start
60                  break;
61               case 2: case 3: case 12: // lose on first roll
62                  gameStatus = LOST;
63                  point.setText( "" );  // clear point text field
64                  firstRoll = true;       // allow new game to start
65                  break;
66               default:                      // remember point
67                  gameStatus = CONTINUE;
68                  myPoint = dieSum;
69                  point.setText( Integer.toString( myPoint ) );
70                  firstRoll = false;
71                  break;
72            }
73         }
74         else {
75            dieSum = rollDice();
76
77            if ( dieSum == myPoint )     // win by making point
78               gameStatus = WON;
79            else
80               if ( dieSum == 7 )          // lose by rolling 7
81                  gameStatus = LOST;
82         }
83
84         if ( gameStatus == CONTINUE )
85            showStatus( "Roll again." );
86         else {
87            if ( gameStatus == WON )
88               showStatus( "Player wins. " +
89                  "Click Roll Dice to play again." );
90            else
91               showStatus( "Player loses. " +
92                  "Click Roll Dice to play again." );
93
94            firstRoll = true;
95         }
96      }
```

Fig. 4.9   Program to simulate the game of craps (part 2 of 4).

```
97
98      // call method play when button is clicked
99      public boolean action( Event e, Object o )
100     {
101        play();
102        return true;
103     }
104
105     // roll the dice
106     int rollDice()
107     {
108        int die1, die2, workSum;
109
110        die1 = 1 + (int) ( Math.random() * 6 );
111        die2 = 1 + (int) ( Math.random() * 6 );
112        workSum = die1 + die2;
113
114        firstDie.setText( Integer.toString( die1 ) );
115        secondDie.setText( Integer.toString( die2 ) );
116        sum.setText( Integer.toString( workSum ) );
117
118        return workSum;
119     }
120  }
121
```

Fig. 4.9   Program to simulate the game of craps (part 3 of 4).

Fig. 4.9   Program to simulate the game of craps (part 4 of 4).

Notice that the player must roll two dice on the first roll, and must do so later on all subsequent rolls. We define a method **rollDice** (line 106) to roll the dice and compute and display their sum. Method **rollDice** is defined once, but it is called from two places in the program (lines 53 and 75). Interestingly, **rollDice** takes no arguments, so we have indicated an empty parameter list. The method **rollDice** does return the sum of the two dice, so a return type of **int** is indicated in the method header.

The game is reasonably involved. The player may win or lose on the first roll, or may win or lose on any subsequent roll. The variable **gameStatus** is used to keep track of this. Variable **gameStatus** is declared to be of type **int**. Line 8 of the program

        final int WON = 0, LOST = 1, CONTINUE = 2;

creates variables that define the three states of a game of craps—game won, game lost, or continue rolling the dice. Keyword ***final*** at the beginning of the declaration indicates that these are *constant variables*. Constant variables must be initialized when they are declared, and cannot be modified thereafter. Constant variables are often called *named constants* or *read-only variables*. The names of **final** variables are capitalized by convention so they stand out in the program. Keyword **final** is discussed in detail in Chapters 5 and 6.

Common Programming Error 4.11

*After a **final** variable has been defined, attempting to assign another value to the variable is a syntax error.*

Good Programming Practice 4.5

*Use only uppercase letters in the names of **final** variables. This makes these constants stand out in a program.*

Good Programming Practice 4.6

*Using **final** variables rather than integer constants (such as 2) makes programs more readable.*

The user clicks the "**Roll Dice**" button to roll the dice. This invokes the **action** method of the applet which then invokes the **play** method. The **play** method checks the **boolean** variable **firstRoll** to determine if it is **true** or **false** (if it is **true**, this is the first roll of the game). After the first roll, if the game is won or lost, the program proceeds to the **if/else** structure at line 87 which displays in the status bar

        Player wins. Click Roll Dice to play again.

if **gameStatus** is equal to **WON** and

        Player loses. Click Roll Dice to play again.

if **gameStatus** is equal to **LOST**.

    After the first roll, if the game is not over, **sum** is saved in **myPoint** and displayed in the **point** text field. The program then waits for the user to click the "**Roll Dice**" button again. Each time the "**Roll Dice**" button is clicked, method **play** is invoked and method **rollDice** is called to produce a new **sum**. If **sum** matches **myPoint**, **gameStatus** is set to **WON**, the **if/else** structure at line 87 is executed, and the game is complete. If **sum** is equal to **7**, **gameStatus** is set to **LOST**, **if/else** structure at line 87 is executed, and the game is complete. Clicking the "**Roll Dice**" button starts a new game. Throughout the program, the four text fields are updated with the new values of the dice and the sum on each roll and the **point** text field is updated each time a new game is started.

    Note the interesting use of the various program control mechanisms we have discussed. The craps program uses four methods—**init**, **action**, **play** and **rollDice**—and the **switch**, **if/else**, and nested **if** structures. In the exercises, we investigate various interesting characteristics of the game of craps.

4.9 Automatic Variables

In Chapters 1 through 3, we used identifiers for variable names. The attributes of variables include name, type, size, and value. In this chapter, we also use identifiers as names for user-defined methods. Actually, each identifier in a program has other attributes including *duration* and *scope*.

    An identifier's *duration* (also called its *lifetime*) determines the period during which that identifier exists in memory. Some identifiers exist briefly, some are repeatedly created and destroyed, and others exist for the entire execution of a program.

    An identifier's *scope* is where the identifier can be referenced in a program. Some identifiers can be referenced throughout a program, while others can be referenced from only limited portions of a program. This section discusses duration of identifiers. Section 4.10 discusses the scope of identifiers.

    Identifiers that represent local variables in a method—i.e., parameters and variables declared in the method body—have *automatic duration*. Automatic duration variables are created when the block in which they are declared is entered, they exist while the block is active, and they are destroyed when the block is exited. For the remainder of the text, we will refer to variables of automatic duration simply as automatic variables.

Performance Tip 4.1

Automatic duration is a means of conserving memory because automatic duration variables are created when the block in which they are declared is entered and are destroyed when the block is exited.

Software Engineering Observation 4.9

Automatic duration is yet another example of the principle of least privilege. Why have variables stored in memory and accessible when they are not needed?

The instance variables of a class are automatically initialized by the compiler if the programmer does not provide initial values. Variables of the primitive data types are initialized to zero except boolean variables which are initialized to **false**. References are initialized to **null**. Unlike instance variables of a class, automatic variables must be initialized by the programmer before they can be used in an expression.

Testing and Debugging Tip 4.1

Automatic variables must be initialized before they are used in a method; otherwise, the compiler issues an error message

Java also has identifiers of *static duration*. Variables and methods of static duration exist from the point at which the class in which they are defined is loaded into memory for execution until the program terminates. For static duration variables, storage is allocated and initialized once when their class is loaded into memory. For static duration methods, the name of the method exists when their class is loaded into memory. Even though the static duration variables and method names exist when their class is loaded into memory, this does not mean that these identifiers can be used throughout the program. Duration and scope (where a name can be used) are separate issues as shown in Section 4.10.

4.10 Scope Rules

The *scope* of an identifier is the portion of the program in which the identifier can be referenced. For example, when we declare a local variable in a block, it can be referenced only in that block or in blocks nested within that block. The scopes for an identifier are *class scope* and *block scope*.

Methods and instance variables of a class have *class scope*. Class scope begins at the opening left brace, **{**, of the class definition and terminates at the closing right brace, **}**, of the class definition. Class scope enables methods of a class to directly invoke all methods defined in the same class or inherited into the class (such as the methods inherited into our applets from the Applet class) and to directly access all instance variables defined in the class. (In Chapter 6, we will see that **static** methods are an exception to this rule.) In a sense, all instance variables and methods of a class are *global* to the methods of the class in which they are defined—i.e., the methods can modify the instance variables directly and invoke other methods of the class.

Identifiers declared inside a block have *block scope*. Block scope begins at the identifier's declaration and ends at the terminating right brace (**}**) of the block. Local variables declared at the beginning of a method have block scope as do method parameters, which are also local variables of the method. Any block may contain variable declarations. When blocks are nested, and an identifier in an outer block has the same name as an identifier in an inner block, the compiler generates a syntax error stating that the variable is already defined. If a local variable in a method has the same name as an instance variable, the instance variable is "hidden" until the block terminates execution. In Chapter 6, we discuss how to access such "hidden" instance variables.

Common Programming Error 4.12

Accidentally using the same name for an identifier in an inner block as is used for an identifier in an outer block results in a syntax error from the compiler.

Good Programming Practice 4.7

Avoid local variable names that hide instance variable names. This can be accomplished by avoiding the use of duplicate identifiers in a program.

The program of Fig. 4.10 demonstrates scoping issues with instance variables and automatic local variables. Note that the main output for the program is sent to the command line (or to the Java console if you are using a browser such as Netscape Navigator).

```
1   // Fig. 4.10: Scoping.java
2   // A scoping example
3   import java.awt.Graphics;
4   import java.applet.Applet;
5
6   public class Scoping extends Applet {
7      int x = 1;       // instance variable
8
9      public void paint( Graphics g )
10     {
11        g.drawString( "See command line for output", 25, 25 );
12
13        int x = 5;    // local variable to paint
14
15        System.out.println( "local x in paint is " + x );
16
17        a();          // a has automatic local x
18        b();          // b uses instance variable x
19        a();          // a reinitializes automatic local x
20        b();          // instance variable x retains its value
21
22        System.out.println( "\nlocal x in paint is " + x );
23     }
24
25     void a()
26     {
27        int x = 25;  // initialized each time a is called
28
29        System.out.println( "\nlocal x in a is " + x +
30                            " after entering a" );
31        ++x;
32        System.out.println( "local x in a is " + x +
33                            " before exiting a" );
34     }
```

Fig. 4.10 A scoping example (part 1 of 2).

```
35
36     void b()
37     {
38        System.out.println( "\ninstance variable x is " + x +
39                            " on entering b" );
40        x *= 10;
41        System.out.println( "instance variable x is " + x +
42                            " on exiting b" );
43     }
44  }
```

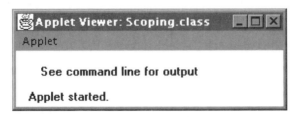

```
local x in paint is 5

local x in a is 25 after entering a
local x in a is 26 before exiting a

instance variable x is 1 on entering b
instance variable x is 10 on exiting b

local x in a is 25 after entering a
local x in a is 26 before exiting a

instance variable x is 10 on entering b
instance variable x is 100 on exiting b

local x in paint is 5
```

Fig. 4.10 A scoping example (part 2 of 2).

An instance variable **x** (line 7) is declared and initialized to 1. This instance variable is hidden in any block (or method) in which a variable named **x** is declared. In **paint**, a local variable **x** is declared and initialized to 5. This variable is printed to show that the instance variable **x** is hidden in **paint**. The program defines two other methods—each takes no arguments and returns nothing. Method **a** defines automatic variable **x** and initializes it to 25. When **a** is called, the variable is printed, incremented, and printed again before exiting the method. Each time this method is called, automatic variable **x** is recreated and initialized to 25. Method **b** does not declare any variables. Therefore, when it refers to variable **x**, the instance variable **x** is used. When **b** is called, the instance variable is printed, multiplied by 10, and printed again before exiting the method. The next time method **b** is called, the instance variable has its modified value, 10. Finally, the program prints the local variable **x** in **paint** again to show that none of the method calls modified the value of **x** because the methods all referred to variables in other scopes.

4.11 Recursion

The programs we have discussed are generally structured as methods that call one another in a disciplined, hierarchical manner. For some problems, it is useful to have methods call themselves. A *recursive method* is a method that calls itself either directly or indirectly through another method. Recursion is an important topic discussed at length in upper-level computer science courses. In this section and the next, simple examples of recursion are presented. This book contains an extensive treatment of recursion. Figure 4.15 (at the end of Section 4.13) summarizes the recursion examples and exercises in the book.

We consider recursion conceptually first, and then examine several programs containing recursive methods. Recursive problem solving approaches have a number of elements in common. A recursive method is called to solve a problem. The method actually knows how to solve only the simplest case(s), or so-called *base case(s)*. If the method is called with a base case, the method simply returns a result. If the method is called with a more complex problem, the method divides the problem into two conceptual pieces: a piece that the method knows how to do and a piece that the method does not know how to do. To make recursion feasible, the latter piece must resemble the original problem, but be a slightly simpler or slightly smaller version of the original problem. Because this new problem looks like the original problem, the method launches (calls) a fresh copy of itself to go to work on the smaller problem—this is referred to as a *recursive call* and is also called the *recursion step*. The recursion step also includes the keyword **return** because its result will be combined with the portion of the problem the method knew how to solve to form a result that will be passed back to the original caller.

The recursion step executes while the original call to the method is still open, i.e., it has not finished executing. The recursion step can result in many more recursive calls, as the method divides each new subproblem into two conceptual pieces. For the recursion to eventually terminate, each time the method calls itself with a slightly simpler version of the original problem, the sequence of smaller and smaller problems must converge on the base case. At that point, the method recognizes the base case, returns a result to the previous copy of the method, and a sequence of returns ensues up the line until the original method call eventually returns the final result to the caller. This sounds exotic compared to the conventional problem solving we performed to this point. As an example of these concepts at work, let us write a recursive program to perform a popular mathematical calculation.

The factorial of a nonnegative integer *n,* written *n!* (and pronounced "*n* factorial"), is the product

$$n \cdot (n - 1) \cdot (n - 2) \cdot \ldots \cdot 1$$

with 1! equal to 1, and 0! defined to be 1. For example, 5! is the product $5 \cdot 4 \cdot 3 \cdot 2 \cdot 1$, which is equal to 120.

The factorial of an integer, **number**, greater than or equal to 0, can be calculated *iteratively* (nonrecursively) using **for** as follows:

```
factorial = 1;
for ( int counter = number; counter >= 1; counter-- )
    factorial *= counter;
```

A recursive definition of the factorial method is arrived at by observing the following relationship:

$$n! = n \cdot (n - 1)!$$

For example, 5! is clearly equal to 5 * 4! as is shown by the following:

$$5! = 5 \cdot 4 \cdot 3 \cdot 2 \cdot 1$$
$$5! = 5 \cdot (4 \cdot 3 \cdot 2 \cdot 1)$$
$$5! = 5 \cdot (4!)$$

The evaluation of 5! would proceed as shown in Fig. 4.11. Figure 4.11a shows how the succession of recursive calls proceeds until 1! is evaluated to be 1, which terminates the recursion. Figure 4.11b shows the values returned from each recursive call to its caller until the final value is calculated and returned.

The program of Fig. 4.12 uses recursion to calculate and print the factorials of the integers 0 to 10 (the choice of the data type **long** will be explained momentarily). The recursive method **factorial** first tests to see if a terminating condition is true, i.e., is **number** less than or equal to 1. If **number** is indeed less than or equal to 1, **factorial** returns 1, no further recursion is necessary, and the program terminates. If **number** is greater than 1, the statement

```
return number * factorial( number - 1 );
```

expresses the problem as the product of **number** and a recursive call to **factorial** evaluating the factorial of **number - 1**. Note that **factorial(number - 1)** is a slightly simpler problem than the original calculation **factorial(number)**.

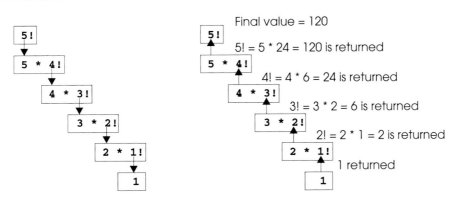

a) Procession of recursive calls.   b) Values returned from each recursive call.

Fig. 4.11 Recursive evaluation of 5!.

```
1   // Fig. 4.12: FactorialTest.java
2   // Recursive factorial method
3   import java.awt.Graphics;
4   import java.applet.Applet;
5
6   public class FactorialTest extends Applet {
7      public void paint( Graphics g )
8      {
9         int yPosition = 25;
10
11        for ( long i = 0; i <= 10; i++ )  {
12           g.drawString( i + "! = " + factorial( i ),
13                         25, yPosition );
14           yPosition += 15;
15        }
16     }
17
18     // Recursive definition of method factorial
19     public long factorial( long number )
20     {
21        if ( number <= 1 )  // base case
22           return 1;
23        else
24           return number * factorial( number - 1 );
25     }
26  }
```

Fig. 4.12 Calculating factorials with a recursive method.

Method **factorial** has been declared to receive a parameter of type **long** and return a result of type **long**. As can be seen in Fig. 4.12, factorial values become large quickly. We have chosen the data type **long** so the program can calculate factorials greater than 20!. Unfortunately, the **factorial** method produces large values so quickly that even **long** does not help us print many factorial values before the size of a **long** variable is exceeded.

As we explore in the exercises, **float** and **double** may ultimately be needed by the user desiring to calculate factorials of larger numbers. This points to a weakness in most programming languages, namely that the languages are not easily extended to handle the unique requirements of various applications. As we will see in the section of the book on object-oriented programming, Java is an extensible language that allows us to create arbitrarily large integers if we wish.

Common Programming Error 4.13

Forgetting to return a value from a recursive method when one is needed results in a syntax error.

Common Programming Error 4.14

Either omitting the base case, or writing the recursion step incorrectly so that it does not converge on the base case, will cause infinite recursion, eventually exhausting memory. This is analogous to the problem of an infinite loop in an iterative (nonrecursive) solution. Infinite recursion can also be caused by providing an unexpected input.

4.12 Example Using Recursion: The Fibonacci Series

The Fibonacci series

$$0, 1, 1, 2, 3, 5, 8, 13, 21, \ldots$$

begins with 0 and 1 and has the property that each subsequent Fibonacci number is the sum of the previous two Fibonacci numbers.

The series occurs in nature and, in particular, describes a form of spiral. The ratio of successive Fibonacci numbers converges on a constant value of $1.618\ldots$. This number, too, repeatedly occurs in nature and has been called the *golden ratio* or the *golden mean.* Humans tend to find the golden mean aesthetically pleasing. Architects often design windows, rooms, and buildings whose length and width are in the ratio of the golden mean. Postcards are often designed with a golden mean length/width ratio.

The Fibonacci series may be defined recursively as follows:

fibonacci(0) = 0
fibonacci(1) = 1
fibonacci(n) = fibonacci(n – 1) + fibonacci(n – 2)

Figure 4.13 calculates the ith Fibonacci number recursively using method **fibonacci**. Notice that Fibonacci numbers tend to become large quickly. Therefore, we have chosen the data type **unsigned long** for the parameter type and the return type in method **fibonacci**. In Fig. 4.13, each pair of output lines shows a separate run of the program.

The call to **fibonacci** from **action** is not a recursive call, but all subsequent calls to **fibonacci** are recursive. Each time **fibonacci** is invoked, it immediately tests for the base case—**n** equal to 0 or 1. If this is true, **n** is returned. Interestingly, if **n** is greater than 1, the recursion step generates *two* recursive calls, each of which is for a slightly simpler problem than the original call to **fibonacci**. Figure 4.14 shows how method **fibonacci** would evaluate **fibonacci(3)**—we abbreviate **fibonacci** simply as **f** to make the figure more readable.

```
1   // Fig. 4.13: FibonacciTest.java
2   // Recursive fibonacci method
3   import java.awt.*;
4   import java.applet.Applet;
5
6   public class FibonacciTest extends Applet {
7      Label numLabel, resultLabel;
8      TextField num, result;
9
10     public void init()
11     {
12       numLabel = new Label( "Enter an integer and press return" );
13        num = new TextField( 10 );
14        resultLabel = new Label( "Fibonacci value is" );
15        result = new TextField( 15 );
16        result.setEditable( false );
17
18        add( numLabel );
19        add( num );
20        add( resultLabel );
21        add( result );
22     }
23
24     public boolean action( Event e, Object o )
25     {
26        long number, fibonacciVal;
27
28        number = Long.parseLong( num.getText() );
29        showStatus( "Calculating ..." );
30        fibonacciVal = fibonacci( number );
31        showStatus( "Done." );
32        result.setText( Long.toString( fibonacciVal ) );
33        return true;
34     }
35
36     // Recursive definition of method fibonacci
37     long fibonacci( long n )
38     {
39        if ( n == 0 || n == 1 )   // base case
40           return n;
41        else
42           return fibonacci( n - 1 ) + fibonacci( n - 2 );
43     }
44  }
```

Fig. 4.13 Recursively generating Fibonacci numbers (part 1 of 3).

Fig. 4.13 Recursively generating Fibonacci numbers (part 2 of 3).

Fig. 4.13 Recursively generating Fibonacci numbers (part 3 of 3).

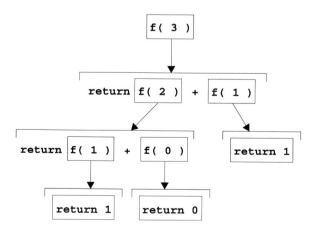

Fig. 4.14 Set of recursive calls to method **fibonacci**.

This figure raises some interesting issues about the order in which Java compilers will evaluate the operands of operators. This is a different issue from the order in which operators are applied to their operands, namely the order dictated by the rules of operator precedence. From Fig. 4.14 it appears that while evaluating **f(3)**, two recursive calls will be made, namely **f(2)** and **f(1)**. But in what order will these calls be made? Most programmers simply assume the operands will be evaluated left to right. In Java this is true.

Strangely, the C and C++ languages (on which many of Java's features are based) do not specify the order in which the operands of most operators (including **+**) are evaluated. Therefore, the programmer may make no assumption in those languages about the order in which these calls execute. The calls could in fact execute **f(2)** first and then **f(1)**, or the calls could execute in the reverse order, **f(1)** then **f(2)**. In this program and in most other programs, it turns out the final result would be the same. But in some programs the evaluation of an operand may have *side effects* that could affect the final result of the expression.

The Java language specifies the order of evaluation of the operands is left-to-right. Thus, the method calls are in fact **f(2)** first, then **f(1)**.

Good Programming Practice 4.8

Do not write expressions that depend on the order of evaluation of the operands of operator. This often results in programs that are difficult to read, debug, modify, and maintain.

A word of caution is in order about recursive programs like the one we use here to generate Fibonacci numbers. Each invocation of the **fibonacci** method that does not match one of the base cases (i.e., 0 or 1) results in two more recursive calls to the **fibonacci** method. This rapidly gets out of hand. Calculating the fibonacci value of 20 using the program in Fig. 4.13 requires 21,891 calls to the **fibonacci** method, calculating the fibonacci value of 30 requires 2,692,537 calls to the **fibonacci** method.

As you try larger values, you will notice that each consecutive fibonacci number you ask the applet to calculate results in a substantial increase in calculation time and number of calls to the **fibonacci** method. For example, the fibonacci value of 31 requires 4,356,617 calls and the fibonacci value of 32 requires 7,049,155 calls. As you can see, the number of calls to fibonacci is increasing quickly—1,664,080 additional calls between fibonacci of 30 and 31, and 2,692,538 additional calls between fibonacci of 31 and 32. This difference in number of calls made between fibonacci of 31 and 32 is more than 1.5 times the difference for fibonacci of 30 and 31. Problems of this nature humble even the world's most powerful computers! Computer scientists study in the field of complexity theory how hard algorithms have to work to do their jobs. Complexity issues are discussed in detail in the upper-level computer science curriculum course generally called "Algorithms."

Performance Tip 4.2

Avoid fibonacci-style recursive programs which result in an exponential "explosion" of calls.

4.13 Recursion vs. Iteration

In the previous sections, we studied two methods that can easily be implemented either recursively or iteratively. In this section we compare the two approaches and discuss why the programmer might choose one approach over the other in a particular situation.

Both iteration and recursion are based on a control structure: Iteration uses a repetition structure (such as **for, while** or **do/while**); recursion uses a selection structure (such as **if, if/else** or **switch**). Both iteration and recursion involve repetition: Iteration explicitly uses a repetition structure; recursion achieves repetition through repeated method calls. Iteration and recursion each involve a termination test: Iteration terminates when the loop-continuation condition fails; recursion terminates when a base case is recognized. Iteration with counter-controlled repetition and recursion each gradually approach termination: Iteration keeps modifying a counter until the counter assumes a value that makes the loop-continuation condition fail; recursion keeps producing simpler versions of the original problem until the base case is reached. Both iteration and recursion can occur infinitely: An infinite loop occurs with iteration if the loop-continuation test never becomes false; infinite recursion occurs if the recursion step does not reduce the problem each time in a manner that converges on the base case.

Recursion has many negatives. It repeatedly invokes the mechanism, and consequently the overhead, of method calls. This can be expensive in both processor time and memory space. Each recursive call causes another copy of the method (actually only the method's variables) to be created; this can consume considerable memory. Iteration normally occurs within a method so the overhead of repeated method calls and extra memory assignment is omitted. So why choose recursion?

Software Engineering Observation 4.10

Any problem that can be solved recursively can also be solved iteratively (nonrecursively). A recursive approach is normally chosen in preference to an iterative approach when the recursive approach more naturally mirrors the problem and results in a program that is easier to understand and debug. Another reason to choose a recursive solution is that an iterative solution may not be apparent.

Performance Tip 4.3

Avoid using recursion in performance situations. Recursive calls take time and consume additional memory.

Common Programming Error 4.15

Accidentally having a nonrecursive method call itself either directly, or indirectly through another method.

Most programming textbooks introduce recursion much later than we have done here. We feel that recursion is a sufficiently rich and complex topic that it is better to introduce it earlier and spread the examples over the remainder of the text. Figure 4.15 summarizes the recursion examples and exercises in the text.

Let us reconsider some observations that we make repeatedly throughout the book. Good software engineering is important. High performance is often important. Unfortunately, these goals are often at odds with one another. Good software engineering is key to making more manageable the task of developing the larger and more complex software systems we need. High performance in these systems is key to realizing the systems of the future that will place ever greater computing demands on hardware. Where do methods fit in here?

Chapter	Recursion Examples and Exercises
Chapter 4	Factorial method
	Fibonacci method
	Greatest common divisor
	Sum of two integers
	Multiply two integers
	Raising an integer to an integer power
	Towers of Hanoi
	Visualizing recursion
Chapter 5	Sum the elements of an array
	Print an array
	Print an array backwards
	Check if a string is a palindrome
	Minimum value in an array
	Selection sort
	Eight Queens
	Linear search
	Binary search
	Quicksort
	Maze traversal
Chapter 8	Printing a string input at the keyboard backwards
Chapter 17	Linked list insert
	Linked list delete
	Search a linked list
	Print a linked list backwards
	Binary tree insert
	Preorder traversal of a binary tree
	Inorder traversal of a binary tree
	Postorder traversal of a binary tree

Fig. 4.15 Summary of recursion examples and exercises in the text.

Software Engineering Observation 4.11

Modularizing programs in a neat, hierarchical manner promotes good software engineering. But it has a price.

Performance Tip 4.4

A heavily modularized program—as compared to a monolithic (i.e., one-piece) program without methods—makes potentially large numbers of method calls and these consume execution time and space on a computer's processor(s). But monolithic programs are difficult to program, test, debug, maintain, and evolve.

So modularize your programs judiciously, always keeping in mind the delicate balance between performance and good software engineering.

4.14 Method Overloading

Java enables several methods of the same name to be defined as long as these methods have different sets of parameters (based on the number of parameters, the types of the parameters and the order of the parameters). This is called *method overloading*. When an overloaded method is called, the Java compiler selects the proper method by examining the number, types, and order of the arguments in the call. Method overloading is commonly used to create several methods of the same name that perform similar tasks, but on different data types.

Good Programming Practice 4.9

Overloading methods that perform closely related tasks can make programs more readable and understandable.

Figure 4.16 uses overloaded method **square** to calculate the square of an **int** and the square of a **double**.

Overloaded methods are distinguished by their *signature*—a combination of the method's name and its parameter types. If the Java compiler only looked at method names during compilation, the code in Fig. 4.16 would be ambiguous—the compiler would not know how to distinguish the two **square** methods. Logically, the compiler uses longer "mangled" or "decorated" names that include the original method name, the types of each parameter and the exact order of the parameters to determine if the methods in a class are unique in that class.

```
1   // Fig. 4.16: MethodOverload.java
2   // Using overloaded methods
3   import java.awt.Graphics;
4   import java.applet.Applet;
5
6   public class MethodOverload extends Applet {
7      public void paint( Graphics g )
8      {
9         g.drawString( "The square of integer 7 is " + square( 7 ),
10                       25, 25 );
11         g.drawString( "The square of double 7.5 is " +
12                       square( 7.5 ), 25, 40 );
13      }
14
15      int square( int x )
16      {
17         return x * x;
18      }
19
20      double square( double y )
21      {
22         return y * y;
23      }
24   }
```

Fig. 4.16 Using overloaded methods (part 1 of 2).

Fig. 4.16 Using overloaded methods (part 2 of 2).

For example in Fig. 4.16, the compiler might use the logical name *"square of int"* for the **square** method that specifies an **int** parameter and *"square of double"* for the **square** method that specifies a **double** parameter. If the definition of a method **foo**'s definition begins as follows

```
    void foo( int a, float b )
```

the compiler might use the logical name *"foo of int and float."* If the parameters are specified as follows

```
    void foo( float a, int b )
```

the compiler might use the logical name *"foo of float and int."* Note that the order of the parameters is important to the compiler. The preceding two **foo** methods are considered to be unique by the compiler.

So far, the logical names of methods used by the compiler did not mention the return types of the methods. This is because methods cannot be distinguished by return type. The program of Fig. 4.17 illustrates the compiler errors generated when two methods have the same signature and different return types. Overloaded methods can have different return types, but must have different parameter lists. Also, overloaded methods need not have the same number of parameters.

Common Programming Error 4.16

Creating overloaded methods with identical parameter lists and different return types causes a syntax error.

4.15 Methods of the Applet Class

We have written many applets to this point in the text, but we have not yet discussed the key methods of the Applet class that are called automatically during the execution of an applet. Figure 4.18 lists the key methods of the **Applet** class, when they get called, and the purpose of each method.

These **Applet** methods are defined by the Java API to do nothing unless you provide a definition in your applet's class definition. If you would like to use one of these methods in an applet you are defining, you *must* define the first line of the method as shown in Fig. 4.18. Otherwise, the method will not get called automatically during the execution of the applet.

```
1   // Fig. 4.17: MethodOverload.java
2   // Overloaded methods with identical signatures and
3   // different return types.
4   import java.awt.Graphics;
5   import java.applet.Applet;
6
7   public class MethodOverload extends Applet {
8       int square( double x )
9       {
10          return x * x;
11      }
12
13      double square( double y )
14      {
15          return y * y;
16      }
17  }
```

```
MethodOverload,java:13: Methods can't be redefined with a
    different return type: double square(double) was
    int square(double)
    double square( double y )
                 ^
1 error
```

Fig. 4.17 Compiler error messages generated from overloaded methods with identical parameter lists and different return types.

Common Programming Error 4.17

Providing a definition for one of the **Applet** *methods* **init, start, paint, stop,** *or* **destroy** *that does not match the method headers shown in Fig. 4.18 results in a method that will not be called automatically during the execution of the applet.*

The **resize** and **repaint** methods are also of interest to many applet programmers. As you know, when an applet is invoked via an HTML page, the applet's width and height in pixels are specified in the HTML code (see Fig. 1.3). The applet' size can be changed during the applet's execution by invoking method **resize**. For example, the statement

```
resize( 200, 400 );
```

makes the applet's width 200 pixels and its height 400 pixels. This statement is normally placed in the applet's **init** method.

The applet's **paint** method is normally called automatically. What if you would like to change the appearance of the applet in response to the user's interactions with the applet? In such situations, you may want to call **paint** directly. However, to call **paint**, we must pass it the **Graphics** parameter it expects. This poses a problem for us. We do not have a **Graphics** object at our disposal to pass to **paint** (we discuss this issue in Chapter 14, Multimedia). For this reason, the **repaint** method is provided for you. The statement

Method	When the method is called and its purpose
`public void init()`	This method is called once by the Appletviewer or browser when an applet is loaded for execution. It performs initialization of an applet. Typical actions performed here are initialization of instance variables and GUI components of the Applet, loading of sounds to play or images to display (Chapter 14, Multimedia), and creation of threads (Chapter 13, Multithreading).
`public void start()`	This method is called after the **init** method completes execution and every time the user of the browser returns to the HTML page on which the applet resides (after browsing another HTML page). This method performs any tasks that must be completed when the applet is loaded for the first time into the Appletviewer or browser and that must be performed every time the HTML page on which the applet resides is revisited. Typical actions performed here include starting an animation (Chapter 14, Multimedia) and starting other threads of execution (Chapter 13, Multithreading).
`public void paint( Graphics g )`	This method is called after the **init** method completes execution and the start method has started executing to draw on the applet. It is also called automatically every time the applet needs to be repainted. For example, if the user of the Appletviewer or browser covers the applet with another open window on his or her computer then uncovers the applet, the **paint** method is called. Typical actions performed here involve drawing with the **Graphics** object **g** that is automatically passed to the **paint** method for you.
`public void stop()`	This method is called when the applet should stop executing—normally when the user of the browser leaves the HTML page on which the applet resides. This method performs any tasks that are required to suspend the applet's execution. Typical actions performed here are to stop execution of animations and threads.
`public void destroy()`	This method is called when the applet is being removed from memory—normally when the user of the browser exits the browsing session. This method performs any tasks that are required to destroy resources allocated to the applet. Typical actions performed here include terminating threads (Chapter 13, Multithreading).

Fig. 4.18 Applet methods called automatically during an applet's execution.

```
repaint();
```

invokes another method called **update** and passes it the **Graphics** object for you. Method **update** erases any drawing that was previously done on the applet then invokes the

paint method and passes it the **Graphics** object for you. The **repaint** and **update** methods are discussed in detail in Chapter 14, Multimedia.

Summary

- The best way to develop and maintain a large program is to divide it into several smaller program modules each of which is more manageable than the original program. Modules are written in Java as classes and methods.

- A method is invoked by a method call. The method call mentions the method by name and provides information (as arguments) that the called method needs to perform its task.

- Methods are invoked in a program by writing the name of the method followed by the arguments of the method followed in parentheses.

- Each argument of a method may be a constant, a variable, or an expression.

- A local variable is known only in a method definition. Methods are not allowed to know the implementation details of any other method (including local variables).

- The general format for a method definition is

  return-value-type method-name **(** *parameter-list* **)**
  {
        declarations and statements
  }

  The return-value-type states the type of the value returned to the calling method. If a method does not return a value, the return-value-type is empty. The method-name is any valid identifier. The parameter-list is a comma-separated list containing the declarations of the variables that will be passed to the method. If a method does not receive any values, parameter-list is declared as void. The method-body is the set of declarations and statements that constitute the method.

- An empty parameter list is specified with empty parentheses.

- The arguments passed to a method should match in number, type, and order with the parameters in the method definition.

- When a program encounters a method, control is transferred from the point of invocation to the called method, the method is executed, and control returns to the caller.

- A called method can return control to the caller in one of three ways. If the method does not return a value, control is returned when the method-ending right brace is reached, or by executing the statement

  return;

  If the method does return a value, the statement

  return *expression***;**

  returns the value of *expression*.

- Method **Math.random** generates a double value from 0.0 up to (but not including) 1.0.

- Values produced by **Math.random** can be scaled and shifted to produce values in a specific range.

- The general equation for scaling and shifting a random number is

  ```
  n = a + (int) ( Math.random() * b );
  ```

  where **a** is the shifting value (which is equal to the first number in the desired range of consecutive integers), and **b** is the scaling factor (which is equal to the width of the desired range of consecutive integers).

- Each variable identifier has the attributes duration (lifetime) and scope. An identifier's duration determines when that identifier exists in memory. An identifier's scope is where the identifier can be referenced in a program.

- Identifiers that represent local variables in a method—i.e., parameters and variables declared in the method body—have automatic duration. Automatic duration variables are created when the block in which they are declared is entered, they exist while the block is active, and they are destroyed when the block is exited.

- Java also has identifiers of *static duration*. Variables and methods of static duration exist from the point at which the class in which they are defined is loaded into memory for execution until the program terminates. For static duration variables, storage is allocated and initialized once when their class is loaded into memory. For static duration methods, the name of the method exists when their class is loaded into memory.

- The scopes for an identifier are class scope and block scope.

- An instance variable declared outside any method has class scope. Such an identifier is "known" in all methods of the class.

- Identifiers declared inside a block have block scope. Block scope ends at the terminating right brace (**}**) of the block.

- Local variables declared at the beginning of a method have block scope as do method parameters, which are considered local variables by the method.

- Any block may contain variable declarations.

- A recursive method is a method that calls itself either directly or indirectly.

- If a recursive method is called with a base case, the method simply returns a result. If the method is called with a more complex problem, the method divides the problem into two or more conceptual pieces: a piece that the method knows how to do and a slightly smaller version of the original problem. Because this new problem looks like the original problem, the method launches a recursive call to work on the smaller problem.

- For recursion to terminate, each time the recursive method calls itself with a slightly simpler version of the original problem, the sequence of smaller and smaller problems must converge on the base case. When the method recognizes the base case, the result is returned to the previous method call, and a sequence of returns ensues all the way up the line until the original call of the method eventually returns the final result.

- Both iteration and recursion are based on a control structure: Iteration uses a repetition structure; recursion uses a selection structure.

- Both iteration and recursion involve repetition: Iteration explicitly uses a repetition structure; recursion achieves repetition through repeated method calls.

- Iteration and recursion each involve a termination test: Iteration terminates when the loop-continuation condition fails; recursion terminates when a base case is recognized.

- Iteration and recursion can occur infinitely: An infinite loop occurs with iteration if the loop-continuation test never becomes false; infinite recursion occurs if the recursion step does not reduce the problem in a manner that converges on the base case.

- Recursion repeatedly invokes the mechanism, and consequently the overhead, of method calls. This can be expensive in both processor time and memory space.

- A method that does not return a value is declared with a **void** return type. If an attempt is made either to return a value from the method or to use the result of the method invocation in the calling method, the compiler reports an error.

- The **final** qualifier creates "constant variables." A constant variable must be initialized when the variable is declared, and cannot be modified thereafter. Constant variables are often called named constants or read-only variables.

- It is possible to define methods with the same name but with different parameter lists (based on the types of the parameters, the number of parameters and the order of the parameters). This is called method overloading. When an overloaded method is called, the compiler selects the proper method by examining the arguments in the call.

- Overloaded methods can have different return values, and must have different parameter lists. Two methods differing only by return type will result in a compilation error.

- The applet's **init** method is called once by the Appletviewer or browser when an applet is loaded for execution. It performs initialization of an applet. The applet's **start** method is called after the **init** method completes execution and every time the user of the browser returns to the HTML page on which the applet resides (after browsing another HTML page).

- The applet's **paint** method is called after the **init** method completes execution and the start method has started executing to draw on the applet. It is also called automatically every time the applet needs to be repainted.

- The applet's **stop** method is called when the applet should suspend execution—normally when the user of the browser leaves the HTML page on which the applet resides.

- The applet's **destroy** method is called when the applet is being removed from memory—normally when the user of the browser exits the browsing session.

Terminology

argument in a method call	base case in recursion
automatic duration	block
automatic variable	block scope

call a method
called method
caller
calling method
class
class scope
coercion of arguments
constant variable
copy of a value
destroy method
divide and conquer
duration
element of chance
factorial method
file scope
final
init method
invoke a method
iteration
Java API (Java class library)
local variable
Math class methods
Math.E
Math.PI
Math.random method
method
method call
method declaration
method definition
method overloading
mixed-type expression
modular program

named constant
overloading
paint method
parameter in a method definition
programmer-defined method
promotion rules
random number generation
read-only variable
recursion
recursion step
recursive call
recursive method
reference parameter
reference types
repaint method
resize method
return
return-value-type
scaling
scope
shifting
side effects
signature
simulation
software engineering
software reusability
start method
static storage duration
stop method
update method
void

Common Programming Errors

4.1   Forgetting to invoke a **Math** class method by preceding the method name with the class
name **Math** and a dot operator (**.**) results in a syntax error.

4.2   Defining a method outside the braces of a class definition results in a syntax error.

4.3   Omitting the return-value-type in a method definition causes a syntax error.

4.4   Forgetting to return a value from a method that is supposed to return a value is a syntax error.
If a return-value-type other than **void** is specified, the method must contain a **return**
statement.

4.5   Returning a value from a method whose return type has been declared **void** causes a syntax
error.

4.6   Declaring method parameters of the same type as **float x, y** instead of **float x, float y**. The parameter declaration **float x, y** would actually report a compilation error because types are required for each parameter in the parameter list.

4.7   Placing a semicolon after the right parenthesis enclosing the parameter list of a method definition is a syntax error.

4.8   Defining a method parameter again as a local variable in the method is a syntax error.

4.9   Defining a method inside another method is a syntax error.

4.10   Converting a primitive-data-type value to another primitive data type that is not in the original type's list of allowed promotions can change the data value.

4.11   After a **final** variable has been defined, attempting to assign another value to the variable is a syntax error.

4.12   Accidentally using the same name for an identifier in an inner block as is used for an identifier in an outer block results in a syntax error from the compiler.

4.13   Forgetting to return a value from a recursive method when one is needed results in a syntax error.

4.14   Either omitting the base case, or writing the recursion step incorrectly so that it does not converge on the base case, will cause infinite recursion, eventually exhausting memory. This is analogous to the problem of an infinite loop in an iterative (nonrecursive) solution. Infinite recursion can also be caused by providing an unexpected input.

4.15   Accidentally having a nonrecursive method call itself either directly, or indirectly through another method.

4.16   Creating overloaded methods with identical parameter lists and different return types causes a syntax error.

4.17   Providing a definition for one of the **Applet** methods **init**, **start**, **paint**, **stop**, or **destroy** that does not match the method headers shown in Fig. 4.18 results in a method that will not be called automatically during the execution of the applet.

Good Programming Practices

4.1   Familiarize yourself with the rich collection of classes and methods in the Java API and with the rich collections of classes available in various class libraries.

4.2   Place a blank line between method definitions to separate the methods and enhance program readability.

4.3   Although it is not incorrect to do so, do not use the same names for the arguments passed to a method and the corresponding parameters in the method definition. This helps avoid ambiguity.

4.4   Choosing meaningful method names and meaningful parameter names makes programs more readable and helps avoid excessive use of comments.

4.5   Use only uppercase letters in the names of **final** variables. This makes these constants stand out in a program.

4.6   Using **final** variables rather than integer constants (such as 2) makes programs more readable.

4.7   Avoid local variable names that hide instance variable names. This can be accomplished by avoiding the use of duplicate identifiers in a program.

4.8   Do not write expressions that depend on the order of evaluation of the operands of operator. This often results in programs that are difficult to read, debug, modify, and maintain.

4.9   Overloading methods that perform closely related tasks can make programs more readable and understandable.

Performance Tips

4.1   Automatic duration is a means of conserving memory because automatic duration variables are created when the block in which they are declared is entered and are destroyed when the block is exited.

4.2   Avoid fibonacci-style recursive programs which result in an exponential "explosion" of calls.

4.3   Avoid using recursion in performance situations. Recursive calls take time and consume additional memory.

4.4   A heavily modularized program—as compared to a monolithic (i.e., one-piece) program without methods—makes potentially large numbers of method calls and these consume execution time and space on a computer's processor(s). But monolithic programs are difficult to program, test, debug, maintain, and evolve.

Software Engineering Observations

4.1   Avoid reinventing the wheel. When possible, use Java API classes and methods instead of writing new classes and methods. This reduces program development time.

4.2   It is not necessary to import the **Math** class into a program to use **Math** class methods. The **Math** class is part of the **java.lang** package which is automatically imported by the compiler.

4.3   Each method should be limited to performing a single, well-defined task, and the method name should effectively express that task. This promotes software reusability.

4.4   If you cannot choose a concise name that expresses what the method does, it is possible that your method is attempting to perform too many diverse tasks. It is usually best to break such a method into several smaller methods.

4.5   A method should usually be no longer than one page. Better yet, a method should usually be no longer than half a page. Regardless of how long a method is, it should perform one task well. Small methods promote software reusability.

4.6   Programs should be written as collections of small methods. This makes programs easier to write, debug, maintain and modify.

4.7   A method requiring a large number of parameters may be performing too many tasks. Consider dividing the method into smaller methods that perform the separate tasks. The method header should fit on one line if possible.

4.8   The method header and method calls should all agree in the number, type, and order of arguments and parameters, and in the type of return value.

4.9   Automatic duration is yet another example of the principle of least privilege. Why have variables stored in memory and accessible when they are not needed?

4.10   Any problem that can be solved recursively can also be solved iteratively (nonrecursively). A recursive approach is normally chosen in preference to an iterative approach when the recursive approach more naturally mirrors the problem and results in a program that is easier to understand and debug. Another reason to choose a recursive solution is that an iterative solution may not be apparent.

4.11   Modularizing programs in a neat, hierarchical manner promotes good software engineering. But it has a price.

Testing and Debugging Tip

4.1   Automatic variables must be initialized before they are used in a method; otherwise, the compiler issues an error message

Self-Review Exercises

4.1   Answer each of the following:
a) Program modules in Java are called _____ and_____.
b) A method is invoked with a _____.
c) A variable known only within the method in which it is defined is called a _____.
d) The _____ statement in a called method can be used to pass the value of an expression back to the calling method.
e) The keyword _____ is used in a method header to indicate that a method does not return a value.
f) The _____ of an identifier is the portion of the program in which the identifier can be used.
g) The three ways to return control from a called method to a caller are_____, _____, and _____.
h) The _____ method is invoked once when an applet begins execution.
i) The _____ method is used to produce random numbers.
j) The _____ method is invoked each time the user of a browser revisits the HTML page on which an applet resides.

k) The _____ method is invoked to draw on an applet.

l) Variables declared in a block or in the parameter list of a method are assumed to be of _____ duration.

m) The _____ method is invoked to changes the width and height of an applet during the applet's execution.

n) The _____ method invokes the applet's **update** method which in turn invokes the applet's **paint** method.

o) The _____ method is invoked for an applet each time the user of a browser leaves an HTML page on which the applet resides.

p) A method that calls itself either directly or indirectly is a _____ method.

q) A recursive method typically has two components: one that provides a means for the recursion to terminate by testing for a _____ case, and one that expresses the problem as a recursive call for a slightly simpler problem than the original call.

r) In Java, it is possible to have various methods with the same name that each operate on different types and/or numbers of arguments. This is called method _____.

s) The _____ qualifier is used to declare read-only variables.

4.2   For the following program, state the scope (either class scope or block scope) of each of the following elements.

a) The variable **x**.

b) The variable **y**.

c) The method **cube**.

d) The method **paint**.

e) The variable **yPos**.

```
public class CubeTest extends Applet {
   int x;

   public void paint( Graphics g )
   {
      int yPos = 25;

      for ( x = 1; x <= 10; x++ ) {
         g.drawString( cube( x ), 25, yPos );
         yPos += 15;
      }
   }

   public int cube( int y )
   {
      return y * y * y;
   }
}
```

4.3   Write an application that tests if the examples of the math library method calls shown in Fig. 4.2 actually produce the indicated results.

4.4   Give the method header for each of the following methods.

a) Method **hypotenuse** that takes two double-precision, floating-point arguments, **side1** and **side2**, and returns a double-precision, floating-point result.

b) Method **smallest** that takes three integers, **x**, **y**, **z**, and returns an integer.

c) Method **instructions** that does not receive any arguments and does not return a value. (Note: Such methods are commonly used to display instructions to a user.)

d) Method **intToFloat** that takes an integer argument, **number**, and returns a floating-point result.

4.5   Find the error in each of the following program segments and explain how the error can be corrected:

a)
```java
int g() {
    System.out.println( "Inside method g" );
    int h() {
        System.out.println( "Inside method h" );
    }
}
```

b)
```java
int sum(int x, int y) {
    int result;

    result = x + y;
}
```

c)
```java
int sum( int n ) {
    if ( n == 0 )
        return 0;
    else
        n + sum( n - 1 );
}
```

d)
```java
void f( float a ); {
    float a;

    System.out.println( a );
}
```

e)
```java
void product() {
    int a = 6, b = 5, c = 4, result;
    result = a * b * c;
    System.out.println( "Result is " + result );
    return result;
}
```

4.6   Write a complete Java program to prompt the user for the **double** radius of a sphere and call method **sphereVolume** to calculate and display the volume of that sphere using the assignment

```java
volume = ( 4 / 3 ) * Math.PI * Math.pow( radius, 3 )
```

The user should input the radius through a text field. A string can be converted to a **double** value as follows (assume **o** is the **String** passed to the action method when the user presses the Enter key in the text field):

```
// Create a Double object using the text field value.
Double val = new Double( o.toString() );

// Pull the primitive data type double value out of
// the Double object.
double radius = val.doubleValue();   //
```

The result can be converted to a **String** with method **Double.toString**.

Answers to Self-Review Exercises

4.1   a) Methods and classes. b) Method call. c) Local variable. d) **return**. e) **void**. f) Scope.
g) **return;** or **return** *expression;* or encountering the closing right brace of a method. h) **init**.
i) **Math.random**. j) **start**. k) **paint**. l) Automatic. m) **resize**. n) **repaint**. o) **stop**. p)
Recursive. q) Base. r) Overloading. s) **final**.

4.2   a) Class scope. b) Block Scope. c) Class scope. d) Class scope. f) Block scope.

4.3   The following solution demonstrates the **Math** class methods in Fig. 4.2.

```
1  // Exercise 4.3: MathTest.java
2  // Testing the Math class methods
3
4  public class MathTest {
5     public static void main( String args[] )
6     {
7        System.out.println( "Math.abs( 23.7 ) = " +
8                            Math.abs( 23.7 ) );
9        System.out.println( "Math.abs( 0.0 ) = " +
10                           Math.abs( 0.0 ) );
11       System.out.println( "Math.abs( -23.7 ) = " +
12                           Math.abs( -23.7 ) );
13       System.out.println( "Math.ceil( 9.2 ) = " +
14                           Math.ceil( 9.2 ) );
15       System.out.println( "Math.ceil( -9.8 ) = " +
16                           Math.ceil( -9.8 ) );
17       System.out.println( "Math.cos( 0.0 ) = " +
18                           Math.cos( 0.0 ) );
19       System.out.println( "Math.exp( 1.0 ) = " +
20                           Math.exp( 1.0 ) );
21       System.out.println( "Math.exp( 2.0 ) = " +
22                           Math.exp( 2.0 ) );
23       System.out.println( "Math.floor( 9.2 ) = " +
24                           Math.floor( 9.2 ) );
25       System.out.println( "Math.floor( -9.8 ) = " +
26                           Math.floor( -9.8 ) );
27       System.out.println( "Math.log( 2.718282 ) = " +
28                           Math.log( 2.718282 ) );
29       System.out.println( "Math.log( 7.389056 ) = " +
30                           Math.log( 7.389056 ) );
31       System.out.println( "Math.max( 2.3, 12.7 ) = v +
32                           Math.max( 2.3, 12.7 ) );
33       System.out.println( "Math.max( -2.3, -12.7 ) = " +
34                           Math.max( -2.3, -12.7 ) );
```

```
35        System.out.println( "Math.min( 2.3, 12.7 ) = " +
36                            Math.min( 2.3, 12.7 ) );
37        System.out.println( "Math.min( -2.3, -12.7 ) = " +
38                            Math.min( -2.3, -12.7 ) );
39        System.out.println( "Math.pow( 2, 7 ) = " +
40                            Math.pow( 2, 7 ) );
41        System.out.println( "Math.pow( 9, .5 ) = " +
42                            Math.pow( 9, .5 ) );
43        System.out.println( "Math.sin( 0.0 ) = " +
44                            Math.sin( 0.0 ) );
45        System.out.println( "Math.sqrt( 25.0 ) = " +
46                            Math.sqrt( 25.0 ) );
47        System.out.println( "Math.tan( 0.0 ) = " +
48                            Math.tan( 0.0 ) );
49    }
50  }
```

```
Math.abs( 23.7 ) = 23.7
Math.abs( 0.0 ) = 0
Math.abs( -23.7 ) = 23.7
Math.ceil( 9.2 ) = 10
Math.ceil( -9.8 ) = -9
Math.cos( 0.0 ) = 1
Math.exp( 1.0 ) = 2.71828
Math.exp( 2.0 ) = 7.38906
Math.floor( 9.2 ) = 9
Math.floor( -9.8 ) = -10
Math.log( 2.718282 ) = 1
Math.log( 7.389056 ) = 2
Math.max( 2.3, 12.7 ) = 12.7
Math.max( -2.3, -12.7 ) = -2.3
Math.min( 2.3, 12.7 ) = 2.3
Math.min( -2.3, -12.7 ) = -12.7
Math.pow( 2, 7 ) = 128
Math.pow( 9, .5 ) = 3
Math.sin( 0.0 ) = 0
Math.sqrt( 25.0 ) = 5
Math.tan( 0.0 ) = 0
```

4.4 a) `double hypotenuse( double side1, double side2 )`
  b) `int smallest( int x, int y, int z )`
  c) `void instructions()`
  d) `float intToFloat( int number )`

4.5 a) Error: Method **h** is defined in method **g**.
  Correction: Move the definition of **h** out of the definition of **g**.
  b) Error: The method is supposed to return an integer, but does not.
  Correction: Delete variable **result** and place the following statement in the method:

```
return x + y;
```

c) Error: The result of **n + sum(n - 1)** is not returned; **sum** returns an improper result.
   Correction: Rewrite the statement in the **else** clause as

   ```
   return n + sum(n - 1);
   ```

d) Error: Semicolon after the right parenthesis that encloses the parameter list, and re-defining the parameter **a** in the method definition.
   Correction: Delete the semicolon after the right parenthesis of the parameter list, and delete the declaration **float a;**.

e) Error: The method returns a value when it is not supposed to.
   Correction: Eliminate the **return** statement.

4.6   The following solution calculates the volume of a sphere using the radius entered by the user.

```
1  // Ex. 4.6: SphereTest.java
2  import java.applet.Applet;
3  import java.awt.*;
4
5  public class SphereTest extends Applet {
6     Label prompt;
7     TextField input;
8
9     public void init()
10    {
11       prompt = new Label( "Enter sphere radius: " );
12       input = new TextField( 10 );
13       add( prompt );
14       add( input );
15    }
16
17    public boolean action( Event e, Object o )
18    {
19       Double val = new Double( o.toString() );
20       double radius = val.doubleValue();
21       showStatus( "Volume is " +
22                   Double.toString( sphereVolume( radius ) ) );
23       return true;
24    }
25
26    public double sphereVolume( double radius )
27    {
28       double volume;
29       volume = ( 4 / 3 ) * Math.PI * Math.pow( radius, 3 );
30       return volume;
31    }
32 }
```

Exercises

4.7   Show the value of x after each of the following statements is performed:
   a) **x = Math.abs(7.5);**
   b) **x = Math.floor(7.5);**
   c) **x = Math.abs(0.0);**
   d) **x = Math.ceil(0.0);**
   e) **x = Math.abs(-6.4);**

f) `x = Math.ceil( -6.4 );`
g) `x = Math.ceil( -Math.abs( -8 + Math.floor( -5.5 ) ) );`

4.8 A parking garage charges a $2.00 minimum fee to park for up to three hours. The garage charges an additional $0.50 per hour for each hour *or part thereof* in excess of three hours. The maximum charge for any given 24-hour period is $10.00. Assume that no car parks for longer than 24 hours at a time. Write an applet that calculates and displays the parking charges for each customer who parked their car in this garage yesterday. You should enter the hours parked for each customer. Your program should display the charge for the current customer and should calculate and display the running total of yesterday's receipts. The program should use the method `calculateCharges` to determine the charge for each customer. Use the techniques described in Self-Review Exercise 4.6 to read the double value from a text field.

4.9 An application of method `Math.floor` is rounding a value to the nearest integer. The statement

`y = Math.floor( x + .5 );`

will round the number **x** to the nearest integer and assign the result to **y**. Write an applet that reads double values and uses the preceding statement to round each of these numbers to the nearest integer. For each number processed, display both the original number and the rounded number. Use the techniques described in Self-Review Exercise 4.6 to read the double value from a text field.

4.10 `Math.floor` may be used to round a number to a specific decimal place. The statement

`y =Math.floor( x * 10 + .5 ) / 10;`

rounds **x** to the tenths position (the first position to the right of the decimal point). The statement

`y = Math.floor( x * 100 + .5 ) / 100;`

rounds **x** to the hundredths position (i.e., the second position to the right of the decimal point). Write an applet that defines four methods to round a number **x** in various ways:
   a) `roundToInteger( number )`
   b) `roundToTenths( number )`
   c) `roundToHundredths( number )`
   d) `roundToThousandths( number )`

For each value read, your program should display the original value, the number rounded to the nearest integer, the number rounded to the nearest tenth, the number rounded to the nearest hundredth, and the number rounded to the nearest thousandth.

4.11 Answer each of the following questions.
   a) What does it mean to choose numbers "at random?"
   b) Why is the `Math.random` method useful for simulating games of chance?
   c) Why is it often necessary to scale and/or shift the values produced by `Math.random`?
   d) Why is computerized simulation of real-world situations a useful technique?

4.12 Write statements that assign random integers to the variable n in the following ranges:
   a) $1 \le n \le 2$
   b) $1 \le n \le 100$
   c) $0 \le n \le 9$

    d) $1000 \leq n \leq 1112$
    e) $-1 \leq n \leq 1$
    f) $-3 \leq n \leq 11$

4.13   For each of the following sets of integers, write a single statement that will print a number at random from the set.
    a) 2, 4, 6, 8, 10.
    b) 3, 5, 7, 9, 11.
    c) 6, 10, 14, 18, 22.

4.14   Write a method **integerPower(base, exponent)** that returns the value of

      $base^{\ exponent}$

For example, **integerPower(3, 4) = 3 * 3 * 3 * 3**. Assume that **exponent** is a positive, nonzero integer, and **base** is an integer. Method **integerPower** should use **for** or **while** to control the calculation. Do not use any math library methods. Incorporate this method into an applet that reads integer values for **base** and **exponent** from the user at the keyboard and performs the calculation with the **integerPower** method.

4.15   Define a method **hypotenuse** that calculates the length of the hypotenuse of a right triangle when the other two sides are given. The method should take two arguments of type **double** and return the hypotenuse as a **double**. Incorporate this method into an applet that reads integer values for **side1** and **side2** from the user at the keyboard and performs the calculation with the **hypotenuse** method. Determine the length of the hypotenuse for each of the following triangles.

Triangle	Side 1	Side 2
1	3.0	4.0
2	5.0	12.0
3	8.0	15.0

4.16   Write a method **multiple** that determines for a pair of integers whether the second integer is a multiple of the first. The method should take two integer arguments and return **true** if the second is a multiple of the first, and **false** otherwise. Incorporate this method into an applet that inputs a series of pairs of integers.

4.17   Write an applet that inputs integers and passes them one at a time to method **isEven** which uses the modulus operator to determine if an integer is even. The method should take an integer argument and return **true** if the integer is even and **false** otherwise.

4.18   Write a method **squareOfAsterisks** that displays a solid square of asterisks whose side is specified in integer parameter **side**. For example, if **side** is **4**, the method displays

```
****
****
****
****
```

Incorporate this method into an applet that reads an integer value for **side** from the user at the keyboard and performs the drawing with the **squareOfAsterisks** method. Note that this method should be called from the applet's **paint** method and should be passed the **Graphics** object from **paint**.

4.19   Modify the method created in Exercise 4.18 to form the square out of whatever character is contained in character parameter **fillCharacter**. Thus if **side** is **5** and **fillCharacter** is "**#**" then this method should print

```
#####
#####
#####
#####
#####
```

4.20   Use techniques similar to those developed in Exercises 4.18 and 4.19 to produce a program that graphs a wide range of shapes.

4.21   Modify the program of Exercise 4.18 to draw a solid square with the **fillRect** method of the **Graphics** class. Method **fillRect** receives four arguments—x coordinate, y coordinate, width and height. Allow the user to enter the coordinates at which the square should appear. (See Exercises 1.25-1.28 for more information on **Graphics** class methods.)

4.22   Write program segments that accomplish each of the following:
a) Calculate the integer part of the quotient when integer **a** is divided by integer **b**.
b) Calculate the integer remainder when integer **a** is divided by integer **b**.
c) Use the program pieces developed in a) and b) to write a method **displayDigits** that receives an integer between **1** and **99999** and prints it as a series of digits, each pair of which is separated by two spaces. For example, the integer **4562** should be printed as **4 5 6 2**.
d) Incorporate the method developed in c) into an applet that inputs an integer from the user at the keyboard and invokes **displayDigits** from the applet's **paint** method by passing the method both the integer entered and the **Graphics** object.

4.23   Implement the following integer methods:
a) Method **celsius** returns the Celsius equivalent of a Fahrenheit temperature.
b) Method **fahrenheit** returns the Fahrenheit equivalent of a Celsius temperature.
c) Use these methods to write an applet that enables the user to enter either a Fahrenheit temperature and display the Celsius equivalent or enter a Celsius temperature and display the Fahrenheit equivalent.

4.24   Write a method **minimum3** that returns the smallest of three floating-point numbers. Use the **Math.min** method to implement **minimum3**. Incorporate the method into an applet that reads three values from the user and uses **minimum3** to determine the smallest value. Display the result in the status bar.

4.25   An integer number is said to be a *perfect number* if its factors, including 1 (but not the number itself), sum to the number. For example, 6 is a perfect number because 6 = 1 + 2 + 3. Write a method **perfect** that determines if parameter **number** is a perfect number. Use this method in an applet that determines and prints all the perfect numbers between 1 and 1000. Print the factors of each perfect number to confirm that the number is indeed perfect. Challenge the computing power of your computer by testing numbers much larger than 1000.

4.26   An integer is said to be *prime* if it is divisible only by 1 and itself. For example, 2, 3, 5, and 7 are prime, but 4, 6, 8, and 9 are not.

     a) Write a method that determines if a number is prime.
     b) Use this method in an applet that determines and prints all the prime numbers between 1 and 10,000. How many of these 10,000 numbers do you really have to test before being sure that you have found all the primes?
     c) Initially you might think that $n/2$ is the upper limit for which you must test to see if a number is prime, but you need only go as high as the square root of n. Why? Rewrite the program, and run it both ways. Estimate the performance improvement.

4.27   Write a method that takes an integer value and returns the number with its digits reversed. For example, given the number 7631, the method should return 1367. Incorporate the method into an applet that reads a value from the user. Display the result of the method in the status bar.

4.28   The *greatest common divisor (GCD)* of two integers is the largest integer that evenly divides each of the two numbers. Write a method **gcd** that returns the greatest common divisor of two integers. Incorporate the method into an applet that reads two values from the user. Display the result of the method in the status bar.

4.29   Write a method **qualityPoints** that inputs a student's average and returns 4 if a student's average is 90-100, 3 if the average is 80-89, 2 if the average is 70-79, 1 if the average is 60-69, and 0 if the average is lower than 60. Incorporate the method into an applet that reads a value from the user. Display the result of the method in the status bar.

4.30   Write an applet that simulates coin tossing. Let the program toss the coin each time the user presses the "**Toss**" button. Count the number of times each side of the coin appears. Display the results. The program should call a separate method **flip** that takes no arguments and returns **false** for tails and **true** for heads. *Note:* If the program realistically simulates the coin tossing, then each side of the coin should appear approximately half the time.

4.31   Computers are playing an increasing role in education. Write a program that will help an elementary school student learn multiplication. Use **Math.random** to produce two positive one-digit integers. It should then display a question in the status bar such as:

     How much is 6 times 7?

The student then types the answer into an text field. Your program checks the student's answer. If it is correct, draw the string **"Very good!"** on the applet then ask another multiplication question. If the answer is wrong, draw the string **"No. Please try again."** on the applet; then, let the student try the same question again repeatedly until the student finally gets it right. A separate method should be used to generate each new question. This method should be called once when the applet begins execution and each time the user answers the question correctly. All drawing on the applet should be performed by the **paint** method.

4.32   The use of computers in education is referred to as *computer-assisted instruction* (CAI). One problem that develops in CAI environments is student fatigue. This can be eliminated by varying the computer's dialogue to hold the student's attention. Modify the program of Exercise 4.31 so the various comments are printed for each correct answer and each incorrect answer as follows:

Responses to a correct answer

```
Very good!
Excellent!
Nice work!
Keep up the good work!
```

Responses to an incorrect answer

```
No. Please try again.
Wrong. Try once more.
Don't give up!
No. Keep trying.
```

Use random number generation to choose a number from 1 to 4 that will be used to select an appropriate response to each answer. Use a **switch** structure in the **paint** method to issue the responses.

4.33   More sophisticated computer-aided instructions systems monitor the student's performance over a period of time. The decision to begin a new topic is often based on the student's success with previous topics. Modify the program of Exercise 4.32 to count the number of correct and incorrect responses typed by the student. After the student types 10 answers, your program should calculate the percentage of correct responses. If the percentage is lower than 75 percent, your program should print **Please ask your instructor for extra help** and then terminate.

4.34   Write an applet that plays the "guess the number" game as follows: Your program chooses the number to be guessed by selecting a random integer in the range 1 to 1000. The applet displays the prompt **Guess a number between 1 and 1000** next to a text field. The player types a first guess into the text field and presses the Enter key. If the player's guess is incorrect, your program should display **Too high. Try again.** or **Too low. Try again.** in the status bar to help the player "zero in" on the correct answer and should clear the text field so the user can enter the next guess. When the user enters the correct answer, display **Congratulations. You guessed the number!** in the status bar and clear the text field so the user can play again. Note: The searching technique employed in this problem is called *binary search.*

4.35   Modify the program of Exercise 4.34 to count the number of guesses the player makes. If the number is 10 or fewer, print **Either you know the secret or you got lucky!** If the player guesses the number in 10 tries, then print **Ahah! You know the secret!** If the player makes more than 10 guesses, then print **You should be able to do better!** Why should it take no more than 10 guesses? Well with each "good guess" the player should be able to eliminate half of the numbers. Now show why any number 1 to 1000 can be guessed in 10 or fewer tries.

4.36   Write a recursive method **power (base, exponent)** that when invoked returns

$$base^{\,exponent}$$

Fig. 4.19 The Towers of Hanoi for the case with four disks.

For example, **power(3, 4) = 3 * 3 * 3 * 3**. Assume that **exponent** is an integer greater than or equal to 1. *Hint:* The recursion step would use the relationship

$$base\ ^{exponent} = base \cdot base\ ^{exponent\ -\ 1}$$

and the terminating condition occurs when **exponent** is equal to **1** because

$$base^1 = base$$

Incorporate this method into an applet that enables the user to enter the **base** and **exponent**.

4.37   The Fibonacci series

0, 1, 1, 2, 3, 5, 8, 13, 21, …

begins with the terms 0 and 1 and has the property that each succeeding term is the sum of the two preceding terms. a) Write a *nonrecursive* method **fibonacci(n)** that calculates the nth Fibonacci number. Incorporate this method into an applet that enables the user to enter the value of **n**. b) Determine the largest Fibonacci number that can be printed on your system. Modify the program of part a) to use **double** instead of **int** to calculate and return Fibonacci numbers, and use this modified program to repeat part b).

4.38   *(Towers of Hanoi)* Every budding computer scientist must grapple with certain classic problems, and the Towers of Hanoi (see Fig. 4.19) is one of the most famous of these. Legend has it that in a temple in the Far East, priests are attempting to move a stack of disks from one peg to another. The initial stack had 64 disks threaded onto one peg and arranged from bottom to top by decreasing size. The priests are attempting to move the stack from this peg to a second peg under the constraints that exactly one disk is moved at a time, and at no time may a larger disk be placed above a smaller disk. A third peg is available for temporarily holding disks. Supposedly the world will end when the priests complete their task, so there is little incentive for us to facilitate their efforts.

Let us assume that the priests are attempting to move the disks from peg 1 to peg 3. We wish to develop an algorithm that will print the precise sequence of peg-to-peg disk transfers.

If we were to approach this problem with conventional methods, we would rapidly find ourselves hopelessly knotted up in managing the disks. Instead, if we attack the problem with recursion in mind, it immediately becomes tractable. Moving *n* disks can be viewed in terms of moving only *n* - 1 disks (and hence the recursion) as follows:

a) Move *n* - 1 disks from peg 1 to peg 2, using peg 3 as a temporary holding area.

b) Move the last disk (the largest) from peg 1 to peg 3.

c) Move the *n* - 1 disks from peg 2 to peg 3, using peg 1 as a temporary holding area.

The process ends when the last task involves moving *n* = 1 disk, i.e., the base case. This is accomplished by trivially moving the disk without the need for a temporary holding area.

Write an application to solve the Towers of Hanoi problem. Use a recursive **tower** method with four parameters:

a) The number of disks to be moved

b) The peg on which these disks are initially threaded

c) The peg to which this stack of disks is to be moved

d) The peg to be used as a temporary holding area

Your program should print the precise instructions it will take to move the disks from the starting peg to the destination peg. For example, to move a stack of three disks from peg 1 to peg 3, your program should print the following series of moves:

$1 \rightarrow 3$ (This means move one disk from peg 1 to peg 3.)

$1 \rightarrow 2$

$3 \rightarrow 2$

$1 \rightarrow 3$

$2 \rightarrow 1$

$2 \rightarrow 3$

$1 \rightarrow 3$

Note: Your **tower** method must have the keyword **static** in its function header. This will be explained in detail in Chapter 6.

4.39   Any program that can be implemented recursively can be implemented iteratively, although sometimes with more difficulty and less clarity. Try writing an iterative version of the Towers of Hanoi. If you succeed, compare your iterative version with the recursive version you developed in Exercise 4.38. Investigate issues of performance, clarity, and your ability to demonstrate the correctness of the programs.

4.40   *(Visualizing Recursion)* It is interesting to watch recursion "in action." Modify the factorial method of Fig. 4.12 to print its local variable and recursive call parameter. For each recursive call, display the outputs on a separate line and add a level of indentation. Do your utmost to make the outputs clear, interesting, and meaningful. Your goal here is to design and implement an output format that helps a person understand recursion better. You may want to add such display capabilities to the many other recursion examples and exercises throughout the text.

4.41   The greatest common divisor of integers **x** and **y** is the largest integer that evenly divides both **x** and **y**. Write a recursive method **gcd** that returns the greatest common divisor of **x** and **y**. The **gcd** of **x** and **y** is defined recursively as follows: If **y** is equal to **0**, then **gcd(x, y)** is **x**; otherwise **gcd(x, y)** is **gcd(y, x % y)** where **%** is the modulus operator. Use this method to replace the one you wrote in the applet of Exercise 4.28.

4.42   Exercises 4.31 through 4.33 developed a computer-assisted instruction program to teach an elementary school student multiplication. This exercise suggests enhancements to that program.

a) Modify the program to allow the user to enter a grade-level capability. A grade level of 1 means to use only single-digit numbers in the problems, a grade level of two means to use numbers as large as two-digits, etc.

b) Modify the program to allow the user to pick the type of arithmetic problems he or she wishes to study. An option of 1 means addition problems only, 2 means subtraction problems only, 3 means multiplication problems only, 4 means division problems only, and 5 means to randomly intermix problems of all these types.

4.43 Write method **distance** that calculates the distance between two points (x1, y1) and (x2, y2). All numbers and return values should be of type **double**. Incorporate this method into an applet that enables the user to enter the coordinates of the points.

4.44 What does the following method do?

```
// Parameter b must be a positive
// integer to prevent infinite recursion
int mystery( int a, int b )
{
   if ( b == 1 )
      return a;
   else
      return a + mystery( a, b - 1 );
}
```

4.45 After you determine what the program of Exercise 4.44 does, modify the method to operate properly after removing the restriction of the second argument being nonnegative. Also, incorporate the method into an applet that enables the user to enter two integers and test the method.

4.46 Write an application that tests as many of the math library methods in Fig. 4.2 as you can. Exercise each of these methods by having your program print out tables of return values for a diversity of argument values.

4.47 Find the error in the following recursive method and explain how to correct it:

```
int sum( int n )
{
   if ( n == 0 )
      return 0;
   else
      return n + sum(n);
}
```

4.48 Modify the craps program of Fig. 4.9 to allow wagering. Initialize variable **bankBalance** to 1000 dollars. Prompt the player to enter a **wager**. Check that **wager** is less than or equal to **bankBalance** and if not have the user to reenter **wager** until a valid **wager** is entered. After a correct **wager** is entered, run one game of craps. If the player wins, increase **bankBalance** by **wager** and print the new **bankBalance**. If the player loses, decrease **bankBalance** by **wager**, print the new **bankBalance**, check if **bankBalance** has become zero, and if so print the message **"Sorry. You busted!"** As the game progresses, print various messages to create some "chatter" such as **"Oh, you're going for broke, huh?"**, or **"Aw cmon, take a chance!"**, or **"You're up big. Now's the time to cash in your chips!"**.

4.49 Write an applet that uses a method **circleArea** to prompt the user for the radius of a circle, and to calculate and print the area of that circle.

5

Arrays

Objectives

- To introduce the array data structure.
- To understand the use of arrays to store, sort, and search lists and tables of values.
- To understand how to declare an array, initialize an array, and refer to individual elements of an array.
- To be able to pass arrays to methods.
- To understand basic sorting techniques.
- To be able to declare and manipulate multiple-subscript arrays.

With sobs and tears he sorted out
Those of the largest size …
Lewis Carroll

Attempt the end, and never stand to doubt;
Nothing's so hard, but search will find it out.
Robert Herrick

Now go, write it before them in a table,
and note it in a book.
Isaiah 30:8

'Tis in my memory lock'd,
And you yourself shall keep the key of it.
William Shakespeare

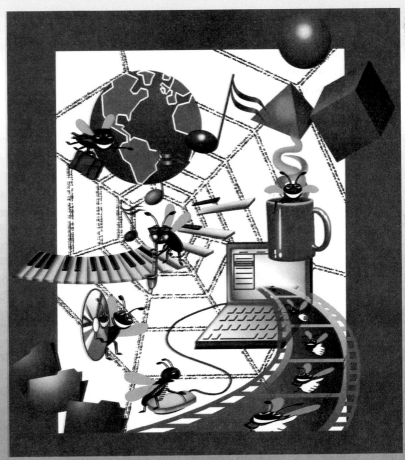

Outline

5.1 Introduction

This chapter serves as an introduction to the important topic of data structures. *Arrays* are data structures consisting of related data items of the same type. Arrays are "static" entities in that they remain the same size once they are created, although an array reference may be reassigned to a new array of a different size. In Chapter 17, "Data Structures," we introduce dynamic data structures such as lists, queues, stacks, and trees that may grow and shrink as programs execute. In Chapter 18, "Utilities and Bit Manipulation," we discuss class **Vector** which is an array-like class whose objects can grow and shrink in response to a Java program's changing storage requirements.

5.2 Arrays

An array is a group of contiguous memory locations that all have the same name and the same type. To refer to a particular location or element in the array, we specify the name of the array and the *position number* of the particular element in the array.

Figure 5.1 shows an integer array called **c**. This array contains twelve *elements*. Any one of these elements may be referred to by giving the name of the array followed by the position number of the particular element in square brackets (**[]**). The first element in every array is the *zeroth element.* Thus, the first element of array **c** is referred to as **c[0]**, the second element of array **c** is referred to as **c[1]**, the seventh element of array **c** is referred to as **c[6]**, and, in general, the *i*th element of array **c** is referred to as **c[i-1]**. Array names follow the same conventions as other variable names.

The position number in square brackets is more formally called a *subscript*. A subscript must be an integer or an integer expression. If a program uses an expression as a subscript, then the expression is evaluated to determine the subscript. For example, if we assume that variable **a** is equal to **5** and that variable **b** is equal to **6**, then the statement

```
c[ a + b ] += 2;
```

Name of array (Note that all
elements of this array have
the same name, c)

c[0]	-45
c[1]	6
c[2]	0
c[3]	72
c[4]	1543
c[5]	-89
c[6]	0
c[7]	62
c[8]	-3
c[9]	1
c[10]	6453
c[11]	78

Position number of the element
within array c

Fig. 5.1   A 12-element array.

adds 2 to array element **c[11]**. Note that a subscripted array name is an *lvalue*—it can be used on the left side of an assignment to place a new value into an array element.

Let us examine array **c** in Fig. 5.1 more closely. The *name* of the array is **c**. The *length* of the array is determined by the following expression:

```
c.length
```

Every array in Java knows its own length. The array's twelve elements are referred to as **c[0], c[1], c[2], ..., c[11]**. The *value* of **c[0]** is **-45**, the value of **c[1]** is **6**, the value of **c[2]** is **0**, the value of **c[7]** is **62**, and the value of **c[11]** is **78**. To calculate the sum of the values contained in the first three elements of array **c** and store the result in variable **sum**, we would write

```
sum = c[ 0 ] + c[ 1 ] + c[ 2 ];
```

To divide the value of the seventh element of array **c** by **2** and assign the result to the variable **x**, we would write

```
x = c[ 6 ] / 2;
```

Common Programming Error 5.1

It is important to note the difference between the "seventh element of the array" and "array element seven." Because array subscripts begin at 0, the "seventh element of the array" has a subscript of 6, while "array element seven" has a subscript of 7 and is actually the eighth element of the array. This confusion is a source of "off-by-one" errors.

The brackets used to enclose the subscript of an array are an operator in Java. Brackets have the same level of precedence as parentheses. The chart in Fig. 5.2 shows the precedence and associativity of the operators introduced to this point in the text. They are shown top to bottom in decreasing order of precedence with their associativity and type.

5.3 Declaring and Allocating Arrays

Arrays occupy space in memory. The programmer specifies the type of the elements and uses the **new** operator to allocate the number of elements required by each array. To allocate 12 elements for integer array **c**, the declaration

```
int c[] = new int[ 12 ];
```

is used. The preceding statement can also be performed in two steps as follows:

```
int c[];              // declares the array
c = new int[ 12 ];    // allocates the array
```

When arrays are allocated, the elements are automatically initialized to zero for the numeric primitive data type variables, to **false** for **boolean** variables or to **null** for references.

Operators						Associativity	Type
( )	[ ]	.				left to right	parentheses
++	--	+	-	!	(*type*)	right to left	unary
*	/	%				left to right	multiplicative
+	-					left to right	additive
<	<=	>	>=			left to right	relational
==	!=					left to right	equality
&						left to right	boolean logical AND
^						left to right	boolean logical exclusive OR
|						left to right	boolean logical inclusive OR
&&						left to right	logical AND
||						left to right	logical OR
?:						right to left	conditional
=	+=	-=	*=	/=	%=	right to left	assignment

Fig. 5.2   Operator precedence and associativity.

Note that unlike C or C++ the number of elements in the array is never specified in the square brackets after the array name. The declaration

```
int c[ 12 ];
```

causes a syntax error.

Memory may be reserved for several arrays with a single declaration. The following declaration reserves 100 elements for integer array **b** and 27 elements for integer array **x**.

```
int b[] = new int[ 100 ], x[] = new int[ 27 ];
```

Arrays may be declared to contain other data types. For example, an array of type **String** can store a set of character strings (**String**s will be discussed in Chapter 8).

5.4 Examples Using Arrays

The program in Fig. 5.3 uses the **new** operator to dynamically allocate an array of 10 elements which are initially zero, then it prints the array in tabular format.

```
1   // Fig. 5.3: InitArray.java
2   // initializing an array
3   import java.awt.Graphics;
4   import java.applet.Applet;
5
6   public class InitArray extends Applet {
7      int n[];          // declare an array of integers
8
9      // initialize instance variables
10     public void init()
11     {
12        n = new int[ 10 ];  // dynamically allocate array
13     }
14
15     // paint the applet
16     public void paint( Graphics g )
17     {
18        int yPosition = 25;  // starting y position on applet
19
20        g.drawString( "Element", 25, yPosition );
21        g.drawString( "Value", 100, yPosition );
22
23        for ( int i = 0; i < n.length; i++ ) {
24           yPosition += 15;
25           g.drawString( String.valueOf( i ), 25, yPosition );
26           g.drawString( String.valueOf( n[ i ] ),
27                         100, yPosition );
28        }
29     }
30  }
```

Fig. 5.3   Initializing the elements of an array to zeros (part 1 of 2).

Fig. 5.3   Initializing the elements of an array to zeros (part 2 of 2).

The first two statements in the **paint** method of Fig. 5.3 display the column headings for the columns printed in the **for** structure. Variable **yPosition** is used to determine the vertical position at which the **drawString** method outputs on the applet. The **String.valueOf** method is used to convert each integer to a string that can be displayed on the applet. Note the expression **n.length** in the **for** structure (line 23) to determine the length of the array.

The elements of an array can be initialized in the array declaration by following the declaration with an equal sign and a comma-separated list (enclosed in braces) of *initializers*. In this case, the array size is determined by the number of elements in the initializer list. For example, the statement

```
int n[] = { 1, 2, 3, 4, 5 };
```

creates a five-element array.

The program in Fig. 5.4 initializes an integer array with ten values (line 7) and prints the array in tabular format.

```
1   // Fig. 5.4: InitArray.java
2   // initializing an array with a declaration
3   import java.awt.Graphics;
4   import java.applet.Applet;
5
6   public class InitArray extends Applet {
7       int n[] = { 32, 27, 64, 18, 95, 14, 90, 70, 60, 37 };
8
```

Fig. 5.4   Initializing the elements of an array with a declaration (part 1 of 2).

```
9        // paint the applet
10       public void paint( Graphics g )
11       {
12          int yPosition = 25;    // starting y position on applet
13
14          g.drawString( "Element", 25, yPosition );
15          g.drawString( "Value", 100, yPosition );
16
17          for ( int i = 0; i < n.length; i++ ) {
18             yPosition += 15;
19             g.drawString( String.valueOf( i ), 25, yPosition );
20             g.drawString( String.valueOf( n[ i ] ),
21                           100, yPosition );
22          }
23       }
24    }
```

Applet Viewer: InitArray.class		
Applet		
Element	Value	
0	32	
1	27	
2	64	
3	18	
4	95	
5	14	
6	90	
7	70	
8	60	
9	37	
Applet started.		

Fig. 5.4   Initializing the elements of an array with a declaration (part 2 of 2).

The program in Fig. 5.5 initializes the elements of a ten-element array **s** to the integers **2, 4, 6, ..., 20**, and prints the array in tabular format. These numbers are generated by multiplying each successive value of the loop counter by **2** and adding **2**.

Line 7

```
final int arraySize = 10;
```

uses the **final** qualifier to declare a so-called *constant variable* **arraySize** whose value is **10**. Constant variables must be initialized with a constant expression when they are declared and cannot be modified thereafter (Fig. 5.6 and Fig. 5.7). If an attempt is made to modify a final variable after it is declared, the compiler produces the error message:

```
Can't assign a value to a final variable
```

```
1   // Fig. 5.5: InitArray.java
2   // initialize array s to the even integers from 2 to 20
3   import java.awt.Graphics;
4   import java.applet.Applet;
5
6   public class InitArray extends Applet {
7      final int arraySize = 10;
8      int s[];
9
10     // initialize instance variables
11     public void init()
12     {
13        s = new int[ arraySize ];
14
15        // Set the values in the array
16        for ( int i = 0; i < s.length; i++ )
17           s[ i ] = 2 + 2 * i;
18     }
19
20     // paint the applet
21     public void paint( Graphics g )
22     {
23        int yPosition = 25;    // starting y position on applet
24
25        g.drawString( "Element", 25, yPosition );
26        g.drawString( "Value", 100, yPosition );
27
28        for ( int i = 0; i < s.length; i++ ) {
29           yPosition += 15;
30           g.drawString( String.valueOf( i ), 25, yPosition );
31           g.drawString( String.valueOf( s[ i ] ),
32                         100, yPosition );
33        }
34     }
35  }
```

Fig. 5.5   Generating the values to be placed into elements of an array (part 1 of 2).

Constant variables are also called *named constants* or *read-only variables*. They are often used to make a program more readable. Note that the term "constant variable" is an oxymoron—a contradiction in terms like "jumbo shrimp" or "freezer burn." (Please send your favorite oxymorons to our email address listed in the Preface. Thanks!)

Common Programming Error 5.2

Assigning a value to a constant variable in an executable statement is a syntax error.

The program of Fig. 5.8 sums the values contained in the ten-element integer array **a**. The statement in the body of the **for** loop does the totaling. It is important to remember that the values being supplied as initializers for array **a** normally would be read into the program. For example, the user could enter the values through a text field in the applet.

Fig. 5.5   Generating the values to be placed into elements of an array (part1 of 2).

```
1    // Fig. 5.6: FinalTest.java
2    // a final object must be initialized
3    import java.applet.Applet;
4
5    public class FinalTest extends Applet {
6       final int x;  // Error: Final variables must be initialized
7    }
```

```
FinalTest.java:7: Final variables must be initialized: int x
    final int x;  // Final variables must be initialized
                ^
1 error
```

Fig. 5.6   A **final** object must be initialized.

```
1    // Fig. 5.7: FinalTest.java
2    // using a properly initialized constant variable
3    import java.awt.Graphics;
4    import java.applet.Applet;
5
6    public class FinalTest extends Applet {
7       final int x = 7;  // initialize constant variable
8
9       public void paint( Graphics g )
10      {
11         g.drawString( "The value of x is: " + x, 25, 25 );
12      }
13   }
```

Fig. 5.7   Correctly initializing and using a constant variable (part 1 of 2).

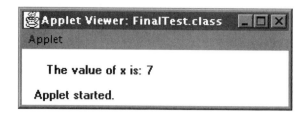

Fig. 5.7 Correctly initializing and using a constant variable (part 2 of 2).

```
1   // Fig. 5.8: SumArray.java
2   // Compute the sum of the elements of the array
3   import java.awt.Graphics;
4   import java.applet.Applet;
5
6   public class SumArray extends Applet {
7      int a[] = { 1, 2, 3, 4, 5, 6, 7, 8, 9, 10 };
8      int total;
9
10     // initialize instance variables
11     public void init()
12     {
13        total = 0;
14
15        for ( int i = 0; i < a.length; i++ )
16           total += a[ i ];
17     }
18
19     // paint the applet
20     public void paint( Graphics g )
21     {
22        g.drawString( "Total of array elements: " + total,
23                     25, 25 );
24     }
25  }
```

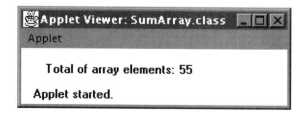

Fig. 5.8 Computing the sum of the elements of an array.

Our next example uses arrays to summarize the results of data collected in a survey. Consider the problem statement:

Forty students were asked to rate the quality of the food in the student cafeteria on a scale of 1 to 10 (1 means awful and 10 means excellent). Place the forty responses in an integer array and summarize the results of the poll.

This is a typical array processing application (see Fig. 5.9). We wish to summarize the number of responses of each type (i.e., 1 through 10). The array **responses** is a 40-element integer array of the students' responses to the survey. We use an eleven-element array **frequency** to count the number of occurrences of each response. We ignore the first element, **frequency[0]**, because it is more logical to have the response 1 increment **frequency[1]** than **frequency[0]**. This allows us to use each response directly as the subscript in the **frequency** array.

```java
1   // Fig. 5.9: StudentPoll.java
2   // Student poll program
3   import java.awt.Graphics;
4   import java.applet.Applet;
5
6   public class StudentPoll extends Applet {
7      int responses[] = { 1, 2, 6, 4, 8, 5, 9, 7, 8, 10,
8                           1, 6, 3, 8, 6, 10, 3, 8, 2, 7,
9                           6, 5, 7, 6, 8, 6, 7, 5, 6, 6,
10                          5, 6, 7, 5, 6, 4, 8, 6, 8, 10 };
11     int frequency[];
12
13     // initialize instance variables
14     public void init()
15     {
16        frequency = new int[ 11 ];
17
18        for ( int answer = 0; answer < responses.length; answer++ )
19           ++frequency[ responses[ answer ] ];
20     }
21
22     // paint the applet
23     public void paint( Graphics g )
24     {
25        int yPosition = 25;    // starting y position on applet
26
27        g.drawString( "Rating", 25, yPosition );
28        g.drawString( "Frequency", 100, yPosition );
29
30        for ( int rating = 1;
31              rating < frequency.length; rating++ ) {
32           yPosition += 15;
33           g.drawString( String.valueOf( rating ),
34                         25, yPosition );
35           g.drawString( String.valueOf( frequency[ rating ] ),
36                         100, yPosition );
37        }
38     }
39  }
```

Fig. 5.9   A simple student poll analysis program (part 1 of 2).

```
Applet Viewer: StudentPoll.cla...  [_][□][X]
Applet

   Rating        Frequency
   1             2
   2             2
   3             2
   4             2
   5             5
   6             11
   7             5
   8             7
   9             1
   10            3
Applet started.
```

Fig. 5.9   A simple student poll analysis program (part 2 of 2).

Good Programming Practice 5.1

Strive for program clarity. It is sometimes worthwhile to trade off the most efficient use of memory or processor time in favor of writing clearer programs.

Performance Tip 5.1

Sometimes performance considerations far outweigh clarity considerations.

The **for** loop on line 18 takes the responses one at a time from the array **response** and increments one of the ten counters (**frequency[1]** to **frequency[10]**) in the **frequency** array. The key statement in the loop is

```
++frequency[ responses[ answer ] ];
```

This statement increments the appropriate **frequency** counter depending on the value of **responses[answer]**.

Let's consider several iterations of the **for** loop. When the counter **answer** is **0**, **responses[answer]** is **1**, so **++frequency[responses[answer]];** is actually interpreted as

```
++frequency[ 1 ];
```

which increments array element one.

When the counter **answer** is **1**, **responses[answer]** is **2**, so the statement **++frequency[responses[answer]];** is actually interpreted as

```
++frequency[ 2 ];
```

which increments array element two.

When the counter **answer** is **2**, **responses[answer]** is **6**, so the statement **++frequency[responses[answer]];** is actually interpreted as

> **++frequency[6];**

which increments array element six, and so on. Note that regardless of the number of responses processed in the survey, only an eleven-element array is required (ignoring element zero) to summarize the results. Also note that the results of this program are correct because the elements of the **frequency** array were automatically initialized to zero when the array was allocated with **new**. If the elements were not initialized to zero, the frequency counts for each response in the survey would be incorrect.

If the data contained invalid values such as 13, the program would attempt to add **1** to **frequency[13]**. This is outside the bounds of the array. In the C and C++ programming languages, such a reference would be allowed by the compiler and at execution time. The program would "walk" past the end of the array to where it thought element number 13 was located and add 1 to whatever happened to be at that location in memory. This could potentially result in modification of another variable in the program or even result in the program terminating prematurely.

Java provides mechanisms to prevent accessing elements outside the bounds of the array. When a Java program is compiled, the compiler checks array element references to be sure they are valid (i.e., all subscripts must be greater than or equal to 0 and less than the length of the array). If there is an invalid reference, the compiler generates an error. Also, if an invalid reference is made to an array element at execution time, Java generates an exception. Exceptions are used to indicate that an error occurred in a program. They enable the programmer to recover from an error and continue the execution of the program instead of abnormally terminating the program. When an invalid array reference is made, an **ArrayIndexOutOfBoundsException** is generated. Chapter 12 covers "Exception Handling" in detail.

Common Programming Error 5.3

Referring to an element outside the array bounds.

Good Programming Practice 5.2

When looping through an array, the array subscript should never go below 0 and should always be less than the total number of elements in the array (one less than the size of the array). Make sure the loop terminating condition prevents accessing elements outside this range.

Good Programming Practice 5.3

Programs should validate the correctness of all input values to prevent erroneous information from affecting a program's calculations.

Our next example (Fig. 5.10) reads numbers from an array and graphs the information in the form of a bar chart or histogram—each number is printed, and then a bar consisting of that many asterisks is printed beside the number. The nested **for** loop (line 26) actually draws the bars.

```
1   // Fig. 5.10: Histogram.java
2   // Histogram printing program
3   import java.awt.Graphics;
4   import java.applet.Applet;
5
6   public class Histogram extends Applet {
7      int n[] = { 19, 3, 15, 7, 11, 9, 13, 5, 17, 1 };
8
9      // paint the applet
10     public void paint( Graphics g )
11     {
12        int xPosition;        // position of * in histogram
13        int yPosition = 25;   // vertical position in applet
14
15        g.drawString( "Element", 25, yPosition );
16        g.drawString( "Value", 100, yPosition );
17        g.drawString( "Histogram", 175, yPosition );
18
19        for ( int i = 0; i < n.length; i++ ) {
20           yPosition += 15;
21           g.drawString( String.valueOf( i ), 25, yPosition );
22           g.drawString( String.valueOf( n[ i ] ),
23                         100, yPosition );
24           xPosition = 175;
25
26           for ( int j = 1; j <= n[i]; j++ ) { // print one bar
27              g.drawString( "*", xPosition, yPosition );
28              xPosition += 7;
29           }
30        }
31     }
32  }
```

Fig. 5.10 A program that prints histograms.

In Chapter 4 we stated that we would show a more elegant method of writing the dice-rolling program of Fig. 4.8. The problem was to roll a single six-sided die 6000 times to test whether the random number generator produces random numbers. An array version of this program is shown in Fig. 5.11.

5.5 References and Reference Parameters

Two ways to pass arguments to methods (or functions) in many programming languages (like C and C++) are *call-by-value* and *call-by-reference*. Normally the programmer spec-

```
1   // Fig. 5.11: RollDie.java
2   // Roll a six-sided die 6000 times
3   import java.awt.Graphics;
4   import java.applet.Applet;
5   import java.util.Random;
6
7   public class RollDie extends Applet {
8       int face;
9       int frequency[];
10      Random r;    // create the random number generator
11
12      // initialize instance variables
13      public void init()
14      {
15          frequency = new int[ 7 ];
16          r = new Random();
17
18          for ( int roll = 1; roll <= 6000; roll++ ) {
19              face = 1 + Math.abs( r.nextInt() % 6 );
20              ++frequency[ face ];
21          }
22      }
23
24      // paint the applet
25      public void paint( Graphics g )
26      {
27          int yPosition = 25;
28
29          g.drawString( "Face", 25, yPosition );
30          g.drawString( "Frequency", 100, yPosition );
31
32          for ( face = 1; face < frequency.length; face++ ) {
33              yPosition += 15;
34              g.drawString( String.valueOf( face ), 25, yPosition );
35              g.drawString( String.valueOf( frequency[ face ] ),
36                            100, yPosition );
37          }
38      }
39  }
```

Fig. 5.11 Dice-rolling program using arrays instead of **switch** (part 1 of 2).

Applet Viewer: RollDie.class

Applet

Face	Frequency
1	1030
2	1049
3	977
4	973
5	988
6	983

Applet started.

Fig. 5.11 Dice-rolling program using arrays instead of **switch** (part 2 of 2).

ifies the particular way each argument will be passed. When an argument is passed call-by-value, a *copy* of the argument's value is made and passed to the called method.

Testing and Debugging Tip 5.1

With call-by-value, changes to the called method's copy do not affect the original variable's value in the calling method. This prevents the accidental side effects that so greatly hinder the development of correct and reliable software systems.

With call-by-reference, the caller gives the called method the ability to directly access the caller's data and to modify that data if the called method so chooses. Call-by-reference can improve performance because it can eliminate the overhead of copying large amounts of data, but call-by-reference can weaken security because the called method can access the caller's data. Java, unlike other languages, does not allow the programmer to choose whether to pass each argument call-by-value or call-by-reference. Primitive data type variables are always passed call-by-value and objects are always passed call-by-reference.

To pass an object call-by-reference, simply specify in the method call the reference to the object by name. Mentioning the object by its parameter name in the body of the called method actually refers to the original object in memory, and the original object can be accessed directly by the called method.

Because arrays are treated as objects by Java, arrays are passed to methods call-by-reference—a called method can access the element values in the callers' original arrays. The name of an array is actually a reference to an object that contains the array elements and the **length** instance variable which indicates the number of elements in the array.

Performance Tip 5.2

Passing arrays by reference makes sense for performance reasons. If arrays were passed by value, a copy of each element would be passed. For large, frequently passed arrays, this would waste time and would consume considerable storage for the copies of the arrays.

When returning information from a method via a **return** statement, primitive data type variables are always returned by value and objects are always returned by reference. In the next section, we demonstrate call-by-value and call-by-reference using arrays.

5.6 Passing Arrays to Methods

To pass an array argument to a method, specify the name of the array without any brackets. For example, if array **hourlyTemperatures** has been declared as

```
int hourlyTemperatures[] = new int[ 24 ];
```

the method call

```
modifyArray( hourlyTemperatures );
```

passes array **hourlyTemperatures** to method **modifyArray**. In Java every array object knows its own size (via the **length** instance variable). Thus, when we pass an array object into a method we do not separately pass the size of the array as an argument.

Although entire arrays are passed call-by-reference, *individual array elements of primitive data types are passed call-by-value exactly as simple variables are* (individual array elements that are not of primitive types are still passed call-by-reference). Such simple single pieces of data are called *scalars* or *scalar quantities.* To pass an array element to a method, use the subscripted name of the array element as an argument in the method call.

For a method to receive an array through a method call, the method's parameter list must specify that an array will be received. For example, the method header for method **modifyArray** might be written as

```
void modifyArray( int b[] )
```

indicating that **modifyArray** expects to receive an integer array in parameter **b**. Because arrays are passed by reference, when the called method uses the array name **b**, it refers to the actual array in the caller (array **hourlyTemperatures** in the preceding call).

The program in Fig. 5.12 demonstrates the difference between passing an entire array and passing an array element. The program first prints the five elements of integer array **a**. Next, **a** is passed to method **modifyArray** where each of **a**'s elements is multiplied by 2. Then **a** is reprinted in **main**. As the output shows, the elements of **a** are indeed modified by **modifyArray**. Now the program prints the value of **a[3]** and passes it to method **modifyElement**. Method **modifyElement** multiplies its argument by 2. Note that when **a[3]** is reprinted in **main**, it has not been modified because individual primitive-data-type array elements are passed call-by-value.

5.7 Sorting Arrays

Sorting data (i.e., placing the data into some particular order such as ascending or descending) is one of the most important computing applications. A bank sorts all checks by account number so that it can prepare individual bank statements at the end of each month. Telephone companies sort their lists of accounts by last name and, within that, by first name to make it easy to find phone numbers. Virtually every organization must sort some data and in many cases massive amounts of data. Sorting data is an intriguing problem which has attracted some of the most intense research efforts in the field of computer science. In this chapter we discuss the simplest sorting scheme. In the exercises and in Chapter 17, we investigate more complex schemes that yield superior performance.

```
1   // Fig. 5.12: PassArray.java
2   // Passing arrays and individual array elements to methods
3   import java.awt.Graphics;
4   import java.applet.Applet;
5
6   public class PassArray extends Applet {
7      int a[] = {0, 1, 2, 3, 4};
8
9      public void paint( Graphics g )
10     {
11        int xPosition = 25, yPosition = 25;
12
13        g.drawString(
14           "Effects of passing entire array call-by-reference:",
15           xPosition, yPosition );
16        yPosition += 15;
17        g.drawString( "The values of the original array are:",
18                      xPosition, yPosition );
19        xPosition += 15;
20        yPosition += 15;
21
22        for ( int i = 0; i < a.length; i++ ) {
23           g.drawString( String.valueOf( a[ i ] ),
24                         xPosition, yPosition );
25           xPosition += 15;
26        }
27
28        xPosition = 25;
29        yPosition += 30;
30
31        modifyArray( a );   // array a passed call-by-reference
32
33        g.drawString( "The values of the modified array are:",
34                      xPosition, yPosition );
35        xPosition += 15;
36        yPosition += 15;
37
38        for ( int i = 0; i < a.length; i++ ) {
39           g.drawString( String.valueOf( a[ i ] ),
40                         xPosition, yPosition );
41           xPosition += 15;
42        }
43
44        xPosition = 25;
45        yPosition += 30;
46
47        g.drawString(
48           "Effects of passing array element call-by-value:",
49           xPosition, yPosition );
50        yPosition += 15;
```

Fig. 5.12 Passing arrays and individual array elements to methods (part 1 of 2).

```
51          g.drawString( "a[3] before modifyElement: " + a[ 3 ],
52                        xPosition, yPosition );
53          yPosition += 15;
54
55          modifyElement( a[ 3 ] );
56
57          g.drawString( "a[3] after modifyElement: " + a[ 3 ],
58                        xPosition, yPosition );
59       }
60
61       public void modifyArray( int b[] )
62       {
63          for ( int j = 0; j < b.length; j++ )
64             b[ j ] *= 2;
65       }
66
67       public void modifyElement( int e )
68       {
69          e *= 2;
70       }
71    }
```

Fig. 5.12 Passing arrays and individual array elements to methods (part 2 of 2).

Performance Tip 5.3

Often, the simplest algorithms perform poorly. Their virtue is that they are easy to write, test and debug. More complex algorithms are often needed to realize maximum performance.

The program in Fig. 5.13 sorts the values of the ten-element array **a** into ascending order. The technique we use is called the *bubble sort* or the *sinking sort* because the smaller values gradually "bubble" their way to the top of the array like air bubbles rising in water, while the larger values sink to the bottom of the array. The technique is to make several passes through the array. On each pass, successive pairs of elements are compared. If a pair is in increasing order (or the values are identical), we leave the values as they are. If a pair is in decreasing order, their values are swapped in the array. Note the use in this program of method **print** (defined on line 31) to output the contents of the array preceded by a string.

```java
1   // Fig. 5.13: BubbleSort.java
2   // This program sorts an array's values into
3   // ascending order
4   import java.awt.Graphics;
5   import java.applet.Applet;
6
7   public class BubbleSort extends Applet {
8      int a[] = { 2, 6, 4, 8, 10, 12, 89, 68, 45, 37 };
9      int hold;   // temporary holding area for swap
10
11     public void paint( Graphics g )
12     {
13        print( g, "Data items in original order", a, 25, 25 );
14
15        sort();
16
17        print( g, "Data items in ascending order", a, 25, 55 );
18     }
19
20     public void sort()
21     {
22        for ( int pass = 1; pass < a.length; pass++ ) // passes
23           for ( int i = 0; i < a.length - 1; i++ ) // one pass
24              if ( a[ i ] > a[ i + 1 ] ) {        // one comparison
25                 hold = a[i];                      // one swap
26                 a[ i ] = a[ i + 1 ];
27                 a[ i + 1 ] = hold;
28              }
29     }
30
31     public void print( Graphics g, String head, int b[],
32                        int x, int y )
33     {
34        g.drawString( head, x, y );
35        x += 15;
36        y += 15;
37
38        for ( int i = 0; i < b.length; i++ ) {
39           g.drawString( String.valueOf( b[ i ] ), x, y );
40           x += 20;
41        }
42     }
43  }
```

Fig. 5.13 Sorting an array with bubble sort (part 1 of 2).

Fig. 5.13 Sorting an array with bubble sort (part 2 of 2).

First the program compares **a[0]** to **a[1]**, then **a[1]** to **a[2]**, then **a[2]** to **a[3]**, and so on until it completes the pass by comparing **a[8]** to **a[9]**. Although there are ten elements, only nine comparisons are performed. Because of the way the successive comparisons are made, a large value may move down the array many positions on a single pass, but a small value may move up only one position. On the first pass, the largest value is guaranteed to sink to the bottom element of the array, **a[9]**. On the second pass, the second largest value is guaranteed to sink to **a[8]**. On the ninth pass, the ninth largest value sinks to **a[1]**. This leaves the smallest value in **a[0]**, so only nine passes are needed to sort a ten-element array.

The sorting is performed by the nested **for** loop in the **sort** method (line 20). If a swap is necessary, it is performed by the three assignments

```
hold = a[ i ];
a[ i ] = a[ i + 1 ];
a[ i + 1 ] = hold;
```

where the extra variable **hold** temporarily stores one of the two values being swapped. The swap cannot be performed with only the two assignments

```
a[ i ] = a[ i + 1 ];
a[ i + 1 ] = a[ i ];
```

If, for example, **a[i]** is **7** and **a[i + 1]** is **5**, after the first assignment both values will be **5** and the value **7** will be lost. Hence the need for the extra variable **hold**.

The chief virtue of the bubble sort is that it is easy to program. However, the bubble sort runs slowly. This becomes apparent when sorting large arrays. In the exercises, we will develop more efficient versions of the bubble sort and investigate some far more efficient sorts than the bubble sort. More advanced courses (often titled "Data Structures" or "Algorithms" or "Computational Complexity") investigate sorting and searching in greater depth.

5.8 Searching Arrays: Linear Search and Binary Search

Often, a programmer will be working with large amounts of data stored in arrays. It may be necessary to determine whether an array contains a value that matches a certain *key value*.

The process of finding a particular element of an array is called *searching*. In this section we discuss two searching techniques—the simple *linear search* technique and the more efficient *binary search* technique. Exercises 5.31 and 5.32 at the end of this chapter ask you to implement recursive versions of the linear search and the binary search.

The linear search (Fig. 5.14) compares each element of the array with the *search key*. Since the array is not in any particular order, it is just as likely that the value will be found in the first element as the last. On average, therefore, the program will have to compare the search key with half the elements of the array.

```
1   // Fig. 5.14: LinearSearch.java
2   // Linear search of an array
3   import java.awt.*;
4   import java.applet.Applet;
5
6   public class LinearSearch extends Applet {
7       int a[];
8       int element;
9       String searchKey;
10      Label enterLabel;
11      TextField enter;
12      Label resultLabel;
13      TextField result;
14
15      public void init()
16      {
17          a = new int[ 100 ];
18
19          for ( int i = 0; i < a.length; i++ ) // create data
20              a[ i ] = 2 * i;
21
22          enterLabel = new Label( "Enter integer search key" );
23          enter = new TextField( 10 );
24          resultLabel = new Label( "Result" );
25          result = new TextField( 25 );
26          result.setEditable( false );
27          add( enterLabel );
28          add( enter );
29          add( resultLabel );
30          add( result );
31      }
32
33      public int linearSearch( int key )
34      {
35          for ( int n = 0; n < a.length; n++ )
36              if ( a[ n ] == key )
37                  return n;
38
```

Fig. 5.14 Linear search of an array (part 1 of 2).

```
39          return -1;
40      }
41
42      public boolean action( Event event, Object o )
43      {
44          if ( event.target == enter ) {
45              searchKey = event.arg.toString();
46            element = linearSearch( Integer.parseInt( searchKey ) );
47
48              if ( element != -1 )
49                result.setText( "Found value in element " + element );
50              else
51                  result.setText( "Value not found" );
52          }
53
54          return true;
55      }
56  }
```

Fig. 5.14 Linear search of an array (part 2 of 2).

The linear search method works well for small arrays or for unsorted arrays. However, for large arrays linear searching is inefficient. If the array is sorted, the high-speed binary search technique can be used.

The binary search algorithm eliminates half of the elements in the array being searched after each comparison. The algorithm locates the middle array element and compares it to the search key. If they are equal, the search key is found and the subscript of that element is returned. Otherwise, the problem is reduced to searching half of the array. If the search key is less than the middle array element, the first half of the array is searched, otherwise the second half of the array is searched. If the search key is not the middle element in the specified subarray (piece of the original array), the algorithm is repeated on one quarter of the original array. The search continues until the search key is equal to the middle element of a subarray or until the subarray consists of one element that is not equal to the search key (i.e., the search key is not found).

In a worst case scenario, searching an array of 1024 elements will take only 10 comparisons using a binary search. Repeatedly dividing 1024 by 2 (because after each comparison we are able to eliminate half of the array) yields the values 512, 256, 128, 64, 32, 16, 8, 4, 2, and 1. The number 1024 (2^{10}) is divided by 2 only ten times to get the value 1. Dividing by 2 is equivalent to one comparison in the binary search algorithm. An array of 1,048,576 (2^{20}) elements takes a maximum of 20 comparisons to find the key. An array of one billion elements takes a maximum of 30 comparisons to find the key. This is a tremendous increase in performance over the linear search that required comparing the search key to an average of half the elements in the array. For a one billion element array, this is a difference between an average of 500 million comparisons and a maximum of 30 comparisons! The maximum number of comparisons needed for the binary search of any sorted array is the exponent of the first power of 2 greater than the number of elements in the array.

Figure 5.15 presents the iterative version of method **binarySearch** (line 64). The method receives two arguments—an integer **key** (the search key) and the **Graphics** object **gg** (used for output). If **key** does not match the middle element of a subarray, the **low** subscript or **high** subscript (both declared in the method) is adjusted so a smaller subarray can be searched. If **key** is less than the middle element, the **high** subscript is set to **middle - 1**, and the search is continued on the elements from **low** to **middle - 1**. If **key** is greater than the middle element, the **low** subscript is set to **middle + 1**, and the search is continued on the elements from **middle + 1** to **high**. The program uses a 15-element array. The first power of 2 greater than the number of array elements is 16 (2^4), so a maximum of 4 comparisons are required to find the **key**. Method **printRow** outputs each subarray during the binary search process. The middle element in each subarray is marked with an asterisk (*****) to indicate the element to which the **key** is compared.

```
1   // Fig. 5.15: BinarySearch.java
2   // Binary search of an array
3   import java.awt.*;
4   import java.applet.Applet;
5
6   public class BinarySearch extends Applet {
7       int a[];
8       int element;
9       String searchKey;
10      int xPosition;  // applet horizontal drawing position
11      int yPosition;  // applet vertical drawing position
12      Label enterLabel;
13      TextField enter;
14      Label resultLabel;
```

Fig. 5.15 Binary search of a sorted array (part 1 of 4).

```
15      TextField result;
16      boolean timeToSearch = false;
17
18      public void init()
19      {
20         a = new int[ 15 ];
21
22         for ( int i = 0; i < a.length; i++ ) // create data
23            a[ i ] = 2 * i;
24
25         enterLabel = new Label( "Enter key" );
26         enter = new TextField( 5 );
27         resultLabel = new Label( "Result" );
28         result = new TextField( 22 );
29         result.setEditable( false );
30         add( enterLabel );
31         add( enter );
32         add( resultLabel );
33         add( result );
34      }
35
36      public void paint( Graphics g )
37      {
38         if ( timeToSearch ) { // prevents search 1st time called
39            element = binarySearch(
40               Integer.parseInt( searchKey ), g );
41
42            if ( element != -1 )
43               result.setText(
44                  "Found value in element " + element );
45            else
46               result.setText( "Value not found" );
47         }
48      }
49
50      public boolean action( Event event, Object o )
51      {
52         if ( event.target == enter ) {
53            timeToSearch = true;
54            xPosition = 25;
55            yPosition = 75;
56            searchKey = event.arg.toString();
57            repaint();  // call paint to start search and output
58         }
59
60         return true;
61      }
62
```

Fig. 5.15 Binary search of a sorted array (part 2 of 4).

```
63    // Binary search
64    public int binarySearch( int key, Graphics gg )
65    {
66       gg.drawString( "Portions of array searched",
67                      xPosition, yPosition );
68       yPosition += 15;
69
70       int low = 0;              // low subscript
71       int high = a.length - 1;  // high subscript
72       int middle;               // middle subscript
73
74       while ( low <= high ) {
75          middle = ( low + high ) / 2;
76
77          printRow( low, middle, high, gg );
78
79          if ( key == a[ middle ] )  // match
80             return middle;
81          else if ( key < a[ middle ] )
82             high = middle - 1;  // search low end of array
83          else
84             low = middle + 1;   // search high end of array
85       }
86
87       return -1;   // searchKey not found
88    }
89
90    // Print one row of output showing the current
91    // part of the array being processed.
92    void printRow( int low, int mid, int high, Graphics gg )
93    {
94       xPosition = 25;
95
96       for ( int i = 0; i < a.length; i++ ) {
97          if ( i < low || i > high )
98             gg.drawString( "", xPosition, yPosition );
99          else if ( i == mid )    // mark middle value
100            gg.drawString( String.valueOf( a[ i ] ) + "*",
101                           xPosition, yPosition );
102         else
103            gg.drawString( String.valueOf( a[ i ] ),
104                           xPosition, yPosition );
105
106         xPosition += 20;
107      }
108
109      yPosition += 15;
110   }
111 }
```

Fig. 5.15 Binary search of a sorted array (part 3 of 4).

Fig. 5.15 Binary search of a sorted array (part 4 of 4).

5.9 Multiple-Subscripted Arrays

Multiple-subscripted arrays with two subscripts are often used to represent *tables* of values consisting of information arranged in *rows* and *columns.* To identify a particular table element, we must specify the two subscripts: The first (by convention) identifies the element's row, and the second (by convention) identifies the element's column. Tables or arrays that require two subscripts to identify a particular element are called *double-subscripted arrays.* Note that multiple-subscripted arrays can have more than two subscripts. Java does not support multiple-subscript directly, but does allow the programmer to specify single-subscript arrays whose elements are also single-subscript arrays, thus achieving the same effect.

Fig. 5.16 illustrates a double-subscripted array, **a**, that contains three rows and four columns, so it is said to be a 3-by-4 array. In general, an array with *m* rows and *n* columns is called an *m-by-n array.*

Every element in array **a** is identified in Fig. 5.16 by an element name of the form **a[i][j]**; **a** is the name of the array, and **i** and **j** are the subscripts that uniquely identify each element in **a**. Notice that the names of the elements in the first row all have a first subscript of **0**; the names of the elements in the fourth column all have a second subscript of **3**.

Multiple-subscripted arrays can be initialized in declarations like a single subscripted arrays. A double-subscripted array **b[2][2]** could be declared and initialized with

```
int b[][] = { { 1, 2 }, { 3, 4 } };
```

The values are grouped by row in braces. So, **1** and **2** initialize **b[0][0]** and **b[0][1]**, and **3** and **4** initialize **b[1][0]** and **b[1][1]**.

Multiple-subscripted arrays are maintained as arrays of arrays. The declaration

```
int b[][] = { { 1, 2 }, { 3, 4, 5 } };
```

creates integer array **b** with row **0** containing two elements (**1** and **2**) and row **1** containing three elements (**3**, **4** and **5**).

Figure 5.17 demonstrates initializing double-subscripted arrays in declarations. The program declares two arrays.

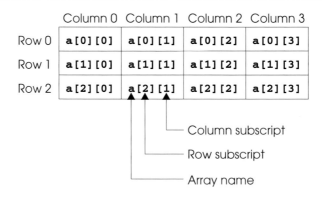

Fig. 5.16 A double-subscripted array with three rows and four columns.

```
1   // Fig. 5.17: InitArray.java
2   // Initializing multidimensional arrays
3   import java.awt.Graphics;
4   import java.applet.Applet;
5
6   public class InitArray extends Applet {
7      int array1[][] = { { 1, 2, 3 }, { 4, 5, 6 } };
8      int array2[][] = { { 1, 2 }, { 4 } };
9
10     // paint the applet
11     public void paint( Graphics g )
12     {
13        g.drawString( "Values in array1 by row are", 25, 25 );
14        printArray( array1, g, 40 );
15
16        g.drawString( "Values in array2 by row are", 25, 70 );
17        printArray( array2, g, 85 );
18     }
19
20     public void printArray( int a[][], Graphics g, int y )
21     {
22        int x = 25;
23
24        for ( int i = 0; i < a.length; i++ ) {
25
26           for ( int j = 0; j < a[ i ].length; j++ )  {
27              g.drawString( String.valueOf( a[ i ][ j ] ), x, y );
28              x += 15;
29           }
30
31           x = 25;
32           y += 15;
33        }
34     }
35  }
```

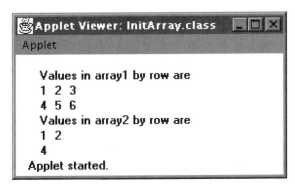

Fig. 5.17 Initializing multidimensional arrays.

The declaration of **array1** provides six initializers in two sublists. The first sublist initializes the first row of the array to the values 1, 2, and 3; and the second sublist initializes the second row of the array to the values 4, 5, and 6. The declaration of **array2** provides three initializers in two sublists. The sublist for the first row explicitly initializes the first row to have two elements with values 1 and 2, respectively. The sublist for the second row initializes the first row to have one element with value 4.

The program calls method **printArray** (lines 14 and 17) to output each array's elements. Notice that the method definition specifies the array parameter as **int a[][]** to indicate that a double-subscripted array will be received as an argument. Also, a **Graphics** reference is passed as an argument to enable the **printArray** method to output the contents of each array on the applet. Note the use of a nested **for** structure to output the rows of each double-subscripted array. In the outer **for** structure, the expression **a.length** determines the number of rows in the array. In the inner **for** structure, the expression **a[i].length** determines the number of columns in each row of the array.

Many common array manipulations use **for** repetition structures. For example, the following **for** structure sets all the elements in the third row of array **a** in Fig. 5.16 to zero:

```
for ( int col = 0; col < a[ 2 ].length; col++)
    a[ 2 ][ col ] = 0;
```

We specified the *third* row, therefore we know that the first subscript is always **2** (**0** is the first row, and **1** is the second row). The **for** loop varies only the second subscript (i.e., the column subscript). The preceding **for** structure is equivalent to the assignment statements:

```
a[ 2 ][ 0 ] = 0;
a[ 2 ][ 1 ] = 0;
a[ 2 ][ 2 ] = 0;
a[ 2 ][ 3 ] = 0;
```

The following nested **for** structure determines the total of all the elements in array **a**.

```
total = 0;

for ( int row = 0; row < a.length; row++ )
    for ( int col = 0; col < a[ row ].length; col++ )
        total += a[ row ][ col ];
```

The **for** structure totals the elements of the array one row at a time. The outer **for** structure begins by setting the **row** subscript to **0** so the elements of the first row may be totaled by the inner **for** structure. The outer **for** structure then increments **row** to **1**, so the second row can be totaled. Then, the outer **for** structure increments **row** to **2**, so the third row can be totaled. The result can be displayed when the nested **for** structure terminates.

The program of Fig. 5.18 performs several other common array manipulations on 3-by-4 array **grades**. Each row of the array represents a student and each column represents a grade on one of the four exams the students took during the semester. The array manipulations are performed by four methods. Method **minimum** determines the lowest grade of any student for the semester. Method **maximum** determines the highest grade of any student for the semester. Method **average** determines a particular student's semester average. Method **printArray** outputs the double-subscripted array in a tabular format.

```
1   // Fig. 5.18: DoubleArray.java
2   // Double-subscripted array example
3   import java.awt.Graphics;
4   import java.applet.Applet;
5
6   public class DoubleArray extends Applet {
7      int grades[][] = { { 77, 68, 86, 73 },
8                         { 96, 87, 89, 81 },
9                         { 70, 90, 86, 81 } };
10      int students, exams;
11      int xPosition, yPosition;
12
13      // initialize instance variables
14      public void init()
15      {
16         students = grades.length;
17         exams = grades[ 0 ].length;
18      }
19
20      // paint the applet
21      public void paint( Graphics g )
22      {
23         xPosition = 25;
24         yPosition = 25;
25
26         g.drawString( "The array is:", xPosition, yPosition );
27         yPosition += 15;
28         printArray( g );
29         xPosition = 25;
30         yPosition += 30;
31         g.drawString( "Lowest grade:", xPosition, yPosition );
32         int min = minimum();
33         g.drawString( String.valueOf( min ),
34                       xPosition + 85, yPosition );
35         yPosition += 15;
36         g.drawString( "Highest grade:", xPosition, yPosition );
37         int max = maximum();
38         g.drawString( String.valueOf( max ),
39                       xPosition + 85, yPosition );
40         yPosition += 15;
41
42         for ( int i = 0; i < students; i++ ) {
43            g.drawString( "Average for student " + i + " is ",
44                          25, yPosition );
45            double ave = average( grades[ i ] );
46            g.drawString( String.valueOf( ave ), 165, yPosition );
47            yPosition += 15;
48         }
49      }
50
```

Fig. 5.18 Example of using double-subscripted arrays (part 1 of 3).

```
51    // find the minimum grade
52    public int minimum()
53    {
54       int lowGrade = 100;
55
56       for ( int i = 0; i < students; i++ )
57          for ( int j = 0; j < exams; j++ )
58             if ( grades[ i ][ j ] < lowGrade )
59                lowGrade = grades[ i ][ j ];
60
61       return lowGrade;
62    }
63
64    // find the maximum grade
65    public int maximum()
66    {
67       int highGrade = 0;
68
69       for ( int i = 0; i < students; i++ )
70          for ( int j = 0; j < exams; j++ )
71             if ( grades[ i ][ j ] > highGrade )
72                highGrade = grades[ i ][ j ];
73
74       return highGrade;
75    }
76
77    // determine the average grade for a particular
78    // student (or set of grades)
79    public double average( int setOfGrades[] )
80    {
81       int total = 0;
82
83       for ( int i = 0; i < setOfGrades.length; i++ )
84          total += setOfGrades[ i ];
85
86       return (double) total / setOfGrades.length;
87    }
88
89    // print the array
90    public void printArray( Graphics g )
91    {
92       xPosition = 80;
93
94       for ( int i = 0; i < exams; i++ ) {
95          g.drawString( "[" + i + "]", xPosition, yPosition );
96          xPosition += 30;
97       }
98
```

Fig. 5.18 Example of using double-subscripted arrays (part 2 of 3).

```
99          for ( int i = 0; i < students; i++ ) {
100            xPosition = 25;
101            yPosition += 15;
102            g.drawString( "grades[" + i + "]",
103                            xPosition, yPosition );
104            xPosition = 80;
105
106            for ( int j = 0; j < exams; j++ )  {
107                g.drawString( String.valueOf( grades[ i ][ j ] ),
108                                xPosition, yPosition );
109                xPosition += 30;
110            }
111        }
112    }
113 }
```

Fig. 5.18 Example of using double-subscripted arrays (part 3 of 3).

Methods **minimum**, **maximum**, and **printArray** each use the **grades** array and the variables **students** (number of rows in the array) and **exams** (number of columns in the array). Each method loops through array **grades** using nested **for** structures. The following nested **for** structure is from the method **minimum** definition:

```
int lowGade = 100;

for ( int i = 0; i < students; i++ )
    for ( int j = 0; j < exams; j++ )
        if ( grades[ i ][ j ] < lowGrade )
            lowGrade = grades[ i ][ j ];
```

The outer **for** structure begins by setting **i** (i.e., the row subscript) to **0** so the elements of the first row can be compared to variable **lowGrade** in the body of the inner **for** structure. The inner **for** structure loops through the four grades of a particular row and compares each grade to **lowGrade**. If a grade is less than **lowGrade, lowGrade** is set to that grade. The outer **for** structure then increments the row subscript by **1**. The elements of the second row are compared to variable **lowGrade**. The outer **for** structure then increments the row subscript to **2**. The elements of the third row are compared to variable **lowGrade**. When execution of the nested structure is complete, **lowGrade** contains the smallest grade in the double-subscripted array. Method **maximum** works similarly to method **minimum**.

Method **average** takes one argument—a single-subscripted array of test results for a particular student. When **average** is called, the argument is **grades[i]** which specifies that a particular row of the double-subscripted array **grades** is to be passed to **average**. For example, the argument **grades[1]** represents the four values (a single-subscripted array of grades) stored in the second row of the double-subscripted array **grades**. Remember that in Java a double-subscripted array is an array with elements that are single-subscripted arrays. Method **average** calculates the sum of the array elements, divides the total by the number of test results, and returns the floating-point result as a **double** value.

Summary

- Java stores lists of values in arrays. An array is a contiguous group of related memory locations. These locations are related by the fact that they all have the same name and the same type. To refer to a particular location or element within the array, we specify the name of the array and the subscript of the element.

- A subscript may be an integer or an integer expression. If a program uses an expression as a subscript, then the expression is evaluated to determine the particular element of the array.

- Java arrays always begin with element 0, thus it is important to note the difference when referring to the seventh element of the array as opposed to array element seven. The seventh element has a subscript of **6**, while array element seven has a subscript of **7** (actually the eighth element of the array). This is a source of "off-by-one" errors.

- Arrays occupy space in memory. To reserve 100 elements for integer array **b** and 27 elements for integer array **x**, the programmer writes

  ```
  int b[] = new int[ 100 ], x[] = new int[ 27 ];
  ```

- The elements of an array can be initialized by declaration, by assignment, and by input.

- Java prevents referencing elements beyond the bounds of an array.

- To pass an array to a method, the name of the array is passed. To pass a single element of an array to a method, simply pass the name of the array followed by the subscript (contained in square brackets) of the particular element.

- Arrays are passed to methods call-by-reference—therefore the called methods can modify the element values in the callers' original arrays. Single elements of arrays are passed to methods call-by-value.

- To receive an array argument, the method's parameter list must specify that an array will be received.

- An array can be sorted using the bubble-sort technique. Several passes of the array are made. On each pass, successive pairs of elements are compared. If a pair is in order (or the values are identical), it is left as is. If a pair is out of order, the values are swapped. For small arrays, the bubble sort is acceptable, but for larger arrays it is inefficient compared to more sophisticated sorting algorithms.

- The linear search compares each element of the array with the search key. If the array is not in any particular order, it is just as likely that the value will be found in the first element as the last. On average, therefore, the program will have to compare the search key with half the elements of the array. Linear search works well for small arrays and is acceptable even for large unsorted arrays.

- For sorted arrays the binary search eliminates from consideration one half of the elements in the array after each comparison. The algorithm locates the middle element of the array and compares it to the search key. If they are equal, the search key is found and the array subscript of that element is returned. Otherwise, the problem is reduced to searching one half of the array that is still under consideration.

- In a worst case scenario, searching a sorted array of 1024 elements will take only 10 comparisons using a binary search.

- Arrays may be used to represent tables of values consisting of information arranged in rows and columns. To identify a particular element of a table, two subscripts are specified: The first identifies the row in which the element is contained, and the second identifies the column in which the element is contained. Tables or arrays that require two subscripts to identify a particular element are called double-subscripted arrays.

- To pass one row of a double-subscripted array to a method that receives a single-subscripted array, simply pass the name of the array followed by the row subscript.

Terminology

`a[i]`
`a[i][j]`
array
array initializer list
binary search of an array
bounds checking
bubble sort
column subscript
constant variable
declare an array
double-subscripted array
element of an array
`final`
initialize an array
initializer

linear search of an array
lvalue
m-by-n array
multiple-subscripted array
name of an array
named constant
off-by-one error
pass-by-reference
pass-by-value
pass of a bubble sort
passing arrays to methods
position number
row subscript
search key
searching an array

single-subscripted array
sinking sort
sorting
sorting an array
square brackets [ ]
subscript

table of values
tabular format
temporary area for exchange of values
value of an element
zeroth element

Common Programming Errors

5.1   It is important to note the difference between the "seventh element of the array" and "array element seven." Because array subscripts begin at 0, the "seventh element of the array" has a subscript of 6, while "array element seven" has a subscript of 7 and is actually the eighth element of the array. This confusion is a source of "off-by-one" errors.

5.2   Assigning a value to a constant variable in an executable statement is a syntax error.

5.3   Referring to an element outside the array bounds.

Good Programming Practices

5.1   Strive for program clarity. It is sometimes worthwhile to trade off the most efficient use of memory or processor time in favor of writing clearer programs.

5.2   When looping through an array, the array subscript should never go below 0 and should always be less than the total number of elements in the array (one less than the size of the array). Make sure the loop terminating condition prevents accessing elements outside this range.

5.3   Programs should validate the correctness of all input values to prevent erroneous information from affecting a program's calculations.

Performance Tips

5.1   Sometimes performance considerations far outweigh clarity considerations.

5.2   Passing arrays by reference makes sense for performance reasons. If arrays were passed by value, a copy of each element would be passed. For large, frequently passed arrays, this would waste time and would consume considerable storage for the copies of the arrays.

5.3   Often, the simplest algorithms perform poorly. Their virtue is that they are easy to write, test and debug. More complex algorithms are often needed to realize maximum performance.

Testing and Debugging Tip

5.1   With call-by-value, changes to the called method's copy do not affect the original variable's value in the calling method. This prevents the accidental side effects that so greatly hinder the development of correct and reliable software systems.

Self-Review Exercises

5.1 Answer each of the following:
a) Lists and tables of values are stored in _____.
b) The elements of an array are related by the fact that they have the same _____ and _____.
c) The number used to refer to a particular element of an array is called its _____.
d) The process of placing the elements of an array in order is called _____ the array.
e) The process of determining if an array contains a certain key value is called _____ the array.
f) An array that uses two subscripts is referred to as a _____ array.

5.2 State whether the following are true or false. If the answer is false, explain why.
a) An array can store many different types of values.
b) An array subscript should normally be of data type **float**.
c) An individual array element that is passed to a method and modified in that method will contain the modified value when the called method completes execution.

5.3 Answer the following questions regarding an array called **fractions**.
a) Define a constant variable **arraySize** initialized to 10.
b) Declare an array with **arraySize** elements of type **float** and initialize the elements to **0**.
c) Name the fourth element from the beginning of the array.
d) Refer to array element 4.
e) Assign the value **1.667** to array element 9.
f) Assign the value **3.333** to the seventh element of the array.
g) Sum all the elements of the array using a **for** repetition structure. Define the integer variable **x** as a control variable for the loop.

5.4 Answer the following questions regarding an array called **table**.
a) Declare the array to be an integer array and to have 3 rows and 3 columns. Assume the constant variable **arraySize** has been defined to be 3.
b) How many elements does the array contain?
c) Use a **for** repetition structure to initialize each element of the array to the sum of its subscripts. Assume the integer variables **x** and **y** are declared as control variables.

5.5 Find the error in each of the following program segments and correct the error.
a) `arraySize = 10;  // arraySize was declared final`
b) Assume `int b[] = new int[ 10 ];`
```
for ( int i = 0; i <= b.length; i++ )
   b[ i ] = 1;
```
c) Assume `int a[][] = { { 1, 2 }, { 3, 4 } };`
```
a[ 1, 1 ] = 5;
```

Answers to Self-Review Exercises

5.1 a) Arrays. b) Name, type. c) Subscript. d) Sorting. e) Searching. f) Double-subscripted.

5.2 a) False. An array can store only values of the same type.
b) False. An array subscript should normally be an integer or an integer expression.

c) False for individual primitive data type elements of an array because they are passed call-by-value. If an entire array is passed to a method, then any modifications to the array elements will be reflected in the original. Also, an individual element of a class type passed to a method is passed call-by-reference and changes to the object will be reflected in the original array element.

5.3   a) `final int arraySize = 10;`
       b) `float fractions[] = new float[ arraySize ];`
       c) `fractions[ 3 ]`
       d) `fractions[ 4 ]`
       e) `fractions[ 9 ] = 1.667;`
       f) `fractions[ 6 ] = 3.333;`
       g) `float total = 0;`
```
for ( int x = 0; x < fractions.length; x++ )
   total += fractions[ x ];
```

5.4   a) `int table[][] = new int[ arraySize ][ arraySize ];`
       b) Nine.
       c)
```
for ( int x = 0; x < table.length; x++ )
   for ( int y = 0; y < table[ x ].length; y++ )
      table[ x ][ y ] = x + y;
```

5.5   a) Error: Assigning a value to a constant variable using an assignment statement.
         Correction: Assign a value to the constant variable in a **final int arraySize** declaration.
       b) Error: Referencing an array element outside the bounds of the array (**b[10]**).
         Correction: Change the **<=** operator to **<**.
       c) Error: Array subscripting done incorrectly.
         Correction: Change the statement to **a[1][1] = 5;**

Exercises

5.6 Fill in the blanks in each of the following:
    a) Java stores lists of values in _____.
    b) The elements of an array are related by the fact that they _____.
    c) When referring to an array element, the position number contained within brackets is called a _____.
    d) The names of the four elements of array **p** are _____, _____, _____, and _____.
    e) Naming an array, stating its type, and specifying the number of elements in the array is called _____ the array.
    f) The process of placing the elements of an array into either ascending or descending order is called _____.
    g) In a double-subscripted array, the first subscript identifies the _____ of an element, and the second subscript identifies the _____ of an element.
    h) An m-by-n array contains _____ rows, _____ columns, and _____ elements.
    i) The name of the element in row 3 and column 5 of array **d** is _____.

5.7 State which of the following are true and which are false; for those that are false, explain why they are false.
    a) To refer to a particular location or element within an array, we specify the name of the array and the value of the particular element.

b) An array declaration reserves space for the array.

c) To indicate that 100 locations should be reserved for integer array **p**, the programmer writes the declaration

```
p[100];
```

d) A Java program that initializes the elements of a 15-element array to zero must contain at least one **for** statement.

e) A Java program that totals the elements of a double-subscripted array must contain nested **for** statements.

5.8 Write Java statements to accomplish each of the following:

a) Display the value of the seventh element of character array **f**.

b) Initialize each of the 5 elements of single-subscripted integer array **g** to **8**.

c) Total the elements of floating-point array **c** of 100 elements.

d) Copy 11- element array **a** into the first portion of array **b** containing 34 elements.

e) Determine and print the smallest and largest values contained in 99-element floating-point array **w**.

5.9 Consider a 2-by-3 integer array **t**.

a) Write a declaration for **t**.

b) How many rows does **t** have?

c) How many columns does **t** have?

d) How many elements does **t** have?

e) Write the names of all the elements in the second row of **t**.

f) Write the names of all the elements in the third column of **t**.

g) Write a single statement that sets the element of **t** in row 1 and column 2 to zero.

h) Write a series of statements that initializes each element of **t** to zero. Do not use a repetition structure.

i) Write a nested **for** structure that initializes each element of **t** to zero.

j) Write a statement that inputs the values for the elements of **t** from the terminal.

k) Write a series of statements that determines and prints the smallest value in array **t**.

l) Write a statement that displays the elements of the first row of **t**.

m) Write a statement that totals the elements of the fourth column of **t**.

n) Write a series of statements that prints the array **t** in neat, tabular format. List the column subscripts as headings across the top and list the row subscripts at the left of each row.

5.10 Use a single-subscripted array to solve the following problem. A company pays its salespeople on a commission basis. The salespeople receive $200 per week plus 9 percent of their gross sales for that week. For example, a salesperson who grosses $5000 in sales in a week receives $200 plus 9 percent of $5000, or a total of $650. Write a program (using an array of counters) that determines how many of the salespeople earned salaries in each of the following ranges (assume that each salesperson's salary is truncated to an integer amount):

a) $200-$299

b) $300-$399

c) $400-$499

d) $500-$599

e) $600-$699

f) $700-$799

g) $800-$899

h) $900-$999

i) $1000 and over

5.11   The bubble sort presented in Fig. 5.13 is inefficient for large arrays. Make the following simple modifications to improve the performance of the bubble sort.

a) After the first pass, the largest number is guaranteed to be in the highest-numbered element of the array; after the second pass, the two highest numbers are "in place," and so on. Instead of making nine comparisons on every pass, modify the bubble sort to make eight comparisons on the second pass, seven on the third pass, and so on.

b) The data in the array may already be in the proper order or near-proper order, so why make nine passes if fewer will suffice? Modify the sort to check at the end of each pass if any swaps have been made. If none has been made, then the data must already be in the proper order, so the program should terminate. If swaps have been made, then at least one more pass is needed.

5.12   Write statements that perform the following single-subscripted array operations:

a) Set the 10 elements of integer array **counts** to zeros.

b) Add 1 to each of the 15 elements of integer array **bonus**.

c) Print the 5 values of integer array **bestScores** in column format.

5.13   Use a single-subscripted array to solve the following problem. Read in 20 numbers, each of which is between 10 and 100, inclusive. As each number is read, print it only if it is not a duplicate of a number already read. Provide for the "worst case" in which all 20 numbers are different. Use the smallest possible array to solve this problem.

5.14   Label the elements of 3-by-5 double-subscripted array **sales** to indicate the order in which they are set to zero by the following program segment:

```
for ( int row = 0; row < sales.length; row++ )
    for ( int col = 0; col < sales[ row ].length; col++ )
        sales[ row ][ col ] = 0;
```

5.15   Write a program to simulate the rolling of two dice. The program should use **Math.random** to roll the first die, and should use **Math.random** again to roll the second die. The sum of the two values should then be calculated. *Note:* Since each die can show an integer value from 1 to 6, the sum of the values will vary from 2 to 12 with 7 being the most frequent sum and 2 and 12 being the least frequent sums. Figure 5.19 shows the 36 possible combinations of the two dice. Your program should roll the dice 36,000 times. Use a single-subscripted array to tally the numbers of times each possible sum appears. Print the results in a tabular format. Also, determine if the totals are reasonable, i.e., there are six ways to roll a 7, so approximately one sixth of all the rolls should be 7.

	1	2	3	4	5	6
1	2	3	4	5	6	7
2	3	4	5	6	7	8
3	4	5	6	7	8	9
4	5	6	7	8	9	10
5	6	7	8	9	10	11
6	7	8	9	10	11	12

Fig. 5.19 The 36 possible outcomes of rolling two dice.

5.16   What does the following program do?

```
1   // Exercise 5.16
2   // What does this program do?
3   import java.awt.*;
4   import java.applet.Applet;
5
6   public class MysteryClass extends Applet {
7      int result;
8
9      public void start()
10     {
11        int a[] = { 1, 2, 3, 4, 5, 6, 7, 8, 9, 10 };
12
13        result = whatIsThis( a, a.length );
14     }
15
16     public void paint( Graphics g )
17     {
18        g.drawString( "Result is " + result, 25, 25 );
19     }
20
21     public int whatIsThis( int b[], int size )
22     {
23        if ( size == 1 )
24           return b[0];
25        else
26           return b[ size - 1 ] + whatIsThis( b, size - 1 );
27     }
28  }
```

5.17   Write a program that runs 1000 games of craps and answers the following questions:

a) How many games are won on the first roll, second roll, ..., twentieth roll, and after the twentieth roll?

b) How many games are lost on the first roll, second roll, ..., twentieth roll, and after the twentieth roll?

c) What are the chances of winning at craps? (*Note:* You should discover that craps is one of the fairest casino games. What do you suppose this means?)

d) What is the average length of a game of craps?

e) Do the chances of winning improve with the length of the game?

5.18   (*Airline Reservations System*) A small airline has just purchased a computer for its new automated reservations system. You have been asked to program the new system. You are to write a program to assign seats on each flight of the airline's only plane (capacity: 10 seats).

Your program should display the following menu of alternatives:

```
Please type 1 for "smoking"
Please type 2 for "nonsmoking"
```

If the person types 1, then your program should assign a seat in the smoking section (seats 1-5). If the person types 2, then your program should assign a seat in the nonsmoking section (seats 6-10). Your program should then print a boarding pass indicating the person's seat number and whether it is in the smoking or nonsmoking section of the plane.

Use a single-subscripted array to represent the seating chart of the plane. Initialize all the elements of the array to 0 to indicate that all seats are empty. As each seat is assigned, set the corresponding elements of the array to 1 to indicate that the seat is no longer available.

Your program should, of course, never assign a seat that has already been assigned. When the smoking section is full, your program should ask the person if it is acceptable to be placed in the nonsmoking section (and vice versa). If yes, then make the appropriate seat assignment. If no, then print the message **"Next flight leaves in 3 hours."**

5.19   What does the following program do?

```
1   // Exercise 5.19
2   // What does this program do?
3   import java.awt.*;
4   import java.applet.Applet;
5
6   public class MysteryClass extends Applet {
7       int yPosition;
8       int a[] = { 1, 2, 3, 4, 5, 6, 7, 8, 9, 10 };
9
10      public void paint( Graphics g )
11      {
12          yPosition = 25;
13          someMethod( a, 0, g );
14      }
15
16      public void someMethod( int b[], int x, Graphics g )
17      {
18          if ( x < b.length ) {
19              someMethod( b, x + 1, g );
20              g.drawString( String.valueOf( b[ x ] ),
21                          25, yPosition );
22              yPosition += 15;
23          }
24      }
25  }
```

5.20   Use a double-subscripted array to solve the following problem. A company has four salespeople (1 to 4) who sell five different products (1 to 5). Once a day, each salesperson passes in a slip for each different type of product sold. Each slip contains:

1. The salesperson number

2. The product number

3. The total dollar value of that product sold that day

Thus, each salesperson passes in between 0 and 5 sales slips per day. Assume that the information from all of the slips for last month is available. Write a program that will read all this information for last month's sales, and summarize the total sales by salesperson by product. All totals should be stored in the double-subscripted array **sales**. After processing all the information for last month, print the results in tabular format with each of the columns representing a particular salesperson and each of the rows representing a particular product. Cross total each row to get the total sales of each product for last month; cross total each column to get the total sales by salesperson for last month. Your tabular printout should include these cross totals to the right of the totaled rows and to the bottom of the totaled columns.

5.21   (*Turtle Graphics*) The Logo language, which is popular among young computer users, made the concept of *turtle graphics* famous. Imagine a mechanical turtle that walks around the room under the control of a Java program. The turtle holds a pen in one of two positions, up or down. While the pen is down, the turtle traces out shapes as it moves; while the pen is up, the turtle moves about freely without writing anything. In this problem you will simulate the operation of the turtle and create a computerized sketchpad as well.

Use a 20-by-20 array **floor** which is initialized to zeros. Read commands from an array that contains them. Keep track of the current position of the turtle at all times and whether the pen is currently up or down. Assume that the turtle always starts at position 0,0 of the floor with its pen up. The set of turtle commands your program must process are as follows:

Command	Meaning
1	Pen up
2	Pen down
3	Turn right
4	Turn left
5,10	Move forward 10 spaces (or a number other than 10)
6	Print the 20-by-20 array
9	End of data (sentinel)

Suppose that the turtle is somewhere near the center of the floor. The following "program" would draw and print a 12-by 12-square leaving the pen in the up position:

```
2
5,12
3
5,12
3
5,12
3
5,12
1
6
9
```

As the turtle moves with the pen down, set the appropriate elements of array **floor** to **1**s. When the **6** command (print) is given, wherever there is a **1** in the array, display an asterisk, or some other character you choose. Wherever there is a zero, display a blank. Write a program to implement the turtle graphics capabilities discussed here. Write several turtle graphics programs to draw interesting shapes. Add other commands to increase the power of your turtle graphics language.

5.22   (*Knight's Tour*) One of the more interesting puzzlers for chess buffs is the Knight's Tour problem, originally proposed by the mathematician Euler. The question is this: Can the chess piece called the knight move around an empty chessboard and touch each of the 64 squares once and only once? We study this intriguing problem in depth here.

The knight makes L-shaped moves (over two in one direction and then over one in a perpendicular direction). Thus, from a square in the middle of an empty chessboard, the knight can make eight different moves (numbered 0 through 7) as shown in Fig. 5.20.

    a)   Draw an 8-by-8 chessboard on a sheet of paper and attempt a Knight's Tour by hand. Put a **1** in the first square you move to, a **2** in the second square, a **3** in the third, etc. Before starting the tour, estimate how far you think you will get, remembering that a full tour consists of 64 moves. How far did you get? Was this close to your estimate?

b) Now let us develop a program that will move the knight around a chessboard. The board is represented by an 8-by-8 double-subscripted array **board**. Each of the squares is initialized to zero. We describe each of the eight possible moves in terms of both their horizontal and vertical components. For example, a move of type 0 as shown in Fig. 5.20 consists of moving two squares horizontally to the right and one square vertically upward. Move 2 consists of moving one square horizontally to the left and two squares vertically upward. Horizontal moves to the left and vertical moves upward are indicated with negative numbers. The eight moves may be described by two single-subscripted arrays, **horizontal** and **vertical**, as follows:

```
horizontal[ 0 ] = 2
horizontal[ 1 ] = 1
horizontal[ 2 ] = -1
horizontal[ 3 ] = -2
horizontal[ 4 ] = -2
horizontal[ 5 ] = -1
horizontal[ 6 ] = 1
horizontal[ 7 ] = 2

vertical[ 0 ] = -1
vertical[ 1 ] = -2
vertical[ 2 ] = -2
vertical[ 3 ] = -1
vertical[ 4 ] = 1
vertical[ 5 ] = 2
vertical[ 6 ] = 2
vertical[ 7 ] = 1
```

Fig. 5.20 The eight possible moves of the knight.

Let the variables **currentRow** and **currentColumn** indicate the row and column of the knight's current position. To make a move of type **moveNumber**, where **moveNumber** is between 0 and 7, your program uses the statements

```
currentRow += vertical[ moveNumber ];
currentColumn += horizontal[ moveNumber ];
```

Keep a counter that varies from **1** to **64**. Record the latest count in each square the knight moves to. Test each potential move to see if the knight already visited that square. Test every potential move to ensure that the knight does not land off the chessboard. Write a program to move the knight around the chessboard. Run the program. How many moves did the knight make?

c) After attempting to write and run a Knight's Tour program, you have probably developed some valuable insights. We will use these to develop a *heuristic* (or strategy) for moving the knight. Heuristics do not guarantee success, but a carefully developed heuristic greatly improves the chance of success. You may have observed that the outer squares are more troublesome than the squares nearer the center of the board. In fact, the most troublesome, or inaccessible, squares are the four corners.

Intuition may suggest that you should attempt to move the knight to the most troublesome squares first and leave open those that are easiest to get to so when the board gets congested near the end of the tour there will be a greater chance of success.

We may develop an "accessibility heuristic" by classifying each of the squares according to how accessible they are, and then always moving the knight to the square (within the knight's L-shaped moves, of course) that is most inaccessible. We label a double-subscripted array **accessibility** with numbers indicating from how many squares each particular square is accessible. On a blank chessboard, each center square is rated as **8**, each corner square is rated as **2**, and the other squares have accessibility numbers of **3**, **4**, or **6** as follows:

```
2  3  4  4  4  4  3  2
3  4  6  6  6  6  4  3
4  6  8  8  8  8  6  4
4  6  8  8  8  8  6  4
4  6  8  8  8  8  6  4
4  6  8  8  8  8  6  4
3  4  6  6  6  6  4  3
2  3  4  4  4  4  3  2
```

Write a version of the Knight's Tour using the accessibility heuristic. The knight should always move to the square with the lowest accessibility number. In case of a tie, the knight may move to any of the tied squares. Therefore, the tour may begin in any of the four corners. (*Note:* As the knight moves around the chessboard, your program should reduce the accessibility numbers as more squares become occupied. In this way, at any given time during the tour, each available square's accessibility number will remain equal to precisely the number of squares from which that square may be reached.) Run this version of your program. Did you get a full tour? Modify the program to run 64 tours, one starting from each square of the chessboard. How many full tours did you get?

d) Write a version of the Knight's Tour program which, when encountering a tie between two or more squares, decides what square to choose by looking ahead to those squares reachable from the "tied" squares. Your program should move to the square for which the next move would arrive at a square with the lowest accessibility number.

5.23   (*Knight's Tour: Brute Force Approaches*) In Exercise 5.22 we developed a solution to the Knight's Tour problem. The approach used, called the "accessibility heuristic," generates many solutions and executes efficiently.

As computers continue increasing in power, we will be able to solve more problems with sheer computer power and relatively unsophisticated algorithms. Let us call this approach "brute force" problem solving.

a) Use random number generation to enable the knight to walk around the chess board (in its legitimate L-shaped moves, of course) at random. Your program should run one tour and print the final chessboard. How far did the knight get?

b) Most likely, the preceding program produced a relatively short tour. Now modify your program to attempt 1000 tours. Use a single-subscripted array to keep track of the number of tours of each length. When your program finishes attempting the 1000 tours, it should print this information in neat tabular format. What was the best result?

c) Most likely, the preceding program gave you some "respectable" tours but no full tours. Now "pull all the stops out" and simply let your program run until it produces a full tour. (*Caution:* This version of the program could run for hours on a powerful computer.) Once again, keep a table of the number of tours of each length, and print this table when the first full tour is found. How many tours did your program attempt before producing a full tour? How much time did it take?

d) Compare the brute force version of the Knight's Tour with the accessibility heuristic version. Which required a more careful study of the problem? Which algorithm was more difficult to develop? Which required more computer power? Could we be certain (in advance) of obtaining a full tour with the accessibility heuristic approach? Could we be certain (in advance) of obtaining a full tour with the brute force approach? Argue the pros and cons of brute force problem solving in general.

5.24   (*Eight Queens*) Another puzzler for chess buffs is the Eight Queens problem. Simply stated: Is it possible to place eight queens on an empty chessboard so that no queen is "attacking" any other, i.e., no two queens are in the same row, the same column, or along the same diagonal? Use the thinking developed in Exercise 5.22 to formulate a heuristic for solving the Eight Queens problem. Run your program. (*Hint:* It is possible to assign a value to each square of the chessboard indicating how many squares of an empty chessboard are "eliminated" if a queen is placed in that square. Each of the corners would be assigned the value 22, as in Fig. 5.21.) Once these "elimination numbers" are placed in all 64 squares, an appropriate heuristic might be: Place the next queen in the square with the smallest elimination number. Why is this strategy intuitively appealing?

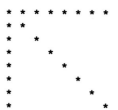

Fig. 5.21 The 22 squares eliminated by placing a queen in the upper left corner.

5.25   (*Eight Queens: Brute Force Approaches*) In this exercise you will develop several brute force approaches to solving the Eight Queens problem introduced in Exercise 5.24.

   a) Solve the Eight Queens exercise, using the random brute force technique developed in Exercise 5.23.

   b) Use an exhaustive technique, i.e., try all possible combinations of eight queens on the chessboard.

   c) Why do you suppose the exhaustive brute force approach may not be appropriate for solving the Knight's Tour problem?

   d) Compare and contrast the random brute force and exhaustive brute force approaches.

5.26   (*Knight's Tour: Closed Tour Test*) In the Knight's Tour, a full tour occurs when the knight makes 64 moves touching each square of the chess board once and only once. A closed tour occurs when the 64th move is one move away from the square in which the knight started the tour. Modify the program you wrote in Exercise 5.22 to test for a closed tour if a full tour has occurred.

5.27   (*The Sieve of Eratosthenes*) A prime integer is any integer that is evenly divisible only by itself and 1. The Sieve of Eratosthenes is a method of finding prime numbers. It operates as follows:

   1) Create an array with all elements initialized to 1 (true). Array elements with prime subscripts will remain 1. All other array elements will eventually be set to zero.

   2) Starting with array subscript 2 (subscript 1 must be prime), every time an array element is found whose value is 1, loop through the remainder of the array and set to zero every element whose subscript is a multiple of the subscript for the element with value 1. For array subscript 2, all elements beyond 2 in the array that are multiples of 2 will be set to zero (subscripts 4, 6, 8, 10, etc.); for array subscript 3, all elements beyond 3 in the array that are multiples of 3 will be set to zero (subscripts 6, 9, 12, 15, etc.); and so on.

When this process is complete, the array elements that are still set to one indicate that the subscript is a prime number. These subscripts can then be printed. Write a program that uses an array of 1000 elements to determine and print the prime numbers between 1 and 999. Ignore element 0 of the array.

5.28   (*Bucket Sort*) A bucket sort begins with a single-subscripted array of positive integers to be sorted, and a double-subscripted array of integers with rows subscripted from 0 to 9 and columns subscripted from 0 to n - 1 where n is the number of values in the array to be sorted. Each row of the double-subscripted array is referred to as a bucket. Write a method **bucketSort** that takes an integer array as an argument and performs as follows:

   1) Place each value of the single-subscripted array into a row of the bucket array based on the value's ones digit. For example, 97 is placed in row 7, 3 is placed in row 3, and 100 is placed in row 0. This is called a "distribution pass."

   2) Loop through the bucket array row-by-row and copy the values back to the original array. This is called a "gathering pass." The new order of the preceding values in the single-subscripted array is 100, 3, and 97.

   3) Repeat this process for each subsequent digit position (tens, hundreds, thousands, etc.).

On the second pass, 100 is placed in row 0, 3 is placed in row 0 (because 3 has no tens digit), and 97 is placed in row 9. After the gathering pass, the order of the values in the single-subscripted array is 100, 3, and 97. On the third pass, 100 is placed in row 1, 3 is placed in row zero and 97 is placed in row zero (after the 3). After the last gathering pass, the original array is now in sorted order.

   Note that the double-subscripted array of buckets is ten times the size of the integer array being sorted. This sorting technique provides better performance than a bubble sort, but requires much more memory. The bubble sort requires space for only one additional element of data. This is an example of the space-time trade-off: The bucket sort uses more memory than the bubble sort, but performs better. This version of the bucket sort requires copying all the data back to the original array on each pass. Another possibility is to create a second double-subscripted bucket array and repeatedly swap the data between the two bucket arrays.

Recursion Exercises

5.29   (*Selection Sort*) A selection sort searches an array looking for the smallest element in the array. Then, the smallest element is swapped with the first element of the array. The process is repeated for the subarray beginning with the second element of the array. Each pass of the array results in one element being placed in its proper location. This sort performs comparably to the bubble sort—for an array of *n* elements, *n* - 1 passes must be made, and for each subarray, *n* - 1 comparisons must be made to find the smallest value. When the subarray being processed contains one element, the array is sorted. Write recursive method **selectionSort** to perform this algorithm.

5.30   (*Palindromes*) A palindrome is a string that is spelled the same way forwards and backwards. Some examples of palindromes are: "radar," "able was i ere i saw elba," and (if blanks are ignored) "a man a plan a canal panama." Write a recursive method **testPalindrome** that returns 1 if the string stored in the array is a palindrome, and 0 otherwise. The method should ignore spaces and punctuation in the string.

5.31   (*Linear Search*) Modify Fig. 5.14 to use recursive method **linearSearch** to perform a linear search of the array. The method should receive an integer array and the size of the array as arguments. If the search key is found, return the array subscript; otherwise, return –1.

5.32   (*Binary Search*) Modify the program of Fig. 5.15 to use a recursive method **binarySearch** to perform the binary search of the array. The method should receive an integer array and the starting subscript and ending subscript as arguments. If the search key is found, return the array subscript; otherwise, return –1.

5.33   (*Eight Queens*) Modify the Eight Queens program you created in Exercise 5.24 to solve the problem recursively.

5.34   (*Print an array*) Write a recursive method **printArray** that takes an array and the size of the array as arguments and returns nothing. The method should stop processing and return when it receives an array of size zero.

5.35   (*Print a string backwards*) Write a recursive method **stringReverse** that takes a character array containing a string as an argument, prints the string backwards, and returns nothing. The method should stop processing and return when the terminating null character is encountered.

5.36   (*Find the minimum value in an array*) Write a recursive method **recursiveMinimum** that takes an integer array and the array size as arguments and returns the smallest element of the array. The method should stop processing and return when it receives an array of 1 element.

5.37   (*Quicksort*) In the examples and exercises of this chapter, we discussed the sorting techniques of bubble sort, bucket sort, and selection sort. We now present the recursive sorting technique called Quicksort. The basic algorithm for a single-subscripted array of values is as follows:

1) *Partitioning Step:* Take the first element of the unsorted array and determine its final location in the sorted array, i.e., all values to the left of the element in the array are less than the element, and all values to the right of the element in the array are greater than the element. We now have one element in its proper location and two unsorted subarrays.
2) *Recursive Step:* Perform step 1 on each unsorted subarray.

Each time step 1 is performed on a subarray, another element is placed in its final location of the sorted array, and two unsorted subarrays are created. When a subarray consists of one element, it must be sorted, therefore that element is in its final location.

The basic algorithm seems simple enough, but how do we determine the final position of the first element of each subarray. As an example, consider the following set of values (the element in bold is the partitioning element—it will be placed in its final location in the sorted array):

37   2   6   4   89   8   10   12   68   45

1) Starting from the rightmost element of the array, compare each element to **37** until an element less than **37** is found, then swap **37** and that element. The first element less than **37** is 12, so **37** and 12 are swapped. The new array is:

12   2   6   4   89   8   10   **37**   68   45

Element 12 is in italic to indicate that it was just swapped with **37**.

2) Starting from the left of the array, but beginning with the element after 12, compare each element to **37** until an element greater than **37** is found, then swap **37** and that element. The first element greater than **37** is 89, so **37** and 89 are swapped. The new array is:

12   2   6   4   **37**   8   10   *89*   68   45

3) Starting from the right, but beginning with the element before 89, compare each element to **37** until an element less than **37** is found, then swap **37** and that element. The first element less than **37** is 10, so **37** and 10 are swapped. The new array is:

12   2   6   4   *10*   8   **37**   89   68   45

4) Starting from the left, but beginning with the element after 10, compare each element to **37** until an element greater than **37** is found, then swap **37** and that element. There are no more elements greater than **37**, so when we compare **37** to itself we know that **37** has been placed in its final location of the sorted array.

Once the partition has been applied on the above array, there are two unsorted subarrays. The subarray with values less than 37 contains 12, 2, 6, 4, 10, and 8. The subarray with values greater than 37 contains 89, 68, and 45. The sort continues with both subarrays being partitioned in the same manner as the original array.

Based on the preceding discussion, write recursive method **quickSort** to sort a single-subscripted integer array. The method should receive as arguments an integer array, a starting subscript, and an ending subscript. Method **partition** should be called by **quickSort** to perform the partitioning step.

5.38   (*Maze Traversal*) The following grid of #s and dots (.) is a double-subscripted array representation of a maze.

In the preceding double-subscripted array, the **#**s represent the walls of the maze and the dots represent squares in the possible paths through the maze. Moves can only be made to a location in the array that contains a dot.

There is a simple algorithm for walking through a maze that guarantees finding the exit (assuming there is an exit). If there is not an exit, you will arrive at the starting location again. Place your right hand on the wall to your right and begin walking forward. Never remove your hand from the wall. If the maze turns to the right, you follow the wall to the right. As long as you do not remove your hand from the wall, eventually you will arrive at the exit of the maze. There may be a shorter path than the one you have taken, but you are guaranteed to get out of the maze if you follow the algorithm.

Write recursive method **mazeTraverse** to walk through the maze. The method should receive as arguments a 12-by-12 character array representing the maze, and the starting location of the maze. As **mazeTraverse** attempts to locate the exit from the maze, it should place the character **X** in each square in the path. The method should display the maze after each move so the user can watch as the maze is solved.

5.39   (*Generating Mazes Randomly*) Write a method **mazeGenerator** that takes as an argument a double-subscripted 12-by-12 character array and randomly produces a maze. The method should also provide the starting and ending locations of the maze. Try your method **mazeTraverse** from Exercise 5.38 using several randomly generated mazes.

5.40   (*Mazes of Any Size*) Generalize methods **mazeTraverse** and **mazeGenerator** of Exercises 5.38 and 5.39 to process mazes of any width and height.

5.41   (*Simulation: The Tortoise and the Hare*) In this problem you will recreate one of the truly great moments in history, namely the classic race of the tortoise and the hare. You will use random number generation to develop a simulation of this memorable event.

Our contenders begin the race at "square 1" of 70 squares. Each square represents a possible position along the race course. The finish line is at square 70. The first contender to reach or pass square 70 is rewarded with a pail of fresh carrots and lettuce. The course weaves its way up the side of a slippery mountain, so occasionally the contenders lose ground.

There is a clock that ticks once per second. With each tick of the clock, your program should adjust the position of the animals according to the following rules:

Animal	Move type	Percentage of the time	Actual move
Tortoise	Fast plod	50%	3 squares to the right
	Slip	20%	6 squares to the left
	Slow plod	30%	1 square to the right
Hare	Sleep	20%	No move at all
	Big hop	20%	9 squares to the right
	Big slip	10%	12 squares to the left
	Small hop	30%	1 square to the right
	Small slip	20%	2 squares to the left

Use variables to keep track of the positions of the animals (i.e., position numbers are 1-70). Start each animal at position 1 (i.e., the "starting gate"). If an animal slips left before square 1, move the animal back to square 1.

Generate the percentages in the preceding table by producing a random integer, i, in the range $1 \leq i \leq 10$. For the tortoise, perform a "fast plod" when $1 \leq i \leq 5$, a "slip" when $6 \leq i \leq 7$, or a "slow plod" when $8 \leq i \leq 10$. Use a similar technique to move the hare.

Begin the race by printing

```
BANG !!!!!
AND THEY'RE OFF !!!!!
```

Then, for each tick of the clock (i.e., each repetition of a loop), print a 70-position line showing the letter **T** in the position of the tortoise and the letter **H** in the position of the hare. Occasionally, the contenders will land on the same square. In this case, the tortoise bites the hare and your program should print **OUCH!!!** beginning at that position. All print positions other than the **T**, the **H**, or the **OUCH!!!** (in case of a tie) should be blank.

After each line is printed, test if either animal has reached or passed square 70. If so, then print the winner and terminate the simulation. If the tortoise wins, print **TORTOISE WINS!!! YAY!!!** If the hare wins, print **Hare wins. Yuch.** If both animals win on the same tick of the clock, you may want to favor the turtle (the "underdog"), or you may want to print **It's a tie**. If neither animal wins, perform the loop again to simulate the next tick of the clock. When you are ready to run your program, assemble a group of fans to watch the race. You'll be amazed at how involved your audience gets!

Special Section: Building Your Own Computer

In the next several problems, we take a temporary diversion away from the world of high-level language programming. We "peel open" a computer and look at its internal structure. We introduce machine language programming and write several machine language programs. To make this an especially valuable experience, we then build a computer (through the technique of software-based *simulation*) on which you can execute your machine language programs!

5.42 (*Machine Language Programming*) Let us create a computer we will call the Simpletron. As its name implies, it is a simple machine, but, as we will soon see, a powerful one as well. The Simpletron runs programs written in the only language it directly understands, that is, Simpletron Machine Language, or SML for short.

The Simpletron contains an *accumulator*—a "special register" in which information is put before the Simpletron uses that information in calculations or examines it in various ways. All information in the Simpletron is handled in terms of *words*. A word is a signed four-digit decimal number such as **+3364**, **-1293**, **+0007**, **-0001**, etc. The Simpletron is equipped with a 100-word memory, and these words are referenced by their location numbers **00**, **01**, …, **99**.

Before running an SML program, we must *load* or place the program into memory. The first instruction (or statement) of every SML program is always placed in location **00**. The simulator will start executing at this location.

Each instruction written in SML occupies one word of the Simpletron's memory (and hence instructions are signed four-digit decimal numbers). We shall assume that the sign of an SML instruction is always plus, but the sign of a data word may be either plus or minus. Each location in the Simpletron's memory may contain either an instruction, a data value used by a program, or an unused (and hence undefined) area of memory. The first two digits of each SML instruction are the *operation code* specifying the operation to be performed. SML operation codes are summarized in Fig. 5.22.

Operation code	Meaning
Input/output operations:	
`static final int READ = 10;`	Read a word from the terminal into a specific location in memory.
`static final int WRITE = 11;`	Write a word from a specific location in memory to the terminal.
Load/store operations:	
`static final int LOAD = 20;`	Load a word from a specific location in memory into the accumulator.
`static final int STORE = 21;`	Store a word from the accumulator into a specific location in memory.
Arithmetic operations:	
`static final int ADD = 30;`	Add a word from a specific location in memory to the word in the accumulator (leave result in accumulator).
`static final int SUBTRACT = 31;`	Subtract a word from a specific location in memory from the word in the accumulator (leave result in accumulator).
`static final int DIVIDE = 32;`	Divide a word from a specific location in memory into the word in the accumulator (leave result in accumulator).
`static final int MULTIPLY = 33;`	Multiply a word from a specific location in memory by the word in the accumulator (leave result in accumulator).
Transfer of control operations:	
`static final int BRANCH = 40;`	Branch to a specific location in memory.
`static final int BRANCHNEG = 41;`	Branch to a specific location in memory if the accumulator is negative.
`static final int BRANCHZERO = 42;`	Branch to a specific location in memory if the accumulator is zero.
`static final int HALT = 43;`	Halt—the program has completed its task.

Fig. 5.22 Simpletron Machine Language (SML) operation codes.

The last two digits of an SML instruction are the *operand*—the address of the memory location containing the word to which the operation applies. Let's consider several simple SML programs.

The first SML program (Example 1) reads two numbers from the keyboard and computes and prints their sum. The instruction **+1007** reads the first number from the keyboard and places it into location **07** (which has been initialized to zero). Then instruction **+1008** reads the next number into location **08**. The *load* instruction, **+2007**, puts the first number into the accumulator, and the *add* instruction, **+3008**, adds the second number to the number in the accumulator. *All SML arithmetic* *instructions leave their results in the accumulator.* The *store* instruction, **+2109**, places the result back into memory location **09** from which the *write* instruction, **+1109**, takes the number and prints it (as a signed four-digit decimal number). The *halt* instruction, **+4300**, terminates execution.

Example 1 Location	Number	Instruction
00	+1007	(Read A)
01	+1008	(Read B)
02	+2007	(Load A)
03	+3008	(Add B)
04	+2109	(Store C)
05	+1109	(Write C)
06	+4300	(Halt)
07	+0000	(Variable A)
08	+0000	(Variable B)
09	+0000	(Result C)

Example 2 Location	Number	Instruction
00	+1009	(Read A)
01	+1010	(Read B)
02	+2009	(Load A)
03	+3110	(Subtract B)
04	+4107	(Branch negative to 07)
05	+1109	(Write A)
06	+4300	(Halt)
07	+1110	(Write B)
08	+4300	(Halt)
09	+0000	(Variable A)
10	+0000	(Variable B)

This SML program reads two numbers from the keyboard and determines and prints the larger value. Note the use of the instruction **+4107** as a conditional transfer of control, much the same as Java's `if` statement. Now write SML programs to accomplish each of the following tasks.

    a) Use a sentinel-controlled loop to read 10 positive numbers and compute and print their sum.

    b) Use a counter-controlled loop to read seven numbers, some positive and some negative, and compute and print their average.

    c) Read a series of numbers and determine and print the largest number. The first number read indicates how many numbers should be processed.

5.43   (*A Computer Simulator*) It may at first seem outrageous, but in this problem you are going to build your own computer. No, you will not be soldering components together. Rather, you will use the powerful technique of *software-based simulation* to create an object-oriented *software model* of the Simpletron. You will not be disappointed. Your Simpletron simulator will turn the computer you are using into a Simpletron, and you will actually be able to run, test, and debug the SML programs you wrote in Exercise 5.42. Your Simpletron will be an event-driven applet—you will click a button to execute each SML instruction and you will be able to see the instruction "in action."

When you run your Simpletron simulator, it should begin by displaying:

```
*** Welcome to Simpletron! ***
*** Please enter your program one instruction   ***
*** (or data word) at a time into the input     ***
*** text field. I will display the location     ***
*** number and a question mark (?). You then    ***
*** type the word for that location. Press the  ***
*** Done button to stop entering your program.  ***
```

The program should display an **input** text field in which the user will type each instruction one at a time and a **Done** button for the user to click when the complete SML program has been entered. Simulate the memory of the Simpletron with a single-subscripted array **memory** that has 100 elements. Now assume that the simulator is running, and let us examine the dialog as we enter the program of Example 2 of Exercise 5.42:

```
00 ? +1009
01 ? +1010
02 ? +2009
03 ? +3110
04 ? +4107
05 ? +1109
06 ? +4300
07 ? +1110
08 ? +4300
09 ? +0000
10 ? +0000
```

Your program should use a text field to display the memory location followed by a question mark. Each of the values to the right of a question mark is typed by the user into the **input** text field. When the **Done** button is clicked, the program should display:

```
*** Program loading completed ***
*** Program execution begins   ***
```

The SML program has now been placed (or loaded) in array **memory**. The Simpletron should provide an "**Execute next instruction**" button the user can click to execute each instruction in your SML program. Execution begins with the instruction in location **00** and, like Java, continues sequentially, unless directed to some other part of the program by a transfer of control.

Use the variable **accumulator** to represent the accumulator register. Use the variable **instructionCounter** to keep track of the location in memory that contains the instruction being performed. Use the variable **operationCode** to indicate the operation currently being performed, i.e., the left two digits of the instruction word. Use the variable **operand** to indicate the memory location on which the current instruction operates. Thus, **operand** is the rightmost two digits of the instruction currently being performed. Do not execute instructions directly from memory. Rather, transfer the next instruction to be performed from memory to a variable called **instructionReg-**

ister. Then "pick off" the left two digits and place them in **operationCode**, and "pick off" the right two digits and place them in **operand**. Each of the preceding registers should have a corresponding text field in which its current value can be displayed at all times. When Simpletron begins execution, the special registers are all initialized to 0.

Now let us "walk through" the execution of the first SML instruction, **+1009** in memory location **00**. This is called an *instruction execution cycle.*

The **instructionCounter** tells us the location of the next instruction to be performed. We *fetch* the contents of that location from **memory** by using the Java statement

```
instructionRegister = memory[ instructionCounter ];
```

The operation code and the operand are extracted from the instruction register by the statements

```
operationCode = instructionRegister / 100;
operand = instructionRegister % 100;
```

Now the Simpletron must determine that the operation code is actually a *read* (versus a *write*, a *load*, etc.). A **switch** differentiates among the twelve operations of SML.

In the **switch** structure, the behavior of various SML instructions is simulated as follows (we leave the others to the reader):

read:	Display the prompt "**Enter an integer.**" Enable the **input** text field so a value can be entered by the user. Read the value entered, convert it to an integer, and store it in location **memory[operand]**.
load:	**accumulator = memory[operand];**
add:	**accumulator += memory[operand];**
branch:	We will discuss the branch instructions shortly.
halt:	This instruction prints the message ***** Simpletron execution terminated *****

When the SML program completes execution, the name and contents of each register as well as the complete contents of memory should be displayed. Such a printout is often called a *computer dump* (and, no, a computer dump is not a place where old computers go). To help you program your dump method, a sample dump format is shown in Fig. 5.23. Note that a dump after executing a Simpletron program would show the actual values of instructions and data values at the moment execution terminated. The sample dump assumes the output will be sent to the display screen with a series of **System.out.print** and **System.out.println** method calls. However, we encourage you to experiment with a version that can be displayed on the applet using the **Graphics** method **drawString** or an array of **TextField** objects.

Let us proceed with the execution of our program's first instruction, namely the **+1009** in location **00**. As we have indicated, the **switch** statement simulates this by prompting the user to enter a value into the **input** text field, reading the value, converting the value to an integer and storing it in memory location **memory[operand]**. Because your Simpletron is event driven, it waits for the user to type a value into the **input** text field and press the *Enter key*. The value is then read into location **09**.

At this point, simulation of the first instruction is completed. All that remains is to prepare the Simpletron to execute the next instruction. Since the instruction just performed was not a transfer of control, we need merely increment the instruction counter register as follows:

```
++instructionCounter;
```

This completes the simulated execution of the first instruction. When the user clicks the **Execute next instruction** button, the entire process (i.e., the instruction execution cycle) begins anew with the fetch of the next instruction to be executed.

Now let us consider how the branching instructions—the transfers of control—are simulated. All we need to do is adjust the value in the instruction counter appropriately. Therefore, the unconditional branch instruction (**40**) is simulated within the **switch** as

```
instructionCounter = operand;
```

The conditional "branch if accumulator is zero" instruction is simulated as

```
if ( accumulator == 0 )
    instructionCounter = operand;
```

At this point you should implement your Simpletron simulator and run each of the SML programs you wrote in Exercise 5.42. You may embellish SML with additional features and provide for these in your simulator.

Your simulator should check for various types of errors. During the program loading phase, for example, each number the user types into the Simpletron's **memory** must be in the range **-9999** to **+9999**. Your simulator should test that each number entered is in this range, and, if not, keep prompting the user to reenter the number until the user enters a correct number.

During the execution phase, your simulator should check for various serious errors, such as attempts to divide by zero, attempts to execute invalid operation codes, accumulator overflows (i.e., arithmetic operations resulting in values larger than **+9999** or smaller than **-9999**), and the like. Such serious errors are called *fatal errors*. When a fatal error is detected, your simulator should print an error message such as:

```
*** Attempt to divide by zero ***
*** Simpletron execution abnormally terminated ***
```

and should print a full computer dump in the format we have discussed previously. This will help the user locate the error in the program.

```
REGISTERS:
accumulator          +0000
instructionCounter      00
instructionRegister  +0000
operationCode           00
operand                 00

MEMORY:
        0     1     2     3     4     5     6     7     8     9
 0  +0000 +0000 +0000 +0000 +0000 +0000 +0000 +0000 +0000 +0000
10  +0000 +0000 +0000 +0000 +0000 +0000 +0000 +0000 +0000 +0000
20  +0000 +0000 +0000 +0000 +0000 +0000 +0000 +0000 +0000 +0000
30  +0000 +0000 +0000 +0000 +0000 +0000 +0000 +0000 +0000 +0000
40  +0000 +0000 +0000 +0000 +0000 +0000 +0000 +0000 +0000 +0000
50  +0000 +0000 +0000 +0000 +0000 +0000 +0000 +0000 +0000 +0000
60  +0000 +0000 +0000 +0000 +0000 +0000 +0000 +0000 +0000 +0000
70  +0000 +0000 +0000 +0000 +0000 +0000 +0000 +0000 +0000 +0000
80  +0000 +0000 +0000 +0000 +0000 +0000 +0000 +0000 +0000 +0000
90  +0000 +0000 +0000 +0000 +0000 +0000 +0000 +0000 +0000 +0000
```

Fig. 5.23 A sample dump.

5.44   (*Modifications to the Simpletron Simulator*) In Exercise 5.43, you wrote a software simulation of a computer that executes programs written in Simpletron Machine Language (SML). In this exercise, we propose several modifications and enhancements to the Simpletron Simulator. In Exercises 17.26 and 17.27, we propose building a compiler that converts programs written in a high-level programming language (a variation of Basic) to Simpletron Machine Language. Some of the following modifications and enhancements may be required to execute the programs produced by the compiler.

a) Extend the Simpletron Simulator's memory to contain 1000 memory locations to enable the Simpletron to handle larger programs.

b) Allow the simulator to perform modulus calculations. This requires an additional Simpletron Machine Language instruction.

c) Allow the simulator to perform exponentiation calculations. This requires an additional Simpletron Machine Language instruction.

d) Modify the simulator to use hexadecimal values rather than integer values to represent Simpletron Machine Language instructions.

e) Modify the simulator to allow output of a newline. This requires an additional Simpletron Machine Language instruction.

f) Modify the simulator to process floating-point values in addition to integer values.

g) Modify the simulator to handle string input. Hint: Each Simpletron word can be divided into two groups, each holding a two-digit integer. Each two-digit integer represents the ASCII decimal equivalent of a character. Add a machine language instruction that will input a string and store the string beginning at a specific Simpletron memory location. The first half of the word at that location will be a count of the number of characters in the string (i.e., the length of the string). Each succeeding half-word contains one ASCII character expressed as two decimal digits. The machine language instruction converts each character into its ASCII equivalent and assigns it to a half-word.

h) Modify the simulator to handle output of strings stored in the format of part (g). Hint: Add a machine language instruction that will print a string beginning at a certain Simpletron memory location. The first half of the word at that location is a count of the number of characters in the string (i.e., the length of the string). Each succeeding half-word contains one ASCII character expressed as two decimal digits. The machine language instruction checks the length and prints the string by translating each two-digit number into its equivalent character.

6

Object-Based Programming

Objectives

- To understand encapsulation and data hiding.
- To understand the notions of data abstraction and abstract data types (ADTs).
- To create Java ADTs, namely classes.
- To be able to create, use and destroy objects.
- To be able to control access to object instance variables and methods.
- To appreciate the value of object orientation.
- To understand class variables and class methods.
- To understand the use of the **this** reference.

My object all sublime
I shall achieve in time.
W. S. Gilbert

Is it a world to hide virtues in?
William Shakespeare, Twelfth Night

Your public servants serve you right.
Adlai Stevenson

But what, to serve our private ends,
Forbids the cheating of our friends?
Charles Churchill

This above all: to thine own self be true.
William Shakespeare, Hamlet

Have no friends not equal to yourself.
Confucius

Outline

6.1 Introduction

Now we investigate object orientation in Java in greater depth. Why have we deferred this until now? First, the objects we will build will be composed in part of structured program pieces, so we needed to establish a basis in structured programming with control structures. Second, we wanted to study methods in depth. Third, we wanted to familiarize the reader with arrays which are Java objects.

Through our discussions of object-oriented Java programs in Chapters 1 through 5, we have introduced many of the basic concepts (i.e., "object think") and terminology (i.e., "object speak") of object-oriented programming in Java. In these chapters, we also discussed our program-development methodology: We analyzed many typical problems that required a program—either a Java applet or a Java application—to be built, determined what classes from the Java API were needed to implement the program, determined what instance variables our applet or application needed to have, determined what methods our applet or application needed to have and specified how an object of our class needed to collaborate with objects of Java API classes to accomplish the overall goals of the program.

Let us briefly review some key concepts and terminology of object orientation. OOP *encapsulates* data (*attributes*) and methods (*behaviors*) into *objects;* the data and methods of an object are intimately tied together. Objects have the property of *information hiding.* This means that although objects may know how to communicate with one another across well-defined *interfaces,* objects normally are not allowed to know how other objects are implemented—implementation details are hidden within the objects themselves. Surely it is possible to drive a car effectively without knowing the details of how engines, transmissions and exhaust systems work internally. We will see why information hiding is so crucial to good software engineering.

In C and other *procedural programming languages,* programming tends to be *action-oriented,* whereas in Java-programming is *object-oriented.* In C, the unit of programming is the *function* (and functions are called *methods* in Java). In Java, the unit of programming is the *class* from which objects are eventually *instantiated* (i.e., created). Functions do not disappear in Java; rather they are encapsulated as methods with the data they process within the "walls" of classes.

C programmers concentrate on writing functions. Groups of actions that perform some task are formed into functions and functions are grouped to form programs. Data is certainly important in C, but the view is that data exists primarily in support of the actions that functions perform. The *verbs* in a system requirements document help the C programmer determine the set of functions that will work together to implement the system.

Java programmers concentrate on creating their own *user-defined types* called *classes.* Classes are also referred to as *programmer-defined types.* Each class contains data as well as the set of methods that manipulate the data. The data components of a class are called *instance variables* (these are called *data members* in C++). Just as an instance of a built-in type such as **int** is called a *variable,* an instance of a user-defined type (i.e., a class) is called an *object.* The focus of attention in Java is on objects rather than methods. The *nouns* in a system requirements document help the Java programmer determine an initial set of classes with which to begin the design process. These classes are then used to instantiate objects that will work together to implement the system.

This chapter explains how to create and use objects, a subject we like to call *object-based programming (OBP).* Chapter 7 introduces *inheritance* and *polymorphism*—the two key technologies that enable true *object-oriented programming (OOP).*

Performance Tip 6.1

All Java objects are passed by reference. Only a memory address is passed, not a copy of a possibly large object (as would be the case in a pass by value).

Software Engineering Observation 6.1

It is important to write programs that are understandable and easy to maintain. Change is the rule rather than the exception. Programmers should anticipate that their code will be modified. As we will see, classes facilitate program modifiability.

6.2 Implementing a Time Abstract Data Type with a Class

Figure 6.1 (part 1) contains a simple definition for class **Time**. Our **Time** class definition begins on line 3. The *body* of the class definition is delineated with left and right braces (**{**

and **}**). Our **Time** class definition contains three integer instance variables—**hour**, **minute** and **second**.

The **public** and **private** keywords are called *member access modifiers*. Any instance variable or method declared with the member access modifier **public** is accessible wherever the program has access to an object of class **Time**. Any instance variable or method declared with member access modifier **private** is accessible only to methods of the class. Every instance variable or method definition must be explicitly preceded by a member access modifier. Member access modifiers can appear multiple times and in any order in a class definition.

```
1   // Fig. 6.1: Time.java
2   // Time class definition
3   public class Time {
4      private int hour;      // 0 - 23
5      private int minute;    // 0 - 59
6      private int second;    // 0 - 59
7
8      // Time constructor initializes each instance variable
9      // to zero. Ensures that each Time object starts in a
10     // consistent state.
11     public Time() { setTime( 0, 0, 0 ); }
12
13     // Set a new Time value using military time. Perform
14     // validity checks on the data. Set invalid values
15     // to zero.
16     public void setTime( int h, int m, int s )
17     {
18        hour = ( ( h >= 0 && h < 24 ) ? h : 0 );
19        minute = ( ( m >= 0 && m < 60 ) ? m : 0 );
20        second = ( ( s >= 0 && s < 60 ) ? s : 0 );
21     }
22
23     // Convert Time to String in military-time format
24     public String toMilitaryString()
25     {
26        return ( hour < 10 ? "0" : "" ) + hour +
27               ( minute < 10 ? "0" : "" ) + minute;
28     }
29
30     // Convert Time to String in standard-time format
31     public String toString()
32     {
33        return ( ( hour == 12 || hour == 0 ) ? 12 : hour % 12 ) +
34               ":" + ( minute < 10 ? "0" : "" ) + minute +
35               ":" + ( second < 10 ? "0" : "" ) + second +
36               ( hour < 12 ? " AM" : " PM" );
37     }
38  }
```

Fig. 6.1   Abstract data type **Time** implementation as a class (part 1 of 3).

```
39    // Fig. 6.1: TimeTest.java
40    // Class TimeTest to exercise class Time
41    import java.awt.Graphics;
42    import java.applet.Applet;
43
44    public class TimeTest extends Applet {
45       private Time t;
46
47       public void init()
48       {
49          t = new Time();
50       }
51
52       public void paint( Graphics g )
53       {
54          g.drawString( "The initial military time is: " +
55                        t.toMilitaryString(), 25, 25 );
56          g.drawString( "The initial standard time is: " +
57                        t.toString(), 25, 40 );
58
59          t.setTime( 13, 27, 6 );
60          g.drawString( "Military time after setTime is: " +
61                        t.toMilitaryString(), 25, 70 );
62          g.drawString( "Standard time after setTime is: " +
63                        t.toString(), 25, 85 );
64
65          t.setTime( 99, 99, 99 );
66          g.drawString( "After attempting invalid settings:",
67                        25, 115 );
68          g.drawString( "Military time: " +
69                        t.toMilitaryString(), 25, 130 );
70          g.drawString( "Standard time: " + t.toString(),
71                        25, 145 );
72       }
73    }
```

Fig. 6.1   Abstract data type **Time** implementation as a class (part 2 of 3).

Good Programming Practice 6.1

Group members by member access modifier in a class definition for clarity and readability.

Class **Time** contains the following **public** methods—**Time**, **setTime**, **toMilitaryString** and **toString**. These are the *public methods,* or *public services* or *public interface* of the class. These methods are used by *clients* (i.e., portions of a program that are users) of the class to manipulate the class's data.

Notice the method with the same name as the class; it is the *constructor* method of that class. A constructor is a special method that initializes the instance variables of a class object. A class's constructor method is called automatically when an object of that class is created. It is common to have several constructors for a class; this is accomplished through method overloading. Constructors can take arguments but cannot return a value.

Fig. 6.1   Abstract data type **Time** implementation as a class (part 3 of 3).

Common Programming Error 6.1

Attempting to declare a return type for a constructor and/or attempting to return a value from a constructor is a syntax error.

The three integer instance variables **hour**, **minute** and **second** are each declared with the **private** member access modifier. This indicates that these instance variables of the class are only accessible to methods of the class. Instance variables are normally declared **private** and methods are normally declared **public**. It is possible to have **private** methods and **public** data as we will see later. The **private** methods are often called *utility methods* or *helper methods* because they can only be called by other methods of that class and are used to support the operation of those methods. Using **public** data is uncommon and is a dangerous programming practice.

Once the class has been defined, it can be used as a type in declarations such as:

```
Time sunset,        // reference to object of type Time
     TimeArray[];    // reference to array of Time objects
```

The class name is a new type specifier. There may be many objects of a class, just as there may be many variables of a primitive data type such as **int**. The programmer can create new class types as needed; this is one of the reasons why Java is an *extensible language*.

Figure 6.1 (part 2) uses the **Time** class. Applet **TimeTest** declares an instance variable of class **Time** called **t** and instantiates it in the **init** method. When the object is instantiated, the **Time** constructor is called automatically and invokes method **setTime** to explicitly initialize each private instance variable to **0**. Next, the applet's **paint** method is automatically invoked and the time is printed in military format (using method **toMilitaryString**) and standard format (using method **toString**) to confirm that the data were initialized properly. The time is then set to another correct value using the **setTime** method and the time is printed again in both formats. Method **setTime** then attempts to set the instance variables to invalid values and the time is again printed in both formats.

Again, note that the instance variables **hour, minute** and **second** are each declared **private**. Private instance variables of a class are not accessible outside the class. The philosophy here is that the actual data representation used within the class is of no concern to the class's clients. For example, it would be perfectly reasonable for the class to represent the time internally as the number of seconds since midnight. Clients could use the same public methods and get the same results without being aware of this. In this sense, the implementation of a class is said to be *hidden* from its clients. Exercise 6.18 asks you to make precisely this modification to the **Time** class of Fig. 6.1 and show that there is no visible change to the clients of the class.

Software Engineering Observation 6.2

Information hiding promotes program modifiability and simplifies the client's perception of a class.

Software Engineering Observation 6.3

Clients of a class can (and should) use the class without knowing the internal details of how the class is implemented. If the class implementation is changed (to improve performance, for example), provided the class's interface remains constant, the class clients' source code need not change. This makes it much easier to modify systems.

In this program, the **Time** constructor simply initializes the instance variables to 0 (i.e., the military time equivalent of 12 AM). This ensures that the object is created in a *consistent state*—i.e., all instance variable values are valid. Invalid values cannot be stored in the instance variables of a **Time** object because the constructor is automatically called when the **Time** object is created and subsequent attempts by a client to modify the instance variables are scrutinized by the method **setTime**.

Instance variables can be initialized where they are declared in the class body, by the class's constructor, or they can be assigned values by "set" methods.

Good Programming Practice 6.2

Initialize instance variables of a class in that class's constructor.

Every class may include a *finalizer* method called **finalize** that does "termination housekeeping" on each class object before the memory for the object is garbage collected by the system. We will discuss garbage collection and finalizers in detail later.

It is interesting that the **toMilitaryString** and **toString** methods take no arguments. This is because these methods implicitly know that they are to manipulate the instance variables of the particular **Time** object for which they are invoked. This makes method calls more concise than conventional function calls in procedural programming. It also reduces the likelihood of passing the wrong arguments, the wrong types of arguments and/or the wrong number of arguments as often happens in C function calls.

Software Engineering Observation 6.4

Using an object-oriented programming approach can often simplify method calls by reducing the number of parameters to be passed. This benefit of object-oriented programming derives from the fact that encapsulation of instance variables and methods within an object gives the methods the right to access the instance variables.

Classes simplify programming because the client (or user of the class object) need only be concerned with the operations encapsulated in the object. Such operations are usually designed to be client-oriented rather than implementation-oriented. Clients need not be concerned with a class's implementation. Interfaces do change, but less frequently than implementations. When an implementation changes, implementation-dependent code must change accordingly. By hiding the implementation we eliminate the possibility of other program parts becoming dependent on the details of the class implementation.

Often, classes do not have to be created "from scratch." Rather, they may be *derived* from other classes that provide operations the new classes can use, or classes can include objects of other classes as members. Such *software reuse* can greatly enhance programmer productivity. Deriving new classes from existing classes is called *inheritance* and is discussed in detail in Chapter 7. Including class objects as members of other classes is called *composition* or *aggregation* and is discussed later in this chapter.

6.3 Class Scope

A class's instance variables and methods belong to that *class's scope*. Within a class's scope, class members are immediately accessible by all of that class's methods and can be referenced simply by name. Outside a class's scope, class members cannot be referenced directly by name. Those class members (such as **public** members) that are visible can only be accessed off a "handle," i.e., primitive data type members can be referred to by **objectReferenceName.primitive_VariableName** and object members can be referenced by **objectReferenceName.objectMemberName**.

Variables defined in a method are known only to that method, i.e., they are local variables to that method. Such variables may be said to have block scope. If a method defines a variable with the same name as a variable with class scope (i.e., an instance variable), the class-scope variable is hidden by the method-scope variable in the method scope. A hidden instance variable can be accessed in the method by preceding its name with the keyword **this** and the dot operator as in **this.x**.

6.4 Controlling Access to Members

The member access modifiers **public** and **private** are used to control access to a class's instance variables and methods. (In Chapter 7, we will introduce the additional access specifier **protected**.)

As we stated previously, the primary purpose of **public** methods is to present to the class's clients a view of the *services* the class provides—i.e., the public interface of the class. Clients of the class need not be concerned with how the class accomplishes its tasks. For this reason, the **private** members of a class as well as the definitions of its **public** methods (i.e., the class's implementation) are not accessible to the clients of a class.

Common Programming Error 6.2

*An attempt by a method which is not a member of a particular class to access a **private** member of that class is a syntax error.*

Figure 6.2 demonstrates that **private** class members are not accessible by name outside the class. Lines 17 and 19 attempt to directly access the **private** instance variables

hour and **minute** of **Time** object **t**. When this program is compiled, the compiler generates two errors stating that the **private** member specified in each statement is not accessible. (Note: This program assumes the **Time** class from Fig. 6.1 is used.)

Good Programming Practice 6.3

*Our preference is to list the **private** members of a class first.*

Good Programming Practice 6.4

*Despite the fact that **private** and **public** members may be repeated and intermixed, list all the **private** members of a class first in one group and then list all the **public** members in another group.*

```java
1   // Fig. 6.2: TimeTest.java
2   // Demonstrate errors resulting from attempts
3   // to access private class members.
4   import java.awt.Graphics;
5   import java.applet.Applet;
6
7   public class TimeTest extends Applet {
8      private Time t;
9
10     public void init()
11     {
12        t = new Time();
13     }
14
15     public void paint( Graphics g )
16     {
17        t.hour = 7;
18
19        g.drawString( "minute = " + t.minute, 25, 25 );
20     }
21  }
```

```
TimeTest.java:17: Variable hour in class Time not
                  accessible from class TimeTest.
      t.hour = 7;
        ^
TimeTest.java:19: Variable minute in class Time not
                  accessible from class TimeTest.
      g.drawString( "minute = " + t.minute, 25, 25 );
                                    ^
2 errors
```

Fig. 6.2   Erroneous attempt to access private members of a class.

Software Engineering Observation 6.5

*Keep all the instance variables of a class **private**. When necessary provide **public** methods to set the values of **private** instance variables and to get the values of **private** instance variables. This architecture helps hide the implementation of a class from its clients, which reduces bugs and improves program modifiability.*

Software Engineering Observation 6.6

*Class designers use **private** and **public members** to enforce the notion of information hiding and the principle of least privilege.*

Access to **private** data should be carefully controlled by the class's methods. For example, to allow clients to read the value of **private** data, the class can provide a *"get" method* (also called an *accessor method*). To enable clients to modify **private** data, the class can provide a *"set" method* (also called a *mutator method*). Such modification would seem to violate the notion of **private** data. But a *set* method can provide data validation capabilities (such as range checking) to ensure that the value is set properly. A *set* method can also translate between the form of the data used in the interface and the form used in the implementation. A *get* method need not expose the data in "raw" format; rather, the *get* method can edit the data and limit the view of the data the client will see.

Software Engineering Observation 6.7

*The class designer need not provide set and/or get methods for each **private** data item; these capabilities should be provided only when it makes sense and after careful thought by the class designer.*

Testing and Debugging Tip 6.1

*Making the instance variables of a class **private** and the methods of the class **public** facilitates debugging because problems with data manipulations are localized to the class's methods.*

6.5 Utility Methods

Not all methods need be made **public** and serve as part of the interface of the class. Some methods can be **private** and serve as *utility methods* to the other methods of the class.

Software Engineering Observation 6.8

*Methods tend to fall into a number of different categories: methods that get the values of **private** instance variables; methods that set the values of **private** instance variables; methods that implement the features of the class; and methods that perform various mechanical chores for the class such as initializing class objects, assigning class objects, converting between classes and built-in types or between classes and other classes.*

Access methods can read or display data. Another common use for access methods is to test the truth or falsity of conditions—such methods are often called *predicate methods*. An example of a predicate method would be an **isEmpty** method for any container class—a class capable of holding many objects—such as a linked list, a stack or a queue (these data structures are discussed in depth in Chapters 17 and 18). A program might test **isEmpty** before attempting to read another item from the container object. A program might test **isFull** before attempting to insert another item into a container object.

Figure 6.3 demonstrates the notion of a *utility method.* A utility method is not part of a class's **public** interface. Rather, it is a **private** method that supports the operation of the class's **public** methods. Utility methods are not intended to be called by clients of a class.

Class **SalesPerson** has an array of 12 monthly sales figures. These figures are automatically initialized to zero by Java when the array is allocated with **new**. Then the figures are set to user-supplied values by method **setSales**. Public method **toString** forms a **String** containing the total sales for the last 12 months. Notice the use of the **private** utility method **totalAnnualSales** (line 34) to total the 12 monthly sales figures for the benefit of method **toString**.

```
1   // Fig. 6.3: SalesPerson.java
2   // Definition of class SalesPerson with a utility method
3   public class SalesPerson {
4      private double sales[];      // 12 monthly sales figures
5
6      // Constructor method allocates sales array
7      public SalesPerson()
8      {
9         sales = new double[ 12 ];
10     }
11
12     // Method to set one of the 12 monthly sales figures
13     public void setSales( int month, double amount )
14     {
15        if ( month >= 1 && month <= 12 && amount > 0 )
16           sales[ month - 1 ] = amount;
17     }
18
19     // Private utility method to total annual sales
20     private double totalAnnualSales()
21     {
22        double total = 0.0;
23
24        for ( int i = 0; i < 12; i++ )
25           total += sales[ i ];
26
27        return total;
28     }
29
30     // Convert the total annual sales figure to a String
31     public String toString()
32     {
33        return "The total annual sales are $" +
34               totalAnnualSales();
35     }
36  }
```

Fig. 6.3   Using a utility method (part 1 of 3).

```
37   // Fig. 6.3: SalesPersonTest.java
38   // Demonstrating class SalesPerson and its utility method
39   import java.awt.*;
40   import java.applet.Applet;
41
42   public class SalesPersonTest extends Applet {
43      private SalesPerson s;
44      private double salesFigure;
45      private int month;
46      private boolean moreInput = true;
47      private String months[] = { "January", "February",
48                         "March", "April", "May", "June",
49                         "July", "August", "September",
50                         "October", "November", "December" };
51
52      // GUI components
53      private Label enterLabel;
54      private TextField currentMonth, enter, total;
55
56      public void init()
57      {
58         s = new SalesPerson();
59         month = 1;
60
61         enterLabel = new Label( "Enter sales for" );
62         currentMonth = new TextField( "January", 10 );
63         currentMonth.setEditable( false );
64         enter = new TextField( 10 );
65         total = new TextField( 30 );
66         total.setEditable( false );
67
68         add( enterLabel );
69         add( currentMonth );
70         add( enter );
71         add( total );
72      }
73
74      public boolean action( Event e, Object o )
75      {
76         if ( e.target == enter ) {
77            if ( moreInput ) {
78               Double val = Double.valueOf( e.arg.toString() );
79               s.setSales( month, val.doubleValue() );
80
81               if ( month == 12 ) {
82                  total.setText( s.toString() );
83
```

Fig. 6.3   Using a utility method (part 2 of 3).

```
84                    // hide GUI components no longer needed
85                    enterLabel.hide();
86                    currentMonth.hide();
87                    enter.hide();
88                    moreInput = false;
89                 }
90              else {
91                 month++;
92                 currentMonth.setText( months[ month - 1 ] );
93                 enter.setText( "" );  // clear the text field
94              }
95           }
96        }
97
98        return true;
99     }
100  }
```

Fig. 6.3   Using a utility method (part 3 of 3).

Class **SalesPersonTest** uses an object of the **SalesPerson** class and several GUI components to obtain the 12 monthly sales figures from the user. When the user supplies a sales figure and presses the Enter key in the text field, the **action** method is invoked automatically and the sales figure is converted from a **String** into a **Double** object. The method **doubleValue** is used to extract the **double** value from the **Double** object **val**. This value is passed to the **setSales** method with the month number to set that month's sales figure.

If the month number is 12 when the user enters a sales figure (i.e., the sales figures have been entered for the whole year), the total annual sales figure is displayed by setting the **total** text field to result of the **SalesPerson**'s **toString** method. Next, the lines

```
enterLabel.hide();
currentMonth.hide();
enter.hide();
```

are executed as part of the **if** structure at line 81. These lines cause the **enterLabel** label, **currentMonth** text field and **enter** text field to be hidden from the user (as shown in the last screen capture of this program containing only the **total** text field). Hiding these elements prevents the user from interacting with them for the rest of the program. If the month number is not 12, the **action** method simply prepares the program to accept the next sales figure by incrementing the month number, displaying the month name and clearing the **enter** text field so the user can type the next sales figure.

6.6 Initializing Class Objects: Constructors

When an object is created, its members can be initialized by a *constructor* method. A constructor is a method with the same name as the class. The programmer provides the constructor which is then invoked automatically each time an object of that class is instantiated. Instance variables can be initialized implicitly, can be initialized in a constructor of the class, or their values may be set later after the object is created. Constructors cannot specify return types or return values. Constructors may be overloaded to provide a variety of means for initializing objects of a class.

Good Programming Practice 6.5

When appropriate (almost always), provide a constructor to ensure that every object is properly initialized with meaningful values.

When an object of a class is created, *initializers* can be provided in parentheses to the right of the class name. These initializers are passed as arguments to the class's constructor. This technique is demonstrated in the next example.

If no constructors are defined for a class, the compiler creates a *default constructor* that takes no arguments. The default constructor for a class calls the constructor for the class that this class extends and proceeds to initialize the instance variables in the manner we discussed previously (i.e., primitive numeric data type variables to **0**, **boolean**s to **false** and references to **null**). It is also possible for the programmer to provide a *no-argument constructor* as we will see in the next example. If any constructors are defined for a class by the programmer, Java will not create a default constructor for the class.

Common Programming Error 6.3

If constructors are provided for a class, but none are no-argument constructors, and an attempt is made to call a no-argument constructor to initialize an object of the class, a syntax error occurs. A constructor may be called with no arguments only if there are no constructors for the class (the default constructor is called) or if there is a no-argument constructor.

6.7 Using Overloaded Constructors

Methods of a class can be overloaded, but only by other methods of the same class. To overload a method of a class, simply provide a separate method definition with the same name for each version of the method. Remember that overloaded methods must have different parameter lists.

Common Programming Error 6.4

Attempting to overload a method of a class with a method not in that class's scope.

The constructor from Fig. 6.1 initialized **hour, minute** and **second** to **0** (i.e., 12 midnight in military time). Figure 6.4 overloads the **Time** constructor method to provide a convenient variety of ways to initialize **Time** objects. The constructors guarantee that every object begins its existence in a consistent state. In this program, each constructor calls method **setTime** with the values passed to the constructor to ensure that the value supplied for **hour** is in the range 0 to 23 and that the values for **minute** and **second** are each in the range 0 to 59. If a value is out of range, it is set to zero by **setTime** (this is an example of ensuring that an instance variable remains in a consistent state). Line 60 shows that the no-argument constructor is invoked by placing an empty set of parentheses after the class name when allocating a **Time** object with **new**. Lines 61 through 64 of the program demonstrate passing arguments to the **Time** constructors. The appropriate constructor is invoked by checking the number, types and order of the arguments specified in the constructor call with the number, types and order of the parameters specified in each method definition. The matching constructor is called automatically.

Good Programming Practice 6.6

Every method that modifies the private instance variables of an object should ensure that the data remains in a consistent state.

Notice that the constructors that do not explicitly receive three values for **hour, minute** and **second** call **setTime** with zeros for the missing values to satisfy **setTime**'s requirement of three arguments.

Note that each **Time** constructor could be written to include a copy of the appropriate statements from method **setTime**. This may be slightly more efficient because the extra call to **setTime** is eliminated. However, coding the **Time** constructors and method **setTime** identically makes maintenance of this program more difficult. If the implementation of method **setTime** changes, the implementation of the **Time** constructors would need to change accordingly. Having the **Time** constructors call **setTime** directly requires any changes to the implementation of **setTime** to be made only once. This reduces the likelihood of a programming error when altering the implementation.

```
 1   // Fig. 6.4: Time.java
 2   // Time class definition
 3   public class Time {
 4      private int hour;      // 0 - 23
 5      private int minute;    // 0 - 59
 6      private int second;    // 0 - 59
 7
 8      // Time constructor initializes each instance variable
 9      // to zero. Ensures that Time object starts in a
10      // consistent state.
11      public Time() { setTime( 0, 0, 0 ); }
12
13      // Time constructor: hour supplied, minute and second
14      // defaulted to 0.
15      public Time( int h ) { setTime( h, 0, 0 ); }
16
17      // Time constructor: hour and minute supplied, second
18      // defaulted to 0.
19      public Time( int h, int m ) { setTime( h, m, 0 ); }
20
21      // Time constructor: hour, minute and second supplied.
22      public Time( int h, int m, int s ) { setTime( h, m, s ); }
23
24      // Set a new Time value using military time. Perform
25      // validity checks on the data. Set invalid values
26      // to zero.
27      public void setTime( int h, int m, int s )
28      {
29         hour = ( ( h >= 0 && h < 24 ) ? h : 0 );
30         minute = ( ( m >= 0 && m < 60 ) ? m : 0 );
31         second = ( ( s >= 0 && s < 60 ) ? s : 0 );
32      }
33
34      // Convert Time to String in military-time format
35      public String toMilitaryString()
36      {
37         return ( hour < 10 ? "0" : "" ) + hour +
38                ( minute < 10 ? "0" : "" ) + minute;
39      }
40
41      // Convert Time to String in standard-time format
42      public String toString()
43      {
44         return ( ( hour == 12 || hour == 0 ) ? 12 : hour % 12 ) +
45                ":" + ( minute < 10 ? "0" : "" ) + minute +
46                ":" + ( second < 10 ? "0" : "" ) + second +
47                ( hour < 12 ? " AM" : " PM" );
48      }
49   }
```

Fig. 6.4   Using overloaded constructors (part 1 of 3).

```
50   // Fig. 6.4: TimeTest.java
51   // Using overloaded constructors
52   import java.awt.Graphics;
53   import java.applet.Applet;
54
55   public class TimeTest extends Applet {
56      private Time t1, t2, t3, t4, t5;
57
58      public void init()
59      {
60         t1 = new Time();
61         t2 = new Time( 2 );
62         t3 = new Time( 21, 34 );
63         t4 = new Time( 12, 25, 42 );
64         t5 = new Time( 27, 74, 99 );
65      }
66
67      public void paint( Graphics g )
68      {
69         g.drawString( "Constructed with:", 25, 25 );
70         g.drawString( "all arguments defaulted:", 25, 40 );
71         g.drawString( "   " + t1.toMilitaryString(),
72                          25, 55 );
73         g.drawString( "   " + t1.toString(), 25, 70 );
74
75         g.drawString( "hour specified; minute " +
76                       "and second defaulted:", 25, 85 );
77         g.drawString( "   " + t2.toMilitaryString(),
78                          25, 100 );
79         g.drawString( "   " + t2.toString(), 25, 115 );
80
81         g.drawString( "hour and minute specified; " +
82                       "second defaulted:", 25, 130 );
83         g.drawString( "   " + t3.toMilitaryString(),
84                          25, 145 );
85         g.drawString( "   " + t3.toString(), 25, 160 );
86
87         g.drawString( "hour, minute, and second specified:",
88                          25, 175 );
89         g.drawString( "   " + t4.toMilitaryString(),
90                          25, 190 );
91         g.drawString( "   " + t4.toString(), 25, 205 );
92
93         g.drawString( "all invalid values specified:",
94                          25, 220 );
95         g.drawString( "   " + t5.toMilitaryString(),
96                          25, 235 );
97         g.drawString( "   " + t5.toString(), 25, 250 );
98      }
99   }
```

Fig. 6.4 Using overloaded constructors (part 2 of 3).

Fig. 6.4 Using overloaded constructors (part 3 of 3).

Software Engineering Observation 6.9

If a method of a class already provides all or part of the functionality required by a constructor (or other method) of the class, call that method from the constructor (or other method). This simplifies the maintenance of the code and reduces the likelihood of an error if the implementation of the code is modified. It is also an effective example of reuse.

6.8 Using *Set* and *Get* Methods

Private instance variables can be manipulated only by methods of the class. A typical manipulation might be the adjustment of a customer's bank balance (e.g., a private instance variable of a class **BankAccount**) by a method **computeInterest**.

Classes often provide **public** methods to allow clients of the class to *set* (i.e., assign values to) or *get* (i.e., obtain the values of) **private** instance variables. These methods need not be called *set* and *get*, but they often are. More specifically, a method that sets instance variable **interestRate** would typically be named **setInterestRate** and a method that gets the **interestRate** would typically be called **getInterestRate**. *Get* methods are also commonly called *accessor methods* or *query methods*.

It would seem that providing *set* and *get* capabilities is essentially the same as making the instance variables **public**. This is another subtlety of Java that makes the language so desirable for software engineering. If an instance variable is **public**, the instance variable may be read or written at will by any method in the program. If an instance variable is **private**, a **public** *get* method certainly seems to allow other methods to read the data at will but the *get* method controls the formatting and display of the data. A **public** *set* method can—and most likely will—carefully scrutinize attempts to modify the instance variable's value. This ensures that the new value is appropriate for that data item. For example, an attempt to *set* the day of the month to 37 would be rejected, an attempt to *set* a person's weight to a negative value would be rejected, and so on.

The benefits of data integrity are not automatic simply because instance variables are made **private**—the programmer must provide validity checking. Java provides the framework in which programmers can design better programs in a convenient manner.

Software Engineering Observation 6.10

*Methods that set the values of **private** data should verify that the intended new values are proper; if they are not, the* set *methods should place the **private** instance variables into an appropriate consistent state.*

A class's *set* methods often return values indicating that an attempt was made to assign invalid data to an object of the class. This enables clients of the class to test the return values of *set* methods to determine if the objects they are manipulating are valid and to take appropriate action if the objects are not valid.

Figure 6.5 extends our **Time** class to include *get* and *set* methods for the **hour**, **minute** and **second private** instance variables. The *set* methods strictly control the setting of the instance variables. Attempts to set any instance variable to an incorrect value cause the instance variable to be set to zero (thus leaving the instance variable in a consistent state). Each *get* method simply returns the appropriate instance variable's value.

```
1   // Fig. 6.5: Time.java
2   // Time class definition
3   public class Time {
4       private int hour;      // 0 - 23
5       private int minute;    // 0 - 59
6       private int second;    // 0 - 59
7
8       // Time constructor initializes each instance variable
9       // to zero. Ensures that Time object starts in a
10      // consistent state.
11      public Time() { setTime( 0, 0, 0 ); }
12
13      // Time constructor: hour supplied, minute and second
14      // defaulted to 0.
15      public Time( int h ) { setTime( h, 0, 0 ); }
16
17      // Time constructor: hour and minute supplied, second
18      // defaulted to 0.
19      public Time( int h, int m ) { setTime( h, m, 0 ); }
20
21      // Time constructor: hour, minute and second supplied.
22      public Time( int h, int m, int s ) { setTime( h, m, s ); }
```

Fig. 6.5　Using set and get methods (part 1 of 6).

```
23
24     // Set Methods
25     // Set a new Time value using military time. Perform
26     // validity checks on the data. Set invalid values
27     // to zero.
28     public void setTime( int h, int m, int s )
29     {
30        setHour( h );      // set the hour
31        setMinute( m );    // set the minute
32        setSecond( s );    // set the second
33     }
34
35     // set the hour
36     public void setHour( int h )
37        { hour = ( ( h >= 0 && h < 24 ) ? h : 0 ); }
38
39     // set the minute
40     public void setMinute( int m )
41        { minute = ( ( m >= 0 && m < 60 ) ? m : 0 ); }
42
43     // set the second
44     public void setSecond( int s )
45        { second = ( ( s >= 0 && s < 60 ) ? s : 0 ); }
46
47     // Get Methods
48     // get the hour
49     public int getHour() { return hour; }
50
51     // get the minute
52     public int getMinute() { return minute; }
53
54     // get the second
55     public int getSecond() { return second; }
56
57     // Convert Time to String in military-time format
58     public String toMilitaryString()
59     {
60        return ( hour < 10 ? "0" : "" ) + hour +
61               ( minute < 10 ? "0" : "" ) + minute;
62     }
63
64     // Convert Time to String in standard-time format
65     public String toString()
66     {
67        return ( ( hour == 12 || hour == 0 ) ? 12 : hour % 12 ) +
68               ":" + ( minute < 10 ? "0" : "" ) + minute +
69               ":" + ( second < 10 ? "0" : "" ) + second +
70               ( hour < 12 ? " AM" : " PM" );
71     }
72  }
```

Fig. 6.5   Using set and get methods (part 2 of 6).

```
73   // Fig. 6.5: TimeTest.java
74   // Demonstrating the Time class set and get methods
75   import java.awt.*;
76   import java.applet.Applet;
77
78   public class TimeTest extends Applet {
79      private Time t;
80      private Label hrLabel, minLabel, secLabel;
81      private TextField hrField, minField, secField, display;
82      private Button tickButton;
83
84      public void init()
85      {
86         t = new Time();
87
88         hrLabel = new Label( "Set Hour" );
89         hrField = new TextField( 10 );
90         minLabel = new Label( "Set Minute" );
91         minField = new TextField( 10 );
92         secLabel = new Label( "Set Second" );
93         secField = new TextField( 10 );
94         display = new TextField( 30 );
95         display.setEditable( false );
96         tickButton = new Button( "Add 1 to Second" );
97
98         add( hrLabel );
99         add( hrField );
100        add( minLabel );
101        add( minField );
102        add( secLabel );
103        add( secField );
104        add( display );
105        add( tickButton );
106        updateDisplay();
107     }
108
109     public boolean action( Event e, Object o )
110     {
111        if ( e.target == tickButton )
112           tick();
113        else if ( e.target == hrField ) {
114           t.setHour( Integer.parseInt( e.arg.toString() ) );
115           hrField.setText( "" );
116        }
117        else if ( e.target == minField ) {
118           t.setMinute( Integer.parseInt( e.arg.toString() ) );
119           minField.setText( "" );
120        }
```

Fig. 6.5   Using set and get methods (part 3 of 6).

```
121            else if ( e.target == secField ) {
122               t.setSecond( Integer.parseInt( e.arg.toString() ) );
123               secField.setText( "" );
124            }
125
126            updateDisplay();
127
128            return true;
129         }
130
131         public void updateDisplay()
132         {
133            display.setText( "Hour: " + t.getHour() +
134               "; Minute: " + t.getMinute() +
135               "; Second: " + t.getSecond() );
136            showStatus( "Standard time is: " + t.toString()+
137               "; Military time is: " + t.toMilitaryString() );
138         }
139
140         public void tick()
141         {
142            t.setSecond( ( t.getSecond() + 1 ) % 60 );
143
144            if ( t.getSecond() == 0 ) {
145               t.setMinute( ( t.getMinute() + 1 ) % 60 );
146
147               if ( t.getMinute() == 0 )
148                  t.setHour( ( t.getHour() + 1 ) % 24 );
149            }
150         }
151      }
```

Fig. 6.5   Using set and get methods (part 4 of 6).

Fig. 6.5 Using set and get methods (part 5 of 6).

Fig. 6.5   Using set and get methods (part 6 of 6).

The **TimeTest** applet provides a graphical user interface that enables the user to exercise the methods of the **Time** class. The user can set the hour, minute or second value by typing a value in the appropriate text field and pressing the Enter key. The user can also click the "**Add 1 to second**" button to increment the time by one second. After each operation, the resulting time is displayed as a string in the status bar of the applet. The output windows illustrate the applet before and after the following operations: setting the hour to 23, setting the minute to 59, setting the second to 58 and incrementing the minute twice with the "**Add 1 to second**" button.

Note that when the "**Add 1 to second**" button is clicked, the applet's **tick** method is called. Method **tick** uses the *set* and *get* methods to increment the second properly.

Although this works, it incurs the performance burden of issuing multiple method calls. In the next chapter, we discuss the notion of friendly access as a means of eliminating this performance burden.

Common Programming Error 6.5

A constructor can call other methods of the class, such as set *or* get *methods, but because the constructor is initializing the object, the instance variables may not yet be in a consistent state. Using instance variables before they have been properly initialized is an error.*

Set methods are certainly important from a software engineering standpoint because they can perform validity checking. *Set* and *get* methods have another important software engineering advantage as discussed in the following Software Engineering Observation.

Software Engineering Observation 6.11

Accessing private data through set *and* get *methods not only protects the instance variables from receiving invalid values, but it also insulates clients of the class from the representation of the instance variables. Thus, if the representation of the data changes (typically to reduce the amount of storage required or to improve performance), only the method implementations need to change—the clients need not change as long as the interface provided by the methods remains the same.*

6.9 Software Reusability

Java programmers concentrate on crafting new classes and reusing existing classes. Many *class libraries* exist and others are being developed worldwide. Software is then constructed from existing, well-defined, carefully tested, well-documented, portable, widely available components. This kind of software reusability speeds the development of powerful, high-quality software. *Rapid applications development (RAD)* is of great interest today.

To realize the full potential of software reusability we need to improve cataloging schemes, licensing schemes, protection mechanisms that ensure master copies of classes are not corrupted, description schemes that system designers use to determine if existing objects meet their needs, browsing mechanisms that determine what classes are available and how closely they meet software developer requirements, and the like. Many interesting research and development problems have been solved and many more need to be solved; these problems will be solved because the potential value of software reuse is enormous.

6.10 Final Instance Variables

We have repeatedly emphasized the *principle of least privilege* as one of the most fundamental principles of good software engineering. Let us see one way in which this principle applies to instance variables.

Some instance variables need to be modifiable and some do not. The programmer may use the keyword **final** to specify that a variable is not modifiable and that any attempt to modify the variable is an error. For example,

```
final int increment = 5;
```

declares a constant instance variable **increment** of type **int** and initializes it to 5.

Software Engineering Observation 6.12

*Declaring an instance variable as **final** helps enforce the principle of least privilege. If an instance variable should not be modified, then declare it to be **final** to expressly forbid modification. Accidental attempts to modify a **final** instance variable are caught at compile time rather than causing execution-time errors.*

Common Programming Error 6.6

*Attempting to modify a **final** instance variable.*

The program of Fig. 6.6 creates a **final** instance variable **increment** of type **int** and initializes it to 5 in its declaration (line 8). A **final** variable cannot be modified by assignment so it *must* be initialized.

```
1   // Fig. 6.6: Increment.java
2   // Initializing a final variable
3   import java.awt.*;
4   import java.applet.Applet;
5
6   public class Increment extends Applet {
7      private int count, total;
8      private final int increment = 5; // constant variable
9      private Button incr;
10
11     public void init()
12     {
13        count = 0;
14        total = 0;
15        incr = new Button( "Click to increment" );
16        add( incr );
17     }
18
19     public boolean action( Event e, Object o )
20     {
21        total += increment;
22        count++;
23        showStatus( "After increment " + count +
24                  ": total = " + total );
25        return true;
26     }
27  }
```

Fig. 6.6   Initializing a **final** variable.

Figure 6.7 illustrates compiler errors produced for the program of Fig. 6.6 if instance variable **increment** is declared **final**, but is not initialized in the declaration.

Common Programming Error 6.7

*Not initializing a **final** instance variable.*

Software Engineering Observation 6.13

*Constant class members (**final** objects and **final** "variables") must be initialized. Assignments are not allowed.*

6.11 Composition: Objects as Instance Variables of Other Classes

An **AlarmClock** class object needs to know when it is supposed to sound its alarm, so why not include a **Time** object as a member of the **AlarmClock** object? Such a capability is called *composition*. A class can have objects of other classes as members.

Software Engineering Observation 6.14

One form of software reuse is composition in which a class has objects of other classes as members.

Figure 6.8 uses class **Employee** and class **MyDate** to demonstrate objects as members of other objects. Class **Employee** contains private instance variables **firstName**, **lastName**, **birthDate** and **hireDate**. Members **birthDate** and **hireDate** are objects of class **MyDate** which contains private instance variables **month**, **day** and **year**. The program instantiates an **Employee** object and initializes and displays its instance variables. The constructor takes eight arguments (**fName**, **lName**, **bMonth**, **bDay**, **bYear**, **hMonth**, **hDay** and **hYear**). Arguments **bMonth**, **bDay** and **bYear** are passed to the **birthDate** constructor and **hMonth**, **hDay** and **hYear** are passed to the **hireDate** constructor.

A member object does not need to be initialized immediately with constructor arguments. If an empty argument list is provided when a member object is created, the object's default constructor (or no-argument constructor if one is available) will be called automatically. Values, if any, established by the default constructor (or no-argument constructor) can then be overridden by *set* methods.

```
Increment.java:8: Final variables must be initialized:
                  int increment
     final int increment; // constant instance variable
                 ^

1 error
```

Fig. 6.7   Compiler error message as a result of not initializing **increment**.

Performance Tip 6.2

Initialize member objects explicitly at constructor time. This eliminates the overhead of doubly initializing member objects—once when the member object's default constructor is called and again when set *methods are used to provide initial values for the member object.*

```
1   // Fig. 6.8: MyDate.java
2   // Declaration of the MyDate class.
3   public class MyDate {
4      private int month;   // 1-12
5      private int day;     // 1-31 based on month
6      private int year;    // any year
7
8      // Constructor: Confirm proper value for month;
9      // call utility method checkDay to confirm proper
10     // value for day.
11     public MyDate( int mn, int dy, int yr )
12     {
13        if ( mn > 0 && mn <= 12 )         // validate the month
14           month = mn;
15        else {
16           month = 1;
17           System.out.println( "Month " + mn +
18                                " invalid. Set to month 1." );
19        }
20
21        year = yr;                        // could also check
22        day = checkDay( dy );             // validate the day
23
24        System.out.println(
25           "MyDate object constructor for date " + toString() );
26     }
27
28     // Utility method to confirm proper day value
29     // based on month and year.
30     private int checkDay( int testDay )
31     {
32        int daysPerMonth[] = { 0, 31, 28, 31, 30,
33                               31, 30, 31, 31, 30,
34                               31, 30, 31 };
35
36        if ( testDay > 0 && testDay <= daysPerMonth[ month ] )
37           return testDay;
38
39        if ( month == 2 &&    // February: Check for leap year
40             testDay == 29 &&
41             ( year % 400 == 0 ||
42               ( year % 4 == 0 && year % 100 != 0 ) ) )
43           return testDay;
```

Fig. 6.8   Demonstrating an object with a member object (part 1 of 5).

```
44
45          System.out.println( "Day " + testDay +
46                              " invalid. Set to day 1." );
47
48          return 1;  // leave object in consistent state
49      }
50
51      // Create a String of the form month/day/year
52      public String toString()
53          { return month + "/" + day + "/" + year; }
54   }
```

Fig. 6.8   Demonstrating an object with a member object (part 2 of 5).

```
55   // Fig. 6.8: Employee.java
56   // Declaration of the Employee class.
57   public class Employee {
58      private String firstName;
59      private String lastName;
60      private MyDate birthDate;
61      private MyDate hireDate;
62
63      public Employee( String fName, String lName,
64                       int bMonth, int bDay, int bYear,
65                       int hMonth, int hDay, int hYear)
66      {
67         firstName = fName;
68         lastName = lName;
69         birthDate = new MyDate( bMonth, bDay, bYear );
70         hireDate = new MyDate( hMonth, hDay, hYear );
71      }
72
73      public String toString()
74      {
75         return lastName + ", " + firstName +
76                " Hired: " + hireDate.toString() +
77                " Birthday: " + birthDate.toString();
78      }
79   }
```

Fig. 6.8   Demonstrating an object with a member object (part 3 of 5).

```
80   // Fig. 6.8: EmployeeTest.java
81   // Demonstrating an object with a member object.
82   import java.awt.Graphics;
83   import java.applet.Applet;
84
85   public class EmployeeTest extends Applet {
86      private Employee e;
```

Fig. 6.8   Demonstrating an object with a member object (part 4 of 5).

302 OBJECT-BASED PROGRAMMING   CHAPTER 6

```
87
88      public void init()
89      {
90         e = new Employee( "Bob", "Jones", 7, 24, 49,
91                           3, 12, 88 );
92      }
93
94      public void paint( Graphics g )
95      {
96         g.drawString( e.toString(), 25, 25 );
97      }
98   }
```

Fig. 6.8   Demonstrating an object with a member object (part 5 of 5).

6.12 Friendly Members

When no access modifier is provided for a method or variable when it is defined in a class, the method or variable is considered to have "friendly" access (also called *package access*). If your program consists of one class definition, this has no specific effects on the program. However, if your program uses multiple classes from the same package (i.e., a group of related classes), these classes can access each other's friendly methods and data directly through a reference to an object. Friendly access enables objects of different classes to interact without the need for *set* and *get* methods that provide access to data, thus eliminating some of the method call overhead.

Let us consider a mechanical example of friendly access. The program of Fig. 6.9 contains two classes—the **FriendlyDataTest** applet class and the **FriendlyData** class. In the **FriendlyData** class definition, the lines

```
int x;     // friendly instance variable
String s;  // friendly instance variable
```

declare the instance variables **x** and **s** with no member access modifiers; therefore, these are friendly instance variables. The **FriendlyDataTest** applet creates an instance of the **FriendlyData** class to demonstrate the ability to modify the **FriendlyData** instance variables directly (as shown on lines 21 and 22). The results of the modification can be seen in the output window.

Note that when this program is compiled, two separate files are produced—a **.class** file for class **FriendlyData** and a **.class** file for class **FriendlyDataTest**. These two files are placed in the same directory automatically and are considered to be part of the same package (they are certainly related by the fact that they are in the same program). Because they are part of the same package, class **FriendlyDataTest** is allowed to modify the friendly data of objects of class **FriendlyData**.

Software Engineering Observation 6.15

Some people in the OOP community feel that friendly access corrupts information hiding and weakens the value of the object-oriented design approach.

```
1   // Fig. 6.9: FriendlyDataTest.java
2   // Classes in the same package (i.e., the same directory)
3   // can access friendly data of other classes in the
4   // same package.
5   import java.awt.Graphics;
6   import java.applet.Applet;
7
8   public class FriendlyDataTest extends Applet {
9      private FriendlyData d;
10
11     public void init()
12     {
13        d = new FriendlyData();
14     }
15
16     public void paint( Graphics g )
17     {
18        g.drawString( "After instantiation: ", 25, 25 );
19        g.drawString( d.toString(), 40, 40 );
20
21        d.x = 77;
22        d.s = new String( "Good bye" );
23        g.drawString( "After changing values: ", 25, 55 );
24        g.drawString( d.toString(), 40, 70 );
25     }
26  }
27
28  class FriendlyData {
29     int x;      // friendly instance variable
30     String s;   // friendly instance variable
31
32     // constructor
33     public FriendlyData()
34     {
35        x = 0;
36        s = new String( "Hello" );
37     }
```

Fig. 6.9   Friendly access to members of a class (part 1 of 2).

```
38
39     public String toString()
40     {
41        return "x: " + x + "      s: " + s;
42     }
43  }
```

Fig. 6.9   Friendly access to members of a class (part 2 of 2).

6.13 Using the this Reference

When a method of a class references another member of that class for a specific object of that class, how does Java ensure that the proper object is referenced? The answer is that each object has access to a reference to itself—called the ***this*** *reference*. The **this** reference is not instance data stored in an object itself. Rather, the **this** reference is passed into the object as an implicit argument in every non-**static** method call (we discuss **static** methods in the next section). Thus, when any non-**static** method of an object is run, that method has access to the **this** reference.

Common Programming Error 6.8

*Explicitly using the **this** reference in a static method is a syntax error.*

The **this** reference is implicitly used to refer to both the instance variables and methods of an object. For now, we show a simple example of using the **this** reference explicitly; later, we show some substantial and subtle examples of using **this**.

Performance Tip 6.3

Java conserves storage by maintaining only one copy of each method per class; this method is invoked by every object of that class. Each object, on the other hand, has its own copy of the class's instance variables.

Figure 6.10 demonstrates the explicit use of the **this** reference to enable a method of class **ThisTest** to print the private data **x** of a **ThisTest** object.

The **toString** method in Fig. 6.10 begins forms a string containing the value of **x**. First **toString** accesses the value of **x** directly, then **toString** refers to **x** through the **this** reference and the dot operator (**.**).

```
1   // Fig. 6.10: ThisTest.java
2   // Using the this reference to refer to
3   // instance variables and methods.
4   import java.awt.Graphics;
5   import java.applet.Applet;
6
7   public class ThisTest extends Applet {
8      private int x = 12;
9
10     public void paint( Graphics g )
11     {
12        g.drawString( this.toString(), 25, 25 );
13     }
14
15     public String toString()
16     {
17        return "x: " + x + "    this.x = " + this.x;
18     }
19  }
```

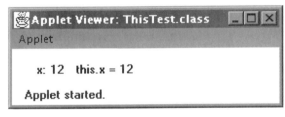

Fig. 6.10 Using the **this** reference.

Another use of the **this** reference is in enabling *concatenated method calls* (also called *cascaded method calls*). Figure 6.11 illustrates returning a reference to a **Time** object to enable method calls of class **Time** to be concatenated. Methods **setTime**, **set-Hour**, **setMinute** and **setSecond** each return **this** with a return type of **Time**.

Why does the technique of returning the **this** reference work? The dot operator (**.**) associates from left to right, so the expression

```
      t.setHour( 18 ).setMinute( 30 ).setSecond( 22 );
```

first evaluates **t.setHour(18)** then returns a reference to object **t** as the value of this method call. The remaining expression is then interpreted as

```
      t.setMinute( 30 ).setSecond( 22 );
```

The **t.setMinute(30)** call executes and returns a reference to **t**. The remaining expression is interpreted as

```
      t.setSecond( 22 );
```

Note the calls

```
      t.setTime( 20, 20, 20 ).toString();
```

```
1   // Fig. 6.11: Time.java
2   // Time class definition
3   public class Time {
4      private int hour;      // 0 - 23
5      private int minute;    // 0 - 59
6      private int second;    // 0 - 59
7
8      // Time constructor initializes each instance variable
9      // to zero. Ensures that Time object starts in a
10     // consistent state.
11     public Time() { setTime( 0, 0, 0 ); }
12
13     // Time constructor: hour supplied, minute and second
14     // defaulted to 0.
15     public Time( int h ) { setTime( h, 0, 0 ); }
16
17     // Time constructor: hour and minute supplied, second
18     // defaulted to 0.
19     public Time( int h, int m ) { setTime( h, m, 0 ); }
20
21     // Time constructor: hour, minute and second supplied.
22     public Time( int h, int m, int s ) { setTime( h, m, s ); }
23
24     // Set Methods
25     // Set a new Time value using military time. Perform
26     // validity checks on the data. Set invalid values
27     // to zero.
28     public Time setTime( int h, int m, int s )
29     {
30        setHour( h );     // set the hour
31        setMinute( m );   // set the minute
32        setSecond( s );   // set the second
33
34        return this;      // enables chaining
35     }
36
37     // set the hour
38     public Time setHour( int h )
39     {
40        hour = ( ( h >= 0 && h < 24 ) ? h : 0 );
41
42        return this;      // enables chaining
43     }
44
45     // set the minute
46     public Time setMinute( int m )
47     {
48        minute = ( ( m >= 0 && m < 60 ) ? m : 0 );
49
50        return this;      // enables chaining
51     }
```

Fig. 6.11 Chaining method calls (part 1 of 3).

```
52
53        // set the second
54        public Time setSecond( int s )
55        {
56            second = ( ( s >= 0 && s < 60 ) ? s : 0 );
57
58            return this;     // enables chaining
59        }
60
61        // Get Methods
62        // get the hour
63        public int getHour() { return hour; }
64
65        // get the minute
66        public int getMinute() { return minute; }
67
68        // get the second
69        public int getSecond() { return second; }
70
71        // Convert Time to String in military-time format
72        public String toMilitaryString()
73        {
74            return ( hour < 10 ? "0" : "" ) + hour +
75                   ( minute < 10 ? "0" : "" ) + minute;
76        }
77
78        // Convert Time to String in standard-time format
79        public String toString()
80        {
81            return ( ( hour == 12 || hour == 0 ) ? 12 : hour % 12 ) +
82                   ":" + ( minute < 10 ? "0" : "" ) + minute +
83                   ":" + ( second < 10 ? "0" : "" ) + second +
84                   ( hour < 12 ? " AM" : " PM" );
85        }
86   }
```

Fig. 6.11 Chaining method calls (part 2 of 3).

also use the concatenation feature. These method calls must appear in this order in this expression because **toString** as defined in the class does not return a reference to **t**. Placing the call to **toString** in the preceding statement before the call to **setTime** causes a syntax error.

Common Programming Error 6.9

In a method in which a method parameter has the same name as one of the class members, use **this** *explicitly if you want to access the class member; otherwise, you will incorrectly reference the method parameter.*

Good Programming Practice 6.7

Avoid using method parameter names that conflict with class member names.

```
87   // Fig. 6.11: TimeTest.java
88   // Chaining method calls together with the this reference
89   import java.awt.Graphics;
90   import java.applet.Applet;
91
92   public class TimeTest extends Applet {
93      private Time t;
94
95      public void init()
96      {
97         t = new Time();
98      }
99
100     public void paint( Graphics g )
101     {
102        t.setHour( 18 ).setMinute( 30 ).setSecond( 22 );
103        g.drawString( "Military time: " +
104                      t.toMilitaryString(), 25, 25 );
105        g.drawString( "Standard time: " + t.toString(),
106                      25, 40 );
107
108        g.drawString( "New standard time: " +
109           t.setTime( 20, 20, 20 ).toString(), 25, 70 );
110     }
111  }
```

Fig. 6.11   Chaining method calls (part 3 of 3).

Good Programming Practice 6.8

*Explicitly using **this** can increase program clarity in some contexts in which **this** is optional.*

6.14 Finalizers

We have seen that constructor methods are capable of initializing data in an object of a class when the class is created. Often, constructors acquire various system resources such as memory (when the **new** operator is used). We need a disciplined way to give resources back to the system when they are no longer needed to avoid resource leaks. The most common resource acquired by constructors is memory. But, in Java we do not have to worry about returning memory to the system because Java performs automatic "garbage collection" of memory. Therefore, memory leaks that are common in other languages like C and C++ cannot happen in Java. However, other resource leaks can occur.

Each class in Java can have a finalizer method that returns resources to the system. The finalizer method for an object is guaranteed to be called to perform *termination house-keeping* on the object just before Java garbage collects the object. A class's finalizer method always has the name **finalize**. A finalizer receives no parameters and returns no value (i.e., its return type is **void**). A class may have only one **finalize** method—finalizer overloading is not allowed.

Finalizers have not been provided for the classes presented so far. Actually, finalizers are rarely used with simple classes. We will see a sample **finalize** method in Fig. 6.12.

6.15 Static Class Members

Each object of a class has its own copy of all the instance variables of the class. In certain cases only one copy of a particular variable should be shared by all objects of a class. A **static** class variable is used for these and other reasons. A **static** class variable represents "class-wide" information. The declaration of a **static** member begins with the keyword **static**.

Let us motivate the need for **static** class-wide data with a video game example. Suppose we have a video game in which we have **Martian**s and other space creatures. Each **Martian** tends to be brave and willing to attack other space creatures when the **Martian** is aware that there are at least 5 **Martian**s present. If there are fewer than five **Martian**s present, each **Martian** becomes cowardly. So each **Martian** needs to know the **martianCount**. We could endow class **Martian** with **martianCount** as instance data. If we do this, then every **Martian** will have a separate copy of the instance data and every time we create a new **Martian** we will have to update the instance variable **martianCount** in every **Martian**. This wastes space with the redundant copies and wastes time in updating the separate copies. Instead, we declare **martianCount** to be **static**. This makes **martianCount** class-wide data. Every **Martian** can see the **martianCount** as if it were instance data of the **Martian**, but only one copy of the static **martianCount** is maintained by Java. This saves space. We save time by having the **Martian** constructor increment the static **martianCount**. Because there is only one copy, we do not have to increment separate copies of **martianCount** for each **Martian** object.

Performance Tip 6.4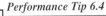

*Use **static** class variables to save storage when a single copy of the data will suffice.*

Although **static** class variables may seem like global variables, **static** class variables have class scope. A class's **public static** class members can be accessed through any object of that class, or they can be accessed through the class name using the dot operator. A class's **private static** class members can be accessed through methods of the class. Actually, **static** class members exist even when no objects of that class exist. To access a **public** or friendly **static** class member when no objects of the class exist, simply prefix the class name and the dot operator to the class member. To access a **pri-**

vate static class member when no objects of the class exist, a **public** or friendly **static** method must be provided and the method must be called by prefixing its name with the class name and dot operator.

The program of Fig. 6.12 demonstrates the use of a **private static** instance variable and a **public static** method. The instance variable **count** is initialized to zero by default. Instance variable **count** maintains a count of the number of objects of class **Employee** that have been instantiated. When objects of class **Employee** exist, member **count** can be referenced through any method of an **Employee** object—in this example, **count** is referenced by the constructor. When no objects of class **Employee** exist, member **count** can still be referenced, but only through a call to **static** method **get-Count** as follows:

```
Employee.getCount()
```

```
1   // Fig. 6.12: Employee.java
2   // Declaration of the Employee class.
3   public class Employee {
4      private String firstName;
5      private String lastName;
6      private static int count;   // # of objects instantiated
7
8      public Employee( String fName, String lName )
9      {
10         firstName = fName;
11         lastName = lName;
12
13         ++count;   // increment static count of employees
14         System.out.println( "Employee object constructor: " +
15                             firstName + " " + lastName );
16      }
17
18      public void finalize()
19      {
20         --count;   // decrement static count of employees
21         System.out.println( "Employee object finalizer: " +
22                             firstName + " " + lastName );
23      }
24
25      public String getFirstName()
26         { return new String( firstName ); }
27
28      public String getLastName()
29         { return new String( lastName ); }
30
31      public static int getCount() { return count; }
32   }
```

Fig. 6.12 Using a **static** class variable to maintain a count of the number of objects of a class (part 1 of 3).

```
33  // Fig. 6.12: EmployeeTest.java
34  // Test Employee class with static class variable,
35  // static class method, and dynamic memory.
36  import java.awt.Graphics;
37  import java.applet.Applet;
38
39  public class EmployeeTest extends Applet {
40     public void paint( Graphics g )
41     {
42        g.drawString( "Employees before instantiation: " +
43                       Employee.getCount(), 25, 25 );
44        Employee e1 = new Employee( "Susan", "Baker" );
45        Employee e2 = new Employee( "Bob", "Jones" );
46
47        g.drawString( "Employees after instantiation: " +
48                       e1.getCount(), 25, 40 );
49
50        g.drawString( "Employee 1: " + e1.getFirstName() +
51                       " " + e1.getLastName(), 25, 70 );
52        g.drawString( "Employee 2: " + e2.getFirstName() +
53                       " " + e2.getLastName(), 25, 85 );
54
55        e1 = null;
56        e2 = null;
57
58        System.gc();  // explicit call to garbage collector
59
60        g.drawString( "Employees after garbage collection: " +
61                       Employee.getCount(), 25, 115 );
62     }
63  }
```

Fig. 6.12 Using a **static** class variable to maintain a count of the number of objects of a class (part 2 of 3).

In this example, method **getCount** is used to determine the number of **Employee** objects currently instantiated. Note that when there are no objects instantiated in the program, the **Employee.getCount()** method call is issued. However, when there are objects instantiated, method **getCount** can also be called through one of the objects as in

        e1.getCount()

Notice that the **Employee** class has a **finalize** method. This method is included to show when it is called in a program. Method **paint** of the applet **EmployeeTest** declares, instantiates and uses two **Employee** objects. When **paint** is done with these objects, the references **e1** and **e2** are set to **null**—i.e., they no longer refer to the objects that were instantiated on lines 44 and 45. This "marks the objects for garbage collection" because there are no more references to the objects in the program. Eventually, the garbage collector reclaims the memory for these objects (or the memory is reclaimed by the operating system when the program terminates). Because we cannot be sure when the garbage collector will execute, we make an explicit call to the garbage collector with the statement

```
Employee object constructor: Susan Baker
Employee object constructor: Bob Jones
Employee object finalizer: Susan Baker
Employee object finalizer: Bob Jones
```

Fig. 6.12 Using a **static** class variable to maintain a count of the number of objects of a class (part 3 of 3).

```
System.gc();  // explicit call to garbage collector
```

This statement invokes the **static** method **gc** of the **System** class to schedule the garbage collector to execute as soon as it can (in this program it executes when the paint method finishes executing). We provided two outputs for this program. The screen dump shows the use of the **Employee** objects, but notice that the last line of text says the number of employees after garbage collection is 2. This is because the garbage collector was called but not executed. The second output shows that the **finalize** methods were called for both **Employee** objects, thus indicating that the garbage collector reclaimed those objects from memory.

A method declared **static** cannot access nonstatic class members. Unlike nonstatic methods, a **static** method has no **this** reference because **static** class variables and **static** class methods exist independent of any objects of a class.

Common Programming Error 6.10

*Referring to the **this** reference within a **static** method is a syntax error.*

Common Programming Error 6.11

*It is a syntax error for a **static** method to call an instance method or to access an instance variable.*

Software Engineering Observation 6.16

*Any **static** class variables and **static** class methods exist and can be used even if no objects of that class have been instantiated.*

6.16 Data Abstraction and Information Hiding

Classes normally hide their implementation details from the clients of the classes. This is called *information hiding*. As an example of information hiding, let us consider a data structure called a *stack*.

Think of a stack in terms of a pile of dishes. When a dish is placed on the pile, it is always placed at the top (referred to as *pushing* the dish onto the stack), and when a dish is removed from the pile, it is always removed from the top (referred to as *popping* the dish off the stack). Stacks are known as *last-in, first-out (LIFO) data structures*—the last item pushed (inserted) on the stack is the first item popped (removed) from the stack.

The programmer may create a stack class and hide from its clients the implementation of the stack. Stacks can easily be implemented with arrays and other methods (such as linked lists; see Chapter 17, "Data Structures" and Chapter 18, "Utilities and Bit Manipulation"). A client of a stack class need not know how the stack is implemented. The client simply requires that when data items are placed in the stack, they will be recalled in last-in, first-out order. This concept is referred to as *data abstraction,* and Java classes define abstract data types (ADTs). Although users may happen to know the details of how a class is implemented, users may not write code that depends on these details. This means that a particular class (such as one that implements a stack and its operations of *push* and *pop*) can be replaced with another version without affecting the rest of the system, as long as the public interface to that class does not change.

The job of a high-level language is to create a view convenient for programmers to use. There is no single accepted standard view—that is one reason why there are so many programming languages. Object-oriented programming in Java presents yet another view.

Most programming languages emphasize actions. In these languages, data exists in support of the actions programs need to take. Data is "less interesting" than actions, anyway. Data is "crude." There are only a few built-in data types, and it is difficult for programmers to create their own new data types.

This view changes with Java and the object-oriented style of programming. Java elevates the importance of data. The primary activity in Java is creating new data types (i.e., classes) and expressing the interactions among objects of those data types.

To move in this direction, the programming-languages community needed to formalize some notions about data. The formalization we consider is the notion of *abstract data types (ADTs)*. ADTs receive as much attention today as structured programming did over the last two decades. ADTs do not replace structured programming. Rather, they provide an additional formalization to further improve the program development process.

What is an abstract data type? Consider the built-in type **int**. What comes to mind is the notion of an integer in mathematics, but **int** on a computer is not precisely what an integer is in mathematics. In particular, computer **int**s are normally quite limited in size. For example, **int** on a 32-bit machine is limited approximately to the range -2 billion to +2 billion. If the result of a calculation falls outside this range, an error occurs and the machine responds in some machine-dependent manner, including the possibility of "quietly" producing an incorrect result. Mathematical integers do not have this problem. So the notion of a computer **int** is really only an approximation to the notion of a real-world integer. The same is true with **float**.

The point is that even the built-in data types provided with programming languages like Java are really only approximations or models of real-world concepts and behaviors. We have taken **int** for granted until this point, but now you have a new perspective to consider. Types like **int**, **float**, **char** and others are all examples of abstract data types. They are essentially ways of representing real-world notions to some satisfactory level of precision within a computer system.

An abstract data type actually captures two notions, namely a *data representation* and the *operations* that are allowed on that data. For example, the notion of **int** defines addition, subtraction, multiplication, division and modulus operations in Java, but division by zero is undefined. Another example is the notion of negative integers whose operations and data representation are clear, but the operation of taking the square root of a negative integer is undefined. In Java, the programmer uses classes to implement abstract data types.

Java has a small set of primitive types. ADTs extend the base programming language.

Software Engineering Observation 6.17

The programmer is able to create new types through the use of the class mechanism. These new types may be designed to be used as conveniently as the built-in types. Thus, Java is an extensible language. Although the language is easy to extend with these new types, the base language itself is not changeable.

New Java classes can be proprietary to an individual, to small groups, to companies, and so on. Many classes are placed in standard *class libraries* intended for wide distribution. This does not necessarily promote standards although de facto standards are emerging. The full value of Java will be realized only when substantial, standardized class libraries become more widely available than they are today. In the United States, such standardization often happens through ANSI, the American National Standards Institute. Regardless of how these libraries ultimately appear, the reader who learns Java and object-oriented programming will be ready to take advantage of the new kinds of rapid, component-oriented software development made possible with class libraries.

6.16.1 Example: Queue Abstract Data Type

Each of us stands in line from time to time. A waiting line is also called a *queue*. We wait in line at the supermarket checkout counter, we wait in line to get gasoline, we wait in line to board a bus, we wait in line to pay a toll on the highway, and students know all too well about waiting in line during registration to get the courses they want. Computer systems use many waiting lines internally, so we need to write programs that simulate what queues are and do.

A queue is a good example of an abstract data type. A queue offers well-understood behavior to its clients. Clients put things in a queue one at a time—using an *enqueue* operation, and the clients get those things back one at a time on demand—using a *dequeue* operation. Conceptually, a queue can become infinitely long. A real queue, of course, is finite. Items are returned from a queue in *first-in, first-out (FIFO)* order—the first item inserted in the queue is the first item removed from the queue.

The queue hides an internal data representation that keeps track of the items currently waiting in line, and it offers a set of operations to its clients, namely *enqueue* and *dequeue*.

The clients are not concerned about the implementation of the queue. Clients merely want the queue to operate "as advertised." When a client enqueues a new item, the queue should accept that item and place it internally in some kind of first-in, first-out data structure. When the client wants the next item from the front of the queue, the queue should remove the item from its internal representation and should deliver the item to the outside world in FIFO order, i.e., the item that has been in the queue the longest should be the next one returned by the next *dequeue* operation.

The queue ADT guarantees the integrity of its internal data structure. Clients may not manipulate this data structure directly. Only the queue ADT has access to its internal data. Clients may cause only allowable operations to be performed on the data representation; operations not provided in the ADT's public interface are rejected by the ADT in some appropriate manner. This could mean issuing an error message, terminating execution, or simply ignoring the operation request.

Summary

- Members of a class are accessed using the member access operator—the dot operator (**.**).
- Classes enable the programmer to model objects with attributes and behaviors. Class types are defined in Java using the keyword **class**.
- Class definitions begin with the keyword **class**. The body of the class definition is delineated with braces (**{** and **}**). Class definitions terminate with a semicolon.
- Any instance variable or method declared **public** in a class is visible to any method with access to an object of the class.
- Any instance variable or method declared **private** is visible only to other members of the class.
- Member access modifiers can appear multiple times and in any order in a class definition.
- A constructor is a special method with the same name as the class that is used to initialize the members of a class object. Constructors are called when objects of their classes are instantiated.
- The set of **public** methods of a class is called the class's public interface.
- Calling methods is more concise than calling functions in procedural programming because most data used by the method is already in the object.
- Within a class's scope, class members may be referenced simply by their names. Outside a class's scope, class members are referenced through a reference to an object.
- The member selection operator **.** is used to access class members.
- Public class members present a view of the services the class provides to the clients of the class.
- To enable clients to read **private** data, the class can provide *get* methods. To enable clients to modify **private** data, the class can provide *set* methods.

- Instance variables of a class are normally made **private** and methods of a class are normally made **public**. Some methods may be **private** and serve as utility methods to the other methods of the class.
- Constructors can be overloaded.
- Once a class object is properly initialized, all methods that manipulate the object should ensure that the object remains in a consistent state.
- When an object of a class is declared, initializers can be provided. These initializers are passed to the class's constructor.
- Constructors may not specify return types, nor may they attempt to return values.
- A finalizer performs termination housekeeping before the system garbage collects an object's storage.
- The keyword **final** specifies that an object is not modifiable.
- A **final** object must be initialized in its declaration.
- Classes can be composed of objects of other classes.
- The **this** reference is implicitly used to reference both methods and instance variables from within an object.
- The **new** operator automatically creates an object of the proper size, and returns a reference of the correct type.
- A static class variable represents "class-wide" information. The declaration of a static member begins with the keyword **static**.
- Static class variables have class scope.
- A method declared **static** cannot access nonstatic class members. A **static** method has no **this** reference because **static** class variables and **static** methods exist independent of any objects of a class.

Terminology

abstract data type (ADT)	consistent state for an instance variable
access method	constructor
aggregation	container class
attribute	data type
behavior	default constructor
cascaded method calls	dot operator (**.**)
class	encapsulation
class definition	extends
class library	extensibility
class method (**static**)	finalizer
class scope	"friendly" access
class variable	get method
client of a class	helper method
composition	implementation of a class
concatenated method calls	information hiding

initialize a class object

instance method

instance of a class

instance variable

instantiate an object of a class

interface to a class

member access control

member access operator (**.**)

member access modifiers

message

method

method calls

mutator method

new operator

no-argument constructor

object

object-based programming (OBP)

object-oriented programming (OOP)

package access

predicate method

principle of least privilege

private

programmer-defined type

public

public interface of a class

query method

rapid applications development (RAD)

reusable code

services of a class

set method

software reusability

static class variable

static method

this reference

user-defined type

utility method

Common Programming Errors

6.1   Attempting to declare a return type for a constructor and/or attempting to return a value from a constructor is a syntax error.

6.2   An attempt by a method which is not a member of a particular class to access a **private** member of that class is a syntax error.

6.3   If constructors are provided for a class, but none are no-argument constructors, and an attempt is made to call a no-argument constructor to initialize an object of the class, a syntax error occurs. A constructor may be called with no arguments only if there are no constructors for the class (the default constructor is called) or if there is a no-argument constructor.

6.4   Attempting to overload a method of a class with a method not in that class's scope.

6.5   A constructor can call other methods of the class, such as set or get methods, but because the constructor is initializing the object, the instance variables may not yet be in a consistent state. Using instance variables before they have been properly initialized is an error.

6.6   Attempting to modify a **final** instance variable.

6.7   Not initialing a **final** instance variable.

6.8   Explicitly using the **this** reference in a static method is a syntax error.

6.9   In a method in which a method parameter has the same name as one of the class members, use **this** explicitly if you want to access the class member; otherwise, you will incorrectly reference the method parameter.

6.10   Referring to the **this** reference within a **static** method is a syntax error.

6.11   It is a syntax error for a **static** method to call an instance method or to access an instance variable.

Good Programming Practices

6.1   Group members by member access modifier in a class definition for clarity and readability.

6.2   Initialize instance variables of a class in that class's constructor.

6.3   Our preference is to list the **private** members of a class first.

6.4   Despite the fact that **private** and **public** members may be repeated and intermixed, list all the **private** members of a class first in one group and then list all the **public** members in another group.

6.5   When appropriate (almost always), provide a constructor to ensure that every object is properly initialized with meaningful values.

6.6   Every method that modifies the private instance variables of an object should ensure that the data remains in a consistent state.

6.7   Avoid using method parameter names that conflict with class member names.

6.8   Explicitly using **this** can increase program clarity in some contexts in which **this** is optional.

Performance Tips

6.1   All Java objects are passed by reference. Only a memory address is passed, not a copy of a possibly large object (as would be the case in a pass by value).

6.2   Initialize member objects explicitly at constructor time. This eliminates the overhead of doubly initializing member objects—once when the member object's default constructor is called and again when set methods are used to provide initial values for the member object.

6.3   Java conserves storage by maintaining only one copy of each method per class; this method is invoked by every object of that class. Each object, on the other hand, has its own copy of the class's instance variables.

6.4   Use **static** class variables to save storage when a single copy of the data will suffice.

Software Engineering Observations

6.1   It is important to write programs that are understandable and easy to maintain. Change is the rule rather than the exception. Programmers should anticipate that their code will be modified. As we will see, classes facilitate program modifiability.

6.2   Information hiding promotes program modifiability and simplifies the client's perception of a class.

6.3   Clients of a class can (and should) use the class without knowing the internal details of how the class is implemented. If the class implementation is changed (to improve performance, for example), provided the class's interface remains constant, the class clients' source code need not change. This makes it much easier to modify systems.

6.4   Using an object-oriented programming approach can often simplify method calls by reducing the number of parameters to be passed. This benefit of object-oriented programming derives from the fact that encapsulation of instance variables and methods within an object gives the methods the right to access the instance variables.

6.5   Keep all the instance variables of a class **private**. When necessary provide **public** methods to set the values of **private** instance variables and to get the values of **private** instance variables. This architecture helps hide the implementation of a class from its clients, which reduces bugs and improves program modifiability.

6.6   Class designers use **private** and **public members** to enforce the notion of information hiding and the principle of least privilege.

6.7   The class designer need not provide set and/or get methods for each **private** data item; these capabilities should be provided only when it makes sense and after careful thought by the class designer.

6.8   Methods tend to fall into a number of different categories: methods that get the values of **private** instance variables; methods that set the values of **private** instance variables; methods that implement the features of the class; and methods that perform various mechanical chores for the class such as initializing class objects, assigning class objects, converting between classes and built-in types or between classes and other classes.

6.9   If a method of a class already provides all or part of the functionality required by a constructor (or other method) of the class, call that method from the constructor (or other method). This simplifies the maintenance of the code and reduces the likelihood of an error if the implementation of the code is modified. It is also an effective example of reuse.

6.10   Methods that set the values of **private** data should verify that the intended new values are proper; if they are not, the set methods should place the **private** instance variables into an appropriate consistent state.

6.11   Accessing private data through set and get methods not only protects the instance variables from receiving invalid values, but it also insulates clients of the class from the representation of the instance variables. Thus, if the representation of the data changes (typically to reduce the amount of storage required or to improve performance), only the method implementations need to change—the clients need not change as long as the interface provided by the methods remains the same.

6.12   Declaring an instance variable as **final** helps enforce the principle of least privilege. If an instance variable should not be modified, then declare it to be **final** to expressly forbid modification. Accidental attempts to modify a **final** instance variable are caught at compile time rather than causing execution-time errors.

6.13   Constant class members (**final** objects and **final** "variables") must be initialized. Assignments are not allowed.

6.14   One form of software reuse is composition in which a class has objects of other classes as members.

6.15   Some people in the OOP community feel that friendly access corrupts information hiding and weakens the value of the object-oriented design approach.

6.16   Any **static** class variables and **static** class methods exist and can be used even if no objects of that class have been instantiated.

6.17   The programmer is able to create new types through the use of the class mechanism. These new types may be designed to be used as conveniently as the built-in types. Thus, Java is an extensible language. Although the language is easy to extend with these new types, the base language itself is not changeable.

Testing and Debugging Tip

6.1   Making the instance variables of a class **private** and the methods of the class **public** facilitates debugging because problems with data manipulations are localized to the class's methods.

Self-Review Exercises

6.1   Fill in the blanks in each of the following:
   a) Class members are accessed via the _____ operator in conjunction with an object of the class.
   b) Members of a class specified as _____ are accessible only to methods of the class.
   c) A _____ is a special method used to initialize the instance variables of a class.
   d) A _____method is used to assign values to **private** instance variables of a class.
   e) Methods of a class are normally made _____ and instance variables of a class are normally made _____.
   f) A _____ method is used to retrieve values of **private** data of a class.
   g) The keyword _____ introduces a class definition.
   h) Members of a class specified as _____ are accessible anywhere an object of the class is in scope.
   i) The _____ operator dynamically allocates memory for an object of a specified type and returns a _____ to that type.
   j) A constant object must be _____; it cannot be modified after it is created.
   k) A _____ instance variable represents class-wide information.
   l) The _____ reference is passed as an implicit first argument into every method of a class.
   m) The keyword _____ specifies that an object or variable is not modifiable after it is initialized.
   n) A method declared **static** cannot access _____ class members.

Answers to Self-Review Exercises

6.1   a) dot (**.**). b) **private**. c) constructor. d) set. e) **public**, **private**. f) get. g) **class**. h) **public**. i) **new**, reference. j) initialized. k) **static**. l) **this**. m) **final**. n) non-**static**.

Exercises

6.2   Create a class called **Complex** for performing arithmetic with complex numbers. Write a driver program to test your class.

   Complex numbers have the form

```
realPart + imaginaryPart * i
```

where *i* is

$$\sqrt{-1}$$

Use floating-point variables to represent the private data of the class. Provide a constructor method that enables an object of this class to be initialized when it is declared. Provide a no-argument constructor with default values in case no initializers are provided. Provide **public** methods for each of the following:

a) Addition of two **Complex** numbers: The real parts are added together and the imaginary parts are added together.

b) Subtraction of two **Complex** numbers: The real part of the right operand is subtracted from the real part of the left operand and the imaginary part of the right operand is subtracted from the imaginary part of the left operand.

c) Printing **Complex** numbers in the form **(a, b)** where **a** is the real part and **b** is the imaginary part.

6.3 Create a class called **Rational** for performing arithmetic with fractions. Write a driver program to test your class.

Use integer variables to represent the **private** instance variables of the class—the **numerator** and the **denominator**. Provide a constructor method that enables an object of this class to be initialized when it is declared. The constructor should store the fraction in reduced form (i.e., the fraction

2/4

would be stored in the object as 1 in the **numerator** and 2 in the **denominator**). Provide a no-argument constructor with default values in case no initializers are provided. Provide **public** methods for each of the following:

a) Addition of two **Rational** numbers. The result of the addition should be stored in reduced form.

b) Subtraction of two **Rational** numbers. The result of the subtraction should be stored in reduced form.

c) Multiplication of two **Rational** numbers. The result of the multiplication should be stored in reduced form.

d) Division of two **Rational** numbers. The result of the division should be stored in reduced form.

e) Printing **Rational** numbers in the form **a/b** where **a** is the **numerator** and **b** is the **denominator**.

f) Printing **Rational** numbers in floating-point format. (Consider providing formatting capabilities that enable the user of the class to specify the number of digits of precision to the right of the decimal point.)

6.4 Modify the **Time** class of Fig. 6.5 to include the **tick** method that increments the time stored in a **Time** object by one second. Also provide method **incrementMinute** to increment the minute and method **incrementHour** to increment the hour. The **Time** object should always remain in a consistent state. Write a driver program that tests the **tick** method, the **incrementMinute** method and the **incrementHour** method to ensure that they work correctly. Be sure to test the following cases:

a) Incrementing into the next minute.

b) Incrementing into the next hour.

c) Incrementing into the next day (i.e., 11:59:59 PM to 12:00:00 AM).

6.5   Modify the **MyDate** class of Fig. 6.8 to perform error checking on the initializer values for instance variables **month, day** and **year**. Also, provide a method **nextDay** to increment the day by one. The **Myate** object should always remain in a consistent state. Write a driver program that tests the **nextDay** method in a loop that prints the date during each iteration of the loop to illustrate that the **nextDay** method works correctly. Be sure to test the following cases:
  a) Incrementing into the next month.
  b) Incrementing into the next year.

6.6   Combine the modified **Time** class of Exercise 6.4 and the modified **MyDate** class of Exercise 6.5 into one class called **DateAndTime** (in Chapter 7 we will discuss inheritance which will enable us to accomplish this task quickly without modifying the existing class definitions). Modify the **tick** method to call the **nextDay** method if the time is incremented into the next day. Modify methods **toString** and **PrintMilitary** to output the date in addition to the time. Write a driver program to test the new class **DateAndTime**. Specifically test incrementing the time to the next day.

6.7   Modify the set methods in the program of Fig. 6.5 to return appropriate error values if an attempt is made to set one of the instance variables **hour, minute** or **second** of an object of class **Time** to an invalid value.

6.8   Create a class **Rectangle**. The class has attributes **length** and **width**, each of which defaults to 1. It has methods that calculate the **perimeter** and the **area** of the rectangle. It has *set* and *get* methods for both **length** and **width**. The *set* methods should verify that **length** and **width** are each floating-point numbers larger than 0.0 and less than 20.0.

6.9   Create a more sophisticated **Rectangle** class than the one you created in Exercise 6.8. This class stores only the Cartesian coordinates of the four corners of the rectangle. The constructor calls a *set* method that accepts four sets of coordinates and verifies that each of these is in the first quadrant with no single *x* or *y* coordinate larger than 20.0. The *set* method also verifies that the supplied coordinates do, in fact, specify a rectangle. Methods calculate the **length, width, perimeter** and **area**. The length is the larger of the two dimensions. Include a predicate method **square** which determines if the rectangle is a square.

6.10   Modify the **Rectangle** class of Exercise 6.9 to include a **draw** method that displays the rectangle inside a 25-by-25 box enclosing the portion of the first quadrant in which the rectangle resides. Use the methods of the **Graphics** class to help output the **Rectangle**. If you feel ambitious you might include methods to scale the size of the rectangle, rotate it and move it around within the designated portion of the first quadrant.

6.11   Create a class **HugeInteger** which uses a 40-element array of digits to store integers as large as 40-digits each. Provide methods **inputHugeInteger, outputHugeInteger, addHugeIntegers** and **substractHugeIntegers**. For comparing **HugeInteger** objects provide methods **isEqualTo, isNotEqualTo, isGreaterThan, isLessThan, IsGreaterThanOrEqualTo** and **isLessThanOrEqualTo**—each of these is a "predicate" method that simply returns **true** if the relationship holds between the two **HugeInteger**s and returns **false** if the relationship does not hold. Provide a predicate method **isZero**. If you feel ambitious, also provide the method **multiplyHugeIntegers**, teh method **divideHugeIntegers** and the method **modulusHugeIntegers**.

6.12   Create a class **TicTacToe** that will enable you to write a complete program to play the game of tic-tac-toe. The class contains as private data a 3-by-3 double array of integers. The constructor should initialize the empty board to all zeros. Allow two human players. Wherever the first player moves, place a 1 in the specified square; place a 2 wherever the second player moves. Each move must be to an empty square. After each move determine if the game has been won, or if the game is a draw. If you feel ambitious, modify your program so that the computer makes the moves for one of the players automatically. Also, allow the player to specify whether he or she wants to go first or second. If you feel exceptionally ambitious, develop a program that will play three-dimensional tic-tac-toe on a 4-by-4-by-4 board (Note: This is a challenging project that could take many weeks of effort!).

6.13   Explain the notion of "friendly" access in Java. Explain the negative aspects of "friendly" access as described in the text.

6.14   What happens when a return type, even **void**, is specified for a constructor or destructor?

6.15   Create a **MyDate** class with the following capabilities:
a) Output the date in multiple formats such as

```
MM/DD/YY
June 14, 1992
DDD YYYY
```

b) Use overloaded constructors to create **MyDate** objects initialized with dates of the formats in part (a).

6.16   Create class **SavingsAccount**. Use a **static** class variable to store the **annualInterestRate** for each of the savers. Each object of the class contains a **private** instance variable **savingsBalance** indicating the amount the saver currently has on deposit. Provide method **calculateMonthlyInterest** to calculate the monthly interest by multiplying the **balance** by **annualInterestRate** divided by 12; this interest should be added to **savingsBalance**. Provide a **static** method **modifyInterestRate** that sets the **annualInterestRate** to a new value. Write a driver program to test class **SavingsAccount**. Instantiate two different **savingsAccount** objects, **saver1** and **saver2**, with balances of $2000.00 and $3000.00, respectively. Set **annualInterestRate** to 4%, then calculate the monthly interest and print the new balances for each of the savers. Then set the **annualInterestRate** to 5% and calculate the next month's interest and print the new balances for each of the savers.

6.17   Create class **IntegerSet**. Each object of the class can hold integers in the range 0 through 100. A set is represented internally as an array of ones and zeros. Array element **a[i]** is 1 if integer i is in the set. Array element **a[j]** is 0 if integer j is not in the set. The no-argument constructor initializes a set to the so-called "empty set," i.e., a set whose array representation contains all zeros.

Provide the following methods: Method **unionOfIntegerSets** creates a third set which is the set-theoretic union of two existing sets (i.e., an element of the third set's array is set to 1 if that element is 1 in either or both of the existing sets, otherwise the element of the third set is set to 0. Method **intersectionOfIntegerSets** creates a third set which is the set-theoretic intersection of two existing sets, i.e., an element of the third set's array is set to 0 if that element is 0 in either or both of the existing sets, otherwise the element of the third set is set to 1. Method **insertElement** inserts a new integer k into a set (by setting **a[k]** to 1). Method **deleteElement** deletes integer m (by setting **a[m]** to 0). Method **setPrint** prints a set as a list of numbers separated by spaces. Print only those elements that are present in the set. Print **- - -** for an empty set. Method **isEqualTo** determines if two sets are equal. Write a program to test your **IntegerSet** class. Instantiate several **IntegerSet** objects. Test that all your methods work properly.

6.18   It would be perfectly reasonable for the **Time** class of Fig. 6.1 to represent the time internally as the number of seconds since midnight rather than the three integer values **hour**, **minute** and **second**. Clients could use the same public methods and get the same Modify the **Time** class of Fig. 6.1 to implement the **Time** as the number of seconds since midnight and show that there is no visible change to the clients of the class.

7

Object-Oriented Programming

Objectives

- To be able to create new classes by inheriting from existing classes.
- To understand inheritance and software reusability.
- To understand superclasses and subclasses.
- To appreciate how polymorphism makes systems extensible and maintainable.
- To understand the distinction between abstract classes and concrete classes.
- To learn how to create abstract classes.

Say not you know another entirely, till you have divided an inheritance with him.
Johann Kasper Lavater

This method is to define as the number of a class the class of all classes similar to the given class.
Bertrand Russell

Good as it is to inherit a library, it is better to collect one.
Augustine Birrell

General propositions do not decide concrete cases.
Oliver Wendell Holmes

A philosopher of imposing stature doesn't think in a vacuum. Even his most abstract ideas are, to some extent, conditioned by what is or is not known in the time when he lives.
Alfred North Whitehead

When creating a new class, instead of writing completely new instance variables and instance methods, the programmer can designate that the new class is to *inherit* the instance variables and instance methods of a previously defined *superclass.* The new class is referred to as a *subclass.* Each subclass itself becomes a candidate to be a superclass for some future subclass.

The *direct superclass* of a subclass is the superclass from which the subclass explicitly inherits. An indirect superclass is inherited from two or more levels up the class hierarchy.

With *single inheritance,* a class is derived from one superclass. Java does not support *multiple inheritance* (as C++ does) but it does support the notion of *interfaces.* Interfaces help Java achieve many of the advantages of multiple inheritance without the associated problems. We will discuss interfaces in Chapter 13, "Multithreading," where we consider both general principles as well as a detailed specific example using the **Runnable** interface with threads.

A subclass normally adds instance variables and instance methods of its own, so a subclass is generally larger than its superclass. A subclass is more specific than its superclass and represents a smaller group of objects. With single inheritance, the subclass starts out essentially the same as the superclass. The real strength of inheritance comes from the ability to define in the subclass additions to, or replacements for, the features inherited from the superclass.

Every object of a subclass is also an object of that subclass's superclass. However, the converse is not true—superclass objects are not objects of that superclass's subclasses. We will take advantage of this "subclass-object-is-a-superclass-object" relationship to perform some powerful manipulations. For example, we can link a wide variety of different objects related to a common superclass through inheritance into a linked list of superclass objects. This allows a variety of objects to be processed in a general way. As we will see in this and the next chapter, this is a key thrust of object-oriented programming.

We add a new form of member access control in this chapter, namely **protected** access. Subclass methods and methods of other classes in the same package as the superclass can access **protected** superclass members.

Experience in building software systems indicates that significant portions of the code deal with closely related special cases. It becomes difficult in such systems to see the "big picture" because the designer and the programmer become preoccupied with the special cases. Object-oriented programming provides several ways of "seeing the forest through the trees"—a process called *abstraction.*

If a procedural program has many closely related special cases, then it is common to see **switch** statements that distinguish among the special cases and provide the processing logic to deal with each case individually. We will show how to use inheritance and polymorphism to replace such **switch** logic with much simpler logic.

We distinguish between the *"is a" relationship* and the *"has a" relationship.* "Is a" is inheritance. In an "is a" relationship, an object of a subclass type may also be treated as an object of the superclass type. "Has a" is composition (as we discussed in Chapter 6). In a "has a" relationship, a class object has one or more objects of other classes as members.

A subclass's methods may need to access certain of its superclass's instance variables and methods.

Software Engineering Observation 7.1

A subclass cannot directly access `private` *members of its superclass.*

This is a crucial aspect of software engineering in Java. If a subclass could access the superclass's `private` members, this would violate information hiding in the superclass.

Testing and Debugging Tip 7.1

Hiding `private` *members is a huge help in testing, debugging and correctly modifying systems. If a subclass could access its superclass's* `private` *members, it would then be possible for classes derived from that subclass to access that data as well, and so on. This would propagate access to what is supposed to be* `private` *data, and the benefits of information hiding would be lost throughout the class hierarchy.*

A subclass can, however, access the ***public***, ***protected*** and "friendly" members of its superclass. Superclass members that should not be accessible to a subclass via inheritance are declared ***private*** in the superclass. A subclass can effect state changes in superclass ***private*** members only through access methods provided in the superclass's ***public***, ***protected*** and "friendly" interfaces.

One problem with inheritance is that a subclass can inherit methods that it does not need or should expressly not have. When a superclass member is inappropriate for a subclass, that member can be *overridden* in the subclass with an appropriate implementation.

Perhaps most exciting is the notion that new classes can inherit from abundant *class libraries.* Organizations develop their own class libraries and can take advantage of other libraries available worldwide. Someday, most software may be constructed from *standardized reusable components* just as hardware is often constructed today. This will help meet the challenges of developing the ever more powerful software we will need in the future.

7.2 Superclasses and Subclasses

Often an object of one class "is an" object of another class as well. A rectangle certainly *is a* quadrilateral (as are squares, parallelograms and trapezoids). Thus, class **Rectangle** can be said to *inherit* from class **Quadrilateral**. In this context, class **Quadrilateral** is a superclass and class **Rectangle** is a subclass. A rectangle *is a* specific type of quadrilateral, but it is incorrect to claim that a quadrilateral *is a* rectangle (the quadrilateral could be a parallelogram). Figure 7.1 shows several simple inheritance examples.

Because inheritance normally produces subclasses with *more* features than their superclasses, the terms superclass and subclass can be confusing. There is another way, however, to view these terms that makes perfectly good sense. Because every subclass object "is an" object of its superclass, and because one superclass can have many subclasses, the set of objects represented by a superclass is normally larger than the set of objects represented by any of that superclass's subclasses.

Inheritance relationships form tree-like hierarchical structures. A superclass exists in a hierarchical relationship with its subclasses. A class can certainly exist by itself, but it is when a class is used with the mechanism of inheritance that the class becomes either a superclass that supplies attributes and behaviors to other classes, or the class becomes a subclass that inherits those attributes and behaviors.

Superclass	Subclasses
Student	GraduateStudent UndergraduateStudent
Shape	Circle Triangle Rectangle
Loan	CarLoan HomeImprovementLoan MortgageLoan
Employee	FacultyMember StaffMember
Account	CheckingAccount SavingsAccount

Fig. 7.1   Some simple inheritance examples.

Let us develop a simple inheritance hierarchy. A typical university community has thousands of people who are community members. These people consist of employees, students and alumni. Employees are either faculty members or staff members. Faculty members are either administrators (such as deans and department chairpersons) or teaching faculty. This yields the inheritance hierarchy shown in Fig. 7.2. Note that the inheritance hierarchy could contain many other classes. For example, students can be graduate students or undergraduate students. Undergraduate students can be freshman, sophomores, juniors, and seniors. And so on.

Another substantial inheritance hierarchy is the **Shape** hierarchy of Fig. 7.3. There are abundant examples of hierarchies in the real world but students are not accustomed to categorizing the real world in this manner, so it takes some adjustment in their thinking. Actually, biology students have had some practice with hierarchies. Everything we study in biology is grouped into a hierarchy headed by living things and these can be plants or animals and so on.

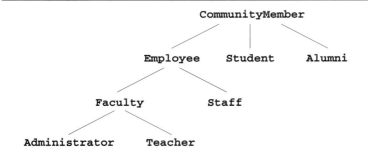

Fig. 7.2   An inheritance hierarchy for university community members.

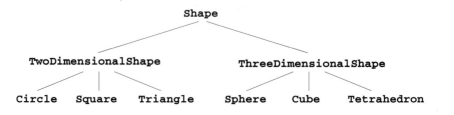

Fig. 7.3   A portion of a **Shape** class hierarchy.

To specify that class **CommissionWorker** is derived from (or inherits from) class **Employee**, class **CommissionWorker** could be defined in Java as follows

```
class CommissionWorker extends Employee { ... }
```

With inheritance only **private** members of a superclass are not accessible from that class's subclasses. All other superclass members become members of the subclass.

It is possible to treat superclass objects and subclass objects similarly; that commonality is expressed in the attributes and behaviors of the superclass. Objects of all classes derived from a common superclass can all be treated as objects of that superclass.

We will consider many examples in which we can take advantage of this relationship with an ease of programming not available in non-object-oriented languages such as C.

7.3 **protected** Members

Public members of a superclass are accessible by all methods in the program. **Private** members of a superclass are accessible only by methods of the superclass.

Protected access serves as an intermediate level of protection between **public** access and **private** access. **Protected** members of a superclass may be accessed only by methods of the superclass, by methods of subclasses and by methods of other classes in the same package.

Subclass methods can normally refer to **public**, **protected** and "friendly" members of the superclass simply by using the member names. When a subclass method overrides a superclass method, the superclass method may be accessed from the subclass by preceding the superclass method name with **super** followed by the dot character (**.**).

7.4 Relationship between Superclass Objects and Subclass Objects

An object of a subclass can be treated as an object of its corresponding superclass. This makes possible some interesting manipulations. For example, despite the fact that objects of a variety of classes derived from a particular superclass may be quite different from one another, we can create an array of them—as long as we treat them as superclass objects. But the reverse is not true: A superclass object is not also automatically a subclass object.

 Common Programming Error 7.1

Treating a superclass object as a subclass object can cause errors.

The programmer may, however, use an explicit cast to convert a superclass reference to a subclass reference. This can only be done when the superclass reference is actually referencing a subclass object, otherwise Java will throw a **ClassCastException**.

Common Programming Error 7.2

Assigning an object of a superclass to a subclass reference (without a cast) is a syntax error.

Software Engineering Observation 7.2

If an object has been assigned to a reference of one of its superclasses, it is acceptable to cast that object back to its own type. In fact, this must be done in order to send that object any of its messages that do not appear in that superclass.

Our first example is shown in Fig. 7.4. Lines 1–26 show a **Point** class definition and **Point** method definitions. Lines 27–63 show a **Circle** class definition and **Circle** method definitions; we will see that class **Circle** inherits from class **Point**. Lines 64–101 show a driver program that demonstrates assigning subclass references to superclass references and casting superclass references to subclass references.

```java
1   // Fig. 7.4: Point.java
2   // Definition of class Point
3
4   public class Point {
5      protected double x, y; // coordinates of the Point
6
7      // constructor
8      public Point( double a, double b ) { setPoint( a, b ); }
9
10     // Set x and y coordinates of Point
11     public void setPoint( double a, double b )
12     {
13        x = a;
14        y = b;
15     }
16
17     // get x coordinate
18     public double getX() { return x; }
19
20     // get y coordinate
21     public double getY() { return y; }
22
23     // convert the point into a String representation
24     public String toString()
25        { return "[" + x + ", " + y + "]"; }
26   }
```

Fig. 7.4   Assigning subclass references to superclass references (part 1 of 4).

```
27   // Fig. 7.4: Circle.java
28   // Definition of class Circle
29
30   public class Circle extends Point {  // inherits from Point
31      protected double radius;
32
33      // no-argument constructor
34      public Circle()
35      {
36         super( 0, 0 );  // call the superclass constructor
37         setRadius( 0 );
38      }
39
40      // Constructor
41      public Circle( double r, double a, double b )
42      {
43         super( a, b );  // call the superclass constructor
44         setRadius( r );
45      }
46
47      // Set radius of Circle
48      public void setRadius( double r )
49         { radius = ( r >= 0.0 ? r : 0.0 ); }
50
51      // Get radius of Circle
52      public double getRadius() { return radius; }
53
54      // Calculate area of Circle
55      public double area() { return 3.14159 * radius * radius; }
56
57      // convert the Circle to a String
58      public String toString()
59      {
60         return "Center = " + "[" + x + ", " + y + "]" +
61                 "; Radius = " + radius;
62      }
63   }
```

Fig. 7.4   Assigning subclass references to superclass references (part 2 of 4).

Let us first examine the **Point** class definition in lines 1–26. The **public** interface to **Point** contains methods **Point**, **setPoint**, **getX**, **getY** and **toString**. The instance variables **x** and **y** of **Point** are specified as **protected**. This prevents clients of **Point** objects from directly accessing the data (unless they are in the same package), but enables classes derived from **Point** to access the inherited instance variables directly. If the data were specified as **private**, the non-**private** methods of **Point** would have to be used to access the data, even by subclasses.

Class **Circle** (lines 27–63) inherits from class **Point**. This is specified in the first line of the class definition

```
Public class Circle extends Point {  // inherits from Point
```

```
64   // Fig. 7.4: Test.java
65   // Casting superclass references to subclass references
66   import java.awt.Graphics;
67   import java.applet.Applet;
68
69   public class Test extends Applet {
70      private Point pointRef, p;
71      private Circle circleRef, c;
72
73      public void init()
74      {
75         p = new Point( 3.5, 5.3 );
76         c = new Circle( 2.7, 1.2, 8.9 );
77      }
78
79      public void paint( Graphics g )
80      {
81         g.drawString( "Point p: " + p.toString(), 25, 25 );
82         g.drawString( "Circle c: " + c.toString(), 25, 40 );
83
84         // Attempt to treat a Circle as a Point
85         pointRef = c;   // assign Circle to pointRef
86         g.drawString( "Circle c (via pointRef): " +
87                        pointRef.toString(), 25, 70 );
88
89         // Treat a Circle as a Circle (with some casting)
90         pointRef = c;   // assign Circle to pointRef
91         circleRef = (Circle) pointRef;  // cast super to sub
92         g.drawString( "Circle c (via circleRef): " +
93                        circleRef.toString(), 25, 100);
94         g.drawString( "Area of c (via circleRef): " +
95                        circleRef.area(), 25, 115 );
96
97         // Attempt to refer to Point object
98         // with Circle reference
99         circleRef = (Circle) p;
100     }
101  }
```

Fig. 7.4   Assigning subclass references to superclass references (part 3 of 4).

Keyword **extends** in the class definition indicates inheritance. All the (non-**private**) members of class **Point** are inherited into class **Circle**. Thus, the **public** interface to **Circle** includes the **Point public** methods as well as the two overloaded **Circle** constructors and **Circle** methods **setRadius, getRadius, area** and **toString**.

The **Circle** constructors (lines 33–38 and lines 40–45) must invoke the **Point** constructor to initialize the superclass portion of a **Circle** object. The first line of the body of each constructor (line 36 and line 43) invokes the **Point** constructor by the reference to **super**. The no-argument constructor passes zeros to initialize superclass members **x** and **y** and the other constructor passes values **a** and **b** to the **Point** constructor to initialize the superclass members **x** and **y**.

```
Applet Viewer: Test.class

Applet

    Point p: [3.5, 5.3]
    Circle c: Center = [1.2, 8.9]; Radius = 2.7

    Circle c (via pointRef): Center = [1.2, 8.9]; Radius = 2.7

    Circle c (via circleRef): Center = [1.2, 8.9]; Radius = 2.7
    Area of c (via circleRef): 22.9022

Applet started.
```

```
Exception in thread "AWT-Callback-Win32"
    java.lang.ClassCastException: Point
        at Test.paint(Test.java:36)
        at sun.awt.win32.MComponentPeer.paint
            (MComponentPeer.java:147)
        at sun.awt.win32.MComponentPeer.handleExpose
            (MComponentPeer.java:268)
        at sun.awt.win32.MToolkit.run(MToolkit.java:57)
```

Fig. 7.4   Assigning subclass references to superclass references (part 4 of 4).

If the **Circle** constructor did not invoke the **Point** constructor explicitly, the **Point** constructor would be invoked with no arguments. Because the **Point** class does not provide a no-argument constructor, the compiler would generate an error.

A subclass can redefine a superclass method using the same signature; this is called *overriding* a superclass method. When that method is mentioned by name in the subclass, the subclass version is automatically selected. The **super** reference followed by the dot operator may be used to access the superclass version of that method from the subclass.

Note that class **Circle** overrides the **Point** class **toString** method (lines 57–62). The **Circle** method **toString** directly accesses the **protected** instance variables **x** and **y** that were inherited from the **Point** class.

Software Engineering Observation 7.3

A redefinition of a superclass method in a subclass need not have the same signature as the superclass method. Such a redefinition is not method overriding but is simply an example of method overloading.

Common Programming Error 7.3

It is a syntax error if a method in a superclass and a method in its subclass have the same signature but a different return type.

The applet (lines 64–101) instantiates **Point** object **p** and **Circle** object **c** (lines 75–76). These objects are output to show that they were initialized correctly (lines 81–82).

Next, **Circle c**, a subclass object, is assigned to **pointRef** (line 85). It is always acceptable in Java to assign a subclass reference to a superclass reference (because of the "is a" relationship of inheritance). The converse of this is dangerous, as we will see. Interestingly, when this **pointRef** is sent the **toString** message, Java knows that the object really is a **Circle**, so it chooses the **Circle toString** method instead of using the **Point toString** method as you might have expected. This is an example of polymorphism and dynamic binding, concepts we treat in depth later in this chapter.

In line 90 we assign **Circle** reference **c** to **pointRef** (again, such assignments are always allowed in Java). In line 91 we cast **pointRef** (which admittedly is referencing a **Circle**) to **circleRef** (this cast would be dangerous if **pointRef** were really referencing a **Point** as we will soon see). Then we use **circleRef** to print successfully the various facts about **Circle circleRef**.

Then we attempt a dangerous cast in line 99. We cast **Point p** to **circleRef**. At execution time when this is attempted, Java determines that **p** really references a **Point**, recognizes the cast to **Circle** as being dangerous, and throws a **ClassCastException**. Because we made no provision to deal with this exception here, the program terminates. We will discuss exception handling in depth in Chapter 12. The second output window shows the error messages displayed when the **ClassCastException** occurs. Such error messages normally include the file name and line number at which the error occurred so you go to that specific line in the program for debugging. Note that the first line number specified—**test.java:36**—is different from the line numbers for file **test.java** shown in the text. This is because the examples in the text are numbered with consecutive line numbers for all files in the same program for discussion purposes. If you open the file **test.java**, you will find that the error did indeed occur at line 36.

7.5 Using Constructors and Finalizers in Subclasses

When an object of a subclass is instantiated, the superclass's constructor should be called to do any necessary initialization of the superclass instance variables of the subclass object. An explicit call to the superclass constructor (via the **super** reference) can be provided as the first statement in the subclass constructor. Otherwise the subclass constructor will call the superclass default constructor (or no-argument constructor) implicitly.

Common Programming Error 7.4

If a subclass constructor invokes a superclass default constructor (or no-argument constructor) and if the superclass does not have a default constructor (or no-argument constructor), a syntax error occurs.

Common Programming Error 7.5

*It is a syntax error if a **super** call by a subclass to its superclass constructor is not the first statement in the subclass constructor.*

Superclass constructors are not inherited by subclasses. Subclass constructors, however, can call superclass constructors via the **super** reference.

Software Engineering Observation 7.4

When an object of a subclass is created, first the superclass constructor executes, then the subclass constructor executes.

Figure 7.5 shows the order in which superclass and subclass constructors and finalizers are called. Class **Point** (lines 1–37) contains a constructor, a finalizer, other **public** methods and **protected** instance variables **x** and **y**. The constructor and finalizer each print that they are executing then display the **Point** for which they are invoked. Class **Circle** (lines 38–86) derives from **Point** and contains two constructors, a finalizer, other **public** methods and **protected** instance variable **radius**. The constructor and finalizer each print that they are executing then display the **Circle** for which they are invoked. The **Circle** constructor also invokes the **Point** constructor via **super** and passes the values **a** and **b** so the superclass instance variables can be initialized. Note that the **Circle** method **toString** invokes **Point**'s **toString** via **super** (line 83).

```
1   // Fig. 7.5: Point.java
2   // Definition of class Point
3   public class Point {
4      protected double x, y; // coordinates of the Point
5
6      // constructor
7      public Point( double a, double b )
8      {
9         setPoint( a, b );
10        System.out.println( "Point constructor: " +
11                            toString() );
12     }
13
14     // finalizer
15     public void finalize()
16     {
17        System.out.println( "Point finalizer: " +
18                            toString() );
19     }
20
21     // Set x and y coordinates of Point
22     public void setPoint( double a, double b )
23     {
24        x = a;
25        y = b;
26     }
27
28     // get x coordinate
29     public double getX() { return x; }
30
31     // get y coordinate
32     public double getY() { return y; }
33
34     // convert the point into a String representation
35     public String toString()
36        { return "[" + x + ", " + y + "]"; }
37  }
```

Fig. 7.5   Order in which constructors and finalizers are called (part 1 of 3).

```
38  // Fig. 7.5: Circle.java
39  // Definition of class Circle
40
41  public class Circle extends Point {   // inherits from Point
42     protected double radius;
43
44     // no-argument constructor
45     public Circle()
46     {
47        super( 0, 0 );  // call the superclass constructor
48        setRadius( 0 );
49        System.out.println( "Circle constructor: " +
50                            toString() );
51     }
52
53     // Constructor
54     public Circle( double r, double a, double b )
55     {
56        super( a, b );  // call the superclass constructor
57        setRadius( r );
58        System.out.println( "Circle constructor: " +
59                            toString() );
60     }
61
62     // finalizer
63     public void finalize()
64     {
65        System.out.println( "Circle finalizer: " +
66                            toString() );
67     }
68
69     // Set radius of Circle
70     public void setRadius( double r )
71        { radius = ( r >= 0 ? r : 0 ); }
72
73     // Get radius of Circle
74     public double getRadius() { return radius; }
75
76     // Calculate area of Circle
77     public double area()
78        { return 3.14159 * radius * radius; }
79
80     // convert the Circle to a String
81     public String toString()
82     {
83        return "Center = " + super.toString() +
84               "; Radius = " + radius;
85     }
86  }
```

Fig. 7.5   Order in which constructors and finalizers are called (part 2 of 3).

```
87   // Fig. 7.5: Test.java
88   // Demonstrate when superclass and subclass
89   // constructors and finalizers are called.
90   import java.awt.Graphics;
91   import java.applet.Applet;
92
93   public class Test extends Applet {
94      private Circle circle1, circle2;
95
96      public void init()
97      {
98         circle1 = new Circle( 4.5, 7.2, 2.9 );
99         circle2 = new Circle( 10, 5, 5 );
100     }
101
102     public void start()
103     {
104        circle2 = null; // Circle can now be garbage collected
105        circle1 = null; // Circle can now be garbage collected
106
107        System.gc();     // call the garbage collector
108     }
109
110     public void paint( Graphics g )
111     {
112        g.drawString(
113           "See command line or Java Console for output",
114           25, 25 );
115     }
116  }
```

Fig. 7.5   Order in constructors and finalizers are called (part 3 of 3).

Common Programming Error 7.6

*When a superclass method is overridden in a subclass, it is common to have the subclass version call the superclass version and do some additional work. Not using the **super** reference to reference the superclass's method causes infinite recursion because the subclass method actually calls itself.*

Common Programming Error 7.7

*Cascading **super** references to refer to a member (method or variable) several levels up the hierarchy (as in **super.super.x**) is a syntax error.*

Lines 87–116 show an applet for testing this **Point/Circle** inheritance hierarchy. The program begins by instantiating **Circle** object **circle1**. This invokes the **Circle** constructor (lines 53–60) which invokes the **Point** constructor (line 56) to perform output with values passed from the **Circle** constructor, then performs the output specified in the **Circle** constructor. **Circle** object **circle2** is instantiated next. Again, the **Point** and **Circle** constructors both execute. Note that the body of the **Point** constructor is performed before the body of the **Circle** constructor showing that objects are constructed "inside out."

In the **start** method, we set **circle2** to **null** then set **circle1** to **null**. Since each of these objects is no longer needed, Java marks the memory occupied by **circle2** and **circle1** for *garbage collection*. Java guarantees that before the garbage collector runs to reclaim the space for each of these objects, the **finalize** methods for each object will be called. The garbage collector is a low-priority thread that runs automatically whenever processor time is available. We choose here to force the garbage collector to run with the call **System.gc()** in line 107. Note that Java does not guarantee the order in which objects will be garbage collected nor the order in which finalizers will be run.

7.6 Implicit Subclass-Object-to-Superclass-Object Conversion

Despite the fact that a subclass object also "is a" superclass object, the subclass type and the superclass type are different. Subclass objects can be treated as superclass objects. This makes sense because the subclass has members corresponding to each of the superclass members—remember that the subclass normally has more members than the superclass has. Assignment in the other direction is not allowed because assigning a superclass object to a subclass reference would leave the additional subclass members undefined.

Common Programming Error 7.8

Assigning a subclass object to a reference to a corresponding superclass, then attempting to reference subclass-only members with that superclass reference is a syntax error.

A reference to a subclass object may be implicitly converted into a reference to a superclass object because a subclass object *is a* superclass object through inheritance.

There are four possible ways to mix and match superclass references and subclass references with superclass objects and subclass objects:

1. Referring to a superclass object with a superclass reference is straightforward.

2. Referring to a subclass object with a subclass reference is straightforward.

3. Referring to a subclass object with a superclass reference is safe because the subclass object *is an* object of its superclass as well. Such code can only refer to superclass members. If this code refers to subclass-only members through the superclass reference, the compiler will report a syntax error.

4. Referring to a superclass object with a subclass reference is a syntax error. The subclass reference must first be cast to a superclass reference.

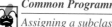

Common Programming Error 7.9

Assigning a subclass object to a superclass reference, and then attempting to reference subclass-only members with the superclass reference, is a syntax error.

As convenient as it may be to treat subclass objects as superclass objects, and to do this by manipulating all these objects with superclass references, there appears to be a problem. In a payroll system, for example, we would like to be able to walk through an array of employees and calculate the weekly pay for each person. But intuition suggests that using superclass references would enable the program to call only the superclass payroll calculation routine (if indeed there is such a routine in the superclass). We need a way to invoke the proper payroll calculation routine for each object, whether it is a superclass object or a subclass object, and to do this simply by using the superclass reference. Actually, this is precisely how Java behaves and is discussed later in this chapter when we consider polymorphism and dynamic binding.

7.7 Software Engineering with Inheritance

We can use inheritance to customize existing software. When we use inheritance to create a new class from an existing class, the new class inherits the attributes and behaviors of an existing class, then we can add attributes and behaviors or override superclass behaviors to customize the class to meet our needs.

It can be difficult for students to appreciate the problems faced by designers and implementors on large-scale software projects in industry. People experienced on such projects will invariably state that a key to improving the software development process is encouraging software reuse. Object-oriented programming in general, and Java in particular, certainly does this.

It is the availability of substantial and useful class libraries that delivers the maximum benefits of software reuse through inheritance. As interest in Java grows, interest in Java class libraries will increase. Just as shrink-wrapped software produced by independent software vendors became an explosive growth industry with the arrival of the personal computer, so, too, will the creation and sale of Java class libraries. Application designers will build their applications with these libraries, and library designers will be rewarded by having their libraries wrapped with the applications. What we see coming is a massive worldwide commitment to the development of Java class libraries for a huge variety of applications arenas.

Software Engineering Observation 7.5

Creating a subclass does not affect its superclass's source code or the superclass's Java byte-codes; the integrity of a superclass is preserved by inheritance.

A superclass specifies commonality. All classes derived from a superclass inherit the capabilities of that superclass. In the object-oriented design process, the designer looks for commonality among a set of classes and factors it out to form desirable superclasses. Subclasses are then customized beyond the capabilities inherited from the superclass.

Software Engineering Observation 7.6

Just as the designer of non-object-oriented systems should avoid unnecessary proliferation of functions, the designer of object-oriented systems should avoid unnecessary proliferation of classes. Proliferating classes creates management problems and can hinder software reusability simply because it is more difficult for a potential reuser of a class to locate that class in a huge collection. The trade-off is to create fewer classes, each providing substantial additional functionality, but such classes might be a bit too rich for certain reusers.

Performance Tip 7.1

If classes produced through inheritance are larger than they need to be, memory and processing resources may be wasted. Inherit from the class "closest" to what you need.

Note that reading a set of subclass declarations can be confusing because inherited members are not shown, but inherited members are nevertheless present in the subclasses. A similar problem can exist in the documentation of subclasses.

Software Engineering Observation 7.7

In an object-oriented system, classes are often closely related. "Factor out" common attributes and behaviors and place these in a superclass. Then use inheritance to form subclasses without having to repeat common attributes and behaviors.

Software Engineering Observation 7.8

Modifications to a superclass do not require subclasses to change as long as the public interface to the superclass remains unchanged.

7.8 Composition Vs. Inheritance

We have discussed *is a* relationships which are implemented by inheritance. We have also discussed *has a* relationships (and seen examples in preceding chapters) in which a class may have objects of other classes as members—such relationships create new classes by *composition* of existing classes. For example, given the classes **Employee**, **BirthDate**, and **TelephoneNumber**, it is improper to say that an **Employee** *is a* **BirthDate** or that an **Employee** *is a* **TelephoneNumber**. But it is certainly appropriate to say that an **Employee** *has a* **BirthDate** and that an **Employee** *has a* **TelephoneNumber**.

7.9 Case Study: Point, Circle, Cylinder

Now let us consider a substantial inheritance example. We consider a point, circle, cylinder hierarchy. First we develop and use class **Point** (Fig. 7.6). Then we present an example in which we derive class **Circle** from class **Point** (Fig. 7.7). Finally, we present an example in which we derive class **Cylinder** from class **Circle** (Fig. 7.8).

Figure 7.6 shows class **Point**. Part 1 is the class **Point** definition. Note that **Point**'s instance variables are **protected**. Thus, when class **Circle** is derived from class **Point**, the methods of class **Circle** will be able to directly reference coordinates **x** and **y** rather than using access methods. This may result in better performance.

Figure 7.6, part 2, shows a **Test** applet for testing class **Point**. Note that the **paint** method must use methods **getX** and **getY** to read the values of **protected** instance variables **x** and **y**; remember that **protected** instance variables are accessible only to methods of their class, to methods of their subclasses and to methods of other classes in the same package.

Our next example is shown in Fig. 7.7. The **Point** class definition and the method definitions from Fig. 7.6 are reused here, so the class definition is not shown again. Part 1 of Fig. 7.7 shows the **Circle** class definition with the **Circle** method definitions. Parts 2 and 3 show a **Test** applet. Note that class **Circle extends** class **Point**. This means that the **public** interface to **Circle** includes the **Point** methods as well as the **Circle** methods **setRadius**, **getRadius**, **area**, **toString** and the two **Circle** constructors. The **Test** applet instantiates an object of class **Circle** (line 49) then uses *get* methods to obtain the information about the **Circle** object. Again, the **Test** applet's **paint** method indirectly references the **protected** data of class **Circle** through method calls. The **Test** applet then uses *set* methods **setRadius** and **setPoint** to reset the radius and coordinates of the center of the circle. Finally, the **paint** displays the new **Circle** object **c** and calculates and prints its area.

```
1   // Fig. 7.6: Point.java
2   // Definition of class Point
3
4   public class Point {
5      protected double x, y; // coordinates of the Point
6
7      // constructor
8      public Point( double a, double b ) { setPoint( a, b ); }
9
10     // Set x and y coordinates of Point
11     public void setPoint( double a, double b )
12     {
13        x = a;
14        y = b;
15     }
16
17     // get x coordinate
18     public double getX() { return x; }
19
20     // get y coordinate
21     public double getY() { return y; }
22
23     // conver the point into a String representation
24     public String toString()
25        { return "[" + x + ", " + y + "]"; }
26  }
```

Fig. 7.6   Testing class **Point** (part 1 of 2).

```
27   // Fig. 7.6: Test.java
28   // Applet to test class Point
29   import java.awt.Graphics;
30   import java.applet.Applet;
31
32   public class Test extends Applet {
33      private Point p;
34
35      public void init()
36      {
37         p = new Point( 7.2, 11.5 );
38      }
39
40      public void paint( Graphics g )
41      {
42         g.drawString( "X coordinate is " + p.getX(), 25, 25 );
43         g.drawString( "Y coordinate is " + p.getY(), 25, 40 );
44
45         p.setPoint( 10, 10 );
46         g.drawString( "The new location of p is " +
47                       p.toString(), 25, 70 );
48      }
49   }
```

Fig. 7.6   Testing class **Point** (part 2 of 2).

Our last example is shown in Fig. 7.8. The **Point** class and **Circle** class definitions Fig. 7.6 and Fig. 7.7 are reused here. Parts 1 and 2 show the **Cylinder** class definition with the **Cylinder** method definitions. Parts 3 and 4 are a **Test** applet to test the **Cylinder** class. Note that class **Cylinder extends** class **Circle**. This means that the **public** interface to **Cylinder** includes the **Circle** methods as well as the **Cylinder** constructor and **Cylinder** methods **setHeight, getHeight, area** (which overrides the **Circle area** method), **volume** and **toString**. The **Test** applet instantiates an object of class **Cylinder** (line 46) then uses *get* methods (lines 51-54) to obtain the information about the **Cylinder** object. Again, the **Test** applet's **paint** method cannot directly reference the **protected** data of class **Cylinder**. The **Test** applet then uses *set* methods **setHeight, setRadius**, and **setPoint** to reset the **height, radius**, and coordinates of the cylinder. The **Test** applet then uses **toString, area**, and **volume** to print the attributes and some facts about the **Cylinder**.

```
1    // Fig. 7.7: Circle.java
2    // Definition of class Circle
3
4    public class Circle extends Point {   // inherits from Point
5       protected double radius;
6
7       // no-argument constructor
8       public Circle()
9       {
10         super( 0, 0 );  // call the superclass constructor
11         setRadius( 0 );
12      }
13
14      // Constructor
15      public Circle( double r, double a, double b )
16      {
17         super( a, b );  // call the superclass constructor
18         setRadius( r );
19      }
20
21      // Set radius of Circle
22      public void setRadius( double r )
23         { radius = ( r >= 0.0 ? r : 0.0 ); }
24
25      // Get radius of Circle
26      public double getRadius() { return radius; }
27
28      // Calculate area of Circle
29      public double area()
30         { return 3.14159 * radius * radius; }
31
32      // convert the Circle to a String
33      public String toString()
34      {
35         return "Center = " + super.toString() +
36                "; Radius = " + radius;
37      }
38   }
```

Fig. 7.7   Testing class **Circle** (part 1 of 3).


```
39   // Fig. 7.7: Test.java
40   // Applet to test class Circle
41   import java.awt.Graphics;
42   import java.applet.Applet;
43
44   public class Test extends Applet {
45      private Circle c;
46
```

Fig. 7.7   Testing class **Circle** (part 2 of 3).

```
47        public void init()
48        {
49           c = new Circle( 2.5, 3.7, 4.3 );
50        }
51
52        public void paint( Graphics g )
53        {
54           g.drawString( "X coordinate is " + c.getX(), 25, 25 );
55           g.drawString( "Y coordinate is " + c.getY(), 25, 40 );
56           g.drawString( "Radius is " + c.getRadius(), 25, 55 );
57
58           c.setRadius( 4.25 );
59           c.setPoint( 2, 2 );
60           g.drawString( "The new location and radius of c are ",
61                         25, 85 );
62           g.drawString( c.toString(), 40, 100 );
63           g.drawString( "Area is " + c.area(), 25, 115 );
64        }
65    }
```

Fig. 7.7 Testing class `Circle` (part 3 of 3).

```
1    // Fig. 7.8: Cylinder.java
2    // Definition of class Cylinder
3    public class Cylinder extends Circle {
4       protected double height;  // height of Cylinder
5
6       // Cylinder constructor calls Circle constructor
7       public Cylinder( double h, double r, double a, double b )
8       {
9          super( r, a, b );
10         setHeight( h );
11      }
12
```

Fig. 7.8 Testing class `Cylinder` (part 1 of 4).

```
13      // Set height of Cylinder
14      public void setHeight( double h )
15         { height = ( h >= 0 ? h : 0 ); }
16
17      // Get height of Cylinder
18      public double getHeight() { return height; }
19
20      // Calculate area of Cylinder (i.e., surface area)
21      public double area()
22      {
23         return 2 * super.area() +
24               2 * 3.14159 * radius * height;
25      }
26
27      // Calculate volume of Cylinder
28      public double volume() { return super.area() * height; }
29
30      // Convert the Cylinder to a String
31      public String toString()
32      {
33         return super.toString() + "; Height = " + height;
34      }
35   }
```

Fig. 7.8   Testing class **Cylinder** (part 2 of 4).

```
36   // Fig. 7.8: Test.java
37   // Applet to test class Cylinder
38   import java.awt.Graphics;
39   import java.applet.Applet;
40
41   public class Test extends Applet {
42      private Cylinder c;
43
44      public void init()
45      {
46         c = new Cylinder( 5.7, 2.5, 1.2, 2.3 );
47      }
48
49      public void paint( Graphics g )
50      {
51         g.drawString( "X coordinate is " + c.getX(), 25, 25 );
52         g.drawString( "Y coordinate is " + c.getY(), 25, 40 );
53         g.drawString( "Radius is " + c.getRadius(), 25, 55 );
54         g.drawString( "Height is " + c.getHeight(), 25, 70 );
55
56         c.setHeight( 10 );
57         c.setRadius( 4.25 );
58         c.setPoint( 2, 2 );
59
```

Fig. 7.8   Testing class **Cylinder** (part 3 of 4).

```
60          g.drawString( "The new location, radius and height" +
61                          " of c are ", 25, 100 );
62          g.drawString( c.toString(), 40, 115 );
63          g.drawString( "Area is " + c.area(), 25, 130 );
64          g.drawString( "Volume is " + c.volume(), 25, 145 );
65      }
66   }
```

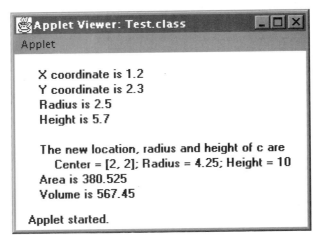

Fig. 7.8   Testing class **Cylinder** (part 4 of 4).

This example nicely demonstrates inheritance and defining and referencing **protected** instance variables. The reader should now be confident with the basics of inheritance. In the next several sections, we show how to program with inheritance hierarchies in a general manner using polymorphism. Data abstraction, inheritance, and polymorphism are the crux of object-oriented programming.

7.10 Introduction to Polymorphism

With *polymorphism,* it is possible to design and implement systems that are more easily *extensible.* Programs can be written to process generically—as superclass objects—objects of all existing classes in a hierarchy. Classes that do not exist during program development can be added with little or no modifications to the generic part of the program—as long as those classes are part of the hierarchy that is being processed generically. The only parts of a program that need modification are those parts that require direct knowledge of the particular class that is added to the hierarchy. We will study two substantial class hierarchies and will show how objects throughout those hierarchies are manipulated polymorphically.

7.11 Type Fields and Switch Statements

One means of dealing with objects of many different types is to use a **switch** statement to take an appropriate action on each object based on that object's type. For example, in a hierarchy of shapes in which each shape has a **shapeType** instance variable, a **switch** structure could determine which **print** method to call based on the object's **shapeType**.

There are many problems with using **switch** logic. The programmer might forget to make such a type test when one is warranted. The programmer may forget to test all possible cases in a **switch**. If a **switch**-based system is modified by adding new types, the programmer might forget to insert the new cases in existing **switch** statements. Every addition or deletion of a class demands that every **switch** statement in the system be modified; tracking these down can be time consuming and error prone.

As we will see, polymorphic programming can eliminate the need for **switch** logic. The programmer can use Java's polymorphism mechanism to perform the equivalent logic automatically, thus avoiding the kinds of errors typically associated with **switch** logic.

Testing and Debugging Tip 7.2

An interesting consequence of using polymorphism is that programs take on a simplified appearance. They contain less branching logic in favor of simpler sequential code. This simplification facilitates testing, debugging, and program maintenance.

7.12 Dynamic Method Binding

Suppose a set of shape classes such as **Circle**, **Triangle**, **Rectangle**, **Square**, etc. are all derived from superclass **Shape**. In object-oriented programming, each of these classes might be endowed with the ability to draw itself. Although each class has its own **draw** method, the **draw** method for each shape is quite different. When drawing a shape, whatever that shape may be, it would be nice to be able to treat all these shapes generically as objects of the superclass **Shape**. Then to draw any shape, we could simply call method **draw** of superclass **Shape** and let the program determine dynamically (i.e., at execution time) which subclass **draw** method to use.

To enable this kind of behavior, we declare **draw** in the superclass, and then we override **draw** in each of the subclasses to draw the appropriate shape.

Software Engineering Observation 7.9

When a subclass chooses not to redefine a method, the subclass simply inherits its immediate superclass's method definition.

If we use a superclass reference to refer to a subclass object and invoke the **draw** method, the program will choose the correct subclass's **draw** method dynamically (i.e., at execution time). This is called *dynamic method binding* which will be illustrated in the case studies later in this chapter.

7.13 **final** Methods and Classes

We saw in Chapter 4 that variables can be declared **final** to indicate that they cannot be modified after they are declared and that they must be initialized when they are declared. It is also possible to define methods and classes with the **final** modifier.

A method that is declared **final** cannot be overridden in a subclass. Methods that are declared **static** and methods that are declared **private** are implicitly **final**. Because a **final** method's definition can never change, the compiler can optimize the program by removing calls to **final** methods and replacing them with the expanded code of their definitions at each method call location—a technique known as *inlining the code*.

A class that is declared **final** cannot be a superclass—i.e., **final** classes cannot be inherited. All methods in a **final** class are implicitly **final**.

Performance Tip 7.2

*The compiler can decide to inline a **final** method call and will do so for small, simple **final** methods. Inlining does not violate encapsulation or information hiding (but does improve performance because it eliminates the overhead of making a method call).*

Performance Tip 7.3

*Pipelined processors are able to improve performance by executing portions of the next several instructions simultaneously, but not if those instructions follow a method call. Thus, inlining (which the compiler can perform on a **final** method) can improve performance in pipelined processors because it eliminates the out-of-line transfer of control associated with a method call.*

Software Engineering Observation 7.10

*A class declared **final** cannot be subclassed. Every method of a **final** class is implicitly **final**.*

7.14 Abstract Superclasses and Concrete Classes

When we think of a class as a type, we assume that objects of that type will be instantiated. However, there are cases in which it is useful to define classes for which the programmer never intends to instantiate any objects. Such classes are called *abstract classes*. Because these are used as superclasses in inheritance situations, we will normally refer to them as *abstract superclasses*. No objects of abstract superclasses can be instantiated.

The sole purpose of an abstract class is to provide an appropriate superclass from which other classes may inherit interface and/or implementation (we will see examples of each shortly). Classes from which objects can be instantiated are called *concrete classes*.

We could have an abstract superclass **TwoDimensionalObject** and derive concrete classes such as **Square**, **Circle**, **Triangle**, etc. We could also have an abstract superclass **ThreeDimensionalObject** and derive concrete classes such as **Cube**, **Sphere**, **Cylinder**, etc. Abstract superclasses are too generic to define real objects; we need to be more specific before we can think of instantiating objects. That is what concrete classes do; they provide the specifics that make it reasonable to instantiate objects.

A class is made abstract by declaring it with the keyword **abstract**.

Software Engineering Observation 7.11

*If a subclass is derived from a superclass with an **abstract** method, and if no definition is supplied in the subclass for that **abstract** method (i.e., if that method is not overridden in the subclass), then that method remains **abstract** in the subclass. Consequently, the subclass is also an **abstract** class and must be explicitly declared as an **abstract** class.*

Software Engineering Observation 7.12

*The ability to declare an **abstract** method gives the class designer considerable power over how subclasses will be implemented in a class hierarchy. Any new class that wants to inherit from this class is forced to override the **abstract** method (either directly or by inheriting from a class that has overridden the method). Otherwise that new class will contain an **abstract** method and thus be an **abstract** class unable to instantiate objects.*

Software Engineering Observation 7.13

Even if a class is **abstract** *it can still have instance data and non-***abstract** *methods subject to the normal rules of inheritance by subclasses.*

Common Programming Error 7.10

Attempting to instantiate an object of an **abstract** *class (i.e., a class that contains one or more* **abstract** *methods) is a syntax error.*

Common Programming Error 7.11

It is a syntax error if a class with one or more **abstract** *methods is not explicitly declared* **abstract***.*

A hierarchy does not need to contain any **abstract** classes, but as we will see, many good object-oriented systems have class hierarchies headed by **abstract** superclasses. In some cases, **abstract** classes constitute the top few levels of the hierarchy. A good example of this is a shape hierarchy. The hierarchy could begin with **abstract** superclass **Shape**. On the next level down we can have two more **abstract** superclasses, namely **TwoDimensionalShape** and **ThreeDimensionalShape**. The next level down would start defining concrete classes for two-dimensional shapes such as **Circle** and **Square**, and concrete classes for three-dimensional shapes such as **Sphere** and **Cube**.

7.15 Polymorphism Examples

Here is an example of polymorphism. If class **Rectangle** is derived from class **Quadrilateral**, then a **Rectangle** object *is a* more specific version of a **Quadrilateral** object. An operation (such as calculating the perimeter or the area) that can be performed on an object of class **Quadrilateral** can also be performed on an object of class **Rectangle**. Such operations can also be performed on other "kinds of" **Quadrilateral**s such as **Square**s, **Parallelogram**s and **Trapezoid**s. When a request is made through a superclass reference to use a method, Java chooses the correct overridden method polymorphically in the appropriate subclass associated with the object.

Here is another example of polymorphism. Suppose we have a video game that manipulates objects of many varieties including objects of class **Martian, Venutian, Plutonian, SpaceShip, LaserBeam**, and the like. A Java screen manager program would simply maintain some kind of container (such as an array) of objects of these various classes. To refresh the screen periodically the screen manager would simply send each object the same message, namely **drawYourself**. Each object would respond in its own unique way. A **Martian** object would draw itself with the appropriate number of antennae. A **SpaceShip** object would draw itself bright and silvery. A **LaserBeam** object would draw itself as a bright red beam across the screen. Thus, the same message sent to a variety of objects would take on many forms—hence the term *polymorphism.*

Such a polymorphic screen manager makes it especially easy to add new types of objects to a system with minimal impact. Suppose we want to add **Mercurian**s to our video game. We certainly have to build a new class **Mercurian**. We would be sure to endow it with a **drawYourself** method. Then when objects of class **Mercurian** appear in the container, the screen manager need not be modified. It simply sends the message **drawYourself** to every object in the container regardless of the object's type, so the new **Mercurian** objects just "fit right in." Thus, with polymorphism, new types of objects not even envisioned when a system is created may be added without modifications to the system (other than the new class itself, of course).

Through the use of polymorphism, one method call can cause different actions to occur depending on the type of the object receiving the call. This gives the programmer tremendous expressive capability. We will see examples of the power of polymorphism in the next several sections.

Software Engineering Observation 7.14

With polymorphism, the programmer can deal in generalities and let the execution-time environment concern itself with the specifics. The programmer can command a wide variety of objects to behave in manners appropriate to those objects without even knowing the types of those objects.

Software Engineering Observation 7.15

Polymorphism promotes extensibility: Software written to invoke polymorphic behavior is written independent of the types of the objects to which messages (i.e., method calls) are sent. Thus, new types of objects that can respond to existing messages can be added into such a system without modifying the base system.

Software Engineering Observation 7.16

*If a method is declared **final** it cannot be overridden in subclasses, so that method calls may not be sent polymorphically to objects of those subclasses. The method call may still be sent to subclasses but they will all respond identically rather than polymorphically.*

Performance Tip 7.4

*A method declared **final** uses static binding rather than dynamic binding. Static binding is faster than dynamic binding.*

Software Engineering Observation 7.17

*An **abstract** class defines a common interface for the various members of a class hierarchy. The **abstract** class contains methods that will be defined in the subclasses. All classes in the hierarchy can use this same interface through polymorphism.*

Although we cannot instantiate objects of **abstract** superclasses, we *can* declare references to **abstract** superclasses. Such references can be used to enable polymorphic manipulations of subclass objects when such objects are instantiated from concrete classes.

Let us consider more applications of polymorphism. A screen manager needs to display a variety of objects, including new types of objects that will be added to the system even after the screen manager is written. The system may need to display various shapes (i.e., the superclass is **Shape**) such as **Square**, **Circle**, **Triangle**, **Rectangle**, and the like (each of these shape classes is derived from the superclass **Shape**). The screen manager uses superclass references (to **Shape**) to manage all the objects to be displayed. To draw any object (regardless of the level at which that object appears in the inheritance hierarchy), the screen manager uses a superclass reference to the object and simply sends a **draw** message to the object. Method **draw** has been declared **abstract** in superclass **Shape** and has been overridden in each of the subclasses. Each **Shape** object knows how to draw itself. The screen manager does not have to worry about what type each object is or whether the screen manager has seen objects of that type before—the screen manager simply tells each object to **draw** itself.

Polymorphism is particularly effective for implementing layered software systems. In operating systems, for example, each type of physical device may operate quite differently from the others. Even so, commands to *read* or *write* data from and to devices can have a certain uniformity. The *write* message sent to a device-driver object needs to be interpreted specifically in the context of that device driver and how that device driver manipulates devices of a specific type. However, the *write* call itself is really no different from the *write* to any other device in the system—simply place some number of bytes from memory onto that device. An object-oriented operating system might use an **abstract** superclass to provide an interface appropriate for all device drivers. Then, through inheritance from that **abstract** superclass, subclasses are formed that all operate similarly. The capabilities (i.e., the **public** interface) offered by the device drivers are provided as **abstract** methods in the **abstract** superclass. The implementations of these **abstract** methods are provided in the subclasses that correspond to the specific types of device drivers.

It is common in object-oriented programming to define an *iterator class* that can walk through all the objects in a container (such as an array). If you want to print a list of objects in a linked list, for example, an iterator object can be instantiated that will return the next element of the linked list each time the iterator is called. Iterators are commonly used in polymorphic programming to walk through an array or a linked list of objects from various levels of a hierarchy. The references in such a list would all be superclass references (see Chapter 17, "Data Structures," for more on linked lists). A list of objects of superclass class **TwoDimensionalShape** could contain objects from the classes **Square**, **Circle**, **Triangle**, etc. Sending a **draw** message to each object in the list would, using polymorphism, draw the correct picture on the screen.

7.16 Case Study: A Payroll System Using Polymorphism

Let us use **abstract** methods and polymorphism to perform payroll calculations based on the type of an employee (Fig. 7.9). We use an **abstract** superclass **Employee**. The subclasses of **Employee** are **Boss**, who gets paid a fixed weekly salary regardless of the number of hours worked, **CommissionWorker**, who gets a flat base salary plus a percentage of sales, **PieceWorker**, who gets paid by the number of items produced, and **HourlyWorker**, who gets paid by the hour and receives overtime pay. Each of the subclasses of **Employee** in this example have been declared **final** because we do not intend to inherit from them again.

An **earnings** method call certainly applies generically to all employees. But the way each person's earnings are calculated depends on the class of the employee, and these classes are all derived from the superclass **Employee**. So **earnings** is declared **abstract** in superclass **Employee** and appropriate implementations of **earnings** are provided for each of the subclasses. Then, to calculate any employee's earnings, the program simply uses a superclass reference to that employee's object and invokes the **earnings** method. In a real payroll system, the various **Employee** objects might be referenced by individual elements in an array of **Employee** references. The program would simply walk through the array one element at a time using the **Employee** references to invoke the **earnings** method of each object.

Let us consider the **Employee** class (Fig. 7.9, lines 1–27). The **public** methods include a constructor that takes the first name and last name as arguments; a **getFirst-Name** method that returns the first name; a **getLastName** method that returns the last name; and an **abstract** method—**earnings**. Why is this method **abstract**? The answer is that it does not make sense to provide an implementation of this method in the **Employee** class. We cannot calculate the earnings for a generic employee—we must first know what kind of employee it is. By making this method **abstract** we are indicating that we will provide an implementation in each subclass, but not in the superclass itself.

Class **Boss** (Fig. 7.9, lines 28–54) is derived from **Employee**. The **public** methods include a constructor that takes a first name, a last name, and a weekly salary as arguments and passes the first name and last name to the **Employee** constructor to initialize the **firstName** and **lastName** members of the superclass part of the subclass object; a **setWeeklySalary** method to assign a new value to **private** instance variable **weeklySalary**; an **earnings** method defining how to calculate a **Boss**'s earnings; and a **toString** method that forms a **String** containing the type of the employee (i.e., **"Boss: "**) followed by the boss's name.

```
1    // Fig. 7.9: Employee.java
2    // Abstract superclass Employee
3
4    public abstract class Employee {
5        private String firstName;
6        private String lastName;
7
8        // Constructor
9        public Employee( String first, String last )
10       {
11           firstName = new String ( first );
12           lastName = new String( last );
13       }
14
15       // Return a copy of the first name
16       public String getFirstName()
17           { return new String( firstName ); }
18
19       // Return a copy of the last name
20       public String getLastName()
21           { return new String( lastName ); }
22
23       // Abstract method that must be implemented for each
24       // derived class of Employee from which objects
25       // are instantiated.
26       abstract double earnings();
27   }
```

Fig. 7.9 **Employee** class hierarchy using an **abstract** superclass (part 1 of 7).

```
28   // Fig. 7.9: Boss.java
29   // Boss class derived from Employee
30
31   public final class Boss extends Employee {
32      private double weeklySalary;
33
34      // Constructor for class Boss
35      public Boss( String first, String last, double s)
36      {
37         super( first, last );   // call base-class constructor
38         setWeeklySalary( s );
39      }
40
41      // Set the Boss's salary
42      public void setWeeklySalary( double s )
43         { weeklySalary = ( s > 0 ? s : 0 ); }
44
45      // Get the Boss's pay
46      public double earnings() { return weeklySalary; }
47
48      // Print the Boss's name
49      public String toString()
50      {
51         return "Boss: " + getFirstName() + ' ' +
52                getLastName();
53      }
54   }
```

Fig. 7.9 **Employee** class hierarchy using an **abstract** superclass (part 2 of 7).

Class **CommissionWorker** (Fig. 7.9, lines 55–95) is derived from **Employee**. The **public** methods include a constructor that takes a first name, a last name, a salary, a commission, and a quantity of items sold as arguments and passes the first name and last name to the **Employee** constructor; *set* methods to assign new values to **private** instance variables **salary**, **commission**, and **quantity**; an **earnings** method defining how to calculate a **CommissionWorker**'s earnings; and a **toString** method that forms a **String** containing the type of the employee (i.e., **"Commission worker: "**) followed by the commission worker's name.

Class **PieceWorker** (Fig. 7.9, lines 96–128) is derived from **Employee**. The **public** methods include a constructor that takes a first name, a last name, a wage per piece, and a quantity of items produced as arguments and passes the first name and last name to the **Employee** constructor; *set* methods to assign new values to private methods **wagePerPiece** and **quantity**; an **earnings** method defining how to calculate a **PieceWorker**'s earnings; and a **toString** method that forms a **String** containing the type of the employee(i.e., **"Piece worker: "**) followed by the piece worker's name.

```
55  // Fig. 7.9: CommissionWorker.java
56  // CommissionWorker class derived from Employee
57
58  public final class CommissionWorker extends Employee {
59      private double salary;      // base salary per week
60      private double commission;  // amount per item sold
61      private int quantity;       // total items sold for week
62
63      // Constructor for class CommissionWorker
64      public CommissionWorker( String first, String last,
65                               double s, double c, int q)
66      {
67          super( first, last );  // call base-class constructor
68          setSalary( s );
69          setCommission( c );
70          setQuantity( q );
71      }
72
73      // Set CommissionWorker's weekly base salary
74      public void setSalary( double s )
75          { salary = ( s > 0 ? s : 0 ); }
76
77      // Set CommissionWorker's commission
78      public void setCommission( double c )
79          { commission = ( c > 0 ? c : 0 ); }
80
81      // Set CommissionWorker's quantity sold
82      public void setQuantity( int q )
83          { quantity = ( q > 0 ? q : 0 ); }
84
85      // Determine CommissionWorker's earnings
86      public double earnings()
87          { return salary + commission * quantity; }
88
89      // Print the CommissionWorker's name
90      public String toString()
91      {
92          return "Commission worker: " +
93                  getFirstName() + ' ' + getLastName();
94      }
95  }
```

Fig. 7.9 **Employee** class hierarchy using an **abstract** superclass (part 3 of 7).

Class **HourlyWorker** (Fig. 7.9, lines 129–162) is derived from **Employee**. The **public** methods include a constructor that takes a first name, a last name, a wage, and the number of hours worked as arguments and passes the first name and last name to the **Employee** constructor to initialize the **firstName** and **lastName** members of the superclass part of the subclass object; *set* methods to assign new values to private methods **wage** and **hours**; an **earnings** method defining how to calculate an **Hourly-Worker**'s earnings; and a **toString** method that forms a **String** containing the type of the employee (i.e., **"Hourly worker: "**) followed by the hourly worker's name.

```
96  // Fig. 7.9: PieceWorker.java
97  // PieceWorker class derived from Employee
98  public final class PieceWorker extends Employee {
99     private double wagePerPiece; // wage per piece output
100    private int quantity;        // output for week
101
102    // Constructor for class PieceWorker
103    public PieceWorker( String first, String last,
104                        double w, int q )
105    {
106       super( first, last );  // call base-class constructor
107       setWage( w );
108       setQuantity( q );
109    }
110
111    // Set the wage
112    public void setWage( double w )
113       { wagePerPiece = ( w > 0 ? w : 0 ); }
114
115    // Set the number of items output
116    public void setQuantity( int q )
117       { quantity = ( q > 0 ? q : 0 ); }
118
119    // Determine the PieceWorker's earnings
120    public double earnings()
121       { return quantity * wagePerPiece; }
122
123    public String toString()
124    {
125       return "Piece worker: " +
126              getFirstName() + ' ' + getLastName();
127    }
128 }
```

Fig. 7.9   **Employee** class hierarchy using an **abstract** superclass (part 4 of 7).

The **Test** applet (Fig. 7.9, lines 163–210) begins by declaring **Employee** reference, **ref**. Each of the types of **Employee**s is handled similarly in **Test**, so we will discuss only the case in which **Test** deals with a **Boss** object.

The line

```
Boss b = new Boss ("John", "Smith", 800.00);
```

instantiates subclass object **b** of class **Boss** and provides various constructor arguments including a first name, a last name, and a fixed weekly salary.

Line 186

```
ref = b;  // superclass reference to subclass object
```

places in superclass reference **ref** a reference to subclass **Boss** object **b**. This is precisely what we must do to effect polymorphic behavior.

```
129  // Fig. 7.9: HourlyWorker.java
130  // Definition of class HourlyWorker
131
132  public final class HourlyWorker extends Employee {
133     private double wage;   // wage per hour
134     private double hours;  // hours worked for week
135
136     // Constructor for class HourlyWorker
137     public HourlyWorker( String first, String last,
138                          double w, double h )
139     {
140        super( first, last );   // call base-class constructor
141        setWage( w );
142        setHours( h );
143     }
144
145     // Set the wage
146     public void setWage( double w )
147        { wage = ( w > 0 ? w : 0 ); }
148
149     // Set the hours worked
150     public void setHours( double h )
151        { hours = ( h >= 0 && h < 168 ? h : 0 ); }
152
153     // Get the HourlyWorker's pay
154     public double earnings() { return wage * hours; }
155
156     public String toString()
157     {
158        return "Hourly worker: " +
159               getFirstName() + ' ' + getLastName();
160     }
161
162  }
```

Fig. 7.9 **Employee** class hierarchy using an **abstract** superclass (part 5 of 7).

The expression in line 187

```
ref.toString()
```

invokes the **toString** method of the object referenced by **ref**. The system invokes the subclass object's **toString** method—precisely what we call polymorphic behavior. This method call is an example of dynamic method binding—the decision as to what method to invoke is deferred until execution time.

The method call in line 188

```
ref.earnings();
```

invokes the **earnings** method of the object referred to by **ref**. The system invokes the subclass object's **earnings** method rather than the superclass's **earnings** method. This is also an example of dynamic method binding.

```
163   // Fig. 7.9: Test.java
164   // Driver for Employee hierarchy
165   import java.awt.Graphics;
166   import java.applet.Applet;
167
168   public class Test extends Applet {
169      private Employee ref;  // base-class reference
170      private Boss b;
171      private CommissionWorker c;
172      private PieceWorker p;
173      private HourlyWorker h;
174
175      public void init()
176      {
177         b = new Boss( "John", "Smith", 800.00 );
178         c = new CommissionWorker( "Sue", "Jones",
179                                   400.0, 3.0, 150);
180         p = new PieceWorker( "Bob", "Lewis", 2.5, 200 );
181         h = new HourlyWorker( "Karen", "Price", 13.75, 40 );
182      }
183
184      public void paint( Graphics g )
185      {
186         ref = b;  // superclass reference to subclass object
187         g.drawString( ref.toString() + " earned $" +
188                       ref.earnings(), 25, 25 );
189         g.drawString( b.toString() + " earned $" +
190                       b.earnings(), 25, 40 );
191
192         ref = c;  // superclass reference to subclass object
193         g.drawString( ref.toString() + " earned $" +
194                       ref.earnings(), 25, 55 );
195         g.drawString( c.toString() + " earned $" +
196                       c.earnings(), 25, 70 );
197
198         ref = p;  // superclass reference to subclass object
199         g.drawString( ref.toString() + " earned $" +
200                       ref.earnings(), 25, 85 );
201         g.drawString( p.toString() + " earned $" +
202                       p.earnings(), 25, 100 );
203
204         ref = h;  // superclass reference to subclass object
205         g.drawString( ref.toString() + " earned $" +
206                       ref.earnings(), 25, 115 );
207         g.drawString( h.toString() + " earned $" +
208                       h.earnings(), 25, 130 );
209      }
210   }
```

Fig. 7.9   **Employee** class hierarchy using an **abstract** superclass (part 6 of 7).

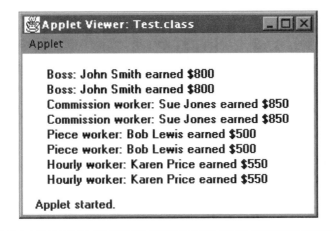

Fig. 7.9 **Employee** class hierarchy using an **abstract** superclass (part 7 of 7).

The call

```
b.toString();
```

explicitly invokes the **Boss** version of method **toString** by using the dot member selection operator off the specific **Boss** object **b**. This is an example of static binding. Because the type of the object **b** is known at compile time and because class **Boss** is a **final** class, the compiler is able to determine that the only possible **toString** method to call in this case is the **Boss** class's **toString** method. This call is included for comparison purposes to ensure that the dynamically bound method invoked with **ref.toString()** was indeed the proper method.

The line

```
b.earnings();
```

explicitly invokes the **Boss** version of method **earnings** by using the dot member selection operator off the specific **Boss** object **b**. This is also an example of static binding. This call is included for comparison purposes to ensure that the dynamically bound method invoked with **ref.earnings()** was indeed the proper method.

7.17 New Classes and Dynamic Binding

Polymorphism certainly works nicely when all possible classes are known in advance. But it also works when new kinds of classes are added to systems.

New classes are accommodated by dynamic method binding (also called *late binding*). An object's type need not be known at compile time for a polymorphic call to be compiled. At execution time, the call is matched with the method of the called object.

A screen manager program can now handle (without recompilation) new display objects as they are added to the system. The **draw** method call remains the same. The new objects themselves each contain a **draw** method implementing the actual drawing capabilities. This makes it easy to add new capabilities to systems with minimal impact. It also promotes software reuse.

Performance Tip 7.5

Polymorphism as implemented with dynamic method binding is efficient.

Performance Tip 7.6

*The kinds of polymorphic manipulations made possible with dynamic binding can also be accomplished by using hand-coded **switch** logic based on type fields in objects. The polymorphic code generated by the Java compiler runs with comparable performance to efficiently coded **switch** logic.*

7.18 Case Study: Inheriting Interface and Implementation

Our next example (Fig. 7.10) re-examines the **Point**, **Circle**, **Cylinder** hierarchy except that we now head the hierarchy with **abstract** superclass **Shape**. **Shape** has an **abstract** method—**getName**—so **Shape** is an **abstract** superclass. **Shape** contains two other methods, **area** and **volume**, each of which has an implementation that returns a value of zero. **Point** inherits these implementations from **Shape**. This makes sense because both the area and volume of a point are zero. **Circle** inherits the **volume** method from **Point**, but **Circle** provides its own implementation for the **area** method. **Cylinder** provides its own implementations for both the **area** (which we interpret as the surface area of the cylinder) and **volume** methods.

Note that although **Shape** is an **abstract** superclass, it still contains implementations of methods **area** and **volume**, and these implementations are inheritable. The **Shape** class provides an inheritable interface in the form of three methods that all classes of the hierarchy will contain. The **Shape** class also provides some implementations that subclasses in the first few levels of the hierarchy will use.

This case study emphasizes that a subclass can inherit interface and/or implementation from a superclass.

Software Engineering Observation 7.18

Hierarchies designed for implementation inheritance tend to have their functionality high in the hierarchy—each new subclass inherits one or more methods that were defined in a superclass and uses the superclass definitions.

```
1  // Fig. 7.10: Shape.java
2  // Definition of abstract superclass Shape
3
4  public abstract class Shape {
5     public double area() { return 0.0; }
6     public double volume() { return 0.0; }
7     public abstract String getName();
8  }
```

Fig. 7.10 Shape, point, circle, cylinder hierarchy (part 1 of 6).

```
9    // Fig. 7.10: Point.java
10   // Definition of class Point
11
12   public class Point extends Shape {
13      protected double x, y; // coordinates of the Point
14
15      // constructor
16      public Point( double a, double b ) { setPoint( a, b ); }
17
18      // Set x and y coordinates of Point
19      public void setPoint( double a, double b )
20      {
21         x = a;
22         y = b;
23      }
24
25      // get x coordinate
26      public double getX() { return x; }
27
28      // get y coordinate
29      public double getY() { return y; }
30
31      // convert the point into a String representation
32      public String toString()
33         { return "[" + x + ", " + y + "]"; }
34
35      // return the class name
36      public String getName() { return "Point"; }
37   }
```

Fig. 7.10 Shape, point, circle, cylinder hierarchy (part 2 of 6).

Software Engineering Observation 7.19

Hierarchies designed for interface inheritance tend to have their functionality lower in the hierarchy—a superclass specifies one or more methods that should be called identically for each object in the hierarchy (i.e., they have the same signature), but the individual subclasses provide their own implementations of the method(s).

Superclass **Shape** (Fig. 7.10, lines 1–8) consists of three **public** methods and does not contain any data. Method **getName** is **abstract**, so it is overridden in each of the subclasses. Methods **area** and **volume** are defined to return **0.0**. These methods are overridden in subclasses when it is appropriate for those classes to have a different **area** calculation and/or a different **volume** calculation.

Class **Point** (Fig. 7.10, lines 9–37) is derived from **Shape**. A **Point** has an area of 0.0 and a volume of 0.0, so the superclass methods **area** and **volume** are not overridden here—they are inherited as defined in **Shape**. Method **getName** is an implementation of the **abstract** method in the superclass. Other methods include **SetPoint** to assign new **x** and **y** coordinates to a **Point** and **getX** and **getY** to return the **x** and **y** coordinates of a **Point**.

```
38   // Fig. 7.10: Circle.java
39   // Definition of class Circle
40
41   public class Circle extends Point {  // inherits from Point
42      protected double radius;
43
44      // no-argument constructor
45      public Circle()
46      {
47         super( 0, 0 );  // call the superclass constructor
48         setRadius( 0 );
49      }
50
51      // Constructor
52      public Circle( double r, double a, double b )
53      {
54         super( a, b );  // call the superclass constructor
55         setRadius( r );
56      }
57
58      // Set radius of Circle
59      public void setRadius( double r )
60         { radius = ( r >= 0 ? r : 0 ); }
61
62      // Get radius of Circle
63      public double getRadius() { return radius; }
64
65      // Calculate area of Circle
66      public double area() { return 3.14159 * radius * radius; }
67
68      // convert the Circle to a String
69      public String toString()
70         { return "Center = " + super.toString() +
71                  "; Radius = " + radius; }
72
73      // return the class name
74      public String getName() { return "Circle"; }
75   }
```

Fig. 7.10 Shape, point, circle, cylinder hierarchy (part 3 of 6).

Class **Circle** (Fig. 7.10, lines 38–75) is derived from **Point**. A **Circle** has a volume of 0.0, so superclass method **volume** is not overridden here—it is inherited from class **Point** which inherited it from **Shape**. A **Circle** has an area different from that of a point, so the **area** method is overridden in this class. Method **getName** is an implementation of the **abstract** method in the superclass. If this method is not overridden here, the **Point** versions of **getName** would be inherited. Other methods include **setRadius** to assign a new **radius** to a **Circle** and **getRadius** to return the **radius** of a **Circle**.

```
76   // Fig. 7.10: Cylinder.java
77   // Definition of class Cylinder
78
79   public class Cylinder extends Circle {
80      protected double height;  // height of Cylinder
81
82      // Cylinder constructor calls Circle constructor
83      public Cylinder( double h, double r, double a, double b )
84      {
85         super( r, a, b );   // call base-class constructor
86         setHeight( h );
87      }
88
89      // Set height of Cylinder
90      public void setHeight( double h )
91         { height = ( h >= 0 ? h : 0 ); }
92
93      // Get height of Cylinder
94      public double getHeight() { return height; }
95
96      // Calculate area of Cylinder (i.e., surface area)
97      public double area()
98      {
99         return 2 * super.area() +
100               2 * 3.14159 * radius * height;
101     }
102
103     // Calculate volume of Cylinder
104     public double volume() { return super.area() * height; }
105
106     // Convert a Cylinder to a String
107     public String toString()
108        { return super.toString() + "; Height = " + height; }
109
110     // Return the class name
111     public String getName() { return "Cylinder"; }
112  }
```

Fig. 7.10 Shape, point, circle, cylinder hierarchy (part 4 of 6).

Class **Cylinder** (Fig. 7.10, lines 76–112) is derived from **Circle**. A **Cylinder** has area and volume different from those of class **Circle**, so the **area** and **volume** methods are both overridden in this class. Method **getName** is an implementation of the **abstract** method in the superclass. If this method had not been overridden here, the **Circle** version of **getName** would be inherited. Other methods include **setHeight** to assign a new **height** to a **Cylinder** and **getHeight** to return the **height** of a **Cylinder**.

```
113  // Fig. 7.10: Test.java
114  // Driver for point, circle, cylinder hierarchy
115  import java.awt.Graphics;
116  import java.applet.Applet;
117
118  public class Test extends Applet {
119     private Point point;
120     private Circle circle;
121     private Cylinder cylinder;
122     private Shape arrayOfShapes[];
123
124     public void init()
125     {
126        point = new Point( 7, 11 );
127        circle = new Circle( 3.5, 22, 8 );
128        cylinder = new Cylinder( 10, 3.3, 10, 10 );
129
130        arrayOfShapes = new Shape[ 3 ];
131
132        // aim arrayOfShapes[0] at subclass Point object
133        // aim arrayOfShapes[1] at subclass Circle object
134        // aim arrayOfShapes[2] at subclass Cylinder object
135        arrayOfShapes[ 0 ] = point;
136        arrayOfShapes[ 1 ] = circle;
137        arrayOfShapes[ 2 ] = cylinder;
138     }
139
140     public void paint( Graphics g )
141     {
142        g.drawString( point.getName() + ": " +
143                      point.toString(), 25, 25 );
144
145        g.drawString( circle.getName() + ": " +
146                      circle.toString(), 25, 40 );
147
148        g.drawString( cylinder.getName() + ": " +
149                      cylinder.toString(), 25, 55 );
150
151        int yPos = 85;
152
153        // Loop through arrayOfShapes and print the name,
154        // area, and volume of each object.
155        for ( int i = 0; i < 3; i++ ) {
156           g.drawString( arrayOfShapes[ i ].getName() +
157              ": " + arrayOfShapes[ i ].toString(),
158              25, yPos );
159           yPos += 15;
160           g.drawString( "Area = " +
161              arrayOfShapes[ i ].area(), 25, yPos );
162           yPos += 15;
```

Fig. 7.10 Shape, point, circle, cylinder hierarchy (part 5 of 6).

```
163              g.drawString( "Volume = " +
164                 arrayOfShapes[ i ].volume(), 25, yPos );
165              yPos += 30;
166          }
167      }
168  }
```

Fig. 7.10 Shape, point, circle, cylinder hierarchy (part 6 of 6).

The **Test** applet (Fig. 7.10, lines 113–168) begins by instantiating **Point** object **point**, **Circle** object **circle**, and **Cylinder** object **cylinder** (lines 126–128). Next, array **arrayOfShapes** is instantiated (line 130). This array of superclass references is used to refer to each of the subclass objects instantiated. Next, a reference to object **point** is assigned to array element **arrayOfShapes[0]**, a reference to object **circle** is assigned to array element **arrayOfShapes[1]**, and a reference to object **cylinder** is assigned to array element **arrayOfShapes[2]** (lines 135–137). Methods **getName** and **toString** are invoked as each object is output to illustrate that the objects are initialized correctly (lines 141–149). Next, a **for** structure walks through **arrayOfShapes** and the following calls are made during each iteration of the loop

```
arrayOfShapes[ i ].getName()
arrayOfShapes[ i ].toString()
arrayOfShapes[ i ].area()
arrayOfShapes[ i ].volume()
```

Each of these method calls is invoked on the object to which **arrayOfShapes[i]** currently refers. The output illustrates that the methods are invoked properly. First, the string

"Point: " and the coordinates of the object **point** are output; the area and volume are both **0**. Next, the string **"Circle: "**, the coordinates of object **circle**, and the radius of object **circle** are output; the area of **circle** is calculated and the volume is **0**. Finally, the string **"Cylinder: "**, the coordinates of object **cylinder**, the radius of object **cylinder** and the height of object **cylinder** are output; the area of **cylinder** is calculated and the volume of **cylinder** is calculated. All the **getName, toString, area**, and **volume** method calls are resolved at run-time with dynamic binding.

7.19 Type Wrapper Classes for Primitive Types

Each of the primitive types has a *type wrapper class*. These classes are called **Integer, Float, Char, Long, Double** and **Boolean**. Each type wrapper class enables you to manipulate primitive types as objects of class **Object**. Many of the classes we will develop or reuse manipulate and share **Object**s. These classes can not manipulate variables of primitive types, but they can manipulate objects of the type wrapper classes, because every class ultimately is derived from class **Object**. Each of the numeric classes—**Integer, Float, Long** and **Double**—inherits from class **Number**. Each of the type wrappers is declared **final**, so their methods are implicitly **final** and may not be overridden. We will use the type wrapper classes in study our data structures in chapters 17 and 18.

Summary

- One of the keys to the power of object-oriented programming is achieving software reusability through inheritance.

- Through inheritance, a new class inherits the instance variables and methods of a previously defined superclass. In this case, the new class is referred to as a subclass.

- With single inheritance, a class is derived from one superclass. With multiple inheritance, a subclass inherits from multiple (possibly unrelated) superclasses. Java does not support multiple inheritance, but Java does provide the notion of interfaces (discussed in Chapter 13, "Multithreading") that offer many of the benefits of multiple inheritance without the associated problems.

- A subclass normally adds instance variables and methods of its own, so a subclass generally is larger than its superclass. A subclass is more specific than its superclass and normally represents fewer objects.

- A subclass cannot access the **private** members of its superclass. A subclass can, however, access the **public, protected** and "friendly" members of its superclass; the subclass must be in the superclass's package to access "friendly" superclass members.

- A subclass constructor always calls the constructor for its superclass first (either explicitly or implicitly) to create and initialize the subclass's superclass members.

- Inheritance enables software reusability which saves time in development and encourages the use of previously proven and debugged high-quality software.

- Someday most software will be constructed from standardized reusable components exactly as hardware often is today.

- An object of a subclass can be treated as an object of its corresponding superclass but the reverse is not true.

- A superclass exists in a hierarchical relationship with its subclasses.

- When a class is used with the mechanism of inheritance, it becomes either a superclass that supplies attributes and behaviors to other classes, or the class becomes a subclass that inherits those attributes and behaviors.

- An inheritance hierarchy can be arbitrarily deep within the physical limitations of a particular system, but most inheritance hierarchies have only a few levels.

- Hierarchies are useful for understanding and managing complexity. With software becoming increasingly complex, Java provides mechanisms for supporting hierarchical structures through inheritance and polymorphism.

- **Protected** access serves as an intermediate level of protection between **public** access and **private** access. **Protected** members of a superclass may be accessed by methods of the superclass, by methods of subclasses and by methods of classes in the same package; no other methods can access the **protected** members of a superclass.

- A superclass may be either a direct superclass of a subclass or an indirect superclass of a subclass. A direct superclass is the class that a subclass explicitly **extends**. An indirect superclass is inherited from several levels up the class hierarchy tree.

- When a superclass member is inappropriate for a subclass, the programmer may override that member in the subclass.

- It is important to distinguish between "is a" relationships and "has a" relationships. In a "has a" relationship, a class object has a reference to an object of another class as a member. In an "is a" relationship, an object of a subclass type may also be treated as an object of the superclass type. "Is a" is inheritance. "Has a" is composition.

- A subclass object can be assigned to a superclass reference. This kind of assignment makes sense because the subclass has members corresponding to each of the superclass members.

- A reference to a subclass object may be implicitly converted into a reference for a superclass object.

- It is possible to convert a superclass reference to a subclass reference by using an explicit cast. If the target is not a subclass object a **classCastException** is thrown.

- A superclass specifies commonality. All classes derived from a superclass inherit the capabilities of that superclass. In the object-oriented design process, the designer looks for commonality and factors it out to form superclasses. Subclasses are then customized beyond the capabilities inherited from the superclass.

- Reading a set of subclass declarations can be confusing because inherited superclass members are not listed in the subclass declarations, but these members are indeed present in the subclasses.

- "Knows a" relationships are examples of objects containing references to other objects so they can be aware of those objects.

- For a subclass object, first a superclass constructor is called either explicitly or implicitly, then the subclass constructor is called.

- With polymorphism, it becomes possible to design and implement systems that are more easily extensible. Programs can be written to process objects of types that may not exist when the program is under development.

- Polymorphic programming can eliminate the need for **switch** logic thus avoiding the kinds of errors associated with **switch** logic.

- An abstract method is declared by preceding the method's definition with the keyword **abstract** in the superclass.

- Subclasses can provide their own implementations of a superclass method if necessary, but if they do not, the superclass's implementation is used.

- There are many situations in which it is useful to define classes for which the programmer never intends to instantiate any objects. Such classes are called **abstract** classes. Because these are used only as superclasses, we will normally refer to them as **abstract** superclasses. No objects of an **abstract** class may be instantiated.

- Classes from which objects can be instantiated are called concrete classes.

- A class is made abstract by declaring one or more of its methods to be **abstract**. Such a class must be explicitly declared abstract.

- If a subclass is derived from a superclass with an **abstract** method without supplying a definition for that **abstract** method in the subclass, then that method remains **abstract** in the subclass. Consequently, the subclass is also an **abstract** class (and cannot instantiate any objects).

- When a request is made through a superclass reference to use a method, Java chooses the correct overridden method in the subclass associated with the object.

- Through the use of polymorphism, one method call can cause different actions to occur depending on the type of the object receiving the call.

- Although we cannot instantiate objects of **abstract** superclasses, we can declare references to **abstract** superclasses. Such references can then be used to enable polymorphic manipulations of subclass objects when such objects are instantiated from concrete classes.

- New kinds of classes are regularly added to systems. New classes are accommodated by dynamic method binding (also called late binding). The type of an object need not be known at compile time for a method call to be compiled. At execution time, the appropriate method of the receiving object is selected.

- With dynamic method binding, at execution time the call to a method is routed to the method version appropriate for the class of the object receiving the call.

- When a superclass provides a method, subclasses can override the method, but they do not have to override it. Thus a subclass can use a superclass's version of a method.

Terminology

abstract class	"knows a" relationship
abstract method	late binding
abstract superclass	**Long** class
abstraction	member access control
base class	member object
Boolean class	method overriding
Char class	method table
class hierarchy	multiple inheritance
client of a class	**Number** class
composition	**Object** class
direct superclass	object-oriented programming (OOP)
Double class	override a method
dynamic method binding	override an **abstract** method
extends	polymorphism
extensibility	overriding vs. overloading
final class	**protected** member of a class
final instance variable	reference to an **abstract** class
final method	single inheritance
"friendly" access	software reusability
garbage collection	standardized software components
"has a" relationship	static binding
hierarchical relationship	subclass
implementation inheritance	subclass constructor
implicit reference conversion	subclass reference
indirect superclass	super
infinite recursion error	superclass
inheritance	superclass constructor
inheritance hierarchy	superclass reference
Integer class	**switch** logic
interface	this
interface inheritance	type wrapper class
"is a" relationship	"uses a" relationship

Common Programming Errors

7.1   Treating a superclass object as a subclass object can cause errors.

7.2   Assigning an object of a superclass to a subclass reference (without a cast) is a syntax error.

7.3   It is a syntax error if a method in a superclass and a method in its subclass have the same signature but a different return type.

7.4   If a subclass constructor invokes a superclass default constructor (or no-argument constructor) and if the superclass does not have a default constructor (or no-argument constructor), a syntax error occurs.

7.5   It is a syntax error if a **super** call by a subclass to its superclass constructor is not the first statement in the subclass constructor.

7.6   When a superclass method is overridden in a subclass, it is common to have the subclass version call the superclass version and do some additional work. Not using the **super** reference to reference the superclass's method causes infinite recursion because the subclass method actually calls itself.

7.7   Cascading **super** references to refer to a member (method or variable) several levels up the hierarchy (as in **super.super.x**) is a syntax error.

7.8   Assigning a subclass object to a reference to a corresponding superclass, then attempting to reference subclass-only members with that superclass reference is a syntax error.

7.9   Assigning a subclass object to a superclass reference, and then attempting to reference subclass-only members with the superclass reference, is a syntax error.

7.10   Attempting to instantiate an object of an **abstract** class (i.e., a class that contains one or more **abstract** methods) is a syntax error.

7.11   It is a syntax error if a class with one or more **abstract** methods is not explicitly declared **abstract**.

Performance Tip

7.1   The compiler can decide to inline a **final** method call and will do so for small, simple **final** methods. Inlining does not violate encapsulation or information hiding (but does improve performance because it eliminates the overhead of making a method call).

7.2   Pipelined processors are able to improve performance by executing portions of the next several instructions simultaneously, but not if those instructions follow a method call. Thus, inlining (which the compiler can perform on a **final** method) can improve performance in pipelined processors because it eliminates the out-of-line transfer of control associated with a method call.

7.3   If classes produced through inheritance are larger than they need to be, memory and processing resources may be wasted. Inherit from the class "closest" to what you need.

7.4   A method declared **final** uses static binding rather than dynamic binding. Static binding is faster than dynamic binding.

7.5   Polymorphism as implemented with dynamic method binding is efficient.

7.6   The kinds of polymorphic manipulations made possible with dynamic binding can also be accomplished by using hand-coded **switch** logic based on type fields in objects. The polymorphic code generated by the Java compiler runs with comparable performance to efficiently coded **switch** logic.

Software Engineering Observations

7.1   A subclass cannot directly access **private** members of its superclass.

7.2   If an object has been assigned to a reference of one of its superclasses, it is acceptable to cast that object back to its own type. In fact, this must be done in order to send that object any of its messages that do not appear in that superclass.

7.3   A redefinition of a superclass method in a subclass need not have the same signature as the superclass method. Such a redefinition is not method overriding but is simply an example of method overloading.

7.4   When an object of a subclass is created, first the superclass constructor executes, then the subclass constructor executes.

7.5   Creating a subclass does not affect its superclass's source code or the superclass's Java bytecodes; the integrity of a superclass is preserved by inheritance.

7.6   Just as the designer of non-object-oriented systems should avoid unnecessary proliferation of functions, the designer of object-oriented systems should avoid unnecessary proliferation of classes. Proliferating classes creates management problems and can hinder software reusability simply because it is more difficult for a potential reuser of a class to locate that class in a huge collection. The trade-off is to create fewer classes, each providing substantial additional functionality, but such classes might be a bit too rich for certain reusers.

7.7   In an object-oriented system, classes are often closely related. "Factor out" common attributes and behaviors and place these in a superclass. Then use inheritance to form subclasses without having to repeat common attributes and behaviors.

7.8   Modifications to a superclass do not require subclasses to change as long as the public interface to the superclass remains unchanged.

7.9   When a subclass chooses not to redefine a method, the subclass simply inherits its immediate superclass's method definition.

7.10 A class declared **final** cannot be subclassed. Every method of a **final** class is implicitly **final**.

7.11 If a subclass is derived from a superclass with an **abstract** method, and if no definition is supplied in the subclass for that **abstract** method (i.e., if that method is not overridden in the subclass), then that method remains **abstract** in the subclass. Consequently, the subclass is also an **abstract** class and must be explicitly declared as an **abstract** class.

7.12 The ability to declare an **abstract** method gives the class designer considerable power over how subclasses will be implemented in a class hierarchy. Any new class that wants to inherit from this class is forced to override the **abstract** method (either directly or by inheriting from a class that has overridden the method). Otherwise that new class will contain an **abstract** method and thus be an **abstract** class unable to instantiate objects.

7.13 Even if a class is **abstract** it can still have instance data and non-**abstract** methods subject to the normal rules of inheritance by subclasses.

7.14 With polymorphism, the programmer can deal in generalities and let the execution-time environment concern itself with the specifics. The programmer can command a wide variety of objects to behave in manners appropriate to those objects without even knowing the types of those objects.

7.15 Polymorphism promotes extensibility: Software written to invoke polymorphic behavior is written independent of the types of the objects to which messages (i.e., method calls) are sent. Thus, new types of objects that can respond to existing messages can be added into such a system without modifying the base system.

7.16 If a method is declared **final** it cannot be overridden in subclasses, so that method calls may not be sent polymorphically to objects of those subclasses. The method call may still be sent to subclasses but they will all respond identically rather than polymorphically.

7.17 An **abstract** class defines a common interface for the various members of a class hierarchy. The **abstract** class contains methods that will be defined in the subclasses. All classes in the hierarchy can use this same interface through polymorphism.

7.18 Hierarchies designed for implementation inheritance tend to have their functionality high in the hierarchy—each new subclass inherits one or more methods that were defined in a superclass and uses the superclass definitions.

7.19 Hierarchies designed for interface inheritance tend to have their functionality lower in the hierarchy—a superclass specifies one or more methods that should be called identically for each object in the hierarchy (i.e., they have the same signature), but the individual subclasses provide their own implementations of the method(s).

Testing and Debugging Tips

7.1 An interesting consequence of using polymorphism is that programs take on a simplified appearance. They contain less branching logic in favor of simpler sequential code. This simplification facilitates testing, debugging, and program maintenance.

7.2 Hiding **private** members is a huge help in testing, debugging and correctly modifying systems. If a subclass could access its superclass's **private** members, it would then be possible for classes derived from that subclass to access that data as well, and so on. This would propagate access to what is supposed to be **private** data, and the benefits of information hiding would be lost throughout the class hierarchy.

Self-Review Exercises

7.1 Fill in the blanks in each of the following:
  a) If the class **Alpha** inherits from the class **Beta**, class **Alpha** is called the _____ class and class **Beta** is called the _____ class.
  b) Inheritance enables _____ which saves time in development, and encourages using previously proven and high-quality software components.
  c) An object of a _____ class can be treated as an object of its corresponding _____ class.
  d) The four member access specifiers are _____, _____, _____, and _____.
  e) A "has a" relationship between classes represents _____ and an "is a" relationship between classes represents _____ .
  f) Using polymorphism helps eliminate _____ logic.
  g) If a class contains one or more **abstract** methods, it is an _____ class.
  h) A method call resolved at compile time is referred to as _____ binding.
  i) A method call resolved at run time is referred to as _____ binding.

7.2   a) A subclass may call any method of its superclass by prepending _____ to the method call.

   b) A superclass typically represents a larger number of objects than its subclass represents
      (T/F).
   c) A subclass typically encapsulates less functionality than does its superclass. (T/F).

Answers to Self-Review Exercises

7.1   a) sub, super. b) software reusability. c) sub, super. d)**public**, **protected**, **private**
and "friendly." e) composition, inheritance. f) **switch**. g) **abstract**. h) static. i) dynamic.

7.2   a) **super**
       b) T
       c) F

Exercises

7.3   Consider the class **bicycle**. Given your knowledge of some common components of bi-
cycles, show a class hierarchy in which the class **bicycle** inherits from other classes, which, in turn,
inherit from yet other classes. Discuss the instantiation of various objects of class **bicycle**. Discuss
inheritance from class **bicycle** for other closely related subclasses.

7.4   Define each of the following terms: single inheritance, multiple inheritance, interface, superclass and subclass.

7.5   Discuss why casting a superclass reference to a subclass reference is potentially dangerous.

7.6   Distinguish between single inheritance and multiple inheritance. Why does Java not support
multiple inheritance? What feature of Java helps realize the benefits of multiple inheritance?

7.7   (True/False) A subclass is generally smaller than its superclass.

7.8   (True/False) A subclass object is also an object of that subclass's superclass.

7.9   Some programmers prefer not to use **protected** access because it breaks information hiding in the superclass. Discuss the relative merits of using **protected** access vs. **private** access
in superclasses.

7.10   Many programs written with inheritance could be solved with composition instead, and vice
versa. Discuss the relative merits of these approaches in the context of the **Point**, **Circle**, **Cylinder** class hierarchy in this chapter. Rewrite the program of Fig. 7.10 (and the supporting classes)
to use composition rather than inheritance. After you do this, reassess the relative merits of the two
approaches both for the **Point**, **Circle**, **Cylinder** problem and for object-oriented programs in
general.

7.11   Rewrite the **Point**, **Circle**, **Cylinder** program of Fig. 7.10 as a **Point**, **Square**,
Cube program. Do this two ways—once with inheritance and once with composition.

7.12   In the chapter, we stated, "When a superclass member is inappropriate for a subclass, that
member can be overridden in the subclass with an appropriate implementation." If this is done, does
the subclass-is-a-superclass-object relationship still hold? Explain your answer.

7.13 Study the inheritance hierarchy of Fig. 7.2. For each class, indicate some common attributes and behaviors consistent with the hierarchy. Add some other classes (i.e., **UndergraduateStudent**, **GraduateStudent**, **Freshman**, **Sophomore**, **Junior**, **Senior**, etc., to enrich the hierarchy.

7.14 Write an inheritance hierarchy for classes **Quadrilateral**, **Trapezoid**, **Parallelogram**, **Rectangle**, and **Square**. Use **Quadrilateral** as the superclass of the hierarchy. Make the hierarchy as deep (i.e., as many levels) as possible. The **private** data of **Quadrilateral** should include the *(x, y)* coordinate pairs for the four endpoints of the **Quadrilateral**. Write a driver program that instantiates and displays objects of each of these classes. [In Chapter 9, "Graphics" you will learn how to use Java's drawing capabilities.]

7.15 Write down all the shapes you can think of—both two-dimensional and three-dimensional—and form those shapes into a shape hierarchy. Your hierarchy should have superclass **Shape** from which class **TwoDimensionalShape** and class **ThreeDimensionalShape** are derived. Once you have developed the hierarchy, define each of the classes in the hierarchy. We will use this hierarchy in the exercises to process all shapes as objects of superclass **Shape**.

7.16 How is it that polymorphism enables you to program "in the general" rather than "in the specific." Discuss the key advantages of programming "in the general."

7.17 Discuss the problems of programming with **switch** logic. Explain why polymorphism is an effective alternative to using **switch** logic.

7.18 Distinguish between static binding and dynamic binding.

7.19 Distinguish between inheriting interface and inheriting implementation. How do inheritance hierarchies designed for inheriting interface differ from those designed for inheriting implementation?

7.20 Distinguish between non-**abstract** methods and **abstract** methods.

7.21 (True/False) All methods in an **abstract** superclass must be declared **abstract**.

7.22 Suggest one or more levels of **abstract** superclasses for the **Shape** hierarchy discussed in the beginning of this chapter (the first level is **Shape** and the second level consists of the classes **TwoDimensionalShape** and **ThreeDimensionalShape**).

7.23 How does polymorphism promote extensibility?

7.24 You have been asked to develop a flight simulator that will have elaborate graphical outputs. Explain why polymorphic programming would be especially effective for a problem of this nature.

7.25 Develop a basic graphics package. Use the **Shape** class inheritance hierarchy from this chapter. Limit yourself to two-dimensional shapes such as squares, rectangles, triangles, and circles. Interact with the user. Let the user specify the position, size, shape, and fill characters to be used in drawing each shape. The user can specify many items of the same shape. As you create each shape, place a **Shape** reference to each new **Shape** object into an array. Each class has its own **draw** method. Write a polymorphic screen manager that walks through the array sending **draw** messages to each object in the array to form a screen image. Redraw the screen image each time the user specifies an additional shape.

7.26   Modify the payroll system of Fig. 7.9 to add **private** instance variables **birthDate** (a **Date** object) and **departmentCode** (an **int**) to class **Employee**. Assume this payroll is processed once per month. Then, as your program calculates the payroll for each **Employee** (polymorphically), add a $100.00 bonus to the person's payroll amount if this is the month in which the **Employee**'s birthday occurs.

7.27   In Exercise 7.15, you developed a **Shape** class hierarchy and defined the classes in the hierarchy. Modify the hierarchy so that class **Shape** is an **abstract** superclass containing the interface to the hierarchy. Derive **TwoDimensionalShape** and **ThreeDimensionalShape** from class **Shape**—these classes should also be **abstract**. Use an **abstract print** method to output the type and dimensions of each class. Also include **area** and **volume** methods so these calculations can be performed for objects of each concrete class in the hierarchy. Write a driver program that tests the **Shape** class hierarchy.

8

Strings

Objectives

- To be able to create and manipulate objects of class **String**.
- To be able to create and manipulate objects of class **StringBuffer**.
- To be able to create and manipulate objects of class **Character**.
- To be able to use a **StringTokenizer** object to break a **String** object into individual components called tokens.

The chief defect of Henry King
Was chewing little bits of string.
Hilaire Belloc

Vigorous writing is concise. A sentence should contain no
unnecessary words, a paragraph no unnecessary sentences.
William Strunk, Jr.

I have made this letter longer than usual, because I lack the
time to make it short.
Blaise Pascal

The difference between the almost-right word & the right word
is really a large matter—it's the difference between the
lightning bug and the lightning.
Mark Twain

Mum's the word.
Miguel de Cervantes, *Don Quixote de la Mancha*

Outline

8.1 Introduction

In this chapter, we introduce Java's string and character processing capabilities. The techniques discussed here are appropriate for developing text editors, word processors, page layout software, computerized typesetting systems, and other kinds of text-processing software. We have already presented several string processing capabilities in the text. In this chapter we discuss in detail the capabilities of class *String*, class *StringBuffer* and class *Character* from the **java.lang** package and class *StringTokenizer* from the **java.util** package.

8.2 Fundamentals of Characters and Strings

Characters are the fundamental building blocks of Java source programs. Every program is composed of a sequence of characters that—when grouped together meaningfully—is interpreted by the computer as a series of instructions used to accomplish a task. A program may contain *character constants*. A character constant is an integer value represented as a character in single quotes. As we stated previously, the value of a character constant is the integer value of the character in the Unicode character set. For example, `'z'` represents the integer value of **z**, and `'\n'` represents the integer value of newline.

A string is a series of characters treated as a single unit. A string may include letters, digits, and various *special characters* such as **+, -, *, /, $**, and others. A string in Java is an object of class **String**. *String literals* or *string constants* (which are often referred to as *anonymous* **String** *objects*) in Java are written as a sequence of characters in double quotation marks as follows:

`"John Q. Doe"`	(a name)
`"9999 Main Street"`	(a street address)
`"Waltham, Massachusetts"`	(a city and state)
`"(201) 555-1212"`	(a telephone number)

Java treats all anonymous **String**s with the same contents as one anonymous **String** object that has many references.

A **String** may be assigned in a declaration to a **String** reference. The declarations

```
String color = "blue";
```

initializes a **String** reference **color** to refer to the anonymous **String** object **"blue"**.

8.3 String Constructors

Class **String** provides seven constructors for initializing **String** objects in a variety of ways. Each of the constructors is demonstrated in Fig. 8.1. All the constructors are used in the **StringConstructors** applet's **init** method. The statement

```
s1 = new String();
```

instantiates a new **String** object and assigns it to reference **s1** using the **String** class's default constructor. The new **String** object contains no characters and has a length of 0.

The statement

```
s2 = new String( s );
```

instantiates a new **String** object and assigns it to reference **s2** using the **String** class's copy constructor. The new **String** object contains a copy of the characters in the **String** object **s** that is passed as an argument to the constructor.

The statement

```
s3 = new String( charArray );
```

instantiates a new **String** object and assigns it to reference **s3** using the **String** class constructor that takes a character array as an argument. The new **String** object contains a copy of the characters in the array.

The statement

```
s4 = new String( charArray, 6, 3 );
```

```
1   // Fig. 8.1: StringConstructors.java
2   // This program demonstrates the String class constructors.
3   import java.awt.Graphics;
4   import java.applet.Applet;
5
6   public class StringConstructors extends Applet {
7      char charArray[] = { 'b', 'i', 'r', 't', 'h', ' ',
8                           'd', 'a', 'y' };
9      byte byteArray[] = { 'n', 'e', 'w', ' ',
10                          'y', 'e', 'a', 'r' };
11     StringBuffer buffer;
12     String s, s1, s2, s3, s4, s5, s6, s7;
13
14     public void init()
15     {
16        s = new String( "hello" );
17        buffer = new StringBuffer();
18        buffer.append( "Welcome to Java Programming!" );
19
20        // use the String constructors
21        s1 = new String();
22        s2 = new String( s );
23        s3 = new String( charArray );
24        s4 = new String( charArray, 6, 3 );
25        s5 = new String( byteArray, 0, 4, 4 );
26        s6 = new String( byteArray, 0 );
27        s7 = new String( buffer );
28     }
29
30     public void paint( Graphics g )
31     {
32        g.drawString( "s1 = " + s1, 25, 25 );
33        g.drawString( "s2 = " + s2, 25, 40 );
34        g.drawString( "s3 = " + s3, 25, 55 );
35        g.drawString( "s4 = " + s4, 25, 70 );
36        g.drawString( "s5 = " + s5, 25, 85 );
37        g.drawString( "s6 = " + s6, 25, 100 );
38        g.drawString( "s7 = " + s7, 25, 115 );
39     }
40  }
```

Fig. 8.1   Demonstrating the **String** class constructors (part 1 of 2).

Fig. 8.1   Demonstrating the **String** class constructors (part 2 of 2).

instantiates a new **String** object and assigns it to reference **s4** using the **String** class constructor that takes a character array and two integers as arguments. The second argument specifies the starting position (the *offset*) from which characters in the array are copied. The third argument specifies the number of characters (the *count*) to be copied from the array. The new **String** object contains a copy of the specified characters in the array. If the **offset** or the **count** specified as arguments result in accessing an element outside the bounds of the character array, a **StringIndexOutOfBoundsException** is thrown. We discuss exceptions in detail in Chapter 12.

The statement

```
s5 = new String( byteArray, 0, 4, 4 );
```

instantiates a new **String** object and assigns it to reference **s5** using the **String** class constructor that receives a byte array and three integers as arguments. The third and fourth arguments specify the **offset** and **count**, respectively. The second argument specifies the *hibyte value*. As you know, characters in Java are two byte Unicode characters. However, each element in a byte array is only one byte. The **hibyte** value is combined with the value in each array element to create a two-byte character that can be stored as part of a **String**. In the two-byte character that is formed, the original **byte** value from the **byte** array is referred to as the *low-order byte* and the **hibyte** value is referred to as the *high-order byte*. Zero is normally specified as the **hibyte** value for English characters (this results in a character from the ASCII character set). The new **String** object contains a copy of the specified bytes in the array. If the **offset** or the **count** specified as arguments result in accessing an element outside the bounds of the character array, a **StringIndexOutOfBoundsException** is thrown.

The statement

```
s6 = new String( byteArray, 0 );
```

instantiates a new **String** object and assigns it to reference **s6** using the **String** class constructor that takes a **byte** array and an integer as arguments. The second argument to the constructor is the **hibyte** value. The new **String** object contains a copy of the bytes in the array.

The statement

```
s7 = new String( buffer );
```

instantiates a new **String** object and assigns it to reference **s7** using the **String** class constructor that receives a **StringBuffer** as an argument. The new **String** object contains a copy of the characters in the **StringBuffer**. A **StringBuffer** is a dynamically resizable string. The lines

```
buffer = new StringBuffer();
buffer.append( "Welcome to Java Programming!" );
```

create a new object of class **StringBuffer**, assign it to **StringBuffer** reference **buffer** and use the **StringBuffer** method **append** to add the string "**Welcome to Java Programming**" to object **buffer**. We discuss **StringBuffer**s in detail later in this chapter.

8.4 String Methods `length`, `charAt`, `getChars`, `getBytes`

This section presents **String** methods **length**, **charAt**, **getChars** and **getBytes**. The methods are used in applet **StringMisc**'s **paint** method (Fig. 8.2). The statement

```
g.drawString( "Length of s1: " + s1.length(), 25, 40 );
```

uses the **String** method **length** to determine the number of characters in **String s1**. Like arrays, **String**s always know their own size. However, unlike arrays, **String**s do not have a **length** instance variable that specifies the number of elements in a **String**.

```
1  // Fig. 8.2: StringMisc.java
2  // This program demonstrates the length, charAt, getChars, and
3  // getBytes methods of the String class.
4  //
5  // Note: Methods getChars and getBytes require a starting point
6  // and ending point in the String. The starting point is the
7  // actual subscript from which copying starts. The ending point
8  // is one past the subscript at which the copying ends.
9  import java.awt.Graphics;
10 import java.applet.Applet;
11
12 public class StringMisc extends Applet {
13     String s1;
14     char charArray[];
15     byte byteArray[];
16
```

Fig. 8.2   The **String** class character manipulation methods (part 1 of 2).

```
17     public void init()
18     {
19        s1 = new String( "hello there" );
20        charArray = new char[ 5 ];
21        byteArray = new byte[ 5 ];
22     }
23
24     public void paint( Graphics g )
25     {
26        // output the string
27        g.drawString( "s1: " + s1, 25, 25 );
28
29        // test the length method
30        g.drawString( "Length of s1: " + s1.length(), 25, 40 );
31
32        // loop through the characters in s1 and display reversed
33        g.drawString( "The string reversed is: ", 25, 55 );
34        int xPosition = 155;
35
36        for ( int i = s1.length() - 1; i >= 0; i-- ) {
37           g.drawString( String.valueOf( s1.charAt( i ) ),
38                         xPosition, 55 );
39           xPosition += 10;
40        }
41
42        // copy characters from string into char array
43        s1.getChars( 0, 5, charArray, 0 );
44        g.drawString( "The character array is: ", 25, 70 );
45        g.drawChars( charArray, 0, charArray.length, 158, 70 );
46
47        // copy characters from string into byte array
48        s1.getBytes( 6, 11, byteArray, 0 );
49        g.drawString( "The byte array is: ", 25, 85 );
50        g.drawBytes( byteArray, 0, byteArray.length, 130, 85);
51     }
52  }
```

Fig. 8.2   The **String** class character manipulation methods (part 2 of 2).

Common Programming Error 8.1

*Attempting to determine the length of a **String** via an instance variable called **length** (e.g., **s1.length**) is a syntax error. The **String** method **length** must be used. (e.g. **s1.length()**).*

The **for** structure at line 36 displays the characters of the **String s1** in reverse order. The **String** method **charAt** is used to select the character at a specific position in the **String**. Method **charAt** receives an integer argument that is used as the *position number* (or *index*) and returns the character at that position. Like arrays, the first element of a **String** is considered to be at position 0 of the **String**. If the index specified as an argument is outside the bounds of the **String**, a **StringIndexOutOfBoundsException** is thrown.

Common Programming Error 8.2

*Attempting to access a character that is outside the bounds of a **String** (i.e., an index less than 0 or an index greater than or equal to the **String**'s length) results in a **StringIndexOutOfBoundsException***

The statement

```
s1.getChars( 0, 5, charArray, 0 );
```

uses the **String** method **getChars** to copy the characters of a **String** into a character array. The first argument is the starting index from which characters are copied in the **String**. The second argument is the index that is one past the last character to be copied from the **String**. The third argument is the character array into which the characters are copied. The last argument is the starting index where the copied characters are placed in the character array. The result of the preceding statement is displayed with the statement

```
g.drawChars( charArray, 0, charArray.length, 158, 70 );
```

which uses **Graphics** method **drawChars** to output the character array. The second argument specifies the index of the first character to be output. The third argument specifies the index one beyond the last character to be output.

The statement

```
s1.getBytes( 6, 11, byteArray, 0 );
```

uses the **String** method **getBytes** to copy the characters of a **String** into a **byte** array. The first argument is the starting index from which characters are copied in the **String**. The second argument is the index that is one past the last character to be copied from the **String**. The third argument is the **byte** array into which the characters are copied. The last argument is the starting index where the copied characters are placed in the character array. Only the low-order byte of each character is copied into the **byte** array This may produce incorrect results for internationalized programs that use characters from languages other than English. The result of the preceding statement is output with the **Graphics** method **drawBytes** outputs a byte array in the same manner as **drawChars** outputs a character array.

8.5 Comparing Strings

Java provides a variety of methods for comparing **String** objects demonstrated in the next two examples. To understand just what it means for one string to be "greater than" or "less than" another string, consider the process of alphabetizing a series of last names. The reader would, no doubt, place "Jones" before "Smith" because the first letter of "Jones" comes before the first letter of "Smith" in the alphabet. But the alphabet is more than just a list of 26 letters—it is an ordered list of characters. Each letter occurs in a specific position within the list. "Z" is more than just a letter of the alphabet; "Z" is specifically the twenty-sixth letter of the alphabet.

How does the computer know that one letter comes before another? All characters are represented inside the computer as numeric codes; when the computer compares two strings, it actually compares the numeric codes of the characters in the strings.

Figure 8.3 shows the **String** methods **equals, equalsIgnoreCase, compareTo** and **regionMatches**, and demonstrates using the equality operator **==** to compare **String** objects.

The condition in the **if** structure at line 27

```
s1.equals( "hello" )
```

uses the **equals** method to compare **String s1** for equality with the anonymous **String "hello"**. Method **equals** (which is inherited by class **String** from its superclass **Object**) is used to test any two objects for equality (i.e., the contents of the two objects are identical). The method returns **true** if the objects are equal and **false** otherwise. The result of the preceding call to **equals** is **true** because **String s1** was initialized with a copy of the anonymous **String "hello"**. Method **equals** uses a *lexicographical comparison*—the integer Unicode values that represent each character in each **String** are compared. Thus, if the **String "hello"** is compared to the **String "HELLO"** the result is **false** because the integer representation of a lowercase letter is different from that of the corresponding uppercase letter.

The condition in the **if** structure at line 34

```
s1 == "hello"
```

uses the equality operator **==** to compare **String s1** for equality with the anonymous **String "hello"**. *Operator **==** actually has different functionality when it is used to compare references and when it is used to compare values of primitive data types.* When primitive data type values are compared with **==**, the result is **true** if both values are identical. When references are compared with **==**, the result is **true** if both references *refer to the same object in memory*. To compare the actual contents (or state information) of objects for equality, methods (such as **equals**) must be invoked. The preceding condition evaluates to **false** in this program because the reference **s1** was initialized with the statement

```
s1 = new String( "hello" );
```

which creates a new **String** object with a copy of anonymous **String "hello"** and assigns the new object to reference **s1**. If **s1** had been initialized with the statement

```
1   // Fig. 8.3: StringCompare
2   // This program demonstrates the methods equals,
3   // equalsIgnoreCase, compareTo, and regionMatches
4   // of the String class.
5   import java.awt.Graphics;
6   import java.applet.Applet;
7
8   public class StringCompare extends Applet {
9      String s1, s2, s3, s4;
10
11     public void init()
12     {
13        s1 = new String( "hello" );
14        s2 = new String( "good bye" );
15        s3 = new String( "Happy Birthday" );
16        s4 = new String( "happy birthday" );
17     }
18
19     public void paint( Graphics g )
20     {
21        g.drawString( "s1 = " + s1, 25, 25 );
22        g.drawString( "s2 = " + s2, 25, 40 );
23        g.drawString( "s3 = " + s3, 25, 55 );
24        g.drawString( "s4 = " + s4, 25, 70 );
25
26        // test for equality
27        if ( s1.equals( "hello" ) )
28           g.drawString( "s1 equals \"hello\"", 25, 100 );
29        else
30           g.drawString( "s1 does not equal \"hello\"",
31                         25, 100 );
32
33        // test for equality with ==
34        if ( s1 == "hello" )
35           g.drawString( "s1 equals \"hello\"", 25, 115 );
36        else
37           g.drawString( "s1 does not equal \"hello\"",
38                         25, 115 );
39
40        // test for equality--ignore case
41        if ( s3.equalsIgnoreCase( s4 ) )
42           g.drawString( "s3 equals s4", 25, 130 );
43        else
44           g.drawString( "s3 does not equal s4", 25, 130 );
45
46        // test compareTo
47        g.drawString( "s1.compareTo( s2 ) is " +
48                      s1.compareTo( s2 ), 25, 160 );
49        g.drawString( "s2.compareTo( s1 ) is " +
50                      s2.compareTo( s1 ), 25, 175 );
```

Fig. 8.3   Demonstrating **String** comparisons (part 1 of 3).

```
51          g.drawString( "s1.compareTo( s1 ) is " +
52                         s1.compareTo( s1 ), 25, 190 );
53          g.drawString( "s3.compareTo( s4 ) is " +
54                         s3.compareTo( s4 ), 25, 205 );
55          g.drawString( "s4.compareTo( s3 ) is " +
56                         s4.compareTo( s3 ), 25, 220 );
57
58          // test regionMatches (case sensitive)
59          if ( s3.regionMatches( 0, s4, 0, 5 ) )
60             g.drawString(
61                "First 5 characters of s3 and s4 match",
62                25, 250 );
63          else
64             g.drawString(
65                "First 5 characters of s3 and s4 do not match",
66                25, 250 );
67
68          // test regionMatches (ignore case)
69          if ( s3.regionMatches( true, 0, s4, 0, 5 ) )
70             g.drawString(
71                "First 5 characters of s3 and s4 match",
72                25, 265 );
73          else
74             g.drawString(
75                "First 5 characters of s3 and s4 do not match",
76                25, 265 );
77       }
78 }
```

Fig. 8.3   Demonstrating **String** comparisons (2 of 3).

```
s1 = "hello";
```

which directly assigns the anonymous **String "hello"** to the reference **s1**, the condition would produce a **true** result. This is because Java treats all anonymous **String**s with the same contents as one anonymous **String** object that has many references. Thus, lines 13, 27 and 34 all refer to the same anonymous **String** object **"hello"** in memory.

If you are sorting **String**s, you may compare them for equality with method **equalsIgnoreCase** which ignores the case of the letters in each **String** when performing the comparison. Thus, the **String "hello"** and the **String "HELLO"** compare as equal. The **if** structure at line 41 uses the condition

```
s3.equalsIgnoreCase( s4 )
```

to compare **String s3**—**Happy Birthday**—for equality with **String s4**—**happy birthday**. The result of this comparison is **true**.

Lines 47 through 56 use the **String** method **compareTo** to compare **String** objects. For example, the expression

```
s1.compareTo( s2 )
```

Applet Viewer: StringCompare.class

Applet

s1 = hello
s2 = good bye
s3 = Happy Birthday
s4 = happy birthday

s1 equals "hello"
s1 does not equal "hello"
s3 equals s4

s1.compareTo(s2) is 1
s2.compareTo(s1) is -1
s1.compareTo(s1) is 0
s3.compareTo(s4) is -32
s4.compareTo(s3) is 32

First 5 characters of s3 and s4 do not match
First 5 characters of s3 and s4 match
Applet started.

Fig. 8.3 Demonstrating **String** comparisons (3 of 3).

on line 48 compares **String s1** to **String s2**. Method **compareTo** returns 0 if the **Strings** are equal, a negative number if the **String** that invokes **compareTo** is less than the **String** that is passed as an argument, and a positive number if the **String** that invokes **compareTo** is greater than the **String** that is passed as an argument. Method **compareTo** uses a lexicographical comparison. The value returned is the difference between the integer representations of the first character that is different in each **String**. When comparing **s4** and **s3**, the first character in each **String** is different and the value returned is 32 because the integer representation of **h** is 104 and the integer representation of **H** is 72.

The condition in the **if** structure at line 59

```
s3.regionMatches( 0, s4, 0, 5 )
```

uses **String** method **regionMatches** to compare portions of two **String** objects for equality. The first argument is the starting index in the **String** that invokes the method. The second argument is a **String** for comparison. The third argument is the starting index in the **String** for comparison. The last argument is the number of characters to compare between the two **String**s. The method returns **true** only if the specified number of characters are lexicographically equal.

Finally, the condition in the **if** structure at line 69

```
s3.regionMatches( true, 0, s4, 0, 5 )
```

uses the second version of **String** method **regionMatches** to compare portions of two **String** objects for equality. If the first argument is **true**, the method ignores the case of the characters being compared. The remaining arguments are identical to those described for the **regionMatches** method with four arguments.

The second example of this section (Fig. 8.4) demonstrates the **startsWith** and **endsWith** methods of class **String**. Applet **StringStartEnd** contains an array of **String**s called **strings** containing **"started"**, **"starting"**, **"ended"** and **"ending"**. The paint method consists of three for structures that test the elements of the array to determine if they start with or end with a particular set of characters.

```
1    // Fig. 8.4: StringStartEnd.java
2    // This program demonstrates the methods startsWith and
3    // endsWith of the String class.
4    import java.awt.Graphics;
5    import java.applet.Applet;
6
7    public class StringStartEnd extends Applet{
8       String strings[] = { "started", "starting",
9                             "ended", "ending" };
10
11      public void paint( Graphics g )
12      {
13         int yPosition = 25;
14
15         // Test method startsWith
16         for ( int i = 0; i < strings.length; i++ )
17            if ( strings[ i ].startsWith( "st" ) ) {
18               g.drawString( "\"" + strings[ i ] +
19                  "\" starts with \"st\"", 25, yPosition );
20               yPosition += 15;
21            }
22
23         yPosition += 15;
24
25         // Test method startsWith starting from position
26         // 2 of the string
27         for ( int i = 0; i < strings.length; i++ )
28            if ( strings[ i ].startsWith( "art", 2 ) ) {
29               g.drawString( "\"" + strings[ i ] +
30                  "\" starts with \"art\" at position 2",
31                  25, yPosition );
32               yPosition += 15;
33            }
34
```

Fig. 8.4   The **String** class **startsWith** and **endsWith** methods (part 1 of 2).

```
35          yPosition += 15;
36
37          // Test method endsWith
38          for ( int i = 0; i < strings.length; i++ )
39             if ( strings[ i ].endsWith( "ed" ) ) {
40                g.drawString( "\"" + strings[ i ] +
41                   "\" ends with \"ed\"", 25, yPosition );
42                yPosition += 15;
43             }
44       }
45    }
```

Fig. 8.4   The **String** class **startsWith** and **endsWith** methods (part 2 of 2).

The first **for** structure (line 16) uses the version of method **startsWith** that takes a **String** argument. The condition in the **if** structure (line 17)

```
strings[ i ].startsWith( "st" )
```

determines if the **String** at location **i** of array **strings** starts with the characters **"st"**. If so, the method returns **true** and the **String** is displayed on the applet.

The second **for** structure (line 27) uses the version of method **startsWith** that takes a **String** and an integer as arguments. The integer argument specifies the index at which the comparison should begin in the **String**. The condition in the **if** structure

```
strings[ i ].startsWith( "art", 2 )
```

determines if the **String** at location **i** of array **strings** starts with the characters **"art"** beginning with the character at index **2** in each **String**. If so, the method returns **true** and the **String** is displayed on the applet.

The third **for** structure (line 38) uses method **endsWith** that takes a **String** argument. The condition in the **if** structure

```
strings[ i ].endsWith( "ed" )
```

determines if the **String** at location **i** of array **strings** ends with the characters **"ed"**. If so, the method returns **true** and the **String** is displayed on the applet.

8.6 **String** Method **hashCode**

Often, it is necessary to store **String**s and other data types in a manner that allows the information to be found quickly. One of the best ways to store information for fast lookup is a hash table. A hash table stores information using a special calculation on the object to be stored that produces a hash code. The hash code is used to choose the location in the table at which to store the object. When the information needs to be retrieved, the same calculation is performed, the hash code is determined and a lookup of that location in the table results in the value that was stored there previously. Every object has the ability to be stored in a hash table. Class **Object** defines method **hashCode** to perform the hash code calculation. This method is inherited into all subclasses of **Object**. Method **hashCode** is overridden by **String** to provide a good hash code distribution based on the contents of the **String**. We will say more about hashing in Chapter 18.

The example in Fig. 8.5 demonstrates the **hashCode** method for two **String**s containing **"hello"** and **"Hello"**.

```
1   // Fig. 8.5: StringHashCode.java
2   // This program demonstrates the method
3   // hashCode of the String class.
4   import java.awt.Graphics;
5   import java.applet.Applet;
6
7   public class StringHashCode extends Applet {
8      String s1 = "hello",
9             s2 = "Hello";
10
11     public void paint( Graphics g )
12     {
13        g.drawString( "The hash code for \"" +
14           s1 + "\" is " + s1.hashCode(), 25, 25 );
15        g.drawString( "The hash code for \"" +
16           s2 + "\" is " + s2.hashCode(), 25, 40 );
17     }
18  }
```

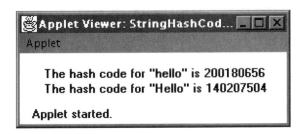

The hash code for "hello" is 200180656
The hash code for "Hello" is 140207504

Fig. 8.5 The **String** class **hashCode** method.

Note that the hash code values for each of the **String**s is different. That is because the **String**s themselves are lexicographically different. We will discuss hash tables in more detail in Chapter 18.

8.7 Locating Characters and Substrings in **Strings**

Often it is useful to search for a character or set of characters in a **String**. For example, if you are creating your own word processor, you may want to provide a capability for searching through the document. The program of Fig. 8.6 demonstrates the many versions of **String** methods **indexOf** and **lastIndexOf** that search for a specified character in a **String**. All the searches in this example are performed on the **String** letters (initialized with **"abcdefghijklmabcdefghijklm"**) in the **paint** method of applet class **StringIndexMethods**.

```java
1   // Fig. 8.6: StringIndexMethods.java
2   // This program demonstrates the String
3   // class index methods.
4   import java.awt.Graphics;
5   import java.applet.Applet;
6
7   public class StringIndexMethods extends Applet {
8      String letters = "abcdefghijklmabcdefghijklm";
9
10     public void paint( Graphics g )
11     {
12        // test indexOf to locate a character in a string
13        g.drawString( "'c' is located at index " +
14           letters.indexOf( (int) 'c' ), 25, 25 );
15
16        g.drawString( "'a' is located at index " +
17           letters.indexOf( (int) 'a', 1 ), 25, 40 );
18
19        g.drawString( "'$' is located at index " +
20           letters.indexOf( (int) '$' ), 25, 55 );
21
22        // test lastIndexOf to find a character in a string
23        g.drawString( "Last 'c' is located at index " +
24           letters.lastIndexOf( (int) 'c' ), 25, 85 );
25
26        g.drawString( "Last 'a' is located at index " +
27           letters.lastIndexOf( (int) 'a', 25 ), 25, 100 );
28
29        g.drawString( "Last '$' is located at index " +
30           letters.lastIndexOf( (int) '$' ), 25, 115 );
31
32        // test indexOf to locate a substring in a string
33        g.drawString( "\"def\" is located at index " +
34           letters.indexOf( "def" ), 25, 145 );
```

Fig. 8.6   The **String** class searching methods (part 1 of 2).

```
35
36        g.drawString( "\"def\" is located at index " +
37           letters.indexOf( "def", 7 ), 25, 160 );
38
39        g.drawString( "\"hello\" is located at index " +
40           letters.indexOf( "hello" ), 25, 175 );
41
42        // test lastIndexOf to find a substring in a string
43        g.drawString( "Last \"def\" is located at index " +
44           letters.lastIndexOf( "def" ), 25, 205 );
45
46        g.drawString( "Last \"def\" is located at index " +
47           letters.lastIndexOf( "def", 25 ), 25, 220 );
48
49        g.drawString( "Last \"hello\" is located at index " +
50           letters.lastIndexOf( "hello" ), 25, 235 );
51     }
52  }
```

Fig. 8.6 The **String** class searching methods (part 2 of 2).

The output statements at lines 13 through 20 use method **indexOf** to locate the first occurrence of a character in a **String**. If the character is found, the index of that character in the **String** is returned; otherwise -1 is returned. There are two versions of **indexOf** that search for characters in a **String**. The expression

```
letters.indexOf( (int) 'c' )
```

uses the version of method **indexOf** that takes one integer argument that is the integer representation of a character—the reason for the integer cast operation in the preceding expression. The expression

```
letters.indexOf( (int) 'a', 1 )
```

uses the second version of method **indexOf** that takes two integer arguments—the integer representation of a character and the starting index at which the search of the **String** should begin.

The output statements at lines 23 through 30 use method **lastIndexOf** to locate the last occurrence of a character in a **String**. The search is performed from the end of the **String** toward the beginning of the **String**. If the character is found, the index of that character in the **String** is returned; otherwise -1 is returned. There are two versions of **lastIndexOf** that search for characters in a **String**. The expression

```
letters.lastIndexOf( (int) 'c' )
```

uses the version of method **lastIndexOf** that takes one integer argument that is the integer representation of a character. The expression

```
letters.lastIndexOf( (int) 'a', 25 )
```

uses the version of method **lastIndexOf** that takes two integer arguments—the integer representation of a character and the highest index at which to begin searching for the character.

Lines 33 through 50 of the program demonstrate the **indexOf** and **lastIndexOf** methods—each of which takes a **String** as its first argument. These versions of the methods perform identically to those described above except that they search for sets of characters (or substrings) that are specified by their **String** arguments.

8.8 Extracting Substrings from **Strings**

Class **String** provides two **substring** methods to enable a new **String** object to be created by copying part of an existing **String** object. Each method returns a **String** object. Both methods are demonstrated in Fig. 8.7.

The expression

```
letters.substring( 20 )
```

uses the **substring** method that takes one integer argument. The argument specifies the starting index from which characters are copied in the original **String**. The substring returned contains copies of the characters from the starting index to the end of the **String**. If the index specified as an argument is outside the bounds of the **String**, a **StringIndexOutOfBoundsException** is generated.

The expression

```
letters.substring( 0, 6 )
```

```
1    // Fig. 8.7: SubString.java
2    // This program demonstrates the String class substring methods.
3    import java.awt.Graphics;
4    import java.applet.Applet;
5
6    public class SubString extends Applet {
7       String letters = "abcdefghijklmabcdefghijklm";
8
9       public void paint( Graphics g )
10      {
11         // test substring methods
12         g.drawString( "Substring from index 20 to end is " +
13            "\"" + letters.substring( 20 ) + "\"", 25, 25 );
14
15         g.drawString( "Substring from index 0 upto 6 is " +
16            "\"" + letters.substring( 0, 6 ) + "\"", 25, 40 );
17      }
18   }
```

Fig. 8.7   The **String** class **substring** methods.

uses the **substring** method that takes two integer arguments. The first argument specifies the starting index from which characters are copied in the original **String**. The second argument specifies the index one beyond the last character to be copied. The substring
returned contains copies of the specified characters from the original **String**. If the arguments are outside the bounds of the **String**, a **StringIndexOutOfBoundsException** is generated.

8.9 Concatenating **Strings**

The **String** method **concat** (Fig. 8.8) concatenates two **String** objects and returns a
new **String** object containing the characters from both original **Strings**. If the argument **String** has no characters in it, the original **String** is returned. The expression

        s1.concat(s2)

adds the characters from the **String s2** to the end of the **String s1**. The original
Strings **s1** and **s2** are not modified.

```
1   // Fig. 8.8: StringConcat.java
2   // This program demonstrates the String class concat method.
3   // Note that the concat method returns a new String object. It
4   // does not modify the object that invoked the concat method.
5   import java.awt.Graphics;
6   import java.applet.Applet;
7
8   public class StringConcat extends Applet {
9       String s1 = new String( "Happy " ),
10             s2 = new String( "Birthday" );
11
12      public void paint( Graphics g )
13      {
14          g.drawString( "s1 = " + s1, 25, 25 );
15          g.drawString( "s2 = " + s2, 25, 40 );
16          g.drawString( "Result of s1.concat( s2 ) = " +
17                         s1.concat( s2 ), 25, 55 );
18          g.drawString( "s1 after concatenation = " + s1,
19                         25, 70 );
20      }
21  }
```

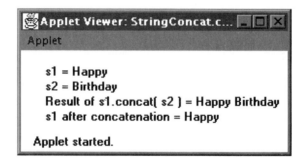

Fig. 8.8   The **String** method **concat**.

The expression

```
s1.replace( 'l', 'L' )
```

from line 21 uses **String** method **replace** to generate a new **String** object in which every occurrence in **String s1** of character **'l'** is replaced with character **'L'**. The method returns a new **String** object containing the converted **String**, or if there were no occurrences of the first argument in the **String**, the original **String** is returned. The **String** object is unchanged.

The expression

```
s1.toUpperCase()
```

from line 25 uses **String** method **toUpperCase** to generate a new **String** object with uppercase letters where corresponding lowercase letters reside in **s1**. The method returns a new **String** object containing the converted **String**, or if there are no characters that have uppercase versions in the **String**, the original **String** is returned. The original **String** is unchanged.

The expression

```
s1.toLowerCase()
```

from line 27 uses **String** method **toLowerCase** to generate a new **String** object with lowercase letters where corresponding uppercase letters reside in **s1**. The method returns a new **String** object containing the converted **String**, or if there are no characters that have lowercase versions in the **String**, the original **String** is returned. The original **String** is unchanged.

The expression

```
s3.trim()
```

from line 30 uses **String** method **trim** to generate a new **String** object that removes all whitespace characters (such as spaces, newlines and tabs) that appear at the beginning or end of the **String** to which the **trim** call is sent. The method returns a new **String** object containing the **String** without leading or trailing whitespace characters. The original **String** is unchanged.

The expression

```
s1.toString()
```

from line 34 returns the **String s1**. Why is the **toString** method provided for class **String**? All objects can be converted to **String**s in Java by using method **toString** which originates in the **Object** class. If a class that inherits from **Object** (such as **String**) does not override method **toString**, the default version from class **Object** is used. The default version creates a **String** consisting of the object's class name and the hash code for the object. The **toString** method is normally used to express the contents of an object as text. Method **toString** is provided in class **String** to ensure that the proper **String** value is returned.

The statement

```
char charArray[] = s1.toCharArray();
```

from line 37 creates a new character array containing a copy of the characters in **String** **s1** and assigns it to **charArray**.

8.10 Miscellaneous **String** Methods

Class **String** provides several methods that return modified copies of **String**s or that return a character array. These methods are demonstrated in the **paint** method of applet class **StringMisc2** in Fig. 8.9.

```
1   // Fig. 8.9: StringMisc2.java
2   // This program demonstrates the String class replace,
3   // toLowerCase, toUpperCase, trim, toString, and toCharArray
4   // methods.
5   import java.awt.Graphics;
6   import java.applet.Applet;
7
8   public class StringMisc2 extends Applet {
9      String s1 = new String( "hello" ),
10            s2 = new String( "GOOD BYE" ),
11            s3 = new String( "   spaces   " );
12
13     public void paint( Graphics g )
14     {
15        g.drawString( "s1 = " + s1, 25, 25 );
16        g.drawString( "s2 = " + s2, 25, 40 );
17        g.drawString( "s3 = " + s3, 25, 55 );
18
19        // test method replace
20        g.drawString( "Replace 'l' with 'L' in s1: " +
21                      s1.replace( 'l', 'L' ), 25, 85 );
22
23        // test toLowerCase and toUpperCase
24        g.drawString( "s1 after toUpperCase = " +
25                      s1.toUpperCase(), 25, 115 );
26        g.drawString( "s2 after toLowerCase = " +
27                      s2.toLowerCase(), 25, 130 );
28
29        // test trim method
30        g.drawString( "s3 after trim = \"" + s3.trim() + "\"",
31                      25, 160 );
32
33        // test toString method
34        g.drawString( "s1 = " + s1.toString(), 25, 190 );
35
36        // test toCharArray method
37        char charArray[] = s1.toCharArray();
38        g.drawString( "s1 as a character array = ", 25, 220 );
39        g.drawChars( charArray, 0, charArray.length, 172, 220 );
40     }
41  }
```

Fig. 8.9   Miscellaneous **String** methods (part 1 of 2).

8.11 Using **String** Method **valueOf**

Class **String** provides a set of **static** class methods that take arguments of various types, convert those arguments to strings and return them as **String** objects. Applet class **StringValueOf** (Fig. 8.10) demonstrates the **String** class **valueOf** methods. The expression

```
String.valueOf( charArray )
```

Fig. 8.9 Miscellaneous **String** methods (part 2 of 2).

```
1   // Fig. 8.10: StringValueOf.java
2   // This program demonstrates the String class valueOf methods.
3   import java.awt.Graphics;
4   import java.applet.Applet;
5
6   public class StringValueOf extends Applet {
7      char charArray[] = { 'a', 'b', 'c', 'd', 'e', 'f' };
8      boolean b = true;
9      char c = 'Z';
10     int i = 7;
11     long l = 10000000;
12     float f = 2.5f;
13     double d = 33.333;
14     Object o = "hello";   // Assign String to Object reference
15
16     public void paint( Graphics g )
17     {
18        g.drawString( "char array = " +
19                      String.valueOf( charArray ), 25, 25 );
20        g.drawString( "part of char array = " +
21                      String.valueOf( charArray, 3, 3 ),
22                      25, 40 );
23
24        g.drawString( "boolean = " + String.valueOf( b ),
25                      25, 70 );
```

Fig. 8.10 The **String** class **valueOf** methods (part 1 of 2).

```
26          g.drawString( "char = " + String.valueOf( c ),
27                         25, 85 );
28          g.drawString( "int = " + String.valueOf( i ),
29                         25, 100 );
30          g.drawString( "long = " + String.valueOf( l ),
31                         25, 115 );
32          g.drawString( "float = " + String.valueOf( f ),
33                         25, 130 );
34          g.drawString( "double = " + String.valueOf( d ),
35                         25, 145 );
36          g.drawString( "Object = " + String.valueOf( o ),
37                         25, 160 );
38      }
39  }
```

Fig. 8.10 The `String` class `valueOf` methods (part 2 of 2).

from line 19 copies the contents of the character array **charArray** into a new **String** object and returns the new **String**.

The expression

```
String.valueOf( charArray, 3, 3 )
```

from line 21 copies a portion of the contents of the character array **charArray** into a new **String** object and returns the new **String**. The second argument specifies the starting index from which the characters are copied. The third argument specifies the number of characters to copy.

There are seven other versions of method **valueOf** that take arguments of type **boolean**, **char**, **int**, **long**, **float**, **double** and **Object**, respectively. These are demonstrated in lines 24 through 37 of the program. Note that the version of **valueOf** that takes an **Object** as an argument can do so because all **Object**s can be converted to **String**s with the **toString** method.

8.12 String Method intern

Comparing large **String** objects is a relatively slow operation. **String** method **intern** can improve **String** comparison performance. The first time **String** method **intern** is invoked on a **String** object it returns a reference to that **String** object in memory. Subsequent invocations of **intern** on different **String** objects that have the same contents as the original **String** object result in multiple references to the original **String** object. This is useful for efficient **String** comparisons of large **String**s. Once **intern** has been performed, the **String** references can be compared with **==** (which simply compares two references—this is a fast operation) rather than using the **String** comparison methods such as **equals** and **equalsIgnoreCase** (which require comparisons of each of the pairs of corresponding characters in each **String**—a time-consuming iterative operation). The program of Fig. 8.11 demonstrates the **intern** method.

```
1   // Fig. 8.11: StringIntern.java
2   // This program demonstrates the intern method
3   // of the String class.
4   import java.awt.Graphics;
5   import java.applet.Applet;
6
7   public class StringIntern extends Applet {
8      String s1, s2, s3, s4;
9
10     public void init()
11     {
12        s1 = new String( "hello" );
13        s2 = new String( "hello" );
14     }
15
16     public void paint( Graphics g )
17     {
18        // Test strings to determine if they are the same
19        // String object in memory.
20        if ( s1 == s2 )
21           g.drawString( "s1 and s2 are the " +
22                         "same object in memory", 25, 25 );
23        else
24           g.drawString( "s1 and s2 are not the " +
25                         "same object in memory", 25, 25 );
26
27        // Test strings for equality of contents
28        if ( s1.equals( s2 ) )
29           g.drawString( "s1 and s2 are equal", 25, 45 );
30        else
31           g.drawString( "s1 and s2 are not equal", 55, 45 );
32
```

Fig. 8.11 The **String** class **intern** method (part 1 of 3).

```
33          // Use String intern method to get a unique copy of
34          // "hello" refered to by both s3 and s4.
35          s3 = s1.intern();
36          s4 = s2.intern();
37
38          // Test strings to determine if they are the same
39          // String object in memory.
40          if ( s3 == s4 )
41             g.drawString( "s3 and s4 are the " +
42                            "same object in memory", 25, 65 );
43          else
44             g.drawString( "s3 and s4 are not the " +
45                            "same object in memory", 25, 65 );
46
47          // Determine if s1 and s3 refer to the same object
48          if ( s1 == s3 )
49             g.drawString( "s1 and s3 are the " +
50                            "same object in memory", 25, 85 );
51          else
52             g.drawString( "s1 and s3 are not the " +
53                            "same object in memory", 25, 85 );
54
55          // Determine if s2 and s4 refer to the same object
56          if ( s2 == s4 )
57             g.drawString( "s2 and s4 are the " +
58                            "same object in memory", 25, 105 );
59          else
60             g.drawString( "s2 and s4 are not the " +
61                            "same object in memory", 25, 105 );
62
63          // Determine if s1 and s4 refer to the same object
64          if ( s1 == s4 )
65             g.drawString( "s1 and s4 are the " +
66                            "same object in memory", 25, 125 );
67          else
68             g.drawString( "s1 and s4 are not the " +
69                            "same object in memory", 25, 125 );
70       }
71    }
```

Fig. 8.11 The **String** class **intern** method (part 2 of 3).

Applet class **StringIntern** declares four **String**s—**s1**, **s2**, **s3** and **s4**. **String**s **s1** and **s2** are initialized with copies of **"hello"**. The first **if** structure uses operator **==** to determine that **String**s **s1** and **s2** are the same object in memory. The second **if** structure uses method **equals** to determine that the contents of **String**s **s1** and **s2** are equal. The statement

```
        s3 = s1.intern();
```

uses method **intern** to get a reference to the **String** object **s1** and assigns the reference to **s3**. The statement

Fig. 8.11 The **String** class **intern** method (part 3 of 3).

```
s4 = s2.intern();
```

also uses method **intern** to get a reference to a **String** object. However, because **String s1** and **String s2** have the same contents, the reference returned by this call to intern is a reference to **String s1** in memory.

The third **if** structure uses operator **==** to determine that **String**s **s3** and **s4** are the same object in memory. The fourth **if** structure uses operator **==** to determine that **String**s **s1** and **s3** are the same object in memory. The fifth **if** structure uses operator **==** to determine that **String**s **s2** and **s4** are *not* the same object in memory (this is because the second **intern** call results in a reference to **String s1** not **String s2**). The sixth **if** structure uses operator **==** to determine that **String**s **s1** and **s4** are, in fact, the same object in memory.

8.13 StringBuffer Class

The **String** class provides many capabilities for processing **String**s. However, once a **String** object is created, its contents never change. The next several sections discuss the features of class **StringBuffer** for creating and manipulating dynamic string information—i.e., modifiable **String**s. Every **StringBuffer** is capable of storing a number of characters as specified by its capacity. If the capacity of a **StringBuffer** is exceeded, the capacity is automatically expanded to accommodate the additional characters. As we will see, class **StringBuffer** is also used to implement operators **+** and **+=** for **String** concatenation.

Performance Tip 8.1

String objects are constant strings and StringBuffer objects are modifiable strings. Java distinguishes constant strings and modifiable strings for optimization purposes; in particular, Java can perform certain optimizations involving String objects (such as sharing one String object among multiple references) because it knows these objects will not change.

Performance Tip 8.2

*When given the choice between using a **String** object to represent a string versus a **StringBuffer** object to represent that string, always using a **String** object if indeed the object will not change; this improves performance.*

Common Programming Error 8.3

*Sending **StringBuffer** methods that are not methods of class **String** to **String** objects is a syntax error.*

8.14 StringBuffer Constructors

Class **StringBuffer** provides three constructors that are demonstrated in Fig. 8.12. The statement

        buf1 = new StringBuffer();

uses the default **StringBuffer** constructor to create a **StringBuffer** with no characters in it and an initial capacity of 16 characters.

The statement

        buf2 = new StringBuffer(10);

uses the **StringBuffer** constructor that takes an integer argument to create a **String-Buffer** with no characters in it and the initial capacity specified in the integer argument.

The statement

        buf3 = new StringBuffer("hello");

uses the **StringBuffer** constructor that takes a **String** argument to create a **StringBuffer** containing the characters of the **String** argument and with an initial capacity which is the number of characters in the **String** argument plus 16.

The output statements on lines 18 through 23 use the **StringBuffer toString** method to convert the three **StringBuffer**s into **String** objects that can be displayed with **drawString**. Note the use of operator **+** to concatenate **String**s for output. In Section 8.17 we discuss how the **StringBuffer** is used to implement the **+** operator and **+=** operator.

8.15 StringBuffer length, capacity, setLength and ensureCapacity Methods

Class **StringBuffer** provides the **length** and **capacity** methods to return the number of characters currently in a **StringBuffer** and the number of characters that can be stored in a **StringBuffer** without allocating more memory, respectively. Method **ensureCapacity** is provided to allow the programmer to guarantee that a **StringBuffer** has a minimum capacity. Method **setLength** is provided to enable the programmer to increase or decrease the length of a **StringBuffer**. The program of Fig. 8.13 demonstrates these methods.

```
1    // Fig. 8.12: StringBufferConstructors.java
2    // This program demonstrates the StringBuffer constructors.
3    import java.awt.Graphics;
4    import java.applet.Applet;
5
6    public class StringBufferConstructors extends Applet {
7       StringBuffer buf1, buf2, buf3;
8
9       public void init()
10      {
11         buf1 = new StringBuffer();
12         buf2 = new StringBuffer( 10 );
13         buf3 = new StringBuffer( "hello" );
14      }
15
16      public void paint( Graphics g )
17      {
18         g.drawString( "buf1 = " + "\"" + buf1.toString() + "\"",
19                       25, 25 );
20         g.drawString( "buf2 = " + "\"" + buf2.toString() + "\"",
21                       25, 40 );
22         g.drawString( "buf3 = " + "\"" + buf3.toString() + "\"",
23                       25, 55 );
24      }
25   }
```

Fig. 8.12 The **StringBuffer** class constructors.

Applet class **StringBufferCapLen** contains one instance variable—**String-Buffer** object **buf**. Line 12 of the program uses the **StringBuffer** constructor that takes a **String** argument to instantiate and initialize the **StringBuffer** with **"hello"**. Notice in the output window that the capacity of the **StringBuffer** is initially 21. Remember that the **StringBuffer** constructor that takes a **String** argument creates a **StringBuffer** object with an initial capacity that is the length of the **String** passed as an argument plus 16.

The statement

```
buf.ensureCapacity( 50 );
```

expands the capacity of the **StringBuffer** to a minimum of 50 characters. Actually, if the original capacity is less than the argument, the method ensures a capacity that is the

greater of the number specified as an argument or twice the original capacity plus 2. If the
StringBuffer's current capacity is more than the specified capacity, the **String-
Buffer**'s capacity remains unchanged.

```
1   // Fig. 8.13: StringBufferCapLen.java
2   // This program demonstrates the length and
3   // capacity methods of the StringBuffer class.
4   import java.awt.Graphics;
5   import java.applet.Applet;
6
7   public class StringBufferCapLen extends Applet {
8      StringBuffer buf;
9
10     public void init()
11     {
12        buf = new StringBuffer( "hello" );
13     }
14
15     public void paint ( Graphics g )
16     {
17        g.drawString( "buf = " + buf.toString(), 25, 25  );
18        g.drawString( "length = " + buf.length(), 25, 40 );
19        g.drawString( "capacity = " + buf.capacity(),
20                      25, 55 );
21
22        buf.ensureCapacity( 50 );
23        g.drawString( "New capacity = " + buf.capacity(),
24                      25, 85 );
25
26        buf.setLength( 10 );
27        g.drawString( "New length = " + buf.length(),
28                      25, 115 );
29     }
30  }
```

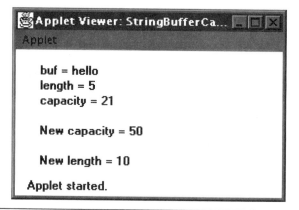

Fig. 8.13 The **StringBuffer** class **length** and **capacity** methods.

The statement

```
buf.setLength( 10 );
```

uses method **setLength** to set the length of the **StringBuffer** to 10. If the specified length is less than the current number of characters in the **StringBuffer**, the characters are truncated to the specified length—i.e., the characters in the **StringBuffer** after the specified length are discarded. If the specified length is greater than the number of characters currently in the **StringBuffer**, null characters (characters with the numeric representation 0) are appended to the **StringBuffer** until the total number of characters in the **StringBuffer** is equal to the specified length.

8.16 StringBuffer charAt, setCharAt and getChars Methods

Class **StringBuffer** provides the **charAt**, **setCharAt** and **getChars** methods to manipulate the characters in a **StringBuffer**. Method **charAt** takes an integer argument and returns the character in the **StringBuffer** at that index. Method **setCharAt** takes an integer and a character argument and sets the character at the specified position to the character argument. The index specified in the **charAt** and **setCharAt** methods must be greater than or equal to 0 and less than the **StringBuffer** length, otherwise a **StringIndexOutOfBoundsException** is generated.

Common Programming Error 8.4

*Attempting to access a character that is outside the bounds of a **StringBuffer** (i.e., an index less than 0 or an index greater than or equal to the **StringBuffer**'s length) results in a **StringIndexOutOfBoundsException***

Method **getChars** returns a character array containing a copy of the characters in the **StringBuffer**. This method takes four arguments—the starting index from which characters should be copied in the **StringBuffer**, the index one past the last character to be copied from the **StringBuffer**, the character array into which the characters are to be copied and the starting location in the character array where the first character should be placed. Each of these methods is demonstrated in Fig. 8.14

```
1   // Fig. 8.14: StringBufferChars.java
2   // The charAt, setCharAt, and getChars methods
3   // of class StringBuffer.
4   import java.awt.Graphics;
5   import java.applet.Applet;
6
7   public class StringBufferChars extends Applet {
8       StringBuffer buf;
9       char charArray[];
10
```

Fig. 8.14 StringBuffer class character manipulation methods (part 1 of 2).

```
11      public void init()
12      {
13          buf = new StringBuffer( "hello there" );
14          charArray = new char[ 100 ];
15      }
16
17      public void paint ( Graphics g )
18      {
19          g.drawString( "buf = " + buf.toString(), 25, 25 );
20          g.drawString( "Character at 0: " + buf.charAt( 0 ),
21                      25, 40 );
22          g.drawString( "Character at 4: " + buf.charAt( 4 ),
23                      25, 55 );
24
25          buf.getChars( 0, buf.length(), charArray, 0 );
26          g.drawString( "The characters are: ", 25, 85 );
27          g.drawChars( charArray, 0, charArray.length, 120, 85 );
28
29          buf.setCharAt( 0, 'H' );
30          buf.setCharAt( 6, 'T' );
31          g.drawString( "buf = " + buf.toString(), 25, 115 );
32      }
33  }
```

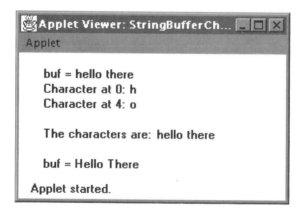

Fig. 8.14 `StringBuffer` class character manipulation methods (part 2 of 2).

8.17 StringBuffer append Methods

Class **StringBuffer** provides 10 overloaded **append** methods to allow various data type values to be added to the end of a **StringBuffer**. Versions are provided for each of the primitive data types and for character arrays, **String**s and **Object**s (remember that method **toString** produces a **String** representation of any **Object**). Each of the methods takes its argument, converts it to a **String** and appends it to the **String-Buffer**. The **append** methods are demonstrated in Fig. 8.15.

Actually, **StringBuffer**s and the **append** methods are used by the compiler to implement the **+** and **+=** operators for concatenating **String**s. For example, the statement

```
1   // Fig. 8.15: StringBufferAppend.java
2   // This program demonstrates the append
3   // methods of the StringBuffer class.
4   import java.awt.Graphics;
5   import java.applet.Applet;
6
7   public class StringBufferAppend extends Applet {
8      Object o = "hello";   // Assign String to Object reference
9      String s = "good bye";
10     char charArray[] = { 'a', 'b', 'c', 'd', 'e', 'f' };
11     boolean b = true;
12     char c = 'Z';
13     int i = 7;
14     long l = 10000000;
15     float f = 2.5f;
16     double d = 33.333;
17     StringBuffer buf;
18
19     public void init()
20     {
21        buf = new StringBuffer();
22     }
23
24     public void start()
25     {
26        buf.append( o );
27        buf.append( ' ' );
28        buf.append( s );
29        buf.append( ' ' );
30        buf.append( charArray );
31        buf.append( ' ' );
32        buf.append( charArray, 0, 3 );
33        buf.append( ' ' );
34        buf.append( b );
35        buf.append( ' ' );
36        buf.append( c );
37        buf.append( ' ' );
38        buf.append( i );
39        buf.append( ' ' );
40        buf.append( l );
41        buf.append( ' ' );
42        buf.append( f );
43        buf.append( ' ' );
44        buf.append( d );
45     }
```

Fig. 8.15 The **StringBuffer** class **append** methods (part 1 of 2).

```
46
47      public void paint( Graphics g )
48      {
49          g.drawString( "buf = " + buf.toString(), 25, 25 );
50      }
51  }
```

Fig. 8.15 The `StringBuffer` class **append** methods (part 2 of 2).

```
String s = "BC" + 22;
```

concatenates **String "BC"** and integer **22**. The concatenation is performed as follows:

```
new StringBuffer().append( "bc" ).append( 22 ).toString();
```

First, an empty **StringBuffer** is created, then the **String "bc"** is appended to the empty **StringBuffer**. Next integer **22** is appended to the end of the **StringBuffer**. Finally, the **StringBuffer** is converted to a **String** with method **toString** and the result is assigned to **String s**. The statement

```
s += "!";
```

is actually performed as follows:

```
s = new StringBuffer().append( s ).append( "!" ).toString()
```

First, an empty **StringBuffer** is created, then the **String s** is appended to the empty **StringBuffer**. Next the **String "!"** is appended to the end of the **StringBuffer**. Finally, the **StringBuffer** is converted to a **String** with method **toString** and the result is assigned to **String s**.

8.18 StringBuffer insert Methods

Class **StringBuffer** provides nine overloaded **insert** methods to allow various data type values to be inserted at any position in a **StringBuffer**. Versions are provided for each of the primitive data types and for character arrays, **String**s and **Object**s (remember that method **toString** produces a **String** representation of any **Object**). Each of the methods takes its second argument, converts it to a **String** and inserts it at the index specified by the first argument. The index specified by the second argument must be greater than or equal to **0** and less than or equal to the length of the **StringBuffer**, otherwise a **StringIndexOutOfBoundsException** is generated. The **insert** methods are demonstrated in Fig. 8.16.

```
1    // Fig. 8.16: StringBufferInsert.java
2    // This program demonstrates the insert
3    // methods of the StringBuffer class.
4    import java.awt.Graphics;
5    import java.applet.Applet;
6
7    public class StringBufferInsert extends Applet {
8       Object o = "hello";   // Assign String to Object reference
9       String s = "good bye";
10      char charArray[] = { 'a', 'b', 'c', 'd', 'e', 'f' };
11      boolean b = true;
12      char c = 'Z';
13      int i = 7;
14      long l = 10000000;
15      float f = 2.5f;
16      double d = 33.333;
17      StringBuffer buf;
18
19      public void init()
20      {
21         buf = new StringBuffer();
22      }
23
24      public void start()
25      {
26         buf.insert( 0, o );
27         buf.insert( 0, ' ' );
28         buf.insert( 0, s );
29         buf.insert( 0, ' ' );
30         buf.insert( 0, charArray );
31         buf.insert( 0, ' ' );
32         buf.insert( 0, b );
33         buf.insert( 0, ' ' );
34         buf.insert( 0, c );
35         buf.insert( 0, ' ' );
36         buf.insert( 0, i );
37         buf.insert( 0, ' ' );
38         buf.insert( 0, l );
39         buf.insert( 0, ' ' );
40         buf.insert( 0, f );
41         buf.insert( 0, ' ' );
42         buf.insert( 0, d );
43      }
44
45      public void paint( Graphics g )
46      {
47         g.drawString( "buf = " + buf.toString(), 25, 25 );
48      }
49   }
```

Fig. 8.16 The **StringBuffer** class **insert** methods (part 1 of 2).

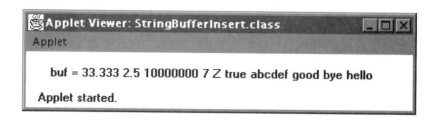

Fig. 8.16 The **StringBuffer** class **insert** methods (part 2 of 2).

8.19 Character Class Examples

Java provides a number of classes that enable the primitive data types to be treated as objects. The classes are **Boolean, Character, Double, Float, Integer** and **Long**. These classes—all derived from **Object**—are known as *type wrappers* and they are part of the **java.lang** package. Objects of these classes can be used anywhere in a program that an **Object** is expected. In this section, we present class **Character**—the type wrapper class for characters.

Most **Character** class method are **static** methods that take at least a character argument and perform either a test or a manipulation of the character. The class also contains a constructor that receives a **char** argument to initialize a **Character** object and several non-**static** methods. Most of the methods of class **Character** are presented in the next three examples. For more information on class **Character** (and all the wrappers classes), see the **java.lang** package in the Java API documentation.

The program of Fig. 8.17 demonstrates the **static** methods that test characters to determine if they are a specific character type and the **static** methods that perform case conversions on characters. Each of the methods is used in the **paint** method of applet class **StaticCharMethods**. The program allows you to enter any character and apply the preceding methods to the character. Several sample outputs are shown.

The expression

```
Character.isDefined( c )
```

uses method **Character.isDefined** to determine if character **c** is defined in the Unicode character set. If so, the method returns **true**; otherwise, it returns **false**.

The expression

```
Character.isDigit( c )
```

uses method **Character.isDigit** to determine if character **c** is a defined Unicode digit. If so, the method returns **true**; otherwise, it returns **false**.

The expression

```
Character.isJavaLetter( c )
```

uses method **Character.isJavaLetter** to determine if character **c** is a character that can be used as the first character of an identifier in Java—i.e., a letter, an underscore (_) or a dollar sign ($). If so, the method returns **true**; otherwise, it returns **false**.

```
1    // Fig. 8.17: StaticCharMethods.java
2    // Demonstrates the static character testing methods
3    // and case conversion methods of class Character
4    // from the java.lang package.
5    import java.awt.*;
6    import java.applet.Applet;
7
8    public class StaticCharMethods extends Applet {
9       char c;
10      Label prompt;
11      TextField input;
12
13      public void init()
14      {
15         c = 'A';
16
17         prompt = new Label( "Enter a character and press Enter" );
18         input = new TextField( "A", 5 );
19         add( prompt );
20         add( input );
21      }
22
23      public void paint( Graphics g )
24      {
25         g.drawString( "is defined: " +
26            Character.isDefined( c ), 25, 40 );
27         g.drawString( "is digit: " +
28            Character.isDigit( c ), 25, 55 );
29         g.drawString( "is Java letter: " +
30            Character.isJavaLetter( c ), 25, 70 );
31         g.drawString( "is Java letter or digit: " +
32            Character.isJavaLetterOrDigit( c ), 25, 85 );
33         g.drawString( "is letter: " +
34            Character.isLetter( c ), 25, 100 );
35         g.drawString( "is letter or digit: " +
36            Character.isLetterOrDigit( c ), 25, 115 );
37         g.drawString( "is lower case: " +
38            Character.isLowerCase( c ), 25, 130 );
39         g.drawString( "is upper case: " +
40            Character.isUpperCase( c ), 25, 145 );
41         g.drawString( "to upper case: " +
42            Character.toUpperCase( c ), 25, 160 );
43         g.drawString( "to lower case: " +
44            Character.toLowerCase( c ), 25, 175 );
45      }
```

Fig. 8.17 **static** character testing methods and case conversion methods of class **Character** (part 1 of 3).

The expression

```
Character.isJavaLetterOrDigit( c )
```

```
46
47    public boolean action( Event e, Object o )
48    {
49        String s = o.toString();
50        c = s.charAt( 0 );
51        repaint();
52        return true;
53    }
54 }
```

Fig. 8.17 **static** character testing methods and case conversion methods of class **Character** (part 2 of 3).

Fig. 8.17 `static` character testing methods and case conversion methods of class `Character` (part 3 of 3).

uses method **Character.isJavaLetter** to determine if character **c** is a character that can be used in an identifier in Java—i.e., a digit, a letter, an underscore (_) or a dollar sign (**$**). If so, the method returns **true**; otherwise, it returns **false**.

The expression

```
Character.isLetter( c )
```

uses method **Character.isLetter** to determine if character **c** is a letter. If so, the method returns **true**; otherwise, it returns **false**.

The expression

```
Character.isLetterOrDigit( c )
```

uses method **Character.isLetterOrDigit** to determine if character **c** is a letter or a digit. If so, the method returns **true**; otherwise, it returns **false**.

The expression

```
Character.isLowerCase( c )
```

uses method **Character.isLowerCase** to determine if character **c** is a lowercase letter. If so, the method returns **true**; otherwise, it returns **false**.

The expression

```
Character.isUpperCase( c )
```

uses method **Character.isUpperCase** to determine if character **c** is an uppercase letter. If so, the method returns **true**; otherwise, it returns **false**.

The expression

```
Character.toUpperCase( c )
```

uses method **Character.toUpperCase** to convert the character **c** to its uppercase equivalent. The method returns the converted character if the character has an uppercase equivalent; otherwise, the method returns its original argument.

The expression

```
Character.toLowerCase( c )
```

uses method **Character.toLowerCase** to convert the character **c** to its lowercase equivalent. The method returns the converted character if the character has a lowercase equivalent; otherwise, the method returns its original argument.

Figure 8.18 demonstrates the **static Character** methods **digit** and **forDigit** to perform conversions between characters and digits in different number systems. Common number systems include decimal (base 10), octal (base 8), hexadecimal (base 16) and binary (base 2). The base of a number is also known as its *radix*. For more information on conversions between number systems, see the appendix "Number Systems."

```
1  // Fig. 8.18: StaticCharMethods2.java
2  // Demonstrates the static character conversion methods
3  // of class Character from the java.lang package.
4  import java.awt.*;
5  import java.applet.Applet;
6
7  public class StaticCharMethods2 extends Applet {
8     char c;
9     int digit, radix;
10    boolean charToDigit;
11    Label prompt1, prompt2;
12    TextField input, radixField;
13    Button toChar, toInt;
14
15    public void init()
16    {
17       c = 'A';
18       radix = 16;
19       charToDigit = true;
20
21       prompt1 = new Label( "Enter a digit or character " );
22       input = new TextField( "A", 5 );
23       prompt2 = new Label( "Enter a radix " );
24       radixField = new TextField( "16", 5 );
25       toChar = new Button( "Convert digit to character" );
26       toInt = new Button( "Convert character to digit" );
27       add( prompt1 );
28       add( input );
```

Fig. 8.18 Character class **static** conversion methods (part 1 of 3).

```
29            add( prompt2 );
30            add( radixField );
31            add( toChar );
32            add( toInt );
33        }
34
35        public void paint( Graphics g )
36        {
37            if ( charToDigit )
38                g.drawString( "Convert character to digit: " +
39                    Character.digit( c, radix ), 25, 125 );
40            else
41                g.drawString( "Convert digit to character: " +
42                    Character.forDigit( digit, radix ), 25, 125 );
43        }
44
45        public boolean action( Event e, Object o )
46        {
47            if ( e.target == toChar ) {
48                charToDigit = false;
49                digit = Integer.parseInt( input.getText() );
50                radix = Integer.parseInt( radixField.getText() );
51                repaint();
52            }
53            else if ( e.target == toInt ) {
54                charToDigit = true;
55                String s = input.getText();
56                c = s.charAt( 0 );
57                radix = Integer.parseInt( radixField.getText() );
58                repaint();
59            }
60
61            return true;
62        }
63    }
```

Fig. 8.18 Character class **static** conversion methods (part 2 of 3).

Fig. 8.18 Character class **static** conversion methods (part 3 of 3).

The expression

```
Character.digit( c, radix )
```

uses method **digit** to convert the character **c** into an integer in the number system specified by the integer **radix** (i.e., the base of the number). For example, the character **'A'** in base 16 (the **radix**) has the integer value 10.

The expression

```
Character.forDigit( digit, radix )
```

uses method **forDigit** to convert the integer **digit** into a character in the number system specified by the integer **radix** (also known as the base of the number). For example, the integer **13** in base 16 (the **radix**) has the character value **'d'**. Note that the lowercase and uppercase letters are equivalent in number systems.

The program of Fig. 8.19 demonstrates the non-**static** methods of class **Character**—the constructor, **charValue**, **toString**, **hashCode** and **equals**.

The statements

```
c1 = new Character( 'A' );
c2 = new Character( 'a' );
```

from the **init** method of class **OtherCharMethods** instantiate two **Character** objects and pass constants of type **char** to the constructor to initialize the **Character** objects.

The expression

```
c1.charValue()
```

uses **Character** method **charValue** (which returns a **char**) to get the value of primitive data type **char** from the **Character** object **c1**.

```
1   // Fig. 8.19: OtherCharMethods.java
2   // Demonstrate the non-static methods of class
3   // Character from the java.lang package.
4   import java.awt.Graphics;
5   import java.applet.Applet;
6
7   public class OtherCharMethods extends Applet {
8      Character c1, c2;
9
10     public void init()
11     {
12        c1 = new Character( 'A' );
13        c2 = new Character( 'a' );
14     }
15
16     public void paint( Graphics g )
17     {
18        g.drawString( "c1 = " + c1.charValue(), 25, 25 );
19        g.drawString( "c2 = " + c2.toString(), 25, 40 );
20        g.drawString( "hash code for c1 = " +
21                      c1.hashCode(), 25, 70 );
22        g.drawString( "hash code for c2 = " +
23                      c2.hashCode(), 25, 85 );
24
25        if (  c1.equals( c2 ) )
26           g.drawString( "c1 and c2 are equal", 25, 115 );
27        else
28           g.drawString( "c1 and c2 are not equal", 25, 115 );
29     }
30  }
```

Fig. 8.19 Non-**static** methods of class **Character**.

The expression

```
c2.toString()
```

returns a **String** representation of the **Character** object **c2** using **Character** method **toString**.

The expressions

```
c1.hashCode()
c2.hashCode()
```

perform **hashCode** calculations on the **Character** objects **c1** and **c2** respectively. Remember that hash code values are used to store objects in hash tables for fast lookup capabilities (see Chapter 18).

The condition

```
c1.equals( c2 )
```

from the **if** structure at line 25 uses the **equals** method to determine if the object **c1** has the same contents as the object **c2** (i.e., the characters inside each object are equal).

8.20 Class **StringTokenizer**

When you read a sentence, your mind breaks the sentence into individual words, or *tokens,* each of which conveys meaning to you. Compilers also perform tokenization. They break up statements into individual pieces like keywords, identifiers, operators and other elements of a programming language. In this section we study Java's **StringTokenizer** class (from package **java.util**) that breaks a string into its component tokens.

Tokens are separated from one another by delimiters, typically *whitespace characters* such as blank, tab, newline and carriage return. Other characters may also be used as delimiters to separate tokens.

The program of Fig. 8.20 demonstrates class **StringTokenizer**. Applet class **TokenTest** displays a **TextField** where the user types a sentence to tokenize. Output in this program is sent to a **TextArea**. Text areas are similar to text fields—they can be used to display or enter text. The text area in this program is instantiated with the statement

```
output = new TextArea( 10, 30 );
```

which specifies that the text area has **10** rows and **30** columns. We discuss text areas in detail in Chapter 11, "Advanced Graphical User Interface Components."

When return is pressed in the text field, the **action** method is invoked. The statement

```
String stringToTokenize = o.toString();
```

creates **String** reference **stringToTokenize** and assigns it **o.toString()**—the text in the text field. Next, a **StringTokenizer** object is created in the statement

```
StringTokenizer tokens =
    new StringTokenizer( stringToTokenize );
```

This statement uses the **StringTokenizer** constructor that takes a **String** argument to create a **StringTokenizer** for **stringToTokenize** that will use the default delimiter string **" \n\t\r"** consisting of a space, a newline, a tab and a carriage return for tokenization. There are two other constructors for **StringTokenizer**. In the version that takes two **String** arguments, the second **String** is the delimiter **String**. In the version that takes three arguments, the second **String** is the delimiter **String** and the third argument (a **boolean**) determines if the delimiters are also returned as tokens (only if the argument is **true**). This is useful if you need to know what the delimiters are

.

```
1   // Fig. 8.20: TokenTest.java
2   // Testing the StringTokenizer class of the java.util package
3   import java.util.*;
4   import java.awt.*;
5   import java.applet.Applet;
6
7   public class TokenTest extends Applet {
8       // GUI components
9       Label prompt;
10      TextField input;
11      TextArea output;
12
13      public void init()
14      {
15          prompt = new Label( "Enter a sentence and press Enter" );
16          input = new TextField( 50 );
17          output = new TextArea( 10, 30 );
18          output.setEditable( false );
19          add( prompt );
20          add( input );
21          add( output );
22      }
23
24      public boolean action( Event e, Object o )
25      {
26          String stringToTokenize = o.toString();
27          StringTokenizer tokens =
28              new StringTokenizer( stringToTokenize );
29
30          output.setText( "" );
31
32          output.appendText( "Number of elements: " +
33              tokens.countTokens() + "\nThe tokens are:\n" );
34
35          while ( tokens.hasMoreTokens() )
36              output.appendText( tokens.nextToken() + "\n" );
37
38          return true;
39      }
40  }
```

Fig. 8.20 Tokenizing strings with a **StringTokenizer** object (part 1 of 2).

Fig. 8.20 Tokenizing strings with a **StringTokenizer** object (part 2 of 2).

The statement

```
output.setText( "" );
```

sets the text in the text area to the null **String** **""** to clear the text area.

The statement

```
output.appendText( "Number of elements: " +
    tokens.countTokens() + "\nThe tokens are:\n" );
```

uses the **TextArea** method **appendText** to append the concatenated **String** specified as its argument to text already in the text area. In the preceding statement, the expression

```
tokens.countTokens()
```

uses the **StringTokenizer** method **countTokens** to determine the number of tokens in the **String** to be tokenized.

The **while** structure at line 35

```
while ( tokens.hasMoreTokens() )
    output.appendText( tokens.nextToken() + "\n" );
```

uses condition **tokens.hasMoreTokens()** to determine if there are more tokens in the **String** being tokenized. If so, the **appendText** method is invoked for the text area **output** to append the next token to the **String** in the text area. The next token is determined with a call to **tokens.nextToken()** which returns a **String**. The token is output followed by a newline character so subsequent tokens output appear on separate lines.

If you would like to change the delimiter **String** while tokenizing a **String**, you may do so by specifying a new delimiter string in a **nextToken** call as follows:

```
tokens.nextToken( newDelimiterString );
```

This feature is not demonstrated in the program.

8.21 A Card Shuffling and Dealing Simulation

In this section, we use random number generation to develop a card shuffling and dealing simulation program. This program can then be used to implement programs that play specific card games.

We develop applet **DeckOfCards** (Fig. 8.21) that creates a deck of 52 playing cards using **Card** objects, then enables the user to deal each card by clicking on a "**Deal card**" button. Each card dealt is displayed in a text field. The user can also shuffle the deck at any time by clicking on a "**Shuffle cards**" button.

```
1   // Fig. 8.21: DeckOfCards.java
2   // Card shuffling and dealing program
3   import java.awt.*;
4   import java.applet.Applet;
5
6   public class DeckOfCards extends Applet {
7      private Card deck[];
8      private int currentCard;
9
10     // GUI components
11     private Button dealButton, shuffleButton;
12     private TextField displayCard;
13
14     public void init()
15     {
16        String faces[] = { "Ace", "Deuce", "Three", "Four",
17                           "Five", "Six", "Seven", "Eight",
18                           "Nine", "Ten", "Jack", "Queen",
19                           "King" };
20        String suits[] = { "Hearts", "Diamonds",
21                           "Clubs", "Spades" };
22
23        deck = new Card[ 52 ];
24        currentCard = -1;
25
26        for ( int i = 0; i < deck.length; i++ )
27           deck[ i ] = new Card( faces[ i % 13 ],
28                                 suits[ i / 13 ] );
29
30        dealButton = new Button( "Deal card" );
31        shuffleButton = new Button( "Shuffle cards" );
```

Fig. 8.21 Card dealing program (part 1 of 3).

```
32          displayCard = new TextField( 20 );
33          displayCard.setEditable( false );
34          add( dealButton );
35          add( shuffleButton);
36          add( displayCard );
37      }
38
39      public boolean action( Event event, Object obj )
40      {
41          if ( event.target == dealButton ) {
42              Card dealt = dealCard();
43
44              if ( dealt != null ) {
45                  displayCard.setText( dealt.toString() );
46                  showStatus( "Card #: " + currentCard );
47              }
48              else {
49                  displayCard.setText( "NO MORE CARDS TO DEAL" );
50                  showStatus( "Shuffle cards to continue" );
51              }
52          }
53          else if ( event.target == shuffleButton ) {
54              displayCard.setText( "SHUFFLING ..." );
55              showStatus( "" );
56              shuffle();
57              displayCard.setText( "DECK IS SHUFFLED" );
58          }
59
60          return true;
61      }
62
63      public void shuffle()
64      {
65          currentCard = -1;
66
67          for ( int i = 0; i < deck.length; i++ ) {
68              int j = (int) ( Math.random() * 52 );
69              Card temp = deck[ i ];
70              deck[ i ] = deck[ j ];
71              deck[ j ] = temp;
72          }
73
74          dealButton.enable();
75      }
76
77      public Card dealCard()
78      {
79          if ( ++currentCard < deck.length )
80              return deck[ currentCard ];
81          else {
82              dealButton.disable();
```

Fig. 8.21 Card dealing program (part 2 of 3).

```
83              return null;
84          }
85      }
86  }
87
88  class Card {
89      private String face;
90      private String suit;
91
92      public Card( String f, String s )
93      {
94          face = f;
95          suit = s;
96      }
97
98      public String toString() { return face + " of " + suit; }
99  }
```

Fig. 8.21   Card dealing program (part 3 of 3).

Class **Card** contains two **String** instance variables—**face** and **suit**—that are used to store references to the face name and suit name for a specific **Card**. The constructor for the class receives two **String**s that it uses to initialize **face** and **suit**. Method **tostring** is provided to create a **String** consisting of the **face** of the card, the **String " of "** and the **suit** of the card.

Class **DeckOfCards** consists of an array **deck** of 52 **Card**s, an integer **current-Card** representing the most recently dealt card in the deck array (-1 if no cards have been dealt yet) and the GUI components used to manipulate the deck of cards. The **init** method of the applet instantiates the **deck** array (line 23) and uses the following for structure

```
for ( int i = 0; i < deck.length; i++ )
    deck[ i ] = new Card( faces[ i % 13 ], suits[ i / 13 ] );
```

to fill the **deck** array with **Card**s. Note that each **Card** is instantiated and initialized with two **String**s—one from the **faces** array (**String**s **"Ace"** through **"King"**) and one from the **suits** array (**"Hearts"**, **"Diamonds"**, **"Clubs"** and **"Spades"**). The calculation **i % 13** always results in a value from 0 to 12 (the thirteen subscripts of the **faces** array) and the calculation **i / 13** always results in a value from 0 to 3 (the four subscripts in the **suits** array). When the **deck** array is initialized, it contains the cards with faces Ace through King in order for each suit.

When the user clicks the "**Deal card**" button, **action** invokes method **dealCard** (line 42) to get the next card in the array. If the **deck** is not empty, a **Card** object is returned; otherwise, **null** is returned. If the reference is not **null**, the statements

```
displayCard.setText( dealt.toString() );
showStatus( "Card #: " + currentCard );
```

are executed to display the **Card** in the text field **displayCard** and to display the card number in the status bar of the applet.

If the reference returned by **dealCard** was **null**, the **String** "NO MORE CARDS TO DEAL" is displayed in the text field and the **String** "Shuffle cards to continue" is displayed in the applet's status bar.

When the user clicks the "**Shuffle cards**" button, the **action** method invokes method **shuffle()** (defined on line 63) to shuffle the cards. The method loops through all 52 cards (array subscripts 0 to 51). For each card, a number between 0 and 51 is picked randomly. Next, the current **Card** object and the randomly selected **Card** object are swapped in the array. A total of only 52 swaps are made in a single pass of the entire array, and the array of **Card** objects is shuffled! When the shuffling is complete, the **String** "DECK IS SHUFFLED" is displayed in the text field.

Summary

- A character constant's value is its integer value in the Unicode character set. Strings may include letters, digits and special characters such as +, -, *, /, and $. A string in Java is an object of class **String**. String literals or string constants are often referred to as anonymous **String** objects and are written in double quotes in a program.

- Class **String** provides seven constructors that initialize a **String** as an empty **String**, as a copy of an existing **String**, as a copy of the characters (or a portion of the characters) from a character array, as a copy of the bytes (or a portion of the bytes in a byte array) or as a copy of the characters in a **StringBuffer**.

- **String** method **length** returns the number of characters in a **String**.

- **String** method **charAt** selects the character at a specific position. Method **get-Bytes** copies the characters of a **String** into a **byte** array.

- Method **equals** (which is inherited by class **String** from its superclass **Object**) is used to test any two objects for equality (i.e., the contents of the two objects are identical). The method returns **true** if the objects are equal and **false** otherwise. Method **equals** uses a lexicographical comparison.

- Operator **==** has different functionality when used to compare references and when used to compare values of primitive data types. When primitive data type values are compared with **==**, the result is **true** if both values are identical. When references are compared with **==**, the result is **true** if both references refer to the same object in memory.

- Java treats all anonymous **String**s with the same contents as one anonymous **String** object that has many references.

- **String** method **equalsIgnoreCase** ignores the case of the letters in each **String** when performing a comparison.

- **String** method **compareTo** returns 0 if the **String**s it is comparing are equal, a negative number if the **String** that invokes **compareTo** is less than the **String** that is passed as an argument, and a positive number if the **String** that invokes **compareTo** is greater than the **String** that is passed as an argument. Method **compareTo** uses a lexicographical comparison.

- **String** method **regionMatches** compares portions of two **String**s for equality.

- **String** method **startsWith** determines if the **String** for which it is called starts with the characters specified as an argument.

- **String** method **endsWith** determines if the **String** for which it is called starts with the characters specified as an argument.

- Method **hashCode** performs a hash code calculation that enables a **String** object to be stored in a hash table. This method is inherited into all subclasses of **Object** and overridden by **String**.

- **String** method **indexOf** locates the first occurrence of a character in a **String**. There is a version of this method that searches for substrings in a **String**. Method **lastIndexOf** locates the last occurrence of a character in a **String**. There is a version of this method that searches for substrings in a **String**.

- **String** method **substring** creates a new **String** by copying part of an existing **String** object.

- **String** method **concat** concatenates two **String** objects and returns a new **String** object containing the characters from both original **String**s.

- **String** method **replace** returns a new **String** object that replaces every occurrence in a **String** of its first character argument with its second character argument. The original **String** is unchanged.

- **String** method **toUpperCase** returns a new **String** object with uppercase letters in the positions where the original **String** had lowercase letters. Method **toLowerCase** returns a new **String** object with lowercase letters in the positions where the original **String** had uppercase letters. The original **String**s are unchanged.

- **String** method **trim** returns a new **String** object in which all whitespace characters (such as spaces, newlines and tabs) have been removed from the beginning or end of a **String**. The original **String** is unchanged.

- **String** method **toCharArray** creates a new character array containing a copy of the characters in a **String** and returns the new array.

- **String** class method **valueOf** is overloaded to take arguments of various types (**boolean**, **char**, **char** arrays, **int**, **long**, **float**, **double** and **Object**), convert those arguments to strings and return them as **String** objects.

- The first time **String** method **intern** is invoked on a **String** object it returns a reference to that **String** object in memory. Subsequent invocations of **intern** on different **String** objects that have the same contents as the original **String** object result in multiple references to the original **String** object.

- Class **StringBuffer** provides three constructors that enable **StringBuffer**s to be initialized with no characters and an initial capacity of 16 characters; with no characters and an initial capacity specified in the integer argument; or with a copy of the characters of the **String** argument and an initial capacity which is the number of characters in the **String** argument plus 16.

- **StringBuffer** method **length** returns the number of characters currently stored in a **StringBuffer**. Method **capacity** returns the number of characters that can be stored in a **StringBuffer** without allocating more memory.

- Method **ensureCapacity** ensures that a **StringBuffer** has a minimum capacity. Method **setLength** increases or decreases the length of a **StringBuffer**.

- **StringBuffer** method **charAt** returns the character at the specified index. Method **setCharAt** sets the character at the specified position. Method **getChars** returns a character array containing a copy of the characters in the **StringBuffer**.

- Class **StringBuffer** provides 10 overloaded **append** methods to allow various data type values to be added to the end of a **StringBuffer**. Versions are provided for each of the primitive data types and for character arrays, **String**s and **Object**s.

- **StringBuffer**s and the **append** methods are used by the Java compiler to implement the **+** and **+=** operators for concatenating **String**s.

- Class **StringBuffer** provides overloaded **insert** methods to allow various data type values to be inserted at any position in a **StringBuffer**. Versions are provided for each of the primitive data types and for character arrays, **String**s and **Object**s.

- Class **Character** provides a constructor that takes a character argument.
- **Character** method **isDefined** determines if a character is defined in the Unicode character set. If so, the method returns **true**; otherwise, it returns **false**.
- **Character** method **isDigit** determines if a character is a defined Unicode digit. If so, the method returns **true**; otherwise, it returns **false**.
- **Character** method **isJavaLetter** determines if a character is a character that can be used as the first character of an identifier in Java—i.e., a letter, an underscore (_) or a dollar sign (**$**). If so, the method returns **true**; otherwise, it returns **false**.
- **Character** method **isJavaLetterOrDigit** determines if a character is a character that can be used in an identifier in Java—i.e., a digit, a letter, an underscore (_) or a dollar sign (**$**). If so, the method returns **true**; otherwise, it returns **false**.Method **isLetter** determine if character **c** is a letter. If so, the method returns **true**; otherwise, it returns **false**. Method **isLetterOrDigit** determines if a character is a letter or a digit. If so, the method returns **true**; otherwise, it returns **false**.
- **Character** method **isLowerCase** determines if a character is a lowercase letter. If so, the method returns **true**; otherwise, it returns **false**.
- **Character** method **isUpperCase** determines if character is an uppercase letter. If so, the method returns **true**; otherwise, it returns **false**.
- **Character** method **toUpperCase** converts a character to its uppercase equivalent. Method **toLowerCase** converts a character to its lowercase equivalent.
- **Character** method **digit** converts its character argument into an integer in the number system specified by its integer argument **radix** (i.e., the base of the number). Method **forDigit** converts its integer argument **digit** into a character in the number system specified by its integer argument **radix**.
- **Character** method **charValue** returns the **char** stored in a **Character** object. Method **toString** returns a **String** representation of a **Character**.
- **Character** method **hashCode** performs a hash code calculation on a **Character**.
- **StringTokenizer**'s default constructor creates a **StringTokenizer** for its **String** argument and that will use the default delimiter string **" \n\t\r"** consisting of a space, a newline, a tab and a carriage return for tokenization.
- In the **StringTokenizer** constructor that takes two **String** arguments, the second **String** is the delimiter **String**. In the **StringTokenizer** constructor that takes three arguments, the second **String** is the delimiter **String** and the third argument (a **boolean**) determines if the delimiters are also returned as tokens.
- **StringTokenizer** method **countTokens** returns the number of tokens in the **String** to be tokenized.
- **StringTokenizer** method **hasMoreTokens()** determines if there are more tokens in the **String** being tokenized.
- **StringTokenizer** method **nextToken()** returns a **String** with the next token.

Terminology

append method of class **StringBuffer**	**isLowerCase** method of class **Character**
appending strings to other strings	**isUpperCase** method of class **Character**
array of strings	**lastIndexOf** method of class **String**
capacity method of class **StringBuffer**	**length** method of class **String**
Character class	**length** method of class **StringBuffer**
character code	length of a string
character constant	literal
character set	low-order byte
charAt method of class **String**	**nextTokens** method of **StringTokenizer**
charAt method of class **StringBuffer**	numeric code representation of a character
charValue method of class **Character**	printing character
compareTo method of class **String**	**regionMatches** method of class **String**
comparing strings	**replace** method of class **String**
concat method of class **String**	search string
concatenation	**setCharAt** method of class **StringBuffer**
copying strings	**startsWith** method of class **String**
countTokens method of **StringTokenizer**	string
delimiter	**String** class
digit method of class **Character**	string concatenation
endsWith method of class **String**	string constant
equals method of class **String**	string literal
equalsIgnoreCase method of class **String**	string processing
forDigit method of class **Character**	**StringBuffer** class
getBytes method of class **String**	**StringIndexOutOfBoundsException**
getChars method of class **String**	**StringTokenizer** class
getChars method of class **StringBuffer**	**substring** method of **String** class
hashCode method of class **Character**	**toCharArray** method of class **String**
hashCode method of class **String**	token
hash table	tokenizing strings
hasMoreTokens method	**toLowerCase** method of class **Character**
hexadecimal digits	**toLowerCase** method of class **String**
high-order byte	**toString** method of class **Character**
indexOf method of class **String**	**toString** method of class **String**
insert method of class **StringBuffer**	**toString** method of class **StringBuffer**
intern method of class **String**	**toUpperCase** method of class **Character**
isDefined method of class **Character**	**toUpperCase** method of class **String**
isDigit method of class **Character**	**trim** method of class **String**
isJavaLetter method of class **Character**	Unicode
isJavaLetterOrDigit method	**valueOf** method of class **String**
isLetter method of class **Character**	white space characters
isLetterOrDigit method of **Character**	word processing

Common Programming Errors

8.1   Attempting to determine the length of a **String** via an instance variable called **length** (e.g., **s1.length**) is a syntax error. The **String** method **length** must be used. (e.g. **s1.length()**).

8.2   Attempting to access a character that is outside the bounds of a **String** (i.e., an index less than 0 or an index greater than or equal to the **String**'s length) results in a **StringIndexOutOfBoundsException.**

8.3   Sending **StringBuffer** methods that are not methods of class **String** to **String** objects is a syntax error.

8.4   Attempting to access a character that is outside the bounds of a **StringBuffer** (i.e., an index less than 0 or an index greater than or equal to the **StringBuffer**'s length) results in a **StringIndexOutOfBoundsException.**

Performance Tips

8.1   **String** objects are constant strings and **StringBuffer** objects are modifiable strings. Java distinguishes constant strings and modifiable strings for optimization purposes; in particular, Java can perform certain optimizations involving **String** objects (such as sharing one **String** object between multiple references) because it knows these objects will not change.

8.2   When given the choice between using a **String** object to represent a string versus a **StringBuffer** object to represent that string, always using a **String** object if indeed the object will not change; this improves performance.

Self-Review Exercises

8.1   State whether the following are true or false. If the answer is false, explain why.
  a) When **String** objects are compared with **==**, the result is **true** if the **String**s contain the same values.
  b) A **String** can be modified after it is created.

8.2   For each of the following, write a single statement that performs the indicated task.
  a) Compare the string in **s1** to the string in **s2** for equality of contents.
  b) Append the string **s2** to the string **s1** using **+=**.
  c) Determine the length of the string in **s1**.

Answers to Self-Review Exercises

8.1   a) False. **String** objects that are compared with operator **==** are actually compared to determine if they are the same object in memory.
  b) False. **String** objects are constant and cannot be modified after they are created.

8.2   a) **s1.equals(s2)**
  b) **s1 += s2;**
  c) **s1.length()**

Exercises

NOTE: Exercises 8.3 through 8.6 are reasonably challenging. Once you have done these problems, you ought to be able to implement most popular card games easily.

8.3   Modify the program in Fig. 8.21 so that the card dealing method deals a five-card poker hand. Then write the following additional methods:

a) Determine if the hand contains a pair.

b) Determine if the hand contains two pairs.

c) Determine if the hand contains three of a kind (e.g., three jacks).

d) Determine if the hand contains four of a kind (e.g., four aces).

e) Determine if the hand contains a flush (i.e., all five cards of the same suit).

f) Determine if the hand contains a straight (i.e., five cards of consecutive face values).

8.4   Use the methods developed in Exercise 8.3 to write a program that deals two five-card poker hands, evaluates each hand, and determines which is the better hand.

8.5   Modify the program developed in Exercise 8.4 so that it can simulate the dealer. The dealer's five-card hand is dealt "face down" so the player cannot see it. The program should then evaluate the dealer's hand and, based on the quality of the hand, the dealer should draw one, two, or three more cards to replace the corresponding number of unneeded cards in the original hand. The program should then reevaluate the dealer's hand. (*Caution:* This is a difficult problem!)

8.6   Modify the program developed in Exercise 8.5 so that it can handle the dealer's hand automatically, but the player is allowed to decide which cards of the player's hand to replace. The program should then evaluate both hands and determine who wins. Now use this new program to play 20 games against the computer. Who wins more games, you or the computer? Have one of your friends play 20 games against the computer. Who wins more games? Based on the results of these games, make appropriate modifications to refine your poker playing program (this, too, is a difficult problem). Play 20 more games. Does your modified program play a better game?

8.7   Write an applet that uses **String** method **compareTo** to compare two strings input by the user. The program should state whether the first string is less than, equal to, or greater than the second.

8.8   Write an applet that uses **String** method **regionMatches** to compare two strings input by the user. The program should input the number of characters to be compared and the starting index of the comparison. The program should state whether the first string is less than, equal to, or greater than the second string. Ignore the case of the characters when performing the comparison.

8.9   Write an applet that uses random number generation to create sentences. Use four arrays of strings called **article**, **noun**, **verb**, and **preposition**. Create a sentence by selecting a word at random from each array in the following order: **article**, **noun**, **verb**, **preposition**, **article**, and **noun**. As each word is picked, concatenate it to the previous words in the sentence. The words should be separated by spaces. When the final sentence is output, it should start with a capital letter and end with a period. The program should generate 20 sentences and output them to a text area.

The arrays should be filled as follows: the **article** array should contain the articles **"the"**, **"a"**, **"one"**, **"some"**, and **"any"**; the **noun** array should contain the nouns **"boy"**, **"girl"**, **"dog"**, **"town"**, and **"car"**; the **verb** array should contain the verbs **"drove"**, **"jumped"**, **"ran"**, **"walked"**, and **"skipped"**; the **preposition** array should contain the prepositions **"to"**, **"from"**, **"over"**, **"under"**, and **"on"**.

After the preceding program is written, modify the program to produce a short story consisting of several of these sentences. (How about the possibility of a random term paper writer!)

8.10   (*Limericks*) A limerick is a humorous five-line verse in which the first and second lines rhyme with the fifth, and the third line rhymes with the fourth. Using techniques similar to those developed in Exercise 8.9, write a Java program that produces random limericks. Polishing this program to produce good limericks is a challenging problem, but the result will be worth the effort!

8.11   Write an applet that encodes English language phrases into pig Latin. Pig Latin is a form of coded language often used for amusement. Many variations exist in the methods used to form pig Latin phrases. For simplicity, use the following algorithm:

To form a pig Latin phrase from an English language phrase, tokenize the phrase into words with an object of class **StringTokenizer**. To translate each English word into a pig Latin word, place the first letter of the English word at the end of the word and add the letters "**ay**." Thus the word "**jump**" becomes "**umpjay**," the word "**the**" becomes "**hetay**," and the word "**computer**" becomes "**omputercay**." Blanks between words remain as blanks. Assume the following: The English phrase consists of words separated by blanks, there are no punctuation marks, and all words have two or more letters. Method **printLatinWord** should display each word. Each token returned from **nextToken** is passed to method **printLatinWord** to print the pig Latin word. Enable the user to input the sentence. Keep a running display of all the converted sentences in a text area.

8.12   Write an applet that inputs a telephone number as a string in the form **(555) 555-5555**. The program should use an object of class **StringTokenizer** to extract the area code as a token, the first three digits of the phone number as a token, and the last four digits of the phone number as a token. The seven digits of the phone number should be concatenated into one string. The program should convert the area code string to **int** (remember **parseInt**!) and convert the phone number string to **long**. Both the area code and the phone number should be printed. Remember that you will have to change delimiter characters during the tokenization process.

8.13   Write an applet that inputs a line of text, tokenizes the line with an object of class **StringTokenizer**, and outputs the tokens in reverse order.

8.14   Use the string comparison methods discussed and the techniques for sorting arrays developed in Chapter 5 to write a program that alphabetizes a list of strings. Allow the user to enter the Strings in a text field. Display the results in a text area.

8.15   Write an applet that inputs text and outputs the text in uppercase and lowercase letters.

8.16   Write an applet that inputs several lines of text and a search character, and uses method **String** method **indexOf** to determine the number of occurrences of the character in the text.

8.17   Write an applet based on the program of Exercise 8.16 that inputs several lines of text and uses **String** method **indexOf** to determine the total number of occurrences of each letter of the alphabet in the text. Uppercase and lowercase letters should be counted together. Store the totals for each letter in an array, and print the values in tabular format after the totals have been determined.

8.18   Write an applet that reads a series of strings and outputs only those strings beginning with the letter "**b**." The results should be output to a text area.

8.19   Write an applet that reads a series of strings and prints only those strings ending with the letters "**ED**." The results should be output to a text area.

8.20   Write an applet that inputs an integer code for a character and displays the corresponding character. Modify this program so that it generates all possible three-digit codes in the range 000 to 255 and attempts to print the corresponding characters. Display the results in a text area.

8.21   Write your own versions of the **String** methods for searching strings.

Special Section: Advanced String Manipulation Exercises

The preceding exercises are keyed to the text and designed to test the reader's understanding of fundamental string manipulation concepts. This section includes a collection of intermediate and advanced string manipulation exercises. The reader should find these problems challenging yet entertaining. The problems vary considerably in difficulty. Some require an hour or two of program writing and implementation. Others are useful for lab assignments that might require two or three weeks of study and implementation. Some are challenging term projects.

8.22   *(Text Analysis)* The availability of computers with string manipulation capabilities has resulted in some rather interesting approaches to analyzing the writings of great authors. Much attention has been focused on whether William Shakespeare ever lived. Some scholars believe there is substantial evidence indicating that Christopher Marlowe or other authors actually penned the masterpieces attributed to Shakespeare. Researchers have used computers to find similarities in the writings of these two authors. This exercise examines three methods for analyzing texts with a computer.

    a) Write an applet that reads several lines of text from the keyboard and prints a table indicating the number of occurrences of each letter of the alphabet in the text. For example, the phrase

        `To be, or not to be: that is the question:`

    contains one "a," two "b's," no "c's," etc.

    b) Write an applet that reads several lines of text and prints a table indicating the number of one-letter words, two-letter words, three-letter words, etc. appearing in the text. For example, the phrase

        `Whether 'tis nobler in the mind to suffer`

    contains

Word length	Occurrences
1	0
2	2
3	2
4	2 (including 'tis)
5	0
6	2
7	1

    c) Write an applet that reads several lines of text and prints a table indicating the number of occurrences of each different word in the text. The first version of your program should include the words in the table in the same order in which they appear in the text. For example, the lines

        `To be, or not to be: that is the question:`
        `Whether 'tis nobler in the mind to suffer`

    contain the words "to" three times, the word "be" two times, the word "or" once, etc. A more interesting (and useful) printout should then be attempted in which the words are sorted alphabetically.

8.23   *(Printing Dates in Various Formats)* Dates are printed in several common formats. Two of the more common formats are:

        `07/21/55 and July 21, 1955`

Write an applet that reads a date in the first format and prints that date in the second format.

8.24 *(Check Protection)* Computers are frequently employed in check-writing systems such as payroll applications and accounts payable applications. Many strange stories circulate regarding weekly paychecks being printed (by mistake) for amounts in excess of $1 million. Incorrect amounts are printed by computerized check-writing systems because of human error and/or machine failure. Systems designers build controls into their systems to prevent such erroneous checks from being issued.

Another serious problem is the intentional alteration of a check amount by someone who intends to cash a check fraudulently. To prevent a dollar amount from being altered, most computerized check-writing systems employ a technique called *check protection.*

Checks designed for imprinting by computer contain a fixed number of spaces in which the computer may print an amount. Suppose a paycheck contains eight blank spaces in which the computer is supposed to print the amount of a weekly paycheck. If the amount is large, then all eight of those spaces will be filled, for example:

```
1,230.60 (check amount)
--------
12345678 (position numbers)
```

On the other hand, if the amount is less than $1000, then several of the spaces would ordinarily be left blank. For example,

```
   99.87
--------
12345678
```

contains three blank spaces. If a check is printed with blank spaces, it is easier for someone to alter the amount of the check. To prevent a check from being altered, many check-writing systems insert *leading asterisks* to protect the amount as follows:

```
***99.87
--------
12345678
```

Write an applet that inputs a dollar amount to be printed on a check, and then prints the amount in check-protected format with leading asterisks if necessary. Assume that nine spaces are available for printing the amount.

8.25 *(Writing the Word Equivalent of a Check Amount)* Continuing the discussion of the previous exercise, we reiterate the importance of designing check-writing systems to prevent alteration of check amounts. One common security method requires that the check amount be written both in numbers, and "spelled out" in words as well. Even if someone is able to alter the numerical amount of the check, it is extremely difficult to change the amount in words.

Many computerized check-writing systems do not print the amount of the check in words. Perhaps the main reason for this omission is the fact that most high-level languages used in commercial applications do not contain adequate string manipulation features. Another reason is that the logic for writing word equivalents of check amounts is somewhat involved.

Write an applet that inputs a numeric check amount and writes the word equivalent of the amount. For example, the amount 112.43 should be written as

ONE HUNDRED TWELVE and 43/100

8.26   *(Morse Code)* Perhaps the most famous of all coding schemes is the Morse code, developed by Samuel Morse in 1832 for use with the telegraph system. The Morse code assigns a series of dots and dashes to each letter of the alphabet, each digit, and a few special characters (such as period, comma, colon, and semicolon). In sound-oriented systems, the dot represents a short sound and the dash represents a long sound. Other representations of dots and dashes are used with light-oriented systems and signal-flag systems.

Separation between words is indicated by a space, or, quite simply, the absence of a dot or dash. In a sound-oriented system, a space is indicated by a short period of time during which no sound is transmitted. The international version of the Morse code appears in Fig. 8.22.

Write an applet that reads an English language phrase and encodes the phrase into Morse code. Also write a program that reads a phrase in Morse code and converts the phrase into the English language equivalent. Use one blank between each Morse-coded letter and three blanks between each Morse-coded word.

8.27   *(A Metric Conversion Program)* Write an applet that will assist the user with metric conversions. Your program should allow the user to specify the names of the units as strings (i.e., centimeters, liters, grams, etc. for the metric system and inches, quarts, pounds, etc. for the English system) and should respond to simple questions such as

```
"How many inches are in 2 meters?"
"How many liters are in 10 quarts?"
```

Character	Code	Character	Code
A	.−	T	−
B	−...	U	..−
C	−.−.	V	...−
D	−..	W	.−−
E	.	X	−..−
F	..−.	Y	−.−−
G	−−.	Z	−−..
H	....		
I	..	**Digits**	
J	.−−−	1	.−−−−
K	−.−	2	..−−−
L	.−..	3	...−−
M	−−	4	....−
N	−.	5	.....
O	−−−	6	−....
P	.−−.	7	−−...
Q	−−.−	8	−−−..
R	.−.	9	−−−−.
S	...	0	−−−−−

Fig. 8.22 The letters of the alphabet as expressed in international Morse code.

Your program should recognize invalid conversions. For example, the question

"How many feet in 5 kilograms?"

is not meaningful because **"feet"** are units of length while **"kilograms"** are units of weight.

Challenging string manipulation projects

8.28 *(Project: A Spelling Checker)* Many popular word processing software packages have built-in spell checkers.

In this project, you are asked to develop your own spell-checker utility. We make suggestions to help get you started. You should then consider adding more capabilities. Use a computerized dictionary (if you have access to one) as a source of words.

Why do we type so many words with incorrect spellings? In some cases, it is because we simply do not know the correct spelling, so we make a "best guess." In some cases, it is because we transpose two letters (e.g., "defualt" instead of "default"). Sometimes we double-type a letter accidentally (e.g., "hanndy" instead of "handy"). Sometimes we type a nearby key instead of the one we intended (e.g., "biryhday" instead of "birthday"). And so on.

Design and implement a spell-checker applet in Java. Your program should maintain an array **wordList** of strings. Enable the user to enter these strings. Note: In Chapters 15 and 16 we introduce file processing and networking. Once you have these capabilities, you can obtain the words for the spell checker from a computerized dictionary.

Your program should ask a user to enter a word. The program should then look up that word in the **wordList** array. If the word is present in the array, your program should print '**Word is spelled correctly**."

If the word is not present in the array, your program should print '**word is not spelled correctly**." Then your program should try to locate other words in **wordList** that might be the word the user intended to type. For example, you can try all possible single transpositions of adjacent letters to discover that the word "default" is a direct match to a word in **wordList**. Of course, this implies that your program will check all other single transpositions such as "edfault," "dfeault," "deafult," "defalut," and "defautl." When you find a new word that matches one in **wordList**, print that word in a message such as, '**Did you mean "default?"**."

Implement other tests such as replacing each double letter with a single letter and any other tests you can develop to improve the value of your spell checker.

8.29 *(Project: A Crossword Puzzle Generator)* Most people have worked a crossword puzzle, but few have ever attempted to generate one. Generating a crossword puzzle is suggested here as a string manipulation project requiring substantial sophistication and effort. There are many issues the programmer must resolve to get even the simplest crossword puzzle generator program working. For example, how does one represent the grid of a crossword puzzle inside the computer? Should one use a series of strings, or should double-subscripted arrays be used? The programmer needs a source of words (i.e., a computerized dictionary) that can be directly referenced by the program. In what form should these words be stored to facilitate the complex manipulations required by the program? The really ambitious reader will want to generate the "clues" portion of the puzzle in which the brief hints for each "across" word and each "down" word are printed for the puzzle worker. Merely printing a version of the blank puzzle itself is not a simple problem.

9

Graphics

Objectives

- To understand graphics contexts and graphics objects.
- To understand and be able to use methods for drawing strings, characters, and bytes.
- To understand and be able to manipulate colors.
- To understand and be able to manipulate fonts.
- To understand and be able to use a methods for drawing lines, rectangles, rectangles with rounded corners, three dimensional rectangles, ovals, arcs and polygons.
- To be able to copy areas of the screen.
- To understand paint modes.

One picture is worth ten thousand words.
Chinese proverb

Treat nature in terms of the cylinder, the sphere, the cone, all in perspective.
Paul Cezanne

Nothing ever becomes real till it is experienced—even a proverb is no proverb to you till your life has illustrated it.
John Keats

A picture shows me at a glance what it takes dozens of pages of a book to expound.
Ivan Sergeyevich

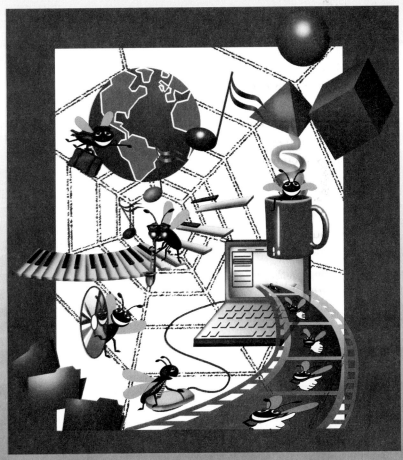

Outline

Summary • Terminology • Common Programming Errors • Portability Tips • Software Engineering Observation • Self-Review Exercises • Answers to Self-Review Exercises • Exercises

9.1 Introduction[1]

We now begin our in-depth treatment of *Java's Abstract Windowing Toolkit (AWT)*—the classes that comprise the **java.awt** *package*. We present the graphics capabilities for drawing on the screen. Figure 9.1 shows a portion of the **java.awt** *class hierarchy* that includes the classes covered in this chapter. Each class in the figure inherits directly from class **Object**. Class **Color** contains methods and constants for manipulating colors. Class **Font** contains methods and constants for manipulating fonts. Class **FontMetrics** contains methods for obtaining font information. Class **Polygon** contains methods for creating polygons. Class **Graphics** contains methods for drawing strings, lines, rectangles and other shapes. Class **Toolkit** provides methods for getting graphical information from a system such as the set of displayable fonts and the display screen resolution.

To begin drawing in Java, we must first understand Java's *coordinate system* (Fig. 9.2) which is a scheme for identifying every possible point on the screen. By default, the upper-left corner of the screen has the coordinates (0, 0). A coordinate pair is composed of an *x coordinate* (the *horizontal coordinate*) and a *y coordinate* (the *vertical coordinate*). The *x* coordinate is the horizontal distance moving right from the upper-left corner. The *y* coordinate is the vertical distance moving down from the upper-left corner. The *x axis* describes every horizontal coordinate and the *y axis* describes every vertical coordinate.

---

1. Chapter 9 on graphics, and Chapters 10 and 11 on basic and advanced graphical user interface components were coauthored with the authors' colleague Mr. Tem Nieto of Deitel & Associates, Inc.

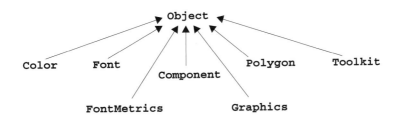

Fig. 9.1   A portion of the **java.awt** hierarchy.

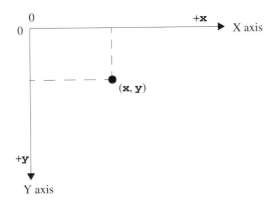

Fig. 9.2   Java coordinate system. Units are measured in pixels.

Text and shapes are displayed on the screen by specifying coordinates. Coordinate units are measured in *pixels*. A pixel is a display monitor's smallest unit of resolution.

Portability Tip 9.1

Different display monitors have different levels of resolution (i.e., the density of pixels vary).

9.2 Graphics Contexts and Graphics Objects

A *graphics context* enables drawing on the screen in Java. A **Graphics** object manages a graphics context by controlling how information is drawn. **Graphics** objects contain methods for drawing, font manipulation, color manipulation, etc. Every applet we have seen in the text that performs drawing on the screen has used the **Graphics** object **g** (the argument to the applet's **paint** method) to manage the applet's graphics context.

A **Graphics** object must be used to draw. The **Graphics** class is an **abstract** class—i.e., **Graphics** objects cannot be instantiated. The reason for this is found in Java's portability. Because drawing is performed differently on each platform that supports Java, there cannot be one class that implements drawing capabilities on all systems. For example, the graphics capabilities that enable a PC running Windows to draw a rectangle are different from the graphics capabilities that enable a UNIX workstation to draw a rectangle— and those are both different from the graphics capabilities that enable a Macintosh to draw a rectangle. When Java is implemented on each platform, a derived class of **Graphics** is created that actually implements all the drawing capabilities. This implementation is hidden from us by the **Graphics** class which supplies the interface that enables us to write programs that use graphics in a platform independent manner.

The **Component** class *paint* method takes a **Graphics** object as an argument. The **Graphics** object is passed to the **paint** method by the system when a paint operation occurs for a **Component**. Class **Component** is the superclass for many of the classes in the AWT. The header for the **paint** method is

```
public void paint( Graphics g )
```

The **Graphics** object **g** receives a reference to an object of the system's derived **Graphics** class. The preceding method header should look familiar to you—it is the same one we have been using in our applet classes. Actually, the **Component** class is an indirect base class of class **Applet** from which every applet inherits. In fact, many of the capabilities of the **Applet** class are inherited from class **Component**. The **paint** method defined in class **Component** does nothing by default—it must be overridden by the programmer.

The **paint** method is seldom called directly by the programmer because drawing graphics is an *event driven process*. When an applet is initially executed, the **paint** method is automatically called (after calls to the **Applet**'s **init** and **start** methods). For **paint** to be called again, an *event*, such as the user resizing the applet, must occur.

If the programmer needs to call **paint**, a call is made to the **Component** class *repaint* method. The **repaint** method calls the **Component** class *update* method to clear the **Component**'s background of any previous drawing, then **update** calls **paint** directly. The **repaint** method is frequently called by the programmer to force a **paint** operation. Method **repaint** should not be overridden. The **update** method is seldom called directly and sometimes overridden. Overriding the **update** method is useful for "smoothing" animations (i.e., reducing "flicker") as we will see in Chapter 14, "Multimedia: Images, Animation, Audio." The headers for **repaint** and **update** are

```
public void repaint()
public void update( Graphics g )
```

Both methods are **public** and have a **void** return type. The **update** method takes a **Graphics** object as an argument which is supplied automatically by method **repaint**.

In this chapter we focus on the **paint** method. In the next chapter we concentrate more on the event-driven nature of graphics and discuss the **repaint** and **update** methods in more detail.

9.3 Drawing Strings, Characters, and Bytes

This section presents the **Graphics** methods for drawing strings, characters, and bytes. The methods and their parameters are summarized in Fig. 9.3.

Graphics methods for drawing strings, characters and bytes

```
public abstract void drawString(
    String string,      // string to be drawn
    int x,              // x coordinate
    int y )             // y coordinate
```
Draws a string in the current font and color at the coordinate (**x**, **y**).

```
public void drawChars(
    char chars[],       // array to be drawn
    int offset,         // starting subscript (index)
    int number,         // number of elements to draw
    int x,              // x coordinate
    int y )             // y coordinate
```
Draws a series of characters in the current font and color at the coordinate (**x**, **y**).

```
public void drawBytes(
    byte bytes[],       // array of bytes
    int offset,         // starting subscript (index)
    int number,         // number of elements to draw
    int x,              // x coordinate
    int y )             // y coordinate
```
Draws a series of bytes in the current font and color at the coordinate (**x**, **y**).

Fig. 9.3   Graphics methods for drawing strings, characters and bytes.

The *drawString* method draws a **String**. The method takes three arguments—the **String** to be drawn, an x coordinate, and a y coordinate. The **String** is drawn in the current color and font. The *current color* is the color in which text or shapes are drawn. The *current font* is the font in which text is drawn (the next two sections discuss how to set the current color and font). *The point (**x**, **y**) corresponds to the lower-left corner of the string*— i.e., the first character in the **String** is drawn above and to the right of the specified pixel coordinate. Therefore, if you draw a **String** at coordinate (0, 0), it will not be visible.

The *drawChars* method draws a series of characters. The **drawChars** method takes five arguments. The first argument is an array of characters. The second argument specifies the subscript in the array of the first character to be drawn. The third argument specifies the number of characters to be drawn. The last two arguments specify the coordinates where drawing is to begin. The point (**x**, **y**) corresponds to the lower-left corner of the first character drawn.

The *drawBytes* method draws a series of bytes. Like the **drawChars** method, the **drawBytes** method takes five arguments. The first argument is an array of bytes. The second argument specifies the subscript in the array of the first byte to be drawn. The third argument specifies the number of elements to be drawn. The last two arguments specify the coordinates where drawing is to begin. The point (**x**, **y**) corresponds to the lower-left corner of the bytes drawn.

The program of Fig. 9.4 uses the **drawString**, **drawChars**, and **drawBytes** methods to draw information on the applet.

```
1  // Fig. 9.4: DrawSCB.java
2  // Demonstrating drawString, drawChars and drawBytes
3  import java.applet.Applet;
4  import java.awt.Graphics;
5
6  public class DrawSCB extends Applet {
7     private String s = "Using drawString!";
8     private char c[] = { 'c', 'h', 'a', 'r', 's', ' ', '8' };
9     private byte b[] = { 'b', 'y', 't', 'e', 1, 2, 3 };
10
11    public void paint( Graphics g )
12    {
13       // draw a string at location (100, 25) on the applet
14       g.drawString( s, 100, 25 );
15
16       // draw a series of characters at location (100, 50)
17       g.drawChars( c, 2, 3,  100, 50 );
18
19       // draw a series of bytes at location (100, 75)
20       g.drawBytes( b, 0, 5, 100, 75 );
21    }
22 }
```

Fig. 9.4 Demonstrating **drawString**, **drawChars**, and **drawBytes**.

In the program, the **drawString** method displays "**Using drawString!**" at location (100, 25). The statement

```
g.drawChars(c, 2, 3, 100, 50);
```

displays "**ars**" at location (100, 50). The second argument, **2**, specifies that drawing is to begin with subscript **2** (the third element) of character array **c**. The third argument, **3**, specifies that three elements will be drawn. Method **drawBytes** displays a set of bytes at location (100, 75). Notice that the characters in the first four elements of array **b** are displayed as characters, but the numeric value 1 in the fifth element is displayed as a vertical black bar. This is because method **drawBytes** takes the numeric value in each element and interprets it as a character for display purposes. On this particular system, the character with the numeric value 1 was not a displayable character so the black bar was printed instead.

Common Programming Error 9.1

Passing an invalid array subscript to the **drawChars** *or* **drawBytes** *method throws an*
ArraySubscriptOutOfBoundsException

9.4 Color Control

This section presents the constants and methods for color control. Colors enhance the appearance of a program. A user's first impression of a program is usually through color. Colors convey meaning. For example, a traffic light has three different color lights—red indicates a stop; yellow indicates caution; and green indicates go.

Color constants and color methods are defined in the ***Color*** *class* which inherits from the **Object** class. The predefined color constants are summarized in Fig. 9.5 and the color methods and constructors are summarized in Fig. 9.6. Note that two of the methods in Fig. 9.6 are **Graphics** methods that are specific to colors.

Every color is created from an *RGB value* (Red/Green/Blue). An RGB value is created from three parts. All three RGB parts can be integers in the range 0 to 255 or all three RGB parts can be floating point values in the range 0.0 to 1.0. The first RGB part defines the amount of red; the second RGB part defines the amount of green; and the third part defines the amount of blue. The larger the RGB value, the greater the amount of that particular color. Java enables the programmer to choose from $256 \times 256 \times 256$ (or approximately 16 million) colors. However, not all computers are capable of displaying all these colors. If this is the case, the computer will display the closest color it can.

Common Programming Error 9.2

Spelling any **static Color** *class constant with an initial capital letter is a syntax error.*

Color constant	Color	RGB value
public final static Color orange	orange	255, 200, 0
public final static Color pink	pink	255, 175, 175
public final static Color cyan	cyan	0, 255, 255
public final static Color magenta	magenta	255, 0, 255
public final static Color yellow	yellow	255, 255, 0
public final static Color black	black	0, 0, 0
public final static Color white	white	255, 255, 255
public final static Color gray	gray	128, 128, 128
public final static Color lightGray	light gray	192, 192, 192
public final static Color darkGray	dark gray	64, 64, 64
public final static Color red	red	255, 0, 0
public final static Color green	green	0, 255, 0
public final static Color blue	blue	0, 0, 255

Fig. 9.5 **Color** class **static** constants and RGB values.

Color methods and color related Graphics methods

```
public Color(
    int r,    // 0 - 255 red content
    int g,    // 0 - 255 green content
    int b)    // 0 - 255 blue content
```
   Creates a color based on red, green, and blue contents.

```
public Color(
    float r, // 0.0 - 1.0 red content
    float g, // 0.0 - 1.0 green content
    float b) // 0.0 - 1.0 blue content
```
   Creates a color based on red, green, and blue contents.

```
public int getRed()        // Color class
```
   Returns a value between 0 and 255 representing the red content.

```
public int getBlue()       // Color class
```
   Returns a value between 0 and 255 representing the blue content.

```
public int getGreen()      // Color class
```
   Returns a value between 0 and 255 representing the green content.

```
public abstract Color getColor()      // Graphics class
```
   Returns a **Color** object representing the current color for the graphics context.

```
public abstract void setColor(Color c) // Graphics class
```
   Sets the current color for drawing with the graphics context.

Fig. 9.6   **Color** methods and color related **Graphics** methods.

Two **Color** constructors are shown in Fig 9.6—one that takes three **int** arguments and one that takes three **float** arguments with each argument specifying the amount of red, green, and blue respectively. Remember that the **int** values are between the 0 and 255 and the float values are between 0.0 and 1.0. The **Color** constructed has the specified amounts of red, green, and blue. **Color** methods *getRed*, *getGreen* and *getBlue* return integer values from 0 to 255 representing the amount of red, green, and blue respectively. **Graphics** method *getColor* returns a **Color** object representing the current drawing color. **Graphics** method *setColor* sets the current drawing color.

The program of Fig. 9.7 changes the current color and draws a **String**. The program uses the version of the **Color** constructor that takes three **int** arguments

The instance variables **red**, **green**, and **blue** are declared and initialized. In the **paint** method, the current color is changed with the statement

```
        g.setColor( new Color( red, green, blue ) );
```

The **setColor** method sets the current color to the **Color** object constructed with the **red**, **green**, and **blue** values. Then, the **drawString** method draws the **String** in the new current color. The statement

```
1   // Fig. 9.7: ShowColors.java
2   // Demonstrating setting and getting a Color.
3   import java.applet.Applet;
4   import java.awt.Graphics;
5   import java.awt.Color;
6
7   public class ShowColors extends Applet {
8      private int red, green, blue;
9
10     public void init()
11     {
12        // set some values
13        red = 100;
14        blue = 255;
15        green = 125;
16     }
17
18     public void paint ( Graphics g )
19     {
20        g.setColor( new Color( red, green, blue ) );
21        g.drawString( "ABCDEFGHIJKLMNOPQRSTUVWXYZ", 50, 33 );
22        showStatus( "Current RGB: " + g.getColor().toString() );
23     }
24  }
```

Fig. 9.7   Demonstrating setting and getting a **Color** .

```
showStatus( "Current RGB: : + g.getColor().toString() );
```

uses the **toString** method on the **Color** object returned by **getColor**; the resulting information is then displayed in the status bar. Notice that method **toString** method converts the **Color** object into a **String** representation of the object containing the class name and package (**java.awt.Color**), and the red, green and blue values.

The program of Fig. 9.8 uses the **Color** constructor that takes three **float** arguments to create a new **Color** object, changes the current color and draws a **String** in the new current color.

The instance variables **red**, **green**, and **blue** are declared and initialized. The current color is changed in the **paint** method with the statement

```
g.setColor( new Color( red, green, blue ) );
```

```
1   // Fig. 9.8: ShowColors2.java
2   // Demonstrating the Color constructor with float arguments
3   import java.applet.Applet;
4   import java.awt.Graphics;
5   import java.awt.Color;
6
7   public class ShowColors2 extends Applet {
8      private float red, green, blue;
9
10     public void init()
11     {
12        red = 0.1f;
13        green = 0.21f;
14        blue = 0.33f;
15     }
16
17     public void paint( Graphics g )
18     {
19        g.setColor( new Color( red, green, blue ) );
20        g.drawString( "ABCDEFGHIJKLMNOPQRSTUVWXYZ", 60, 33 );
21        showStatus( "Current RGB: " + g.getColor().toString() );
22     }
23  }
```

Fig. 9.8   Demonstrating the **Color** constructor with **float** arguments.

The **setColor** method sets the current color to the color constructed from **red**, **green**, and **blue**. The **drawString** method draws the string in the color set by **setColor**. The statement

```
showStatus( "Current RGB: " + g.getColor().toString() );
```

uses the **toString** method on the **Color** object returned by **getColor**; the resulting information is then displayed in the status bar. Note that integer values (not floating point values) are displayed in the status bar for each of the values of the **red**, **green** and **blue** components.

The program of Fig. 9.9 changes the current color to **blue**. In the program, a reference to a **Color** object (instance variable **c**) is created with the line

```
private Color c;
```

```
1   // Fig. 9.9: ShowColors3.java
2   // Using a predefined static Color object to set the color
3   import java.applet.Applet;
4   import java.awt.Graphics;
5   import java.awt.Color;
6
7   public class ShowColors3 extends Applet {
8      private Color c;
9
10     public void init()
11     {
12        c = Color.blue;
13     }
14
15     public void paint( Graphics g )
16     {
17        g.setColor( c );
18        g.drawString( "ABCDEFGHIJKLMNOPQRSTUVWXYZ", 50, 33 );
19        showStatus( "Current RGB: " +
20                   String.valueOf( c.getRed() ) +
21                   " " + String.valueOf( c.getGreen() ) +
22                   " " + String.valueOf( c.getBlue() ) );
23     }
24  }
```

Fig. 9.9   Using a predefined **static Color** object to set the color to **blue**.

The value of **c** is set to the constant **Color.blue** in the **init** method. The current color is changed to **blue** with the statement

```
    g.setColor( c );
```

The **getRed**, **getGreen**, and **getBlue** methods are used to get the RGB values of the current color. The RGB value is displayed in the status bar.

9.5 Font Control

This section introduces the methods and constants for font control. Most font methods and font constants are part of the **Font** class which inherits from class **Object**. The methods are summarized in Fig. 9.10, Fig. 9.12, and Fig. 9.14.

Font constants, Font constructor and Graphics method setFont

```
public final static int PLAIN      // Font class
```
A constant representing a plain font style.

```
public final static int BOLD       // Font class
```
A constant representing a bold font style.

```
public final static int ITALIC     // Font class
```
A constant representing an italic font style.

```
public Font(
    String s,          // font name
    int style,         // font style
    int size)          // font point size
```
Creates a **Font** object with the specified font, style, and size.

```
public abstract void setFont(Font f)  // Graphics class
```
Sets the current font to the font, style, and size specified by the **Font** object **f**.

Fig. 9.10 **Font** constants, **Font** constructor and **Graphics** method **setFont**.

In Fig. 9.10, the **static** constants *PLAIN, BOLD*, and *ITALIC* of class **Font** are used to specify the *font style*. The **Font** constructor takes three arguments—the *font name,* the font style and the *font size*. The font name is any font currently supported by the system where the program is running, such as **Courier, Helvetica** and **TimesRoman**. The font style is either **Font.PLAIN, Font.ITALIC**, or **Font.BOLD** (the **static** constants of the **Font** class). Font styles can also be used in combination (e.g., **Font.ITALIC + Font.BOLD**). The font size is measured in points. A *point* is 1/72 of an inch. The *setFont* method sets the current font—the font in which text will be displayed. The **setFont** method takes a **Font** object as an argument.

Portability Tip 9.2

The number of fonts varies greatly across systems. The JDK guarantees that the fonts **TimesRoman, Courier, Helvetica, Dialog** *and* **DialogInput** *will be available.*

Software Engineering Observation 9.1

If a font is not available on a system, Java will substitute that system's default font.

The program of Fig. 9.11 displays text in three different fonts with each font is a different size. The program uses the **Font** constructor to create **Font** objects **font1, font2** and **font3**. Each call to the **Font** constructor passes a font name (**TimesRoman, Courier**, or **Helvetica**) as a **String**, a font style (**Font.PLAIN, Font.ITALIC**, or **Font.BOLD**) and a font size. The current font is changed using the **setFont** method. Once the **setFont** method is invoked, all text displayed following the call will appear in the new font.

```
1   // Fig. 9.11: DemoFont.java
2   // Demonstrating the Font constants, the Font constructor
3   // and the setFont method
4   import java.applet.Applet;
5   import java.awt.Graphics;
6   import java.awt.Font;
7
8   public class DemoFont extends Applet {
9      private Font font1, font2, font3;
10
11     public void init()
12     {
13        // create a font object: 12-point bold times roman
14        font1 = new Font( "TimesRoman", Font.BOLD, 12 );
15
16        // create a font object: 24-point italic courier
17        font2 = new Font( "Courier", Font.ITALIC, 24 );
18
19        // create a font object: 14-point plain helvetica
20        font3 = new Font( "Helvetica", Font.PLAIN, 14 );
21     }
22
23     public void paint( Graphics g )
24     {
25        // set the current font to font1
26        g.setFont( font1 );
27
28        // draw a string in font font1
29        g.drawString( "TimesRoman 12 point bold.", 20, 20 );
30
31        // change the current font to font2
32        g.setFont( font2 );
33
34        // draw a string in font font2
35        g.drawString( "Courier 24 point italic.", 20, 40 );
36
37        // change the current font to font3
38        g.setFont( font3 );
39
40        // draw a string in font font3
41        g.drawString( "Helvetica 14 point plain.", 20, 60 );
42     }
43  }
```

Fig. 9.11 Setting fonts with **Font** objects and the **Graphics setFont** method (part 1 of 2).

Often it is necessary to get information about the current font such as the font name, the font style and the font size. The **Font** methods used to get font information are summarized in Fig. 9.12. The *getStyle* method returns an integer value representing the current style. The integer value returned is either **Font.PLAIN**, **Font.ITALIC**, **Font.BOLD** or any combination of **Font.PLAIN**, **Font.ITALIC** and **Font.BOLD**.

Fig. 9.11 Setting fonts with **Font** objects and the **Graphics setFont** method (part 2 of 2).

Font methods for retrieving font information

public int getStyle()   // Font class
    Returns an integer value indicating the current font style.

public int getSize()   // Font class
    Returns an integer value indicating the current font size.

public String getName()   // Font class
    Returns the current font name as a string.

public String getFamily() // Font class
    Returns the font's family name as a string.

Fig. 9.12 Font methods for retrieving font information.

Method *getSize* returns the font size in points. Method *getName* returns the current font name as a **String**. Method *getFamily* returns the name of the font family to which the current font belongs. The name of the font family is platform specific.

 Portability Tip 9.3

Java uses standardized font names and maps these into system-specific font names for portability. This is transparent to the programmer.

The program of Fig. 9.13 creates a **Font** object **f** that is 24-point **Courier** bold italic. The current font is changed to **f** with the **setFont** method. The statement

        style = f.getStyle();

uses **getStyle** to determine the current font style. The integer returned is compared with the **Font** constants to display a **String** with the font's style. The statement

        size = f.getSize();

determines the current font size. The font name (**Courier**) is determined with a call to method **getName**. The font family (**Courier**) is displayed with the statement

```
            g.drawString( "Font family is " + f.getFamily(), 20, 60 );
```

Method **drawString** displays the text at location (20, 60). Note again that the **get-Style, getName, getSize**, and **getFamily** methods belong to the **Font** class.

```
1    // Fig. 9.13: DemoFont2.java
2    // Demonstrating the Font methods for
3    // retrieving font information
4    import java.applet.Applet;
5    import java.awt.Graphics;
6    import java.awt.Font;
7
8    public class DemoFont2 extends Applet {
9       private Font f;
10
11      public void init()
12      {
13         // create a font object: 24-point bold italic courier
14         f = new Font( "Courier", Font.ITALIC + Font.BOLD, 24 );
15      }
16
17      public void paint( Graphics g )
18      {
19         int style, size;
20         String s, name;
21
22         g.setFont( f );          // set the current font to f
23         style = f.getStyle();    // determine current font style
24
25         if ( style == Font.PLAIN )
26            s = "Plain ";
27         else if ( style == Font.BOLD )
28            s = "Bold ";
29         else if ( style == Font.ITALIC )
30            s = "Italic ";
31         else    // bold + italic
32            s = "Bold italic ";
33
34         size = f.getSize();      // determine current font size
35         s += size + " point ";
36         name = f.getName();      // determine current font name
37         s += name;
38         g.drawString( s, 20, 40 );
39
40         // display font family
41         g.drawString( "Font family is " + f.getFamily(), 20, 60 );
42      }
43   }
```

Fig. 9.13 Demonstrating **getName, getStyle, getSize**, and **getFamily** (part 1 of 2).

Fig. 9.13 Demonstrating **getName**, **getStyle**, **getSize**, and **getFamily** (part 2 of 2).

Font methods are also available for testing the style of the current font and are summarized in Fig. 9.14. The *isPlain* method returns **true** if the current font style is plain. The *isBold* method returns **true** if the current font style is bold. The *isItalic* method returns **true** if the current font style is italic.

The program of Fig. 9.15 demonstrates the use of the **isPlain**, **isBold**, and **isItalic** methods. The **Font** object **f** is created with the statement

```
f = new Font( "Courier", Font.ITALIC + Font.BOLD, 24 );
```

and is set as the current font with the **setFont** method. The **isBold**, **isItalic**, and **isPlain** methods are used in an **if/else** to test the font style of **f**. A **String** is drawn on the applet describing the font style.

Sometimes precise information about a font's metrics must be known—such as *height*, *descent* (the amount a character dips below the baseline), *ascent* (the amount a character rises above the baseline), *leading* (the difference between the height and the ascent), etc. Fig. 9.16 illustrates some of the common *font metrics*. Note that the coordinate passed to **drawString** corresponds to the lower-left corner.

Font methods for testing font styles

```
public boolean isPlain()      // Font class
```
   Tests a font for a plain font style. Returns **true** if the font is plain.

```
public boolean isBold()       // Font class
```
   Tests a font for a bold font style. Returns **true** if the font is bold.

```
public boolean isItalic()     // Font class
```
   Tests a font for an italic font style. Returns **true** if the font is italic.

Fig. 9.14 **Font** methods for testing font styles.

```
1   // Fig. 9.15: DemoFont3.java
2   // Demonstrating isPlain, isBold and isItalic
3   import java.applet.Applet;
4   import java.awt.Graphics;
5   import java.awt.Font;
6
7   public class DemoFont3 extends Applet {
8      private Font f;
9
10     public void init()
11     {
12        // create a font object: 24-point bold italic courier
13        f = new Font( "Courier", Font.ITALIC + Font.BOLD, 24 );
14     }
15
16     public void paint( Graphics g )
17     {
18        String s;
19
20        g.setFont( f );              // set the current font to f
21
22        if ( f.isPlain() == true )
23           s = "Font is plain.";
24        else if ( f.isBold() == true && f.isItalic() == false )
25           s = "Font is bold.";
26        else if ( f.isItalic() == true && f.isBold() == false )
27           s = "Font is italic.";
28        else    // bold + italic
29           s = "Font is bold italic.";
30
31        g.drawString( s, 20, 40 );
32     }
33  }
```

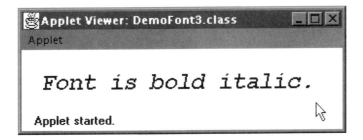

Fig. 9.15 Demonstrating `isPlain`, `isBold`, and `isItalic`.

Some methods for obtaining font metrics are defined in the ***FontMetrics*** class—which inherits from the **Object** class. The **FontMetrics** methods as well as other useful methods from the **Graphics** class and the **Toolkit** class are summarized in Fig. 9.17.

Fig. 9.16 Font metrics.

Methods useful for obtaining font metrics

`public abstract Font getFont()`   `// Graphics class`
    Returns a Font object representing the current font.

`public abstract String[] getFontList()`   `// Toolkit class`
    Creates a list of the available fonts for a system.

`public int getAscent()`   `// FontMetrics class`
    Returns a value representing the ascent of a font in points.

`public int getDescent()`   `// FontMetrics class`
    Returns a value representing the descent of a font in points.

`public int getLeading()`   `// FontMetrics class`
    Returns a value representing the leading of a font in points.

`public int getHeight()`   `// FontMetrics class`
    Returns a value representing the height of a font in points.

`public FontMetrics getFontMetrics()`   `// Graphics class`
    Returns the current font metrics. Used with **getAscent**, **getDescent**, **getLeading**, and **getHeight**.

Fig. 9.17 Methods from class **Graphics**, class **Toolkit** and class **FontMetrics** useful for obtaining font metrics.

The program of Fig. 9.18 uses the methods of Fig. 9.17 to obtain font metric information. The program creates two fonts—one that is **Courier** bold 14-point and one that is **TimesRoman** 10-point. The object **font1** is set as the current font. The statement

```
showStatus( g.getFont().toString() );
```

uses the **toString** method to convert the **Font** object returned by **getFont** to a **String**. The converted **String** is then displayed in the status bar. The ascent, height, leading and descent for **font1** are determined with the four lines

```
int ascent = g.getFontMetrics().getAscent();
int descent = g.getFontMetrics().getDescent();
```

```
1   // Fig. 9.18: Metrics.java
2   // Demonstrating methods of the FontMetrics class, Graphics
3   // class and Toolkit class useful for obtaining font metrics
4   import java.applet.Applet;
5   import java.awt.Graphics;
6   import java.awt.Font;
7   import java.awt.Toolkit;
8
9   public class Metrics extends Applet {
10     private Font font1, font2;
11
12     public void init()
13     {
14        font1 = new Font( "Courier", Font.BOLD, 14 );
15        font2 = new Font( "TimesRoman", Font.PLAIN, 10 );
16     }
17
18     public void paint( Graphics g )
19     {
20        g.setFont( font1 );    // set the current font
21
22        // display the current font in the status bar
23        showStatus( g.getFont().toString() );
24
25        // get information about the current font font1
26        int ascent = g.getFontMetrics().getAscent();
27        int descent = g.getFontMetrics().getDescent();
28        int height = g.getFontMetrics().getHeight();
29        int leading = g.getFontMetrics().getLeading();
30
31        String s1 = "Ascent of Font font1 is    " +
32                    String.valueOf( ascent );
33
34        String s2 = "Descent of Font font1 is   " +
35                    String.valueOf( descent );
36
37        String s3 = "Height of Font font1 is    " +
38                    String.valueOf( height );
39
40        String s4 = "Leading of Font font1 is   " +
41                    String.valueOf( leading );
42
43        g.drawString( s1, 10, 10 );
44        g.drawString( s2, 10, 20 );
45        g.drawString( s3, 10, 30 );
46        g.drawString( s4, 10, 40 );
47
48        // get information about the font font2
49        ascent = g.getFontMetrics( font2 ).getAscent();
50        descent = g.getFontMetrics( font2 ).getDescent();
```

Fig. 9.18 Program that demonstrates obtaining font metric information and obtaining a list of the system's available fonts (part 1 of 3).

```
51      height = g.getFontMetrics( font2 ).getHeight();
52      leading = g.getFontMetrics( font2 ).getLeading();
53
54      s1 = "Ascent of Font font2 is    " +
55          String.valueOf( ascent );
56
57      s2 = "Descent of Font font2 is    " +
58          String.valueOf( descent );
59
60      s3 = "Height of Font font2 is    " +
61          String.valueOf( height );
62
63      s4 = "Leading of Font font2 is    " +
64          String.valueOf( leading );
65
66      g.drawString( s1, 10, 60 );
67      g.drawString( s2, 10, 70 );
68      g.drawString( s3, 10, 80 );
69      g.drawString( s4, 10, 90 );
70
71      g.drawString( "    Font list:", 10, 110 );
72
73      // get the list of fonts
74      String fonts[] =
75          Toolkit.getDefaultToolkit().getFontList();
76
77      for ( int i = 0; i < fonts.length; i++ )
78          g.drawString( fonts[ i ], 10, i * 10 + 120 );
79   }
80  }
```

Fig. 9.18 Program that demonstrates obtaining font metric information and obtaining a list of the system's available fonts (part 2 of 3).

```
int height = g.getFontMetrics().getHeight();
int leading = g.getFontMetrics().getLeading();
```

The font metric information from the above lines is drawn on the applet. The ascent, height, leading, and descent information for **font2** is gathered in a similar manner and drawn on the applet. The statement

```
String fonts[] = Toolkit.getDefaultToolkit().getFontList();
```

gets the fonts on the system from the toolkit and stores them in an array. The *toolkit* interacts between Java and the system to get information about the system. The ***getDefault-Toolkit*** method is a **static** method of the ***Toolkit*** class (**Toolkit** inherits from the **Object** class). The **getDefaultToolkit** method gets the default toolkit for the current system (i.e., returns a **Toolkit** object). The ***getFontList*** method of class **Toolkit** returns the names of the system's available fonts as an array of **String**s. A **for** loop is used to display the available fonts for the system.

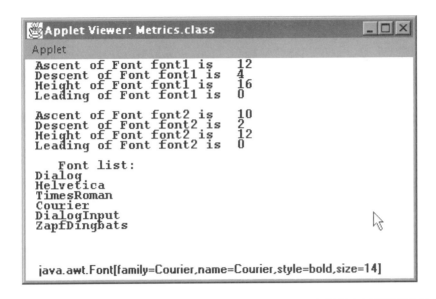

Fig. 9.18 Program that demonstrates obtaining font metric information and obtaining a list of the system's available fonts (part 3 of 3).

9.6 Drawing Lines

This section presents the **Graphics** method *drawLine* for drawing lines. The **drawLine** method's parameters are summarized in Fig. 9.19. The **drawLine** method takes four integer arguments. The first two arguments specify the coordinates of one point and the last two arguments specify the coordinates of a second point. The line is drawn between the two points in the current color.

The program of Fig. 9.20 uses the **drawLine** method to draw a line on the applet. The line is drawn between the points (10, 10) and (230, 95).

Graphics method drawLine

```
public abstract void drawLine(    // Graphics class
    int x1,     // x coordinate first point
    int y1,     // y coordinate first point
    int x2,     // x coordinate second point
    int y2 )    // y coordinate second point
```
Draws a line between the point (**x1, y1**) and the point (**x2, y2**) in the current color.

Fig. 9.19 Graphics method **drawLine**.

```
1   // Fig. 9.20: Line.java
2   // Demonstrating drawLine
3   import java.applet.Applet;
4   import java.awt.Graphics;
5
6   public class Line extends Applet {
7
8       public void paint( Graphics g )
9       {
10          // draw a line from (10, 10) to (230, 95)
11          g.drawLine( 10, 10, 230, 95 );
12      }
13  }
```

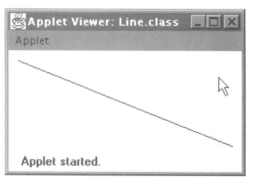

Fig. 9.20 Demonstrating `Graphics` method `drawLine`.

9.7 Drawing Rectangles

This section presents the **Graphics** methods for drawing rectangles. The methods are summarized in Fig. 9.21.

The **drawRect** method draws a rectangle. The first two arguments specify the coordinates of the upper-left corner of the rectangle. The third and fourth arguments specify the **width** and **height** of the rectangle.

The **fillRect** method draws a filled rectangle. The current color is used to fill the rectangle. The **fillRect** method takes four arguments: an **x** coordinate, a **y** coordinate, a **width** and a **height**. The point (**x, y**) specifies the upper-left corner of the filled rectangle.

The **clearRect** method draws a rectangle in the current *background color* over the specified rectangle. The method takes the upper-left coordinates, the **width** and **height** of the rectangle to erase.

The program of Fig. 9.22 draws a rectangle and a filled rectangle using the **drawRect** and **fillRect** methods. The **drawRect** method is used to draw a rectangle at the coordinates (10, 15). The rectangle has a width of 100 pixels and a height of 100 pixels. The **fillRect** method is used to draw a filled rectangle at the coordinates (150, 15). The filled rectangle has a width of 100 pixels and a height of 100 pixels.

Graphics methods for drawing rectangles

```
public void drawRect(          // Graphics class
   int x,           // top-left x coordinate
   int y,           // top-left y coordinate
   int width,       // width
   int height )     // height
```
Draws a rectangle of the specified **width** and **height**. The top-left corner of the rectangle has the coordinates (**x**, **y**). The rectangle is drawn in the current color.

```
public abstract void fillRect(     // Graphics class
   int x,           // top-left x coordinate
   int y,           // top-left y coordinate
   int width,       // width
   int height )     // height
```
Draws a solid rectangle in the current color with the specified **width** and **height**. The top-left corner of the rectangle has the coordinate (**x**, **y**).

```
public abstract void clearRect(  // Graphics class
   int x,           // top-left x coordinate
   int y,           // top-left y coordinate
   int width,       // width
   int height )     // height
```
Draws a rectangle in the current background color.

Fig. 9.21 Graphics methods for drawing rectangles.

```
1    // Fig. 9.22: Rectangle.java
2    // Demonstrating drawRect and fillRect
3    import java.applet.Applet;
4    import java.awt.Graphics;
5
6    public class Rectangle extends Applet {
7
8       public void paint( Graphics g )
9       {
10         // draw a rectangle at location ( 10, 15 )
11         g.drawRect( 10, 15, 100, 100 );
12
13         // draw a filled rectangle at location ( 150, 15 )
14         g.fillRect( 150, 15, 100, 100 );
15      }
16   }
```

Fig. 9.22 Drawing rectangles with **Graphics** methods **drawRect** and **fillRect** (part 1 of 2).

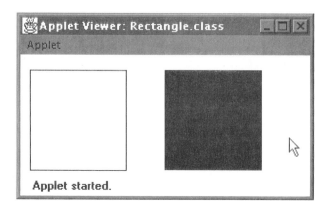

Fig. 9.22 Drawing rectangles with **Graphics** methods **drawRect** and **fillRect** (part 2 of 2).

9.8 Drawing Rounded Rectangles

This section presents the **Graphics** methods for drawing rectangles with rounded corners. The methods and their parameters are summarized in Fig. 9.23.

Graphics methods for drawing rounded rectangles

```
public abstract void drawRoundRect(       // Graphics class
    int x,              // x coordinate
    int y,              // y coordinate
    int width,          // width
    int height,         // height
    int arcWidth,       // arc width
    int arcHeight )     // arc height
```
Draws a rectangle with rounded corners in the current color with the specified **width** and **height**.

```
public abstract void fillRoundRect(       // Graphics class
    int x,              // x coordinate
    int y,              // y coordinate
    int width,          // width
    int height,         // height
    int arcWidth,       // arc width
    int arcHeight )     // arc height
```
Draws a solid rectangle with rounded corners in the current color with the specified **width** and **height**.

Fig. 9.23 Graphics methods for drawing rounded rectangles.

The ***drawRoundRect*** method draws a rectangle with rounded corners. The first two arguments specify the coordinates of the upper-left corner of the *bounding rectangle*—the area in which the rounded rectangle will be drawn. Note that the upper-left corner coordinates are not the edge of the rounded rectangle, but the coordinates of where the edge would be if the rectangle were not rounded. The next two arguments specify the **width** and **height**. The last two arguments specify how round the rectangle corners are. The **arcWidth** argument specifies the horizontal component and the **arcHeight** argument specifies the vertical component. Using the same value for **arcWidth** and **arcHeight** produces a quarter circle at the corner.

Figure 9.24 labels the arc width, arc height, width, and height. Note that a circle is produced when **width**, **height**, **arcWidth** and **arcHeight** have the same values. If the values for **width** and **height** are the same and the values of **arcWidth** and **arcHeight** are 0, a square is produced.

The ***fillRoundRect*** method draws a filled rectangle with rounded corners. The current color is used to fill the rectangle. The **fillRoundRect** method takes the same six arguments as the **drawRoundRect** method: an **x** coordinate, a **y** coordinate, a **width**, a **height**, an arc width and an arc height. The point (**x**, **y**) specifies the upper-left corner of the bounding rectangle.

The program of Fig. 9.25 draws three rounded rectangles and two filled rounded rectangles using the **drawRoundRect** and **fillRoundRect** methods. The first rounded rectangle is drawn at (10, 35) with a width of 50 and a height of 50. The arc width and arc height are 10 and 20, respectively. The second rounded rectangle is drawn at (80, 15) and is filled. The width and height of the filled rounded rectangle are 60 and 80, respectively. The third rounded rectangle forms an ellipse. The ellipse is drawn at (150, 55) and has a height of 80 and a width of 20. The arc width and arc height are both 70. The fourth rounded rectangle forms a filled square. The square is drawn at (240, 15) and has a width of 80 and a height of 80. The arc width and arc height are both 0. The last rounded rectangle drawn forms a circle. The circle is drawn at (330, 15) and has a width, height, arc width, and arc height of 80.

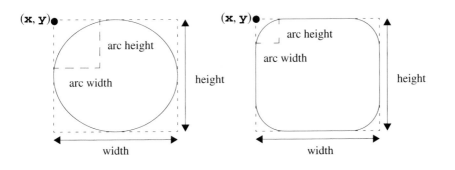

Fig. 9.24 Rounded rectangles.

```
1   // Fig. 9.25: Rectangle2.java
2   // Drawing rounded rectangles
3   import java.applet.Applet;
4   import java.awt.Graphics;
5
6   public class Rectangle2 extends Applet {
7
8      public void paint( Graphics g )
9      {
10        // draw a rounded rectangle at (10, 35)
11        g.drawRoundRect( 10, 35, 50, 50, 10, 20 );
12
13        // draw a filled rounded rectangle at (80, 15)
14        g.fillRoundRect( 80, 15, 60, 80, 50, 10 );
15
16        // draw a rounded rectangle at (150, 55)
17        g.drawRoundRect( 150, 55, 80, 20, 70, 70 );
18
19        // draw a filled square at (240, 15)
20        g.fillRoundRect( 240, 15, 80, 80, 0, 0 );
21
22        // draw a circle at (330, 15)
23        g.drawRoundRect( 330, 15, 80, 80, 80, 80 );
24     }
25  }
```

Fig. 9.25 Demonstrating **drawRoundRect** and **fillRoundRect**.

9.9 Drawing 3-Dimensional Rectangles

This section presents the **Graphics** methods for drawing three-dimensional rectangles. The methods are summarized in Fig. 9.26. Both **draw3DRect** and **fill3DRect** take the same arguments. The first two arguments specify the top-left corner coordinates of the rectangle. The next two arguments specify the **width** and **height** of the rectangle, respectively. The last argument determines whether or not the rectangle is raised or lowered. A **true** value specifies that the rectangle is to be raised and a **false** value specifies that the rectangle is to be lowered. Three-dimensional rectangles are drawn in the current color. The three-dimensional effect is difficult to see in certain colors.

Graphics methods for drawing 3-D rectangles

```
public void draw3DRect(       // Graphics class
   int x,          // x coordinate top-left corner
   int y,          // y coordinate top-left corner
   int width,      // width of rectangle
   int height,     // height of rectangle
   Boolean b )     // raised when true
```
Draws a three-dimensional rectangle in the current color with the specified **width** and **height**. The top-left corner of the rectangle has the coordinates (**x**, **y**). The rectangle is raised when **b** is **true** and is lowered when **b** is **false**.

```
public void fill3DRect(       // Graphics class
   int x,          // x coordinate top-left corner
   int y,          // y coordinate top-left corner
   int width,      // width of rectangle
   int height,     // height of rectangle
   Boolean b )     // raised when true
```
Draws a filled three-dimensional rectangle in the current color with the specified **width** and **height**. The top-left corner of the rectangle has the coordinates (**x**, **y**). The rectangle is raised when **b** is **true** and is lowered when **b** is **false**.

Fig. 9.26 **Graphics** methods for drawing 3-D rectangles.

The program of Fig. 9.27 demonstrates the **draw3DRect** and **fill3DRect** methods. The three-dimensional rectangles are drawn in yellow to enhance the three dimensional effect. Both raised and lowered rectangles are demonstrated.

```
1  // Fig. 9.27: Draw3D.java
2  // Drawing 3-D rectangles
3  import java.applet.Applet;
4  import java.awt.Graphics;
5  import java.awt.Color;
6
7  public class Draw3D extends Applet {
8
9     public void paint( Graphics g )
10    {
11       g.setColor( Color.yellow );
12
13       // draw a raised 3D rectangle at location (10, 10)
14       g.draw3DRect( 10, 10, 100, 100, true );
15
16       // draw a sunk 3D at location (130, 10)
17       g.draw3DRect( 130, 10, 100, 100, false );
18
```

Fig. 9.27 Demonstrating **draw3DRect** and **fill3DRect** (part 1 of 2).

```
19        // draw a filled raised 3D rectangle at (10, 120)
20        g.fill3DRect( 10, 120, 100, 100, true );
21
22        // draw a filled sunk 3D rectangle at (130, 120)
23        g.fill3DRect( 130, 120, 100, 100, false );
24    }
25  }
```

Fig. 9.27 Demonstrating **draw3DRect** and **fill3DRect** (part 2 of 2).

9.10 Drawing Ovals

This section presents the **Graphics** methods for drawing ovals. The methods are summarized in Fig. 9.28.

Both the **drawOval** and **fillOval** methods take the same two arguments. The first two arguments specify the top-left coordinate of the bounding rectangle that contains the oval. The last two arguments specify the **width** and **height**, respectively. Figure 9.29 shows an oval bounded by a rectangle.

The program of Fig. 9.30 demonstrates the **drawOval** and **fillOval** methods. The program draws two ovals on the applet—one of which is filled.

9.11 Drawing Arcs

This section presents **Graphics** methods for drawing arcs. An *arc* is a portion of a circle. Arc angles are measured in degrees. An arc is drawn between two angles—a *starting angle* and an *arc angle*. The starting angle is the degree where the arc begins. The arc angle is the last degree of the arc. Arcs *sweep* between their starting angle and their arc angle.

Graphics methods for drawing ovals

```
public abstract void drawOval(        // Graphics class
    int x,          // x coordinate
    int y,          // y coordinate
    int width,      // width
    int height ) // height
```
Draws an oval in the current color with the specified width and height. The bounding rectangle's top-left corner is at the coordinates (**x, y**).

```
public abstract void fillOval(        // Graphics class
    int x,          // x coordinate
    int y,          // y coordinate
    int width,      // width
    int height ) // height
```
Draws a filled oval in the current color with the specified width and height. The bounding rectangle's top-left corner is at the coordinates (**x, y**).

Fig. 9.28 Graphics methods for drawing ovals.

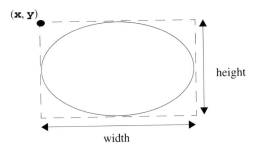

Fig. 9.29 An oval bounded by a rectangle.

```
1   // Fig. 9.30: DrawOval.java
2   // Drawing ovals
3   import java.applet.Applet;
4   import java.awt.Graphics;
5
6   public class DrawOval extends Applet {
7      public void paint( Graphics g )
8      {
9         // draw an oval at location (10, 15)
10        g.drawOval( 10, 15, 100, 70 );
11
12        // draw an oval at location (160, 15)
13        g.fillOval( 160, 15, 70, 130 );
14     }
15  }
```

Fig. 9.30 Demonstrating **drawOval** and **fillOval** (part 1 of 2).

Fig. 9.30 Demonstrating **drawOval** and **fillOval** (part 2 of 2).

Fig. 9.31 illustrates two arcs. The left set of axes shows an arc sweeping from zero degrees to approximately 110 degrees. Arcs that sweep in a counter-clockwise direction are measured in *positive degrees*. The right set of axes shows an arc sweeping from zero degrees to approximately -110 degrees. Arcs that sweep in a clockwise direction are measured in *negative degrees*. The **Graphics** methods for drawing arcs are summarized in Fig. 9.32.

Both the **drawArc** and **fillArc** methods take six arguments. The first two arguments specify the top-left corner coordinates for the bounding rectangle that encloses the arc. The third and fourth arguments specify the arc width and arc height. The fifth argument specifies the starting angle. The last argument specifies the arc angle. The arc is drawn in the current color. Figure 9.33 shows an arc bounded by a rectangle. The arc angle starts at approximately 20° and sweeps to approximately −110°.

The program of Fig. 9.34 demonstrates the arc methods of Fig. 9.32. Five different arcs are drawn, three of which are filled.

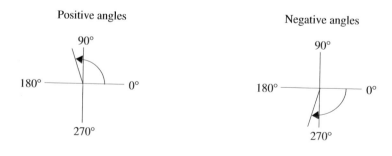

Fig. 9.31 Positive and negative arc angles.

Graphics methods for drawing arcs

```
public abstract void drawArc(         // Graphics class
    int x,           // x coordinate
    int y,           // y coordinate
    int width,       // arc width
    int height,      // arc height
    int startAngle,  // beginning angle
    int arcAngle )   // arc angle
```
Draws an arc in the current color relative to the bounding rectangle's top-left coordinates (**x**, **y**) with the specified **width** and **height**. The arc segment is drawn from the starting angle to the arc angle.

```
public abstract void fillArc(         // Graphics class
    int x,           // x coordinate
    int y,           // y coordinate
    int width,       // arc width
    int height,      // arc height
    int startAngle,  // beginning angle
    int arcAngle )   // arc angle
```
Draws a solid arc in the current color relative to the bounding rectangle's top-left coordinates (**x**, **y**) with the specified width and height. The arc segment is drawn from the starting angle to the arc angle.

Fig. 9.32 Graphics methods for drawing arcs.

Fig. 9.33 An arc bounded by a rectangle.

9.12 Drawing Polygons

Polygons are multisided shapes. Polygons are drawn with the **Graphics** methods described in Fig. 9.35. Note that some methods require a **Polygon** object—which is created with the **Polygon** class. The **Polygon** class constructors are also described in Fig. 9.35.

The first **drawPolygon** method of Fig. 9.35 takes three arguments: an array of integers containing *x* coordinates, an array of integers containing *y* coordinates, and the number of points in the polygon. Specifying a last point different than the first point results in an *open polygon*—the last point is not connected to the first point.

```
1   // Fig. 9.34: DrawArcs.java
2   // Drawing arcs
3   import java.applet.Applet;
4   import java.awt.Graphics;
5
6   public class DrawArcs extends Applet {
7
8       public void paint( Graphics g )
9       {
10          // draw an arc
11          g.drawArc( 15, 15, 80, 80, 0, 180 );
12
13          // draw an arc
14          g.drawArc( 100, 100, 80, 80, 0, 110 );
15
16          // draw a solid arc
17          g.fillArc( 100, 15, 70, 80, 0, 270 );
18
19          // draw a solid arc
20          g.fillArc( 15, 70, 70, 80, 0, -110 );
21
22          // draw a solid arc
23          g.fillArc( 190, 15, 80, 140, 0, -360 );
24      }
25  }
```

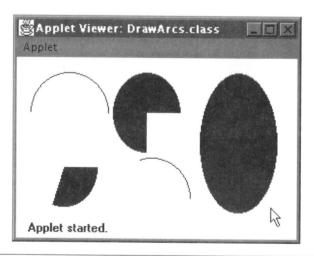

Fig. 9.34 Demonstrating **drawArc** and **fillArc**.

The second **drawPolygon** method of Fig. 9.35 requires a **Polygon** object as an argument. The **Polygon** class inherits from class **Object**.

Solid polygons or *filled polygons* are drawn with the ***fillPolygon*** method. The first **fillPolygon** method of Fig. 9.35 takes three arguments: an array of integers containing *x* coordinates, an array of integers containing *y* coordinates, and the number of points in the polygon. The current color is used to fill the polygon.

Graphics methods for drawing polygons and the `Polygon` constructors

```
public abstract void drawPolygon(     // Graphics class
   int xPoints[],    // x coordinates
   int yPoints[],    // y coordinates
   int points )      // number of points
```
Draws a polygon of **points** points in the current color. The x-coordinate of each point is specified in the **xPoints** array and the y-coordinate of each point is specified in the **yPoints** array.

```
public void drawPolygon( Polygon p ) // Graphics class
```
Draws a polygon in the current color.

```
public abstract void fillPolygon(     // Graphics class
   int xPoints[],    // x coordinates
   int yPoints[],    // y coordinates
   int points )      // number of points
```
Draws a solid polygon of **points** in the current color. The x-coordinate of each point is specified in the **xPoints** array and the y-coordinate of each point is specified in the **yPoints** array.

```
public void fillPolygon( Polygon p ) // Graphics class
```
Draws a filled polygon in the current color.

```
public Polygon()          // Polygon class
```
Constructs a new polygon object. The polygon does not contain any points.

```
public Polygon(          // Polygon class
   int xValues[],        // x coordinates
   int yValues[],        // y coordinates
   int numberOfPoints )  // number of points
```
Constructs a new polygon object. The polygon has **numberOfPoints** sides with each point consisting of an x-coordinate from **xValues** and a y-coordinate from **yValues**.

Fig. 9.35 `Graphics` methods for drawing polygons and the `Polygon` constructors.

The second **fillPolygon** method of Fig. 9.35 requires a **Polygon** object. Filled polygons are always *closed polygons*—the last point does not have to match the first (i. e., the last point is automatically connected to the first point).

Common Programming Error 9.3

*It is a logic error if the number of points specified in the third argument to method **draw-Polygon** or method **fillPolygon** is less than the number of elements in the arrays of coordinates that define the polygon to display.*

Common Programming Error 9.4

*An **ArrayIndexOutOfBoundsException** is thrown if the number of points specified in the third argument to method **drawPolygon** or method **fillPolygon** is greater than the number of elements in the arrays of coordinates that define the polygon to display.*

The program of Fig. 9.36 draws four polygons, two of which are filled. Each of the four methods and each of the constructors of Fig. 9.35 is used.

```java
// Fig. 9.36: DrawPoly.java
// Drawing polygons
import java.applet.Applet;
import java.awt.Graphics;
import java.awt.Polygon;

public class DrawPoly extends Applet {
   // coordinates for first polygon
   private int xValues[] = { 20, 40, 50, 30, 20, 15, 20 };
   private int yValues[] = { 20, 20, 30, 50, 50, 30, 20 };

   // coordinates for second polygon
   private int xValues2[] = { 70, 90, 100, 80, 70, 65,
                              60, 70 };

   private int yValues2[] = { 70, 70, 80, 100, 100, 80,
                              60, 70 };

   // coordinates for third polygon
   private int xValues3[] = { 120, 140, 150, 190 };
   private int yValues3[] = { 10, 40, 50, 30 };

   // create references to polygons
   private Polygon p4, p5, p6;

   public void init()
   {
      // instantiate polygon objects
      p4 = new Polygon( xValues, yValues, 7 );
      p5 = new Polygon();
      p6 = new Polygon();

      // add points to p5
      p5.addPoint( 165, 105 );
      p5.addPoint( 175, 120 );
      p5.addPoint( 270, 170 );
      p5.addPoint( 200, 190 );
      p5.addPoint( 130, 150 );
      p5.addPoint( 165, 105 );

      // add points to p6
      p6.addPoint( 240, 50 );
      p6.addPoint( 260, 70 );
      p6.addPoint( 250, 90 );
   }
```

Fig. 9.36 Demonstrating **drawPolygon** and **fillPolygon** (part 1 of 2).

```
46
47        public void paint( Graphics g )
48        {
49            // draw a polygon of 8 points
50            g.drawPolygon( xValues2, yValues2, 8 );
51
52            // draw a polygon object
53            g.drawPolygon( p4 );
54
55            // draw a filled polygon object
56            g.fillPolygon( p5 );
57
58            // draw a filled polygon object
59            g.fillPolygon( p6 );
60
61            // draw a filled polygon of 4 points
62            g.fillPolygon( xValues3, yValues3, 4 );
63        }
64    }
```

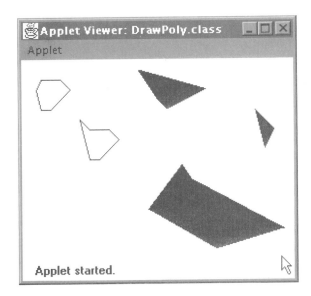

Fig. 9.36 Demonstrating **drawPolygon** and **fillPolygon** (part 2 of 2).

Six integer arrays are declared and initialized. The arrays **xValues**, **xValues2**, and **xValues3** represent the *x* coordinates for three of the polygons. The *y* coordinates are represented with the arrays **yValues**, **yValues2**, and **yValues3**.

The **Polygon** class is used to create three objects. The line

        private Polygon p4, p5, p6;

creates **Polygon** references **p4**, **p5**, and **p6**. The statements

```
p4 = new Polygon( xValues, yValues, 7 );
p5 = new Polygon();
p6 = new Polygon();
```

construct **Polygon** objects and assign them to the references **p4**, **p5** and **p6**. Points are added to **p5** and **p6** with the **Polygon** method **addPoint**. The **addPoint** method takes two arguments an *x* coordinate and a *y* coordinate. The statement

```
g.drawPolygon( xValues2, yValues2, 8 );
```

draws the first polygon. The second polygon is drawn with the statement

```
g.drawPolygon( p4 );
```

The third, fourth, and fifth polygons are drawn with the statements

```
g.fillPolygon( p5 );
g.fillPolygon( p6 );
g.fillPolygon( xValues3, yValues3, 4 );
```

9.13 Screen Manipulation

This section presents a **Graphics** method for screen manipulation—*copyArea*. The **copyArea** method copies a rectangular area of the screen places the copy in another location on the screen. The **copyArea** method is summarized in Fig. 9.37.

The **copyArea** method takes six arguments. The first two arguments specify the top-left corner of the area to copy. The third and fourth arguments specify the **width** and **height** of the area to copy. The fifth and six arguments specify the offset where the copy will be placed relative to the first two values.

The program of Fig. 9.38 uses the **copyArea** method to copy a rectangular area (100 by 100) to the point (140,10).

Graphics method copyArea

```
public abstract void copyArea(     // Graphics class
    int x,          // top-left x coordinate
    int y,          // top-left y coordinate
    int width,      // width of area to copy
    int height,     // height of area to copy
    int dx,         // horizontal distance
    int dy )        // vertical distance
```

Copies a screen area of the specified **width** and **height**. The coordinate (**x**, **y**) is the upper-left corner of the area to be copied. The values of **dx** and **dy** specify the horizontal and vertical offset from (**x**, **y**). The copy is placed relative to (**x**, **y**).

Fig. 9.37 Graphics method for copying an area of the screen.

```
1    // Fig. 9.38: DemoCopyArea.java
2    // Demonstrate copying one area of the screen to another
3    // area of the screen
4    import java.applet.Applet;
5    import java.awt.Graphics;
6
7    public class DemoCopyArea extends Applet {
8
9        // coordinates for first polygon
10       int xValues[] = { 20, 40, 50, 30, 20, 15, 20 };
11       int yValues[] = { 20, 20, 30, 50, 50, 30, 20 };
12
13       // coordinates for second polygon
14       int xValues2[] = { 70, 90, 100, 80, 70, 65, 60, 70 };
15       int yValues2[] = { 70, 70, 80, 100, 100, 80, 60, 70 };
16
17       public void paint( Graphics g )
18       {
19           // draw a polygon of 7 points
20           g.drawPolygon( xValues, yValues, 7 );
21
22           // draw a filled polygon of 8 points
23           g.fillPolygon( xValues2, yValues2, 8 );
24
25           // copy 100 x 100 area of applet to (140, 10)
26           g.copyArea( 0, 0, 100, 100, 140, 10 );
27       }
28   }
```

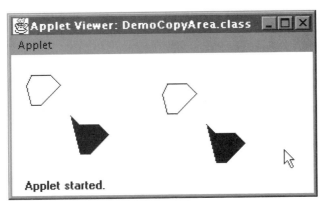

Fig. 9.38 Demonstrating **copyArea**.

The program draws two polygons. A rectangular area 100 by 100 starting at (0, 0) is copied to the location (140, 10) with the statement

```
g.copyArea( 0, 0, 100, 100, 140, 10 );
```

The horizontal offset of **140** is added to the *x* coordinate of **0** and the vertical offset of **10** is added to the *y* coordinate of **0**.

9.14 Paint Modes

A *paint mode* describes how graphics are drawn. The default paint mode is *overwrite paint mode*—shapes are drawn on top of each other. When a shape is drawn, the shape overwrites anything beneath it. The other paint mode is *XOR paint mode* which allows all shapes that overlap to be seen. XOR paint mode is set with the **Graphics** method *setXORMode*. The header for method **setXORMode** is

```
public abstract void setXORMode( Color c )
```

The **setXORMode** method takes a **Color** object as an argument. This color is referred to as the *XORMode color*. When overlapping objects are drawn in the same color, the overlapping part will be drawn in the XORMode color.

The program of Fig. 9.39 demonstrates both paint modes by drawing six shapes. Each shape overlaps with at least one other shape. A pink oval is the first shape drawn. A yellow rectangle is drawn next. The yellow rectangle is drawn in overpaint mode and covers part of the pink oval. The next shape drawn is an orange rectangle. The orange rectangle is drawn in overpaint mode and covers part of the yellow rectangle. The XOR mode is then set with the statement

```
g.setXORMode( Color.yellow );
```

The XORMode color is yellow. The next shape drawn is an oval in XOR mode. The current color is orange. Drawing an orange oval on the orange rectangle results in the XOR mode color being used. The oval is drawn in yellow. The portion of the oval that overlaps with the yellow rectangle is drawn in orange. A blue circle (a 360° arc) and a red square are also drawn on the yellow rectangle.

Summary

- The **java.awt** package contains the classes necessary to work with graphics.
- Class **Color** contains methods and constants for manipulating colors.
- Class **Font** contains methods and constants for manipulating fonts.
- Class **FontMetrics** contains methods for getting information about a font.
- Class **Polygon** contains methods for creating polygons.
- Class **Graphics** contains methods for drawing various shapes.
- The **Toolkit** class contains tools used by the AWT.
- A coordinate system describes every point on the screen. The upper-left corner of the screen has the coordinates (0, 0). Coordinates are composed an *x* coordinate (the horizontal distance from the upper-left corner) and a *y* coordinate (the vertical distance from the upper-left corner).
- The *x* axis describes every *x* coordinate and the *y* axis describes every *y* coordinate. Text and shapes are precisely drawn using coordinates. Units are measured in pixels. A pixel is a monitor's smallest unit of resolution.

```
1   // Fig. 9.39: PaintMode.java
2   // Demonstrating the XOR paint mode
3   import java.applet.Applet;
4   import java.awt.Graphics;
5   import java.awt.Color;
6
7   public class PaintMode extends Applet {
8
9       public void paint( Graphics g )
10      {
11          // draw pink oval
12          g.setColor( Color.pink );
13          g.fillOval( 20, 10, 100, 50 );
14
15          // draw a yellow rectangle over part of the oval
16          g.setColor( Color.yellow );
17          g.fillRect( 100, 10, 100, 50 );
18
19          // draw an orange rectangle
20          g.setColor( Color.orange );
21          g.fillRect( 190, 10, 80, 50 );
22
23          // set XOR mode to yellow
24          g.setXORMode( Color.yellow );
25          g.fillOval( 180, 25, 60, 20 );
26
27          // draw a blue arc
28          g.setColor( Color.blue );
29          g.fillArc( 150, 20, 20, 20, 0, 360 );
30
31          // draw a red square
32          g.setColor( Color.red );
33          g.fillRect( 120, 25, 20, 20 );
34      }
35  }
```

Fig. 9.39 Program that demonstrates the **setXORMode** method.

- A graphics context enables drawing. A **Graphics** object manages a graphics context by controlling how information is drawn. **Graphics** objects contain methods for drawing, font manipulation, color manipulation, etc.

- Class **Graphics** is an **abstract** class—**Graphics** objects cannot be instantiated.

- The **repaint** method calls the **Component** class **update** method which in turn calls **paint**. The **repaint** method is frequently called by the programmer to force a call to **paint**. The **update** method is sometimes overridden for "smoothing" animations (i.e., reducing "flicker").

- **Graphics** method **drawString** takes three arguments—the string to be drawn, an *x* coordinate and a *y* coordinate. The **String** is drawn in the current color and font. The point (**x**, **y**) corresponds to the lower-left corner of the **String**.

- **Graphics** method **drawChars** takes five arguments—an array of characters, the starting subscript in the array, the number of characters to be drawn and the coordinates at which the characters should be displayed. The point (**x**, **y**) corresponds to the lower-left corner of the characters drawn.

- **Graphics** method **drawBytes** takes five arguments. The arguments are the same as method **drawChars** except that a **byte** array is passed as the first argument.

- Color constants and color methods are defined in the **Color** class. Every color is created from an RGB value (Red/Green/Blue). An RGB value is created from three integer or three floating-point parts. Each RGB part is either an integer value between 0 and 255 or a floating point value between 0.0 and 1.0. The first RGB part defines the amount of red; the second RGB part defines the amount of green; and the third part defines the amount of blue. The larger the RGB value; the greater the amount of that particular color.

- The **Color** methods **getRed**, **getGreen**, **getBlue** return integer values between 0 and 255 representing the amount of red, green, and blue respectively. The **Graphics** method **getColor** returns a **Color** object representing the current color. The **Graphics** method **setColor** sets the current color.

- Most font methods and font constants are part of the **Font** class which inherits from the **Object** class. The **static** constants **PLAIN**, **BOLD**, and **ITALIC** are used to specify the font style and are defined in the **Font** class.

- The **Font** constructor takes three arguments—font name, font style and font size.

- The **Graphics** method **setFont** sets the current font.

- The **Font** method **getStyle** returns an integer value representing the current style. The integer value returned is either **Font.PLAIN**, **Font.ITALIC**, **Font.BOLD**, or any combination of **Font.PLAIN**, **Font.ITALIC**, and **Font.BOLD**.

- The **Font** method **getSize** returns the font size. The integer value returned represents the size of the font in points. The **Font** method **getName** returns the current font name as a **String**.

- The **Font** method **getFamily** returns the name of the font family to which the current font belongs. The name of the font family is platform specific.

- The **Font** method **isPlain** returns **true** if the current font style is plain. The **is-Bold** method returns **true** if the current font style is bold. The **isItalic** method returns **true** if the current font style is italic.

- Font metrics include height, descent (the amount a character dips below the baseline), ascent (the amount a character rises above the baseline) and leading (the difference between the height and the ascent).

- Methods for getting font metrics are defined in the **FontMetric** class.

- The toolkit interacts between Java and the system to get information about the system. The **getDefaultToolkit** method is a **static** method of the **Toolkit** class. The **getDefaultToolkit** method gets the default toolkit for the current system (i.e., returns a **Toolkit** object). The **Toolkit** method **getFontList** returns the names of the system's available fonts.

- The **Graphics** method **drawLine** draws a line between the two specified points in the current color.

- The **Graphics** method **drawRect** draws a rectangle with the specified upper-left corner, width and height.

- The **Graphics** method **fillRect** draws a filled rectangle with the specified upper-left corner, width and height. The current color is used to fill the rectangle.

- The **Graphics** method **clearRect** draws a rectangle in the current background color or over the specified rectangle.

- The **Graphics** method **drawRoundRect** draws a rectangle with rounded corners with the specified upper-left corner, width, height, arc width and arc height.

- The **Graphics** method **fillRoundRect** draws a filled rectangle with rounded corners with the specified upper-left corner, width, height, arc width and arc height. The current color is used to fill the rectangle.

- The **Graphics** method **draw3DRect** draws a three dimensional rectangle and the **fill3DRect** method draws a filled three dimensional rectangle. Both **draw3DRect** and **fill3DRect** take the same arguments. The last argument determines whether or not the rectangle is raised or lowered. A **true** value specifies that the rectangle is to be raised and a **false** value specifies that the rectangle is to be lowered.

- An arc is a portion of a circle. Arc angles in Java are measured in degrees. An arc is drawn between two angles—a starting angle and an arc angle. The starting angle is the degree where the arc begins. The arc angle is the last degree of the arc. The arc sweeps between the starting angle and the arc angle.

- Arcs that sweep in a counter-clockwise direction are measured in positive degrees. Arcs that sweep in a clockwise direction are measured in negative degrees.

- The **Graphics** method **drawArc** draws an arc and the **fillArc** method draws a filled arc. Both the **drawArc** and **fillArc** methods take six arguments—the top-left corner x and y coordinates, the arc width, the arc height, the starting angle and the arc angle.

- Polygons are multisided shapes. A **Polygon** object is created with the **Polygon** class. One version of the **Graphics** method **drawPolygon** takes three arguments: an array of integers containing *x* coordinates, an array of integers containing *y* coordinates, and the number of points in the polygon. Specifying a last point different than the first point results in an open polygon—the last point is not connected to the first point. The other version of the **drawPolygon** method takes one **Polygon** object.

- Solid polygons or filled polygons are drawn with the **Graphics** method **fillPolygon** method. Filled polygons are always closed polygons—the last point does not have to match the first (i. e., the last point is always connected to the first point).

- The **Polygon** method **addPoint** adds a point to a polygon and takes two arguments an *x* coordinate and a *y* coordinate.

- The **Graphics** method **copyArea** copies a rectangular area of the screen draws the copied area on another area of the screen.

- A paint mode describes how graphics are drawn. The default paint mode is overwrite paint mode—when a shape is drawn, the shape overwrites anything beneath it. The other paint mode is XOR paint mode—which allows all shapes that overlap to be seen. XOR paint mode is set with the **Graphics** method **setXORMode**. The **setXORMode** method takes a **Color** object as an argument.

Terminology

addPoint method	**Color** constructor
angle	**Color** object
arc bounded by a rectangle	**Component** class
arc height	coordinate
arc sweeping through an angle	coordinate system
arc width	**copyArea** method
ascent	**Courier** font
awt hierarchy	current color
awt package	current font
background color	degree
baseline	descent
bounding rectangle	**draw3DRect** method
clearRect method	**drawArc** method
closed polygon	**drawBytes** method
Color.black	**drawChars** method
Color.blue	drawing arc
Color.cyan	drawing bytes
Color.darkGray	drawing strings
Color.gray	**drawLine** method
Color.green	**drawOval** method
Color.lightGray	**drawRect** method
Color.magenta	**drawPolygon** method
Color.orange	**drawRoundRect** method
Color.pink	**drawString** method

`Color.red`

`Color.white`

`Color.yellow`

`Color` class

filled polygon

`fillOval` method

`fillPolygon` method

`fillRect` method

`fillRoundRect` method

`Font.BOLD`

`Font.ITALIC`

`Font.PLAIN`

font

`Font` class

`Font` constructor

font metrics

font name

font style

`FontMetrics` class

`getAscent` method

`getBlue` method

`getDescent` method

`getGreen` method

`getFamily` method

`getFont` method

`getFontList` method

`getFontMetrics` method

`getHeight` method

`getLeading` method

`getName` method

`getRed` method

`getSize` method

`getStyle` method

`Graphics` class

graphics context

graphics object

height

event

event-driven process

`fill3DRect` method

`fillArc` method

`Helvetica` font

horizontal component

`isBold` method

`isItalic` method

`isPlain` method

leading

negative degrees

open polygon

overwrite paint mode

`paint` method

paint mode

pixel

point

polygon

`Polygon` class

`Polygon` constructor

positive degrees

`repaint` method

RGB value

`setColor` method

`setFont` method

`setXORMode` method

solid polygons

`TimesRoman` font

toolkit

`Toolkit` class

`update` method

vertical component

x axis

x coordinate

XOR paint mode

y axis

y coordinate

Common Programming Errors

9.1 Passing an invalid array subscript to the **drawChars** or **drawBytes** method throws an **ArraySubscriptOutOfBoundsException**

9.2 Spelling any **static Color** class constant with an initial capital letter is a syntax error.

9.3   It is a logic error if the number of points specified in the third argument to method **draw-Polygon** or method **fillPolygon** is less than the number of elements in the arrays of coordinates that define the polygon to display.

9.4   An **ArrayIndexOutOfBoundsException** is thrown if the number of points specified in the third argument to method **drawPolygon** or method **fillPolygon** is greater than the number of elements in the arrays of coordinates that define the polygon to display.

Portability Tips

9.1   Different display monitors have different levels of resolution (i.e., the density of pixels vary).

9.2   The number of fonts varies greatly across systems. The JDK guarantees that the fonts **TimesRoman**, **Courier**, **Helvetica**, **Dialog** and **DialogInput** will be available.

9.3   Java uses standardized font names and maps these into system-specific font names for portability. This is transparent to the programmer.

Software Engineering Observation

9.1   If a font is not available on a system, Java will substitute that system's default font.

Self-Review Exercises

9.1   Fill in the blanks in each of the following:
   a) The return type of **getName** is _____.
   b) A rectangular area of the screen can be copied with the _____ method.
   c) The _____ method draws a line between two points.
   d) RGB is short for _____, _____, and _____.
   e) Font sizes are measured in units called _____.
   f) The _____ method draws a series of bytes.

9.2   State which of the following statements are true and which are false. If a statement is false, explain why.
   a) The first two arguments of **drawOval(x, y, 50, 100)** specify the center coordinate of the oval.
   b) In the Java coordinate system, *x* values increase from left to right.
   c) The **fillPolygon** method draws a solid polygon in the current color.
   d) The **drawArc** method allows negative angles.
   e) The **drawRoundRect** method can be used to draw a circle.
   f) The **getSize** method returns the size of the current font in centimeters.
   g) The pixel coordinate (0, 0) is located at the exact center of the monitor.

9.3   Find the error(s) in each of the following and explain how to correct the error(s). Assume **g** is a **Graphics** object.
   a) `char x[] = { '1', '2', '0', '2', '*', '*', 'P', 'C', 'M' };`
       `g.drawChars( x, 6, 8, 435, 80 );  // draw chars PCM`
   b) `g.setFont( "Helvetica" );`

```
c) g.erase( x, y, w, h );     // clear rectangle at (x, y)
d) Font fish = new Font( "Carp", Font.BOLDITALIC, 12 );
e) g.setColor( Color.Yellow );   // change color to yellow
```

Answers to Self-Review Exercises

9.1   a) `String` b) `copyArea` c) `drawLine` d) red, green, blue e) points f) `drawBytes`

9.2   a) False. The first two arguments specify the upper-left corner of the rectangle.
b) True.
c) True.
d) True.
e) True.
f) False. Font sizes are measured in points.
g) False. The coordinate (0,0) corresponds to the upper-left corner of the monitor.

9.3   a) The last valid subscript is exceeded. The `drawChars` method attempts to draw eight characters—from the sixth subscript. The **8** should be changed to a **3**.
b) The `setFont` method takes a **Font** object as an argument—not a **String**
c) The **Graphics** class does not have an **erase** method. The **clearRect** method should be used
d) **Carp** is not a valid font. A font such as **Courier**, **TimesRoman**, etc. should be used
e) **Yellow** should begin with a lowercase letter: `g.setColor( Color.yellow );`

Exercises

9.4   Fill in the blanks in each of the following:
a) The `getSize` method belongs to the _____ class.
b) The return type of `isBold` is _____.
c) The three constants that specify font style are _____, _____, and _____.
d) The _____ method returns an integer representing a color's RGB green value.

9.5   State which of the following statements are true and which are false. If a statement is false, explain why.
a) The `drawPolygon` method automatically connects the endpoints of the polygon.
b) The `drawLine` method draws a line between two points.
c) The `fillArc` method uses degrees to specify the angle.
d) In the Java coordinate system, *y* values increase from top to bottom.
e) The **Graphics** class inherits directly from class **Object**.
f) The **Graphics** class is an **abstract** class.
g) The **Font** class inherits directly from class **Graphics**.

9.6   Find the error(s) in each of the following. Explain how to correct the error(s).
a) `String listOfFonts[] = Toolkit.getFontList();`
b) `Toolkit.setXORMode( green );`
c) `String x = graphicsObject.getAscent();`
d) `Graphics myGraphics = new Graphics();`

9.7   Write a program that draws a series of eight concentric circles. The circles should be separated by 10 pixels. Use the `drawRoundRect` method.

9.8   Write a program that draws a series of eight concentric circles. The circles should be separated by 10 pixels. Use the **drawArc** method.

9.9   Write a program that uses the **drawArc** method to draw a spiral.

9.10   Write a program that uses the **fillArc** method to draw a spiral.

9.11   Write a program that draws lines of random lengths.

9.12   Write a program that draws lines in random colors.

9.13   Write a program that combines the capabilities of the programs you wrote for Exercise 9.11 and Exercise 9.12.

9.14   Write a program that gets a list of fonts from your system and draws a 12-point bold string in each font.

9.15   Write a program that displays five triangles of different sizes. Each triangle should be filled with a different color.

9.16   Write a program that randomly draws characters in different font sizes.

9.17   Write a program that randomly draws characters in different colors.

9.18   Write a program that draws an 8-by-8 grid. Use the **drawLine** method.

9.19   Write a program that draws an 10-by-10 grid. Use the **drawRect** method.

9.20   Write a program that draws a tetrahedron (a pyramid) on the applet.

9.21   Write a program that draws a cube on the applet.

9.22   Modify the program of Fig. 9.18 to display each font name in that font. The program should also print the metrics for each font.

9.23   In Exercise 1.21, you wrote an applet that input the radius of a circle from the user and displayed the circle's diameter, circumference and area. Modify your solution to Exercise 1.21 to read a set of coordinates in addition to the radius. Then, draw the circle and display the circle's diameter, circumference and area.

9.24   Write an applet that simulates a screen saver. The applet should randomly draw lines. After drawing 100 lines, the applet should clear itself and start drawing lines again.

9.25   Modify your solution to exercise 9.24 to enable the user to enter the number of random lines that should be drawn before the applet clears itself and starts drawing lines again. Use a text field to obtain the value. The user should be able to type a new number into the text field at any time during the program's execution.

9.26   Modify your solution to exercise 9.25 to randomly choose different shapes to display.

9.27   Write a graphical version of your solution to Exercise 4.38—the *Towers of Hanoi*. After studying Chapter 14, you will be able to implement a version of this exercise using Java's image, animation and audio capabilities.

9.28   Modify the die-rolling program of Fig. 5.11 so that it updates the counts for each side of the die after each roll. Use **Graphics** method **drawString** to output the totals.

9.29   Modify your solution to Exercise 5.21—*Turtle Graphics*—to add a graphical user interface using text fields and buttons. Also, draw lines rather than drawing asterisks (*****). When the turtle graphics program specifies a move, translate the number of positions into a number of pixels on the screen by multiplying the number of positions by 10 (or any value you wish).

9.30   Produce a graphical version of the Knight's Tour problem (Exercise 5.22, 5.23, 5.26). As each move is made, the appropriate cell of the chessboard should be updated with the proper move number. If the result of the program is a *full tour* or a *closed tour*, the program should display an appropriate message.

9.31   Produce a graphical version of the *Tortoise and the Hare* simulation (Exercise 5.41). Simulate the mountain by drawing an arc that extends from the bottom-left of the applet to the top-right of the applet. The tortoise and the hare should race up the mountain. Try to implement the graphical output so the tortoise and the hare are actually printed on the arc every move.

9.32   Produce a graphical version of the Maze Traversal problem (Exercises 5.38-5.40). Use the mazes you produced as guides for creating the graphical versions. While the maze is being solved, a small circle should be displayed in the maze indicating the current position.

9.33   Produce a graphical version of the Bucket Sort (Exercise 5.28) that shows each value being placed into the appropriate bucket and eventually being copied back to the original array.

10

Basic Graphical User Interface Components

Objectives

- To understand the design principles of graphical user interfaces.
- To understand the **java.awt** class hierarchy.
- To be able to build graphical user interfaces.
- To be able to create and manipulate labels, lists, text fields, text areas and panels.
- To understand and handle mouse events and keyboard events.
- To understand and be able to use layout managers.

All the better to see you with my dear.
The Big Bad Wolf to Little Red Riding Hood

...The user should feel in control of the computer, not the other way around. This is achieved in applications that embody three qualities: responsiveness, permissiveness, and consistency.
Inside Macintosh, Volume 1 Apple Computer, Inc. 1985

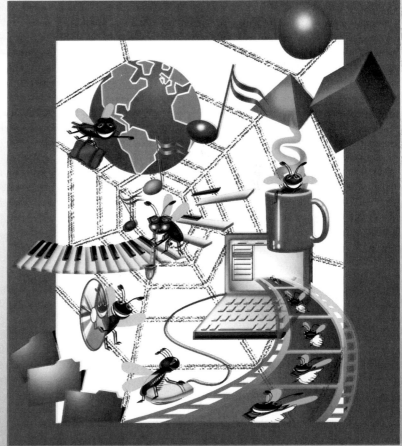

Outline

10.1 Introduction[1]

A *graphical user interface (GUI)* presents a pictorial interface to a program. A GUI (pronounced "GOO-EE") gives a program a distinctive "look" and "feel." GUIs allow the user to spend less time trying to remember which keystroke sequences do what and spend more time using the program in a productive manner. Interaction between the user and the program is through the GUI. A GUI resembling a telephone keypad is shown in Fig. 10.1.

GUIs are built from *GUI components* (sometimes called *widgets*). A GUI component is a visual object with which the user may interact via the mouse or the keyboard. Several GUI components are listed in Fig 10.2. In the sections that follow, we discuss each of these GUI components in detail. In the next chapter, we discuss more advanced GUI components.

The classes that are used to create the GUI components of Fig. 10.2 are part of the **java.awt** *(Another Windowing Toolkit) package*. The **java.awt** package is sometimes called the *Abstract Windowing Toolkit*. The line

```
import java.awt.*;
```

is used to import the classes in the **java.awt** package. The asterisk is a *wild card* that specifies multiple classes in the package are to be imported. Figure 10.3 shows the inheritance hierarchy for the components listed in Fig. 10.2. Each arrow indicates that the class "pointed from" **extend**s the class "pointed to."

---

1. Chapter 9 on graphics, and Chapters 10 and 11 on basic and advanced graphical user interface components were coauthored with the authors' colleague Mr. Tem Nieto of Deitel & Associates, Inc.

Fig. 10.1 A GUI resembling a telephone keypad.

GUI Component	Description
Label	An area where non-editable text can be displayed.
Button	An area that triggers an event when clicked.
List	An area where a list of items is displayed.
Text field	An area in which the user inputs data from the keyboard. The area can also display information.
Panel	A container in which components can be placed.

Fig. 10.2 Basic GUI components.

In order to effectively use GUI components, the **awt** inheritance hierarchy must be understood—especially the **Component** *class* and the **Container** *class*. Much of each GUI component's functionality is derived from one or both of these classes. Any class that inherits from the **Component** class is a *component*. The **Label** class inherits from the **Component** class and the **Component** class inherits from **Object**. Thus a **Label** is a **Component** and an **Object** but a **Component** is only an **Object**. Likewise, any class that inherits from the **Container** class is a *container*. A container is an area where components can be placed.

Portability Tip 10.1

The look of a particular GUI component may vary across platforms. Java "ties" into the "local" GUI which varies from platform to platform.

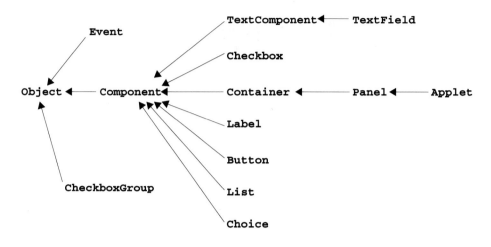

Fig. 10.3 A portion of the **java.awt** inheritance hierarchy.

10.2 Labels

One way of providing text instructions or information on a GUI is with *labels*. A label provides an area where a single line of *static* (read-only) *text* is displayed. Text displayed in labels is said to be "static" because the user cannot modify it. Labels are created with class **Label** which inherits directly from class **Component**. Like other objects, a label must be instantiated with a call to a constructor. Two **Component** constructors are shown in Fig. 10.4.

The program of Fig. 10.5 creates two labels and adds them to the applet. The two **Label** constructors of Fig. 10.4 are used.

Label objects are created with the **Label** class and a **Label** constructor. The line

```
private Label noLabel, textLabel;
```

creates two label references using the **Label** class. Both **Label** objects are instantiated in the **init** method. The object **noLabel** is instantiated with the statement

```
noLabel = new Label();
```

Class **Label** constructors

---

public Label()
    Constructs an empty label—text is not displayed.

public Label(String s)   **// label text**
    Constructs a label that displays the text **s**.

Fig. 10.4 Class **Label** constructors.

```
1   // Fig. 10.5: MyLabel.java
2   // Demonstrating the Label class constructors.
3   import java.applet.Applet;
4   import java.awt.*;
5
6   public class MyLabel extends Applet {
7      private Font f;
8      private Label noLabel, textLabel;
9
10     public void init()
11     {
12        f = new Font( "Courier", Font.BOLD, 14 );
13
14        // call label constructor with no text
15        noLabel = new Label();
16
17        // call label constructor with a string argument
18        textLabel = new Label( "This is read-only text" );
19
20        // set font for text displayed in label
21        textLabel.setFont( f );
22
23        // add label components to applet container
24        add( noLabel );
25        add( textLabel );
26     }
27  }
```

Fig. 10.5 Program that demonstrates the `Label` class constructors.

which creates a label that does not contain any text. These types of label objects are useful for labels that do not need to display any text initially. However, later in the program information may need to be displayed. In the next example—Fig. 10.7, we explain how to set the text for these types of labels.

The object **textLabel** is created with the statement

```
textLabel = new Label( "This is read-only text" );
```

that creates a label with the text **"This is read-only text"**.

The font in which the label text is displayed is set with **Component**'s method **set-Font** that takes a **Font** object as an argument.

In order for the label objects to be visible, they must be *added* to a container with the ***add*** *method*. As mentioned earlier, a container is an area where components may be placed.

The two containers discussed in this chapter are applets and panels. Panels are discussed in Section 10.8. We present more containers in the next chapter. Components are placed on containers with **Container** *method* **add**. Thus the line

```
add( noLabel );
```

adds **noLabel** to the applet. Note that the **Label** object **noLabel** does not contain any text.

Common Programming Error 10.1

Forgetting to add a component to a container is a run-time logic error.

Common Programming Error 10.2

Adding to a container a component that has not been instantiated throws a **NullPointer-Exception***.*

Labels have several methods associated with them. These are summarized in Fig. 10.6. The **getText** *method* returns a label's text. If a label does not contain any text, the null string is returned. The **setText** *method* sets the text for a label. Any text that the label is currently displaying is replaced with the new text.

The program of Fig. 10.7 demonstrates the two methods of Fig. 10.6. The program creates a **Label** object that does not display any text. The label text is then set with the **set-Text** method. The **getText** method is used to get the label's text. The label's text is displayed in the status bar.

Initially, object **noLabel** does not contain any text. The text to be displayed in **noLabel** is passed as an argument to the **setText** method.

The statement

```
showStatus( "Label is displaying: " + noLabel.getText() );
```

displays **noLabel**'s text in the status bar. Method **getText** is used to get **noLabel**'s text. The statement is written in the **paint** method so the **showStatus** method can be used to display **noLabel**'s text after the applet is initialized. If the statement had been placed in **init**, **"Applet started."** would overwrite the information being displayed by the **showStatus** method.

Class Label methods getText and setText

```
public String getText()
```
    Returns the label text.

```
public void setText( String s )   // read-only string to display
```
    Sets the label text.

Fig. 10.6 Class **Label** methods **getText** and **setText**.

```
1   // Fig. 10.7: MyLabel2
2   // Demonstrating Label methods getText and setText.
3   import java.applet.Applet;
4   import java.awt.*;
5
6   public class MyLabel2 extends Applet {
7      private Font f;
8      private Label noLabel;
9
10     public void init()
11     {
12        f = new Font( "Courier", Font.BOLD, 14 );
13
14        // call label constructor with no text
15        noLabel = new Label();
16
17        // set text in noLabel
18        noLabel.setText( "new text!" );
19
20        // set font for noLabel
21        noLabel.setFont( f );
22
23        // add label component
24        add( noLabel );
25     }
26
27     public void paint( Graphics g )
28     {
29        // get noLabel's text
30        showStatus( "Label is displaying: " + noLabel.getText() );
31     }
32  }
```

Fig. 10.7 Program that demonstrates **getText** and **setText**.

10.3 Push Buttons

A *button* is a component the user clicks to trigger a specific action. Three types of buttons exist: *push buttons*, *choice buttons* and *checkboxes*. We discuss choice buttons and checkboxes in later sections.

A push button is a button that triggers an action when clicked with the mouse. Push buttons are created with the ***Button*** *class* that inherits directly from the **Component** class. The **Button** class constructors are summarized in Fig. 10.8.

Class **Button** constructors

```
public Button()              // no button label
```
  Constructs an unlabeled push button.

```
public Button( String s )  // button label
```
  Constructs a labeled push button.

Fig. 10.8 Class **Button** constructors.

The text on the face of a button is called a *button label*. A GUI can have many buttons, but each button label should be unique. The reason each button label should be unique has to do with *event handling*. When a button is clicked a *button event* is generated. The button label is often used to determine which button was pressed. Buttons with the same labels are ambiguous to the user.

Common Programming Error 10.3

Having more than one button with the same button label is a logic error. The buttons appear to be ambiguous to the user.

Good Programming Practice 10.1

Provide a unique name for each button label.

In the previous section, we did not discuss event handling because clicking on a label does not generate an event. GUIs are *event driven*, i.e., they respond to events. An *event* is an *asynchronous action* such as the user moving the mouse, clicking the mouse, etc. Events are sent to a Java program by the windowing system. Events are stored in objects of the **Event** class which inherits directly from class **Object**. These events are processed by methods of class **Component**. Class **Event** is part of the **java.awt** package. The components of Fig. 10.2, with the exception of labels and panels, generate events. We will discuss the event handling for each component as it is introduced.

The program of Fig. 10.9 creates three push buttons and adds them to the applet. Two of the buttons have button labels. Event handling code is provided in the applet's **action** method for each of the two buttons that performs an action when pressed. The statement

```
private Button pushButton1, pushButton2, pushButton3;
```

creates three **Button** references. Each **Button** reference is instantiated with **new** and a call to a **Button** constructor. The statements

```
pushButton1 = new Button( "Click here" );
pushButton2 = new Button( "Sorry I don't do anything" );
```

instantiate **pushButton1** and **pushButton2**. The string passed to the **Button** constructor is used as the button label. Object **pushButton3** does not have a label. The buttons are attached to the applet with the **Container** class's **add** method. The statements

```
1   // Fig. 10.9: MyButtons.java
2   // Creating push buttons.
3   import java.applet.Applet;
4   import java.awt.*;
5
6   public class MyButtons extends Applet {
7      private Button pushButton1, pushButton2, pushButton3;
8
9      public void init()
10     {
11        pushButton1 = new Button( "Click here" );
12        pushButton2 = new Button( "Sorry I don't do anything" );
13        pushButton3 = new Button();  // no button label
14
15        // add buttons
16        add( pushButton1 );
17        add( pushButton2 );
18        add( pushButton3 );
19     }
20
21     // handle the button events
22     public boolean action( Event e,  Object o )
23     {
24        // check to see if a button triggered the event
25        if ( e.target instanceof Button ) {
26
27           // check to see if pushButton1 or pushButton3
28           // was pressed. Nothing will be done if
29           // pushButton2 was pressed.
30           if ( e.target == pushButton1 )
31              showStatus( "You pressed: " + o.toString() );
32           else if ( e.target == pushButton3 )
33              showStatus( "You pressed: " + e.arg );
34
35           return true;   // event was handled here
36        }
37
38        return true;
39     }
40  }
```

Fig. 10.9 Program that creates three push buttons (part 1 of 2).

```
add( pushButton1 );
add( pushButton2 );
add( pushButton3 );
```

place the three buttons on the applet. Clicking any of the three buttons generates an event.

When a button is clicked, the **action** method is called. The **action** method returns a **boolean** value and received two arguments—an **Event** and **Object**. The **Event** stores specific information about the component that generated the event and the event that occurred.

Fig. 10.9   Program that creates three push buttons (part 2 of 2).

The **Object** parameter stores component-specific information for the event (for a **Button** it is the **Button**'s label). For buttons to perform specific tasks, method **action** must be overridden. Class **MyButtons** overrides class **Component**'s **action** method.

In the **action** method, the first **if** structure's condition

        e.target instanceof Button

tests whether a push button generated the event. The **Event** class instance variable **target** identifies the component that generated the event. The **instanceof** operator tests **e.target** to determine if it is a **Button** object. If **so**, the condition evaluates to **true**. Because the program includes several buttons, we want to know which button was pressed. The next **if** structure's condition

```
e.target == pushButton1
```

checks whether **pushButton1** generated the event. The statement

```
showStatus( "You pressed: " + o.toString() );
```

displays the string **"You pressed: Click here"**. The object **o** stores the button label. No other information is stored in **o**. The last **if** structure's condition

```
e.target == pushButton3
```

checks whether **pushButton3** generated the event. The statement

```
showStatus( "You pressed: " + e.arg );
```

displays the string **"You pressed: "**. The **Event** class instance variable *arg* (which is of data type **Object**) contains the button label. The value **e.arg** is always identical to **o**. We will use **e.arg** in the examples that follow.

The last **if** condition could also be rewritten using **e.arg** as

```
e.arg.equals( pushButton3.getLabel() )
```

The **Button** class **getLabel** *method* returns a button's label as a **String** object. The **Object** class **equals** method is used to compare the button label in **arg** to **pushButton3**'s button label.

The **action** method in this program is written to handle only **Button** events. Specifically, method **action** handles events from **pushButton1** and **pushButton3**. When **pushButton2** is clicked, the button does trigger an event, but code has not been provided to handle the event. If a **Button** generated the event, a value of **true** is returned indicating that this **action** method has handled the event. We discuss event handling in greater detail in the next chapter.

10.4 Text Fields

Text fields are single-line areas that receive user inputs from the keyboard. The user types data into the text field and presses the Enter key. The data can then be used in the program. Text fields can also be used to display information. Text fields are created with the ***Text-Field* class** which inherits directly from the ***TextComponent* class**. The **TextField** constructors are summarized in Fig. 10.10.

Common Programming Error 10.4

*Using a lowercase f in **TextField** is a compilation error.*

The program of Fig. 10.11 uses class **TextField** and the **TextField** constructors to create four text fields. The program does not override the **action** method to handle text field events—we demonstrate this in the next program. Entering information in any of the four text fields has no effect.

Class `TextField` constructors

```
public TextField()
```
Constructs a **TextField** object.

```
public TextField( int columns ) // number of columns
```
Constructs an empty **TextField** object with the specified number of columns.

```
public TextField( String s )    // text displayed in text field
```
Constructs a **TextField** object displaying **s**.

```
public TextField(
    String s,                       // text displayed in text field
    int columns )                   // number of columns
```
Constructs a **TextField** object displaying **s** in the specified number of columns.

Fig. 10.10 Class **TextField** constructors.

```
1   // Fig. 10.11: MyTextField.java
2   // Demonstrating the TextField class constructors.
3   import java.applet.Applet;
4   import java.awt.*;
5
6   public class MyTextfield extends Applet {
7      private TextField text1, text2, text3, text4;
8
9      public void init()
10     {
11        // construct text field with default sizing
12        text1 = new TextField();
13
14        // construct text field with default text
15        text2 = new TextField( "Some text " );
16
17        // construct text field with 25 elements visible
18        text3 = new TextField( 25 );
19
20        // construct text field with default text and
21        // 40 visible elements
22        text4 = new TextField( "Yet some more text", 40 );
23
24        // add text fields to applet
25        add( text1 );
26        add( text2 );
27        add( text3 );
28        add( text4 );
29     }
30  }
```

Fig. 10.11 Program that demonstrates the **TextField** constructors (part 1 of 2).

Fig. 10.11 Program that demonstrates the **TextField** constructors (part 2 of 2).

The **TextField** object **text1** is instantiated with the statement

```
text1 = new TextField();
```

The text field created does not display any text and has a default size of two columns. The size of a column is the average width of a character. Although **text1** has only two columns, the user can enter information consisting of more than two characters, but only two columns will be visible at a time. The arrow keys can be used to scroll through any text field regardless of the number of visible columns. The **TextField** object **text2** is instantiated with the statement

```
text2 = new TextField( "Some Text " );
```

The number of visible columns is the minimum number of columns required to display the text. The **TextField** object **text3** is instantiated with the statement

```
text3 = new TextField( 25 );
```

This text field has 25 visible columns and does not display any text. The **TextField** object **text4** has 40 visible columns and displays the text "**Yet some more text**". The text fields are added to the applet with the **Component** method **add**.

The program of Fig. 10.12 consists of three text fields. Two of the text fields are used to display text and the other is used to get input from the user. The text field used for input masks the character being typed.

The three **TextField** objects are instantiated and initialized with **TextField** constructors. The statements

```
message.setEditable( false );
message2.setEditable( false );
```

use method **setEditable** to make **message** and **message2** read-only. The masking character used by **passwordField** is set with **TextField** method **setEchoCharacter**. In this program an asterisk appears for each character typed in **passwordField**. When the Enter key is pressed in any **TextField** an event is triggered.

```
1   // Fig. 10.12: MyTextField2.java
2   // Demonstrating TextField events.
3   import java.applet.Applet;
4   import java.awt.*;
5
6   public class MyTextField2 extends Applet {
7      private TextField message, passwordField, message2;
8      private String password;
9
10     public void init()
11     {
12        password = "Marak954";   // set password
13        message = new TextField( "Enter password: " );
14        message.setEditable( false );   // read only
15
16        passwordField = new TextField( 12 );
17        passwordField.setEchoCharacter( '*' );   // masking char
18
19        message2 = new TextField( 30 );
20        message2.setEditable( false );
21
22        // add text fields to applet
23        add( message );
24        add( passwordField );
25        add( message2 );
26     }
27
28     public boolean action( Event e, Object o )
29     {
30        // check to see if a text field triggered the event
31        if ( e.target instanceof TextField )
32
33           // check to see it it was the text field passwordField
34           if ( e.target == passwordField )
35
36              // check for correct password
37              if ( e.arg.equals( password ) )
38                 message2.setText( "Access Granted" );
39              else
40                 message2.setText( "Invalid password. " +
41                                   "Access Denied" );
42
43        return true;    // event was handled here
44     }
45  }
```

Fig. 10.12 Program that demonstrates **TextField** events (part 1 of 2).

The **action** method is overridden for this applet to process events generated by text fields. Any text field can generate a text field event—even the read-only ones. Although **message** and **message2** cannot be modified, the user can still press the Enter key in either text field and generate an event.

Fig. 10.12 Program that demonstrates **TextField** events (part 2 of 2).

When a **TextField** event is generated, the **Event** instance variable **arg** and the **Object** passed to the **action** method each contain a **String** representing the text in the **TextField** that generated the event.

The condition

```
e.target == passwordField
```

tests whether **passwordField** generated the event. If so, the condition

> e.arg.equals(password)

is tested. This condition tests for the correct password. The **arg** instance variable contains the text the user typed in the text field. If a correct password is entered, the string "**Access Granted**" is displayed in **message2**. Otherwise **message2** displays "**Invalid Password. Access Denied**"

10.5 Choice Buttons

A *choice button* provides a list of items from which the user can make a selection. **Choice** buttons are created with class ***Choice*** which inherits directly from class **Component**. The **Choice** class constructor is not overloaded and takes no arguments. Some common methods of class **Choice** are listed in Fig. 10.13.

The program of Fig. 10.14 uses a choice button to provide a list of three fonts. When a font is selected, the text in a text field is changed to that font. The program uses the methods of Fig. 10.13.

The statement

> choiceButton = new Choice();

uses the **Choice** constructor to create a **Choice** button object. Items are added to a **Choice** button with method ***addItem*** which adds a single **String** item to the choice button. Items appear in the order in which they are added. A numeric *index* keeps track of the ordering of items. The first item is added at index 0; the next item is added at index 1, and so forth. The first item added to a **Choice** button is displayed when the **Choice** button is added to a container. Other items are selected by clicking the down arrow. When clicked, the down arrow expands into a list from which the user can make a selection.

Methods of class Choice

```
public int countItems()
```
  Returns the number of items in the **Choice** button.

```
public String getItem( int index )
```
  Returns the **Choice** item at index.

```
public synchronized void addItem( String s )
```
  Adds an item to a **Choice** button.

```
public String getSelectedItem()
```
  Returns the selected **Choice** item.

```
public int getSelectedIndex()
```
  Returns the index of the selected **Choice** item.

Fig. 10.13 Method of class **Choice**.

```
1   // Fig. 10.14: MyChoice.java
2   // Using a Choice button to select a font.
3   import java.applet.Applet;
4   import java.awt.*;
5
6   public class MyChoice extends Applet {
7       private Choice choiceButton;
8       private TextField t;
9       private Font f;
10
11      public void init()
12      {
13          choiceButton = new Choice();
14          t = new TextField( "Sample Text", 16 );
15          t.setEditable( false );
16
17          // add items to choiceButton
18          choiceButton.addItem( "TimesRoman" );
19          choiceButton.addItem( "Courier" );
20          choiceButton.addItem( "Helvetica" );
21
22          f = new Font( choiceButton.getItem( 0 ),
23                        Font.PLAIN, 14 );
24          t.setFont( f );
25          add( choiceButton );
26          add( t );
27      }
28
29      public boolean action( Event e, Object o )
30      {
31          String s;
32
33          // Check for Choice button event
34          if ( e.target instanceof Choice ) {
35              f = new Font( choiceButton.getSelectedItem(),
36                            Font.PLAIN, 14 );
37
38              t.setFont( f );
39
40              s = "Number of items: " +
41                  choiceButton.countItems();
42
43              s += "      Current index: " +
44                  choiceButton.getSelectedIndex();
45
46              showStatus( s );
47          }
48
49          return true;
50      }
51  }
```

Fig. 10.14 Program that uses a **Choice** button to select a font (part 1 of 2).

Fig. 10.14 Program that uses a **Choice** button to select a font (part 2 of 2).

The **Font** object **f** is instantiated with the line

```
f = new Font( choiceButton.getItem( 0 ), Font.PLAIN, 14 );
```

Method *getItem* is used to return the item at index 0, which is **"TimesRoman"**. The font is set for the text field with the **setFont** method.

The **action** method is overridden for this applet. Selecting an item from the **Choice** button generates an event. The **Font** object **f** is instantiated with the statement

```
f = new Font( choiceButton.getSelectedItem(),
              Font.PLAIN, 14 );
```

The *getSelectedItem* method returns the selected item, which is used to change the font. The preceding statement could also have been written as

```
f = new Font( e.arg, Font.PLAIN, 14 );
```

The **Event** instance **arg** is a **String** representing the item selected. The number of items in the choice button is displayed in the status bar using method *countItems*. The index of the selected item is also displayed in the status bar using methof *getSelectedIndex*.

10.6 Checkboxes and Radio Buttons

Class ***Checkbox*** is used to create *checkbox buttons* and *radio buttons*; these are *state buttons* (i.e., buttons that have on/off or true/false values). We first discuss checkbox buttons.

Class **Checkbox** inherits directly from class **Component**. The **Checkbox** class constructors are summarized in Fig. 10.15.

The program of Fig. 10.16 uses **Checkbox** objects to change the font style of the text displayed in a text field. One checkbox applies a bold style and the other applies an italic style. When the program is initially run, neither checkbox is checked. The applet was sized in the HTML file at 290 by 70.

Class Checkbox constructors

`public Checkbox()`
    Constructs a **Checkbox** object no label. The **Checkbox** object is initially unchecked.

`public Checkbox( String s )`
    Constructs a **Checkbox** object with label **s**. The **Checkbox** object is initially unchecked.

Fig. 10.15 Class **Checkbox** constructors.

```
1   // Fig. 10.16: MyCheckbox.java
2   // Creating Checkbox buttons.
3   import java.applet.Applet;
4   import java.awt.*;
5
6   public class MyCheckbox extends Applet {
7       private Font f;
8       private TextField t;
9       private Checkbox checkBold, checkItalic;
10
11      public void init()
12      {
13          t = new TextField( "Sample Text", 30 );
14
15          // instantiate checkbox objects
16          checkBold = new Checkbox( "Bold" );
17          checkItalic = new Checkbox();
18          checkItalic.setLabel( "Italic" );   // set checkbox label
19
20          f = new Font( "TimesRoman", Font.PLAIN, 14 );
21          t.setFont( f );
22
23          add( t );
24          add( checkBold );       // unchecked (false) by default
25          add( checkItalic );     // unchecked (false) by default
26      }
```

Fig. 10.16 Program that creates a set of two checkbox buttons (part 1 of 3).

```
27
28      public boolean action( Event e, Object o )
29      {
30         int b, i;
31
32         // Check for Checkbox event
33         if ( e.target instanceof Checkbox ) {
34
35            // test state of bold checkbox
36            if ( checkBold.getState() == true  )
37               b = Font.BOLD;
38            else
39               b = Font.PLAIN;    // value of 0
40
41            // test state of italic checkbox
42            if ( checkItalic.getState() == true )
43               i = Font.ITALIC;
44            else
45               i = Font.PLAIN;    // value of 0
46
47            f = new Font( "TimesRoman", b + i, 14 );
48            t.setFont( f );
49         }
50
51         return true;
52      }
53   }
```

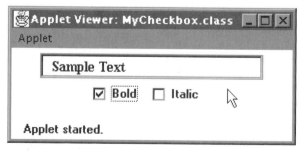

Fig. 10.16 Program that creates a set of two checkbox buttons (part 2 of 3).

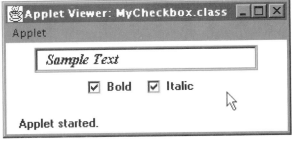

Fig. 10.16 Program that creates a set of two checkbox buttons (part 3 of 3).

The **Checkbox** references are created with the line

```
private Checkbox checkBold, checkItalic;
```

The object **checkBold** is constructed with the statement

```
checkBold = new Checkbox( "Bold" );
```

The **String** passed to the constructor is the *checkbox label*. The checkbox label appears to the right of **Checkbox**. The object **checkItalic** is instantiated and given a label with the statements

```
checkItalic = new Checkbox();
checkItalic.setLabel( "Italic" );
```

When **checkItalic** is constructed, it does not have a label. The label is set using the **Checkbox** class method *setLabel* method. The purpose of constructing **checkItal-ic** in this manner is to demonstrate the no-argument constructor and method **setLabel**. The text field and checkboxes are added to the applet with the **add** method.

The **action** method is overridden for this applet. When a **Checkbox** object is clicked, an event is triggered. The **Event** class instance variable **target** is tested for an instance of **Checkbox**. A **Checkbox** is always either **true** if a checkmark is in the box and **false** if the box is empty. The state of each **Checkbox** object is tested with an **if/else** structure. Two **if/else** structures are necessary because the checkboxes are independent of each other and checking one has no effect on the other. Thus any combination of checkboxes may be checked at any time. The condition

```
checkItalic.getState() == true
```

tests the state of **checkItalic**. The **Checkbox** class method **getState** returns a **boolean** value representing a checkbox's state. The **Event** class instance **arg** could have been used here; **arg** for a **Checkbox** is a **Boolean** object. The value would have to be converted to **boolean** using **Boolean** method **booleanValue**. Once the state of a the **Checkbox** that generated the event is determined, the text in the text field is updated to the appropriate font style.

Checkboxes can also be grouped together to form *radio buttons*—a group of buttons where only one button in the group can be **true** and selecting that button forces all other buttons in the group to **false** (i.e., unchecked). A set of radio buttons is created with the **CheckboxGroup** class and the **Checkbox** class. Class **CheckboxGroup** inherits directly from class **Object** and is not a **Component**. *This means that CheckboxGroup objects cannot be added to a container.* Remember that only objects of classes derived from **Component** can be added to a container. The constructors used to create radio buttons are summarized in Fig. 10.17.

Common Programming Error 10.5

*Using an uppercase b for box in **Checkbox** or **CheckboxGroup** is a syntax error.*

Common Programming Error 10.6

*Adding a **CheckboxGroup** object to a container is a compilation error.*

The program of Fig. 10.18 is similar to the previous program. The user can alter the font style of a text field's text. The program uses radio buttons, which permit only a single selection.

Checkbox and CheckboxGroup Constructors for creating radio buttons

---

```
public Checkbox(
    String s,          // radio button label
    CheckboxGroup c,   // CheckboxGroup owning radio button
    boolean state )    // state of radio button
```
Constructs a single radio button with the label **s** and the state **state**. The radio button is added to the existing **CheckboxGroup c**.

```
public CheckboxGroup()
```
Constructs a **CheckboxGroup** object.

Fig. 10.17 **Checkbox** and **CheckboxGroup** constructors for creating radio buttons.

```
1   // Fig. 10.18: RadioButton.java
2   // Creating radio buttons using CheckboxGroup and Checkbox.
3   import java.applet.Applet;
4   import java.awt.*;
5
6   public class RadioButton extends Applet {
7      private TextField t;
8      private Font f;
9      private CheckboxGroup radio;
10     private Checkbox radioBold, radioItalic,
11                      radioPlain;
12
13     public void init()
14     {
15        t = new TextField( "Sample Text", 40 );
16
17        // instantiate checkbox group (i.e. radio buttons)
18        radio = new CheckboxGroup();
19
20        add( t );   // add text field
21
22        // instantiate radio button objects
23        add( radioPlain = new Checkbox( "Plain", radio, true ) );
24        add( radioItalic = new Checkbox( "Italic", radio,
25                                         false ) );
26
27        add( radioBold = new Checkbox( "Bold", radio, false ) );
28     }
29
30     public boolean action( Event e, Object o )
31     {
32        int style;
33
34        // Check for Checkbox event
35        if ( e.target instanceof Checkbox) {
36
37           // test state of radio buttons
38           if ( radioPlain.getState() == true  )
39              style = Font.PLAIN;
40           else if ( radioItalic.getState() == true )
41              style = Font.ITALIC;
42           else
43              style = Font.BOLD;
44
45           f = new Font( "TimesRoman", style, 14 );
46           t.setFont( f );
47        }
48
49        return true;
50     }
51  }
```

Fig. 10.18 Creating radio buttons (part 1 of 2).

Fig. 10.18 Creating radio buttons (part 2 of 2).

The line

```
private CheckboxGroup radio;
```

creates a reference to a **CheckboxGroup** named **radio**. Three **Checkbox** references are also created. The statement

```
radio = new CheckboxGroup();
```

instantiates **radio**. The object **radio** cannot be added to the applet because the **CheckboxGroup** class does not inherit from the **Component** class. Only **Component** class objects can be added to **Container** class objects. Instead, the object **radio** is the "glue" that binds the three **Checkbox**es together to form three radio buttons. Each **Checkbox** is a component and therefore can be added to the applet. The statements

```
add( radioPlain = new Checkbox( "Plain", radio, true ) );
add( radioItalic = new Checkbox( "Italic", radio, false ) );
add( radioBold = new Checkbox( "Bold", radio, false ) );
```

add the radio buttons to the applet. The checkboxes are now radio buttons belonging to the **CheckboxGroup** object **radio**. The first argument passed to the constructor is the *radio button label*, the second argument is the **CheckboxGroup** that will own the radio button, and the last argument is the initial button state—only one radio button can be set to **true**, but all radio buttons can be set to **false** initially. If more than one radio button in the same **CheckboxGroup** is set to **true**, the last one set to **true** is the only one checked.

> *Common Programming Error 10.7*
>
> *When instantiating radio buttons, setting more than one radio button to **true** is a run-time logic error.*

The **action** method has been overridden for this class. The **Event** class instance **target** is tested against a **Checkbox** because a radio button is still a form of **Checkbox**. The **Checkbox** class method **getState** gets the state of a radio button. The **Event** class instance **arg** could have been used in the **action** method. The **arg** instance variable contains a **Boolean** object when a radio button generates the event. Once the radio button state is determined, the font is set for the text field.

10.7 Lists

Lists display a series of items from which the user may select one or more items. Lists are created with the *List* class which inherits directly from class **Component**. The **List** class constructors are summarized in Fig. 10.19.

The program of Fig. 10.20 creates a list of four colors. When a color name is double-clicked in the **List**, the applet's background changes to that color. The statement

```
private List colorList;
```

creates a reference called **colorList**. The **colorList** object is instantiated with the statement

---

List class constructors

```
public List()
```
Constructs a **List** object that allows one item to be selected.

```
public List(
    int items,        // number of items visible
    boolean ms )      // multiple selections
```
Constructs a **List** object with **items** lines visible. If **ms** is **true**, multiple items may be selected from the list.

Fig. 10.19 **List** class constructors.

```
1   // Fig. 10.20: MyList.java
2   // Creating a List.
3   import java.applet.Applet;
4   import java.awt.*;
5
6   public class MyList extends Applet {
7      private List colorList;
8
9      public void init()
10     {
11        // create a list with 5 items visible
12        // do not allow multiple selections
13        colorList = new List( 5, false );
14
15        // add four items to the list
16        colorList.addItem( "White" );
17        colorList.addItem( "Black" );
18        colorList.addItem( "Yellow" );
19        colorList.addItem( "Green" );
20
21        // add list to applet
22        add( colorList );
23     }
24
25     public boolean action( Event e, Object o )
26     {
27        // test for a list
28        if ( e.target instanceof List ) {
29
30           if ( e.arg.equals( "Yellow" ) )
31              setBackground( Color.yellow );
32           else if ( e.arg.equals( "White" ) )
33              setBackground( Color.white );
34           else if ( e.arg.equals( "Black" ) )
35              setBackground( Color.black );
36           else
37              setBackground( Color.green );
38
39           repaint();      // update applet
40        }
41
42        return true;
43     }
44  }
```

Fig. 10.20 Program that creates a **List** (part 1 of 2).

```
colorList = new List( 5, false );
```

The constructor arguments indicate that object **colorList** has five lines visible and does not allow multiple selections. Items are added to the list with **List** method **addItem**. Only **String**s can be added to a list. The **List** is added to the applet with method **add**.

Fig. 10.20 Program that creates a **List** (part 2 of 2).

Common Programming Error 10.8

Attempting to add an item that is not a string to a list is a syntax error.

Double clicking a list item triggers an event. The **action** method is overridden for this class. The **Event** instance variable **target** is tested for a **List**. The **arg** instance variable for a **List** is the **String** representing the double-clicked item. The **arg** instance is tested against each **String** in the list. The background color of the applet is then changed with method **setBackground**.

In Chapter 9, we discussed the **paint** method and briefly mentioned the **repaint** method. The **repaint** method schedules a call to **Component** method **update**. The **update** method redraws or refreshes the applet by filling the background of the applet with the current background color and calling method **paint**. Method **repaint** s useful because it automatically supplies the **Graphics** object that both **update** and **paint** require to do their jobs.

The program of Fig. 10.21 uses a multiple-selection **List** to copy items from one **List** to another. Several **List** items can be copied at a time by selecting the desired items and clicking the button between the **List** objects. Note that the items selected can be from anywhere in the **List**.

The object **stateList** is instantiated with the statement

```
stateList = new List( 5, true );
```

The constructor arguments indicate that five items are visible in the **List** at a time and that multiple selections are allowed. Five items are also visible for object **copyList**. Multiple selections are not allowed for object **copyList**. A push button object **copy** is also instantiated. This is used to initiate the copying of items from one **List** to the other.

The **stateList** object has eight items added to it with the **addItem** method. Only five list items are visible at a time, so a *scrollbar* automatically appears at the right side the list. The scrollbar allows the entire list to be viewed by clicking the up arrow at the top of the bar or the down arrow at the bottom of the bar to scroll through the items. A scrollbar only appears when the number of items in the list exceeds the number of visible items.

```
1   // Fig. 10.21: MyList2.java
2   // Copying items from one List to another.
3   import java.applet.Applet;
4   import java.awt.*;
5
6   public class MyList2 extends Applet {
7      private List stateList, copyList;
8      private Button copy;
9
10     public void init()
11     {
12        // create a list with 5 items visible
13        // allow multiple selections
14        stateList = new List( 5, true );
15
16        // create a list with 5 items visible
17        // do not allow multiple selections
18        copyList = new List( 5, false );
19
20        // create copy button
21        copy = new Button( "Copy >>>" );
22
23        // add some data to stateList
24        stateList.addItem( "Texas" );
25        stateList.addItem( "Alaska" );
26        stateList.addItem( "Florida" );
27        stateList.addItem( "Montana" );
28        stateList.addItem( "Mississippi" );
29        stateList.addItem( "Delaware" );
30        stateList.addItem( "New Mexico" );
31        stateList.addItem( "South Dakota" );
32        stateList.addItem( "West Virginia" );
33
34        // add list to applet
35        add( stateList );
36        add( copy );
37        add( copyList );
38     }
39
40     public boolean action( Event e, Object o )
41     {
42        String states[];
43
44        // test for a button event
45        if ( e.target == copy ) {
46
47           // get the selected states
48           states = stateList.getSelectedItems();
```

Fig. 10.21 Using a multiple-selection **List** (part 1 of 2).

```
49
50            // copy them to copyList
51            for ( int i = 0; i < states.length; i++ )
52                copyList.addItem( states[ i ] );
53         }
54
55         return true;
56    }
57 }
```

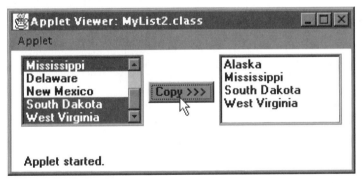

Fig. 10.21 Using a multiple-selection **List** (part 2 of 2).

The **action** method for this applet is overridden. To capture items from a multiple-selection **List**, an external event must be triggered (i.e., some other component should be used to indicate that multiple selections were made in a **List**). In this program, a push button is used to trigger the event. The **Event** class instance variable **target** is tested for the **copy** button to process the event in this program. Note: It is possible to generate an event on a multiple-selection **List** by double-clicking one of the **List** items.

The **states** array stores the selected list items. The statement

```
states = stateList.getSelectedItems();
```

uses method **getSelectedItems** to get the Strings representing the selected items in the **List**. A **for** loop is used to add each element of **states** into **copyList**.

10.8 Panels

As mentioned earlier, a *panel* is a container. Class **Panel** inherits from class **Container** and class **Applet** inherits from **Panel**. Thus **Panel**s and **Applet**s are containers and may have components, including other panels, added to them. The **Panel** constructor takes no arguments and is not overloaded.

The program of Fig. 10.22 creates two panels and adds them to the applet. We emphasize each panel by changing its background color. One panel is changed to pink and the other is changed to yellow using **Component** method **setBackgound**.

```
1   // Fig. 10.22: TwoPanels.java
2   // Creating Panel objects.
3   import java.applet.Applet;
4   import java.awt.*;
5
6   public class TwoPanels extends Applet {
7      private Panel p1, p2;
8      private Label label1, label2;
9
10     public void init()
11     {
12        p1 = new Panel();   // create a panel object
13        p2 = new Panel();   // create a second panel object
14        label1 = new Label( " first panel" );
15        label2 = new Label( "second panel" );
16
17        // change p1's background to yellow
18        p1.setBackground( Color.yellow );
19
20        // change p2's background to pink
21        p2.setBackground( Color.pink );
22
23        p1.add( label1 );   // add label to p1
24        p2.add( label2 );   // add label to p2
25
26        add( p1 );   // add panel to applet
27        add( p2 );   // add panel to applet
28     }
29  }
```

Fig. 10.22 Program that creates two **Panel** objects.

Two **Panel** objects **p1** and **p2** are created. Two **Label** objects are also created. Each label is added to a panel using the **add** method. The statement

```
p1.add( label1 );
```

adds **label1** to panel **p1**. Each panel is then added to the applet. The statement

```
add( p1 );
```

adds **p1** to the applet.

Note that the panels in Fig. 10.22 are only sized to the label component they contain. The **Panel**s have no effect on the applet size. Applets with multiple **Panel**s allow complex GUIs to be built. The layout managers presented in Section 10.11 arrage a **Panel**'s components more precisely. **Panel**s do not generate events, so event handling is not necessary for **Panel**s.

Common Programming Error 10.9

Adding a component to a container that has not been instantiated throws a **NullPointer-Exception**.

10.9 Mouse Events

This section presents the **Component** *class* methods and constants for handling *mouse events*. A mouse event occurs when the user interacts with the mouse. The methods are summarized in Fig. 10.23 and the constants are summarized in Fig. 10.28. We discuss each method and constant below.

Each of the mouse methods takes three arguments—an event, an *x* coordinate and a *y* coordinate. The *x* and *y* coordinates specify where the event occurred. The **mouseDown** method (Fig. 10.24) is called whenever a mouse button is pressed. The **mouseUp** method (Fig. 10.24) is called whenever a mouse button is released. The **mouseMove** method (Fig. 10.25) is called when the mouse is moved. The **mouseEnter** method (Fig. 10.26) is called when the mouse pointer enters the physical boundaries of a component. The *mouse pointer* is the small arrow that represents the mouse location on the screen. The **mouseExit** method (Fig. 10.26) is called when the mouse pointer leaves the physical boundary of a component. The **mouseDrag** method (Fig. 10.27) is called when the mouse button is pressed and held, and the mouse is moved (a process known as *clicking and dragging*). The **mouseDrag** event is preceded by a **mouseDown** event and followed by a **mouseUp** event.

The program of Fig. 10.24 overrides methods **mouseDown** and **mouseUp**. When the user presses the mouse button at a particular location, the **mouseDown** event occurs and the coordinates of the mouse are displayed in the status bar. When the mouse button is released, the coordinates are drawn on the form.

In the program, the coordinates where a **mouseUp** event occurred are stored in the variables **xUp** and **yUp**. The **boolean** variable **first** determines whether or not the mouse button has been released for the first time.

In the **init** method, **first** is set to **true** indicating that the applet is running for the first time. The **if** statement in the **paint** method prevents the statements

---

Component class mouse methods

```
public boolean mouseDown(
    Event e,           // Event object
    int x,             // x coordinate of mouse
    int y )            // y coordinate of mouse
```
Handles a mouse-down event. A mouse-down event occurs when a mouse button is pressed.

```
public boolean mouseUp(
    Event e,           // Event object
    int x,             // x coordinate of mouse
    int y )            // y coordinate of mouse
```
Handles a mouse-up event. A mouse-up event occurs when a mouse button is released.

```
public boolean mouseMove(
    Event e,           // Event object
    int x,             // x coordinate
    int y )            // y coordinate
```
Handles a mouse-move event. A mouse-move event occurs when the mouse is moved.

```
public boolean mouseExit(
    Event e,           // Event object
    int x,             // x coordinate
    int y )            // y coordinate
```
Handles a mouse-exit event. A mouse-exit event occurs when the mouse pointer leaves the area of a component.

```
public boolean mouseEnter(
    Event e,           // Event object
    int x,             // x coordinate
    int y )            // y coordinate
```
Handles a mouse-enter event. A mouse-enter event occurs when the mouse pointer enters the area of a component.

```
public boolean mouseDrag(
    Event e,           // Event object
    int x,             // x coordinate
    int y )            // y coordiante
```
Handles a mouse-drag event. A mouse-drag event occurs when the mouse button is pressed and the mouse is moved.

Fig. 10.23 Component class mouse methods.

```
String s = "MouseUp at ";
g.setFont( f );
s += "(" + xUp + ", " + yUp + ")!";
g.drawString( s, xUp, yUp );
```

from executing the first time the applet is run. When a **mouseDown** event occurs, the co-ordinates are displayed in the status bar. Releasing the mouse button generates a **mouseUp** event. The variable **first** is set to **true** to enable the statements in **paint**; the coordinates are stored in **xUp** and **yUp**; and **repaint** is called to schedule a call to **paint**. The coordinates of the **mouseUp** are then drawn on the applet.

```
1   // Fig. 10.24: MouseUpAndDown.java
2   // Demonstrating methods mouseUp and mouseDown.
3   import java.applet.Applet;
4   import java.awt.*;
5
6   public class MouseUpAndDown extends Applet {
7      private int xUp, yUp;
8      private boolean first;
9      private Font f;
10
11     public void init()
12     {
13        // disable statements in paint initially
14        first = true;
15
16        f = new Font( "TimesRoman", Font.BOLD, 14 );
17     }
18
19     public void paint( Graphics g )
20     {
21        // these statements will not execute
22        // on the first call to paint
23        if ( first == false ) {
24           String s = "MouseUp at ";
25           g.setFont( f );
26           s += "(" + xUp + ", " + yUp + ")!";
27           g.drawString( s, xUp, yUp );
28        }
29     }
30
31     public boolean mouseDown( Event e, int x, int y )
32     {
33        showStatus( "mouseDown at (" + x + ", " + y + ")" );
34        return true;    // event has been handled
35     }
36
37     public boolean mouseUp( Event e, int x, int y )
38     {
39        first = false;  // enable statements in paint
40        xUp = x;
41        yUp = y;
42        repaint();
43        return true;    // event has been handled
44     }
45   }
```

Fig. 10.24 Program that demonstrates **mouseUp** and **mouseDown** (part 1 of 2).

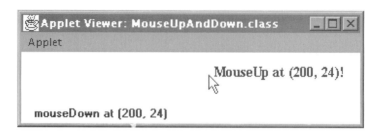

Fig. 10.24 Program that demonstrates **mouseUp** and **mouseDown** (part 2 of 2).

The program of Fig. 10.25 demonstrates the **mouseMove** method. The program consists of an applet with no GUI components. The **mouseMove** event is overridden to display the coordinates of the mouse in the status bar. The coordinates are continuously updated as the mouse moves. When the mouse pointer is outside the applet, **mouseMove** events are not generated as the mouse moves.

The program of Fig. 10.26 demonstrates the **mouseEnter** and **mouseExit** events. When the mouse enters the applet, a **mouseEnter** event is triggered. When the mouse exits the applet, a **mouseExit** event is triggered. A **mouseEnter** event is triggered when the mouse pointer enters the applet space. A **mouseExit** event is triggered when the mouse pointer exits the applet space.

```
1   // Fig. 10.25: MoveTheMouse.java
2   // Demonstrating method mouseMove.
3   import java.applet.Applet;
4   import java.awt.*;
5
6   public class MoveTheMouse extends Applet {
7
8      public boolean mouseMove( Event e, int x, int y )
9      {
10         showStatus( "mouse at (" + x + ", " + y + ")" );
11         return true;    // event has been handled
12     }
13  }
```

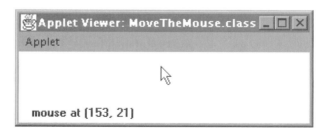

Fig. 10.25 Program that demonstrates method **mouseMove**.

```
1    // Fig. 10.26: MouseEnterExit.java
2    // Demonstrating methods mouseEnter and mouseExit.
3    import java.applet.Applet;
4    import java.awt.*;
5
6    public class MouseEnterExit extends Applet {
7        private Label 1;
8        private List t;
9
10       public void init()
11       {
12           t = new List( 3, false );
13           1 = new Label( "Measure in: " );
14
15           t.addItem( "Metric system" );
16           t.addItem( "Marak system" );
17           t.addItem( "English system" );
18
19           add( 1 );
20           add( t );
21       }
22
23       public boolean mouseEnter( Event e, int x, int y )
24       {
25           showStatus( "Entered area of applet" );
26           return true;   // event has been handled
27       }
28
29       public boolean mouseExit( Event e, int x, int y )
30       {
31           showStatus( "Exited area of applet" );
32           return true;   // event has been handled
33       }
34   }
```

Fig. 10.26 Program that demonstrates methods **mouseEnter** and **mouseExit**.

The program of Fig. 10.27 uses the **mouseDrag** event to create a simple drawing program. The user can draw pictures with the mouse by clicking and dragging.

```
1   // Fig. 10.27: Drag.java
2   // Demonstrating method mouseDrag.
3   import java.applet.Applet;
4   import java.awt.*;
5
6   public class Drag extends Applet {
7      private int xValue, yValue;
8      private boolean firstTime;
9
10     public void init()
11     {
12        // first running of program
13        firstTime = true;
14     }
15
16     public void paint( Graphics g )
17     {
18        // do not draw the first time
19        if ( !firstTime )
20           g.fillOval( xValue, yValue, 4, 4 );
21     }
22
23     // override Component class update
24     public void update( Graphics g )
25     {
26        // do not clear background
27        // only call paint
28        paint( g );
29     }
30
31     public boolean mouseDrag( Event e, int x, int y )
32     {
33        xValue = x;
34        yValue = y;
35
36        // enable drawing
37        firstTime = false;
38
39        repaint();      // call repaint
40        showStatus( "Event: mouseDrag" );
41
42        return true;    // event handled
43     }
44  }
```

Fig. 10.27 Program that demonstrates method **mouseDrag** (part 1 of 2).

The variables **xValue** and **yValue** store the coordinates of the **mouseDrag** event. The **boolean** variable **firstTime** determines whether or not the **paint** method has been executed the first time. The value of **firstTime** is set to **true** in the **init** method; this prevents a filled oval from being drawn at the coordinates (0, 0). The **paint**, **update**, and **mouseDrag** methods have been overridden for this class.

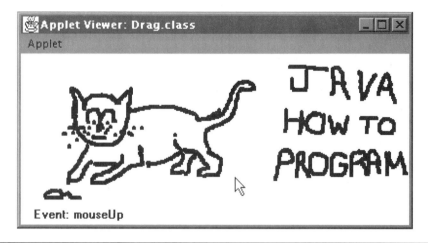

Fig. 10.27 Program that demonstrates method **mouseDrag** (part 2 of 2).

Inside the **mouseDrag** method, the variables **xValue** and **yValue** are assigned the values of **x** and **y** respectively. The variable **firstTime** is set to **false**. Drawing can now be enabled because the applet will be properly initialized before the **mouseDrag** event occurs. Method **repaint** is called to schedule a call to **paint** via **update**.

The **update** method is overridden to call **paint** without clearing the applet's background. This enables everything the user draws to be preserved. If **update** is not overridden, only the most recent circle is displayed on the applet. The **paint** method draws an oval at the coordinates (**xValue**, **yValue**). The width and height of the oval are set to 4.

Figure 10.28 describes the **Event** class mouse constants. The program of Fig. 10.29 uses these constants to test for mouse events. For each event, the applet adds to a **List** a **String** indicating which mouse event occurred.

Component class mouse constants

`public final static int MOUSE_DOWN`
    A constant integer value representing the mouse-down event.

`public final static int MOUSE_UP`
    A constant integer value representing the mouse-up event.

`public final static int MOUSE_MOVE`
    A constant integer value representing the mouse-move event.

`public final static int MOUSE_EXIT`
    A constant integer value representing the mouse-exit event.

Fig. 10.28 Component class mouse constants (part 1 of 2).

Component class mouse constants

---

public final static int MOUSE_ENTER

A constant integer value representing the mouse-enter event.

public final static int MOUSE_DRAG

A constant integer value representing the mouse-drag event.

Fig. 10.28 **Component** class mouse constants (part 2 of 2).

The program overrides the **Component** class *handleEvent* method. Method **handleEvent** takes one **Event** argument and returns a **boolean** value. The default behavior of **handleEvent** is to identify the event (**mouseMove**, **mouseExit**, etc.) and call the appropriate handler (**mouseMove** method, **mouseExit** method, etc.). Each event has a unique number that identifies the event. This number is stored in the **Event** instance variable **id**. We discuss **handleEvent** in greater detail in Chapter 11.

Event instance variable **id** is tested against the mouse event constants in method **handleEvent**. When a mouse event is identified, a string is either added to the **List** or written to the status bar. A value of **true** is returned indicating that the event has been handled. Any non-mouse event is unhandled and **true** is returned to indicate that no further processing should occur for non-mouse events in this example.

```
1   // Fig. 10.29: MouseEvents.java
2   // Demonstrating mouse Event constants.
3   import java.applet.Applet;
4   import java.awt.*;
5
6   public class MouseEvents extends Applet {
7      private List eventList;
8
9      public void init()
10     {
11        eventList = new List( 6, false );
12        add( eventList );
13     }
14
15     public boolean handleEvent( Event e )
16     {
17        // determine which mouse event occurred
18        switch ( e.id ) {
19           case Event.MOUSE_UP:
20              eventList.addItem( "Mouse up" );
21              return true;
22
```

Fig. 10.29 Program that demonstrates the mouse **Event** constants (part 1 of 2).

```
23              case Event.MOUSE_DOWN:
24                  eventList.addItem( "Mouse down" );
25                  return true;
26
27              case Event.MOUSE_MOVE:
28                  showStatus( "Mouse move" );
29                  return true;
30
31              case Event.MOUSE_ENTER:
32                  eventList.addItem( "Mouse enter");
33                  return true;
34
35              case Event.MOUSE_EXIT:
36                  eventList.addItem( "Mouse exit" );
37                  return true;
38
39              case Event.MOUSE_DRAG:
40                  showStatus( "Mouse drag" );
41                  return true;
42          }
43
44          // not one of our mouse events
45          showStatus( "Not one of the mouse events!" );
46          return true;   // done processing
47      }
48  }
```

Fig. 10.29 Program that demonstrates the mouse **Event** constants (part 2 of 2).

10.10 Keyboard Events

Keyboard events are generated when keys are pressed and released. The **Component** class contains methods **keyUp** and **keyDown** to handle keyboard events. These methods are summarized in Fig. 10.30.

The **keyDown** event is triggered when a key is pressed and the **keyUp** event is triggered when a key is released.

Component class keyboard methods

```
public boolean keyDown(
   Event e,    // event
   int key )   // Unicode value of key pressed
```
Handles a key-down event. A key-down event occurs when a key is pressed.

```
public boolean keyUp(
   Event e,    // event
   int key )   // Unicode value of key released
```
Handles a key-up event. A key-up event occurs when a key is released.

Fig. 10.30 **Component** class keybord methods.

The program of Fig. 10.31 demonstrates the **keyDown** and **keyUp** methods. The character representation of the key and a message indicating if the key was pressed or released are displayed in the status bar. The program also draws the character representation of the key pressed on the applet.

```
1   // Fig. 10.31: Key.java
2   // Demonstrating methods keyUp and keyDown.
3   import java.applet.Applet;
4   import java.awt.*;
5
6   public class Key extends Applet {
7      private Font f;
8      private String letter;
9      private boolean first;
10
11     public void init()
12     {
13        f = new Font( "Courier", Font.BOLD, 72 );
14        first = true;
15     }
16
17     public void paint( Graphics g )
18     {
19        g.setFont( f );
20
21        if ( !first )
22           g.drawString( letter, 75, 70 );
23     }
24
25     public boolean keyDown( Event e, int key )
26     {
27        showStatus( "keyDown: the " + ( char ) key +
```

Fig. 10.31 Program that demonstrates methods **keyDown** and **keyUp** (part 1 of 2).

```
28                     " was pressed." );
29
30         letter = String.valueOf( ( char ) key );
31         first = false;
32         repaint();
33
34         return true;    // event has been handled
35      }
36
37      public boolean keyUp( Event e, int key )
38      {
39         showStatus( "keyUp: the " + ( char ) key +
40                     " was released." );
41
42         return true;    // event has been handled
43      }
44   }
```

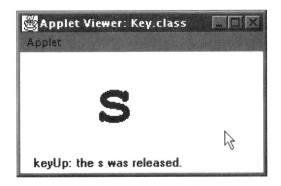

Fig. 10.31 Program that demonstrates methods **keyDown** and **keyUp** (part 2 of 2).

The **Event** instance variable **key** contains the Unicode value of the key pressed or released. The Unicode value is cast to **char** to show the character representation.

Keyboard constants are defined in class **Event** for some of the special-purpose keys such as **Home** and **End**. These **Event** class constants are summarized in Fig. 10.32.

Event class special-purpose keyboard constant

public final static int UP
A constant integer value representing the up-arrow key.

public final static int DOWN
A constant integer value representing the down-arrow key.

Fig. 10.32 **Event** class special-purpose keyboard constants (part 1 of 2).

Event class special-purpose keyboard constant

public final static int LEFT
    A constant integer value representing the left-arrow key.

public final static int RIGHT
    A constant integer value representing the right-arrow key.

public final static int END
    A constant integer value representing the end key.

public final static int HOME
    A constant integer value representing the home key.

public final static int PGDN
    A constant integer value representing the page-down key.

public final static int PGUP
    A constant integer value representing the page-up key.

public final static int F1
    A constant integer value representing the **F1** key. Keyboard constants also exist for **F2** through **F12**.

Fig. 10.32 **Event** class special-purpose keyboard constants (part 2 of 2).

The program of Fig. 10.33 determines whether one of the special-purpose keys (as summarized in Fig. 10.32) was pressed. Each time a special-purpose key is pressed, an item is added to a list box identifying which special key was pressed.

The program overrides the **Component** class **handleEvent** method. A **switch** structure uses the **Event** instance variable **key** to determine which of the special keys was pressed. A description is then displayed in a text field.

```
1   // Fig. 10.33: KeyEvents.java
2   // Demonstrating the keyboard Event constants.
3   import java.applet.Applet;
4   import java.awt.*;
5
6   public class KeyEvents extends Applet {
7      private TextField t;
8
9      public void init()
10     {
11        t = new TextField( 25 );
12        t.setEditable( false );
13        add( t );
14     }
```

Fig. 10.33 Program that demonstrates the keyboard **Event** constants (part 1 of 3).

```
15
16    public boolean handleEvent( Event e )
17    {
18       // determine which key event occured
19       switch ( e.key ) {
20          case Event.PGUP:
21             t.setText( "PageUp key" );
22             return true;
23
24          case Event.PGDN:
25             t.setText( "PageDown key" );
26             return true;
27
28          case Event.END:
29             t.setText( "End key" );
30             return true;
31
32          case Event.RIGHT:
33             t.setText( "Right arrow key");
34             return true;
35
36          case Event.LEFT:
37             t.setText( "Left arrow key");
38             return true;
39
40          case Event.UP:
41             t.setText( "Up arrow key" );
42             return true;
43
44          case Event.DOWN:
45             t.setText( "Down arrow key" );
46             return true;
47
48          case Event.HOME:
49             t.setText( "Home key" );
50             return true;
51
52          case Event.F1: case Event.F2: case Event.F3:
53          case Event.F4: case Event.F5: case Event.F6:
54          case Event.F7: case Event.F8: case Event.F9:
55          case Event.F10: case Event.F11: case Event.F12:
56             t.setText( "A function key ( F1 - F12 )" );
57             return true;
58       }
59
60       // not one of our key events
61       t.setText( "Not a special key!" );
62       return true;   // done processing
63    }
64 }
```

Fig. 10.33 Program that demonstrates the keyboard **Event** constants (part 2 of 3).

Fig. 10.33 Program that demonstrates the keyboard **Event** constants (part 3 of 3).

The status of the control, meta, and shift keys can also be tested. The **Event** class methods **controlDown**, **metaDown**, and **shiftDown** are summarized in Fig. 10.34.

The program of Fig. 10.35 demonstrates the **controlDown**, **metaDown** and **shiftDown** methods. Three non-editable text fields are used to display the name of each key. Any combination of the **Ctrl** key, **Shift** key and **Meta** keys can be pressed.

Event methods controlDown, metaDown and shiftDown

---

public boolean controlDown()
    Returns a true value if the control key is pressed.

public boolean metaDown()
    Returns a true value if the meta key is pressed.

public boolean shiftDown()
    Returns a true value if the shift key is pressed.

Fig. 10.34 Methods for testing the state of the control, meta and shift keys.

```
1   // Fig. 10.35: MetaShiftCtrl.java
2   // Demonstrating methods controlDown, metaDown and shiftDown.
3   import java.applet.Applet;
4   import java.awt.*;
5
6   public class MetaShiftCtrl extends Applet {
7      private TextField meta, shift, ctrl;
8
9      public void init()
10     {
11        meta = new TextField( 10 );
12        shift = new TextField( 10 );
13        ctrl = new TextField( 10 );
14
```

Fig. 10.35 Demonstrating methods **controlDown**, **metaDown** and **shiftDown** (part 1 of 2).

```
15            meta.setEditable( false );
16            ctrl.setEditable( false );
17            shift.setEditable( false );
18
19            add( meta );
20            add( shift );
21            add( ctrl );
22        }
23
24        public boolean handleEvent( Event e )
25        {
26            if ( e.metaDown() )
27                meta.setText( " META" );
28
29            if ( e.controlDown() )
30                ctrl.setText( " CTRL" );
31
32            if ( e.shiftDown() )
33                shift.setText( "SHIFT" );
34
35            return true;    // event has been handled
36        }
37    }
```

Fig. 10.35 Demonstrating methods **controlDown**, **metaDown** and
shiftDown (part 2 of 2).

10.11 FlowLayout Layout Manager

Complex GUIs (like Fig. 10.1) require that each component be placed in an exact location.
They usually consist of multiple panels with each panel's components arranged in a specific order. *Layout managers* arrange components on a container. Figure 10.36 lists the layout
managers we discuss in this chapter. We discuss more layout managers in the next chapter.

The previous examples have been using the *FlowLayout* layout manager—which is
the default for panels and applets. Class *FlowLayout* inherits from class **Object** and
implements the *LayoutManger* interface. The **LayoutManager** interface defines the
methods that each layout manager uses to arrange components on a container.

FlowLayout is the most basic layout manager. GUI components are placed on a container from left to right in the order in which they are added to the container. When the edge
of the container is reached, components are continued on the next line. The **FlowLayout**
class constructors and constants are summarized in Fig. 10.37.

Layout manager	Description
FlowLayout	Default for applets and panels. Places components sequentially (left to right) in the order they were added.
BorderLayout	Arranges the components into five areas: **North, South, East, West**, and **Center**.
GridLayout	Arranges the components into rows and columns.

Fig. 10.36 Layout managers.

FlowLayout contructors and constants

```
public final static int CENTER
```
A constant value representing center alignment in **FlowLayout**. Components are aligned center by default.

```
public final static int LEFT
```
A constant value representing left alignment in **FlowLayout**.

```
public final static int RIGHT
```
A constant value representing right alignment in **FlowLayout**.

```
public FlowLayout()
```
Constructs a **FlowLayout** with center alignment.

```
public FlowLayout( int alignment ) // component alignment
```
Constructs a **FlowLayout** with a specified alignment. The value for alignment is either **FlowLayout.RIGHT, FlowLayout.LEFT**, or **FlowLayout.CENTER**.

```
public FlowLayout(
    int alignment,        // component alignment
    int horizontal_gap,   // horizontal distance between components
    int vertical_gap )    // vertical distance between components
```
Constructs a **FlowLayout** with a specified alignment. The value for alignment is either **FlowLayout.RIGHT, FlowLayout.LEFT**, or **FlowLayout.CENTER**. The distance in pixels between components is specified by the last two arguments.

Fig. 10.37 FlowLayout constructors and constants.

The program of Fig. 10.38 creates four **TextField** objects and adds them to the applet using the default **FlowLayout** layout manager. The components are automatically center aligned on the applet.

The program of Fig. 10.39 creates four **TextField** objects and adds them to the applet. The components are center aligned in **FlowLayout**. The layout of the program is the same as Fig. 10.38.

```
1   // Fig. 10.38: FlowDefault.java
2   // Demonstrating FlowLayout default alignment.
3   import java.applet.Applet;
4   import java.awt.*;
5
6   public class FlowDefault extends Applet {
7      private TextField t1, t2, t3, t4;
8
9      public void init()
10     {
11        // use the default layout manager
12        // for the applet which is FlowLayout
13
14        t1 =  new TextField( "Default " );
15        t1.setEditable( false );
16        add( t1 );
17
18        t2 = new TextField( "Default " );
19        t2.setEditable( false );
20        add( t2 );
21
22        t3 =  new TextField( "Default " );
23        t3.setEditable( false );
24        add( t3 );
25
26        t4 = new TextField( "Default " );
27        t4.setEditable( false );
28        add( t4 );
29     }
30  }
```

Fig. 10.38 Program that demonstrates the default alignment in **FlowLayout**.

A container's layout is set with the **setLayout** *method* of the **Container** class. The statement

```
setLayout( new FlowLayout( FlowLayout.CENTER ) );
```

constructs a new center aligned **FlowLayout** layout manager, which is then set for the applet using method **setLayout**. As each component is added the applet, the component is placed according to the **FlowLayout** layout manager.

```
1   // Fig. 10.39: FlowCenter.java
2   // Demonstrating FlowLayout center alignment.
3   import java.applet.Applet;
4   import java.awt.*;
5
6   public class FlowCenter extends Applet {
7      private TextField t1, t2, t3, t4;
8
9      public void init()
10     {
11        // set layout
12        setLayout( new FlowLayout( FlowLayout.CENTER ) );
13
14        t1 =  new TextField( "Center " );
15        t1.setEditable( false );
16        add( t1 );
17
18        t2 = new TextField( "Center " );
19        t2.setEditable( false );
20        add( t2 );
21
22        t3 =  new TextField( "Center " );
23        t3.setEditable( false );
24        add( t3 );
25
26        t4 = new TextField( "Center " );
27        t4.setEditable( false );
28        add( t4 );
29     }
30  }
```

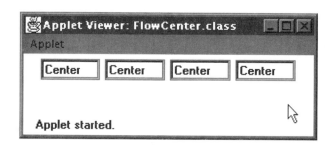

Fig. 10.39 Program that demonstrates the center alignment in **FlowLayout**.

The program of Fig. 10.40 creates four **TextField** objects and adds them to the applet. The components are right aligned in **FlowLayout**. The **FlowLayout** object was initialized with the constant **FlowLayout.RIGHT**.

```
1  // Fig. 10.40: FlowRight.java
2  // Demonstrating FlowLayout right alignment.
3  import java.applet.Applet;
4  import java.awt.*;
5
6  public class FlowRight extends Applet {
7     private TextField t1, t2, t3, t4;
8
9     public void init()
10    {
11       // set layout
12       setLayout( new FlowLayout( FlowLayout.RIGHT ) );
13
14       t1 =  new TextField( "Right " );
15       t1.setEditable( false );
16       add( t1 );
17
18       t2 = new TextField( "Right " );
19       t2.setEditable( false );
20       add( t2 );
21
22       t3 =  new TextField( "Right " );
23       t3.setEditable( false );
24       add( t3 );
25
26       t4 = new TextField( "Right " );
27       t4.setEditable( false );
28       add( t4 );
29    }
30 }
```

Fig. 10.40 Program that demonstrates the right alignment in **FlowLayout**.

The program of Fig. 10.41 creates four **TextField** objects and adds them to the applet. The components are left aligned in **FlowLayout**. The **FlowLayout** object was initialized with the constant **FlowLayout.LEFT**.

```
1   // Fig. 10.41: FlowLeft.java
2   // Demonstrating FlowLayout left alignment.
3   import java.applet.Applet;
4   import java.awt.*;
5
6   public class FlowLeft extends Applet {
7      private TextField t1, t2, t3, t4;
8
9      public void init()
10     {
11        // set layout
12        setLayout( new FlowLayout( FlowLayout.LEFT ) );
13
14        t1 =  new TextField( "Left " );
15        t1.setEditable( false );
16        add( t1 );
17
18        t2 = new TextField( "Left " );
19        t2.setEditable( false );
20        add( t2 );
21
22        t3 =  new TextField( "Left " );
23        t3.setEditable( false );
24        add( t3 );
25
26        t4 = new TextField( "Left " );
27        t4.setEditable( false );
28        add( t4 );
29     }
30  }
```

Fig. 10.41 Program that demonstrates the left alignment in **FlowLayout**.

The program of Fig. 10.42 creates three **Panel** objects and adds two **Textfield** objects to each. One panel uses a **FlowLayout** that specifies right alignment with a horizontal spacing of 0 pixels and a vertical spacing of 10 pixels. Another panel uses a **Flow-Layout** that specifies left alignment with a horizontal spacing of 10 pixels and a vertical spacing of 0 pixels. The third panel uses a **FlowLayout** that specifies center alignment with a horizontal spacing of 10 pixels and a vertical spacing of 10 pixels. The background color of each panel is changed for emphasis.

```
1   // Fig. 10.42: Flow.java
2   // Demonstrating FlowLayout component spacing.
3   import java.applet.Applet;
4   import java.awt.*;
5
6   public class Flow extends Applet {
7      private TextField t1, t2, t3, t4, t5, t6;
8      private Panel p1, p2, p3;
9
10     public void init()
11     {
12        p1 = new Panel();
13        p2 = new Panel();
14        p3 = new Panel();
15
16        // set layout for panel p1
17        p1.setLayout( new FlowLayout( FlowLayout.RIGHT,
18                                      0, 10 ) );
19
20        t1 = new TextField( "Text " );
21        t2 = new TextField( "Field " );
22        p1.add( t1 );
23        p1.add( t2 );
24
25        // set layout for panel p2
26        p2.setLayout( new FlowLayout( FlowLayout.LEFT,
27                                      10, 0 ) );
28
29        t3 = new TextField( "Text " );
30        t4 = new TextField( "Field " );
31        p2.add( t3 );
32        p2.add( t4 );
33
34        p3.setLayout( new FlowLayout( FlowLayout.CENTER,
35                                      10, 10 ) );
36
37        t5 = new TextField( "Text " );
38        t6 = new TextField( "Field " );
39        p3.add( t5 );
40        p3.add( t6 );
41
42        // change background colors of panels
43        p1.setBackground( Color.pink );
44        p2.setBackground( Color.red );
45        p3.setBackground( Color.orange );
46        add( p1 );
47        add( p2 );
48        add( p3 );
49     }
50  }
```

Fig. 10.42 Demonstrating space between components (part 1 of 2).

Fig. 10.42 Demonstrating space between components (part 2 of 2).

The statement

```
p1.setLayout( new FlowLayout( FlowLayout.RIGHT, 0, 10 ) );
```

sets the layout manager of **p1** to right aligned **FlowLayout**. Each component will be separated by zero pixels horizontally and ten pixels vertically. Panel objects **p2** and **p3** have their layouts set to **FlowLayout** in a similar manner. Note that the panels are center aligned on the applet because the applet's default layout was not changed.

10.12 BorderLayout Layout Manager

The **BorderLayout** layout manager arranges components into five areas: **North**, **South**, **East**, **West**, and **Center** (**North** corresponds to the top of the container). Class **BorderLayout** class inherits from **Object** and implements the **LayoutManager** interface. The **BorderLayout** class constructors are summarized in Fig. 10.43.

The program of Fig. 10.44 demonstrates the **BorderLayout** layout manager using five buttons.

The **setLayout** method is used to specify **BorderLayout**. Notice the difference in the **add** method's arguments. For example, the statement

---

BorderLayout constructors

---

public BorderLayout()
    Constructs a **BorderLayout**.

public BorderLayout(int horizontalGap, int verticalGap)
    Constructs a **BorderLayout** with horizontal components separated by **horizontalGap** pixels and each vertical component separated by **verticalGap** pixels.

Fig. 10.43 **BorderLayout** class constructors.

```
1    // Fig. 10.44: Border.java
2    // Demonstrating BorderLayout.
3    import java.applet.Applet;
4    import java.awt.*;
5
6    public class Border extends Applet {
7        private Button centerButton, eastButton, northButton,
8                       westButton, southButton;
9
10       public void init()
11       {
12           // instantiate button objects
13           centerButton = new Button( "center Button" );
14           westButton = new Button( "west Button" );
15           eastButton = new Button( "east Button" );
16           southButton = new Button( "south Button" );
17           northButton = new Button( "north Button");
18
19           // set layout to border layout
20           setLayout( new BorderLayout() );
21
22           // order not important
23           add( "South", southButton );     // South position
24           add( "North", northButton );     // North position
25           add( "East", eastButton );       // East position
26           add( "Center", centerButton );   // Center position
27           add( "West", westButton );       // West position
28       }
29   }
```

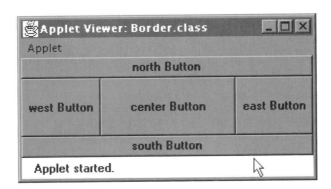

Fig. 10.44 Program that demonstrates **BorderLayout**.

```
add( "South", southButton );
```

specifies that the button named **southButton** is to be placed in the **South** position. Since the position must be specified as the first argument, the components can be added in any order.

The **North** and **South** positions are the first to be sized. They extend to each container side. The **East** and **West** positions are sized next. They extend from **North** to **South** and extend to one container side. The **Center** component is sized last. The **Center** area is bounded by the **North**, **South**, **East**, and **West** positions.

In **BorderLayout**, up to five components can be used—one for each position. When a position is not used (except **Center**), the position is occupied by one or more of the other components. For example, if the **North** position is unoccupied, the **East**, **Center**, and **West** components extend to the top of the container.

The program of Fig. 10.45 uses a **BorderLayout** with four components. The **East** position is not used. The **Center** component extends to occupy the **East** position.

The program of Fig. 10.46 uses a **BorderLayout** with five buttons. Each button is separated horizontally by 20 pixels and vertically by 15 pixels.

The statement

```
setLayout( new BorderLayout( 20, 15 ) );
```

sets the applet's layout manager to **BorderLayout**. Each component is separated by 20 pixels horizontally and 15 pixels vertically.

```
1   // Fig. 10.45: Border2.java
2   // Demonstrating BorderLayout with four components.
3   import java.applet.Applet;
4   import java.awt.*;
5
6   public class Border2 extends Applet {
7      private Button centerButton, northButton,
8                     westButton, southButton;
9
10     public void init()
11     {
12        // instantiate button objects
13        centerButton = new Button( "center Button" );
14        westButton = new Button( "west Button" );
15        southButton = new Button( "south Button" );
16        northButton = new Button( "north Button");
17
18        // set layout to border layout
19        setLayout( new BorderLayout() );
20
21        // order not important
22        add( "South", southButton );    // South position
23        add( "North", northButton );    // North position
24        add( "Center", centerButton );  // Center position
25        add( "West", westButton );      // West position
26     }
27  }
```

Fig. 10.45 Program that demonstrates a **BorderLayout** with four components (part 1 of 2).

Fig. 10.45 Program that demonstrates a **BorderLayout** with four components (part 2 of 2).

```
1   // Fig. 10.46: Border3.java
2   // Demonstrating BorderLayout component spacing.
3   import java.applet.Applet;
4   import java.awt.*;
5
6   public class Border3 extends Applet {
7       private Button centerButton, eastButton, northButton,
8                      westButton, southButton;
9
10      public void init()
11      {
12          // instantiate button objects
13          centerButton = new Button( "center Button" );
14          westButton = new Button( "west Button" );
15          eastButton = new Button( "east Button" );
16          southButton = new Button( "south Button" );
17          northButton = new Button( "north Button");
18
19          // set layout to border layout
20          setLayout( new BorderLayout( 20, 15 ) );
21
22          // order not important
23          add( "South", southButton );     // South position
24          add( "North", northButton );     // North position
25          add( "East", eastButton );       // East position
26          add( "Center", centerButton );   // Center position
27          add( "West", westButton );       // West position
28      }
29  }
```

Fig. 10.46 Demonstrating **BorderLayout** component spacing (part 1 of 2).

Fig. 10.46 Demonstrating **BorderLayout** component spacing (part 2 of 2).

Common Programming Error 10.10

*In **BorderLayout**, passing to the **add** method either **"north"**, **"south"**, **"east"**, **"west"**, or **"center"** results in a run time logic error. In some cases, the component may not be displayed at all. The name of each direction must begin with a capital letter.*

10.13 GridLayout Layout Manager

The **GridLayout** layout manager divides the container into a grid so components can be placed in rows and columns. Class **GridLayout** inherits directly from class **Object** and implements the **LayoutManager** interface. Each component is given the same size. Components are added to a **GridLayout** starting at the top-left cell of the grid proceding left-to-right until the row is full. Then, the process continues left-to-right on the next row, etc. The **GridLayout** class's constructors are summarized in Fig. 10.47.

GridLayout constructors

```
public GridLayout(
    int rows,          // number of rows
    int columns)       // number of columns
```
Constructs a **GridLayout** of **rows** rows and **columns** columns.

```
public GridLayout(
    int rows,          // number of rows
    int columns,       // number of columns
    int h,             // horizontal spacing between components
    int v)             // vertical spacing between components
```
Constructs a **GridLayout** with each component separated horizontally by **h** pixels and separated vertically by **v** pixels.

Fig. 10.47 GridLayout constructors.

The program of Fig. 10.48 demonstrates the **GridLayout** layout manager using five buttons. The **Button** objects are arranged in a grid with two rows and three columns. Method *setLayout* specifies a **GridLayout**. The first component is added to the first column of the first row. The next component is added to the second column of the first row, etc. Because there are only five components, the third column in the second row is empty.

```
1   // Fig. 10.48: Grid.java
2   // Demonstrating GridLayout.
3   import java.applet.Applet;
4   import java.awt.*;
5
6   public class Grid extends Applet {
7       private Button button1, button2, button3,
8                      button4, button5;
9
10      public void init()
11      {
12          // instantiate button objects
13          button1 = new Button( "one" );
14          button2 = new Button( "two" );
15          button3 = new Button( "three" );
16          button4 = new Button( "four" );
17          button5 = new Button( "five");
18
19          // set layout to grid layout
20          setLayout( new GridLayout( 2, 3 ) );
21
22          // order is important
23          add( button1 );      // row 1 column 1
24          add( button2 );      // row 1 column 2
25          add( button3 );      // row 1 column 3
26          add( button4 );      // row 2 column 1
27          add( button5 );      // row 2 column 2
28      }
29  }
```

Fig. 10.48 Program that demonstrates **GridLayout**.

The program of Fig. 10.49 places six buttons into a 2-by-3 grid in which components are separated by 20 pixels horizontally and 25 pixels vertically. The grid is set with the following statement

```
setLayout( new GridLayout( 2, 3, 20, 25 ) );
```

```
1   // Fig. 10.49: Grid2.java
2   // Demonstrating GridLayout component spacing.
3   import java.applet.Applet;
4   import java.awt.*;
5
6   public class Grid2 extends Applet {
7      private Button button1, button2, button3,
8                     button4, button5, button6;
9
10     public void init()
11     {
12        // instantiate button objects
13        button1 = new Button( "one" );
14        button2 = new Button( "two" );
15        button3 = new Button( "three" );
16        button4 = new Button( "four" );
17        button5 = new Button( "five");
18        button6 = new Button( "six" );
19
20        // set layout to grid layout
21        setLayout( new GridLayout( 2, 3, 20, 25 ) );
22
23        // order is important
24        add( button1 );     // row 1 column 1
25        add( button2 );     // row 1 column 2
26        add( button3 );     // row 1 column 3
27        add( button4 );     // row 2 column 1
28        add( button5 );     // row 2 column 2
29        add( button6 );     // row 2 column 3
30     }
31  }
```

Fig. 10.49 Program that demonstrates **GridLayout** component spacing

Summary

- Graphical user interfaces (GUIs) present a program as a picture allowing the user to get a "look" and "feel" for a program.

- Classes used to create GUI components are part of the **java.awt** package.

- Labels provide an area where a single line of static (read-only) text is displayed.

- A container is an area where components may be placed with the **Container** class **add** method. When a component is added, the component appears on the screen.

- **Label** method **getText** returns a label's text.

- **Label** method **setText** method sets the text for a label.

- A button is a component that the user can click to trigger a specific event.

- Push buttons are created with class **Button**. The text on the face of a button is called a button label.

- GUIs are event driven. An event is an asynchronous process such as the user moving the move, clicking the mouse, etc. Events are sent to a program by the windowing system.

- Events are stored in **Event** objects. Class **Event** is part of the **java.awt** package.

- When a button is clicked, the **action** method is called. The **action** method returns a **boolean** value and receives two arguments: **Event** and **Object**. The **Event** stores specific information about the event. The **Object** component-specific information. **Event** instance variable **target** identifies the component that generated the event. For **Button**, the **Event** class's instance variable **arg** contains the button label.

- **TextField**s are single-line areas that receive user inputs from the keyboard.

- **TextField** method **setEditable**, when passed a **false** value, specifies that a text field is read-only.

- **TextField** method **setEchoCharacter** takes a single character argument and uses it as a masking character for the specified text field.

- For **TextField**s, **Event** instance variable **arg** contains the text in the text field when the enter key is pressed.

- **Choice** buttons enable the user to select from a list of items. Items are added to a **Choice** button with method **addItem**. A numeric index keeps track of the ordering of items. The first item is added at index 0. The first item added is displayed when the **Choice** button is added to a container. Other items are selected by clicking the down arrow which expands into a list from which the user can make a selection. For a **Choice** button, **Event** instance variable **arg** is the **String** item selected.

- **Choice** method **getItem** returns the item at a specified index. **Choice** method **getSelectedItem** returns the selected item from a **Choice** button. **Choice** method **countItems** returns the number of items in a choice button. **Choice** method **getSelectedIndex** index returns the index of a selected item.

- **Checkbox** buttons and radio buttons are state buttons **true/false** values.

- **Checkbox** method **setLabel** sets the label for a checkbox. A checkbox is always either **true** or **false**—**true** if a checkmark is in the box and **false** if the box is empty. **Checkbox** method **getState** returns a **boolean** representing a checkbox's state. **Event** instance variable **arg** for a **Checkbox** is a **Boolean** object.

- Checkboxes can be grouped together to form radio buttons. A set of radio buttons is created with the **CheckboxGroup** class and the **Checkbox** class. **CheckboxGroup**s are not components.

- **Checkbox** method **getState** is used to get the state of a radio button.

- **List**s display a series of items from which the user may select one or more items. **String**s are added to the list with **List** method **addItem**.

- Double clicking a **List** item triggers an event. **Event** instance variable **arg** for a **List** is the item double clicked.

- Multiple-selection **List**s can have more than one item selected at a time. Multiple selection is enabled by passing **true** as the second argument in the **List** constructor.

- A scrollbar appears when the number of list items exceeds the number of visible items. The number of visible lines is specified as the first argument in the constructor call.

- To capture items from a multiple-selection **List**, an external event must be triggered. A **Button** is commonly used to trigger the event. Method **getSelectedItems** returns the selected items in the list.

- Class **Panel** class inherits from **Container** and **Applet** inherits from **Panel**. The **Panel** constructor takes no arguments and is not overloaded. Panels are sized based on the components they contain.

- Method **mouseDown** is called when a mouse button is pressed. Method **mouseUp** is called when a mouse button is released. Method **mouseMove** is called when the mouse moves. Method **mouseEnter** is called when the mouse enters the physical boundaries of a component. Method **mouseExit** is called when the mouse leaves the physical boundary of a component. Method **mouseDrag** is called when the mouse button is pressed and held, and the mouse is moved (a process known as clicking and dragging).

- **Component** method **handleEvent** takes an **Event** argument and returns a **boolean** value. The default behavior of **handleEvent** is to identify the event and call the appropriate handler method. Each event has a unique number that identifies it. This number is stored in the **Event** instance variable **id**.

- Keyboard events are generated when keys are pressed and released. **Component** methods **keyUp** and **keyDown** handle keyboard events. The **keyDown** event is triggered when a key is pressed and the **keyUp** event is triggered when a key is released.

- **Event** instance variable **key** contains the unicode value of the key pressed or released.

- Keyboard constants are defined for some of the special purpose keys such as **Home**, **End**, **PgDn**, **PgUp**, **F1**, etc.

- **Event** methods **controlDown**, **metaDown** and **shiftDown** test the status of the control, meta and shift key.

- Layout managers are used to arrange components on a container. The default for panels and applets is the **FlowLayout** layout manager.

- **FlowLayout** is the most basic layout manager. GUI components are placed on a container from left to right—one after the other. A **Flowlayout** may be right, left, or center aligned. Center is the default alignment.

- The **BorderLayout** layout manager arranges components into five areas: **North**, **South**, **East**, **West**, and **Center**.

- Container method **setLayout** specifies a new layout for a container.

- In **BorderLayout**, up to five components can be used—one for each position. When a position is not used, the position is occupied by one or more of the other components.

- The **GridLayout** layout manager places components into rows and columns.Each component is given the same size. When components are added, the order is important. The first component added will be placed in the first column of the first row. The next component added will be placed in the second column of the first row and so forth.

Terminology

action method	container
add method	**Container** class
addItem method	control key
Applet class	**controlDown** method
arg	**countItems** method
attach a component to a container	default text in a text field
AWT (another/abstract windowing toolkit)	**East** in **BorderLayout**
awt package	**Event.DOWN**
BorderLayout class	**Event.END**
BorderLayout constructor	**Event.F1 - Event.F12**
BorderLayout layout manager	**Event.HOME**
button	**Event.LEFT**
button event	**Event.MOUSE_DOWN**
button label	**Event.MOUSE_DRAG**
Button class	**Event.MOUSE_ENTER**
Center in **BorderLayout**	**Event.MOUSE_EXIT**
checkbox button	**Event.MOUSE_MOVE**
Checkbox class	**Event.MOUSE_UP**
Checkbox constructor	**Event.PGDN**
checkbox label	**Event.PGUP**
CheckboxGroup class	**Event.RIGHT**
CheckboxGroup constructor	Event.UP
choice button	**Event** class
Choice class	event driven
Choice constructor	event handling
clicking and dragging	**FlowLayout.CENTER**
Component	**FlowLayout.LEFT**
Component class	**FlowLayout.RIGHT**

Common Programming Errors

10.1   Forgetting to add a component to a container is a run-time logic error.

10.2   Adding to a container a component that has not been instantiated throws a **NullPointer-Exception**.

10.3 Having more than one button with the same button label is a logic error. The buttons appear to be ambiguous to the user.

10.4 Using a lowercase f in **TextField** is a compilation error.

10.5 Using an uppercase b for box in **Checkbox** or **CheckboxGroup** is a syntax error.

10.6 Adding a **CheckboxGroup** object to a container is a compilation error.

10.7 When instantiating radio buttons, setting more than one radio button to **true** is a run-time logic error.

10.8 Attempting to add an item that is not a string to a list is a syntax error.

10.9 Adding a component to a container that has not been instantiated throws a **NullPointer-Exception**.

10.10 In **BorderLayout**, passing to the **add** method either **"north"**, **"south"**, **"east"**, **"west"**, or **"center"** results in a run time logic error. In some cases, the component may not be displayed at all. The name of each direction must begin with a capital letter.

Good Programming Practices

10.1 Provide a unique name for each button label.

Portability Tip

10.1 The look of a particular GUI component may vary across platforms. Java "ties" into the "local" GUI which varies from platform to platform.

Self-Review Exercises

10.1 Fill in the blanks in each of the following:
  a) A _____ event occurs when the mouse is moved.
  b) Text that cannot be modified by the user is called _____.
  c) A _____ arranges GUI components on an applet or panel.
  d) The **add** method is a _____ class method.
  e) GUI is an acronym for _____.
  f) The _____ method is used to set the layout manager for a container.
  g) A **mouseDrag** event triggers a _____ event and a _____ event.

10.2 State which of the following statements are true and which are false. If a statement is false, explain why.
  a) **BorderLayout** is the default layout manager for a panel.
  b) When the mouse pointer is on top of a GUI component, a **mouseOver** event occurs.
  c) A panel cannot be added to another panel.
  d) When building a GUI, one or more classes must be imported from the **awt** package.
  e) In a **BorderLayout** with five buttons, the **Center** button is the last component to be sized.
  f) When using **BorderLayout**, a maximum of five components may be used.

10.3 Find the error(s) in each of the following and explain how to correct it (them).

a) `buttonName = Button( "Caption" );`

b) `Label aLabel, Label;      // create references`

c) `txtField = new TextField( 50, "Default Text" );`

d)
```
public class radioButtons extends Applet {
    RadioButton rb;      // awt class RadioButton
    public void init()
    {
        this.rb = new RadioGroup();
        // other statements
     }
}
```

e)
```
public void init()
{
    setLayout( new GridLayout( 9, 9 ) );
    button1 = new Button( "North Star" );
    button2 = new Button( "South Pole" );
    add( "North", button1 );
    add( "South", button2 );
}
```

10.4 Briefly answer the following.

a) Explain what the asterisk (*****) means in the following statement:

`import java.awt.*;`.

b) Explain difference between a text field and a label.

Answers to Self-Review Exercises

10.1 a) **mouseMove**. b) static (read-only). c) Layout manager. d) **Container**. e) graphical user interface. f) **setLayout**. g) **mouseDown, mouseUp**.

10.2
a) False. The default is **FlowLayout**.
b) False. A **mouseEnter** event occurs.
c) False. A panel can be added to another panel.
d) True.
e) True.
f) True

10.3
a) **new** is needed to instantiate the object.
b) **Label** is a keyword and cannot be used as an identifier
c) The arguments passed to the constructor are reversed.
d) The **RadioGroup** class does not exist, the **CheckBoxGroup** class should be used.
e) **GridLayout** has been set and components are being adding with **BorderLayout** positions.

10.4
a) The asterisk is a wildcard that specifies multiple classes are to be imported.
b) A label is a component that displays a non-modifiable text. A text field is a component with a border that displays either modifiable text or non-modifiable text. A text field can also accept user input—where as a label cannot.

Exercises

10.5   Fill in the blanks in each of the following:
   a)   The **TextField** class inherits directly from _____
   b)   The layout managers discussed in this chapter are _____, _____, and _____.
   c)   The _____ method attaches a GUI component to a panel or to an applet.
   d)   A _____ event occurs when a mouse button is released.
   e)   The _____ class is used to create the a radio button group.

10.6   State which of the following statements are true and which are false. If a statement is false, explain why.
   a)   Only one layout manager can be used per applet (each panel added to the applet must use same layout manager as the applet).
   b)   GUI components can be added to a panel, in any order, with the **BorderLayout** layout manager.
   c)   The **addItem** method adds items to a choice button.
   d)   Radio buttons provide a series of mutually exclusive buttons (only one can be **true** at a time).
   e)   The **Graphics** object's **setFont** method is used to set the font for text fields.
   f)   A **List** object always displays a scrollbar.
   g)   The data type of **Event** instance **target** is always **Object**.
   h)   A **Mouse** object contains a method called **mouseDrag**.
   i)   The **BorderLayout** layout manager implements **LayoutManager**.
   j)   The **GridLayout** layout manager implements **LayoutManager**.
   k)   The **FlowLayout** layout manager does not implement **LayoutManager**.

10.7   State which of the following statements are true and which are false. If a statement is false, explain why.
   a)   An applet is a container.
   b)   A panel is a component.
   c)   A label is a container.
   d)   A list is a panel.
   e)   A button is a component.
   f)   A text field is an object.
   g)   **LayoutManager** inherits from **Object**.
   h)   **CheckboxGroup** inherits from **Component**.

10.8   Find any error(s) in each of the following and explain how to correct it (them).

```
a) import java.awt.*       // include AWT package
b) panelObject.GridLayout( 8, 8 ); // set GridLayout
c) button94.add( "Click here!" );  // add button label
d) setLayout( new FlowLayout( FlowLayout.DEFAULT ) );
e) if ( o.target instance of Choice )  // o is of type Object
f) add( east, eastButton );  // BorderLayout
g) CheckboxGroup c = new CheckboxGroup();
   add(c.Checkbox( "Gold", false ) );
   add(c.Checkbox( "Silver", true ) );
h) public boolean mouseMove( Event e, int x, int y )
   {
       ShowStatus("mouseMove...");
   }
```

10.9   Create the following GUI (Note you do not have to provide any functionality):

10.10 Create the following GUI (Note you do not have to provide any functionality):

10.11 Create the following GUI: (Note you do not have to provide any functionality)

10.12   Create the following GUI: (Note you do not have to provide any functionality)

10.13   Create the GUI of Fig. 10.1. The left-most component is a textarea. We discuss textareas in the next chapter. The textarea is created with the **TextArea** class and a call to the textarea constructor:

```
TextArea a = new TextArea( "Notepad", 5, 12 );
```

Note you do not have to provide any functionality for this GUI.

10.14   Write a temperature conversion program that converts from Fahrenheit to Celsius. The Fahrenheit temperature should be entered from the keyboard (via a text field). A text field should be used to display the converted temperature. Use the following formula for the conversion:
$$Celsius = 5/9 \times (Fahrenheit - 32)$$

10.15   Enhance the temperature conversion program of Exercise 10.14 by adding the Kelvin temperature scale. The program should also allow the user to make conversions between any two scales. Use the following formula (in addition to the one in Exercise 10.14): $Kelvin = Celsius + 273$.

10.16   Write a program that allows the user to draw a rectangle on an applet with the mouse. The upper-left coordinate should be the location where the user clicked and the lower-right coordinate should be the location where the user released the mouse button. Also display the area of the rectangle in the status bar. Use the formula: $Area = width \times height$.

10.17   Modify the program of Fig. 10.16 to draw different shapes. The user should be allowed to choose from an oval, an arc, a line, a rectangle with rounded corners, and a predefined polygon. Also display the mouse coordinates in the status bar.

10.18   Write a program that will allow the user to draw a shape on an applet with the mouse. The shape drawn should be determined by the following keys: c draws a circle, o draws an oval, r draws a rectangle, and l draws a line. The size and placement of the shape should be determined by the **mouseDrag** event. Display the current shape in the status bar. The initial shape should default to a circle.

10.19   Create an applet that enables the user to paint a picture. The user should be able to choose the shape to draw, the color in which the shape should appear and whether the shape should be filled with color. Use the graphical user interface components we discussed in this chapter such as **Choice** buttons, radio buttons and **Checkbox**es to allow the user to select various options. The program should override the **update** method so the user can draw several shapes and see all the shapes at the same time on the applet. The program should provide a **Button** object that allows the user to erase the applet. If you feel ambitious, try to provide a "rubber-banding" effect as the user drags the mouse to draw a shape (i.e., the user should be able to see the outline of the shape. (Note: You may have to remove the overridden **update** for this to work. Techniques from Chapter 14 will allow you to have both capabilities.)

10.20   Write a program that uses **System.out.println** statements to print out events. Provide a choice button with a minimum of four or five different events. The user should be able to choose an event to "monitor" from the choice button. When that particular event occurs, display information about the event in the status bar. Use the **toString** method on the event.

10.21   Write a program that draws a square. As the mouse is moved on the applet, the upper-left corner of the square should "float" to the mouse pointer. The square should follow the exact path of the mouse pointer.

10.22   Modify the program of Fig. 10.27 to incorporate colors. Provide a "toolbar" at the bottom of the applet that lists the following six colors: red, black, magenta, blue, green, and yellow. The toolbar should consist of six buttons, each with the appropriate color name. When a button is clicked, drawing should occur in the new color. Display the current drawing color in the status bar.

10.23   Modify the program of Fig. 10.27 to allow the user to erase. Erasing is done by drawing over a information in the background color. When the shift key is held, the drawing should be done in the background color.

10.24   Write a program that plays "guess the number" as follows: Your program chooses the number to be guessed by selecting an integer at random in the range 1-1000. The program then displays in a label:

> **I have a number between 1 and 1000 can you guess my number? Please enter your first guess.**

A text field should be used to input the guess. As each guess is input the background color should change to either red or blue. Red indicates that the user is getting "warmer" and blue indicates that the user is getting "colder." A second non-editable text field should display either "**Too High**" or "**Too Low**" to help the user zero in on the correct answer. When the user gets the correct answer "**Correct!**" should be displayed. When the user guesses the correct answer, the text field used for input should be changed to non-editable.

A button should be provided to allow the user to play the game again. When the button is clicked, a new random number should be generated and the first text field changed to editable.

10.25   It is often useful to display the events that occur druing the execution of a program to help understand when the events occur and how they are generated. Write an applet that enables the user to generate and process every event discussed in this chapter. The applet should override methods **action, mouseUp, mouseDown, mouseMove, mouseDrag, mouseEnter, mouseExit, keyUp** and **keyDown** to display messages when the events occur. Use **Event** method **toString** to convert the **Event** into a **String** that can be displayed. Method **toString** creates a **String** containing all the information in the **Event** object.

10.26   Modify your solution to exercise 10.19 to enable the user to select a font and a font size, then type text into a **TextField**. When the user presses enter, the text should be displayed on the applet in the chosen font and size. Modify the applet further to allow the user to specify the exact position at which the text should be dsplayed.

11

Advanced Graphical User Interface Components

Objectives

- To extend the graphical user interface.
- To be able to create and manipulate text areas.
- To be able to create and manipulate canvases.
- To be able to create and manipulate scrollbars.
- To be able to create custom components.
- To be able to create and manipulate frames.
- To be able to create and manipulate menus.
- To be able to create and manipulate dialog boxes.
- To be able to use advanced layout managers.

I claim not to have controlled events, but confess plainly that events have controlled me.
Abraham Lincoln

A good symbol is the best argument, and is a missionary to persuade thousands.
Ralph Waldo Emerson

Capture its reality in paint!
Paul Cézanne

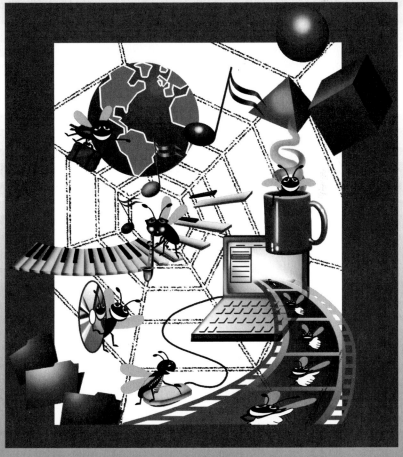

Outline

11.1 Introduction

In this chapter (also co-authored with our colleague, Mr. Tem Nieto of Deitel & Associates, Inc.) we continue our study of *graphical user interfaces* (GUIs). We discuss more advanced components and layout managers and lay the groundwork for building complex GUIs. Figure 11.1 shows the inheritance hierarchy for the components discussed in this chapter.

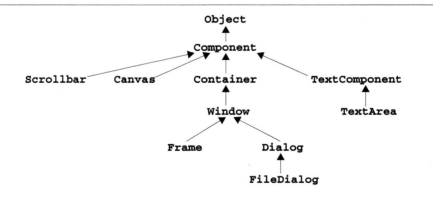

Fig. 11.1 Hierarchy of **java.awt** components discussed in this chapter.

11.2 TextAreas

Text areas provide an area for manipulating multiple lines of text. Like class **TextField**, class *TextArea* class inherits from *TextComponent*. Two **TextArea** class constructors are summarized in Fig. 11.2.

The program of Fig. 11.3 demonstrates the two constructors of Fig. 11.2. One text area displays text that cannot be modified by the user and the other text area allows the user to type information into the text area.

TextArea class constructors

```
public TextArea(
    int rows,       // number of visible rows
    int columns )   // number of visible columns
```
Constructs a text area with the specified number of rows and columns.

```
public TextArea(
    String s,
    int rows,
    int columns )
```
Constructs a text area containing the text **s** and the specified number of rows and columns.

Fig. 11.2 TextArea class constructors.

```
1   // Fig. 11.3: MyTextArea.java
2   // Creating TextArea objects.
3   import java.applet.Applet;
4   import java.awt.*;
5
6   public class MyTextArea extends Applet {
7      private TextArea t1, t2;
8
9      public void init()
10     {
11         t1 = new TextArea( "This text is read-only!",
12                            10, 20 );   // 10 x 20
13         t2 = new TextArea( 10, 20 );
14
15         t1.setEditable( false );      // read-only
16
17         // set layout
18         setLayout( new FlowLayout( FlowLayout.LEFT ) );
19
20         add( t1 );
21         add( t2 );
22      }
23   }
```

Fig. 11.3 Creating **TextArea** objects (part 1 of 2).

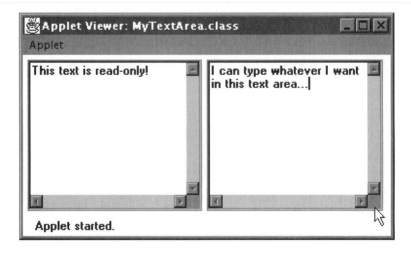

Fig. 11.3 Creating **TextArea** objects (part 2 of 2).

TextArea references **t1** and **t2** are created with class **TextArea**. The statement

```
t1 = new TextArea( "This text is read-only!", 10, 20 );
```

constructs a text area with **10** visible rows and **20** visible columns. The text **"This text is read-only!"** is displayed in the text area. The statement

```
t2 = new TextArea( 10, 20 );
```

instantiates object **t2**. **TextArea** object **t2** has **10** visible rows and **20** visible columns and initially does not display any text.

Method **setEditable** is used to make **TextArea t1** a non-editable **TextArea**. **TextArea t2** can be modified by the user. The applet's layout manager is set to a left-justified **FlowLayout** and each text area is placed on the applet with method **add**.

A text area always has a vertical scrollbar and horizontal scrollbar. The scrollbars are not capable of scrolling unless text extends beyond the visible rows or visible columns. The programmer does not have direct control over either of the scrollbars. We will discuss creating scrollbar components that the programmer can control in Section 11.4.

Unlike text fields in which pressing Enter generates an **action** event, text areas do not generate any events for processing by method **handleEvent** or method **action**. Retrieving text from a text area requires an external event—such as a button press. The process is similar to retrieving multiple items from a list (see Chapter 10).

The program of Fig. 11.4 copies the text selected in one text area to another text area. The text is copied when the button is pressed.

Text area objects **t1** and **t2** are instantiated. Each text area has **5** visible rows and **20** visible columns. The text contained in **String s** is placed in **t1** with the statement

```
t1.setText( s );
```

```
1   // Fig. 11.4: MyTextArea2.java
2   // Copying selected text from one text area to another.
3   import java.applet.Applet;
4   import java.awt.*;
5
6   public class MyTextArea2 extends Applet {
7      private TextArea t1, t2;
8      private Button b;
9
10     public void init()
11     {
12        String s = "The big bad boy stepped up\n" +
13                   "to the microphone. The crowd\n" +
14                   "sat on the edge of their seats\n" +
15                   "and waited...";
16
17        t1 = new TextArea( 5, 20 );
18        t1.setText( s );     // add text to t1
19
20        t2 = new TextArea( 5, 20 );
21        b = new Button( "Copy >>>" );
22
23        // set layout
24        setLayout( new FlowLayout( FlowLayout.LEFT, 5, 5 ) );
25
26        add( t1 );
27        add( b );
28        add( t2 );
29     }
30
31     public boolean action( Event e, Object o )
32     {
33        if ( e.target == b ) {
34           t2.setText( t1.getSelectedText() );
35           return true;
36        }
37
38        return false;
39     }
40  }
```

Fig. 11.4 Copying selected text from one text area to another (part 1 of 2).

which uses the **TextComponent** class method *setText*. The button object **b** is instantiated and given the label **"Copy>>>"**. The layout manager for the applet is set to **FlowLayout** left justified with **5** pixels of horizontal spacing and **5** pixels of vertical spacing around each component. Each component is placed on the applet with the **add** method.

The **action** method is overridden for this class. When the button is clicked, any selected text in **t1** is placed in **t2**. The statement

```
t2.setText( t1.getSelectedText() );
```

Fig. 11.4 Copying selected text from one text area to another (part 2 of 2).

performs the copying. The **TextComponent** class method *getSelectedText* returns the selected text as a **String** which is then placed in **t2** with method **setText**. Copying does not occur if text is not selected in **t1** when the button is clicked. Text is selected by highlighting it with the mouse.

11.3 Canvases

A *canvas* is a component where graphics can be drawn and that can receive mouse events. Class *Canvas* class inherits from **Component**. A canvas has its own graphics context.

 Software Engineering Observation 11.1

Graphics drawn directly on an applet can be covered by components. Canvases eliminate this problem by providing a dedicated area for graphics.

The program of Fig. 11.5 creates the simplest possible canvas. The **Component** class method *setBackground* is used to change the canvas background to green. The program does nothing other than display a green canvas.

Canvas object **c** is instantiated with the statement

```
c = new Canvas();
```

which calls the **Canvas** constructor. The background color of **c** is changed to green with method **setBackground**.

A canvas has no default size when it is created. The statement

```
c.resize( 250, 60 );
```

uses the **Component** method *resize* to size the canvas to the specified width and height. The **Canvas** object is placed on the applet with the **add** method.

 Common Programming Error 11.1

*Forgetting to call the **resize** method on a canvas is a run-time logic error. The canvas cannot be seen.*

```
1   // Fig. 11.5: CreateCanvas.java
2   // Creating a Canvas.
3   import java.applet.Applet;
4   import java.awt.*;
5
6   public class CreateCanvas extends Applet {
7      private Canvas c;
8
9      public void init()
10     {
11        c = new Canvas();  // instantiate object
12        c.setBackground( Color.green );
13        c.resize( 250, 60 );
14
15        add( c );
16     }
17  }
```

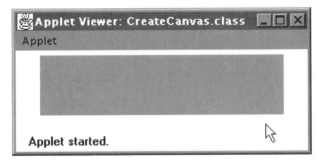

Fig. 11.5 Program that creates a canvas.

Class **NewCanvas** contains one instance variable **shape** that keeps track of which shape is to be drawn. The **paint** method is overridden in class **NewCanvas** to draw a shape on the canvas. If **shape** is **1**, method **fillOval** draws a solid circle. Otherwise method **fillRect** draws a solid rectangle. Method **setShape** sets the **private** instance variable **shape** and calls **repaint** to refresh the applet. When **paint** is called, the appropriate shape is drawn on the canvas.

The **Canvas** instantiated in Fig. 11.5 is not capable of drawing because the **Canvas**'s **paint** method (which is inherited from class **Component**) does nothing by default. The **paint** method for a **Canvas** must be overridden to draw on the **Canvas**. This is accomplished by creating a subclass of **Canvas**. Drawing on a **Canvas** is performed with coordinates that are measured from the upper-left corner of the **Canvas**. The coordinates of the upper-left corner are (0, 0).

The program of Fig. 11.6 creates class **NewCanvas** that extends class **Canvas**. The program draws either a solid circle or a solid square on the canvas depending on which button the user presses.

Class **MyCanvas** declares a reference to a **Panel**, a reference to a **NewCanvas** and two references to **Button** objects. The **Panel** object **p** is instantiated with a call to the **Panel** constructor. The line

```
1   // Fig. 11.6: MyCanvas.java
2   // Extending the Canvas class.
3   import java.applet.Applet;
4   import java.awt.*;
5
6   class NewCanvas extends Canvas {
7      private int shape;
8
9      public void paint( Graphics g )
10     {
11        if ( shape == 1 )
12           g.fillOval( 50, 10, 60, 60 );
13        else  // shape == 2
14           g.fillRect( 50, 10, 60, 60 );
15     }
16
17     public void setShape( int s )
18     {
19        shape = s;
20        repaint();
21     }
22  }
23
24  public class MyCanvas extends Applet {
25     private Panel p;
26     private NewCanvas c;
27     private Button circleButton, squareButton;
28
29     public void init()
30     {
31        p = new Panel();
32        c = new NewCanvas();   // instantiate canvas
33
34        c.resize( 185, 125 );  // resize canvas
35
36        squareButton = new Button( "Square" );
37        circleButton = new Button( "Circle" );
38
39        p.setLayout( new BorderLayout() );
40        p.add( "North", circleButton );
41        p.add( "South", squareButton );
42
43        setLayout( new BorderLayout() );
44        add( "West", p );
45        add( "East", c );      // add canvas
46     }
47
```

Fig. 11.6 Extending the **Canvas** class (part 1 of 2).

```
48        public boolean action( Event e, Object o )
49        {
50            if ( e.target == circleButton )
51                c.setShape( 1 );
52            else    // squareButton
53                c.setShape( 2 );
54
55            return true;
56        }
57    }
```

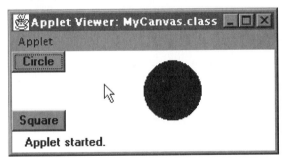

Fig. 11.6 Extending the **Canvas** class (part 2 of 2).

```
    c = new NewCanvas();
```

calls the constructor for **NewCanvas**. The canvas is resized to **185** by **125** pixels. The objects **squareButton** and **circleButton** are instantiated with calls to the **Button** constructor. The layout manager for the panel is changed to **BorderLayout** and both button objects are added to the panel. The layout manager for the applet is also changed to **BorderLayout** and the panel and canvas are added.

The **action** method is overridden for the applet. If **circleButton** is pressed **NewCanvas** method **setShape** is passed a value of **1**, otherwise a value of **2** is passed. The **NewCanvas** is then updated with the proper shape.

Canvases do not generate any events but are capable of recognizing mouse events. The program of Fig. 11.7 allows the user to draw an oval on a canvas with the mouse.

```
1   // Fig. 11.7: MyCanvas.java
2   // Capturing mouse events with a Canvas.
3   import java.applet.Applet;
4   import java.awt.*;
5
6   class NewCanvas extends Canvas {
7      private int width, height;
8      private int x1, y1;
9
10     public void paint( Graphics g )
11     {
12        g.drawOval( x1, y1, width, height );
13     }
14
15     public boolean mouseDown( Event e, int x, int y )
16     {
17        x1 = x;
18        y1 = y;
19        return true;
20     }
21
22     public boolean mouseUp( Event e, int x, int y )
23     {
24        width = Math.abs( x - x1 );
25        height = Math.abs( y - y1 );
26
27        // determine the upper left point of
28        // the bounding rectangle
29        x1 = Math.min( x1, x );
30        y1 = Math.min( y1, y );
31
32        repaint();
33        return true;
34     }
35  }
36
37  public class MyCanvas extends Applet {
38     private NewCanvas c;
39
40     public void init()
41     {
42        c = new NewCanvas();
43        c.resize( 185, 70 );  // resize canvas
44        c.setBackground( Color.yellow );
45
46        add( c );     // add canvas to applet
47     }
48  }
```

Fig. 11.7 Capturing mouse events with a **Canvas** (part 1 of 2).

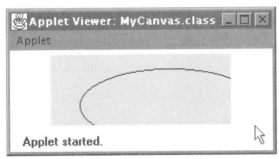

Fig. 11.7 Capturing mouse events with a **Canvas** (part 2 of 2).

The **NewCanvas** class extends the **Canvas** class. The instance variables **width** and **height** store the oval's width and height respectively. The other two instance variables store the *x* coordinate and *y* coordinate where the mouse was pressed.

The **paint** method has been overridden for this class. The **paint** method draws an oval of the specified width and height with the upper-left corner of the rectangle that bounds the oval at the coordinate (**xDown, yDown**). Drawing is strictly confined to the canvas. Anything drawn off the canvas is *clipped*.

The **mouseDown** method and **mouseUp** method have been overridden for this class. The instance variables **x1** and **y1** are set in **mouseDown**. The **mouseUp** method sets **width** and **height** with the statements

```
width = Math.abs( x - x1 );
height = Math.abs( y - y1 );
```

The **x1** value is subtracted from **x** of the **mouseUp** event and the **y1** value is subtracted from **y** of the **mouseUp** event. The oval's width and height must be positive values or the oval cannot be displayed. The **Math** class method **abs** returns the absolute value of the subtraction. The upper-left corner of the bounding rectangle should be the lowest *x* coordinate and the lowest *y* coordinate. The **static Math** class method **min** is used to get the lowest coordinate for **x1** and **y1**. The **repaint** method is called to schedule a repaint of the canvas.

Class **MyCanvas** instantiates a **NewCanvas** object **c**. The canvas is resized and the background color is set to yellow. The canvas is then added to the applet.

11.4 Scrollbars

A *scrollbar* is a component that "scrolls" through a range of integer values. Stand-alone scrollbars are created with class **Scrollbar** which inherits from **Component**. Figure 11.8 shows a stand-alone horizontal scrollbar.

Scrollbars have either a *horizontal orientation* or a *vertical orientation*. The *scroll arrows* for a horizontal scrollbar point right-left with the minimum value being the extreme left and the maximum value being the extreme right. The scroll arrows for a vertical scrollbar point up-down—with the minimum value being the extreme upward position and the maximum value being the extreme downward position. The relative position of the *scroll box* (also called a *slider*) indicates the current value of the scrollbar.

The **Scrollbar** class has three constructors one of which is presented here. The orientation of a **Scrollbar** is specified by one of two **static** class variables. These constants and the **Scrollbar** constructor are summarized in Fig. 11.9.

scroll arrow   scroll box

Fig. 11.8 A scrollbar component.

Scrollbar constants and a **Scrollbar** constructor

public final static int HORIZONTAL
    Constant that specifies a horizontal orientation for a scrollbar.

public final static int VERTICAL
    Constant that specifies a vertical orientation for a scrollbar.

```
public Scrollbar(
    int orientation,      // HORIZONTAL or VERTICAL
    int initialValue,     // initial value of scrollbar
    int visibleArea,      // scroll box size
    int minimumValue,     // minimum value of scrollbar
    int maximumValue )    // maximum value of scrollbar
```
    Constructs a scrollbar with the specified orientation (**HORIZONTAL** or **VERTICAL**), initial value, visible area, minimum value, and maximum value.

Fig. 11.9 **Scrollbar** constants and a **Scrollbar** constructor.

The constructor takes five integer arguments. The first argument, **Scrollbar.HOR-IZONTAL** or **Scrollbar.VERTICAL**, specifies the orientation. The second argument specifies the *initial value* of the scrollbar. The scroll box is initially at this position. The third argument specifies the *visible area* of the scroll box. This value is used when the user clicks between a scroll arrow and a scroll box on a **Scrollbar** to determine how far the scroll box should move. The fourth argument specifies the *minimum value* of the scrollbar. If the initial value is less than the minimum value, the initial value is changed to the minimum value. The fifth argument specifies the *maximum value* the scrollbar can have. If the initial value is larger than the maximum value, the initial value is set to the maximum value.

Common Programming Error 11.2

*Passing a value to the **Scrollbar** constructor of Fig. 11.9 other than **Scrollbar.HOR-IZONTAL** or **Scrollbar.VERTICAL** throws an* **IllegalArgumentException**

The program of Fig. 11.10 allows the user to size an oval drawn on a canvas. The sizing is done with a horizontal scrollbar and a vertical scrollbar.

```
1   // Fig. 11.10: Scroll.java
2   // Using Scrollbars to size an oval.
3   import java.applet.Applet;
4   import java.awt.*;
5
6   public class Scroll extends Applet {
7       private Scrollbar upDown, leftRight;
8       private MyCanvas theCanvas;
9       private Panel thePanel;
10
11      public void init()
12      {
13          // create scrollbars
14          upDown = new Scrollbar( Scrollbar.VERTICAL, 100,
15                                  0, 0, 200 );
16
17          leftRight = new Scrollbar( Scrollbar.HORIZONTAL, 100,
18                                     0, 0, 200 );
19
20          // create canvas
21          theCanvas = new MyCanvas();
22          theCanvas.resize( 200, 200 );
23          theCanvas.setBackground( Color.yellow );
24
25          thePanel = new Panel();  // create panel
26
27          // set layouts
28          setLayout( new BorderLayout() );
29          thePanel.setLayout( new BorderLayout() );
30
```

Fig. 11.10 Using **Scrollbar**s to size an oval (part 1 of 3).

```
31          // layout components
32          add( "West", upDown );
33          thePanel.add( "South", leftRight );
34          thePanel.add( "Center", theCanvas );
35          add( "Center", thePanel );
36       }
37
38    public boolean handleEvent( Event e )
39    {
40       if ( e.target instanceof Scrollbar ) {
41
42          if ( e.target == upDown )
43             theCanvas.setHeight( upDown.getValue() );
44          else   // leftRight
45             theCanvas.setWidth( leftRight.getValue() );
46
47          showStatus( "e.arg is " + String.valueOf( e.arg ) );
48          theCanvas.repaint();   // repaint canvas
49          return true;
50       }
51
52       // not one of our scroll bars
53       // do the default handling ( base class )
54       return super.handleEvent( e );
55    }
56 }
57
58 class MyCanvas extends Canvas {
59    private int width, height;
60
61    public MyCanvas()
62    {
63       setWidth( 100 );
64       setHeight( 100 );
65    }
66
67    public void setWidth( int w )
68    {   width = w;   }
69
70    public void setHeight( int h )
71    {   height = h;   }
72
73    public void paint( Graphics g )
74    {
75       g.setColor( Color.black );
76       g.drawOval( 0, 0, width, height );
77    }
78 }
```

Fig. 11.10 Using **Scrollbar**s to size an oval (part 2 of 3).

Fig. 11.10 Using **Scrollbar**s to size an oval (part 3 of 3).

Two **Scrollbar** references **upDown** and **leftRight** are created. The statement

```
upDown = new Scrollbar( Scrollbar.VERTICAL, 100, 0, 0, 200 );
```

instantiates **upDown**. The orientation of **upDown** is vertical with an initial value of **100**. The scroll box visible area is set to **0**. The minimum value is **0** and the maximum value is **200**. The horizontal scrollbar object **leftRight** is constructed in a similar manner.

The **Canvas** class **MyCanvas** contains a constructor, a **setWidth** method, a **set-Height** method and a **paint** method. Methods **setWidth** and **setHeight** set the **private** instance variables **width** and **height** respectively. The **paint** method sets the current color to black and draws the oval. When **MyCanvas** object **theCanvas** is instantiated, it is resized and the background color is set to yellow.

Panel **thePanel** is instantiated. The layout manager for the applet and the layout manager for **thePanel** are set to **BorderLayout**. The scrollbar **upDown** is added to the **West** position of the applet. The scrollbar **leftRight** is added to the **South** position of **thePanel**. Canvas **theCanvas** is added to the **Center** position of **thePanel**. Panel **thePanel** is then added to the **"Center"** position of the applet.

The **handleEvent** method is overridden for the **Scroll** class. *Scrollbar events* are generated when either a scroll arrow is clicked, the scroll box is moved, or the area between a scroll arrow and the scroll box is clicked. **Scrollbar** events are processed in method **handleEvent**. The statement

```
if ( e.target instanceof Scrollbar )
```

tests whether a **Scrollbar** generated the event. If so, an **if/else** determines which **Scrollbar** it was. If **upDown** generated the event, the statement

```
theCanvas.setHeight( upDown.getValue() );
```

is executed. Method **setHeight** is passed the integer value of the scrollbar **upDown**. **Scrollbar** method **getValue** returns the current value of a scrollbar. If **leftRight** generated the event, the statement

```
theCanvas.setWidth( leftRight.getValue() );
```

is executed. Method **setWidth** is passed the integer value of the scrollbar **leftRight**.

For a **Scrollbar**, the **Event** instance variable **arg** is an **Integer** object containing the value of the **Scrollbar**. Method **showStatus** displays the value of **e.arg** in the status bar. Method **repaint** cause the components on the applet to be refreshed.

The **handleEvent** method returns **true** if a scrollbar generated the event. Otherwise the superclass **handleEvent** is called to do the default event handling. This passes the **Event** to the orignal **handleEvent** method that was inherited into class **Scroll**. The original **handleEvent** method is defined to receive an **Event**, determine the type of **Event** that occurred and send the event to one of the other event handling methods like **action**, **mouseUp**, **keyDown**, etc.

11.5 Custom Components

Java allows programmers to create their own custom components. A *custom component* is a component created by the programmer rather than a "built in" component.

In general, custom components are created by extending either class **Canvas** or class **Panel**. The **Component** class cannot be used because it does not have a **public** constructor. The **Canvas** class should be extended if the custom component does not need the methods of the **Container** class.

If the custom component contains other components, the **Panel** class should be extended. The **Container** class methods are needed to add multiple components. Custom components that contain more than one component are said to be *composite components*. We focus on composite components in this section.

Software Engineering Observation 11.2

The ability to create custom components contributes to Java's extensibility. This is one of Java's most appealing attributes.

Good Programming Practice 11.1

*Extend class **Canvas** rather than class **Panel** when **Container** methods are not required to implement a custom component.*

The program of Fig. 11.11 creates a composite component for a "labeled text field." The **Panel** class is extended to create a custom component called **LabelTextField** which contains a **Label** component and a **TextField** component. The program takes the text entered in the text field and displays it in the label. When the button is clicked, the text in the text field is displayed in the status bar.

The **Test** class creates a reference to a **LabelTextField** object **customComponent** and a reference to a **Button** object **button1**. The **LabelTextField** object is instantiated with the statement

```
customComponent = new LabelTextField( "label text" );
```

The **String "label text"** is passed to the **LabelTextField** constructor. The
Button object **button1** is instantiated with a call to the **Button** constructor. Both
button1 and **customComponent** are added to the applet with the **add** method.

The **action** method is overridden for the applet. When the button is clicked, the
event is handled in the **action** method. The statements

```
1  // Fig. 11.11: Test.java
2  // Creating a custom component.
3  import java.applet.Applet;
4  import java.awt.*;
5
6  public class Test extends Applet {
7      private LabelTextField customComponent;
8      private Button button1;
9
10     public void init()
11     {
12         customComponent = new LabelTextField( "label text" );
13         button1 = new Button( "Button" );
14
15         add( button1 );
16         add( customComponent );
17     }
18
19     // button event is handled here
20     public boolean action( Event e, Object o )
21     {
22         String s = "Textfield text: ";
23         showStatus( s + customComponent.getFieldText() );
24         return true;
25     }
26  }
27
28  class LabelTextField extends Panel {
29      private Label theLabel;
30      private TextField theTextField;
31
32      public LabelTextField( String s )
33      {
34          setLayout( new BorderLayout() );
35          theLabel = new Label( s );
36          theTextField = new TextField( 10 );
37
38          add( "North", theLabel );
39          add( "South", theTextField );
40      }
41
```

Fig. 11.11 Creating a custom component (part 1 of 2).

```
42      // handles its own text field event
43      public boolean action( Event e, Object o )
44      {
45          setLabelText( e.arg.toString() );
46          return true;
47      }
48
49      // setLabelText is programmer-defined
50      public void setLabelText( String s )
51      {
52          theLabel.setText( s );
53      }
54
55      // getFieldText is programmer-defined
56      public String getFieldText()
57      {
58          return theTextField.getText();
59      }
60  }
```

Fig. 11.11 Creating a custom component (part 2 of 2).

```
String s = "Textfield text: ";
showStatus( s + v.getFieldText() );
```

display **s** and the **String** returned from **LabelTextField** method **getFieldText** in the status bar. The applet's **action** method does not handle the events generated from the text field; these events are handled by class **LabelTextField**'s **action** method.

Class **LabelTextField** extends **Panel**, thus **LabelTextField** is a type of **Container**. **LabelTextField** has a **Label** and a **TextField** instance variable.

The **LabelTextField** constructor takes one **String** argument that is displayed in the **Label**. The layout manager for the container is set to **BorderLayout** and the instance variables **theLabel** and **theTextField** are instantiated. Object **theText-Field** has ten columns visible. The label is added to the container in the **"North"** position and the text field is added in the **"South"** position.

LabelTextField method **setLabelText** sets the text for the **Label** component. The statement

```
theLabel.setText( s );
```

uses the **Label** class method **setText** to set the text for the label. Note that the label object **theLabel** is **private** and therefore inaccessible to objects outside the class. The **setLabelText** provides a **public** interface for setting the label text.

LabelTextField also provides a **getFieldText** method which returns the text in the **private** text field. The statement

```
return theTextField.getText();
```

uses the **TextComponent** method **getText** to return the text field's text.

The **LabelTextField** class handles its own action events by overriding the **action** method. The statement

```
setLabelText( e.arg.toString() );
```

passes a **String** representation of **e.arg** to the **setLabelText** method. The **action** method returns **true** indicating that the event has been successfully handled.

If the **action** method returned **false**, the event would be sent to the applet container. The **handleEvent** method for the applet would route the event to the applet's **action** method. Returning **false** is useful if the custom component partially handles the event or selectively handles certain component events.

Good Programming Practice 11.2

Extending the ***Canvas*** *class instead of the* ***Panel*** *class when a custom component does not need the methods of the* ***Container*** *class.*

Good Programming Practice 11.3

Providing get and set methods to access ***private*** *data in a custom component.*

11.6 Frames

A *frame* is a window with a title bar and a border. Frames are created with class ***Frame*** that extends class ***Window*** which inherits from **Container**. Class **Window** contains methods for window management. **Window** objects do not have title bars or borders. The default layout manager for windows and frames is **BorderLayout**.

Common Programming Error 11.3

The default layout manager for windows and frames is ***BorderLayout***. *Forgetting to specify* **"North"**, **"South"**, **"East"**, **"West"** *or* **"Center"** *when adding a component to a* ***Window*** *or* ***Frame*** *is a run-time logic error. The component may not appear.*

Frames are typically used to build windowed applications (programs that do not require a browser to run). Frames are occasionally used with applets. We will discuss both applets that use Frames and Frame-based applications in this section.

The program of Fig. 11.12 creates an applet with a single button. When the button is clicked, a frame with a label is displayed.

```
1   // Fig. 11.12: MyFrame.java
2   // Creating a Frame from an applet.
3   import java.applet.Applet;
4   import java.awt.*;
5
6   public class MyFrame extends Applet {
7       private Frame f;
8       private Font x;
9       private String s;
10      private Label l;
11      private Button showFrame;
12
13      public void init()
14      {
15          String s2 = "Click here to see a Frame";
16
17          s = "FRAME";
18          x = new Font( "Courier", Font.BOLD, 36 );
19          showFrame = new Button( s2 );
20          add( showFrame );
21      }
22
23      public boolean action( Event e, Object o )
24      {
25          if ( e.target == showFrame ) {
26
27              if ( f != null ) {
28                  f.hide();       // hide frame
29                  f.dispose();  // free resources
30              }
31
32              // create frame
33              f = new Frame( "A Frame!" );
34
35              // create label
36              l = new Label( s );
37              l.setFont( x );
38
39              // change layout
40              f.setLayout( new FlowLayout() );
41
42              // add label to frame
43              f.add( l );
```

Fig. 11.12 Creating a Frame from an applet (part 1 of 2).

```
44
45              // size and show frame
46              f.resize( 300, 100 );
47              f.show();   // display frame
48          }
49
50          return true;
51      }
52  }
```

Fig. 11.12 Creating a **Frame** from an applet (part 2 of 2).

Class **MyFrame** creates a references to a **Frame** object, a **Font** object, a **String** object, a **Label** object and a **Button** object.

The **String** objects **s2** and **s** are assigned values with the two statements

```
String s2 = "Click here to see a Frame";
s = "Frame";
```

A 36-point bold Courier font is constructed. **String s2** is passed to the **Button** constructor as the label for **showFrame**. The button is added to the applet with method **add**.

The **action** method is overridden for this applet. A test determines if the **show-Frame** button generated the event. If so, an **if** statement tests the condition

```
f != null
```

to determine if **f** refers to an existing **Frame** object. If so, the statements

```
f.hide();
f.dispose();
```

are executed. **Component** method *hide* (which is inherited into class **Frame**) removes the **Frame** from the screen so the **Frame** is no longer visible. **Frame** method *dispose* frees the resources that were allocated to the **Frame** by the windowing system. The preceding statements from the **action** method are provided so only one frame exists at a time in the program.

Good Programming Practice 11.4

*Hide a **Frame** before calling the **dispose** method. Sometimes resources may not be freed properly resulting in the bitmap image of the **Frame** still being displayed.*

Performance Tip 11.1

Disposing a frame releases windowing system resources.

The statement

```
f = new Frame( "A Frame!" );
```

instantiates a **Frame** object with a call to the **Frame** constructor. The string **"A Frame!"** is the text that appears in the frame's title bar (the bar at the top of the window).

Label object **l** is instantiated with a call to the **Label** constructor. The **String s** is passed to the constructor as the value to be displayed on the label. The label's font is set with the **setFont** method. The layout for the **Frame** is set to a **FlowLayout**, then the **Label** is added to the frame with

```
f.add( l );
```

Frames must be sized before being displayed. A frame has no default size other than the minimum size required to display the title bar. The **Component** method **resize** is used to size the frame to the specified width and height. The statement

```
f.show();
```

displays the frame on the screen. **Component** method **show** displays a component. Frames are not visible by default. The programmer must explicitly call **show** to display a frame. Most other components are displayed automatically when they are added to an applet or application.

Common Programming Error 11.4

*Forgetting to call the **resize** method on a **Frame** is a run-time logic error; usually only the title bar of the **Frame** is visible.*

Common Programming Error 11.5

*Forgetting to call the **show** method on a **Frame** is a run-time logic error; the **Frame** is not displayed.*

Most windows have an icon at the top-left or top-right corner that enable a user to close the window and terminate a program. Clicking this icon (also known as the *exit icon*) for a Java **Frame** has no effect unless the programmer writes the code to close the **Frame**. In this example, the **Frame** can be closed only if the applet terminates (by exiting the appletviewer, for example). We will write the code to dispose of the frame when the exit icon is clicked in the next example.

The program of Fig. 11.12 demonstrated how to construct a frame, display it and remove it. The newly created frame had no functionality. Like class **Canvas**, class **Frame** is typically extended to perform a task. The program of Fig. 11.13 creates an applet with a single button. When the button is clicked, a **Frame** with four buttons around the edges is displayed. The **Frame** created extends the **Frame** class. When a button on the **Frame** is clicked, the background of the **Frame** changes to the color specified on the button.

```
1   // Fig. 11.13: MyFrame2.java
2   // Creating a subclass of Frame.
3   import java.applet.Applet;
4   import java.awt.*;
5
6   public class MyFrame2 extends Applet {
7      private DemoFrame f;
8      private Button showFrame;
9
10     public void init()
11     {
12        String s = "Click here to see the Frame";
13
14        showFrame = new Button( s );
15        add( showFrame );
16     }
17
18     public boolean action( Event e, Object o )
19     {
20        if ( e.target == showFrame ) {
21           String s = "This frame does something!";
22
23           if ( f != null ) {
24              f.hide();      // hide frame
25              f.dispose();   // free resources
26           }
27
28           f = new DemoFrame( s );  // instantiate frame
29           f.resize( 300, 200 );    // resize frame
30
31           // do not allow the frame to be resized
32           f.setResizable( false );
33
34           f.show();   // display frame
35        }
36
37        return true;
38     }
39  }
```

Fig. 11.13 Creating a subclass of **Frame** (part 1 of 3).

```
40
41   class DemoFrame extends Frame {
42      private Button a, b, c, d;
43
44      public DemoFrame( String s )
45      {
46         // call base class constructor
47         super( s );
48
49         a = new Button( "yellow" );
50         b = new Button( "red" );
51         c = new Button( "blue" );
52         d = new Button( "green" );
53
54         // default layout is border layout
55         add( "North", a );
56         add( "East", b );
57         add( "South", c );
58         add( "West", d );
59      }
60
61      public boolean handleEvent( Event e )
62      {
63         if ( e.id == Event.WINDOW_DESTROY ) {
64            hide();      // hide frame
65            dispose();   // free resources
66            return true;
67         }
68
69         return super.handleEvent( e );
70      }
71
72      public boolean action( Event e, Object o )
73      {
74         if ( e.target == a )
75            setBackground( Color.yellow );
76         else if ( e.target == b )
77            setBackground( Color.red );
78         else if ( e.target == c )
79            setBackground( Color.blue );
80         else    // d button
81            setBackground( Color.green );
82
83         repaint();  // update color change
84         return true;
85      }
86   }
```

Fig. 11.13 Creating a subclass of **Frame** (part 2 of 3).

Fig. 11.13 Creating a subclass of **Frame** (part 3 of 3).

Applet class **MyFrame2** creates a reference to a **DemoFrame** object and a reference to a **Button** object. The **init** method constructs the **Button** and places the button on the applet.

The **action** method is overridden for the applet. A test determines if the **show-Frame** button generated the event. If the **showFrame** button generated the event, an **if** statement tests the condition

```
f != null
```

to determine if **f** refers to an existing **Frame** object. If this condition is **true**, the frame is hidden and its resources are released with methods **hide** and **dispose**, respectively.

The statement

```
f = new DemoFrame( s );
```

instantiates the **DemoFrame** object **f** with a call to the **DemoFrame** constructor.

The frame is resized with a call to the **resize** method. The statement

```
f.setResizable( false );
```

passes a value of **false** to the **Frame *setResizable*** method. The **setResizable** method determines whether a frame can be resized by the user. Frames are resizable by default unless **false** is passed to the **setResizable** method. The **show** method displays the frame.

Class **DemoFrame** extends **Frame**. Class **DemoFrame** contains four references to **Button** objects. The class constructor takes one **String** argument. The statement

```
super( s );
```

passes the **String** object **s** to the superclass (i.e., **Frame**) constructor. The constructor instantiates the button objects and adds them to the frame. The default layout manager is **BorderLayout** so the position of each button is specified.

The **handleEvent** method is overridden for this applet. The **if** tests for a *window destroy event* with the condition

```
e.id == Event.WINDOW_DESTROY
```

The **e.id** is tested against the **Event** constant *WINDOW_DESTROY*. A window destroy event occurs when the exit icon is clicked on the window. Method **handleEvent** invokes the **hide** method and **dispose** method for the frame. If the event received by **handleEvent** is not the **WINDOW_DESTROY** event, the superclass **handleEvent** is called to send the event to the appropriate event handling method.

The **action** method is overridden for **DemoFrame**. When a button on the frame is clicked, the event is sent by **DemoFrame**'s **handleEvent** to **DemoFrame**'s **action** method. The **action** method determines which button was pressed and changes the background color of the frame with the **setBackground** method. The call to **repaint** updates frame with the color change.

Frames can also be used to create *frame-based applications*. The frame provides the space in which the application GUI is built. The program of Fig.11.14 is the frame-based application equivalent of the applet program of Fig. 11.13.

```
1   // Fig. 11.14: MyFrame3.java
2   // Creating a Frame-based application.
3   import java.awt.*;
4
5   public class MyFrame3 extends Frame {
6       private Button showFrame;
7       private DemoFrame f;
8       private int number;
9       private String frameTitle, title;
10
11      // default constructor
12      public MyFrame3()
13         {  this( "Frame" );   }
14
```

Fig. 11.14 Creating a **Frame**-based application (part 1 of 4).

```
15      public MyFrame3( String t )
16      {
17         super( "Application" );
18         String s = "Click here to see the Frame";
19
20         number = 0;
21         title = t;
22         showFrame = new Button( s );
23         add( "South", showFrame );
24
25         resize( 300, 100 );
26         show();
27      }
28
29      public boolean handleEvent( Event e )
30      {
31         if ( e.id == Event.ACTION_EVENT ) {
32            action( e, e.arg );
33            return true;
34         }
35         else if ( e.id == Event.WINDOW_DESTROY ) {
36            removeFrame( this );
37            System.exit( 0 );   // terminate program
38            return true;
39         }
40
41         return super.handleEvent( e );
42      }
43
44      public boolean action( Event e, Object o )
45      {
46         if ( e.target == showFrame ) {
47
48            if ( f != null )
49               removeFrame( f );
50
51            number++;
52            frameTitle = title + " " +
53                         String.valueOf( number );
54
55            f = new DemoFrame( frameTitle );
56         }
57
58         return true;
59      }
60
61      public void removeFrame( Frame w )
62      {
63         w.hide();      // hide frame
64         w.dispose();   // free resources
65      }
```

Fig. 11.14 Creating a **Frame**-based application (part 2 of 4).

```
66
67     public static void main( String args[] )
68     {
69        MyFrame3 myself;
70
71        if ( args.length == 0 )
72           myself = new MyFrame3();
73        else
74           myself = new MyFrame3( args[ 0 ] );
75     }
76  }
77
78  class DemoFrame extends Frame {
79     private Button a, b, c, d;
80
81     public DemoFrame( String s )
82     {
83        super( s );
84        a = new Button( "yellow" );
85        b = new Button( "red" );
86        c = new Button( "blue" );
87        d = new Button( "green" );
88
89        // default layout is border
90        add( "North", a );
91        add( "East", b );
92        add( "South", c );
93        add( "West", d );
94
95        resize( 200, 200 );
96        show();   // display frame
97     }
98
99     public boolean handleEvent( Event e )
100    {
101       if ( e.id == Event.WINDOW_DESTROY ) {
102          hide();    // hide frame
103          dispose(); // free resources
104          return true;
105       }
106
107       return super.handleEvent( e );
108    }
109
110    public boolean action( Event e, Object o )
111    {
112       if ( e.target == c )
113          setBackground( Color.blue );
114       else if ( e.target == b )
115          setBackground( Color.red );
```

Fig. 11.14 Creating a **Frame**-based application (part 3 of 4).

```
116        else if ( e.target == d )
117            setBackground( Color.green );
118        else  // a button
119            setBackground( Color.yellow );
120
121        repaint();
122        return true;
123    }
124 }
```

Fig. 11.14 Creating a **Frame**-based application (part 4 of 4).

Class **DemoFrame** of Fig. 11.14 is virtually identical to class **DemoFrame** of Fig. 11.13. Class **DemoFrame** contains four button objects arranged in a **BorderLayout**. When one of the buttons is clicked, the background color of the **Frame** changes.

Class **MyFrame3** has two constructors. The first constructor is the default constructor. The default constructor calls the other constructor with the statement

```
    this( "Frame" );
```

The second constructor takes one **String** argument. The string **"Application"** is passed to the superclass constructor to be set as the text in the title bar of the **Frame**. The instance variables **number** and **title** are initialized. The **Button** object is instantiated and added to the **South** position of the frame. The frame is then resized and shown.

The **handleEvent** method is overridden for class **MyFrame3**. The **Event** instance variable **id** is checked for a **WINDOW_DESTROY** event. If the **id** is for a **WINDOW_DESTROY** event, the statement

```
removeFrame( this );
```

is executed. Method **removeFrame** is a programmer-defined method that hides and disposes of a frame. The method takes as its argument the frame to dispose. Argument **this** is the **MyFrame3** object. If the event received by method **handleEvent** is not **WINDOW_DESTROY**, the superclass **handleEvent** is called.

The **action** method is overridden for class **MyFrame3**. A test determines if the **showFrame** button was clicked. If so, the second **if** structure determines if a frame already exists and, if necessary, invokes method **removeFrame** to hide and dispose of the existing **DemoFrame** object. Next, instance variable **number** is incremented by one and the **frameTitle** string is built. A new **DemoFrame** is constructed with the statement

```
f = new DemoFrame( frameTitle );
```

Method **main** creates a reference to a **MyFrame3** object. An **if/else** determines whether command-line arguments were provided in **String** array **args**. If no command-line arguments were provided, the default constructor is called. Otherwise the second constructor is called. Once the **MyFrame3** object is instantiated, the user can interact with the program.

11.7 Menus

Menus are an integral part of GUIs. *Menus* allow the user to perform direct or indirect actions, without unneccessarily "cluttering" up a container with extra GUI components. Currently, menus can only be used with **Frame**s. Figure 11.15 shows the **java.awt** hierarchy for menus and their related classes.

Class *MenuComponent* is the superclass for **MenuBar** and **MenuItem**. Class **MenuComponent** contains several methods including **setFont** and **getFont**.

Class *MenuItem* contains the constructor and methods necessary to manage menu items. A *menu item* is a string inside a menu that when selected causes an action to be performed. A menu item can be a command to execute a method or it can be another menu called a *submenu*.

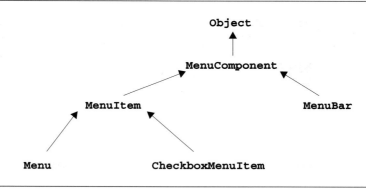

Fig. 11.15 Class hierarchy for the **awt Menu** class.

Class ***MenuBar*** contains the constructor and methods necessary to manage the menu bar. A *menu bar* is a container for menus.

Class ***Menu*** contains the constructors and methods necessary for managing menus. Menus contain menu items and are added to menu bars. When a menu is clicked, the menu expands to show a listing of menu items. Clicking a menu item generates an action event.

The **CheckboxMenuItem** *class* contains the constructor and methods necessary to manage checkbox menu items. A *checkbox menu item* is a menu item that is a toggle. When the checkbox item is selected, a check appears to the left of the menu item name. When the checkbox item is selected again, the check to the left of the menu item name is removed.

Software Engineering Observation 11.3

Menus simplify GUIs by reducing the number of components the user views.

The program of Fig. 11.16 creates a simple notepad application. The **Frame**-based application consists of a single frame, a text area and a menubar with a single menu. The menu contains three menu items each specifying a different font. When a menu item is selected by the user, the text in the text area is changed to the selected font.

The class creates references to a **TextArea** object and to a **Font** object. The class has one constructor. The superclass constructor is called to set the title and the **TextArea** object is instantiated and added to the **Center** position of the frame. The **Font** object **f** is also instantiated. The statement

```
Menubar bar = new MenuBar();
```

constructs the menu bar object with the **MenuBar** constructor. The **Font** menu is constructed with the statement

```
Menu fontMenu = new Menu( "Font" );
```

The **String** passed to the **Menu** constructor is the *menu name*. The statements

```
fontMenu.add( new MenuItem( "Times Roman" ) );
fontMenu.add( new MenuItem( "Courier" ) );
fontMenu.add( new MenuItem( "Helvetica" ) );
```

construct three menu items and add them to the **fontMenu**. Menu items are constructed with the **MenuItem** constructor. The **String** passed to the **MenuItem** constructor is the *menu item name*. The **Menu** class method **add** adds a menu item to a menu. The **fontMenu** is added to the menu bar with the statement

```
bar.add( fontMenu );
```

The menu bar class method **add** adds a menu to the menu bar. The statement

```
setMenuBar( bar );
```

uses the **Frame** method **setMenuBar** to place the menu bar on the frame. The frame is then sized and shown.

```
1   // Fig. 11.16: ScratchPad.java
2   // Incorporating menus into a Frame-based application.
3   import java.awt.*;
4
5   public class ScratchPad extends Frame {
6       private TextArea t;
7       private Font f;
8
9       public ScratchPad()
10      {
11          super( "ScratchPad Application" );
12
13          t = new TextArea();
14          add( "Center", t );
15
16          f = new Font( "TimesRoman", Font.PLAIN, 12 );
17          setFont( f );
18
19          // create menubar
20          MenuBar bar = new MenuBar();
21
22          // create font menu
23          Menu fontMenu = new Menu( "Font" );
24
25          // add some items to the menu
26          fontMenu.add( "Times Roman" );
27          fontMenu.add( "Courier" );
28          fontMenu.add( "Helvetica" );
29
30          // add menu to menu bar
31          bar.add( fontMenu );
32
33          // set the menubar for the frame
34          setMenuBar( bar );
35
36          resize( 300, 200 );
37          show();
38      }
39
40      public boolean handleEvent( Event e )
41      {
42          if ( e.id == Event.WINDOW_DESTROY ) {
43              hide();        // hide frame
44              dispose();     // free resources
45              System.exit( 0 );  // terminate
46              return true;
47          }
48
49          return super.handleEvent( e );
50      }
```

Fig. 11.16 Incorporating menus into a **Frame**-based application (part 1 of 2).

```
51
52      public boolean action( Event e, Object o )
53      {
54         if ( e.target instanceof MenuItem ) {
55
56            if ( e.arg.equals( "Times Roman" ) )
57               f = new Font( "TimesRoman", Font.PLAIN, 12 );
58            else if ( e.arg.equals( "Courier" ) )
59               f = new Font( "Courier", Font.PLAIN, 12 );
60            else  // Helvetica
61               f = new Font( "Helvetica", Font.PLAIN, 12 );
62
63            t.setFont( f );
64         }
65
66         return true;
67      }
68
69      public static void main( String args[] )
70      {
71         ScratchPad e;
72
73         e = new ScratchPad();
74      }
75   }
```

Fig. 11.16 Incorporating menus into a **Frame**-based application (part 2 of 2).

Common Programming Error 11.6

*Forgetting to set the menu bar with **Frame** method **setMenuBar** results in the menu bar not being displayed on the **Frame**.*

Common Programming Error 11.7

Attempting to use menus with applets results in compilation errors.

The **handleEvent** method is overridden for this class. A test is made for the **WINDOW_DESTROY** event. If this event occurs the frame is removed from the screen and method **exit** is called to terminate the program. Other events are passed to the superclass **handleEvent**.

The **action** method is overridden for this class. The condition

```
e.target instanceof MenuItem
```

tests to determine if a menu item generated the event. An **if/else** structure determines which menu item generated the event. **Event** instance variable **arg** is a **String** containing the name of the selected menu item. A **Font** object is created based on the selected menu item. The text area font is changed with the **setFont** method.

The conditions used to test each menu item are similar to

```
e.arg.equals( "Courier" )
```

which uses the **equals** method. This type of testing is fine if each menu item is unique. If multiple menu items have the same name (possibly in separate menus), the condition should be rewritten as

```
e.target == item2
```

where **item2** is a **MenuItem** object. Otherwise, if two menu items have the same name then they will perform the same action.

Menus are the last item we introduce that are capable of generating events. Figure 11.17 summarizes the events for the GUI components.

Component handler	Event generated by	arg instance variable value	arg data type	Event handling method
Button	pressing button	button label	**String**	**action**
Canvas	none	none	none	none
Checkbox or radio button	clicking checkbox	checkbox state	**Boolean**	**action**
Choice	selecting item	item selected	**String**	**action**
Label	none	none	none	none
List	double-clicking item	item selected	**String**	**action**
MenuItem	selecting item	item selected	**String**	**action**
Panel	none	none	none	none
Scrollbar	clicking scrollbar	scrollbar value	**Integer**	**handleEvent**
TextArea	none	none	none	none
TextField	pressing return	text in text field	**String**	**action**

Fig. 11.17 Summary of events for GUI components.

Common Programming Error 11.8

*Using a lowercase **i** in **MenuItem** or **CheckboxMenuItem** is a syntax error.*

Common Programming Error 11.9

*Using a lowercase **b** in class name **MenuBar** is a syntax error.*

Common Programming Error 11.10

*Using an uppercase **b** in class name **CheckboxMenuItem** is a syntax error.*

Common Programming Error 11.11

Forgetting to add a menu item to a menu is a run-time logic error. The menu item will not appear in the menu.

Common Programming Error 11.12

*Attempting to use a **Checkbox** component instead of a **CheckboxMenuItem** in a menu is a syntax error.*

The frame-based application of Fig. 11.18 enhances the program of Fig. 11.16 by adding color and the option to make the text area read-only. This program demonstrates how to use submenus.

```
1    // Fig. 11.18: Scratch2.java
2    // Using submenus in a menu.
3    import java.awt.*;
4
5    public class Scratch2 extends Frame {
6        private TextArea t;
7        private Font f;
8        private Color c;
9        private CheckboxMenuItem x;
10
11       public Scratch2()
12       {
13           super( "ScratchPad Application 2" );
14
15           t = new TextArea();
16           add( "Center", t );
17
18           f = new Font( "TimesRoman", Font.PLAIN, 12 );
19           t.setFont( f );
20
21           t.setForeground( Color.black );
22
23           // create menubar
24           MenuBar bar = new MenuBar();
```

Fig. 11.18 Using submenus in a menu (part 1 of 4).

```
25
26          // create menus
27          Menu viewMenu = new Menu( "View" );
28          Menu fontMenu = new Menu( "Font" );
29          Menu colorMenu = new Menu( "Color" );
30
31          // build color menu
32          colorMenu.add( new MenuItem( "Black" ) );
33          colorMenu.add( new MenuItem( "Blue" ) );
34
35          // build font menu
36          fontMenu.add( new MenuItem( "Times Roman" ) );
37          fontMenu.add( new MenuItem( "Courier" ) );
38
39          // build view menu
40          viewMenu.add( fontMenu );
41          viewMenu.add( new MenuItem( "-" ) );
42          viewMenu.add( colorMenu );
43          viewMenu.add( new MenuItem( "-" ) );
44
45          x = new CheckboxMenuItem( "Read-only" );
46          viewMenu.add( x );
47          x.setState( false );
48
49          // add menu to menu bar
50          bar.add( viewMenu );
51
52          // set the menubar for the frame
53          setMenuBar( bar );
54
55          resize( 300, 200 );
56          show();
57       }
58
59       public boolean handleEvent( Event e )
60       {
61          if ( e.id == Event.WINDOW_DESTROY ) {
62             hide();        // hide frame
63             dispose();   // free resources
64             System.exit( 0 );  // terminate
65             return true;
66          }
67
68          return super.handleEvent( e );
69       }
70
```

Fig. 11.18 Using submenus in a menu (part 2 of 4).

```
71       public boolean action( Event e, Object o )
72       {
73          if ( e.target instanceof MenuItem ) {
74
75             if ( e.arg.equals( "Times Roman" ) )
76                f = new Font( "TimesRoman", Font.PLAIN, 12 );
77             else if ( e.arg.equals( "Courier" ) )
78                f = new Font( "Courier", Font.PLAIN, 12 );
79             else if ( e.arg.equals( "Black" ) )
80                c = Color.black;
81             else if ( e.arg.equals( "Blue" ) )
82                c = Color.blue;
83             else if ( e.arg.equals( x.getLabel() ) )
84                   t.setEditable( !x.getState() );
85
86             t.setForeground( c );
87             t.setFont( f );
88          }
89
90          return true;
91       }
92
93       public static void main( String args[] )
94       {
95          Scratch2 e;
96
97          e = new Scratch2();
98       }
99    }
```

Fig. 11.18 Using submenus in a menu (part 3 of 4).

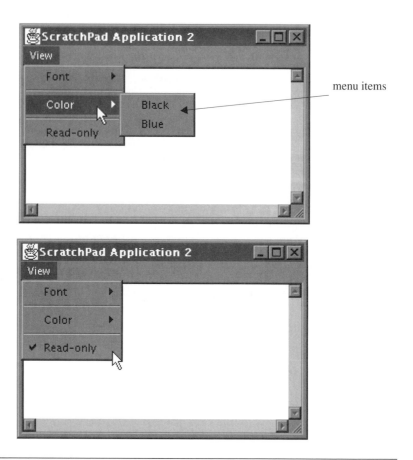

Fig. 11.18 Using submenus in a menu (part 4 of 4).

The class contains references to a **TextArea**, a **Font**, a **Color** and a **Checkbox-MenuItem**. The class constructor sets the frame title with a call to the superclass constructor; instantiates the **TextArea** object and adds it to the frame; instantiates the **Font** object and sets the **TextArea** object to that font; builds the menus; sets the menu bar; resizes the frame; and finally displays the frame.

The menu bar is created with a call to the **MenuBar** constructor. Three menus are created with the statements

```
viewMenu = new Menu( "View" );
fontMenu = new Menu( "Font" );
colorMenu = new Menu( "Color" );
```

The **colorMenu** object and the **fontMenu** object each have two menu items added to them. The **fontMenu** object is added to the **viewMenu** with the statement

```
viewMenu.add( fontMenu );
```

When **fontMenu** is added to **viewMenu**, a submenu is created. Selecting the submenu displays the menu items for that submenu. Note that submenus have an arrow head pointing to the right to indicate that there are submenu items.

The statement

```
viewMenu.add( new MenuItem( "-" ) );
```

uses a special case of the **MenuItem** constructor to create a *separator bar*—a line that visually separates menu items. Passing a hyphen (**-**) to the **MenuItem** constructor creates a separator bar. Separator bars do not generate events when clicked. The **colorMenu** is also added to **viewMenu** as well as another separator bar.

The statement

```
x = new CheckboxMenuItem( "Read-only" );
```

uses the **CheckboxMenuItem** constructor to create a checkbox menu item. The checkbox menu item is added to **viewMenu** with the statement

```
viewMenu.add( x );
```

The state of the checkbox menu item is set to **false** with the statement

```
x.setState( false );
```

which uses **CheckboxMenuItem** method *setState* to set the **boolean** state for a checkbox menu item. When a checkbox menu item is set to **false**, a check does not appear next to the checkbox menu item.

The **viewMenu** is added to the menu bar with the **add** method. The menu bar is set for the frame. The frame is then resized and shown.

The **handleEvent** method is overridden for this class. A test is made for the window-destroy event. If a window-destroy event occurs, the frame is removed from the screen and the **exit** method is called to terminate the program. Other events are passed to the superclass **handleEvent**.

The **action** method is overridden for this class. The condition

```
e.target instanceof MenuItem
```

determines if a menu item generated the event. If so, an **if/else** structure determines which menu item generated the event. The **Event** instance variable **arg** is the name of the menu item selected. The **Font** object and **Color** object are created based on the menu item selected. The text area foreground color is changed with the *setForeground* method and the text area font is changed to **f** with the **setFont** method.

If the checkbox menu item generated the event the statement

```
t.setEditable( !x.getState() );
```

uses **CheckboxMenuItem** method *getState* to get the **boolean** state of a checkbox menu item. If the value returned is **true**, the text area's **setEditable** method is passed **false**—and vice versa.

11.8 Dialogs

A *dialog box* is a borderless window with a title bar. Dialog boxes are commonly used to gather information from the user or to show information to the user. Dialog boxes are created with the **Dialog** class which inherits from **Window**.

Dialog boxes can either be modal or modeless. A *modal dialog box* does not allow any other window in the application to be accessed until the dialog box is dismissed. A *modeless dialog box* allows other windows to be accessed while the dialog is displayed. **BorderLayout** is the default layout manager for dialog boxes.

The program of Fig. 11.19 displays a dialog box when the user selects the **About...** menu item from the **Help** menu. The dialog box is modeless so the frame and its menus can be accessed while the dialog box is visible. The dialog box displays the text **"Java How To Program"** and an **Ok** button. While the dialog box is visible, the **About...** menu is *grayed*—clicking it does not generate an event.

```
1   // Fig. 11.19: DialogBoxes.java
2   // Demonstrating modeless Dialog boxes.
3   import java.awt.*;
4
5   public class DialogBoxes extends Frame {
6       private About a;
7       private MenuItem item, item2;
8
9       public DialogBoxes()
10      {
11          super( "Dialog boxes" );
12
13          MenuBar bar = new MenuBar();
14          Menu helpMenu = new Menu( "Help" );
15          Menu fileMenu = new Menu( "File" );
16
17          item = new MenuItem( "About..." );
18          item2 = new MenuItem( "Exit" );
19
20          helpMenu.add( item );
21          fileMenu.add( item2 );
22
23          bar.setHelpMenu( helpMenu );
24          bar.add( helpMenu );
25          bar.add( fileMenu );
26
27          setMenuBar( bar );
28          resize( 200, 100 );
29          show();
30      }
31
```

Fig. 11.19 Application that creates a modeless dialog box (part 1 of 4).

```
32      public static void main( String args[] )
33      {
34         DialogBoxes d;
35
36         d = new DialogBoxes();
37      }
38
39      public boolean action( Event e, Object o )
40      {
41         if ( e.target instanceof MenuItem )
42
43            if ( e.arg.equals( item.getLabel() ) ) {
44               a = new About( this );
45               setItemState( false );
46            }
47            else
48               removeFrame();
49
50         return true;
51      }
52
53      public boolean handleEvent( Event e )
54      {
55         if ( e.id == Event.WINDOW_DESTROY ) {
56            removeFrame();
57            return true;
58         }
59
60         return super.handleEvent( e );
61      }
62
63      // setItemState is programmer-defined
64      public void setItemState( boolean state )
65      {
66         if ( state == true )
67            item.enable();
68         else
69            item.disable();
70      }
71
72      // removeFrame is programmer-defined
73      public void removeFrame()
74      {
75         hide();
76         dispose();
77         System.exit( 0 );
78      }
79   }
80
```

Fig. 11.19 Application that creates a modeless dialog box (part 2 of 4).

```
81   class About extends Dialog {
82      private Button b;
83      private Label l;
84      private Panel p, p2;
85      private DialogBoxes parent;
86
87      public About( Frame f )
88      {
89         super( f, "About", false );
90         parent = ( DialogBoxes ) f;
91
92         b = new Button( "Ok" );
93         p = new Panel();
94         p2 = new Panel();
95         l = new Label( "Java How To Program" );
96
97         p.add( l );
98         p2.add( b );
99
100        add( "Center", p );
101        add( "South", p2 );
102        resize( 200, 100 );
103        show();
104     }
105
106     public boolean handleEvent( Event e )
107     {
108        if ( e.id == Event.WINDOW_DESTROY ) {
109           removeDialog();
110           return true;
111        }
112
113        return super.handleEvent( e );
114     }
115
116     public boolean action( Event e, Object o )
117     {
118        if ( e.target == b )
119           removeDialog();
120
121        return true;
122     }
123
124     // removeDialog is user-defined
125     public void removeDialog()
126     {
127        hide();
128        dispose();
129        parent.setItemState( true );
130     }
131  }
```

Fig. 11.19 Application that creates a modeless dialog box (part 3 of 4).

Fig. 11.19 Application that creates a modeless dialog box (part 4 of 4).

The **DialogBoxes** class creates references to **About** and to **MenuItem**s. The class constructor calls the superclass constructor, creates the menu bar, creates menus **File** and **Help**, adds the menus to the menu bar, sets the menu bar and finally sizes and displays the frame.

The statement

```
bar.setHelpMenu( helpMenu );
```

sets the help menu for the menu bar with the **MenuBar** method *setHelpMenu*. When a help menu is set, the help menu automatically appears as the rightmost menu on the menu bar. Note that the **File** menu is actually added after the **Help** menu but the **Help** menu is still the rightmost menu.

The **action** method is overridden for this class. If the **About...** menu item generates the event, the statements

```
a = new About( this );
setItemState( false );
```

are executed. The current **Frame** object **this** is passed to the **About** constructor that constructs an **About** dialog box object. Dialog boxes can be attached to a **Frame** by passing a **Frame** reference (such as **this**) to the **Dialog** constructor. The **setItemState** method either enables or disables the **About...** menu item. The **setItemState** method uses the **MenuItem** methods *enable* and *disable*. When a menu item is enabled, the menu item generates an **action** event when selected. A menu item that is disabled is grayed—selecting a grayed menu does not generate an event.

The **handleEvent** method is overridden for this class. The **handleEvent** method tests for window destroy events. If the event is a window-destroy event, the **remove-Frame** method is called. The **removeFrame** method hides the frame, calls **dispose**, and calls **exit** to terminate the program. Other events are passed to the superclass **handleEvent**.

To create a dialog box, the **Dialog** class should be extended. Like the **Frame** class, the **Dialog** class does not do enough on its own to be useful. The class **About** extends **Dialog**.

The **About** class creates five references—a **Button**, a **Label**, two **Panel**s and a **DialogBoxes** reference to refer to an object of the **DialogBoxes** application class. The constructor takes as its **Frame** argument the parent container of the dialog box. Events not processed by the dialog box will be sent to the dialog box's parent frame.

The superclass constructor is called with the statement

```
super( f, "About", false );
```

The superclass constructor takes three arguments—the parent frame, the title, and a **boolean** value indicating whether the dialog should be modal. A value of **false** for the third argument indicates that the dialog box should be modeless.

The **About** object's parent is instantiated with the statement

```
parent = ( DialogBoxes ) f;
```

The **About** class can interact with the **public** methods of the parent frame through **parent**. The **Button** object, **Panel** objects and **Label** object are instantiated. The **Label** object is added to one panel and the **Button** object is added to the other panel. Both panels are added to the dialog—one in the **Center** position and the other in the **South** position. The dialog box is then sized and displayed. Like frames, dialog boxes have no default size and are not visible. The **resize** method is used to size the dialog box and the **show** method is used to display the dialog box.

Common Programming Error 11.13

*Forgetting to call the **resize** method on a dialog box is a run-time logic error. The dialog box usually cannot be seen because it has no default size.*

Common Programming Error 11.14

*Forgetting to call the **show** method is a run-time logic error. The dialog box is not displayed because dialogs are hidden by default.*

The **action** method is overridden for this class. When the **Ok** button is pressed by the user, the **removeDialog** method is called. The **removeDialog** method calls the **hide** method and **dispose** method to remove the dialog from the screen, then calls the **setItemState** method of **parent**. The boolean value **true** is passed to **setItemState** to enable the **About...** menu item.

The **handleEvent** method is overridden for this class. The **handleEvent** method tests for a window-destroy event. If a window-destroy event occurs, method **removeDialog** is called. If an action event occurs, the **action** method is called by the superclass **handleEvent** method.

The **java.awt** contains a specialized dialog class, *FileDialog*, for file processing. The **FileDialog** class inherits from the **Dialog** class. The "look" of the file dialog box is predefined by the windowing system. File dialog boxes are modal by default. Two types of file dialogs can be used—an *open file dialog* and a *save file dialog*. We demonstrate how to create file dialog boxes. We will not write the code necessary to open a file or to save a file. File processing is discussed in Chapter 15.

The program of Fig. 11.20 displays a file dialog box when either the **Open...** menu item or the **Save...** menu item is selected. The file dialog boxes have some built in capabilities such as being able to navigate the directory tree.

```
1   // Fig. 11.20: DialogBoxes2.java
2   // Demonstrating the "Open" and "Save" dialog boxes.
3   import java.awt.*;
4
5   public class DialogBoxes2 extends Frame
6   {
7       private MyFiles m;
8       private MenuItem item, item2;
9
10      public DialogBoxes2()
11      {
12          super( "Dialog boxes 2" );
13
14          MenuBar bar = new MenuBar();
15          Menu fileMenu = new Menu( "File" );
16
17          item = new MenuItem( "Open..." );
18          item2 = new MenuItem( "Save As ..." );
19
20          fileMenu.add( item );
21          fileMenu.add( item2 );
22
23          bar.add( fileMenu );
24          setMenuBar( bar );
25          resize( 200, 100);
26          show();
27      }
28
29      public static void main( String args[] )
30      {
31          DialogBoxes2 d = new DialogBoxes2();
32      }
33
```

Fig. 11.20 **Frame**-based application that displays a file dialog box (part 1 of 3).

```
34      public boolean action( Event e, Object o )
35      {
36          if ( e.target instanceof MenuItem )
37
38              if ( e.arg.equals( item.getLabel() ) )
39                  m = new MyFiles( this, FileDialog.LOAD );
40              else if ( e.arg.equals( item2.getLabel() ) )
41                  m = new MyFiles( this, FileDialog.SAVE );
42
43          return true;
44      }
45
46      public boolean handleEvent( Event e )
47      {
48          if ( e.id == Event.WINDOW_DESTROY ) {
49              hide();
50              dispose();
51              System.exit( 0 );
52              return true;
53          }
54
55          return super.handleEvent( e );
56      }
57  }
58
59  class MyFiles extends FileDialog
60  {
61      public MyFiles( Frame f, int type )
62      {
63          super( f, ( type == FileDialog.LOAD ? "Open "
64                      : "Save " ) + "Dialog", type );
65
66          resize( 400, 250 );
67          show();
68      }
69  }
```

Fig. 11.20 Frame-based application that displays a file dialog box (part 2 of 3).

The **DialogBoxes2** class constructor calls the superclass constructor, builds the menu, sets the menu bar, sizes the frame, and displays the frame.

The **handleEvent** method is overridden for the class. A window-destroy event hides the frame, disposes of the frame and calls **exit** to terminate the program. An action event results in a call to the **action** method.

Fig. 11.20 Frame-based application that displays a file dialog box (part 3 of 3).

The **action** method is overridden for this class. If the **Open...** menu item generated the event, the statement

```
m = new MyFiles( this, FileDialog.LOAD );
```

is executed. The arguments **this** and **FileDialog.LOAD** are passed to the **MyFiles** constructor. The **static** constants *FileDialog.SAVE* and *FileDialog.LOAD* specify the type of file dialog to create.

Class **MyFiles** extends class **FileDialog**. Class **MyFiles** consists of a single constructor which takes one **Frame** argument and one **int** argument. The superclass constructor is called with the statement

```
super( f, ( type == FileDialog.LOAD ? "Open " : "Save " ) +
       "Dialog", type );
```

The first argument specifies the parent frame of the file dialog box. The second argument is the file dialog box title. The third argument is either **FileDialog.SAVE** or **FileDialog.LOAD**. At the time of this publication, the **resize** method must be used with file dialogs. However, the values passed to the **resize** method have no effect on the file dialog box. To be visible, file dialog boxes must be displayed with the **show** method.

Common Programming Error 11.15

*Forgetting to call the **show** method for a **FileDialog** object is a run-time logic error— the file dialog is not displayed.*

11.9 Advanced Layout Managers

In the previous chapter, we introduced three layout managers—**FlowLayout**, **BorderLayout** and **GridLayout**. This section presents four additional layout managers (summarized in Fig. 11.21). We discuss these layout managers in the sections that follow.

11.10 CardLayout Layout Manager

The *CardLayout layout manager* arranges components into a "deck" of cards where only the top card is visible. Any card in the deck can be placed at the top of the deck with one or more method calls. Each card is usually a container such as a panel. The card can use any layout manager. Class **CardLayout** inherits from **Object** and implements the **LayoutManager** interface. We will say more about interfaces in Chapter 13.

The program of Fig. 11.22 creates five panels. One of these uses the **CardLayout** layout manager by controlling which card is displayed and the other three panels are used as cards. The program does nothing other than display a GUI.

Layout manager	Description
CardLayout	A layout manager that stacks components like a deck of cards. Each container in the stack can use any layout manager. Only the container at the "top" of the deck is visible.
GridBagLayout	A layout manager similar to **GridLayout**. Unlike **GridLayout** each component size can vary and components can be added in any order.
none	A layout manager is not being used. Each component is manually placed.
user-defined	A custom layout manager created by the programmer.

Fig. 11.21 Advanced layout managers.

```
1    // Fig. 11.22: CardDeck.java
2    // Demonstrating CardLayout.
3    import java.applet.Applet;
4    import java.awt.*;
5
6    public class CardDeck extends Applet {
7       private Canvas c;
8       private CardLayout cardManager;
9       private Panel deck, p1, p2, p3, p4;
10      private Button b1, b2, b3,
11                      prevButton, nextButton,
12                      lastButton, firstButton;
13
14      public void init()
15      {
16         setLayout( new BorderLayout() );     // applet
17
18         b1 = new Button( "card one   " );
19         b2 = new Button( "card two   " );
20         b3 = new Button( "card three" );
21
22         // create and customize a canvas
23         c = new Canvas();
24         c.setBackground( Color.green );
25         c.resize( 80, 80 );
26
27         deck = new Panel();
28         cardManager = new CardLayout();   // instantiate object
29         deck.setLayout( cardManager );    // set cardLayout
30         add( "East", deck );
31
32         // use the default layout for p1
33         p1 = new Panel();
34         p1.add( b1 );        // add a button
35         deck.add( b1.getLabel(), p1 );   // add card to deck
36
37         // set up second card
38         p2 = new Panel();
39         p2.add( b2 );        // add a button
40         p2.add( c );         // add a canvas
41         deck.add( b2.getLabel(), p2 );   // add card to deck
42
43         // set up last card
44         p3 = new Panel();
45         p3.setLayout( new BorderLayout() );   // set layout
46         p3.add( "North", new Button( "North Pole" ) );
47         p3.add( "West", new Button( "The West" ) );
48         p3.add( "East", new Button( "Far East" ) );
49         p3.add( "South", new Button( "South Pole" ) );
50         p3.add( "Center", b3 );
51         deck.add( b3.getLabel(), p3 );   // add card to deck
```

Fig. 11.22 Demonstrating the **CardLayout** layout manager (part 1 of 3).

```
52
53          // create and layout panel that will control deck
54          p4 = new Panel();
55          p4.setLayout ( new GridLayout( 2, 2 ) );
56          p4.add( firstButton = new Button( "First" ) );
57          p4.add( nextButton = new Button( "Next" ) );
58          p4.add( prevButton = new Button( "Previous" ) );
59          p4.add( lastButton = new Button( "Last" ) );
60          add( "West", p4 );
61       }
62
63    public boolean action( Event e, Object o )
64    {
65       if ( e.target == firstButton )
66          cardManager.first( deck );     // show first card
67       else if ( e.target == prevButton )
68          cardManager.previous( deck ); // show previous card
69       else if ( e.target == nextButton )
70          cardManager.next( deck );      // show next card
71       else if ( e.target == lastButton )
72          cardManager.last( deck );      // show last card
73
74       return true;
75    }
76 }
```

Fig. 11.22 Demonstrating the **CardLayout** layout manager (part 2 of 3).

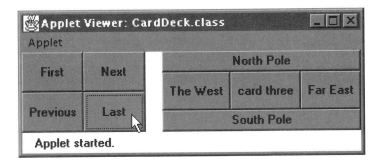

Fig. 11.22 Demonstrating the **CardLayout** layout manager (part 3 of 3).

The **CardDeck** class creates references to **Panel**s, references to **Button**s, and a reference to a **Canvas**. The line

```
private CardLayout cardManager;
```

creates a reference to a **CardLayout** object. Having a **CardLayout** object allows the deck to be traversed with the **CardLayout** class methods. The **CardDeck** class contains two methods—**init** and **action**.

The **init** method builds the GUI. The layout manager for the applet is set to **BorderLayout**. The three **Button** objects and the **Canvas** are instantiated. The background color of the canvas is changed to green. The canvas is also sized. The statements

```
deck = new Panel();
cardManager = new CardLayout();
deck.setLayout( cardManager );
```

instantiate a **Panel** object called **deck**, instantiate the **CardLayout** object **cardManager**, and set the layout manager of **deck** to **CardLayout**. As we set up each card, we will add the card to **deck**. The **deck** panel is added to the applet's **East** position.

The statements

```
p1 = new Panel();
p1.add( b1 );
deck.add( b1.getLabel(), p1 );
```

instantiate a panel **p1**, add button **b1** to the panel, and add the panel to **deck**. The first argument is used to identify the component added and the second argument is the card to add. Panels **p2** and **p3** are created in a similar way and added to **deck**. Note that **p3** arranges its components in **BorderLayout**.

Panel **p4** contains the buttons that will allow the user to traverse the deck. The name of each button specifies which card in the deck is displayed when that button is clicked. When the program runs, the first card added, **p1**, is displayed. Panel **p4** occupies the **West** position of the applet.

The **action** method is overridden for this class. A test is made to determine which button on **p4** clicked. The **CardLayout** methods *first*, *previous*, *next*, and *last* are used to show a particular card. The **first** method displays the first card added to the deck. The **previous** method displays the previous card in the deck. The **next** method displays the next card in the deck. The **last** method displays the last card in the deck. Note that **deck** is passed to each of these methods.

11.11 GridBagLayout Layout Manager

The most complex of the predefined layout managers is *GridBagLayout*. The **Grid-BagLayout** layout manager is similar to the **GridLayout** layout manager because **GridBagLayout** also arranges components in a grid. However **GridBagLayout** is more flexible. The components can vary in size and can be added in any order.

The first step in using **GridBagLayout** is to determine the appearance of the GUI. This step does not involve any programming; all that is needed is a piece of paper. The GUI should be drawn first. Next a grid should be drawn over the GUI dividing the components into rows and columns. The initial row and column should start with 0 which is necessary for the **GridBagLayout** manager to properly place the components. The coordinates from the rows and columns will be used to place the component in an exact position. Figure. 11.23 demonstrates drawing the lines for the rows and columns over a GUI.

In order to use the **GridBagLayout** layout manager, a *GridBagConstraints* object must be constructed. The **GridBagConstraints** object specifies how a component is laid out with **GridBagLayout**. Several important **GridBagConstraints** instance variables are summarized in Fig. 11.24.

The *gridx* and *gridy* variables specify where the upper-left corner of the component is placed. The **gridx** variable corresponds to the column and the **gridy** variable corresponds to the row. In Fig. 11.23, the choice button (displaying **"Linden"**) has a **gridx** value of 1 and a **gridy** value 2.

Fig. 11.23 Designing a GUI that will use **GridBagLayout**.

GridBagConstraints instance variable	Description
gridx	The column in which the component will be placed.
gridy	The row in which the component will be placed.
gridwidth	The number of columns the component occupies.
gridheight	The number of rows the component occupies.
weightx	The portion of extra space to allocate vertically. The components in a row can become "taller" when extra space is available.
weighty	The portion of extra space to allocate horizontally. The components in a column can become "wider" when extra space is available.

Fig. 11.24 GridBagConstraints instance variables.

The **gridwidth** variable specifies the number of columns a component occupies. In Fig. 11.23, the choice button occupies two columns. The **gridheight** variable specifies the number of rows a component occupies. In Fig. 11.23, the text area occupies three rows.

The **weightx** variable specifies how to distribute extra space vertically to a component when the container is resized. A value of zero indicates that the component will not grow vertically. The **weighty** variable specifies how to distribute extra space horizontally to a component when the container is resized. A value of zero indicates that the component will not grow horizontally.

Common Programming Error 11.16

*Using a negative value for either **weightx** or **weighty** is a logic error.*

In Fig. 11.23, the affects of **weighty** and **weightx** cannot be seen. When the container is resized, the additional space becomes available. Components with larger weight values will occupy more of the additional space than components with smaller weight values. In the exercises, we explore the effects of varying **weightx** and **weighty**.

Components should be given non-zero positive weight values—otherwise the components will "huddle" together in the middle of the container. Figure 11.25 shows the GUI of Fig. 11.23—where all weights have been set to zero.

The **GridBagConstraints** instance variable **fill** specifies how much of the components area is occupied. The variable **fill** is assigned one of the following **Grid-BagConstraints** class **static** constants: *NONE*, *VERTICAL*, *HORIZONTAL*, or *BOTH*. The default value is **GridBagConstraints.NONE**.

The **GridBagConstraints** instance variable **anchor** specifies where the component is placed in the area when the component does not fill the entire area. The variable **anchor** is assigned one of the following **GridBagConstraints** class **static** constants: *NORTH*, *NORTHEAST*, *EAST*, *SOUTHEAST*, *SOUTH*, *SOUTHWEST*, *WEST*, *NORTHWEST*, or *CENTER*. The default value is **GridBagConstraints.CENTER**.

Fig. 11.25 `GridBagLayout` with the weights set to zero.

The program of Fig. 11.26 uses the **GridBagLayout** manager to arrange the components in the GUI of Fig. 11.23. The program does nothing other than display the GUI.

```
1   // Fig. 11.26: GridBagDemo.java
2   // Demonstrating GridBagLayout.
3   import java.applet.Applet;
4   import java.awt.*;
5
6   public class GridBagDemo extends Applet {
7       private Canvas c;
8       private Choice cb;
9       private TextArea ta;
10      private TextField tf;
11      private Button b1, b2, b3;
12      private GridBagLayout gbLayout;
13      private GridBagConstraints gbConstraints;
14
15      public void init()
16      {
17          gbLayout = new GridBagLayout();
18          setLayout( gbLayout );    // applet
19
20          // instantiate gridbag constraints
21          gbConstraints = new GridBagConstraints();
22
23          ta = new TextArea( "Text Area", 5, 10 );
24          cb = new Choice( );
25          cb.addItem( "Linden" );
26          cb.addItem( "Birch" );
27          cb.addItem( "Ceder" );
28          tf = new TextField( "TextField" );
```

Fig. 11.26 Demonstrating the **GridBagLayout** layout manager (part 1 of 4).

```
29          b1 = new Button( "Button 1" );
30          b2 = new Button( "Button 2" );
31          b3 = new Button( "Button 3" );
32          c = new Canvas();
33          c.setBackground( Color.blue );
34          c.resize( 10, 5 );
35
36          // text area
37          // weightx and weighty are both 0: the default
38          // anchor for all components is CENTER: the default
39          gbConstraints.fill = GridBagConstraints.BOTH;
40          addComponent( ta, gbLayout, gbConstraints, 0, 0, 1, 3 );
41
42          // button b1
43          // weightx and weighty are both 0: the default
44          gbConstraints.fill = GridBagConstraints.HORIZONTAL;
45          addComponent( b1, gbLayout, gbConstraints, 0, 1, 2, 1 );
46
47          // choice button
48          // weightx and weighty are both 0: the default
49          // fill is HORIZONTAL
50          addComponent( cb, gbLayout, gbConstraints, 2, 1, 2, 1 );
51
52          // button b2
53          gbConstraints.weightx = 1000;  // can grow taller
54          gbConstraints.weighty = 1;     // can grow wider
55          gbConstraints.fill = GridBagConstraints.BOTH;
56          addComponent( b2, gbLayout, gbConstraints, 1, 1, 1, 1 );
57
58          // button b3
59          // fill is BOTH
60          gbConstraints.weightx = 0;
61          gbConstraints.weighty = 0;
62          addComponent( b3, gbLayout, gbConstraints, 1, 2, 1, 1 );
63
64          // text field
65          // weightx and weighty are both 0: fill is BOTH
66          addComponent( tf, gbLayout, gbConstraints, 3, 0, 2, 1 );
67
68          // canvas
69          // weightx and weighty are both 0: fill is BOTH
70          addComponent( c, gbLayout, gbConstraints, 3, 2, 1, 1 );
71       }
72
```

Fig. 11.26 Demonstrating the `GridBagLayout` layout manager (part 2 of 4).

The GUI consists of three buttons, a text area, a choice button, a canvas and a text field. The layout manager used is **GridBagLayout**. The statements

```
gbLayout = new GridBagLayout();
setLayout( gbLayout );
```

```
73    // addComponent is programmer defined
74    private void addComponent( Component c, GridBagLayout g,
75                               GridBagConstraints gc, int row,
76                               int column, int width, int height )
77    {
78       // set gridx and gridy
79       gc.gridx = column;
80       gc.gridy = row;
81
82       // set gridwidth and gridheight
83       gc.gridwidth = width;
84       gc.gridheight = height;
85
86       g.setConstraints( c, gc );   // set constraints
87       add( c );        // add component to applet
88    }
89 }
```

Fig. 11.26 Demonstrating the **GridBagLayout** layout manager (part 3 of 4).

instantiates **gbLayout** with a call to the **GridBagLayout** constructor and sets the layout manager for the applet to **gbLayout**. The **GridBagConstraints** object is instantiated with the statement

```
gbConstraints = new GridBagConstraints()
```

that calls the **GridBagConstraints** constructor. The next several lines of code instantiate each of the components.

The text area is the first component added to the **GridBagLayout**. Since the **weightx** and **weighty** values are not specified, the default value for each is zero. The component will not resize itself if space is available—however the text area spans multiple rows so the vertical resizing is subject to the **weightx** values of **b2** and **b3**. When either **b2** or **b3** is resized vertically, the text area is resized as well. The **fill** variable has been set to **BOTH**—the text area will always fill its entire area. An **anchor** value is not specified, so the default of **CENTER** is used. We do not use the **anchor** variable in this program, so all components will use **CENTER** by default. The statement

Fig. 11.26 Demonstrating the **GridBagLayout** layout manager (part 4 of 4).

```
addComponent( ta, gbLayout, gbConstraints, 0, 0, 1, 3 );
```

calls the programmer-defined **addComponent** method. The **TextArea** object, **Grid-BagLayout** object and **GridBagConstraints** object are passed as the first three arguments. The last four arguments specify the row, column, number of columns to span, and the number of rows to span.

The ***addComponent*** method declares a **Component** reference **c**, a **GridBag-Layout** reference **g**, a **GridBagConstraints** reference **gc** and integers **row**, **column**, **width** and **height**. The statements

```
gc.gridx = column;
gc.gridy = row;
```

set the **GridBagConstraints** variables **gridx** and **gridy**. The **gridx** variable is assigned the column value and the **gridy** value is assigned the row value. The statements

```
gc.gridwidth = width;
gc.gridheight = height;
```

set the **GridBagConstraints** variables **gridwidth** and **gridheight**. The **gridwidth** variable specifies the number of columns to span and the **gridheight** variable specifies the number of rows to span. The statement

```
g.setConstraints( c, gc );
```

sets the **GridBagConstraints** for a component **GridBagLayout**. The **GridBagLayout** method **setConstraints** takes a **Component** argument and a **GridBagConstraints** argument. Method **add** is used to add the component to the applet.

The **Button** object **b1** is the next component added. The values of **weightx** and **weighty** are still zero. The **fill** variable is set to **HORIZONTAL**—the component will always fill its area in the horizontal direction. The vertical direction is not filled. Since the **weighty** value is zero, the button can never become taller. Resizing the applet in the vertical direction has no effect on **b1**. Button **b1** is located at row 0, column 1. One row and two columns are occupied.

The choice button **cb** is the next component added. The **weightx** and **weighty** values are zero and the **fill** variable is set to **HORIZONTAL**. The choice button will grow only in the horizontal directions. Note that the **weightx**, **weighty**, and **fill** variables remain set until they are changed. The choice button is placed at row 2, column 1. Two rows and one column are occupied.

Button **b2** is given a **weightx** value of **1000** and a **weighty** value of **1**. The area occupied by the button is capable of growing in the vertical and horizontal direction. The **fill** variable is set to **BOTH** which specifies that the button will always fill the entire area. When the applet is resized, **b2** will grow. The button is placed at row 1, column 1. One row and one column are occupied.

Button **b3** is added next. Both the **weightx** value and **weighty** value are set to zero and the value of **fill** is **BOTH**. Button **b3** will grow if the applet is resized; it is affected by the weight values of **b2**. Note that the **weightx** value for **b2** is much larger than **b3**. When resizing occurs, **b2** will occupy a much larger percentage of the new space. The button is placed at row-1 column-2. One row and one column are occupied.

Both the text field and canvas have a **weightx** value of 0 and a **weighty** value of 0. The value of **fill** is **BOTH**. The text field is placed at row 3, column 0 and the canvas is placed at row 3, column 2. The text field occupies one row and two columns. The canvas occupies one row and one column.

Java also provides a variation of **GridBagLayout**. The **gridx**, **gridy**, **gridwidth** and **gridheight** variables are not used; constants are used in their place. The **GridbagConstraints** constants are *RELATIVE* and *REMAINDER*. **RELATIVE** specifies that the component is placed next to the previous component. **REMAINDER** specifies that a component is the last component in the row. Figure 11.27 uses these constants to lay out components in **GridBagLayout**. The program only creates the GUI.

```
1    // Fig. 11.27: GridBagDemo2.java
2    // Demonstrating GridBagLayout constants.
3    import java.applet.Applet;
4    import java.awt.*;
5
6    public class GridBagDemo2 extends Applet {
7       private Choice cb;
8       private TextField tf;
9       private List m;
10      private Button b1, b2, b3, b4;
11      private GridBagLayout gbLayout;
12      private GridBagConstraints gbConstraints;
13
14      public void init()
15      {
16         gbLayout = new GridBagLayout();
17         setLayout( gbLayout );    // applet
18
19         // instantiate gridbag constraints
20         gbConstraints = new GridBagConstraints();
21
22         // create some components
23         cb = new Choice();
24         cb.addItem( "Pine" );
25         cb.addItem( "Ash" );
26         cb.addItem( "Pecan" );
27         tf = new TextField( "TextField" );
28         m = new List( 3, false );
29         m.addItem( "Java" );
30         b1 = new Button( "eins" );
31         b2 = new Button( "zwei" );
32         b3 = new Button( "drei" );
33         b4 = new Button( "vier" );
34
35         // text field
36         gbConstraints.weightx = 1;
37         gbConstraints.weighty = 1;
38         gbConstraints.fill = GridBagConstraints.BOTH;
39         gbConstraints.gridwidth = GridBagConstraints.REMAINDER;
40         addComponent( tf, gbLayout, gbConstraints );
41
42         // button b1
43         // weightx and weighty are 1: fill is BOTH
44         gbConstraints.gridwidth = GridBagConstraints.RELATIVE;
45         addComponent( b1, gbLayout, gbConstraints );
46
47         // button b2
48         // weightx and weighty are 1: fill is BOTH
49         gbConstraints.gridwidth = GridBagConstraints.REMAINDER;
50         addComponent( b2, gbLayout, gbConstraints );
```

Fig. 11.27 Demonstrating the **GridBagConstrants** constants **RELATIVE** and **REMAINDER** (part 1 of 2).

```
51
52          // choicebox
53          // weightx is 1: fill is BOTH
54          gbConstraints.weighty = 0;
55          gbConstraints.gridwidth = GridBagConstraints.REMAINDER;
56          addComponent( cb, gbLayout, gbConstraints );
57
58          // button b3
59          // weightx is 1: fill is BOTH
60          gbConstraints.weighty = 1;
61          gbConstraints.gridwidth = GridBagConstraints.REMAINDER;
62          addComponent( b3, gbLayout, gbConstraints );
63
64          // button b4
65          // weightx and weighty are 1: fill is BOTH
66          gbConstraints.gridwidth = GridBagConstraints.RELATIVE;
67          addComponent( b4, gbLayout, gbConstraints );
68
69          // list
70          // weightx and weighty are 1: fill is BOTH
71          gbConstraints.gridwidth = GridBagConstraints.REMAINDER;
72          addComponent( m, gbLayout, gbConstraints );
73       }
74
75       // addComponent is programmer-defined
76       private void addComponent( Component c, GridBagLayout g,
77                                  GridBagConstraints gc )
78       {
79          g.setConstraints( c, gc );
80          add( c );        // add component to applet
81       }
82    }
```

Fig. 11.27 Demonstrating the **GridBagConstrants** constants **RELATIVE** and **REMAINDER** (part 2 of 2).

The statements

```
gbLayout = new GridBagLayout();
setLayout( gbLayout );
```

construct the **GridBagLayout** and set the layout manager to **GridBagLayout**.

The components that are placed in **GridBagLayout** are each constructed. The components are four buttons, one text field, one list, and one choice button.

The text field is added first. The **weightx** and **weighty** values are set to one. The **fill** variable is set to **BOTH**. The statement

```
gbConstraints.gridwidth = GridBagConstraints.REMAINDER;
```

specifies that the text field is the last component on the line. The text field is added to the applet with a call to programmer-defined method **addComponent**.

The **addComponent** method takes a **Component** argument, a **GridBagLayout** argument and a **GridBagConstraints** argument. The **GridBagLayout** method **setConstraints** sets the constraints for the component. The **add** method then adds the component to the applet.

Button **b1** has **weightx** and **weighty** values of one. The **fill** variable is **BOTH**. The statement

```
gbConstraints.gridwidth = GridBagConstraints.RELATIVE;
```

specifies that the button is to be placed relative to the previous component. The button is added to the applet with a call to **addComponent**.

Button **b2** has **weightx** and **weighty** values of one. The **fill** variable is **BOTH**. This button is the last component on the line, so **REMAINDER** is used. The button is added to the applet with a call to **addComponent**.

The choice button has a **weightx** of 1 and a **weighty** of 0. The choice button will not grow in the vertical direction. This button is the only component on the line, so **REMAINDER** is used. Method **addComponent** adds the choice button to the applet.

Button **b3** has **weightx** and **weighty** values of one. The **fill** variable is **BOTH**. This button is the only component on the line, so **REMAINDER** is used. The button is added to the applet with a call to **addComponent**.

Button **b4** has **weightx** and **weighty** values of one. The **fill** variable is **BOTH**. This button is not the last component on the line, so **RELATIVE** is used. The button is added to the applet with a call to **addComponent**.

The list component has **weightx** and **weighty** values of one. The **fill** variable is **BOTH**. The list is the last component on the line, so **REMAINDER** is used. The list is added to the applet with a call to **addComponent**.

11.12 Not Using a Layout Manager

Java allows the programmer to not use a layout manager. If a layout manager is not being used, each individual component must be manually placed by the programmer. The program of Fig. 11.28 does not use a layout manager. Three buttons and one choice button are placed on the applet. The program does nothing other than displaying the GUI.

```
1    // Fig. 11.28: NoLayout.java
2    // Demonstrating the null layout manager.
3    import java.applet.Applet;
4    import java.awt.*;
5
6    public class NoLayout extends Applet {
7       private Choice cb;
8       private Button b1, b2, b3;
9
10      public void init()
11      {
12         // do not use a layout manager
13         setLayout( null );
14
15         cb = new Choice();
16         cb.addItem( "Item 1" );
17         cb.addItem( "Item 2" );
18         cb.addItem( "Item 3" );
19
20         b1 = new Button( "Button" );
21         b2 = new Button( "Another Button" );
22         b3 = new Button( "Last Button" );
23
24         add( cb );
25         add( b1 );
26         add( b2 );
27         add( b3 );
28
29         b1.reshape( 15, 9, 60, 26 );
30         b2.reshape( 100, 40, 90, 22 );
31         b3.reshape( 220, 20, 70, 55);
32         cb.reshape( 50, 80, 70, 17);
33      }
34   }
```

Fig. 11.28 Program that does not use a layout manager.

The **NoLayout** class creates a reference to a **Choice** button and three references to **Button**. The statement

```
setLayout( null );
```

specifies that no layout manager is to be used. Next the choice button is instantiated and three items are added. The buttons are then instantiated and added to the applet. The statements

```
b1.reshape( 15, 9, 60, 26 );
b2.reshape( 100, 40, 90, 22 );
b3.reshape( 220, 20, 70, 55 );
cb.reshape( 50, 80, 70, 17 );
```

place and size the components. The **Component** class method **reshape** specifies the component's *x* coordinate, *y* coordinate, the width, and the height.

Common Programming Error 11.17

Placing a component at a location off the container space is a logic error. The component will either be clipped or not seen.

Common Programming Error 11.18

Forgetting to place the component manually on the container is a logic error. The component is usually not visible.

Portability Tip 11.1

Using no layout manager (i.e., manually placing components) may affect a program's platform independence.

11.13 Programmer-defined Layout Managers

If any of the layout managers presented do not layout components in the desired order, Java allows programmers to create their own layout manager. Programmer-defined layout managers are created by implementing the **LayoutManager** interface.

Good Programming Practice 11.5

Creating a programmer-defined layout manager can complicate a program, so whenever possible the predefined layout managers should be used.

We present a program that uses a programmer-defined layout manager to place up to five components in a "V" shape. The program is shown in Fig. 11.29. The example provides enough information to demonstrate how a programmer-defined layout manager is created and provides a foundation for creating more complex layout managers.

Software Engineering Observation 11.4

The ability to create a programmer-defined layout manager is another example of Java's extensibility.

```
1   // Fig. 11.29: UserLayout.java
2   // Demonstrating a programmer-defined layout manager.
3   import java.applet.Applet;
4   import java.awt.*;
5
6   public class UserLayout extends Applet {
7      private Choice cb1, cb2;
8      private Button b1, b2, b3;
9
10     public void init()
11     {
12        // use the v layout manager
13        setLayout( new VLayout() );
14
15        cb1 = new Choice();
16        cb1.addItem( "Item 1" );
17        cb1.addItem( "Item 2" );
18
19        cb2 = new Choice();
20        cb2.addItem( "Choice 1" );
21        cb2.addItem( "Choice 2" );
22
23        b1 = new Button( "Button 1" );
24        b2 = new Button( "Button 2" );
25        b3 = new Button( "Button 3" );
26
27        // order is important
28        add( cb1 );
29        add( b1 );
30        add( b2 );
31        add( b3 );
32        add( cb2 );
33     }
34  }
35
36  // create class for user defined layout
37  class VLayout implements LayoutManager {
38
39     public void layoutContainer( Container c )
40     {
41        int numberOfComponents = c.countComponents();
42
43        if ( numberOfComponents > 5 )
44           numberOfComponents = 5;
45
46        Insets i = c.insets();
47        int w = c.size().width - i.left - i.right;
48        int h = c.size().height - i.bottom - i.top;
49        int x = 0, y = 0;
```

Fig. 11.29 Demonstrating a programmer-defined layout manager (part 1 of 3).

```
50
51          // calculate x and y values for each component
52          for ( int j = 0; j < numberOfComponents; j++ ) {
53             Component comp = c.getComponent( j );
54             Dimension d = comp.preferredSize();
55
56             switch ( j ) {
57                case 0:  // first component
58                   x = ( int ) ( 0.2 * w );
59                   y = ( int ) ( 0.25 * h );
60                   break;
61                case 1:  // second component
62                   x = ( int ) ( 0.3 * w );
63                   y = ( int ) ( 0.5 * h );
64                   break;
65                case 2:  // third component
66                   x = ( int ) ( 0.4 * w );
67                   y = ( int ) ( 0.75 * h );
68                   break;
69                case 3:  // fourth component
70                   x = ( int ) ( 0.5 * w );
71                   y = ( int ) ( 0.5 * h );
72                   break;
73                case 4:  // fifth component
74                   x = ( int ) ( 0.6 * w );
75                   y = ( int ) ( 0.25 * h );
76                   break;
77             }
78
79             // size the component
80             comp.reshape( x, y, d.width, d.height );
81          }
82       }
83
84       // These last four methods must be overridden
85       // However our layout manager does not use them
86       public void addLayoutComponent( String s, Component c )
87       { } // empty
88
89       public void removeLayoutComponent( Component c )
90       { } // empty
91
92       public Dimension preferredLayoutSize( Container c )
93       { return minimumLayoutSize( c ); }
94
95       public Dimension minimumLayoutSize( Container c )
96       { return new Dimension( 0, 0 ); }
97    }
```

Fig. 11.29 Demonstrating a programmer-defined layout manager (part 2 of 3).

Fig. 11.30 Demonstrating a programmer-defined layout manager (part 3 of 3).

The **UserLayout** class creates five components, sets the layout to **VLayout** with the statement

```
setLayout( new VLayout() );
```

and adds the components to the applet. The **VLayout** constructor is called to construct the layout manager.

The **VLayout** class implements **LayoutManager** that contains five methods that must be overridden. The five methods are *addLayoutComponent*, *layoutContainer*, *minimumLayoutSize*, *preferredLayoutSize* and *removeLayoutComponent*. Method **addLayoutComponent** specifies how to add a specific component to the layout. Method **layoutContainer** specifies how to lay out the container. Method **minimumLayoutSize** specifies the minimum size needed for the layout. Method **preferredLayoutSize** specifies the preferred layout size for the container. Method **removeLayoutComponent** removes a specified component from the layout. The only method for which we provide significant functionality is **layoutContainer**.

The **layoutContainer** method takes one argument, the container to lay out. The statement

```
int numberOfComponents = c.countComponents();
```

uses the **Container** class method **countComponents** to get the number of components in the container. If the number of components exceeds five, the **numberOfComponents** variable is set to five. The statement

```
Insets i = c.insets();
```

uses the **Container** class method *insets* to get the *insets* for the container. The **Inset** object stores the measurements of the container border. The statements

```
int w = c.size().width - i.left - i.right;
int h = c.size().height - i.bottom - i.top;
```

calculate the width and height of the nonbordered area. Both **w** and **h** are used to precisely position the components. The **Component** class method *size* returns a *Dimension* object. A **Dimension** object contains an instance variable *width* and an instance variable *height*. The **Inset** class contains four instance variables—*left*, *right*, *top*, and *bottom*. These variables correspond to the measurements for the *left border*, *right border*, *top border*, and *bottom border*.

The **for** loop lays out one component at a time. The statement

```
Component comp = c.getComponent( j );
```

gets each component in the order in which they were added. The **Container** class method *getComponent* returns the specified component. The statement

```
Dimension d = comp.preferredSize();
```

instantiates the **Dimension** object **d**. The **Dimension** returned from the **preferred-Size** method is assigned to **d**. Note that we did not do much with the **preferredSize** method other than return a **Dimension** object with a zero width and a zero height.

Common Programming Error 11.19

*Passing a value to the **getComponent** method that is larger than the actual number of components throws an **ArrayIndexOutOfBoundsException***

The **switch** structure sets the **x** and **y** location for each component. The first component is placed at a location twenty percent of the width and twenty-five percent of the height. The second component is placed at thirty percent of the width and fifty percent of the height. The third component is placed at forty percent of the width and seventy-five percent of the height. The fourth component is placed at fifty percent of the width and fifty percent of the height. The fifth component is placed at sixty percent of the width and twenty-five percent of the height. Each component is positioned and sized with the **reshape** method.

Summary

- Text areas provide an area for manipulating multiple lines of text. A text area always has a vertical scrollbar and horizontal scrollbar. The scrollbars are not capable of scrolling unless text extends beyond the visible rows or visible columns. Retrieving text from a text area requires an external event such as a button press.

- **TextComponent** method **setText** places text in a text area. Method **getSelectedText** returns a text area's selected text.

- A canvas is a component where graphics can be drawn and mouse events are recognized. Class **Canvas** inherits from **Component**. A canvas has its own graphics context.

- **Component** method **resize** resizes a component.

- For a **Canvas** to draw, its **paint** method must be overridden. The coordinates on a canvas are relative to the upper left corner of the canvas which is (0, 0).

- A **Scrollbar** is a component that "scrolls" through a range of integer values.

- The orientation of a scrollbar is specified with constant **Scrollbar.HORIZONTAL** or constant **Scrollbar.VERTICAL**. **Scrollbar** events are generated when a scroll arrow is clicked, the scroll box is moved or the area between a scroll arrow and the scroll box is clicked. Scrollbar events are handled in **handleEvent**.

- Custom components are created by extending the **Canvas** class or the **Panel** class. Custom components that contain other components should extend the **Panel** class.

- A **Frame** is a window with a title bar and a border. Class **Frame** extends class **Window**. Class **Window** contains methods for window management. The default layout manager for windows and frames is **BorderLayout**.

- **Frame** method **dispose** frees the resources allocated to a frame. Frames must be sized before being displayed. Frames are not visible by default. The programmer must explicitly call **show** to display a frame.

- **Frame** method **setResizable** determines whether a frame can be resized by the user. Frames are resizable by default.

- A window destroy event occurs when the frame's exit icon is clicked.

- Menus allow the user to perform direct or indirect actions, without "cluttering" a container with extra GUI components. Menus can only be used with frames.

- Class **MenuComponent** is the base class for **MenuBar** and **MenuItem**.

- Class **MenuBar** contains the constructor and methods necessary to manage the menu bar. A menu bar is a container for menus.

- Class **Menu** contains the constructors and methods necessary for managing menus. When a menu is clicked, the menu expands to show a list of menu items. Clicking a menu item generates an action event.

- A **CheckboxMenuItem** is a menu item that toggles. When the checkbox item is selected, a check appears to the left of the menu item name. When the checkbox item is selected again, the check to the left of the menu item is removed.

- **Menu** method **add** inserts a menu item in a menu. **MenuBar** method **add** adds a menu to the menu bar. **Frame** method **setMenuBar** attaches the menu bar on the frame.

- A separator bar is a line that visually separates menu items. Passing a hyphen (-) to the **MenuItem** constructor creates a separator bar.

- **CheckboxMenuItem** method **setState** sets the **boolean** state for a checkbox menu item. Method **getState** returns the **boolean** state of a checkbox menu item.

- A dialog box is a borderless window with a title bar. Dialog boxes are commonly used to gather information from the user or to show information to the user. Dialog boxes are created with the **Dialog** class—which inherits from **Window**. Dialog boxes can be modal or modeless. A modal dialog box does not allow any other window in the application to be accessed until the dialog box is dismissed. A modeless dialog box allows other windows to be accessed while the dialog is displayed. **BorderLayout** is the default layout manager for dialog boxes.

- **MenuBar** method **setHelpMenu** sets the help menu on the menu bar.

- **MenuItem** methods **enable** and **disable** enable and disable a menu item. When a menu item is enabled, the menu item generates an action event when selected. A menu item that is disabled is grayed—selecting a grayed menu does not generate an event.

- **FileDialog** boxes are modal by default. The two types of **FileDialog**s are an open file dialog and a save file dialog.

- The **CardLayout** layout manager arranges components into a "deck" of cards where only the top card is visible. Each card is usually a container such as a panel. The cards can use any layout manager. **CardLayout** methods **first**, **previous**, **next**, and **last** are used to show a particular card.

- The **GridBagLayout** layout manager is similar to the **GridLayout** layout manager because components are arranged in a grid. However **GridBagLayout** is more flexible. The components can vary in size and can be added in any order. **GridBagConstraints** specify how components are laid out with **GridBagLayout**.

- Java allows the programmer to not use a layout manager by passing **null** to the **setLayout** method. If a layout manager is not being used, each individual component must be manually placed and sized by the programmer.

- **Component** method **reshape** specifies the component's *x* coordinate, *y* coordinate, the width and the height.

- Programmer-defined layout managers are created by implementing the **LayoutManager** interface. The **LayoutManager** interface contains five methods that must be overridden—**addLayoutComponent**, **layoutContainer**, **minimumLayoutSize**, **preferredLayoutSize** and **removeLayoutComponent**.

- **Container** method **countComponents** gets the number of components in the container. **Container** method **insets** gets the insets for a container.

- **Component** method **size** returns a **Dimension** object containing an instance variable **width** and an instance variable **height**.

Terminology

action method	canvas
ACTION_EVENT	**Canvas** class
add method	**Canvas** constructor
addLayoutContainer method	**CardLayout** class
anchor	**CardLayout** layout manager
arrow head symbol	**CardLayout** object
bottom	**CardLayout** reference
bottom border	checkbox menu item

`Scrollbar.HORIZONTAL`
scrollbar orientation
`Scrollbar` reference
`Scrollbar.VERTICAL`
scroll box
separator bar
`setBackground` method
`setConstraints` method
`setEditable` method
`setFont` method
`setHelpMenu` method
`setLayout( null );`
`setMenuBar` constructor
`setResizable` method
`setState` method
`setText` method
`show` method
`size` method
slider

submenu
`super`
text area
`TextArea` class
`TextArea` constructor
`TextArea` object
`TextArea` reference
`TextComponent` class
title bar
`top`
top border
`weightx`
`weighty`
width
`Window` class
`Window` object
`WINDOW_DESTROY`
window destroy events

Common Programming Errors

11.1   Forgetting to call the `resize` method on a canvas is a run-time logic error. The canvas cannot be seen.

11.2   Passing a value to the `Scrollbar` constructor of Fig. 11.9 other than `Scrollbar.HORIZONTAL` or `Scrollbar.VERTICAL` throws an `IllegalArgumentException`.

11.3   The default layout manager for windows and frames is `BorderLayout`. Forgetting to specify `"North"`, `"South"`, `"East"`, `"West"` or `"Center"` when adding a component to a `Window` or `Frame` is a run-time logic error. The component may not appear.

11.4   Forgetting to call the `resize` method on a `Frame` is a run-time logic error; usually only the title bar of the `Frame` is visible.

11.5   Forgetting to call the `show` method on a `Frame` is a run-time logic error; the `Frame` is not displayed.

11.6   Forgetting to set the menu bar with `Frame` method `setMenuBar` results in the menu bar not being displayed on the `Frame`.

11.7   Attempting to use menus with applets results in compilation errors.

11.8   Using a lowercase `i` in `MenuItem` or `CheckboxMenuItem` is a syntax error.

11.9   Using a lowercase `b` in class name `MenuBar` is a syntax error.

11.10 Using an uppercase `b` in class name `CheckboxMenuItem` is a syntax error.

11.11 Forgetting to add a menu item to a menu is a run-time logic error. The menu item will not appear in the menu.

11.12   Attempting to use a **Checkbox** component instead of a **CheckboxMenuItem** in a menu is a syntax error.

11.13   Forgetting to call the **resize** method on a dialog box is a run-time logic error. The dialog box usually cannot be seen because it has no default size.

11.14   Forgetting to call the **show** method is a run-time logic error. The dialog box is not displayed because dialogs are hidden by default.

11.15   Forgetting to call the **show** method for a **FileDialog** object is a run-time logic error—the file dialog is not displayed.

11.16   Using a negative value for either **weightx** or **weighty** is a logic error.

11.17   Placing a component at a location off the container space is a logic error. The component will either be clipped or not seen.

11.18   Forgetting to place the component manually on the container is a logic error. The component is usually not visible.

11.19   Passing a value to the **getComponent** method that is larger than the actual number of components throws an **ArrayIndexOutOfBoundsException**.

Good Programming Practices

11.1   Extend class **Canvas** rather than class **Panel** when **Container** methods are not required to implement a custom component.

11.2   Extending the **Canvas** class instead of the **Panel** class when a custom component does not need the methods of the **Container** class.

11.3   Providing get and set methods to access **private** data in a custom component.

11.4   Hide a **Frame** before calling the **dispose** method. Sometimes resources may not be freed properly resulting in the bitmap image of the **Frame** still being displayed.

11.5   Creating a programmer-defined layout manager can complicate a program, so whenever possible the predefined layout managers should be used.

Performance Tips

11.1   Disposing a frame releases windowing system resources.

Portability Tips

11.1   Using no layout manager (i.e., manually placing components) may affect a program's platform independence.

Software Engineering Observations

11.1   Graphics drawn directly on an applet can be covered by components. Canvases eliminate this problem by providing a dedicated area for graphics.

11.2   The ability to create custom components contributes to Java's extensibility. This is one of Java's most appealing attributes.

11.3   Menus simplify GUIs by reducing the number of components the user views.

11.4   The ability to create a programmer-defined layout manager is another example of Java's extensibility.

Self-Review Exercises

11.1   Fill in the blanks in each of the following:
a) The _____ class is used to create a menu object.
b) The _____ constructor must be used to create a separator bar.
c) Passing **true** to a text area's _____ method allows text to be modified by the user.
d) Scrollbar events are handled by the _____ method.
e) The value of the **Event** class instance **arg** for a menu item is _____.
f) The **GridBagConstraints** instance variable _____ is set to **CENTER** by default.

11.2   State which of the following statements are true and which are false. If a statement is false, explain why.
a) When the programmer creates a dialog box, a minimum of one menu must be created and added to the dialog.
b) When the programmer creates a frame, a minimum of one menu must be created and added to the dialog.
c) The **static** instance variable **fill** belongs to the **GridBagLayout** class.
d) Frames and applets cannot be used together in the same program.
e) The top left corner of a frame or applet has a coordinate of (0, 0).
f) A text area's text is always static (read-only).

11.3   Find the error(s) in each of the following and explain how to correct the error(s).
a) `if ( x instanceof TextArea )   // check for text area event`
b) `Menubar b;   // create menubar reference`
c) `myScroll = Scrollbar( 1000, 0, 222, 100, 450 );`
d) `gbc.fill = GridBagConstraints.NORTHWEST;   // set fill`
e) `ml.add( new Checkbox( "Snap to grid" ) ); // ml is a Menu`
f) `// call Java's HelpMenu constructor to create a help Menu`
    `help = new HelpMenu( "Help" );`
g) `y.reshape( x, y, w, h, c ); // size and place component`

Answers to Self-Review Exercises

11.1   a) **Menu** b) **MenuItem** c) **setEditable** d) **handleEvent** e) menu item selected (string) f) **anchor**

11.2   a) False. A dialog box does not have to have any menus.
b) False. A frame does not have to have any menus.
c) False. The variable **fill** belongs to the **GridBagConstraints** class.
d) False. They can be used together.
e) True.
f) False. Text areas are editable by default.

11.3 a) Text areas do not generate events on their own. An external event such as a button would have to be used.

  b) **Menubar** should be **MenuBar**.

  c) The first argument should be either **Scrollbar.HORIZONTAL** or **Scrollbar.VERTICAL**.

  d) The constant should be either **BOTH, HORIZONTAL, VERTICAL** or **NONE**.

  e) Checkboxes cannot be added to menus. A **CheckboxMenuItem** should be used.

  f) Java does not have a **HelpMenu** class constructor—**setHelpMenu** should set the menu that is the designated help menu.

  g) The **reshape** method should have four arguments passed—not five.

Exercises

11.4 Fill in the blanks in each of the following:

  a) _____ are created by inheriting from the **Canvas** class.

  b) A menu item that is a menu is called a _____.

  c) Both text fields and text areas inherit directly from the _____ class.

  d) The _____ constructor displays a menubar.

  e) A _____ must be passed to the **MenuItem** constructor to create a separator bar.

  f) The **size** method belongs to the _____ class.

  g) The _____ interface must be implemented to create a programmer-defined layout manager.

  h) The _____ class inherits from the **Dialog** class.

11.5 State which of the following statements are true and which are false. If a statement is false, explain why.

  a) Menus require a **MenuBar** object.

  b) A **Canvas** object is capable of handling mouse events.

  c) **CardLayout** is the default layout manager for a frame.

  d) The **setEditable** method is a **TextComponent** class method.

  e) The **GridBagLayout** layout manager implements **LayoutManager**.

  f) **Canvas** objects cannot be used with any of the layout managers.

  g) Class **Frame** inherits directly from class **Window**.

  h) File dialog boxes are modal by default.

11.6 Find the error(s) in each of the following. Explain how to correct the error(s).

  a) `x.add( new MenuItem( "Submenu Color" ) ); // create submenu`

  b) `setLayout( m = new GridbagLayout() );`

  c) `if ( u instanceof Canvas )`
     `    System.out.println( "It was a canvas!" );`

  d) `int weightValue = i.weightx;   // i is an Inset object`

  e) `String s = TextArea.getText();`

  f) `Dialog d = new Dialog( a, "Dialog", true ); // a is an applet`

  g) `int width = z.width();   // z is a Dimension object`

11.7 Write a program that displays a circle of a random size and calculates and displays the area, radius, diameter, and circumference. Use the following equations: $diameter = 2 \times radius$, $area = \pi \times radius^2$, $circumference = 2 \times \pi \times radius$. Use the constant **Math.PI** for Pi (π). All drawing should be done on a canvas and the results of the calculations should be displayed in a read-only text area.

11.8   Enhance the program of Exercise 11.7 by allowing the user to alter the radius with a scrollbar. The program should work for all radii in the range of 100 to 200. As the radius changes, the diameter, area, and circumference should be updated and displayed. The initial radius should be 150. Use the equations of Exercise 11.7. All drawing should be done on a canvas and the results of the calculations should be displayed in a read-only text area.

11.9   Explore the effects of varying the **weightx** and **weighty** values of the program of Fig. 11.26. What happens when a component has a non-zero weight, but is not allowed to fill the whole area (i.e., the **fill** value is not **BOTH**)?

11.10   Write your own programmer-defined layout manager. Use the program of Fig. 11.29 as a starting point. Consult the Java API for additional information.

11.11   Write a program that uses the **paint** method to draw the current value of a scrollbar on a canvas. In addition, provide a text field where a specific value can be entered. The text field should display the current value of the scrollbar at all times. A label should be used to identify the text field. The **Scrollbar** class methods **setValue** and **getValue** should be used. Note: The **setValue** method is a **public** method that does not return a value and takes one integer argument—the scroll-bar value.

11.12   Modify the program of Fig. 11.22 to use a single **Choice** button instead of the four separate buttons. Each "card" should not be modified.

11.13   Modify the program of Fig. 11.22 by adding a minimum of two new "cards" to the deck.

11.14   Write a program that allows the user to view a custom color. The program should consist of three non-editable text fields, one canvas, and three scrollbars. The canvas should be used to display the color. The scrollbars should be used to adjust the red, green, and blue values respectively. The three text fields should display the current values of their respective scrollbars.

11.15   Create your own custom component. If possible, the custom component created should handle its own events.

11.16   Write a program that demonstrates the other **TextArea** class constructors. How do these constructors differ from the two introduced in this chapter?

12

Exception Handling

Objectives

- To understand exception and error handling.
- To be able to use **try** blocks to delineate code in which an exception may occur.
- To be able to **throw** exceptions.
- To use **catch** blocks to specify exception handlers.
- To use the **finally** block to release resources.
- To understand the Java exception hierarchy.
- To create programmer-defined exceptions.

It is common sense to take a method and try it. If it fails, admit it frankly and try another. But above all, try something.
Franklin Delano Roosevelt

O! throw away the worser part of it,
And live the purer with the other half.
William Shakespeare

If they're running and they don't look where they're going
I have to come out from somewhere and catch them.
Jerome David Salinger

And oftentimes excusing of a fault
Doth make the fault the worse by the excuse.
William Shakespeare

I never forget a face, but in your case I'll make an exception.
Groucho (Julius Henry) Marx

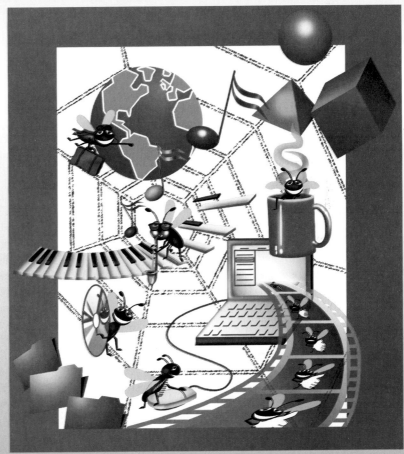

Outline

12.1 Introduction

In this chapter, we introduce *exception handling*. The extensibility of Java can increase the number and types of errors that can occur. Every new class can add its own error possibilities. The features presented here enable programmers to write clearer, more robust, more fault-tolerant programs. We also consider when exception handling should not be used.

The style and details of exception handling in Java as presented in this chapter are based in part on the work of Andrew Koenig and Bjarne Stroustrup as presented in their paper, "Exception Handling for C++ (revised)," published in the *Proceedings of the USENIX C++ Conference* held in San Francisco in April, 1990. Their work forms the basis of the ANSI (draft) standard version of C++ exception handling. Java's designers chose to implement an exception-handling mechanism similar to that used in C++.

Error-handling code varies in nature and quantity among software systems depending on the application and whether the software is a product for release. Products tend to contain far more error-handling code than "casual" software does.

There are many popular means for dealing with errors. Most commonly, error-handling code is interspersed throughout a system's code. Errors are dealt with at the places in the code where the errors can occur. The advantage to this approach is that a programmer reading code can see the error processing in the immediate vicinity of the code and determine if the proper error checking has been implemented.

The problem with this scheme is that the code in a sense becomes "polluted" with the error processing. It becomes more difficult for a programmer concerned with the application itself to read the code and determine if it is functioning correctly. This can make it difficult to understand and maintain the application.

Some common examples of exceptions are an out-of-bounds array subscript, arithmetic overflow (i.e., a value outside the representable range of values), division by zero, invalid method parameters and memory exhaustion.

Good Programming Practice 12.1

Using Java exception handling enables the programmer to remove the error-handling code from the "main line" of the program's execution. This improves program clarity and enhances modifiability.

Separating error-handling code from the main line of program code is consistent with the virtues of separability we have discussed in the contexts of both structured programming and object-oriented programming.

Java exception handling enables a program to catch all types of exceptions, or to catch all exceptions of a certain type, or to catch all exceptions of related types. This makes programs more robust by reducing the likelihood that errors will not be caught by a program.

Exception handling is provided to enable programs to catch and handle errors rather than letting them occur and suffering the consequences. Exception handling is designed for dealing with *synchronous errors* such as an attempt to divide by zero (that occurs as the program executes the divide instruction). Exception handling is not designed to deal with *asynchronous* events such as disk I/O completions, network message arrivals, mouse clicks, keystrokes and the like; these are best handled through other means, such as interrupt processing.

Exception handling is used in situations in which the system can recover from the malfunction causing the exception. The recovery procedure is called an *exception handler*.

Exception handling is typically used in situations in which a malfunction will be dealt with in a different scope from that which detected the malfunction. For example, a program that carries on an interactive dialog with a user should not use exceptions to process keyboard input problems.

Good Programming Practice 12.2

Use exceptions for malfunctions that must be processed in a different scope from where they occur. Use conventional error-handling techniques for local error-processing in which a program is able to deal with its own errors.

Good Programming Practice 12.3

Avoid using exception handling for purposes other than error handling because this can reduce program clarity.

There is another reason to avoid using exception handling techniques for conventional program control. Exception handling is designed for error processing which is an infrequent activity that is often used because a program is about to terminate. It is not required that Java implement exception handling for the kind of optimal performance that might be expected of regular application code.

Performance Tip 12.1

Although it is possible to use exception handling for purposes other than error handling, this can reduce program performance.

Performance Tip 12.2

When an exception does not occur, little or no overhead is imposed by the presence of exception-handling code. When exceptions happen, they do incur execution-time overhead.

Testing and Debugging Tip 12.1

Exception handling helps improve a program's fault tolerance. It becomes "more pleasant" to write error-processing code, so programmers are more likely to provide it.

Good Programming Practice 12.4

Using Java's standardized exception handling rather than having programmers use a diversity of "home-grown" techniques can improve program clarity on large projects.

Most programs written today support only a single thread of execution. The techniques discussed in this chapter apply even for multithreaded programs. We discuss multithreading in Chapter 13.

We will see that exceptions are objects of classes that are derived from superclass **Exception**. We will show how to deal with "uncaught" exceptions. We will consider how unexpected exceptions are handled by Java. We will show how related exception types can be represented by exception subclasses that are derived from a common exception superclass.

Exception handling can be viewed as another means of returning control from a method or exiting a block of code. Normally, when an exception occurs, the exception will be handled by a caller of the method generating the exception, by a caller of that caller, or however far back in the call chain it becomes necessary to go to find a handler for that exception.

Software Engineering Observation 12.1

Exception handling is particularly well-suited to systems of separately developed components. Such systems are typical of real-world software systems and products. Exception handling makes it easier to combine the components and have them work together effectively.

Software Engineering Observation 12.2

With other programming languages that do not support exception handling, programmers often delay writing error-processing code, and sometimes programmers simply forget to include it. This often results in less-robust, and thus inferior, software products. Java forces the programmer to deal with exception handling from the inception of a project. Still, the programmer must put considerable effort into incorporating an exception handling strategy into software projects.

Software Engineering Observation 12.3

It is best to incorporate your exception handling strategy into a system from the inception of the design process. It is difficult to add effective exception handling after a system has been implemented.

12.2 When Exception Handling Should Be Used

Exception handling should be used

- to process only exceptional situations.
- to process exceptions from program components that are not geared to handling those exceptions directly.
- to process exceptions from software components such as methods, libraries, and classes that are likely to be widely used, and where it does not make sense for those components to handle their own exceptions.
- on large projects to handle error processing in a uniform manner project-wide.

Software Engineering Observation 12.4

The client of a library class will likely have unique error processing in mind for an exception generated in the library class. It is unlikely that a library class will perform error processing that would meet the unique needs of all clients. Exceptions are an appropriate means for dealing with errors produced by library classes.

12.3 Other Error-Handling Techniques

We have presented various ways of dealing with exceptional situations prior to this chapter. A program can ignore the exceptions. This can be devastating for software products released to the general public, or for special-purpose software needed for mission-critical situations. But for software developed for your own purposes, it is common to ignore many kinds of errors. A program could be directed to abort upon encountering an exceptional situation. This prevents a program from running to completion and producing incorrect results. For many types of errors this is a good strategy. Such a strategy is inappropriate for mission-critical applications. Resource issues are also important here. If a program obtains a resource, the program should normally return that resource before program termination.

Common Programming Error 12.1

Aborting a program could leave a resource in a state in which other programs would not be able to acquire the resource, and hence we would have a so-called "resource leak."

Good Programming Practice 12.5

If your method is capable of handling a given type of exception then handle it rather than passing the exception on to other regions of your program. This makes programs clearer.

Performance Tip 12.3

If an error can be processed locally instead of throwing an exception, do so. This will improve program speed. Exception handling is slow compared to simple local processing.

12.4 The Basics of Java Exception Handling

Java exception handling is geared to situations in which the method that detects an error is unable to deal with it. Such a method will *throw an exception*. There is no guarantee that there will be "anything out there" (i.e., an *exception handler*—code that executes when an exception has been detected) specifically geared to processing that kind of exception. If there is, the exception will be *caught* and *handled*. The following Testing and Debugging Tip describes what happens if no appropriate exception handler can be found.

Testing and Debugging Tip 12.2

All Java applets and certain Java applications are GUI-based. Some Java applications are not GUI-based; these are often called command-line applications (or console applications). When an exception is not caught in a command-line application the program terminates (i.e., Java exits) after the default exception handler runs. When an exception is not caught in an applet or a GUI-based application, the GUI is still displayed and the user can continue using the applet or application even after the default exception handler runs. However, the GUI may be in an inconsistent state.

The programmer encloses in a **try** block the code that may generate an exception. The **try** block is immediately followed by one or more **catch** blocks. Each **catch** block specifies the type of exception it can catch and contains an exception handler. After the last **catch** block, an optional **finally** block provides code that always executes regardless of whether or not an exception occurs; as we will see the **finally** block is an ideal place for code that releases resources to prevent "resource leaks."

When an exception is thrown, program control leaves the **try** block and the **catch** blocks are searched in order for an appropriate handler (we will soon discuss what makes a handler "appropriate"). If the type of the thrown exception matches the parameter type in one of the **catch** blocks, the code for that **catch** block is executed. If no exceptions are thrown in the **try** block, the exception handlers for that block are skipped and the program resumes execution after the last **catch** block. If a **finally** block appears after the last **catch** block, it is executed regardless of whether or not an exception is thrown.

We can specify with a **throws** clause the exceptions a method throws. An exception can be thrown from a **try** block in the method, or the exception can be thrown from a method called directly or indirectly from the **try** block. The point at which the **throw** is executed is called the *throw point*.

Once an exception is thrown, the block in which the exception is thrown expires and control cannot return to the throw point. Thus Java uses the *termination model of exception handling* rather than the *resumption model of exception handling*. In the resumption model, control would return to the point at which the exception was thrown and resume execution.

When an exception occurs, it is possible to communicate information to the exception handler from the vicinity in which the exception occurred. That information is the type of the thrown object itself or information can be harvested from the vicinity in which the exception occurs and placed into the thrown object.

Software Engineering Observation 12.5

A key to Java-style exception handling is that the portion of a program or system that handles the exception can be distant from the portion of the program that generates the exception.

12.5 A Simple Exception Handling Example: Divide by Zero

Now let us consider a simple example of exception handling. The program of Fig. 12.1 uses **try**, **throw**, and **catch** to detect, indicate, and handle a divide-by-zero exception.

```
1    // Fig. 12.1: DivideByZeroException.java
2    // Definition of class DivideByZeroException.
3    // Used to throw an exception when a
4    // divide-by-zero is attempted.
5    public class DivideByZeroException
6                   extends ArithmeticException {
7       public DivideByZeroException()
8       {
9          super( "Attempted to divide by zero" );
10      }
11   }
```

Fig. 12.1 A simple exception handling example with divide by zero (part 1 of 4).

```
12   // Fig. 12.1: DivideByZeroTest.java
13   // A simple exception handling example.
14   // Checking for a divide-by-zero-error.
15   import java.awt.*;
16   import java.applet.Applet;
17
18   public class DivideByZeroTest extends Applet {
19      Label prompt1, prompt2;
20      TextField input1, input2;
21      int number1, number2;
22      double result;
23
24      // Initialization
25      public void init()
26      {
27         prompt1 = new Label( "Enter numerator" );
28         input1 = new TextField( 10 );
29         prompt2 = new Label( "Enter denominator and " +
30                              "press Enter" );
31         input2 = new TextField( 10 );
32         add( prompt1 );
33         add( input1 );
34         add( prompt2 );
35         add( input2 );
36      }
37
38      // Process GUI events
39      public boolean action( Event event, Object object )
40      {
41         if ( event.target == input2 ) {
42            number1 = Integer.parseInt( input1.getText() );
43            input1.setText( "" );
44            number2 = Integer.parseInt( input2.getText() );
45            input2.setText( "" );
46
```

Fig. 12.1 A simple exception handling example with divide by zero (part 2 of 4).

```
47              try {
48                 result = quotient( number1, number2 );
49                 showStatus( number1 + " / " + number2 + " = " +
50                          Double.toString( result ) );
51              }
52              catch ( DivideByZeroException exception ) {
53                 showStatus( exception.toString() );
54              }
55           }
56
57           return true;
58        }
59
60        // Definition of method quotient. Used to demonstrate
61        // throwing an exception when a divide-by-zero error
62        // is encountered.
63        public double quotient( int numerator, int denominator )
64           throws DivideByZeroException
65        {
66           if ( denominator == 0 )
67              throw new DivideByZeroException();
68
69           return ( double ) numerator / denominator;
70        }
71     }
```

Fig. 12.1 A simple exception handling example with divide by zero (part 3 of 4).

Consider the two sample executions shown in the four output windows. The first two windows show a successful execution. In the last two windows, a zero denominator is entered and the program detects the problem, throws an exception and issues an appropriate diagnostic message.

Fig. 12.1 A simple exception handling example with divide by zero (part 4 of 4).

First we must either find an appropriate **Exception** class for a divide-by-zero situation or we must create one. When we search the **Exception** classes of the **java.lang** package we find a whole set of **RuntimeException** classes. The one that most closely matches our needs is **ArithmeticException**. We could use this class directly, but instead we choose to create our own more specific class **DivideByZeroException** (lines 1–11).

Good Programming Practice 12.6

Associating each type of serious execution-time malfunction with an appropriately named **Exception** *class improves program clarity.*

Class **DivideByZeroException** is formed by extending class **ArithmeticException**. The constructor (lines 7–10) uses a **super** call to the constructor for **ArithmeticException** passing it the string **"Attempted to divide by zero"**.

Now consider the **DivideByZeroTest** applet (lines 12–71). The applet's **init** method (lines 24–36) builds a graphical user interface with two **Label**s and two **TextField**s.

After the user enters the denominator, the **action** method (lines 38–58) determines that the **Event** target was the second **TextField** (line 41) and therefore that input is complete for our purposes. The contents of the two **TextField**s are read into **number1** and **number2**.

Next, the **action** method proceeds with a **try** block (lines 47–51) which encloses the code that may **throw** an exception. The division that can cause the error is not explicitly listed in the **try** block. Rather, the call to method **quotient** invokes the code that attempts the division. Method **quotient** (lines 60–70) **throw**s the **DivideByZe-**

roException object as we will see momentarily. In general, errors may surface through explicitly mentioned code in a **try** block, through calls to a method, or even through deeply nested method calls initiated by code in a **try** block.

The **try** block is immediately followed by a **catch** block (lines 52–54) containing the exception handler for the **DivideByZeroException**. In general, when an exception is thrown within a **try** block, the exception is caught by a **catch** block that specifies an appropriate type that matches the thrown exception. In Fig. 12.1, the **catch** block specifies that it will catch exception objects of type **DivideByZeroException**; this type indeed matches the type of the object thrown in method **quotient**. In this case our exception handler simply issues an error message, but exception handlers can be more elaborate than this. After executing, the exception-handler control proceeds to the first statement after the last **catch** block (there is only one **catch** block here, but there could be several).

If, when executed, the code in the **try** block does not **throw** an exception, then the **catch** handler is skipped and execution resumes with the first line of code after the **catch** handlers. In Fig. 12.1 a **return** statement is executed that returns **true**, but the program could simply continue executing.

Testing and Debugging Tip 12.3

With exception handling, a program can continue executing after dealing with a problem. This helps ensure robust applications that contribute to what is called mission-critical computing *or* business-critical computing.

Now let us examine method **quotient**. When the **if** statement determines that **denominator** is zero, the body of the **if** issues a **throw** statement that creates and throws a **new DivideByZeroException** object. This object will be caught by the **catch** block specifying type **DivideByZeroException** after the **try** block. The thrown object is received in parameter **exception** (line 52) specified in the **catch** handler, and the message is printed there by converting **exception** to a **String** via **toString** and then passing this **String** to **showStatus**.

If **denominator** is not zero, no exception is thrown, the division is performed and the result of the division is returned to the point of invocation of method **quotient** in the **try** block (line 48). We then use **showStatus** to display the calculation and its result. The catch block is skipped and the **action** method executes the **return true;** statement.

Note that when **quotient** throws the **DivideByZeroException**, **quotient**'s block expires. This would cause any of its objects to be marked for garbage collection and the finalizers for these objects would run before garbage collection takes place. If this exception is thrown, the **try** block also expires before the **showStatus** in line 49 can execute. Here, too, if there were any automatic object references created in the **try** prior to the exception being thrown, these objects would be marked for eventual garbage collection and their finalizers would be run before garbage collection occurs.

12.6 Try Blocks

An exception that occurs in a **try** block is normally caught by a handler specified by a **catch** block immediately following that **try** block.

```
try {
    ...
}
catch(  ) {
    ...
}
```

A **try** block can be followed by zero or more **catch** blocks.

Common Programming Error 12.2

It is a syntax error to separate with other code the **catch** *handlers that correspond to a particular* **try** *block.*

If a **try** block executes and no exceptions are thrown, all the exception handlers are skipped and control resumes with the first statement after the last exception handler. If a **finally** block follows the last **catch** block, the code in the **finally** block executes regardless of whether or not an exception is thrown.

Testing and Debugging Tip 12.4

A **finally** *block is an excellent place in which to place code that will release resources acquired in a* **try** *block. This strategy is an effective way to avoid resource leaks.*

12.7 Throwing an Exception

The **throw** statement is executed to indicate that an exception has occurred. This is called *throwing an exception*. A **throw** statement specifies an object to be thrown. The operand of a **throw** can be of any class derived from class **Throwable**. The two immediate subclasses of class **Throwable** are **Exception** and **Error**. **Error**s are particularly serious system problems that generally should not be caught. **Exception**s are caused by problems most Java programmers will want to deal with. If the operand is an object of class **Exception**, we call it an *exception object*.

Testing and Debugging Tip 12.5

When **toString** *is invoked on any* **Throwable** *object, its printout includes the* **String** *that was supplied to the constructor.*

Testing and Debugging Tip 12.6

If it is necessary to pass information about the malfunction that caused an exception, such information can be placed in the thrown object. That information can then be referenced through the parameter name in the **catch** *handler.*

Testing and Debugging Tip 12.7

An object can be thrown without containing information to be passed; in this case, knowledge that an exception of this type has been raised may provide sufficient information for the handler to do its job correctly.

When an exception is thrown, control exits the current **try** block and proceeds to an appropriate **catch** handler (if one exists) after that **try** block. It is possible that the **throw** point could be in a deeply nested scope within a **try** block; control will still proceed to the **catch** handler. It is also possible that the **throw** point could be in a deeply nested method call; still, control will proceed to the **catch** handler.

A **try** block may appear to contain no error checking and include no **throw** statements, but code referenced in the **try** block could certainly cause error-checking code in constructors to execute and possibly throw exceptions. Code in a **try** block may perform array subscripting on an array object. If an invalid array subscript is specified, the system throws an **ArrayIndexOutOfBoundsException**. Any method call can invoke code that might **throw** an exception or call another method that throws an exception.

Although an exception can terminate program execution, it need not do this. However, an exception does terminate at least the block in which the exception occurred.

12.8 Catching an Exception

Exception handlers are contained in **catch** blocks. Each **catch** block starts with the keyword **catch** followed by parentheses containing a class name (specifying the type of exception to be caught) and a parameter name. The object caught by the handler can be referenced through this parameter. This is followed by a block delineating the exception-handling code. When an exception is caught, the code in the **catch** block is executed.

Common Programming Error 12.3

*Assuming that after an exception is processed, control will return to the first statement after the **throw** can lead to errors.*

Common Programming Error 12.4

Specifying a comma-separated list of **catch** *arguments is a syntax error. A* **catch** *can have only a single argument.*

Common Programming Error 12.5

It is a syntax error to **catch** *the same type in two different* **catch** *blocks associated with a particular* **try** *block.*

A **catch** that catches an **Exception** object

```
catch( Exception e )
```

means to catch all exceptions.

Common Programming Error 12.6

Placing **catch(Exception e)** *before other* **catch** *blocks would prevent those blocks from ever being executed;* **catch(Exception e)** *should always be placed last in the list of handlers following a* **try** *block, or a syntax error occurs.*

Software Engineering Observation 12.6

If you catch all exceptions with **catch(Exception e)** *you can use the* **instanceof** *operator to probe the type of the exception. For example, the boolean condition* **x instanceof Y** *evaluates to* **true** *if object* **x** *is an instance of class* **Y**, *and* **false** *otherwise.*

It is possible that no handler will match a particular thrown object. This causes the search for a match to continue in the next enclosing **try** block. As this process continues, it may eventually be determined that there is no handler in the program that matches the type of the thrown object; in this case a non-GUI-based application terminates—applets and GUI-based applications return to their regular event processing.

It is possible that several exception handlers will provide an acceptable match to the type of the exception. This can happen for several reasons. First, there can be a "catch-all" handler **catch(Exception e)** that will catch any exception. Second, because of inheritance relationships, it is possible that a subclass object can be caught either by a handler specifying the subclass type, or by handlers specifying the types of any superclasses of that subclass. In this case, the first exception handler that matches the exception type is executed.

Software Engineering Observation 12.7

If several handlers match the type of an exception, and if each of these handles the exception differently, then the order of the handlers will affect the manner in which the exception is handled.

Common Programming Error 12.7

*It is a syntax error if a **catch** that catches a superclass object is placed before a **catch** that catches an object of a subclass of that superclass.*

Sometimes a program may process many closely related types of exceptions. Instead of providing separate exception classes and **catch** handlers for each, a programmer can provide a single exception class and **catch** handler for a group of exceptions. As each exception occurs, the exception object can be created with different instance data such as a type code. The **catch** handler can examine this data to distinguish the type of the exception. Actually, this style of programming is discouraged in object-oriented languages like Java because inheritance takes care of this situation more elegantly.

By default, if no handler is found for an exception, a non-GUI-based application terminates. Although this may seem like the right thing to do, it is not what programmers using other languages without exception-handling features are used to doing. Rather, errors often simply happen and then program execution continues, possibly only "hobbling" along.

A **try** block followed by several exception handlers resembles a **switch** statement, but a **break** statement is not used to exit an exception handler in a manner that skips over the remaining exception handlers. Each **catch** block defines a distinct scope whereas all the cases in a **switch** statement are contained within the single scope of the **switch**.

An exception cannot access objects defined within its **try** block because the **try** block has expired when the handler begins executing.

What happens when an exception occurs in an exception handler? The **try** block that noticed the exception has expired when the exception handler begins running, so exceptions occurring in an exception handler need to be processed outside the **try** block in which the original exception was thrown. The outer **try** block watches for errors occurring in the original **try** block's **catch** handlers.

Exception handlers can be written in a variety of ways. They could simply rethrow an exception (we will see how to do this in the next section). They could convert one type of exception into another by throwing a different type of exception. They could perform any necessary recovery and resume execution after the last exception handler. They could look at the situation causing the error, remove the cause of the error, and retry by calling the original method that caused an exception. They could simply return some status value to their environment, etc.

It is not possible to return to the **throw** point by issuing a **return** statement in a **catch** handler. Such a **return** simply returns to the method that called the method containing the **catch** block. Again, the **throw** point is in a block that has expired, so returning via a **return** statement would not make sense.

Software Engineering Observation 12.8

Another reason not to use exceptions for conventional flow of control is that these "additional" exceptions can "get in the way" of genuine error-type exceptions. It becomes more difficult for the programmer to keep track of the larger number of exception cases. Exceptional situations should be rare, not commonplace.

Common Programming Error 12.8

*Assuming that an exception thrown from a **catch** handler will be processed by that handler or any other handler associated with the same **try** block can lead to logic errors.*

12.9 Rethrowing an Exception

It is possible that the **catch** handler that catches an exception may decide it cannot process the exception or it may want to let some other **catch** handler handle it. In this case, the handler that received **Exception e** can simply rethrow the exception with the statement

```
throw e;
```

Such a **throw** rethrows the exception to the next enclosing **try** block.

Even if a handler can process an exception, and regardless of whether it does any processing on that exception, the handler can still rethrow the exception for further processing outside the handler. A rethrown exception is detected by the next enclosing **try** block and is handled by an exception handler listed after that enclosing **try** block.

12.10 Throws Clause

A **throws** clause lists the exceptions that can be thrown by a method.

```
int g( float h ) throws a, b, c
{
    // method body
}
```

The types of exceptions that are thrown by a method are specified in the method definition with a **throws** clause. A method can **throw** objects of the indicated classes, or it can **throw** objects of subclasses.

Some exceptions occur because something that could have been avoided went wrong. These are *run-time exceptions* and they derive from class **RuntimeException**. If your program attempts to access an out-of-range array subscript, an exception of type **ArrayIndexOutOfBoundsException** (derived from **RuntimeException**) is thrown. Your program can clearly avoid such a problem; hence, it is a run-time exception.

Another run-time exception occurs when your program has created an object reference but has not yet created on object and attached it to the reference. Attempting to use such a

null reference causes a **NullPointerException** to be thrown. Clearly, your program could have avoided this circumstance; hence, it, too, is a run-time exception.

Another kind of run-time exception is an invalid cast which throws a **ClassCast-Exception** (see Chapter 7).

There are a variety of exceptions that are not **RuntimeException**s. Two of the most common are **InterruptedException**s (see Chapter 13, "Multithreading") and **IOException**s (see Chapter 15, "Files and Streams").

Not all errors and exceptions that can be thrown from a method are listed in the **throws** clause. **Error**s do not need to be listed, nor do **RuntimeException**s (avoidable exceptions). **Error**s are serious system problems that can occur almost anywhere and most users will not have the need to deal with them. You should be dealing with **RuntimeException**s directly rather than passing them on to other regions of your program. Non-**RuntimeException**s a method explicitly throws and non-**RuntimeException**s thrown by methods the method calls must be listed in the method's **throws** clause.

Software Engineering Observation 12.9

*If a non-**RuntimeException** is thrown by a method, or if that method calls methods that throw non-**RuntimeException**s, each of those exceptions must be declared in the **throws** clause of that method or caught in a **try/catch** in that method.*

Java distinguishes *checked **Exception**s* versus *unchecked **Exception**s* and **Error**s. A method's checked exceptions need to be listed in that method's **throws** clause. Because **Error**s and **RuntimeException**s can be thrown from almost any method, it would be cumbersome for programmers to be required to list them; these are not required to be listed in a method's **throws** clause, and hence are said to be "unchecked." All non-**RuntimeException**s a method can **throw** must be listed in that method's **throws** clause, and hence are said to be "checked."

Common Programming Error 12.9

*It is a syntax error if a method throws a checked exception not in that method's **throws** clause.*

Common Programming Error 12.10

*Attempting to throw a checked exception from a method that has no **throws** clause is a syntax error.*

Software Engineering Observation 12.10

*If your method calls other methods that explicitly **throw** checked exceptions, those exceptions must be listed in the **throws** clause of your method, unless your method catches those exceptions. This is Java's "**catch**-or-declare" requirement.*

Common Programming Error 12.11

*If a subclass method overrides a superclass method, it is an error for the subclass method to list more exceptions in its **throws** list than the overridden superclass method does. A subclass **throws** list can contain a subset of a superclass's **throws** list.*

Java's **catch**-or-declare requirement demands that the programmer either **catch** each checked exception or place it in the **throws** clause of a method. Of course placing a checked exception in the **throws** clause would force other methods to deal with the checked exception as well. If a programmer feels a particular checked exception is unlikely to occur, the programmer might elect to catch that checked exception and do nothing with it to avoid the annoyance of being forced to deal with it later. This can of course come back to haunt you because as a program evolves it may become important to deal with this checked exception.

Testing and Debugging Tip 12.8

Do not try to circumvent Java's **catch**-*or-declare requirement by simply catching exceptions and doing nothing with them. Exceptions are generally of a serious enough nature that they need to be dealt with rather than suppressed.*

Testing and Debugging Tip 12.9

The Java compiler, through the **throws** *list used with exception handling, forces programmers to deal with the exceptions that can be thrown from each method a program calls. This helps avoid bugs that arise in programs when programmers ignore the fact that things can go wrong and make no provisions for these problems.*

Software Engineering Observation 12.11

Subclass methods that do not override their corresponding superclass methods exhibit the same exception handling behavior of the inherited superclass methods. The **throws** *list of a subclass method that overrides a superclass method may not have more exceptions than the* **throws** *list of the overridden superclass method.*

Common Programming Error 12.12

The Java compiler requires that a method either catch any checked exceptions thrown in the method (either directly from the method's code itself or indirectly through called methods), or declare checked **Exception**s *the method can* **throw** *to other methods; otherwise the Java compiler issues a syntax error.*

Testing and Debugging Tip 12.10

Suppose a method **throws** *all subclasses of a particular superclass. You may be tempted to list only the superclass in the* **throws** *clause. Instead, explicitly list all the subclasses. This focuses the programmer's attention on the specific* **Exception**s *that must be dealt with and will often help avoid bugs caused by processing* **Exception**s *in too general a manner.*

Figures 12.2 through 12.7 list Java's **Error**s and **Exception**s hierarchically. We show Java's **Error** hierarchy in Fig. 12.2. Most Java programmers will simply ignore **Error**s. They are serious but rare events.

Figure 12.3 is particularly important because it lists almost all of Java's **Runtime-Exception**s. Although Java programmers will not declare these exceptions in **throws** clauses, there are the kinds of exceptions that will commonly be caught and handled in Java applications. All but two of Java's **RuntimeException**s are in the **java.lang** package.

Figure 12.4 lists Java's other two **RuntimeException**s data types. We will encounter these exceptions in Chapter 18 when we study the **Vector** class. A **Vector** is a dynamic array that can grow and shrink to accommodate a program's varying storage requirements.

The `java.lang` package errors

Error (all in **`java.lang`** except for **`AWTError`** which is in **`java.awt`**)

    LinkageError

        ClassCircularityError
        ClassFormatError
        IncompatibleClassChangeError

            AbstractMethodError
            IllegalAccessError
            InstantiationError
            NoSuchFieldError
            NoSuchMethodError

        NoClassDefFoundError
        UnsatisfiedLinkError
        VerifyError

    ThreadDeath

    VirtualMachineError (Abstract class)

        InternalError
        OutOfMemoryError
        StackOverflowError
        UnknownError

    AWTError (in **`java.awt`**)

Fig. 12.2 The **`java.lang`** package errors .

Figure 12.5 lists Java's **IOException**s. These are all checked exceptions that can occur during input/output and file processing.

Figure 12.6 lists the **`java.awt`** package's only **Exception**, the **AWTException**. This is a checked exception that is thrown by various abstract windowing toolkit methods.

Figure 12.7 lists the **IOException**s of the **`java.net`** package. These are all checked **Exception**s that indicate various networking problems.

12.11 Constructors, Finalizers, and Exception Handling

First, let us deal with an issue we have mentioned, but that has yet to be satisfactorily resolved. What happens when an error is detected in a constructor? The problem is that a constructor cannot return a value, so how do we let the program know that an object has not been properly constructed? One scheme is simply to return the improperly constructed object and hope that anyone using the object would make appropriate tests to determine that the object is in fact bad. Another scheme is to set some global variable outside the constructor but this is a poor programming practice. A thrown exception passes to the outside world the information about the failed constructor and the responsibility to deal with the failure.

The `java.lang` package exceptions

```
Exception

    ClassNotFoundException
    CloneNotSupportedException
    IllegalAccessException
    InstantiationException
    InterruptedException
    NoSuchMethodException

    RuntimeException

        ArithmeticException
        ArrayStoreException
        ClassCastException

        IllegalArgumentException

            IllegalThreadStateException
            NumberFormatException

        IllegalMonitorStateException

        IndexOutOfBoundsException

            ArrayIndexOutOfBoundsException
            StringIndexOutOfBoundsException

        NegativeArraySizeException
        NullPointerException
        SecurityException
```

Fig. 12.3 The `java.lang` package exceptions .

Exceptions thrown in constructors cause objects built as part of the object being constructed to be marked for eventual garbage collection. Before each object is garbage collected, its finalizer will be called. Once again, Java does not guarantee the order in which objects will be garbage collected and therefore it does not guarantee the order in which finalizers will be called.

The `java.util` package exceptions

`Exception`

   `RuntimeException`

      `EmptyStackException`
      `NoSuchElementException`

Fig. 12.4 The `java.util` package exceptions.

The `java.io` package exceptions

`Exception`

   `IOException`

      `EOFException`
      `FileNotFoundException`
      `InterruptedIOException`
      `UTFDataFormatException`

Fig. 12.5 The `java.io` package exceptions.

The `java.awt` package exceptions

`Exception`

      `AWTException`

Fig. 12.6 The `java.awt` package exceptions.

The java.net package exceptions

```
Exception

    IOException

        MalformedURLException
        ProtocolException
        SocketException
        UnknownHostException
        UnknownServiceException
```

Fig. 12.7 The **java.net** package exceptions .

12.12 Exceptions and Inheritance

Various exception classes can be derived from a common superclass. If a **catch** is written
to catch exception objects of a superclass type, it can also catch all objects of subclasses of
that superclass. This can allow for polymorphic processing of related errors.

Using inheritance with exceptions enables an exception handler to catch related errors
with a concise notation. One could certainly catch each subclass exception object individually, but it is more concise to catch the superclass exception object instead. This only
makes sense of the handling behavior would be the same for all subclasses of course. Otherwise, use the subclasses.

Testing and Debugging Tip 12.11

*Catching subclass exception objects individually is subject to error if the programmer forgets
to explicitly test for one or more of the subclass types; catching the superclass guarantees
that objects of all subclasses will be caught.*

12.13 **finally** Block

Programs that obtain certain types of resources must explicitly return those resources to the
system to avoid so-called *resource leaks.* In programming languages like C and C++ the
most common kind of resource leak is a memory leak. Java performs automatic garbage
collection of memory no longer needed by programs, thus avoiding most memory leaks.
But other kinds of resource leaks can occur in Java.

Software Engineering Observation 12.12

*A **finally** block typically contains code to release resources acquired in its corresponding
try block; this is an effective way to eliminate resource leaks. For example, the **finally**
block should close any files opened in the **try** block that threw the exception.*

Testing and Debugging Tip 12.12

*Actually, Java does not completely eliminate memory leaks. There is a subtle issue here. Java
will not garbage collect an object until there are no more references to the object. Thus, mem-*

ory leaks can occur, but only if programmers erroneously keep references to unwanted objects. Most *memory leak problems are solved by Java's garbage collection.*

The **finally** block is optional; if it is present it is placed after the last of a **try** block's **catch** blocks as follows

```
try {
    statements;
    resource-acquire statements;
}
catch ( AKindOfException ex1 ) {
    exception-handling statements;
}
catch (AnotherKindOfException ex2) {
    exception-handling statements;
}
finally {
    statement;
    resource-release statement;
}
```

Java guarantees that a **finally** block (if one is present) will be executed regardless of whether or not any exception is thrown in a **try** block or any of its corresponding **catch** blocks. Java also guarantees that a **finally** block (if one is present) will be executed if a **try** block is exited via a **return**, **break** or **continue** statement. Resource-release code is placed in a **finally** block. Suppose a resource is allocated in a **try** block. If no exception occurs, the **catch** handlers are skipped and control proceeds to the **finally** block which frees the resource and control proceeds to the first statement after the **finally** block.

If an exception occurs, the rest of the **try** block is skipped and if the exception is caught by one of the **catch** handlers, the exception is handled and control still proceeds to the **finally** block which releases the resource and control proceeds to the first statement after the **finally** block.

If an exception that occurs in the **try** block cannot be caught by one of the **catch** handlers, the rest of the **try** block is skipped (as the **try** block expires) and control proceeds to the **finally** block which releases the resource and then the exception is passed up the call chain until some calling method chooses to **catch** it. If no method chooses to deal with it, a non-GUI-based application terminates.

If a **catch** handler throws an exception, the **finally** block is still executed and the exception is passed up the call chain for a calling method to **catch** and handle.

The Java application of Figure 12.8 demonstrates that the **finally** block (if one is present) executes even if an exception is not thrown in the corresponding **try** block. The figure contains methods **main**, **throwException**, and **doesNotThrowException**. Method **main** begins executing, enters its **try** block and immediately calls **throwException**. Method **throwException** throws an **Exception** (line 23), catches it (line 25) and rethrows it. The rethrown exception will be handled in **main**, but first the **finally** block (lines 31–33) executes. The rethrown exception is detected in the **try** block in **main** (lines 7–9) and handled by the **catch** block (lines 10–13).

```
1   // Fig. 12.8: UsingExceptions.java
2   // Demonstration of the try-catch-finally
3   // exception handling mechanism.
4   public class UsingExceptions {
5      public static void main( String args[] )
6      {
7         try {
8            throwException();
9         }
10        catch ( Exception e )
11        {
12           System.err.println( "Exception handled in main" );
13        }
14
15        doesNotThrowException();
16     }
17
18     public static void throwException() throws Exception
19     {
20        // Throw an exception and immediately catch it.
21        try {
22           System.out.println( "Method throwException" );
23           throw new Exception();   // generate exception
24        }
25        catch( Exception e )
26        {
27           System.err.println( "Exception handled in " +
28                               "method throwException" );
29           throw e;   // rethrow exception for further processing
30        }
31        finally {
32           System.err.println( "Finally is always executed" );
33        }
34     }
35
36     public static void doesNotThrowException()
37     {
38        try {
39           System.out.println( "Method doesNotThrowException" );
40        }
41        catch( Exception e )
42        {
43           System.err.println( e.toString() );
44        }
45        finally {
46           System.err.println( "Finally is always executed." );
47        }
48     }
49  }
```

Fig. 12.8 Demonstration of the **try-catch-finally** exception handling mechanism (part 1 of 2).

```
Method throwException
Exception handled in method throwException
Finally is always executed
Exception handled in main
Method doesNotThrowException
Finally is always executed.
```

Fig. 12.8 Demonstration of the **try-catch-finally** exception handling mechanism (part 1 of 2).

Method **doesNotThrowException** is called. No exception is thrown in its **try** block, so the **catch** block is skipped, but the **finally** block nevertheless executes. Control proceeds past the **finally** block. Because there are no statements following **finally** control returns to **main** which also terminates.

The Java application in Fig. 12.9 demonstrates that when an exception thrown in a **try** block is not caught in a corresponding **catch** block, the exception will be detected in the next outer **try** block and will be handled by an appropriate **catch** block (if one is present) associated with that outer **try** block.

A **finally** block as we have seen may be entered for a variety of reasons such as a **try** completing successfully, an exception being thrown and then handled by a local **catch**, an exception being thrown for which no local **catch** is available, or a program control statement like a **return**, **break** or **continue** being issued. Normally, the **finally** block will execute then behave appropriately (we will call this **finally**'s "continuation action") depending on the reason it was entered. It is possible, however, for the **finally** block to perform some action that would cause the "continuation action" to be overridden. For example, if an exception is thrown in the **finally** block, the continuation action will be for *that* exception to be dealt with in the next enclosing block. Unfortunately, the first exception is lost. This is dangerous.

Common Programming Error 12.13

*If an exception is thrown for which no local **catch** is available, when control enters the local **finally** block the **finally** block could also **throw** an exception. If this happens the first exception will be lost.*

Testing and Debugging Tip 12.13

*Avoid placing code that can **throw** an exception in a **finally** block.*

Good Programming Practice 12.7

*Java's exception-handling mechanism is intended to remove error processing code from the main line of a program's code to improve program clarity. Do not place **try-catch-finally** around every statement that may throw an exception. This makes programs difficult to read. Rather, place one **try** block around a significant portion of your code, then follow that **try** block with **catch** blocks that handle each of the things that can go wrong, then follow the **catch** blocks with a single **finally** block.*

```
1   // Fig. 12.9: UsingExceptions.java
2   // Demonstration of stack unwinding.
3   public class UsingExceptions {
4      public static void main( String args[] )
5      {
6         try {
7            throwException();
8         }
9         catch ( Exception e )
10        {
11           System.err.println( "Exception handled in main" );
12        }
13     }
14
15     public static void throwException() throws Exception
16     {
17        // Throw an exception and catch it in main.
18        try {
19           System.out.println( "Method throwException" );
20           throw new Exception();   // generate exception
21        }
22        catch( OtherException e )
23        {
24           System.err.println( "Exception handled in " +
25                                "method throwException" );
26        }
27        finally {
28           System.err.println( "Finally is always executed" );
29        }
30     }
31  }
32
33  class OtherException extends Exception {
34     public OtherException()
35     {
36        super( "Another exception type" );
37     }
38  }
```

```
Method throwException
Finally is always executed
Exception handled in main
```

Fig. 12.9 Demonstration of stack unwinding.

 Software Engineering Observation 12.13

As a rule, resources should be released as soon as it is apparent that they are no longer need-ed. This makes these resources immediately available for reuse and can improve perfor-mance.

Software Engineering Observation 12.14

*If a **try** block has a corresponding **finally** block, the **finally** block will be executed even if the **try** block is exited with **return**, **break** or **continue**; then the effect of the **return**, **break** or **continue** will occur.*

12.14 Using **printStackTrace** and **getMessage**

Exceptions derive from class **Throwable**. Class **Throwable** offers a **printStack-Trace** method that prints the method call stack. By sending this method to an **Exception** object that has been caught, a program can print the method call stack. This is often helpful in testing and debugging. In this section, we consider an example that exercises the **printStackTrace** method and another useful method, **getMessage**.

Testing and Debugging Tip 12.14

*All **Throwable** objects contain a **printStackTrace** method that prints a stack trace for the object.*

Testing and Debugging Tip 12.15

An exception that is not caught eventually causes Java's default exception handler to run. This displays the name of the exception, the optional character string that was supplied when the exception was constructed, and a complete execution stack trace. The stack trace shows the complete method call stack. This lets the programmer see the path of execution that led to the exception file-by-file (and thus class-by-class) and method-by-method. This information is normally very helpful in debugging a program.

There are two constructors for class **Exception**. The first constructor

```
public Exception()
```

takes no arguments. The second constructor

```
public Exception( String informationString )
```

takes an argument **informationString** which is descriptive information about this kind of **Exception** that will be carried in every object of this class. The **informationString** stored in the **Exception** may be queried with method **getMessage**.

Testing and Debugging Tip 12.16

***Exception** classes have a constructor that accepts a **String**. Using this form of the constructor is helpful in determining the source of the exception via method **getMessage()**.*

Figure 12.10 demonstrates **getMessage** and **printStackTrace**. Method **getMessage** returns the descriptive **String** stored in an exception. Method **printStackTrace** outputs to the standard error stream (normally the command line or console) an error message with the class name of the exception, the descriptive **String** stored in the exception and a list of the methods that had not completed execution when the exception was thrown (i.e., all methods currently residing on the method call stack).

In the program, **main** invokes **method1**, **method1** invokes **method2** and **method2** invokes **method3**. At this point, the method call stack for the program is

```
method3
method2
method1
main
```

with the last method called (**method3**) at the top and the first method called (**main**) at the bottom. When **method3** throws a **UserException** (line 30), the stack unwinds to the first method in which the exception can be caught (i.e., **main** because it contains a **catch** handler for **UserException**). The **catch** handler then uses **getMessage** and **printStackTrace** on the **UserException** object **e** to produce the output.

Summary

- Some common examples of exceptions are memory exhaustion, an out-of-bounds array subscript, arithmetic overflow, division by zero, and invalid method parameters.

- Exception handling is designed for dealing with synchronous malfunction, i.e., those that occur as the result of a program's execution.

- Exception handling is typically used in situations in which a malfunction will be dealt with by a different scope from that which detected the malfunction.

- Exceptions should not be used as an alternate mechanism for specifying flow of control.

- Exception handling should be used to process exceptions from software components such as methods, libraries, and classes that are likely to be widely used, and where it does not make sense for those components to handle their own exceptions.

- Exception handling should be used on large projects to handle error processing in a standardized manner for the entire project.

- Java exception handling is geared to situations in which the method that detects an error is unable to deal with it. Such a method will **throw** an exception. If the exception matches the type of the parameter in one of the **catch** blocks, the code for that **catch** block is executed.

- The programmer encloses in a **try** block the code that may generate an error that will produce an exception. The **try** block is immediately followed by one or more **catch** blocks. Each **catch** block specifies the type of exception it can catch and handle. Each **catch** block is an exception handler.

- If no exceptions are thrown in the **try** block, the exception handlers for that block are skipped and the program resumes execution after the last **catch** block, possibly executing a **finally** block if one is provided.

- Exceptions are thrown in a **try** block in a method or from a method called directly or indirectly from the **try** block.

- It is possible to communicate information to the exception handler from the point of the exception. That information is the type of thrown object or it is information harvested from the vicinity and placed into the thrown object.

- The operand of a **throw** can be of any class derived from **Throwable**. The immediate subclasses of **Throwable** are **Error** and **Exception**.

```
1   // Fig. 12.10: UsingExceptions.java
2   // Demonstrating the getMessage and printStackTrace
3   // methods inherited into all exception classes.
4   public class UsingExceptions {
5      public static void main( String args[] )
6      {
7         try {
8            method1();
9         }
10        catch ( UserException e )
11        {
12           System.err.println( e.getMessage() +
13                               "\nThe stack trace is:" );
14           e.printStackTrace();
15        }
16     }
17
18     public static void method1() throws UserException
19     {
20        method2();
21     }
22
23     public static void method2() throws UserException
24     {
25        method3();
26     }
27
28     public static void method3() throws UserException
29     {
30        throw new UserException();
31     }
32  }
33
34  class UserException extends Exception {
35     public UserException()
36     {
37        super( "This is a user defined exception." );
38     }
39  }
```

```
This is a user defined exception.
The stack trace is:
UserException: This is a user defined exception.
    at UsingExceptions.method3(UsingExceptions.java:31)
    at UsingExceptions.method2(UsingExceptions.java:26)
    at UsingExceptions.method1(UsingExceptions.java:21)
    at UsingExceptions.main(UsingExceptions.java:8)
```

Fig. 12.10 Using `getMessage` and `printStackTrace`.

- **RuntimeException**s and **Error**s are said to be "unchecked." Non-**RuntimeException**s are said to be "checked." The checked exceptions thrown by a particular method must be specified in that method's **throws** clause.
- Exceptions are caught by the closest exception handler (for the **try** block from which the exception was thrown) specifying an appropriate type.
- An exception terminates the block in which the exception occurred.
- A handler may rethrow the object to an outer try block.
- **catch(Exception e)** catches all **Exception**s.
- **catch(Error err)** catches all **Error**s.
- **catch(Throwable t)** catches all **Exception**s and **Error**s.
- If no handler matches a particular thrown object the search for a match continues in an enclosing **try** block.
- Exception handlers are searched in order for an appropriate match based on type. The first handler that matches is executed. When that handler finishes executing, control resumes with the first statement after the last **catch** block.
- The order of the exception handlers affects how an exception is handled.
- A subclass object can be caught either by a handler specifying that subclass type or by handlers specifying the types of any direct or indirect superclasses of that subclass.
- If no handler is found for an exception, a non-GUI-based application terminates; an applet or a GUI-based application will return to its regular event handling.
- An exception handler cannot access variables in the scope of its **try** block because by the time the exception handler begins executing the **try** block has expired. Information the handler needs is normally passed in the thrown object.
- Exception handlers can rethrow an exception. They can convert one type of exception into another by throwing a different exception. They can perform any necessary recovery and resume execution after the last exception handler. They can look at the situation causing the error, remove the cause of the error, and retry by calling the original method that caused an exception. They can simply return some status value to their environment.
- A handler that catches a subclass object should be placed before a handler that catches a superclass object. If the superclass handler were first, it would catch superclass objects and the objects of subclasses of that superclass.
- When an exception is caught, it is possible that resources may have been allocated but not yet released in the **try** block. A **finally** block should release these resources.
- It is possible that the handler that catches an exception may decide it cannot process the exception. In this case, the handler can simply rethrow the exception. A **throw** followed by the exception object name rethrows the exception.
- Even if a handler can process an exception, and regardless of whether it does any processing on that exception, the handler can rethrow the exception for further processing outside the handler. A rethrown exception is detected by the next enclosing **try** block

(normally in a calling method) and is handled by an appropriate exception handler (if there is one) listed after that enclosing **try** block.

- A **throws** clause lists the checked exceptions that may be thrown from a method. A method may **throw** the indicated exceptions, or it may **throw** subclass types. If a checked exception not listed in the **throws** clause is thrown, a syntax error occurs.

- A powerful reason for using inheritance with exceptions is to **catch** a variety of related errors easily with concise notation. One could certainly **catch** each type of subclass exception object individually, but it is more concise to simply **catch** the superclass exception object.

Terminology

ArithmeticException

array exceptions

ArrayIndexOutOfBoundsException

business-critical computing

catch a group of exceptions

catch all exceptions

catch an exception

catch block

catch(Exception e)

catch-or-declare requirement

checked **Exception**s

ClassCastException

declare exceptions that can be thrown

default exception handler

EmptyStackException

Error class

Error class hierarchy

error handling

exception

Exception class

Exception class hierarchy

exception handler

exception handling

exception object

fault tolerance

FileNotFoundException

finally block

getMessage() method of **Throwable** class

handle an exception

IllegalAccessException

IncompatibleClassChangeException

instanceof operator

InstantiationException

InternalException

InterruptedException

IOException

library exception classes

memory exhaustion

mission-critical computing

NegativeArraySizeException

NoClassDefFoundException

nonruntime exception

null reference

NullPointerException

OutOfMemoryException

resource leak

resumption model of exception handling

rethrow an exception

RuntimeException

stack unwinding

synchronous error

termination model of exception handling

throw an exception

throw point

throw statement

Throwable class

throws clause

try block

unchecked **Exception**s

UnsatisfiedLinkException

Common Programming Errors

12.1   Aborting a program could leave a resource in a state in which other programs would not be able to acquire the resource, and hence we would have a so-called "resource leak."

12.2   It is a syntax error to separate with other code the **catch** handlers that correspond to a particular **try** block.

12.3   Assuming that after an exception is processed, control will return to the first statement after the **throw** can lead to errors.

12.4   Specifying a comma-separated list of **catch** arguments is a syntax error. A **catch** can have only a single argument.

12.5   It is a syntax error to **catch** the same type in two different **catch** blocks associated with a particular **try** block.

12.6   Placing **catch(Exception e)** before other **catch** blocks would prevent those blocks from ever being executed; **catch(Exception e)** should always be placed last in the list of handlers following a **try** block, or a syntax error occurs.

12.7   It is a syntax error if a **catch** that catches a superclass object is placed before a **catch** that catches an object of a subclass of that superclass.

12.8   Assuming that an exception thrown from a **catch** handler will be processed by that handler or any other handler associated with the same **try** block can lead to logic errors.

12.9   It is a syntax error if a method throws a checked exception not in that method's **throws** clause.

12.10   Attempting to throw a checked exception from a method that has no **throws** clause is a syntax error.

12.11   If a subclass method overrides a superclass method, it is an error for the subclass method to list more exceptions in its **throws** list than the overridden superclass method does. A subclass **throws** list can contain a subset of a superclass's **throws** list.

12.12   The Java compiler requires that a method either catch any checked exceptions thrown in the method (either directly from the method's code itself or indirectly through called methods), or declare checked **Exception**s the method can **throw** to other methods; otherwise the Java compiler issues a syntax error.

12.13   If an exception is thrown for which no local **catch** is available, when control enters the local **finally** block the **finally** block could also **throw** an exception. If this happens the first exception will be lost.

Good Programming Practices

12.1   Using Java exception handling enables the programmer to remove the error-handling code from the "main line" of the program's execution. This improves program clarity and enhances modifiability.

12.2   Use exceptions for malfunctions that must be processed in a different scope from where they occur. Use conventional error-handling techniques for local error-processing in which a program is able to deal with its own errors.

12.3   Avoid using exception handling for purposes other than error handling because this can reduce program clarity.

12.4   Using Java's standardized exception handling rather than having programmers use a diversity of "home-grown" techniques can improve program clarity on large projects.

12.5   If your method is capable of handling a given type of exception then handle it rather than passing the exception on to other regions of your program. This makes programs clearer.

12.6   Associating each type of serious execution-time malfunction with an appropriately named **Exception** class improves program clarity.

12.7   Java's exception-handling mechanism is intended to remove error processing code from the main line of a program's code to improve program clarity. Do not place **try-catch-finally** around every statement that may throw an exception. This makes programs difficult to read. Rather, place one **try** block around a significant portion of your code, then follow that **try** block with **catch** blocks that handle each of the things that can go wrong, then follow the **catch** blocks with a single **finally** block.

Performance Tips

12.1   Although it is possible to use exception handling for purposes other than error handling, this can reduce program performance.

12.2   When an exception does not occur, little or no overhead is imposed by the presence of exception-handling code. When exceptions happen, they do incur execution-time overhead.

12.3   If an error can be processed locally instead of throwing an exception, do so. This will improve program speed. Exception handling is slow compared to simple local processing.

Software Engineering Observations

12.1   Exception handling is particularly well-suited to systems of separately developed components. Such systems are typical of real-world software systems and products. Exception handling makes it easier to combine the components and have them work together effectively.

12.2   With other programming languages that do not support exception handling, programmers often delay writing error-processing code, and sometimes programmers simply forget to include it. This often results in less-robust, and thus inferior, software products. Java forces the programmer to deal with exception handling from the inception of a project. Still, the programmer must put considerable effort into incorporating an exception handling strategy into software projects.

12.3   It is best to incorporate your exception handling strategy into a system from the inception of the design process. It is difficult to add effective exception handling after a system has been implemented.

12.4   The client of a library class will likely have unique error processing in mind for an exception generated in the library class. It is unlikely that a library class will perform error processing that would meet the unique needs of all clients. Exceptions are an appropriate means for dealing with errors produced by library classes.

12.5   A key to Java-style exception handling is that the portion of a program or system that handles the exception can be distant from the portion of the program that generates the exception.

12.6   If you catch all exceptions with `catch(Exception e)` you can use the `instanceof` operator to probe the type of the exception. For example, the boolean condition `x instanceof Y` evaluates to `true` if object `x` is an instance of class `Y`, and `false` otherwise.

12.7   If several handlers match the type of an exception, and if each of these handles the exception differently, the order of the handlers affects the manner in which the exception is handled.

12.8   Another reason not to use exceptions for conventional flow of control is that these "additional" exceptions can "get in the way" of genuine error-type exceptions. It becomes more difficult for the programmer to keep track of the larger number of exception cases. Exceptional situations should be rare, not commonplace.

12.9   If a non-`RuntimeException` is thrown by a method, or if that method calls methods that throw non-`RuntimeException`s, each of those exceptions must be declared in the `throws` clause of that method or caught in a `try/catch` in that method.

12.10   If your method calls other methods that explicitly `throw` checked exceptions, those exceptions must be listed in the `throws` clause of your method, unless your method catches those exceptions. This is Java's "`catch`-or-declare" requirement.

12.11   Subclass methods that do not override their corresponding superclass methods exhibit the same exception handling behavior of the inherited superclass methods. The `throws` list of a subclass method that overrides a superclass method may not have more exceptions than the `throws` list of the overridden superclass method.

12.12   A `finally` block typically contains code to release resources acquired in its corresponding `try` block; this is an effective way to eliminate resource leaks. For example, the `finally` block should close any files opened in the `try` block that threw the exception.

12.13   As a rule, resources should be released as soon as it is apparent that they are no longer needed. This makes these resources immediately available for reuse and can improve performance.

12.14   If a `try` block has a corresponding `finally` block, the `finally` block will be executed even if the `try` block is exited with `return`, `break` or `continue`; then the effect of the `return`, `break` or `continue` will occur.

Testing and Debugging Tips

12.1   Exception handling helps improve a program's fault tolerance. It becomes "more pleasant" to write error-processing code, so programmers are more likely to provide it.

12.2   All Java applets and certain Java applications are GUI-based. Some Java applications are not GUI-based; these are often called command-line applications (or console applications). When an exception is not caught in a command-line application the program terminates (i.e., Java exits) after the default exception handler runs. When an exception is not caught in an applet or a GUI-based application, the GUI is still displayed and the user can continue using the applet or application even after the default exception handler runs. However, the GUI may be in an inconsistent state.

12.3   With exception handling, a program can continue executing after dealing with a problem. This helps ensure robust applications that contribute to what is called mission-critical computing or business-critical computing.

12.4   A **finally** block is an excellent place in which to place code that will release resources acquired in a **try** block. This strategy is an effective way to avoid resource leaks.

12.5   When **toString** is invoked on any **Throwable** object, its printout includes the **String** that was supplied to the constructor.

12.6   If it is necessary to pass information about the malfunction that caused an exception, such information can be placed in the thrown object. That information can then be referenced through the parameter name in the **catch** handler.

12.7   An object can be thrown without containing information to be passed; in this case, knowledge that an exception of this type has been raised may provide sufficient information for the handler to do its job correctly.

12.8   Do not try to circumvent Java's **catch**-or-declare requirement by simply catching exceptions and doing nothing with them. Exceptions are generally of a serious enough nature that they need to be dealt with rather than suppressed.

12.9   The Java compiler, through the **throws** list used with exception handling, forces programmers to deal with the exceptions that can be thrown from each method a program calls. This helps avoid bugs that arise in programs when programmers ignore the fact that things can go wrong and make no provisions for these problems.

12.10   Suppose a method **throws** all subclasses of a particular superclass. You may be tempted to list only the superclass in the **throws** clause. Instead, explicitly list all the subclasses. This focuses the programmer's attention on the specific **Exception**s that must be dealt with and will often help avoid bugs caused by processing **Exception**s in too general a manner.

12.11   Catching subclass exception objects individually is subject to error if the programmer forgets to explicitly test for one or more of the subclass types; catching the superclass guarantees that objects of all subclasses will be caught.

12.12   Actually, Java does not completely eliminate memory leaks. There is a subtle issue here. Java will not garbage collect an object until there are no more references to the object. Thus, memory leaks can occur, but only if programmers erroneously keep references to unwanted objects. Most memory leak problems are solved by Java's garbage collection.

12.13   Avoid placing code that can **throw** an exception in a **finally** block.

12.14   All **Throwable** objects contain a **printStackTrace** method that prints a stack trace for the object.

12.15   An exception that is not caught eventually causes Java's default exception handler to run. This displays the name of the exception, the optional character string that was supplied when the exception was constructed, and a complete execution stack trace. The stack trace shows the complete method call stack. This lets the programmer see the path of execution that led to the exception file-by-file (and thus class-by-class) and method-by-method. This information is normally very helpful in debugging a program.

12.16   **Exception** classes have a constructor that accepts a **String** argument. Using this form of the constructor is helpful in determining the source of the exception via method **getMessage()**.

Self-Review Exercises

12.1   List five common examples of exceptions.

12.2   Why should exception handling techniques not be used for conventional program control?

12.3   Why are exceptions particularly appropriate for dealing with errors produced by library classes and methods?

12.4   What is a "resource leak?"

12.5   If no exceptions are thrown in a **try** block, where does control proceed to when the **try** block completes execution?

12.6   What happens if an exception occurs and an appropriate exception handler cannot be found?

12.7   Give a key advantage of using **catch(Exception e)**.

12.8   Should a conventional applet or application catch **Error** objects?

12.9   What happens if several handlers match the type of the thrown object?

12.10   Why would a programmer specify a superclass type as the type of a **catch** handler and then throw objects of subclass types?

12.11   How might a **catch** handler be written to process related types of errors without using inheritance among exception classes?

12.12   What is the key reason for using **finally** blocks?

12.13   Does throwing an **Exception** have to cause program termination?

12.14   What happens when a **catch** handler throws an **Exception**?

12.15   What happens to the automatic objects that have been constructed in a **try** block when that block throws an **Exception**?

Answers to Self-Review Exercises

12.1   Memory exhaustion, array subscript out of bounds, arithmetic overflow, division by zero, invalid method parameters.

12.2   (a) **Exception** handling is designed to handle infrequently occurring situations that often result in program termination, so compiler writers are not required to implement exception handling to perform optimally. (b) Flow of control with conventional control structures is generally clearer and more efficient than with exceptions. (c) Problems can occur because the stack is unwound when an exception occurs and resources allocated prior to the exception may not be freed. (d) The "additional" exceptions can get in the way of genuine error-type exceptions. It becomes more difficult for the programmer to keep track of the larger number of exception cases.

12.3   It is unlikely that library classes and methods could perform error processing that would meet the unique needs of all users.

12.4   An aborting program could leave a resource in a state in which other programs would not be able to acquire the resource.

12.5   The exception handlers (in the **catch** blocks) for that **try** block are skipped and the program resumes execution after the last **catch** block. If there is a **finally** block, it is executed and the program resumes execution after the **finally** block.

12.6   A non-GUI-based application terminates; an applet or a GUI-based application resumes regular event processing.

12.7   The form **catch(Exception e)** catches any type of exception thrown in a **try** block. An advantage is that no thrown **Exception** can slip by.

12.8   **Error**s are usually serious problems with the underlying Java system; most programs will not want to catch **Error**s.

12.9   The first matching **Exception** handler after the **try** block is executed.

12.10   This is a nice way to catch related types of exceptions, but is should only be used carefully.

12.11   Provide a single **Exception** subclass and **catch** handler for a group of exceptions. As each exception occurs, the exception object can be created with different instance data. The **catch** handler can examine this data to distinguish the type of the **Exception**.

12.12   The **finally** block is the preferred means for preventing resource leaks.

12.13   No, but it does terminate the block in which the **Exception** is thrown.

12.14   The exception will be processed by a **catch** handler (if one exists) associated with the **try** block (if one exists) enclosing the **catch** handler that caused the exception.

12.15   The objects are marked for garbage collection. A finalizer is called for each object before the object is garbage collected.

Exercises

12.16   Under what circumstances would you use the following statement?

```
catch(Exception e) { throw e; }
```

12.17   List the benefits of exception handling over conventional means of error-processing.

12.18   Describe an object-oriented technique for handling related exceptions.

12.19   Until this chapter, we have found that dealing with errors detected by constructors is a bit awkward. Explain why exception handling is an effective means for dealing with constructor failure.

12.20   Suppose a program throws an exception and the appropriate exception handler begins executing. Now suppose that the exception handler itself throws the same exception. Does this create an infinite recursion? Explain your answer.

12.21   Use inheritance to create an exception superclass and various exception subclasses. Write a program to demonstrate that the **catch** specifying the superclass catches subclass exceptions.

12.22   Write a Java program which shows that all finalizers for objects constructed in a block are called after an exception is thrown from that block.

12.23   Write a Java program that demonstrates how various exceptions are caught with **catch(Exception e)**.

12.24   Write a Java program which shows that the order of exception handlers is important. The first matching handler is the one that executes. Compile and run your program two different ways to show that two different handlers execute with two different effects.

12.25   Write a Java program that shows a constructor passing information about constructor failure to an exception handler after a **try** block.

12.26   Write a Java program that illustrates rethrowing an exception.

12.27   Write a Java program which shows that a method with its own **try** block does not have to catch every possible error generated within the **try**. Some exceptions can slip through to, and be handled in other scopes.

13

Multithreading

Objectives

- To understand the notion of multithreading.
- To appreciate how multithreading can improve performance.
- To understand how to create, manage, and destroy threads.
- To understand the life-cycle of a thread.
- To study several examples of thread synchronization.
- To understand thread priorities and scheduling.
- To understand daemon threads and thread groups.

The spider's touch, how exquisitely fine!
Feels at each thread, and lives along the line.
Alexander Pope

A person with one watch knows what time it is; a person with
two watches is never sure.
Proverb

Conversation is but carving!
Give no more to every guest,
Then he's able to digest.
Johathan Swift

Learn to labor and to wait.
Henry Wadsworth Longfellow

The most general definition of beauty ... Multeity in Unity.
Samuel Taylor Coleridge

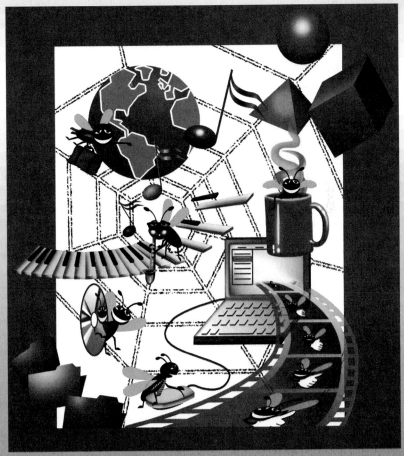

Outline

13.1 Introduction

It would be nice if we could "do one thing at a time" and "do it well." But that is simply not how the world works. The human body performs a great variety of operations *in parallel,* or as we will say throughout this chapter, *concurrently.* Respiration, blood circulation, and digestion for example, can occur concurrently. All of the senses—seeing, touching, smelling, tasting, and hearing—can occur concurrently. An automobile can be accelerating, turning, air conditioning, and playing music concurrently. Computers, too, perform operations concurrently. It is common today for desktop personal computers to be compiling a program, printing a file, and receiving electronic mail messages over a network concurrently.

Concurrency is important in our lives. Ironically, though, most programming languages do not enable programmers to specify concurrent activities. Rather, programming languages generally provide only a simple set of control structures that enable programmers to perform one action at a time and then proceed to the next action after the previous one is finished. The kind of concurrency that computers perform today is normally implemented as operating systems "primitives" available only to highly experienced "systems programmers."

The *Ada* programming language developed by the United States Department of Defense made concurrency primitives widely available to defense contractors building command and control systems. But Ada has not been widely used in universities and commercial industry.

Java is unique among popular general-purpose programming languages in that it makes concurrency primitives available to the personal computer applications programmer. The programmer specifies that applications contain *threads of execution,* each thread designating a portion of a program that may execute concurrently with other threads. This capability, called *multithreading,* gives the Java programmer powerful capabilities not available in C and C++, the languages on which Java is based. C and C++ are called *single-threaded* languages.

Software Engineering Observation 13.1

*Unlike many languages that do not have built-in multithreading (such as C and C++) and must therefore make calls to operating system multithreading primitives, Java includes multithreading primitives as a part of the language itself (actually in classes **Thread**, **ThreadGroup** and **ThreadDeath** of the **java.lang** package). This encourages the use of multithreading among a larger part of the applications programming community.*

We will discuss many applications of concurrent programming. When programs download large files such as audio clips or video clips from the World Wide Web, we do not want to wait until an entire clip is downloaded before starting the playback. So we can put multiple threads to work, one that downloads a clip, and another that plays the clip so that these activities, or *tasks,* may proceed concurrently. To avoid choppy playback, we will coordinate the threads so that the player thread does not begin until there is a sufficient amount of the clip in memory to keep the player thread busy.

Another example of multithreading is Java's automatic garbage collection. C and C++ place with the programmer the responsibility for reclaiming dynamically allocated memory. Java provides a *garbage collector thread* that automatically reclaims dynamically allocated memory that is no longer needed.

Testing and Debugging Tip 13.1

In C and C++, programmers must explicitly provide statements for reclaiming dynamically allocated memory. When memory is not reclaimed (because a programmer forgets to do so, or because of a logic error or because an exception diverts program control), this results in an all-to-common error called a memory leak *that can eventually exhaust the supply of free memory and may cause program termination. Java's automatic garbage collection eliminates the vast majority of memory leaks, i.e., those that are due to orphaned (unreferenced) objects.*

Java's garbage collector runs as a low-priority thread. When Java determines that there are no longer any references to an object, it marks the object for eventual garbage collection. The garbage collector runs when processor time is available and when there are no higher-priority runnable threads. The garbage collector will, however, run immediately when the system is out of memory.

Performance Tip 13.1

Java's garbage collection is not as efficient as the dynamic memory management code the best C and C++ programmers write, but it is relatively efficient and much safer for the programmer..

Performance Tip 13.2

*Setting an object reference to **null** marks that object for garbage collection (if there are no other references to the object). This can help conserve memory in a system in which an automatic object is not going out of scope because the method it is in will execute for a lengthy period.*

Writing multithreaded programs can be tricky. Although the human mind can perform many functions concurrently, humans find it difficult to jump between parallel "trains of thought." To see why multithreading can be difficult to program and understand, try the following experiment: Open three books to page 1. Now try reading the books concurrently. Read a few words from the first book, then read a few words from the second book, then read a few words from the third book, then loop back and read the next few words from the first book, and so on. After a brief time you will rapidly appreciate the challenges of multithreading: switching between books, reading briefly, remembering your place in each book, moving the book you are reading closer so you can see it, pushing books you are not reading aside, and amidst all this chaos, trying to comprehend the content of the books!

Performance Tip 13.3

One problem with single-threaded applications is that possibly lengthy activities must complete before other activities can begin. Users feel they already spend too much time waiting with Internet and World Wide Web applications, so multithreading is immediately appealing.

Although Java is perhaps the world's most portable programming language, certain portions of the language are nevertheless platform dependent. In particular, there are differences among the first three Java platforms implemented, namely the Solaris implementation and the Windows-based implementations for Windows 95 and Windows NT.

The early Solaris Java platform runs a thread of a given priority to completion or until a higher-priority thread becomes ready. At that point *preemption* occurs, i.e., the processor is given to the higher-priority thread while the previously running thread must wait.

In the 32-bit Java implementations for Windows 95 and Windows NT, threads are *timesliced*. This means that each thread is given a limited amount of time (called a time *quantum*) to execute on a processor, and when that time expires the thread is made to wait while all other threads of equal priority get their chances to use their quantum in *round-robin* fashion. Then the original thread resumes execution. Thus, on Windows 95 and Windows NT, a running thread can be preempted by a thread of equal priority whereas on the early Solaris implementation, a running Java thread can only be preempted by a higher-priority thread. Future Solaris Java systems are expected to perform timeslicing as well.

Portability Tip 13.1

Java multithreading is platform dependent. Thus, a multithreaded application could behave differently on different Java implementations.

13.2 Class Thread: An Overview of the Thread Methods

In this section we overview the various thread-related methods in the Java API. We use many of these methods in live-code examples throughout the chapter. The reader should refer to the Java API directly for more details on using each method, especially the exceptions thrown by each method.

Class **Thread** has several constructors. The constructor

```
public Thread( String threadName )
```

constructs a **Thread** whose name is **threadName**. The constructor

```
public Thread()
```

constructs a **Thread** whose name is **"Thread"** concatenated with a digit, like **Thread1**, **Thread2**, and so on.

The code that "does the real work" of a thread is placed in its **run** method. The **run** method can be overridden in a subclass of **Thread** or it may be overridden in a **Runnable** object; **Runnable** is an important Java *interface* that we study in Section 13.10.

A program launches a thread's execution by calling the thread's **start** method which, in turn, calls the **run** method. When **start** launches the thread, **start** returns to its caller immediately. The caller then executes concurrently with the launched thread. The **start** method throws an **IllegalThreadStateException** if the thread it is trying to start has already been started.

The **static sleep** method is called with an argument specifying how long the currently executing thread should sleep (in milliseconds); while a thread sleeps, it does not contend for the processor, so other threads can execute. This can give lower-priority threads a chance to run.

The **interrupt** method is called to interrupt a thread. The **interrupted** method (a **static** method) returns **true** if a thread has been interrupted and **false** otherwise. Method call **isInterrupted** (a non-**static** method) is sent to some other thread to determine if it has been interrupted.

Method **suspend** suspends a thread's execution. Method **resume** resumes the execution of a suspended thread. An attempt to **resume** a thread that is not suspended lets it continue to execute.

Method **stop** stops a thread by throwing a **ThreadDeath** object. Most users will call the version of **stop** that takes no arguments.

Method **isAlive** returns **true** if **start** has been called for a given thread but **stop** has not.

We will discuss the **yield** method in detail after we have considered thread priorities and thread scheduling.

Method **setName** sets the name of the **Thread**. Method **getName** returns the name of the **Thread**. Method **toString** returns a **String** consisting of the name of the thread, the priority of the thread and the thread's thread group.

The **static** method **currentThread** returns a reference to the current **Thread**.

Method **join** (which takes as an argument some number of **milliSeconds**) waits for the **Thread** to which the message is sent to die before the current **Thread** can proceed; no argument or an argument of 0 milliseconds indicates that the current **Thread** will wait forever for the target **Thread** to die before the current **Thread** proceeds. Such waiting can be dangerous; it can lead to two particularly serious problems called *deadlock* and *indefinite postponement*. We will discuss these momentarily.

Testing and Debugging Tip 13.2

*Methods **dumpStack** and **countStackFrames** are useful for debugging multithreaded applications. A program calls **static** method **dumpStack** (with the call **Thread.dumpStack**) to print a method-call stack trace for the current **Thread**. A program calls non-**static** method **countStackFrames** to determine the number of method call stack frames in a suspended **Thread**.*

13.3 Thread States: Life-Cycle of a Thread

At any time, a thread is said to be in one of several *thread states* (illustrated in Fig. 13.1). Let us say that a thread that was just created is in the *born* state. The thread remains in this state until the thread's **start** method is called; this causes the thread to enter the *ready* state. The highest-priority *ready* thread enters the *running* state when the system assigns a processor to the thread (i.e., the thread begins executing). A thread enters the *dead* state when its **run** method completes, or when its **stop** method is called; a *dead* thread will eventually be disposed of by the system.

A *running* thread enters the *blocked* state when the thread issues an input/output request. A *blocked* thread becomes *ready* when the I/O it is waiting for completes. A *blocked* thread cannot use a processor even if one is available.

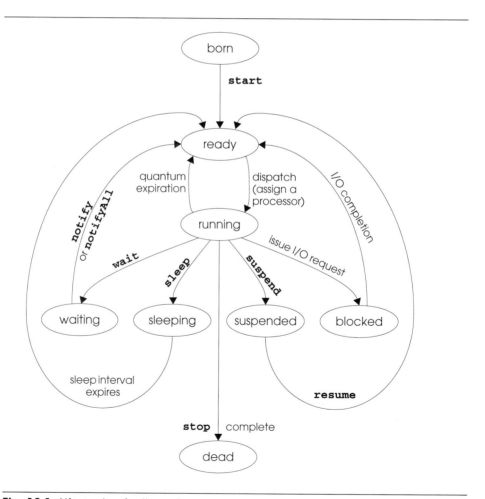

Fig. 13.1 Life cycle of a thread.

When a *running* thread's **sleep** method is called, that thread enters the *sleeping* state. A *sleeping* thread becomes *ready* after the designated sleep time expires. A *sleeping* thread cannot use a processor even if one is available.

> *Performance Tip 13.4*
>
> *One way to delay a thread is to loop some appropriate number of times doing nothing in the body of the loop. This is called a* busy wait *and leads to poor performance; while the processor is busy doing nothing for this thread, other runnable threads may be kept waiting. A better technique is to call the thread's* **sleep** *method. A sleeping thread does not use the processor.*

When a *running* thread's **suspend** method is called, that thread enters the *suspended* state. A *suspended* thread becomes ready when its **resume** method is called by another thread. A *suspended* thread cannot use a processor even if one is available.

When a *running* thread calls **wait** the thread enters a *waiting* state where it waits in a queue associated with the particular object on which **wait** was called. The first thread in the *wait* queue for a particular object becomes *ready* on a call to **notify** issued by another thread associated with that object. Every thread in the *wait* queue for a given object becomes ready on a call to **notifyAll** by another thread associated with that object. The **wait**, **notify**, and **notifyAll** methods will be discussed in more depth shortly when we consider monitors.

A thread enters the *dead state* when its **run** method completes or its **stop** method is called. The **stop** method sends a **ThreadDeath** object to the thread. **ThreadDeath** is a subclass of class **Error**.

> *Common Programming Error 13.1*
>
> ***ThreadDeath** is an **Error**, not an **Exception**. Ordinarily, user programs should not catch **Error** objects. If you choose to catch a **ThreadDeath** object, be sure to rethrow it or the thread may not die "properly."*

13.4 Thread Priorities and Thread Scheduling

Every Java applet or application is multithreaded. Every Java thread has a priority in the range **Thread.MIN_PRIORITY** (a constant of 1) and **Thread.MAX_PRIORITY** (a constant of 10). By default, each thread is given priority **Thread.NORM_PRIORITY** (a constant of 5). Each new thread inherits the priority of the thread that creates it.

Some Java platforms support a concept called *timeslicing* and some do not. Without timeslicing, each thread of a set of equal-priority threads runs to completion before that thread's peers get a chance to execute. With timeslicing, each thread receives a brief burst of processor time called a *quantum* during which that thread can execute. At the completion of the quantum, even if that thread has not finished executing, the processor is taken away from that thread and given to the next thread of equal priority if one is available.

The job of the Java *scheduler* is to keep a highest-priority thread running at all times, and if timeslicing is available, to ensure that several equally high-priority threads each execute for a quantum in *round-robin* fashion (i.e., these threads can be timesliced). Figure 13.2 illustrates Java's multilevel priority queue for threads. In the figure, threads A and B each execute for a quantum in round-robin fashion until both threads complete execution. Next, thread C runs to completion. Then, threads D, E and F each execute for a quantum in round-robin fashion until they all complete execution. This process continues until all threads run to completion. Note that new higher-priority threads could postpone—possibly indefinitely—the execution of lower-priority threads. Such *indefinite postponement* is often referred to more colorfully as *starvation*.

A thread's priority can be adjusted with the **setPriority** method which takes an **int** argument. If the argument is not in the range 1 through 10 inclusive, then method **setPriority** throws an **IllegalArgumentException**. Method **getPriority** returns the thread's priority.

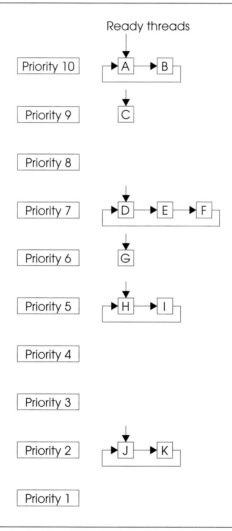

Fig. 13.2 Java thread priority scheduling.

A thread can call the **yield** method to give other threads a chance to execute. Actually, whenever a higher-priority thread becomes ready, the current thread is preempted, so a thread cannot **yield** to a higher-priority thread because the first thread will have been preempted when the higher-priority thread became ready. Similarly, **yield** always allows the highest-priority *ready* thread to run, so if only lower-priority threads are ready at the time of a **yield** call, the current thread will be the highest-priority thread and will continue executing. Therefore, a thread **yield**s to give threads of an equal priority a chance to run. On a timesliced system this is unnecessary because threads of equal priority will each execute for their quantum (or until they lose the processor for some other reason) and other threads of equal priority will execute in round-robin fashion. Thus **yield** is appropriate for non-timesliced systems in which a thread would ordinarily run to completion before another thread of equal priority would have an opportunity to run.

Performance Tip 13.5

On non-timesliced systems, cooperating threads of equal priority should periodically call **yield** *to enable their peers to proceed smoothly.*

Portability Tip 13.2

Applets should be programmed to work on all Java platforms to realize Java's goal of true portability.

A thread executes unless it dies, it becomes blocked for input/output, it calls **sleep**, it calls **yield**, it is preempted by a thread of higher priority or its quantum expires. A thread with a higher priority than the running thread can become ready (and hence preempt the running thread) if a *suspended* thread is resumed, if a *sleeping* thread finishes sleeping, if I/O completes for a thread waiting for that I/O, or if either **notify** or **notifyAll** is called on a thread that called **wait**.

The application of Fig. 13.3 demonstrates basic threading techniques including creation of a derived class from **Thread**, construction of a **Thread** and using the **Thread** class **sleep** method. Each thread of execution we create in the program displays its name after sleeping for a random amount of time between 0 and 5 seconds. The program consists of two classes—**PrintThread** and **PrintTest**.

```
1   // Fig. 13.3: PrintTest.java
2   // Show multiple threads printing at different intervals.
3
4   public class PrintTest {
5      public static void main( String args[] )
6      {
7         PrintThread thread1, thread2, thread3, thread4;
8
9         thread1 = new PrintThread( "1" );
10        thread2 = new PrintThread( "2" );
11        thread3 = new PrintThread( "3" );
12        thread4 = new PrintThread( "4" );
```

Fig. 13.3 Multiple threads printing at random intervals (part 1 of 2).

```
13
14          thread1.start();
15          thread2.start();
16          thread3.start();
17          thread4.start();
18       }
19    }
20
21    class PrintThread extends Thread {
22       int sleepTime;
23
24       // PrintThread constructor assigns name to thread
25       // by calling Thread constructor
26       public PrintThread( String id )
27       {
28          super( id );
29
30          // sleep between 0 and 5 seconds
31          sleepTime = (int) ( Math.random() * 5000 );
32
33          System.out.println( "Name: " + getName() +
34                              "; sleep: " + sleepTime );
35       }
36
37       // execute the thread
38       public void run()
39       {
40          // put thread to sleep for a random interval
41          try {
42             sleep( sleepTime );
43          }
44          catch ( InterruptedException exception ) {
45             System.err.println( "Exception: " +
46                                 exception.toString() );
47          }
48
49          // print thread name
50          System.out.println( "Thread " + getName() );
51       }
52    }
```

```
Name: 1;   sleep: 4297
Name: 2;   sleep: 672
Name: 3;   sleep: 27
Name: 4;   sleep: 2090
Thread 3
Thread 2
Thread 4
Thread 1
```

Fig. 13.3 Multiple threads printing at random intervals (part 2 of 2).

Class **PrintThread**—which inherits from **Thread**—consists of instance variable **sleepTime**, a constructor and a **run** method. Instance variable **sleepTime** stores a random integer value chosen when a **PrintThread** object is constructed. Each **PrintThread** object will sleep for the amount of time specified by **sleepTime** then output its name. The **PrintThread** constructor takes a **String** argument representing the name of the thread and invokes the superclass **Thread** constructor with the **String**. The **Thread** class constructor uses the **String** to set the thread's name. Next, the **PrintThread** constructor initializes **sleepTime** to a random integer between 0 and 5000 (0 to 5 seconds). Then, the name and **sleepTime** are output to show the values for the particular **PrintThread** being constructed. When a **PrintThread**'s **start** method (inherited from **Thread**) is invoked, the **PrintThread** object enters the *ready* state. When the system assigns a processor to the **PrintThread** object, it enters the *running* state and its **run** method begins execution. Method **run** invokes the **sleep** method (line 42) that immediately puts the object into a *sleeping* state. When the object awakens, it is placed into a *ready* state again until it is assigned a processor. When the **PrintThread** object enters the *running* state again, it outputs its name, its **run** method terminates and the thread object enters the *dead* state. Note that the **sleep** method can throw an **InterruptedException**, therefore **sleep** must be called in a **try** block or the exception must be declared in the **throws** clause of the **run** method.

Class **PrintTest**'s **main** method instantiates four **PrintThread** objects and invokes the **Thread** class **start** method on each one to place all four **PrintThread** objects in a *ready* state.

13.5 Thread Synchronization

Java uses *monitors* (as discussed by C.A.R. Hoare in his 1974 paper we cite in Exercise 13.24) to perform synchronization. Every object with **synchronized** methods is a monitor. The monitor lets only one thread at a time execute a **synchronized** method on the object. This is accomplished by *locking* the object when the **synchronized** method is invoked—also known as *obtaining the lock*. If there are several **synchronized** methods, only one **synchronized** method may be active on an object at once; all other threads attempting to invoke **synchronized** methods must wait. When a **synchronized** method finishes executing, the lock on the object is released and the monitor lets the highest-priority *ready* thread attempting to invoke a **synchronized** method proceed.

A thread executing in a **synchronized** method may determine that it cannot proceed, so the thread voluntarily calls **wait**. This removes the thread from contention for the processor and from contention for the monitor object. The thread now waits in a queue while other threads try to enter the object. When a thread executing **synchronized** method completes, the object can **notify** a waiting thread to become *ready* again so it can attempt to obtain the lock on the monitor object again and execute. The **notify** acts as a signal to the waiting thread that the condition the waiting thread has been waiting for is now satisfied, so it is acceptable for that thread to reenter the monitor. If a thread calls **notifyAll**, then all threads waiting for the object become eligible to reenter the monitor (i.e., they are all placed in a *ready* state). Remember that only one of those threads can obtain the lock on the object at a time.

Common Programming Error 13.2

Threads waiting for a monitor object must eventually be awakened explicitly with a **notify** *or the thread will wait forever. This is a simple example of deadlock.*

Testing and Debugging Tip 13.3

Be sure that every call to **wait** *has a corresponding call to* **notify** *that will eventually end the waiting.*

Performance Tip 13.6

Synchronization to achieve correctness in multithreaded programs can make programs run slower as threads wait. There is not much to say, however, for highly efficient, incorrect programs!

Testing and Debugging Tip 13.4

The locking that occurs with the execution of **synchronized** *methods could lead to deadlock if the locks are never released. When exceptions occur, Java's exception mechanism coordinates with Java's synchronization mechanism to release appropriate synchronization locks to avoid these kinds of deadlocks.*

Monitor objects queue all threads waiting to enter the object to execute **synchronized** methods. A thread gets enqueued and waits for the object if that thread calls a **synchronized** method of the object while another thread is already executing in a **synchronized** method of that object. A thread also gets enqueued if the thread calls **wait** while operating inside the object. However, it is important to distinguish waiting threads that blocked because the monitor was busy vs. threads that explicitly called **wait** inside the monitor. Upon completion of a **synchronized** method, outside threads that blocked because the monitor was busy can proceed to enter the object. Threads that explicitly invoked **wait** can only proceed when notified via a call by another thread to **notify** or **notifyAll**. When it is acceptable for an enqueued thread to proceed, the scheduler selects the thread with the highest priority.

Common Programming Error 13.3

It is an error if a thread executing outside a monitor issues a **wait**, *a* **notify**, *or a* **notifyAll**. *This causes an* **IllegalMonitorStateException** *to be thrown.*

13.6 Producer/Consumer Relationship without Thread Synchronization

In a *producer/consumer relationship*, a *producer thread* calling a *produce* method may see that the consumer thread has not read the last message from a shared region of memory called a *buffer*, so the producer thread will call **wait**. When a *consumer thread* reads the message, it will call **notify** to allow a waiting producer to proceed. When a consumer thread enters the monitor and finds the buffer empty, it calls **wait**. A producer finding the buffer empty, writes to the buffer then calls **notify** so a waiting consumer can proceed.

Shared data can get corrupted if we do not synchronize access among multiple threads. Consider a simple producer/consumer relationship in which a producer thread deposits a sequence of numbers (we will use 0, 1, 2, ...) into a slot of shared memory. The consumer thread reads this data from the shared memory slot and prints the data. We will print what the producer produces as it produces it and what the consumer consumes as it consumes it. The application of Fig. 13.4 demonstrates a producer and a consumer accessing a shared cell of memory without any synchronization. Because these threads are not synchronized data can be lost if the producer places new data into the slot before the consumer consumes the previous data and data can be "doubled" if the consumer consumes data again before the producer produces the next data item.

```
1   // Fig. 13.4: SharedCell.java
2   // Show multiple threads modifying shared object.
3
4   public class SharedCell {
5      public static void main( String args[] )
6      {
7         HoldInteger h = new HoldInteger();
8         ProduceInteger p = new ProduceInteger( h );
9         ConsumeInteger c = new ConsumeInteger( h );
10
11        p.start();
12        c.start();
13     }
14  }
15
16  class ProduceInteger extends Thread {
17     private HoldInteger pHold;
18
19     public ProduceInteger( HoldInteger h )
20     {
21        pHold = h;
22     }
23
24     public void run()
25     {
26        for ( int count = 0; count < 10; count++ ) {
27           pHold.setSharedInt( count );
28           System.out.println( "Producer set sharedInt to " +
29                               count );
30
31           // sleep for a random interval
32           try {
33              sleep( (int) ( Math.random() * 3000 ) );
34           }
35           catch( InterruptedException e ) {
36              System.err.println( "Exception " + e.toString() );
37           }
38        }
39     }
40  }
```

Fig. 13.4 Threads modifying a shared object without synchronization (part 1 of 3).

```
41
42   class ConsumeInteger extends Thread {
43      private HoldInteger cHold;
44
45      public ConsumeInteger( HoldInteger h )
46      {
47         cHold = h;
48      }
49
50      public void run()
51      {
52         int val;
53
54         val = cHold.getSharedInt();
55         System.out.println( "Consumer retrieved " + val );
56
57         while ( val != 9 ) {
58            // sleep for a random interval
59            try {
60               sleep( (int) ( Math.random() * 3000 ) );
61            }
62            catch( InterruptedException e ) {
63               System.err.println( "Exception " + e.toString() );
64            }
65
66            val = cHold.getSharedInt();
67            System.out.println( "Consumer retrieved " + val );
68         }
69      }
70   }
71
72   class HoldInteger {
73      private int sharedInt;
74
75      public void setSharedInt( int val ) { sharedInt = val; }
76
77      public int getSharedInt() { return sharedInt; }
78   }
```

Fig. 13.4 Threads modifying a shared object without synchronization (part 2 of 3).

The program consists of four classes—**SharedCell**, **ProduceInteger**, **ConsumeInteger** and **HoldInteger**. Class **SharedCell**'s **main** method (line 5) instantiates the shared **HoldInteger** object **h** and uses it as the argument to the constructors for the **ProduceInteger** object **p** and the **ConsumeInteger** object **c**. Method **main** then invokes the **Thread** class **start** method on the **ProduceInteger** object **p** and the **ConsumeInteger** object **c** to place them in the *ready* state. This essentially launches these threads

```
Producer set sharedInt to 0
Consumer retrieved 0
Producer set sharedInt to 1
Consumer retrieved 1
Producer set sharedInt to 2
Producer set sharedInt to 3
Consumer retrieved 3
Producer set sharedInt to 4
Producer set sharedInt to 5
Consumer retrieved 5
Consumer retrieved 5
Producer set sharedInt to 6
Consumer retrieved 6
Consumer retrieved 6
Producer set sharedInt to 7
Producer set sharedInt to 8
Producer set sharedInt to 9
Consumer retrieved 9
```

Fig. 13.4 Threads modifying a shared object without synchronization (part 2 of 3).

Class **ProduceInteger**—which inherits from **Thread**—consists of instance variable **pHold**, a constructor and a **run** method. Instance variable **pHold** is initialized in the constructor (line 21) to refer to the **HoldInteger** object **h** that was passed as an argument. Class **ProduceInteger**'s **run** method (line 24) consists of a **for** structure that loops 10 times. Each iteration of the loop invokes class **HoldInteger**'s **setSharedInt** method with the value of **count** to set the shared object's instance variable **sharedInt**. Next, the value passed to **setSharedInt** is displayed. Then, method **sleep** is called to put the **ProduceInteger** object into the *sleeping* state for a random time interval between 0 and 3 seconds.

Class **ConsumeInteger**—which inherits from **Thread**—consists of instance variable **cHold**, a constructor and a **run** method. Instance variable **cHold** is initialized in the constructor (line 47) to refer to the **HoldInteger** object **h** that was passed as an argument. Class **ConsumeInteger**'s **run** method (line 50) consists of a **while** structure that executes until it reads the value **9** from the shared memory cell. Each iteration of the loop invokes method **sleep** to put the **ConsumeInteger** object into the *sleeping* state for a random time interval between 0 and 3 seconds. Next, class **HoldInteger**'s **getSharedInt** method is called to get the value of the shared object's instance variable **sharedInt**. Then, the value returned by **getSharedInt** is displayed.

Class **HoldInteger**'s **setSharedInt** method (line 75) and a **getSharedInt** method (line 77) do not synchronize access to instance variable **sharedInt**. Ideally, we would like every value produced by the **ProduceInteger** object **p** to be consumed exactly once by the **ConsumeInteger** object **c**. However, when we study the output of Fig. 13.4 we see that the values 2, 4, 7 and 8 are lost (i.e., never seen by the consumer) and the values 5 and 6 are incorrectly doubled (i.e., retrieved twice) by the consumer. This example clearly demonstrates that access to shared data by concurrent threads must be carefully controlled or a program may produce incorrect results.

To solve the problems of lost data and doubled data in the previous example, we will *synchronize* access of the concurrent producer and consumer threads to the shared data. Each method used by a producer or consumer to access the shared data is declared with the **synchronized** keyword. When a method declared **synchronized** is running in an object, the object is *locked* so no other **synchronized** method can run in that object at the same time.

13.7 Producer/Consumer Relationship with Thread Synchronization

The application in Fig. 13.5 demonstrates a producer and a consumer accessing a shared cell of memory with synchronization so that the consumer only consumes after the producer produces a value. Class **HoldInteger** (line 74) has been redefined for this example. It now contains two instance variables—**sharedInt** and **writeable**—and we have made methods **setSharedInt** and **getSharedInt synchronized** methods. Because **HoldInteger** now contains **synchronized** methods, objects of class **Hold-Integer** are considered to be monitors. Instance variable **writeable**—known as the monitor's *condition variable*—is used by the **setSharedInt** method to determine if it can write to the shared memory location and is used by the **getSharedInt** method to determine if it can read from the shared memory location.

```
1   // Fig. 13.5: SharedCell.java
2   // Show multiple threads modifying shared object.
3   // Use synchronization to ensure that both threads
4   // access the shared cell properly.
5
6   public class SharedCell {
7      public static void main( String args[] )
8      {
9         HoldInteger h = new HoldInteger();
10        ProduceInteger p = new ProduceInteger( h );
11        ConsumeInteger c = new ConsumeInteger( h );
12
13        p.start();
14        c.start();
15     }
16  }
17
18  class ProduceInteger extends Thread {
19     private HoldInteger pHold;
20
21     public ProduceInteger( HoldInteger h )
22     {
23        pHold = h;
24     }
```

Fig. 13.5 Threads modifying a shared object with synchronization (part 1 of 4).

```
25
26    public void run()
27    {
28       for ( int count = 0; count < 10; count++ ) {
29          pHold.setSharedInt( count );
30          System.out.println( "Producer set sharedInt to " +
31                                count );
32
33          // sleep for a random interval
34          try {
35             sleep( (int) ( Math.random() * 3000 ) );
36          }
37          catch( InterruptedException e ) {
38             System.err.println( "Exception " + e.toString() );
39          }
40       }
41    }
42 }
43
44 class ConsumeInteger extends Thread {
45    private HoldInteger cHold;
46
47    public ConsumeInteger( HoldInteger h )
48    {
49       cHold = h;
50    }
51
52    public void run()
53    {
54       int val;
55
56       val = cHold.getSharedInt();
57       System.out.println( "Consumer retrieved " + val );
58
59       while ( val != 9 ) {
60          // sleep for a random interval
61          try {
62             sleep( (int) ( Math.random() * 3000 ) );
63          }
64          catch( InterruptedException e ) {
65             System.err.println( "Exception " + e.toString() );
66          }
67
68          val = cHold.getSharedInt();
69          System.out.println( "Consumer retrieved " + val );
70       }
71    }
72 }
73
```

Fig. 13.5 Threads modifying a shared object with synchronization (part 2 of 4).

```
74   class HoldInteger {
75      private int sharedInt;
76      private boolean writeable = true;
77
78      public synchronized void setSharedInt( int val )
79      {
80         while ( !writeable ) {
81            try {
82               wait();
83            }
84            catch ( InterruptedException e ) {
85               System.err.println( "Exception: " + e.toString() );
86            }
87         }
88
89         sharedInt = val;
90         writeable = false;
91         notify();
92      }
93
94      public synchronized int getSharedInt()
95      {
96         while ( writeable ) {
97            try {
98               wait();
99            }
100           catch ( InterruptedException e ) {
101              System.err.println( "Exception: " + e.toString() );
102           }
103        }
104
105        writeable = true;
106        notify();
107        return sharedInt;
108     }
109  }
```

Fig. 13.5 Threads modifying a shared object with synchronization (part 3 of 4).

Instance variable **writeable** is a **boolean** variable used by both methods of class **HoldInteger**. If **writeable** is **true**, **setShareInt** can place a value into variable **sharedInt** because the variable currently does not contain information. However, this means **getSharedInt** currently cannot read the value of **sharedInt**. If **writeable** is **false**, **getShareInt** can read a value from variable **sharedInt** because the variable currently does contain information. However, this means **setSharedInt** currently cannot place a value into **sharedInt**.

```
Producer set sharedInt to 0
Consumer retrieved 0
Producer set sharedInt to 1
Consumer retrieved 1
Producer set sharedInt to 2
Consumer retrieved 2
Producer set sharedInt to 3
Consumer retrieved 3
Producer set sharedInt to 4
Consumer retrieved 4
Producer set sharedInt to 5
Consumer retrieved 5
Producer set sharedInt to 6
Consumer retrieved 6
Producer set sharedInt to 7
Consumer retrieved 7
Producer set sharedInt to 8
Consumer retrieved 8
Producer set sharedInt to 9
Consumer retrieved 9
```

Fig. 13.5 Threads modifying a shared object with synchronization (part 4 of 4).

When the **ProduceInteger** object invokes method **setSharedInt**, a lock is acquired on the **HoldInteger** object. The **while** structure at line 80 tests the **writeable** variable with the condition **!writeable**. If this condition is **true**, the **wait** method is invoked. This places the **ProduceInteger** object that called method **setSharedInt** into the *wait queue* for the **HoldInteger** object and releases the lock on it so other **synchronized** methods can be invoked on the object. The **ProduceInteger** object remains in the *wait queue* until it is *notified* that it may proceed—at which point it enters the *ready* state and waits for a processor to be assigned to it. When the **ProduceInteger** object re-enters the *running* state, the lock on the **HoldInteger** object is reacquired implicitly and the **setSharedInt** method continues executing in the **while** structure with the next statement after **wait**. There are no more statements, so the **while** condition is tested again. If the condition is **false**, **sharedInt** is assigned **val** (the argument passed to **setSharedInt**), **writeable** is set to **false** to indicate that the shared memory is now full and method **notify** is invoked. If there are any *waiting* threads, the first thread in the *wait queue* is placed into the *ready* state indicating that the thread can now attempt its task again (as soon as it is assigned a processor). The **notify** method returns immediately and method **setSharedInt** returns to its caller.

Methods **getSharedInt** and **setSharedInt** are implemented similarly. When the **ConsumeInteger** object invokes method **getSharedInt**, a lock is acquired on the **HoldInteger** object. The **while** structure at line 96 tests the **writeable** variable. If **writeable** is **true** (i.e., there is nothing to consume), the **wait** method is invoked. This places the **ConsumeInteger** object that called method **getSharedInt** into the *wait queue* for the **HoldInteger** object and releases the lock on it so other **synchro-**

nized methods can be invoked on the object. The **ConsumeInteger** object remains in the *wait queue* until it is *notified* that it may proceed—at which point it enters the *ready* state and waits for a processor to be assigned to it. When the **ConsumeInteger** object re-enters the *running* state, the lock on the **HoldInteger** object is re-acquired and the **setSharedInt** method continues executing in the **while** structure with the next statement after **wait**. There are no more statements, so the **while** condition is tested again. If the condition is **false, writeable** is set to **true** to indicate that the shared memory is now empty and method **notify** is invoked. If there are any *waiting* threads, the first thread in the *wait queue* is placed into the *ready* state indicating that the thread can now attempt its task again (as soon as it is assigned a processor). The **notify** method returns immediately and the value of **sharedInt** is returned to its caller.

When we study the output in Fig. 13.5, we observe that every integer produced is consumed once—no values are lost and no values are doubled.

13.8 Producer/Consumer Relationship: The Circular Buffer

The program of Fig. 13.5 does access the shared data correctly, but it may not perform optimally. Because the threads are running asynchronously, we cannot predict their relative speeds. If the producer wants to produce faster than the consumer can consume, it cannot do so. To enable the producer to continue producing we can use a *circular buffer* which has enough extra cells to handle the "extra" production. The program of Fig. 13.6 demonstrates a producer and a consumer accessing a circular buffer (in this case, a shared array of 5 cells) with synchronization so that the consumer only consumes a value when there are one or more values in the array and the producer only produces a value when there are one or more available cells in the array. This program is implemented as an applet that sends its output to a text area. Class **SharedCell**'s **start** method creates the **HoldInteger**, **ProduceInteger** and **ConsumeInteger** objects. The **HoldInteger** object **h** is passed a **TextArea** object in which the program's output will be displayed.

```
1   // Fig. 13.6: SharedCell.java
2   // Show multiple threads modifying shared object.
3   // Use synchronization to ensure that both threads
4   // access the shared cell properly.
5   import java.awt.*;
6   import java.applet.Applet;
7
8   public class SharedCell extends Applet {
9       private TextArea output;
10
11      public void init()
12      {
13          output = new TextArea( 28, 48 );
14          add( output );
15      }
```

Fig. 13.6 Multiple threads modifying shared object containing an array of cells with synchronization (part 1 of 5).

```
16
17      public void start()
18      {
19          HoldInteger h = new HoldInteger( output );
20          ProduceInteger p = new ProduceInteger( h );
21          ConsumeInteger c = new ConsumeInteger( h );
22
23          p.start();
24          c.start();
25      }
26  }
27
28  class ProduceInteger extends Thread {
29      private HoldInteger pHold;
30      private TextArea output;
31
32      public ProduceInteger( HoldInteger h )
33      {
34          pHold = h;
35      }
36
37      public void run()
38      {
39          for ( int count = 0; count < 10; count++ ) {
40              pHold.setSharedInt( count );
41
42              // sleep for a random interval
43              try {
44                  sleep( (int) ( Math.random() * 500 ) );
45              }
46              catch( InterruptedException e ) {
47                  System.err.println( "Exception " + e.toString() );
48              }
49          }
50      }
51  }
52
53  class ConsumeInteger extends Thread {
54      private HoldInteger cHold;
55
56      public ConsumeInteger( HoldInteger h )
57      {
58          cHold = h;
59      }
60
61      public void run()
62      {
63          int val;
64
65          val = cHold.getSharedInt();
```

Fig. 13.6 Multiple threads modifying shared object containing an array of cells with synchronization (part 2 of 5).

```
66
67          while ( val != 9 ) {
68             // sleep for a random interval
69             try {
70                sleep( (int) ( Math.random() * 3000 ) );
71             }
72             catch( InterruptedException e ) {
73                System.err.println( "Exception " + e.toString() );
74             }
75
76             val = cHold.getSharedInt();
77          }
78       }
79    }
80
81    class HoldInteger {
82       private int sharedInt[] = { 9, 9, 9, 9, 9 };
83       private boolean writeable = true;
84       private boolean readable = false;
85       private int readLoc = 0, writeLoc = 0;
86       private TextArea output;
87
88       public HoldInteger( TextArea out )
89       {
90          output = out;
91       }
92
93       public synchronized void setSharedInt( int val )
94       {
95          while ( !writeable ) {
96             try {
97                output.appendText( " WAITING TO PRODUCE " + val );
98                wait();
99             }
100            catch ( InterruptedException e ) {
101               System.err.println( "Exception: " + e.toString() );
102            }
103         }
104
105         sharedInt[ writeLoc ] = val;
106         readable = true;
107
108         output.appendText( "\nProduced " + val +
109                            " into cell " + writeLoc );
110
111         writeLoc = ++writeLoc % 5;
112
113         output.appendText( "\twrite " + writeLoc +
114                            "\tread " + readLoc );
115         printBuffer( output, sharedInt );
```

Fig. 13.6 Multiple threads modifying shared object containing an array of cells with synchronization (part 3 of 5).

```
116
117
118        if ( writeLoc == readLoc ) {
119            writeable = false;
120            output.appendText( "\nBUFFER FULL" );
121        }
122
123        notify();
124    }
125
126    public synchronized int getSharedInt()
127    {
128        int val;
129
130        while ( !readable ) {
131            try {
132                output.appendText( " WAITING TO CONSUME" );
133                wait();
134            }
135            catch ( InterruptedException e ) {
136                System.err.println( "Exception: " + e.toString() );
137            }
138        }
139
140        writeable = true;
141        val = sharedInt[ readLoc ];
142
143        output.appendText( "\nConsumed " + val +
144                           " from cell " + readLoc );
145
146        readLoc = ++readLoc % 5;
147
148        output.appendText( "\twrite " + writeLoc +
149                           "\tread " + readLoc );
150        printBuffer( output, sharedInt );
151
152        if ( readLoc == writeLoc ) {
153            readable = false;
154            output.appendText( "\nBUFFER EMPTY" );
155        }
156
157        notify();
158        return val;
159    }
160
```

Fig. 13.6 Multiple threads modifying shared object containing an array of cells with synchronization (part 4 of 5).

```
161    public void printBuffer( TextArea out, int buf[] )
162    {
163       output.appendText( "\tbuffer: " );
164
165       for ( int i = 0; i < buf.length; i++ )
166          out.appendText( " " + buf[ i ] );
167    }
168 }
```

Fig. 13.6 Multiple threads modifying shared object containing an array of cells with synchronization (part 5 of 5).

Once again, the main changes in this example are to the definition of class **HoldInteger**. The class now contains six instance variables—**sharedInt** is a 5-element integer array that is used as the circular buffer, **writeable** indicates if a producer can write into the circular buffer, **readable** indicates if a consumer can read from the circular buffer, **readLoc** indicates the current position from which the next value can be read by a consumer, **writeLoc** indicates the next location in which a value can be placed by a producer and **output** is the **TextArea** used for displaying output.

Method **setSharedInt** performs the same tasks as it did in Fig. 13.5 with a few modifications. When execution continues at line 105 after the **while** loop, the produced value is placed into the circular buffer at location **writeLoc**. Next, **readable** is set to **true** because there is at least one value in the buffer to be read. The value produced and the cell where the value was placed are appended to the text area with method **append-Text**. Then, **writeLoc** is updated for the next call to **setSharedInt**. The output in the text area is continued with the current **writeLoc** and **readLoc** values and the values in the circular buffer. If the **writeLoc** is equal to the **readLoc**, the circular buffer is currently full, so **writeable** is set to **false** and the string **BUFFER FULL** is displayed. Finally, method **notify** is invoked to place the next waiting thread into the ready state.

Method **getSharedInt** also performs the same tasks in this example as it did in Fig. 13.5 with a few minor modifications. When execution continues at line 139 after the **while** loop, **writeable** is set to **true** because there is at least one open position in the buffer in which a value can be placed. Next, **val** is assigned the value at location **readLoc** in the circular buffer. The value consumed and the cell from which the value was read are appended to the text area with method **appendText**. Then, **readLoc** is updated for the next call to method **getSharedInt**. The output line in the text area is continued with the current **writeLoc** and **readLoc** values and the current values in the circular buffer. If the **readLoc** is equal to the **writeLoc**, the circular buffer is currently empty, so **readable** is set to **false** and the string **BUFFER EMPTY** is displayed. Finally, method **notify** is invoked to place the next waiting thread into the *ready* state.

In the program of Fig. 13.6, the outputs have been augmented to include the current **writeLoc** and **readLoc** values. Also, the current contents of the buffer **sharedInt** are displayed. The elements of the **sharedInt** array were initialized to 9 for output purposes so you can see each value inserted into the buffer. Notice that after the fifth value is placed in fifth element of the buffer, the sixth value is inserted at the beginning of the array—thus providing the *circular buffer* effect. All output statements have been removed from the **ProduceInteger** and **ConsumeInteger** classes.

13.9 Daemon Threads

A *daemon thread* is a thread that runs for the benefit of other threads. Daemon threads run in the background (i.e., when processor time is available that would otherwise go to waste). The garbage collector is a daemon thread. Non-daemon threads are conventional user threads. We designate a thread as a daemon with the method call

```
setDaemon( true );
```

An argument of **false** means that the thread is not a daemon thread. A program can include a mixture of daemon threads and non-daemon threads. When only daemon threads remain in a program, Java exits. If a thread is to be a daemon, it must be set as such before its **start** method is called or an **IllegalThreadStateException** will be thrown. Method **isDaemon** returns **true** if a thread is a daemon thread and **false** otherwise.

13.10 Runnable Interface

C++ supports multiple inheritance in which a subclass can inherit from multiple superclasses. Multiple inheritance is a powerful capability but it is complex to use and suffers from ambiguity and performance problems. Java does not support multiple inheritance. This choice is consistent with Java's omission of a number of other complex C++ topics. Java does, however, support the notion of *interfaces,* a simpler scheme that delivers some of the key advantages of multiple inheritance.

Until now we have been extending class **Thread** to create new classes that support multithreading. We overrode the **run** method to specify the tasks to be performed concurrently.

One problem with this scheme is that it created some rather strange relationships because with **extend** we are really performing inheritance indicating that a subclass object "is an" object of its superclass.

If we want multithreading supported in a class derived from some class other than **Thread**, we **implement** the *Runnable* interface in that class. Class **Thread** itself implements the **Runnable** interface as expressed in the class header

```
public class Thread extends Object implements Runnable
```

Implementing the **Runnable** interface gives us the ability to treat our new class as a **Runnable** object (just like inheriting from a class allows us to treat our subclass as an object of its superclass). As with deriving from the **Thread** class, the code that controls the thread is placed in the **run** method.

We create a thread with the new class by passing to the following **Thread** class constructor

```
public Thread( Runnable runnableObject )
```

a reference to an object of the class that implements the **Runnable** interface. The **Thread** constructor registers the **run** method of the **runnableObject** as the method to be invoked when the thread begins execution.

The constructor

```
public Thread( Runnable runnableObject, String threadName )
```

constructs a **Thread** with name **threadName** and registers the **run** method of its argument called **runnableObject** as the method to be invoked when the thread begins execution.

The program of Fig. 13.7 demonstrates an applet that implements the **Runnable** interface. The applet class **RandomCharacters** displays three text fields and three buttons. A separate thread of execution is associated with each text field and button pair. The applet also defines the **String alphabet** that contains the letters from A to Z. This string is shared among the three threads. The applet's **start** method (line 38) instantiates three **Thread** objects and initializes each with **this**—i.e., the applet object—then invokes the **Thread** class **start** method on each **Thread** placing the threads in the *ready* state.

```
1   // Fig. 13.7: RandomCharacters.java
2   // Demonstrating the Runnableinterface
3   import java.awt.*;
4   import java.applet.Applet;
5
6   public class RandomCharacters extends Applet
7                                 implements Runnable {
8
9       String alphabet;
10      TextField output1, output2, output3;
11      Button button1, button2, button3;
12
13      Thread thread1, thread2, thread3;
14
15      boolean suspend1, suspend2, suspend3;
16
17      public void init()
18      {
19          alphabet = new String( "ABCDEFGHIJKLMNOPQRSTUVWXYZ" );
20          output1 = new TextField( 10 );
21          output1.setEditable( false );
22          output2 = new TextField( 10 );
23          output2.setEditable( false );
24          output3 = new TextField( 10 );
25          output3.setEditable( false );
26          button1 = new Button( "Suspend/Resume 1" );
27          button2 = new Button( "Suspend/Resume 2" );
28          button3 = new Button( "Suspend/Resume 3" );
29
30          add( output1 );
31          add( button1 );
32          add( output2 );
33          add( button2 );
34          add( output3 );
35          add( button3 );
36      }
37
38      public void start()
39      {
40          // create threads and start every time start is called
41          thread1 = new Thread( this, "Thread 1" );
42          thread2 = new Thread( this, "Thread 2" );
43          thread3 = new Thread( this, "Thread 3" );
44
45          thread1.start();
46          thread2.start();
47          thread3.start();
48      }
49
```

Fig. 13.7 Demonstrating the **Runnable** interface (part 1 of 3).

```
50      public void stop()
51      {
52         // stop threads every time stop is called
53         // as the user browses another Web page
54         thread1.stop();
55         thread2.stop();
56         thread3.stop();
57      }
58
59      public boolean action( Event event, Object obj )
60      {
61         if ( event.target == button1 )
62            if ( suspend1 ) {
63               thread1.resume();
64               suspend1 = false;
65            }
66            else {
67               thread1.suspend();
68               output1.setText( "suspended" );
69               suspend1 = true;
70            }
71         else if ( event.target == button2 )
72            if ( suspend2 ) {
73               thread2.resume();
74               suspend2 = false;
75            }
76            else {
77               thread2.suspend();
78               output2.setText( "suspended" );
79               suspend2 = true;
80            }
81         else if ( event.target == button3 )
82            if ( suspend3 ) {
83               thread3.resume();
84               suspend3 = false;
85            }
86            else {
87               thread3.suspend();
88               output3.setText( "suspended" );
89               suspend3 = true;
90            }
91
92         return true;
93      }
94
95      public void run()
96      {
97         int location;
98         char display;
99         String executingThread;
100
```

Fig. 13.7 Demonstrating the **Runnable** interface (part 2 of 3).

```
101          while ( true ) {
102             // sleep from 0 to 5 seconds
103             try {
104                Thread.sleep( (int) ( Math.random() * 5000 ) );
105             }
106             catch ( InterruptedException e ) {
107                e.printStackTrace();
108             }
109
110             location = (int) ( Math.random() * 26 );
111             display = alphabet.charAt( location );
112
113             executingThread = Thread.currentThread().getName();
114
115             if ( executingThread.equals( "Thread 1" ) )
116                output1.setText( "Thread 1: " + display );
117             else if ( executingThread.equals( "Thread 2" ) )
118                output2.setText( "Thread 2: " + display );
119             else if ( executingThread.equals( "Thread 3" ) )
120                output3.setText( "Thread 3: " + display );
121          }
122       }
123    }
```

Fig. 13.7 Demonstrating the **Runnable** interface (part 3 of 3).

The **run** method (line 95) contains an infinite loop. In each iteration of the loop, the thread sleeps for a random interval from 0 to 5 seconds. Next, a random character is chosen from the **alphabet** string. The statement

```
executingThread = Thread.currentThread().getName();
```

uses the **Thread.currentThread** method to determine the currently executing **Thread** object, then uses the **getName** method to get its name. The string returned from **getName** is used in the nested **if/else** structure to pick the text field in which the character is displayed.

If the user clicks the **Suspend/Resume** button next to a particular text field, the **action** method (line 59) is invoked. The **action** method determines which button received the event, then determines if the corresponding thread is currently suspended by testing one of the **boolean** variables **suspend1**, **suspend2** or **suspend3** (one for each thread). If the appropriate **boolean** variable is **true**, the thread's **resume** method is invoked and the **boolean** variable is set to **false**. Otherwise, the thread's **suspend** method is invoked, the string "**suspended**" is displayed in the text field for the thread and the **boolean** variable is set to **true**.

The applet's stop method is provided to stop all three threads' execution if the user leaves the Web page on which this applet resides. If the user returns to the Web page, the three threads will be instantiated again because the applet's **start** method is invoked when the Web page is revisited.

Performance Tip 13.7

*Stopping applet threads when leaving a Web page is a polite programming practice because it prevents your applet from using processor time (which can reduce performance) on the browser's machine when the applet is not being viewed. The threads can be restarted from the applet's **start** method which is automatically invoked when the Web page is revisited by the user.*

13.11 Thread Groups

It is sometimes useful to identify various threads as belonging to a *thread group,* class **ThreadGroup** contains the methods for creating and manipulating thread groups. At constructor time the group is given a unique name via a **String** argument.

The threads in a thread group can be dealt with as a group. It may, for example, be desirable to **suspend** all the threads in a group, **resume** all the threads in a group, or even kill all the threads in a group. A thread group can be the *parent thread group* to a *child thread group.* Method calls sent to a parent thread group are also sent to all the threads in that parent's child thread groups.

Class **ThreadGroup** provides two constructors. The constructor

```
public ThreadGroup( String stringName )
```

constructs a **ThreadGroup** with name **stringName**. The constructor

```
public ThreadGroup( ThreadGroup parentThreadGroup,
                    String stringName )
```

constructs a child **ThreadGroup** of **parentThreadGroup** called **stringName**.

Class **Thread** provides three constructors that enable the programmer to instantiate a **Thread** and associate it with a **ThreadGroup**. The constructor

```
    public Thread( ThreadGroup threadGroup, String stringName )
```

constructs a **Thread** that belongs to **threadGroup** and has the name **stringName**. This constructor is normally invoked for derived classes of **Thread** whose objects should be associated with a **ThreadGroup**.

The constructor

```
    public Thread( ThreadGroup threadGroup,
                   Runnable runnableObject )
```

constructs a **Thread** that belongs to **threadGroup** and that invokes the **run** method of **runnableObject** when the thread is assigned a processor to begin execution.

The constructor

```
    public Thread( ThreadGroup threadGroup,
                   Runnable runnableObject,
                   String stringName )
```

constructs a **Thread** that belongs to **threadGroup** and that invokes the **run** method of **runnableObject** when the thread is assigned a processor to begin execution. The name of this **Thread** is indicated by **stringName**.

Class **ThreadGroup** contains many methods for processing groups of threads. Some of these methods are summarized here. For more information on these methods, see the Java API documentation.

1. Method **activeCount** reports the number of active threads in a thread group plus the number of active threads in all its child thread groups. [Note: At the time of this writing one of our Sun reviewers indicated that this method has been replaced by **allThreadsCount**.]

2. Method **enumerate** has four versions. Two versions copy into an array of **Thread** references the active threads in the **ThreadGroup** (one of these also allows you to recursively get copies of all the active threads in child **Thread-Group**). Two versions copy into an array of **ThreadGroup** references the active child thread groups in the **ThreadGroup** (one of these also allows you to recursively get copies of all the active thread groups in all the child **Thread-Group**s). [Note: At the time of this writing one of our Sun reviewers indicated: "This has been replaced by **allGroups** that returns an array of all **Thread-Group** objects for all descendent thread groups, or **groups** that returns an array of all immediate child groups."]

3. Method **getMaxPriority** returns the maximum priority of a **ThreadGroup**. Method **setMaxPriority** sets a new maximum priority for a **ThreadGroup**.

4. Method **getName** returns as a **String** the **ThreadGroup**'s name.

5. Method **getParent** determines the parent of a thread group.

6. Method **parentOf** returns **true** if the **ThreadGroup** to which the message is sent is the parent of, or the same as, the **ThreadGroup** supplied as an argument and returns **false** otherwise.

7. Method **stop** stops every **Thread** in the **ThreadGroup** and in every subgroup of that **ThreadGroup**.

8. Method **suspend** suspends every **Thread** in the **ThreadGroup** and in every subgroup of that **ThreadGroup**.

9. Method **resume** resumes every **Thread** in the **ThreadGroup** and in every subgroup.

10. Method **destroy** destroys a **ThreadGroup** and its child **ThreadGroup**s.

Testing and Debugging Tip 13.5

---

*Method **list** lists the **ThreadGroup**. This can help in debugging.*

Summary

- Computers perform operations concurrently such as compiling a program, printing a file, and receiving electronic mail messages over a network.

- Programming languages generally provide only a simple set of control structures that enable programmers to perform one action at a time and then proceed to the next action after the previous one is finished.

- The concurrency that computers perform today is normally implemented as operating systems "primitives" available only to highly experienced "systems programmers."

- Java makes concurrency primitives available to the programmer.

- Applications contain threads of execution, each thread designating a portion of a program that may execute concurrently with other threads. This capability is called multithreading.

- Java provides a low priority garbage collector thread that automatically reclaims dynamically allocated memory that is no longer needed. The garbage collector runs when processor time is available and there are no higher-priority runnable threads. The garbage collector runs immediately when the system is out of memory to try to reclaim memory.

- Method **run** contains the code that controls the thread's execution.

- A program launches a thread's execution by calling the thread's **start** method which, in turn, calls the **run** method.

- Method **interrupt** is called to interrupt a thread. The **interrupted** method returns **true** if the current thread has been interrupted and **false** otherwise. Method **isInterrupted** determines if a thread has been interrupted.

- Method **stop** stops a thread by throwing a **ThreadDeath** object into it; **ThreadDeath** is a subclass of **Error**.

- Method **isAlive** returns **true** if **start** has been called but **stop** has not.

- Method **setName** sets the name of the **Thread**. Method **getName** returns the name of the **Thread**. Method **toString** returns a **String** consisting of the name of the thread, the priority of the thread and the thread's group.

- Method **currentThread** returns a reference to the current **Thread**.

- Method **join** waits for the **Thread** to which the message is sent to die before the current **Thread** can proceed.

- Waiting can be dangerous; it can lead to two particularly serious problems called deadlock and indefinite postponement; indefinite postponement is also called starvation.

- A thread that was just created is in the born state. The thread remains in this state until the thread's **start** method is called; this causes the thread to enter the ready state.

- A highest-priority ready thread enters the running state when the system assigns a processor to the thread.

- A thread enters the dead state when its **run** method completes, or when its **stop** method is called; a dead thread will eventually be disposed of by the system.

- A running thread enters the blocked state when the thread issues an input/output request. A blocked thread becomes ready when the I/O it is waiting for completes. A blocked thread cannot use a processor even if one is available.

- When a running thread's **sleep** method is called, that thread enters the sleeping state. A sleeping thread becomes ready after the designated sleep time expires. A sleeping thread cannot use a processor even if one is available.

- When a running thread's **suspend** method is called, that thread enters the suspended state. A suspended thread becomes ready when its **resume** method is called by another thread. A suspended thread cannot use a processor even if one is available.

- When a running method calls **wait** the thread enters a waiting state where it waits in a queue associated with the particular object in which the thread was running. The first thread in the wait queue for a particular object becomes ready on a call to **notify** issued by another thread associated with that object.

- Every thread in the wait queue for a given object becomes ready on a call to **notifyAll** by another thread associated with that object.

- Every Java thread has a priority in the range **Thread.MIN_PRIORITY** (a constant of 1) and **Thread.MAX_PRIORITY** (a constant of 10). By default, each thread is given priority **Thread.NORM_PRIORITY** (a constant of 5).

- Some Java platforms support a concept called timeslicing and some do not. Without timeslicing, threads of equal priority run to completion before their peers get a chance to execute. With timeslicing, each thread receives a brief burst of processor time called a quantum during which that thread can execute. At the completion of the quantum, even if that thread has not finished executing, the processor is taken away from that thread and given to the next thread of equal priority if one is available.

- The job of the Java scheduler is to keep a highest-priority thread running at all times, and if timeslicing is available, to ensure that several equally high-priority threads each execute for a quantum in round-robin fashion.

- A thread's priority can be adjusted with the **setPriority** method. Method **getPriority** returns the thread's priority.

- A thread can call the **yield** method to give other threads a chance to execute.
- Every object that has **synchronized** methods has a monitor. The monitor lets only one thread at a time execute a **synchronized** method on the object.
- A thread executing in a **synchronized** method may determine that it cannot proceed, so the thread voluntarily calls **wait**. This removes the thread from contention for the processor and from contention for the object.
- A thread that has called **wait** is awakened by a thread that calls **notify**. The **notify** acts as a signal to the waiting thread that the condition the waiting thread has been waiting for is now satisfied, so it is acceptable for that thread to reenter the monitor.
- A daemon thread serves other threads. When only daemon threads remain in a program, Java will exit. If a thread is to be a daemon, it must be set as such before its **start** method is called.
- To support multithreading in a class derived from some class other than **Thread**, **implement** the **Runnable** interface in that class.
- Implementing the **Runnable** interface gives us the ability to treat the new class as a **Runnable** object (just like inheriting from a class allows us to treat our subclass as an object of its superclass). As with deriving from the **Thread** class, the code that controls the thread is placed in the **run** method.
- A thread with a **Runnable** class is created by passing to the **Thread** class constructor a reference to an object of the class that implements the **Runnable** interface. The **Thread** constructor registers the **run** method of the **runnableObject** as the method to be invoked when the thread begins execution.
- Class **ThreadGroup** contains the methods for creating and manipulating groups of related threads in a program.

Terminology

asynchronous threads
blocked on I/O
blocked (state of a thread)
busy wait
child thread group
circular buffer
concurrency
concurrent execution of threads
condition variable
consumer
consumer thread
context
countStackFrames method
currentThread method
daemon thread
dead (state of a thread)

death of a thread
deadlock
destroy method
dumpStack method
Error class **ThreadDeath** is a subclass
execution context
fixed-priority scheduling
garbage collection by a low-priority thread
getName method
getParent method of **ThreadGroup** class
getThreadGroup()
highest-priority runnable thread
IllegalArgumentException
IllegalMonitorStateException
IllegalThreadStateException
indefinite postponement

Common Programming Errors

13.1   **ThreadDeath** is an **Error**, not an **Exception**. Ordinarily, user programs should not catch **Error** objects. If you choose to catch a **ThreadDeath** object, be sure to rethrow it or the thread may not die "properly."

13.2   Threads waiting for a monitor object must eventually be awakened explicitly with a **notify** or the thread will wait forever. This is a simple example of deadlock.

13.3   It is an error if a thread executing outside a monitor issues a **wait**, a **notify**, or a **notifyAll**. This causes an **IllegalMonitorStateException** to be thrown.

Performance Tips

13.1   Java's garbage collection is not as efficient as the dynamic memory management code the best C and C++ programmers write, but it is relatively efficient and much safer for the programmer.

13.2   Setting an object reference to **null** marks that object for garbage collection (if there are no other references to the object). This can help conserve memory in a system in which an automatic object is not going out of scope because the method it is in will execute for a lengthy period.

13.3   One problem with single-threaded applications is that possibly lengthy activities must complete before other activities can begin. Users feel they already spend too much time waiting with Internet and World Wide Web applications, so multithreading is immediately appealing.

13.4   One way to delay a thread is to loop some appropriate number of times doing nothing in the body of the loop. This is called a busy wait and leads to poor performance; while the processor is busy doing nothing for this thread, other runnable threads may be kept waiting. A better technique is to call the thread's **sleep** method. A sleeping thread does not use the processor.

13.5   On non-timesliced systems, cooperating threads of equal priority should periodically call **yield** to enable their peers to proceed smoothly.

13.6   Synchronization to achieve correctness in multithreaded programs can make programs run slower as threads wait. There is not much to say, however, for highly efficient, incorrect programs!

13.7   Stopping applet threads when leaving a Web page is a polite programming practice because it prevents your applet from using processor time (which can reduce performance) on the browser's machine when the applet is not being viewed. The threads can be restarted from the applet's **start** method which is automatically invoked when the Web page is revisited by the user.

Portability Tips

13.1   Java multithreading is platform dependent. Thus, a multithreaded application could behave differently on different Java implementations.

13.2   Applets should be programmed to work on all Java platforms to realize Java's goal of true portability.

Software Engineering Observation

13.1   Unlike many languages that do not have built-in multithreading (such as C and C++) and must therefore make calls to operating system multithreading primitives, Java includes multithreading primitives as a part of the language itself (actually in classes **Thread**, **Thread-Group** and **ThreadDeath** of the **java.lang** package). This encourages the use of multithreading among a larger part of the applications programming community.

Testing and Debugging Tips

13.1   In C and C++, programmers must explicitly provide statements for reclaiming dynamically allocated memory. When memory is not reclaimed (because a programmer forgets to do so, or because of a logic error or because an exception diverts program control), this results in an all-to-common error called a memory leak that can eventually exhaust the supply of free memory and may cause program termination. Java's automatic garbage collection eliminates the vast majority of memory leaks, i.e., those that are due to orphaned (unreferenced) objects.

13.2   Methods **dumpStack** and **countStackFrames** are useful for debugging multithreaded applications. A program calls **static** method **dumpStack** (with the call **Thread.dumpStack**) to print a method-call stack trace for the current **Thread**. A program calls non-**static** method **countStackFrames** to determine the number of method call stack frames in a suspended **Thread**.

13.3   Be sure that every call to **wait** has a corresponding call to **notify** that will eventually end the waiting.

13.4   The locking that occurs with the execution of **synchronized** methods could lead to deadlock if the locks are never released. When exceptions occur, Java's exception mechanism coordinates with Java's synchronization mechanism to release appropriate synchronization locks to avoid these kinds of deadlocks.

13.5   Method **list** lists the **ThreadGroup**. This can help in debugging.

Self-Review Exercises

13.1   Fill in the blanks in each of the following:
   a) C and C++ are _____-threaded languages whereas Java is a _____-threaded language.
   b) Java provides a _____ thread that automatically reclaims dynamically allocated memory.
   c) Java eliminates most _____ errors that occur commonly in languages like C and C++ when dynamically allocated memory is not explicitly reclaimed by the program.
   d) The _____ method is used to terminate a **Thread**'s execution.
   e) Four reasons a thread could be not runnable (i.e., blocked) are _____, _____, _____, and _____.
   f) Two reasons a thread could enter the dead state are _____ and _____.
   g) A thread's priority can be changed with the _____ method.
   h) A thread may give up the processor to a thread of the same priority by calling the _____ method.
   i) To wait for a designated number of milliseconds and then resume execution, a thread should call the _____ method.
   j) A _____ thread may be made active again by calling the **resume** method.

k) The _____ method places the first thread in the object's wait queue into the ready state.

13.2 State whether each of the following is **true** or **false**. For those that are **false**, state why.
a) A thread is not runnable if it is dead.
b) In Java, a higher-priority runnable thread will preempt threads of lower priority.
c) The Windows and Windows NT Java systems use timeslicing. Therefore they can enable threads to preempt threads of the same priority.
d) Threads may **yield** to threads of lower priority.

Answers to Self-Review Exercises

13.1 a) single, multi. b) garbage collector. c) memory leak. d) **stop**. e) waiting, sleeping, suspended, blocked for I/O. f) its **run** method terminates, **stop** is called on the thread. g) **setPriority**. h) **yield**. i) **sleep**. j) suspended. k) **notify**.

13.2 a) True
b) True.
c) False. Timeslicing allows a thread to execute until its time slice (or quantum) expires. Then other threads of equal priority can execute.
d) False. Threads can only yield to threads of equal priority.

Exercises

13.3 State whether each of the following is **true** or **false**. For those that are **false**, state why.
a) The **sleep** method does not consume processor time while a thread sleeps.
b) Declaring a method **synchronized** guarantees that deadlock cannot occur.
c) Java provides a powerful capability called multiple inheritance.

13.4 Define each of the following terms.
a) thread
b) multithreading
c) ready state
d) blocked state
e) preemptive scheduling
f) **Runnable** interface
g) monitor
h) **notify** method
i) producer/consumer relationship

13.5 a) List each of the reasons stated in this chapter for using multithreading.
b) List additional reasons for using multithreading.

13.6 List each of the four reasons given in the text for entering the blocked state. For each of these, describe how the program will normally leave the blocked state and enter the runnable state.

13.7 Distinguish between preemptive scheduling and nonpreemptive scheduling. Which does Java use?

13.8   What is timeslicing? Give a fundamental difference in how scheduling is performed on Java systems that support timeslicing vs. on Java systems that do not support timeslicing.

13.9   Why would a thread ever want to call **yield**?

13.10   What aspects of developing Java applets for the World Wide Web encourage applet designers to use **yield** and **sleep** abundantly?

13.11   If you choose to write your own **start** method, what must you be sure to do to make sure that your threads start up properly?

13.12   Distinguish among each of the following means of pausing threads:
   a) busy wait.
   b) sleep.
   c) suspend.

13.13   Write a Java statement that tests if a thread is alive.

13.14   a) What is multiple inheritance?
   b) Explain why Java does not offer multiple inheritance.
   c) What feature does Java offer instead of multiple inheritance?
   d) Explain the typical usage of this feature.
   e) How does this feature differ from abstract classes.

13.15   Distinguish between the notions of **extends** and **implements**.

13.16   Discuss each of the following terms in the context of monitors:
   a) monitor.
   b) producer.
   c) consumer.
   d) **wait**.
   e) **notify**.
   f) **InterruptedException**.
   g) **synchronized**.

13.17   *(Tortoise and the Hare)* In the Chapter 5 exercises you were asked to simulate the legendary race of the tortoise and the hare. Implement a new version of that simulation this time placing each of the animals in separate threads. At the start of the race call the **start** methods for each of the threads. Use **wait** and **notify**, and **notifyAll** to synchronize the animals' activities.

13.18   *(Multithreaded, Networked, Collaborative Applications)* In Chapter 16 we will cover networking in Java. A multithreaded Java application can communicate concurrently with several host computers. This creates the possibility of being able to build some interesting kinds of collaborative applications. In anticipation of studying networking in Chapter 16, develop proposals for several possible multithreaded networked applications. After studying Chapter 16, implement some of those applications.

13.19   Write a Java program to demonstrate that as a high-priority thread executes, it will delay the execution of all lower-priority threads.

13.20 If your system supports timeslicing, write a Java program that demonstrates timeslicing among several equal-priority threads. Show that a lower-priority thread's execution is deferred by the time-slicing of the higher-priority threads.

13.21 Write a Java program that demonstrates a high-priority thread using **sleep** to give lower-priority threads a chance to run.

13.22 If your system does not support timeslicing, write a Java program that demonstrates two threads using **yield** to enable one another to execute.

13.23 Two problems that can occur in systems, like Java, that allow threads to wait are deadlock in which one or more threads will wait forever for an event that cannot occur and indefinite postponement in which one or more threads will be delayed for some unpredictably long time. Give an example of how each of these problems can occur in a multithreaded Java program.

13.24 *(Readers and Writers)* This exercise asks you to develop a Java monitor to solve a famous problem in concurrency control. This problem was first discussed and solved by P. J. Courtois, F. Heymans and D. L. Parnas in their research paper, "Concurrent Control with Readers and Writers," *Communications of the ACM,* Vol. 14, No. 10, October 1971, pp. 667–668. The interested student might also want to read C. A. R. Hoare's seminal research paper on monitors, "Monitors: An Operating System Structuring Concept," *Communications of the ACM,* Vol. 17, No. 10, October 1974, pp. 549–557. Corrigendum, *Communications of the ACM,* Vol. 18, No. 2, February 1975, p. 95. [The readers and writers problem is discussed at length in Chapter 5 of the author's book: Deitel, H. M., *Operating Systems*, Reading, MA: Addison Wesley, 1990.]

With multithreading, many threads can access shared data; as we have seen, access to shared data needs to be carefully synchronized to avoid corrupting the data.

Consider an airline reservation system in which may clients are attempting to book seats on particular flights between particular cities. All of the information about flights and seats is stored in a common database in memory. The database consists of many entries each representing a seat on a particular flight for a particular day between particular cities. In a typical airline reservation scenario, the client will probe around in the database looking for the "optimal" flight to meet that client's needs. So a client may probe the database many times before deciding to try and book a particular flight. A seat that was available during this probing phase could easily be booked by someone else before the client has a chance to book it after deciding on it. In that case, when the client attempts to make the reservation, the client will discover that the data has changed and the flight is no longer available.

The client probing around the database is called a *reader*. The client attempting to book the flight is called a *writer*. Clearly, any number of readers can be probing shared data at once, but each writer needs exclusive access to the shared data to prevent the data from being corrupted.

Write a multithreaded Java program that launches multiple reader threads and multiple writer threads, each attempting to access a single reservation record. A writer thread has two possible transactions, **makeReservation** and **cancelReservation**. A reader has one possible transaction, **queryReservation**.

First implement a version of your program that allows unsynchronized access to the reservation record. Show how the integrity of the database can be corrupted. Next implement a version of your program that uses Java monitor synchronization with **wait** and **notify** to enforce a disciplined protocol for readers and writers accessing the shared reservation data. In particular, your program should allow multiple readers to access the shared data simultaneously when no writer is active. But if a writer is active, then no readers should be allowed to access the shared data.

Be careful. This problem has many subtleties. For example, what happens when there are several active readers and a writer wants to write? If we allow a steady stream of readers to arrive and share the data, they could indefinitely postpone the writer (who may become tired of waiting and take his or her business elsewhere). To solve this problem, you might decide to favor writers over readers. But here, too, there is a trap, because a steady stream of writers could then indefinitely postpone the waiting readers, and they, too, might choose to take their business elsewhere! Implement your monitor with the following methods: **startReading** which is called by any reader that wants to begin accessing the reservation, **stopReading** to be called by any reader that has finished reading the reservation, **startWriting** to be called by any writer that wants to make a reservation and **stop-Writing** to be called by any writer that has finished making a reservation.

13.25 Write a program that bounces a blue ball inside an applet. The ball should be initiated with a **mouseDown** event. When the ball hits the edge of the applet, the ball should bounce off the edge at a randomly selected angle between 20 and 60 degrees.

13.26 Modify the program of Exercise 13.25 to allow the user to draw up to five lines on the applet while the ball is bouncing. When the ball hits a line, it should bounce off the line at a randomly selected angle between 20 and 60 degrees.

14

Multimedia: Images, Animation, Audio

Objectives

- To understand how to get and display images.
- To be able to create animations from sequences of images; to control animation speed and flicker.
- To be able to get, play, loop and stop sounds.
- To be able to monitor the loading of images with the **MediaTracker**; to create image maps.
- To customize applets with the **param** tag.

The wheel that squeaks the loudest... gets the grease.
John Billings (Henry Wheeler Shaw)

Noise proves nothing. Often a hen who has merely laid an egg cackles as if she had laid an asteroid.
Mark Twain, *Following the Equator*

We'll use a signal I have tried and found far-reaching and easy to yell. Waa-hoo!
Zane Grey

A wide screen just makes a bad film twice as bad.
Samuel Goldwyn

There is a natural hootchy-kootchy motion to a goldfish.
Walt Disney

Between the motion and the act falls the shadow.
Thomas Stearns Eliot, *The Hollow Men*

What we experience of nature is in models, and all of nature's models are so beautiful.
Richard Buckminster Fuller

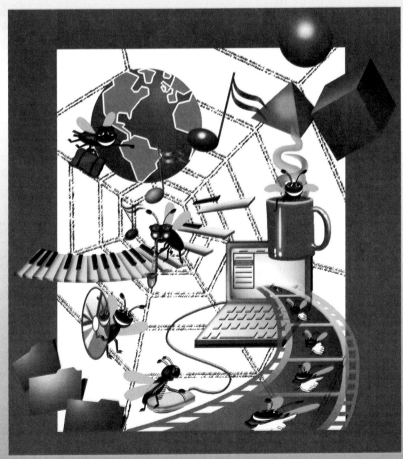

Outline

14.1 Introduction

Welcome to what may well become the largest revolution in the history of the computer field. Those of us who entered the field decades ago were primarily interested in using computers to do arithmetic calculations at high-speed. But as the computer field evolves, we are beginning to realize that the data manipulation capabilities of computers are now equally important. The "sizzle" of Java is *multimedia*, the use of *sound*, *images*, *graphics*, and *video* to make applications "come alive." Today many people consider two-dimensional color video to be the "ultimate" in multimedia. But within the decade, we expect all kinds of exciting new three-dimensional applications. Multimedia programming offers many new challenges. The field is already enormous and will grow rapidly.

People are rushing to equip their computers for multimedia. Most new computers are being sold "multimedia ready" with CD-ROM drives, audio boards and sometimes with special video capabilities.

Among those users who want graphics, two-dimensional graphics no longer suffice. Now many people want three-dimensional, high-resolution, color graphics. True three-dimensional imaging may become available within the next decade. Imagine having ultra-high-resolution, "theater-in-the-round," three-dimensional television. Sporting and entertainment events will take place on your living room floor! Medical students worldwide will see operations being performed thousands of miles away as if they were occurring in the same room. People will be able to learn how to drive with extremely realistic driving simulators in their homes before they get behind the wheel. The possibilities are exciting and endless.

Multimedia demands extraordinary computing power. Until recently, affordable computers with this kind of power were not available. But today's ultra-fast processors like the SPARC Ultra from Sun Microsystems, the Pentium from Intel, the Alpha from Digital Equipment Corporation and the R8000 from MIPS/Silicon Graphics (among others) are making effective multimedia possible. The computer and communications industries will be primary beneficiaries of the multimedia revolution. Users will be willing to pay more for the faster processors, larger memories and wider communications bandwidths that will be needed to support multimedia applications. Ironically, users may not have to pay more as the fierce competition in these industries forces prices down.

We also need programming languages that make creating multimedia easy. Most programming languages do not have built-in multimedia capabilities. But Java, through the packages of classes that are an integral part of the Java programming world, provides extensive multimedia facilities that will enable you to start developing powerful multimedia applications immediately

In this chapter we present a series of "live-code" examples that cover many of the interesting multimedia features you will need to build useful applications. We will cover the basics of manipulating images, creating smooth animations, playing sounds, creating image maps that can sense when the cursor is over them even without a mouse click, and customizing applets via parameters supplied from the HTML file that invokes an applet. The chapter exercises suggest dozens of challenging and interesting projects and even mention some "million-dollar" ideas that may help you make your fortune! When we were creating these exercises it seemed that the ideas just kept flowing. Multimedia seems to leverage creativity in ways that we have not experienced with "conventional" computer capabilities.

14.2 Loading, Displaying and Scaling Images

Java's multimedia capabilities include graphics, images, animations, sounds and shortly video. We begin our multimedia discussion with images.

The program of Fig. 14.1 loads an image into an applet, displays the image in its original size and displays the image scaled to twice its original width and twice its original height. **Image** reference **deitel** is initialized with the statement

```
deitel = getImage( getDocumentBase(), "deitel0.gif" );
```

which uses **Applet** method **getImage** to load an image into the applet. This version of **getImage** takes two arguments—a location where the image is stored and the file name of the image. In the first argument, **Applet** method **getDocumentBase** is used to determine the location of the image on the Internet (or on your computer if that is where the applet came from). We assume that the image to be loaded is stored in the same location as the HTML file that invoked the applet. Method **getDocumentBase** returns the location of the HTML file on the Internet as an object of class **URL**. A **URL** stores a *Uniform Resource Locator*—a standard format for an address of a piece of information on the Internet. We discuss **URL**s in more depth in Chapter 16. The second argument specifies an image file name. Java currently supports two image formats—*Graphics Interchange Format (GIF)* and *Joint Photographic Experts Group (JPEG)*. File names for each of these types end with **.gif** or **.jpg**, respectively.

When method **getImage** is invoked, it launches a separate thread of execution in which the image is loaded (or downloaded from the Internet). This enables the program to continue execution while the image is loaded.

```java
1   // Fig. 14.1: LoadImageAndScale.java
2   // Load an image and display it in its original size
3   // and scale it to twice its original width and height.
4   import java.applet.Applet;
5   import java.awt.*;
6
7   public class LoadImageAndScale extends Applet {
8      private Image deitel;
9
10     // load the image when the applet begins executing
11     public void init()
12     {
13        deitel = getImage( getDocumentBase(),
14                           "deitel0.gif" );
15     }
16
17     // display the image
18     public void paint( Graphics g )
19     {
20        // draw the original image
21        g.drawImage( deitel, 1, 1, this );
22
23        // draw the image with its width and height doubled
24        int width = deitel.getWidth( this );
25        int height = deitel.getHeight( this );
26        g.drawImage( deitel, 1, 90, width * 2,
27                     height * 2, this );
28     }
29  }
```

Fig. 14.1 Loading and displaying an image in an applet (part 1 of 2).

The applet's **paint** method displays the image using **Graphics** method **drawImage**. This applet uses two versions of **drawImage**. The statement

```java
g.drawImage( deitel, 1, 1, this );
```

uses the **drawImage** method that takes four arguments. The first argument is a reference to the **Image** object in which the image is stored. The second and third arguments are the *x* and *y* coordinates where the image should be displayed on the applet (the coordinates indicate the upper-left corner of the image). The last argument is a reference to an **ImageObserver** object. Normally, the **ImageObserver** is the object on which the image is displayed—we used **this** to indicate the applet. An **ImageObserver** can be any object that implements the **ImageObserver** interface. Class **ImageObserver** is an interface that is implemented by class **Component** (one of class **Applet**'s indirect superclasses). This argument is important when displaying large images that require a long time to download from the Internet. It is possible that a program will display the image before it is completely downloaded. The **ImageObserver** is automatically notified to update the image that was displayed as the remainder of the image is loaded. When you run this applet, watch carefully as pieces of the image are displayed while the image loads.

Fig. 14.1 Loading and displaying an image in an applet (part 2 of 2).

The statement

```
g.drawImage( deitel, 1, 90, width * 2, height * 2, this );
```

uses method **drawImage** to output a scaled version of the image. The fourth and fifth arguments specify the width and height of the image for display purposes. Java automatically scales the image to fit the specified width and height. We specified that the width and height of the scaled image should be twice the original image's width and height. These values are determined with **Image** methods **getWidth** and **getHeight**. Each method receives an **ImageObserver** as an argument. This enables the **ImageObserver** to be updated as the **Image** loads into the applet.

14.3 Introduction to Animation: An Image Loop

The applet of Fig. 14.2 demonstrates a simple animation. The applet uses the same techniques to load images and display images as used in Fig. 14.1. The next several examples demonstrate various techniques for smoothing animations. They also represent the steps that lead to the animation we currently display on the Deitel & Associates, Inc. World Wide Web site **http://www.deitel.com/JavaCurriculum.html**.

Class **DeitelLoop** maintains an array of **Image**s that are loaded in the applet's **init** method. The **getImage** method is used to load each individual image (there are 30 in the animation) with the statement

```
1   // Fig. 14.2: DeitelLoop.java
2   // Load an array of images, loop through the array,
3   // and display each image.
4   import java.applet.Applet;
5   import java.awt.*;
6
7   public class DeitelLoop extends Applet {
8      private Image deitel[];
9      private int totalImages = 30,   // total number of images
10                 currentImage = 0,   // current image subscript
11                 sleepTime = 40;     // milliseconds to sleep
12
13     // load the images when the applet begins executing
14     public void init()
15     {
16        deitel = new Image[ totalImages ];
17
18        for ( int i = 0; i < deitel.length; i++ )
19           deitel[ i ] = getImage( getDocumentBase(),
20              "images/deitel" + i + ".gif" );
21     }
22
23     // start the applet
24     public void start()
25     {
26        currentImage = 0;  // always start with 1st image
27     }
28
29     // display the image in the Applet's Graphics context
30     // then sleep and call repaint
31     public void paint( Graphics g )
32     {
33        g.drawImage( deitel[ currentImage ], 1, 1, this );
34
35        // fix to help load images in Netscape Navigator
36        // makes browser "think" there is a mouse event
37        postEvent( new Event( this, Event.MOUSE_ENTER, "" ) );
38
39        currentImage = ++currentImage % totalImages;
40
41        try {
42           Thread.sleep( sleepTime );
43        }
44        catch ( InterruptedException e ) {
45           showStatus( e.toString() );
46        }
47
48        repaint();
49     }
50  }
```

Fig. 14.2 Demonstrating a simple animation using an image loop (part 1 of 2).

Fig. 14.2 Demonstrating a simple animation using an image loop (part 2 of 2).

```
deitel[ i ] = getImage( getDocumentBase(),
    "images/deitel" + i + ".gif" );
```

The second argument assembles the file name from the pieces **"images/deitel"**, **i**, and **".gif"**. Each of the images in the animation is in one of the files "**deitel0.gif**" through "**deitel29.gif**." The value of the control variable in the **for** structure is used to select one of the 30 images. Remember that **getImage** launches a separate thread of execution for each image it loads.

Performance Tip 14.1

*It is more efficient to load the frames of the animation as one image than to load each image separately (a painting program can be used to combine the frames of the animation into one image). Every **getImage** method call requires a separate connection to the World Wide Web site where the images are stored.*

Performance Tip 14.2

Loading all the frames of an image as one large image may force your program to wait to begin displaying the animation.

The work of displaying the animation is this example is performed by the **Applet**'s **paint** method. Instance variable **currentImage** keeps track of the image to display. First, method **drawImage** is used to display one frame, then the applet sleeps for a fraction of a second with the statement

```
Thread.sleep( sleepTime );
```

Next, method **repaint** is invoked which, in turn, invokes the applet's **update** method to clear the background of the applet. Then, **update** invokes the **paint** method to display the next image.

The statement

```
postEvent( new Event( this, Event.MOUSE_ENTER, "" ) );
```

is a fix we discovered to help the animation images load properly in a popular browser. Often when loading many images in this browser, the applet freezes and does not load anything. However, if you move the mouse pointer in and out of the applet on the screen, the images load and the animation begins executing! As we saw in Chapter 10, when the mouse pointer moves in and out of the applet, **MOUSE_ENTER** and **MOUSE_EXIT** events are generated by the system. The preceding statement uses method **postEvent** (inherited indirectly from class **Component**) to make the applet "think" that a **MOUSE_ENTER** event occurred. This causes the images to load properly in the browser. This statement is not required to execute the applet in Java's appletviewer. The new **Event** object that is instantiated in the preceding statement takes three constructor arguments—the component on which the event occurred (i.e., the applet), the event ID (**Event.MOUSE_ENTER**) and a reference to an **Object** (we chose to use the empty **String**) where information about the event is stored.

When you execute this applet, notice that the images take time to load. This often results in partial images being displayed. Watch carefully as each image is displayed. You may be able to see that each image appears to display in pieces (similar to what happened in the example of Fig. 14.1). This is often the result of the image format that is used. For example, GIF images can be stored in interlaced and non-interlaced formats. The format indicates the order in which the pixels of the image are stored. The pixels of a non-interlaced image are stored in the same order that the pixels appear on the screen. As a non-interlaced image is displayed, it appears in chunks from top to bottom as the pixel information is read. The pixels of an interlaced image are stored in rows of pixels, but the rows are out of order. For example, the rows of pixels in the image may be stored in the order 1, 5, 9, 13, ..., followed by 2, 6, 10, 14, ..., and so on. When the image is displayed, it appears to fade in as the first batch of rows presents a rough outline of the picture and the subsequent batches of rows refine the displayed image until the entire image is complete.

Also, note that the animation flickers as each image is displayed. This is due to the applet's **update** method being called. When **update** clears the applet, it does so by drawing a filled rectangle the size of the applet in the current background color. This covers the image that was just drawn. Thus, the applet draws an image, sleeps for a fraction of a second, clears the background (causing a flicker) and draws the next image.

This applet seems to have infinite recursion in it—**paint** calls **repaint**, **repaint** calls **update**, **update** calls **paint** and **paint** calls **repaint** again. Actually, each call to **repaint** starts a separate thread of execution (which creates a separate method call stack) in which the repainting of the applet is performed. The "infinite recursion" is really happening as follows: **repaint** starts a new thread in which **update** is called, **update** calls **paint**, **paint** calls **repaint**, **repaint** starts a new thread of execution in which **update** is called and the last repainting thread terminates. The method call stack for each thread never has more than three methods in the stack. Also, each stack is garbage collected automatically when its thread is garbage collected. The problem with this apparent infinite recursion is that if the user moves to another Web page, this applet will continue to use processor time on the computer and possibly degrade that computer's performance.

Performance Tip 14.3

*An animation applet that uses a call to **repaint** from the applet's **paint** method to implement animation occupies processor time even after the user leaves the Web page on which the animation applet resides. This may cause performance degradation on the user's computer.*

Software Engineering Observation 14.1

When creating an animation be sure to provide a mechanism for disabling the animation when the user browses a new Web page separate from the page on which the animation applet resides.

We will discuss several techniques over the next few examples to eliminate each of the animation deficiencies described above.

14.4 Graphics Double Buffering

If you want to develop multimedia-based applications, your users will want smooth sound and animations. Choppy presentations are unacceptable. This often happens when you write applications that draw directly to the screen. With the technique of *graphics double buffering*, while the program renders one image on the screen, it can build the next image in an off-screen buffer. Then, when it is time for that next image to be displayed, it can be placed on the screen smoothly. Of course, there is a space-time tradeoff. The extra memory required can be substantial, but the improved display performance may be well worth it.

Graphics double buffering is also useful in programs that need to use drawing capabilities in methods other than **paint** (where we have done all our drawing to this point). The off-screen buffer can be passed between methods or even between objects of different classes to allow other methods or objects to draw on the off-screen buffer. The results of the drawing can then be displayed at a later time.

Performance Tip 14.4

Double buffering can reduce or eliminate flicker in an animation, but it can visibly slow the speed at which the animation runs.

When all the pixels of an image do not display at once, an animation has more flicker. When an image is drawn using graphics double buffering, by the time the image is displayed, it will have already been drawn off the screen and the fading or chunking of the image will be hidden from the user. All the pixels will be displayed for the user in one "blast" so the flicker is reduced tremendously or eliminated.

The basic concept of a graphics double buffer is as follows: create a blank **Image**, draw on the blank **Image** (using methods of the **Graphics** class) and display the image.

The applet of Fig. 14.3 extends the animation of Fig. 14.2 by adding graphics double buffering. There are two key pieces to implementing a graphics double buffer—an **Image** reference (called **buffer** in this program) and a **Graphics** reference (called **gContext** in this program). The **Image** is where the actual pixels to be displayed are stored. The **Graphics** reference is used to draw the pixels. Every image has an associated graphics context—i.e., an object of class **Graphics** that enables drawing to be performed. The **Image** and **Graphics** references used for graphics double buffering are often referred to as the *offscreen image* and the *offscreen graphics context* because they are not actually manipulating screen pixels.

The graphics double buffer is created with the statements

```
buffer = createImage( 160, 80 ); // create image buffer
gContext = buffer.getGraphics(); // get graphics context
```

```java
1   // Fig. 14.3: DeitelLoop2.java
2   // Load an array of images, loop through the array,
3   // and display each image.
4   import java.applet.Applet;
5   import java.awt.*;
6
7   public class DeitelLoop2 extends Applet {
8      private Image deitel[];
9      private int totalImages = 30,   // total number of images
10                 currentImage = 0,   // current image subscript
11                 sleepTime = 40;     // milliseconds to sleep
12
13     // The next two objects are for double-buffering
14     private Graphics gContext; // off-screen graphics context
15     private Image buffer;      // buffer in which to draw image
16
17     // load the images when the applet begins executing
18     public void init()
19     {
20        deitel = new Image[ totalImages ];
21        buffer = createImage( 160, 80 ); // create image buffer
22        gContext = buffer.getGraphics(); // get graphics context
23
24        // set background of buffer to white
25        gContext.setColor( Color.white );
26        gContext.fillRect( 0, 0, 160, 80 );
27
28        for ( int i = 0; i < deitel.length; i++ )
29           deitel[ i ] = getImage( getDocumentBase(),
30              "images/deitel" + i + ".gif" );
31     }
32
33     // start the applet
34     public void start()
35     {
36        // always start with 1st image
37        gContext.drawImage( deitel[ 0 ], 0, 0, this );
38        currentImage = 1;
39     }
40
41     // display the image in the Applet's Graphics context
42     public void paint( Graphics g )
43     {
44        g.drawImage( buffer, 0, 0, this );
45
46        // clear previous image from buffer
47        gContext.fillRect( 0, 0, 160, 80 );
48
49        // draw new image in buffer
50        gContext.drawImage( deitel[ currentImage ], 0, 0, this );
```

Fig. 14.3 Using graphics double buffering to reduce animation flicker (part 1 of 2).

```
51
52          // fix to help load images in Netscape Navigator
53          // makes browser "think" there is a mouse event
54          postEvent( new Event( this, Event.MOUSE_ENTER, "" ) );
55
56          currentImage = ++currentImage % totalImages;
57
58          try {
59             Thread.sleep( sleepTime );
60          }
61          catch ( InterruptedException e ) {
62             showStatus( e.toString() );
63          }
64
65          repaint();  // display buffered image
66       }
67    }
```

Fig. 14.3 Using graphics double buffering to reduce animation flicker (part 2 of 2).

from the applet's **init** method. The first statement uses the applet's **createImage** method (inherited indirectly from class **Component**) to ask the system to create an image that is 160 pixels wide and 80 pixels tall (this is the size of each image we display in the animation). Class **Image** is an abstract class, so **Image** objects cannot be created directly. To achieve platform independence, the Java implementation on each platform provides its own subclass of **Image** to store image information. Class **Image** provides the programmer with a uniform set of methods used to process images. Method **createImage** instantiates an object of the platform's subclass of **Image**. The second statement uses **Image** method **getGraphics** to get the graphics context (i.e., the **Graphics** object) associated with the **Image** object referenced by **buffer**. The **gContext** reference will be used to draw to the offscreen image. The statements

```
gContext.setColor( Color.white );
gContext.fillRect( 0, 0, 160, 80 );
```

set the drawing color for the offscreen graphics context to white (any shapes are drawn in the drawing color) and draw a filled rectangle in white to the offscreen image. This prepares the offscreen image to have the first animation image drawn.

The **start** method specifies that the first image in the array of images should be drawn using **gContext**. The image is stored in the **Image** object to which **buffer** refers. The **paint** method displays whatever image happens to be stored in **buffer** currently, then prepares the next image to be displayed. First, **fillRect** is used to clear the offscreen image. Then the next image is drawn to the offscreen image. After sleeping for a fraction of a second, method **repaint** is called. This causes a separate thread of execution in which **update** is invoked, **update** calls **paint**, **paint** displays the image that was just prepared and **paint** prepares the next image to be displayed.

When you execute this applet, notice that the animation is still choppy while the images load. However, once the images are completely loaded, most of the flicker from the previous animation applet has been eliminated. This version of the applet still issues a **repaint** call from **paint** which means this applet will occupy processor time on the user's computer when the user moves to another Web page. In the next example, we will eliminate all the flicker.

14.5 Using the **MediaTracker** to Monitor Image Loading

As you have seen in the first two animations, when the images are loading, they are frequently displayed as partial images. This makes the animation appear choppy at first. In the applet of Fig. 14.4 we extend the animation to use Java's **MediaTracker** to determine when an image is completely loaded. Once an image is completely loaded it is displayed as part of the animation.

```
1   // Fig. 14.4: DeitelLoop3.java
2   // Load an array of images, loop through the array,
3   // and display each image.
4   import java.applet.Applet;
5   import java.awt.*;
6
7   public class DeitelLoop3 extends Applet {
8       private Image deitel[];
9       private int totalImages = 30,   // total number of images
10                  currentImage = 0,   // current image subscript
11                  sleepTime = 40;     // milliseconds to sleep
12
13      // The next two objects are for double-buffering
14      private Graphics gContext; // off-screen graphics context
15      private Image buffer;      // buffer in which to draw image
16
17      private MediaTracker imageTracker; // used to track images
18
19      // load the images when the applet begins executing
20      public void init()
21      {
```

Fig. 14.4 Using the **MediaTracker** to smooth animation startup and overriding **update** to eliminate animation flicker (part 1 of 3).

```
22          deitel = new Image[ totalImages ];
23          buffer = createImage( 160, 80 ); // create image buffer
24          gContext = buffer.getGraphics(); // get graphics context
25
26          // set background of buffer to white
27          gContext.setColor( Color.white );
28          gContext.fillRect( 0, 0, 160, 80 );
29
30          imageTracker = new MediaTracker( this );
31
32          for ( int i = 0; i < deitel.length; i++ ) {
33             deitel[ i ] = getImage( getDocumentBase(),
34                "images/deitel" + i + ".gif" );
35
36             // track loading image
37             imageTracker.addImage( deitel[ i ], i );
38          }
39
40          try {
41             imageTracker.waitForID( 0 );
42          }
43          catch( InterruptedException e ) { }
44       }
45
46       // start the applet
47       public void start()
48       {
49          // always start with 1st image
50          gContext.drawImage( deitel[ 0 ], 0, 0, this );
51          currentImage = 1;
52       }
53
54       // display the image in the Applet's Graphics context
55       public void paint( Graphics g )
56       {
57          g.drawImage( buffer, 0, 0, this );
58
59          if ( imageTracker.checkID( currentImage, true ) ) {
60             // clear previous image from buffer
61             gContext.fillRect( 0, 0, 160, 80 );
62
63             // draw new image in buffer
64             gContext.drawImage(
65                deitel[ currentImage ], 0, 0, this );
66
67             currentImage = ++currentImage % totalImages;
68          }
69          else    // fix to help load images in Netscape Navigator
70             postEvent( new Event( this, Event.MOUSE_ENTER, "" ) );
71
```

Fig. 14.4 Using the **MediaTracker** to smooth animation startup and overriding **update** to eliminate animation flicker (part 2 of 3).

```
72          try {
73              Thread.sleep( sleepTime );
74          }
75          catch ( InterruptedException e ) {
76              showStatus( e.toString() );
77          }
78
79          repaint();  // display buffered image
80      }
81
82      // override update to eliminate flicker
83      public void update( Graphics g )
84      {
85          paint( g );
86      }
87  }
```

Fig. 14.4 Using the **MediaTracker** to smooth animation startup and overriding **update** to eliminate animation flicker (part 3 of 3).

Performance Tip 14.5

*Some people experienced with **MediaTracker** objects have reported that they can have a detrimental effect on performance. Keep this in mind as an area to scrutinize if you need to tune your multimedia applications.*

When loading images into a program, the images can be registered with an object of class **MediaTracker** to enable the program to determine when an image is loaded completely. Class **MediaTracker** also provides the ability to wait for an image or several images to load before allowing a program to continue and to determine if an error occurred while loading an image.

The **MediaTracker** is instantiated with the statement

```
imageTracker = new MediaTracker( this );
```

The argument to the constructor is an **ImageObserver** (the object on which the images will be drawn). In this case, the applet (**this**) is the **ImageObserver**. After method **getImage** is invoked to load each image, the statement

```
imageTracker.addImage( deitel[ i ], i );
```

is executed to register the loading image with the **MediaTracker** object **imageTracker**. The first argument to method **addImage** is the **Image** reference to the image being loaded. The second argument is an integer ID that can be used to query the **MediaTracker** on the status of that image. The ID does not have to be unique. To track multiple images as a group, simply give them the same ID number.

Once all the images have been registered with the **imageTracker**, the statement

```
imageTracker.waitForID( 0 );
```

is executed to force the program to wait until the image identified as 0 is completely loaded. This is a blocking call—the program does not continue executing until the image is completely loaded. Class **MediaTracker** also provides a **waitForAll** method that blocks until all the images registered are completely loaded.

Performance Tip 14.6

*Using **MediaTracker** method **waitForAll** to wait for all registered images to completely load may result is a long delay between when the applet begins execution and when the images are actually displayed. The more images and the larger the images, the more time the user will have to wait. Use **MediaTracker** method **waitForAll** only to wait for small numbers of images to load completely.*

Good Programming Practice 14.1

Always display something while images load. The longer a user must wait to see information appear on the screen, the more likely they will leave the Web page before the information appears.

Once the first image has completely loaded it is prepared to display in the start method, then it is displayed in the **paint** method. The preparing of the next image to display is now accomplished by an **if** structure in the **paint** method. The condition

```
imageTracker.checkID( currentImage, true )
```

performs two tasks. First, method **checkID** checks the image registered as **currentImage** to determine if the image has completely loaded. If so, the method returns **true** and the **if** structure's body is executed to prepare the next image for display. If the image is not completely loaded, the method returns **false** and the **else** part of the **if/else** structure is executed to perform our browser fix. If the image has not started to load when **checkID** is invoked to check the image, the second argument indicates that the image should start loading now.

The **MediaTracker** does not eliminate flicker—it simply smooths the beginning of the animation as the images are loaded so no partial images are displayed. To eliminate all flicker, we have provided our own definition of the applet's **update** method. Previously we stated that **update** clears the applet, then calls **paint**. Clearing the applet causes the flicker. Our definition of **update** overrides the one that was indirectly inherited from class **Component**. The new version simply calls **paint**—no clearing of the applet is performed. But how do we clear the image that is on the applet so the next image can be displayed? The answer is that we already do so. Every time we prepare an image to be displayed, we clear the offscreen image so the background is all white. Then we draw the next image on the white background. When the offscreen image is displayed, the white background of the image being displayed hides the entire image that was already on the applet.

When you execute this applet, notice that there is no more flicker! Also, notice that the first pass of the animation (when each image is displayed for the first time) is slower than the subsequent passes. This is due to our use of the **MediaTracker** to wait for each image to load. In the next example, we add a separate thread to execute the animation so we have control over when the animation executes and when it stops.

14.6 Using a Separate Thread to Run an Animation

The applet of Fig. 14.5 does not add any new multimedia or animation techniques. Rather it shows a better way to construct an animation to make it "browser-friendly." As we mentioned previously, our animations will continue to execute and occupy processor time on the user's computer even after they leave the Web page. In this example, we extend the applet to implement interface **Runnable** so we can run the animation as a separate thread and have control over the execution of the thread.

```
1    // Fig. 14.5: DeitelLoop4.java
2    // Load an array of images, loop through the array,
3    // and display each image.
4    import java.applet.Applet;
5    import java.awt.*;
6
7    public class DeitelLoop4 extends Applet implements Runnable {
8        private Image deitel[];
9        private int totalImages = 30,   // total number of images
10                   currentImage = 0,   // current image subscript
11                   sleepTime = 40;     // milliseconds to sleep
12
13       // The next two objects are for double-buffering
14       private Graphics gContext; // off-screen graphics context
15       private Image buffer;      // buffer in which to draw image
16
17       private MediaTracker imageTracker; // used to track images
18
19       private Thread animate;       // animation thread
20       private boolean suspended;    // toggle on/off
21
22       // load the images when the applet begins executing
23       public void init()
24       {
25           deitel = new Image[ totalImages ];
26           buffer = createImage( 160, 80 ); // create image buffer
27           gContext = buffer.getGraphics(); // get graphics context
28
```

Fig. 14.5 Using a separate thread to run an animation (part 1 of 4).

```
29          // set background of buffer to white
30          gContext.setColor( Color.white );
31          gContext.fillRect( 0, 0, 160, 80 );
32
33          imageTracker = new MediaTracker( this );
34
35          for ( int i = 0; i < deitel.length; i++ ) {
36             deitel[ i ] = getImage( getDocumentBase(),
37                "images/deitel" + i + ".gif" );
38
39             // track loading image
40             imageTracker.addImage( deitel[ i ], i );
41          }
42
43          try {
44             imageTracker.waitForID( 0 );
45          }
46          catch( InterruptedException e ) { }
47       }
48
49       // start the applet
50       public void start()
51       {
52          // always start with 1st image
53          gContext.drawImage( deitel[ 0 ], 0, 0, this );
54          currentImage = 1;
55
56          // create a new animation thread when user visits page
57          if ( animate == null ) {
58             animate = new Thread( this );
59             animate.start();
60          }
61       }
62
63       // terminate animation thread when user leaves page
64       public void stop()
65       {
66          if ( animate != null ) {
67             animate.stop();
68             animate = null;
69          }
70       }
71
72       // display the image in the Applet's Graphics context
73       public void paint( Graphics g )
74       {
75          g.drawImage( buffer, 0, 0, this );
76       }
77
```

Fig. 14.5 Using a separate thread to run an animation (part 2 of 4).

```
78      // override update to eliminate flicker
79      public void update( Graphics g )
80      {
81         paint( g );
82      }
83
84      public void run()
85      {
86         while ( true ) {
87            if ( imageTracker.checkID( currentImage, true ) ) {
88               // clear previous image from buffer
89               gContext.fillRect( 0, 0, 160, 80 );
90
91               // draw new image in buffer
92               gContext.drawImage(
93                  deitel[ currentImage ], 0, 0, this );
94
95               currentImage = ++currentImage % totalImages;
96            }
97            else    // browser fix: help load images
98               postEvent(
99                  new Event( this, Event.MOUSE_ENTER, "" ) );
100
101           try {
102              Thread.sleep( sleepTime );
103           }
104           catch ( InterruptedException e ) {
105              showStatus( e.toString() );
106           }
107
108           repaint();  // display buffered image
109        }
110     }
111
112     public boolean mouseDown( Event e, int x, int y )
113     {
114        if ( suspended ) {
115           animate.resume();
116           suspended = false;
117        }
118        else {
119           animate.suspend();
120           suspended = true;
121        }
122
123        return true;
124     }
125  }
```

Fig. 14.5 Using a separate thread to run an animation (part 3 of 4).

Fig. 14.5 Using a separate thread to run an animation (part 4 of 4).

Thread object **animate** is used to run the animation and **boolean** variable **suspended** indicates whether or not the applet is currently in a suspended state. When the applet's **start** method executes it draws the first image on the offscreen graphics context, then creates a **Thread** (initialized with the applet) and invokes the thread's **start** method. This launches the animation thread. The applet's **run** method is invoked to control the animation. Everything that used to be accomplished by the **paint** method is now accomplished by the infinite loop in **run** with the exception of the actual display of the image on the applet—this is still performed by **paint**.

There are two other key features—method **stop** and method **mouseDown**. Remember that method **stop** is invoked automatically on an applet when the user leaves the Web page on which the applet resides. Method **stop** is defined to invoke the thread's **stop** method which terminates the thread. Thus, the applet is not executing the animation when the user moves to another Web page. Method **start** is invoked automatically if the user revisits the Web page containing the applet, so **start** can create a new thread to run the animation. If this occurs, the animation begins immediately because the images are still loaded in memory. Method **mouseDown** allows the user to click on the applet to suspend the animation and to click again to resume the animation. This is accomplished with the **Thread** methods **suspend** and **resume**, respectively. Both these additions make the animation applet more browser-friendly. Notice the **boolean** variable **suspended** has not been initialized, so we rely on the Java default initialization to **false**.

14.7 Loading and Playing Audio Clips

Java programs can manipulate and play audio clips. It is easy for users to capture their own audio clips and there is a huge variety of clips available in software products and over the Internet. Your system will need to be equipped with audio hardware, typically speakers and a sound board.

Java provides two mechanisms for playing sounds in an applet—the **Applet**'s *play* method and the *play* method from the **AudioClip** *interface*. If you would like to play a sound once in a program, the **Applet** method **play** will load the sound and play it for you once; the sound is marked for garbage collection when it is done playing. The **Applet** method **play** method has two forms:

```
public void play( URL location, String soundFileName );
public void play( URL soundURL );
```

The first version loads the audio clip stored in file **soundFileName** from **location** and plays the sound. The first argument is normally a call to the applet's **getDocument-Base** or *getCodeBase method*. Method **getDocumentBase** indicates where to locate the HTML file that loaded the applet. Method **getCodeBase** indicates where the **.class** file for the applet is located. The second version of method **play** takes a **URL** that contains the location and the file name of the audio clip. The statement

```
public void play( getDocumentBase(), "hi.au" );
```

loads the audio clip in file **hi.au** and plays it once.

The program of Fig. 14.6 demonstrates loading and playing an **AudioClip**. This technique is more flexible. It allows the audio to be stored in the program so the audio can be reused throughout the program's execution. The **Applet** method **getAudioClip** has two forms that take the same arguments as the **play** method described above. Method **getAudioClip** returns a reference to an **AudioClip**. Once an **AudioClip** is loaded, three methods can be invoked for the object—**play**, **loop** and **stop**. Method **play** plays the audio once. Method **loop** continuously loops the audio clip in the background. Method **stop** terminates an audio clip that is currently playing. In the program, each of these methods is associated with a button on the applet.

14.8 Customizing Applets via the HTML `param` Tag

When browsing the World Wide Web you will often come across applets that are in the public domain—you can use them free of charge on your own Web pages (normally in exchange for crediting the applet's creator). One common feature of such applets is the ability to customize the applet via parameters that are supplied from the HTML file that invokes the applet. For example, the following HTML file

```
<html>
<applet code="DeitelLoop5.class" width=400 height=400>
<param name="totalimages" value="30">
<param name="imagename" value="deitel">
<param name="sleeptime" value="500">
</applet>
</html>
```

invokes the applet **DeitelLoop5** (Fig. 14.7) and specifies three parameters. The **param** tag lines must appear between the starting **applet** tag and the ending **applet** tag. These values can then be used to customize the applet. Any number of **param** tags can appear between the starting and ending **applet** tags. Each parameter has a **name** and a **value**. The **Applet** method **getParameter** is used to get the **value** associated with a specific parameter and return the **value** as a **String**. The argument passed to **getParameter** is a **String** containing the name of the parameter in the **param** tag. For example, the statement

```
1   // Fig. 14.6: LoadAudioAndPlay.java
2   // Load an audio clip and play it.
3   import java.applet.*;
4   import java.awt.*;
5
6   public class LoadAudioAndPlay extends Applet {
7      private AudioClip sound;
8      private Button playSound, loopSound, stopSound;
9
10     // load the image when the applet begins executing
11     public void init()
12     {
13        sound = getAudioClip( getDocumentBase(), "hi.au" );
14        playSound = new Button( "Play" );
15        loopSound = new Button( "Loop" );
16        stopSound = new Button( "Stop" );
17        add( playSound );
18        add( loopSound );
19        add( stopSound );
20     }
21
22     public boolean action( Event e, Object o )
23     {
24        if ( e.target == playSound )
25           sound.play();
26        else if ( e.target == loopSound )
27           sound.loop();
28        else if ( e.target == stopSound )
29           sound.stop();
30
31        return true;
32     }
33  }
```

Fig. 14.6 Loading and playing an audio clip.

```
parameter = getParameter( "sleeptime" );
```

gets the value associated with the **sleeptime** parameter and assigns it to **String** reference **parameter**. If there is not a **param** tag containing the specified parameter, **get-Parameter** returns **null**.

This version of our animation applet allows users to customize the animation to use their own images. Three parameters are provided. Parameter **sleeptime** is the number of milliseconds to sleep between images being displayed. This value will be converted to an integer and used as the value for instance variable **sleepTime**. Parameter **image-Name** is the base name of the images to be loaded. This **String** will be assigned to instance variable **imageName**. The applet assumes that the images are in a subdirectory named **images** that can be found in the same directory as the applet. The applet also assumes that the image file names are numbered from 0. Parameter **totalimages** represents the total number of images in the animation. Its value will be converted to an integer and assigned to instance variable **totalImages**.

The applet also provides a text field that displays the sleep time and allows the user to vary the sleep time by typing a new value in the text field. This is an extended version of our animation applet that uses a separate thread to run the animation.

```
1   // Fig. 14.7: DeitelLoop5.java
2   // Load an array of images, loop through the array,
3   // and display each image. This version is customizeable.
4   //
5   // HTML parameter "sleeptime" is an integer indicating the
6   // number of milliseconds to sleep between images.
7   //
8   // HTML parameter "imagename" is the base name of the images
9   // that will be displayed (i.e., "deitel" is the base name
10  // for images "deitel0.gif," "deitel1.gif," etc.). The applet
11  // assumes that images are in an "images" subdirectory of
12  // the directory in which the applet resides.
13  //
14  // HTML parameter "totalimages" is an integer representing the
15  // total number of images in the animation. The applet assumes
16  // images are numbered from 0 to totalimages - 1.
17
18  import java.applet.Applet;
19  import java.awt.*;
20
21  public class DeitelLoop5 extends Applet implements Runnable {
22      private Image images[];
23      private int totalImages,          // total number of images
24                  currentImage = 0,     // current image subscript
25                  sleepTime;            // milliseconds to sleep
26      private String imageName;   // base name of images
27
28      // The next two objects are for double-buffering
29      private Graphics gContext; // off-screen graphics context
30      private Image buffer;       // buffer in which to draw image
31
32      private MediaTracker imageTracker;  // used to track images
33
34      private Thread animate;         // animation thread
35      private boolean suspended;      // toggle on/off
36
37      private int width, height;
```

Fig. 14.7 Customizing an applet via the **param** HTML tag (part 1 of 5).

```
38
39      // GUI Components to allow dynamic speed changing
40      private Label sleepLabel;
41      private TextField sleepDisplay;
42      private Panel sleepStuff;
43
44      // load the images when the applet begins executing
45      public void init()
46      {
47         processHTMLParameters();
48
49         if ( totalImages == 0 || imageName == null ) {
50            showStatus( "Invalid parameters" );
51            destroy();
52         }
53
54         images = new Image[ totalImages ];
55         imageTracker = new MediaTracker( this );
56
57         for ( int i = 0; i < images.length; i++ ) {
58            images[ i ] = getImage( getDocumentBase(),
59               "images/" + imageName + i + ".gif" );
60
61            // track loading image
62            imageTracker.addImage( images[ i ], i );
63         }
64
65         try {
66            imageTracker.waitForID( 0 );
67         }
68         catch( InterruptedException e ) { }
69
70         width = images[ 0 ].getWidth( this );
71         height = images[ 0 ].getHeight( this );
72         resize( width, height + 30 );
73
74         buffer = createImage( width, height );
75         gContext = buffer.getGraphics();
76
77         // set background of buffer to white
78         gContext.setColor( Color.white );
79         gContext.fillRect( 0, 0, 160, 80 );
80
81         setLayout( new BorderLayout() );
82         sleepLabel = new Label( "Sleep time" );
83         sleepDisplay = new TextField( 5 );
84         sleepDisplay.setText( String.valueOf( sleepTime ) );
85         sleepStuff = new Panel();
86         sleepStuff.add( sleepLabel );
87         sleepStuff.add( sleepDisplay );
```

Fig. 14.7 Customizing an applet via the **param** HTML tag (part 2 of 5).

```
88            add( "South", sleepStuff );
89        }
90
91        // start the applet
92        public void start()
93        {
94            // always start with 1st image
95            gContext.drawImage( images[ 0 ], 0, 0, this );
96            currentImage = 1;
97
98            // create a new animation thread when user visits page
99            if ( animate == null ) {
100                animate = new Thread( this );
101                animate.start();
102            }
103        }
104
105        // terminate animation thread when user leaves page
106        public void stop()
107        {
108            if ( animate != null ) {
109                animate.stop();
110                animate = null;
111            }
112        }
113
114        // display the image in the Applet's Graphics context
115        public void paint( Graphics g )
116        {
117            g.drawImage( buffer, 0, 0, this );
118        }
119
120        // override update to eliminate flicker
121        public void update( Graphics g )
122        {
123            paint( g );
124        }
125
126        public void run()
127        {
128            while ( true ) {
129                if ( imageTracker.checkID( currentImage, true ) ) {
130                    // clear previous image from buffer
131                    gContext.fillRect( 0, 0, 160, 80 );
132
133                    // draw new image in buffer
134                    gContext.drawImage(
135                        images[ currentImage ], 0, 0, this );
136
137                    currentImage = ++currentImage % totalImages;
138                }
```

Fig. 14.7 Customizing an applet via the **param** HTML tag (part 3 of 5).

```
139            else    // browser fix: help load images
140               postEvent(
141                  new Event( this, Event.MOUSE_ENTER, "" ) );
142
143            try {
144               Thread.sleep( sleepTime );
145            }
146            catch ( InterruptedException e ) {
147               showStatus( e.toString() );
148            }
149
150            repaint();   // display buffered image
151         }
152      }
153
154      public boolean action( Event e, Object o )
155      {
156         try {
157            int i = Integer.parseInt( o.toString() );
158            sleepTime = i;
159         }
160         catch( NumberFormatException nfe ) {
161            showStatus( "Sleep time must be an integer" );
162         }
163
164         return true;
165      }
166
167      public boolean mouseDown( Event e, int x, int y )
168      {
169         if ( suspended ) {
170            animate.resume();
171            suspended = false;
172         }
173         else {
174            animate.suspend();
175            suspended = true;
176         }
177
178         return true;
179      }
180
181      public void processHTMLParameters()
182      {
183         String parameter;
184
185         parameter = getParameter( "sleeptime" );
186         sleepTime = ( parameter == null ? 50 :
187                         Integer.parseInt( parameter ) );
188
189         imageName = getParameter( "imagename" );
```

Fig. 14.7 Customizing an applet via the **param** HTML tag (part 4 of 5).

```
190
191        parameter = getParameter( "totalimages" );
192        totalImages = ( parameter == null ? 0 :
193                        Integer.parseInt( parameter ) );
194    }
195 }
```

Fig. 14.7 Customizing an applet via the **param** HTML tag (part 5 of 5).

14.9 Image Maps

A common technique for creating more interesting Web pages is the use of *image maps*. An image map is an image that has *hot areas* that the user can click to accomplish a task such as loading a different Web page into a browser. When the user positions the mouse pointer over a hot area, normally a descriptive message is displayed in the status area of the browser. This technique can be used to implement a *bubble help* system. When the user positions the mouse pointer over a particular element on the screen, a system with bubble help usually displays a message in a small window that appears automatically over the screen element. In Java, the message can be displayed in the status bar.

The program of Fig. 14.8 loads an image containing the icons from the *Java Multimedia Cyber Classroom*—the interactive-CD, multimedia version of this text. These icons may look familiar; they are designed to mimic the icons used in this book. The program allows the user to position the mouse pointer over an icon and display a descriptive message for the icon. Method **mouseMove** takes the coordinates of the mouse and passes them to method **translateLocation**. The coordinates are tested to determine in which icon the coordinates are located. Method **translateLocation** then displays a message in the status bar of the applet indicating what the icon represents.

Clicking in this applet will not cause any action. In Chapter 16, "Networking," we discuss the techniques required to load another Web page into a browser. Once we have these networking capabilities, we can modify this applet to enable each icon to be associated with a different URL.

```
1    // Fig. 14.8: ImageMap.java
2    // Demonstrating an image map.
3    import java.awt.*;
4    import java.applet.Applet;
5
6    public class ImageMap extends Applet {
7        Image mapImage;
8        MediaTracker trackImage;
9        int width, height;
10
11       public void init()
12       {
13           trackImage = new MediaTracker( this );
14           mapImage = getImage( getDocumentBase(), "icons2.gif" );
15           trackImage.addImage( mapImage, 0 );
16
17           try {
18               trackImage.waitForAll();
19           }
20           catch( InterruptedException e ) { }
21
22           width = mapImage.getWidth( this );
23           height = mapImage.getHeight( this );
24           resize( width, height );
25       }
26
27       public void paint( Graphics g )
28       {
29           g.drawImage( mapImage, 0, 0, this );
30       }
31
32       public boolean mouseMove( Event e, int x, int y )
33       {
34           showStatus( translateLocation( x, y ) );
35           return true;
36       }
37
38       public boolean mouseExit( Event e, int x, int y )
39       {
40           showStatus( "Pointer outside ImageMap applet" );
41           return true;
42       }
43
44       public String translateLocation( int x, int y )
45       {
46           // determine width of each icon (there are 6)
47           int iconWidth = width / 6;
48
49           if ( x >= 0 && x <= iconWidth)
50               return "Common Programming Error";
```

Fig. 14.8 Demonstrating an image map (part 1 of 3).

```
51        else if ( x > iconWidth && x <= iconWidth * 2 )
52           return "Good Programming Practice";
53        else if ( x > iconWidth * 2 && x <= iconWidth * 3 )
54           return "Performance Tip";
55        else if ( x > iconWidth * 3 && x <= iconWidth * 4 )
56           return "Portability Tip";
57        else if ( x > iconWidth * 4 && x <= iconWidth * 5 )
58           return "Software Engineering Observation";
59        else if ( x > iconWidth * 5 && x <= iconWidth * 6 )
60           return "Testing and Debugging Tip";
61
62        return "";
63     }
64  }
```

Fig. 14.8 Demonstrating an image map (part 2 of 3).

Fig. 14.8 Demonstrating an image map (part 3 of 3).

Summary

- **Applet** method **getImage** loads an image into an applet.

- **Applet** method **getDocumentBase** returns the location on the Internet of the HTML file that invoked the applet as an object of class **URL**.

- A **URL** stores a Uniform Resource Locator—a standard format for an address of a piece of information on the Internet.

- Java currently supports two image formats—Graphics Interchange Format (GIF) and Joint Photographic Experts Group (JPEG). File names for each of these types end with **.gif** or **.jpg**, respectively.

- Method **getImage** launches a separate thread of execution in which an image is loaded (or downloaded from the Internet). This enables the program to continue execution while the image is loaded.

- **Graphics** method **drawImage** displays an image on an applet.

- Class **ImageObserver** is an interface that is implemented by class **Component**. The **ImageObserver** is automatically notified to update an image that was displayed as the remainder of the image is loaded.

- **Image** methods **getWidth** and **getHeight** each receive an **ImageObserver** as an argument and return the width and height of the image, respectively. The **ImageObserver** argument enables updating of the image information as the **Image** loads.

- An animation often flickers as each image is displayed. This is due to the applet's **update** method being called. When **update** clears the applet, it does so by drawing a filled rectangle the size of the applet in the current background color. This covers the image that was just drawn causing a flicker.

- Each call to **repaint** starts a separate thread of execution (which creates a separate method call stack) in which the repainting of the applet is performed.

- With the technique of graphics double buffering, while the program renders one image on the screen, it can be building the next image in an off-screen buffer. Then, when it is time for that next image to be displayed, it can be placed on the screen smoothly.

- Graphics double buffering is useful in programs that draw in methods other than **paint**. The off-screen buffer can be passed between methods or even between objects of different classes to allow other methods or objects to draw on the off-screen buffer.

- GIF images can be stored in interlaced and non-interlaced formats. As a non-interlaced image is displayed, it appears in chunks from top to bottom as the pixel information is read. As an interlaced image is displayed, it appears to fade in as the first batch of rows presents a rough outline of the picture and the subsequent batches of rows refine the displayed image until the entire image is complete.

- There are two key pieces to implementing a graphics double buffer—an **Image** reference and a **Graphics** reference. The **Image** is where the actual pixels to be displayed are stored. The **Graphics** reference is used to draw the pixels.

- Every image has an associated graphics context—i.e., an object of class **Graphics** that enables drawing to be performed.

- The **Image** and **Graphics** references used for graphics double buffering are often referred to as the off-screen image and the off-screen graphics context because they are not actually manipulating screen pixels.

- Applet method **createImage** asks the system to create an empty image by instantiating an object of the system-specific subclass of **Image**. The method receives two integer arguments—the width and height of the empty image.

- **Image** method **getGraphics** gets the graphics context (i.e., the **Graphics** object) associated with an **Image** object.

- Images can be registered with a **MediaTracker** object to enable the program to determine when an image is loaded completely. Class **MediaTracker** also provides the ability to wait for an image or several images to load before allowing a program to continue and to determine if an error occurred while loading an image.

- The **MediaTracker** constructor takes one argument—an **ImageObserver** (normally the object on which the images will be drawn).

- **MediaTracker** method **addImage** registers an image with a **MediaTracker** object. The first argument is an **Image** reference. The second argument is an integer ID that can be used to query the **MediaTracker** on the status of that image. To track multiple images as a group, give them the same ID number.

- **MediaTracker** method **waitForID** forces the program to wait until the image specified by the integer argument is completely loaded. **MediaTracker** method **waitForAll** blocks until all registered images are loaded completely.

- To eliminate all flicker, override the applet's **update** method to call **paint** without clearing the applet.

- To make an animation "browser-friendly" run the animation as a separate thread in the applet. The applet's **start** method should instantiate a **Thread** and launch the animation. The applet's **stop** method should stop the thread to terminate the animation when the user browses a different Web page. **Thread** methods **suspend** and **resume** can also be used to let the user suspend and resume the applet.

- Java provides two mechanisms for playing sounds in an applet—the **Applet**'s **play** method and the **play** method from the **AudioClip** interface.

- To play a sound once in a program, use the **Applet** method **play** to load the sound and play it; the sound is marked for garbage collection when it is done playing.

- **Applet** method **getDocumentBase** indicates where to locate the HTML file that loaded the applet.

- **Applet** method **getCodeBase** indicates where the applet's **.class** file is located.

- The HTML **param** tag specifies a parameter for an applet. The **param** tag lines appear between the starting **applet** tag and the ending **applet** tag. Each parameter has a **name** and a **value**.

- **Applet** method **getParameter** is used to get the **value** associated with a specific parameter and return the **value** as a **String**. If there is not a **param** tag containing the specified parameter, **getParameter** returns **null**.

- An image map is an image that has hot areas that the user can click to accomplish a task such as loading a different Web page.

Terminology

addImage method
animation
animation loop
animation speed
.au file format for sound files
audio
AudioClip class
audio clips
checkID period
display an image
double buffering to reduce flicker
drawImage method of Graphics class
fetch an image from a server
flicker
flicker reduction
frame of an animation
frames order
getAudioClip method
getCodeBase method
getDocumentBase method
getGraphics method
getImage method of Applet class
getParameter method
.gif image file
graphics
Graphics class
graphics context

graphics double buffering
image
Image class
ImageObserver class
imageUpdate method of an applet
JPEG image format
load an audio clip
load an image
loop method of AudioClip class
loop on an audio clip
MediaTracker class
multimedia
play method of AudioClip class
play method of class Applet
restart an animation
smooth animation
sound
sound clip
sound loop
sound track
stop an animation
stop method of AudioClip class
stop an audio clip
URL of an image
waitForAll method
waitForID method

Good Programming Practice

14.1 Always display something while images load. The longer a user must wait to see information appear on the screen, the more likely they will leave the Web page before the information appears.

Performance Tips

14.1 It is more efficient to load the frames of the animation as one image than to load each image separately (a painting program can be used to combine the frames of the animation into one image). Every getImage method call requires a separate connection to the World Wide Web site where the images are stored.

14.2 Loading all the frames of an image as one large image may force your program to wait to begin displaying the animation.

14.3 An animation applet that uses a call to repaint from the applet's paint method to implement animation occupies processor time even after the user leaves the Web page on which the animation applet resides. This may cause performance degradation on the user's computer.

14.4   Double buffering can reduce or eliminate flicker in an animation, but it can visibly slow the speed at which the animation runs.

14.5   Some people experienced with **MediaTracker** objects have reported that they can have a detrimental effect on performance. Keep this in mind as an area to scrutinize if you need to tune your multimedia applications.

14.6   Using **MediaTracker** method **waitForAll** to wait for all registered images to completely load may result is a long delay between when the applet begins execution and when the images are actually displayed. The more images and the larger the images, the more time the user will have to wait. Use **MediaTracker** method **waitForAll** only to wait for small numbers of images to load completely.

Software Engineering Observation

14.1   When creating an animation be sure to provide a mechanism for disabling the animation when the user browses a new Web page separate from the page on which the animation applet resides.

Self-Review Exercises

14.1   Fill in the blanks in each of the following:
   a) **Applet** method _____ loads an image into an applet.
   b) **Applet** method _____ returns the location on the Internet of the HTML file that invoked the applet as an object of class **URL**.
   c) A _____ is a standard format for an address of a piece of information on the Internet.
   d) **Graphics** method _____ displays an image on an applet.
   e) An animation often flickers as each image is displayed. This is due to the applet's _____ method being called. When this method clears the applet, it does so by drawing a filled rectangle the size of the applet in the current background color. This covers the image that was just drawn causing a flicker.
   f) With the technique of _____, while the program renders one image on the screen, it can be building the next image in an off-screen buffer. Then, when it is time for that next image to be displayed, it can be placed on the screen smoothly.
   g) As an _____ image is displayed, it appears to fade in as the first batch of rows presents a rough outline of the picture and the subsequent batches of rows refine the displayed image until the entire image is complete.
   h) There are two key pieces to implementing a graphics double buffer—an _____ reference and a _____ reference. The first is where the actual pixels to be displayed are stored; the second is used to draw the pixels.
   i) Images can be registered with a _____ object to enable the program to determine when an image is loaded completely.
   j) Java provides two mechanisms for playing sounds in an applet—the **Applet**'s **play** method and the **play** method from the _____ interface.
   k) An _____ is an image that has hot areas that the user can click to accomplish a task such as loading a different Web page.

14.2   State whether each of the following is true or false. If false, explain why.
   a) Java currently supports two image formats. File names for each of these types end with **.jif** or **.gpg**, respectively.

b) Overriding the applet's **update** method to call **paint** without clearing the applet will significantly reduce animation flicker.

c) A sound will be garbage collected as soon as it is done playing.

d) The Java **param** tag specifies a parameter for an applet. The **param** tag lines appear between the starting **applet** tag and the ending **applet** tag. Each parameter has a **name** and a **value**.

Answers to Self-Review Exercises

14.1   a) **getImage**. b) **getDocumentBase**. c) **URL**. d) **drawImage**. e) **update**. f) graphics double buffering. g) interlaced. h) **Image**, **Graphics**. i) **MediaTracker**. j) **AudioClip**. k) image map.

14.2   a) False; should be **.gif** or **.jpg** b) True. c) False, the sound will be marked for garbage collection and will be garbage collected when the garbage collector is able to run, possibly not immediately. d) False. The **param** tag is HTML not Java.

Exercises

14.3   Describe how to make an animation "browser friendly."

14.4   Discuss the various aspects of flicker elimination in Java.

14.5   Explain the technique of graphics double buffering.

14.6   Describe the Java methods for playing and manipulating audio clips.

14.7   How can Java applets be customized with information from an HTML file?

14.8   How is a **MediaTracker** object used? What cautions should you keep in mind when using a **MediaTracker**?

14.9   Explain how image maps are used. List ten applications of image maps.

14.10   *(Animation)* Create a a general-purpose Java animation applet. Your applet should allow the user to specify the sequence of frames to be display, the speed at which the images are displayed, audios that should be played while the animation is running and so on.

14.11   *(Story Teller)* Record audio for a large number of nouns, verbs, articles, prepositions, etc. Then use random number generation to forms sentences and have your program speak the sentences.

14.12   *(Limericks)* Modify the limerick writing program you wrote in Exercise 8.10 to sing the limericks your program creates.

14.13   *(Screensaver)* Use animation of a series of your favorite images to create a screensaver program. Create various special effects that explode the images, spin the images, fade them in and out, move them off the edge of the screen, and the like

14.14   *(Randomly Erasing an Image)* Suppose an image is displayed in a rectangular screen area. One way to erase the image is simply to set every pixel to the same color immediately, but this is a dull visual effect. Write a Java applet that displays an image then erases it by using random number generation to select individual pixels to erase. After most of the image is erased, erase all of the remaining pixels at once. You can refer to individual pixels by having a line that starts and ends at the same point. You might try several variants of this problem. For example, you might display lines randomly or you might display shapes randomly to erase regions of the screen.

14.15   *(Random Inter-Image Transition)* Here is a nice visual effect. If you are displaying one image in a given area on the screen and you would like to transition to another image in the same screen area, Store the new screen image in an off-screen buffer and randomly copy pixels from the new image to the display area overlaying the previous pixels at those locations. When the vast majority of the pixels have been copied, copy the entire new image to the display area to be sure you are displaying the complete new image. To implement this program you may need to use the **PixelGrabber** and **MemoryImageSource** classes (see the Java API documentation for descriptions of these classes). You might try several variants of this problem. For example, you might select all the pixels in a randomly selected straight line or shape in the new image and overlay those pixels above the corresponding positions of the old image.

14.16   *(Background Audio)* Add background audio to one of your favorite applications by using the **loop** method of class **AudioClip** to play the sound in the background while you interact with your application in the normal way.

14.17   *(Project: Multimedia Aerobics)* Here a product idea that could help you make your fortune! Millions of people do aerobics exercises every day to help stay fit. Develop a Java aerobics applet that displays animated sequences of exercises with appropriate background music, sounds, instructions and words of encouragement. Internationalize your program by offering the instructions in several languages and by playing music appropriate for each region. Allow the users to customize their exercise programs to meet their particular exercise needs. Allow the users to customize their exercise programs for beginner, intermediate and advanced levels. Add other features as appropriate.

14.18   *(Project: Multimedia Authoring System)* Develop a general-purpose multimedia authoring system. Your program should allow the user to form multimedia presentations consisting of text, audios, images, animations and eventually, videos. Your program lets the user weave together a presentation consisting of any of these multimedia elements that are selected from a catalog your program displays. Provide controls to allow the user to customize the presentation dynamically as the presentation is delivered

14.19   *(Video Games)* Video games have become wildly popular. Develop your own Java video game program. Have a contest with your classmates to develop the best original video game.

14.20   *(Scrolling Marquee Sign)* Create a Java applet that scrolls dotted characters right-to-left (or left-to-right if that is appropriate for your language) across a Marquee-like display sign. As an option, display the text in a continuous loop so that after the text goes off the sign at one end it reappears at the other end.

14.21   *(Text Flasher)* Create a Java applet that repeatedly flashes text on the screen. Do this by interspersing the text with a plain background color image. Allow the user to control the "blink speed" and the background color or pattern.

14.22   *(Image Flasher)* Create a Java applet that repeatedly flashes an image on the screen. Do this by interspersing the image with a plain background color image.

14.23   *(Scrolling Image Marquee)* Create a Java applet that scrolls an image across a Marquee screen.

14.24   *(Physics Demo: Bouncing Ball)* Develop an animated applet that shows a bouncing ball. Give the ball a constant horizontal velocity. Allow the user to specify the coefficient of restitution, e.g., a coefficient of restitution of 75% means that after the ball bounces it returns to only 75% of its height before it was bounced. Your demo should take gravity into effect—this will cause the bouncing ball to trace a parabolic path. Track down a "boing" sound (like a spring bouncing) and play the sound every time the ball hits the ground.

14.25 *(Pendulum)* Develop an animated applet that shows a pendulum swinging. Allow the user to specifying a damping factor that gradually slows the pendulum to an eventual stop.

14.26 *(Project: Flight Simulator)* Develop your own flight simulator Java applet. This is a very challenging project. It is also an excellent candidate for a contest with your classmates.

14.27 *(Towers of Hanoi)* Write an animated version of the Towers of Hanoi problem we presented in Exercise 4.38. As each disk is lifted off a peg or slid onto a peg play a "whooshing" sound. As each disk lands on the pile play a "clunking" sound. Play some appropriate background music.

14.28 *(Tortoise and the Hare)* Develop a multimedia version of the Tortoise and Hare simulation we presented in Exercise 5.41. You might record an announcer's voice calling the race, "The contenders are at the starting line." "And they're off!" "The Hare pulls out in front." "The Tortoise is coming on strong." etc. As the race proceeds, play the appropriate recorded audios. Play sounds to simulate the animals' running, and don't forget the crowd cheering! Do an animation of the animals racing up the side of slippery mountain.

14.29 *(Bubble Help)* Use an image map to implement a "bubble help" facility. When the mouse cursor passes over a given image, display some appropriate text to assist your user who may not be sure what a particular image is supposed to designate. You might build in a bit of a delay so that the help messages are only displayed when the mouse cursor lingers over an image.

14.30 *(Digital Clock)* Implement an applet that displays a digital clock on the screen. You might add options to scale the clock; display day, month and year; issue an alarm; play certain audios at designated times and the like.

14.31 *(Analog Clock)* Create a Java applet that displays an analog clock with hour, minute and second hands that move appropriately as the time changes.

14.32 *(Dynamic Stock Portfolio Evaluator)* Create a Java applet that will read a file describing an investor's stock portfolio. For each stock the investor owns, the file contains the stock ticker symbol and the number of shares of that stock the investor owns. The applet then accesses some stock quotation service available over the Internet and filters out only those stock transactions for the stocks in the investor's portfolio. As the applet fetches new stock prices, it displays a speadsheet on the screen and dynamically updates the spreadsheet. The spreadsheet shows each stock symbol, the latest price of that stock, the number of shares and the latest total value of shares of that stock. The spreadsheet also totals the latest value of the investor's entire portfolio. An investor could run your Java applet in a small portion of his or her screen while proceeding with other work.

14.33 *(Dynamic Customized Newsletter)* After you complete Chapter 16 you will understand how to develop Internet-based Java applications that access the World Wide Web. Develop a "newspaper of the future" in which your user uses a graphical user interface to design a customized dynamic newspaper which meets that user's unique information needs. Then have your application harvest information from the World Wide Web at the designated intervals, possibly continuously. You'll be amazed to see how many popular publications offer computerized versions at no charge on the Web.

14.34 *(Dynamic Audio and Graphical Kaleidoscope)* Develop a kaleidoscope applet that displays reflected graphics to simulate the popular children's toy. Incorporate audio effects that "mirror" your applet's dynamically changing graphics.

14.35 *(Automatic Jigsaw Puzzle Generator)* Create a Java jigsaw puzzle generator and manipulator. Your user specifies an image. Your applet loads and displays the image. Then your applet breaks the image into randomly selected shapes. Then it shuffles the shapes. Your user then uses the mouse to move the puzzle pieces around until the puzzle is solved. Add appropriate audio sounds as the pieces are being shuffled around and snapped back into place. You might keep tabs on each piece and where it really belongs and then use audio effects to help the user get the pieces into correct positions.

14.36 *(Teaching Juggling)* If you've ever tried juggling, you know how difficult it is. It is especially difficult to learn from a book, because books cannot possibly display the dynamics of juggling. Develop a multimedia-based Java applet that will help frustrated juggling students (like the older author) learn how to juggle. In particular, your simulation should show the detail of juggling various numbers of items. You should probably read a good book on juggling before you begin this assignment.

14.37 *(Maze Generator and Walker)* Develop a multimedia-based maze generator and traverser applet based on the maze programs you wrote in Exercises 5.38, 5.39 and 5.40. Let the user customize the maze by specifying the number of rows and columns and by indicating the level of difficulty. Have an animated mouse walk the maze. Use audio to dramatize the movement of your mouse character.

14.38 *(Knight's Tour Walker)* Develop multimedia-based versions of the Knight's Tour programs you wrote in Exercises 5.22 and 5.23.

14.39 *(Pinball Machine)* Here's another contest problem. Develop a Java applet that simulates a pinball machine of your own design. Have a contest with your classmates to develop the best original multimedia pinball machine. Use every possible multimedia trick you can think of to add "pizzazz" to your pinball game. Try to keep the game mechanisms close to those of real pinball games.

14.40 *(Roulette)* Study the rules for the game of roulette and implement a multimedia-based version of the game. Create an animated spinning roulette wheel. Use audio to simulate the sound of the ball jumping the various compartments that correspond to each of the numbers. Use an audio to simulate the sound of the ball falling into its final slot. While the roulette wheel is spinning, allow multiple players to place their bets. When the ball lands in its final slot, you should update the bank accounts of each of the players with the appropriate wins or losses.

14.41 *(Craps)* Simulate the complete game of craps. Use a graphical representation of a craps table. Allow multiple players to place their bets. Use an animation of the player who is rolling the dice and show the animated dice rolling eventually to a stop. Use audio to simulate some of the chatter around the craps table. After each roll, the system should automatically update the bank accounts of each of the players depending on the bets they have made.

14.42 *(One-Armed Bandit)* Develop a multimedia simulation of a one-armed bandit. Have three spinning wheels. Place various fruits and symbols on each wheel. Use true random number generation to simulate the spinning of each wheel and the stopping of each wheel on a symbol.

14.43 *(Horse Race)* Create a Java simulation of a horse race. Have multiple contenders. Use audios for a race announcer. Play the appropriate audios to indicate the correct status of each of the contenders throughout the race. Use audios to announce the final results. You might try to simulate the kind of horse race games that are often played at carnivals. The players get turns at the mouse and have to perform some skill-oriented manipulation with the mouse to advance their horses.

14.44 *(Shuffleboard)* Develop a multimedia-based simulation of the game of shuffleboard. Use appropriate audio and visual effects.

14.45 *(Game of Pool)* Create a multimedia-based simulation of the game of pool. Each player takes turns using the mouse to position a pool stick and to hit the stick against the ball at the appropriate angle to try to get the pool balls to fall into the pockets. You applet should keep score.

14.46   *(Fashion Designer)* Develop a multimedia-based fashion design tool that will help a fashion designer design high-fashion clothing. Your tool should allow the designer to choose colors, shapes, decorative accents and the like to create clothing designs.

14.47   *(Artist)* Design a Java art applet that will give an artist a great variety of capabilities to draw, use images, use animations and the like to create a dynamic multimedia art display.

14.48   *(Fireworks Designer).* Create a Java applet that someone might use to create a fireworks display. Create a variety of fireworks demonstrations. Then orchestrate the firing of the fireworks for maximum effect.

14.49   *(Floor Planner)* Develop a Java applet that will help someone arrange his or her furniture in his or her home. Add features that help the person achieve the best possible arrangement.

14.50   *(Crossword)* Crossword puzzles are among the most popular pastimes. Develop a multimedia-based crossword puzzle program. Your program should enable the player to place and erase words easily. Tie your program to a large computerized dictionary. Your applet should be able to suggest words based on which letters have already been filled in. Provide other features that will make the crossword puzzle enthusiast's job easier.

14.51   *(15 Puzzle)* Write a multimedia-based Java applet that enables the user to play the game of 15. There is a 4-by-4 board for a total of 16 slots. One of the slots is empty. The other slots are occupied by 15 tiles numbered 1 through 15. Any tile next to the currently empty slot can be moved into the currently empty slot by clicking on the tile. Your applet should create the board with the tiles out of order. The goal is to arrange the tiles into sequential order row by row.

14.52   *(Synthesizer)* Develop a multimedia-based Java applet that simulates a synthesizer musical instrument. Your applet should display a keyboard along with a variety of sound options. The user plays music by pressing the appropriate keys in sequence and for the proper duration. The user can select from a variety of instrument sounds like piano, clarinet, drums, cymbals and the like.

14.53   *(Player Piano)* Create a Java applet that functions as a player piano. Your applet receives encoded sheet music in a file indicating what notes or combinations of notes are to be played for what durations. You can prerecord audios for each of the 88 notes on the piano.

14.54   *(Sheet Music Generator/Player)* Write a Java applet that displays sheet music for the files you created in the previous exercise.

14.55   *(Music Teacher)* Develop a Java applet that will help a student learn to play the piano. Your applet should display the keyboard and use a variety of visual and audio techniques.

14.56   *(Arithmetic Tutor)* Develop a multimedia version of the Computer-Assisted Instruction (CAI) systems you developed in Exercises 4.31, 4.32 and 4.33.

14.57   *(Karaoke)* Create a Karaoke system that plays the music for a song and displays the words for your user to sing at the appropriate time.

14.58   *(Calling Attention to an Image)* If you want to emphasize an image, you might place a row of simulated light bulbs around your image. You can let the light bulbs flash in unison or you can let them fire on and off in sequence one after the other.

14.59   *(Physics Demo: Kinetics)* If you have taken physics, implement a Java applet that will demo concepts like energy, inertia, momentum, velocity, acceleration, friction, coefficient of restitution, gravity and others. Create visual effects and use audios where appropriate for emphasis and realism.

14.60   *(On-Line Product Catalog)* Companies are rapidly realizing the potential for doing business on the Web. Develop an on-line multimedia catalog from which your customers may select products to be shipped. After reading Chapter 16, you will be able to handle the networking aspects of this problem. If you have an actual company, you should read the latest articles on secure transmission of credit card IDs over the Internet.

14.61   *(Reaction Time/Reaction Precision Tester)* Create a Java applet that moves a randomly created shape around the screen. The user moves the mouse to catch and click on the shape. The shape's speed and size can be varied. Keep statistics on how much time the user typically takes to catch a shape of a given size. The user will probably have more difficulty catching faster moving smaller shapes.

14.62   *(Image Zooming)* Create a Java applet that enables you to zoom in on, or away from, an image.

14.63   *(Calendar/Tickler File)* Create a general purpose calendar and "tickler" file. Use audio and images. For example, the applet should sing "Happy Birthday" to you when you use it on your birthday. Have the applet display images and play audios associated with important events. Have the applet remind you in advance of important events. It would be nice, for example, to have the applet give you a week's warning so you can pick up an appropriate greeting card for that special person.

14.64   *(Rotating Images)* Create a Java applet that lets you rotate an image through some number of degrees (out of a maximum of 360 degrees). As an option, the applet should let you specify that you want to spin the image continuously. The applet should let you adjust the spin speed dynamically.

14.65   *(Coloring Black and White Photographs and Images)* Create a Java applet that lets you paint a black and white photograph with color. Provide a color palette for selecting colors. Your applet should let you apply different colors to different regions of the image.

14.66   *(Project: Automated Teller Machine) [Note: This project will require that you use advanced Java techniques from Chapters 14, 15 and 16. We suggest that you do as much as you can now with the Java graphics, GUI, multithreading and multimedia technologies you studied in Chapters 9 through 14. Then incorporate file processing after you complete Chapter 15 and incorporate client/ server networking after you complete Chapter 16. This is an excellent group project.]* One of the authors had the privilege of teaching at the division of one of the largest banks in the United States that builds the hardware and software for the automated teller machines that the bank deploys worldwide. During this teaching engagement the author got a behind-the-scenes peek at the "automated teller machine of the future." Develop the framework of a Java *application* that implements an automated teller machine and simulates its interaction with a bank's accounts maintained by another computer. The first version of your applet should simulate automated teller machines pretty much as they operate today. Then let your creative juices flow and try to design your own version of the "automated teller machine of the future." Use graphics, animation, sound and any other capabilities of Java, the World Wide Web and the Internet that you wish to employ.

14.67   *(Multimedia-Based Simpletron Simulator)* Modify the Simpletron simulator that you developed in the exercises in the previous chapters to include multimedia features. Add computer-like sounds to indicate that the Simpletron is executing instructions. Add a breaking glass sound when a fatal error occurs. Use flashing lights to indicate which cells of memory and/or which registers are currently being manipulated. Use other multimedia techniques as appropriate to make your Simpletron simulator more valuable as an educational tool to its users.

15

Files and Streams

Objectives

- To be able to create, read, write and update files.
- To understand the Java streams class hierarchy.
- To be able to use the **FileInputStream** and **FileOutputStream** classes.
- To be able to use the **DataInputStream** and **DataOutputStream** classes.
- To become familiar with sequential-access and random-access file processing.
- To build a transaction-processing program with random-access files.
- To be able to use the **File** class.

I can only assume that a "Do Not File" document is filed in a "Do Not File" file.
Senator Frank Church
Senate Intelligence Subcommittee Hearing, 1975

Consciousness ... does not appear to itself chopped up in bits. ... A "river" or a "stream" are the metaphors by which it is most naturally described.
William James

I read part of it all the way through.
Samuel Goldwyn

It is quite a three-pipe problem.
Sir Athur Conan Doyle

Outline

15.1 Introduction

Storage of data in variables and arrays is temporary—the data is lost when a local variable "goes out of scope" or when the program terminates, for example. *Files* are used for long-term retention of large amounts of data, even after the program that created the data terminates. Data maintained in files is often called *persistent data*. Computers store files on *secondary storage devices* such as magnetic disks, optical disks and magnetic tapes. In this chapter, we explain how data files are created, updated, and processed by Java programs. We consider both "sequential-access" files and "random-access" files and indicate the kinds of applications for which each is best suited.

File processing is one of the most important capabilities a language must have to support commercial applications that typically process massive amounts of persistent data. In this chapter we discuss Java's powerful and abundant file-processing and stream input/output features.

Software Engineering Observation 15.1

It would be dangerous to enable applets arriving from anywhere on the World Wide Web to be able to read and write files on the client system. Most web browsers prevent applets from performing file processing on the client system. Therefore, file-processing programs are generally implemented as Java applications.

15.2 The Data Hierarchy

Ultimately, all data items processed by a computer are reduced to combinations of zeros and ones. This occurs because it is simple and economical to build electronic devices that can assume two stable states—one state represents **0** and the other state represents **1**. It is remarkable that the impressive functions performed by computers involve only the most fundamental manipulations of **0**s and **1**s.

The smallest data item in a computer can assume the value **0** or the value **1**. Such a data item is called a *bit* (short for "*b*inary dig*it*"—a digit that can assume one of two values). Computer circuitry performs various simple bit manipulations such as examining the value of a bit, setting the value of a bit, and reversing a bit (from **1** to **0** or from **0** to **1**).

It is cumbersome for programmers to work with data in the low-level form of bits. Instead, programmers prefer to work with data in forms such as *decimal digits* (i.e., 0, 1, 2, 3, 4, 5, 6, 7, 8, and 9), *letters* (i.e., A through Z, and a through z), and *special symbols* (i.e., $, @, %, &, *, (,), -, +, ", :, ?, /, and many others). Digits, letters, and special symbols are referred to as *characters*. The set of all characters used to write programs and represent data items on a particular computer is called that computer's *character set*. Since computers can process only **1**s and **0**s, every character in a computer's character set is represented as a pattern of **1**s and **0**s (characters in Java are *Unicode* characters composed of 2 *bytes*). Bytes are most commonly composed of eight bits. Programmers create programs and data items with characters; computers manipulate and process these characters as patterns of bits.

Just as characters are composed of bits, *fields* are composed of characters. A field is a group of characters that conveys meaning. For example, a field consisting solely of upper-case and lowercase letters can be used to represent a person's name.

Data items processed by computers form a *data hierarchy* in which data items become larger and more complex in structure as we progress from bits, to characters (bytes), to fields, and so on.

A *record* (i.e., a **class** in Java) is composed of several fields (called instance variables in Java). In a payroll system, for example, a record for a particular employee might consist of the following fields:

1. Employee identification number

2. Name

3. Address

4. Hourly salary rate

5. Number of exemptions claimed

6. Year-to-date earnings

7. Amount of federal taxes withheld, etc.

Thus, a record is a group of related fields. In the preceding example, each of the fields belongs to the same employee. Of course, a particular company may have many employees, and will have a payroll record for each employee. A *file* is a group of related records. A company's payroll file normally contains one record for each employee. Thus, a payroll file for a small company might contain only 22 records, whereas a payroll file for a large company might contain 100,000 records. It is not unusual for a company to have many files, each containing millions of characters of information. Figure 15.1 illustrates the *data hierarchy*.

To facilitate the retrieval of specific records from a file, at least one field in each record is chosen as a *record key*. A record key identifies a record as belonging to a particular person or entity that is unique from all other records in the file. In the payroll record described previously, the employee identification number would normally be chosen as the record key.

There are many ways of organizing records in a file. The most common type of organization is called a *sequential file* in which records are typically stored in order by the record key field. In a payroll file, records are usually placed in order by employee identification number. The first employee record in the file contains the lowest employee identification number, and subsequent records contain increasingly higher employee identification numbers.

Most businesses utilize many different files to store data. For example, companies may have payroll files, accounts receivable files (listing money due from clients), accounts payable files (listing money due to suppliers), inventory files (listing facts about all the items handled by the business), and many other types of files. A group of related files is sometimes called a *database*. A collection of programs designed to create and manage databases is called a *database management system* (DBMS).

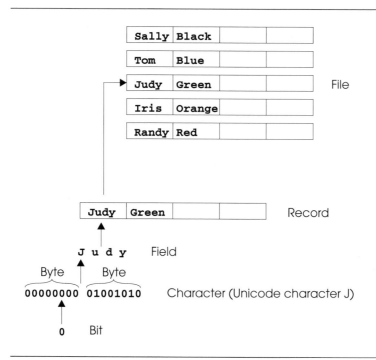

Fig. 15.1 The data hierarchy.

15.3 Files and Streams

Java views each file simply as a sequential stream of bytes (Fig. 15.2). Each file ends either with an *end-of-file marker* or at a specific byte number recorded in a system-maintained administrative data structure. When a file is *opened*, an object is created and a stream is associated with the object. Three stream objects are created for us automatically when we begin executing a Java application or applet—**System.in**, **System.out**, and **System.err**. The streams associated with these objects provide communication channels between a program and a particular file or device. For example, the **System.in** object (*standard input stream object*) enables a program to input bytes from the keyboard, the **System.out** object (*standard output stream object*) enables a program to output data to the screen, and the **System.err** object (*standard error stream object*) enables a program to output error messages to the screen.

To perform file processing in Java, the package **java.io** must be imported. This package includes the definitions for the stream classes such as **FileInputStream** (for input from a file) and **FileOutputStream** (for output to a file). Files are opened by creating objects of these stream classes that are derived from (i.e., inherit the functionality of) classes **InputStream** and **OutputStream**, respectively. Thus, the methods of these stream classes can all be applied to file streams as well. To perform input and output of primitive data types, objects of class **DataInputStream** and **DataOutputStream** will be used together with the file stream classes. The inheritance relationships of the Java I/O classes are summarized in Fig. 15.3. The following discussion overviews the capabilities of each of the classes in Fig. 15.3.

Java offers many classes for performing input/output. In this section we give a brief overview of each and explain how they relate to one another. In the rest of the chapter, we put several key stream classes to work as we implement a variety of file-processing programs that create, manipulate and destroy sequential-access files and random-access files. We also include a detailed example on the **File** class which is useful for obtaining information about files and directories. In Chapter 16, Networking," we use stream classes extensively to implement networking applications.

InputStream (a subclass of **Object**) and *OutputStream* (a subclass of **Object**) are abstract classes that define methods for performing input and output respectively; their derived classes override these methods.

File input/output is done with *FileInputStream* (a subclass of **InputStream**) and *FileOutputStream* (a subclass of **OutputStream**). We use these classes extensively in the examples in this chapter.

Fig. 15.2 Java's view of a file of *n* bytes.

```
Java Streams Class Hierarchy
```

```
Object
    File
    FileDescriptor
    StreamTokenizer
    InputStream
        ByteArrayInputStream
        SequenceInputStream
        StringBufferInputStream
        PipedInputStream
        FileInputStream
        FilterInputStream
            DataInputStream
            BufferedInputStream
            PushBackInputStream
            LineNumberInputStream
    OutputStream
        ByteArrayOutputStream
        PipedOutputStream
        FileOutputStream
        FilterOutputStream
            DataOutputStream
            BufferedOutputStream
            PrintStream
    RandomAccessFile
```

Fig. 15.3 Class hierarchy of the **java.io** package.

Pipes are synchronized communication channels between threads. A pipe is established between two threads. One thread sends data to another by writing to a *PipedOutputStream* (a subclass of **OutputStream**). The target thread reads information from the pipe via a *PipedInputStream* (a subclass of **InputStream**).

A *PrintStream* (a subclass of **FilterOutputStream**) is used for performing output to the screen (or the "standard output" as defined by your local operating system). Actually, we have been using **PrintStream** output throughout the text to this point; **System.out** is a **PrintStream** (as is **System.err**).

A **FilterInputStream** *filters* an **InputStream** and a **FilterOutStream** *filters* an **OutputStream**; filtering simply means that the filter stream provides additional functionality such as buffering, monitoring line numbers or aggregating data bytes into meaningful primitive-data-type units.

Reading data as raw bytes is fast but crude. Usually programs want to read data as aggregates of bytes that form an **int**, a **float**, a **double**, and so on. To accomplish this we use a **DataInputStream** (a subclass of class **FilterInputStream**).

The **DataInput** interface is implemented by class **DataInputStream** and class **RandomAccessFile** (discussed below) that each need to read primitive data types from a stream. **DataInputStream**s enable a program to read binary data from an **InputStream**. We would typically chain a **DataInputStream** to a **FileInputStream**; we will explain chaining shortly. The **DataInput** interface includes methods **read** (for byte arrays), **readBoolean**, **readByte**, **readChar**, **readDouble**, **readFloat**, **readFully** (for byte arrays) **readInt**, **readLine**, **readLong**, **readShort**, **readUnsignedByte**, **readUnsignedShort**, **readUTF** (for Unicode format strings) and **skipBytes**.

The **DataOutput** interface is implemented by class **DataOutputStream** (a subclass of class **FilterOutputStream**) and class **RandomAccessFile** that each need to write primitive data types to an **OutputStream**. **DataOutputStream**s enable a program to write binary data to an **OutputStream**. We would typically chain a **DataOutputStream** to a **FileOutputStream**. The **DataOutput** interface includes methods **flush**, **size**, **write** (for a byte), **write** (for a byte array), **writeBoolean**, **writeByte**, **writeBytes**, **writeChar**, **writeChars** (for Unicode Strings), **writeDouble**, **writeFloat**, **writeInt**, **writeLong**, **writeShort** and **writeUTF**.

Buffering is an I/O-performance-enhancement technique. With a ***BufferedOutputStream*** (a subclass of class **FilterOutputStream**) each output statement does not necessarily result in an actual physical transfer of data to the output device. Rather, each output operation is directed to a region in memory called a *buffer* that is large enough to hold the data of many output operations. Then actual output to the output device is performed in one large *physical output operation* each time the buffer fills. The output operations directed to the output buffer in memory are often called *logical output operations*.

Performance Tip 15.1

Because typical physical output operations are extremely slow compared to typical processor speeds, buffering outputs normally yields significant performance improvements over unbuffered outputs.

With a ***BufferedInputStream*** (a subclass of class **FilterInputStream**) many "logical" chunks of data from a file are read as one large *physical input operation* into a memory buffer. As a program requests each new chunk of data, it is taken from the buffer (this is sometimes referred to as a *logical input operation*). When the buffer becomes empty, the next actual physical input operation from the input device is performed to read in the next group of "logical" chunks of data. Thus, the number of actual physical input operations is small compared with the number of read requests issued by the program.·

Performance Tip 15.2

Because typical input operations are extremely slow compared to typical processor speeds, buffering inputs normally yields significant performance improvements over unbuffered inputs.

With a **BufferedOutputStream** a partially filled buffer can be forced out to the device at any time with an explicit **flush** as follows:

```
testBufferedOutputStream.flush();
```

A *PushBackInputStream* (a subclass of class **FilterInputStream**) is used for more exotic applications than most users will need. Essentially, the application reading a **PushBackInputStream** reads bytes from the stream and forms aggregates consisting of several bytes. Sometimes, to determine that one aggregate is complete, the application must read the first character the "past the end" of the first aggregate. Once the program has determined that the current aggregate is complete, the extra character is "pushed back" onto the stream. **PushBackInputStream**s are used by programs like compilers that *parse* their inputs, i.e., break them into meaningful units (such as the keywords, identifiers and operators that the Java compiler must recognize).

A *StreamTokenizer* (a subclass of **Object**) is helpful for breaking up a stream of text from an input text file into meaningful pieces called *tokens*. The behavior of the **StreamTokenizer** class is similar to that of the **StringTokenizer** class we discussed in Chapter 8.

A *RandomAccessFile* (a subclass of **Object**) is useful for *direct-access applications* such as *transaction-processing applications* like airline-reservations systems and point-of-sale systems. With a *sequential-access file* each successive input/output request reads or writes the next consecutive set of data in the file. With a *random-access file*, each successive input/output request may be directed to any part of the file, perhaps widely separated from the part of the file referenced in the previous request. Direct-access applications provide rapid access to specific data items in large files; such applications are often used while people are waiting for answers—these answers must be made available quickly or the people may become impatient and "take their business elsewhere."

Java stream I/O includes capabilities for inputting from byte arrays in memory and outputting to byte arrays in memory. A **ByteArrayInputStream** (a subclass of abstract class **InputStream**) performs its inputs from a byte array in memory. A **ByteArray-OutputStream** (a subclass of abstract class **OutputStream**) outputs to a byte array in memory. An application of byte-array I/O is data validation. A program can input an entire line at a time from the input stream into a byte array. Then a validation routine can scrutinize the contents of the byte array and correct the data, if necessary. The program can now proceed to input from the byte array, knowing that the input data is in the proper format. Outputting to a byte array is a nice way to take advantage of the powerful output formatting capabilities of Java streams. Data can be prepared in a character array to mimic the edited screen format. That array could then be written to a disk file to preserve the screen image.

A **StringBufferInputStream** (a subclass of abstract class **InputStream**) inputs from a **StringBuffer** object.

A **SequenceInputStream** (a subclass of abstract class **InputStream**) enables several **InputStream**s to be concatenated so that the program sees the group as one continuous **InputStream**. As the end of each input stream is reached, the stream is closed and the next stream in the sequence is opened.

A **LineNumberInputStream** (a subclass of class **FilterInputStream**) always knows what line number of the file is being read.

Objects of the **FileDescriptor** class are ordinarily not manipulated by most Java users, so we omit a discussion of class **FileDescriptor**.

Class **File** enables programs to obtain information about a file or directory. We discuss class **File** extensively in Section 15.12

15.4 Creating a Sequential-Access File

Java imposes no structure on a file. Thus, notions like "record" do not exist in Java files. Therefore, the programmer must structure files to meet the requirements of applications. In the following example, we see how the programmer can impose a simple record structure on a file. First we present the program, then we analyze it in detail.

Figure 15.4 creates a simple sequential-access file that might be used in an accounts receivable system to help manage the money owed by a company's credit clients. For each client, the program obtains an account number, the client's first name, the client's last name, and the client's balance (i.e., the amount the client still owes the company for goods and services received in the past). The data obtained for each client constitutes a record for that client. The account number is used as the record key in this application; that is, the file will be created and maintained in account number order. This program assumes the user enters the records in account number order. In a comprehensive accounts receivable system, a sorting capability would be provided so the user could enter the records in any order—the records would then be sorted and written to the file.

```
1   // Fig. 15.4: CreateSeqFile.java
2   // This program uses TextFields to get information from the
3   // user at the keyboard and writes the information to a
4   // sequential file.
5   import java.io.*;
6   import java.awt.*;
7
8   public class CreateSeqFile extends Frame {
9
10      // Application window components
11      TextField account,    // where user enters account number
12              fName,        // where user enters first name
13              lName,        // where user enters last name
14              balance;      // where user enters balance
15      Button enter,         // send record to file
16            done;           // quit program
17      Label acctLabel,      // account label
18          fNameLabel,       // first name label
19          lNameLabel,       // last name label
20          balLabel;         // balance label
21
22      // Application other pieces
23      DataOutputStream output;  // enables output of data to file
24
```

Fig. 15.4 Creating a sequential file (part 1 of 4).

```
25       // Constructor -- intialize the Frame
26       public CreateSeqFile()
27       {
28          super( "Create Client File" );
29       }
30
31       public void addRecord()
32       {
33          int acct = 0;
34          Double d;
35
36          acct = (new Integer( account.getText() )).intValue();
37
38          // output the values to the file
39          try {
40             if ( acct > 0 ) {
41                output.writeInt( acct );
42                output.writeUTF( fName.getText() );
43                output.writeUTF( lName.getText() );
44                d = new Double ( balance.getText() );
45                output.writeDouble( d.doubleValue() );
46             }
47          }
48          catch ( IOException e ) {
49             System.err.println( "Error during write to file\n" +
50                                 e.toString() );
51             System.exit( 1 );
52          }
53
54          // clear the TextFields
55          account.setText( "" );
56          fName.setText( "" );
57          lName.setText( "" );
58          balance.setText( "" );
59       }
60
61       // Setup the window for the application with
62       // TextFields and Buttons
63       public void setup()
64       {
65          resize( 300, 150 );
66          setLayout( new GridLayout( 5, 2 ) );
67
68          // create the components of the Frame
69          account = new TextField( 20 );
70          acctLabel = new Label( "Account Number" );
71          fName = new TextField( 20 );
72          fNameLabel = new Label( "First Name" );
73          lName = new TextField( 20 );
```

Fig. 15.4 Creating a sequential file (part 2 of 4).

```
74          lNameLabel = new Label( "Last Name" );
75          balance = new TextField( 20 );
76          balLabel = new Label( "Balance" );
77          enter = new Button( "Enter" );
78          done = new Button( "Done" );
79
80          // add the components to the Frame
81          add( acctLabel );    // add label
82          add( account );      // add TextField
83          add( fNameLabel );   // add label
84          add( fName );        // add TextField
85          add( lNameLabel );   // add label
86          add( lName );        // add TextField
87          add( balLabel );     // add label
88          add( balance );      // add TextField
89          add( enter );        // add button
90          add( done );         // add button
91
92          show();              // show the Frame
93
94          // Open the file
95          try {
96             output = new DataOutputStream(
97                      new FileOutputStream( "client.dat" ) );
98          }
99          catch ( IOException e ) {
100            System.err.println( "File not opened properly\n" +
101                                e.toString() );
102            System.exit( 1 );
103         }
104      }
105
106      // Cleanup--add the current information (if valid),
107      // flush remaining output to file and close file.
108      public void cleanup()
109      {
110         if ( !account.getText().equals("") )
111            addRecord();
112
113         try {
114            output.flush();
115            output.close();
116         }
117         catch ( IOException e ) {
118            System.err.println( "File not closed properly\n" +
119                                e.toString() );
120            System.exit( 1 );
121         }
122      }
123
```

Fig. 15.4 Creating a sequential file (part 3 of 4).

```
124     // Process the event when the user closes the window
125     // or presses the "Done" button
126     public boolean handleEvent( Event event )
127     {
128         // User closed the window or clicked the done button--
129         // be sure info is written to file and exit program
130         if ( event.id == Event.WINDOW_DESTROY ||
131              event.target == done ) {
132             cleanup();   // write data, close file, etc.
133
134             hide();
135             dispose();   // release system resources
136             System.exit( 0 );
137             return true;
138         }
139
140         // User clicked Enter button to send record to file
141         if ( event.target instanceof Button ) {
142             if ( event.arg.equals( "Enter" ) ) {
143                 addRecord();
144                 return true;
145             }
146         }
147
148         return super.handleEvent( event );
149     }
150
151     // Instantiate a CreateSeqFile object and start the program
152     public static void main( String args[] )
153     {
154         CreateSeqFile accounts = new CreateSeqFile();
155
156         accounts.setup();
157     }
158 }
```

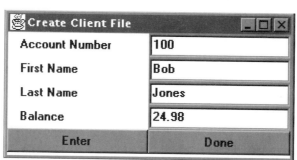

Fig. 15.4 Creating a sequential file (part 4 of 4).

Now let us examine this program. As stated previously, files are opened by creating objects of stream classes **FileInputStream** and **FileOutputStream**. In Fig. 15.4, the file is to be opened for output, so a **FileOutputStream** object is created. One argument is passed to the object's constructor—the *filename*. Existing files opened for output are *truncated*—all data in the file is discarded. If the specified file does not yet exist, then a file is created with that filename.

In this program, we output data in using a **DataOutputStream** that is connected to a **FileOutputStream** via a technique called *chaining of stream objects*. For example, when the **DataOutputStream** object **output** is created, its constructor is supplied a **FileOutputStream** object as an argument as shown in lines 96 and 97 of Fig. 15.4:

```
output = new DataOutputStream(
            new FileOutputStream( "client.dat" ) );
```

The preceding statement creates a **DataOutputStream** object named **output** associated with the file **client.dat**. The argument **"client.dat"** is passed to the **FileOutputStream** constructor which opens the file. This establishes a "line of communication" with the file.

Common Programming Error 15.1

Opening an existing file for output when, in fact, the user wants to preserve the file; the contents of the file are discarded without warning.

Common Programming Error 15.2

*Using an incorrect **FileOutputStream** object to refer to a file.*

Common Programming Error 15.3

Not opening a file before attempting to reference it in a program.

When creating a **FileOutputStream** object and attempting to open a file, the program tests whether the open operation was successful. If the operation fails, an **IOException** is generated that must be caught by the program as shown in the following lines (95 through 104) from Fig. 15.4:

```
try {
   output = new DataOutputStream(
               new FileOutputStream( "client.dat" ) );
}
catch ( IOException e ) {
   System.err.println( "File not opened properly\n" +
                          e.toString() );
   System.exit( 1 );
}
```

If an **IOException** is generated because the open attempt was unsuccessful, the error message "**File not opened properly**" is output followed by the error message in the exception object, and the **exit** method of the **System** class is called to end the program. The argument to **exit** is returned to the environment from which the program was invoked. Argument **0** indicates that the program terminated normally; any other value indicates that the program terminated due to an error. The value returned by **exit** is used by the calling environment (most likely the operating system) to respond appropriately to the error. Some possible reasons for **IOException**s while opening files are attempting to open a nonexistent file for reading, attempting to open a file for reading without permission, and opening a file for writing when no disk space is available.

If the file is opened successfully, the program is ready to process data. The following window appears to enable the user to enter data:

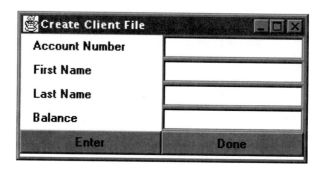

The program assumes data is input correctly and in the proper record number order. When a record is complete, the user clicks the **Enter** button to write the record to the file. This invokes the **addRecord** method of our **CreateSeqFile** class to perform the write operation. In this method, each field of the record is written separately with calls to the **writeInt** (write an integer value), **writeUTF** (write a string) and **writeDouble** (write a double value) methods of class **DataOutputStream**. Lines 41 through 46 of the **addRecord** method input each set of data from the user and write the data immediately to the file. The user clicks the **Done** button to inform the program that there is no more data to be processed. The data may be retrieved by a program designed to read the file (see Section 15.5).

Once the user clicks the "Done" button, the program will terminate. However, before terminating, the program determines if there is a record to write to disk, flushes the output stream to be sure that all the data is sent to the file and closes the output stream. A **FileOutputStream** object can be closed explicitly by the programmer using the method **close** as follows:

```
output.close();
```

or the file will be closed implicitly when Java garbage collects the object.

Performance Tip 15.3

Always release resources explicitly and at the earliest possible moment at which it is determined that the resource is no longer needed. This makes the resource immediately available to be reused by your program or by another program, thus improving resource utilization

When using chained stream objects, the outermost object (the **DataOutputStream** in this example) should be used to close the file.

Performance Tip 15.4

Explicitly close each file as soon as it is known that the program will not reference the file again. This can reduce resource usage in a program that will continue executing long after it no longer needs to be referencing a particular file. This practice also improves program clarity.

In the sample execution for the program of Fig. 15.4, we entered information for five accounts (see Fig. 15.5), and then signaled that data entry was complete by clicking the "Done" button. The program does not show how the data records actually appear in the file. To verify that the file has been created successfully, in the next section we create a program to read the file.

15.5 Reading Data from a Sequential-Access File

Data are stored in files so that they may be retrieved for processing when needed. The previous section demonstrated how to create a file for sequential access. In this section, we discuss how to read data sequentially from a file.

The program of Fig. 15.6 reads records from the file **"client.dat"** created by the program of Fig. 15.4 and prints the contents of the records. Files are opened for input by creating an **FileInputStream** object. The name of the file to open is passed as an argument to the **FileInputStream** constructor. In Fig. 15.4, we wrote data to the file **"client.dat"** using a **DataOutputStream** object. Data must be read from the file in the same format in which it was written to the file. Therefore, we use a **DataInput-Stream** chained to a **FileInputStream** in this program to read the data as shown in lines 66 and 67 of Fig. 15.6:

```
input = new DataInputStream(
        new FileInputStream( "client.dat" ) );
```

The preceding statement creates a **DataInputStream** object named **input** associated with the file **client.dat**. The argument **"client.dat"** is passed to the **FileInputStream** constructor which opens the file. This establishes a "line of communication" with the file.

Sample Data			
100	Bob	Jones	24.98
200	Steve	Doe	345.67
300	Pam	White	0.00
400	Sam	Stone	-42.16
500	Sue	Rich	224.62

Fig. 15.5 Sample data for the program of Fig. 15.4.

```
1    // Fig. 15.6: ReadSeqFile.java
2    // This program reads a file sequentially and displays each
3    // record in text fields.
4    import java.io.*;
5    import java.awt.*;
6
7    public class ReadSeqFile extends Frame {
8
9       // Application window components
10      TextField acct,        // displays account number
11               fName,        // displays first name
12               lName,        // displays last name
13               bal;          // displays balance
14      Button next,           // display next record
15             done;           // quit program
16      Label acctLabel,       // account label
17            fNameLabel,      // first name label
18            lNameLabel,      // last name label
19            balLabel;        // balance label
20
21      // Application other pieces
22      DataInputStream input;  // file from which data is read
23      boolean moreRecords = true;
24
25      // Constructor -- intialize the Frame
26      public ReadSeqFile()
27      {
28         super( "Read Client File" );
29      }
30
31      public void readRecord()
32      {
33         int account;
34         String first, last;
35         double balance;
36
37         // input the values from the file
38         try {
39            account = input.readInt();
40            first = input.readUTF();
41            last = input.readUTF();
42            balance = input.readDouble();
43
44            acct.setText( String.valueOf( account ) );
45            fName.setText( String.valueOf( first ) );
46            lName.setText( String.valueOf( last ) );
47            bal.setText( String.valueOf( balance ) );
48         }
```

Fig. 15.6 Reading a sequential file (part 1 of 4).

```
49          catch ( EOFException eof ) {
50              moreRecords = false;
51          }
52          catch ( IOException e ) {
53              System.err.println( "Error during read from file\n" +
54                                  e.toString() );
55              System.exit( 1 );
56          }
57      }
58
59      // Setup the window for the application with TextFields
60      // and Buttons
61      public void setup()
62      {
63
64          // Open the file
65          try {
66              input = new DataInputStream(
67                      new FileInputStream( "client.dat" ) );
68          }
69          catch ( IOException e ) {
70              System.err.println( "File not opened properly\n" +
71                                  e.toString() );
72              System.exit( 1 );
73          }
74
75          resize( 300, 150 );
76          setLayout( new GridLayout( 5, 2 ) );
77
78          // create the components of the Frame
79          acct = new TextField( 20 );
80          acctLabel = new Label( "Account Number" );
81          fName = new TextField( 20 );
82          fNameLabel = new Label( "First Name" );
83          lName = new TextField( 20 );
84          lNameLabel = new Label( "Last Name" );
85          bal = new TextField( 20 );
86          balLabel = new Label( "Balance" );
87          next = new Button( "Next" );
88          done = new Button( "Done" );
89
90          // add the components to the Frame
91          add( acctLabel );      // add label
92          add( acct );           // add TextField
93          add( fNameLabel );     // add label
94          add( fName );          // add TextField
95          add( lNameLabel );     // add label
96          add( lName );          // add TextField
```

Fig. 15.6 Reading a sequential file (part 2 of 4).

```
 97          add( balLabel );      // add label
 98          add( bal );           // add TextField
 99          add( next );          // add button
100          add( done );          // add button
101
102          show();               // show the Frame
103       }
104
105       // Cleanup--close the input file.
106       public void cleanup()
107       {
108          try {
109             input.close();
110          }
111          catch ( IOException e ) {
112             System.err.println( "File not closed properly\n" +
113                                   e.toString() );
114             System.exit( 1 );
115          }
116       }
117
118       public boolean action( Event event, Object o )
119       {
120          if ( event.target instanceof Button )
121             if ( event.arg.equals( "Next" ) )
122                readRecord();
123
124          return true;
125       }
126
127       // Process the event when the user closes the window
128       // or presses the "Done" button
129       public boolean handleEvent( Event event )
130       {
131          // End of file reached, user closed window, or
132          // user clicked the Done button.
133          if ( moreRecords == false ||
134               event.id == Event.WINDOW_DESTROY ||
135               event.target == done ) {
136             cleanup();   // close file
137
138             hide();
139             dispose();   // release system resources
140             System.exit( 0 );
141             return true;
142          }
143
144          // May need to process event still
145          return super.handleEvent( event );
146       }
147
```

Fig. 15.6 Reading a sequential file (part 3 of 4).

```
148      // Instantiate a ReadSeqFile object and start the program
149      public static void main( String args[] )
150      {
151          ReadSeqFile accounts = new ReadSeqFile();
152
153          accounts.setup();
154      }
155  }
```

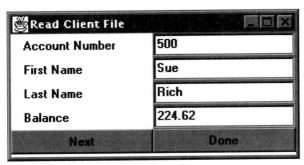

Fig. 15.6 Reading a sequential file (part 4 of 4).

When creating a **FileInputStream** object and attempting to open a file, the program tests whether the open operation was successful. If the operation fails, an **IOException** is generated that must be caught by the program as shown in the following lines (65 through 73) from Fig. 15.6:

```
try {
    input = new DataInputStream(
                new FileInputStream( "client.dat" ) );
}
catch ( IOException e ) {
    System.err.println( "File not opened properly\n" +
                        e.toString() );
    System.exit( 1 );
}
```

If an **IOException** is generated because the open attempt was unsuccessful, the error message "**File not opened properly**" is output followed by the error message in the exception object, and the **exit** method of the **System** class is called to end the program. If the file is opened successfully, the program is ready to process data.

The program will read a record each time the user clicks the "Next" button. This action causes the **readRecord** method of the **ReadSeqFile** class to be invoked. The lines

```
account = input.readInt();
first = input.readUTF();
last = input.readUTF();
balance = input.readDouble();
```

read one record of information from the file. If the end-of-file marker is reached while reading, an **EndOfFileException** is thrown which causes the **moreRecords** flag to be set to **false**. If the user attempts to read another record by clicking the "Next" button, the program terminates.

After the preceding code is executed the first time, **account** has the value **100**, **first** has the value **"Bob"**, **last** has the value **"Jones"**, and **balance** has the value **24.98**. Each time the preceding code is executed, another record is read from the file into the variables **account**, **first**, **last**, and **balance**. The records are displayed in text fields by the following lines:

```
acct.setText( String.valueOf( account ) );
fName.setText( String.valueOf( first ) );
lName.setText( String.valueOf( last ) );
bal.setText( String.valueOf( balance ) );
```

If the user clicks the "Done" button (or the **moreRecords** flag is **false** and the user clicks "Next"), the file is closed by invoking the **cleanUp** method which calls the close method on the **DataInputStream** object **input**. The program terminates with a call to the **exit** method of the **System** class.

To retrieve data sequentially from a file, programs normally start reading from the beginning of the file, and read all the data consecutively until the desired data are found. It may be necessary to process the file sequentially several times (from the beginning of the file) during the execution of a program. Currently in Java, there is no method for repositioning the *file-position pointer* (the byte number of the next byte in the file to be read or written) in a **FileInputStream** or **FileOutputStream** for the next input or output operation. Therefore, a **FileInputStream** object can only be repositioned to the beginning of a file by closing the file and reopening the file.

Performance Tip 15.5

The process of closing a file and reopening a file for the purpose of positioning the file-position pointer back to the beginning of a file is a time consuming task for the computer. If this is done frequently, it may slow the performance of your program.

The program of Fig. 15.7 enables a credit manager to display the account information for those customers with zero balances (i.e., customers who do not owe the company any money), credit balances (i.e., customers to whom the company owes money), and debit balances (i.e., customers who owe the company money for goods and services received in the past).

```
1  // Fig. 15.7: CreditInquiry.java
2  // This program reads a file sequentially and displays the
3  // contents in a text area based on the type of account the
4  // user requests (credit balance, debit balance or zero balance.
5  import java.io.*;
6  import java.awt.*;
7
```

Fig. 15.7 Credit inquiry program (part 1 of 4).

```
 8   public class CreditInquiry extends Frame {
 9       // Application window components
10       TextArea recordDisplay;      // where records are displayed
11       Button done;                 // quit program
12       Button credit,               // account type to display
13              debit,                // account type to display
14              zero;                 // account type to display
15       Panel buttonPanel;           // panel for buttons
16       String accountType;          // Account type to display
17
18       // Application other pieces
19       File file;
20       DataInputStream input;  // file from which data is read
21
22       // Constructor -- intialize the Frame
23       public CreditInquiry()
24       {
25           super( "Credit Inquiry Program" );
26       }
27
28       public void readRecords()
29       {
30           int acct;
31           String first, last;
32           double bal;
33
34           // input the values from the file
35           try {
36               recordDisplay.setText( accountType + ":\n" );
37
38               while ( true ) {
39                   acct = input.readInt();
40                   first = input.readUTF();
41                   last = input.readUTF();
42                   bal = input.readDouble();
43
44                   if ( shouldDisplay( bal ) )
45                       recordDisplay.appendText( acct +
46                           "\t" + first + "\t" + last +
47                           "\t" + bal + "\n" );
48               }
49           }
50           catch ( EOFException eof ) {
51               // do nothing on EOF exception
52           }
53           catch ( IOException e ) {
54               System.err.println( "Error during read from file\n" +
55                                   e.toString() );
56               System.exit( 1 );
57           }
58       }
```

Fig. 15.7 Credit inquiry program (part 2 of 4).

```
59
60      public boolean shouldDisplay( double balance )
61      {
62         if ( accountType.equals( "Credit balances" ) &&
63              balance < 0 )
64           return true;
65
66         if ( accountType.equals( "Debit balances" ) &&
67              balance > 0 )
68           return true;
69
70         if ( accountType.equals( "Zero balances" ) &&
71              balance == 0 )
72           return true;
73
74         return false;
75      }
76
77      // Setup the window for the application with TextArea
78      // and Buttons
79      public void setup()
80      {
81         resize( 400, 150 );
82
83         // create the components of the Frame
84         recordDisplay = new TextArea( 4, 40 );
85         buttonPanel = new Panel();
86         done = new Button( "Done" );
87         credit = new Button( "Credit balances" );
88         debit = new Button( "Debit balances" );
89         zero = new Button( "Zero balances" );
90         buttonPanel.add( credit );
91         buttonPanel.add( debit );
92         buttonPanel.add( zero );
93         buttonPanel.add( done );
94
95         // add the components to the Frame
96         add( "Center", recordDisplay );     // add TextArea
97         add( "South", buttonPanel );        // add Button
98
99         show();                             // show the Frame
100     }
101
102     // Process the event when the user closes the window
103     // or presses the "Done" button
104     public boolean handleEvent( Event event )
105     {
106        // User closed the window or clicked the Done button
107        // Clean up window and exit program
```

Fig. 15.7 Credit inquiry program (part 3 of 4).

```
108          if ( event.id == Event.WINDOW_DESTROY ||
109              event.target == done ) {
110           hide();
111           dispose();  // release system resources
112           System.exit( 0 );
113           return true;
114          }
115
116          // User selected type of account to display
117          if ( event.target instanceof Button ) {
118           accountType = event.arg.toString();
119
120           // Open the file
121           try {
122              input = new DataInputStream(
123                        new FileInputStream( "client.dat" ) );
124           }
125           catch ( IOException e ) {
126              System.err.println( e.toString() );
127              System.exit( 1 );
128           }
129
130           readRecords();
131
132           // Close the file
133           try {
134              input.close();
135           }
136           catch ( IOException e ) {
137              System.err.println( "File not closed properly\n" +
138                                 e.toString() );
139              System.exit( 1 );
140           }
141          }
142
143       return super.handleEvent( event );
144    }
145
146    // Instantiate a CreditInquiry object and start the program
147    public static void main( String args[] )
148    {
149       CreditInquiry accounts = new CreditInquiry();
150
151       accounts.setup();
152       accounts.show();
153    }
154 }
```

Fig. 15.7 Credit inquiry program (part 4 of 4).

Fig. 15.8 Sample outputs of the credit inquiry program of Fig. 15.7.

The program displays buttons that allow the credit manager to obtain credit information. The "Credit balances" button produces a list of accounts with credit balances. The "Debit balances" button produces a list of accounts with debit balances. The "Zero balances" button produces a list of accounts with zero balances. The "Done" button terminates program execution. Sample outputs are shown in Fig. 15.8.

The records of a particular type are displayed in the **TextArea** called **recordDisplay**. The record information is collected by reading through the entire file and determining if each record satisfies the criteria for the account type selected by the credit manager by clicking one of the buttons. Clicking a button other than the "Done" button causes the **handleEvent** method to set **accountType** to the appropriate type, open the **client.dat** file and invoke the **readRecords** method. The **readRecords** method loops through the file and reads every record. The **shouldDisplay** method is invoked to determine if the current record satisfies the account type requested. If the method returns **true**, the account information for the current record is appended to the **StringBuffer** called **records**. When the end-of-file marker is reached, the **setText** method is invoked for **recordDisplay** with the result of **records.toString()** as the string to be displayed.

15.6 Updating Sequential-Access Files

Data that is formatted and written to a sequential-access file as shown in Section 15.4 cannot be modified without reading and writing all the data in the file. For example, if the name "**White**" needed to be changed to "**Worthington**", the old name cannot simply be overwritten.

Such updating can be done, but it is awkward. For example, to make the preceding name change, the records before **White** in a sequential-access file could be copied to a new file, the updated record would then be written to the new file, and the records after **White** would be copied to the new file. This requires processing every record in the file to update one record. If many records are being updated in one pass of the file, then this technique can be acceptable.

15.7 Random-Access Files

So far, we have seen how to create sequential-access files and to search through them to locate particular information. Sequential-access files are inappropriate for so-called "*instant-access*" *applications* in which a particular record of information must be located immediately. Some popular instant access applications are airline reservation systems, banking systems, point-of-sale systems, automated teller machines and other kinds of *transaction-processing systems* that require rapid access to specific data. The bank at which you have your account may have hundreds of thousands or even millions of other customers, yet when you use an automated teller machine, your account is checked for sufficient funds in seconds. This kind of instant access is possible with *random-access files*. Individual records of a random-access file can be accessed directly (and quickly) without searching through other records.

As we have said, Java does not impose structure on a file. So the application that wants to use random-access files must literally create them. A variety of techniques can be used to create random-access files. Perhaps the simplest is to require that all records in a file are of the same fixed length.

Using fixed-length records makes it easy for a program to calculate (as a function of the record size and the record key) the exact location of any record relative to the beginning of the file. We will soon see how this facilitates immediate access to specific records, even in large files.

Figure 15.9 illustrates Java's view of a random-access file composed of fixed-length records (each record is 100 bytes long). A random-access file is like a railroad train with many cars—some empty and some with contents.

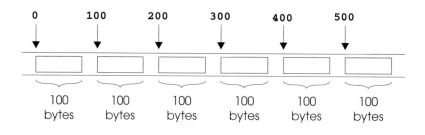

Fig. 15.9 Java's view of a random-access file.

Data can be inserted in a random-access file without destroying other data in the file. Data stored previously also can be updated or deleted without rewriting the entire file. In the following sections we explain how to create a random-access file, enter data, read the data both sequentially and randomly, update the data, and delete data no longer needed.

15.8 Creating a Random-Access File

RandomAccessFile objects have all the capabilities of **DataInputStream** and **DataOutputStream** objects discussed in the preceding sections. When a **RandomAccessFile** stream is associated with a file, data is read or written beginning at the location in the file specified by the file-position pointer and all data is read or written as primitive data types. When writing an **int** value, 4 bytes are output to the file. When reading a **double** value, 8 bytes are input from the file. The size of the various data types is guaranteed because Java has fixed sizes for all primitive data types regardless of the computing platform.

Random-access file-processing programs rarely write a single field to a file. Normally, they write one object at a time, as we show in the following examples.

Consider the following problem statement:

Create a transaction-processing program capable of storing up to 100 fixed-length records for a company that can have up to 100 customers. Each record should consist of an account number that will be used as the record key, a last name, a first name, and a balance. The program should be able to update an account, insert a new account, and delete an account.

The next several sections introduce the techniques necessary to create this credit processing program. Figure 15.10 contains the **Record** class that is used by the next four programs for both reading records from and writing records to the **credit.dat** file.

The **Record** class contains four instance variables—**account**, **lastName**, **firstName** and **balance**—that define the contents of a record of information and three methods to manipulate records. The **write** method outputs one record of information from the **RandomAccessFile** object passed in as an argument to the method. It uses the **writeInt** method to output the account number, the **write** method to output the last name and first name as arrays of bytes (15 bytes each) and the **writeDouble** method to output the balance.

```java
1   // Fig. 15.10: Record.java
2   // Record class for the RandomAccessFile programs.
3   import java.io.*;
4
5   public class Record {
6      int account;
7      String lastName;
8      String firstName;
9      double balance;
10
11     // Read a record from the specified RandomAccessFile
12     public void read( RandomAccessFile file ) throws IOException
13     {
14        account = file.readInt();
15        byte b1[] = new byte[ 15 ];
16        file.readFully( b1 );
17        firstName = new String( b1, 0 );
18        byte b2[] = new byte[ 15 ];
19        file.readFully( b2 );
20        lastName = new String( b2, 0 );
21        balance = file.readDouble();
22     }
23
24     // Write a record to the specified RandomAccessFile
25     public void write( RandomAccessFile file ) throws IOException
26     {
27        file.writeInt( account );
28
29        byte b1[] = new byte[ 15 ];
30
31        if ( firstName != null )
32           firstName.getBytes( 0, firstName.length(), b1, 0 );
33
34        file.write( b1 );
35
36        byte b2[] = new byte[ 15 ];
37
38        if ( lastName != null )
39           lastName.getBytes( 0, lastName.length(), b2, 0 );
40
41        file.write( b2 );
42        file.writeDouble( balance );
43     }
44
45     // NOTE: This method contains a hard coded value for the
46     // size of a record of information.
47     public int size() { return 42; }
48  }
```

Fig. 15.10 **Record** class used in the random-access file programs.

The **read** method inputs one record of information from the **RandomAccessFile** object passed in as an argument to the method. The **RandomAccessFile readInt** and **readDouble** methods are used to input the account number and balance, respectively. The **readFully** method is used to read the last name and first name into arrays of 15 bytes each. These arrays are used as the initial values for the **String** objects assigned to the **firstName** and **lastName** objects, respectively. The **size** method returns the size of the record in bytes. This method is defined to explicitly return 42 which is the number of bytes occupied on disk for each record (4 bytes for the **int** account, 15 bytes for the first name converted to an array of bytes, 15 bytes for the last name converted to an array of bytes, and 8 bytes for the **double** balance).

Figure 15.11 illustrates opening a random-access file and writing data to the disk. This program initializes all 100 records of the file **"credit.dat"** with empty objects using the **write** method of our **Record** class. Each empty object contains **0** for the account number, the null string (represented by empty quotation marks) for the last name, the null string for the first name, and **0.0** for the balance. The file is initialized to create the proper amount of empty space in which the account data will be stored and to enable us to determine in subsequent programs if each record is empty or contains data.

In Fig. 15.11, the lines

```
try {
    file = new RandomAccessFile( "credit.dat", "rw" );
}
catch( IOException e ) {
    System.err.println( "File not opened properly\n" +
                        e.toString() );
    System.exit( 1 );
}
```

attempt to open the file **credit.dat** for use in this program. Two arguments are passed to the **RandomAccessFile** constructor—the file name and the *file open mode*. The file open mode for a **RandomAccessFile** is either **"r"** to open the file for reading or **"rw"** to open the file for reading and writing. If an **IOException** occurs during the open process, the program terminates. If the file is opened properly, the program uses a for structure to execute the following line 100 times:

```
blank.write( file );
```

This statement causes the object **blank** to be written to the **credit.dat** file associated with **RandomAccessFile** object **file**.

15.9 Writing Data Randomly to a Random-Access File

The program of Fig. 15.12 writes data to the file **"credit.dat"** which is opened with the **"rw"** mode for reading and writing. It uses the **RandomAccessFile** method **seek** to determine the exact location in the file at which a record of information is stored. Method **seek** sets the file-position pointer to a specific position in the file relative to the beginning of the file, and the **Record** class **write** method outputs the data.

```java
1   // Fig. 15.11: CreateRandFile.java
2   // This program creates a random access file sequentially
3   // by writing 100 empty records to disk.
4   import java.io.*;
5
6   public class CreateRandFile {
7       private Record blank;
8       RandomAccessFile file;
9
10      public CreateRandFile()
11      {
12          blank = new Record();
13
14          try {
15              file = new RandomAccessFile( "credit.dat", "rw" );
16          }
17          catch( IOException e ) {
18              System.err.println( "File not opened properly\n" +
19                                  e.toString() );
20              System.exit( 1 );
21          }
22      }
23
24      public void create()
25      {
26          try {
27              for ( int i = 0; i < 100; i++ )
28                  blank.write( file );
29          }
30          catch ( IOException e ) {
31              System.err.println( e.toString() );
32          }
33      }
34
35      public static void main( String args[] )
36      {
37          CreateRandFile accounts = new CreateRandFile();
38
39          accounts.create();
40      }
41  }
```

Fig. 15.11 Creating a random-access file sequentially.

```
1    // Fig. 15.12: WriteRandFile.java
2    // This program uses TextFields to get information from the
3    // user at the keyboard and writes the information to a
4    // random access file.
5    import java.io.*;
6    import java.awt.*;
7
8    public class WriteRandFile extends Frame {
9
10       // Application window components
11       TextField acct,        // where user enters account number
12                  fName,       // where user enters first name
13                  lName,       // where user enters last name
14                  bal;         // where user enters balance
15       Button enter,          // send record to file
16              done;           // quit program
17       Label acctLabel,       // account label
18             fNameLabel,      // first name label
19             lNameLabel,      // last name label
20             balLabel;        // balance label
21
22       // Application other pieces
23       RandomAccessFile output;  // file for output
24       Record data;
25
26       // Constructor -- intialize the Frame
27       public WriteRandFile()
28       {
29          super( "Write to random access file" );
30
31          data = new Record();
32
33          // Open the file
34          try {
35             output = new RandomAccessFile( "credit.dat", "rw" );
36          }
37          catch ( IOException e ) {
38             System.err.println( e.toString() );
39             System.exit( 1 );
40          }
41
42          setup();
43       }
44
45       public void addRecord()
46       {
47          int acctNum = 0;
48          Double d;
49
50          acctNum = ( new Integer( acct.getText() ) ).intValue();
```

Fig. 15.12 Writing data randomly to a random-access file (part 1 of 4).

```
51
52              // output the values to the file
53              try {
54                 if ( acctNum > 0 && acctNum <= 100 ) {
55                    data.account = acctNum;
56                    data.firstName = fName.getText();
57                    data.lastName = lName.getText();
58                    d = new Double ( bal.getText() );
59                    data.balance = d.doubleValue();
60                    output.seek( (long) ( acctNum-1 ) * data.size() );
61                    data.write( output );
62
63                    // clear the TextFields
64                    acct.setText( "" );
65                    fName.setText( "" );
66                    lName.setText( "" );
67                    bal.setText( "" );
68                 }
69                 else {
70                    acct.setText( "Enter valid account (1-100)" );
71                    acct.selectAll();
72                 }
73              }
74              catch ( IOException e ) {
75                 System.err.println( "Error during write to file\n" +
76                                     e.toString() );
77                 System.exit( 1 );
78              }
79           }
80
81           // Setup the window for the application with TextFields
82           // and Buttons
83           public void setup()
84           {
85              resize( 300, 150 );
86              setLayout( new GridLayout( 5, 2 ) );
87
88              // create the components of the Frame
89              acct = new TextField( 20 );
90              acctLabel = new Label( "Account Number" );
91              fName = new TextField( 20 );
92              fNameLabel = new Label( "First Name" );
93              lName = new TextField( 20 );
94              lNameLabel = new Label( "Last Name" );
95              bal = new TextField( 20 );
96              balLabel = new Label( "Balance" );
97              enter = new Button( "Enter" );
98              done = new Button( "Done" );
99
100             // add the components to the Frame
101             add( acctLabel );    // add label
```

Fig. 15.12 Writing data randomly to a random-access file (part 2 of 4).

```
102        add( acct );          // add TextField
103        add( fNameLabel );    // add label
104        add( fName );         // add TextField
105        add( lNameLabel );    // add label
106        add( lName );         // add TextField
107        add( balLabel );      // add label
108        add( bal );           // add TextField
109        add( enter );         // add button
110        add( done );          // add button
111
112        show();               // show the Frame
113     }
114
115     // Cleanup--add the current information (if valid),
116     // flush remaining output to file and close file.
117     public void cleanup()
118     {
119        if ( !acct.getText().equals("") )
120           addRecord();
121
122        try {
123           output.close();
124        }
125        catch ( IOException e ) {
126           System.err.println( "File not closed properly\n" +
127                               e.toString() );
128           System.exit( 1 );
129        }
130     }
131
132     // Process the event when the user closes the window
133     // or presses the "Done" button
134     public boolean handleEvent( Event event )
135     {
136        // User closed the window or clicked Done button
137        if ( event.id == Event.WINDOW_DESTROY ||
138             event.target == done ) {
139           cleanup();  // write data, close file, etc.
140           hide();
141           dispose();  // release system resources
142           System.exit( 0 );
143           return true;
144        }
145
146        // User clicked Enter button to send record to file
147        if ( event.target instanceof Button ) {
148           if ( event.arg.equals( "Enter" ) ) {
149              addRecord();
150              return true;
151           }
152        }
```

Fig. 15.12 Writing data randomly to a random-access file (part 3 of 4).

```
153
154         return super.handleEvent( event );
155      }
156
157      // Instantiate a CreateSeqFile object and start the program
158      public static void main( String args[] )
159      {
160         WriteRandFile accounts = new WriteRandFile();
161
162
```

Fig. 15.12 Writing data randomly to a random-access file (part 4 of 4).

The user enters values for the account number, first name, last name and balance. When the user clicks the **Enter** button, method **addRecord** of the **WriteRandFile** class is invoked to retrieve the data from the text fields, store the data in the **Record** class object called **data**, and call the **write** method of the **Record** class to output the data.

The statement

```
output.seek( (long) ( acctNum - 1 ) * data.size();
```

positions the file-position pointer for object **output** to the byte location calculated by **(long) (acctNum - 1) * data.size()**. Since the account number is between 1 and 100, 1 is subtracted from the account number when calculating the byte location of the record. Thus, for record 1, the file-position pointer is set to byte 0 of the file. The calculation result is cast to **long** because the **seek** method requires a **long** value as an argument.

When the user clicks the **Done** button, the program calls method **cleanUp** of class **WriteRandFile** to add the last record to the file (if there is one waiting to be output), closes the file, and terminates the program. This program assumes the user does not enter duplicate account numbers and that the user enters appropriate data in each text field.

15.10 Reading Data Sequentially from a Random-Access File

In the previous sections, we created a random-access file and wrote data to that file. In this section, we develop a program (Fig. 15.13) that opens a **RandomAccessFile** for reading with the **"r"** file open mode, reads through the file sequentially and displays only those records containing data. This program produces an additional benefit. See if you can determine what it is; we will reveal it at the end of this section.

Good Programming Practice 15.1

Open a file with the "r" file open mode for input if the contents of the file should not be modified. This prevents unintentional modification of the file's contents. This is an example of the principle of least privilege.

```
1   // Fig. 15.13: ReadRandFile.java
2   // This program reads a random access file sequentially and
3   // displays the contents one record at a time in text fields.
4   import java.io.*;
5   import java.awt.*;
6
7   public class ReadRandFile extends Frame {
8
9      // Application window components
10     TextField acct,        // displays account number
11               fName,       // displays first name
12               lName,       // displays last name
13               bal;         // displays balance
14     Button next,           // display next record
15            done;           // quit program
16     Label acctLabel,       // account label
17           fNameLabel,      // first name label
18           lNameLabel,      // last name label
19           balLabel;        // balance label
20
21     // Application other pieces
22     RandomAccessFile input;  // file from which data is read
23     Record data;
24     boolean moreRecords = true;
25
26     // Constructor -- intialize the Frame
27     public ReadRandFile()
28     {
29        super( "Read Client File" );
30
31        // Open the file
32        try {
33           input = new RandomAccessFile( "credit.dat", "r" );
34        }
35        catch ( IOException e ) {
36           System.err.println( e.toString() );
37           System.exit( 1 );
38        }
39
40        data = new Record();
41
42        setup();
43     }
```

Fig. 15.13 Reading a random-access file sequentially (part 1 of 4).

```
44
45      // Read a record and display it on the screen
46      public void readRecord()
47      {
48         // read a record and display
49         try {
50            do {
51               data.read( input );
52            } while ( input.getFilePointer() < input.length() &&
53                      data.account == 0 );
54         }
55         catch( IOException e ) {
56            moreRecords = false;
57         }
58
59         if ( data.account != 0 ) {
60            acct.setText( String.valueOf( data.account ) );
61            fName.setText( data.firstName );
62            lName.setText( data.lastName );
63            bal.setText( String.valueOf( data.balance ) );
64         }
65      }
66
67      // Setup the window for the application with TextFields
68      // and Buttons
69      public void setup()
70      {
71         resize( 300, 150 );
72         setLayout( new GridLayout( 5, 2 ) );
73
74         // create the components of the Frame
75         acct = new TextField( 20 );
76         acctLabel = new Label( "Account Number" );
77         fName = new TextField( 20 );
78         fNameLabel = new Label( "First Name" );
79         lName = new TextField( 20 );
80         lNameLabel = new Label( "Last Name" );
81         bal = new TextField( 20 );
82         balLabel = new Label( "Balance" );
83         next = new Button( "Next" );
84         done = new Button( "Done" );
85
86         // add the components to the Frame
87         add( acctLabel );    // add label
88         add( acct );         // add TextField
89         add( fNameLabel );   // add label
90         add( fName );        // add TextField
91         add( lNameLabel );   // add label
92         add( lName );        // add TextField
93         add( balLabel );     // add label
94         add( bal );          // add TextField
```

Fig. 15.13 Reading a random-access file sequentially (part 2 of 4).

```
95          add( next );          // add button
96          add( done );          // add button
97
98          show();               // show the Frame
99       }
100
101      // Cleanup--close the file.
102      public void cleanup()
103      {
104         try {
105            input.close();
106         }
107         catch ( IOException e ) {
108            System.err.println( e.toString() );
109            System.exit( 1 );
110         }
111      }
112
113      // Process the Next button
114      public boolean action( Event event, Object o )
115      {
116         // Determine if the next record should be displayed
117         if ( event.target instanceof Button )
118            if ( event.arg.equals( "Next" ) )
119               readRecord();
120
121         return true;
122      }
123
124      // Process the event when the user closes the window
125      // or presses the done button
126      public boolean handleEvent( Event event )
127      {
128         // User closed the window or clicked Done
129         if ( moreRecords == false ||
130              event.id == Event.WINDOW_DESTROY ||
131              event.target == done ) {
132            cleanup();  // close file.
133
134            hide();
135            dispose();  // release system resources
136            System.exit( 0 );
137            return true;
138         }
139
140         return super.handleEvent( event );
141      }
142
```

Fig. 15.13 Reading a random-access file sequentially (part 3 of 4).

```
143     // Instantiate a ReadSeqFile object and start the program
144     public static void main( String args[] )
145     {
146         ReadRandFile accounts = new ReadRandFile();
147     }
148 }
```

Fig. 15.13 Reading a random-access file sequentially (part 4 of 4).

When the user clicks the "Next" button to read the next record in the file, the **readRecord** method of class **ReadRandFile** is invoked. This method loops and invokes the **Record** class **read** method to input the data into **Record** class object **data readRecord** loops and reads from the **"credit.dat"** file until it reads a record containing information. It checks each record to see if it contains data by determining if the account number is 0 (its initial value for all records). If the record contains a valid account number (i.e., a non-zero value), the loop terminates and the data is displayed in text fields. When the user clicks the "Done" button, the **cleanUp** method is invoked to close the file and the program terminates. If the end-of-file marker is encountered while reading, the moreRecords flag is set to false and the program terminates when the user clicks the "Next" button again.

What about that additional benefit we promised? If you examine the output window as the program executes, you will notice that the records are listed in sorted order (by account number)! This is a simple consequence of the way we stored these records in the file using direct access techniques. Compared to the bubble sort we have seen (Chapter 5), sorting with direct access techniques is blazingly fast. The speed is achieved by making the file large enough to hold every possible record that might be created. This, of course, means that the file could be sparsely occupied most of the time, a waste of storage. So here is yet another example of the space-time trade-off: By using large amounts of space, we are able to develop a much faster sorting algorithm.

15.11 Example: A Transaction-Processing Program

We now present a substantial transaction-processing program (Fig. 15.14) using a random-access file to achieve "instant" access processing. The program maintains a bank's account information. The program updates existing accounts, adds new accounts, deletes accounts, and stores a formatted listing of all the current accounts in a text file for printing. We assume that the program of Fig. 15.11 has been executed to create the file **credit.dat** and that the program of Fig. 15.12 has been executed to insert the initial data.

The program has four buttons to select various tasks as shown here:

The "Update Record" button displays the **Update Record** dialog box to update an account. The method will only update an existing record, so the user must first enter an account number and press Enter at the keyboard. The **action** method of the **UpdateRec** class checks that the account number is valid, then reads the record into object **data** with **Record** method **read**. Next, **data.account** is compared to zero to determine if the record contains information. If **data.account** is zero, a message is displayed in the account number text field stating that the record does not exist. If there is a valid record, the information is displayed in text fields as follows:

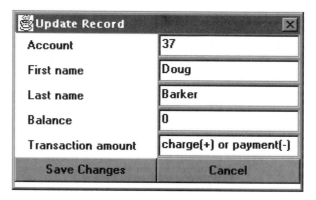

Note that the "Transaction amount" text field contains the string "**charge(+) or payment(-)**." The user enters the transaction amount by selecting this text, typing the transaction amount (a positive value for a charge or a negative value for a payment) and presses the Enter key on the keyboard. The action method takes the transaction amount, adds it to the current balance and displays the new balance in the "Balance" text field. The user can click "Save Changes" to output the updated record to the file or "Cancel" to ignore the transaction and return to the main application window. The result of a transaction being entered is shown below.

The "New Record" button displays the **New Record** dialog box to add a new account to the file. The user first types an account number in the Account text field and presses Enter on the keyboard. The **action** method of the **NewRec** class checks the account number to determine if it is valid. If so, it reads the record into the object **data**. If the account number is for an existing account, a message is displayed in the "Account number" text field stating that the account exists. Otherwise, the user is prompted in the "First name," "Last name" and "Balance" text fields to enter data. This is accomplished by highlighting the prompt in each field and typing over the prompt. When the data is complete, the user clicks the "Save Changes" button to output the data to the file. A typical output for the "New Record" option is:

The "Delete Record" button displays the **Delete Record** dialog box to delete a record from the file. The user enters the account number in the "Account" text field. To get immediate feedback as to whether the account exists, the user can press the Enter key which causes the **action** method of the **DeleteRec** class to read the record into the object **data** and check for valid information. Only an existing record may be deleted, so if the specified account is empty, an error message is issued. The user clicks the "Delete Record" button to reinitialize the record on disk, thus erasing the data. A typical output for the "Delete Record" option is:

The "Done" button terminates program execution. The program is shown in Fig. 15.14. The file **"credit.dat"** is opened by creating a **RandomAccessFile** object with the **"rw"** file open mode.

```java
// Fig. 15_14: TransactionProcessor.java
// Transaction processing program using RandomAccessFiles.

// This program reads a random access file sequentially,
// updates data already written to the file, creates new
// data to be placed in the file, and deletes data
// already in the file.
import java.awt.*;
import java.io.*;

public class TransactionProcessor extends Frame {
   // Application window components
   Button updateButton, // update record
          newButton,    // add new record
          deleteButton, // delete record
          done;         // quit program
   UpdateRec update;    // dialog box for record update
   NewRec    newRec;    // dialog box for new record
   DeleteRec deleteRec; // dialog box for delete record

   // Application other pieces
   RandomAccessFile file;  // file from which data is read
   Record data;

   // Constructor -- intialize the Frame
   public TransactionProcessor()
   {
      super( "Transaction Processor" );

      // Open the file
      try {
         file = new RandomAccessFile( "credit.dat", "rw" );
      }
      catch ( IOException e ) {
         System.err.println( e.toString() );
         System.exit( 1 );
      }
```

Fig. 15.14 Transaction-processing program (part 1 of 9).

```
38
39          data = new Record();
40
41          setup();
42       }
43
44       // Setup the window for the application with TextFields
45       // and Buttons
46       public void setup()
47       {
48          resize( 300, 80 );
49          setLayout( new GridLayout( 2, 2 ) );
50
51          updateButton = new Button( "Update Record" );
52          newButton = new Button( "New Record" );
53          deleteButton = new Button( "Delete Record" );
54          done = new Button( "Done" );
55
56          add( updateButton );
57          add( newButton );
58          add( deleteButton );
59          add( done );
60
61          show();                    // show the Frame
62
63          // Create dialog boxes
64          update = new UpdateRec( file );
65          newRec = new NewRec( file );
66          deleteRec = new DeleteRec( file );
67       }
68
69       // Process actions
70       public boolean action( Event event, Object o )
71       {
72          if ( event.target instanceof Button ) {
73             String current = (String) event.arg;
74
75             if ( current.equals( "Update Record" ) )
76                update.show();
77             else if ( current.equals( "New Record" ) )
78                newRec.show();
79             else if ( current.equals( "Delete Record" ) )
80                deleteRec.show();
81          }
82
83          return true;
84       }
85
```

Fig. 15.14 Transaction-processing program (part 2 of 9).

```
86        // Process the event when the user closes the window
87        // or presses the "Done" button
88        public boolean handleEvent( Event event )
89        {
90           // User closed the window or clicked Done
91           if ( event.id == Event.WINDOW_DESTROY ||
92                event.target == done ) {
93              cleanup();
94              hide();
95              dispose();  // release system resources
96              System.exit( 0 );
97              return true;
98           }
99
100          // May need to process other events in action
101          return super.handleEvent( event );
102       }
103
104       public void cleanup()
105       {
106          try {
107             file.close();
108          }
109          catch ( IOException e ) {
110             System.err.println( e.toString() );
111             System.exit( 1 );
112          }
113       }
114
115       public static void main( String args[] )
116       {
117          TransactionProcessor teller = new TransactionProcessor();
118       }
119 }
120
121 class UpdateRec extends Dialog {
122    RandomAccessFile file;
123    TextField acct,
124              fName,
125              lName,
126              bal,
127              transaction;
128    Label acctLabel,
129          fNameLabel,
130          lNameLabel,
131          balLabel,
132          transLabel;
133    Button cancel,
134           save;
135    Record data;
136    int account;
```

Fig. 15.14 Transaction-processing program (part 3 of 9).

```
137
138     public UpdateRec( RandomAccessFile f )
139     {
140         super( new Frame(), "Update Record", true );
141         resize( 300, 180 );
142         setLayout( new GridLayout( 6, 2 ) );
143         file = f;
144
145         acct = new TextField( 10 );
146         fName = new TextField( 10 );
147         lName = new TextField( 10 );
148         bal = new TextField( 10 );
149         transaction = new TextField( 10 );
150         acctLabel = new Label( "Account" );
151         fNameLabel = new Label( "First name" );
152         lNameLabel = new Label( "Last name" );
153         balLabel = new Label( "Balance" );
154         transLabel = new Label( "Transaction amount" );
155         save = new Button( "Save Changes" );
156         cancel = new Button( "Cancel" );
157
158         add( acctLabel);
159         add( acct );
160         add( fNameLabel );
161         add( fName );
162         add( lNameLabel );
163         add( lName );
164         add( balLabel );
165         add( bal );
166         add( transLabel );
167         add( transaction );
168         add( save );
169         add( cancel );
170
171         data = new Record();
172     }
173
174     public boolean action( Event event, Object o )
175     {
176         if ( event.target == acct )  {
177             account = Integer.parseInt( acct.getText() );
178
179             if ( account < 1 || account > 100 ) {
180                 acct.setText( "Invalid account" );
181                 return true;
182             }
183
184             try {
185                 file.seek( ( account - 1 ) * data.size() );
186                 data.read( file );
187             }
```

Fig. 15.14 Transaction-processing program (part 4 of 9).

```
188          catch ( IOException e ) {
189             acct.setText( "Error reading file" );
190          }
191
192          if ( data.account != 0 ) {
193             acct.setText( String.valueOf( data.account ) );
194             fName.setText( data.firstName );
195             lName.setText( data.lastName );
196             bal.setText( String.valueOf( data.balance ) );
197             transaction.setText( "charge(+) or payment(-)" );
198          }
199          else
200             acct.setText( String.valueOf( account ) +
201                             " does not exist" );
202       }
203       else if ( event.target == save ) {
204          try {
205             file.seek( ( account - 1 ) * data.size() );
206             data.write( file );
207          }
208          catch ( IOException e ) {
209             acct.setText( "Error writing file" );
210             return true;
211          }
212
213          hide();
214          clear();
215       }
216       else if ( event.target == cancel ) {
217          hide();
218          clear();
219       }
220       else if ( event.target == transaction ) {
221          Double trans =
222                    Double.valueOf( transaction.getText() );
223          data.balance += trans.doubleValue();
224          bal.setText( String.valueOf( data.balance ) );
225       }
226
227       return true;
228    }
229
230    private void clear()
231    {
232       acct.setText( "" );
233       fName.setText( "" );
234       lName.setText( "" );
235       bal.setText( "" );
236       transaction.setText( "" );
237    }
238 }
```

Fig. 15.14 Transaction-processing program (part 5 of 9).

```
239
240  class NewRec extends Dialog {
241     RandomAccessFile file;
242     TextField acct,
243                fName,
244                lName,
245                bal;
246     Label acctLabel,
247           fNameLabel,
248           lNameLabel,
249           balLabel;
250     Button cancel,
251            save;
252
253     Record data;
254     int account;
255
256     public NewRec( RandomAccessFile f )
257     {
258        super( new Frame(), "New Record", true );
259        resize( 300, 150 );
260        setLayout( new GridLayout( 5, 2 ) );
261        file = f;
262
263        acctLabel = new Label( "Account" );
264        acct = new TextField( 10 );
265        fName = new TextField( 10 );
266        lName = new TextField( 10 );
267        bal = new TextField( 10 );
268        fNameLabel = new Label( "First name" );
269        lNameLabel = new Label( "Last name" );
270        balLabel = new Label( "Balance" );
271        save = new Button( "Save Changes" );
272        cancel = new Button( "Cancel" );
273
274        add( acctLabel);
275        add( acct );
276        add( fNameLabel );
277        add( fName );
278        add( lNameLabel );
279        add( lName );
280        add( balLabel );
281        add( bal );
282        add( save );
283        add( cancel );
284
285        data = new Record();
286     }
287
```

Fig. 15.14 Transaction-processing program (part 6 of 9).

```
288      public boolean action( Event event, Object o )
289      {
290         if ( event.target == acct )  {
291            account = Integer.parseInt( acct.getText() );
292
293            if ( account < 1 || account > 100 ) {
294               acct.setText( "Invalid account" );
295               return true;
296            }
297
298            try {
299               file.seek( ( account - 1 ) * data.size() );
300               data.read( file );
301            }
302            catch ( IOException e ) {
303               acct.setText( "Error reading file" );
304            }
305
306            if ( data.account == 0 ) {
307               fName.setText( "Enter first name" );
308               lName.setText( "Enter last name" );
309               bal.setText( "Enter balance" );
310            }
311            else {
312               acct.setText( String.valueOf( data.account ) +
313                                 " already exists" );
314               fName.setText( "" );
315               lName.setText( "" );
316               bal.setText( "" );
317            }
318         }
319         else if ( event.target == save ) {
320            try {
321               data.account = account;
322               data.lastName = lName.getText();
323               data.firstName = fName.getText();
324               data.balance = ( Double.valueOf(
325                                  bal.getText() ) ).doubleValue();
326               file.seek( ( account - 1 ) * data.size() );
327               data.write( file );
328            }
329            catch ( IOException e ) {
330               acct.setText( "Error writing file" );
331               return true;
332            }
333
334            hide();
335            clear();
336         }
```

Fig. 15.14 Transaction-processing program (part 7 of 9).

```
337
338
339
340          else if ( event.target == cancel ) {
341             hide();
342             clear();
343          }
344
345          return true;
346       }
347
348       private void clear()
349       {
350          acct.setText( "" );
351          fName.setText( "" );
352          lName.setText( "" );
353          bal.setText( "" );
354       }
355    }
356
357    class DeleteRec extends Dialog {
358       RandomAccessFile file;
359       TextField acct;
360       Label acctLabel;
361       Button cancel,
362              delete;
363
364       Record data;
365       int account;
366
367       public DeleteRec( RandomAccessFile f )
368       {
369          super( new Frame(), "Delete Record", true );
370          resize( 300, 80 );
371          setLayout( new GridLayout( 2, 2 ) );
372          file = f;
373
374          acctLabel = new Label( "Account" );
375          acct = new TextField( 10 );
376          delete = new Button( "Delete Record" );
377          cancel = new Button( "Cancel" );
378
379          add( acctLabel);
380          add( acct );
381          add( delete );
382          add( cancel );
383
384          data = new Record();
385       }
386
```

Fig. 15.14 Transaction-processing program (part 8 of 9).

```
387        public boolean action( Event event, Object o )
388        {
389           if ( event.target == acct )  {
390              account = Integer.parseInt( acct.getText() );
391
392              if ( account < 1 || account > 100 ) {
393                 acct.setText( "Invalid account" );
394                 return true;
395              }
396
397              try {
398                 file.seek( ( account - 1 ) * data.size() );
399                 data.read( file );
400              }
401              catch ( IOException e ) {
402                 acct.setText( "Error reading file" );
403              }
404
405              if ( data.account == 0 )
406                 acct.setText( String.valueOf( account ) +
407                               " does not exist" );
408           }
409           else if ( event.target == delete ) {
410              try {
411                 file.seek( ( account - 1 ) * data.size() );
412                 data.account = 0;
413                 data.firstName = "";
414                 data.lastName = "";
415                 data.balance = 0.0;
416                 data.write( file );
417              }
418              catch ( IOException e ) {
419                 acct.setText( "Error writing file" );
420                 return true;
421              }
422
423              hide();
424              acct.setText( "" );
425           }
426           else if ( event.target == cancel ) {
427              hide();
428              acct.setText( "" );
429           }
430
431           return true;
432        }
433     }
```

Fig. 15.14 Transaction-processing program (part 9 of 9).

15.12 Class `File`

As we stated at the beginning of this chapter, the `java.io` package contains an abundance of classes for processing input and output. We have concentrated on the classes for processing sequential files (`FileInputStream` and `FileOutputStream`), for processing data streams (`DataInputStream` and `DataOutputStream`) and for processing random-access files (`RandomAccessFile`). In this section we introduce class *`File`* which is particularly useful for retrieving from disk information about a file or a directory. Objects of class `File` do not actually open a file or provide any file-processing capabilities.

One example using a `File` object is checking if a file exists. In Common Programming Error 15.1, we warned that opening an existing file for output using a `FileOutput-Stream` object discards the contents of that file *without warning*. A `File` object can be used to determine of the file already exists. If so, you can open it with a `RandomAccess-File` object instead of a `FileOutputStream` object, or you can at least warn the user that they are about to discard the original file's contents.

Good Programming Practice 15.2

*Use a **`File`** object to determine if a file exists before opening the file with a **`FileOutput-Stream`** object.*

A `File` object is initialized using one of three constructors. The constructor

```
public File( String name )
```

stores the **`String`** argument **`name`** in the object. The **`name`** can contain *path information* as well as a file or directory name. A file or directory's path leads you to the file or directory on disk. The path includes some or all of the directories leading to the file or directory. An *absolute path* contains all the directories starting with the *root directory* that lead to a specific file or directory. Every file or directory on a particular disk drive has the same root directory in its path. A *relative path* contains a subset of the directories leading to a specific file or directory. Relative paths start from the current directory in which you are working.

The constructor

```
public File( String pathToName, String name )
```

uses argument **`pathToName`** (an absolute or relative path) to locate the file or directory specified by **`name`**.

The constructor

```
public File( File directory, String name )
```

uses the previously created **`File`** object **`directory`** (an absolute or relative path) to locate the file or directory specified by **`name`**.

Some commonly used **`public`** methods of class **`File`** are shown in Fig. 15.15. See the Java API for other **`File`** methods.

Method	Description
`boolean canRead()`	Returns **true** if a file is readable; **false** otherwise.
`boolean canWrite()`	Returns **true** if a file is writeable; **false** otherwise.
`boolean exists()`	Returns **true** if the name specified as the argument to the **File** constructor is a file or directory in the specified path; **false** otherwise.
`boolean isFile()`	Returns **true** if the name specified as the argument to the **File** constructor is a file; **false** otherwise.
`boolean isDirectory()`	Returns true if the name specified as the argument to the **File** constructor is a directory; **false** otherwise.
`boolean isAbsolute()`	Returns **true** if the arguments specified to the **File** constructor indicate an absolute path to a file or directory; **false** otherwise.
`String getAbsolutePath()`	Returns a **String** with the absolute path of the file or directory.
`String getName()`	Returns a **String** with the name of the file or directory.
`String getPath()`	Returns a **String** with the path of the file or directory.
`String getParent()`	Returns a **String** with the parent directory of the file or directory—i.e., the directory in which the file or directory can be found.
`long length()`	Returns the length of the file in bytes. If the **File** object represents a directory, **0** is returned.
`long lastModified()`	Returns a system-dependent representation of the time at which the file or directory was last modified. The value returned is only useful for comparison with other values returned by this method.
`String[] list()`	Returns an array of **String**s representing the contents of a directory.

Fig. 15.15 Some commonly used **File** methods.

The application of Fig. 15.16 demonstrates class **File**. Class **FileTest** creates a graphical user interface containing a **TextField enter** and a **TextArea output**. The user types a file name or directory name into the **enter** text field and presses the Enter key. The **action** method of class **FileTest** creates a new **File** object and assigns it to name. Next, the condition in the **if** structure at line 41—**name.exists()**—is tested. If name the user typed does not exist, the **action** method proceeds to line 80 and outputs the name the user typed followed by "**does not exist**." Otherwise, the body of the if structure is executed. The program outputs the name of the file or directory, then outputs the results of testing the **File** object with **isFile**, **isDirectory** and **isAbsolute**. Next, the values returned by **lastModified**, **length**, **getPath**, **getAbsolute-Path** and **getParent** are displayed. Finally, if the **File** object represents a file, the contents of the file are read into the program and displayed in the text area. A **RandomAc-cessFile** object is used so we can open the file for reading and read the file one line at a time with the **getLine** method (line 64). Note that the **RandomAccessFile** object was initialized with the **File** object **name** (line59) If the **File** object represents a directory, the contents of the directory are read into the program using **File** method **list**, then the directory contents are displayed in the text area.

The first output of this program demonstrates a **File** object associated with the **README** file from the Java Developer's Kit. The second output demonstrates a **File** object associated with the **demo** directory from the Java Developer's Kit. In both cases, we specified an absolute path on our personal computer. Note that the **** *separator character* is used is a to separate directories and files in the path. On a UNIX workstation, the separator character would be a **/** character. Java actually processes both characters as identical in a path name. So, if we specified the path **c:\java/README** which uses one of each separator character, Java still processes the file properly.

```
1   // Fig. 15.16: FileTest.java
2   // Demonstrating the File class.
3   import java.awt.*;
4   import java.io.*;
5
6   public class FileTest extends Frame {
7       File name;
8       TextField enter;
9       TextArea output;
10
11      public FileTest()
12      {
13          super( "Testing class File" );
14          setLayout( new BorderLayout() );
15          enter = new TextField(
16              "Enter file or directory name here", 40 );
17          output = new TextArea( 20, 30 );
18          add( "North", enter );
19          add( "Center", output );
20          resize( 400, 400 );
21          show();
22      }
23
24      public boolean handleEvent( Event e )
25      {
26          if ( e.id == Event.WINDOW_DESTROY ) {
27              hide();
28              dispose();
29              System.exit( 0 );
30          }
31
32          return super.handleEvent( e );
33      }
34
```

Fig. 15.16 Demonstrating class **File** (part 1 of 4).

```
35      public boolean action( Event e, Object o )
36      {
37         output.setText( "" );
38
39         name = new File( o.toString() );
40
41         if ( name.exists() ) {
42            output.appendText(
43               name.getName() + " exists\n" +
44               ( name.isFile() ? "is a file\n" :
45                                 "is not a file\n" ) +
46               ( name.isDirectory() ? "is a directory\n" :
47                                      "is not a directory\n" ) +
48               ( name.isAbsolute() ? "is absolute path\n" :
49                                     "is not absolute path\n" ) +
50               "Last modified: " + name.lastModified() +
51               "\nLength: " + name.length() +
52               "\nPath: " + name.getPath() +
53               "\nAbsolute path: " + name.getAbsolutePath() +
54               "\nParent: " + name.getParent() );
55
56            if ( name.isFile() ) {
57               try {
58                  RandomAccessFile r =
59                     new RandomAccessFile( name, "r" );
60
61                  output.appendText( "\n\n" );
62
63                  do {
64                     output.appendText( r.readLine() + "\n" );
65                  } while( r.getFilePointer() < r.length() );
66               }
67               catch( IOException e2 ) {
68               }
69            }
70            else if ( name.isDirectory() ) {
71               String dir[] = name.list();
72
73               output.appendText( "\n\nDirectory contents:\n");
74
75               for ( int i = 0; i < dir.length; i++ )
76                  output.appendText( dir[ i ] + "\n" );
77            }
78         }
79         else {
80            output.appendText( o.toString() +
81                               " does not exist\n" );
82         }
83
84         return true;
85      }
```

Fig. 15.16 Demonstrating class **File** (part 2 of 4).

```
86
87      public static void main( String args[] )
88      {
89          FileTest f = new FileTest();
90      }
91  }
```

Fig. 15.16 Demonstrating class **File** (part 3 of 4).

15.13 Input/Output of Objects

In this chapter we discussed Java's object-oriented style of input/output, but our examples concentrated on I/O of traditional data types rather than objects of user-defined classes.

When object instance variables are output to a disk file, in a sense we lose the object's type information. We only have data, not type information, on a disk. If the program that is going to read this data knows what object type it corresponds to, then the data is simply read into objects of that type.

An interesting problem occurs when we store objects of different types in the same file. How can we distinguish them (or their instance variables) as we read them into a program?

Fig. 15.16 Demonstrating class `File` (part 4 of 4).

One approach would be to have each output method output a type code preceding each collection of instance variable data that represent one object. The input methods would always begin by reading the type-code field and using a **switch** statement to invoke the input method for the proper object. Although this solution lacks the elegance of polymorphic programming, it provides a workable mechanism for retaining objects in files and retrieving them as needed.

Summary

- All data items processed by a computer are reduced to combinations of zeros and ones.

- The smallest data item in a computer can assume the value **0** or the value **1**. Such a data item is called a bit.

- Digits, letters, and special symbols are referred to as characters. The set of all characters used to write programs and represent data items on a particular computer is called that computer's character set. Every character in a computer's character set is represented as a pattern of **1**s and **0**s (characters in Java are Unicode characters composed of 2 bytes).

- A field is a group of characters (or bytes) that conveys meaning.
- A record is a group of related fields.
- At least one field in a record is chosen as a record key to identify a record as belonging to a particular person or entity that is unique from all other records in the file.
- Java imposes no structure on a file. Thus, notions like "record" do not exist in Java. The programmer must structure a file appropriately to meet the requirements of a particular application.
- A collection of programs designed to create and manage databases is called a database management system (DBMS).
- Java views each file as a sequential stream of bytes.
- Each file ends in some machine-dependent form of end-of-file marker.
- Streams provide communication channels between files and programs.
- The package **java.io** must be imported into a program to perform Java file I/O. This package includes the definitions for the stream classes such as **FileInputStream**, **FileOutputStream**, **DataInputStream**, and **DataOutputStream**.
- Files are opened by instantiating objects of stream classes **FileInputStream**, **FileOutputStream**, and **RandomAccessFile**.
- **InputStream** (a subclass of **Object**) and **OutputStream** (a subclass of **Object**) are abstract classes that define methods for performing input and output respectively; their derived classes override these methods.
- File input/output is done with **FileInputStream** (a subclass of **InputStream**) and **FileOutputStream** (a subclass of **OutputStream**).
- Pipes are synchronized communication channels between threads. A pipe is established between two threads. One thread sends data to another by writing to a **PipedOutput-Stream** (a subclass of **OutputStream**). The target thread reads information from the pipe via a **PipedInputStream** (a subclass of **InputStream**).
- A **PrintStream** (a subclass of **FilterOutputStream**) is used for performing output to the screen (or the "standard output" as defined by your local operating system). **System.out** is a **PrintStream** (as is **System.err**).
- A **FilterInputStream** filters an **InputStream** and a **FilterOutStream** filters an **OutputStream**; filtering simply means that the filter stream provides additional functionality such as buffering, monitoring line numbers or aggregating data bytes into meaningful primitive-data-type units.
- Reading data as raw bytes is fast but crude. Usually programs want to read data as aggregates of bytes that form an **int**, a **float**, a **double**, and so on. To accomplish this we use a **DataInputStream** (a subclass of class **FilterInputStream**).
- The **DataInput** interface is implemented by class **DataInputStream** and class **RandomAccessFile** (discussed below) that each need to read primitive data types from a stream.

- **DataInputStream**s enable a program to read binary data from an **InputStream**.
- The **DataInput** interface includes methods **read** (for byte arrays), **readBoolean**, **readByte**, **readChar**, **readDouble**, **readFloat**, **readFully** (for byte arrays) **readInt**, **readLine**, **readLong**, **readShort**, **readUnsignedByte**, **readUnsignedShort**, **readUTF** (for Unicode) and **skipBytes**.
- The **DataOutput** interface is implemented by class **DataOutputStream** (a subclass of class **FilterOutputStream**) and class **RandomAccessFile** that each need to write primitive data types to an **OutputStream**.
- **DataOutputStream**s enable a program to write binary data to an **OutputStream**. The **DataOutput** interface includes methods **flush**, **size**, **write** (for a byte), **write** (for a byte array), **writeBoolean**, **writeByte**, **writeBytes**, **write-Char**, **writeChars** (for Unicode **String**s), **writeDouble**, **writeFloat**, **writeInt**, **writeLong**, **writeShort** and **writeUTF**.
- Buffering is an I/O-performance-enhancement technique.
- With a **BufferedOutputStream** (a subclass of class **FilterOutputStream**) each output statement does not necessarily result in an actual physical transfer of data to the output device. Rather, each output operation is directed to a region in memory called a buffer that is large enough to hold the data of many output operations. Then actual output to the output device is performed in one large physical output operation each time the buffer fills. The output operations directed to the output buffer in memory are often called logical output operations.
- With a **BufferedInputStream** (a subclass of class **FilterInputStream**) many "logical" chunks of data from a file are read as one large physical input operation into a memory buffer. As a program requests each new chunk of data, it is taken from the buffer (this is sometimes referred to as a logical input operation). When the buffer becomes empty, the next physical input operation from the input device is performed to read in the next group of "logical" chunks of data. Thus, the number of physical input operations is small compared with the number of read requests issued by the program.
- With a **BufferedOutputStream** a partially filled buffer can be forced out to the device at any time with an explicit **flush**
- A **PushBackInputStream** is a subclass of class **FilterInputStream**. The application reading a **PushBackInputStream** reads bytes from the stream and forms aggregates consisting of several bytes. Sometimes, to determine that one aggregate is complete, the application must read the first character the "past the end" of the first aggregate. Once the program has determined that the current aggregate is complete, the extra character is "pushed back" onto the stream.
- **PushBackInputStream**s are used by programs like compilers that parse their inputs, i.e., break them into meaningful units (such as the keywords, identifiers and operators that the Java compiler must recognize).
- A **StreamTokenizer** (a subclass of **Object**) is helpful for breaking up a stream of text from an input text file into meaningful pieces called tokens.

- A **RandomAccessFile** (a subclass of **Object**) is useful for direct-access applications such as transaction-processing applications like airline-reservations systems and point-of-sale systems.

- With a sequential-access file each successive input/output request reads or writes the next consecutive set of data in the file.

- With a random-access file, each successive input/output request may be directed to any part of the file, perhaps widely separated from the part of the file referenced in the previous request.

- Direct-access applications provide rapid access to specific data items in large files; such applications are often used while people are waiting for answers—these answers must be made available quickly or the people may become impatient and "take their business elsewhere."

- A **ByteArrayInputStream** (a subclass of abstract class **InputStream**) performs its inputs from a byte array in memory.

- A **ByteArrayOutputStream** (a subclass of abstract class **OutputStream**) outputs to a byte array in memory.

- An application of byte-array input/output is data validation. A program can input an entire line at a time from the input stream into a byte array. Then a validation routine can scrutinize the contents of the byte array and correct the data, if necessary. The program can now proceed to input from the byte array, knowing that the input data is in the proper format.

- A **StringBufferInputStream** (a subclass of abstract class **InputStream**) inputs from a **StringBuffer** object.

- A **SequenceInputStream** (a subclass of abstract class **InputStream**) enables several **InputStream**s to be concatenated so that the program sees the group as one continuous **InputStream**. As the end of each input stream is reached, the stream is closed and the next stream in the sequence is opened.

- A **LineNumberInputStream** (a subclass of class **FilterInputStream**) always knows what line number of the file is being read.

- Objects of the **FileDescriptor** class are ordinarily not manipulated by most Java users.

- Class **File** enables programs to obtain information about a file or directory.

- Files are opened for output by creating a **FileOutputStream** class object. One argument is passed to the constructor—the filename. Existing files are truncated and all data in the file is lost. Nonexistent files are created.

- Programs may process no files, one file, or several files. Each file has a unique name and is associated with an appropriate file stream object. All file-processing methods must refer to a file with the appropriate object.

- A file-position pointer indicates the position in the file from which the next input is to occur or at which the next output is to be placed.

- A convenient way to implement random-access files is by using only fixed-length records. Using this technique, a program can quickly calculate the exact location of a record relative to the beginning of the file.

- Data can be inserted in a random-access file without destroying other data in the file. Data can be updated or deleted without rewriting the entire file.

- The **RandomAccessFile** class has the same capabilities for input and output as the **DataInputStream** and **DataOutputStream** classes and also supports seeking to a specific byte position in the file with method **seek**.

Terminology

absolute path	**FileInputStream** class
alphabetic field	file name
binary digit	file-position pointer
bit	**FileInputStream** class
buffer	**FileOutputStream** class
BufferedInputStream class	**FilterInputStream** class
BufferedOutputStream class	**FilterOutputStream** class
buffering	**flush**
byte	**getAbsolutePath** method of **File** class
ByteArrayInputStream class	**getName** method of **File** class
BytArrayOutputStream class	**getParent** method of **File** class
canRead method of **File** class	**getPath** method of **File** class
canWrite method of **File** class	input stream
chaining stream objects	**InputStream** class
character field	instant-access application
character set	**IOException**
close a file	**isAbsolute** method of **File** class
close method	**isDirectory** method of **File** class
data hierarchy	**isFile** method of **File** class
database	**lastModified** method of **File** class
database management system (DBMS)	**list** method of **File** class
DataInput interface	**length** method of **File** class
DataInputStream class	**LineNumberInputStream** class
DataOutput interface	logical input operation
DataOutputStream class	logical output operation
data validation	memory buffer
decimal digit	numeric field
direct-access applications	open a file
directory	output stream
end-of-file	OutputStream class
end-of-file marker	partially filled buffer
exists method of **File** class	persistent data
field	physical input operation
file	physical output operation
File class	pipe
FileDescriptor class	PipedInputStream class

PipedOutputStream class
PrintStream class
PushBackInputStream class
r file open mode
random-access file
RandomAccessFile class
read
readBoolean
readByte
readChar
readDouble
readFloat
readFully
readInt
readLine
readLong
readShort
readUnsignedByte
readUnsignedShort
readUTF
record
record key
relative path
root directory
rw file open mode
SequenceInputStream class

sequential-access file
size
skipBytes stream
standard output
StreamTokenizer class
StringBufferInputStream class
System.err (standard error stream)
System.in (standard input stream)
System.out (standard output stream)
token
transaction-processing systems
truncate an existing file
Unicode character set
write
writeBoolean
writeByte
writeBytes
writeChar
writeChars
writeDouble
writeFloat
writeInt
writeLong
writeShort
writeUTF

Common Programming Errors

15.1 Opening an existing file for output when, in fact, the user wants to preserve the file; the contents of the file are discarded without warning.

15.2 Using an incorrect **FileOutputStream** object to refer to a file.

15.3 Not opening a file before attempting to reference it in a program.

Good Programming Practices

15.1 Open a file with the **"r"** file open mode for input if the contents of the file should not be modified. This prevents unintentional modification of the file's contents. This is an example of the principle of least privilege.

15.2 Use a **File** object to determine if a file exists before opening the file with a **FileOutputStream** object.

Performance Tips

15.1 Because typical physical output operations are extremely slow compared to typical processor speeds, buffering outputs normally yields significant performance improvements over unbuffered outputs.

15.2   Because typical input operations are extremely slow compared to typical processor speeds, buffering inputs normally yields significant performance improvements over unbuffered inputs.

15.3   Explicitly close each file as soon as it is known that the program will not reference the file again. This can reduce resource usage in a program that will continue executing long after it no longer needs to be referencing a particular file. This practice also improves program clarity.

15.4   The process of closing a file and reopening a file for the purpose of positioning the file-position pointer back to the beginning of a file is a time consuming task for the computer. If this is done frequently, it may slow the performance of your program.

Software Engineering Observation

15.1   It would be dangerous to enable applets arriving from anywhere on the World Wide Web to be able to read and write files on the client system. Most web browsers prevent applets from performing file processing on the client system. Therefore, file-processing programs are generally implemented as Java applications.

Self-Review Exercises

15.1   Fill in the blanks in each of the following:
   a) Ultimately, all data items processed by a computer are reduced to combinations of _____and _____.
   b) The smallest data item a computer can process is called a _____.
   c) A _____ is a group of related records.
   d) Digits, letters, and special symbols are referred to as _____.
   e) A group of related files is called a _____.
   f) Method _____ of the file stream classes **FileOutputStream**, **FileInput-Stream**, and **RandomAccessFile** closes a file.
   g) The **DataInputStream** method _____ reads an integer from the specified stream.
   h) The **DataInputStream** method _____ reads a string from the specified stream.
   i) Method _____ of the **RandomAccessFile** class sets the file-position pointer to a specific location in a file for input or output.

15.2   State which of the following are true and which are false (for those that are false, explain why):
   a) The programmer must explicitly create the **System.in**, **System.out**, and **System.err** objects.
   b) If the file-position pointer points to a location in a sequential file other than the beginning of the file, the file must be closed and reopened to read from the beginning of the file.
   c) It is not necessary to search through all the records in a random-access file to find a specific record.
   d) Records in random-access files must be of uniform length.
   e) Method **seek** must seek relative to the beginning of a file.

15.3   Assume that each of the following statements applies to the same program.
   a) Write a statement that opens file **"oldmast.dat"** for input; use **DataInput-Stream** object **inOldMaster** chained to a **FileInputStream** object.

b) Write a statement that opens file **"trans.dat"** for input; use **DataInputStream** object **inTransaction** chained to a **FileInputStream** object.

c) Write a statement that opens file **"newmast.dat"** for output (and creation); use **DataOutputStream** object **outNewMaster** chained to a **FileOutputStream**.

d) Write a set of statements that read a record from the file **"oldmast.dat"**. The record consists of integer **accountNum**, string **name**, and floating point **currentBalance**; use **DataInputStream** object **inOldMaster**.

e) Write a set of statements that read a record from the file **"trans.dat"**. The record consists of integer **accountNum** and floating point **dollarAmount**; use **DataInputStream** object **inTransaction**.

f) Write a set of statements that output a record to the file **"newmast.dat"**. The record consists of integer **accountNum**, string **name**, and floating point **currentBalance**; use **DataOutputStream** object **outNewMaster**.

15.4 Find the error and show how to correct it in each of the following.

a) File **"payables.dat"** referred to by **DataOutputStream** object **outPayable** has not been opened.

```
outPayable.writeInt( account );
outPayable.writeUTF( company );
outPayable.writeDouble( amount );
```

b) The following statement should read a record from the file **"payables.dat"**. The **FileInputStream** object **inPayable** refers to this file, and **DataInputStream** object **inReceivable** refers to the file **"receivables.dat"**.

```
account = inReceivable.readInt();
company = inReceivable.readUTF();
amount = inReceivable.readDouble();
```

Answers to Self-Review Exercises

15.1 a) 1s, 0s. b) Bit. c) File. d) Characters. e) Database. f) **close**. g) **readInt**. h) **readUTF**. i) **seek**.

15.2 a) False. These three streams are created automatically for the programmer.
b) True.
c) True.
d) False. Records in a random-access file are normally of uniform length.
e) True.

15.3 a) **DataInputStream inOldMaster;**
inOldMaster = new DataInputStream(
new FileInputStream("oldmast.dat"));

b) **DataInputStream inTransaction;**
inTransaction = new DataInputStream(
new FileInputStream("trans.dat"));

c) **DataOutputStream outNewMaster;**
outNewMaster = new DataOutputStream(
new FileOutputStream("newmast.dat"));

d) `accountNum = inOldMaster.readInt();`
`name = inOldMaster.readUTF();`
`currentBalance = inOldMaster.readDouble();`
e) `accountNum = inTransaction.readInt();`
`dollarAmount = inTransaction.readDouble();`
f) `outNewMaster.writeInt( accountNum );`
`outNewMaster.writeUTF( name );`
`outNewMaster.writeDouble( currentBalance );`

15.4   a) Error: The file **"payables.dat"** has not been opened before the attempt is made to output data to the stream.
Correction: Create a new **DataOutputStream** object chained to a **FileOutputStream** object to open **"payables.dat"** for output.

b) Error: The incorrect **DataInputStream** object is being used to read a record from file **"payables.dat"**.
Correction: Use object **inPayable** to refer to **"payables.dat"**.

Exercises

15.5   Fill in the blanks in each of the following:
a) Computers store large amounts of data on secondary storage devices as _____.
b) A _____ is composed of several fields.
c) A field that may contain only digits, letters, and blanks is called an_____ field.
d) To facilitate the retrieval of specific records from a file, one field in each record is chosen as a _____.
e) The vast majority of information stored in computer systems is stored in _____ files.
f) A group of related characters that conveys meaning is called a _____.
g) The standard stream objects are _____ , _____ , and_____ .

15.6   State which of the following are true and which are false (and for those that are false, explain why):
a) The impressive functions performed by computers essentially involve the manipulation of zeros and ones.
b) People prefer to manipulate bits instead of characters and fields because bits are more compact.
c) People specify programs and data items as characters; computers then manipulate and process these characters as groups of zeros and ones.
d) A person's 5-digit zip code is an example of a numeric field.
e) A person's street address is generally considered to be an alphabetic field in computer applications.
f) Data items represented in computers form a data hierarchy in which data items become larger and more complex as we progress from fields to characters to bits, etc.
g) A record key identifies a record as belonging to a particular field.
h) Most organizations store all their information in a single file to facilitate computer processing.
i) Each statement that processes a file in a Java program explicitly refers to that file by name.
j) When a program creates a file, the file is automatically retained by the computer for future reference.

15.7   Exercise 15.3 asked the reader to write a series of single statements. Actually, these statements form the core of an important type of file-processing program, namely, a file-matching program. In commercial data processing, it is common to have several files in each application system. In an accounts receivable system, for example, there is generally a master file containing detailed information about each customer such as the customer's name, address, telephone number, outstanding balance, credit limit, discount terms, contract arrangements, and possibly a condensed history of recent purchases and cash payments.

As transactions occur (i.e., sales are made and cash payments arrive in the mail), they are entered into a file. At the end of each business period (i.e., a month for some companies, a week for others, and a day in some cases) the file of transactions (called `"trans.dat"` in Exercise 15.3) is applied to the master file (called `"oldmast.dat"` in Exercise 15.3), thus updating each account's record of purchases and payments. During an updating run, the master file is rewritten as a new file (`"newmast.dat"`), which is then used at the end of the next business period to begin the updating process again.

File-matching programs must deal with certain problems that do not exist in single-file programs. For example, a match does not always occur. A customer on the master file may not have made any purchases or cash payments in the current business period, and therefore no record for this customer will appear on the transaction file. Similarly, a customer who did make some purchases or cash payments may have just moved to this community, and the company may not have had a chance to create a master record for this customer.

Use the statements written in Exercise 15.3 as a basis for writing a complete file-matching accounts receivable program. Use the account number on each file as the record key for matching purposes. Assume that each file is a sequential file with records stored in increasing account number order.

When a match occurs (i.e., records with the same account number appear on both the master file and the transaction file), add the dollar amount on the transaction file to the current balance on the master file, and write the `"newmast.dat"` record. (Assume that purchases are indicated by positive amounts on the transaction file, and that payments are indicated by negative amounts.) When there is a master record for a particular account but no corresponding transaction record, merely write the master record to `"newmast.dat"`. When there is a transaction record but no corresponding master record, print the message `"Unmatched transaction record for account number ..."` (fill in the account number from the transaction record).

15.8   After writing the program of Exercise 15.7, write a simple program to create some test data for checking out the program. Use the following sample account data:

Master file

Account number	Name	Balance
100	Alan Jones	348.17
300	Mary Smith	27.19
500	Sam Sharp	0.00
700	Suzy Green	-14.22

Transaction file

Account number	Balance
100	27.14
300	62.11
400	100.56
900	82.17

Run the program of Exercise 15.7 using the files of test data created in Exercise 15.8. Print the new master file. Check that the accounts have been updated correctly.

15.9   It is possible (actually common) to have several transaction records with the same record key. This occurs because a particular customer might make several purchases and cash payments during a business period. Rewrite your accounts receivable file-matching program of Exercise 15.7 to provide for the possibility of handling several transaction records with the same record key. Modify the test data of Exercise 15.8 to include the following additional transaction records:

Account number	Dollar amount
300	83.89
700	80.78
700	1.53

15.10   Write a series of statements that accomplish each of the following. Assume the structure

```
class Person {
    char lastName[15];
    char firstName[15];
    char age[2];
}
```

has been defined, and that the random-access file has been opened properly.
   a) Initialize the file **"nameage.dat"** with 100 records containing **lastName** = "un-assigned"**, firstName** = " ", and **age** = **"0"**.
   b) Input 10 last names, first names, and ages, and write them to the file.
   c) Update a record that has information in it, and if there is none tell the user **"No info"**.
   d) Delete a record that has information by reinitializing that particular record.

15.11   You are the owner of a hardware store and need to keep an inventory that can tell you what different tools you have, how many of each you have on hand, and the cost of each one. Write a program that initializes the random-access file **"hardware.dat"** to one hundred empty records, lets you input the data concerning each tool, enables you to list all your tools, lets you delete a record for a tool that you no longer have, and lets you update *any* information in the file. The tool identification number should be the record number. Use the following information to start your file:

Record #	Tool name	Quantity	Cost
3	Electric sander	7	57.98
17	Hammer	76	11.99
24	Jig saw	21	11.00
39	Lawn mower	3	79.50
56	Power saw	18	99.99
68	Screwdriver	106	6.99
77	Sledge hammer	11	21.50
83	Wrench	34	7.50

15.12 Modify the telephone number word generating program you wrote in Chapter 4 so that it writes its output to a file. This allows you to read the file at your convenience. If you have a computerized dictionary available, modify your program to look up the thousands of seven-letter words in the dictionary. Some of the interesting seven-letter combinations created by this program may consist of two or more words. For example, the phone number 8432677 produces "THEBOSS." Modify your program to use the computerized dictionary to check each possible seven-letter word to see if it is a valid one-letter word followed by a valid six-letter word, a valid two-letter word followed by a valid five-letter word, etc.

16

Networking

Objectives

- To understand the elements of Java networking.
- To implement Java networking applications.
- To understand how to implement Java clients and servers that communicate with one another.
- To understand how to implement network-based collaborative applications.
- To be able to write programs that "walk the web"
- To construct a multithreaded server.

If the presence of electricity can be made visible in any part of a circuit, I see no reason why intelligence may not be transmitted instantaneously by electricity.
Samuel F. B. Morse

Mr. Watson, come here, I want you.
Alexander Graham Bell

What networks of railroads, highways and canals were in another age, the networks of telecommunications, information and computerization ... are today.
Bruno Kreisky, Austrian Chancellor

Science may never come up with a better office-communication system than the coffee break.
Earl Wilson

It's currently a problem of access to gigabits through punybaud.
J. C. R. Licklider

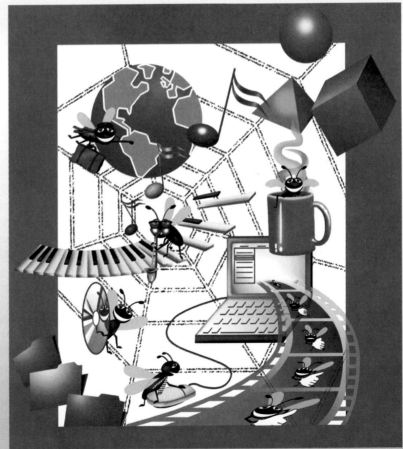

Outline

16.1 Introduction

There is much excitement over the Internet and the World Wide Web. The Internet ties the "information world" together. The World Wide Web makes the Internet easy to use and gives it the flair and sizzle of multimedia. Organizations see the Internet and the Web as crucial to their information systems strategies. In its early implementation Java provides a number of built-in networking capabilities that make it easy to develop Internet-based and Web-based applications. Not only can Java specify parallelism through multithreading, but it can enable programs to search the world for information and to collaborate with programs running on other computers internationally, nationally, or just within the organization. Java can even enable applets and applications running on the same computer to communicate with one another.

Networking introduces many security risks, so browsers may limit the capabilities of applets. We discuss some of these limitations in section 16.9.

Java is evolving quickly. In Section 16.10 we briefly overview some of the forthcoming APIs that enhance Java's networking and security capabilities.

Networking is a massive and complex topic. Computer Science and Computer Engineering students will typically take a full-semester, upper-level course in computer networking and continue with further study at the graduate level. Java provides a rich complement of networking capabilities and will likely be used as an implementation vehicle in computer networking courses. In *Java How to Program* we introduce basic Java networking concepts and capabilities. We provide five live-code examples that will help the reader frame out a great variety of typical networking applications. Java's networking capabilities are centralized in the ***java.net*** *package*. The reader is encouraged to further explore these classes and methods.

Java offers *socket-based communications* that enable applications to view networking as if it were file I/O—a program can read from a *socket* or write to a socket as simply as reading from a file or writing to a file. We show how to create and manipulate sockets.

Java provides *stream sockets* and *datagram sockets*. With *stream sockets* a process establishes a connection to another process. While the connection is in place, data flows between the processes in one continuous stream. Stream sockets are said to provide a *connection-oriented service*. The protocol used for transmission is the popular *TCP (Transmission Control Protocol)*.

With *datagram sockets*, individual *packets* of information are transmitted. This is not the right protocol for everyday users because unlike TCP, the protocol used, *UDP*—the *User Datagram Protocol*—is a *connectionless service*, and does not guarantee that packets arrive in any particular way. In fact, packets can be lost, can be duplicated, and can even arrive out of sequence. So with UDP, significant extra programming is required on the user's part to deal with these problems (if the user chooses to do so). Stream sockets and the TCP protocol will be the most desirable for the vast majority of Java programmers.

Performance Tip 16.1

Connectionless services generally offer greater performance but less reliability than connection-oriented services.

Portability Tip 16.1

The TCP protocol and its related set of protocols enable a great variety of heterogeneous computer systems (i.e., computer systems with different processors and different operating systems) to intercommunicate.

Our discussion of networking focuses on both sides of a *client-server relationship*. The *client* requests that some action be performed and the *server* performs the action returning the result (if any) to the client. The client first attempts to establish a *connection* to the server. The server can *accept* or *deny* the connection. If the connection is accepted, then the client and server communicate through *sockets* in much the same manner as if they were doing file I/O. When the communication connection is no longer needed, the client and server each close the connection. Our networking example programs will make use of the input/output streams facilities we discussed in Chapter 15.

16.2 Manipulating URLs

The Internet offers many protocols. The **http** protocol (HyperText Transfer Protocol) that forms the basis of the World Wide Web uses URLs (*Uniform Resource Locators*, also called *Universal Resource Locators*) to locate data on the Internet. If you know the URL of publicly available HTML files anywhere on the World Wide Web, you can access that data through **http**. Java makes it easy to manipulate URLs. By using a URL as an argument to the **showDocument** method of class **AppletContext**, this will open the URL.

The program of Fig. 16.1 enables the user to click on a button and go to a corresponding World Wide Web site. The applet contains two buttons—"**Java Home**" and "**Deitel Home**." When the user clicks on a specific button, the **action** method of applet **SiteSelector** determines which button was pressed, gets the URL associated with that button and displays the new World Wide Web page.

```
1    // Fig. 16.1: SiteSelector.java
2    // This program uses a button to load a document from a URL.
3    import java.awt.*;
4    import java.net.*;
5    import java.applet.Applet;
6
7    public class SiteSelector extends Applet {
8       Site siteList[];   // array of sites
9
10      public void init()
11      {
12         siteList = new Site[ 2 ];
13         siteList[ 0 ] = new Site ( " Java Home ",
14                     "http://www.javasoft.com/index.html" );
15         siteList[ 1 ] = new Site ( "Deitel Home",
16                     "http://www.deitel.com/index.html" );
17
18         for ( int i = 0; i < siteList.length; i++ )
19            add( new Button( siteList[ i ].getTitle() ) );
20      }
21
22      public boolean action( Event e, Object arg )
23      {
24         if ( e.target instanceof Button ) {
25            String title;
26            URL location;
27
28            for ( int i = 0; i < siteList.length; i++ ) {
29               title = siteList[ i ].getTitle();
30               location =
31                  siteList[ i ].getLocation();
32
33               if ( title.equals( arg.toString() ) ) {
34                  gotoSite( location );
35                  return true;   // event handled
36               }
37            }
38         }
39
40         return false;     // event not handled yet
41      }
42
43      public void gotoSite( URL loc )
44      {
45         // this must be executed in a browser such as Netscape
46         getAppletContext().showDocument( loc );
47      }
48   }
49
```

Fig. 16.1 Loading a document from a URL into a browser (part 1 of 2).

```
50   class Site extends Button {
51       private String title;
52       private URL location;
53
54       public Site( String siteTitle, String siteLocation )
55       {
56           title = siteTitle;
57
58           try {
59               location = new URL( siteLocation );
60           }
61           catch ( MalformedURLException e ) {
62               System.err.println( "Invalid URL: " + siteLocation );
63           }
64       }
65
66       public String getTitle() { return title; }
67
68       public URL getLocation() { return location; }
69   }
```

Fig. 16.1 Loading a document from a URL into a browser (part 2 of 2).

Class **SiteSelector** contains an array of **Site** objects. Each object of class **Site** (defined on line 50) contains two instance variables—a **title** of type **String** and a **location** of type **URL**. When the applet's **init** method creates a **Site** object, two **String**s are passed to the constructor. The first is assigned to the **String title** directly. The second **String** is passed to the constructor for class **URL** that takes a single **String** argument. The **URL** constructor determines if the **String** passed as an argument represents a valid Uniform Resource Locator. If so, the **URL** object is initialized to contain the Uniform Resource Locator; otherwise a **MalformedURLException** is generated. Notice that the **URL** constructor must be called in a **try** block or the **MalformedURLException** must be declared in the **throws** clause of the **Site** constructor.

Common Programming Error 16.1

*A **MalformedURLException** is thrown when a **String** that is not in proper URL format is passed to a **URL** constructor.*

After the two **Site** objects are created in the applet's **init** method, the **for** structure at line 18 creates two **Button** objects. Each button is labeled with the **title** of the **Site** to which the button corresponds. The **title** is determined with a call to the **Site** method **getTitle**.

When the user clicks one of the buttons, the **action** method is called. The **for** structure (line 28) compares the title of each **Site** in the array to the label on the button that was pressed. If the **title** matches the button label, the applet's **gotoSite** method is invoked and is passed the **URL** location for the new World Wide Web site that should be displayed.

The statement

```
getAppletContext().showDocument( loc );
```

from method **gotoSite** uses the applet's **getAppletContext** method (inherited from class **Applet**) to get a reference to an **AppletContext** object that represents the applet's environment—i.e., the browser in which the applet is executing. This reference is then used to invoke the **AppletContext** method **showDocument** which receives a **URL** object as an argument and displays in the browser the World Wide Web resource associated with that **URL**. In this example, both resources are World Wide Web sites.

Note: The output window associated with this applet shows the applet executing in the Appletviewer. This applet must be run from a World Wide Web browser such as Netscape Navigator to see the results of displaying another Web page. The Appletviewer is only capable of executing applets, so all other HTML text will be ignored. If the sites in the program had Java applets on the Web pages we used, only those applets would appear in the Appletviewer when one of the buttons on the applet is clicked.

16.3 Using a URL Stream Connection to Read a File on a Server

The program of Fig. 16.2 uses a **URL** object to open an **InputStream** from a file on a server, read the contents of the file and display the contents in a text area on the applet. The applet class **ReadServerFile** contains a **URL** object called **fileURL** which is initialized with a Uniform Resource Locator that refers to a test file on the Deitel & Associates, Inc. World Wide Web site. The test file (**"test.txt"**) contains some sample text.

```
1   // Fig. 16.2: ReadServerFile.java
2   // This program uses a URL connection to read a file
3   // on the server.
4   import java.awt.*;
5   import java.net.*;
6   import java.io.*;
7   import java.applet.Applet;
8
9   public class ReadServerFile extends Applet {
10      URL fileURL;
11      TextArea contents;
12      InputStream input;
13      DataInputStream dataInput;
14
```

Fig. 16.2 Reading a file through a URL connection (part 1 of 3).

```
15        public void init()
16        {
17            contents = new TextArea( "Please wait...", 10, 40 );
18            add( contents );
19
20            try {
21                fileURL = new URL(
22                    "http://www.deitel.com/test/test.txt" );
23            }
24            catch ( MalformedURLException e ) {
25                showStatus( "Exception: " + e.toString() );
26            }
27        }
28
29        public void start()
30        {
31            String text;
32
33            try {
34                input = fileURL.openStream();
35                dataInput = new DataInputStream( input );
36                contents.setText( "The file contents are:\n" );
37
38                while ( ( text = dataInput.readLine() ) != null )
39                    contents.appendText( text + "\n" );
40
41                dataInput.close();
42            }
43            catch ( IOException e ) {
44                showStatus( "Exception: " + e.toString() );
45            }
46        }
47    }
```

Fig. 16.2 Reading a file through a URL connection (part 2 of 3).

The applet's **init** method creates a text area and displays it, then creates the **URL** object associated with the test file. The applet's **start** method opens a stream connection to the file on the server with the statement

```
    input = fileURL.openStream();
```

which uses the **URL** method **openStream** to get an **InputStream** object associated with the file on the server and assign it to reference **input**. Next, we chain a **DataInputStream** onto the **InputStream** object input so we can use **DataInputStream** method **readLine** to get a line of text from the file.

The **while** structure at line 38 reads one line of text from the file at a time and assigns to reference **text** the **String** returned from **dataInput.readline()**. The **String text** is then appended to the data displayed in the text area. When the complete file has been read, the input stream is closed with the call **dataInput.close()**.

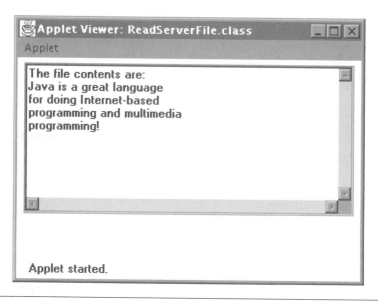

Fig. 16.2 Reading a file through a URL connection (part 3 of 3).

16.4 Establishing a Simple Server (Using Stream Sockets)

To establish a simple server, we create a **ServerSocket** and a **Socket**. The server *registers* an available *port number*. The client will ask to connect to the server on this *port*. The **ServerSocket** establishes the port where the server waits for connections from clients. Each connection is managed with a **Socket**. We also need to create an **OutputStream** over which the server will send data and possibly an **InputStream** through which the server can receive data. The service then needs to be registered with a call like

```
ServerSocket s = new ServerSocket( port, queueLength );
```

The **queueLength** specifies the number of clients that can wait for a connection and be processed by the server. If the queue is full, client connections are automatically refused. Once the **ServerSocket** is established, the server listens indefinitely (or *blocks*) for an attempt by a client to connect. This is accomplished with the **ServerSocket** method call

```
Socket connection = s.accept();
```

which returns a **Socket** object when a connection is established.

Software Engineering Observation 16.1

With sockets, network I/O appears to Java programs to be virtually identical to file I/O. Sockets hide much of the complexity of network programming from the programmer.

Software Engineering Observation 16.2

With Java's multithreading, we can create multithreaded servers that can manage many simultaneous connections with many clients; this multithreaded-server architecture is precisely what is used in popular UNIX, Windows NT and OS/2 network servers.

Software Engineering Observation 16.3

*A multithreaded server can be implemented to take the **Socket** returned by each call to **accept** and create a new thread that would manage network I/O across that **Socket**, or a multithreaded server can be implemented to maintain a pool of threads ready to manage network I/O across the new **Socket**s as they are created.*

Performance Tip 16.2

*In high-performance systems in which memory is abundant, a multithreaded server can be implemented to create a pool of threads that can be assigned quickly to handle network I/O across each new **Socket** as it is created. Thus, when a connection is received, the server need not suffer the overhead of thread creation.*

The server invokes method **getOutputStream** on the **Socket** to get a reference to the **OutputStream** associated with the **Socket**. If necessary, the server also invokes method **getInputStream** on the **Socket** to get a reference to the **InputStream** associated with the **Socket**. The **OutputStream** and **InputStream** objects can be used to send or receive individual bytes or sets of bytes with the **OutputStream** method **write** and the **InputStream** method **read**, respectively. Often it is useful to send or receive values of data types like **int**, **double** and **String** rather than sending bytes. In this case, we can use the techniques of Chapter 15, "Files and Streams" to *chain* other stream types (such as **DataOutputStream** and **DataInputStream**) to the **OutputStream** and **InputStream** associated with the **Socket**. For example,

```
DataInputStream input =
    new DataInputStream( connection.getInputStream() );

DataOutputStream output =
    new DataOutputStream( connection.getOutputStream() );
```

The beauty of establishing these relationships is that whatever the server writes to the **DataOutputStream** is sent via the **OutputStream** and is available at the client's **InputStream** and whatever the client writes to its **OutputStream** (possibly with a corresponding **DataOutputStream**) is available via the server's **InputStream**.

Another common method of sending information is via a **PrintStream** chained to an **OutputStream**. This can be done as follows:

```
PrintStream output =
    new PrintStream( connection.getOutputStream() );
```

When the transmission is complete, the server closes the connection by issuing the **close** method on the **Socket**.

16.5 Establishing a Simple Client (Using Stream Sockets)

To establish a client we use a **Socket** to connect to the server, an **InputStream** to receive information from the server and an **OuputStream** (if necessary) to send information back to the server. The connection to the server is established with a statement like

```
Socket connection = new Socket( "serverName", port );
```

This returns a **Socket**. A connection attempt that fails throws an **IOException**, so many programs simply catch **IOException**.

Common Programming Error 16.2

An **UnknownHostException** *is thrown when a server address indicated by a client can not be resolved.*

The methods **getInputStream** and **getOutputStream** are used to get references to the **Socket**'s associated **InputStream** and **OutputStream**, respectively. **InputStream** method **read** can be used to input individual bytes or sets of bytes from the server. **OutputStream** method **write** can be used to output individual bytes or sets of bytes to the server. As we mentioned in the previous section, often it is useful to send or receive values of data types like **int**, **double** and **String** rather than sending bytes. If the server is sending information in the form of actual data types, the client should receive the information in the same format. Thus, if the server sends values with a **DataOutput-Stream**, the client should read those values with a **DataInputStream**.

When processing information sent by a server, the client must determine when the server is done sending information so the client can call **close** to close the **Socket** connection. For example, the **InputStream** method **read** returns -1 when end-of-stream (also called EOF—end-of-file) is detected. If a **DataInputStream** is used to read information from the server, an **EOFException** is generated when the client attempts to read a value (with a method other than **readLine**) from a stream on which end-of-stream is detected. Method **readLine** returns **null** if end-of-stream is detected (see Fig. 16.2).

When the client closes the **Socket**, an **IOException** may be thrown. The **get-InputStream** and **getOutputStream** methods may also throw **IOException**s.

16.6 Client/Server Interaction with Stream Socket Connections

The programs of Fig. 16.3 and Fig. 16.4 use *stream sockets* to demonstrate a *client/server application*. The client application connects to the server, the server application sends data to the client and the client displays the data received. The definition of class **Server** is in Fig. 16.3. The definition of class **Client** is in Fig. 16.4.

Class **Server** extends class **Frame**, so a constructor is provided to set up the graphical components of the window that is displayed. The **Server** object displays its output in a text area. Also, a **handleEvent** method is provided to enable the user to close the window associated with the application when the application terminates.

Method **runServer** (line 21) of class **Server** does the work of setting up the server to receive a connection and processing the connection when it is received. The method declares a **ServerSocket** called **server** to wait for connections, a **Socket** called **connection** to process the connection from a client and an **OutputStream** called **output** to send data to the client via the **Socket** called **connection**. In the **try** block, the **ServerSocket** is set up to listen for a connection from a client at port **5000**. Port numbers below 1024 are reserved for the system and may not be specified as connection ports in user programs. The second argument to the constructor is the number of connections that can wait in a queue to connect to the server (**100** in this example). If the queue is full when a connection is attempted, the connection is refused automatically.

```
1    // Fig. 16.3: Server.java
2    // Set up a Server that will receive a connection
3    // from a client, send a string to the client,
4    // and close the connection.
5    import java.io.*;
6    import java.net.*;
7    import java.awt.*;
8
9    public class Server extends Frame {
10      TextArea display;
11
12      public Server()
13      {
14         super( "Server" );
15         display = new TextArea( 20, 5 );
16         add( "Center", display );
17         resize( 300, 150 );
18         show();
19      }
20
21      public void runServer()
22      {
23         ServerSocket server;
24         Socket connection;
25         OutputStream output;
26
27         try {
28            server = new ServerSocket( 5000, 100 );
29            connection = server.accept();
30            display.setText( "Connection received...\n" );
31            display.appendText( "Sending data...\n" );
32            output = connection.getOutputStream();
33            String s = new String( "Connection successful\n");
34
35            for ( int i = 0; i < s.length(); i++ )
36               output.write( (int) s.charAt( i ) );
37
38            display.appendText(
39               "Transmission complete. Closing socket.\n" );
40            connection.close();
41         }
42         catch ( IOException e ) {
43            e.printStackTrace();
44         }
45      }
46
```

Fig. 16.3 Demonstrating the server portion of a stream socket connection between a client and a server (part 1 of 2).

```
47      public boolean handleEvent( Event e )
48      {
49         if ( e.id == Event.WINDOW_DESTROY ) {
50            hide();
51            dispose();
52            System.exit( 0 );
53         }
54
55         return super.handleEvent( e );
56      }
57
58      public static void main( String args[] )
59      {
60         Server s = new Server();
61
62         s.runServer();
63      }
64   }
```

Fig. 16.3 Demonstrating the server portion of a stream socket connection between a client and a server (part 2 of 2).

The statement

```
connection = server.accept();
```

uses **ServerSocket** method **accept** to wait for a connection. This method blocks until a connection is received. Once a connection is received, **connection** is assigned a **Socket** object that will be used to manage the connection. The statement

```
output = connection.getOutputStream();
```

assigns to **output** a reference to the **OutputStream** associated with **connection**.

The **for** structure at line 35 uses **output** to send the individual characters in the **String** "Connection successful\n" to the client. Notice that each character is cast to an integer. This is because the **OutputStream** method **write** requires an integer argument. When the transmission is complete, the **Socket** is closed with the statement

```
connection.close();
```

Notice that the **main** method (line 58) creates an object of the **Server** class and invokes the **runServer** method on it. Also, note that the **Server** receives a connection, processes the connection and terminates execution. A more likely scenario would be a **Server** that receives a connection, sets up that connection to be processed as a separate thread of execution, then waits for new connections. The separate threads that process existing connections can continue to execute while the **Server** concentrates on new connection requests.

```
1    // Fig. 16.4: Client.java
2    // Set up a Client that will read information sent
3    // from a Server and display the information.
4    import java.io.*;
5    import java.net.*;
6    import java.awt.*;
7
8    public class Client extends Frame {
9        TextArea display;
10
11       public Client()
12       {
13           super( "Client" );
14           display = new TextArea( 20, 10 );
15           add( "Center", display );
16           resize( 300, 150 );
17           show();
18       }
19
20       public void runClient()
21       {
22           Socket client;
23           InputStream input;
24
25           try {
26               client = new Socket( InetAddress.getLocalHost(),
27                                    5000 );
28               display.appendText( "Created Socket\n" );
29
30               input = client.getInputStream();
31               display.appendText( "Created input stream\n" );
32
33               display.appendText(
34                   "The text from the server is:\n\t");
35               char c;
36
37               while ( ( c = (char) input.read() ) != '\n' )
38                   display.appendText( String.valueOf( c ) );
39
```

Fig. 16.4 Demonstrating the client portion of a stream socket connection between a client and a server (part 1 of 2).

```
40              display.appendText( "\n" );
41              client.close();
42          }
43          catch ( IOException e ) {
44              e.printStackTrace();
45          }
46      }
47
48      public boolean handleEvent( Event e )
49      {
50          if ( e.id == Event.WINDOW_DESTROY ) {
51              hide();
52              dispose();
53              System.exit( 0 );
54          }
55
56          return super.handleEvent( e );
57      }
58
59      public static void main( String args[] )
60      {
61          Client c = new Client();
62
63          c.runClient();
64      }
65  }
```

Fig. 16.4 Demonstrating the client portion of a stream socket connection between a client and a server (part 2 of 2).

Like class **Server**, class **Client** extends class **Frame**, so a constructor is provided to set up the window that will be displayed. Class **Client** displays its output in a text area. Also, a **handleEvent** method is provided to enable the user to close the window associated with the application when the application terminates.

The **Client** method **runClient** performs the work necessary to connect to the **Server** and to receive data from the **Server**. In the **try** block, **Socket client** is instantiated with two arguments to the constructor—**InetAddress.getLocal-Host()** and **5000**. The first argument returns an **InetAddress** object containing the local host name of the computer on which this program is executing. *We have chosen in* *this example to demonstrate the client/server relationship by connecting between programs executing on the same computer. Normally, this first argument would be the Internet address of another computer.* The second argument is the port number on the server. This number must exactly match the port number at which the server is waiting for connections (sometimes called the *handshake point*).

Once the connection is made, a message is displayed in the text area and the statement

```
input = client.getInputStream();
```

is executed to get a reference to the **InputStream** associated with **Socket client** and assign it to reference **input**. The reference **input** is used to process the data sent from the **Server** to the **Client**. The **while** structure at line 37 uses the **InputStream** method **read** to read one byte at a time (as an **int**) from the stream. Note that the byte is converted to a **char** with a cast operation so the byte can be output as a character. In this example, we know that the **Server** is sending a set of characters that ends with the new-line character (**'\n'**), so we explicitly test for that character in the condition of the **while** structure to terminate the loop. When the **Socket** is no longer needed to get information, we close it with the statement

```
client.close();
```

Note that in this example only the **Server** sent information and only the **Client** received information. It is certainly possible that the client and the server in a client/server relationship will each send and receive data.

16.7 Connectionless Client/Server Interaction with Datagrams

We have been discussing *connection-oriented, streams-based transmission.* Now we consider *connectionless transmission with datagrams.*

Connection-oriented transmission is like the telephone system in which you dial and are given a *connection* to the telephone you wish to communicate with; the connection is maintained for the duration of your phone call, even when you are not talking.

Connectionless transmission with *datagrams* is more like the way mail is carried via the postal service. If a large message will not fit in one envelope, you break it into separate message pieces that you place in separate, sequentially numbered envelopes. Each of the letters is then mailed at once. The letters may arrive in order, out of order or not at all (although the last case is rare, it does happen). The person at the receiving end reassembles the message pieces into sequential order before attempting to make sense of the message. If your message is small enough to fit in one envelope, you do not have to worry about the "out-of-sequence" problem, but it is still possible that your message may not arrive.

The programs of Fig. 16.5 and 16.6 use datagrams to send packets of information between a client application and a server application. In this program, the user types a message into a textfield on the client application and presses *Enter*. The message is converted into a **byte** array and placed in a datagram packet that is sent to the server. The server receives the packet and displays the information in the packet, then *echoes* the packet back to the client. When the client receives the packet, the client displays the information in the packet. In this program, the **Client** and **Server** classes are implemented similarly.

```
1   // Fig. 16.5: Server.java
2   // Set up a Server that will receive packets from a
3   // client and send packets to a client.
4   import java.io.*;
5   import java.net.*;
6   import java.awt.*;
7
8   public class Server extends Frame {
9      TextArea display;
10
11     DatagramPacket sendPacket, receivePacket;
12     DatagramSocket sendSocket, receiveSocket;
13
14     public Server()
15     {
16        super( "Server" );
17        display = new TextArea( 20, 10 );
18        add( "Center", display );
19        resize( 400, 300 );
20        show();
21
22        try {
23           sendSocket = new DatagramSocket();
24           receiveSocket = new DatagramSocket( 5000 );
25        }
26        catch( SocketException se ) {
27           se.printStackTrace();
28           System.exit( 1 );
29        }
30     }
31
32     public void waitForPackets()
33     {
34        while ( true ) {
35           try {
36              // set up packet
37              byte array[] = new byte[ 100 ];
38              receivePacket =
39                 new DatagramPacket( array, array.length );
40
41              // wait for packet
42              receiveSocket.receive( receivePacket );
43
44              // process packet
45              display.appendText( "\nPacket received:" +
46                 "\nFrom host: " + receivePacket.getAddress() +
47                 "\nHost port: " + receivePacket.getPort() +
48                 "\nLength: " + receivePacket.getLength() +
49                 "\nContaining:\n\t" );
```

Fig. 16.5 Demonstrating the server side of connectionless client/server computing with datagrams (part 1 of 3).

```
50              byte data[] = receivePacket.getData();
51              String received = new String( data, 0 );
52              display.appendText( received );
53
54              // echo information from packet back to client
55              display.appendText( "\n\nEcho data to client...");
56              sendPacket = new DatagramPacket( data, data.length,
57                  receivePacket.getAddress(), 5001 );
58              sendSocket.send( sendPacket );
59              display.appendText( "Packet sent\n" );
60           }
61           catch( IOException exception ) {
62              display.appendText( exception.toString() + "\n" );
63              exception.printStackTrace();
64           }
65        }
66     }
67
68     public boolean handleEvent( Event e )
69     {
70        if ( e.id == Event.WINDOW_DESTROY ) {
71           hide();
72           dispose();
73           System.exit( 0 );
74        }
75
76        return super.handleEvent( e );
77     }
78
79     public static void main( String args[] )
80     {
81        Server s = new Server();
82
83        s.waitForPackets();
84     }
85  }
```

Fig. 16.5 Demonstrating the server side of connectionless client/server computing
with datagrams (part 2 of 3).

Class **Server** (Fig. 16.5) defines two **DatagramPacket**s that are used to create the
packets to send and receive information, and two **DatagramSocket**s that are used to
send and receive these packets. The constructor for class **Server** first creates the graphical
user interface where the packets of information will be displayed. Next, the **Datagram-
Socket**s are created in the **try** block. The statement

```
sendSocket = new DatagramSocket();
```

uses the **DatagramSocket** constructor that takes no arguments to set up a socket for
sending packets out over the network. The computer will assign an available port to the
sendSocket object automatically. The statement

Fig. 16.5 Demonstrating the server side of connectionless client/server computing with datagrams (part 3 of 3).

```
receiveSocket = new DatagramSocket( 5000 );
```

uses the **DatagramSocket** constructor that takes an integer port number argument to set up a port for receiving packets from the network. We have specified port number **5000**. **Client**s sending packets to this **Server** specify port **5000** in the packets they send. If either of the constructor calls fails to set up a **DatagramSocket** properly, a **Socket-Exception** is thrown.

 Common Programming Error 16.3

Specifying a port that is already in use or specifying an invalid port number when creating a **DatagramSocket** *results in a* **SocketException**

The **Server** method **waitForPackets** loops forever and waits for packets to arrive at the **Server**. First, it creates a **DatagramPacket** (lines 37 through 39) in which a received packet of information can be stored. Next, the statement

```
receiveSocket.receive( receivePacket );
```

is executed to wait for a packet to arrive at the **Server**. The **receive** method blocks until a packet arrives then stores the packet in its argument (**receivePacket**).

Once a packet is received, lines 45 through 52 output the packet's contents. **DatagramPacket** method **getAddress** returns an **InetAddress** object containing the name of the host from which the packet was sent. Method **getPort** returns an integer specifying the port number through which the host sent the packet. Method **getLength** returns an integer representing the number of bytes of data that were sent. Method **get-Data** returns a byte array containing the data that was sent. The byte array is used to initialize a **String** in our program so the data can be output to the text area.

Next, **sendPacket** (the one to be sent back to the client) is instantiated and four arguments are passed to the **DatagramPacket** constructor. The first argument specifies the **byte** array to be sent. The second argument specifies the number of bytes to be sent. The third argument specifies the client address to which the packet will be sent. The fourth argument specifies the port where the client is waiting to receive packets. The statement

```
sendSocket.send( sendPacket );
```

sends the packet out over the network. If an error occurs either receiving or sending a packet, an **IOException** is thrown.

Class **Client** (Fig. 16.6) works similarly to class **Server** except that the **Client** sends packets when it is told to do so by the user typing a message in a text field and pressing return in the text field. When this occurs, the **action** method (line 81) is invoked, the **String** the user entered in the text field is converted into a **byte** array and the **byte** array is used to create a **DatagramPacket**. The **DatagramPacket** is initialized with the **byte** array, the length of the **String** that was entered by the user, the Internet address to which the packet is to be sent (**InetAddress.getLocalHost()** in this example) and the port number at which the **Server** is waiting for packets. Then the packet is sent. If an error occurs while sending a packet, an **IOException** is thrown.

```
1   // Fig. 16.6: Client.java
2   // Set up a Client that will send packets to a
3   // server and receive packets from a server.
4   import java.io.*;
5   import java.net.*;
6   import java.awt.*;
7
8   public class Client extends Frame {
9       TextField enter;
10      TextArea display;
11      Panel enterPanel;
12      Label enterLabel;
13
14      DatagramPacket sendPacket, receivePacket;
15      DatagramSocket sendSocket, receiveSocket;
16
17      public Client()
18      {
19          super( "Client" );
20          enterPanel = new Panel();
21          enterLabel = new Label( "Enter message:" );
22          enter = new TextField( 20 );
```

Fig. 16.6 Demonstrating the client side of connectionless client/server computing with datagrams (part 1 of 4).

```
23          enterPanel.add( enterLabel );
24          enterPanel.add( enter );
25          add( "North", enterPanel );
26          display = new TextArea( 20, 10 );
27          add( "Center", display );
28          resize( 400, 300 );
29          show();
30
31          try {
32             sendSocket = new DatagramSocket();
33             receiveSocket = new DatagramSocket( 5001 );
34          }
35          catch( SocketException se ) {
36             se.printStackTrace();
37             System.exit( 1 );
38          }
39       }
40
41       public void waitForPackets()
42       {
43          while ( true ) {
44             try {
45                // set up packet
46                byte array[] = new byte[ 100 ];
47                receivePacket =
48                   new DatagramPacket( array, array.length );
49
50                // wait for packet
51                receiveSocket.receive( receivePacket );
52
53                // process packet
54                display.appendText( "\nPacket received:" +
55                   "\nFrom host: " + receivePacket.getAddress() +
56                   "\nHost port: " + receivePacket.getPort() +
57                   "\nLength: " + receivePacket.getLength() +
58                   "\nContaining:\n\t" );
59                byte data[] = receivePacket.getData();
60                String received = new String( data, 0 );
61                display.appendText( received );
62             }
63             catch( IOException exception ) {
64                display.appendText( exception.toString() + "\n" );
65                exception.printStackTrace();
66             }
67          }
68       }
69
```

Fig. 16.6 Demonstrating the client side of connectionless client/server computing with datagrams (part 2 of 4).

```
70      public boolean handleEvent( Event e )
71      {
72         if ( e.id == Event.WINDOW_DESTROY ) {
73            hide();
74            dispose();
75            System.exit( 0 );
76         }
77
78         return super.handleEvent( e );
79      }
80
81      public boolean action( Event event, Object o )
82      {
83         try {
84            display.appendText( "\nSending packet containing: " +
85                                o.toString() + "\n" );
86            String s = o.toString();
87            byte data[] = new byte[ 100 ];
88            s.getBytes( 0, s.length(), data, 0 );
89            sendPacket = new DatagramPacket( data, s.length(),
90               InetAddress.getLocalHost(), 5000 );
91            sendSocket.send( sendPacket );
92            display.appendText( "Packet sent\n" );
93         }
94         catch ( IOException exception ) {
95            display.appendText( exception.toString() + "\n" );
96            exception.printStackTrace();
97         }
98
99         return true;
100     }
101
102     public static void main( String args[] )
103     {
104        Client c = new Client();
105
106        c.waitForPackets();
107     }
108 }
```

Fig. 16.6 Demonstrating the client side of connectionless client/server computing with datagrams (part 3 of 4).

Client method **waitForPackets** loops forever and waits for packets using the statement

```
receiveSocket.receive( receivePacket );
```

which blocks until a packet is received. Note that this does not prevent the user from sending a packet. It only prevents the **while** loop from continuing until a packet arrives at the **Client**.

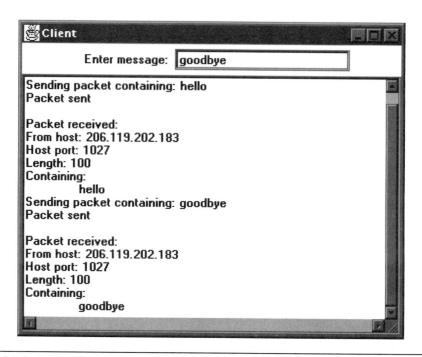

Fig. 16.6 Demonstrating the client side of connectionless client/server computing with datagrams (part 4 of 4).

When a packet arrives, it is stored in **receivePacket** and its contents are displayed in the text area. If an error occurs while receiving a packet an **IOException** is thrown. The user can type information into the **Client** window's text field and press the Enter key at any time; even while a packet is being received. The **action** method processes the text field event and sends the packet containing the data in the text field.

Note that the client in this example must know that the server is receiving packets at port 5000 and is echoing the packets back to the client's port 5001.

16.8 Client/Server Tic-Tac-Toe Using a Multithreaded Server

In this section, we present our capstone networking exercise—the popular game Tic-Tac-Toe implemented using client/server techniques with stream sockets. The program consists of a **TicTacToeServer** application (Fig. 16.7) that allows two **TicTacToeClient** applets (Fig. 16.8) to connect to the server and play Tic-Tac-Toe (outputs shown in Fig. 16.9). As each client connection is received by the server, a **Player** object is created to process the client in a separate thread of execution. This enables the clients to play the game independently. The first client to connect is automatically assigned Xs (X makes the first move) and the second client to connect is automatically assigned Os. The server maintains the information about the board so it can determine if a requested move by one of the players is a valid or invalid move. Each **TicTacToeClient** applet maintains its own version of the Tic-Tac-Toe board on which the state of the game is displayed. The clients can only place a mark in an empty square on the board. Class **Square** is used to implement each of the nine squares on the board. Class **TicTacToeServer** and class **Player** are implemented in file **TicTacToeServer.java**. Class **TicTacToeClient** and class **Square** are implemented in file **TicTacToeClient.java**.

When the **TicTacToeServer** application is executed, the **main** method creates a **TicTacToeServer** object called game. The constructor attempts to set up a **Server-Socket**. If successful, the server window is displayed and the **TicTacToeServer** method **execute** is invoked. Method **execute** loops twice waiting each time for a connection from a client. When a connection is received, a new **Player** object is created to manage the connection as a separate thread and that object's **start** method is invoked.

```
1    // Fig. 16.7: TicTacToeServer.java
2    // This class maintains a game of Tic-Tac-Toe for two
3    // client applets.
4    import java.awt.*;
5    import java.net.*;
6    import java.io.*;
7
8    public class TicTacToeServer extends Frame {
9        private byte board[];
10       private boolean xMove;
11       private TextArea output;
12       private Player players[];
13       private ServerSocket server;
14       private int numberOfPlayers;
15       private int currentPlayer;
16
17       public TicTacToeServer()
18       {
19           super( "Tic-Tac-Toe Server" );
20           board = new byte[ 9 ];
21           xMove = true;
22           players = new Player[ 2 ];
23           currentPlayer = 0;
24
25           // set up ServerSocket
26           try {
27               server = new ServerSocket( 5000, 2 );
28           }
29           catch( IOException e ) {
30               e.printStackTrace();
31               System.exit( 1 );
32           }
33
34           output = new TextArea();
35           add( "Center", output );
36           resize( 300, 300 );
37           show();
38       }
```

Fig. 16.7 Server side of client/server Tic-Tac-Toe program (part 1 of 5).

```
39
40     // wait for two connections so game can be played
41     public void execute()
42     {
43        for ( int i = 0; i < players.length; i++ ) {
44           try {
45              players[ i ] =
46                 new Player( server.accept(), this, i );
47              players[ i ].start();
48              ++numberOfPlayers;
49           }
50           catch( IOException e ) {
51              e.printStackTrace();
52              System.exit( 1 );
53           }
54        }
55     }
56
57     public int getNumberOfPlayers() { return numberOfPlayers; }
58
59     public void display( String s )
60     {
61        output.appendText( s + "\n" );
62     }
63
64     // Determine if a move is valid.
65     // This method is synchronized because only one move can be
66     // made at a time.
67     public synchronized boolean validMove( int loc, int player )
68     {
69        boolean moveDone = false;
70
71        while ( player != currentPlayer ) {
72           try {
73              wait();
74           }
75           catch( InterruptedException e ) {
76           }
77        }
78
79        if ( !isOccupied( loc ) ) {
80           board[ loc ] =
81              (byte)( currentPlayer == 0 ? 'X' : 'O' );
82           currentPlayer = ++currentPlayer % 2;
83           players[ currentPlayer ].otherPlayerMoved( loc );
84           notify();    // tell waiting player to continue
85           return true;
86        }
87        else
88           return false;
89     }
```

Fig. 16.7 Server side of client/server Tic-Tac-Toe program (part 2 of 5).

```
90
91       public boolean isOccupied( int loc )
92       {
93          if ( board[ loc ] == 'X' || board [ loc ] == 'O' )
94             return true;
95          else
96             return false;
97       }
98
99       public boolean gameOver()
100      {
101         return false;
102      }
103
104      public boolean handleEvent( Event event )
105      {
106         if ( event.id == Event.WINDOW_DESTROY ) {
107            hide();
108            dispose();
109
110            for ( int i = 0; i < players.length; i++ )
111               players[ i ].stop();
112
113            System.exit( 0 );
114         }
115
116         return super.handleEvent( event );
117      }
118
119      public static void main( String args[] )
120      {
121         TicTacToeServer game = new TicTacToeServer();
122
123         game.execute();
124      }
125 }
126
127 // Player class to manage each Player as a thread
128 class Player extends Thread {
129      Socket connection;
130      DataInputStream input;
131      DataOutputStream output;
132      TicTacToeServer control;
133      int number;
134      char mark;
135
136      public Player( Socket s, TicTacToeServer t, int num )
137      {
138         mark = ( num == 0 ? 'X' : 'O' );
139
140         connection = s;
```

Fig. 16.7 Server side of client/server Tic-Tac-Toe program (part 3 of 5).

```
141
142         try {
143            input = new DataInputStream(
144                      connection.getInputStream() );
145            output = new DataOutputStream(
146                      connection.getOutputStream() );
147         }
148         catch( IOException e ) {
149            e.printStackTrace();
150            System.exit( 1 );
151         }
152
153         control = t;
154         number = num;
155      }
156
157      public void otherPlayerMoved( int loc )
158      {
159         try {
160            output.writeUTF( "Opponent moved" );
161            output.writeInt( loc );
162         }
163         catch ( IOException e ) {}
164      }
165
166      public void run()
167      {
168         boolean done = false;
169
170         try {
171            control.display( "Player " +
172               ( number == 0 ? 'X' : 'O' ) + " connected" );
173            output.writeChar( mark );
174            output.writeUTF( "Player " +
175               ( number == 0 ? "X connected\n" :
176                               "O connected, please wait\n" ) );
177
178            // wait for another player to arrive
179            if ( control.getNumberOfPlayers() < 2 ) {
180               output.writeUTF( "Waiting for another player" );
181
182               while (control.getNumberOfPlayers() < 2 )
183                  ;
184
185               output.writeUTF(
186                  "Other player connected. Your move." );
187            }
188
189            // Play game
190            while ( !done ) {
191               int location = input.readInt();
```

Fig. 16.7 Server side of client/server Tic-Tac-Toe program (part 4 of 5).

```
192
193              if ( control.validMove( location, number ) ) {
194                 control.display( "loc: " + location );
195                 output.writeUTF( "Valid move." );
196              }
197              else
198                 output.writeUTF( "Invalid move, try again" );
199
200              if ( control.gameOver() )
201                 done = true;
202           }
203
204        connection.close();
205        }
206     catch( IOException e ) {
207        e.printStackTrace();
208        System.exit( 1 );
209     }
210   }
211 }
```

Fig. 16.7 Server side of client/server Tic-Tac-Toe program (part 5 of 5).

When the **Player** is created, its constructor takes the **Socket** object representing the connection to the client and gets the associated input and output streams. The Player's **run** method controls the information that is sent to the client and the information that is received from the client. First, it tells the client that the client's connection has been made, then it passes the client the character that the client will place on the board when a move is made. Next, if there are not currently two clients, the **run** method loops until a second client connects. At this point the game can be played and the **run** method begins executing its second **while** structure. Each iteration of this **while** structure, reads an integer representing the location where the client wants to place a mark and invokes the **TicTacToeServer** method **validMove** to check the move. A message is sent to the client indicating if the move was valid.

Method **validMove** is a **synchronized** method that allows only one move to be attempted at a time. This prevents both players from modifying the state information of the game simultaneously. If the **Player** attempting to validate a move is not the current player (i.e., the one allowed to make a move), the **Player** is placed in a *wait* state until it is his or her turn to move. If the position for the move being validated is already occupied on the board, **false** is returned. Otherwise, the server places a mark for the player in its local representation of the board, notifies the other **Player** object that a move has been made (so the client can be sent a message), invokes the **notify** method so the waiting **Player** (if there is one) can validate a move and returns **true** to indicate that the move is valid.

When a **TicTacToeClient** applet begins execution, it creates a text area in which messages from the server are displayed and a representation of the board using nine **Square** objects. The applet's **start** method opens a connection to the server and gets the associated input and output streams from the **Socket** object. Class **TicTacToe-Client** implements the **Runnable** interface so that a separate thread can be used to continually read messages that are sent from the server to the client. After the connection to the server is established, the **Thread** object **outputThread** is created and initialized with the applet, then the thread's **start** method is invoked. The applet's **run** method controls the separate thread of execution. The method first reads the mark character (X or O) from the server, then loops continually and reads messages from the server. The messages are passed to the applet's **processMessage** method for processing.

```
1   // Fig. 16.8: TicTacToeClient.java
2   // Client for the TicTacToe program
3   import java.applet.Applet;
4   import java.awt.*;
5   import java.net.*;
6   import java.io.*;
7
8   // Client class to let a user play Tic-Tac-Toe with
9   // another user across a network.
10  public class TicTacToeClient extends Applet
11                              implements Runnable {
12     TextField id;
13     TextArea display;
14     Panel boardPanel, panel2;
15     Square board[][], currentSquare;
16     Socket connection;
17     DataInputStream input;
18     DataOutputStream output;
19     Thread outputThread;
20     char myMark;
21
22     // Set up user-interface and board
23     public void init()
24     {
25         setLayout( new BorderLayout() );
```

Fig. 16.8 Client side of client/server Tic-Tac-Toe program (part 1 of 4).

```
26          display = new TextArea( 4, 30 );
27          display.setEditable( false );
28          add( "South", display );
29
30          boardPanel = new Panel();
31          boardPanel.setLayout( new GridLayout( 3, 3, 0, 0 ) );
32          board = new Square[ 3 ][ 3 ];
33
34          for ( int row = 0; row < board.length; row++ )
35             for ( int col = 0; col < board[ row ].length; col++ ) {
36                board[ row ][ col ] = new Square();
37                boardPanel.add( board[ row ][ col ] );
38             }
39
40          id = new TextField();
41          id.setEditable( false );
42          add( "North", id );
43
44          panel2 = new Panel();
45          panel2.add( boardPanel );
46          add( "Center", panel2 );
47       }
48
49       // Make connection to server and get associated streams.
50       // Start separate thread to allow this applet to
51       // continually update its output in text area display.
52       public void start()
53       {
54          try {
55             connection =
56                new Socket( InetAddress.getLocalHost(), 5000 );
57             input = new DataInputStream(
58                connection.getInputStream() );
59             output = new DataOutputStream(
60                connection.getOutputStream() );
61          }
62          catch ( IOException e ) {
63             e.printStackTrace();
64          }
65
66          outputThread = new Thread( this );
67          outputThread.start();
68       }
69
70       // When user clicks mouse and releases in a square,
71       // send an integer representing the clicked square
72       // to the server. The integer is a number from 0 to 8
73       // where the first row contains positions 0, 1 and 2,
74       // the second row contains positions 3, 4 and 5 and
75       // the third row contains positions 6, 7 and 8.
```

Fig. 16.8 Client side of client/server Tic-Tac-Toe program (part 2 of 4).

```
76     public boolean mouseUp( Event e, int x, int y )
77     {
78        for ( int row = 0; row < board.length; row++ ) {
79           for ( int col = 0; col < board[ row ].length; col++ ) {
80              try {
81                 if ( e.target == board[ row ][ col ] ) {
82                    currentSquare = board[ row ][ col ];
83                    output.writeInt( row * 3 + col );
84                 }
85              }
86              catch ( IOException ie ) {
87                 ie.printStackTrace();
88              }
89           }
90        }
91        return true;
92     }
93
94     // Control thread that allows continuous update of the
95     // text area display.
96     public void run()
97     {
98        // First get player's mark (X or O)
99        try {
100          myMark = input.readChar();
101          id.setText( "You are player \"" + myMark + "\"" );
102       }
103       catch ( IOException e ) {
104          e.printStackTrace();
105       }
106
107       // Receive messages sent to client
108       while ( true ) {
109          try {
110             String s = input.readUTF();
111             processMessage( s );
112          }
113          catch ( IOException e ) {
114             e.printStackTrace();
115          }
116       }
117    }
118
119    // Process messages sent to client
120    public void processMessage( String s )
121    {
122       if ( s.equals( "Valid move." ) ) {
123          display.appendText( "Valid move, please wait.\n" );
124          currentSquare.setMark( myMark );
125          currentSquare.repaint();
126       }
```

Fig. 16.8 Client side of client/server Tic-Tac-Toe program (part 3 of 4).

```
127          else if ( s.equals( "Invalid move, try again" ) ) {
128             display.appendText( s + "\n" );
129          }
130          else if ( s.equals( "Opponent moved" ) ) {
131             try {
132                int loc = input.readInt();
133
134                done:
135                for ( int row = 0; row < board.length; row++ )
136                   for ( int col = 0;
137                         col < board[ row ].length; col++ )
138                      if ( row * 3 + col == loc ) {
139                         board[ row ][ col ].setMark(
140                            ( myMark == 'X' ? 'O' : 'X' ) );
141                         board[ row ][ col ].repaint();
142                         break done;
143                      }
144
145                display.appendText(
146                   "Opponent moved. Your turn.\n" );
147             }
148             catch ( IOException e ) {
149                e.printStackTrace();
150             }
151          }
152          else {
153             display.appendText( s + "\n" );
154          }
155       }
156 }
157
158 // Maintains one square on the board
159 class Square extends Canvas {
160    char mark;
161
162    public Square()
163    {
164       resize ( 30, 30 );
165    }
166
167    public void setMark( char c ) { mark = c; }
168
169    public void paint( Graphics g )
170    {
171       g.drawRect( 0, 0, 29, 29 );
172       g.drawString( String.valueOf( mark ), 11, 20 );
173    }
174 }
```

Fig. 16.8 Client side of client/server Tic-Tac-Toe program (part 4 of 4).

Fig. 16.9 Sample outputs from the client/server Tic-Tac-Toe program (part 1 of 4).

If the message received is the string "**Valid move.**", the message "**Valid move, please wait.**" is displayed, the client's mark is set in the current square (the one in which the user clicked) and the square is repainted. If the message received is "**Invalid move, try again**", the message is displayed so the user can click a different square. If the message received is "**Opponent moved**", an integer is read from the server indicating where the opponent moved and a mark is placed in that square of the board. If any other message is received, the message is simply displayed.

Fig. 16.9 Sample outputs from the client/server Tic-Tac-Toe program (part 2 of 4).

16.9 Security and the Network

As much as we look forward to writing a great variety of powerful network-based applications, our efforts will be crimped because of limitations imposed on Java because of security concerns.

Fig. 16.9 Sample outputs from the client/server Tic-Tac-Toe program (part 3 of 4).

Many Web browsers like Netscape Navigator prohibit Java applets from doing file processing on the machines on which they execute. Think about it. A Java applet is designed to be sent to your browser via an HTML document that could be downloaded from any Web server in the world. Often you will know very little about the sources of Java applets that will execute on your system. To allow these applets free reign with your files could be disastrous.

Fig. 16.9 Sample outputs from the client/server Tic-Tac-Toe program (part 4 of 4).

A more subtle situation occurs with limiting the machines to which executing applets can connect. To build truly collaborative applications, we would ideally like to have our applets communicate with machines almost anywhere. But Web browsers often restrict an applet so that it can only communicate with the machine from which it was originally downloaded.

These restrictions may seem too harsh. Java is a new programming language. It needs time to evolve and mature. We need to get more experience with Java applets and applications. Java developers need time to create solutions to some of the problems posed by Java's intriguing architecture and environment.

16.10 Forthcoming Networking and Security APIs

The Java practitioner needs to keep in touch with the rapidly evolving world of Java APIs. Just before this book went to press, we received a copy of the document

`http://java.sun.com/products/apiOverview.html`

that listed nine major new APIs scheduled for implementation and release in the near future. These included the Java RMI API, Java Server API and Java Security API.

The *Java RMI (Remote Method Invocation) API* enables remote method invocation between two Java applications. This can be accomplished in a client/server manner or in a peer-to-peer manner in which applets and applications on different machines can communicate with each other directly by invoking each other's methods.

The *Java Server API* facilitates the creation of Java-based servers for the Internet and for intranets. Having such a uniform set of calls will be of great value to organizations with many departments developing their own Java networking solutions.

The *Java Security API* will help developers secure their network transmissions through the use of encryption and "digital signatures." This will make possible the kind of authentication that will enable browsers to loosen some of the rather tight restrictions currently placed on Java applets.

Summary

- Java's networking capabilities are centralized in the **java.net** package.
- Stream sockets provide a connection-oriented service. The protocol used for transmission is the popular TCP (Transmission Control Protocol).
- UDP—the User Datagram Protocol—is a connectionless service that does not guarantee that packets will arrive in any particular order. UDP packets can be lost, can be duplicated, and can even arrive out of sequence.
- The **http** protocol uses URLs (Uniform Resource Locators, also called Universal Resource Locators) to locate data on the Internet.
- The **URL** constructor determines if the **String** passed as an argument represents a valid Uniform Resource Locator. If so, the **URL** object is initialized to contain the Uniform Resource Locator; otherwise a **MalformedURLException** is generated.
- The applet's **getAppletContext** method (inherited from class **Applet**) gets a reference to an **AppletContext** object that represents the applet's environment—i.e., the browser in which the applet is executing.
- The **AppletContext** method **showDocument** takes a **URL** object as an argument and displays in the browser the World Wide Web resource associated with that **URL**.

- A **URL** object can be used to open an **InputStream** from a file on a server with the **URL** method **openStream**.

- A **ServerSocket** object establishes the port where a server waits for connections from clients. The second argument to the **ServerSocket** constructor specifies the number of clients that can wait for a connection and be processed by the server. If the queue of clients is full, client connections are automatically refused.

- Stream-based connections are managed with **Socket** objects.

- The **ServerSocket** method **accept** waits indefinitely (i.e., blocks) for a connection from a client and returns a **Socket** object when a connection is established.

- The **Socket** method **getOutputStream** gets a reference to the **OutputStream** associated with a **Socket**. The **Socket** method **getInputStream** gets a reference to the **InputStream** associated with the **Socket**.

- When transmission over a **Socket** connection is complete, the server closes the connection by issuing the **close** method on the **Socket**.

- A **Socket** object is used to connect a client to a server by specifying the server name and port number when the Socket object is instantiated. A connection attempt that fails throws an **IOException** object.

- **UnknownHostException** is a subclass of **IOException**.

- The **InputStream** method **read** returns -1 when end-of-stream is detected.

- An **EOFException** is generated when a **DataInputStream** attempts to read a value (with a method other than **readLine**) from a stream on which end-of-stream is detected.

- **InetAddress** method **getLocalHost** returns an **InetAddress** object containing the local host name of the computer on which the program is executing.

- The port where a client connects to a server is sometimes called the handshake point.

- Connection-oriented transmission is like the telephone system in which you dial and are given a connection to the telephone you wish to communicate with; the connection is maintained for the duration of your phone call, even when you are not talking.

- Connectionless transmission with datagrams is like the way mail is carried via the postal service. A large message that will not fit in one envelope can be broken into separate message pieces that are placed in separate, sequentially numbered envelopes. Each of the letters is then mailed at once. The letters may arrive in order, out of order or not at all.

- **DatagramPacket**s are used to create the packets to send and receive information.

- **DatagramSocket**s are used to send and receive **DatagramPacket**s.

- The **DatagramSocket** constructor that takes no arguments sets up a socket for sending packets out over the network. The computer assigns an available port to the **sendSocket** object automatically.

- The **DatagramSocket** constructor that takes an integer port number argument sets up a port for receiving packets from the network.

- If a **DatagramSocket** constructor fails to set up a **DatagramSocket** properly, a **SocketException** is thrown.

- **DatagramSocket** method **receive** waits until a packet arrives then stores the packet in its argument.

- **DatagramPacket** method **getAddress** returns an **InetAddress** object containing the name of the host from which the packet was sent.

- **DatagramPacket** method **getPort** returns an integer specifying the port number through which the host sent the **DatagramPacket**.

- **DatagramPacket** method **getLength** returns an integer representing the number of bytes of data in a **DatagramPacket**.

- **DatagramPacket** method **getData** returns a byte array containing the data in a **DatagramPacket**.

- The **DatagramPacket** constructor for a packet to be sent takes four arguments—the **byte** array to be sent, the number of bytes to be sent, the client address to which the packet will be sent and the port number where the client is waiting to receive packets.

- **DatagramSocket** method **send** sends a **DatagramPacket** out over the network.

- If an error occurs either receiving or sending a **DatagramPacket**, an **IOException** is thrown.

- Many Web browsers like Netscape Navigator prohibit Java applets from doing file processing on the machines on which they execute.

- Web browsers often restrict an applet so that it can only communicate with the machine from which it was originally downloaded.

Terminology

accept a connection
accept method of **ServerSocket** class
AppletContext
client
client connects to a server
client-side socket
client-server relationship
collaborative computing
computer networking
connectionless transmission with datagrams
close a connection
close method
close a **Socket**
close method of **DataInputStream**
connect method
connect to a port
connect to a World Wide Web site
connection

connectionless service
connection-oriented service
connection request
datagram
DatagramPacket class
datagram socket
DatagramSocket class
DataInputStream
deny a connection
duplicated packets
getAddress method of **DatagramPacket**
getAppletContext
getData method of class **DatagramPacket**
getInputStream method of class **Socket**
getLength method of **DatagramPacket**
getLocalHost method of **DatagramPacket**
getOutputStream method of class **Socket**
getPort method of class **DatagramPacket**

handshake point
heterogeneous computer systems
host
import **java.net**
InputStream
Internet
Internet address
InetAddress class
InetAddress.getLocalHost()
IOException
java.net package
Java RMI (Remote Method Invocation) API
Java Security API
Java Server API
java.sun.com
lost packets
MalformedURLException
multithreaded server
Netscape Navigator
network programming
networking
open a socket
open a **URL** connection
openStream method of class **URL**
out-of-sequence packets
OutputStream
packet

packet length
port
port number on a server
read from a socket
readLine method of **DataInputStream**
receive method of class **DatagramSocket**
register an available port number
send method of class **DatagramSocket**
server
server-side socket
ServerSocket class
showDocument method of **AppletContext**
socket
socket-based communications
Socket class
SocketException
stream socket
TCP (Transmission Control Protocol)
UDP (User Datagram Protocol)
UnknownHostException
URL (Uniform Resource Locator)
URL class
wait for a connection
wait for a packet
Web browser
Web server
World Wide Web

Common Programming Errors

16.1   A **MalformedURLException** is thrown when a **String** that is not in proper URL format is passed to a **URL** constructor.

16.2   An **UnknownHostException** is thrown when a server address indicated by a client can not be resolved.

16.3   Specifying a port that is already in use or specifying an invalid port number when creating a **DatagramSocket** results in a **SocketException**.

Performance Tip

16.1   Close a socket immediately after a network connection is no longer needed.

16.2   In high-performance systems in which memory is abundant, a multithreaded server can be implemented to create a pool of threads that can be assigned quickly to handle network I/O across each new **Socket** as it is created. Thus, when a connection is received, the server need not suffer the overhead of thread creation.

Portability Tip

16.1 The TCP protocol and its related set of protocols enable a great variety of *heterogeneous computer systems* (i.e., computer systems with different processors and different operating systems) to intercommunicate.

Software Engineering Observations

16.1 With sockets, network I/O appears to Java programs to be virtually identical to file I/O. Sockets hide much of the complexity of network programming from the programmer.

16.2 With Java's multithreading, we can create *multithreaded servers* that can manage many simultaneous connections with many clients; this multithreaded-server architecture is precisely what is used in popular UNIX, Windows NT and OS/2 network servers.

16.3 A multithreaded server can be implemented to take the **Socket** returned by each call to **accept** and create a new thread that would manage network I/O across that **Socket**, or a multithreaded server can be implemented to maintain a pool of threads ready to manage network I/O across the new **Socket**s as they are created.

Self-Review Exercises

16.1 Fill in the blanks in each of the following:
   a) An _____ is thrown when an I/O error occurs when closing a socket.
   b) An _____ is thrown when a server address indicated by a client cannot be resolved.
   c) If a **DatagramSocket** constructor fails to set up a **DatagramSocket** properly, a _____ is thrown.
   d) The **URL** constructor determines if the **String** passed as an argument represents a valid Uniform Resource Locator. If so, the **URL** object is initialized to contain the Uniform Resource Locator; otherwise, a _____ is generated.
   e) Java's networking classes are contained in the _____ package
   f) Class _____ is used to create a socket for unreliable datagram transmission.
   g) An object of class _____ contains an Internet address.
   h) The two types of sockets we discussed in this chapter are _____ sockets and _____ sockets.
   i) The acronym URL stands for _____.
   j) The key protocol that forms the basis of the World Wide Web is _____.
   k) **AppletContext** method _____ receives a URL object as an argument and displays in a browser the World Wide Web resource associated with that URL.
   l) **InetAddress** method **getLocalHost** returns an _____ object containing the local host name of the computer on which the program is executing.

16.2 State whether the following true or false. If the answer is false, explain why.
   a) A **URL** object once created cannot be changed.
   b) UDP is a connection-oriented protocol.
   c) With stream sockets a process establishes a connection to another process.
   d) A server waits at a port for connections from a client.
   e) Datagram transmission is reliable—packets are guaranteed to arrive in sequence.

f) For security reasons, many Web browsers like Netscape Navigator allow Java applets to do file processing only on the machines on which they execute.

g) Web browsers often restrict an applet so that it can only communicate with the machine from which it was originally downloaded.

Answers to Self-Review Exercises

16.1   a) `IOException`. b) `UnknownHostException`. c) `SocketException`. d) `Mal-formedURLException`. e) `java.net`. f) `DatagramSocket`. g) `InetAddress`. h) stream, datagram. i) Uniform Resource Locator. j) `http`. k) `showDocument`. l) `InetAddress`.

16.2   a) true. b) false; UDP is a connectionless protocol and TCP is a connection-oriented protocol. c) true. d) true. e) false; packets could be lost and packets can arrive out of order. f) false; most browsers prevent applets from doing file processing on the client machine. g) true.

Exercises

16.3   Distinguish between connection-oriented network services and connectionless network services.

16.4   How does a client determine the host name of the client computer?

16.5   Under what circumstances would a **SocketException** be thrown?

16.6   How can a client get a line of text from a server?

16.7   Describe how a client can read a file from a server through a URL connection.

16.8   Describe how a client connects to a server.

16.9   Describe how a server sends data to a client.

16.10   Describe how to prepare a server to receive a streams-based connection request from a single client.

16.11   Describe how to prepare a server to receive connection requests from multiple clients where each client that connects should be processed in parallel with all other connected clients.

16.12   How does a server listen for connections at a port?

16.13   What determines how many connect requests from clients can wait in a queue to connect to a server?

16.14   As described in the text, what reasons might cause a server refuse a connection request from a client?

16.15   Use a socket connection to allow a client to specify a file name and have the server send the contents of the file or indicate that the file does not exist.

16.16   Modify the preceding exercise to allow the client to modify the contents of the file and send the file back to the server for storage. The user can edit the file in a text area then click a *save changes* button to send the file back to the server.

16.17   Modify program of Fig. 16.1 to show a list of sites in a **List** object. Allow uses to add their own sites to the list and remove sites from the list.

16.18   Multithreaded servers are quite popular today, especially because of the increasing use of multiprocessing servers. Modify the simple server presented in Section 16.6 to be a multithreaded server. Then use several clients and have each of them connect to the server simultaneously.

16.19   In the text we presented a tic-tac-toe program controlled by a multithreaded server. Develop a checkers program modeled after the tic-tac-toe program. The two users should alternate making moves. Your program should mediate the players moves determining whose turn it is and allowing only valid moves. The players themselves will determine when the game is over.

16.20   Develop a chess playing program modeled after the checkers program in the previous exercises.

16.21   Develop a black jack card game program in which the server deals cards to each of the clients. The server should deal additional cards (as per the rules of the game) to each player as requested.

16.22   Develop a poker card game in which the server deals cards to each of the clients. The server should deal additional cards (as per the rules of the game) to each player as requested.

16.23   *(Modifications to the Multithreaded Tic-Tac-Toe Program)* The programs of Fig. 16.7 and 16.8 implemented a multithreaded, client/server version of the game Tic-Tac-Toe. Our goal in developing this game was to demonstrate a multithreaded server that could process multiple connections from clients at the same time. The server in the example is really a mediator between the two client applets—it makes sure that each move is valid and that each client moves in the proper order. The server does not determine who won or lost or if there was a draw. Also, there is no capability to allow a new game to be played or to terminate an existing game. The following is a list of suggested modifications to the existing program.

    a) Modify class **TicTacToeServer** to test for a win, loss or draw. Send a message to each client that indicates the result of the game when the game is over.

    b) Modify class **TicTacToeClient** to display a button that when clicked allows the client to play another game. The button should only be enabled when a game completes. Note that both class **TicTacToeClient** and class **TicTacToeServer** must be modified to reset the board and all state information. Also, the other **TicTacToeClient** should be notified that a new game is about to begin so its board and state can be reset.

    c) Modify class **TicTacToeClient** to provide a button that allows a client to terminate the program at any time. When the button is clicked, the server and the other client should be notified. The server should then wait for a connection from another client so a new game can begin.

    d) Modify the class **TicTacToeClient** and class **TicTacToeServer** so the winner of a game can choose X or O for the next game. Remember: X always goes first.

    e) If you would like to be ambitious, allow a client to play against the server while the server waits for a connection from another client.

16.24 *(3-D Multithreaded Tic-Tac-Toe)* Modify the multithreaded, client/server Tic-Tac-Toe program to implement a three-dimensional, 4-by-4-by-4 version. Implement the server to simply mediate between the two clients. Display the three-dimensional board as four boards containing four rows and four columns each. If you would like to be ambitious, try the following modifications:

a) Draw the board in a three dimensional manner.

b) Allow the server to test for a win, loss or draw. Beware! There are many possible ways to win on a 4-by-4-by-4 board!

17

Data
Structures

Objectives

- To be able to form linked data structures using references, self-referential classes, and recursion.
- To be able to create and manipulate dynamic data structures such as linked lists, queues, stacks, and binary trees.
- To understand various important applications of linked data structures.
- To understand how to create reusable data structures with classes, inheritance, and composition.

Much that I bound, I could not free;
Much that I freed returned to me.
Lee Wilson Dodd

'Will you walk a little faster?' said a whiting to a snail,
'There's a porpoise close behind us, and he's treading on my tail.'
Lewis Carroll

There is always room at the top.
Daniel Webster

Push on — keep moving.
Thomas Morton

I think that I shall never see
A poem lovely as a tree.
Joyce Kilmer

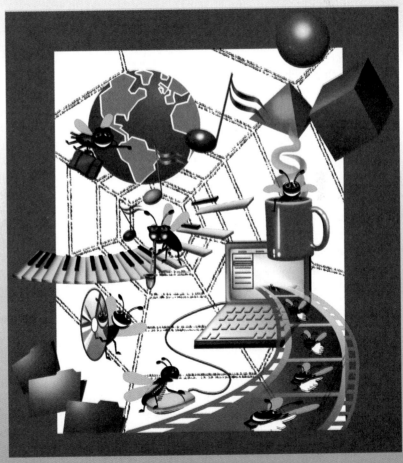

Outline

17.1 Introduction

We have studied fixed-size *data structures* such as single-subscripted arrays and double-subscripted arrays. This chapter introduces *dynamic data structures* that grow and shrink at execution time. *Linked lists* are collections of data items "lined up in a row"—insertions and deletions are made anywhere in a linked list. *Stacks* are important in compilers and operating systems—insertions and deletions are made only at one end of a stack—its *top*. *Queues* represent waiting lines; insertions are made at the back (also referred to as the *tail*) of a queue, and deletions are made from the front (also referred to as the *head*) of a queue. *Binary trees* facilitate high-speed searching and sorting of data, efficient elimination of duplicate data items, representing file system directories, and compiling expressions into machine language. These data structures have many other interesting applications.

   We will discuss each of the major types of data structures and implement programs that create and manipulate these data structures. We use classes, inheritance, and composition to create and package these data structures for reusability and maintainability.

   The chapter examples are practical programs that you will be able to use in more advanced courses and in industry applications. The programs are especially heavy on reference manipulation. The exercises include a rich collection of useful applications.

   We encourage you to attempt the major project described in the special section entitled "Building Your Own Compiler." You have been using a compiler to translate your Java programs to bytecodes so that you could execute these programs on your computer. In this project, you will actually build your own compiler. It will read a file of statements written in a simple, yet powerful, high-level language similar to early versions of the popular language Basic. Your compiler will translate these statements into a file of Simpletron Machine Language (SML) instructions—SML is the language you learned in the Chapter 5 special section, "Building Your Own Computer." Your Simpletron Simulator program will then execute the SML program produced by your compiler! Implementing this project using an object-oriented approach will give you a wonderful opportunity to exercise most of what you have learned in this book. The special section carefully walks you through the specifications of the high-level language, and describes the algorithms you will need to convert each type of high-level language statement into machine language instructions. If you enjoy being challenged, you might attempt the many enhancements to both the compiler and the Simpletron Simulator suggested in the Exercises.

17.2 Self-Referential Classes

A *self-referential class* contains a reference member that refers to a class object of the same class type. For example, the definition

```
class Node {
    private int data;
    private Node next;

    Node( int d ) { /* method body */ }
    void setData( int d ) { /* method body */ }
    int getData() { /* method body */ }
    void setNext( Node nextNode ) { /* method body */ }
    Node getNext() { /* method body */ }
}
```

defines a type, **Node**. Type **Node** has two private instance variables—integer **data** and **Node** reference **next**. Member **next** references an object of type **Node**—an object of the same type as the one being declared here, hence the term "self-referential class." Member **next** is referred to as a *link*—i.e., **next** can be used to "tie" an object of type **Node** to another object of the same type. Type **Node** also has five methods: a constructor that receives an integer to initialize **data**, a **setData** method to set the value **data**, a **getData** method to return the value of **data**, a **setNext** method to set the value of **next**, and a **getNext** method to return the value of member **next**.

Self-referential objects can be linked together to form useful data structures such as lists, queues, stacks and trees. Figure 17.1 illustrates two self-referential objects linked together to form a list. A slash—representing a **null** reference—is placed in the link member of the second self-referential object to indicate that the link does not refer to another object. The slash is for illustration purposes; it does not correspond to the backslash character in Java. A **null** reference normally indicates the end of a data structure.

Common Programming Error 17.1

*Not setting the link in the last node of a list to **null**.*

17.3 Dynamic Memory Allocation

Creating and maintaining dynamic data structures requires *dynamic memory allocation*— the ability for a program to obtain more memory space at execution time to hold new nodes

Fig. 17.1 Two self-referential class objects linked together.

and to release space no longer needed. Java programs do not explicitly release dynamically allocated memory. Rather, Java performs automatic garbage collection. The limit for dynamic memory allocation can be as large as the amount of available physical memory in the computer or the amount of available virtual memory in a virtual memory system. Often, the limits are much smaller because the computer's available memory must be shared among many users.

Operator **new** is essential to dynamic memory allocation. Operator **new** takes as an argument the type of the object being dynamically allocated and returns a reference to an object of that type. For example, the statement

```
Node nodeToAdd = new Node( 10 );
```

allocates the appropriate number of bytes to store a **Node** and stores a reference to this memory in **nodeToAdd**. If no memory is available, **new** throws an **OutOfMemoryException**. The 10 is the **Node** object's data.

The following sections discuss lists, stacks, queues, and trees. These data structures are created and maintained with dynamic memory allocation and self-referential classes.

Good Programming Practice 17.1

*When using **new**, test for an **OutOfMemoryException**. Perform appropriate error processing if the requested memory is not allocated.*

17.4 Linked Lists

A *linked list* is a linear collection of self-referential class objects, called *nodes,* connected by reference *links*—hence, the term "linked" list. A linked list is accessed via a reference to the first node of the list. Subsequent nodes are accessed via the link-reference member stored in each node. By convention, the link reference in the last node of a list is set to **null** to mark the end of the list. Data are stored in a linked list dynamically—each node is created as necessary. A node can contain data of any type including objects of other classes. Stacks and queues are also linear data structures, and, as we will see, are constrained versions of linked lists. Trees are nonlinear data structures.

Lists of data can be stored in arrays, but linked lists provide several advantages. A linked list is appropriate when the number of data elements to be represented in the data structure at one time is unpredictable. Linked lists are dynamic, so the length of a list can increase or decrease as necessary. The size of a "conventional" Java array, however, cannot be altered, because the array size is fixed at creation time. "Conventional" arrays can become full. Linked lists become full only when the system has insufficient memory to satisfy dynamic storage allocation requests. The **java.util** package of the Java API contains class **Vector** for implementing and manipulating dynamic arrays that can grow and shrink during the execution of the program. We will discuss class **Vector** in Chapter 18, "Utilities and Bit Manipulation."

Performance Tip 17.1

An array can be declared to contain more elements than the number of items expected, but this can waste memory. Linked lists can provide better memory utilization in these situations. Linked lists allow the program to adapt at run time.

Performance Tip 17.2

Insertion into a linked list is fast—only two references have to be modified. All existing nodes remain at their current locations in memory.

Linked lists can be maintained in sorted order simply by inserting each new element at the proper point in the list. Existing list elements do not need to be moved.

Performance Tip 17.3

Insertion and deletion in a sorted array can be time consuming—all the elements following the inserted or deleted element must be shifted appropriately.

Performance Tip 17.4

The elements of an array are stored contiguously in memory. This allows immediate access to any array element because the address of any element can be calculated directly based on its position relative to the beginning of the array. Linked lists do not afford such immediate access to their elements.

Linked list nodes are normally not stored contiguously in memory. Logically, however, the nodes of a linked list appear to be contiguous. Figure 17.2 illustrates a linked list with several nodes.

Performance Tip 17.5

Using dynamic memory allocation (instead of arrays) for data structures that grow and shrink at execution time can save memory. Keep in mind, however, that references occupy space, and that dynamic memory allocation incurs the overhead of method calls.

The program of Fig. 17.3 (whose output is shown in Fig. 17.4) uses a **List** class to manipulate a list of miscellaneous object types. The main method of the **ListTest** class creates a list of objects, inserts objects at the beginning of the list using method **insertAtFront**, inserts objects at the end of the list using method **insertAtBack**, deletes objects from the front of the list using method **removeFromFront**, and deletes objects from the end of the list using method **removeFromBack**. After each insertion and deletion operation, the **print** method is invoke to display the contents of the list. A detailed discussion of the program follows. If an attempt is made to remove an item from an empty list, an **EmptyListException** (defined on line 140 of Fig. 17.3) is thrown. Exercise 17.20 asks you to implement a recursive method that prints a linked list backwards, and Exercise 17.21 asks you to implement a recursive method that searches a linked list for a particular data item.

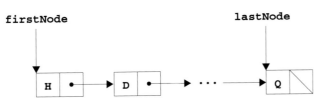

Fig. 17.2 A graphical representation of a list.

```
1    // Class ListNode definition (File: List.java)
2    class ListNode {
3       // friendly data so class List can access it directly
4       Object data;
5       ListNode next;
6
7       // Constructor: Create a ListNode that refers to Object o.
8       ListNode( Object o )
9       {
10         data = o;      // this node refers to Object o
11         next = null;   // set next to null
12      }
13
14      // Constructor: Create a ListNode that refers to Object o and
15      // to the next ListNode in the List.
16      ListNode( Object o, ListNode nextNode )
17      {
18         data = o;           // this node refers to Object o
19         next = nextNode;    // set next to refer to next
20      }
21
22      // Return the Object in this node
23      Object getObject() { return data; }
24
25      // Return the next node
26      ListNode getnext() { return next; }
27   }
28
29   // Class List definition
30   class List {
31      private ListNode firstNode;
32      private ListNode lastNode;
33      private String name;   // String like "list" used in printing
34
35      // Constructor: Construct an empty List with s as the name
36      public List( String s )
37      {
38         name = s;
39         firstNode = lastNode = null;
40      }
41
42      // Constructor: Construct an empty List with
43      // "list" as the name
44      public List() { this( "list" ); }
45
46      // Insert an Object at the front of the List
47      // If List is empty, firstNode and lastNode refer to
48      // same Object. Otherwise, firstNode refers to new node.
49      public void insertAtFront( Object insertItem )
50      {
```

Fig. 17.3 Manipulating a linked list (part 1 of 4).

```
51          if ( isEmpty() )
52              firstNode = lastNode = new ListNode( insertItem );
53          else
54              firstNode = new ListNode( insertItem, firstNode );
55      }
56
57      // Insert an Object at the end of the List
58      // If List is empty, firstNode and lastNode refer to
59      // same Object. Otherwise, lastNode's next instance
60      // variable refers to new node.
61      public void insertAtBack( Object insertItem )
62      {
63          if ( isEmpty() )
64              firstNode = lastNode = new ListNode( insertItem );
65          else
66              lastNode = lastNode.next = new ListNode( insertItem );
67      }
68
69      // Remove the first node from the List.
70      public Object removeFromFront() throws EmptyListException
71      {
72          Object removeItem = null;
73
74          if ( isEmpty() )
75              throw new EmptyListException( name );
76
77          removeItem = firstNode.data;   // retrieve the data
78
79          // reset the firstNode and lastNode references
80          if ( firstNode.equals( lastNode ) )
81              firstNode = lastNode = null;
82          else
83              firstNode = firstNode.next;
84
85          return removeItem;
86      }
87
88      // Remove the last node from the List.
89      public Object removeFromBack() throws EmptyListException
90      {
91          Object removeItem = null;
92
93          if ( isEmpty() )
94              throw new EmptyListException( name );
95
96          removeItem = lastNode.data;   // retrieve the data
97
98          // reset the firstNode and lastNode references
99          if ( firstNode.equals( lastNode ) )
100             firstNode = lastNode = null;
```

Fig. 17.3 Manipulating a linked list (part 2 of 4).

```
101          else {
102             ListNode current = firstNode;
103
104             while ( current.next != lastNode )
105                current = current.next;
106
107             lastNode = current;
108             current.next = null;
109          }
110
111          return removeItem;
112       }
113
114       // Return true if the List is empty
115       public boolean isEmpty() { return firstNode == null; }
116
117       // Output the List contents
118       public void print()
119       {
120          if ( isEmpty() ) {
121             System.out.println( "Empty " + name );
122             return;
123          }
124
125          System.out.print( "The " + name + " is: " );
126
127          ListNode current = firstNode;
128
129          while ( current != null ) {
130             System.out.print( current.data.toString() + " " );
131             current = current.next;
132          }
133
134          System.out.println();
135          System.out.println();
136       }
137    }
138
139    // Class EmptyListException definition
140    class EmptyListException extends RuntimeException {
141       public EmptyListException( String name )
142       {
143          super( "The " + name + " is empty" );
144       }
145    }
```

Fig. 17.3 Manipulating a linked list (part 3 of 4).

```
146  // Class ListTest (File: ListTest.java)
147  public class ListTest {
148     public static void main( String args[] )
149     {
150        List objList = new List();  // create the List container
151
152        // Create objects to store in the List
153        Boolean b = new Boolean( true );
154        Character c = new Character( '$' );
155        Integer i = new Integer( 34567 );
156        String s = new String( "hello" );
157
158        // Use the List insert methods
159        objList.insertAtFront( b );
160        objList.print();
161        objList.insertAtFront( c );
162        objList.print();
163        objList.insertAtBack( i );
164        objList.print();
165        objList.insertAtBack( s );
166        objList.print();
167
168        // Use the List remove methods
169        Object removedObj;
170
171        try {
172           removedObj = objList.removeFromFront();
173           System.out.println( removedObj.toString() +
174                               " removed" );
175           objList.print();
176           removedObj = objList.removeFromFront();
177           System.out.println( removedObj.toString() +
178                               " removed" );
179           objList.print();
180           removedObj = objList.removeFromBack();
181           System.out.println( removedObj.toString() +
182                               " removed" );
183           objList.print();
184           removedObj = objList.removeFromBack();
185           System.out.println( removedObj.toString() +
186                               " removed" );
187           objList.print();
188        }
189        catch ( EmptyListException e ) {
190           System.err.println( "\n" + e.toString() );
191        }
192     }
193  }
```

Fig. 17.3 Manipulating a linked list (part 4 of 4).

```
The list is: true

The list is: $ true

The list is: $ true 34567

The list is: $ true 34567 hello

$ removed
The list is: true 34567 hello

true removed
The list is: 34567 hello

hello removed
The list is: 34567

34567 removed
Empty list
```

Fig. 17.4 Sample output for the program of Fig. 17.3.

The program of Fig. 17.3 consists of three classes—**ListNode**, **List**, and **EmptyListException**. Encapsulated in each **List** object is a linked-list of **ListNode** objects. The **ListNode** class consists of friendly members **data** and **next**. **ListNode** member **data** can refer to any **Object**. **ListNode** member **next** stores a reference to the next **ListNode** object in the linked list.

The **List** class consists of private members **firstNode** (a reference to the first **ListNode** in a list object) and **lastNode** (a reference to the last **ListNode** in a **List** object). The default constructor initializes both references to null. The primary methods of the **List** class are **insertAtFront**, **insertAtBack**, **removeFromFront**, and **removeFromBack**. Method **isEmpty** is called a *predicate method*—it does not alter the list in any way; rather, it determines if the list is empty (i.e., the reference to the first node of the list is **null**). If the list is empty, **true** is returned; otherwise, **false** is returned. Method **print** displays the list's contents.

Over the next several pages, we will discuss each of the methods of the **List** class in detail. Method **insertAtFront** (Fig. 17.5 illustrates the operation) places a new node at the front of the list. The method consists of several steps:

1. Call **isEmpty** to determine if the list is empty (line 51).

2. If the list is empty, both **firstNode** and **lastNode** are set to the **ListNode** allocated with **new** and initialized with **insertItem** (line 52). The **ListNode** constructor (line 8) sets instance variable **data** to refer to the **insertItem** passed as an argument and sets the **next** reference to **null**.

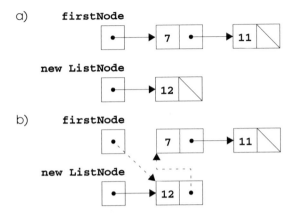

Fig. 17.5 The **insertAtFront** operation.

3. If the list is not empty, the new node is threaded into the list by setting **first-Node** to the **ListNode** object that was allocated with **new** and initialized with **insertItem** and **firstNode** (line 54). When the **ListNode** constructor (line 16) executes, it sets instance variable **data** to refer to the **insertItem** passed as an argument and sets the **next** reference to the **ListNode** passed as an argument which performs the insertion.

Figure 17.5 illustrates method **insertAtFront**. Part a) of the figure shows the list and the new node during the **insertAtFront** operation and before the new node has been threaded into the list. The dotted arrows in part b) illustrate step 3 of the **insertAt-Front** operation that enables the node containing **12** to become the new list front.

Method **insertAtBack** (Fig. 17.6 illustrates the operation) places a new node at the back of the list. The method consists of several steps:

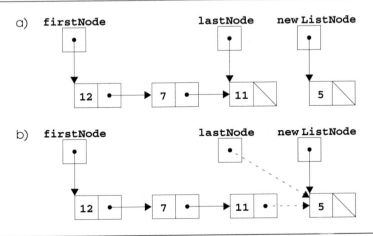

Fig. 17.6 A graphical representation of the **insertAtBack** operation.

1. Call **isEmpty** to determine if the list is empty (line 63).
2. If the list is empty, both **firstNode** and **lastNode** are set to the **ListNode** allocated with **new** and initialized with **insertItem** (line 64). The **ListNode** constructor (line 8) sets instance variable **data** to refer to the **insertItem** passed as an argument and sets the **next** reference to **null**.
3. If the list is not empty, the new node is threaded into the list by setting **LastNode** and **lastNode.next** to the **ListNode** that was allocated with **new** and initialized with **insertItem** (line 66). When the **ListNode** constructor (line 8) executes, it sets instance variable **data** to refer to the **insertItem** passed as an argument and sets the **next** reference to **null**.

Figure 17.6 illustrates an **insertAtBack** operation. Part a) of the figure shows the list and the new node during the **insertAtBack** operation and before the new node has been threaded into the list. The dotted arrows in part b) illustrate the steps of method **insertAtBack** that enable a new node to be added to the end of a list that is not empty.

Method **removeFromFront** (illustrated in Fig. 17.7) removes the front node of the list and returns a reference to the removed data. The method throws an **EmptyListException** (lines 74 and 75) if an attempt is made to remove a node from an empty list. Otherwise, a reference to the removed data is returned. The method consists of several steps:

1. Assign **removeItem** to refer to **firstNode.data** (the data being removed from the list).
2. If **firstNode** is equal to **lastNode** (line 80), i.e., if the list has only one element prior to the removal attempt, then set **firstNode** and **lastNode** to **null** (line 81) to de-thread that node from the list (leaving the list empty).

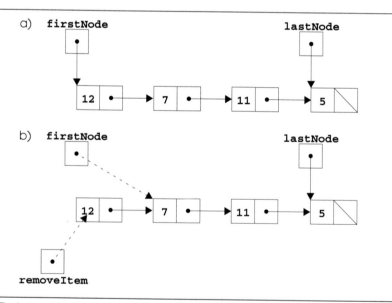

Fig. 17.7 A graphical representation of the **removeFromFront** operation.

3. If the list has more than one node prior to removal, then leave **lastNode** as is and simply set **firstNode** to **firstNode.next** (line 83), i.e., modify **firstNode** to reference what was the second node prior to removal (and now, the new first node).

4. Return the **removeItem** reference.

Figure 17.7 illustrates method **removeFromFront**. Part a) illustrates the list before the removal operation. Part b) shows actual reference manipulations.

Method **removeFromBack** (Fig. 17.8 illustrates the operation) removes the last node of the list and returns a reference to the removed data. Method **removeFromBack** throws an **EmptyListException** (lines 93 and 94) if an attempt is made to remove a node from an empty list. Otherwise, a reference to the removed data is returned. The method consists of several steps:

1. Assign **removeItem** to refer to **lastNode.data** (the data being removed from the list).

2. If **firstNode** is equal to **lastNode** (line 99), i.e., if the list has only one element prior to the removal attempt, then set **firstNode** and **lastNode** to **null** (line 100) to dethread that node from the list (leaving the list empty).

3. If the list has more than one node prior to removal, then create the **Listnode** reference **current** and initialize it to **firstNode**.

4. Now "walk the list" with **current** until it references the node before the last node. This is done with a **while** loop that keeps replacing **current** by **current.next** while **current.next** is not **lastNode**.

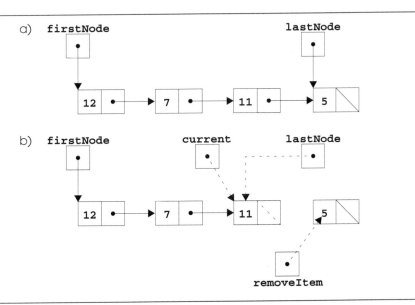

Fig. 17.8 A graphical representation of the **removeFromBack** operation.

5. Copy **current** to **lastNode** to dethread the back node from the list.

6. Set the **current.next** to **null** in the new last node of the list.

7. Return the **removedItem** reference.

Figure 17.8 illustrates method **removeFromBack**. Part a) illustrates the list before the removal operation. Part b) shows the actual reference manipulations.

Method **print** first determines if the list is empty. If so, **print** displays **"The list is empty"** and terminates. Otherwise, it prints the data in the list. The method prints a string consisting of the string **"The "**, the **String** object **name**, and the string **" is: "**. Then the **ListNode** reference **current** is created and initialized with **firstNode**. While **current** is not **null**, **current.data.toString()** is printed and **current.next** is assigned to **current**. Note that if the link in the last node of the list is not null, the printing algorithm will erroneously print past the end of the list. The printing algorithm is identical for linked lists, stacks, and queues.

17.5 Stacks

A *stack* is a constrained version of a linked list—new nodes can be added to a stack and removed from a stack only at the top. For this reason, a stack is referred to as a *last-in, first-out (LIFO)* data structure. The link member in the last node of the stack is set to null to indicate the bottom of the stack.

Common Programming Error 17.2

Not setting the link in the bottom node of a stack to **null**.

The primary methods used to manipulate a stack are *push* and *pop*. Method **push** adds a new node to the top of the stack. Method **pop** removes a node from the top of the stack and returns the **data** object from the popped node.

Stacks have many interesting applications. For example, when a method call is made, the called method must know how to return to its caller, so the return address is pushed onto a stack. If a series of method calls occurs, the successive return values are pushed onto the stack in last-in, first-out order so that each method can return to its caller. Stacks support recursive method calls in the same manner as conventional nonrecursive method calls.

Stacks contain the space created for automatic variables on each invocation of a method. When the method returns to its caller, the space for that method's automatic variables is popped off the stack, and those variables are no longer known to the program.

Stacks are used by compilers in the process of evaluating expressions and generating machine language code. The exercises explore several applications of stacks, including using them to develop a complete working compiler.

We will take advantage of the close relationship between lists and stacks to implement a stack class primarily by reusing a list class. We use two different forms of reusability. First, we implement the stack class through inheritance of the **List** class. Then we implement an identically performing stack class through composition by including a **List** object as a **private** member of a stack class. The list, stack and queue data structures in this chapter are implemented to store **Object** references to encourage further reusability. Thus, any object type can be stored in a list, stack or queue.

Figure 17.9 (output in Fig. 17.10) creates a stack class through inheritance from class **List** of Fig. 17.3. We want the stack to have methods **push**, **pop**, **isEmpty**, and **print**. These are essentially the **insertAtFront**, **removeFromFront**, **isEmpty**, and **print** methods of class **List**. Of course, class **List** contains other methods (i.e., **insertAtBack** and **removeFromBack**) that we would rather not make accessible through the public interface to the stack class. It is important to remember that all methods in the public interface of the **List** class are also **public** methods of the derived class **StackInheritance**. We demonstrate another way to build the stack using our **List** class in Fig. 17.11. When we implement the stack's methods, we have each **StackInheritance** method call the appropriate **List** method—**push** calls **insertAtFront**, **pop** calls **removeFromFront**, **isEmpty** calls **super.isEmpty** to invoke the base class version, and **print** calls **super.print** to invoke the base class version.

```
1   // Class StackInheritance definition
2   // Derived from class List
3   class StackInheritance extends List {
4       public StackInheritance() { super( "stack" ); }
5       public void push( Object o ) { insertAtFront( o ); }
6       public Object pop() throws EmptyListException
7           { return removeFromFront(); }
8       public boolean isEmpty() { return super.isEmpty(); }
9       public void print() { super.print(); }
10  }
```

Fig. 17.9 A simple stack program (part 1 of 3).

```
11  // Class StackInheritanceTest
12  public class StackInheritanceTest {
13      public static void main( String args[] )
14      {
15          StackInheritance objStack = new StackInheritance();
16
17          // Create objects to store in the stack
18          Boolean b = new Boolean( true );
19          Character c = new Character( '$' );
20          Integer i = new Integer( 34567 );
21          String s = new String( "hello" );
22
23          // Use the push method
24          objStack.push( b );
25          objStack.print();
26          objStack.push( c );
27          objStack.print();
28          objStack.push( i );
29          objStack.print();
30          objStack.push( s );
31          objStack.print();
```

Fig. 17.9 A simple stack program (part 2 of 3).

```
32
33              // Use the pop method
34              Object removedObj = null;
35
36              try {
37                 while ( true ) {
38                    removedObj = objStack.pop();
39                    System.out.println( removedObj.toString() +
40                                        " popped" );
41                    objStack.print();
42                 }
43              }
44              catch ( EmptyListException e ) {
45                 System.err.println( "\n" + e.toString() );
46              }
47           }
48        }
```

Fig. 17.9 A simple stack program (part 3 of 3).

```
The stack is: true

The stack is: $ true

The stack is: 34567 $ true

The stack is: hello 34567 $ true

hello popped
The stack is: 34567 $ true

34567 popped
The stack is: $ true

$ popped
The stack is: true

true popped
Empty stack

EmptyListException: The stack is empty
```

Fig. 17.10 Sample output from the program of Fig. 17.9.

The **StackInheritance** class is used in **StackInheritanceTest**'s **main** method to instantiate a stack of **Object**s called **objStack**. A **Boolean** object containing **true**, a **Character** object containing **$**, an **Integer** object containing **34567** and a **String** object containing **hello** are pushed onto **objStack** and then popped off **objStack**. The objects are popped from the stack in an infinite **while** loop. When there are no objects left to pop, an **EmptyListException** is thrown and a message is displayed stating that the stack is empty.

Another way to implement a stack class is by reusing a list class through composition. The program of Fig. 17.11 uses a private object of the **List** class (line 3) in the definition of class **StackComposition**. Composition enables us to hide the methods of class **List** that should not be in the interface to our stack by providing public interface methods only to the required **List** methods. This technique of implementing each stack method as a call to a **List** method is called *forwarding*—the stack method invoked *forwards* the call to the appropriate **List** method. The **StackCompositiondTest** class uses an identical **main** method to the **StackInheritanceTest** class, except an object of class **StackComposition** is instantiated instead. The output is also the same.

17.6 Queues

Another common data structure is the *queue*. A queue is similar to a checkout line in a supermarket—the first person in line is serviced first, and other customers enter the line only at the end and wait to be serviced. Queue nodes are removed only from the *head* of the queue, and are inserted only at the *tail* of the queue. For this reason, a queue is referred to as a *first-in, first-out (FIFO)* data structure. The insert and remove operations are known as *enqueue* and *dequeue*.

Queues have many applications in computer systems. Most computers have only a single processor, so only one user at a time can be serviced. Entries for the other users are placed in a queue. The entry at the front of the queue is the next to receive service. Each entry gradually advances to the front of the queue as users receive service.

Queues are also used to support print spooling. A multiuser environment may have only a single printer. Many users may be generating outputs to be printed. If the printer is busy, other outputs may still be generated. These are "spooled" to disk (much as thread is wound onto a spool) where they wait in a queue until the printer becomes available.

Information packets also wait in queues in computer networks. Each time a packet arrives at a network node, it must be routed to the next node on the network along the path to the packet's final destination. The routing node routes one packet at a time, so additional packets are enqueued until the router can route them.

```
1   // Class StackComposition definition with composed List object
2   class StackComposition {
3       private List s;
4
5       public StackComposition() { s = new List( "stack" ); }
6       public void push( Object o ) { s.insertAtFront( o ); }
7       public Object pop() throws EmptyListException
8           { return s.removeFromFront(); }
9       public boolean isEmpty() { return s.isEmpty(); }
10      public void print() { s.print(); }
11  }
```

Fig. 17.11 A simple stack program using composition.

A file server in a computer network handles file access requests from many clients throughout the network. Servers have a limited capacity to service requests from clients. When that capacity is exceeded, client requests wait in queues.

 Common Programming Error 17.3

Not setting the link in the last node of a queue to **null**.

The program of Fig. 17.12 (whose output is shown in Fig. 17.13) creates a queue class through inheritance from a list class. We want the **QueueInh** class to have methods **enqueue**, **dequeue**, **isEmpty**, and **print**. We note that these are essentially the **insertAtBack**, **removeFromFront**, **isEmpty**, and **print** methods of class **List**.

```
1   // Class QueueInheritance definition
2   // Derived from List
3   class QueueInheritance extends List {
4       public QueueInheritance() { super( "queue" ); }
5       public void enqueue( Object o ) { insertAtBack( o ); }
6       public Object dequeue() throws EmptyListException
7          { return removeFromFront(); }
8       public boolean isEmpty() { return super.isEmpty(); }
9       public void print() { super.print(); }
10  }
```

Fig. 17.12 Processing a queue (part 1 of 3).

```
11  // Class QueueInheritanceTest
12  public class QueueInheritanceTest {
13      public static void main( String args[] )
14      {
15          QueueInheritance objQueue = new QueueInheritance();
16
17          // Create objects to store in the queue
18          Boolean b = new Boolean( true );
19          Character c = new Character( '$' );
20          Integer i = new Integer( 34567 );
21          String s = new String( "hello" );
22
23          // Use the enqueue method
24          objQueue.enqueue( b );
25          objQueue.print();
26          objQueue.enqueue( c );
27          objQueue.print();
28          objQueue.enqueue( i );
29          objQueue.print();
30          objQueue.enqueue( s );
31          objQueue.print();
32
```

Fig. 17.12 Processing a queue (part 2 of 3).

```
33          // Use the dequeue method
34          Object removedObj = null;
35
36          try {
37             while ( true ) {
38                removedObj = objQueue.dequeue();
39                System.out.println( removedObj.toString() +
40                                         " dequeued" );
41                objQueue.print();
42             }
43          }
44          catch ( EmptyListException e ) {
45             System.err.println( "\n" + e.toString() );
46          }
47       }
48    }
```

Fig. 17.12 Processing a queue (part 3 of 3).

```
The queue is: true

The queue is: true $

The queue is: true $ 34567

The queue is: true $ 34567 hello

true dequeued
The queue is: $ 34567 hello

$ dequeued
The queue is: 34567 hello

34567 dequeued
The queue is: hello

hello dequeued
Empty queue

EmptyListException: The queue is empty
```

Fig. 17.13 Sample output from the program in Fig. 17.12.

Of course, the list class contains other methods (i.e., **insertAtFront** and **removeFromBack**) that we would rather not make accessible through the public interface to the queue class. Remember that all methods in the **public** interface of the **List** class are also **public** methods of the derived class **QueueInheritance**. When we implement the queue's methods, we have each **QueueInheritance** method call the appropriate **List** method—**enqueue** calls **insertAtBack**, **dequeue** calls **remove-**

FromFront, isEmpty calls **super.isEmpty** to invoke the base class version and **print** calls **super.print** to invoke the base class version.

The **QueueInheritance** class is used in **QueueInheritanceTest**'s **main** method to instantiate a queue of **Object**s called **objQueue**. A **Boolean** object containing **true**, a **Character** object containing **$**, an **Integer** object containing **34567** and a **String** object containing **hello** are enqueued in **objQueue** and then dequeued from **objQueue** in first-in-first-out order. The objects are dequeued from the queue in an infinite **while** loop. When there are no objects left to dequeue, an **EmptyListException** is thrown and a message is displayed stating that the queue is empty.

17.7 Trees

Linked lists, stacks, and queues are *linear data structures*. A tree is a nonlinear, two-dimensional data structure with special properties. Tree nodes contain two or more links. This section discusses *binary trees* (Fig. 17.14)—trees whose nodes all contain two links (none, one, or both of which may be **null**). The *root node* is the first node in a tree. Each link in the root node refers to a *child*. The *left child* is the first node in the *left subtree,* and the *right child* is the first node in the *right subtree.* The children of a node are called *siblings.* A node with no children is called a *leaf node.* Computer scientists normally draw trees from the root node down—exactly the opposite of the way most trees grow in nature.

Common Programming Error 17.4

*Not setting to **null** the links in leaf nodes of a tree.*

In this section, a special binary tree called a *binary search tree* is created. A binary search tree (with no duplicate node values) has the characteristic that the values in any left subtree are less than the value in its parent node, and the values in any right subtree are greater than the value in its parent node. Figure 17.15 illustrates a binary search tree with 12 integer values. Note that the shape of the binary search tree that corresponds to a set of data can vary, depending on the order in which the values are inserted into the tree.

Figure 17.16 (output in Fig. 17.17) creates a binary search tree of integers and traverses it (i.e., walks through all its nodes) three ways—using recursive *inorder, preorder* and *postorder traversals.* The program generates 10 random numbers and inserts each in the tree.

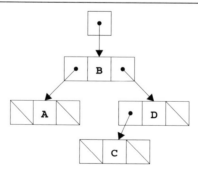

Fig. 17.14 A graphical representation of a binary tree.

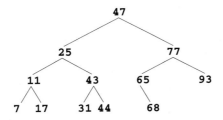

Fig. 17.15 A binary search tree.

```
1   // Class TreeNode definition
2   class TreeNode {
3      TreeNode left;    // left node
4      int data;         // data item
5      TreeNode right;   // right node
6
7      // Constructor: initialize data to d and make a leaf node
8      public TreeNode( int d )
9      {
10        data = d;
11        left = right = null;  // this node has no children
12     }
13
14     // Insert a TreeNode into a Tree that contains nodes.
15     // Ignore duplicate values.
16     public void insert( int d )
17     {
18        if ( d < data ) {
19           if ( left == null )
20              left = new TreeNode( d );
21           else
22              left.insert( d );
23        }
24        else if ( d > data ) {
25           if ( right == null )
26              right = new TreeNode( d );
27           else
28              right.insert( d );
29        }
30     }
31  }
32
33  // Class Tree definition
34  public class Tree {
35     private TreeNode root;
36
37     // Construct an empty Tree of integers
38     public Tree() { root = null; }
39
```

Fig. 17.16 Creating and traversing a binary tree (part 1 of 4).

```
40    // Insert a new node in the binary search tree.
41    // If the root node is null, create the root node here.
42    // Otherwise, call the insert method of class TreeNode.
43    public void insertNode( int d )
44    {
45       if ( root == null )
46          root = new TreeNode( d );
47       else
48          root.insert( d );
49    }
50
51    // Preorder Traversal
52    public void preorderTraversal() { preorderHelper( root ); }
53
54    // Recursive method to perform preorder traversal
55    private void preorderHelper( TreeNode node )
56    {
57       if ( node == null )
58          return;
59
60       System.out.print( node.data + " " );
61       preorderHelper( node.left );
62       preorderHelper( node.right );
63    }
64
65    // Inorder Traversal
66    public void inorderTraversal() { inorderHelper( root ); }
67
68    // Recursive method to perform inorder traversal
69    private void inorderHelper( TreeNode node )
70    {
71       if ( node == null )
72          return;
73
74       inorderHelper( node.left );
75       System.out.print( node.data + " " );
76       inorderHelper( node.right );
77    }
78
79    // Postorder Traversal
80    public void postorderTraversal() { postorderHelper( root ); }
81
82    // Recursive method to perform postorder traversal
83    private void postorderHelper( TreeNode node )
84    {
85       if ( node == null )
86          return;
87
```

Fig. 17.16 Creating and traversing a binary tree (part 2 of 4).

```
88          postorderHelper( node.left );
89          postorderHelper( node.right );
90          System.out.print( node.data + " " );
91       }
92    }
```

Fig. 17.16 Creating and traversing a binary tree (part 3 of 4).

```
93    // This program tests the Tree class.
94    import java.util.*;
95
96    // Class TreeTest definition
97    public class TreeTest {
98       public static void main( String args[] )
99       {
100         Tree tree = new Tree();
101         int intVal;
102
103         System.out.println( "Inserting the following values: " );
104
105         for ( int i = 1; i <= 10; i++ ) {
106            intVal = (int) ( Math.random() * 100 );
107            System.out.print( intVal + " " );
108            tree.insertNode( intVal );
109         }
110
111         System.out.println ( "\n\nPreorder traversal" );
112         tree.preorderTraversal();
113
114         System.out.println ( "\n\nInorder traversal" );
115         tree.inorderTraversal();
116
117         System.out.println ( "\n\nPostorder traversal" );
118         tree.postorderTraversal();
119         System.out.println();
120      }
121   }
```

Fig. 17.16 Creating and traversing a binary tree (part 4 of 4).

Let us walk through the binary tree program of Fig. 17.16. Method **main** or class **TreeTest** begins by instantiating object **tree** of type **Tree** (line 100). The program randomly generates 10 integers, each of which is inserted in the binary tree through a call to **insertNode** (line 108). The program then performs preorder, inorder, and postorder traversals (these will be explained shortly) of **tree**.

```
Inserting the following values:
39 69 94 47 50 72 55 41 97 73

Preorder traversal
39 69 47 41 50 55 94 72 73 97

Inorder traversal
39 41 47 50 55 69 72 73 94 97

Postorder traversal
41 55 50 47 73 72 97 94 69 39
```

Fig. 17.17 Sample output from the program of Fig. 17.16.

Now, let us walk through the class definitions and methods. We begin with the **TreeNode** class (line 1) which declares as friendly data the node's **data** value, and references **left** (to the node's left subtree) and **right** (to the node's right subtree). The constructor (line 8) sets the **data** value to the value supplied as a constructor argument, and sets references **left** and **right** to **null** (thus initializing this node to be a leaf node). Method **insert** is invoked by the **Tree** class **insertNode** method to insert data into a tree that is not empty. This method will be discussed in detail shortly.

Class **Tree** has as private data **root**—a reference to the root node of the tree. The class has public methods **insertNode** (insert a new node in the tree) and **preorderTraversal**, **inorderTraversal** and **postorderTraversal**, each of which walks the tree in the designated manner. Each of these methods calls its own separate recursive utility method to perform the appropriate operations on the internal representation of the tree. The **Tree** constructor initializes **root** to **null** because the tree is initially empty.

The **Tree** class's method **insertNode** (line 43) first determines if the tree is empty. If so, it allocates a new **TreeNode**, initializes the node with the integer being inserted in the tree, and assigns the new node to the **root** reference. If the tree is not empty, the **TreeNode** method **insert** is called to recursively insert a node into the tree. *A node can only be inserted as a leaf node in a binary search tree.*

The **TreeNode** method **insert** compares the value to be inserted with the **data** value in the root node. If the insert value is less than or equal to the root node data, the program determines if the left subtree is empty (line 19). If so, a new **TreeNode** is allocated and initialized with the integer being inserted and the **left** reference is set to the new node (line 20). Otherwise, **insert** recursively calls itself (line 22) for the left subtree to insert the value in the left subtree. If the insert value is greater than the root node data, the program determines if the right subtree is empty (line 25). If so, a new **TreeNode** is allocated and initialized with the integer being inserted and the **right** reference is set to the new node (line 26). Otherwise, **insert** recursively calls itself (line 28) for the right subtree to insert the value in the right subtree.

Methods **inorderTraversal**, **preorderTraversal** and **postorderTraversal** call helper methods **inorderHelper**, **preorderHelper** and **postorderHelper**, respectively to traverse the tree (Fig. 17.18) and print the node values.

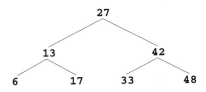

Fig. 17.18 A binary search tree.

The steps for an **inorderTraversal** (line 66) are:

1. Traverse the left subtree with a call to **inorderHelper** (line 69)
2. Process the value in the node (i.e., print the node value).
3. Traverse the right subtree with a call to **inorderHelper**.

The value in a node is not processed until the values in its left subtree are processed. The **inorderTraversal** of the tree in Fig. 17.18 is:

        6 13 17 27 33 42 48

Note that the **inorderTraversal** of a binary search tree prints the node values in ascending order. The process of creating a binary search tree actually sorts the data—and thus this process is called the *binary tree sort*.

The steps for a **preorderTraversal** (line 52) are:

1. Process the value in the node.
2. Traverse the left subtree with a call to **preorderHelper** (line 55)
3. Traverse the right subtree with a call to **preorderHelper**.

The value in each node is processed as the node is visited. After the value in a given node is processed, the values in the left subtree are processed, then the values in the right subtree are processed. The **preorderTraversal** of the tree in Fig. 17.18 is:

        27 13 6 17 42 33 48

The steps for a **postorderTraversal** (line 80) are:

1. Traverse the left subtree with a **postorderHelper** (line 83).
2. Traverse the right subtree with a **postorderHelper**.
3. Process the value in the node.

The value in each node is not printed until the values of its children are printed. The **postorderTraversal** of the tree in Fig. 17.18 is:

        6 17 13 33 48 42 27

The binary search tree facilitates *duplicate elimination.* As the tree is created, attempts to insert a duplicate value are recognized because a duplicate follows the same "go left" or "go right" decisions on each comparison as the original value did. Thus, the duplicate eventually is compared with a node containing the same value. The duplicate value may simply be discarded at this point.

Searching a binary tree for a value that matches a key value is also fast especially for *tightly packed* trees. In a tightly packed tree, each level contains about twice as many elements as the previous level. Figure 17.18 is a tightly packed binary tree. So a binary search tree with n elements has a minimum of $\log_2 n$ levels, and thus as few as $\log_2 n$ comparisons would have to be made either to find a match or to determine that no match exists. This means, for example, that when searching a (tightly packed) 1000-element binary search tree, approximately 10 comparisons need to be made because $2^{10} > 1000$. When searching a (tightly packed) 1,000,000 element binary search tree, approximately 20 comparisons need to be made because $2^{20} > 1,000,000$.

In the Exercises, algorithms are presented for several other binary tree operations, such as deleting an item from a binary tree, printing a binary tree in a two-dimensional tree format, and performing a level-order traversal of a binary tree. The level-order traversal of a binary tree visits the nodes of the tree row-by-row starting at the root node level. On each level of the tree, the nodes are visited from left to right. Other binary tree exercises include allowing a binary search tree to contain duplicate values, inserting string values in a binary tree, and determining how many levels are contained in a binary tree.

Summary

- Self-referential classes contain members called links that reference objects of the same class type.

- Self-referential classes enable many class objects to be linked together in stacks, queues, lists, and trees.

- Dynamic memory allocation reserves a block of bytes in memory to store an object during program execution.

- A linked list is a linear collection of self-referential class objects.

- A linked list is a dynamic data structure—the length of the list can increase or decrease as necessary.

- Linked lists can continue to grow until memory is exhausted.

- Linked lists provide a mechanism for simple insertion and deletion of data by reference manipulation.

- Stacks and queues are constrained versions of linked lists.

- New stack nodes are added to a stack and are removed from a stack only at the top of the stack. For this reason, a stack is referred to as a last-in, first-out (LIFO) data structure.

- The link in the last node of the stack is set to null to indicate the bottom of the stack.

- The two primary operations used to manipulate a stack are **push** and **pop**. The **push** operation creates a new node and places it on the top of the stack. The **pop** operation removes a node from the top of the stack and returns the popped value.

- In a queue data structure, nodes are removed from the head and added to the tail. For this reason, a queue is referred to as a first-in, first-out (FIFO) data structure. The add and remove operations are known as **enqueue** and **dequeue**.

- Trees are two-dimensional data structures requiring two or more links per node.

- Binary trees contain two links per node.

- The root node is the first node in the tree.

- Each of the references in the root node refers to a child. The left child is the first node in the left subtree, and the right child is the first node in the right subtree. The children of a node are called siblings. Any tree node that does not have any children is called a leaf node.

- A binary search tree has the characteristic that the value in the left child of a node is less than the value in its parent node, and the value in the right child of a node is greater than or equal to the value in its parent node. If there are no duplicate data values, the value in the right child is simply greater than the value in its parent node.

- An inorder traversal of a binary tree traverses the left subtree inorder, processes the value in the root node, then traverses the right subtree inorder. The value in a node is not processed until the values in its left subtree are processed.

- A preorder traversal processes the value in the root node, traverses the left subtree preorder, then traverses the right subtree preorder. The value in each node is processed as the node is encountered.

- A postorder traversal traverses the left subtree postorder, traverses the right subtree postorder, then processes the value in the root node. The value in each node is not processed until the values in both its subtrees are processed.

Terminology

binary search tree
binary tree
binary tree sort
child node
children
delete a node
dequeue
duplicate elimination
dynamic data structures
enqueue
FIFO (first-in, first-out)
head of a queue
inorder traversal of a binary tree
insert a node
leaf node
left child
left subtree
level-order traversal of a binary tree
LIFO (last-in, first-out)
linear data structure
linked list

node
nonlinear data structure
null reference
parent node
pop
postorder traversal of a binary tree
preorder traversal of a binary tree
push
queue
recursive tree traversal algorithms
right child
right subtree
root node
self-referential class
stack
subtree
tail of a queue
top of a stack
traversal
tree
visit a node

Common Programming Errors

17.1 Not setting the link in the last node of a list to **null**.

17.2 Not setting the link in the bottom node of a stack to **null**.

17.3 Not setting the link in the last node of a queue to **null**.

17.4 Not setting to **null** the links in leaf nodes of a tree.

Good Programming Practices

17.1 When using **new**, test for an **OutOfMemoryException**. Perform appropriate error processing if the requested memory is not allocated.

Performance Tips

17.1 An array can be declared to contain more elements than the number of items expected, but this can waste memory. Linked lists can provide better memory utilization in these situations. Linked lists allow the program to adapt at run time.

17.2 Insertion into a linked list is fast—only two references have to be modified. All existing nodes remain at their current locations in memory.

17.3 Insertion and deletion in a sorted array can be time consuming—all the elements following the inserted or deleted element must be shifted appropriately.

17.4 The elements of an array are stored contiguously in memory. This allows immediate access to any array element because the address of any element can be calculated directly based on its position relative to the beginning of the array. Linked lists do not afford such immediate access to their elements.

17.5 Using dynamic memory allocation (instead of arrays) for data structures that grow and shrink at execution time can save memory. Keep in mind, however, that references occupy space, and that dynamic memory allocation incurs the overhead of method calls.

Self-Review Exercises

17.1 Fill in the blanks in each of the following:
  a) A self-_____ class is used to form dynamic data structures. that can grow and shrink at execution time.
  b) Operator _____ is used to dynamically allocate memory; this operator returns a reference to the allocated memory.
  c) A _____ is a constrained version of a linked list in which nodes can be inserted and deleted only from the start of the list; this data structure returns node values in last-in-first-out order.
  d) A method that does not alter a linked list, but simply looks at the list to determine if it is empty is referred to as a _____method.
  e) A queue is referred to as a _____ data structure because the first nodes inserted are the first nodes removed.

f) The reference to the next node in a linked list is referred to as a _____.

g) Automatically reclaiming dynamically allocated memory in Java is called _____.

h) A _____ is a constrained version of a linked list in which nodes can be inserted only at the end of the list and deleted only from the start of the list.

i) A _____ is a nonlinear, two-dimensional data structure that contains nodes with two or more links.

j) A stack is referred to as a _____ data structure because the last node inserted is the first node removed.

k) The nodes of a _____ tree contain two link members.

l) The first node of a tree is the _____ node.

m) Each link in a tree node refers to a _____ or _____ of that node.

n) A tree node that has no children is called a _____ node.

o) The four traversal algorithms we mentioned in the text for binary search trees are _____, _____, _____ and _____.

17.2   What are the differences between a linked list and a stack?

17.3   What are the differences between a stack and a queue?

17.4   Perhaps a more appropriate title for this chapter would have been "Reusable Data Structures." Comment on how each of the following entities or concepts contributes to the reusability of data structures:

a) classes

b) inheritance

c) composition.

17.5   Manually provide the inorder, preorder, and postorder traversals of the binary search tree of Fig. 17.19.

Answers to Self-Review Exercises

17.1   a) referential.   b) **new**.   c) stack.   d) predicate.   e) first-in-first-out (FIFO).   f) link.
g) garbage collection.   h) queue.   i) tree.   j) last-in-first-out (LIFO).   k) binary.
l) root.   m) child or subtree.   n) leaf.   o) inorder, preorder, postorder, and level-order.

17.2   It is possible to insert a node anywhere in a linked list and remove a node from anywhere in a linked list. Nodes in a stack may only be inserted at the top of the stack and removed from the top of a stack.

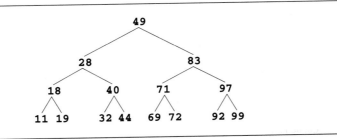

Fig. 17.19 A 15-node binary search tree.

17.3   A queue has references to both its head and its tail so that nodes may be inserted at the tail and deleted from the head. A stack has a single reference to the top of the stack where both insertion and deletion of nodes are performed.

17.4   a) Classes allow us to instantiate as many data structure objects of a certain type (i.e., class) as we wish.

   b) Inheritance enables us to reuse code from a superclass in a subclass so that the derived class data structure is also a base class data structure.

   c) Composition enables us to reuse code by making a class object data structure a member of a composed class; if we make the class object a private member of the composed class, then the class object's public methods are not available through the composed object's interface.

17.5   The inorder traversal is:

   11 18 19 28 32 40 44 49 69 71 72 83 92 97 99

The preorder traversal is:

   49 28 18 11 19 40 32 44 83 71 69 72 97 92 99

The postorder traversal is:

   11 19 18 32 44 40 28 69 72 71 92 99 97 83 49

Exercises

17.6   Write a program that concatenates two linked list objects of characters. Class **ListConcat** should include method **concatenate** that takes references to both list objects as arguments and concatenates the second list to the first list.

17.7   Write a program that merges two ordered list objects of integers into a single ordered list object of integers. Method **merge** or class **ListMerge** should receive references to each of the list objects to be merged, and should return a reference to the merged list object.

17.8   Write a program that inserts 25 random integers from 0 to 100 in order in a linked list object. The program should calculate the sum of the elements, and the floating-point average of the elements.

17.9   Write a program that creates a linked list object of 10 characters, then creates a second list object containing a copy of the first list, but in reverse order.

17.10   Write a program that inputs a line of text and uses a stack object to print the line reversed.

17.11   Write a program that uses a stack to determine if a string is a palindrome (i.e., the string is spelled identically backwards and forwards). The program should ignore spaces and punctuation.

17.12   Stacks are used by compilers to help in the process of evaluating expressions and generating machine language code. In this and the next exercise, we investigate how compilers evaluate arithmetic expressions consisting only of constants, operators, and parentheses.

Humans generally write expressions like **3 + 4** and **7 / 9** in which the operator (**+** or **/** here) is written between its operands—this is called *infix notation*. Computers "prefer" *postfix notation* in which the operator is written to the right of its two operands. The preceding infix expressions would appear in postfix notation as **3 4 +** and **7 9 /**, respectively.

To evaluate a complex infix expression, a compiler would first convert the expression to postfix notation, and then evaluate the postfix version of the expression. Each of these algorithms requires only a single left-to-right pass of the expression. Each algorithm uses a stack object in support of its operation, and in each algorithm the stack is used for a different purpose.

In this exercise, you will write a Java version of the infix-to-postfix conversion algorithm. In the next exercise, you will write a Java version of the postfix expression evaluation algorithm. Later in the chapter, you will discover that code you write in this exercise can help you implement a complete working compiler.

Write class **InfixToPostfixConverter** to convert an ordinary infix arithmetic expression (assume a valid expression is entered) with single digit integers such as

   (6 + 2) * 5 - 8 / 4

to a postfix expression. The postfix version of the preceding infix expression is

   6 2 + 5 * 8 4 / -

The program should read the expression into **StringBuffer infix**, and use one of the stack classes implemented in this chapter to help create the postfix expression in **Stringbuffer postfix**. The algorithm for creating a postfix expression is as follows:

1) Push a left parenthesis **' ('** on the stack.
2) Append a right parenthesis **') '** to the end of **infix**.
3) While the stack is not empty, read **infix** from left to right and do the following
   If the current character in **infix** is a digit, append it to **postfix**.
   If the current character in **infix** is a left parenthesis, push it on the stack.
   If the current character in **infix** is an operator,
      Pop operators (if there are any) at the top of the stack while they have equal or higher precedence than the current operator, and append the popped operators to **postfix**.
      Push the current character in **infix** on the stack.
   If the current character in **infix** is a right parenthesis
      Pop operators from the top of the stack and append them to **postfix** until a left parenthesis is at the top of the stack.
      Pop (and discard) the left parenthesis from the stack.

The following arithmetic operations are allowed in an expression:
   + addition
   - subtraction
   * multiplication
   / division
   ^ exponentiation
   % modulus

The stack should be maintained with stack nodes that each contain an instance variable and a reference to the next stack node.

Some of the methods you may want to provide are:
   a) Method **convertToPostfix** that converts the infix expression to postfix notation.
   b) Method **isOperator** that determines if **c** is an operator.
   c) Method **precedence** that determines if the precedence of **operator1** (from the infix expression) is less than, equal to, or greater than the precedence of **operator2** (from

the stack). The method returns **true** if **operator1** has lower precedence than **operator2**. Otherwise, **false** is returned.

d) Method **stackTop** (this should be added to the stack class) that returns the top value of the stack without popping the stack.

17.13   Write class **PostfixEvaluator** that evaluates a postfix expression (assume it is valid) such as

        6 2 + 5 * 8 4 / -

The program should read a postfix expression consisting of digits and operators into a **String-Buffer**. Using modified versions of the stack methods implemented earlier in this chapter, the program should scan the expression and evaluate it. The algorithm is as follows:

1) Append a right parenthesis (**')'**) to the end of the postfix expression. When the right parenthesis character is encountered, no further processing is necessary.

2) While right parenthesis character has not been encountered, read the expression from left to right.

   If the current character is a digit

   Push its integer value on the stack (the integer value of a digit character is its value in the computer's character set minus the value of **'0'** in the computer's character set)

   Otherwise, if the current character is an *operator*,

   Pop the two top elements of the stack into variables **x** and **y**.

   Calculate **y** *operator* **x**.

   Push the result of the calculation onto the stack.

3) When the right parenthesis is encountered in the expression, pop the top value of the stack. This is the result of the postfix expression.

Note: In 2) above, if the operator is **'/'**, the top of the stack is **2**, and the next element in the stack is **8**, then pop **2** into **x**, pop **8** into **y**, evaluate **8 / 2**, and push the result, **4**, back on the stack. This note also applies to operator **'-'**. The arithmetic operations allowed in an expression are:

    +addition
    -subtraction
    *multiplication
    /division
    ^exponentiation
    %modulus

The stack should be maintained with one of the stack classes introduced in this chapter. You may want to provide the following methods:

a) Method **evaluatePostfixExpression** that evaluates the postfix expression.
b) Method **calculate** that evaluates the expression **op1 operator op2**.
c) Method **push** that pushes a value on the stack.
d) Method **pop** that pops a value off the stack.
e) Method **isEmpty** that determines if the stack is empty.
f) Method **printStack** that prints the stack.

17.14   Modify the postfix evaluator program of Exercise 17.13 so that it can process integer operands larger than 9.

17.15   *(Supermarket simulation)* Write a program that simulates a check-out line at a supermarket. The line is a queue object. Customers (i.e., customer objects) arrive in random integer intervals of 1 to 4 minutes. Also, each customer is serviced in random integer intervals of 1 to 4 minutes. Obviously, the rates need to be balanced. If the average arrival rate is larger than the average service rate, the queue will grow infinitely. Even with "balanced" rates, randomness can still cause long lines. Run the supermarket simulation for a 12-hour day (720 minutes) using the following algorithm:

1) Choose a random integer between 1 and 4 to determine the minute at which the first customer arrives.

2) At the first customer's arrival time
   Determine customer's service time (random integer from 1 to 4);
   Begin servicing the customer;
   Schedule the arrival time of the next customer (random integer 1 to 4 added to the current time).

3) For each minute of the day:
       If the next customer arrives,
           Say so,
           Enqueue the customer;
           Schedule the arrival time of the next customer;
       If service was completed for the last customer;
           Say so
           Dequeue next customer to be serviced
           Determine customer's service completion time (random integer from 1 to 4
              added to the current time).

Now run your simulation for 720 minutes and answer each of the following:

a) What is the maximum number of customers in the queue at any time?

b) What is the longest wait any one customer experiences?

c) What happens if the arrival interval is changed from 1-to-4 minutes to 1-to-3 minutes?

17.16   Modify the program of Fig. 17.16 to allow the binary tree object to contain duplicates.

17.17   Write a program based on the program of Fig. 17.16 that inputs a line of text, tokenizes the sentence into separate words (you may want to use the **StreamTokenizer** class from the **java.io** package), inserts the words in a binary search tree, and prints the inorder, preorder, and postorder traversals of the tree.

17.18   In this chapter, we saw that duplicate elimination is straightforward when creating a binary search tree. Describe how you would perform duplicate elimination using only a single-subscripted array. Compare the performance of array-based duplicate elimination with the performance of binary-search-tree-based duplicate elimination.

17.19   Write a method **depth** that receives a binary tree and determines how many levels it has.

17.20   (*Recursively print a list backwards*) Write a method **printListBackwards** that recursively outputs the items in a linked list object in reverse order. Write a test program that creates a sorted list of integers and prints the list in reverse order.

17.21   (*Recursively search a list*) Write a method **searchList** that recursively searches a linked list object for a specified value. The method should return a reference to the value if it is found; otherwise, null should be returned. Use your method in a test program that creates a list of integers. The program should prompt the user for a value to locate in the list.

17.22   (*Binary tree delete*) In this exercise, we discuss deleting items from binary search trees. The deletion algorithm is not as straightforward as the insertion algorithm. There are three cases that are encountered when deleting an item—the item is contained in a leaf node (i.e., it has no children), the item is contained in a node that has one child, or the item is contained in a node that has two children.

If the item to be deleted is contained in a leaf node, the node is deleted and the reference in the parent node is set to null.

If the item to be deleted is contained in a node with one child, the reference in the parent node is set to reference the child node and the node containing the data item is deleted. This causes the child node to take the place of the deleted node in the tree.

The last case is the most difficult. When a node with two children is deleted, another node in the tree must take its place. However, the reference in the parent node cannot simply be assigned to reference one of the children of the node to be deleted. In most cases, the resulting binary search tree would not adhere to the following characteristic of binary search trees (with no duplicate values): *The values in any left subtree are less than the value in the parent node, and the values in any right subtree are greater than the value in the parent node.*

Which node is used as a *replacement node* to maintain this characteristic? Either the node containing the largest value in the tree less than the value in the node being deleted, or the node containing the smallest value in the tree greater than the value in the node being deleted. Let us consider the node with the smaller value. In a binary search tree, the largest value less than a parent's value is located in the left subtree of the parent node and is guaranteed to be contained in the rightmost node of the subtree. This node is located by walking down the left subtree to the right until the reference to the right child of the current node is null. We are now referencing the replacement node which is either a leaf node or a node with one child to its left. If the replacement node is a leaf node, the steps to perform the deletion are as follows:

1) Store the reference to the node to be deleted in a temporary reference variable.
2) Set the reference in the parent of the node being deleted to reference the replacement node.
3) Set the reference in the parent of the replacement node to null.
4) Set the reference to the right subtree in the replacement node to reference the right subtree of the node to be deleted.

The deletion steps for a replacement node with a left child are similar to those for a replacement node with no children, but the algorithm also must move the child in to the replacement node's position in the tree. If the replacement node is a node with a left child, the steps to perform the deletion are as follows:

1) Store the reference to the node to be deleted in a temporary reference variable.
2) Set the reference in the parent of the node being deleted to reference the replacement node.
3) Set the reference in the parent of the replacement node reference to the left child of the replacement node.
4) Set the reference to the right subtree in the replacement node reference to the right subtree of the node to be deleted.

Write method `deleteNode` which takes as its argument the value to be deleted. The method should locate in the tree the node containing the value to be deleted and use the algorithms discussed here to delete the node. If the value is not found in the tree, the method should print a message that indicates whether or not the value is deleted. Modify the program of Fig. 17.16 to use this method. After deleting an item, call the methods `inorderTraversal`, `preorderTraversal`, and `postorderTraversal` methods to confirm that the delete operation was performed correctly.

17.23   (*Binary tree search*) Write method `binaryTreeSearch` that attempts to locate a specified value in a binary search tree object. The method should take as an argument a search key to be located.

If the node containing the search key is found, the method should return a reference to that node; otherwise, the method should return a null reference.

17.24 (*Level-order binary tree traversal*) The program of Fig. 17.16 illustrated three recursive methods of traversing a binary tree—inorder, preorder, and postorder traversals. This exercise presents the *level-order traversal* of a binary tree in which the node values are printed level-by-level starting at the root node level. The nodes on each level are printed from left to right. The level-order traversal is not a recursive algorithm. It uses a queue object to control the output of the nodes. The algorithm is as follows:

    1) Insert the root node in the queue
    2) While there are nodes left in the queue,
            Get the next node in the queue
            Print the node's value
            If the reference to the left child of the node is not null
                    Insert the left child node in the queue
            If the reference to the right child of the node is not null
                    Insert the right child node in the queue.

      Write method **levelOrder** to perform a level-order traversal of a binary tree object. Modify the program of Fig 17.16 to use this method. (Note: You will also need to use queue processing methods of Fig. 17.12 in this program.)

17.25 (*Printing trees*) Write a recursive method **outputTree** to display a binary tree object on the screen. The method should output the tree row-by-row with the top of the tree at the left of the screen and the bottom of the tree toward the right of the screen. Each row is output vertically. For example, the binary tree illustrated in Fig. 17.19 is output as follows:

Note the rightmost leaf node appears at the top of the output in the rightmost column and the root node appears at the left of the output. Each column of output starts five spaces to the right of the previous column. Method **outputTree** should receive an argument **totalSpaces** representing the number of spaces preceding the value to be output (this variable should start at zero so the root node is output at the left of the screen). The method uses a modified inorder traversal to output the tree—it starts at the rightmost node in the tree and works back to the left. The algorithm is as follows:

While the reference to the current node is not null

    Recursively call **outputTree** with the right subtree of the current node and **totalSpaces** + 5

    Use a **for** structure to count from 1 to **totalSpaces** and output spaces

    Output the value in the current node

    Set the reference to the current node to refer to the left subtree of the current node

    Increment **totalSpaces** by 5.

Special Section: Building Your Own Compiler

In Exercises 5.42 and 5.43, we introduced Simpletron Machine Language (SML) and you implemented a Simpletron computer simulator to execute programs written in SML. In this section, we build a compiler that converts programs written in a high-level programming language to SML. This section "ties" together the entire programming process. You will write programs in this new high-level language, compile these programs on the compiler you build, and run the programs on the simulator you built in Exercise 7.43. You should make every effort to implement your compiler in an object-oriented manner.

17.26 (*The Simple Language*) Before we begin building the compiler, we discuss a simple, yet powerful, high-level language similar to early versions of the popular language Basic. We call the language *Simple*. Every Simple *statement* consists of a *line number* and a Simple *instruction*. Line numbers must appear in ascending order. Each instruction begins with one of the following Simple *commands*: **rem**, **input**, **let**, **print**, **goto**, **if/goto**, or **end** (see Fig. 17.20). All commands except **end** can be used repeatedly. Simple evaluates only integer expressions using the **+**, **-**, *****, and **/** operators. These operators have the same precedence as in Java. Parentheses can be used to change the order of evaluation of an expression.

Command	Example statement	Description
rem	50 rem this is a remark	Any text following the command **rem** is for documentation purposes only and is ignored by the compiler.
input	30 input x	Display a question mark to prompt the user to enter an integer. Read that integer from the keyboard and store the integer in **x**.
let	80 let u = 4 * (j - 56)	Assign **u** the value of **4 * (j - 56)**. Note that an arbitrarily complex expression can appear to the right of the equal sign.
print	10 print w	Display the value of **w**.
goto	70 goto 45	Transfer program control to line **45**.
if/goto	35 if i == z goto 80	Compare **i** and **z** for equality and transfer program control to line **80** if the condition is true; otherwise, continue execution with the next statement.
end	99 end	Terminate program execution.

Fig. 17.20 Simple commands.

Our Simple compiler recognizes only lowercase letters. All characters in a Simple file should be lowercase (uppercase letters result in a syntax error unless they appear in a **rem** statement in which case they are ignored). A *variable name* is a single letter. Simple does not allow descriptive variable names, so variables should be explained in remarks to indicate their use in a program. Simple uses only integer variables. Simple does not have variable declarations—merely mentioning a variable name in a program causes the variable to be declared and initialized to zero automatically. The syntax of Simple does not allow string manipulation (reading a string, writing a string, comparing strings, etc.). If a string is encountered in a Simple program (after a command other than **rem**), the compiler generates a syntax error. The first version of our compiler will assume that Simple programs are entered correctly. Exercise 17.29 asks the student to modify the compiler to perform syntax error checking.

Simple uses the conditional **if/goto** statement and the unconditional **goto** statement to alter the flow of control during program execution. If the condition in the **if/goto** statement is true, control is transferred to a specific line of the program. The following relational and equality operators are valid in an **if/goto** statement: **<**, **>**, **<=**, **>=**, **==**, or **!=**. The precedence of these operators is the same as in Java.

Let us now consider several programs that demonstrate Simple's features. The first program (Fig. 17.21) reads two integers from the keyboard, stores the values in variables **a** and **b**, and computes and prints their sum (stored in variable **c**).

The program of Fig. 17.22 determines and prints the larger of two integers. The integers are input from the keyboard and stored in **s** and **t**. The **if/goto** statement tests the condition **s >= t**. If the condition is true, control is transferred to line **90** and **s** is output; otherwise, **t** is output and control is transferred to the **end** statement in line **99** where the program terminates.

Simple does not provide a repetition structure (such as Java's **for**, **while**, or **do/while**). However, Simple can simulate each of Java's repetition structures using the **if/goto** and **goto** statements. Figure 17.23 uses a sentinel-controlled loop to calculate the squares of several integers. Each integer is input from the keyboard and stored in variable **j**. If the value entered is the sentinel **-9999**, control is transferred to line **99** where the program terminates. Otherwise, **k** is assigned the square of **j**, **k** is output to the screen, and control is passed to line **20** where the next integer is input.

Using the sample programs of Fig. 17.21, Fig. 17.22, and Fig. 17.23 as your guide, write a Simple program to accomplish each of the following:

```
1    10 rem     determine and print the sum of two integers
2    15 rem
3    20 rem     input the two integers
4    30 input a
5    40 input b
6    45 rem
7    50 rem     add integers and store result in c
8    60 let c = a + b
9    65 rem
10   70 rem     print the result
11   80 print c
12   90 rem     terminate program execution
13   99 end
```

Fig. 17.21 Simple program that determines the sum of two integers.

```
1    10 rem    determine and print the larger of two integers
2    20 input s
3    30 input t
4    32 rem
5    35 rem    test if s >= t
6    40 if s >= t goto 90
7    45 rem
8    50 rem    t is greater than s, so print t
9    60 print t
10   70 goto 99
11   75 rem
12   80 rem    s is greater than or equal to t, so print s
13   90 print s
14   99 end
```

Fig. 17.22 Simple program that finds the larger of two integers.

```
1    10 rem    calculate the squares of several integers
2    20 input j
3    23 rem
4    25 rem    test for sentinel value
5    30 if j == -9999 goto 99
6    33 rem
7    35 rem    calculate square of j and assign result to k
8    40 let k = j * j
9    50 print k
10   53 rem
11   55 rem    loop to get next j
12   60 goto 20
13   99 end
```

Fig. 17.23 Calculate the squares of several integers.

a) Input three integers, determine their average, and print the result.
b) Use a sentinel-controlled loop to input 10 integers and compute and print their sum.
c) Use a counter-controlled loop to input 7 integers, some positive and some negative, and compute and print their average.
d) Input a series of integers and determine and print the largest. The first integer input indicates how many numbers should be processed.
e) Input 10 integers and print the smallest.
f) Calculate and print the sum of the even integers from 2 to 30.
g) Calculate and print the product of the odd integers from 1 to 9.

17.27 (*Building A Compiler; Prerequisite: Complete Exercises 5.42, 5.43, 17.12, 17.13, and 17.26*) Now that the Simple language has been presented (Exercise 17.26), we discuss how to build a Simple compiler. First, we consider the process by which a Simple program is converted to SML and executed by the Simpletron simulator (see Fig. 17.24). A file containing a Simple program is read by the compiler and converted to SML code. The SML code is output to a file on disk, in which SML instructions appear one per line. The SML file is then loaded into the Simpletron simulator, and the re-

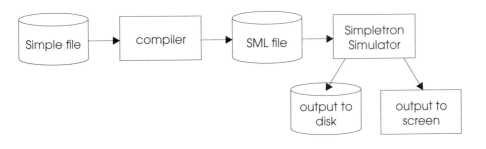

Fig. 17.24 Writing, compiling, and executing a Simple language program.

sults are sent to a file on disk and to the screen. Note that the Simpletron program developed in Exercise 5.19 took its input from the keyboard. It must be modified to read from a file so it can run the programs produced by our compiler.

The Simple compiler performs two *passes* of the Simple program to convert it to SML. The first pass constructs a *symbol table* (object) in which every *line number* (object), *variable name* (object) and *constant* (object) of the Simple program is stored with its type and corresponding location in the final SML code (the symbol table is discussed in detail below). The first pass also produces the corresponding SML instruction object(s) for each of the Simple statements (object, etc.). If the Simple program contains statements that transfer control to a line later in the program, the first pass results in an SML program containing some "unfinished" instructions. The second pass of the compiler locates and completes the unfinished instructions, and outputs the SML program to a file.

First Pass

The compiler begins by reading one statement of the Simple program into memory. The line must be separated into its individual *tokens* (i.e., "pieces" of a statement) for processing and compilation (the **StreamTokenizer** class from the **java.io** package can be used). Recall that every statement begins with a line number followed by a command. As the compiler breaks a statement into tokens, if the token is a line number, a variable, or a constant, it is placed in the symbol table. A line number is placed in the symbol table only if it is the first token in a statement. The **symbolTable** object is an array of **tableEntry** objects representing each symbol in the program. There is no restriction on the number of symbols that can appear in the program. Therefore, the **symbolTable** for a particular program could be large. Make the **symbolTable** a 100-element array for now. You can increase or decrease its size once the program is working.

Each **tableEntry** object contains three members. Member **symbol** is an integer containing the Unicode representation of a variable (remember that variable names are single characters), a line number or a constant. Member **type** is one of the following characters indicating the symbol's type: **'C'** for constant, **'L'** for line number, or **'V'** for variable. Member **location** contains the Simpletron memory location (**00** to **99**) to which the symbol refers. Simpletron memory is an array of 100 integers in which SML instructions and data are stored. For a line number, the location is the element in the Simpletron memory array at which the SML instructions for the Simple statement begin. For a variable or constant, the location is the element in the Simpletron memory array in which the variable or constant is stored. Variables and constants are allocated from the end of Simpletron's memory backwards. The first variable or constant is stored at location **99**, the next at location **98**, etc.

The symbol table plays an integral part in converting Simple programs to SML. We learned in Chapter 5 that an SML instruction is a four-digit integer comprised of two parts—the *operation code* and the *operand*. The operation code is determined by commands in Simple. For example, the simple command **input** corresponds to SML operation code **10** (read), and the Simple command **print** corresponds to SML operation code **11** (write). The operand is a memory location containing the data on which the operation code performs its task (e.g., operation code **10** reads a value from the keyboard and stores it in the memory location specified by the operand). The compiler searches **symbolTable** to determine the Simpletron memory location for each symbol so the corresponding location can be used to complete the SML instructions.

The compilation of each Simple statement is based on its command. For example, after the line number in a **rem** statement is inserted in the symbol table, the remainder of the statement is ignored by the compiler because a remark is for documentation purposes only. The **input**, **print**, **goto** and **end** statements correspond to the SML *read*, *write*, *branch* (to a specific location) and *halt* instructions. Statements containing these Simple commands are converted directly to SML (note that a **goto** statement may contain an unresolved reference if the specified line number refers to a statement further into the Simple program file; this is sometimes called a forward reference).

When a **goto** statement is compiled with an unresolved reference, the SML instruction must be *flagged* to indicate that the second pass of the compiler must complete the instruction. The flags are stored in 100-element array **flags** of type **int** in which each element is initialized to **-1**. If the memory location to which a line number in the Simple program refers is not yet known (i.e., it is not in the symbol table), the line number is stored in array **flags** in the element with the same subscript as the incomplete instruction. The operand of the incomplete instruction is set to **00** temporarily. For example, an unconditional branch instruction (making a forward reference) is left as **+4000** until the second pass of the compiler. The second pass of the compiler will be described shortly.

Compilation of **if/goto** and **let** statements is more complicated than other statements—they are the only statements that produce more than one SML instruction. For an **if/goto** statement, the compiler produces code to test the condition and to branch to another line if necessary. The result of the branch could be an unresolved reference. Each of the relational and equality operators can be simulated using SML's *branch zero* and *branch negative* instructions (or possibly a combination of both).

For a **let** statement, the compiler produces code to evaluate an arbitrarily complex arithmetic expression consisting of integer variables and/or constants. Expressions should separate each operand and operator with spaces. Exercises 17.12 and 17.13 presented the infix-to-postfix conversion algorithm and the postfix evaluation algorithm used by compilers to evaluate expressions. Before proceeding with your compiler, you should complete each of these exercises. When a compiler encounters an expression, it converts the expression from infix notation to postfix notation, then evaluates the postfix expression.

How is it that the compiler produces the machine language to evaluate an expression containing variables? The postfix evaluation algorithm contains a "hook" where the compiler can generate SML instructions rather than actually evaluating the expression. To enable this "hook" in the compiler, the postfix evaluation algorithm must be modified to search the symbol table for each symbol it encounters (and possibly insert it), determine the symbol's corresponding memory location, and *push the memory location on the stack (instead of the symbol)*. When an operator is encountered in the postfix expression, the two memory locations at the top of the stack are popped and machine language for effecting the operation is produced using the memory locations as operands. The result of each subexpression is stored in a temporary location in memory and pushed back onto the stack so the evaluation of the postfix expression can continue. When postfix evaluation is complete, the memory location containing the result is the only location left on the stack. This is popped and SML instructions are generated to assign the result to the variable at the left of the **let** statement.

Second Pass

The second pass of the compiler performs two tasks: resolve any unresolved references and output the SML code to a file. Resolution of references occurs as follows:

a) Search the **flags** array for an unresolved reference (i.e., an element with a value other than **-1**).

b) Locate the object in array **symbolTable** containing the symbol stored in the **flags** array (be sure that the type of the symbol is **'L'** for line number).

c) Insert the memory location from member **location** into the instruction with the unresolved reference (remember that an instruction containing an unresolved reference has operand **00**).

d) Repeat steps 1, 2, and 3 until the end of the **flags** array is reached.

After the resolution process is complete, the entire array containing the SML code is output to a disk file with one SML instruction per line. This file can be read by the Simpletron for execution (after the simulator is modified to read its input from a file). Compiling your first Simple program into an SML file and then executing that file should give you a real sense of personal accomplishment.

A Complete Example

The following example illustrates a complete conversion of a Simple program to SML as it will be performed by the Simple compiler. Consider a Simple program that inputs an integer and sums the values from 1 to that integer. The program and the SML instructions produced by the first pass of the Simple compiler are illustrated in Fig. 17.25. The symbol table constructed by the first pass is shown in Fig. 17.26.

Most Simple statements convert directly to single SML instructions. The exceptions in this program are remarks, the **if/goto** statement in line **20**, and the **let** statements. Remarks do not translate into machine language. However, the line number for a remark is placed in the symbol table in case the line number is referenced in a **goto** statement or an **if/goto** statement. Line **20** of the program specifies that if the condition **y == x** is true, program control is transferred to line **60**. Because line **60** appears later in the program, the first pass of the compiler has not as yet placed **60** in the symbol table (statement line numbers are placed in the symbol table only when they appear as the first token in a statement). Therefore, it is not possible at this time to determine the operand of the SML *branch zero* instruction at location **03** in the array of SML instructions. The compiler places **60** in location **03** of the **flags** array to indicate that the second pass completes this instruction.

We must keep track of the next instruction location in the SML array because there is not a one-to-one correspondence between Simple statements and SML instructions. For example, the **if/goto** statement of line **20** compiles into three SML instructions. Each time an instruction is produced, we must increment the *instruction counter* to the next location in the SML array. Note that the size of Simpletron's memory could present a problem for Simple programs with many statements, variables and constants. It is conceivable that the compiler will run out of memory. To test for this case, your program should contain a *data counter* to keep track of the location at which the next variable or constant will be stored in the SML array. If the value of the instruction counter is larger than the value of the data counter, the SML array is full. In this case, the compilation process should terminate and the compiler should print an error message indicating that it ran out of memory during compilation. This serves to emphasize that although the programmer is freed from the burdens of managing memory by the compiler, the compiler itself must carefully determine the placement of instructions and data in memory, and must check for such errors as memory being exhausted during the compilation process.

Simple program	SML location and instruction	Description
5 rem sum 1 to x	*none*	**rem** ignored
10 input x	00 +1099	read **x** into location **99**
15 rem check y == x	*none*	**rem** ignored
20 if y == x goto 60	01 +2098	load **y** (**98**) into accumulator
	02 +3199	sub **x** (**99**) from accumulator
	03 +4200	*branch zero to unresolved location*
25 rem increment y	*none*	**rem** ignored
30 let y = y + 1	04 +2098	load **y** into accumulator
	05 +3097	add **1** (**97**) to accumulator
	06 +2196	store in temporary location **96**
	07 +2096	load from temporary location **96**
	08 +2198	store accumulator in **y**
35 rem add y to total	*none*	**rem** ignored
40 let t = t + y	09 +2095	load **t** (**95**) into accumulator
	10 +3098	add **y** to accumulator
	11 +2194	store in temporary location **94**
	12 +2094	load from temporary location **94**
	13 +2195	store accumulator in **t**
45 rem loop y	*none*	**rem** ignored
50 goto 20	14 +4001	branch to location **01**
55 rem output result	*none*	**rem** ignored
60 print t	15 +1195	output **t** to screen
99 end	16 +4300	terminate execution

Fig. 17.25 SML instructions produced after the compiler's first pass.

A Step-by-Step View of the Compilation Process

Let us now walk through the compilation process for the Simple program in Fig. 17.25. The compiler reads the first line of the program

```
5 rem sum 1 to x
```

into memory. The first token in the statement (the line number) is determined using the **StreamTo-kenizer** class (see Chapter 8 for a discussion of Java's string manipulation methods). The token returned by the **StreamTokenizer** is converted to an integer using **Integer.parseInt()** so the symbol **5** can be located in the symbol table. If the symbol is not found, it is inserted in the symbol table.

Symbol	Type	Location
5	L	00
10	L	00
'x'	V	99
15	L	01
20	L	01
'y'	V	98
25	L	04
30	L	04
1	C	97
35	L	09
40	L	09
't'	V	95
45	L	14
50	L	14
55	L	15
60	L	15
99	L	16

Fig. 17.26 Symbol table for program of Fig. 17.25.

Since we are at the beginning of the program and this is the first line, no symbols are in the table yet. So, **5** is inserted into the symbol table as type **L** (line number) and assigned the first location in SML array (**00**). Although this line is a remark, a space in the symbol table is still allocated for the line number (in case it is referenced by a **goto** or an **if/goto**). No SML instruction is generated for a **rem** statement, so the instruction counter is not incremented

The statement

        10 input x

is tokenized next. The line number **10** is placed in the symbol table as type **L** and assigned the first location in the SML array (**00** because a remark began the program so the instruction counter is currently **00**). The command **input** indicates that the next token is a variable (only a variable can appear in an **input** statement). Because **input** corresponds directly to an SML operation code, the compiler simply has to determine the location of **x** in the SML array. Symbol **x** is not found in the symbol table. So, it is inserted into the symbol table as the Unicode representation of **x**, given type **V**, and assigned location **99** in the SML array (data storage begins at **99** and is allocated backwards). SML code can now be generated for this statement. Operation code **10** (the SML read operation code) is multiplied by 100, and the location of **x** (as determined in the symbol table) is added to complete the instruction. The instruction is then stored in the SML array at location **00**. The instruction counter is incremented by 1 because a single SML instruction was produced.

The statement

```
15 rem    check y == x
```

is tokenized next. The symbol table is searched for line number **15** (which is not found). The line number is inserted as type **L** and assigned the next location in the array, **01** (remember that **rem** statements do not produce code, so the instruction counter is not incremented).

The statement

```
20 if y == x goto 60
```

is tokenized next. Line number **20** is inserted in the symbol table and given type **L** with the next location in the SML array **01**. The command **if** indicates that a condition is to be evaluated. The variable **y** is not found in the symbol table, so it is inserted and given the type **V** and the SML location **98**. Next, SML instructions are generated to evaluate the condition. Since there is no direct equivalent in SML for the **if/goto**, it must be simulated by performing a calculation using **x** and **y** and branching based on the result. If **y** is equal to **x**, the result of subtracting **x** from **y** is zero, so the *branch zero* instruction can be used with the result of the calculation to simulate the **if/goto** statement. The first step requires that **y** be loaded (from SML location **98**) into the accumulator. This produces the instruction **01 +2098**. Next, **x** is subtracted from the accumulator. This produces the instruction **02 +3199**. The value in the accumulator may be zero, positive, or negative. Since the operator is **==**, we want to *branch zero*. First, the symbol table is searched for the branch location (**60** in this case), which is not found. So, **60** is placed in the **flags** array at location **03**, and the instruction **03 +4200** is generated (we cannot add the branch location because we have not assigned a location to line **60** in the SML array yet). The instruction counter is incremented to **04**.

The compiler proceeds to the statement

```
25 rem    increment y
```

The line number **25** is inserted in the symbol table as type **L** and assigned SML location **04**. The instruction counter is not incremented.

When the statement

```
30 let y = y + 1
```

is tokenized, the line number **30** is inserted in the symbol table as type **L** and assigned SML location **04**. Command **let** indicates that the line is an assignment statement. First, all the symbols on the line are inserted in the symbol table (if they are not already there). The integer **1** is added to the symbol table as type **C** and assigned SML location **97**. Next, the right side of the assignment is converted from infix to postfix notation. Then the postfix expression (**y 1 +**) is evaluated. Symbol **y** is located in the symbol table and its corresponding memory location is pushed onto the stack. Symbol **1** is also located in the symbol table and its corresponding memory location is pushed onto the stack. When the operator **+** is encountered, the postfix evaluator pops the stack into the right operand of the operator and pops the stack again into the left operand of the operator, then produces the SML instructions

```
04 +2098    (load y)
05 +3097    (add 1)
```

The result of the expression is stored in a temporary location in memory (**96**) with instruction

```
06 +2196    (store temporary)
```

and the temporary location is pushed on the stack. Now that the expression has been evaluated, the result must be stored in **y** (i.e., the variable on the left side of **=**). So, the temporary location is loaded into the accumulator and the accumulator is stored in **y** with the instructions

```
07 +2096     (load temporary)
08 +2198     (store y)
```

The reader will immediately notice that SML instructions appear to be redundant. We will discuss this issue shortly.

When the statement

```
35 rem    add y to total
```

is tokenized, line number **35** is inserted in the symbol table as type **L** and assigned location **09**.

The statement

```
40 let t = t + y
```

is similar to line **30**. The variable **t** is inserted in the symbol table as type **V** and assigned SML location **95**. The instructions follow the same logic and format as line **30**, and the instructions **09 +2095, 10 +3098, 11 +2194, 12 +2094**, and **13 +2195** are generated. Note that the result of **t + y** is assigned to temporary location **94** before being assigned to **t** (**95**). Once again, the reader will note that the instructions in memory locations **11** and **12** appear to be redundant. Again, we will discuss this shortly.

The statement

```
45 rem    loop y
```

is a remark, so line **45** is added to the symbol table as type **L** and assigned SML location **14**.

The statement

```
50 goto 20
```

transfers control to line **20**. Line number **50** is inserted in the symbol table as type **L** and assigned SML location **14**. The equivalent of **goto** in SML is the *unconditional branch* (**40**) instruction that transfers control to a specific SML location. The compiler searches the symbol table for line **20** and finds that it corresponds to SML location **01**. The operation code (**40**) is multiplied by 100 and location **01** is added to it to produce the instruction **14 +4001**.

The statement

```
55 rem    output result
```

is a remark, so line **55** is inserted in the symbol table as type **L** and assigned SML location **15**.

The statement

```
60 print t
```

is an output statement. Line number **60** is inserted in the symbol table as type **L** and assigned SML location **15**. The equivalent of **print** in SML is operation code **11** (*write*). The location of **t** is determined from the symbol table and added to the result of the operation code multiplied by 100.

The statement

99 end

is the final line of the program. Line number **99** is stored in the symbol table as type **L** and assigned SML location **16**. The **end** command produces the SML instruction **+4300** (**43** is *halt* in SML) which is written as the final instruction in the SML memory array.

This completes the first pass of the compiler. We now consider the second pass. The **flags** array is searched for values other than **–1**. Location **03** contains **60**, so the compiler knows that instruction **03** is incomplete. The compiler completes the instruction by searching the symbol table for **60**, determining its location, and adding the location to the incomplete instruction. In this case, the search determines that line **60** corresponds to SML location **15**, so the completed instruction **03 +4215** is produced replacing **03 +4200**. The Simple program has now been compiled successfully.

To build the compiler, you will have to perform each of the following tasks:

a) Modify the Simpletron simulator program you wrote in Exercise 5.43 to take its input from a file specified by the user (see Chapter 15). The simulator should output its results to a disk file in the same format as the screen output. Convert the simulator to be an object-oriented program. In particular, make each part of the hardware an object. Arrange the instruction types into a class hierarchy using inheritance. Then execute the program polymorphically simply by telling each instruction to execute itself with an **executeInstruction** message.

b) Modify the infix-to-postfix evaluation algorithm of Exercise 17.12 to process multi-digit integer operands and single-letter variable name operands. Hint: Class **StreamTokenizer** can be used to locate each constant and variable in an expression, and constants can be converted from strings to integers using **Integer** class method **parseInt**. (Note: The data representation of the postfix expression must be altered to support variable names and integer constants.)

c) Modify the postfix evaluation algorithm to process multi-digit integer operands and variable name operands. Also, the algorithm should now implement the "hook" discussed above so that SML instructions are produced rather than directly evaluating the expression. Hint: Class **StreamTokenizer** can be used to locate each constant and variable in an expression, and constants can be converted from strings to integers using **Integer** class method **parseInt**. (Note: The data representation of the postfix expression must be altered to support variable names and integer constants.)

d) Build the compiler. Incorporate parts (b) and (c) for evaluating expressions in **let** statements. Your program should contain a method that performs the first pass of the compiler and a method that performs the second pass. Both methods can call other methods to accomplish their tasks. Make your compiler as object oriented as possible.

17.28 (*Optimizing the Simple Compiler*) When a program is compiled and converted into SML, a set of instructions is generated. Certain combinations of instructions often repeat themselves, usually in triplets called *productions*. A production normally consists of three instructions such as *load, add*, and *store*. For example, Fig. 17.27 illustrates five of the SML instructions that were produced in the compilation of the program in Fig. 17.25 The first three instructions are the production that adds **1** to **y**. Note that instructions **06** and **07** store the accumulator value in temporary location **96**, then load the value back into the accumulator so instruction **08** can store the value in location **98**. Often a production is followed by a load instruction for the same location that was just stored. This code can be *optimized* by eliminating the store instruction and the subsequent load instruction that operate on the same memory location, thus enabling the Simpletron to execute the program faster. Figure 17.28 il-

```
1   04   +2098   (load)
2   05   +3097   (add)
3   06   +2196   (store)
4   07   +2096   (load)
5   08   +2198   (store)
```

Fig. 17.27 Unoptimized code from the program of Fig. 17.25.

lustrates the optimized SML for the program of Fig. 17.25. Note that there are four fewer instructions in the optimized code—a memory-space savings of 25%.

Modify the compiler to provide an option for optimizing the Simpletron Machine Language code it produces. Manually compare the non-optimized code with the optimized code, and calculate the percentage reduction.

17.29 (*Modifications to the Simple compiler*) Perform the following modifications to the Simple compiler. Some of these modifications may also require modifications to the Simpletron Simulator program written in Exercise 5.43.

Simple program	SML location and instruction	Description
5 rem sum 1 to x	*none*	**rem** ignored
10 input x	00 +1099	read **x** into location **99**
15 rem check y == x	*none*	**rem** ignored
20 if y == x goto 60	01 +2098	load **y** (**98**) into accumulator
	02 +3199	sub **x** (**99**) from accumulator
	03 +4211	branch to location **11** if zero
25 rem increment y	*none*	**rem** ignored
30 let y = y + 1	04 +2098	load **y** into accumulator
	05 +3097	add **1** (**97**) to accumulator
	06 +2198	store accumulator in **y** (**98**)
35 rem add y to total	*none*	**rem** ignored
40 let t = t + y	07 +2096	load **t** from location (**96**)
	08 +3098	add **y** (**98**) accumulator
	09 +2196	store accumulator in **t** (**96**)
45 rem loop y	*none*	**rem** ignored
50 goto 20	10 +4001	branch to location **01**
55 rem output result	*none*	**rem** ignored
60 print t	11 +1196	output **t** (**96**) to screen
99 end	12 +4300	terminate execution

Fig. 17.28 Optimized code for the program of Fig. 17.25.

a) Allow the modulus operator (**%**) to be used in **let** statements. Simpletron Machine Language must be modified to include a modulus instruction.

b) Allow exponentiation in a **let** statement using **^** as the exponentiation operator. Simpletron Machine Language must be modified to include an exponentiation instruction.

c) Allow the compiler to recognize uppercase and lowercase letters in Simple statements (e.g., **'A'** is equivalent to **'a'**). No modifications to the Simpletron Simulator are required.

d) Allow **input** statements to read values for multiple variables such as **input x, y**. No modifications to the Simpletron Simulator are required.

e) Allow the compiler to output multiple values in a single **print** statement such as **print a, b, c**. No modifications to the Simpletron Simulator are required.

f) Add syntax-checking capabilities to the compiler so error messages are output when syntax errors are encountered in a Simple program. No modifications to the Simpletron Simulator are required.

g) Allow arrays of integers. No modifications to the Simpletron Simulator are required.

h) Allow subroutines specified by the Simple commands **gosub** and **return**. Command **gosub** passes program control to a subroutine and command **return** passes control back to the statement after the **gosub**. This is similar to a method call in Java. The same subroutine can be called from many **gosub** commands distributed throughout a program. No modifications to the Simpletron Simulator are required.

i) Allow repetition structures of the form

```
for x = 2 to 10 step 2
    Simple statements
next
```

This **for** statement loops from **2** to **10** with an increment of **2**. The **next** line marks the end of the body of the **for** line. No modifications to the Simpletron Simulator are required.

j) Allow repetition structures of the form

```
for x = 2 to 10
    Simple statements
next
```

This **for** statement loops from **2** to **10** with a default increment of **1**. No modifications to the Simpletron Simulator are required.

k) Allow the compiler to process string input and output. This requires the Simpletron Simulator to be modified to process and store string values. Hint: Each Simpletron word can be divided into two groups, each holding a two-digit integer. Each two-digit integer represents the Unicode decimal equivalent of a character. Add a machine language instruction that will print a string beginning at a certain Simpletron memory location. The first half of the word at that location is a count of the number of characters in the string (i.e., the length of the string). Each succeeding half word contains one Unicode character expressed as two decimal digits. The machine language instruction checks the length and prints the string by translating each two-digit number into its equivalent character.

l) Allow the compiler to process floating-point values in addition to integers. The Simpletron Simulator must also be modified to process floating-point values.

17.30 (*A Simple interpreter*) An interpreter is a program that reads a high-level language program statement, determines the operation to be performed by the statement, and executes the operation immediately. The high-level language program is not converted into machine language first. Interpreters execute slower than compilers do because each statement encountered in the program being interpreted must first be deciphered at execution time. If statements are contained in a loop, the statements are deciphered each time they are encountered in the loop. Early versions of the Basic programming language were implemented as interpreters. Most Java programs are run interpretively.

Write an interpreter for the Simple language discussed in Exercise 17.26. The program should use the infix-to-postfix converter developed in Exercise 17.12 and the postfix evaluator developed in Exercise 17.13 to evaluate expressions in a **let** statement. The same restrictions placed on the Simple language in Exercise 17.26 should be adhered to in this program. Test the interpreter with the Simple programs written in Exercise 17.26. Compare the results of running these programs in the interpreter with the results of compiling the Simple programs and running them in the Simpletron Simulator built in Exercise 5.43.

17.31 *(Insert/Delete Anywhere in a Linked List)* Our linked list class allowed insertions and deletions at only the front and the back of the linked list. These capabilities were convenient for us when we used inheritance or composition to produce a stack class and a queue class with a minimal amount of code simply by reusing the list class. Linked lists are normally more general that those we provided. Modify the linked list class we developed in this chapter to handle insertions and deletions anywhere in the list.

17.32 *(List and Queues without Tail References)* Our implementation of a linked list (Fig. 17.3) used both a **firstNode** and a **lastNode**. The **lastNode** was useful for the **insertAtBack** and **removeFromBack** methods of the **List** class. The **insertAtBack** method corresponds to the **enqueue** method of the **Queue** class. Rewrite the **List** class so that it does not use a **lastNode**. Thus, any operations on the tail of a list must begin searching the list from the front. Does this affect our implementation of the **Queue** class (Fig. 17.12)?

17.33 *(Performance of Binary Tree Sorting and Searching)* One problem with the binary tree sort is that the order in which the data is inserted affects the shape of the tree—for the same collection of data, different orderings can yield binary trees of dramatically different shapes. The performance of the binary tree sorting and searching algorithms is sensitive to the shape of the binary tree. What shape would a binary tree have if its data were inserted in increasing order? in decreasing order? What shape should the tree have to achieve maximal searching performance?

17.34 *(Indexed Lists)* As presented in the text, linked lists must be searched sequentially. For large lists, this can result in poor performance. A common technique for improving list searching performance is to create and maintain an index to the list. An index is a set of references to various key places in the list. For example, an application that searches a large list of names could improve performance by creating an index with 26 entries—one for each letter of the alphabet. A search operation for a last name beginning with 'Y' would then first search the index to determine where the 'Y' entries begin, and then "jump into" the list at that point and search linearly until the desired name is found. This would be much faster than searching the linked list from the beginning. Use the **List** class of Fig. 17.3 as the basis of an **IndexedList** class. Write a program that demonstrates the operation of indexed lists. Be sure to include methods **insertInIndexedList**, **searchIndexedList**, and **deleteFromIndexedList**.

18

Java Utilities Package and Bit Manipulation

Objectives

- To understand containers such as classes **Vector** and **Stack**, and the **Enumeration** interface.
- To be able to create **Hashtable** objects and persistent hash tables called **Properties** objects.
- To use bit manipulation and **BitSet** objects.
- To build a popular OO-design pattern with **Observable** objects and the **Observer** interface

Nothing can have value without being an object of utility.
Karl Marx

I've been in Who's Who, and I know what's what, but this is the first time I ever made the dictionary.
Mae West

... what we observe is not nature in itself
but nature exposed to our method of questioning.
Werner Karl Heisenberg

You can observe a lot by just watching.
Yogi Berra

O! Thou hast damnable iteration,
and art indeed able to corrupt a saint.
William Shakespeare, Henry IV, Part I

I am going in search of a great perhaps.
Francois Rebelais

Outline

18.1 Introduction

In this chapter we discuss a variety of utility classes in the **java.util** package. We examine the **Vector** class which enables us to create array-like objects that can grow and shrink dynamically as a program's data storage requirements change. We consider the **Enumeration** interface which we use in conjunction with class **Vector** to allow a program to iterate its way through the elements of a container such as a **Vector**.

We discuss the **Stack** class that offers the conventional stack operations **push** and **pop** along with several others we did not consider in Chapter 17.

We present class **Dictionary** which is an abstract class that gives us the framework for storing keyed data in tables and retrieving that data. We explain the theory of "hashing," a technique for rapidly storing and retrieving information from tables, and we demonstrate the construction and manipulation of hash tables with Java's **Hashtable** class. We consider the **Properties** class that enables us to create persistent hash tables, i.e., hashtables that can be written to a file with an output stream and eventually read back into the system on demand from an input stream.

We review the **Date** class for manipulating dates and times. We overview class **Random** that provides a richer collection of random-number capabilities than is available with **Math.random**.

We discuss a popular design pattern in object-oriented systems, namely having one object inform other objects when the first object's state changes; we implement this pattern with class **Observable** and the **Observer** interface.

We present an extensive discussion of bit manipulation operators and then discuss class **BitSet** that enables the creation of bit-array-like objects for setting and getting individual bits.

18.2 **Vector** Class and **Enumeration** Interface

In most programming languages, including Java, conventional arrays are fixed in size—they cannot grow or shrink in response to an application's changing storage requirements. Java class **Vector** provides the capabilities of array-like data structures that can dynamically resize themselves.

At any time the **Vector** contains a certain number of elements which is less than or equal to its *capacity*. The capacity is the space that has been reserved for the array.

Performance Tip 18.1

Inserting additional elements into an array whose current size is less than its capacity is a relatively fast operation.

If a **Vector** needs to grow, it grows by an increment that you specify or by a default assumed by the system.

Performance Tip 18.2

It is a relatively slow operation to insert an element into an array that needs to grow larger to accommodate the new element.

If you do not specify a capacity increment, the system will automatically double the size of the **Vector** each time additional capacity is needed.

Performance Tip 18.3

*The default capacity increment of doubling the size of the **Vector** may seem wasteful of storage, but it is actually an efficient way for many **Vector**s to grow quickly to be "about the right size." This is much more efficient time-wise than growing the **Vector** each time by only as much space as it takes to hold a single element. But it can waste space.*

Performance Tip 18.4

*If storage is at a premium, use the **trimToSize** method of the **Vector** class to trim a **Vector** to its exact size. This will optimize a **Vector**'s use of storage. But be careful. If an additional element needs to be inserted in the **vector**, this will be slow because it will force the **Vector** to grow dynamically—trimming leaves no room for growth.*

Vectors are designed to store references to **Object**s. Thus, a reference to an object of any class type can be stored in a **Vector**. If you would like to store values of primitive data types in **Vector**s, you must use the type wrapper classes (**Integer, Long, Float, Double, Boolean** and **Character**) from the **java.lang** package to create objects containing the primitive data type values.

The applet of Fig. 18.1 demonstrates class **Vector** and many of its methods. A button is provided for each of the methods. The user can type a **String** into the provided text field, then press a button to see what the method does. Messages are displayed in the status area of the applet to indicate the results of each operation.

The applet's **init** method creates a **Vector** with the statement

```
Vector v = new Vector( 1 );
```

which creates a **Vector** with an initial capacity of 1 element. This **Vector** will double in size automatically each time it needs to grow to accommodate more elements.

```
1   // Fig. 18.1: VectorTest.java
2   // Testing the Vector class of the java.util package
3   import java.util.*;
4   import java.awt.*;
5   import java.applet.Applet;
6
7   public class VectorTest extends Applet {
8      Vector v;
9
10     // GUI components
11     Label prompt;
12     TextField input;
13     Button addBtn, removeBtn, firstBtn, lastBtn,
14            emptyBtn, containsBtn, locationBtn,
15            trimBtn, statsBtn, displayBtn;
16
17     public void init()
18     {
19        v = new Vector( 1 );
20
21        prompt = new Label( "Enter a string" );
22        input = new TextField( 10 );
23        addBtn = new Button( "Add" );
24        removeBtn = new Button( "Remove" );
25        firstBtn = new Button( "First" );
26        lastBtn = new Button( "Last" );
27        emptyBtn = new Button( "Is Empty?" );
28        containsBtn = new Button( "Contains" );
29        locationBtn = new Button( "Location" );
30        trimBtn = new Button( "Trim" );
31        statsBtn = new Button( "Statistics" );
32        displayBtn = new Button( "Display" );
33
34        add( prompt );
35        add( input );          // value to add, remove or locate
36        add( addBtn );         // add the input value
37        add( removeBtn );      // remove the input value
38        add( firstBtn );       // look at the first element
39        add( lastBtn );        // look at the last element
40        add( emptyBtn );       // check if stack is empty
41        add( containsBtn );    // does vector contain input value?
42        add( locationBtn );    // location of input value
43        add( trimBtn );        // trim vector to number of elements
44        add( statsBtn );       // display statistics
45        add( displayBtn );     // display the stack contents
46     }
47
```

Fig. 18.1   Demonstrating class **Vector** of the **java.util** package (part 1 of 3).

```
48      public boolean action( Event e, Object o )
49      {
50         if ( e.target == addBtn ) {
51            v.addElement( input.getText() );
52            showStatus( "Added to end: " + input.getText() );
53         }
54         else if ( e.target == removeBtn ) {
55            if ( v.removeElement( input.getText() ) )
56               showStatus( "Removed: " + input.getText() );
57            else
58               showStatus( input.getText() + " not in vector" );
59         }
60         else if ( e.target == firstBtn ) {
61            try {
62               showStatus( "First element: " + v.firstElement() );
63            }
64            catch ( NoSuchElementException exception ) {
65               showStatus( exception.toString() );
66            }
67         }
68         else if ( e.target == lastBtn ) {
69            try {
70               showStatus( "Last element: " + v.lastElement() );
71            }
72            catch ( NoSuchElementException exception ) {
73               showStatus( exception.toString() );
74            }
75         }
76         else if ( e.target == emptyBtn ) {
77            showStatus( v.isEmpty() ? "Vector is empty" :
78                                      "Vector is not empty" );
79         }
80         else if ( e.target == containsBtn ) {
81            String searchKey = input.getText();
82
83            if ( v.contains( searchKey ) )
84               showStatus( "Vector contains " + searchKey );
85            else
86              showStatus( "Vector does not contain " + searchKey );
87         }
88         else if ( e.target == locationBtn ) {
89            showStatus( "Element is at location " +
90                        v.indexOf( input.getText() ) );
91         }
92         else if ( e.target == trimBtn ) {
93            v.trimToSize();
94            showStatus( "Vector trimmed to size" );
95         }
```

Fig. 18.1 Demonstrating class **Vector** of the **java.util** package (part 2 of 3).

```
96             else if ( e.target == statsBtn ) {
97                showStatus( "Size = " + v.size() +
98                            "; capacity = " + v.capacity() );
99             }
100            else if ( e.target == displayBtn ) {
101               Enumeration enum = v.elements();
102               StringBuffer buf = new StringBuffer();
103
104               while ( enum.hasMoreElements() )
105                  buf.append( enum.nextElement() ).append( " " );
106
107               showStatus( buf.toString() );
108            }
109
110            input.setText( "" );
111            return true;
112      }
113 }
```

Fig. 18.1   Demonstrating class **Vector** of the **java.util** package (part 3 of 3).

Class **Vector** provides two other constructors. The no-argument constructor creates an empty **Vector** with an *initial capacity* of 10 elements. The constructor that takes two arguments creates a **Vector** with an *initial capacity* specified by the first argument and a *capacity increment* specified by the second argument. Each time this **Vector** needs to grow, it will add space for the specified number of elements in the capacity increment.

The statement

```
v.addElement( input.getText() );
```

uses **Vector** method **addElement** to add its argument to the end of the **Vector**. The **Vector**'s capacity is increased automatically (if necessary) to accommodate the new element. Class **Vector** also provides method **insertElementAt** to insert an element (the method's first argument) at a specified position (the method's second argument) in the **Vector** and method **setElementAt** to set the element (the method's first argument) at a specific position (the method's second argument) in the **Vector**. Method **insertEle-**

mentAt makes room for the new element by shifting elements. Method **setElementAt** replaces the element at the specified position with its argument.

The expression

```
v.removeElement( input.getText() )
```

uses **Vector** method **removeElement** to remove the first occurrence of its argument from the **Vector**. The method returns **true** if the element was found in the **Vector**; otherwise, **false** is returned. If the element is removed, all elements after that element in the **Vector** are shifted one position toward the beginning of the **Vector** to fill in the position of the removed element. Class **Vector** also provides method **removeAllElements** to remove every element from the **Vector** and method **removeElementAt** to remove the element at the index specified as an argument.

The expression

```
v.firstElement()
```

uses **Vector** method **firstElement** to return a reference to the first element in the **Vector**. This method throws a **NoSuchElementException** if there are no elements currently in the **Vector**.

The expression

```
v.lastElement()
```

uses **Vector** method **lastElement** to return a reference to the last element in the **Vector**. This method throws a **NoSuchElementException** if there are no elements currently in the **Vector**.

The expression

```
v.isEmpty()
```

uses **Vector** method **isEmpty** to determine if the **Vector** is empty. The method returns **true** if there are no elements in the **Vector**; otherwise, **false** is returned.

The expression

```
v.contains( searchKey )
```

uses **Vector** method **contains** to determine if the **Vector** contains the **searchKey** specified as an argument. The method returns **true** if **searchKey** is in the **Vector**; otherwise, **false** is returned. Method **contains** uses **Object** method **equals** to determine if the **searchKey** is equal to one of the **Vector**'s elements.

The expression

```
v.indexOf( input.getText() )
```

uses **Vector** method **indexOf** to get the index of the first location of the argument in the **Vector**. The method returns -1 if the argument is not found in the **Vector**. There is a version of this method that takes a second argument specifying the index in the **Vector** where the search should begin.

The statement

```
v.trimToSize();
```

uses **Vector** method **trimToSize** to cut the capacity of the **Vector** to the current number of elements in the **Vector** (i.e., the size of the **Vector**).

The expressions

```
v.size()
v.capacity()
```

use **Vector** methods **size** and **capacity** to determine the number of elements currently in the **Vector** and the number of elements that can be stored in the **Vector** without allocating more memory, respectively.

The statement

```
Enumeration enum = v.elements();
```

uses **Vector** method **elements** to return a reference to an **Enumeration** containing the elements of the **Vector**. An **Enumeration** provides two methods that allow a program to walk through a set of elements one element at a time. The expression

```
enum.hasMoreElements();
```

returns **true** as long as there are more elements in the **Enumeration**. The expression

```
enum.nextElement();
```

returns a reference to the next element in the **Enumeration**. If there are no more elements, a **NoSuchElementException** is thrown.

For more information on the **Vector** methods, see the Java API documentation.

18.3 Stack Class

In Chapter 17, "Data Structures," we learned how to build fundamental data structures like linked lists, stacks, queues, and trees. In a world of "reuse, reuse, reuse," instead of building data structures as we need them, we will often be able to take advantage of existing data structures classes. In this section, we investigate the **Stack** class in the Java utilities package (**java.util**).

We have already discussed class **Vector** that implements a dynamically resizable array. Class **Stack** extends class **Vector** to implement a stack data structure. Like **Vector**, class **Stack** is designed to store **Object**s; to store primitive data types, you must use the appropriate type wrapper class (**Boolean**, **Character**, **Integer**, **Long**, **Float** or **Double**).

The applet of Fig. 18.2 provides a graphical user interface that enables you to test each of the **Stack** methods. The statement

```
s = new Stack();
```

creates an empty **Stack**.

```java
1    // Fig. 18.2: StackTest.java
2    // Testing the Stack class of the java.util package
3    import java.util.*;
4    import java.awt.*;
5    import java.applet.Applet;
6
7    public class StackTest extends Applet {
8       Stack s;
9
10      // GUI components
11      Label prompt;
12      TextField input;
13      Button pushBtn, popBtn, peekBtn,
14              emptyBtn, searchBtn, displayBtn;
15
16      public void init()
17      {
18         s = new Stack();
19
20         prompt = new Label( "Enter a string" );
21         input = new TextField( 10 );
22         pushBtn = new Button( "Push" );
23         popBtn = new Button( "Pop" );
24         peekBtn = new Button( "Peek" );
25         emptyBtn = new Button( "Is Empty?" );
26         searchBtn = new Button( "Search" );
27         displayBtn = new Button( "Display" );
28         add( prompt );
29         add( input );        // value to push or search for
30         add( pushBtn );      // push the input value
31         add( popBtn );       // pop a value
32         add( peekBtn );      // peek at the top
33         add( emptyBtn );     // check if stack is empty
34         add( searchBtn );    // search for input value
35         add( displayBtn ); // display the stack contents
36      }
37
38      public boolean action( Event e, Object o )
39      {
40         if ( e.target == pushBtn ) {
41            showStatus( "Pushed: " + s.push( input.getText() ) );
42         }
43         else if ( e.target == popBtn ) {
44            try {
45               showStatus( "Popped: " + s.pop() );
46            }
47            catch ( EmptyStackException exception ) {
48               showStatus( exception.toString() );
49            }
50         }
```

Fig. 18.2 Demonstrating class **Stack** of the **java.util** package (part 1 of 2).

```
51          else if ( e.target == peekBtn ) {
52             try {
53                showStatus( "Top: " + s.peek() );
54             }
55             catch ( EmptyStackException exception ) {
56                showStatus( exception.toString() );
57             }
58          }
59          else if ( e.target == emptyBtn ) {
60             showStatus( s.empty() ? "Stack is empty" :
61                                     "Stack is not empty" );
62          }
63          else if ( e.target == searchBtn ) {
64             String searchKey = input.getText();
65             int result = s.search( searchKey );
66
67             if ( result == -1 )
68                showStatus( searchKey + " not found" );
69             else
70                showStatus( searchKey + " found at element " +
71                            result );
72          }
73          else if ( e.target == displayBtn ) {
74             Enumeration enum = s.elements();
75             StringBuffer buf = new StringBuffer();
76
77             while ( enum.hasMoreElements() )
78                buf.append( enum.nextElement() ).append( " " );
79
80             showStatus( buf.toString() );
81          }
82
83          return true;
84       }
85    }
```

Fig. 18.2   Demonstrating class **Stack** of the **java.util** package (part 2 of 2).

The expression

```
s.push( input.getText() )
```

uses **Stack** method **push** to add its argument to the top of the stack. The method returns an **Object** reference to its argument.

The expression

```
s.pop()
```

uses **Stack** method **pop** to remove the top element of the stack. The method returns an **Object** reference to the element that was removed. If there are no elements in the **Stack**, an **EmptyStackException** is thrown.

The expression

```
s.peek()
```

uses **Stack** method **peek** to look at the top element of the stack without removing it. The method returns an **Object** reference to the element.

The expression

```
s.empty()
```

uses **Stack** method **empty** to determine if the stack is empty. If so, **true** is returned; otherwise, **false** is returned.

The expression

```
int result = s.search( searchKey );
```

uses **Stack** method **search** to determine if its argument is in the stack. If so, the position of the element in the stack is returned. *The top element is position 1.* If the element is not in the stack, -1 is returned.

Please note that the entire public interface of class **Vector** is actually part of class **Stack** because **Stack** inherits from **Vector**. To prove this, our example provides a button to display the contents of the stack. This button invokes method elements to get an **Enumeration** containing the contents of the stack. The **Enumeration** is then used to walk through the elements of the stack.

 Testing and Debugging Tip 18.1

*Because **Stack** inherits from **Vector**, the user may perform operations on **Stack** objects that are ordinarily not allowed on conventional stack data structures. This could corrupt the elements of the **Stack** and destroy the integrity of the **Stack**.*

18.4 Dictionary Class

A **Dictionary** transforms *keys* to *values*. A key is supplied and the **Dictionary** returns a value. **Dictionary** is an abstract class. In particular, it is the superclass of the **Hashtable** class we will discuss shortly. Class **Dictionary** provides the public interface methods required to maintain a table of *key/value pairs* where the keys represent the "rows" of the table and the values are "columns" in the table.

The **size** method returns the number of occupied slots in the **Dictionary** object. Method **isEmpty** returns **true** if the **Dictionary** is empty, **false** otherwise. The **keys** method returns an **Enumeration** that iterates through **Dictionary**'s keys. The

elements method enumerates the **Dictionary**'s elements. The **get** method returns the object that corresponds to a given key value. The **put** method puts an object into the table; the object is associated with a given key. The **remove** method removes an element corresponding to a given key and returns a reference to it.

18.5 Hashtable Class

Object-oriented programming languages make it easy to create new types. When a program creates objects of new or existing types, it then needs to manage those objects efficiently. This includes storing and retrieving objects. Storing and retrieving information with arrays is efficient if some aspect of your data directly matches the key value and if those keys are unique and tightly packed. If you have 100 employees with 9-digit Social Security numbers and you want to store and retrieve employee data by using the Social Security number as a key, it would nominally require an array with 999,999,999 elements, because there are 999,999,999 unique 9-digit numbers. This is impractical for virtually all applications that key on Social Security numbers. But if you could have an array that large, you could get very high performance storing and retrieving employee records by simply using the Social Security number as the array index.

There are a huge variety of applications that have this problem, namely that either the keys are of the wrong type (i.e., not nonnegative integers), or they may be of the right type but sparsely spread over a huge range.

What is needed is a high-speed scheme for converting keys like Social Security numbers, inventory part numbers, and the like into unique array subscripts. Then, when an application needs to store something, the scheme could rapidly convert the application key into a subscript and the record of information could be stored at that slot in the array. Retrieval is accomplished the same way: Once the application has a key value for which it wants to retrieve the data record, the application simply applies the conversion to the key—this produces the array subscript for the data where the array is stored and the data is retrieved.

The scheme we describe here is the basis of a technique called *hashing*. Why the name? Because when we convert a key into an array subscript we literally scramble the bits forming a kind of "mish-mashed" number. The number actually has no real significance beyond its usefulness in storing and retrieving this particular number data record.

A glitch in the scheme occurs when *collisions* occur; i.e., two different keys "hash into" the same cell (or element) in the array. Since we cannot store two different data records in the same space, we need to find an alternate home for all records beyond the first that hash to a particular array subscript. There are many schemes for doing this. One is to "hash again," i.e., to reapply the hashing transformation to the key to provide a next candidate cell in the array. The hashing process is designed to be quite random, so the assumption is that with just a few hashes an available cell will be found.

Another scheme uses one hash to locate the first candidate cell. If that cell is occupied, successive cells are searched linearly until an available cell is found. Retrieval works the same way: The key is hashed once, the cell pointed to is checked to see if it contains the desired data. If it does, the search is finished. If it does not then successive cells are searched linearly until the desired data is found.

The most popular solution to hash table collisions is to have each cell of the table be a hash "bucket," typically a linked list of all the key/value pairs that hash to that cell. This is the solution that Java's **Hashtable** class (from package **java.util**) uses for its implementation.

One factor that affects the performance of hashing schemes is called the *load factor*. This is the ratio of the number of occupied cells in the hash table to the size of the hash table. The closer this ratio gets to 1.0, the greater the chance of collisions.

Performance Tip 18.5

The load factor in a hash table is a classic example of a space-time trade-off: By increasing the load factor, we get better memory utilization, but the program runs slower due to increased hashing collisions. By decreasing the load factor, we get better program speed because of reduced hashing collisions, but we get poorer memory utilization because a larger portion of the hash table remains empty.

The complexity of using hash tables properly is too much for most casual programmers. Computer science students study hashing schemes thoroughly in courses called "Data Structures" and/or "Algorithms." Recognizing the value of hashing to most programmers, Java provides the **Hashtable** class and some related features to enable programmers to take advantage of hashing without having to worry about the messy details.

Actually, the previous sentence is profoundly important in our study of object-oriented programming. Classes encapsulate and hide complexity (i.e., implementation details) and offer friendly user interfaces. Crafting classes to do this properly is one of the most valued skills in the field of object-oriented programming.

The applet of Fig. 18.3 provides a graphical user interface that enables you to test each of the **Hashtable** methods. The statement

```
table = new Hashtable();
```

creates an empty **Hashtable** with a default capacity of 101 elements and a default load factor of .75. When the number of occupied slots in the **Hashtable** becomes more than the capacity times the load factor, the table will automatically grow larger. Class **Hashtable** also provides a constructor that takes one argument specifying the capacity and a constructor that takes two arguments specifying the capacity and load factor, respectively.

The statement

```
Object val = table.put( lName.getText(), emp );
```

uses **Hashtable** method **put** to add a *key* (the first argument) and a *value* (the second argument) into the **Hashtable**. If there was no value in the **Hashtable** for the specified key, **null** is returned. If there was a value in the **Hashtable** for the specified key, the original value in the **Hashtable** is returned; this helps the program manage cases in which it intends to replace the value stored for a given key. If either the key or the value is **null**, a **NullPointerException** is thrown. The value can be located in the **Hashtable** with the statement

```
Object val = table.get( lName.getText() );
```

```
 1    // Fig. 18.3: HashtableTest.java
 2    // Demonstrates class Hashtable of the java.util package.
 3    import java.util.*;
 4    import java.awt.*;
 5    import java.applet.Applet;
 6
 7    public class HashtableTest extends Applet {
 8       Hashtable table;
 9
10       Label name1, name2;
11       TextField fName, lName;
12       TextArea display;
13       Button put, get, remove, empty, containsKey, containsObj,
14              clear, listElems, listKeys;
15
16       public void init()
17       {
18          table = new Hashtable();
19
20          name1 = new Label( "First name" );
21          fName = new TextField( 10 );
22          name2 = new Label( "Last name (key)" );
23          lName = new TextField( 10 );
24          display = new TextArea( 4, 45 );
25          put = new Button( "Put" );
26          get = new Button( "Get" );
27          remove = new Button( "Remove" );
28          empty = new Button( "Empty" );
29          containsKey = new Button( "Contains key" );
30          containsObj = new Button( "Contains object" );
31          clear = new Button( "Clear table" );
32          listElems = new Button( "List objects" );
33          listKeys = new Button( "List keys" );
34          add( name1 );
35          add( fName );
36          add( name2 );
37          add( lName );
38          add( display );
39          add( put );
40          add( get );
41          add( remove );
42          add( empty );
43          add( containsKey );
44          add( containsObj );
45          add( clear );
46          add( listElems );
47          add( listKeys );
48       }
49
50       public boolean action( Event e, Object o )
```

Fig. 18.3   Demonstrating class **Hashtable** (part 1 of 3).

```
51          {
52              if ( e.target == put ) {
53                  Employee emp = new Employee( fName.getText(),
54                                                lName.getText() );
55                  Object val = table.put( lName.getText(), emp );
56
57                  if ( val == null )
58                      showStatus( "Put: " + emp.toString() );
59                  else
60                      showStatus( "Put: " + emp.toString() +
61                                  "; Replaced: " + val.toString() );
62              }
63              else if ( e.target == get ) {
64                  Object val = table.get( lName.getText() );
65
66                  if ( val != null )
67                      showStatus( "Get: " + val.toString() );
68                  else
69                      showStatus( "Get: " + lName.getText() +
70                                  " not in table" );
71              }
72              else if ( e.target == remove ) {
73                  Object val = table.remove( lName.getText() );
74
75                  if ( val != null )
76                      showStatus( "Remove: " + val.toString() );
77                  else
78                      showStatus( "Remove: " + lName.getText() +
79                                  " not in table" );
80              }
81              else if ( e.target == empty ) {
82                  showStatus( "Empty: " + table.isEmpty() );
83              }
84              else if ( e.target == containsKey ) {
85                  showStatus( "Contains key: " +
86                      table.containsKey( lName.getText() ) );
87              }
88              else if ( e.target == containsObj ) {
89                  showStatus( "Contains object: " +
90                      table.contains( new Employee( fName.getText(),
91                                       lName.getText() ) ) );
92              }
93              else if ( e.target == clear ) {
94                  table.clear();
95                  showStatus( "Clear: Table is now empty" );
96              }
97              else if ( e.target == listElems ) {
98                  StringBuffer buf = new StringBuffer();
99
100                 for ( Enumeration enum = table.elements();
101                     enum.hasMoreElements(); )
```

Fig. 18.3   Demonstrating class **Hashtable** (part 2 of 3).

```
102                 buf.append( enum.nextElement() ).append( '\n' );
103
104             display.setText( buf.toString() );
105         }
106         else if ( e.target == listKeys ) {
107             StringBuffer buf = new StringBuffer();
108
109             for ( Enumeration enum = table.keys();
110                     enum.hasMoreElements(); )
111                 buf.append( enum.nextElement() ).append( '\n' );
112
113             display.setText( buf.toString() );
114         }
115
116         return true;
117     }
118 }
119
120 class Employee {
121     private String first;
122     private String last;
123
124     public Employee( String fName, String lName )
125     {
126         first = fName;
127         last = lName;
128     }
129
130     public String toString() { return first + " " + last; }
131 }
```

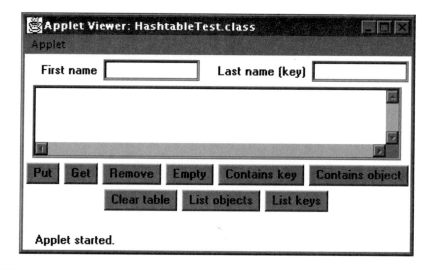

Fig. 18.3   Demonstrating class **Hashtable** (part 3 of 3).

which uses **Hashtable** method **get** to locate the value that is associated with the key specified as an argument. The method returns an **Object** reference to the value if it is located; otherwise, **null** is returned.

The statement

```
Object val = table.remove( lName.getText() );
```

uses **Hashtable** method **remove** to remove from the table the value associated with the key specified as an argument. The method returns an **Object** reference to the removed value. If there is no value mapped to the specified key, the method returns **null**.

The expression

```
table.isEmpty()
```

returns **true** if the **Hashtable** is empty; **false** otherwise.

The expression

```
table.containsKey( lName.getText() )
```

uses **Hashtable** method **containsKey** to determine if the key specified as an argument is in the **Hashtable** (i.e., a value is associated with that key). If so, the method returns **true**; otherwise, **false** is returned. Class **Hashtable** also provides method **contains** to determine if the **Object** specified as its argument is in the **Hashtable**.

The statement

```
table.clear();
```

empties the **Hashtable**.

The expression

```
table.elements()
```

uses **Hashtable** method elements to obtain an **Enumeration** of the values in the **Hashtable**.

The expression

```
table.keys()
```

uses **Hashtable** method **keys** to obtain an **Enumeration** of the keys in the **Hashtable**.

For more information on the methods of class **Hashtable**, see the Java API documentation.

18.6 Date Class

Managing dates and times is a much more sophisticated task than most programmers realize. Java provides class **Date** to help programmers standardize and ensure the completeness of their treatments of dates and times. We will only show a simple example here. The reader is encouraged to explore the Java API in depth.

The **Date** class contains a variety of constructors to initialize **Date** objects. **Date** contains many obvious methods such as **getYear, setYear, getMonth, setMonth, getDate, setDate, getDay, getHours, setHours, getMinutes, setMinutes, getSeconds, setSeconds** and others. Methods **before** and **after** check whether the **Date** object for which they are invoked comes before or after another **Date** specified as an argument. Method **equals** compares the **Date** object to another **Date**. Method **hashCode** computes a hash code for inserting and retrieving **Date**s in **Hashtables**. Method **toString** converts a **Date** object to a **String**.

The applet of Fig. 18.4 demonstrates a **Date** object constructed with the no-argument constructor which uses the system date and time as initial values and a **Date** object constructed with the constructor that takes three integer arguments—year, month and day. Note that the month value for January is 0 and the month value for December is 11. Method **toString** is used to convert the **Date**s to **String** objects for display on the applet.

```
1   // Fig. 18.4: DateTest.java
2   // Test class Date of the java.util package.
3   import java.util.Date;
4   import java.awt.Graphics;
5   import java.applet.Applet;
6
7   public class DateTest extends Applet {
8      Date system, user;
9
10     public void init()
11     {
12        system = new Date();
13        user = new Date( 96, 6, 4 );
14     }
15
16     public void paint( Graphics g )
17     {
18        g.drawString( "System date: " +
19                       system.toString(), 25, 25 );
20        g.drawString( "User defined date: " +
21                       user.toString(), 25, 40 );
22     }
23  }
```

Fig. 18.4   Demonstrating class **Date** from the **java.util** package.

18.7 Observable Class and Observer Interface

There are a number of architectural patterns that appear repeatedly in object-oriented systems. One of the most common is a situation in which an object changes state for some reason and needs to notify several other objects about this state change. The object that changes state should be a subclass of class **Observable**. The objects that need to be notified are called *observers* and their classes implement the **Observer** interface. The **Observable** object maintains an editable list of its observers. When the **Observable** object changes state it notifies each of its observers by calling their **update** methods.

The applet of Fig. 18.5 demonstrates the interaction between an **Observable** object and a single **Observer**. The program consists of applet class **ObserverTest** which extends class **Applet** and implements the **Observer** interface. Class **ObserverTest** defines the **Observer** interface's **update** method which will be called automatically to notify the applet of a change in the state of an object of class **Clock**. Class **Clock** extends class **Observable** and implements the **Runnable** interface so it can execute as a separate thread.

```
1   // Fig. 18.5: ObserverTest.java
2   // Test of class Observable and interface Observer
3   // from the java.util package.
4   import java.util.*;
5   import java.awt.*;
6   import java.applet.Applet;
7
8   public class ObserverTest extends Applet implements Observer {
9       Clock c;
10      Label currentLabel;
11      TextField current;
12      Button alarmOn;
13      Thread clockThread;
14
15      public void init()
16      {
17          c = new Clock();
18          c.addObserver( this );
19          clockThread = new Thread( c );
20
21          currentLabel = new Label( "Current date and time: " );
22          current = new TextField( c.getDate(), 25 );
23          current.setEditable( false );
24          alarmOn = new Button( "Alarm on" );
25          add( currentLabel );
26          add( current );
27          add( alarmOn );
28
29          clockThread.start();
30      }
```

Fig. 18.5   Using class **Observable** and interface **Observer** (part 1 of 3).

```
31
32     public boolean action( Event e, Object o )
33     {
34        showStatus( "Alarm set at " + c.setAlarm() );
35        return true;
36     }
37
38     public void update( Observable ob, Object arg )
39     {
40        current.setText( arg.toString() );
41        showStatus( "Alarm sounded, see new time" );
42     }
43  }
44
45  class Clock extends Observable implements Runnable {
46     Date d;
47     boolean alarmSet;
48
49     public Clock() { d = new Date(); }
50
51     public String setAlarm()
52     {
53        alarmSet = true;
54        d = new Date();
55        return d.toString();
56     }
57
58     public String getDate()
59     {
60        return d.toString();
61     }
62
63     public void run()
64     {
65        while ( true ) {
66           if ( alarmSet ) {
67              try {
68                 Thread.sleep( 10000 );
69              }
70              catch( InterruptedException e ) {
71                 System.err.println( "Sleep interrupted" );
72              }
73
74              alarmSet = false;
75              d = new Date();  // get new time
76              setChanged();
77              notifyObservers( d.toString() );
78           }
79        }
80     }
81  }
```

Fig. 18.5   Using class **Observable** and interface **Observer** (part 2 of 3).

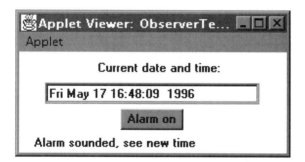

Fig. 18.5   Using class **Observable** and interface **Observer** (part 3 of 3).

When the applet is executed, a graphical user interface with a text field and a button is displayed. The applet's **init** method instantiates **Clock** object **c**. The statement

```
c.addObserver( this );
```

adds the applet into **Clock** object **c**'s list of **Observers**.

The thread **clockThread** is instantiated and initialized with **Clock** object **c** so the **Clock** can execute as a separate thread. When the text field is instantiated, it is initialized with the value of **c.getDate()** which returns a **String** containing the date and time when the **Clock** object was created. When the user clicks the button, the **Clock** object **c**'s **setAlarm** method is invoked. This sets the **Clock** object's **alarmSet** instance variable to **true** to indicate that in 10 seconds the alarm should "sound." When the **Clock** object awakens from its sleep, the current date and time are captured by creating a new **Date** object, then the **Observable** class's **setChanged** method is invoked to indicate that the state of the **Clock** object has changed. Next the **Observable** class's **notify-Observers** method is invoked and passed a **String** representation of the new date and time. This method automatically invokes the **update** method of all its observers (i.e., the applet in this program).

Observer method **update** takes two arguments—a reference to the **Observable** object for which state information changed and a reference to the **Object** that was passed to the **Observable** object's **notifyObservers** method. The **Object** type is typically dependent on the particular program. In this program it is the **String** representing the new date and time. Method **update** in this example displays the new date and time in the text field and a message in the status bar area indicating that the alarm sounded.

Class **Observable** provides several methods that are not used in Fig. 18.5. The following is a brief overview of the other methods using our **Clock** object **c** as the **Observable** object. The statement

```
c.notifyObservers()
```

notifies all of the observers in **c**'s observer list that a state change in **c** has occurred. This results in a call to each **Observer** object's **update** method. In this case, the second argument to the **update** method is **null**. The statement

```
c.deleteObservers()
```

deletes the observers in **c**'s observer list. The statement

```
c.countObservers()
```

returns the number of observers in **c**'s observer list.

The statement

```
c.clearChanged()
```

resets the state flag that indicates that the **Observable** object changed. This method is invoked automatically by the **notifyObservers** method. The statement

```
c.hasChanged()
```

returns **true** if **c**'s state change flag has been set, **false** otherwise.

18.8 Properties Class

A **Properties** object is a persistent **Hashtable** object. By persistent, we mean that the **Hashtable** object can be written to an output stream and directed to a file then read back in through an input stream. The **Properties** class extends class **Hashtable**, so the methods we discussed in Fig. 18.3 can be used for **Properties** objects also. The keys and values in a **Properties** object must be of type **String**. Class **Properties** provides some additional methods that are demonstrated in the application of Fig. 18.6.

```
1   // Fig. 18.6: PropertiesTest.java
2   // Demonstrates class Properties of the java.util package.
3   import java.io.*;
4   import java.util.*;
5   import java.awt.*;
6
7   public class PropertiesTest extends Frame {
8      Properties table;
9      FileInputStream input;
10     FileOutputStream output;
11
12     Label prompt1, prompt2;
13     TextField propName, propVal, result;
14     TextArea display;
15     Button put, clear, getProperty, save, load;
16
17     public PropertiesTest()
18     {
19        super( "Properties Test" );
20        table = new Properties();
21
22        prompt1 = new Label( "Property name (key)" );
23        propName = new TextField( 10 );
24        prompt2 = new Label( "Property value" );
25        propVal = new TextField( 10 );
26        display = new TextArea( 4, 35 );
27        put = new Button( "Put" );
28        clear = new Button( "Clear" );
29        getProperty = new Button( "Get property" );
30        save = new Button( "Save" );
31        load = new Button( "Load" );
32        result = new TextField( 35 );
33        result.setEditable( false );
34        setLayout( new FlowLayout() );
35        add( prompt1 );
36        add( propName );
37        add( prompt2 );
38        add( propVal );
39        add( display );
40        add( put );
41        add( clear );
42        add( getProperty );
43        add( save );
44        add( load );
45        add( result );
46        resize( 330, 225 );
47        show();
48     }
```

Fig. 18.6 Demonstrating class **Properties** (part 1 of 4)

```
49
50    public boolean handleEvent( Event e )
51    {
52       if ( e.id == Event.WINDOW_DESTROY ) {
53          hide();
54          dispose();
55          System.exit( 0 );
56       }
57
58       return super.handleEvent( e );
59    }
60
61    public boolean action( Event e, Object o )
62    {
63       if ( e.target == put ) {
64          Object val = table.put( propName.getText(),
65                                  propVal.getText() );
66
67          if ( val == null )
68             showStatus( "Put: " + propName.getText() + " " +
69                         propVal.getText() );
70          else
71             showStatus( "Put: " + propName.getText() + " " +
72                         propVal.getText() + "; Replaced: " +
73                         val.toString() );
74       }
75       else if ( e.target == clear ) {
76          table.clear();
77          showStatus( "Table in memory cleared" );
78       }
79       else if ( e.target == getProperty ) {
80          Object val = table.getProperty( propName.getText() );
81
82          if ( val != null )
83             showStatus( "Get property: " + propName.getText() +
84                         " " + val.toString() );
85          else
86             showStatus( "Get: " + propName.getText() +
87                         " not in table" );
88       }
89       else if ( e.target == save ) {
90          try {
91             output = new FileOutputStream( "props.dat" );
92             table.save( output, "Sample Properties" );
93             output.close();
94          }
95          catch( IOException ex ) {
96             showStatus( ex.toString() );
97          }
98       }
```

Fig. 18.6   Demonstrating class **Properties** (part 2 of 4)

```
99          else if ( e.target == load ) {
100             try {
101                input = new FileInputStream( "props.dat" );
102                table.load( input );
103                input.close();
104             }
105             catch( IOException ex ) {
106                showStatus( ex.toString() );
107             }
108          }
109
110          listProperties();
111          return true;
112       }
113
114       public void listProperties()
115       {
116          StringBuffer buf = new StringBuffer();
117          String pName, pVal;
118
119          for ( Enumeration enum = table.propertyNames();
120                enum.hasMoreElements(); ) {
121             pName = enum.nextElement().toString();
122             pVal = table.getProperty( pName );
123             buf.append( pName ).append( '\t' );
124             buf.append( pVal ).append( '\n' );
125          }
126
127          display.setText( buf.toString() );
128       }
129
130       public void showStatus( String s )
131       {
132          result.setText( s );
133       }
134
135       public static void main( String args[] )
136       {
137          PropertiesTest p = new PropertiesTest();
138       }
139    }
```

Fig. 18.6 Demonstrating class **Properties** (part 3 of 4)

The statement

```
table = new Properties();
```

uses the no-argument constructor to create an empty **Properties** table with no default properties. There is also a constructor that is passed a reference to a default **Properties** object containing default property values. This version is useful for maintaining a set of default values for use with the **getProperty** method later.

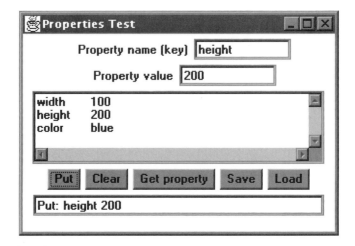

Fig. 18.6   Demonstrating class **Properties** (part 4 of 4)

The statement

```
Object val = table.getProperty( propName.getText() );
```

uses **Properties** method **getProperty** to locate the value of the key specified as an argument. If the key is not found in this **Properties** object, the default **Properties** object (if there is one) is used. The process continues recursively until there are no more default **Properties** objects (remember that every **Properties** object can be initialized with a default **Properties** object) at which point **null** is returned. A second version of this method is provided that takes two arguments, the second of which is the default value to return if **getProperty** cannot locate the key.

The statement

```
table.save( output, "Sample Properties" );
```

uses **Properties** method **save** to save the contents of the **Properties** object to the **OutputStream** object specified as the first argument (in this case a **FileOutput-Stream**). The **String** argument is a description of the **Properties** object. Class properties also provides method list that takes a **PrintStream** argument. This method is useful for displaying the set of properties.

Testing and Debugging Tip 18.2

*Use **Properties** method **list** to display the contents of a **Properties** object for debugging purposes.*

The statement

```
table.load( input );
```

uses **Properties** method **load** to restore the contents of the **Properties** object from the **InputStream** specified as the first argument (in this case a **FileInputStream**).

The expression

```
table.propertyNames()
```

uses **Properties** method **propertyNames** to obtain an **Enumeration** of the property names. The value of each property can be determined using method **getProperty**.

18.9 Random Class

We discussed random number generation in Chapter 4, "Methods," where we used the **random** method of the **Math** class. Java provides extensive additional random number generation capabilities in class **Random**. We briefly walk through the API calls here.

A new random number generator can be created by using

```
Random r = new Random();
```

This form uses the time to seed its random number generator differently each time it is called and thus generate different sequences of random numbers each time.

To create a pseudo-random number generator with "repeatability" use

```
Random r = new Random(seedValue);
```

Each time this form is used with the same **long seedValue**, the same sequence of random numbers will be generated subsequently.

Testing and Debugging Tip 18.3

*The repeatability of random numbers that occurs when the same seed value is used is useful for testing and debugging. While a program is under development, use the form **Random(seedValue)** that produces a repeatable sequence of random numbers. If a bug occurs, fix the bug and test with the same **seedValue**; this allows you to reconstruct the exact same sequence of random numbers that caused the bug. Once the bugs have been removed, use the form **Random()** that generates a new sequence of random numbers each time the program is run.*

The call

```
r.setSeed(seedValue);
```

resets **r**'s seed value at any time.

The calls

```
r.nextInt()
r.nextLong()
```

generate uniformly distributed random integers. You can use **Math.abs** to take the absolute value of the number produced by **nextInt**, thus giving a number in the range zero through approximately two billion. Then use the **%** operator to scale the number. For example, to roll a die from 1 to 6, if you scale with a 6, you will get a number in the range 0 through 5. Then simply shift this value by adding 1 to produce a number in the range 1 through 6. The expression is as follows

```
Math.abs( r.nextInt() ) % 6 + 1
```

The calls

```
r.nextFloat()
r.nextDouble()
```

generate uniformly distributed values in the range $0.0 <= x < 1.0$.
  The call

```
r.nextGaussian()
```

generates a double value with a probability density of a Gaussian (i.e., "normal") distribution (mean of 0.0 and standard deviation of 1.0).

18.10 Bit Manipulation and the Bitwise Operators

Java provides extensive bit manipulation capabilities for programmers who need to get down to the so-called "bits-and-bytes" level. Operating systems, test equipment software, networking software, and many other kinds of software require that the programmer communicate "directly with the hardware." In this and the next section, we discuss Java's bit manipulation capabilities. We introduce Java's many bitwise operators and we demonstrate their use in live-code examples.

  All data is represented internally by computers as sequences of bits. Each bit can assume the value **0** or the value **1**. On most systems, a sequence of 8 bits forms a byte—the standard storage unit for a variable of type **byte**. Other data types are stored in larger numbers of bytes. The bitwise operators are used to manipulate the bits of integral operands (**byte**, **char**, **short**, **int**, and **long**).

  Note that the bitwise operator discussions in this section show the binary representations of the integer operands. For a detailed explanation of the binary (also called base 2) number system see the appendix "Number Systems".

  The bitwise operators are: *bitwise AND (&), bitwise inclusive OR (|), bitwise exclusive OR (^), left shift (<<), right shift with sign extension (>>), right shift with zero extension (>>>) and complement (~).* The bitwise AND, bitwise inclusive OR, and bitwise exclusive OR operators compare their two operands bit-by-bit. The bitwise AND operator sets each bit in the result to 1 if the corresponding bit in both operands is 1. The bitwise inclusive OR operator sets each bit in the result to 1 if the corresponding bit in either (or both) operand(s) is 1. The bitwise exclusive OR operator sets each bit in the result to 1 if the corresponding bit in exactly one operand is 1. The left shift operator shifts the bits of its left operand to the left by the number of bits specified in its right operand. The right shift operator with sign extension shifts the bits in its left operand to the right by the number of bits specified in its right operand—if the left operand is negative **1**s are shifted in from the left; otherwise, **0**s are shifted in from the left. The right shift operator with zero extension shifts the bits in its left operand to the right by the number of bits specified in its right operand—**0**s are shifted in from the left. The bitwise complement operator sets all **0** bits in its operand to **1** in the result and sets all **1** bits to **0** in the result. Detailed discussions of each bitwise operator appear in the following examples. The bitwise operators are summarized in Fig. 18.7.

Operator	Name	Description
&	bitwise AND	The bits in the result are set to **1** if the corresponding bits in the two operands are both **1**.
|	bitwise inclusive OR	The bits in the result are set to **1** if at least one of the corresponding bits in the two operands is **1**.
^	bitwise exclusive OR	The bits in the result are set to **1** if exactly one of the corresponding bits in the two operands is **1**.
<<	left shift	Shifts the bits of the first operand left by the number of bits specified by the second operand; fill from the right with **0** bits.
>>	right shift with sign extension	Shifts the bits of the first operand right by the number of bits specified by the second operand. If the first operand is negative, **1**s are shifted in from the left; otherwise **0**s are shifted in from the left.
>>>	right shift with zero extension	Shifts the bits of the first operand right by the number of bits specified by the second operand; **0**s are shifted in from the left.
~	one's complement	All **0** bits are set to **1** and all **1** bits are set to **0**.

Fig. 18.7 The bitwise operators.

When using the bitwise operators, it is useful to display values in their binary representation to illustrate the effects of these operators. The applet of Fig. 18.8 allows the user to enter an integer into a text field and press Enter. The applet's action method reads the **String** from the text field, converts it to an integer and invokes method **getBits** (line 33) to obtain **String** representation of the integer in bits. The result is displayed in the output text field. The integer is displayed in its binary representation in groups of eight bits each. Method **displayBits** uses the bitwise AND operator to combine variable **value** with variable **displayMask**. Often, the bitwise AND operator is used with an operand called a *mask*—an integer value with specific bits set to **1**. Masks are used to hide some bits in a value while selecting other bits. In **getBits**, mask variable **displayMask** is assigned the value **1 << 31** (**10000000 00000000 00000000 00000000**). The left shift operator shifts the value **1** from the low-order (rightmost) bit to the high-order (leftmost) bit in **displayMask**, and fills in **0** bits from the right. The statement

```
buf.append( ( value & displayMask ) == 0 ? '0' : '1' );
```

determines whether a **1** or a **0** should be appended to **StringBuffer buf** for the current leftmost bit of variable **value**. Assume **value** contains **4000000000** (**11101110 01101011 00101000 00000000**). When **value** and **displayMask** are combined using **&**, all the bits except the high-order bit in variable **value** are "masked off" (hidden) because any bit "ANDed" with **0** yields **0**. If the leftmost bit is **1**, **value & displayMask** evaluates to **1**, and **1** is appended—otherwise, **0** is appended. Variable **value** is then left shifted one bit by the expression **value <<= 1** (this is equivalent to **value =**

value << 1). These steps are repeated for each bit in variable **value**. At the end of method **getBits**, the **StringBuffer** is converted to a **String** with the statement

          buf.toString();

then returned from the method. Figure 18.9 summarizes the results of combining two bits with the bitwise AND (**&**) operator.

 Common Programming Error 18.1

*Using the logical AND operator (**&&**) for the bitwise AND operator (**&**).*

```
1   // Fig. 18.8: PrintBits.java
2   // Printing an unsigned integer in bits
3   import java.awt.*;
4   import java.applet.Applet;
5
6   public class PrintBits extends Applet {
7      Label prompt, result;
8      TextField input, output;
9
10     public void init()
11     {
12        prompt = new Label( "Enter an integer " );
13        input = new TextField( 10 );
14        result = new Label( "The integer in bits is" );
15        output = new TextField( 32 );
16        output.setEditable( false );
17        add( prompt );
18        add( input );
19        add( result );
20        add( output );
21     }
22
23     public boolean action( Event e, Object o )
24     {
25        if ( e.target == input ) {
26           int val = Integer.parseInt( o.toString() );
27           output.setText( getBits( val ) );
28        }
29
30        return true;
31     }
32
33     public String getBits( int value )
34     {
35        int displayMask = 1 << 31;
36        StringBuffer buf = new StringBuffer( 35 );
```

Fig. 18.8   Displaying the bit representation of an integer (part 1 of 2).

```
37
38          for ( int c = 1; c <= 32; c++ ) {
39             buf.append(
40                ( value & displayMask ) == 0 ? '0' : '1' );
41             value <<= 1;
42
43             if ( c % 8 == 0 )
44                buf.append( ' ' );
45          }
46
47          return buf.toString();
48      }
49  }
```

Fig. 18.8 Displaying the bit representation of an integer (part 2 of 2).

Bit 1	Bit 2	Bit 1 & Bit 2
0	0	0
1	0	0
0	1	0
1	1	1

Fig. 18.9   Results of combining two bits with the bitwise AND operator **&**.

The program of Fig. 18.10 demonstrates the use of the bitwise AND operator, the bitwise inclusive OR operator, the bitwise exclusive OR operator and the bitwise complement operator. The program uses method **getBits** to get a **String** representation of the integer values. The program allows the user to enter values into text fields and press Enter (for the binary operators, two values must be entered). The user can then press the button representing the operation they would like to test and the result is displayed in both integer and bit representations.

```
1   // Fig. 18.10: MiscBitOps.java
2   // Using the bitwise AND, bitwise inclusive OR, bitwise
3   // exclusive OR, and bitwise complement operators.
4   import java.awt.*;
5   import java.applet.Applet;
6
7   public class MiscBitOps extends Applet {
8       Label prompt1, prompt2, in1, in2, res, bitsLabel;
9       TextField input1, input2, result, bits1, bits2, bits3;
10      Button and, inclusiveOr, exclusiveOr, complement;
11      Panel inputPanel, bitsPanel, buttonPanel;
12
13      public void init()
14      {
15          setLayout( new BorderLayout() );
16          inputPanel = new Panel();
17          inputPanel.setLayout( new GridLayout( 4, 2 ) );
18          prompt1 = new Label( "Enter 2 ints" );
19          prompt2 = new Label( "" );
20          in1 = new Label( "Value 1" );
21          input1 = new TextField( 8 );
22          in2 = new Label( "Value 2" );
23          input2 = new TextField( 8 );
24          res = new Label( "Result" );
25          result = new TextField( 8 );
26          result.setEditable( false );
27          inputPanel.add( prompt1 );
```

Fig. 18.10 Demonstrating the bitwise AND, bitwise inclusive OR, bitwise exclusive OR and bitwise complement operators (part 1 of 4).

```
28              inputPanel.add( prompt2 );
29              inputPanel.add( in1 );
30              inputPanel.add( input1 );
31              inputPanel.add( in2 );
32              inputPanel.add( input2 );
33              inputPanel.add( res );
34              inputPanel.add( result );
35              bitsPanel = new Panel();
36              bitsPanel.setLayout( new GridLayout( 4, 1 ) );
37              bitsLabel = new Label( "Bit representations" );
38              bits1 = new TextField( 30 );
39              bits1.setEditable( false );
40              bits2 = new TextField( 30 );
41              bits2.setEditable( false );
42              bits3 = new TextField( 30 );
43              bits3.setEditable( false );
44              bitsPanel.add( bitsLabel );
45              bitsPanel.add( bits1 );
46              bitsPanel.add( bits2 );
47              bitsPanel.add( bits3 );
48              buttonPanel = new Panel();
49              and = new Button( "AND" );
50              inclusiveOr = new Button( "Inclusive OR" );
51              exclusiveOr = new Button( "Exclusive OR" );
52              complement = new Button( "Complement" );
53              buttonPanel.add( and );
54              buttonPanel.add( inclusiveOr );
55              buttonPanel.add( exclusiveOr );
56              buttonPanel.add( complement );
57              add( "West", inputPanel );
58              add( "East", bitsPanel );
59              add( "South", buttonPanel );
60          }
61
62      public boolean action( Event e, Object o )
63      {
64          if ( e.target == complement ) {
65              input2.setText( "" );
66              bits2.setText( "" );
67              int val = Integer.parseInt( input1.getText() );
68              result.setText( Integer.toString( ~val ) );
69              bits1.setText( getBits( val ) );
70              bits3.setText( getBits( ~val ) );
71          }
72          else {
73              int val1 = Integer.parseInt( input1.getText() );
74              int val2 = Integer.parseInt( input2.getText() );
75
76              bits1.setText( getBits( val1 ) );
77              bits2.setText( getBits( val2 ) );
```

Fig. 18.10 Demonstrating the bitwise AND, bitwise inclusive OR, bitwise exclusive OR and bitwise complement operators (part 2 of 4).

```
78
79          if ( e.target == and ) {
80              result.setText( Integer.toString( val1 & val2 ) );
81              bits3.setText( getBits( val1 & val2 ) );
82          }
83          else if ( e.target == inclusiveOr ) {
84              result.setText( Integer.toString( val1 | val2 ) );
85              bits3.setText( getBits( val1 | val2 ) );
86          }
87          else if ( e.target == exclusiveOr ) {
88              result.setText( Integer.toString( val1 ^ val2 ) );
89              bits3.setText( getBits( val1 ^ val2 ) );
90          }
91      }
92
93      return true;
94   }
95
96   public String getBits( int value )
97   {
98      int displayMask = 1 << 31;
99      StringBuffer buf = new StringBuffer( 35 );
100
101     for ( int c = 1; c <= 32; c++ ) {
102        buf.append( ( value & displayMask ) == 0 ? '0' : '1' );
103        value <<= 1;
104
105        if ( c % 8 == 0 )
106           buf.append( ' ' );
107     }
108
109     return buf.toString();
110   }
111 }
```

Fig. 18.10 Demonstrating the bitwise AND, bitwise inclusive OR, bitwise exclusive OR and bitwise complement operators (part 3 of 4).

Fig. 18.10 Demonstrating the bitwise AND, bitwise inclusive OR, bitwise exclusive OR and bitwise complement operators (part 4 of 4).

The first output window for Fig. 18.10 shows the results of combining the value **65535** and the value **1** with the bitwise AND operator (**&**). All the bits except the low-order bit in the value **65535** are "masked off" (hidden) by "ANDing" with the value **1**.

The bitwise inclusive OR operator is used to set specific bits to 1 in an operand. The second output window for Fig. 18.10 shows the results of combining the value **15** and the value **241** using the bitwise OR operator—the result is **255**. Figure 18.11 summarizes the results of combining two bits with the bitwise inclusive OR operator.

Common Programming Error 18.2

Using the logical OR operator (| |) for the bitwise OR operator (|).

The bitwise exclusive OR operator (**^**) sets each bit in the result to 1 if *exactly* one of the corresponding bits in its two operands is 1. The third output of Fig. 18.10 shows the results of combining the value **139** and the value **199** using the exclusive OR operator—the result is **76**. Figure 18.12 summarizes the results of combining two bits with the bitwise exclusive OR operator.

The *bitwise* complement operator (**~**) sets all **1** bits in its operand to **0** in the result and sets all **0** bits to **1** in the result—otherwise referred to as "taking the *one's complement* of the value." The fourth output window for Fig. 18.10 shows the results of taking the one's complement of the value **21845**. The result is **-21846**.

The program of Fig. 18.13 demonstrates the left shift operator (**<<**), the right shift operator with sign extension (**>>**) and the right shift operator with zero extension (**>>>**). Method **getBits** obtains a **String** representation of the integer values. The program allows the user to enter an integer in a text field and press Enter. The bit representation of the integer is displayed in another text field.

Bit 1	Bit 2	Bit 1 | Bit 2
0	0	0
1	0	1
0	1	1
1	1	1

Fig. 18.11 Results of combining two bits with the bitwise inclusive OR operator |.

Bit 1	Bit 2	Bit 1 ^ Bit 2
0	0	0
1	0	1
0	1	1
1	1	0

Fig. 18.12 Results of combining two bits with the bitwise exclusive OR operator ^.

A button is provided for each shift operator. As the user clicks each button, the bits in the integer shift left or right by one bit. The new integer value and new bit representation are displayed in the text fields.

```java
1   // Fig. 18.13: BitShift.java
2   // Using the bitwise shift operators.
3   import java.awt.*;
4   import java.applet.Applet;
5
6   public class BitShift extends Applet {
7       Label prompt;
8       TextField value, bits;
9       Button left, rightSign, rightZero;
10
11      public void init()
12      {
13          prompt = new Label( "Integer to shift " );
14          value = new TextField( 8 );
15          bits = new TextField( 30 );
16          bits.setEditable( false );
17          left = new Button( "<<" );
18          rightSign = new Button( ">>" );
19          rightZero = new Button( ">>>" );
20          add( prompt );
21          add( value );
22          add( bits );
23          add( left );
24          add( rightSign );
25          add( rightZero );
26      }
27
28      public boolean action( Event e, Object o )
29      {
30          int val = Integer.parseInt( value.getText() );
31
32          if ( e.target instanceof Button ) {
33              if ( e.target == left )
34                  val <<= 1;
35              else if ( e.target == rightSign )
36                  val >>= 1;
37              else if ( e.target == rightZero )
38                  val >>>= 1;
39
40              value.setText( Integer.toString( val ) );
41          }
42
43          bits.setText( getBits( val ) );
44          return true;
45      }
```

Fig. 18.13 Demonstrating the bitwise shift operators (part 1 of 4).

```
46
47        public String getBits( int value )
48        {
49           int displayMask = 1 << 31;
50           StringBuffer buf = new StringBuffer( 35 );
51
52           for ( int c = 1; c <= 32; c++ ) {
53              buf.append( ( value & displayMask ) == 0 ? '0' : '1' );
54              value <<= 1;
55
56              if ( c % 8 == 0 )
57                 buf.append( ' ' );
58           }
59
60           return buf.toString();
61        }
62     }
```

Fig. 18.13 Demonstrating the bitwise shift operators (part 2 of 4).

The left shift operator (<<) shifts the bits of its left operand to the left by the number of bits specified in its right operand. Bits vacated to the right are replaced with **0**s; **1**s shifted off the left are lost. The first four output windows of Fig. 18.13 demonstrate the left shift operator. Starting with the value 1, the left shift button was pressed twice resulting in the values 2 and 4, respectively. The fourth output window shows the result of the value1 being shifted 31 times. Note that the result is a negative value. That is because a 1 in the high-order bit is used to indicate a negative value in an integer.

Fig. 18.13 Demonstrating the bitwise shift operators (part 3 of 4).

Fig. 18.13 Demonstrating the bitwise shift operators (part 4 of 4).

The right shift operator with sign extension (**>>**) shifts the bits of its left operand to the right by the number of bits specified in its right operand. Performing a right shift causes the vacated bits at the left to be replaced by **0**s if the number is positive and **1**s if the number is negative. Any **1**s shifted off the right are lost. The fifth and sixth output windows show the results of right shifting (with sign extension) the value in the fourth output window two times.

The right shift operator with zero extension (**>>>**) shifts the bits of its left operand to the right by the number of bits specified in its right operand. Performing a right shift causes the vacated bits at the left to be replaced by **0**s. Any **1**s shifted off the right are lost. The eighth and ninth output windows show the results of right shifting (with zero extension) the value in the seventh output window two times.

Each bitwise operator (except the bitwise complement operator) has a corresponding assignment operator. These *bitwise assignment operators* are shown in Fig. 18.14 and are used in a similar manner to the arithmetic assignment operators introduced in Chapter 2.

18.11 **BitSet** Class

The **BitSet** class makes it easy to create and manipulate *bit sets*. Bit sets are useful for representing a set of boolean flags. **BitSet**s are dynamic. More bits can be added as needed and a **BitSet** object will grow to accommodate the additional bits.

```
BitSet b = new BitSet();
```

creates **BitSet** which is initially empty.

```
BitSet b = new BitSet( size );
```

creates a **BitSet** with **size** bits.

```
b.set( bitNumber );
```

sets bit **bitNumber** of **BitSet b** "on."

```
b.clear( bitNumber );
```

sets bit **bitNumber** of **BitSet b** "off."

```
b.get( bitNumber );
```

gets bit **bitNumber** of **BitSet b**. The result is returned as true if the bit is on or false if the bit is off.

```
b.and( b1 );
```

performs a bit-by-bit logical AND between **BitSet**s **b** and **b1**. The result is stored in **b**. Bitwise logical OR and bitwise logical XOR are performed by

```
b.or( b1 );
b.xor( b2 );
```

Bitwise assignment operators	
&=	Bitwise AND assignment operator.
|=	Bitwise inclusive OR assignment operator.
^=	Bitwise exclusive OR assignment operator.
<<=	Left shift assignment operator.
>>=	Right shift with sign extension assignment operator.
>>>=	Right shift with zero extension assignment operator.

Fig. 18.14 The bitwise assignment operators.

The expression

```
b.size()
```

returns the size of **BitSet b**.
The expression

```
b.equals( b1 )
```

compares the two **BitSet**s for equality.

```
b.clone()
```

clones a **BitSet** and returns an **Object** reference to the new **BitSet**.

```
b.toString()
```

converts **BitSet b** to a **String**. This is helpful for debugging.
The expression

```
b.hashCode()
```

provides a hash code useful for storing and retrieving **BitSet** objects in hash tables.

The program of Fig. 18.15 revisits the Sieve of Eratosthenes for finding prime numbers we discussed in Exercise 5.27. A **BitSet** is used instead of an array to implement the algorithm. The program displays all the prime numbers from 1 to 1023 in a text area and provides a text field in which the user can type any number from 1 to 1023 to determine if that number is prime (in which case a message is displayed in the status area of the applet).

```
1   // Fig. 18.15: BitSetTest.java
2   // Using a BitSet to demonstrate the Sieve of Eratosthenes.
3   import java.applet.Applet;
4   import java.awt.*;
5   import java.util.*;
6
7   public class BitSetTest extends Applet {
8      BitSet sieve;
9      Panel inputPanel;
10     Label inputLabel;
11     TextField input;
12     TextArea primes;
13
14     public void init()
15     {
16        sieve = new BitSet( 1024 );
17
18        setLayout( new BorderLayout() );
19        inputLabel = new Label( "Enter a value from 1 to 1023" );
20        input = new TextField( 10 );
```

Fig. 18.15 Demonstrating the Sieve of Eratosthenes using a **BitSet** (part 1 of 3).

```
21            inputPanel = new Panel();
22            inputPanel.add( inputLabel );
23            inputPanel.add( input );
24            add( "North", inputPanel );
25
26            primes = new TextArea();
27            add( "Center", primes );
28
29            // set all bits from 1 to 1023
30            int size = sieve.size();
31
32            for ( int i = 1; i < size; i++ )
33               sieve.set( i );
34
35            // perform Sieve of Eratosthenes
36            int finalBit = (int) Math.sqrt( sieve.size() );
37
38            for ( int i = 2; i < finalBit; i++ )
39               if ( sieve.get( i ) )
40                  for ( int j = 2 * i; j < size; j += i )
41                     sieve.clear( j );
42
43            int counter = 0;
44
45            for ( int i = 1; i < size; i++ )
46               if ( sieve.get( i ) ) {
47                  primes.appendText( String.valueOf( i ) );
48                  primes.appendText(
49                     ++counter % 7 == 0 ? "\n" : "\t" );
50               }
51
52         }
53
54         public boolean action( Event e, Object o )
55         {
56            int val = Integer.parseInt( input.getText() );
57
58            if ( sieve.get( val ) )
59               showStatus( val + " is a prime number" );
60            else
61               showStatus( val + " is not a prime number" );
62
63            return true;
64         }
65      }
```

Fig. 18.15 Demonstrating the Sieve of Eratosthenes using a **BitSet** (part 2 of 3).

Fig. 18.15 Demonstrating the Sieve of Eratosthenes using a **BitSet** (part 3 of 3).

The statement

```
sieve = new BitSet( 1024 );
```

creates a **BitSet** of 1024 bits. We ignore the bit at position 0 in this program. After the
init method sets all the bits on in the **BitSet**, the code

```
// perform Sieve of Eratosthenes
int finalBit = (int) Math.sqrt( sieve.size() );

for ( int i = 2; i < finalBit; i++ )
   if ( sieve.get( i ) )
      for ( int j = 2 * i; j < size; j += i )
         sieve.clear( j );
```

determines all the prime numbers from 1 to 1023. The integer **finalBit** is used to determine when the algorithm is complete. The basic algorithm is that a number is prime if it has no divisors other than 1 and itself. The number 1 is prime. Starting with the number 2, once we know a number is prime, we can eliminate all multiples of that number. The number 2 is only divisible by 1 and itself, so it is prime. Therefore, we can eliminate 4, 6, 8, and so on. The number 3 is divisible by 1 and itself. Therefore, we can eliminate all multiples of 3 (keep in mind that all even numbers have already been eliminated).

Summary

- Class **Vector** provides the capabilities of dynamically resizable arrays.

- At any time the **Vector** contains a certain number of elements which is less than or equal to its *capacity*. The capacity is the space that has been reserved for the array.

- If a **Vector** needs to grow, it grows by an increment that you specify or by a default assumed by the system.

- If you do not specify a capacity increment, the system will automatically double the size of the Vector each time additional capacity is needed.

- **Vector**s are designed to store references to **Object**s. If you would like to store values of primitive data types in **Vector**s, you must use the type wrapper classes (**Integer**, **Long**, **Float**, **Double**, **Boolean** and **Character**) to create objects containing the primitive data type values.

- Class **Vector** provides three constructors. The no-argument constructor creates an empty **Vector**. The constructor that takes one argument creates a **Vector** with an initial capacity specified by the argument. The constructor that takes two arguments creates a **Vector** with an *initial capacity* specified by the first argument and a *capacity increment* specified by the second argument.

- **Vector** method **addElement** adds its argument to the end of the **Vector**. Method **insertElementAt** inserts an element at the specified position. Method **setElementAt** sets the element at a specific position.

- **Vector** method **removeElement** removes the first occurrence of its argument. Method **removeAllElements** removes every element from the **Vector**. Method **removeElementAt** removes the element at the specified index.

- **Vector** method **firstElement** returns a reference to the first element. Method **lastElement** returns a reference to the last element.

- **Vector** method **isEmpty** determines if the **Vector** is empty. Method **contains** determines if the **Vector** contains the **searchKey** specified as an argument. Method **indexOf** gets the index of the first location of its argument. The method returns -1 if the argument is not found in the **Vector**.

- **Vector** method **trimToSize** cuts the capacity of the **Vector** to the **Vector**'s size. Methods **size** and **capacity** determine the number of elements currently in the **Vector** and the number of elements that can be stored in the **Vector** without allocating more memory, respectively.

- **Vector** method **elements** returns a reference to an **Enumeration** containing the elements of the **Vector**.

- **Enumeration** method **hasMoreElements** determines if there are more elements. Method **nextElement** returns a reference to the next element.

- Class **Stack** extends class **Vector**. **Stack** method **push** adds its argument to the top of the stack. Method **pop** removes the top element of the stack. Method **peek** returns an **Object** reference to the top element of the stack without removing the element. **Stack** method **empty** determines if the stack is empty.

- A **Dictionary** transforms keys to values.

- Hashing is a high-speed scheme for converting keys into unique array subscripts for storage and retrieval of information. The load factor is the ratio of the number of occupied cells in a hash table to the size of the hash table. The closer this ratio gets to 1.0, the greater the chance of collisions.

- The no-argument **Hashtable** constructor creates a **Hashtable** with a default capacity of 101 elements and a default load factor of .75. The **Hashtable** constructor that takes one argument specifies the initial capacity and the constructor that takes two arguments specifies the initial capacity and load factor, respectively.

- **Hashtable** method **put** adds a key and a value into a **Hashtable**. Method **get** locates the value associated with the specified key. Method **remove** deletes the value associated with the specified key. Method **isEmpty** determines if the table is empty.

- **Hashtable** method **containsKey** determines if the key specified as an argument is in the **Hashtable** (i.e., a value is associated with that key). Method **contains** determines if the **Object** specified as its argument is in the **Hashtable**. Method **clear** empties the **Hashtable**. Method **elements** obtains an **Enumeration** of the values. Method **keys** obtains an **Enumeration** of the keys.

- Class **Date** provides a variety of constructors to initialize dates. **Date** contains methods **getYear**, **setYear**, **getMonth**, **setMonth**, **getDate**, **setDate**, **getDay**, **getHours**, **setHours**, **getMinutes**, **setMinutes**, **getSeconds**, **setSeconds** and others. **Date** methods **before** and **after** check whether the **Date** object for which they are invoked comes before or after another **Date** specified as an argument. **Date** method **toString** converts a **Date** object to a **String**.

- A common architectural pattern that appears repeatedly in object-oriented systems is a situation in which an object changes state and needs to notify other objects about this change. The object that changes state should be a subclass of class **Observable**. The objects that need to be notified implement the **Observer** interface.

- **Observable** method **addObserver** adds an **Observer** to an **Observable** object's list of observers. Method **setChanged** indicates that the state of the **Observable** object has changed.

- **Observable** method **notifyObservers** automatically invokes **update** for all its observers. Method **update** takes two arguments—a reference to the **Observable** object for which state information changed and a reference to the **Object** that was passed to the **Observable** object's **notifyObservers** method. Method **deleteObservers** deletes the observers of an **Observable** object.

- **Observable** method **clearChanged** resets the state flag that indicates that the **Observable** object changed and is automatically called by the **notifyObservers** method. Method **hasChanged** determines if an **Observable** object's state has changed. Method **countObservers** returns the number of observers.

- A **Properties** object is a persistent **Hashtable** object. Class **Properties** extends **Hashtable**. Keys and values in a **Properties** object must be **String**s.

- The **Properties** no-argument constructor creates an empty **Properties** table with no default properties. There is also a constructor that is passed a reference to a default **Properties** object containing default property values.

- **Properties** method **getProperty** locates the value of the key specified as an argument. Method **save** saves the contents of the **Properties** object to the **OutputStream** object specified as the first argument. Method **load** restores the contents of the **Properties** object from the **InputStream** object specified as the argument. Method **propertyNames** obtains an **Enumeration** of the property names.

- Java provides extensive random number generation capabilities in class **Random**. Class **Random**'s no-argument constructor uses the time to seed its random number generator differently each time it is called. To create a pseudo-random number generator with repeatability use the **Random** constructor that takes a seed argument.

- **Random** method **setSeed** sets the seed. Methods **nextInt** and **nextLong** generate uniformly distributed random integers. Methods **nextFloat** and **nextDouble** generate uniformly distributed values in the range $0.0 <= x < 1.0$.

- The bitwise AND (**&**) operator sets each bit in the result to 1 if the corresponding bit in both operands is 1.

- The bitwise inclusive OR (**|**) operator sets each bit in the result to 1 if the corresponding bit in either (or both) operand(s) is 1.

- The bitwise exclusive OR (**^**) operator sets each bit in the result to 1 if the corresponding bit in exactly one operand is 1.

- The left shift (**<<**) operator shifts the bits of its left operand to the left by the number of bits specified in its right operand.

- The right shift operator with sign extension (**>>**) shifts the bits in its left operand to the right by the number of bits specified in its right operand—if the left operand is negative **1**s are shifted in from the left; otherwise, **0**s are shifted in from the left.

- The right shift operator with zero extension (**>>>**) shifts the bits in its left operand to the right by the number of bits specified in its right operand—**0**s are shifted in from the left.

- The bitwise complement (**~**) operator sets all **0** bits in its operand to **1** in the result and sets all **1** bits to **0** in the result.

- Each bitwise operator (except complement) has a corresponding assignment operator.

- The no-argument **BitSet** constructor creates an empty **BitSet**. The one-argument **BitSet** constructor creates a **BitSet** the number of bits specified by its argument.

- **BitSet** method **set** sets the specified bit "on." Method **clear** sets the specified bit "off." Method **get** returns true if the bit is on or false if the bit is off.

- **BitSet** method **and** performs a bit-by-bit logical AND between **BitSet**s. The result is stored in the **BitSet** that invoked the method. Bitwise logical OR and bitwise logical XOR are performed by methods **or** and **xor**.

- **BitSet** method **size** returns the size of a **BitSet**. Method **clone** clones a **BitSet** and returns an **Object** reference to the new **BitSet**. Method **toString** converts a **BitSet** to a **String**.

Terminology

addElement method of class **Vector**
addObserver method of **Observable**
after method of class **Date**
and method of class **BitSet**
ArrayIndexOutOfBoundsException
before method of class **Date**
bit set
BitSet class
capacity increment of a **Vector**
capacity of a **Vector**
capacity method of class **Vector**
clear method of class **Hashtable**
clearChanged method of **Observable**
clone method of class **BitSet**
collision in hashing
contains method of class **Vector**
containsKey method of class **Hashtable**
countObservers method of **Observable**
Date class
defaults
deleteObserver method of **Observable**
deleteObservers method of **Observable**
delimiter set
Dictionary class
dynamically resizeable array
elementAt method of class **Vector**
elements method of class **Dictionary**
elements method of class **Vector**
empty method of class **Vector**
EmptyStackException class
enumerate successive elements
Enumeration interface
equals method of class **Object**

firstElement method of class **Vector**
get method of class **Dictionary**
getDate method of class **Date**
getDay method of class **Date**
getHours method of class **Date**
getMinutes method of class **Date**
getMonth method of class **Date**
getProperty method of class **Properties**
getSeconds method of class **Date**
getTime method of class **Date**
getYear method of class **Date**
hasChanged method of class **Observable**
hashing
Hashtable class
hashCode method of class **Object**
hasMoreElements method of **Enumeration**
IllegalArgumentException
indexOf method of class **Vector**
initial capacity of a **Vector**
insertElementAt method of class **Vector**
IOException
isEmpty method of class **Dictionary**
isEmpty method of class **Vector**
iterator operations
java.util
key in a **Dictionary**
keys method of class **Dictionary**
lastElement method of class **Vector**
lastIndexOf method of class **Vector**
last-in-first-out (LIFO) stack
list method of class **Properties**
load method of class **Properties**
load factor in hashing

nextDouble method of class **Random**
nextElement method of class **Random**
nextFloat method of class **Random**
nextInt method of class **Random**
nextLong method of class **Random**
nextToken method of class **Random**
NoSuchElementException class
notifyObservers method of **Observable**
NullPointerException
Observable class
observable list
observer
Observer interface
or method of class **BitSet**
peek method of class **Stack**
pop method of class **Stack**
propertyNames method of **Properties**
Properties class
pseudo-random numbers
push method of class **Stack**
put method of class **Dictionary**
Random class
rehash method of class **Hashtable**
remove method of class **Dictionary**
removeAllElements method of **Vector**
removeElement method of class **Vector**

removeElementAt method of class **Vector**
save method of class **Properties**
search method of class **Stack**
seed of a random number generator
set method of class **BitSet**
setChanged method of class **Observable**
setDate method of class **Date**
setElementAt method of class **Vector**
setMinutes method of class **Date**
setMonth method of class **Date**
setSeconds method of class **Date**
setSeed method of class **Random**
setSize method of class **Vector**
setTime method of class **Date**
setYear method of class **Date**
size method of class **Dictionary**
size method of class **Vector**
Stack class
toString method of class **Date**
trim a **Vector** to its exact size
trimToSize method of class **Vector**
update method of interface **Observer**
Vector class
whitespace characters
xor method of class **BitSet**

Common Programming Errors

18.1   Using the logical AND operator (**&&**) for the bitwise AND operator (**&**).

18.2   Using the logical OR operator (**| |**) for the bitwise OR operator (**|**).

Performance Tips

18.1   Inserting additional elements into an array whose current size is less than its capacity is a relatively fast operation.

18.2   It is a relatively slow operation to insert an element into an array that needs to grow larger to accommodate the new element.

18.3   The default capacity increment of doubling the size of the **Vector** may seem wasteful of storage, but it is actually an efficient way for many **Vector**s to grow quickly to be "about the right size." This is much more efficient time-wise than growing the Vector each time by only as much space as it takes to hold a single element. But it can waste space.

18.4   If storage is at a premium, use the **trimToSize** method of the **Vector** class to trim a **Vector** to its exact size. This will optimize a **Vector**'s use of storage. But be careful. If an additional element needs to be inserted in the **Vector**, this will be slow because it will force the array to grow dynamically—trimming leaves no room for growth.

18.5   The load factor in a hash table is a classic example of a space-time trade-off: By increasing the load factor, we get better memory utilization, but the program runs slower due to increased hashing collisions. By decreasing the load factor, we get better program speed because of reduced hashing collisions, but we get poorer memory utilization because a larger portion of the hash table remains empty.

Testing and Debugging Tips

18.1   Because **Stack** inherits from **Vector**, the user may perform operations on **Stack** objects that are ordinarily not allowed on conventional stack data structures. This could corrupt the elements of the **Stack** and destroy the integrity of the **Stack**.

18.2   Use **Properties** method **list** to display the contents of a **Properties** object for debugging purposes.

18.3   The repeatability of random numbers that occurs when the same seed value is used is useful for testing and debugging. While a program is under development, use the form **Random(seedValue)** that produces a repeatable sequence of random numbers. If a bug occurs, fix the bug and test with the same **seedValue**; this allows you to reconstruct the exact same sequence of random numbers that caused the bug. Once the bugs have been removed, use the form **Random()** that generates a new sequence of random numbers each time the program is run.

Self-Review Exercises

18.1   Fill in the blanks in each of the following:
   a) Java class _____ provides the capabilities of array-like data structures that can dynamically resize themselves.
   b) If you do not specify a capacity increment, the system will automatically _____ the size of the **Vector** each time additional capacity is needed.
   c) If storage is at a premium use the _____ method of the **Vector** class to trim a **Vector** to its exact size.

18.2   State whether each of the following statements is true or false. If false, explain why.
   a) Values of primitive data types may be directly stored in a **Vector**.
   b) With hashing, as the load factor increases, the chance of collisions decreases.

18.3   Under what circumstances is an **EmptyStackException** thrown.

18.4   Fill in the blanks in each of the following:
   a) Bits in the result of an expression using operator _____ are set to 1 if the corresponding bits in each operand are set to 1. Otherwise, the bits are set to zero.
   b) Bits in the result of an expression using operator _____ are set to 1 if at least one of the corresponding bits in either operand is set to 1. Otherwise, the bits are set to zero.
   c) Bits in the result of an expression using operator _____ are set to 1 if exactly one of the corresponding bits in either operand is set to 1. Otherwise, the bits are set to zero.

d) The bitwise AND operator **&** is often used to _____ bits, that is to select certain bits from a bit string while zeroing others.

e) The _____ operator is used to shift the bits of a value to the left.

f) The _____ operator is used to shift the bits of a value to the right with sign extension and the _____ operator is used to shift the bits of a value to the right with zero extension.

Answers to Self-Review Exercises

18.1   a) **Vector**. b) double. c) **trimToSize**

18.2   a) False; a **Vector** stores only **Object**s. You must use the type wrapper classes (**Integer, Long, Float, Double, Boolean** and **Character**) from the **java.lang** package to create **Object**s containing the primitive data type values. b) False; as the load factor increases, there are fewer available slots relative to the total number of slots so the chance of selecting an occupied slot with a hashing operation (i.e., a collision) increases.

18.3   **pop** an empty **Stack** object; **peek** an empty **Stack** object.

18.4   a) bitwise AND (**&**).   b) bitwise inclusive OR (**|**). c) bitwise exclusive OR (**^**).   d) mask. e) left shift operator (**<<**). f) right shift operator with sign extension (**>>**), right shift operator with zero extension (**>>>**).

Exercises

18.5   Define each of the following terms in the context of hashing:

a) application key.

b) collision.

c) hashing transformation.

d) load factor.

e) space-time trade-off.

f) **Hashtable** class.

g) capacity of a Hashtable.

18.6   Explain briefly the operation of each of the following methods of class **Vector**:

a) **addElement**.

b) **insertElementAt**.

c) **setElementAt**.

d) **removeElement**.

e) **removeAllElements**.

f) **removeElementAt**.

g) **firstElement**.

h) **lastElement**.

i) **isEmpty**.

j) **contains**.

k) **indexOf**.

l) **trimToSize**.

m) **size**.

n) **capacity**.

18.7   Explain why inserting additional elements into a **Vector** object whose current size is less than its capacity is a relatively fast operation and why inserting additional elements into a **Vector** object whose current size is at capacity is a relatively slow operation.

18.8   In the text we state that the default capacity increment of doubling the size of a **Vector** may seem wasteful of storage, but it is actually an efficient way for vectors to grow quickly to be "about the right size." Explain this statement. Explain the pros and cons of this doubling algorithm. What can a program do when it determines that the doubling is wasting space?

18.9   Explain the use of the **Enumeration** interface with objects of class **Vector**.

18.10   By extending class **Vector**, Java's designers were able to form a **Stack** class quickly. What are the negative aspects of this kind of class construction by inheritance, particularly for class **Stack**?

18.11   Explain briefly the operation of each of the following methods of class **Hashtable**:
   a) **put**.
   b) **get**.
   c) **remove**.
   d) **isEmpty**.
   e) **containsKey**.
   f) **contains**.
   g) **clear**.
   h) **elements**.
   i) **keys**.

18.12   Explain how to use the **Random** class to create pseudo-random numbers with the kind of repeatability we need for debugging.

18.13   By reusing class **Date** instead of writing your own date-processing code, you can save time and avoid costly errors. Investigate the methods of class **Date**. Develop a familiarity with the class. Write a Java applet that demonstrates all of the methods of class **Date** in a way that would teach someone how to use the class.

18.14   Explain the use of the "observers and observable objects" design pattern. List five significant examples of this type of interaction that occur in the real world. Explain the operation of each of the following methods that might be used to implement an observer/observable interaction:
   a) **addObserver**.
   b) **deleteObserver**.
   c) **notifyObservers**.
   d) **deleteObservers**.
   e) **setChanged**.
   f) **clearChanged**.
   g) **hasChanged**.
   h) **countObservers**.

18.15   What does it mean when we state that a **Properties** object is a "persistent" **Hashtable** object? Explain the operation of each of the following methods of the **Properties** class:
   a) **load**.
   b) **save**.
   c) **getProperty**.

    d) **propertyNames**.

    e) **list**.

18.16   Why might you want to use objects of class **BitSet**? Explain the operation of each of the following methods of class **BitSet**:

    a) **set**.

    b) **clear**.

    c) **get**.

    d) **and**.

    e) **or**.

    f) **xor**.

    g) **size**.

    h) **equals**.

    i) **clone**.

    j) **toString**

    k) **hashCode**.

18.17   Write a program that right shifts an integer variable 4 bits with sign extension and then right shifts the same integer variable 4 bits with zero extension. The program should print the integer in bits before and after each shift operation. Run your program once with a positive integer and run it again with a negative integer.

18.18   Show how shifting an integer left by 1 can be used to simulate multiplication by 2 and how shifting an integer right by 2 can be used to simulate division by 2. Be careful to consider issues related to the sign of an integer.

18.19   Write a program that reverses the order of the bits in an integer value. The program should input the value from the user and call method **reverseBits** to print the bits in reverse order. Print the value in bits both before and after the bits are reversed to confirm that the bits are reversed properly. You might want to implement both a recursive and an iterative solution.

Appendix A
Java Demos

A.1 Demos

[Note: Appendices A and B were written by Abbey Deitel, a recent graduate of the Industrial Management program at Carnegie Mellon University.] As a student at Carnegie Mellon, I was able to use one of the largest university computer networks in the United States. Although I was not a Computer Science major or an Information Systems major, nearly every course I took required me to use the campus network extensively. I handed in assignments electronically, participated in discussions and debates outside the classroom and scanned electronic bulletin boards for information.

My contribution to this textbook is as a World Wide Web surfer. In this appendix, I list some of the best Java demos I was able to find on the Web.

I began my journey at **http://www.gamelan.com**. This site is an incredible Java resource and has some of the best Java demos including a huge compilation of games written in Java. The code ranges from basic to complex. Many of the authors of these games and other resources have provided source code. I hope you enjoy surfing these sites as much as I did.

May I ask a favor? I will be keeping this appendix up to date on the Prentice Hall/Deitel Web site

http://www.prenhall.com/deitel

I would appreciate it if you would send me your favorite sites that you want to share with others. I will post your suggestions promptly. Please send me email at

deitel@deitel.com

A.2 The Sites

`http://ariel.cobite.com/ultram/tetris/tetris.html`

Dethtris by Ultramaster Group. One of the Gamelan featured applets, this site is rumored to be one of the more exciting games on the web. The source code is provided. You can win Ultramaster merchandise. Join networked multiplayer games and compete with people all over the world.

`http://reality.sgi.com/employees/sameers_csd/puzzle.html`

The 15 Puzzle. Similar to the puzzle under the Apple menu of every Macintosh, this game allows you to move around 15 tiles to arrange a number sequence or an image. The source code is provided.

`http://www.csiro.au:8000/steve/stuff/slider/Slider.html`

Java Slider. This Java applet was voted top 25% of all applets by JARS, the Java Applet Rating Service (located at `http://www.jars.com`). This is an animated woodblock puzzle with audio. The source code is provided.

`http://k2.scl.cwru.edu/~ptb/ataxx/`

Ataxx. This board game made the JARS top 1% of all Java applets. You can play against yourself or play against the computer. The source code is provided.

`http://www.awinc.com/users/rreichle/puzzle/index.html`

Jigsaw Puzzle. Listed as "what's cool" by Gamelan, this puzzle includes animation. You simply drag each piece into the workspace to solve the puzzle. The picture changes each time you load the puzzle. The source code is provided.

`http://w3.gwis.com/~thorn/Solitaire.html`

Solitaire. Listed as "what's cool" by Gamelan, this solitaire game allows you to see what is possible with the simplest of Java code. It is a simple click and drag game. Source code is provided.

`http://www.cosmix.com/playground/java/solitaire/`

The Marble Solitaire Game. This game incorporates a bit of animation. Rather than the point-and-click method used for similar games, this allows you to drag the marbles across the screen. This made Gamelan's "what's cool" list.

`http://www.tdb.uu.se/~karl/java/rubik.html`

Rubik's Cube. Listed as "what's cool" by Gamelan, this is a Java take on Rubik's Cube, the puzzle we all tried our hand at in the 1980's. The source code is provided.

`http://www.tdb.uu.se/~karl/java/iceblox.html`

The Iceblox game. This game, featured on Gamelan, is a fun game which uses a little animation. The source code is provided.

`http://www-itg.lbl.gov/vbart/`

San Francisco Subway Map. This is a simulated map of the San Francisco subway system. This shows the subway as it moves along various routes. I connected to this through the Gamelan animation site.

`http://test.neog.com/~patrick/own_html/bits/java/BoomButton.html`

Animation. Click on the button and the screen blows up (figuratively, that is).

`http://www.mines.edu/students/d/drferrin/Cool_Beans/`

Cool Beans Java Programming. This is a web page designed by a student at the Colorado School of Mines. The student shows examples of his experiments with Java programming.

http://www.best.com/~daney/piano.html
> *Java Piano.* This is an example of audio incorporated in a Java applet. You can play the piano by clicking on the keys with your mouse or by using the mapped keys on the keyboard. The source code is provided.

http://teamball.sdsu.edu/~boyns/java/
> This is an excellent source for Java demos. There are a number of fun and interesting games. There is also a list of Java resources, however this is not as significant as the lists on most of the other sites mentioned. Several of the teamball site demos follow.

http://teamball.sdsu.edu/~boyns/java/miata/
> *Mazda Miata Animation.* This is a an example of animation using a Mazda Miata. The car cruises across the screen and flashes it's headlights.

http://teamball.sdsu.edu/~boyns/java/centipedo/
> *Centipedo* is similar to the old Centipede video game. The source code is provided.

http://teamball.sdsu.edu/~boyns/java/crazycounter/
> *The Crazy Counter* is a page access counter which counts the number of hits on a page. The source code is provided so that you may install the Crazy Counter on your web page.

http://teamball.sdsu.edu/~boyns/java/logo/
> *Animated SDSU Logo.* View the source code provided here and learn how to create animated Java applets.

http://teamball.sdsu.edu/~boyns/java/nsanim/
> *Animated Netscape Logo.* This site allows you to animate the Netscape logo using designated control keys. The source code is provided.

http://teamball.sdsu.edu/~boyns/java/slot/
> *Slot Machine.* This simple slot machine game allows you to play the slots with just a click of the mouse. Unfortunately, this one-arm-bandit does not pay-up! The source code is provided.

http://teamball.sdsu.edu/~boyns/java/starbase/
> *Starbase* is an animated video game with sound effects. The source code is provided.

http://teamball.sdsu.edu/~boyns/java/mc/
> *Missile Commando* is another video game with sound effects. The source code is provided.

http://www.efd.lth.se/~d93ct/Tanks96/
> *Drive a tank* around and try to avoid hitting buildings.

http://users.aimnet.com/~foureyes/clickboard/fish1.html
> *The Angry Fish.* This is an animated applet that is activated by placing the mouse in the coral reef. The source code is provided.

http://www.crocker.com/~sigelman/java/aster/
> *ASTERNOID!* resembles Asteroids. The author calls this "a GREAT example of object-oriented programming." The source code is provided.

http://www.demonsys.com/jorkin/CelebrityPainter/
> *Celbrity Painter.* This applet made the JARS Top 1% list. You choose from a variety of celebrity faces and alter their looks using a variety of different paint brushes. You can put one celebrity's smile on another's face.

`http://militzer.me.tuns.ca/graffiti/graffitiinfo.html`
Graffitti. JARS Top 1% Java applet. Paint graffiti on the wall without getting arrested. Unfortunately, source code is not provided.

`http://sdcc8.ucsd.edu/~jelwell/java/potato/`
Mr. Potato Head on Java. Give the spud some new duds.

`http://www-elec.enst.fr/java/n/test.html`
3-D Cube. This site has a 3-D cube you can rotate with your mouse. The source code is provided.

`http://www.sover.net/~manx/hyprcube.html`
Stereoscopic Animated Hypercube. If you happen to possess the old red and blue 3D glasses, check this site out. The programmer was able to create a 3D image using Java. It isn't really a complicated image, just some cubes, however the idea that you can create images that will jump off your screen is a great concept!

`http://www.vaxxine.com/candleweb/java/jvgames.html`
If you like to check out new games or some of Java's capabilities, Candle-Web is an excellent page to visit. I found a great list of games and applets including some of the following sites.

`http://www.sfc.keio.ac.jp/~t93034ei/tennis.html`
Tennis served Java-style. This is a mesmerizing game. Use the mouse as your racket and try to concentrate on more than one tennis ball at a time.

`http://www.metamor.com/pages/_play_pages/billpong.html`
Pong. Play ping pong with the president using Bill as your ball. Bounce the president's portrait off your racket, or if you are from the other side of the political spectrum, there is a Newt version, too!

`http://www.well.com/user/yimmit/BlackJack.html`
Black Jack. Play a game of "21" without the risk of losing your money. Just like in the casinos, this game can be addictive.

`http://dmawww.epfl.ch/~kuonen/Java/4.html`
Connect4. Try to get four of your checkers in a row. The computer analyzes your moves with the help of Java programming.

`http://www.spacestar.com/users/hamer/odeax/froggie/example1.html`
Froggie. This game is a take off of Atari's Frogger. You can adjust the game according to the speed of your computer, so if you have a slower system, you will still be able to play this game without the frustration of lag time. The source code, audio files and image files are all provided.

`http://www.delorie.com/game-room/chess/free-game.html`
Chess. Play a game of chess against the computer.

`http://www.ludd.luth.se/users/jonte/ImageTape_audio.java`
Audio. This program allows you play a sequence of audio files. The source code is provided.

`http://seagal.lanl.gov:8090/~liuke/traffic/traffic.html`
Traffic Simulation. This is a traffic simulation using Java.

`http://www.uvision.com/shop/index.html`
Chat. A real-time Java chat room.

`http://www.ludd.luth.se/users/jonte/santa.html`
The Christmas spirit lasts all year at this site. This audio site uses Java to spread Santa's jolly laughter over the web. This site also uses Java to send Santa and his reindeer across the page.

`http://www.earthweb.com/java/Netris/`
> *3D Tetris.* You can change the view and play the game from any angle.

`http://www.npac.syr.edu/projects/vishuman/VisibleHuman.html`
> This site was featured by Gamelan and has won various awards. You can look at different cross sections of the human body. The Java source code is provided.

`http://www.lm.com/~snafu/board.html`
> *Knight's Tour.* This site demonstrates the Knight's Tour example discussed in the exercises of Chapter 5 of this book.

`http://beams.colorado.edu/~sveta/applets/Sveta.java`
> This applet demonstrates a "live" and interactive page. The source code is included

`http://www.twilightgames.com/`
> This site maintains a list of five featured games of the week.

`http://www.arealaudio.com/`
> This site is loaded with audio files. You can listen to clips from some of the latest albums and movies. The site has links to download the software required to listen to the files.

`http://www.voxware.com/`
> Another great site for audio files. You will need to download some software to listen.

`http://www.macromedia.com/index_unshocked.html`
> Audio and video movie clips. This site requires you to download software.

Appendix B
Java Resources

B.1 Java Resources

[Note: Appendices A and B were written by Abbey Deitel, a recent graduate of the Industrial Management program at Carnegie Mellon University.] There is a bounty of Java information on the World Wide Web. Many people are experimenting with Java and sharing their thoughts, discoveries, ideas and source code with each other via the Internet. If you would like to recommend other sites, please send me email at

deitel@deitel.com

and we will put links to the sites you suggest on our Web site

http://www.prenhall.com/deitel.

http://www.javasoft.com
> Another one of Sun Microsystems' Java sites, JavaSoft has links to various newsgroups, mailing lists and resources. You can find the latest Java news at this site.

http://java.sun.com
> Run by Sun Microsystems, this is an important Java Resource. You will find Java and Hot Java documentation, products, news and information.

http://www.javaworld.com
> *Java World* magazine is an excellent resource for current Java information. You will find news clips, conference information and lists of interesting Java sites.

http://www.gamelan.com
> One of the largest resources for Java on the web, Gamelan, has games, puzzles, arts and entertainment, demos, current information and lists of what is new and cool in Java. Gamelan has links to numerous Java resources. From Gamelan you can connect to Java World, Sun Microsystems and hundreds of other sites.
>
> Gamelan has a list of over 1700 resources for Java. Under the heading "Programming in Java," there are hundreds of resources. The subcategories are as follows: class libraries, databases, development tools, documents about Java, examples, graphics, learning Java, projects and user interface.

`http://www.acme.com/java/`

This page has an animated Java applet with the source code provided. This site is an excellent resource for information on Java. The page provides software, notes and a list of other resources. Under "software" you will find some animated applets, utility classes and applications.

`http://www.sunsite.unc.edu/javafaq`

This site provides the latest Java news. It also has some helpful Java resources including the following: the Java FAQ List, a tutorial called Brewing Java, Java User Groups, Java Links, the Java Book List, Java Trade Shows, Java Training, and Exercises.

`http://www.JARS.com/`

The Java Applet Rating Service. You will see their icon on some of the best Java applets. Go directly to this site for a list of the hottest new sites.

`http://www.xm.com/cafe/applets.html`

Café Del Sol is an excellent Java resource. Experts from Sun have put together a live chat session, applets, resources, and FAQs. You can download applets from the café.

`http://www.vaxxine.com/candleweb/java/java.html`

Candle-Web is an excellent resource with links to Java related sites. You can find information on documentation, resources, applets, and software.

`http://wco.com/~linnins/internet.htm`

This is an excellent resource for some interesting Java sites including audio and video.

`http://www.dimensionx.com/products/lr/index.html`

A fun Java resource, this site has audio, video, a live chat room, demos, FAQs, documentation, downloading capabilities and more.

`http://www.cybercom.net/~frog/javaide.html`

This resource has extensive links. There is product information, IDE (Integrated Development Environments) reviews, Java tools, mailings lists, books, tutorials, examples and FAQs.

`http://www.teamjava.com`

Team Java assists Java consultants in search of contracts and helps to promote Java. They have also listed some resourceful sites. A few of the sites are included in this list of resources.

`http://www.qoi.com`

Diva for Java is QOI's fully integrated development environment that seamlessly integrates Sun's Java Development Kit (JDK) for the creation of Java applets for Internet web pages and standalone programs. Diva for Java provides developers with class and project management capabilities within a graphical development environment.

`http://www.io.org/~mentor/DigitalEspresso.html`

Digital Espresso is a synopsis of the information from various Java resources. You can find anything from news and events to applets to technical information about Java.

`http://www.digitalfocus.com/digitalfocus/faq/index.html`

This source provides links to Java resources. You can also find FAQs (frequently asked questions) and a live "Java conference room."

`http://www.Sun.COM/sunworldonline/`

This is SunWorld magazine online. This is a Sun resource that also provides Java information.

`http://www.netscape.com/comprod/products/navigator/version_2.0/`
`java_applets/index.html`

Contains a list of Java applets, demos, and resources.

`http://www.roaster.com/javalinks.html`
This is a great Java resource to get Java news and information or links to other useful Java sites.

`http://www.rssi.com/info/java-info.html`
Another substantial list of Java resources and demos.

`http://porthos.phoenixat.com/~warreng/WWWBoard/wwwboard.html`
Java message exchange center for Java programmers (a bulletin board of sorts).

`news:comp.lang.java`
The Java newsgroup. This is a great place to find detailed answers to technical questions on Java.

`http://www.december.com/works/java.html`
This site is another Java resource. You will find demos with source code, Java news, and information on books.

`http://www.yahoo.com/Computers_and_Internet/Languages/Java/`
Yahoo, a popular World Wide Web search engine, provides a complete Java resource. You can initiate a search using key words or explore the categories listed at the site including games, contests, events, tutorials and documentation, mailing lists, security and more.

`http://home.netscape.com/comprod/products/navigator/version_2.0`
A great resource for Java applets.

`http://www.acm.org/~ops/java.html`
A Java resource with information about the language, reference materials, books, tutorials, a developer's kit and examples.

`http://www.aqui.ibm.com/aqui/help/whatsaqui2.html`
It creates links to web pages.

`http://www.acm.org/~ops/java.html`
There is information about the Java language, resources, events, examples, references, FAQs, and publications.

`http://www.applets.com/cgi-bin-applets/`
Search for applets using key words. Type in "java games" and you get URLs for many applets.

`http://www.inch.com/~nyjava/`
This is the site of a New York based Java group. They post information about their meetings and events. You may also join the mailing list.

`http://www.digitalfocus.com/digitalfocus/faq/`
"The Java Developer." This web site has links to a variety of Java resources. There is also a list of books and newsletters.

`http://rendezvous.com/java/hierarchy/index.html`
"Java Class Hierarchy Diagrams."

B.2 Java Frequently Asked Questions (FAQs)

If you have questions about Java, these sites will enable you to get answers from the experts. You will also find the answers to questions asked by other programmers.

```
http://www.digitalfocus.com/digitalfocus/faq
http://sunsite.unc.edu/javafaq/javafaq.html
http://www.webcity.co.jp/info/andoh/java/javafaq.html
http://www.city-net.com/~krom/java-faq.html
```

B.3 Tutorials for Learning Java

```
http://www.javasoft.com/tutorial/index.html
http://ugweb.cs.ualberta.ca/~nelson/java/JavaTutorial.html
http://www.digitalfocus.com/digitalfocus/faq/howdoi.html
http://users.aol.com/thingtone/workshop/index.html
http://rummelplatz.uni-mannheim.de/~skoch/javatut/kneedeep.htm
```

B.4 Java Books

```
http://lightyear.ncsa.uiuc.edu/~srp/java/javabooks.html
http://www.aw.com/cp/javaseries.html
http://www.clbooks.com/cgi-bin/browsed
http://jollyroger.com/java.html
```

B.5 Java Newsgroups

Those who are interested in contacting a local Java Users Group (JUG), you can find information at **http://www.sug.org/java-groups.html**. JUGs hold discussion groups, seminars and they are a means of distributing the latest Java information. If there is not a JUG in your area, many of the groups have mailing lists.

news:comp.lang.java
   Java newsgroup.

alt.www.hotjava
   The HotJava newsgroup.

mailto:java@java.sun.com
   Get help directly from Sun Microsystems.

B.6 Virtual Reality Modeling Language (VRML)

You may want to look at the following sites that support VRML three-dimensional graphics. Java will be supporting VRML in the near future.

http://www.aereal.com/
   Aereal is an excellent resource for Java and VRML. Download a VRML browser.

http://www.virtpark.com/theme/proteinman/home.html
   A top ten list of some of the best VRML sites.

http://www.hyperion.com/planet9/worlds/vrsoma.wrl
   Very cool animation. You can manipulate the image of a street block.

Appendix C
Operator Precedence Chart

Operators are shown in decreasing order of precedence from top to bottom.

Operator	Type	Associativity
( )	parentheses	left to right
[ ]	array subscript	
.	member selection	
++	unary preincrement	right to left
++	unary postincrement	
--	unary predecrement	
--	unary postdecrement	
+	unary plus	
-	unary minus	
!	unary logical negation	
~	unary bitwise complement	
(*type*)	unary cast	
*	multiplication	left to right
/	division	
%	modulus	
+	addition	left to right
-	subtraction	
<<	bitwise left shift	left to right
>>	bitwise right shift with sign extension	
>>>	bitwise right shift with zero extension	

Fig. C.1   Operator precedence chart (part 1 of 2).

Operator	Type	Associativity
`<`	relational less than	left to right
`<=`	relational less than or equal to	
`>`	relational greater than	
`>=`	relational greater than or equal to	
`instanceof`	type comparison	
`==`	relational is equal to	left to right
`!=`	relational is not equal to	
`&`	bitwise AND	left to right
`^`	bitwise exclusive OR	left to right
	boolean logical exclusive OR	
`|`	bitwise inclusive OR	left to right
	boolean logical inclusive OR	
`&&`	logical AND	left to right
`||`	logical OR	left to right
`?:`	ternary conditional	right to left
`=`	assignment	right to left
`+=`	addition assignment	
`-=`	subtraction assignment	
`*=`	multiplication assignment	
`/=`	division assignment	
`%=`	modulus assignment	
`&=`	bitwise AND assignment	
`^=`	bitwise exclusive OR assignment	
`|=`	bitwise inclusive OR assignment	
`<<=`	bitwise left shift assignment	
`>>=`	bitwise right shift with sign extension assignment	
`>>>=`	bitwise right shift with zero extension assignment	

Fig. C.1   Operator precedence chart (part 2 of 2).

Appendix D
ASCII Character Set

	0	1	2	3	4	5	6	7	8	9
0	nul	soh	stx	etx	eot	enq	ack	bel	bs	ht
1	nl	vt	ff	cr	so	si	dle	dc1	dc2	dc3
2	dc4	nak	syn	etb	can	em	sub	esc	fs	gs
3	rs	us	sp	!	"	#	$	%	&	`
4	(	)	*	+	,	-	.	/	0	1
5	2	3	4	5	6	7	8	9	:	;
6	<	=	>	?	@	A	B	C	D	E
7	F	G	H	I	J	K	L	M	N	O
8	P	Q	R	S	T	U	V	W	X	Y
9	Z	[	\	]	^	_	'	a	b	c
10	d	e	f	g	h	i	j	k	l	m
11	n	o	p	q	r	s	t	u	v	w
12	x	y	z	{	|	}	~	del		

The digits at the left of the table are the left digits of the decimal equivalent (0-127) of the character code, and the digits at the top of the table are the right digits of the character code. For example, the character code for 'F' is 70, and the character code for '&' is 38.

Appendix E
Number Systems

Objectives

- To understand basic number systems concepts such as base, positional value, and symbol value.
- To understand how to work with numbers represented in the binary, octal, and hexadecimal number systems
- To be able to abbreviate binary numbers as octal numbers or hexadecimal numbers.
- To be able to convert octal numbers and hexadecimal numbers to binary numbers.
- To be able to covert back and forth between decimal numbers and their binary, octal, and hexadecimal equivalents.
- To understand binary arithmetic, and how negative binary numbers are represented using two's complement notation.

Here are only numbers ratified.
William Shakespeare

Nature has some sort of arithmetic-geometrical coordinate system, because nature has all kinds of models. What we experience of nature is in models, and all of nature's models are so beautiful.
It struck me that nature's system must be a real beauty, because in chemistry we find that the associations are always in beautiful whole numbers—there are no fractions.
Richard Buckminster Fuller

Outline

E.1 Introduction

In this appendix, we introduce the key number systems that Java programmers use, especially when they are working on software projects that require close interaction with "machine-level" hardware. Projects like this include operating systems, computer networking software, compilers, database systems, and applications requiring high performance.

When we write an integer such as 227 or -63 in a Java program, the number is assumed to be in the *decimal (base 10) number system*. The *digits* in the decimal number system are 0, 1, 2, 3, 4, 5, 6, 7, 8, and 9. The lowest digit is 0 and the highest digit is 9—one less than the *base* of 10. Internally, computers use the *binary (base 2) number system*. The binary number system has only two digits, namely 0 and 1. Its lowest digit is 0 and its highest digit is 1—one less than the base of 2.

As we will see, binary numbers tend to be much longer than their decimal equivalents. Programmers who work in assembly languages and in high-level languages like Java that enable programmers to reach down to the "machine level," find it cumbersome to work with binary numbers. So two other number systems the *octal number system (base 8)* and the *hexadecimal number system (base 16)*— are popular primarily because they make it convenient to abbreviate binary numbers.

In the octal number system, the digits range from 0 to 7. Because both the binary number system and the octal number system have fewer digits than the decimal number system, their digits are the same as the corresponding digits in decimal.

The hexadecimal number system poses a problem because it requires sixteen digits—a lowest digit of 0 and a highest digit with a value equivalent to decimal 15 (one less than the base of 16). By convention, we use the letters A through F to represent the hexadecimal digits corresponding to decimal values 10 through 15. Thus in hexadecimal we can have numbers like 876 consisting solely of decimal-like digits, numbers like 8A55F consisting of digits and letters, and numbers like FFE consisting solely of letters. Occasionally, a hexadecimal number spells a common word such as FACE or FEED—this can appear strange to programmers accustomed to working with numbers.

Each of these number systems uses *positional notation*—each position in which a digit is written has a different *positional value*. For example, in the decimal number 937 (the 9, the 3, and the 7 are referred to as *symbol values*), we say that the 7 is written in the *ones position*, the 3 is written in the *tens position*, and the 9 is written in the *hundreds position*. Notice that each of these positions is a power of the base (base 10), and that these powers begin at 0 and increase by 1 as we move left in the number (Fig. E.3).

Binary digit	Octal digit	Decimal digit	Hexadecimal digit
0	0	0	0
1	1	1	1
	2	2	2
	3	3	3
	4	4	4
	5	5	5
	6	6	6
	7	7	7
		8	8
		9	9
			A (decimal value of 10)
			B (decimal value of 11)
			C (decimal value of 12)
			D (decimal value of 13)
			E (decimal value of 14)
			F (decimal value of 15)

Fig. E.1   Digits of the binary, octal, decimal, and hexadecimal number systems.

Attribute	Binary	Octal	Decimal	Hexadecimal
Base	2	8	10	16
Lowest digit	0	0	0	0
Highest digit	1	7	9	F

Fig. E.2   Comparison of the binary, octal, decimal, and hexadecimal number systems.

Positional values in the decimal number system			
Decimal digit	9	3	7
Position name	Hundreds	Tens	Ones
Positional value	100	10	1
Positional value as a power of the base (10)	10^2	10^1	10^0

Fig. E.3   Positional values in the decimal number system.

For longer decimal numbers, the next positions to the left would be the *thousands position* (10 to the 3rd power), the *ten-thousands position* (10 to the 4th power), the *hundred-thousands position* (10 to the 5th power), the *millions position* (10 to the 6th power), the *ten-millions position* (10 to the 7th power), and so on.

In the binary number 101, we say that the rightmost 1 is written in the *ones position*, the 0 is written in the *twos position*, and the leftmost 1 is written in the *fours position*. Notice that each of these positions is a power of the base (base 2), and that these powers begin at 0 and increase by 1 as we move left in the number (Fig E.4).

For longer binary numbers, the next positions to the left would be the *eights position* (2 to the 3rd power), the *sixteens position* (2 to the 4th power), the *thirty-twos position* (2 to the 5th power), the *sixty-fours position* (2 to the 6th power), and so on.

In the octal number 425, we say that the 5 is written in the *ones position*, the 2 is written in the *eights position*, and the 4 is written in the *sixty-fours position*. Notice that each of these positions is a power of the base (base 8), and that these powers begin at 0 and increase by 1 as we move left in the number (Fig. E.5).

For longer octal numbers, the next positions to the left would be the *five-hundred-and-twelves position* (8 to the 3rd power), the *four-thousand-and-ninety-sixes position* (8 to the 4th power), the *thirty-two-thousand-seven-hundred-and-sixty eights position* (8 to the 5th power), and so on.

In the hexadecimal number 3DA, we say that the A is written in the *ones position*, the D is written in the *sixteens position*, and the 3 is written in the *two-hundred-and-fifty-sixes position*. Notice that each of these positions is a power of the base (base 16), and that these powers begin at 0 and increase by 1 as we move left in the number (Fig. E.6).

Positional values in the binary number system			
Binary digit	**1**	**0**	**1**
Position name	Fours	Twos	Ones
Positional value	**4**	**2**	**1**
Positional value as a power of the base (2)	2^2	2^1	2^0

Fig. E.4 Positional values in the binary number system.

Positional values in the octal number system			
Decimal digit	**4**	**2**	**5**
Position name	Sixty-fours	Eights	Ones
Positional value	**64**	**8**	**1**
Positional value as a power of the base (8)	8^2	8^1	8^0

Fig. E.5 Positional values in the octal number system.

Positional values in the hexadecimal number system			
Decimal digit	3	D	A
Position name	Two-hundred-and-fifty-sixes	Sixteens	Ones
Positional value	256	16	1
Positional value as a power of the base (16)	16^2	16^1	16^0

Fig. E.6 Positional values in the hexadecimal number system.

For longer hexadecimal numbers, the next positions to the left would be the *four-thousand-and-ninety-sixes position* (16 to the 3rd power), the *sixty-five-thousand-five-hundred-and-thirty-six position* (16 to the 4th power), and so on.

E.2 Abbreviating Binary Numbers as Octal Numbers and Hexadecimal Numbers

The main use for octal and hexadecimal numbers in computing is for abbreviating lengthy binary representations. Figure E.7 highlights the fact that lengthy binary numbers can be expressed concisely in number systems with higher bases than the binary number system.

Decimal number	Binary representation	Octal representation	Hexadecimal representation
0	0	0	0
1	1	1	1
2	10	2	2
3	11	3	3
4	100	4	4
5	101	5	5
6	110	6	6
7	111	7	7
8	1000	10	8
9	1001	11	9
10	1010	12	A
11	1011	13	B
12	1100	14	C
13	1101	15	D
14	1110	16	E
15	1111	17	F
16	10000	20	10

Fig. E.7 Decimal, binary, octal, and hexadecimal equivalents.

A particularly important relationship that both the octal number system and the hexadecimal number system have to the binary system is that the bases of octal and hexadecimal (8 and 16 respectively) are powers of the base of the binary number system (base 2). Consider the following 12-digit binary number and its octal and hexadecimal equivalents. See if you can determine how this relationship makes it convenient to abbreviate binary numbers in octal or hexadecimal. The answer follows the numbers.

Binary Number	Octal equivalent	Hexadecimal equivalent
100011010001	**4321**	**8D1**

To see how the binary number converts easily to octal, simply break the 12-digit binary number into groups of three consecutive bits each, and write those groups over the corresponding digits of the octal number as follows

100	**011**	**010**	**001**
4	**3**	**2**	**1**

Notice that the octal digit you have written under each group of thee bits corresponds precisely to the octal equivalent of that 3-digit binary number as shown in Fig. E.7.

The same kind of relationship may be observed in converting numbers from binary to hexadecimal. In particular, break the 12-digit binary number into groups of four consecutive bits each and write those groups over the corresponding digits of the hexadecimal number as follows

1000	**1101**	**0001**
8	**D**	**1**

Notice that the hexadecimal digit you have written under each group of four bits corresponds precisely to the hexadecimal equivalent of that 4-digit binary number as shown in Fig. E.7.

E.3 Converting Octal Numbers and Hexadecimal Numbers to Binary Numbers

In the previous section, we saw how to convert binary numbers to their octal and hexadecimal equivalents by forming groups of binary digits and simply rewriting these groups as their equivalent octal digit values or hexadecimal digit values. This process may be used in reverse to produce the binary equivalent of a given octal or hexadecimal number.

For example, the octal number 653 is converted to binary simply by writing the 6 as its 3-digit binary equivalent 110, the 5 as its 3-digit binary equivalent 101, and the 3 as its 3-digit binary equivalent 011 to form the 9-digit binary number 110101011.

The hexadecimal number FAD5 is converted to binary simply by writing the F as its 4-digit binary equivalent 1111, the A as its 4-digit binary equivalent 1010, the D as its 4-digit binary equivalent 1101, and the 5 as its 4-digit binary equivalent 0101 to form the 16-digit 1111101011010101.

E.4 Converting from Binary, Octal, or Hexadecimal to Decimal

Because we are accustomed to working in decimal, it is often convenient to convert a binary, octal, or hexadecimal number to decimal to get a sense of what the number is "really" worth. Our diagrams in Section E.1 express the positional values in decimal. To convert a number to decimal from another base, multiply the decimal equivalent of each digit by its positional value, and sum these products. For example, the binary number 110101 is converted to decimal 53 as shown in Fig. E.8.

Converting a binary number to decimal					
Positional values:	32	16	8	4	2	1
Symbol values:	1	1	0	1	0	1
Products:	1*32=32	1*16=16	0*8=0	1*4=4	0*2=0	1*1=1
Sum:	= 32 + 16 + 0 + 4 + 0 + 1 = 53					

Fig. E.8   Converting a binary number to decimal.

To convert octal 7614 to decimal 3980, we use the same technique, this time using appropriate octal positional values as shown in Fig. E.9.

To convert hexadecimal AD3B to decimal 44347, we use the same technique, this time using appropriate hexadecimal positional values as shown in Fig. E.10.

E.5 Converting from Decimal to Binary, Octal, or Hexadecimal

The conversions of the previous section follow naturally from the conventions of positional notation. Converting from decimal to binary, octal, or hexadecimal also follows these conventions.

Suppose we wish to convert decimal 57 to binary. We begin by writing the positional values of the columns right to left until we reach a column whose positional value is greater than the decimal number. We do not need that column, so we discard it. Thus, we first write:

Converting an octal number to decimal			
Positional values:	512	64	8	1
Symbol values:	7	6	1	4
Products	7*512=3584	6*64=384	1*8=8	4*1=4
Sum:	= 3584 + 384 + 8 + 4 = 3980			

Fig. E.9   Converting an octal number to decimal.

Converting a hexadecimal number to decimal			
Positional values:	4096	256	16	1
Symbol values:	A	D	3	B
Products	A*4096=40960	D*256=3328	3*16=48	B*1=11
Sum:	= 40960 + 3328 + 48 + 11 = 44347			

Fig. E.10   Converting a hexadecimal number to decimal.

Positional values: **64   32   16   8   4   2   1**

Then we discard the column with positional value 64 leaving:

Positional values: **32   16   8   4   2   1**

Next we work from the leftmost column to the right. We divide 32 into 57 and observe that there is one 32 in 57 with a remainder of 25, so we write 1 in the 32 column. We divide 16 into 25 and observe that there is one 16 in 25 with a remainder of 9 and write 1 in the 16 column. We divide 8 into 9 and observe that there is one 8 in 9 with a remainder of 1. The next two columns each produce quotients of zero when their positional values are divided into 1 so we write 0s in the 4 and 2 columns. Finally, 1 into 1 is 1 so we write 1 in the 1 column. This yields:

Positional values:	**32**	**16**	**8**	**4**	**2**	**1**
Symbol values:	**1**	**1**	**1**	**0**	**0**	**1**

and thus decimal 57 is equivalent to binary 111001.

To convert decimal 103 to octal, we begin by writing the positional values of the columns until we reach a column whose positional value is greater than the decimal number. We do not need that column, so we discard it. Thus, we first write:

Positional values: **512 64   8   1**

Then we discard the column with positional value 512, yielding:

Positional values: **64   8   1**

Next we work from the leftmost column to the right. We divide 64 into 103 and observe that there is one 64 in 103 with a remainder of 39, so we write 1 in the 64 column. We divide 8 into 39 and observe that there are four 8s in 39 with a remainder of 7 and write 4 in the 8 column. Finally, we divide 1 into 7 and observe that there are seven 1s in 7 with no remainder so we write 7 in the 1 column. This yields:

Positional values:	**64**	**8**	**1**
Symbol values:	**1**	**4**	**7**

and thus decimal 103 is equivalent to octal 147.

To convert decimal 375 to hexadecimal, we begin by writing the positional values of the columns until we reach a column whose positional value is greater than the decimal number. We do not need that column, so we discard it. Thus, we first write

Positional values: **4096 256 16   1**

Then we discard the column with positional value 4096, yielding:

Positional values: **256 16   1**

Next we work from the leftmost column to the right. We divide 256 into 375 and observe that there is one 256 in 375 with a remainder of 119, so we write 1 in the 256 column. We divide 16 into 119 and observe that there are seven 16s in 119 with a remainder of 7 and write 7 in the 16 column. Finally, we divide 1 into 7 and observe that there are seven 1s in 7 with no remainder so we write 7 in the 1 column. This yields:

Positional values: **256 16   1**
Symbol values: **1   7   7**

and thus decimal 375 is equivalent to hexadecimal 177.

E.6 Negative Binary Numbers: Two's Complement Notation

The discussion in this appendix has been focussed on positive numbers. In this section, we explain how computers represent negative numbers using *two's complement notation*. First we explain how the two's complement of a binary number is formed, and then we show why it represents the negative value of the given binary number.

Consider a machine with 32-bit integers. Suppose

```
int value = 13;
```

The 32-bit representation of **value** is

```
00000000 00000000 00000000 00001101
```

To form the negative of **value** we first form its *one's complement* by applying Java's bitwise complement operator (**~**):

```
onesComplementOfValue = ~value;
```

Internally, **~value** is now **value** with each of its bits reversed—ones become zeros and zeros become ones as follows:

```
value:
00000000 00000000 00000000 00001101

~value  (i.e., value's ones complement):
11111111 11111111 11111111 11110010
```

To form the two's complement of **value** we simply add one to **value**'s one's complement. Thus

```
Two's complement of value:]\
11111111 11111111 11111111 11110011
```

Now if this is in fact equal to -13, we should be able to add it to binary 13 and obtain a result of 0. Let us try this:

```
 00000000 00000000 00000000 00001101
+11111111 11111111 11111111 11110011
-------------------------------------
 00000000 00000000 00000000 00000000
```

The carry bit coming out of the leftmost column is discarded and we indeed get zero as a result. If we add the one's complement of a number to the number, the result would be all 1s. The key to getting a result of all zeros is that the twos complement is 1 more than the one's complement. The addition of 1 causes each column to add to 0 with a carry of 1. The carry keeps moving leftward until it is discarded from the leftmost bit, and hence the resulting number is all zeros.

Computers actually perform a subtraction such as

```
x = a - value;
```

by adding the two's complement of **value** to **a** as follows:

```
x = a + (~value + 1);
```

Suppose **a** is 27 and **value** is 13 as before. If the two's complement of **value** is actually the negative of **value**, then adding the two's complement of value to a should produce the result 14. Let us try this:

```
a  (i.e., 27)         00000000 00000000 00000000 00011011
+(~value + 1)        +11111111 11111111 11111111 11110011
                     ------------------------------------
                      00000000 00000000 00000000 00001110
```

which is indeed equal to 14.

Summary

- When we write an integer such as 19 or 227 or -63 in a Java program, the number is automatically assumed to be in the decimal (base 10) number system. The digits in the decimal number system are 0, 1, 2, 3, 4, 5, 6, 7, 8, and 9. The lowest digit is 0 and the highest digit is 9—one less than the base of 10.

- Internally, computers use the binary (base 2) number system. The binary number system has only two digits, namely 0 and 1. Its lowest digit is 0 and its highest digit is 1—one less than the base of 2.

- The octal number system (base 8) and the hexadecimal number system (base 16) are popular primarily because they make it convenient to abbreviate binary numbers.

- The digits of the octal number system range from 0 to 7.

- The hexadecimal number system poses a problem because it requires sixteen digits—a lowest digit of 0 and a highest digit with a value equivalent to decimal 15 (one less than the base of 16). By convention, we use the letters A through F to represent the hexadecimal digits corresponding to decimal values 10 through 15.

- Each number system uses positional notation—each position in which a digit is written has a different positional value.

- A particularly important relationship that both the octal number system and the hexadecimal number system have to the binary system is that the bases of octal and hexadecimal (8 and 16 respectively) are powers of the base of the binary number system (base 2).

- To convert an octal number to a binary number, simply replace each octal digit with its three-digit binary equivalent.

- To convert a hexadecimal number to a binary number, simply replace each hexadecimal digit with its four-digit binary equivalent.

- Because we are accustomed to working in decimal, it is convenient to convert a binary, octal or hexadecimal number to decimal to get a sense of the number's "real" worth.

- To convert a number to decimal from another base, multiply the decimal equivalent of each digit by its positional value, and sum these products.

- Computers represent negative numbers using two's complement notation.
- To form the negative of a value in binary, first form its one's complement by applying Java's bitwise complement operator (~). This reverses the bits of the value. To form the two's complement of a value, simply add one to the value's one's complement.

Terminology

base	digit
base 2 number system	hexadecimal number system
base 8 number system	negative value
base 10 number system	octal number system
base 16 number system	one's complement notation
binary number system	positional notation
bitwise complement operator (~)	positional value
conversions	symbol value
decimal number system	two's complement notation

Self-Review Exercises

E.1   The bases of the decimal, binary, octal, and hexadecimal number systems are _____, _____, _____, and _____ respectively.

E.2   In general, the decimal, octal, and hexadecimal representations of a given binary number contain (more/fewer) digits than the binary number contains.

E.3   (True/False) A popular reason for using the decimal number system is that it forms a convenient notation for abbreviating binary numbers simply by substituting one decimal digit per group of four binary bits.

E.4   The (octal / hexadecimal / decimal) representation of a large binary value is the most concise (of the given alternatives).

E.5   (True/False) The highest digit in any base is one more than the base.

E.6   (True/False) The lowest digit in any base is one less than the base.

E.7   The positional value of the rightmost digit of any number in either binary, octal, decimal, or hexadecimal is always _____.

E.8   The positional value of the digit to the left of the rightmost digit of any number in binary, octal, decimal, or hexadecimal is always equal to _____.

E.9   Fill in the missing values in this chart of positional values for the rightmost four positions in each of the indicated number systems:

decimal	1000	100	10	1
hexadecimal	...	256	...	...
binary	...	...	...	...
octal	512	...	8	...

E.10   Convert binary **110101011000** to octal and to hexadecimal.

E.11   Convert hexadecimal **FACE** to binary.

E.12   Convert octal **7316** to binary.

E.13   Convert hexadecimal **4FEC** to octal. (Hint: First convert 4FEC to binary then convert that binary number to octal.)

E.14   Convert binary **1101110** to decimal.

E.15   Convert octal **317** to decimal.

E.16   Convert hexadecimal **EFD4** to decimal.

E.17   Convert decimal **177** to binary, to octal, and to hexadecimal.

E.18   Show the binary representation of decimal **417**. Then show the one's complement of **417**, and the two's complement of **417**.

E.19   What is the result when the one's complement of a number is added to itself?

Self-Review Answers

E.1   **10, 2, 8, 16**.

E.2   Fewer.

E.3   False.

E.4   Hexadecimal.

E.5   False. The highest digit in any base is one less than the base.

E.6   False. The lowest digit in any base is zero.

E.7   **1** (the base raised to the zero power).

E.8   The base of the number system.

E.9   Fill in the missing values in this chart of positional values for the rightmost four positions in each of the indicated number systems:

decimal		**1000**	**100**	**10**	1
hexadecimal	**4096**	**256**	**16**		1
binary			**8**	**4**	**2**	1
octal		**512**	**64**	**8**	1

E.10   Octal **6530**; Hexadecimal **D58**.

E.11   Binary **1111 1010 1100 1110**.

E.12   Binary **111 011 001 110**.

E.13   Binary **0 100 111 111 101 100**; Octal **47754**.

E.14   Decimal **2+4+8+32+64=110**.

E.15   Decimal **7+1*8+3*64=7+8+192=207**.

E.16   Decimal **4+13*16+15*256+14*4096=61396**.

E.17   Decimal **177**
         to binary:

```
256 128 64 32 16 8 4 2 1
128 64 32 16 8 4 2 1
(1*128)+(0*64)+(1*32)+(1*16)+(0*8)+(0*4)+(0*2)+(1*1)
10110001
```

to octal:

```
512 64 8 1
64 8 1
(2*64)+(6*8)+(1*1)
261
```

to hexadecimal:

```
256 16 1
16 1
(11*16)+(1*1)
(B*16)+(1*1)
B1
```

E.18   Binary:

```
512 256 128 64 32 16 8 4 2 1
256 128 64 32 16 8 4 2 1
(1*256)+(1*128)+(0*64)+(1*32)+(0*16)+(0*8)+(0*4)+(0*2)+
(1*1)
110100001
```

One's complement: `001011110`
Two's complement: `001011111`
Check: Original binary number + its two's complement

```
110100001
001011111
---------
000000000
```

E.19   Zero.

Exercises

E.20   Some people argue that many of our calculations would be easier in the base **12** number system because **12** is divisible by so many more numbers than **10** (for base **10**). What is the lowest digit in base **12**? What might the highest symbol for the digit in base **12** be? What are the positional values of the rightmost four positions of any number in the base **12** number system?

E.21   How is the highest symbol value in the number systems we discussed related to the positional value of the first digit to the left of the rightmost digit of any number in these number systems?

E.22   Complete the following chart of positional values for the rightmost four positions in each of the indicated number systems:

	1000	100	10	1
decimal	1000	100	10	1
base 6	...	...	6	...
base 13	...	169	...	...
base 3	27	...	...	...

E.23   Convert binary **100101111010** to octal and to hexadecimal.

E.24   Convert hexadecimal **3A7D** to binary.

E.25   Convert hexadecimal **765F** to octal. (Hint: First convert **765F** to binary, then convert that binary number to octal.)

E.26   Convert binary **1011110** to decimal.

E.27   Convert octal **426** to decimal.

E.28   Convert hexadecimal **FFFF** to decimal.

E.29   Convert decimal **299** to binary, to octal, and to hexadecimal.

E.30   Show the binary representation of decimal **779**. Then show the one's complement of **779**, and the two's complement of **779**.

E.31   What is the result when the two's complement of a number is added to itself?

E.32   Show the two's complement of integer value **-1** on a machine with 32-bit integers.

Appendix F

Object-Oriented Elevator Simulator

Objectives

- To introduce the elements of object orientation in parallel with the early text discussion. This will enable students to begin working on their term projects from the beginning of their introductory computer science and computer engineering courses.
- To introduce students to the elements of the object-oriented design process.
- To enable students to pursue an object-oriented design of a reasonably substantial application.
- To implement a substantial term project using Java's more advanced features including graphics, graphical user interfaces, exception handling, multithreading, and multimedia including audios, images and animation.
- To suggest a number of challenging modifications to the project for the more advanced students.

F.1 Introduction

In this appendix, you will perform the various steps of an object-oriented design (OOD). You will implement an elevator simulator using the techniques of object-oriented programming (OOP). For now, this assignment may seem a bit complex. Please do not be concerned. You will attempt only a small portion of the problem at a time. The elevator simulator is a large project suitable for a term project. It is also suitable as a group project.

We begin with an introduction to object orientation. We will see that object orientation is a natural way of thinking about the world and of writing computer programs.

We start by introducing some of the key terminology of object orientation. Look around you in the real world. Everywhere you look you see them—*objects*! People, animals, plants, computers, cars, buildings, books, planes, lawnmowers, furniture and the like. Humans think in terms of objects. We have the marvelous ability of *abstraction* that enables us to view screen images as objects such as mountains, trees, helicopters, and clouds rather than individual dots of color (i.e., pixels). We can, if we wish, think in terms of beaches instead of grains of sand, forests rather than trees, and houses rather than bricks.

We might be inclined to divide objects into two categories—animate objects and inanimate objects. Animate objects are "alive" in some sense. They move around and do things. Inanimate objects, like rocks, seem not to do much at all. They just kind of "sit around." All these objects, however, do have some things in common. They all have *attributes* like size, shape, color, mass, and the like. And they all exhibit various *behaviors*, e.g., a ball rolls, bounces, inflates, and deflates; a baby sleeps, cries, crawls, walks, drools, and blinks; a car accelerates, brakes and turns, etc.

Humans learn about objects by studying their attributes and observing their behaviors. Different objects can have many of the same attributes and exhibit similar behaviors. Comparisons can be made, for example, between babies and adults, and between humans and chimpanzees. Cars, trucks, little red wagons and roller skates have much in common.

Object oriented programming (OOP) models real-world objects with software counterparts. It takes advantage of *class* relationships where objects of a certain class—such as a class of vehicles—have the same characteristics. It takes advantage of *inheritance* relationships where newly created classes of objects are derived by inheriting characteristics of existing classes, yet contain unique characteristics of their own. Objects of class convertible certainly have the characteristics of class automobile, but the roof goes up and down.

Object-oriented programming gives us a more natural and intuitive way to view the programming process, namely by *modeling* real-world objects, their attributes, and their behaviors. OOP also models communication between objects. Just as people send messages to one another (e.g., a person standing on a corner and signaling a taxicab driver for a ride), objects also communicate via messages.

OOP *encapsulates* (or "wraps") data (attributes) and methods (behavior) into units called *objects.*; the data and methods of an object are intimately tied together. Objects have the property of *information hiding*. This means that although objects may know how to communicate with one another across well-defined interfaces, objects normally are not allowed to know how other objects are implemented—implementation details are hidden within the objects themselves. Surely it is possible to drive a car effectively without knowing the intricate details of how engines, alternators, batteries, transmissions and exhaust systems work internally. We will see why information hiding is so crucial to good software engineering.

In C and other procedural programming languages, programming tends to be *action-oriented*, whereas in Java, programming is object-oriented. In C, the unit of programming is the *function*. In Java the unit of programming is the *class* from which objects are eventually *instantiated* (i.e., created).

C programmers concentrate on writing functions. Groups of actions that perform some common task are formed into functions, and functions are grouped to form programs. Data is certainly important in C, but the view is that data exists primarily in support of the actions that programs perform. The *verbs* in a system specification help the C programmer determine the set of functions that work together to implement the system.

Java programmers concentrate on creating their own *user-defined types* called classes. Each class contains data as well as the set of methods that manipulate the data. The data components of a class are called *instance variables*. Just as an instance of a built-in type such as **int** is called a *variable*, an instance of a user-defined type (i.e., a class) is called an *object*. The programmer uses built-in types as the building blocks for constructing user-defined types. The focus of attention in Java is on objects rather than methods. The *nouns* in a system specification help the Java programmer determine the set of classes from which objects will be created that will work together to implement a system.

F.2 Problem Statement

A company intends to build a two-story office building and equip it with the "latest" in elevator technology. The company wants you to develop a Java applet that simulates the operation of the elevator to determine if it will meet their needs.

The elevator, which has a capacity of one person, is designed to conserve energy, so it only moves when necessary. The elevator starts the day waiting with its door closed on the building's first floor. The elevator, of course, alternates directions—first up, then down.

Your simulator has a simple graphical user interface—an applet with a single "Create Person" push button. When the button is clicked, the simulator creates a "new" person and places that person on a floor (i.e., floor one or floor two). The arrival floor of the person is randomly determined. The person then presses the floor's call button. The person's destination floor is never equal to the floor on which that person is created.

If the first person of the day arrives on floor one, the person can immediately get on the elevator (after pressing the call button, and waiting for the floor door and the elevator door to open, of course!). If the first person arrives at floor two, the elevator should proceed to floor two and "pick up" the person. For simplicity, in this version of the simulation, the elevator moves between the floors in zero time. This will be made more realistic in future versions of your elevator applet.

The elevator's arrival at a floor is signaled by turning on a light on that floor above the door and by ringing a bell in the elevator. The floor button and the elevator button are reset, the elevator's door opens, the floor's door opens, and the passenger gets out of the elevator. If a passenger is waiting on that floor the passenger boards the elevator and presses a destination button. If the elevator needs to begin moving, it determines in which direction it should go (a simple decision on a two-story elevator!), and begins moving to the other floor. For simplicity, assume that all the events that happen once the elevator reaches a floor and until the floor's door is closed, take zero time. The elevator always knows its current floor and its destination floor.

Due to the fact that all events in this version of the simulation take zero time, only one person can be in the simulation at a time. The simulator should process each person completely before the next person arrives in the simulation. In other words, when a person is created, that person should press the call button, be picked up by the elevator, be moved to the opposite floor and should exit the elevator before the next person walks onto a floor to wait for the elevator.

F.3 Elevator Laboratory Assignment 1

(Prerequisites: Chapters 1–3)

In this and the next few assignments, you will perform the separate steps of an object-oriented design. The first step is to identify the classes in the problem. You will eventually describe these classes in a formal way and implement them. For this assignment, you should do the following:

1. Identify the classes in the simulation problem. The problem statement specifies many class objects working together to simulate the elevator and its interactions with the passenger, the floors, the bell, etc. Locate the *nouns* from the problem statement; with high likelihood, these represent most of the classes necessary to implement the elevator simulation.

2. For each class identified, write one briefly, precisely worded paragraph that captures the facts about that class from the problem statement.

Notes

1. This is a good team exercise. Ideally you should work in a group of two to four people. You and your teammates will reinforce one another's efforts, challenge and refine each other's design and implementation approaches.

2. Your group should compete with other groups in your class to develop the "best" design and implementation.

3. In Chapter 4, "Methods", we discuss how to use random number generation. You will learn how to use the **static Math** class method **random** to randomly select the floor onto which a person walks when the "Create Person" button is pushed by the simulator user.

4. We have made a number of simplifying assumptions. You may choose to supply additional details.

5. Because the real world is so object oriented, it will be quite natural for you to pursue this project even though you probably have not formally studied object-orientation.

6. Do not worry about perfection. System design is not a perfect and complete process, so you should pursue this project on a best-efforts basis.

7. Java is fun. Java inspires creativity. Go beyond the basic description presented here, by adding your own enhancements to the elevator simulator. If you would like to share your simulators with us, please email them to us at **deitel@deitel.com**

F.4 Elevator Laboratory Assignment 2

(Prerequisite: Chapter 4)

In the previous assignment, we began the first phase of an object-oriented design for our elevator simulator, namely identifying the classes needed to implement the simulator. As a starting point, you were encouraged to list the nouns in the problem statement. In doing so, you discovered that some of the classes in your simulator were the elevator itself, people, floors, the building, various buttons and so on.

   Classes have attributes and behaviors. Class attributes are represented in Java programs by data; class behaviors are represented by methods. In this assignment we concentrate on determining the attributes of the classes needed to implement the elevator simulator. In the next assignment we will concentrate on behaviors. In Assignment 4, we will concentrate on the interactions between the objects in the elevator simulator.

Let us discuss attributes of real-world objects before we begin the assignment. A person's attributes include height and weight. A radio's attributes include whether it is set to AM or FM, station setting, and current volume setting. A car's attributes include current speedometer and odometer readings. A house's attributes include style ("colonial," "ranch," etc.), number of rooms, square footage, and lot size. A computer's attributes include manufacturer (Apple, Compaq, Digital, IBM, Sun, etc.), type of screen (monochrome or color), main memory size (in megabytes), hard disk size (in megabytes or gigabytes), etc.

1. To get the process started, type into a word processor or editor program the text of the problem statement for the elevator simulation presented in *Elevator Laboratory Assignment 1*.

2. Extract all the *facts* from the problem. Eliminate all irrelevant text and place each fact on a separate line of your text file (there are several dozen facts in the problem statement). Here is a portion of what your fact file might look like:

   Fact File
   two-story office building
   elevator
   person
   floor doors
   elevator door
   directions-up and down
   floor is occupied
   person on elevator
   person on floor
   person's destination floor
   person gets on elevator
   elevator closes its door

3. Group all your facts by class. This will help confirm that you properly identified the classes in *Assignment 1*. Use an outline form in which the class listed at the left margin of the page and the facts related to a class are listed below that class and indented one tab. Some facts mention only one class while other facts mention several classes. Each fact should initially be listed under every class the fact mentions. Note that some facts like "directions-up and down" do not explicitly mention a class but should nevertheless be grouped with a class (in this case the direction is clearly the direction in which the elevator is moving). This outline file will be used in this assignment and in the next several assignments.

4. Now separate the facts for each class into two groups. Label the first group *Attributes* and the second group *Other Facts*. For now, actions (behaviors) should be grouped under *Other Facts*. As you place an action under *Other Facts* consider creating an additional entry under Attributes if appropriate. For example, the fact "elevator closes its door" is an action that for now is grouped under *Other Facts*, but it indicates that an attribute of "door" is that it is either open or shut. The fact "floor is occupied" is an attribute of the floor, more specifically, floor is either occupied (by one person—the stated capacity of each floor) or unoccupied at any time. Some attributes of the elevator are: whether it is "moving" or "stopped," whether it does or does not have a passenger, and if it is moving—whether it is moving "up" or "down." An attribute of the floor button is whether it is "on" or "off." An attribute of a person is the person's destination floor. And so on.

Notes

1. Begin by listing the class attributes that are explicitly mentioned in the problem statement. Then list attributes that are directly implied by the problem statement.

2. Add appropriate attributes as it becomes apparent that they are needed.

3. System design is not a perfect process; simply do the best you can for now. Be prepared to modify your design as you proceed with this exercise in subsequent sections.

4. A class object (actually—a reference to a class object) can be an attribute of another class. This is called *composition*. For example, there are button object references for floor one and floor two inside class elevator—the person presses one of these buttons to select a destination floor. For the purposes of this exercise, treat all the objects as peers—do not allow composition (we will do this later).

5. In Chapter 4, you learned about random number generation. When you eventually implement the elevator simulator, the statement

   ```
   int arrivalFloor = ( int ) ( 1 + Math.random() * 2 );
   ```

   can be used to randomly choose the floor (1 or 2) where a person is "created."

F.5 Elevator Laboratory Assignment 3

(Prerequisite: Chapter 6)

In the previous two assignments, we performed the first two phases of an object-oriented design for our elevator simulator, namely identifying the classes needed to implement the simulator and identifying the attributes of those classes. In this assignment we concentrate on determining the behaviors of the classes needed to implement the elevator simulator. In the next section we concentrate on the interactions between the classes.

Let us consider the behaviors of some real-world objects. A radio's behaviors include having its station set and having its volume set. A car's behaviors include accelerating (by pressing the gas pedal) decelerating (by pressing the brake pedal) and setting the direction (by turning the wheel).

Objects do not ordinarily perform their behaviors spontaneously. Rather, a specific behavior is normally invoked when a method call is sent to the object, requesting that the object perform that specific behavior.

1. Continue working with the facts file you created in *Assignment 2*. You had separated the facts relating to each class into two groups—*Attributes* and *Other Facts*.

2. For each object, add a third group called *Behaviors*. Place in this group every behavior of a class that can be invoked by telling an object of that class to do something, i.e., by sending a method call to the object. For example, a button can be pressed (by a person), so list **pressButton** as a behavior of the **Button** class. The class's attributes (such as whether a **Button** object is "on" or "off") are instance variables of the **Button** class. A class's methods typically manipulate the class's instance variables (such as **pressButton** changing one of class **Button**'s attributes to "on"). Methods often send method calls to objects of other classes (such as a **Button** object sending a **comeGetMe** method call to summon the **Elevator** object). Assume that the elevator has "thermal" buttons that become illuminated when someone presses them. When the elevator arrives at a floor, the elevator will want to send a **resetButton** method call to turn the button's light off. The elevator may want to determine if a particular button has been pressed, so we can provide another behavior called **isButtonOn** that simply examines a button and returns **true** or

false to indicate that the button is currently "on" or "off." You will probably want the elevator's door to respond to method calls **openDoor** and **closeDoor**. And so on.

3. For each behavior you assign to an object, provide a brief description of what the behavior does. List any attribute changes the behavior causes, and list any method calls the behavior sends to other objects.

F.6 Elevator Laboratory Assignment 4

(Prerequisite: Chapter 6)
This is the last of the initial design assignments before you begin writing the code for your elevator simulator. In this section we concentrate on the interactions between class objects. This section will help you "tie it all together." You will probably make some additions to the list of classes, their attributes and their behaviors that you developed in the previous assignments.

We have learned that objects do not ordinarily do things spontaneously. Rather, the objects respond to stimuli in the form of method calls.

Let us consider several of the interactions among the classes in the elevator simulation. The problem statement says, "Person presses the floor's "call button." The "subject" of that clause is person and the object is button. This is an example of an interaction between objects. The person object sends a method call i.e., **pressButton**, to the button object. In the last assignment, we made **pressButton** a method of the **Button** class.

At this point, under *Other Facts* for each of the classes in your simulation, about all you should have left are interactions between classes. Consider a statement like

"person waits for elevator door to open"

In the last assignment, we listed two behaviors of the elevator's door, namely **openDoor** and **closeDoor**. Now we want to determine which classes *send* these method calls. This is not *explicitly* stated in the preceding quoted phrase. So we think about this a bit and we realize that the elevator itself sends these messages to the door. These interactions between classes are *implicit* in the problem statement and are more difficult to recognize than *explicit* interactions.

Now continue refining the *Other Facts* sections for each of the classes in your elevator simulator. These sections should now contain mostly interactions among classes. View each of these interactions as

1. a *sending class*

2. sending a particular method call

3. to a particular receiving class.

Under each class, add the section *Method Calls Sent to Other Classes* and list the remaining interactions between classes, i.e., under the **Person** class, include the entry

Person *sends* **pressButton** *method call to the* **Button**

For the **Button** class under *Method Calls Sent to Other Classes,* place the message

Button *sends* **comeGetMe** *message to* **Elevator**

From the perspective of the sending class, a method call sent to another class is a *collaboration.* From the perspective of the receiving class, a method call invokes a behavior.

As you make these entries, you may add attributes and behaviors to your classes. This is perfectly natural. As you complete this assignment, you will have a reasonably complete listing of the classes you will need to implement your elevator simulator. For each class, you will have a reasonably complete listing of that class's attributes and behaviors, and the method calls that class sends to other classes.

F.7 Elevator Laboratory Assignment 5

(Prerequisite: Chapter 6)

In the previous assignments, we introduced the fundamentals of object orientation and walked you through a basic, object-oriented design for your elevator simulator. At this point, you are ready (and probably eager!) to begin programming your simulator.

1. For each of the classes you identified in the previous assignments, write an appropriate class definition. Each class definition should be written in a separate file with the `.java` extension.

2. Write a driver applet that tests each of these classes and attempts to run the complete elevator simulation. *CAUTION:* You will probably need to complete the next assignment before you will be able to create a reasonable working version of your simulator, so be patient and implement only those portions of the elevator simulator that you can with the knowledge you have gained so far. In the next assignment, we will discuss composition, i.e., creating classes that contain references to objects of other classes as instance variables; this technique might help you represent the button objects inside the elevator as members of the elevator, for example.

3. For the first version of your simulator, design only a simple, text-oriented output that displays a message for each significant event that occurs. Your messages might include strings such as: "Person 1 arrives on Floor 1," "Person 1 presses Call Button on Floor 1," "Elevator moved to Floor 1," etc. We suggest that you capitalize the words that represent objects in your simulation. Note also that you may choose to defer this portion of the lab assignment until you have read the next assignment.

F.8 Elevator Laboratory Assignment 6

(Prerequisite: Chapter 6)

In the last assignment you began programming your elevator simulator. In this assignment we discuss composition, a capability that allows you to create classes that have as members references to objects. Composition enables you to create a building class that contains references to the elevator and to the floors, and, in turn, create an elevator class that contains references to buttons.

1. Each time a person enters the simulator, you should use **new** to create a **Person** object to represent that person. Note that **new** will be used with a constructor call that will initialize the object properly.

2. List the composition relationships among the classes you have implemented for your elevator simulator. Modify the class definitions you created in the last assignment to reflect these composition relationships.

3. Complete the implementation of a working simulator program. We will suggest enhancements and refine the problem statement in the next assignment.

F.9 Elevator Laboratory Assignment 7

(Prerequisites: Chapters 9–11)

At this point you should have version 1 of your elevator simulator working. Over the next several assignments, we will make the elevator simulator more realistic by having the elevator take time to move between the floors, by allowing more than one person in the simulation at once, by using graphical representations of the elevator and the other objects, by animating the motion of the elevator and the people, and the like. This assignment will focus on enhancing the elevator's graphical user interface. Figure F.1 shows the basic GUI design for this assignment.

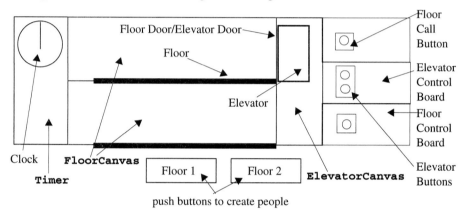

Fig. F.1   Graphical representation of the elevator simulator GUI.

1. Create another push button and add it to the applet. Name one button "Floor 1" and the other button "Floor 2." These buttons will be used to create a new person who wants to board the elevator specifically on that floor.

2. Create a new class called **FloorCanvas** that extends the **Canvas** class. The **Floor-Canvas** class **paint** method should draw a single line representing the floor. A **Floor-Canvas** object should be created for each floor.

3. Create a new class called **ElevatorCanvas** that extends the **Canvas** class. The **ElevatorCanvas** class **paint** method should draw a solid rectangle representing the elevator.

4. Create a new class called **Timer** that extends the **Canvas** class. The **Timer** class **paint** method should draw a circle representing a clock. The clock should have a line inside it representing a "hand."

Notes

1. Try to place the components in the layout of Fig. F.1.

2. At this point, do not worry about "tying in" the GUI to what is occurring in the code. We will discuss how to do this in subsequent assignments.

3. When this assignment is completed, your elevator should work the same as before, except the GUI should display the components created above.

F.10 Elevator Laboratory Assignment 8

(Prerequisites: Chapters 9–11)

This assignment builds on the GUI you developed in Assignment 7. In this assignment, you will add to the GUI and begin graphically representing the events occurring in your simulation.

1. Create a new class called **ElevatorControlBoard** that extends the **Canvas** class. The **ElevatorControlBoard** class **paint** method should draw a rectangle containing two circles. Each circle represents a button inside the elevator.

2. Create a new class called **FloorControlBoard** that extends the **Canvas** class. The **FloorControlBoard** class **paint** method should draw a rectangle containing a circle. The circle represents the floor call button. Two **FloorControlBoard** objects should be instantiated.

3. Write the code that shows the visual interactions between the text output and the buttons. In other words, when a button is pressed in the simulation the appropriate button should "light up." For example, if a person presses a call button on floor one, then the **FloorControlBoard** canvas should paint the circle representing the button yellow.

F.11 Elevator Laboratory Assignment 9

(Prerequisite: Chapter 13)

This assignment covers the steps necessary to provide interaction between the GUI and events generated by your simulator. The interaction in many cases will be done with multithreading.

1. Modify your simulator to allow multiple people to be in the building at once. Remember there can be a maximum of one person in the elevator and one person on each floor at the same time; thus there can be 0, 1, 2, or 3 people active in your simulator at once. When the a push button is clicked, a new person should enter the simulation (assuming that the target floor is not already occupied). Each person should be represented as a thread.

2. Modify the elevator to be a thread. The elevator should continuously monitor the call button actions of each floor.

3. Modify the clock to be a thread. The elevator should take one cycle of the clock (i.e., allow the hand to move one complete 360 degree rotation) to move between floors. The clock is only applicable to the elevator. Provide a text output to indicate when the clock has completed one cycle. A cycle is approximately 60 calls to the **Timer** class **paint** method.

Notes

1. The elevator is now "smarter;" it "knows" when to move.

2. Your program should still print information to the console. This will help you confirm that your elevator is behaving properly.

3. The elevator does not have to move graphically between the floors in this assignment. We ask you to animate the movement of the elevator in the next assignment.

4. The clock hand does not have to move. We ask you to animate the movement of the clock hand in the next assignment.

F.12 Elevator Laboratory Assignment 10

(Prerequisite: Chapter 13)

This assignment covers the steps necessary to provide animation for your simulator.

1. Modify the simulator to animate the clock. When the elevator begins moving between floors, the clock hand should also begin moving. When the clock hand reaches its original position, the elevator should arrive at the next floor.

2. Modify the elevator to move graphically between floors. When the clock hand begins moving, the "box" representing the elevator should begin moving between floors. The elevator should stop on the next floor when the clock hand completes one rotation.

3. Modify your simulator to animate the opening and closing of each floor door and the elevator door.

Notes

1. The floor doors and elevator door open or close on each floor in unison so only one line is necessary for this representation.

F.13 Elevator Laboratory Assignment 11

(Prerequisite: Chapter 14)

This assignment covers the steps necessary to provide additional animation as well some audio for your simulator. Figure F.2 shows the placement of animation objects in the GUI.

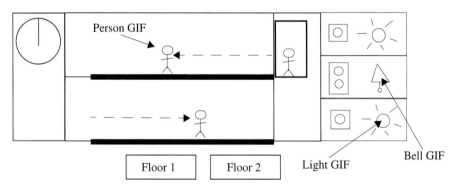

Fig. 6.2 Graphical representation of the elevator simulator GUI.

1. Modify the simulator to display a person walking onto the floor. Use a GIF file for the animation. The same GIF file should also be displayed to show the person leaving the floor.

2. Modify the simulator to show a passenger riding inside the elevator. The same GIF file used in part 1 above should be used.

3. Add a GIF image to the **FloorControlBoard** to represent the floor light. The GIF image should appear "lighted" when the elevator reaches a floor and should then turn off.

4. Add a GIF image to the **ElevatorControlBoard** that represents a bell.

5. Add audio to play a "clicking" sound when a button is pressed.

6. Add audio to play a "stepping" sound when someone walks on a floor.

7. Add audio to play "soft" elevator music when the elevator moves between floors (hard rock is OK, too!).

8. Add audio to play a "ringing" sound (or a "gong") when the bell rings.

Notes

1. You will probably need two GIF images to represent a floor light. One image in which the floor light is on and one image in which the floor light is off.

2. You may want to give the user the option of "isolating" a particular sound such as the bell ringing. Too many sounds playing at once could be unpleasant.

F.14 Elevator Laboratory Assignment 12

(Prerequisite: Chapter 14)
This assignment enhances the animation of the previous assignment.

1. Use a variety of GIF images to represent people in the simulation.

Notes

1. Search for public domain images and audio files on the Internet; you may want to use several of these in your elevator simulator.

2. To make the simulator more realistic, the GIF file used to represent a person can be randomly selected.

Questions

1. How might you decide if the elevator is able to handle the anticipated traffic volume?

2. Why is it more complicated to implement a three-story (or higher) building?

3. Once we have created one elevator object, it is easy to create as many as we want. What problems do you foresee in having several elevators, each of which may pick up and discharge passengers at every floor in the building?

4. For simplicity, we have given our elevator and each of the floors a capacity of one person. What problems do you foresee in being able to increase these capacities?

F.15 Recommended Modifications

1. (Prerequisite: Chapter 17) Modify the simulator to allow a maximum of three people to "queue up" on each floor. Each floor should implement a **Queue** class object.

2. (Prerequisite: Chapter 14) Use a series of GIF images to show a person "walking" across the floor (i.e., with the person's legs moving and the person's arms swinging).

3. Change the number of floors in the simulation from 2 floors to 3 or more.

4. After completing the previous modification, add one or more elevators to the simulator.

5. After completing the previous two modifications, modify the floor ranges each elevator covers. One elevator should be an "express" elevator, which goes from floor one to the top floor without stopping on any floor in between.

6. Increase the capacity of each floor to six or more people. Also increase the capacity of the elevator to three or more people.

7. Modify the elevator simulator to incorporate client-server capabilities, such that when the user clicks on either floor push button the simulator connects to the "person server" and requests information about the person (i.e., person number and the necessary GIF images).

8. Modify the simulator to use the class **Observable** and the **Obeserver** interface. As a suggestion, you might have a person "observe" the elevator. Note: the previous modifications are not required for implementation.

9. Modify the simulator to write, at regular intervals (such as every minute), "vital statistics" to a file. The statistics should include the total number of people in the building, the number of people waiting on each floor, the number of people in the elevator, etc.

Appendix G

Getting Started with Microsoft Visual J++

Objectives

- To understand how Java and Visual J++ relate to each other.
- To use Visual J++ to create Java programs.
- To understand the Microsoft Developer Studio integrated development environment.
- To compile and execute programs developed with Visual J++.
- To use the Applet Wizard to create Java programs rapidly.
- To use the debugger to locate and correct bugs in a program.
- To understand what COM is and how it relates to Java.
- To understand how Visual J++ enables you to integrate Java and ActiveX to develop powerful Java programs.
- To understand the concept of visual programming.
- To be able to use the dialog editor and Java Resource Wizard to create graphical user interfaces.
- To locate World Wide Web resources and demos for Visual J++, Java, and ActiveX.

If you build it, he will come.
William P. Kinsella

Here Skugg lies snug
As a bug in a rug.
Benjamin Franklin

Change the environment; do not try to change man.
Richard Buckminster Fuller

Black as the devil, Hot as hell,
Pure as an angel, Sweet as love.
Recipe for coffee
Charles Maurice de Talleyrand-Périgord

Outline

G.1 Introduction

Welcome to Visual J++! In this appendix (co-authored with our colleague, Mr. Tem Nieto of Deitel & Associates, Inc.), you will learn how to create, execute, debug and evolve Java programs using the powerful Java development environment from Microsoft—Visual J++. When you complete this appendix, you will be able to use Visual J++ to take full advantage of Java as you build substantial Java applets and applications. As you will see, Visual J++ also enables programmers to take advantage of other powerful Microsoft technologies such as *ActiveX controls*. ActiveX controls are cross-platform components written in C++, Java, or other programming languages that can be "plugged" into a program to provide access to a wide variety of preexisting or user-defined capabilities.

We have included the Publisher's Edition of Microsoft's Visual J++ for you on the CD-ROM in the back cover of this book. The CD-ROM also contains the 200 applets and applications from the main portion of the text in which we explain Java concepts that apply to all Java programming environments. This appendix covers the materials specific to Java programming with Visual J++. The full documentation for the Visual J++ Publisher's Edition software is included on the CD-ROM. We think you will enjoy programming in Java with this powerful environment.

G.2 Microsoft Developer Studio Environment Overview: Visual J++

Figure G.1 shows a screen image of the *Microsoft Developer Studio*—the integrated development environment for Visual J++. This environment contains everything you need to create Java programs—an *editor* (for typing and correcting your Java programs), a *compiler* (for translating your Java programs into Java bytecodes—a highly portable program format that can be understood on every major type of computer system that provides a *Java Virtual Machine*), a *debugger* (for finding logic errors in your Java programs after they are compiled), and much more. The environment contains many menus and buttons that facil-

InfoView pane

Fig. G.1   Microsoft Developer Studio (Visual J++).

itate editing, compiling, and debugging your Java applets and applications. We discuss the features associated with many of these menus and buttons in subsequent sections.

G.3 On-line Visual J++ Information

Microsoft Developer Studio provides on-line documentation for Java and Visual J++ in the *InfoView pane (Fig. G.1)*. Information about all aspects of Visual J++ is available—from the Java Language Specification to Microsoft's enhancements to Java. Topics are displayed in *tree-view format*. Click the left mouse button on the plus (**+**) sign next to a topic to expand the topic's subcategories (Fig. G.2). Note: For the rest of this appendix, we refer to "clicking the left mouse button" simply as *clicking*. Notice the enlarged **InfoView** pane. The **InfoView** pane is resized by clicking and dragging its bottom edge or its right edge.

On-line information is divided into categories. Each category is preceded by a book icon. The *Read This First* category contains information about installing Visual J++ on your computer, creating Java applets and Java applications, and getting help.

The *Test Drive* category contains a subcategory named *Introduction to Visual J++* with information about building a sample applet, creating applets rapidly with the Applet Wizard, using the Resource Wizard to create graphical user interfaces (GUIs), and modifying Java programs previously created in Visual J++.

The *User's Guide* contains information about working with projects, working with editors, and customizing the look and feel of the Microsoft Developer Studio environment (such as windows, toolbars, keyboard shortcuts to commands, and adding your own tools to the *Tools* menu). The User's Guide also provides references for several utility programs that come with Visual J++.

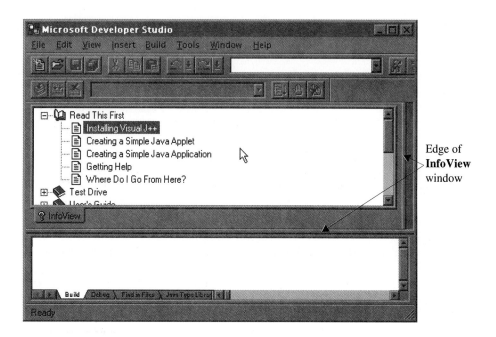

Edge of
InfoView
window

Fig. G.2   Resized **InfoView** window with subcategories.

The *Java API, Volume 1: Core Packages* contains the complete details of several packages. *Packages* are groups of related *classes* (reusable software components that enable Java programmers to assemble software quickly) that provide Java's built-in functionality. The **java.lang** package includes basic language capabilities. The **java.io** package includes all Java's stream processing capabilities for interpreting bytes input into a program and output from a program. The **java.util** package includes data structure classes and miscellaneous other classes. The **java.net** package provides capabilities for implementing client-server networking applications.

The *Java API, Volume 2: Window Toolkit and Applets* contains complete details about the remaining packages of the Java API. The **java.awt** package includes all Java's capabilities for manipulating graphics, fonts, colors and GUI components. The **java.applet** package includes the basic capabilities of Java applets that enable applets to execute in a Java-enabled World Wide Web browser such as *Microsoft Internet Explorer* or *Netscape Navigator*. The **java.awt.image** package includes the image processing capabilities of Java. The **java.awt.peer** package enables Java programmers to use GUI components without knowing specific implementation details of the GUI components on each computer platform. Many classes in package **java.awt** use classes in package **java.awt.peer**. Typically, the **java.awt.peer** package is not used directly by the programmer.

The *Java API Hierarchy Chart* contains a visual hierarchy illustrating how all the core Java classes are related. This will be one of your favorite reference sources.

The *Java Language Specification* category contains the implementation details of the Java language such as language syntax, program structure, data types, expression syntax, multithreading capabilities, exception handling capabilities, and a reference manual for the packages **java.lang**, **java.io** and **java.util**—the required packages for all general purpose Java systems.

The *Java and COM* category contains information about using Java and COM together. COM is Microsoft's *Component Object Model*. We discuss COM in more detail in section G.7.

The *Samples* category contains demos and sample code from both Sun Microsystems (the creator of Java) and Microsoft. In the *Sun Samples*, there are demonstration programs illustrating many of Java's capabilities such as graphics, animation, audio, GUIs, multithreading, and GUI event handling. In the *Microsoft Samples*, there are demonstration programs illustrating Microsoft-specific capabilities that can be incorporated into Java programs for the Microsoft Windows 95 and Windows NT platforms. It is often helpful to mimic the example code when writing your own Java programs that require similar capabilities to those programs in the samples.

The *Build Errors* category contains descriptions of the various errors that can occur when you compile a Java applet or application.

The *Miscellaneous* category contains a glossary of terminology for the Microsoft Developer Studio, copyright information for the Visual J++ product, a **Readme** file containing an overview of the Visual J++ product, and accessibility information for people with disabilities.

G.4 Creating and Executing a Java Applet

This section demonstrates how to create and execute a Java applet—a program that executes in a Java-enabled World Wide Web browser such as Microsoft Internet Explorer or Netscape Navigator. The first step in writing an applet is to click the *New Source File* button (Fig. G.3)—this opens a window entitled **Text1**. Also, note that resting the mouse pointer over a button displays a *tool tip* indicating the button's name. An example of a tool tip can be seen in Fig. G.19.

The next step is to type the Java code into the **Text1** window. Click anywhere in the **Text1** window to begin typing. For the purposes of this example, type the program of Fig. 1.2. In Fig. G.4, notice that an asterisk (*****) appears to the right of **Text1**. The asterisk indicates that the file has been modified (unsaved). To save the program, select **Save** from the **File** menu as shown in Fig. G.4.

Although you selected **Save**, the **Save As** dialog appears (Fig. G.5). The first time a file is saved, the **Save As** dialog is displayed. This dialog is used to specify the file name and the directory in which to save the file. Type the file's name into the *File name* textfield. After you specify the directory and file name, click the *Save* button. *Note*: Remember that your file name should be the name of your class followed by the **.java** extension (i.e., **Welcome.java** for this program). You must specify the file's directory in the *Save in* drop-down list. We created the directory **J++ project** to store our program—you may specify any directory you wish.

Fig. G.3   Displaying a **Text** window.

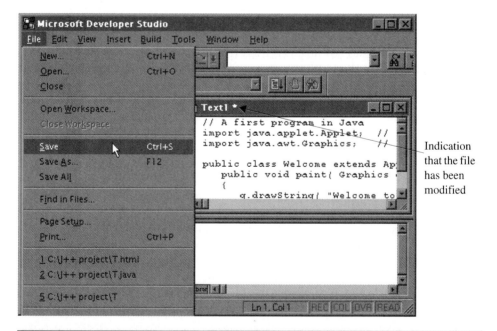

Fig. G.4   Selecting **Save** from the **File** menu.

Fig. G.5   Save As dialog.

When the file is saved, the title of the text window containing the program changes from **Text1** to the file name **Welcome.java**. Microsoft Developer Studio now recognizes this file as a *Java source file* (a file with extension **.java**) and imposes a coloring scheme (called *syntax color highlighting*) on the program elements in the file (Fig. G.6). If you save the file before typing any code, syntax color highlighting is applied as you type your code.

In Fig. G.6, notice that the comment at the beginning of the program and some of the Java keywords are lighter than the class names and the method names. The colors help the user differentiate between keywords, comments, and other text. Keywords normally appear in blue, comments in green, and other text in black, but you can set your own color preferences.

> *Testing and Debugging Tip G.1*
>
> *Microsoft Developers Studio's syntax color highlighting helps the programmer avoid using keywords accidentally as variable names.*

To customize the syntax color highlighting, select the **Options...** menu item from the **Tools** menu. In the *Options* dialog, click the right arrow at the right side of the dialog next to the file folder tabs until the *Format* tab appears and click the **Format** tab. All syntax coloring aspects of the entire Microsoft Developer Studio can be customized here. To change the syntax coloring for your Java source code, select *Source Windows* from the *Category* box in the upper-left corner of the dialog. In the right side of the dialog, the *Font*, *Size*, *Foreground* and *Background* areas enable you to customize each language element. Simply click the element in the *Colors* area, then use the **Font**, **Size**, **Foreground** and **Background** areas to customize the language element. Click the **OK** button when you are done customizing.

Fig. G.6   Saved source file with syntax color highlighting.

Because this is an applet, an *HTML (Hypertext Markup Language)* file is required so the applet can be loaded into a World Wide Web browser. We discuss the required elements of HTML for the purpose of loading an applet in Fig. 1.3. To create an HTML file, open a new **Text** window and type the HTML code. Figure G.7 displays a new text window that was opened by clicking the **New Source File** button (see Fig. G.3). Notice that the new window's title is **Text2**—Microsoft Developer Studio keeps a running total of the number of text windows opened. Enter the following HTML code in the window

```
<applet code="Welcome.class" width=275 height=35>
</applet>
```

If you do not create an HTML file, Visual J++ creates a default HTML file for your applet.

To save the HTML file, click the *Save* button (Fig. G.7) or select **Save** or **Save As** from the **File** menu. The **Save As** dialog (Fig. G.8) appears. Type **Welcome.html** in the *File name* textfield and click the **Save** button. Note: If you do not name the HTML file with the same base name as the Java file (i.e., **Welcome**), Visual J++ creates a default HTML file.

The Java program is now ready to be translated into Java bytecodes. Click the *Compile* button (Fig. G.9) to begin the compilation process (i.e., the translation process). Note: The **Compile** button is disabled unless a Java source file window has the *focus*. A window with focus is the active window and is indicated by a darker title bar (where the window's title is displayed) than other windows. You can click a window to activate it and give it the focus. When the **Compile** button is clicked, the dialog shown in Fig. G.10 appears.

Save button

Fig. G.7   Creating an HTML file.

Fig. G.8   Saving an HTML file.

Fig. G.9 Environment after the HTML file has been saved.

Fig. G.10 Dialog displayed when the **Compile** button is clicked.

Compiling a program requires a project. A *project* is a group of classes and files that is normally in its own directory. Projects enable the programmer to manage as one unit all the files required for a particular applet or application. The user does not explicitly have to create a project because Microsoft Developer Studio gives the user the option of using a *default project*. For this example we use the default project (in subsequent sections we discuss projects in more detail). Click the **Yes** button to create a default project and compile the project's Java source files. Figure G.11 shows the environment after compilation.

Any compiler errors or compiler warnings appear in the ***Output*** window (Fig. G.11) at the bottom of the Developer Studio. A *compiler error* indicates that code in the program violates the syntax of Java (also known as a *syntax error*). A program cannot execute if it contains compiler errors—the errors must first be corrected and the program must be recompiled. A *compiler warning* indicates that a statement is syntactically correct but may cause a problem at run time. Compiler warnings are not as severe as compiler errors—programs with warnings normally can execute.

Fig. G.11 Environment after compilation.

Testing and Debugging Tip G.2

If your program contains compiler errors, double click on an error message in the output window to point out the offending line of code. Visual J++ places a blue arrow next to the line of code in the source file.

Once the Java source file has been successfully compiled (no compiler errors), the program is ready for execution. Select ***Execute*** from the ***Build*** menu (Fig. G.12) to display the ***Information For Running Class*** dialog (Fig. G.13). This dialog is used the first time you execute your program to specify the name of the program's compiled class and whether you are executing the class as an applet or an application. Type the name `Welcome.class` in the **Class file name** textfield.

The *OK* button in the **Information For Running Class** dialog is initially grayed (or disabled) until the class file name is typed into the ***Class file name*** textfield. For applets, click the ***Browser*** radio button in the ***Run project under*** area of the **Information For Running Class** dialog (the radio buttons are indicated in Fig. G.13). The path in the textfield need not be changed by the user. Click the *OK* button to dismiss the **Information For Running Class** dialog. Internet Explorer, automatically launches to execute the applet (Fig. G.14). Once your program completes execution, close Internet Explorer by selecting *Exit* from the **File** menu or by clicking the ∞ button in the upper-right corner of the window.

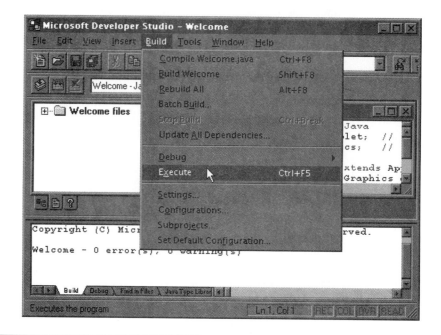

Fig. G.12   Selecting **Execute** from the **Build** menu.

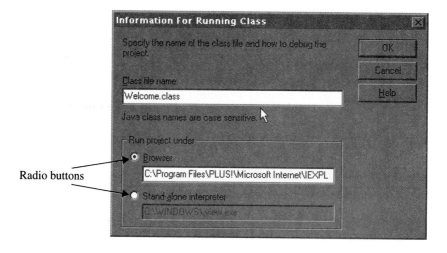

Fig. G.13   **Information For Running Class** dialog.

Fig. G.14 Applet running inside Microsoft's Internet Explorer.

Applets running in Internet Explorer that use **System.out** or **System.err** for standard output write the output to a file named **javalog.txt**. This file is only created if *Java logging* is enabled in Internet Explorer. To enable Java logging, select the **View** menu's *Options* menu item. Click the *Advanced* tab of **Options** dialog. In the bottom right corner of the dialog, click the **Enable Java logging** option (a check should appear in the checkbox). Click the **OK** button to dismiss the dialog. The file **javalog.txt** can be found in a subdirectory (named **java**) of the directory in which windows is installed (usually called **windows**). Note: if you cannot find the file use **Find** from window's **Start** menu to search for it.

Testing and Debugging Tip G.3

*Forgetting to check the **Enable Java logging** checkbox results in the file **javalog.txt** not being created by Internet Explorer.*

Testing and Debugging Tip G.4

*Add **javalog.txt** to your project. This allows you to view information from Visual J++ as it is written to the file. The file can be added by using the **Insert** menu's **Insert Files into Project** dialog.*

G.5 Creating and Executing a Java Application

Applications are programs that require only a Java Virtual Machine to execute (i.e., applications do not require a browser to execute). Visual J++ provides the capability to create and execute Java applications. In this section, we create a simple application and execute it. For demonstration purposes, we use the program of Fig. 2.18.

To begin creating an application, first select **New** from the **File** menu to display the *New Project Workspace* dialog (Fig. G.15). The default selection *Java Workspace* appears highlighted. Select the directory in which the program should be stored and name the project **EscapeSequences**. Notice that the name of the project is added to the directory path in the Location textfield. Your project is stored in its own directory. Click the **Create** button to create the project. Note that the **Create** button is grayed unless a name is specified in the *Name* textfield.

Next, click the **New Source File** button (Fig. G.3) to display a **Text** window (also called a *source window*). Save the file as **EscapeSequences.java** by selecting **Save** from the **File** menu. Since the file does not have a name, the *Save As* dialog pops-up (Fig. G.16). Enter the name **EscapeSequences.java** in the **File name** textfield and click the **Save** button.

Now type the program of Fig. 2.18. Note that as the Java code is typed, the environment imposes the syntax coloring highlighting. Figure G.17 shows the environment after the file has been entered.

Fig. G.15 New Project Workspace dialog.

Fig. G.16 Save As dialog.

Fig. G.17 Microsoft Developer Studio environment after the application is entered.

The file is not currently part of the project. Therefore, it must be added to the project so it can be compiled. Select *Files into Project* from the **Insert** menu to open the *Insert Files into Project* dialog (Fig. G.18). Select the file **EscapeSequences.java** and click the *Add* button. Note: If a project consists of multiple source files, each file must be inserted into the project using the **Insert Files into Project** dialog. The Shift and Ctrl keys can be used to select multiple files at once for insertion.

Fig. G.18 Insert Files into Project dialog.

The project is now ready to be compiled. Click the ***Build*** button (Fig. G.19) to *build* (i.e. compile) the project. Building the project recompiles all Java source files changed since the last build operation. Note the tool tip identifying the **Build** button. The **Build** pane displays the result of the build.

The program is now ready for execution. Select **Execute** from the **Build** menu to display the **Information For Running Class** dialog (Fig. G.20). Enter the name **EscapeSequences** in the **Class file name** textfield. Note that the **OK** button is grayed unless a name is specified in the **Class file name** textfield. Select the ***Stand-alone interpreter*** radio button and click the **OK** button.

Fig. G.19 Environment after the build.

Fig. G.20 **Information For Running Class** dialog.

The application is executed in the *JView* window (Fig. G.21). The **JView** window is a DOS window that displays the program output. Any input required by the program is entered in the **JView** window as well. If your application contains a graphical user interface (GUI), both the **JView** window and the GUI are displayed on the screen. In this case, most input and output is controlled through the GUI. Control returns to the Microsoft Developer Studio environment when the application finishes execution.

Application output that is normally directed to the **Jview** window also can be displayed in the **Output** window of the Microsoft Developer Studio. The following steps explain how to redirect application output to the **Output** window.

1. Select *Customize* from the **Tools** menu. This displays the *Customize* dialog.
2. In the **Customize** dialog select the *Tools* tab.
3. Click the *Add* button. This displays the *Add Tool* dialog.
4. In the **Add Tool** dialog, enter **jview** in the *Command* textfield. Click the **OK** button. Control returns to the **Tools** tab.
5. In the **Tools** tab's *Menu text* textfield is **Jview** and in the **Command** textfield is **jview.EXE**. Enter *$(FileName)* in the *Arguments* textfield and enter *$(FileDir)* in the *Initial Directory* textfield.
6. Check the *Redirect to Output Window* checkbox.
7. Click the **Close** button. Control returns to the environment.

Selecting **Jview** from the **Tools** menu displays the application output in the **Output** window. Note: The **Output** window now contains a *Jview* tab.

If **Redirect to Output Window** in step 6 is not checked, then output for the application continues to go to the **Jview** window rather than the **Output** window. In this case, the **Jview** window closes automatically when the program terminates—possibly before you can look at the results of your application. However, if you select the **Jview** tool from the **Tools** menu to execute your application, the **Jview** window does not close until you press a key to dismiss the window. This enables you to view your results.

Fig. G.21 JView window.

G.6 Creating an Applet with the Applet Wizard

The *Applet Wizard* helps programmers create applets quickly. The Applet Wizard gener-ates a skeleton Java applet source file according to preferences set by the user. The user fills in the appropriate sections of code or adds additional code. The example in this section walks through creating an applet that does an animation of the Earth spinning (the default animation provided by Visual J++). We use the default values specified by the Applet Wiz-ard including the default images for the animation. Programmers can substitute their own animation images for the default images.

Java currently supports two image formats—*GIF (Graphics Interchange Format)* and *JPEG (Joint Photographic Experts Group)*. These can be created with most graphics soft-ware. If you create images, they can simply be substituted for the images supplied by the Applet Wizard. You should name the files the same as Visual J++ does (i.e., **img####.gif** where **####** starts as **0000** and is incremented by 1 for each consecutive image in the animation; you may also edit the applet source code to change the names of the files). By default, the images are placed in a directory called **images** in your project's directory.

Creating an applet with the Applet Wizard involves several steps. First select the *New* menu item from the **File** menu (Fig. G.22). The **New** dialog appears as shown in Fig. G.23. Select the *Project Workspace* in the **New** dialog and click the **OK** button to display the **New Project Workspace** dialog.

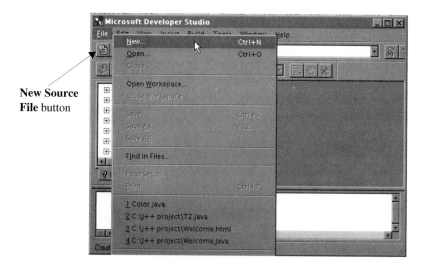

Fig. G.22 Selecting the **New** menu item from the **File** menu.

Fig. G.23 New dialog.

In the left part of the **New Project Workspace** dialog (Fig. G.24) is a list box entitled *Type*. The **Type** list box contains two items—**Java Workspace** and **Java Applet Wizard** (if you have Visual C++ installed on your machine, you will have more than two items in the list). Select **Java Applet Wizard**. The name of the project must be entered in the *Name* textfield. For this example, enter **T3**. The *Location* textfield displays the directory path for the project. We use a directory called **J++ Project**. Notice that the project name is added to the directory path in the **Location** textfield. Once the name and location are specified, click the *Create* button to launch the **Java Applet Wizard**.

Next the *Java Applet Wizard Step 1 of 5* dialog appears as shown in Fig. G.25. Radio buttons for the *How would you like to be able to run your program?* option specify the type of program to create. You can create an applet that executes only in a World Wide Web browser (i.e., the *As an applet only* option), or you can create an applet that executes either in a World Wide Web browser or as a standalone application (as in Section G.3) using the Java interpreter (i.e., the *As an applet and as an application* option). Use the default setting **applet only**. Specify the name of applet in the *What would you like to name your applet class?* textfield. The default name, **T3**, is the same as the project name.

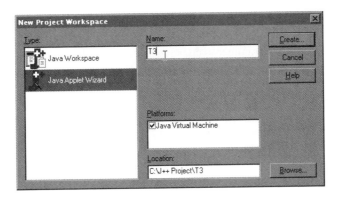

Fig. G.24 New Project Workspace dialog.

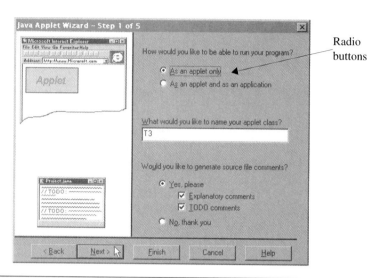

Radio
buttons

Fig. G.25 Java Applet Wizard Step 1 of 5 dialog.

Radio buttons are also used to specify whether or not comments should be generated by the Applet Wizard in the source file. These comments help programmers determine what code they should add to an applet produced with Applet Wizard. The default setting is *Yes, please* with both the **Explanatory comments** and **TODO comments** checkboxes checked. *Explanatory comments* describe all the variables and methods that are automatically generated. *TODO comments* are provided in areas where the programmer may need to write code. Click the *Next>* button to proceed to the next dialog.

The next dialog that appears is the *Java Applet Wizard Step 2 of 5* dialog (Fig. G.26). The dialog contains two radio buttons and two textfields. The radio buttons specify whether or not the user wants an HTML file to be generated automatically. The default is *Yes, please*. The two textfields specify the applet width and height, respectively. The default values are shown in Fig. G.26. Click the **Next>** button.

In the *Java Applet Wizard Step 3 of 5* dialog (Fig. G.27) there are two sets of radio buttons and three checkboxes. The first set of radio buttons specifies whether or not the applet should be multithreaded (multithreading is discussed in detail in Chapter 13). Multithreading enables the programmer to create independent paths of execution in a program. For example, you could have an animation running in one thread of execution and process input from the user in a separate thread of execution. The default is *Yes, please*. Keep the multithreading option selected if you want an animation on your applet or if you intend to add your own multithreading capabilities to the applet. We use multithreading in this example for the default animation created by the Applet Wizard.

The second set of radio buttons specify whether or not the applet supports animation. We use the default *Yes, please*. Note that Visual J++ supplies a default set of images for the animation. The three checkboxes at the bottom of the window specify whether or not the applet processes mouse events with the mouse methods. The mouse methods are discussed in Chapter 10. All three checkboxes are unselected by default. If you plan to add mouse

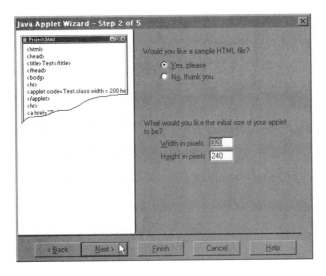

Fig. G.26 Java Applet Wizard Step 2 of 5 dialog.

support to your applet, click the checkbox next to the methods you want to include. The Applet Wizard will supply the skeleton of the mouse methods you select so you can add your processing code later. Click the **Next>** button.

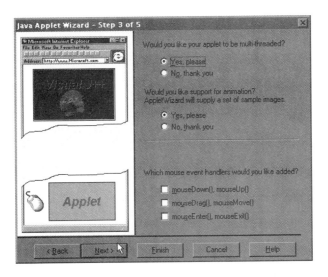

Fig. G.27 Java Applet Wizard Step 3 of 5 dialog.

In the **Java Applet Wizard Step 4 of 5** dialog (Fig. G.28), information returned by the ***getParameterInfo*** *method* about HTML parameters for an applet is specified (for more information on applet HTML parameters, see Chapter 14). Applet parameters are supplied in an HTML file that invokes an applet to customize the applet. Information returned by **getParameterInfo** indicates the name, type and description of each HTML parameter for the applet. This example does not have HTML parameters. Click the **Next>** button.

In the **Java Applet Wizard Step 5 of 5** dialog (Fig. G.29), information returned by the ***getAppletInfo*** *method* is specified. This method returns information about the applet, such as the applet name, the applet author, the applet creator, etc. You can edit this information if you like. When you are done, click the ***Finish*** button.

Next the ***New Project Information*** dialog appears (Fig. G.30) with a summary of the applet that will be created. Click the **OK** button to finish creating the applet.

The environment now displays the project created in the **Project Workspace** window (Fig. G.31). Three tabs are available in the Project Workspace: **ClassView**, **FileView**, and **InfoView**. *ClassView* allows the user to see all the classes associated with the current project. Each class's methods and variables can be listed by clicking the plus sign (**+**) next to the class name. The figure illustrates the expanded view of the methods in class **T3**.

The *FileView* tab displays all the files associated with the project. In Fig. G.32, the **T3.java** file was opened by double clicking the file in the **FileView** tab. The code can be viewed and edited. Double clicking an image file (Fig. G.33) displays an *image editor*, a *toolbox*, and a *color palette*. The image editor allows individual pieces of an image to be edited. This is useful for customizing an image to suit your program's needs. The toolbox contains the tools used to edit the image. Image colors can be changed by selecting a color from the color palette.

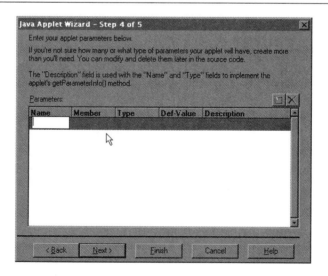

Fig. G.28   Java Applet Wizard Step 4 of 5 dialog.

Fig. G.29   Java Applet Wizard Step 5 of 5 dialog.

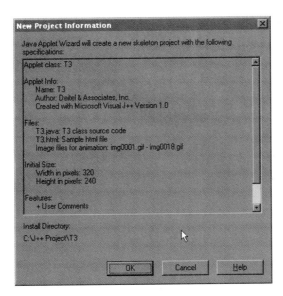

Fig. G.30   New Project Information dialog.

Class
Methods
FileView tab
ClassView tab
Current project
Project Workspace window

Fig. G.31   Viewing the project in **ClassView**.

Fig. G.32   Viewing the code in **FileView**.

Figure G.34 shows the explanatory comments and the TODO comments inserted in the code by the Applet Wizard. Explanatory comments explain variables and methods generated by the Applet Wizard. The Applet Wizard places TODO comments in areas where programmers may need to write code. Programmers are not required to provide code in these areas.

Fig. G.33 Viewing a GIF file.

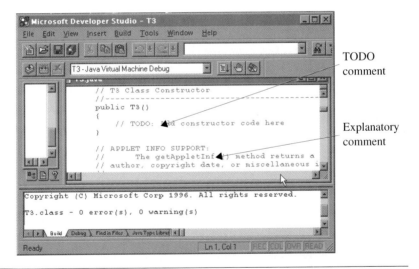

Fig. G.34 Explanatory comments and TODO comments in the Java file.

Software Engineering Observation G.1

Instance and class variables generated by the Applet Wizard are friendly by default.

Good Programming Practice G.1

*Change the access modifier of instance or class variables generated by the Applet Wizard to either **private** or **protected** when the default friendly is not required.*

Figure G.35 shows the applet executing after **Execute** is selected from the **Build** menu. The applet provides an animation of the Earth rotating.

G.7 Java, COM and ActiveX: Using a COM Object in a Java Program

In addition to the Java language, Visual J++ enables programmers to create and use *ActiveX controls*. ActiveX controls are cross platform components written in C++, Java, or other languages that can be "plugged" into a program. A *cross-platform component* can be executed on multiple platforms (e.g. PC, Macintosh, Unix, etc.). Note: ActiveX controls were formerly called *Object Linking and Embedding* (*OLE*) controls.

ActiveX controls are built using the *Component Object Model* (*COM*). COM is a *binary level specification* that describes the procedure by which objects communicate. Binary specifications can be implemented in just about any programming language. The programmer writing a COM object is responsible for following the rules of COM.

ActiveX controls make use of COM, existing OLE technologies, and *Application Programming Interfaces* (*APIs*) such as Win32 (an API for developing 32-bit Microsoft Windows applications for Windows 95 and Windows NT).

COM allows a component to communicate with another component of a potentially different type. COM is language independent, compiler independent, and location independent—COM can be used remotely or locally. Java programs created with Visual J++ can access COM components and vice versa. COM components can access the `public` methods of a Java program created with Visual J++.

Visual J++ allows COM objects to be treated as Java classes. To use a COM object, the programmer creates a reference of the proper type and makes a constructor call to initialize the object. A COM object's `public` methods are called using the dot (`.`) operator.

Portability Tip G.1

COM is language independent, compiler independent, and location independent.

Fig. G.35   Applet created with the Applet Wizard running in Internet Explorer.

Performance Tip G.1

COM objects consist of native windows executable code that executes much faster than interpreted bytecode classes.

In this section, we present a simple example of using an ActiveX control. We write a program (Fig. G.36) that sounds a beep through the computer's speaker every time the user clicks a button. The beeping is performed by an ActiveX control.

We first discuss the Java code in Fig. G.36. Line 3 of the program imports the **beeper** package, which consists of the **class** files generated by the *Java Type Library Wizard* from the *beeper.dll* file. We explain how to generate these **class** files shortly. A file with a **.dll** extension is a *dynamic link library*—a prepackaged component that is usually written in C or C++. The **beeper.dll** file can be found on the Microsoft Visual J++ Publisher's Edition CD-ROM (**msdev\samples\microsoft**). You must copy this file to your project's directory.

```
1   import java.applet.Applet;
2   import java.awt.*;
3   import beeper.*;    // beeper class files
4
5   public class MyBeep extends Applet {
6       private Button beepButton;
7       private IBeeper beeper;    // interface reference
8
9       public void init()
10      {
11          beepButton = new Button( "Beep" );
12          beeper = ( IBeeper ) new Beeper();   // COM object
13          add( beepButton );
14      }
15
16      public boolean action( Event e, Object o )
17      {
18          try {
19              beeper.Beep();   // call Beep method
20          }
21          catch ( ms.com.ms.ComException ex ) {
22              float r = ( float ) Math.random();
23              float g = ( float ) Math.random();
24              float b = ( float ) Math.random();
25
26              setBackground( new Color( r, g, b ) );
27              repaint();
28          }
29
30          return true;
31      }
32  }
```

Fig. G.36 Java program that uses the ActiveX beeper control.

Line 7 declares a reference to an object of type ***IBeeper***—an interface that allows our Java program to communicate with the ActiveX beeper control. Note: An ActiveX interface (i.e., **IBeeper**) is not the same as a Java interface. ActiveX interfaces contain functionality, whereas Java interfaces do not. ActiveX interfaces are like a Java class. Line 12 instantiates the ***beeper*** object by calling the ***Beeper*** constructor. The **IBeeper** interface interacts with the **beeper** object to generate the beep. Line 19 calls the **beeper** object's ***Beep*** *method*, which sounds a beep through the system speaker.

Notice that the **Beep** method is called from a **try** block. Microsoft intentionally introduced an exception into the beeper control. Every sixth beep generates a *COM exception*. In the **catch** handler we catch exception type ***com.ms.com.ComException***, and then change the applet's background color to a random color to indicate that the exception occurred.

Before writing the program of Fig. G.36, the programmer must know how to use the COM object. As mentioned earlier, the **beeper.dll** file must be copied from the CD-ROM to your hard drive. This DLL is not known to operating system yet, so it is considered an *unregistered DLL*.

The beeper DLL is *registered* using the ***regsvr32*** program. This program is located in the **windows\system** directory and is available on all Win32 platforms (Note: Your windows directory may be named differently. If so, replace **windows** with the appropriate directory name). Figure G.37 shows the **beeper.dll** being registered and Fig. G.38 shows the dialog displayed when the DLL is registered. Note: We copied the file **beeper.dll** into the directory **c:\j++ project\beeper** on our system (you may choose to name your directory differently).

Fig. G.37 Registering the beeper DLL.

Fig. G.38 Dialog displayed when the beeper DLL is registered.

Once the DLL is registered, information about that COM object can be viewed by the programmer. Select *OLE Object View* from the **Tools** menu to display the *OLE 2 Object View (Win32)* dialog (Fig. G.39). Information about ActiveX controls and other COM objects can be viewed in this dialog. A small icon to the left of the name indicates the object type. The two primary object types are ActiveX controls and *type libraries*. Note: An *OCX control* is a type of ActiveX control. The beeper control is an example of a type library. A type library contains information about an ActiveX control. Type libraries are files usually ending in either `.DLL`, `.TLB`, or `.OLB`.

If the `beeper.dll` is unregistered, the beeper type library is not be listed. Note that items listed in the **OLE 2 Object View** dialog may be different on your system. Some of the items shown are from other products that are not necessarily on your system.

Double clicking on a type library pops-up the *ITypeLib dialog*, which displays information about the selected type library. Figure G.40 shows the **ITypeLib** dialog for the **beeper** type library.

The *Typeinfo combo box* lists *interfaces* and *coclasses*. Interfaces are used to describe methods and object references. The programmer uses the interface to access the object's methods. Select the *IBeeper(1)* item from the **Typeinfo** combo box. The *Functions list box* lists the object's functions (a function is a method). Select the **Beep** function in the **Functions** list box. The *Function Prototype list box* describes how to use the function. For example, **Beep** has a **void** return type and does not take any arguments.

To use the **Beep** method, we must first declare a reference to the **IBeeper** interface type (line 7 of Fig. G.36) and create a **Beeper** coclass object (line 12 of Fig. G.36). A coclass is a COM class which does not contain methods or variables; but implements the capabilities of a COM object. Other than a constructor call, coclasses are not directly used by the programmer. Rather, the corresponding interface interacts with the coclass to perform a task.

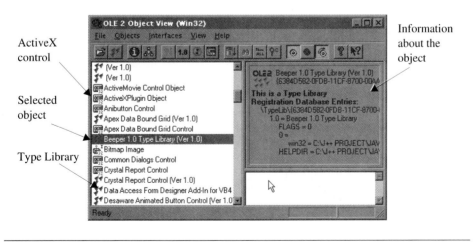

Fig. G.39   OLE 2 Object View (Win32) dialog.

Typeinfo
combo box

Functions
list box

**Function
Prototype**
list box

Fig. G.40   ITypeLib dialog.

How did we know to import the **beeper** package? Where is the **beeper** package? The answer is that it does not exist. The Visual J++ compiler does not know what **IBeeper** is and cannot find any class files in support of this object. Microsoft Developer Studio provides the *Java Type Library Wizard* for generating Java class files for COM components. Select the **Java Type Library Wizard** item in the **Tools** menu to display the **Java Type Library Wizard** dialog (Fig. G.41).

Fig. G.41   Java Type Library Wizard dialog.

Click the checkbox to the left of **Beeper 1.0 Type Library** to specify that class files should be generated for this item. Note that the beeper DLL must be registered; otherwise, the **Beeper 1.0 Type Library** is not listed in this dialog. Also note that the items listed in the **Java Type Library Wizard** may differ on your system.

Click the **OK** button to generate the class files. The `import` statement needed to use the beeper control is specified in the *Java Type Library Wizard pane* (Fig. G.42). This pane can be viewed by clicking the *Java Type Library Wizard tab* on the **Output** window.

Also, the location of the file `summary.txt` is specified in the **Java Type Library Wizard** pane. This file contains a listing of the interfaces and classes for the COM object for the Java package produced by the **Java Type Library Wizard**. The path preceding the file name specifies where this file and the class files generated for the COM object are placed (`\windows\java\trustlib`). You can read this file in any text editor. Note: Double-click `summary.txt` in the **Output** window to open the file (you can do this with any file name displayed in the **Output** window).

Using a COM object in Java is a straight forward process. Writing COM objects and using Java objects in COM objects is more involved. For more information on COM refer to the on-line Visual J++ documentation and visit Microsoft's World Wide Web site:

`http://www.microsoft.com`

Software Engineering Observation G.2

Calling a local or remote COM object is not allowed for applets unless the COM object has a secure digital signature—i.e., the COM object came from a trusted source.

Java Type Library Wizard pane

Java Type Library Wizard tab

Fig. G.42   Java Type Library Wizard pane.

G.8 Using the Debugger

Microsoft Developer Studio contains a built-in debugger. The debugger is useful for finding logic errors in programs. A debugging session is started by selecting the **Build** menu's *Debug* submenu (Fig. G.43). We discuss each of the menu items in this submenu. The debugger is not used for syntax checking—that is the job of the compiler. A program must compile successfully before the debugger can be used. The debugger is most commonly used to step through the lines of code on a line-by-line basis, set variable watches to view the values of individual variables, and set *breakpoints* (lines of code selected by the programmer at which execution is halted so the programmer can examine the code and the current state—such as variable values—of the program's execution).

Breakpoints are used in areas where the programmer wants to examine program execution in more detail. A program can have multiple breakpoints. Breakpoints are set by clicking the line where the breakpoint is desired and clicking the *Insert/Remove Breakpoint* button (Fig. G.44). Program execution halts when a breakpoint is encountered. When a breakpoint is set, a small red dot appears to the left of the line. To set the breakpoint, the cursor must be in the window containing the Java code; otherwise, the **Insert/Remove Breakpoint** button is grayed. An individual breakpoint can be removed by clicking the line with the breakpoint and clicking the **Insert/Remove Breakpoint** button. All breakpoints can be removed by clicking the *Remove All Breakpoints* button. These buttons and a breakpoint are illustrated in Fig. G.44.

Fig. G.43 Build menu's **Debug** submenu.

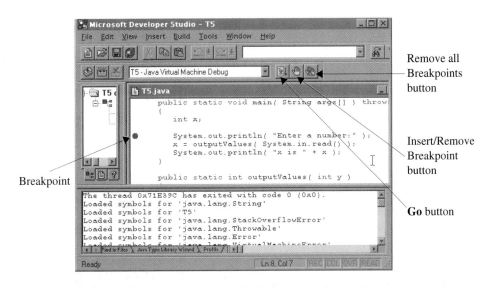

Fig. G.44 Debugger buttons and a breakpoint.

Selecting the *Go* menu item or clicking the *Go* button (Fig. G.44) executes the program. We have chosen to debug an application, so the *jview.exe* window appears as shown in Fig. G.45. Program input is entered in this window and program output is displayed in this window. Note that if we were debugging an applet, Internet Explorer would be displayed. Program execution halts for input and at breakpoints.

Figure G.46 shows the execution being halted by a breakpoint. Notice the arrow to the left of the **System.out.println** statement. This arrow indicates the next line of code to execute. The bottom portion of the window is divided into two parts—the *Variables* window on the left side with three tabs and the *Watch* window on the right side with three tabs. Note that the **Debug** menu has replaced the **Build** menu in Developer Studio.

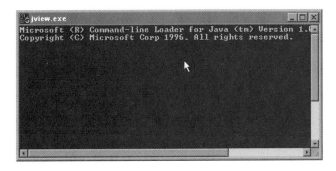

Fig. G.45 The **jview.exe** window.

Next line
of code to
execute

Debug menu

Variables
window

Watch window

Fig. G.46 The **Variables** window and **Watch** window.

Testing and Debugging Tip G.5

*Loops that iterate many times can be skipped by placing a breakpoint after the loop and clicking the **Go** button.*

The **Variables** window contains a list of the program's variables. Note that different variables can be viewed at different times, by clicking either the *Auto*, *Local*, or *this* tabs. The **Auto** tab displays the name and value of the variables or objects used in both the previous statement and the current statement. The **Local** tab displays the name and current value for all the local variables or objects in the current method's scope. The **this** tab displays data for the object to which the currently executing method belongs.

The variable names listed in the **Variables** window cannot be modified by the user. Often certain variables are monitored by the programmer during the debugging process—a process known as *setting a watch*. The **Watch** window allows the user to watch variables. When the value of a particular variable changes, the user can immediately see the new value in the **Watch** window. Variables can be typed directly into the **Watch** window or dragged from the **Variables** window and dropped into the **Watch** window. A variable can be deleted from the **Watch** window by highlighting the variable name and pressing the Delete key. Watch variables can be grouped by the programmer using the **Watch** window's tabs.

Figure G.47 shows a watch set for the variable **x**. Note that the *Debug toolbar* is displayed in Fig. G.47. The **Debug** toolbar contains a series of buttons that facilitate the debugging process. These buttons perform the same actions as the **Debug** menu items. Each button is labeled in Fig. G.48. Note: The **Debug** toolbar can be displayed at any time by positioning the mouse pointer over any toolbar, clicking the right mouse button, and selecting the **Debug** option in the popup menu.

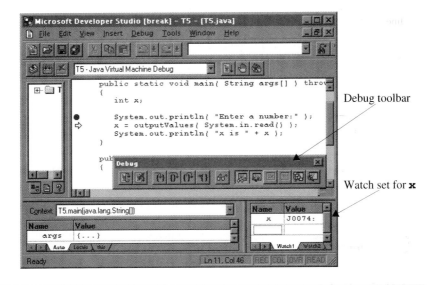

Debug toolbar

Watch set for **x**

Fig. G.47 Watch for the variable **x**.

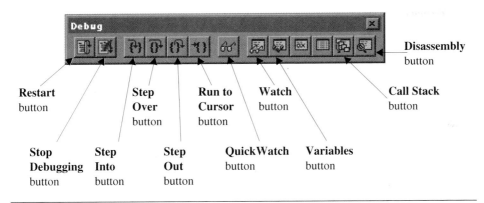

Fig. G.48 Debug toolbar buttons.

The value of a watch variable can be changed by the programmer for testing purposes. Click in the area displaying the current value in **Watch** window and type the new value. The new value appears in red to indicate that the value has changed since the program last stopped at a breakpoint.

The ***Restart*** button restarts execution of the program. Control stops at the first break-point or executable line requiring input. The ***Stop Debugging*** button ends the debugging session. The environment changes back to a state like Fig. G.31.

The ***Step Over*** button executes the next executable line of code. If the line of code contains a method call, the method is not entered (*stepped into*), rather it is executed in its entirety. The ***Step Into*** button allows methods to be stepped into—such that the user can confirm the proper execution for the method. The *Step Out* button allows the user to *step out* of the current method and return control back to the line of the method call. Click the *Run to Cursor* button to execute all code up to the line where the cursor resides.

Testing and Debugging Tip G.6

The debugger allows the user to "step into" Java API methods.

Testing and Debugging Tip G.7

Loops that iterate many times can be skipped by placing the cursor after the loop and clicking the ***Run to Cursor*** *button.*

The *QuickWatch* button displays the *QuickWatch* dialog that is useful for monitoring expressions and variable values. We discuss using the **QuickWatch** dialog in more detail shortly. The *Variable* button displays the **Variable** window. The *Watch* button displays the **Watch** window.

The *Call Stack* button displays a window containing the program's method *call stack*. A method call stack is a list of the methods that were called to get to the current line in the program.

The *Disassembler* button displays the disassembled program code. Analyzing a program that has been disassembled is a complex process and is likely to be used by only the most advanced users of Visual J++. We do not discuss the **Disassembler** button in this appendix.

Select the **Debug** menu's *Step Over* menu item (or click the **Step Over** button) to execute the current instruction and advance the yellow arrow to the next executable line (Fig. G.47) in the program. This process allows the user to execute the program on a line-by-line basis and follow the execution of the program.

Methods can be "stepped into" by selecting the **Debug** menu's *Step Into* menu item or by clicking the **Step Into** button (Fig. G.48). Note the yellow arrow must point to a line of code containing a method call as in Fig. G.47. The results of the "step into" operation are shown in Fig. G.49. Methods that can be stepped into include programmer-defined methods and Java API methods.

Methods can be "stepped out" of by selecting the **Debug** menu item *Step Out*. Control is returned to the calling method.

Selecting the **Debug** menu's **QuickWatch** menu item (or clicking the **QuickWatch** button) displays the **QuickWatch** dialog as shown in Fig. G.50. The **QuickWatch** dialog is used to get a "snap shot" of one or more variable values. The variable name or expression is entered into the *Expression* textfield and the Return key pressed. Note that the *Recalculate* button can be clicked instead of pressing the Return key. If the user wants to maintain a longer watch, the *Add Watch* button is clicked to add the variable to the **Watch** window. Once the **QuickWatch** dialog is dismissed, variables in the dialog are not preserved. The next time the **QuickWatch** dialog is displayed, both the *name* and *value* fields are empty.

If you close a project and reopen it, notice that the breakpoints you set during the debugging session are still there. Breakpoints are persistent. You can gather information about breakpoints by accessing the **Edit** menu's *Breakpoints* menu item. When selected, the **Breakpoints** menu item displays the *Breakpoints* dialog (Fig. G.51).

Fig. G.49 Stepping into a method.

Fig. G.50 **QuickWatch** dialog.

The **Breakpoints** dialog displays all the breakpoints currently set for the program. A checkbox appears next to each breakpoint. If the breakpoint is active, the checkbox contains a check. If the breakpoint is disabled, the checkbox is empty. Clicking the checkbox allows the user to toggle the breakpoint. Additional breakpoints can be added by entering the desired line number into the ***Break at*** text field. Figure G.52 shows a new breakpoint set for line 10. To specify an exact line number for a breakpoint, type the number preceded by a period in the **Break at** textfield.

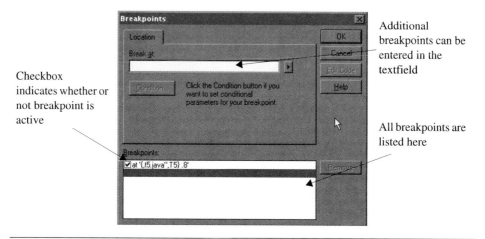

Additional breakpoints can be entered in the textfield

Checkbox indicates whether or not breakpoint is active

All breakpoints are listed here

Fig. G.51   Breakpoints dialog.

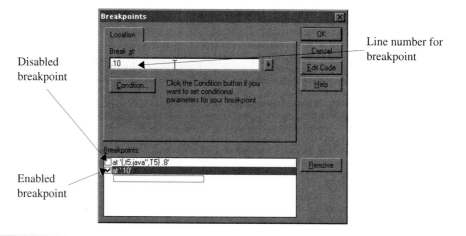

Line number for breakpoint

Disabled breakpoint

Enabled breakpoint

Fig. G.52   Breakpoints dialog with a disabled breakpoint.

Figure G.53 shows the debugging environment with two breakpoints—one active and one disabled. Notice that the disabled breakpoint is still visible but it appears as a hollow dot. To make the breakpoint active, click the empty checkbox in the **Breakpoints** dialog.

Testing and Debugging Tip G.8

Disabled breakpoints allow the programmer to maintain breakpoints in key locations in the program so they can be used again when they are needed. Disabled breakpoints are always visible.

Testing and Debugging Tip G.9

When using the debugger, placing the mouse pointer over a variable name displays the variable's value.

Disabled breakpoint

Active breakpoint

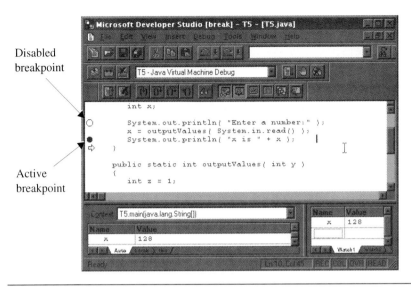

Fig. G.53 Debugging environment with a disabled breakpoint.

Testing and Debugging Tip G.10

*When using the debugger to trace through a program, certain problems such as infinite loops can arise. These problems can usually be interrupted by selecting **Break** from the **Debug** menu.*

When you have finished your debugging session, select ***Stop Debugging*** from the **Debug** menu. The environment changes back to the pre-debugging setup. You should refer to the on-line documentation for more details on using the debugger.

G.9 Using the Dialog Editor and the Java Resource Wizard to Design a Graphical User Interface (GUI)

Note: You should be familiar with the GUI components discussed in Chapter 10 and Chapter 11 before proceeding with this section.

Microsoft Developer Studio provides the *dialog editor* and the *Java Resource Wizard* to enable programmers to design GUIs that can be used with any applet or application. In this section, we show how to use the dialog editor and Resource Wizard to design the user interface for the applet **Comparison** that reads two integers from the user, compares the integers and displays whether or not the numbers are equal.

Figure G.54 contains the final program and a sample execution. We are showing the results first so you have an idea of what to expect from the steps you will perform to create a program with a graphical user interface. The file **Comparison.java** was constructed with the Applet Wizard and modified to suit our needs for this program. The file **InterfaceComponents.java** was generated by the Java Resource Wizard. Another file, **DialogLayout.java**, was also produced by the Java Resource Wizard. We did not show it here because we do not need to know the contents of the code in this file.

```
1    // Comparison.java
2    import java.applet.*;
3    import java.awt.*;
4    import InterfaceComponents;
5
6    public class Comparison extends Applet
7    {
8        private InterfaceComponents gui;
9
10       public String getAppletInfo()
11       {
12           return "Name: Comparison\r\n" +
13                  "Author: Paul Deitel\r\n" +
14                  "Created with Microsoft Visual J++ Version 1.0";
15       }
16
17       public void init()
18       {
19           gui = new InterfaceComponents( this );
20           gui.CreateControls();
21       }
22
23       public boolean action( Event e, Object o )
24       {
25           int num1 = Integer.parseInt( gui.IDC_EDIT1.getText() );
26           int num2 = Integer.parseInt( gui.IDC_EDIT2.getText() );
27
28           if ( num1 == num2 )
29               showStatus( num1 + " is equal to " + num2 );
30           else
31               showStatus( num1 + " is not equal to " + num2 );
32
33           return true;
34       }
35   }


36   //-------------------------------------------------------------
37   // InterfaceComponents.java:
38   //      Implementation of "control creator"
39   //      class InterfaceComponents
40   //-------------------------------------------------------------
41   import java.awt.*;
42   import DialogLayout;
43
44   public class InterfaceComponents
45   {
46       Container    m_Parent       = null;
47       boolean      m_fInitialized = false;
48       DialogLayout m_Layout;
```

Fig. G.54 The comparison applet containing a GUI designed with the dialog editor (Part 1 of 4).

```
49
50          // Control definitions
51          //------------------------------------------------------------
52          Label          IDC_STATIC1;
53          Label          IDC_STATIC2;
54          TextField      IDC_EDIT1;
55          TextField      IDC_EDIT2;
56
57
58          // Constructor
59          //------------------------------------------------------------
60          public InterfaceComponents (Container parent)
61          {
62              m_Parent = parent;
63          }
64
65          // Initialization.
66          //------------------------------------------------------------
67          public boolean CreateControls()
68          {
69              // CreateControls should be called only once
70              //--------------------------------------------------------
71              if (m_fInitialized || m_Parent == null)
72                  return false;
73
74              // m_Parent must be extended from the Container class
75              //--------------------------------------------------------
76              if (!(m_Parent instanceof Container))
77                  return false;
78
79              // Since a given font may not be supported across all
80              // platforms, it is safe to modify only the size of the
81              // font, not the typeface.
82              //--------------------------------------------------------
83              Font OldFnt = m_Parent.getFont();
84              if (OldFnt != null)
85              {
86                  Font NewFnt = new Font(OldFnt.getName(),
87                               OldFnt.getStyle(), 8);
88
89                  m_Parent.setFont(NewFnt);
90              }
91
92              // All position and sizes are in dialog logical units,
93              // so we use a DialogLayout as our layout manager.
94              //--------------------------------------------------------
95              m_Layout = new DialogLayout(m_Parent, 186, 95);
96              m_Parent.setLayout(m_Layout);
97              m_Parent.addNotify();
98
```

Fig. G.54 The comparison applet containing a GUI designed with the dialog editor (Part 2 of 4).

```
99              Dimension size    = m_Layout.getDialogSize();
100             Insets     insets = m_Parent.insets();
101
102             m_Parent.resize(
103                     insets.left + size.width  + insets.right,
104                     insets.top  + size.height + insets.bottom);
105
106             // Control creation
107             //-----------------------------------------------------
108             IDC_STATIC1 = new Label ("Enter an integer", Label.LEFT);
109             m_Parent.add(IDC_STATIC1);
110             m_Layout.setShape(IDC_STATIC1, 58, 10, 51, 8);
111
112             IDC_STATIC2 =
113                new Label ("Enter an integer and press Enter",
114                   Label.LEFT);
115             m_Parent.add(IDC_STATIC2);
116             m_Layout.setShape(IDC_STATIC2, 7, 25, 102, 8);
117
118             IDC_EDIT1 = new TextField ("");
119             m_Parent.add(IDC_EDIT1);
120             m_Layout.setShape(IDC_EDIT1, 115, 7, 40, 14);
121
122             IDC_EDIT2 = new TextField ("");
123             m_Parent.add(IDC_EDIT2);
124             m_Layout.setShape(IDC_EDIT2, 115, 22, 40, 14);
125
126             m_fInitialized = true;
127             return true;
128          }
129       }
```

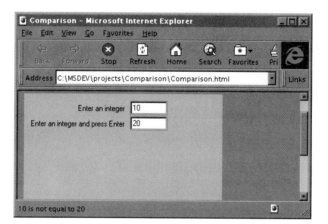

Fig. G.54 The comparison applet containing a GUI designed with the dialog editor (Part 3 of 4).

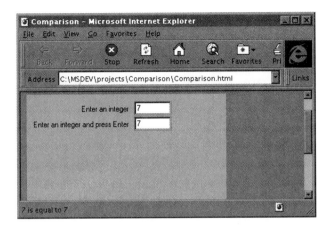

Fig. G.54 The comparison applet containing a GUI designed with the dialog editor (Part 4 of 4).

There are several steps required to create a GUI. The resulting class definition produced by the Java Resource Wizard is reusable with any applet or application. The first step is to create the applet or application. For the purposes of our demo, we create a simple applet using the Applet Wizard. To create the **Comparison** applet for this example, perform the following steps:

1. Select **New...** from the **File** menu.

2. Select **Project Workspace** and click **OK**.

3. In the **New Project Workspace** dialog, select the **Java Applet Wizard** option in the **Type** box and enter the name **Comparison** in the **Name** textfield. Click the **Create...** button to create the applet.

4. In Step 1 of the **Applet Wizard** dialog, select the **No, thank you** option for source file comments, then click **Next >**.

5. In Step 2 of the **Applet Wizard** dialog, click **Next >**.

6. In Step 3 of the **Applet Wizard** dialog, select the **No, thank you** option for multithreading, then click **Finish**. The **New Project Information** dialog appears. This dialog contains information about the Java applet that is about to be created. Click **OK** to dismiss this dialog.

7. Open the source file for **Comparison.java** and delete the following methods: **Comparison**, **paint**, **destroy**, **start** and **stop**. These methods are not used in this applet.

8. Position the cursor at the top of the file and type the comment:

    ```
    // Comparison.java
    ```

9. Delete the comments and the code that were supplied by the Applet Wizard in the **init** method.

Once you have the basic applet in place, the next step is to create a *resource template file* (file names end in the **.rct** extension). Resource template files contain the graphical user interface designed by the programmer in a format that can be translated into Java using the **Java Resource Wizard**. To create a resource template file for the **Comparison** applet, perform the following steps:

1. Select **New...** from the **File** menu.

2. Select **Resource Template** and click **OK**. A window entitled **Templ1** appears.

3. Select **Resource...** from the **Insert** menu. The **Insert Resource** dialog appears.

4. In the **Insert Resource** dialog, select **Dialog** and click **OK**. This opens the *dialog editor* (Fig. G.55). In the dialog editor, it appears that you are editing a window. However, you are actually creating a generic GUI that can be attached to any Java GUI container (i.e., an **Applet**, a **Frame**, a **Dialog**, or a **Panel** in the Java abstract windowing toolkit).

5. Click in the area containing the **OK** and **Cancel** buttons and press the **Alt + Enter** key combination. This displays the *property page* for the GUI.

6. In the **ID** field of the property page (where IDD_DIALOG1 is currently displayed), type the name **InterfaceComponents** (Fig. G.56). This is the name of the class in which your GUI components are created.

7. Remove the **OK** button by clicking on it in the dialog editor window and pressing the Delete key.

8. Remove the **Cancel** button by clicking on it in the dialog editor window and pressing the Delete key.

Fig. G.55 The dialog editor window.

Fig. G.56 The property page for dialog **InterfaceComponents**.

9. Add two **Label** objects and two **TextField** objects to the dialog. Figure G.57 shows the icons for the **Label** and **TextField** objects in the *Controls toolbar*. To add a **Label** to the dialog, click on the **Label** icon in the **Controls toolbar** and click on the dialog where you would like the component to appear (you may also click on the **Label** icon and drag it from the **Controls toolbar** onto the dialog editor). To add a **TextField** to the dialog, click on the **TextField** icon in the **Controls toolbar** and click in the dialog where you would like the component to appear.

10. Double click on the top **Label** and type "**Enter an integer**" in the **Caption** field of the property page.

11. Double click on the bottom **Label** and type "**Enter an integer and press Enter**" in the **Caption** field of the property page.

12. The GUI components should be arranged as shown in Fig. G.58. You can use the options in the **Layout** menu to help align the components. For example, to align both **Label**s at their right sides (i.e., right justify the **Label**s), hold the Shift key and click on each **Label**. From the **Layout** menu, position the mouse over **Align Controls** and select **Right** from the popup menu.

Fig. G.57 The **TextField** and **Label** components in the **Controls** toolbar.

Fig. G.58 Component layout for the **Comparison** applet.

13. When you are done aligning your components, select **Save** from the **File** menu. This opens the **Save As** dialog.

14. From the **Save in** drop-down list, change to the directory in which your applet is stored.

15. In the **File name** field, type **InterfaceComponents.rct** and click the **Save** button. This resource template file is used by the **Java Resource Wizard** to write the Java files that implement the GUI.

At this point, your resource template file is ready to be translated into Java. The **Java Resource Wizard** performs this step for you. To use the **Java Resource Wizard**, perform the following steps:

1. Select **Java Resource Wizard...** from the **Tools** menu.

2. In Step 1 of the **Java Resource Wizard**, click the **Browse** button, select your **InterfaceComponents.rct** file and click the **Open** button.

3. Click the **Finish** button. In the dialog that lists the created files, click **OK**.

You now have the file **InterfaceComponents.java** that contains the class definition for **InterfaceComponents**. This class is used to create the GUI components and attach them to your applet. There is also a separate file called **DialogLayout.java**. The class **DialogLayout** helps lay out the GUI components on the applet (or other Java container).

The next step is to use the **InterfaceComponents** class created by **Java Resource Wizard** to attach your GUI to the applet. The following steps enable you to use your new GUI class:

1. First, add the new Java files into our project. From the **Insert** menu, select **Files into Project...** to open the **Insert Files into Project** dialog. Notice that there are now three Java files—your **Comparison.java** file and the two new files produced by the **Java Resource Wizard** (**DialogLayout.java** and **InterfaceComponents.java**).

2. Hold the Shift key and click on the files **DialogLayout.java** and **Inter-faceComponents.java**, then click the **Add** button.

3. Next, we must add code to the applet that uses the **InterfaceComponents** class. From the **Window** menu, select **Comparison.java** to bring the window containing your program into the foreground.

4. Now import the **InterfaceComponents** class into your applet. Type the statement:

```
import InterfaceComponents;
```

after the **import** statements that were added by the Applet Wizard.

5. Declare an instance of the **InterfaceComponents** class. After the opening curly brace of the **Comparison** class definition, add the declaration:

```
private InterfaceComponents gui;
```

This reference is used to access the individual components attached to the GUI.

6. In the **init** method, add the following statements:

```
gui = new InterfaceComponents( this );
gui.CreateControls();
```

These statements attach the GUI to the applet. The first statement creates the **In-terfaceComponents** object and passes a reference to the **Comparison** applet into the constructor. This indicates to class **InterfaceComponents** that the GUI components should be attached to the applet. The second statement causes the **InterfaceComponents** object to create the GUI components and attach them to the applet.

Your GUI has now been attached to the applet. To prove that the GUI is attached to the applet properly, build and execute the applet.

Next we add the processing capabilities for the applet. Remember that we are going to input two integers from the user, compare the values and display whether or not they are equal in the status bar of the browser. Add the following method definition to the applet:

```
1   public boolean action( Event e, Object o )
2   {
3       int num1 = Integer.parseInt( gui.IDC_EDIT1.getText() );
4       int num2 = Integer.parseInt( gui.IDC_EDIT2.getText() );
5
6       if ( num1 == num2 )
7           showStatus( num1 + " is equal to " + num2 );
8       else
9           showStatus( num1 + " is not equal to " + num2 );
10
11      return true;
12  }
```

In the preceding **action** method, we read the **String** values from the **Text-Fields gui.IDC_EDIT1** and **gui.IDC_EDIT2** and convert the **String**s to **int** values. These values are compared for equality in the **if/else** structure and a **show-Status** method is called to display the results in the status bar area of the browser. Note that the names of the **TextField**s were assigned by the dialog editor. You can see the names of all your GUI components by opening the **InterfaceComponents.java** file created by the **Java Resource Wizard** or by double-clicking the individual component in the dialog editor and displaying the property page for the component.

To test the applet's functionality, build and execute the applet. When the GUI appears in the browser, enter an integer in the first **TextField**, then enter an integer in the second **TextField** and press Enter. The result appears in the status bar area at the bottom-left corner of the browser window.

G.10 Resources and Demos

[Note: This section was written by Abbey Deitel, a recent graduate of the Industrial Management program at Carnegie Mellon University.] There is a bounty of Java information on the World Wide Web. Many people are experimenting with Java and sharing their thoughts, discoveries, ideas and source code with each other via the Internet. If you would like to recommend other sites, please send us email at

   deitel@deitel.com

and we will put links to the sites you suggest on our Web site

   http://www.prenhall.com/deitel

The following World Wide Web sites provide information regarding Visual J++, ActiveX, other Microsoft technologies and development tools, and Java.

http://www.microsoft.com/visualj/

The best place to begin searching for Visual J++ information is the site where the platform was developed. Microsoft's Visual J++ site is one of the most comprehensive sites I have found on Visual J++. You can learn more about Visual J++, check out some great links, gather answers to your questions from the FAQ (frequently asked questions) sheet, find useful product and technical information, or get help from Microsoft online. The following is a walk-through of the Microsoft Visual J++ site.

The *Start Page* provides a brief background on Visual J++ and a section titled "What's New," which lists the latest Visual J++ related products and events.

The *Starter Information* describes how you can use Visual J++ to create more powerful Java™ programs. Organized in bullet-list form, you can quickly browse the list to discover the advantages of using Visual J++. This is also where you can find the system requirements for this platform.

What's New in Visual J++ has detailed information on the latest Visual J++ products.

If you are already using Microsoft's Visual J++ products, the *Product Enhancements* page has the latest product updates which can be downloaded.

Do your research on Microsoft's Visual J++ by visiting *The Library*. Topics in The Library include the following: Introduction to Java Development, Product Feature Overview, Data Sheets, Companion Products, and Technical Documentation including Java™ and COM, Remote Data Objects (RDO), and Data Access Objects (DAO).

Get the *FAQs* (frequently asked questions) and all the answers. Microsoft has an extensive list of answers to frequently asked questions about Visual J++.

If you are having trouble with Visual J++ or have a question for the experts, go to the *Troubleshooting* section. This section links you to the Microsoft Visual J++ Support Online.

The latest Visual J++ news can be found in the *Press* section. Press releases and articles are listed by date and topic.

Finally, for related links, check out *Cool Links*. You can find a few links under each of the following topics: Training for Java and Visual J++™, Magazines and Publications, Java Applets, Cool Tools, and Internet Explorer.

http://www.microsoft.com/mind/1296/visualjava/visualj.htm

Visit this site if you want to begin using Microsoft's Visual J++. This site provides all of the information you need to install the product and get started.

http://www-c.gamelan.com/index.shtml

The Gamelan web site is one of the best Java resources. This site has extensive links to information, news, FAQs, and the coolest Java sites on the World Wide Web. One of the topics on this site, titled "related technologies," has information on ActiveX and Javascript.

http://www-personal.engin.umich.edu/~premise/java/index.html

If you are looking for an extensive list of Java related links, this site is the place to visit. You can find news, product specifications and information, books, tutorials, FAQs, and more.

http://www.davecentral.com/javaanim.html

Visit this site to download Java animation editors, databases, applet distribution systems, development environments, GUI designers, and language translators.

http://www.javaworld.com/

The Java World site has the latest Java news and information. News related to Microsoft's Visual J++ can also be found at this site.

http://www.ncompasslabs.com/

Ncompass Labs has created a site dedicated to ActiveX and related products. This is a great resource for product information.

http://www.oogie.com/leweb/cutedge.html

This site by the Web Developer provides an extensive number of links to Java related sites including Microsoft Visual J++ and Symantec Visual Café.

http://www.microsoft.com/kb/softlib/

This is Microsoft's Online technical support site. You can also download software and sample files related to Visual J++ and other Microsoft products.

http://www.clubie.com/

ClubIE is one of the hot links on Microsoft's Visual J++ site. This is a great resource for Visual J++ technical information, free software, and lists of related sites.

http://www.pla-net.net/~jwapienn/scripts.html

This site has free ActiveX and Java code.

http://www.activex.com/
   Cnet devotes this site to ActiveX. You can connect to the latest ActiveX news and information.

http://www.activex.com/vb5.html
   This site provides news and information about VB 5.0 Control Creation Edition which creates ActiveX controls.

http://www.activex.com/library/248.html
   Visual Basic 5.0 Control Creation Edition downloadable software.

http://www.microsoft.com/icp/us/icpmain/icpfaq.htm
   Microsoft's ActiveX FAQ site.

http://www.active-x.com/
   The ActiveX Resource Center. This site requires Microsoft Internet Explorer 3.0.

http://mach1.threedgraphics.com/compadre/comp_live.html
   This site is an example of how you can use Microsoft's PowerPoint and ActiveX to create multimedia presentations on the web.

http://www.folkarts.com/journals/activex/
   The ActiveX Journal is an excellent on-line source of ActiveX news and information.

http://www.dcs.gla.ac.uk/~greigrg/Java/Jscript/toc.html
   This is a great resource for Jscript information. The site is broken down into Javascript basics, language concepts and references.

http://www.mihelson.com/mihels2.html
   This is one of the best resources I have found for Java and Javascript information. There are games, cool sites, a dictionary, and free listings for related sites. It also has the capability to conduct searches using multiple search engines simultaneously.

http://www.tripnet.se/home/brodd/calct2.html
   This site uses Javascript for two examples. The first computes the cost of an automobile based on a few variables. The second example has a list of colors. Simply point the mouse at any color and the background color changes.

http://www.javacats.com/US/search/dir108.html
   This is an extensive resource for Javascript information and examples. You can find examples of Javascript in multimedia, graphics, games, related sites and games.

http://www.datamation.com/PlugIn/issues/1996/may15/
      DCOMDistributesObjectsButOnlyasfarasMicrosoft9.html
   This site is a developing resource for DCOM information.

http://www.dbms.mfi.com/9611d14.html
   This is one of the most informative resources I found. It describes the relationship between DBMS, OLE, ActiveX, and DCOM.

http://www.neca.com/~vmis/durl.htm
   If you are looking for information on DCOM, this site provides an extensive list of relevant links.

http://www.sigs.com/graphics/sigsnav.map?46,18
   This SIGS Publications home page provides information on upcoming conferences, books and magazines.

`http://www.sigs.com/publications/docs/jro/guide/9611/`
`guide9611.toc.html`
> This SIGS Publications resource is an alphabetized list of over 800 companies that provide Java related services and products. Each listing has an email address and a description of services provided.

`http://www.wcmh.com/lantimes/96may/605b001d.html`
> LAN Times describes Microsoft's Distributed Component Object Model (DCOM) in an article titled "DCOM Could Ease OLE Apps Networking."

`http://www.microsoft.com/intdev/sdk/docs/com/comintro.htm`
> This is an excellent COM resource provided by Microsoft and Digital Equipment Corporation. You can download the COM specifications in a few different formats.

`http://www.microsoft.com/intdev/`
> This Microsoft site has great information on ActiveX controls and links to ActiveX related sites.

`http://www.microsoft.com/intdev/controls/controls-f.htm`
> Microsoft devotes this page to ActiveX controls. You can find a definition of ActiveX controls, examples from Microsoft and other companies, instructions on how to write your own controls, and a list of FAQs.

Terminology

`\windows\java\trustlib` path
`.DLL` file
`.GIF` file
`.HTML` file
`.JAVA` file
`.JPEG` file
`.RCT` file
$(FileDir)
$(FileName)
ActiveX control
Add button
Add Tools dialog
Add Watch button in debugger
Advanced tab
animation images
API
applet
Applet Wizard
application
Application Programming Interface (API)
Arguments textfield
Auto tab
Background area
`Beep` method

Beeper coclass
Beeper 1.0 Type Library
binary level specification
breakpoint
Breakpoints menu item
Breakpoints dialog
Build button
build
Build menu
Call Stack button in debugger
Category box
checkbox
class
ClassView pane
clicking
coclass
color palette
Colors area
`com.ms.com.ComException`
Command textfield
Compile button
compiler
compiler error
compiler warning

Component Object Model (COM)
Controls toolbar
cross-platform component
Customize dialog
debugger
debugger toolbar
default animation images
default project
dialog editor
disabled
Disassembly button in debugger
Dynamic Link Library (DLL)
editor
Enable Java logging checkbox
explanatory comments
Execute menu item in **Build** menu
Exit menu item
File menu
Files into Project menu item
FileView pane
focus
Font area
Foreground area
Format tab
function
Functions list box
Functions Prototype list box
`getAppletInfo` method
`getParameterInfo` method
GIF (Graphics Interchange Format)
HTML (Hypertext Markup Language)
`IBeeper` interface
image editor
`import` statement
Information For Running Class dialog
InfoView pane
Initial Directory textfield
Insert Files into Project dialog
Insert menu
interface
Insert Resource dialog
Internet Explorer
ITypeLib dialog
Java
Java Resource Wizard
Java source file
Java Type Library Wizard
Java Type Library Wizard dialog

Java Type Wizard
Java Type Wizard pane
Java Virtual Machine (JVM)
`javalog.txt`
JPEG (Joint Photographic Experts Group)
Jview tab
JView window
left mouse button
Local tab
Menu text textfield
method
Microsoft Developer Studio
Name field
Netscape Navigator
New dialog
New menu item of **File** menu
New Project Information dialog
New Project Workspace dialog
New Source File button
Next> button
OCX control (**ActiveX** control)
OK button
Object Linking and Embedding (OLE)
OLE control
OLE Object View menu item
OLE2 Object View (Win32) dialog
Options dialog
Options menu item
Output window
package
project
Project Workspace item in **New** dialog
property page
QuickWatch button in debugger
QuickWatch dialog
radio button
Redirect to Output Window checkbox
registered DLL
resource template file
Resource Wizard
Run to Cursor button in debugger
Save As dialog
Save button
Save in textfield
Save menu item
setting a watch
Size area
Source window

Stand-alone interpreter radio button
Step Into button in debugger
Step Out button in debugger
Step Over button in debugger
syntax color highlighting
syntax error
this tab
title bar of a window
TODO comments
tool bar
tool tip
toolbox
Tools menu

Tools tab
tree-view format
Typeinfo combo box
type library
unregistered DLL
Value field
Variables window in debugger
View menu
Visual J++
visual programming
Watch window in debugger
Watch window tab
World Wide Web (WWW) browser

Good Programming Practice

G.1   Change the access modifier of instance or class variables generated by the Applet Wizard to either **private** or **protected** when the default friendly is not required.

Performance Tip

G.1   COM objects consist of native windows executable code that executes much faster than interpreted bytecode classes.

Portability Tip

G.1   COM is language independent, compiler independent, and location independent.

Software Engineering Observations

G.1   Instance and class variables generated by the Applet Wizard are friendly by default.

G.2   Calling a local or remote COM object is not allowed for applets unless the COM object has a secure digital signature—i.e., the COM object came from a trusted source.

Testing and Debugging Tips

G.1   Microsoft Developers Studio's syntax color highlighting helps the programmer avoid using keywords accidentally as variable names.

G.2   If your program contains compiler errors, double click on an error message in the output window to point out the offending line of code. Visual J++ places a blue arrow next to the line of code in the source file.

G.3   Forgetting to check the **Enable Java logging** checkbox results in the file `javalog.txt` not being created by Internet Explorer.

G.4   Add `javalog.txt` to your project. This allows you to view information from Visual J++ as it is written to the file. The file can be added by using the **Insert** menu's **Insert Files into Project** dialog.

G.5   Loops that iterate many times can be skipped by placing a breakpoint after the loop and clicking the **Go** button.

G.6   The debugger allows the user to "step into" Java API methods.

G.7   Loops that iterate many times can be skipped by placing the cursor after the loop and clicking the **Run to Cursor** button.

G.8   Disabled breakpoints allow the programmer to maintain breakpoints in key locations in the program so they can be used again when they are needed. Disabled breakpoints are always visible.

G.9   When using the debugger, placing the mouse pointer over a variable name displays the variable's value.

G.10   When using the debugger to trace through a program, certain problems such as infinite loops can arise. These problems can usually be interrupted by selecting **Break** from the **Debug** menu.

H

CD-ROM Installation Guide

H.1 Installing the Contents of the CD-ROM

As soon as you put the CD in your drive, Microsoft Visual J++ will appear on your screen, offering the opportunity to install it. Follow the prompts within the Visual J++ software to install it on your hard drive.

You can install the source code onto your hard drive so that you can manipulate and compile it. To install the source code so that it will work properly you should use the setup programs provided. The code is split into three sections so that it is not necessary to install it all at once.

To install the examples from Chapters 1-6 run the setup.exe program in d:\code\install1.

To install the examples from Chapters 7-11 run setup.exe in d:\code\install2.

To install the examples from Chapters 12-18 run setup.exe in d:\code\install3.

If your CD-ROM is not drive D, substitute the appropriate drive letter in the commands above.

H.2 Installing and Running Microsoft Visual J++

Microsoft Visual J++ can be installed at any time by following the installation steps included on the CD-ROM. Once you have installed it, you can launch the program as you would any other application in Windows® 95 or Windows NT®.

Once you are running Visual J++, refer to the description in Appendix G to compile and run programs with it.

All code examples from this book are included in the 'CODE' directory of the CD-ROM. They are organized by chapter and figure number, and may be compiled using the Visual J++ software as directed in Appendix G.

H.3 Using the Hot Links on the CD-ROM

The CD-ROM also contains links to the applets from this book, and to all the Internet sites mentioned in Appendices A, B, and G.

To take advantage of these features, launch your Internet browser (Microsoft Internet Explorer is included on this CD) and open the file 'INDEX.HTML' in the 'CODE' directory. You can then view the applets in action and connect to a variety of Internet links for Java and Visual J++.

Bibliography

(Ai96)   Aitken, G., "Moving from C++ to Java," *Dr. Dobb's Journal,* March 1996, pp. 52–56.

(An96)   Anuff, E., *Java Source Book,* New York, NY: John Wiley & Sons, Inc., 1996.

(Ar96)   Arnold, K., and J. Gosling, *The Java Programming Language,* Reading, MA: Addison-Wesley Publishing Company, 1996.

(Ba96)   Bandarpalle, R., and R. Ratnakar, "Distributed Business Applications Using Java: An Implementation Framework," *Java Report,* July/August, 1996. pp. 46–50, 64.

(Be96)   Berg, C., "How Do I Send e-mail from a Java Applet?" *Dr. Dobb's Journal,* August 1996, pp. 111–113.

(Bo96)   Boone, B., "Multitasking in Java," *Java Report,* May/June 1996, pp. 27–33.

(Cg96)   Cargill, T., "An Overview of Java for C++ Programmers," *C++ Report,* February 1996, pp. 46–50.

(Ca96)   Caron, J., "Java: A Status Report," *Web Techniques,* June 1996, pp. 30–37.

(Ch96)   Chaffee, A. D., "Enhancing the Web," *Java Report,* March/April 1996, pp. 24–26.

(Co96)   Cornell, G., and C. S. Horstmann, *Core Java,* The SunSoft Press, Upper Saddle River, NJ: Prentice Hall, 1996.

(Dc96)   Daconta, M. C., *Java for C/C++ Programmers,* New York, NY: John Wiley & Sons, Inc., 1996.

(Da96)   Danesh, A., *Teach Yourself JavaScript in a Week,* Indianapolis, IN: Sams.net Publishing, 1996.

(De95)   December, J., *Presenting Java,* Indianapolis, IN: Sams.net Publishing, 1996.

(Fl96)   Flanagan, D., Java *in a Nutshell,* Sebastopol, CA: O'Reilly & Associates, Inc., 1996.

(Fr96)   Freeman, A., and D. Ince, *Active Java,* Reading, MA: Addison-Wesley Publishing Company, 1996.

(Fr96a)   Freeman, A., and D. Ince, "The java.net Library," *Java Report,* May/June 1996, pp. 35–41.

(Fi96)   Fitzgerald, P., "Becoming a JavaScript Author," *Java Report,* May/June 1996, pp. 55–56.

(Fl96)   Flynn, J., and B. Clarke, "The World Wakes up to Java!" *Computer Technology Review,* 1996, pp. 33–37.

(Fl96a)   Flynn J., and B. Clarke, "How Java Makes Network-Centric Computing REAL," *Datamation,* March 1, 1996, pp. 42–43.

(Ga96)   Gabler, C., "Java: Adding Interactivity in HTML Pages," *Web Techniques,* April 1996, pp. 57–61.

(Go96)   Goodman, D., *JavaScript Handbook,* Foster City, CA: IDG Books, 1996.

(Go96)   Gosling, J.; F. Yellin; and The Java Team, *The Java Application Programming Interface,* Volume 1: Core Packages, Reading, MA: Addison-Wesley Publishing Company, 1996.

(Gr96)   Greenbaum, J., "Java Fever!" *Software Magazine,* May 1996, pp. 36–44.

(Gl96)   Gulbransen, D., and K. Rawlings, *Creating Web Applets with Java,* Indianapolis, IN: Sams.net Publishing, 1996.

(Gu96)   Gurewich, N. and O. Gurewich, *Java Manual of Style,* Emeryville, CA: Ziff-Davis Press, 1996.

(Ha96)   Harms, D., et. al., *Web Site Programming with Java,* New York, NY: McGraw-Hill, Inc., 1996.

(Hy96)   Hayashi, A. M., "Reality Behind the Java Hype," Application Development Trends, February 1996, pp. 78–85.

(He96)   Hemrajani, A., "Examining Symantec's Cafe," *Dr. Dobb's Journal,* August 1996, pp. 78–82.

(Ho96)   Hof, R. D., and J. Verity, "Scott McNealy's Rising Sun," Cover Story, *Business Week,* January 22, 1996, pp. 66–73.

(Ja96)   Jackson, J. R., and A. L. McClellan, *Java by Example,* The SunSoft Press, Upper Saddle River, NJ: Prentice Hall, 1996.

(Jo96)   Johnston, S. J., and J. Swenson, "Microsoft Buys a Cup of Java," *Information Week,* April 29, 1996, pp. 14–16.

(Jv96)   Jovin, D., "Developing Database-Driven Applications in Java," *Java Report,* July/August, 1996. pp.53–56.

(Ko96)   Korzenowski, P., "Java: Cross-Platform OO Language for Distributed Development," *Application Development Trends: Advertising Supplement,* February 1996, pp. S-15–S-21.

(La96)   Lalani, S., and K. Jamsa, *Java Programmer's Library,* Las Vegas, NV: Jamsa Press, 1996.

(Le96)   Lemay, L., and C. L. Perkins, *Teach Yourself Java in 21 Days,* Indianapolis, IN: Sams.net Publishing, 1996.

(Le96a)   Lemay, L., and C. Perkins, "Yes, Java's Secure. Here's Why," *Datamation,* March 1, 1996, pp. 47–49.

(Lo96)   Lorenzo, J., "Exploring Java's Animator Applet," *Web Developer,* Spring 1996, pp. 9–10.

(Me96) Meese, P. D., "The Java Tutor: Creating Your Own First APP," *Java Report,* March/April 1996, pp. 37–46.

(Me96a) Meese, P. D., "The Java Tutor," *Java Report,* May/June 1996, pp. 43–48.

(Me96b) Meese, P. D., "Improving Marquees with Double Buffering," *Java Report,* July/August, 1996. pp. 35–39.

(Me96a) Meese, P. D., "The One Hour Java Applet," *Datamation,* March 1, 1996, pp. 51–61.

(My96) Meyer, M., "True, Online Multimedia," *Java Report,* July/August, 1996. pp. 58–59.

(Na96) Naughton, P., *The Java Handbook,* Berkeley, CA: Osborne-McGraw Hill, 1996.

(Ne96) Newman, A., et. al., *Using Java: Special Edition,* Indianapolis, IN: Que Corporation, 1996.

(Ni96) Niemeyer, P., and J. Peck, *Exploring Java,* Sebastopol, CA: O'Reilly & Associates, Inc., 1996.

(Oa96) Oaks, S., "How Do I Create My Own UI Component?" *Java Report,* March/April 1996, pp. 64, 63.

(Oa96a) Oaks, S., "Two Techniques for Handling Events," July/August, 1996. p. 80.

(Pr96) Perkins, C. L., "The Big Picture," *Java Report,* March/April 1996, pp. 47–53. 56.

(Pe96) Pew, J. A., *Instant Java,* The SunSoft Press, Upper Saddle River, NJ: Prentice Hall, 1996.

(Re96) Reynolds, M. C., "Java Programming from the Grounds Up," *Web Developer,* Spring1996, pp. 30–40.

(Ro96) Rodley, J., "Java Applets and Netscape," *Web Techniques,* April 1996, pp. 70–72.

(Sn96) Sams.net Publishing, *Java Unleashed,* Indianapolis, IN: Sams.net Publishing, 1996

(Sr96) Sarna, D. E., and G. J. Febish, "Java's Place in the Wide OLE World," *Datamation,* February 1, 1996, pp. 25–27.

(Sv96) Savetz, K. M., "Jiving with Javascript," *Web Developer,* May/June 1996, pp. 58–59.

(Sc96) Scotkin, J., "Three Tiers for Java," *Java Report,* May/June 1996, pp. 59–62.

(Sc96a) Scotkin, J., "Business Uses for Java," *Datamation,* March 1, 1996, pp. 40–41.

(Sc96b) Scotkin, J., "Java in the Corporate Environment," *Java Report,* March/April 1996, pp. 54–56.

(Sc96c) Scotkin, J., "Myths, Reality, and When to Use Java," July/August, 1996. pp.74–77.

(So96) Scott, A., "VRML and JavaScript," *Java Report,* July/August, 1996. pp. 41–45.

(Se96) Semich, B., and D. Fisco, "Java: Internet Toy or Enterprise Tool?" *Datamation,* March 1, 1996, pp. 28–37.

(Si96) Singleton, A., "Wired on the Web," *BYTE,* January 1996, p. 77–80.

(Su96) Sun Microsystems, Inc., *Introduction to Java Programming,* Course SL-230, Sun Educational Services SunService Division, Sun Microsystems, Inc., MS UMIL07–14, Part Number 802-6281-02, Revision B, March 1996.

(Su96a) Sun Microsystems, Inc., Java Application Programming, Course SL-270, Sun Educational Services SunService Division, Sun Microsystems, Inc., MS UMIL07–14, Part Number 802-6282-02, Revision B, March 1996.

(Te96)   Tessier, T., "Using JavaScript to Create Interactive Web Pages," *Dr. Dobb's Journal,* March 1996, pp. 84–96.

(Ti95)   Tillel, E., and M. Gaither, *60 Minute Guide to Java,* Foster City, CA: IDG Books, 1995.

(Tr96)   Tropeano, D., "Getting into OT," *Java Report,* March/April 1996, pp. 27–29, 46.

(Tr96a) Tropeano, D., "Class Design," *Java Report,* July/August, 1996. pp. 31–34.

(Ty96)   Tyma, P., "Tuning Java Performance," *Dr. Dobb's Journal,* April 1996, pp. 52, 55–57, 90, 92.

(Vd96)   Valdes, R., "Methods for Motion: Revisiting Animation on Web Pages," *Web Techniques,* June 1996, pp. 45–49.

(Vh96)   van Hoff, A.; S. Shaio; and O. Starbuck, *Hooked on Java,* Reading, MA: Addison-Wesley Publishing Company, 1996.

(Vh96a) van Hoff, A. S.; S. Shaio; and O. Starbuck, "What is this Thing Called Java?" *Datamation,* March 1, 1996, pp. 45–46.

(Vh96b) van Hoff, A., "Believing the Hype,' *Java Report,* March/April 1996, pp. 31–34.

(Vl96)   van der Linden, P., *Just Java,* The SunSoft Press, Upper Saddle River, NJ: Prentice Hall, 1996.

(Vn96)   Venditto, G., "Java: It's Hot, But Is It Ready to Serve?" *Internet World,* February 1996, pp. 78–80.

(Ve96)   Vermeulen, A., "An Asynchronous Design Pattern," *Dr. Dobb's Journal,* June 1996, pp. 42–44.

(Wl96)   Waldo, J., "Programming with Java," *UNIX Review,* May 1996, pp. 31–37.

(Wa96)   Walter, S. J., and A. Weiss, *The Complete Idiot's Guide to JavaScript,* Indianapolis, IN: Que Corporation, 1996.

(Wi96)   Wilson, A., "Porting Windows Applications to Java: Part I," *Web Techniques,* June 1996, pp. 39–43.

(Wo96)   Wong, H., "A Look at Layout Managers," *Java Report,* May/June 1996, pp. 49–51.

(Wo96a) Wong, H., "Writing Your Own Layout Managers," July/August, 1996. pp. 65–73.

Index

A

<= (relational less than or
equal to), 38–39, 116,
131, 134, 974

"abbreviated" assignment
operators, 91
abbreviating binary numbers
as octal numbers and
hexadecimal numbers,
980
abnormally terminating a program, 227
About dialog box, 599
About menu item, 599–600
abs method, 159
absolute path, 799, 801
absolute values, 159
abstract, 66
abstract class, 349, 721,
912, 921
abstract data type (ADT),
313–314
abstract data type **Time**, 276,
278
abstract method, 349,
352–353, 360, 374
AbstractMethodError,
649
abstract superclass, 349,
351–352, 354–355
abstract superclass
Shape, 350, 360
Abstract Windowing Toolkit
(AWT), 440, 649
Abstract Windowing Toolkit
Image Package, 167
Abstract Windowing Toolkit
Package, 167
Abstract Windowing Toolkit
Peer Package, 167
abstraction, 327, 991
accept, 824–825, 827–828,
840
accept or deny a connection,
819, 824

access modifier, 276
access to shared data by concurrent threads, 684
"accessibility heuristic", 259–
260
accessor method, 282, 290
accounts payable file, 754
accounts receivable file, 754,
759
accumulator register, 265–
266, 268
action, 3, 25, 6–8, 127, 141,
144
action, 29, 497, 512, 514,
560, 572, 578
action/decision model of programming, 67, 68
action event, 560, 600
action method, 31–33, 39,
124, 163, 495–497, 500–
501, 504, 507, 511, 513,
515, 641, 698
action-oriented, 991
action-oriented programming,
275
action symbol, 65
actions to be executed, 63
active content, 22
activeCount, 699
ActiveX beeper control,
1029–1030
ActiveX control, 1028–1029
ActiveX interface, 1030
Ada programming language,
14, 670
Ada Lovelace, 14
add, 269
add, 29, 40, 499, 512, 514
addImage, 723–725, 727,
733, 737
add instruction, 266
addItem method, 502–503,
512–515
addLayoutComponent,
622
add method, 32, 491–492,
494, 507, 517
addition, 7, 35, 36, 37
addition program, 29, 30

additional assignment operator **+=**, 90
additional text and examples,
6
addObserver, 929, 931
addPoint, 474
address, 275
"administrative" section of
the computer, 7
Advanced Graphical User
Interface Components,
18
advanced layout managers,
604
advanced string manipulation
exercises, 433
after method of **Date**, 928
aggregation, 280
Airline Reservation System,
255, 708, 758, 775
alarm sounded, 932
algebra, 38
algebraic expressions, 35, 44
algebraic notation, 35
algorithm, 63, 68, 74, 118,
126–127, 187
algorithm for binary tree operations, 886
algorithm for walking through
a maze, 264
algorithms course, 235
allGroups, 699
allocate number of elements
required by an array, 218
allThreadsCount, 699
Alpha, 712
alphabetizing, 385
ALU, 7, 8
American National Standards
Committee on Informa-
tion Processing (X3), 11
American National Standards
Institute, 314
Analog Clock exercise, 746
Analytical Engine, 14
anchor, 609, 612
"ANDing", 946
angry fish, 966
animate objects, 991

End-User License Agreement for Microsoft Software

MICROSOFT VISUAL J++, Publisher's Edition

IMPORTANT--READ CAREFULLY: This Microsoft End-User License Agreement ("EULA") is a legal agreement between you (either an individual or a single entity) and Microsoft Corporation for the Microsoft software product identified above and Microsoft Internet Explorer, which include computer software and associated media and printed materials, and may include "online" or electronic documentation (together, the "SOFTWARE PRODUCT" or "SOFTWARE"). By installing, copying, or otherwise using the SOFTWARE PRODUCT, you agree to be bound by the terms of this EULA. If you do not agree to the terms of this EULA, promptly return the unused SOFTWARE PRODUCT to the place from which you obtained it for a full refund.

SOFTWARE PRODUCT LICENSE

The SOFTWARE PRODUCT is protected by copyright laws and international copyright treaties, as well as other intellectual property laws and treaties. The SOFTWARE PRODUCT is licensed, not sold.

1. **GRANT OF LICENSE.** This EULA grants you the following rights:

    a. You may use one copy of the Microsoft Software Product identified above on a single computer. The SOFTWARE is in "use" on a computer when it is loaded into temporary memory (i.e., RAM) or installed into permanent memory (e.g., hard disk, CD-ROM, or other storage device) of that computer. However, installation on a network server for the sole purpose of internal distribution to one or more other computer(s) shall not constitute "use" for which a separate license is required, provided you have a separate license for each computer to which the SOFTWARE is distributed.

    b. You may only use copies of the Microsoft Internet Explorer software only in conjunction with a validly licensed copy of Microsoft operating system products (e.g., Windows® 95 or Windows NT®). You may make copies of the SOFTWARE PRODUCT for use on all computers for which you have licensed Microsoft operating system products.

c. Solely with respect to electronic documents included with the SOFTWARE, you may make an unlimited number of copies (either in hardcopy or electronic form), provided that such copies shall be used only for internal purposes and are not republished or distributed to any third party.

2. **UPGRADES.** If the SOFTWARE is an upgrade, whether from Microsoft or another supplier, you may use or transfer the SOFTWARE only in conjunction with upgraded product. If the SOFTWARE is an upgrade from a Microsoft product, you may now use that upgraded product only in accordance with this EULA.

3. **COPYRIGHT.** All title and copyrights in and to the SOFTWARE PRODUCT (including but not limited to any images, photographs, animations, video, audio, music, text, and "applets" incorporated into the SOFTWARE PRODUCT), the accompanying printed materials, and any copies of the SOFTWARE PRODUCT are owned by Microsoft or its suppliers. The SOFTWARE PRODUCT is protected by copyright laws and international treaty provisions. Therefore, you must treat the SOFTWARE PRODUCT like any other copyrighted material except that you may either (a) make one copy of the SOFTWARE PRODUCT solely for backup or archival purposes or (b) install the SOFTWARE PRODUCT on a single computer provided you keep the original solely for backup or archival purposes. You may not copy the printed materials accompanying the SOFTWARE PRODUCT.

4. **DESCRIPTION OF OTHER RIGHTS AND LIMITATIONS.**

    a. **Limitations on Reverse Engineering, Decompilation, and Disassembly.** You may not reverse engineer, decompile, or disassemble the SOFTWARE PRODUCT, except and only to the extent that such activity is expressly permitted by applicable law notwithstanding this limitation.

    b. **No Separation of Components.** The SOFTWARE PRODUCT is licensed as a single product and neither the software programs making up the SOFTWARE PRODUCT nor any UPDATE may be separated for use by more than one user at a time.

    c. **Rental.** You may not rent or lease the SOFTWARE PRODUCT.

    d. **Software Transfer.** You may permanently transfer all of your rights under this EULA, provided that you retain no copies, you transfer all of the SOFTWARE PRODUCT (including all component parts, the media and printed materials, any upgrades, this EULA, and, if applicable, the Certificate of Authenticity), and the recipient agrees to the terms of this EULA. If the SOFTWARE PRODUCT is an upgrade, any transfer must include all prior versions of the SOFTWARE PRODUCT. Notwithstanding the foregoing, you may permanently transfer all your rights under this EULA that pertain to the Microsoft Internet Explorer only in conjunction with a permanent transfer of your validly licensed copy of a Microsoft operating system product.

    e. **Termination.** Without prejudice to any other rights, Microsoft may terminate this EULA if you fail to comply with the terms and conditions of this EULA. In such event, you must destroy all copies of the SOFTWARE PRODUCT. In addition, your rights under this EULA that pertain to the Microsoft Internet Explorer software shall terminate upon termination of your Microsoft operating system product EULA

5. **REDISTRIBUTABLE COMPONENTS.**

    a. **Redistributable Files.** In addition to the license granted in Section 1, Microsoft grants you a nonexclusive, royalty-free right to reproduce and distribute the object code version of those portions of the SOFTWARE designated in the SOFTWARE as: (i) the files identified in the REDISTRB.WRI file located in the \MSDev\Redist subdirectory on the "Microsoft Visual J++ version 1.00" CD-ROM; and (ii) SAMPLE CODE (collectively, "REDISTRIBUTABLES"), <u>provided</u> you comply with Section 6.c (and Section 6.d if applicable).

b. **Redistribution Requirements.** If you redistribute the REDISTRIBUTABLES, you agree to: (i) distribute the REDISTRIBUTABLES in object code form only in conjunction with and as a part of your software application product which adds significant and primary functionality and which is designed, developed, and tested to operate in the Microsoft Windows and/or Windows NT environments; (ii) not use Microsoft's name, logo, or trademarks to market your software application product; (iii) include a valid copyright notice on your software product; (iv) indemnify, hold harmless, and defend Microsoft from and against any claims or lawsuits, including attorney's fees, that arise or result from the use or distribution of your software application product; and (v) not permit further distribution of the REDISTRIBUTABLES by your end user.Contact Microsoft for the applicable royalties due and other licensing terms for all other uses and/or distribution of the REDISTRIBUTABLES.

6. **U.S. GOVERNMENT RESTRICTED RIGHTS.** The SOFTWARE PRODUCT and documentation are provided with RESTRICTED RIGHTS. Use, duplication, or disclosure by the Government is subject to restrictions as set forth in subparagraph (c)(1)(ii) of the Rights in Technical Data and Computer Software clause at DFARS 252.227-7013 or subparagraphs (c)(1) and (2) of the Commercial Computer Software-Restricted Rights at 48 CFR 52.227-19, as applicable. Manufacturer is Microsoft Corporation/One Microsoft Way/Redmond, WA 98052-6399.

7. **EXPORT RESTRICTIONS.**

You agree that you will not export or re-export the SOFTWARE PRODUCT to any country, person, entity or end user subject to U.S.A. export restrictions. Restricted countries currently include, but are not necessarily limited to Cuba, Iran, Iraq, Libya, North Korea, Syria, and the Federal Republic of Yugoslavia (Serbia and Montenegro, U.N. Protected Areas and areas of Republic of Bosnia and Herzegovina under the control of Bosnian Serb forces). You warrant and represent that neither the U.S.A. Bureau of Export Administration nor any other federal agency has suspended, revoked or denied your export privileges.

8. **NOTE ON JAVA SUPPORT.** THE SOFTWARE PRODUCT CONTAINS SUPPORT FOR PROGRAMS WRITTEN IN JAVA. JAVA TECHNOLOGY IS NOT FAULT TOLERANT AND IS NOT DESIGNED, MANUFACTURED OR INTENDED FOR USE OR RESALE AS ONLINE CONTROL EQUIPMENT IN HAZARDOUS ENVIRONMENTS REQUIRING FAIL-SAFE PERFORMANCE, SUCH AS IN THE OPERATION OF NUCLEAR FACILITIES, AIRCRAFT NAVIGATION OR COMMUNICATIONS SYSTEMS, AIR TRAFFIC CONTROL, DIRECT LIFE SUPPORT MACHINES, OR WEAPONS SYSTEMS, IN WHICH THE FAILURE OF JAVA TECHNOLOGY COULD LEAD DIRECTLY TO DEATH, PERSONAL INJURY, OR SEVERE PHYSICAL OR ENVIRONMENTAL DAMAGE.

MISCELLANEOUS

If you acquired this product in the United States, this EULA is governed by the laws of the State of Washington.

If you acquired this product in Canada, this EULA is governed by the laws of the Province of Ontario, Canada. Each of the parties hereto irrevocably attorns to the jurisdiction of the courts of the Province of Ontario and further agrees to commence any litigation which may arise hereunder in the courts located in the Judicial District of York, Province of Ontario.

If this product was acquired outside the United States, then local law may apply.

Should you have any questions concerning this EULA, or if you desire to contact Microsoft for any reason, please contact the Microsoft subsidiary serving your country, or write: Microsoft Sales Information Center/One Microsoft Way/Redmond, WA 98052-6399.

If you have a specific question regarding the licensing of redistributables, you may call the Microsoft Developer Services Team at (800) 426-9400 (United States only) or send inquiries via fax to Microsoft Visual J++ Licensing Administrator, (206) 936-7329 (United States).

LIMITED WARRANTY

LIMITED WARRANTY. Except with respect to Microsoft Internet Explorer and the REDIS-TRIBUTABLES, which are provided "as is," without warranty of any kind, Microsoft warrants that (a) the SOFTWARE PRODUCT will perform substantially in accordance with the accompanying written materials for a period of ninety (90) days from the date of receipt, and (b) any hardware accompanying the SOFTWARE PRODUCT will be free from defects in materials and workmanship under normal use and service for a period of one (1) year from the date of receipt. Some states and jurisdictions do not allow limitations on duration of an implied warranty, so the above limitation may not apply to you. To the extent allowed by applicable law, implied warranties on the SOFT-WARE PRODUCT and hardware, if any, are limited to ninety (90) days and one year, respectively.

CUSTOMER REMEDIES. Microsoft's and its suppliers' entire liability and your exclusive remedy shall be, at Microsoft's option, either (a) return of the price paid, or (b) repair or replacement of the SOFTWARE PRODUCT or hardware that does not meet Microsoft's Limited Warranty and which is returned to Microsoft with a copy of your receipt. This Limited Warranty is void if failure of the SOFTWARE PRODUCT or hardware has resulted from accident, abuse, or misapplication. Any replacement SOFTWARE PRODUCT or hardware will be warranted for the remainder of the original warranty period or thirty (30) days, whichever is longer. **Outside the United States, neither these remedies nor any product support services offered by Microsoft are available without proof of purchase from an authorized international source.**

NO OTHER WARRANTIES. TO THE MAXIMUM EXTENT PERMITTED BY APPLICABLE LAW, MICROSOFT AND ITS SUPPLIERS DISCLAIM ALL OTHER WARRANTIES, EITHER EXPRESS OR IMPLIED, INCLUDING, BUT NOT LIMITED TO, IMPLIED WARRANTIES OF MERCHANTABILITY AND FITNESS FOR A PARTICULAR PURPOSE, WITH REGARD TO THE SOFTWARE PRODUCT, AND ANY ACCOMPANYING HARDWARE. THIS LIMITED WARRANTY GIVES YOU SPECIFIC LEGAL RIGHTS. YOU MAY HAVE OTHERS, WHICH VARY FROM STATE/JURISDICTION TO STATE/JURISDICTION.

NO LIABILITY FOR CONSEQUENTIAL DAMAGES. TO THE MAXIMUM EXTENT PERMITTED BY APPLICABLE LAW, IN NO EVENT SHALL MICROSOFT OR ITS SUPPLIERS BE LIABLE FOR ANY SPECIAL, INCIDENTAL, INDIRECT, OR CONSEQUENTIAL DAMAGES WHATSOEVER (INCLUDING, WITHOUT LIMITATION, DAMAGES FOR LOSS OF BUSINESS PROFITS, BUSINESS INTERRUPTION, LOSS OF BUSINESS INFORMATION, OR ANY OTHER PECUNIARY LOSS) ARISING OUT OF THE USE OF OR INABILITY TO USE THE SOFTWARE PRODUCT, EVEN IF MICROSOFT HAS BEEN ADVISED OF THE POSSIBILITY OF SUCH DAMAGES. BECAUSE SOME STATES AND JURISDICTIONS DO NOT ALLOW THE EXCLUSION OR LIMITATION OF LIABILITY FOR CONSEQUENTIAL OR INCIDENTAL DAMAGES, THE ABOVE LIMITATION MAY NOT APPLY TO YOU.

LICENSE AGREEMENT AND LIMITED WARRANTY

8.   **LIMITED WARRANTY AND DISCLAIMER OF WARRANTY:** The Company warrants that the SOFTWARE, when properly used in accordance with the Documentation, will operate in substantial conformity with the description of the SOFTWARE set forth in the Documentation. The Company does not warrant that the SOFTWARE will meet your requirements or that the operation of the SOFTWARE will be uninterrupted or error-free. The Company warrants that the media on which the SOFTWARE is delivered shall be free from defects in materials and workmanship under normal use for a period of thirty (30) days from the date of your purchase. Your only remedy and the Company's only obligation under these limited warranties is, at the Company's option, return of the warranted item for a refund of any amounts paid by you or replacement of the item. Any replacement of SOFTWARE or media under the warranties shall not extend the original warranty period. The limited warranty set forth above shall not apply to any SOFTWARE which the Company determines in good faith has been subject to misuse, neglect, improper installation, repair, alteration, or damage by you. EXCEPT FOR THE EXPRESSED WARRANTIES SET FORTH ABOVE, THE COMPANY DISCLAIMS ALL WARRANTIES, EXPRESS OR IMPLIED, INCLUDING WITHOUT LIMITATION, THE IMPLIED WARRANTIES OF MERCHANTABILITY AND FITNESS FOR A PARTICULAR PURPOSE. EXCEPT FOR THE EXPRESS WARRANTY SET FORTH ABOVE, THE COMPANY DOES NOT WARRANT, GUARANTEE, OR MAKE ANY REPRESENTATION REGARDING THE USE OR THE RESULTS OF THE USE OF THE SOFTWARE IN TERMS OF ITS CORRECTNESS, ACCURACY, RELIABILITY, CURRENTNESS, OR OTHERWISE.

IN NO EVENT, SHALL THE COMPANY OR ITS EMPLOYEES, AGENTS, SUPPLIERS, OR CONTRACTORS BE LIABLE FOR ANY INCIDENTAL, INDIRECT, SPECIAL, OR CONSEQUENTIAL DAMAGES ARISING OUT OF OR IN CONNECTION WITH THE LICENSE GRANTED UNDER THIS AGREEMENT, OR FOR LOSS OF USE, LOSS OF DATA, LOSS OF INCOME OR PROFIT, OR OTHER LOSSES, SUSTAINED AS A RESULT OF INJURY TO ANY PERSON, OR LOSS OF OR DAMAGE TO PROPERTY, OR CLAIMS OF THIRD PARTIES, EVEN IF THE COMPANY OR AN AUTHORIZED REPRESENTATIVE OF THE COMPANY HAS BEEN ADVISED OF THE POSSIBILITY OF SUCH DAMAGES. IN NO EVENT SHALL LIABILITY OF THE COMPANY FOR DAMAGES WITH RESPECT TO THE SOFTWARE EXCEED THE AMOUNTS ACTUALLY PAID BY YOU, IF ANY, FOR THE SOFTWARE.

SOME JURISDICTIONS DO NOT ALLOW THE LIMITATION OF IMPLIED WARRANTIES OR LIABILITY FOR INCIDENTAL, INDIRECT, SPECIAL, OR CONSEQUENTIAL DAMAGES, SO THE ABOVE LIMITATIONS MAY NOT ALWAYS APPLY. THE WARRANTIES IN THIS AGREEMENT GIVE YOU SPECIFIC LEGAL RIGHTS AND YOU MAY ALSO HAVE OTHER RIGHTS WHICH VARY IN ACCORDANCE WITH LOCAL LAW.

ACKNOWLEDGMENT

YOU ACKNOWLEDGE THAT YOU HAVE READ THIS AGREEMENT, UNDERSTAND IT, AND AGREE TO BE BOUND BY ITS TERMS AND CONDITIONS. YOU ALSO AGREE THAT THIS AGREEMENT IS THE COMPLETE AND EXCLUSIVE STATEMENT OF THE AGREEMENT BETWEEN YOU AND THE COMPANY AND SUPERSEDES ALL PROPOSALS OR PRIOR AGREEMENTS, ORAL, OR WRITTEN, AND ANY OTHER COMMUNICATIONS BETWEEN YOU AND THE COMPANY OR ANY REPRESENTATIVE OF THE COMPANY RELATING TO THE SUBJECT MATTER OF THIS AGREEMENT.

Should you have any questions concerning this Agreement or if you wish to contact the Company for any reason, please contact in writing at the address below.

Robin Short
Prentice Hall
One Lake Street
Upper Saddle River, New Jersey 07458

The program on the enclosed CD-ROM was reproduced by Prentice Hall under a special agreement with Microsoft Corporation. For this reason, Prentice Hall is responsible for the product warranty and for support. If your disk is defective, return it to Prentice Hall, which will arrange for its replacement. Any product support will be provided, if at all, by Prentice Hall. PLEASE DO NOT CONTACT MICROSOFT CORPORATION FOR PRODUCT SUPPORT. End users of this Microsoft program shall not be considered "registered owners" of a Microsoft product and therefore shall not be eligible for upgrades, promotions or other benefits available to "registered owners" of Microsoft products.